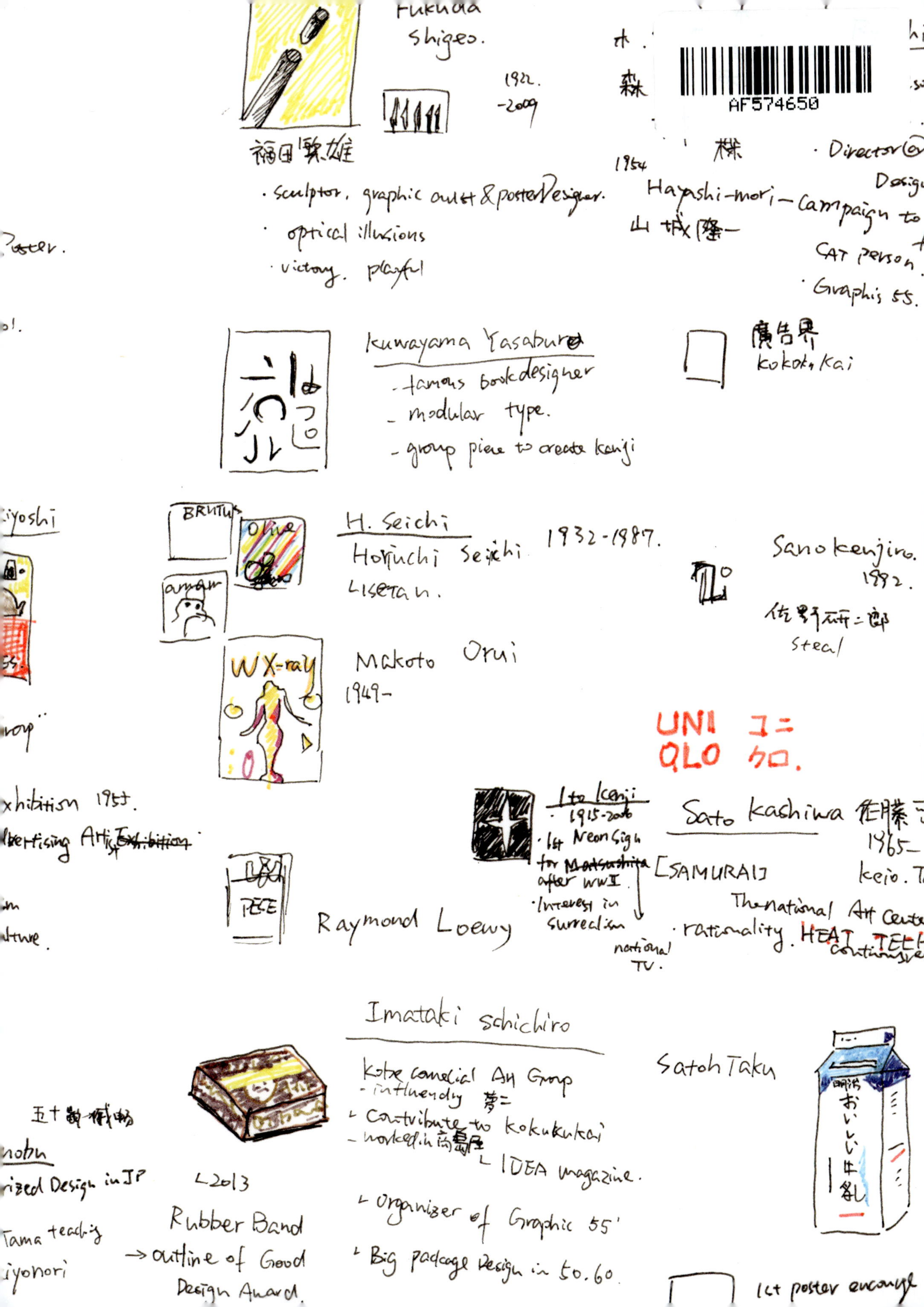

Fukuda Shigeo.
1932. -2009
福田繁雄
· sculptor, graphic artist & posterDesigner.
· optical illusions
· victory. playful
AF574650
1954
Hayashi-mori — Campaign to
山城隆一
· Director @ Design
CAT person
· Graphis 55.
Kuwayama Yasaburo
- famous bookdesigner
- modular type.
- group piece to create kanji
廣告界
kokokukai
H. Seichi
Horiuchi Seichi
1932-1987.
Lisetan.
BRUTUS
Olive
Sano kenjiro.
1982.
佐野研二郎
steal
Makoto Orui
1949-
WX-ray
UNI QLO ユニクロ.
Ito kenji
· 1915-2006
· 1st Neon Sign for Matsushita after WWII
· Interest in surrealism
national TV.
Sato kashiwa 佐藤可
1965-
[SAMURAI]
keio. Ta
The national Art Center
· rationality. HEAT TECH continuous
Raymond Loewy
PEACE
Imataki schichiro
Kobe comercial Art Group
- influenced by 夢二
└ Contribute to kokukukai
- worked in 高島屋
└ IDEA magazine.
└ Organizer of Graphic 55'
└ Big package Design in 50.60
Satoh Taku
おいしい牛乳
1st poster encourage
五十嵐威暢
└2013
Rubber Band
→ outline of Good Design Award.

fra
jap
gr
d
1875

Ian Lynam

cture:
inese
aphic
esign
5–1975

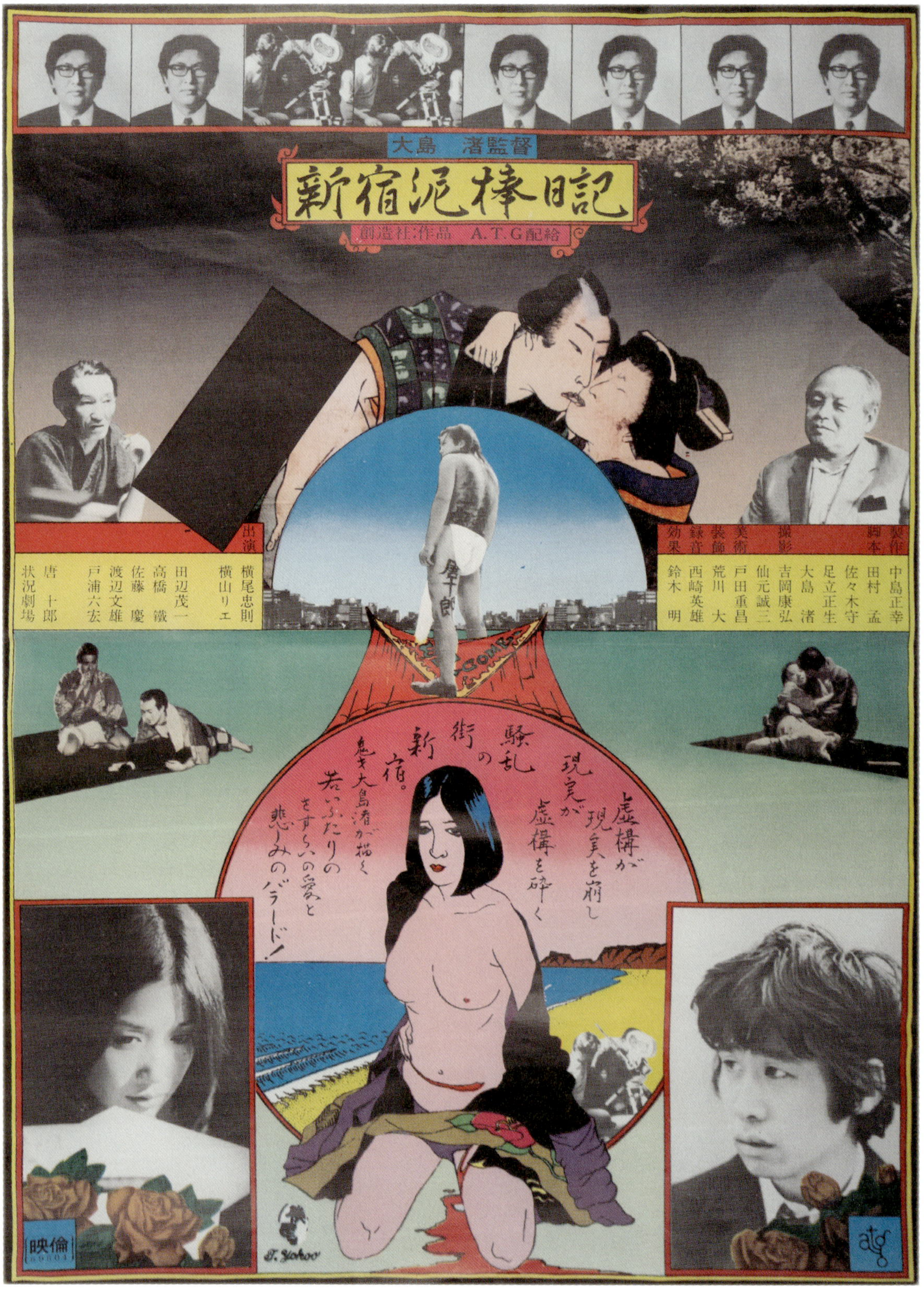

Above: Yokoo Tadanori-designed offset-printed poster for the divisive 1968 agitprop film ***Diary of a Shinjuku Thief* 新宿泥棒日記 directed by Nagisa Ōshima 大島渚.** The poster combines photography of the movie's stars and supporting cast members, censored historical pornographic *shunga* ukiyo-e printmaking, and Yokoo's then contemporary, ukiyo-e-informed illustration.

Opposite: ***Main Street* 本町通り (メインストリート)**, Sinclair Lewis シンクレーア・ルイス, **Shinchosha 新潮社 Tokyo: 1931. Designer: unknown.** A purely typographic slipcase design with hand lettering that mixes horizontal and vertical orthographies.

fracture: japanese graphic design 1875–1975

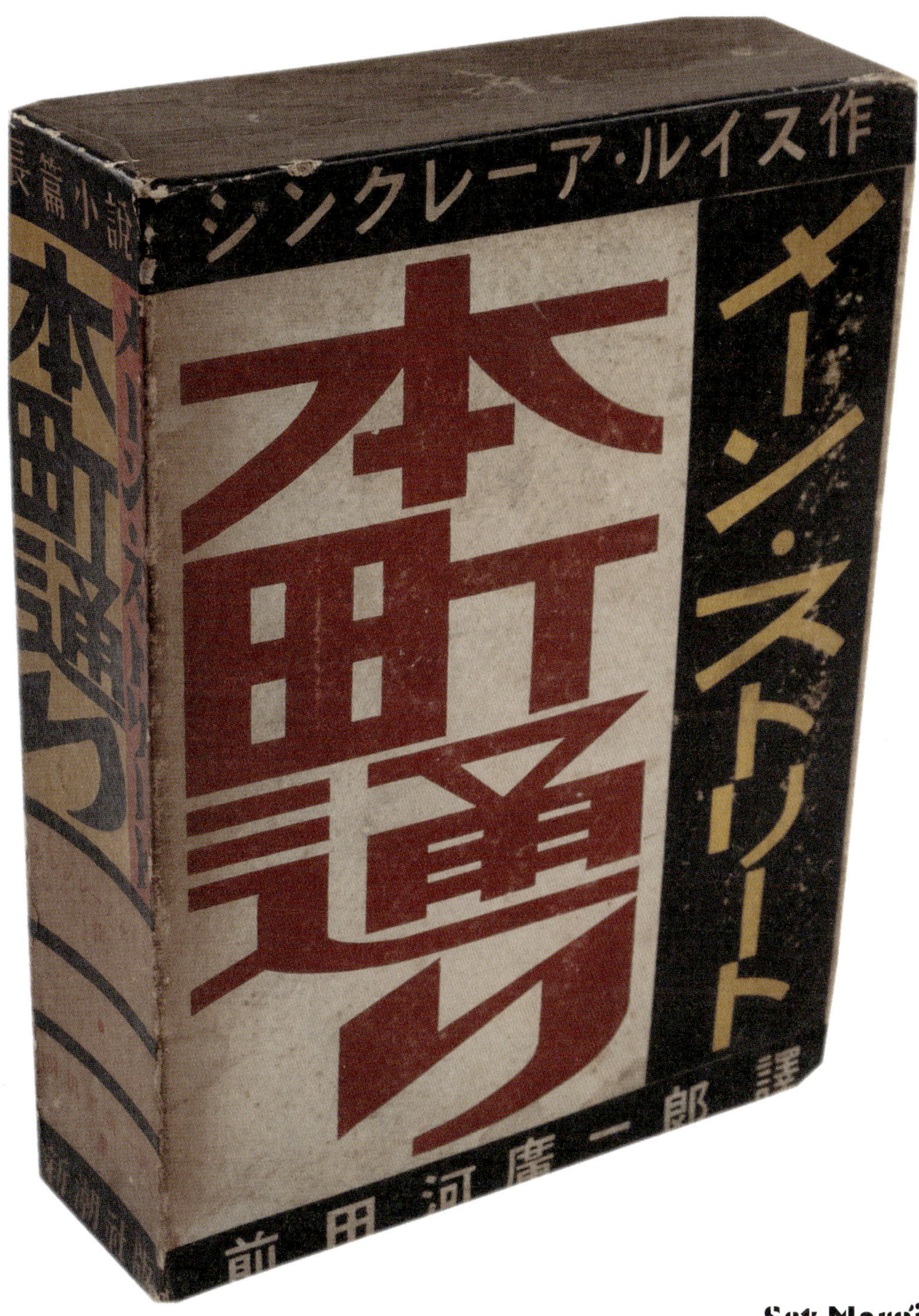

Set Margins' 54

TABLE OF CONTENTS:

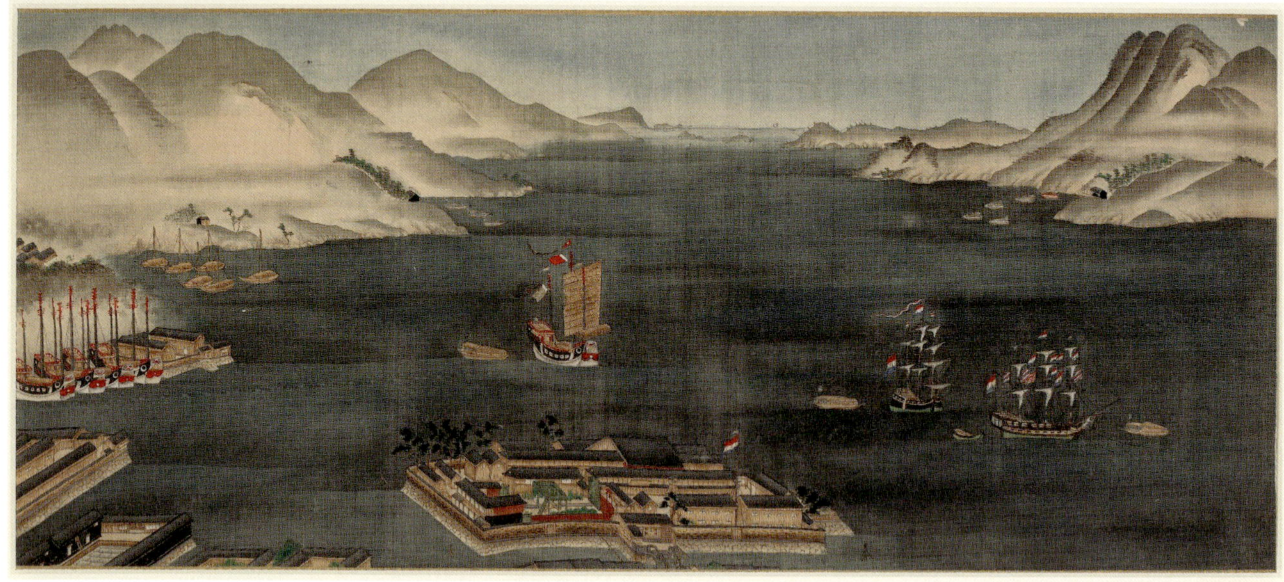

***Painting of Japanese and Dutch trade on Dejima (in Nagasaki)* 出島における日蘭貿易, 1820.** Painting, section of handscroll. © The Trustees of the British Museum. Courtesy of the British Museum. A rendering of one of Japan's port communities open to trade with foreigners, notably the Dutch.

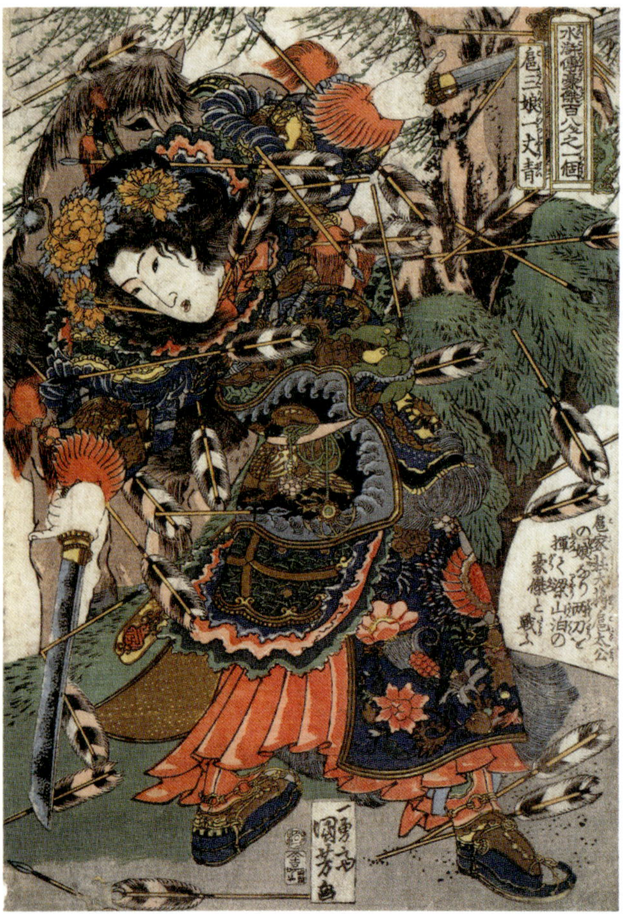

***Honcho Suikoden Gōketsu* 本朝水滸伝豪傑, Utagawa Kuniyoshi 歌川国芳 Utagawa Kunisada 歌川国貞, 1830.** An ukiyo-e portrait of Kosanjō Ichijōsei 扈三娘一丈青 from the 1827–1830 series *One Hundred Eight Heroes of a Popular Water Margin* 通俗水滸伝豪傑百八人之一個. © The Trustees of the British Museum. Courtesy of the British Museum. A classic example of ukiyo-e printmaking.

Introduction

Japan has a rich history of words and images. This history culminated in a host of art and graphic craft forms prior to the Meiji Restoration, when the country opened to the world after centuries of self-isolation, and many still exist today.

These include *ukiyo-e* 浮世絵 printmaking and *sōsaku hanga* 創作版画 printmaking. (The term *hanga* was not coined until 1904—the term *surimono* 摺物 was in common use prior to describe assorted forms of printing.) Craftspeople and artists involved in the production of these forms of printmaking were some of Japan's earliest graphic craftspeople. Other forms of commercial printing included decorative *pochibukuro* ポチ袋, money gift-giving envelopes and *senjafuda* 千社札, honorific proto-graffiti seals produced by woodblock carvers and printers. Senjafuda were made for *kō* 講, groups of male pilgrims, to note their presence on shrines throughout the country. (At the time, women largely were not allowed to travel unless they had special permission or were en route to engage in an arranged marriage.) Each of these specific forms of visual communication was mass produced and distributed in printed formats.

In these artifacts, we can perhaps locate the origins of Japanese graphic design. Global histories of Japan point to the Meiji Restoration as the birthplace of modernity (largely due to the buildup of a colonial-oriented Japanese military and imperialist expansion). Yet if we inhabit a lay-understanding of modernity, this specific era's social and cultural evolution surpassed that of prior eras'. During the Edō period (1603–1868), the urban merchant class emerged as a monied, pleasure-seeking, and aesthetics-embracing force intimately engaged with visual representations of the secular world. Design-rich books were printed in editions of up to 10,000 copies using woodblocks carved with nuanced forms, including calligraphy translated into regulated form and abundant decoration and ornamentation.

The Meiji Restoration and the re-opening of Japan's borders and peoples to the world after two hundred years of isolation is significant, as it provides a rich context for students of history to investigate the social conditions in which modern graphic design in Japan sprung forth, both prior to and after opening.

Japan did not undertake the project of *global* modernity (read: expansionism) in earnest until the mid-nineteenth century, yet even during the *sakoku* 鎖国 period of closure to international relations and trade imposed by the Tokugawa regime from 1603 to 1868, Japan still had access to imported technology from China, Korea, and Holland. These imports did not spark widespread technological, social, or cultural change during that time—these shifts would be kickstarted by the forced opening of Japan's ports in the 1850s.

It was around the time of the country's opening that Japanese people developed the basis for a scalable system of typography and the use of movable, modular, recombinant typographic characters that allowed for the reproduction of both long-form and short-form typographic materials for the masses. Movable metal type in East Asia predates Gutenberg, and Japan had certainly made forays into the process during the Edo period.

In the decade before, many Chinese port cities and regions had succumbed to Western colonizing powers, as had most of Southeast Asia. Russia was also strengthening to the north, and the leaders of Japan sought to modernize and industrialize rapidly in order to avoid a similar fate. With the restoration of the emperor as head of state in 1868, Japanese leaders concentrated on building a modern, technological, bureaucratic nation with the emperor as the central pillar of culture and politics, and thus the initial *Meiji* period (1868–1912) saw Western-style executive, judiciary, and legislature grafted onto a historically feudal structure.

The Meiji period is largely considered the advent of "Modern Japan," with the Emperor being restored to symbolic head of state, the newly formed parliament—made up of middle-ranking Samurai—abolishing the Neo-Confucian class structure of Japanese society, and rapid urbanization. This period also saw the formation of Japan's modern military and the start of aggressive imperialism in which Japan would wage war with nations throughout Asia and Russia and annex large swaths of surrounding countries. The Japanese imperialist tendency would continue through the *Taishō* (1912–1926) and *Shōwa* (1926–1989) periods, with the goal being to create the *Greater East Asia Co-Prosperity Sphere* 大東亜共栄圏, a vast pan-Asian empire under Japanese governance and control.

"THE GOOD OLD CANON"

There are a number of books about Japanese graphic design history in Japanese, but few in English save ones covering

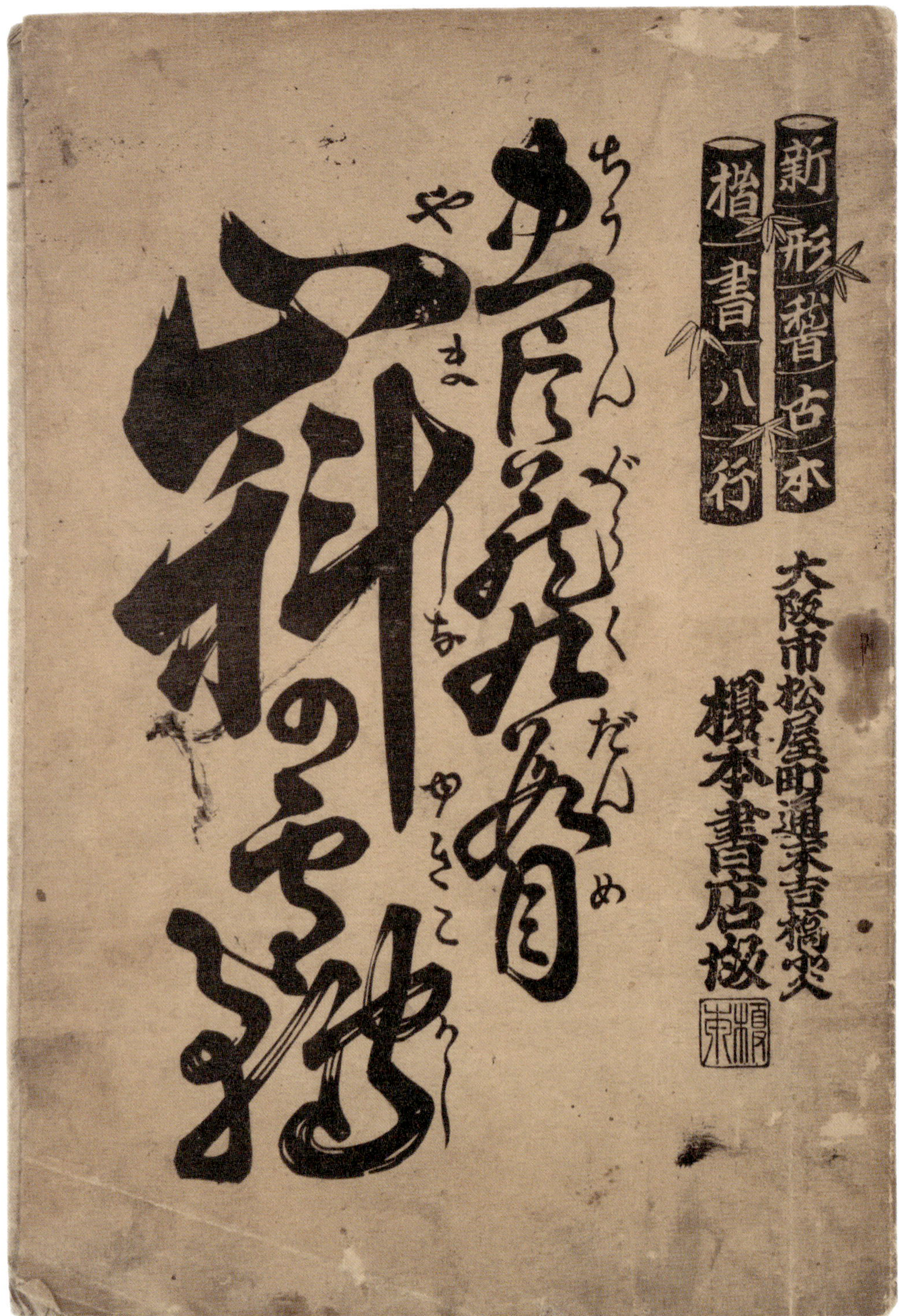

Chūshingura kudanme yamashina no yukikokashi **忠臣蔵九段目山科の雪転**
(Osaka: Enomoto Shoten 榎本書店, 1908).
The script of a kabuki play which debuted in 1748, printed using wood blocks and notable for the dense expressive calligraphy utilized on the cover, the integration of which would not be possible using metal type in that era.

narrow slices in time or monographs devoted to individual designers. My hope is that this book helps make Japanese graphic design more understandable and less "exotic" to readers, and with the draining of said exoticism, that readers might gain a greater understanding of the development of Japanese graphic design.

Most design historians and students of design outside of Japan do not have a robust understanding of Japanese graphic design history, and there are a number of reasons for this: The Japanese visual and spoken language is difficult to pick up as a second language, and Japan boasts the world's fourth-largest economy in the current moment, meaning that there is little need or desire for the majority of the Japanese populace to understand languages other than Japanese. If one consumes Japanese television today, the bulk of the programming is in Japanese, with foreign content subtitled or overdubbed in Japanese. It is the same if one heads to most bookstores, libraries, or cineplexes. The needs and desires of the Japanese populace are served to them in the Japanese language, so it remains a largely monolingual culture. This is reinforced by a cultural legacy of isolationism and an insistence upon the appearance of economic, cultural, and social self-reliance in Japan.

Due to the difficulty of learning the language and the social/cultural conditions that have maintained Japan as separate from much of the rest of the world in many ways, there have been no overarching histories of Japanese graphic design written in English to date, other than Richard Thornton's *The Graphic Spirit of Japan*. *Graphic Spirit* is a problematic book, as it was colored by Thornton's lack of deep research and reliance upon a single curatorial force in Japan—design tastemaker Katsumi Masaru—as to whose works and biographies were included. As such, the book pays scant attention to history and cultural context and skews heavily towards Katsumi's advertising-oriented view of design.

It is here that I would like to quote historian and scholar Natalia Ilyin as to the historiography (the study of the writing of history and of written histories) of graphic design. In conversation at Vermont College of Fine Arts in a workshop held by fellow historian N. Silas Munro, Ilyin stated that "the problem with how graphic design history has been written is that it has been contextualized in a context of 'no context,'" which sounds overly complicated but alludes to the vacuum space where writing on graphic design history is staged. Graphic design history is often reduced to single images and captions including a work's title, author, and date.

Additionally, as the term "graphic design" was only coined in 1922, the histories that we have are not very deep, are much less rich, are incredibly depoliticized, and seem to exist outside of a greater understanding of cultural continuums, which is problematic.

In this book, I have attempted to bridge these gaps between world history and graphic design history, though this entire production is colored by my perspective as a white American cisgender heterosexual male living in Tokyo—in short, there can be no objectivity—and I ask readers to examine this book critically, as all histories are authored. It is also worth considering Japan-as-site: a place of *fracture*. Japan is a nation which took over large parts of Asia, lost it all, and has since turned inward, both pondering and shouting its schizophrenic place in history both quietly and aloud.

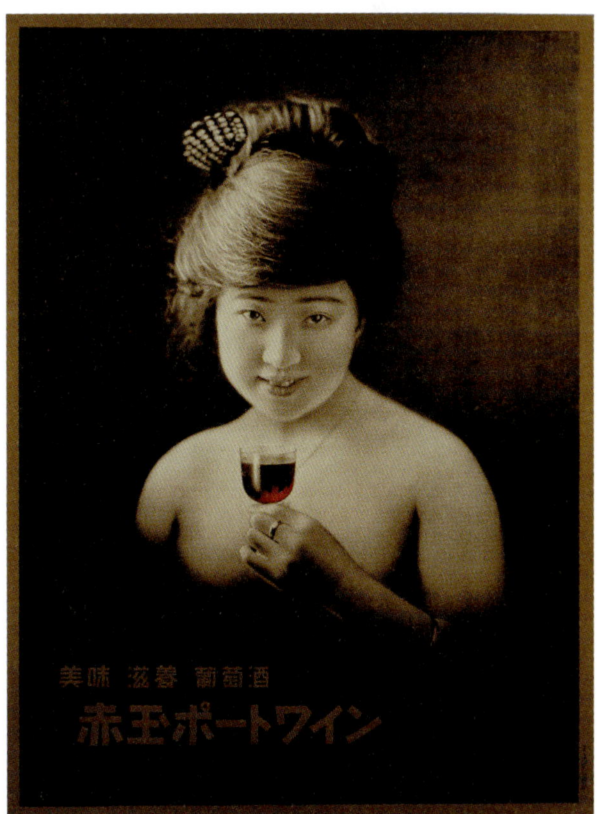

Poster for Akadama Port Wine designed by Kataoka Toshirō 片岡敏郎, 1922. This was the first Japanese poster featuring photographic reproduction of a near-naked woman, and the ensuing public moral upheaval caused the model, actress Matsushima Emiko 松島栄美子, much distress. The poster won the World Poster Contest in Germany the following year.

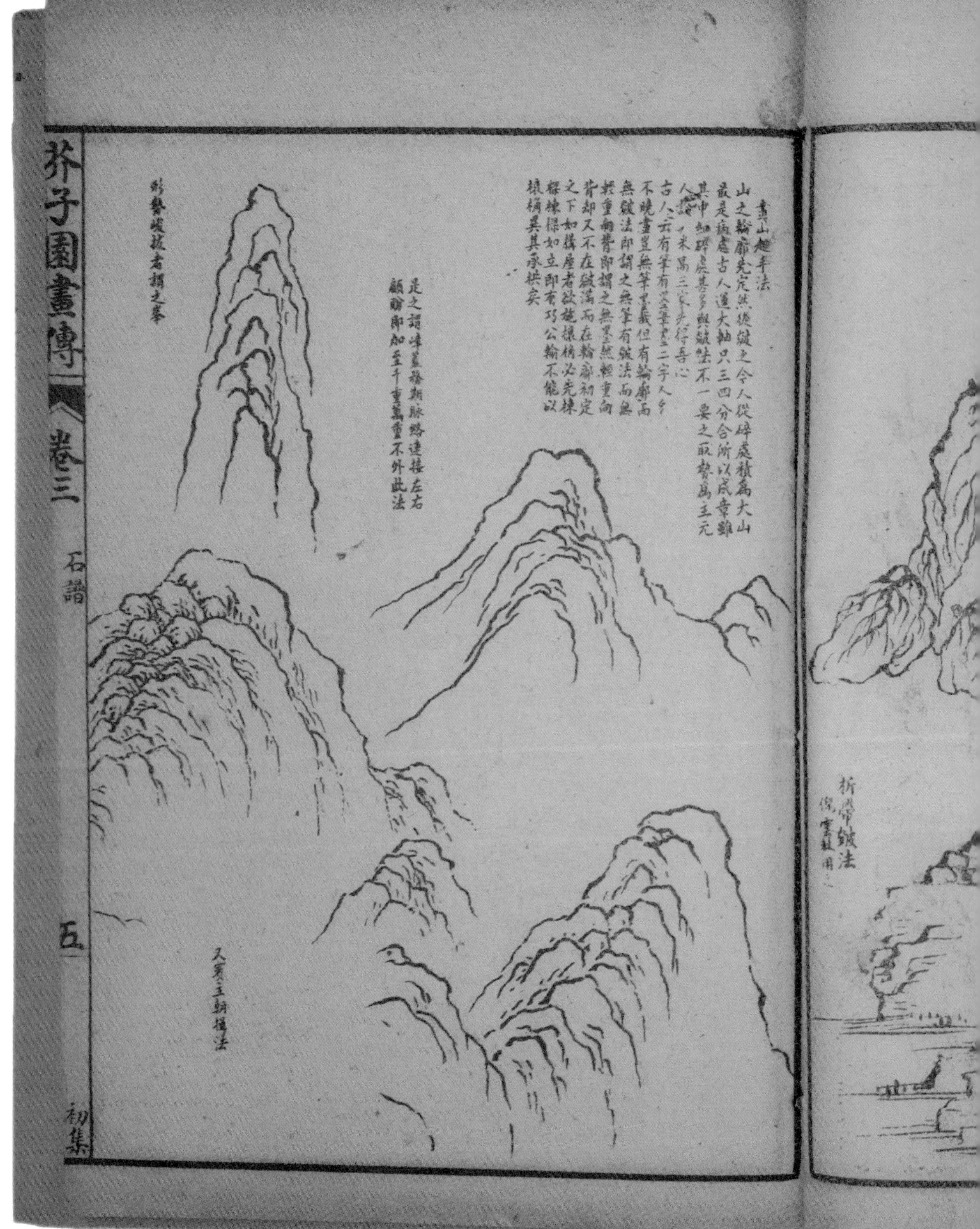

芥子園畫傳 卷三 石譜 五 初集

畫山起手法

山之輪廓先定然後皴之今人從碎處積為大山最是病處古人通大軸只三四分合所以成章雖其中細碎處甚多無皴法不一要之取勢為主元人論〻米高三家先得吾心古人云有筆有墨筆墨二字人多不曉畫豈無筆墨哉但有輪廓而無皴法即謂之無筆有皴法而無輕重向背明晦即謂之無墨然輕重向背却又不在皴法而在輪廓初定之下如構屋者欲施椽桷必先棟樑棟樑得立即有巧公輸不能以椽桷異其承接矣

形勢峻拔者謂之峯

走之謂峰蓋發朝脈絡連接左右顧盼即加至千重萬疊不外此法

又寫主朝揖法

折帶皴法 倪雲林用之

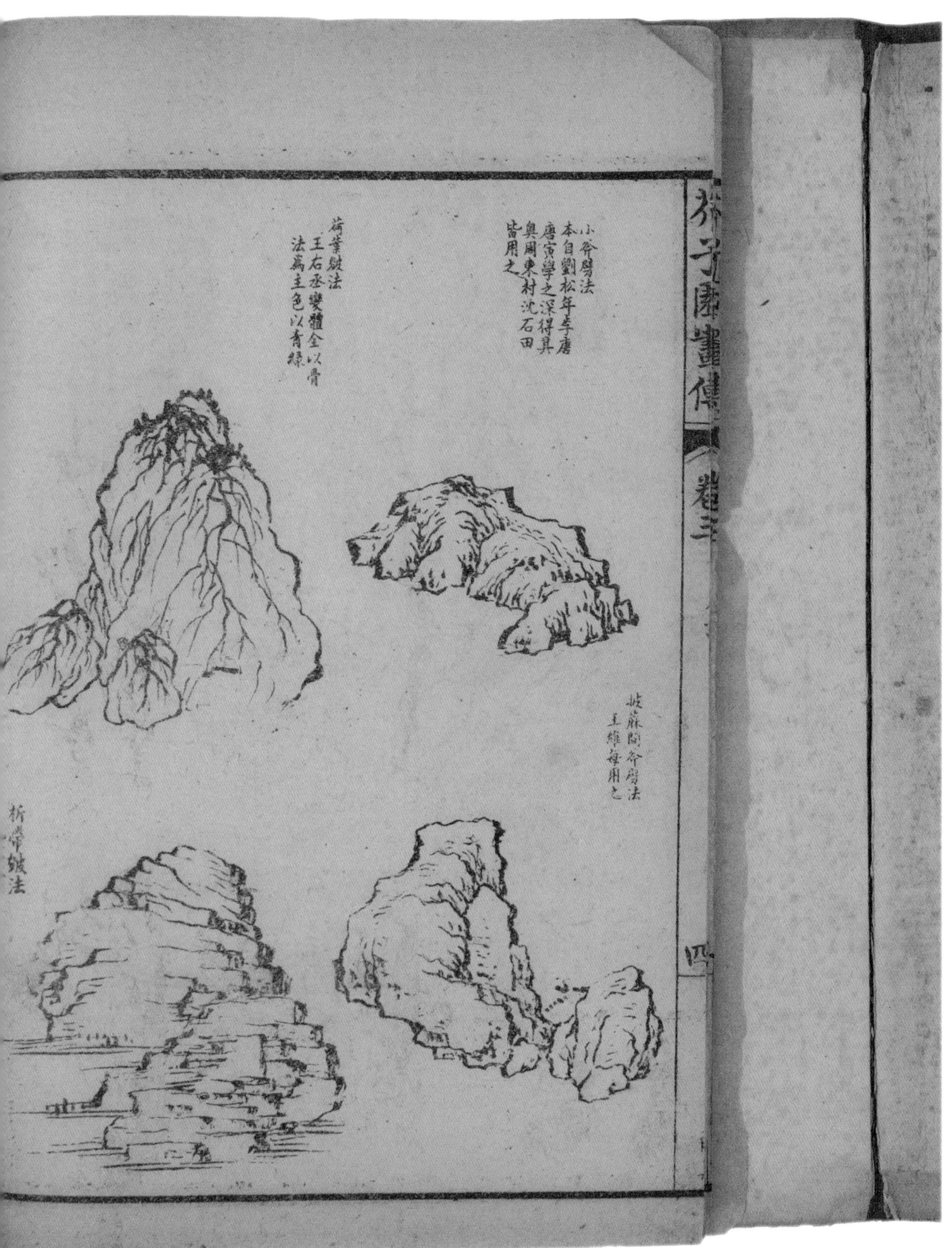

***Kaishien gahaku shoshū* 芥子園画博初集** (Kyoto: Gosharo / Hishiya Sonbei 上海天寶書局, 1812).
A woodblock-printed Chinese painting manual printed in Japan, filled with renderings of rock formations and wildlife, that exemplifies the dynamism and spatiality that could be achieved without metal typesetting.

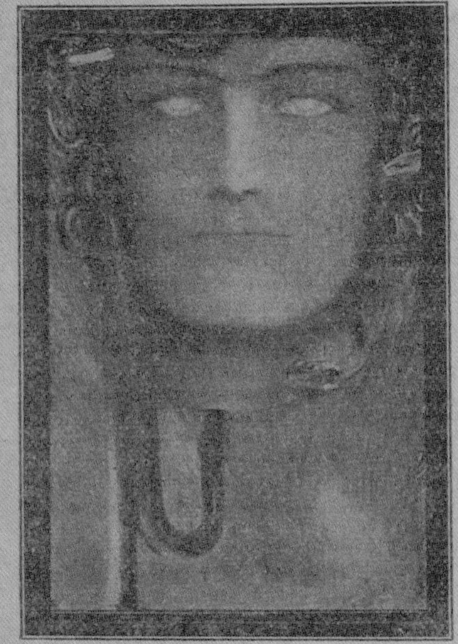

Belgian Art in Exile

Paper 3.50

Vellum Cover. 11.50

流竄中の 白國美術

（着彩版三十六面 寫眞版五十七面）

!!! 着・荷・近・き・に・あ・り !!!

白耳義の過去の美術は破壞されたり。左れど追はれたる白國美術家は爰に新らしき光輝を發したり。

此帖や文明の破壞者に對する沈痛なるクライたると同時に如何なる暴力にも犯されざる藝術の輝ける誇なり白耳義の任俠義勇なる精神の籠れる此の輝きある藝術の光に浴せよ。

着荷一千部中豫約を登錄したるもの既に其の半ばを越えたり。急いで申込まれよ。

滿卷清新の畫趣は如何なる炎熱をも忘れて兩腋清風の感あらん。

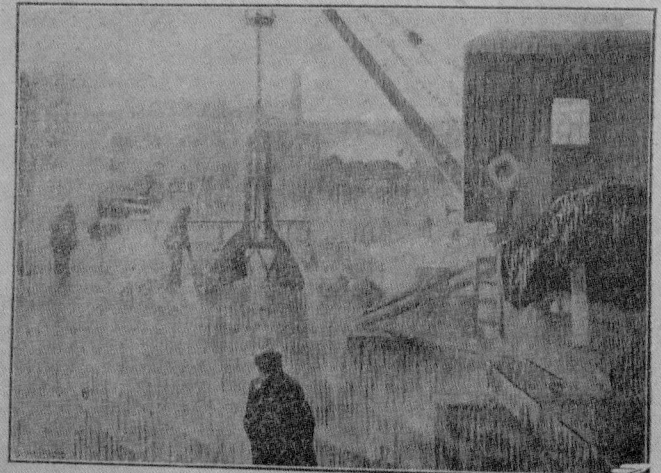

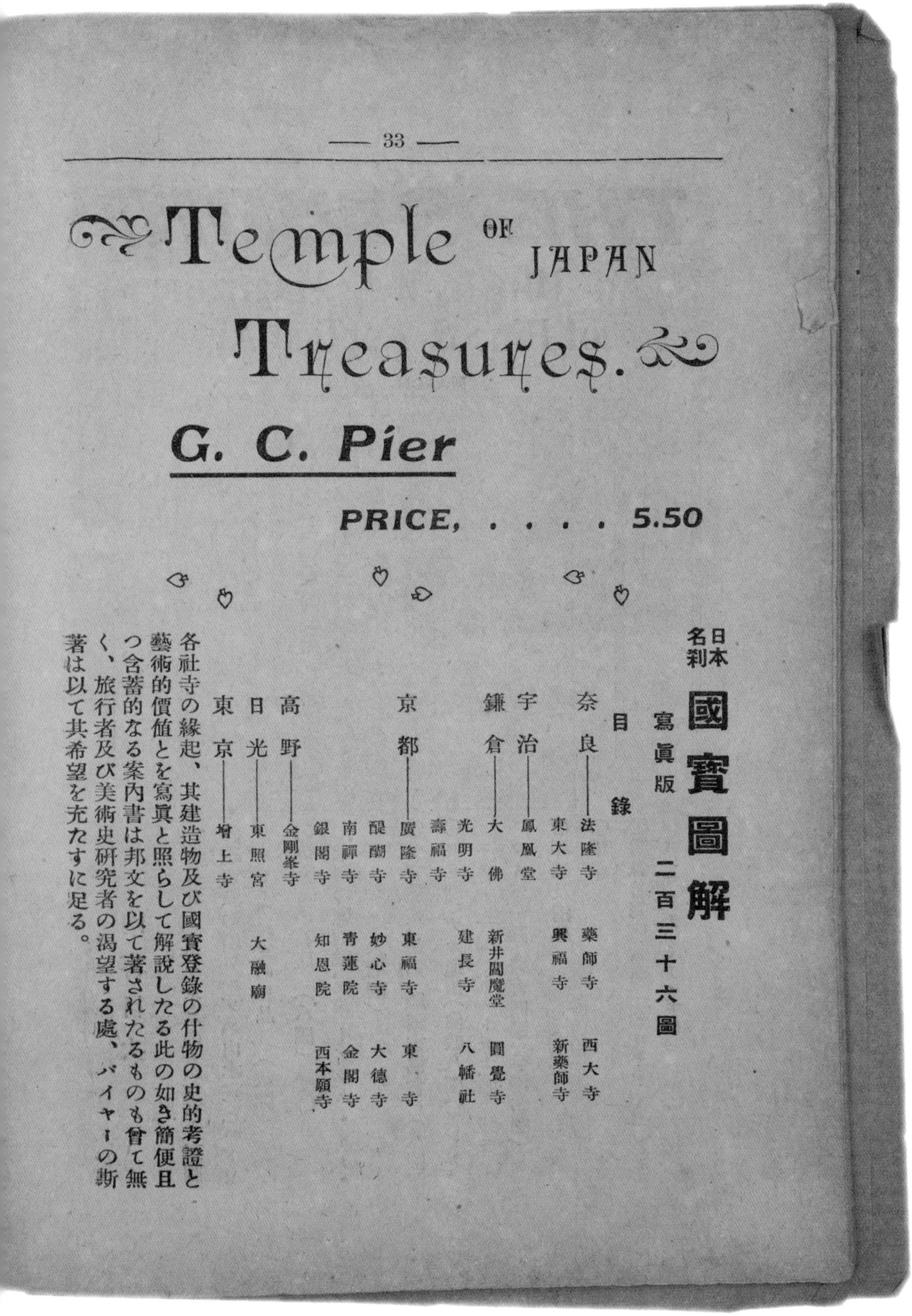

Temple OF JAPAN Treasures.

G. C. Pier

PRICE, ... 5.50

日本名刹 **國寶圖解**

寫眞版 二百三十六圖

目錄

奈良——法隆寺　藥師寺　西大寺
　　　　東大寺　興福寺　新藥師寺
宇治——鳳凰堂
鎌倉——大佛　新井閻魔堂　圓覺寺
　　　　光明寺　建長寺　八幡社
　　　　壽福寺
京都——廣隆寺　東福寺　東寺
　　　　醍醐寺　妙心寺　大德寺
　　　　南禪寺　青蓮院　金閣寺
　　　　銀閣寺　知恩院　西本願寺
高野——金剛峯寺
日光——東照宮　大融廟
東京——增上寺

各社寺の縁起、其建造物及び國寶登錄の什物の史的考證と藝術的價値とを寫眞と照らして解説したる此の如き簡便且つ含蓄的なる案内書は邦文を以て著されたるものも曾て無く、旅行者及び美術史研究者の渇望する處、バイヤーの斯著は以て其希望を充たすに足る。

Gakutō 学燈 (Tokyo: Hakubunkan 博文館 / Kyoto: Maruzen Shoten 丸善書店, July 1916).
Mail-order book catalog of foreign publications from one of Japan's early leading booksellers. A stunning example of multiplex bilingual typography with multiple levels of visual hierarchy.

before “design”

Before "Design": The DNA of Japanese Aesthetics

In its early development, Japanese graphic design drew from the visual themes and means of production of traditional Japanese arts and crafts, imparting multiple aesthetic attributes. An examination of each of these aspects of visual production is formative in understanding indigenous Japanese aesthetics. Additionally, it clarifies how the seismic shifts of modernity in Japan created an aesthetic that utilized pre-existing visual tropes as much as it adopted and adapted new approaches to visual expression in the development of modern Japanese graphic design.

WRITING SYSTEMS

The Japanese language has a rich calligraphic tradition that reaches back almost two millennia, when Japanese was written wholly using Chinese characters, at first in a transliterative way: grammatical reversals and inflections were annotated along with an unadulterated Chinese text with many encodings and markings, called *kanbun kundoku* 漢文訓読. Later, a laborious phonetic use of Chinese characters was tried, called *man'yōgana* 万葉仮名. The pictogram content was ignored in favor of sounds. It was dropped due to massive redundancy, but one can still see occasional glimpses of it in contemporary soba shops and other contexts. In the tenth century, two simplified syllabic character sets were developed in Japanese, and in time these became a formalized part of the written language. Centuries later, after regular contact with the West was established, the use of Latin lettering and numerals came into popular use in Japan, along with a score of analphabetic symbols and extended punctuation developed domestically and abroad that have made for a polyphonic written language. The contemporary Japanese writing system includes a number of discrete scripts which are used concurrently, each with its own timeline, provenance, and aesthetic.

Derived from simplified Chinese characters, hiragana and *katakana*, known together as "kana," are perhaps the most easily identifiable parts of the Japanese visual language to foreign eyes, as *kanji* are a fairly direct import from the Chinese written language, with the first movable Japanese typefaces being derived from Song (Ming) Era calligraphic designs.

HIRAGANA 平仮名 & KATAKANA 片仮名

Hiragana is mostly used to indicate prefixes and grammatical word endings, but also to represent entire words (usually of Japanese, rather than Chinese, origin) in place of kanji. Hiragana are composed of five singular vowels, thirty-nine distinct consonant-vowel unions, one double vowel (を wo, though pronounced "o"), and one singular consonant (ん pronounced "n"). Distinct combinations and reduced-size digraph modifiers are used to emphasize pronunciation and vocal stops and glides.

Hiragana are used exclusively for innate Japanese particles such as で de and と to. Particles are the cement of the Japanese language—they hold nouns and verbs together and often function as prepositions. Also, hiragana characters are used for verb endings in order to indicate tense (past/present/future), as well as for grammatical words. Some kanji are too difficult to memorize for common usage, and the hiragana version is substituted instead.

In the Heian Period (794 to 1185), women used hiragana for diaries, correspondence, and composing poetry and literature. The Chinese writing system of kanji was considered too difficult for women, as it required years of study, and women were forced to utilize the syllabic form of hiragana instead. Elite men had their heads stuck in books studying law, science, and philosophy, and memorizing thousands of rare kanji. As a result, the greatest pieces of literature of the Heian era were written in hiragana by women, most prominently the classic text *The Tale of Genji* 源氏物語. Hiragana was utilized by all for informal writing, but it was women who did the most to develop Hiragana as a meaningful applied language.

Hiragana has gone through reforms in spelling and orthographic rules, first in 1900, and then again in 1946. Rare character combinations and obsolete characters (ゑ "e," ゐ "i") were made obsolete and characters for pronouncing words outside of the Japanese syllabary (such as ゔ "v") were added.

With a corpus of forty-six characters each, hiragana and katakana are easier to memorize than kanji, which maxes out somewhere north of 50,000 characters, though only 2,000 to 3,000 are in regular use.

As hiragana is a syllabary (a phonetic syllable-based character set) and signifies the total range of sounds used in the Japanese language, children and foreigners are taught to read and write hiragana first.

HIRAGANA
KATAKANA

A	あ	ア	I	い	イ	U	う	ウ	E	え	エ	O	お	オ
KA	か	カ	KI	き	キ	KU	く	ク	KE	け	ケ	KO	こ	コ
SA	さ	サ	SHI	し	シ	SU	す	ス	SE	せ	セ	SO	そ	ソ
TA	た	タ	CHI	ち	チ	TSU	つ	ツ	TE	て	テ	TO	と	ト
NA	な	ナ	NI	に	ニ	NU	ぬ	ヌ	NE	ね	ネ	NO	の	ノ
HA	は	ハ	HI	ひ	ヒ	HU	ふ	フ	HE	へ	ヘ	HO	ほ	ホ
MA	ま	マ	MI	み	ミ	MU	む	ム	ME	め	メ	MO	も	モ
YA	や	ヤ				YU	ゆ	ユ				YO	よ	ヨ
RA	ら	ラ	RI	り	リ	RU	る	ル	RE	れ	レ	RO	ろ	ロ
WA	わ	ワ										WO	を	ヲ
N	ん	ン												
GA	が	ガ	GI	ぎ	ギ	GU	ぐ	グ	GE	げ	ゲ	GO	ご	ゴ
ZA	ざ	ザ	JI	じ	ジ	ZU	ず	ズ	ZE	ぜ	ゼ	ZO	ぞ	ゾ
DA	だ	ダ	JI	ぢ	ヂ	ZU	づ	ヅ	DE	で	デ	DO	ど	ド
BA	ば	バ	BI	び	ビ	BU	ぶ	ブ	BE	べ	ベ	BO	ぼ	ボ
PA	ぱ	パ	PI	ぴ	ピ	PU	ぷ	プ	PE	ぺ	ペ	PO	ぽ	ポ
KYA	きゃ	キャ				KYU	きゅ	キュ				KYO	きょ	キョ
SHA	しゃ	シャ				SHU	しゅ	シュ				SHO	しょ	ショ
CHA	ちゃ	チャ				CHU	ちゅ	チュ				CHO	ちょ	チョ
NYA	にゃ	ニャ				NYU	にゅ	ニュ				NYO	にょ	ニョ
HYA	ひゃ	ヒャ				HYU	ひゅ	ヒュ				HYO	ひょ	ヒョ
MYA	みゃ	ミャ				MYU	みゅ	ミュ				MYO	みょ	ミョ
RYA	りゃ	リャ				RYU	りゅ	リュ				RYO	りょ	リョ
GYA	ぎゃ	ギャ				GYU	ぎゅ	ギュ				GYO	ぎょ	ギョ
JA	じゃ	ジャ				JU	じゅ	ジュ				JO	じょ	ヂョ
JA	ぢゃ	ヂャ				JU	ぢゅ	ヅュ				JO	ぢょ	ヂョ
BYA	びゃ	ビャ				BYU	びゅ	ビュ				BYO	びょ	ビョ
PYA	ぴゃ	ピャ				PYU	ぴゅ	ピュ				PYO	ぴょ	ピョ

Hepburn romanization chart.
The main system of romanization for the Japanese language.

Heian-era male Japanese students of Buddhism found difficulty in keeping up with the boggling number of Chinese characters and it is to them that the Japanese credit the second phonetic or syllabic writing system, katakana. Most likely, students taking notes during lectures often had a difficult time with the pronunciations and meanings of unfamiliar kanji and had to develop a phonetic shorthand. Instead of adopting the already established (though then female-gendered) hiragana, katakana, another purely phonetic visual syllabary, was developed. Katakana's anatomy is much more angular than that of hiragana, making it more streamlined and harder-edged.

In contemporary times, katakana is used for foreign loanwords, country names, and proper names of foreigners. Katakana is also used for onomatopoeic words—words that describe sounds and movements. Names of plants, animals, and multinational corporations are often written using katakana, and writers occasionally will utilize katakana for emphasis, as well.

KANJI 漢字

Kanji is the writing system imported to Japan from China starting in the fourth century BC. Japan had no known written form of language prior to the adoption of Chinese hanzi. There are now significant differences between kanji used in Japanese and hanzi used in traditional written Chinese (still in use in Taiwan, Macau, and Hong Kong), due to the past nearly-2,000 years of domestic linguistic development in Japan. Over the past two millennia, there has been a proliferation of characters created in Japan, characters that have taken on different meanings in Japanese than the original Chinese, and simplified kanji due to orthographic reforms following World War II. Similar linguistic reform in mainland China in the 1950s created a systematic simplification from the original in that geographic area, as well.

Kanji include huge numbers of compound characters—some kanji can have up to ten different readings (base meanings/morphemes). Small *ruby* characters called *furigana* ふり仮名 are often used in text layouts to help annotate kanji if a kanji is obscure, or if the target audience is thought to be unfamiliar with the kanji. Furigana are usually formed of hiragana characters, but on occasion katakana and Latin characters are utilized.

Japanese names are usually written in kanji, but because there are so many possible readings for them, furigana characters are often used to sound out the readings of names. On official Japanese forms where one's name is to be written, there is always an adjacent column for the name to be written in furigana.

CALLIGRAPHIC ORTHOGRAPHY

The development of calligraphic expressions of the Japanese visual language formed the basis for Japanese movable type, from the earliest Song Dynasty-inspired Japanese typefaces through the effects of calligraphic orthography on the readability of the most deconstructed Japanese characters of the Postmodern era. When handwritten, each character or *moji* 文字 in the hiragana, katakana, and kanji systems is reliant upon stroke order for proper construction, giving each an innately visual form.

Kanji, hiragana, and katakana were used independently into the 1800s, lending each a developed formal quality. In contemporary usage, all three are mixed with Latin characters (*romaji* ローマ字), and each has a distinctive rhythm and density, yet the four aspects of Japanese visual language work together fluidly. The makeshift nature of the Japanese writing system means that the same word may be written in different ways. While this can be a source of great confusion, it can also offer writers and designers a unique stylistic choice and plurality of emphasis. The same word may be written in either Chinese characters, Hiragana, katakana, or Latin letterforms depending on the situation, the type of text, and the writer's preference.

The Japanese visual language reached dizzying heights of calligraphic expression during its centuries of development, with varying degrees of flourish, decoration, and readability in the approaches utilized. There are three primary forms of calligraphy now in common use:

- *kaisho* 楷書, a formal geometric script used largely for official documents;
- *gyōsho* 行書, a more humanist script;
- *sōsho* 草書, an expressive script using fluid strokes that often trail from character to character.

A variety of other specialized forms of calligraphy and lettering are also used, from *tensho* 篆書 (a script used for decorative engraving, largely for seals) to *higemoji* 髭文字 (a form of display lettering used as a specific calligraphic expression of Nichiren temples, yet also found on the labels of alcohol products). Higemoji exploits and emphasizes the brush tracks left behind by the calligrapher.

These different approaches to calligraphy and lettering were applied in woodblock-based book design prior to the Meiji Restoration and the resultant adoption of movable type. Due to the large number of individual characters in the Japanese visual language, calligraphy and lettering remain an important component of graphic design today, particularly for display lettering. Because the creation of Japanese typefaces is so expensive and labor-intensive, designers are highly reliant upon custom display lettering.

Japanese was written vertically from right to left (*tategaki* 縦書き) until 1885, when the Meiji-era shift toward modernization led to right-to-left horizontal writing (*migi yokogaki* 右横書き) being adopted nationally for a handful of years, before settling into left-to-right horizontal writing (*hidari yokogaki* 左横書き) after World War II.

IDENTITY & SYMBOLISM: MON 紋

Nearly every family of Japanese origin has a meaning-laden *kamon* 家紋, or family crest, with over 5,000 belonging to the official registry in contemporary times. Kamon are a subset of mon, heraldic emblems used to denote and identify clans, associations, businesses, religious groups or sites, guilds, neighborhoods, city wards, and assorted other groups. They most likely originated as identifying marks to distinguish clan or organization affiliation, to signify social status and alliances during times of strife and war. Mon were essential to the Japanese prior to widespread literacy, as they signified caste and rank.

Many mon are representations of plants, animals, natural phenomena (e.g., waves), designed objects, celestial bodies, kanji, geometric shapes, and abstract shapes. Mon are single-color and vary compositionally, though many are rendered in rounded or rectangular compositions.

Mon did not start out being such widespread and pervasive familial symbols. Instead, they were first created as identification devices for household objects by the aristocracy during the Heian Period (tenth century), then spread to become identification devices by assorted *daimyō* (lords) and were applied to battlefield regalia, weapons, vehicle liveries, businesses, and gravestones, and as decorative signifying elements on kimono during the Kamakura and Muromachi eras (1192–1568). The use of mon helped warriors identify sides during battle, branded property, and were applied in countless ways as architectural ornamentation. During the Ēdo period (1603–1868), much of the feuding between assorted clans in Japan stopped, and mon were taken up by the emerging and powerful merchant class, various associations, and trade groups. Slowly, mon became democratized during this time, with the general populace adopting them to signify family association for both private and public use. Mon were integrated into signage designs such as *kanban* (carved and painted wooden business signs), on *noren* (decorative curtains hung in front of businesses to signify that they were open), used as logos for businesses, and utilized by civic groups such as fire companies. Often, mon were designed by individual merchants period for their businesses and families.

Mon are integrated into the design of kimono as a standalone element, in a group of three for semi-formal occasions, and in a group of five for formal occasions such as weddings or funerals. In contemporary times, mon are utilized by corporations as logos (e.g., Mitsubishi) and are emblazoned on the covers of Japanese passports in the form of a sixteen-petal chrysanthemum which signifies the Japanese emperor.

The reductive graphic and widespread communicative qualities of mon are an essential part of Japan's visual DNA, transmitting tradition and identity, both concretely and abstractly.

PICTORIAL ART: UKIYO-E 浮世絵

The development of pictorial art was a major influence on graphic design in Japan. The legacy of painting in Japan has traversed numerous schools and movements—from colorful *Yamato-e* 大和絵 decorative painting on temple walls to the *e-maki* 絵巻 scroll paintings of the 1100s and 1200s, depicting famous literature such as the *Tale of Genji* 源氏物語. During the Muromachi era (1338–1573), the influence of Chinese paintings became prevalent, with Japanese painting shifting to largely monochromatic works often executed with an economy of visual form. In the turbulent Azuchi-Momoyama period of 1573 to 1603, the shogunate-supported Kanō School of painters worked with gold leaf, paint, and ink to master approaches to decorating screen doors with sacred and heavenly subject matter in the various castles and residencies of the ruling class.

The Ēdo period, lasting from 1603 to 1868, saw continued refinement in Chinese-inspired *nanga* 南画 and *bunjinga* 文人画 painting. *Ukiyo-e* 浮世絵 painting and printmaking came to the fore among the merchant and working classes whose numbers were growing rapidly in Ēdo. Ukiyo-e is the name of the genre, dominated by a flattened depth of field, with artists highlighting

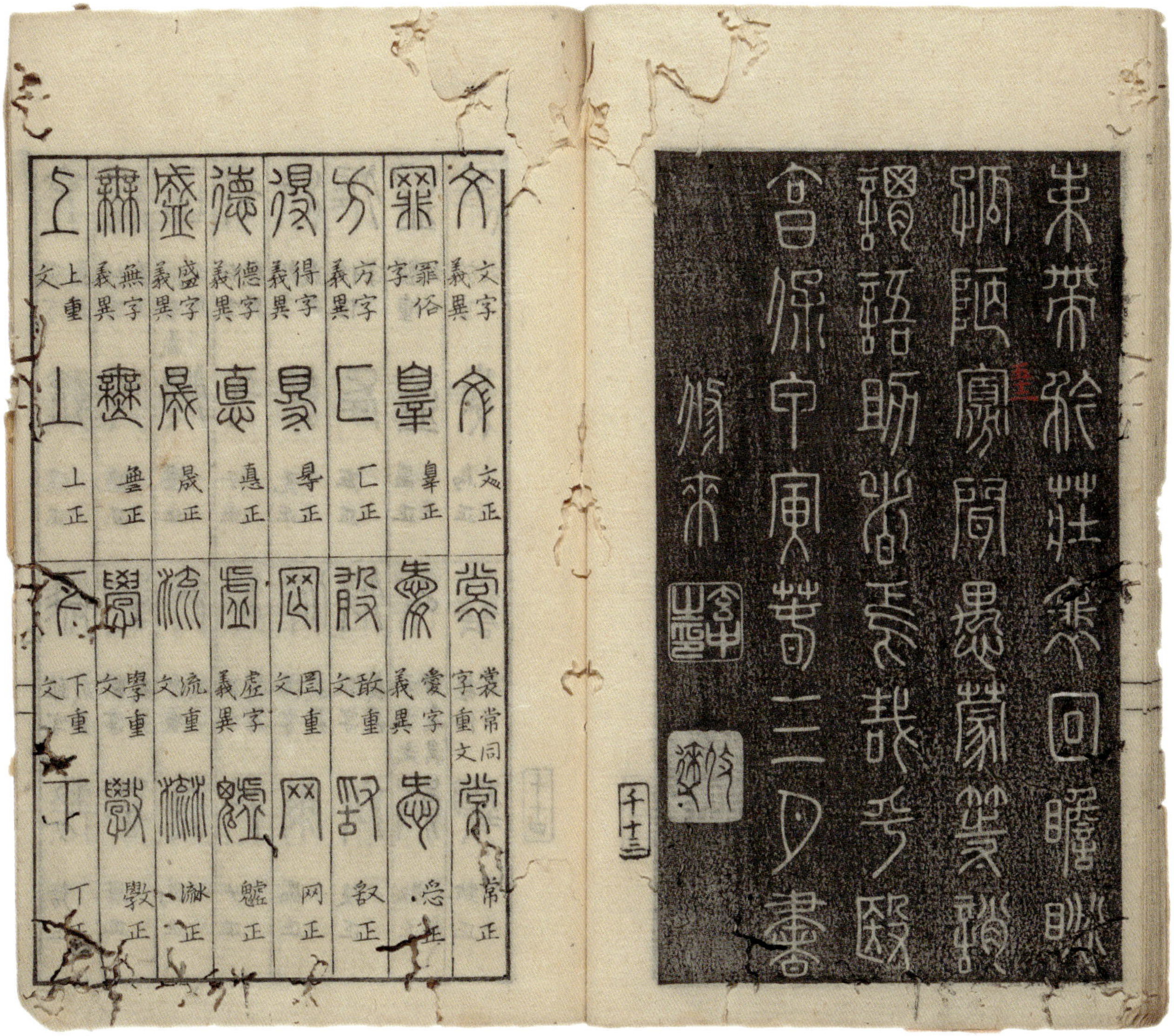

An example of tensho 篆書 script in ***Tensho Senjimon* 篆書千字文**, Tsujimoto Shiyu 辻本史邑 (Osaka: Shinshindoshuppan 駸々堂出版, 1934).

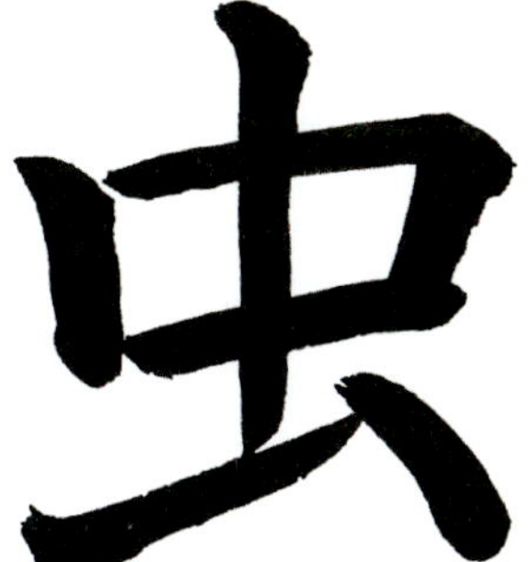

kaisho 楷書 script

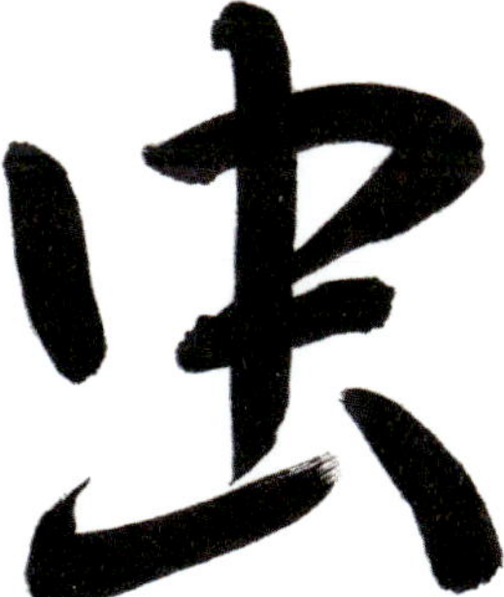

gyōsho 行書 script

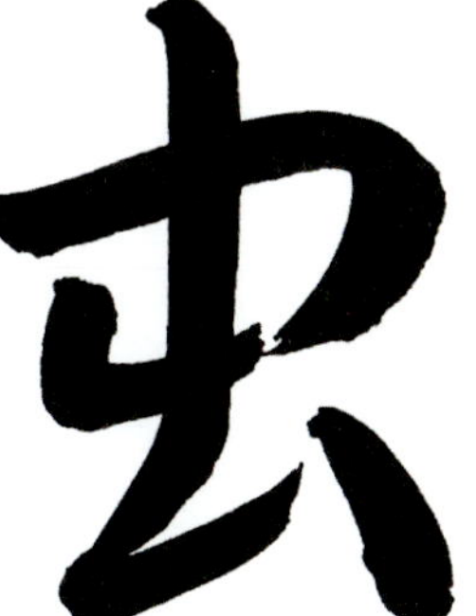

sōsho 草書 script

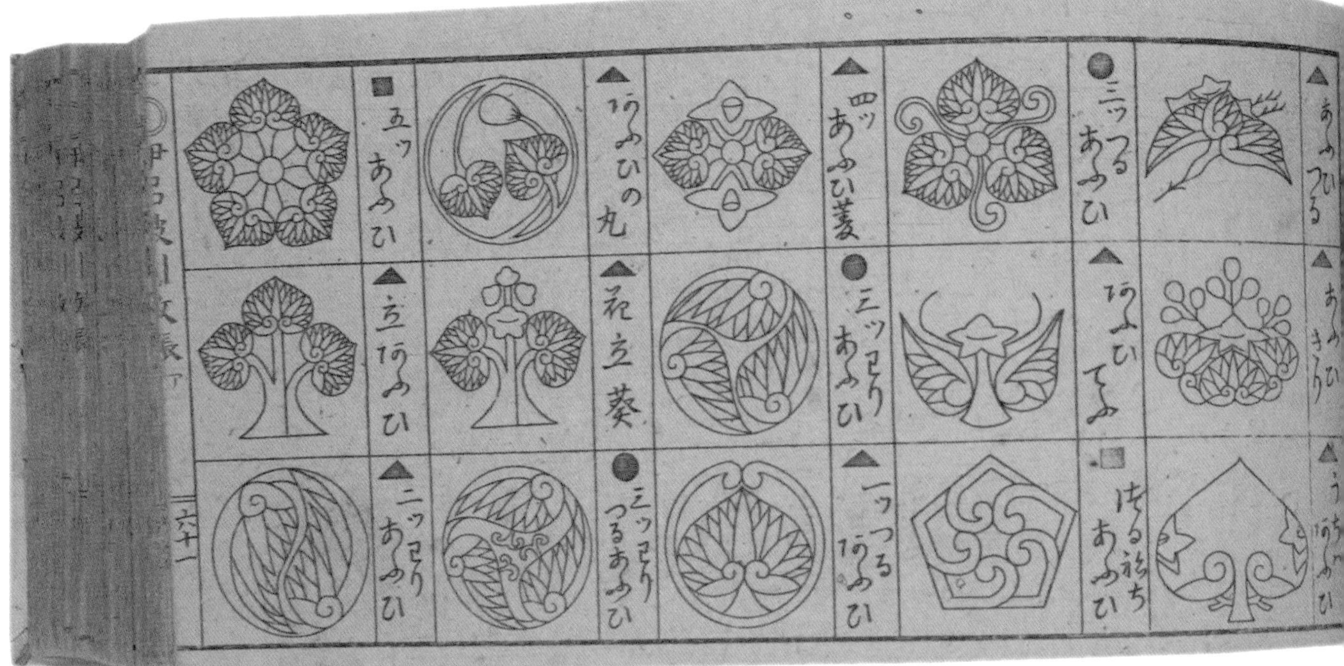

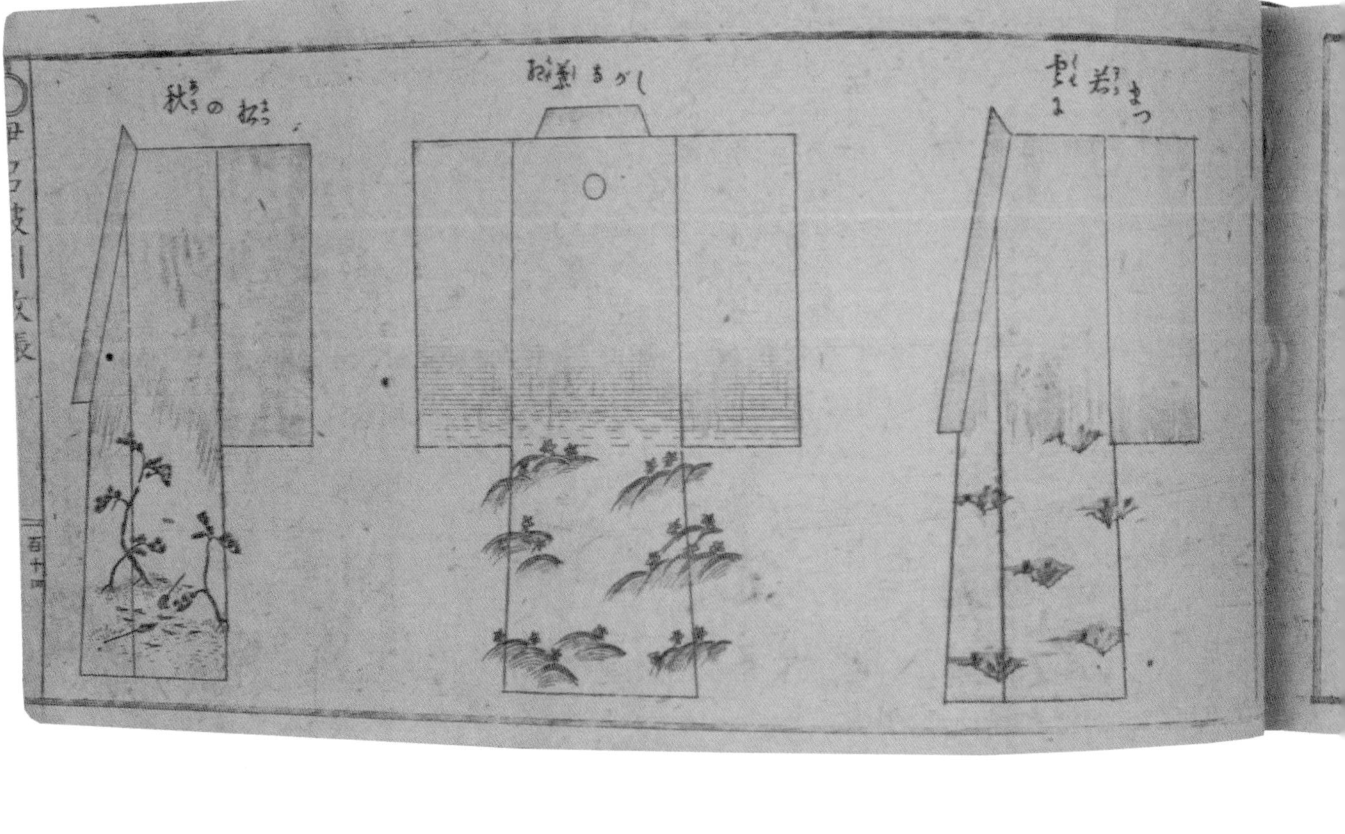

Untitled Seal Print Collection, circa 1890s.
A collection of kamon family seal designs, associated ornamentation, and application to kimono and assorted accoutrements.

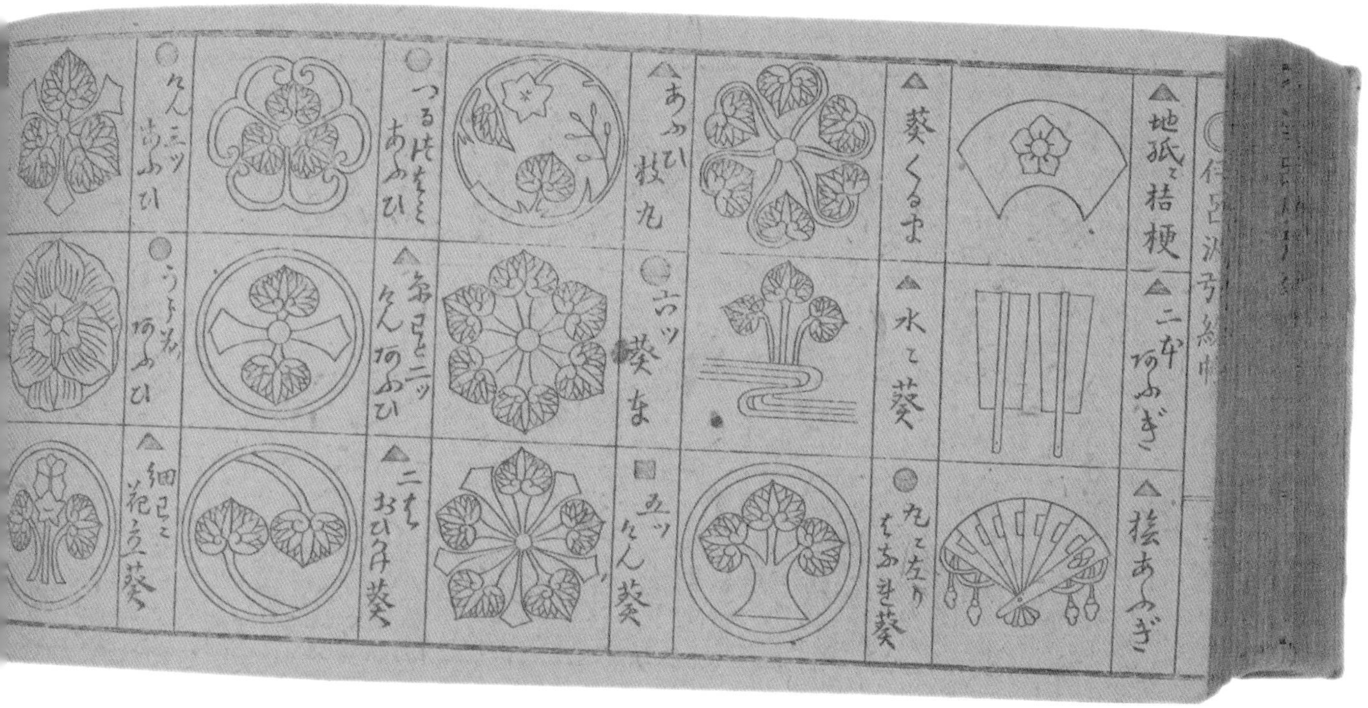

伊呂波引紋帳

△地紙に桔梗
△二本あふぎ
△桧あふぎ
△葵くるま
△水に葵
●丸に左りたち葵
△あふひ枝丸
●六ツ葵くるま
■五ツくん葵
●つる付きとあふひ
△糸巻に二ツくんあふひ
△二ちおひ丹葵
●くん三ツあふひ
●うら葵あふひ
△細丸に花立葵

伊呂波引紋帳

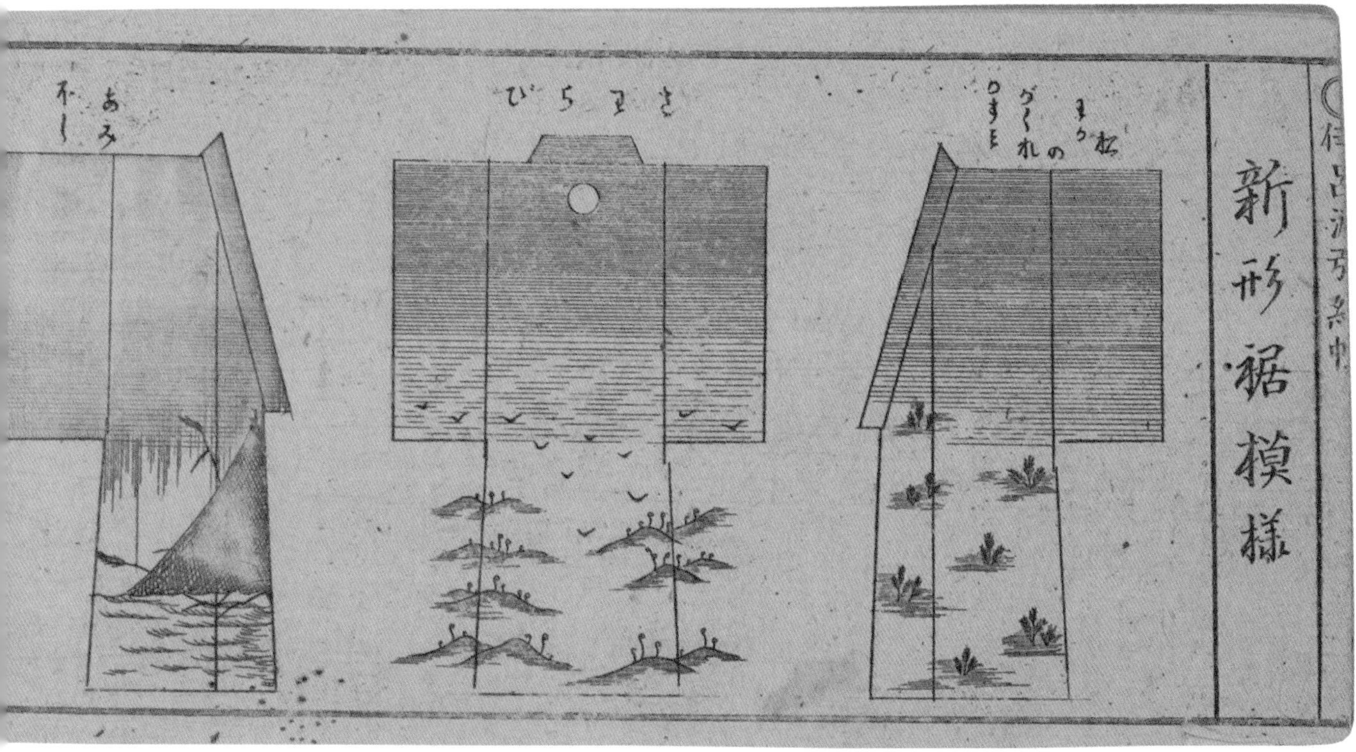

新形裾模様

松のむらくれかすみ

さまちび

あみ干し

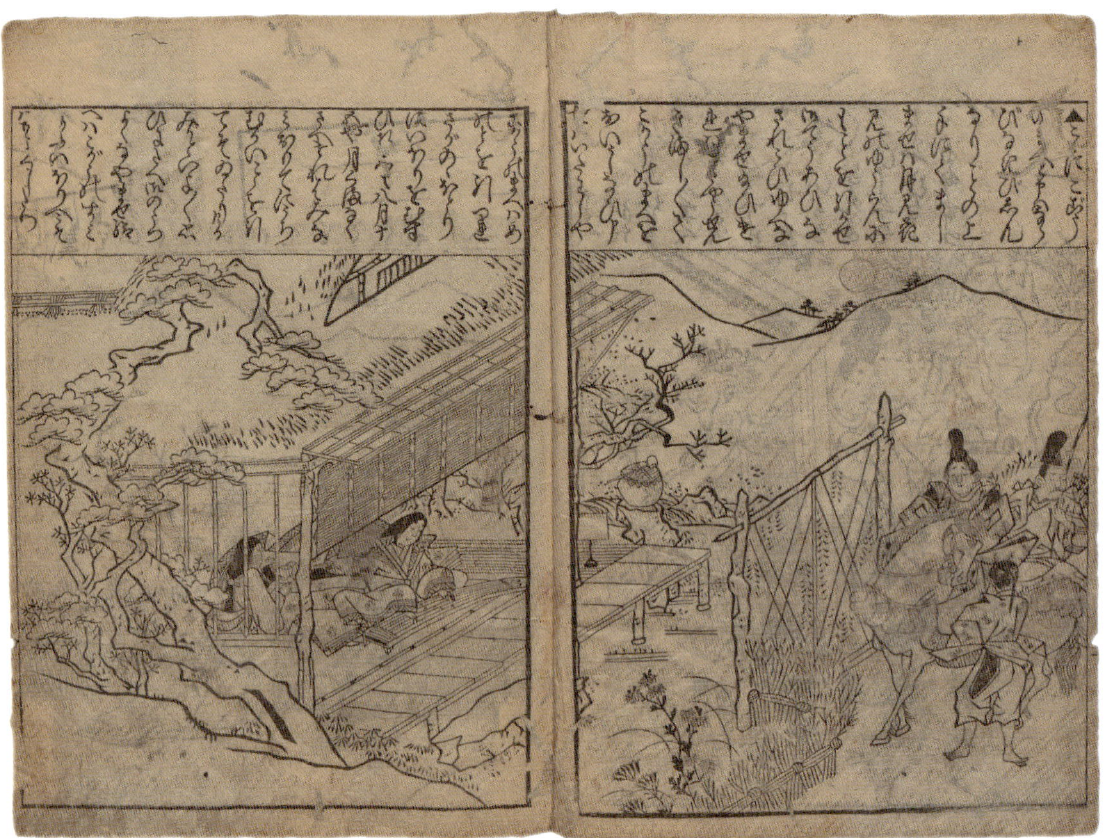

***Yamato-e zukushi* 大和絵つくし** (Compendium of Yamato-e Painting Themes), 1686, courtesy of The Metropolitan Museum of Art, The Howard Mansfield Collection. An example of the tight integration of text and illustration made possible using woodblock printing.

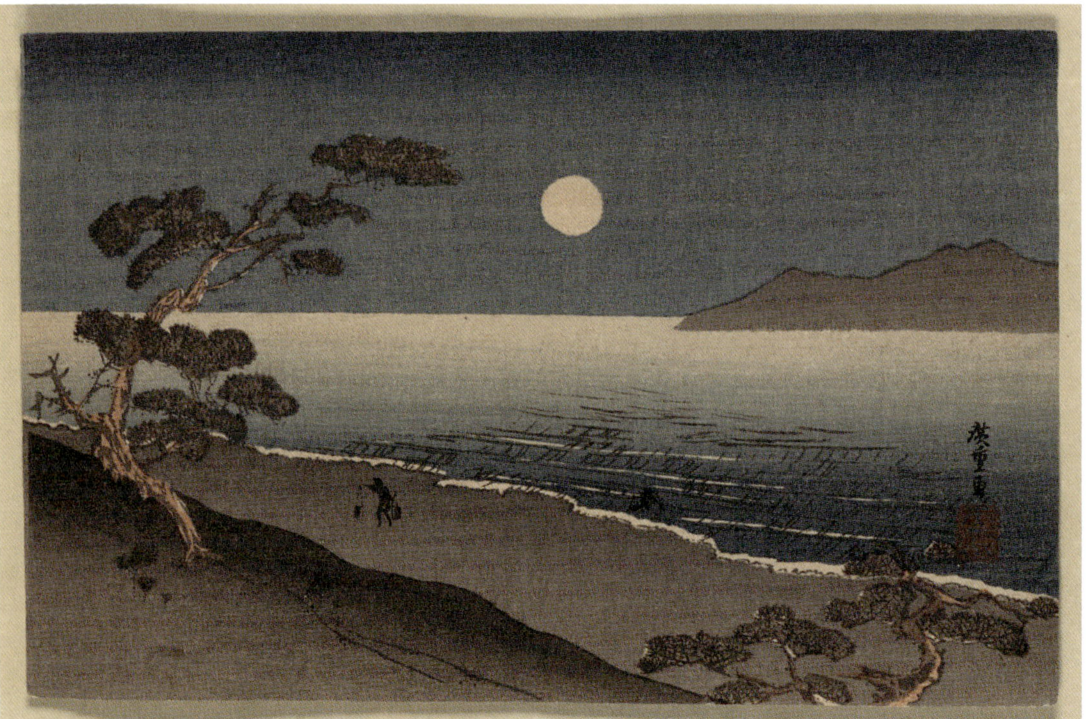

A fairy moon and a lonely shore, Utagawa Hiroshige 歌川広重 (Tokyo: Matsumoto Do, 1910), , courtesy of US Library of Congress. A stunning specimen of ukiyo-e that utilized multiple instances of *bokashi* ぼかし gradated printing, one of the primary visual tropes of ukiyo-e.

the foreground and extreme background only. By removing the middle ground, ukiyo-e expressed a foreshortened sense of perspective as exemplified in the works of Katsushika Hokusai 葛飾北斎, Utagawa Hiroshige 歌川広重, and Kitagawa Utamaro 喜多川歌麿. Ukiyo-e prints were widely disseminated globally before and after the Meiji Restoration of 1868. Depictions of life in the 'floating world' (*ukiyo* 浮世) of urban pleasure quarters, erotica (*shunga* 春画), travel prints, and landscapes were fraught with social commentary. Additionally, depictions of beautiful women, scenes and actors from popular kabuki plays, sports such as sumo wrestling, flora and fauna, folktales, and scenes from historical legend dominated ukiyo-e printmaking. In short, the subject matter reflected the worldly concerns and lives of the clientele purchasing them, as opposed to prior painting forms.

Created using a division of labor between artists, woodblock carvers, printers, and publishers, ukiyo-e were incredibly popular. Rather than using a press, works were printed by hand using a baren—a disc-shaped object made from hand-woven cord wrapped in lacquered paper and a bamboo leaf—to press handmade mulberry sheets of paper onto a printing surface. Printers were able to achieve dazzling multicolor shading and tonal effects. Many created gradations of color known as *bokashi* ぼかし, which became one of the most popular and enduring aspects of the ukiyo-e aesthetic. With the mass export of ukiyo-e in the Meiji period, the influence of these prints echoed widely in Europe, with Japonisme inspiring European artists from the Post-Impressionists, the Vienna Secession, and the Arts and Crafts Movement. Art Nouveau artists adopted and iterated the "whiplash line" prevalent in much ukiyo-e—a sinuous, dynamic motif of linework that intimates motion as much as the forms of plants. The European adaptation of Japanese aesthetics would return to Japan through the prints of British illustrator Aubrey Beardsley, France's Edgar Degas, and Paris-based Czech painter and illustrator Alphonse Mucha, to be reinterpreted by later Japanese designers such as Sugiura Hisui 杉浦非水 and Yamana Ayao 山名文夫 in the early twentieth century.

With the Meiji Restoration and the subsequent reopening of Japan to international trade, there was a rush to incorporate western approaches to painting, yet simultaneously this led to the formation of schools which would teach traditional Japanese themes, techniques, and approaches to art-making, as well. This tension led to the creation of the terms *nihonga* 日本画 for Neo Traditional Japanese painting and *yōga* 洋画 for Western painting. It is precisely at the time of this aesthetic and etymological split that early forms of Japanese graphic design, then called *zuan* 図案, emerged.

COLOR & PATTERN: CHIYOGAMI & KIMONO 着物と千代紙

The primary objective of kimono's appearance is the expression of the surface design. Though they are often confused for "traditional" dress, the history of kimono is actually one of fashion—to this day, there is a giant kimono industry in Japan releasing the very latest designs. Throughout the evolution of kimono, the focus has been on the shape and pattern of the kimono itself, not upon the wearer, a reversal of Western norms regarding attire.

Kimono were known prior to 1868 as *kosode* 小袖, garments with arm openings just large enough to allow one's hands to pass through (though incorporated sleeve pockets that gave the appearance of wider sleeves). They evolved into *ōsode* 大袖, the more familiar garment with wide arm-holes, and it was in the Ēdo period that the widespread adoption of the term "kimono" or "thing that is worn" was popularized. Kimono have not changed greatly in cut since the Ēdo period but have instead changed to reflect trends through materials, dyeing, pattern, and applied form and imagery.

The Ēdo period saw an explosion of sartorial expression through the woven, dyed, embroidered, and embellished kimono. These were the culmination of centuries of exploration of materials including silk, crepe, hemp, and cotton, and of natural dyeing using a dizzying array of resist techniques including stencil dyeing, freehand dyeing, and the use of clamping, sewing, and tying cloths prior to dye immersion to affect the distribution of dyes. Kimono reached new heights under Miyazaki Yūzensai 宮崎友禅斎, a kimono surface pattern designer and painter after whom a whole form of kimono decoration techniques is named today. Previously employed as a painter of decorative fans, Yūzen provided his clientele with both the surface decoration and the overall design of the kimono he worked on.

In the Ēdo period, kimono pattern designs for men and women tended to be quite similar, but by the end of the seventeenth century, the previously dominant geometric, even patterning gave way to graphic disruptions, and in the case of a form of kimono known as *chōnin* 町人, the graphic elements tended to pool at kimono's hems in lieu of even distribution. Motifs

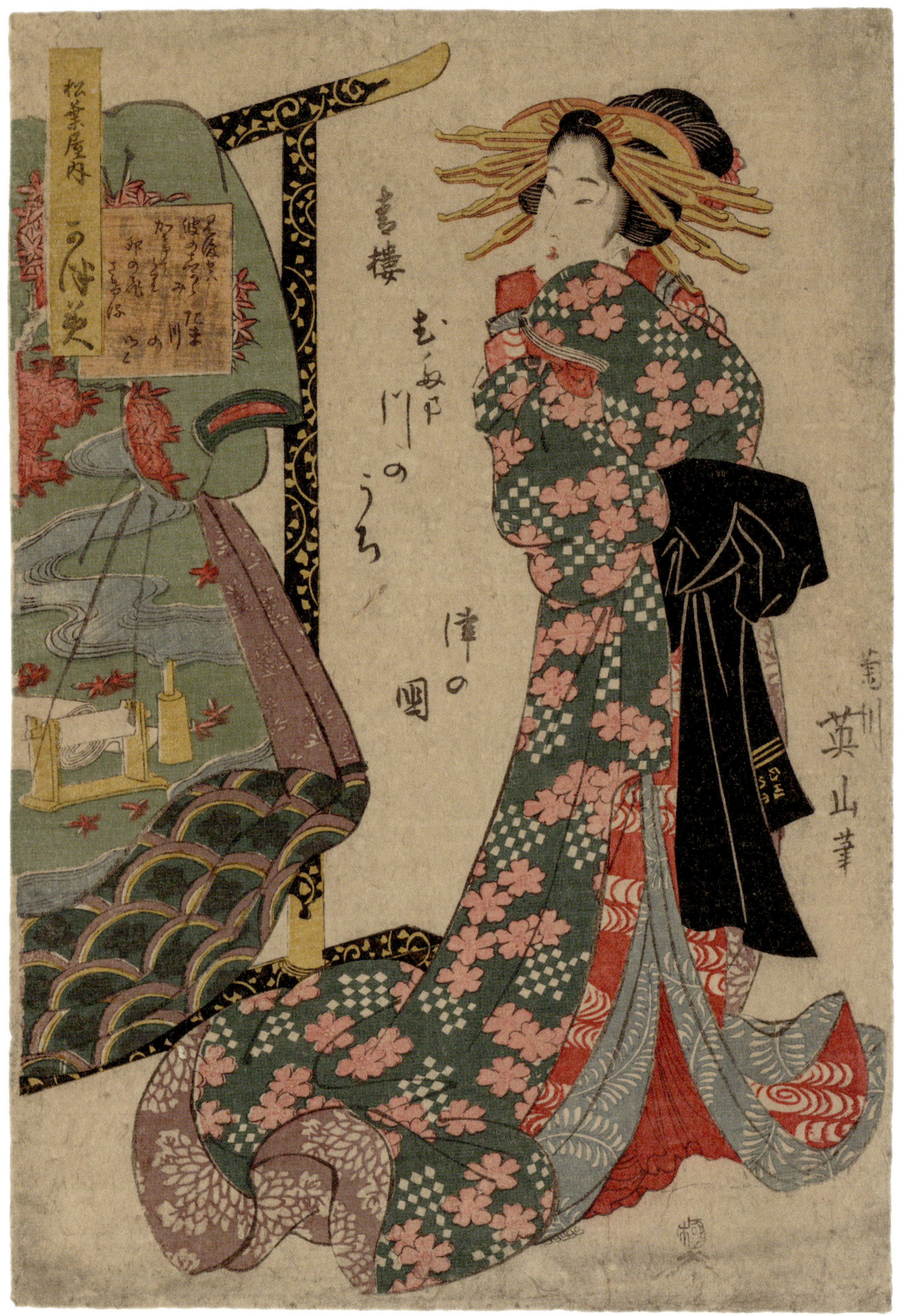

Courtesan Beside Kimono Rack, Kikugawa Eizan 菊川英山, 1787, courtesy of Cleveland Museum of Art. An ukiyo-e print that showcases multiple kimono designs. A fact little known outside of Japan is that kimono cannot be washed (traditionally, underlayers are worn to protect kimono from the wearer's sweat) and must be aired instead, as washing would distort the warp and weft of the garment.

for kimono pulled strongly from nature, calligraphy, designed objects, and abstract patterning. Ordered kimono were delivered in lavish patterned *furoshiki* 風呂敷 fabric wrappings, and kimono fabricators such as Daimaru (today a department store chain) produced pattern books for consumers to peruse the latest fashions.

The Ēdo period also saw a shift in economic power from the higher shogun class to the merchant class. Merchants would periodically be chastised by the ruling daimyō lords for flaunting their wealth through opulent dress. Punishments for daring to challenge the imposed class/caste structure involved the occasional confiscation of merchants' holdings and property. The offending sartorial displays of the merchant class included wearing fabrics more sumptuous than the daimyō, but also the display of dazzling colors such as *beni*-red, a highly expensive pigment derived from safflowers. In turn, the merchant class opted for non-offensive fabric colors such as blue and white. Yet, when the shogunate published edicts regarding dress, they made no mention of undergarments, so women made haste in adopting red for collar linings and undergarment linings—the deployment of which made for public insinuations of danger and resistance, but just as much allure.

Appearing during the Ēdo period, chiyogami are patterned papers influenced by the pattern of kimono fabrics. Used for interior decoration, candy wrappers, and paper crafts such as origami, pochibukuro envelopes, and other forms of stationery, chiyogami is another ancestor of Japanese graphic design in the form of printmaking. The patterns used in the production of classic chiyogami were often inspired by kimono surface designs, through which a rich, deep history has developed.

The surface designs on kimono and the resultant chiyogami are essential aspects of Japanese aesthetics, and they have been reflected in graphic design artifacts since the Meiji Restoration. From the endpapers of books to wrapping paper to posters, the influence of kimono patterns and graphics echoes throughout Japan's print culture.

A CULMINATION & AN ERASURE

The extant development of each of these forms of graphic expression formed the foundations of Japanese aesthetics, and with the opening of Japan to the world, these aesthetics became aspects of culture which the denizens of Japan would define themselves both with and against. The history of Japanese graphic design, as elsewhere, has its roots in the cradle of traditional craft forms and how they were perceived both domestically and globally.

Simultaneously, the decorative traditions of the Ainu, Japan's indigenous population, were largely scrubbed from Japanese culture and excluded from the visual lexicon representing Japanese national identity. In 1899, the Hokkaido Former Aborigine Protection Laws were enacted, calling for the Ainu to assimilate into Japanese culture. The Ainu people were forbidden from speaking their native language, were forced to adopt Japanese names, and were discouraged from expressions of Ainu cultural identity, visual and otherwise. It was not until 1997 that a Japanese court acknowledged the cultural rights of the Ainu, and the Ainu were not legally designated as indigenous peoples of Japan until 2008. The colors, patterns, and forms that are the output of Ainu culture are an intrinsic part of Japanese visual history that have been largely isolated and exotified as "non-Japanese" until very recently in history. Ainu aesthetics include a vast array of visual attributes that are singular in nature, especially the wholly abstract whorl-ornamented surface designs of Ainu robes and clothing.

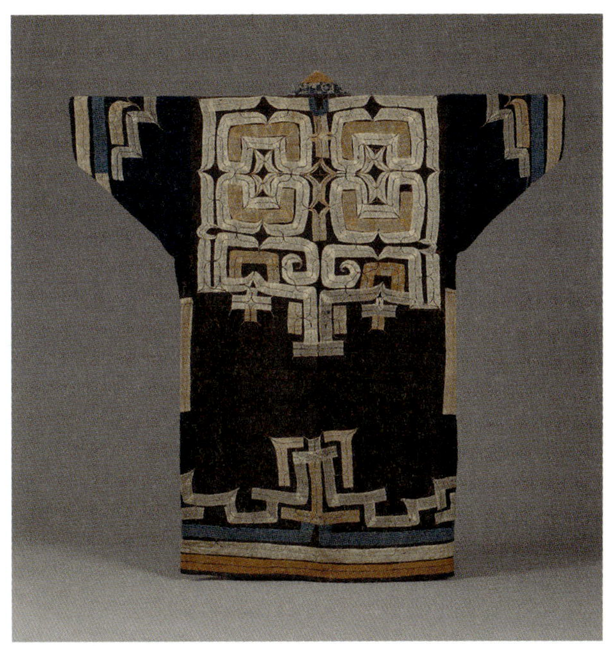

Traditional Ainu cotton garment displaying deceptively asymmetric Ainu ornamentation. Image courtesy of Shoto Museum of Art.

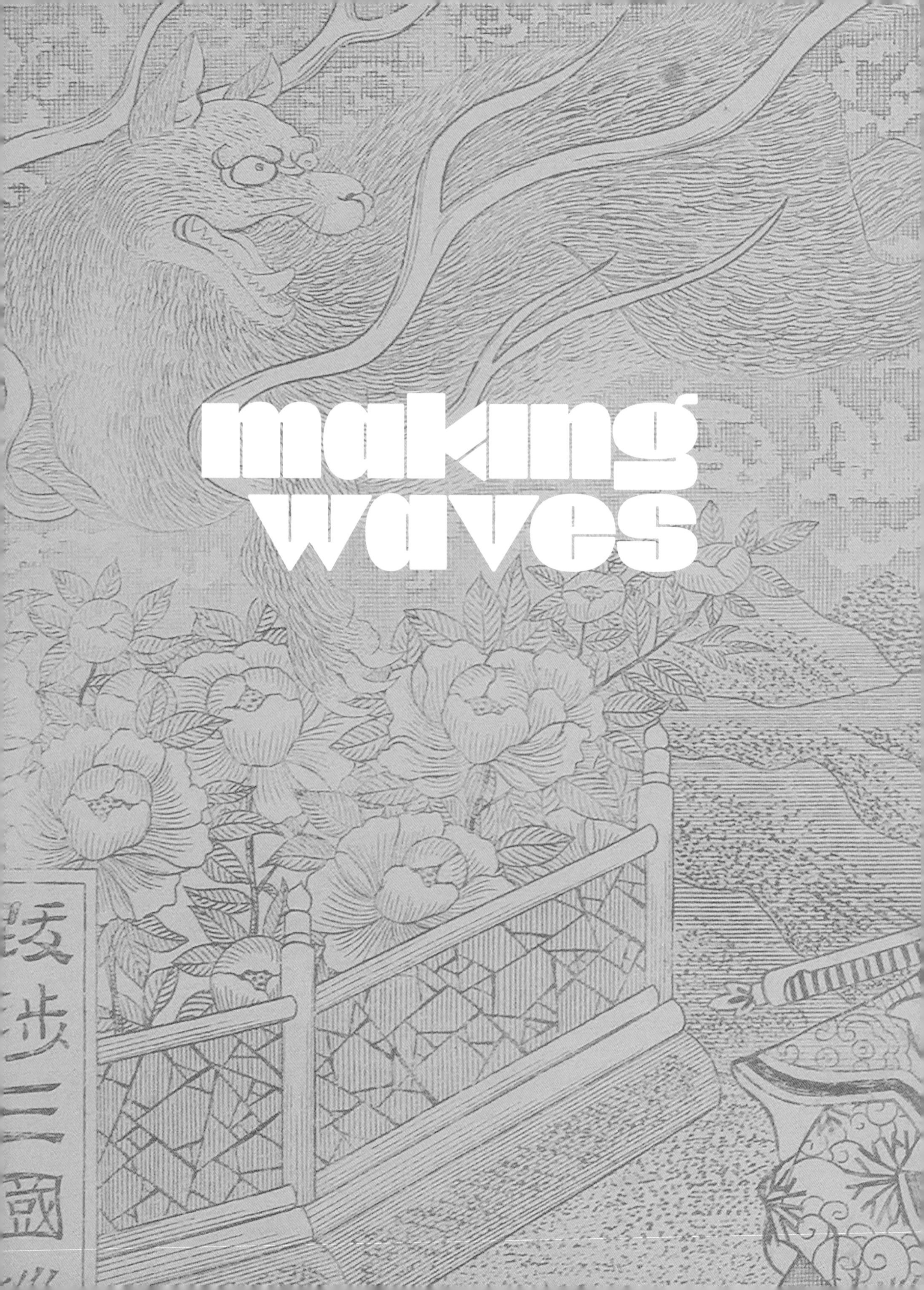
making
waves

Making Waves: The Establishment of Japanese Graphic Design

ONCE UPON A TIME

What is Japanese graphic design, and how did it come into its full form? What defines it other than a specific geographic locale? How did it develop locally, as well as in conjunction with other forms of graphic design globally?

Perhaps the best initial step is to try to define what graphic design *itself* is.

Many people have tried to define graphic design over the years and have settled on some conventions throughout the world. At its most rudimentary, one can define graphic design as visual communication created in multiples or in media for mass audiences. Going a bit further, graphic design is a sector of cultural production in which conceptual and thematic thinking drive the synthesis of visual form and typography in an applied setting. The output of graphic design results in media which are disseminated in multiples or in broadcast form. Furthermore, graphic design embodies a *mass* communicative function.

Japanese graphic design is this range of activities and processes as they developed in the nation of Japan. Modern Japanese graphic design is often defined as graphic design starting after the Meiji Restoration through the mid-to-late 1970s. Japanese graphic design from the 1920s through the early 1960s tended to be more direct than the preceding traditional Japanese graphic craft forms, used systematic approaches to composition, and clearly integrated form and content.

There was often an insistence upon contrast, planned visual hierarchy, and typographic continuity. These characteristics are shared with the development of European and North American Modern graphic design. In large part, this is due to intercultural exchange between Europe, Russia, the Americas, and Japan that has occurred since the Meiji Restoration of 1868.

EARLY TYPOGRAPHY IN JAPAN

Japan has a long history of both printing and movable typography—movable type was utilized by private presses from the early seventeenth century, was discarded when block printing was reestablished as the dominant medium in the 1650s, and then was adopted again in the nineteenth century.

Until the 1880s, the majority of books printed in Japan were block printed. To prepare a block for printing, a handwritten manuscript (often but not always made by a specialist calligrapher) was adhered to a wooden block, and the areas not containing writing were carved away by hand. In this way, the gesture of original handwriting was preserved in printed materials in lieu of the standardized aesthetic of movable typographic design.

The first movable type in the world was ceramic type made in China in the tenth century. The Chinese would adopt wooden movable type later, but not en masse. These examples, along with Korea's initial forays into metal movable type in the early thirteenth century, preceded Gutenberg's investigations into movable type by several decades. The Korean Court created their official Printing Office in 1392, first printing with metal type and later with indigenous wooden type.

The first record of movable type brought to Japan was in 1590, when the Italian Jesuit missionary Alessandro Valignani ordered the installation of the first European press in Nagasaki to create Christian reading materials locally. The press was brought to Japan in 1590 by a group known as Tenshō Embassy 天正の使節, which had been sent by the Christian daimyō Ōtomo Sōrin 大友宗麟 to the Pope and the kings of Europe in 1582. The group comprised the Portuguese missionary Diogo de Mesquita alongside four young Japanese missionaries from the Christian daimyō of Kyushu and Ōmura: Nakaura Julião 中浦ジュリアン, Chijiwa Miguel 千々石ミゲル, Hara Martino 原マルチノ, and their leader, Itō Mancio 伊東マンショ. The missionaries were accompanied by a young Japanese Christian man named Constantino Dourado コンスタンチノドラード who served as their assistant. Dourado trained in the printing arts in Lisbon in 1586, after the group acquired the press and type founding equipment.[1]

During their eight years abroad, the missionaries wrote Japanese translations of the work of ascetic friar Luis de Granada and presented their works to de Granada in person while in Europe. Upon their return, they created a set of matrices to produce katakana typefaces in three sizes, later adding hiragana and kanji types. The Jesuits conducted the typesetting, printing approximately forty works, though few survive today. They printed a number of Japanese-language books devoted to the biographies of Christian figures, alongside Luis de Granada's *Libro de Fide* and the *Guia de Pecadores* and

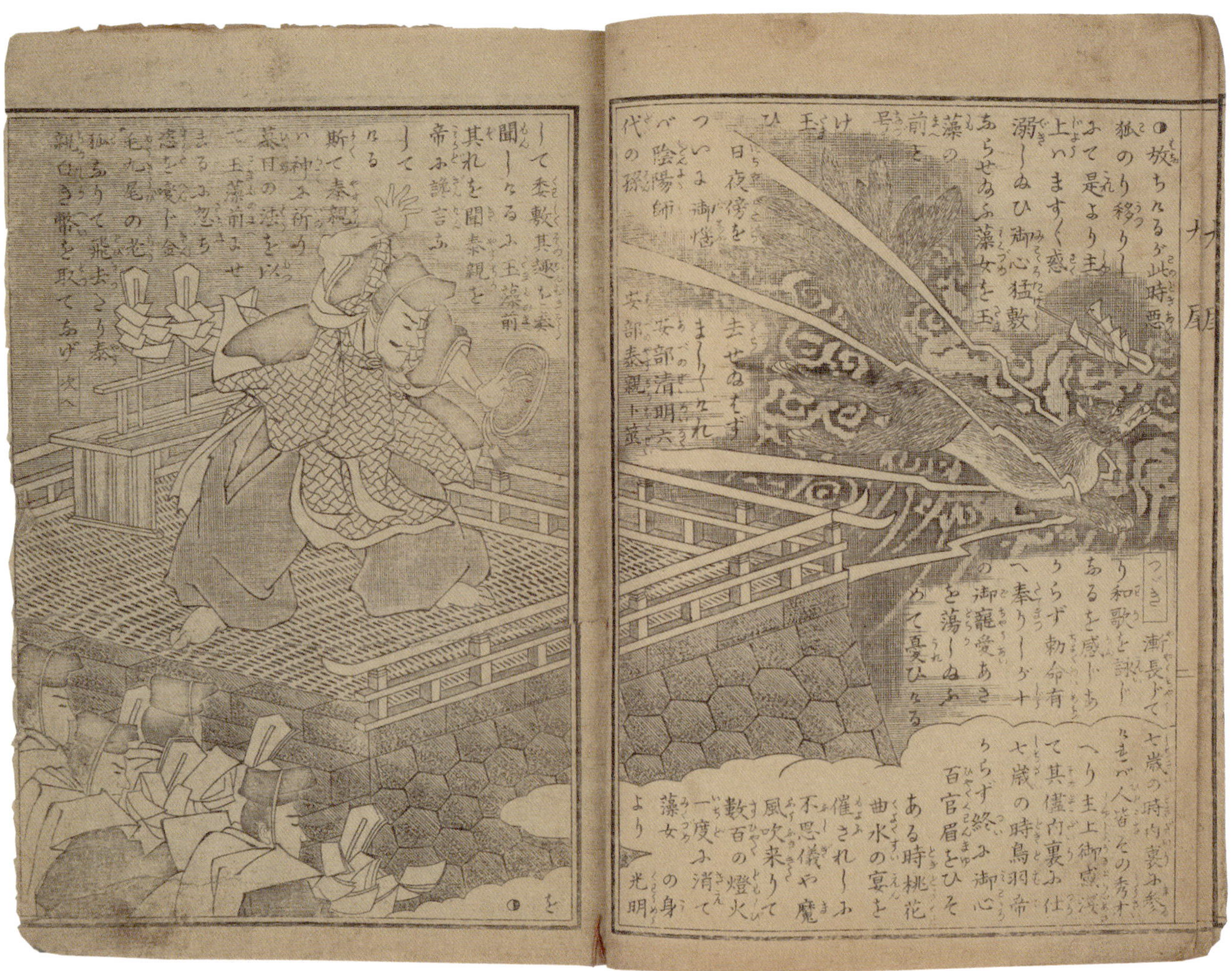

Picture Book Three of the Nine Tailed Story 絵本三国九尾傳,
Kichibei Tsutsumi 堤吉兵衛, Tokyo: Hoeidō 保永堂版, 1893.
Illustrated storybook.

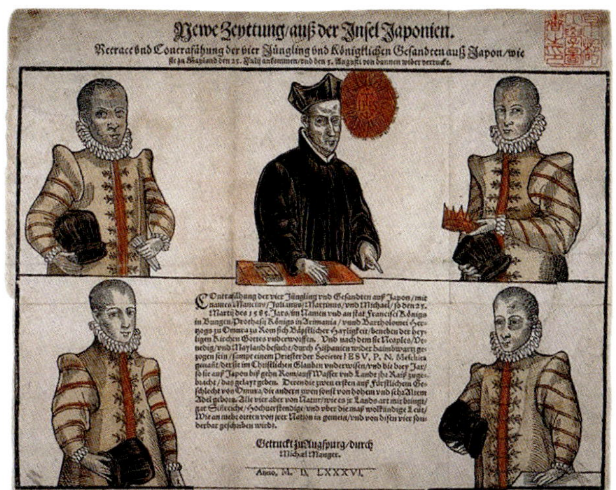

Newe Zeyttung/auß der Insel Japonien.

Retract vnd Conterafähung der vier Jüngling vnd Königlichen Gesandten auß Japon/wie sie zu Mayland den 25. Julij ankommen/vnd den 3. Augusti von dannen wider verruckt.

Getruckt zu Augspurg/durch Michael Manger.

Anno, M. D. LXXXVI.

Newe Zeyttung, a German proto-newspaper describing the Japanese "embassy" organized by the Society of Jesus. The Japanese members were carefully selected sons of Japanese noblemen: (top, from left to right) Julião Nakaura, Father Mesquita, Mancio Ito; (bottom) Martinão Hara, Miguel Chijiwa. This paper was printed in Augsburg, Germany, in 1586, shortly after the embassy stayed in Milano. The highlight of their journey through Catholic Europe was an audience in Rome. This copy is kept by Kyōto University.

Thomas à Kempis's *The Imitation of Christ* or *Contempus Mundi*. The Jesuits also printed excerpts from *The Tale of Heike*, the first known example of Japanese literature being offered using Japanese typography. Valignani wrote in a 1595 letter that the Jesuits had printed a Japanese dictionary containing over 32,000 terms.

It is estimated that approximately one hundred *kirishtan-ban* キリシタン版 (Christian books) were produced by the press, but as of 1990, only thirty-one have been identified. Each used a mix of *romaji* (Latin characters) in upright roman and sloped italic; squared, cursive, and semi-cursive kanji; and hiragana, from 1585 to 1605 in black ink, and from 1605 onward in red and black inks. The books explored Christian literature of that age, intercultural exchange, interfaith exchange, and a history of education.

The Jesuit press would not be long-lasting, however. The shogunate demanded that the missionaries leave its Nagasaki fiefdom. Hara Martino took the press with him to Macau in exile in 1614 and continued printing Christian works in Japanese.

When the *samurai* and *daimyō* lord Toyotomi Hideyoshi 豊臣秀吉 ordered an invasion of the Korean Peninsula from 1592 through 1598, one of the looted treasures from two excursions was a Korean printing press and set of type which was given to the then-emperor Go-Yōzei 後陽成天皇.

The Korean Dynasty had a lengthy prior history of creating movable type. Korea's first typecasting operation was initiated in 1403, and the result was the Kyemicha, Korea's first metal type based on the calligraphic models of the Sung Dynasty. The Kyemicha was in use until Sejong—the fourth King of the Korean dynasty and leader of the development of Hangul, the indigenous Korean visual language—ordered that Kyonsucha and the more developed Kabincha types be created to help standardize Korean typesetting. Initially, 200,000 pieces were cast, with multiple re-castings over the following decades, and they were used to print official government publications distributed throughout the Korean peninsula.

The Korean-acquired press was used to print the *Xiao Jing*, or *Classic of Filial Piety*, in Japan. In Peter Kornicki's masterpiece, *The Book in Japan*, he writes that, "In 1597, in the postface to another work printed in Japan with movable type, a monk who was present at Hideyoshi's headquarters

1 Diego Pacheco, "Diogo De Mesquita, S. J. and the Jesuit Mission Press," *Monumenta Nipponica* 26, no. 3/4 (1971): 431. https://doi.org/10.2307/2383655.

acknowledged that typography in Japan had come from Korea." For five decades, movable type was used widely in Japan for book printing alongside block-printed books, just as was occurring simultaneously in Korea.

The production of movable type was encouraged by those in power, notably the shogun Tokugawa Ieyasu 徳川家康. Tokugawa ordered the carving of 100,000 characters of wooden type, which were used to print a number of books in the Kyoto region. Additionally, Tokugawa called upon the expertise of Lin Gokan / Lin Wuguan (historical records differ), a Chinese man who arrived in Japan via a shipwreck, for the casting of copper type. Using sand-based molds informed by extant Korean casting methods, Lin created the type that would become known as Suruga-ban 駿河版.

Printing with movable type was limited to the realm of temples, for the production of Buddhist texts, and of politicians, for the production of secular texts. Until the 1620s, primarily Chinese texts were produced, but in that decade the tide shifted and more Japanese publications—notably Japanese classical texts—were released.

Some private presses using movable type were established in the 1600s, including the joint press operated by the calligrapher Hon'ami Koetsu 本阿弥光悦 and the intellectual Suminokura Soan 角倉素庵 in the Saga region of Kyoto. Known as Sagabon 嵯峨本 (Books from Saga), Koetsu and Soan contributed to the proliferation of Japanese literature at that time, though their print runs were limited. Koetsu was a master calligrapher whose writing was informed by the court of the Heian Period. The type produced by the press was most likely derived from his handwriting. As each character was carved separately, there are variations in the orthography that appealed to readers at the time, as the type mimicked the output of the human hand. The press released books such as the *Ise Monogatari* 伊勢物語 (*The Tales of Ise*), a collection of *waka* 和歌 poems and associated narratives that was originally written in the eighth century.

Movable type all but disappeared by the end of the 1650s. Reprinting was incredibly important, and being able to print new editions at will according to market demands made block-printing overtake movable type until the late eighteenth century. Blocks could be pulled out of storage, inked, and printed, whereas type had to be composed from scratch for reprints, as the high number of Japanese characters required that typesetters reuse characters for different projects.

Another advantage to woodblock composition is that the margins in vertically typeset Japanese often contain *kunten* 訓点: circular, square, triangular, and derivative marks which are used to suggest the pronunciation and meaning of lesser-known characters. Kunten were far easier to hand-write and carve than typeset, and they were especially difficult to typeset with movable type. Woodblock-printed books often featured an intense integration of the pictorial and the typographic, and it took many years after the popularization of movable type for Japanese books to approximate this synthesis of form and text.

While the amount of printed matter using typography dwindled, movable type didn't completely die out—a smattering of calendar and book projects were printed using movable type throughout the 1700s and 1800s, primarily through certain Buddhist sects and academies affiliated with the ruling shogunate.

IMPORTS & EXPORTS

Beginning in the early 1600s, influences from abroad on aesthetics and printing technology slowed to a trickle following a series of shogunate edicts meant to control trade with foreign nations and minimize Christian influence. The Sakoku Edict of 1635 ordered that Japanese people were not allowed to leave Japan, and if any citizen managed to leave and somehow return, they would be immediately executed. The practice of Christianity was also outlawed in reaction to legitimate concerns over the opium wars and colonization sweeping through Asia. Trade with Japan was limited to the Dutch and Chinese in designated areas around Nagasaki, most notably the Dutch trading post on the artificial island of Dejima. Every aspect of Japanese interaction with foreigners on Dejima was intensely monitored and controlled from its establishment in 1641 until the island fell out of use as a trading post in the mid-1800s.

Japan remained culturally isolated for over 200 years and did not open to foreign trade or visitation until 1854. The previous year, the American Commodore Matthew Perry led an expedition to Japan and demonstrated the might of American firepower, demanding that Japan establish relations with the United States. The incursion led to a series of treaties opening Japan to foreign trade in the cities of Ēdo (Tokyo), Kobe, Nagasaki, Niigata, and Yokohama in 1859.

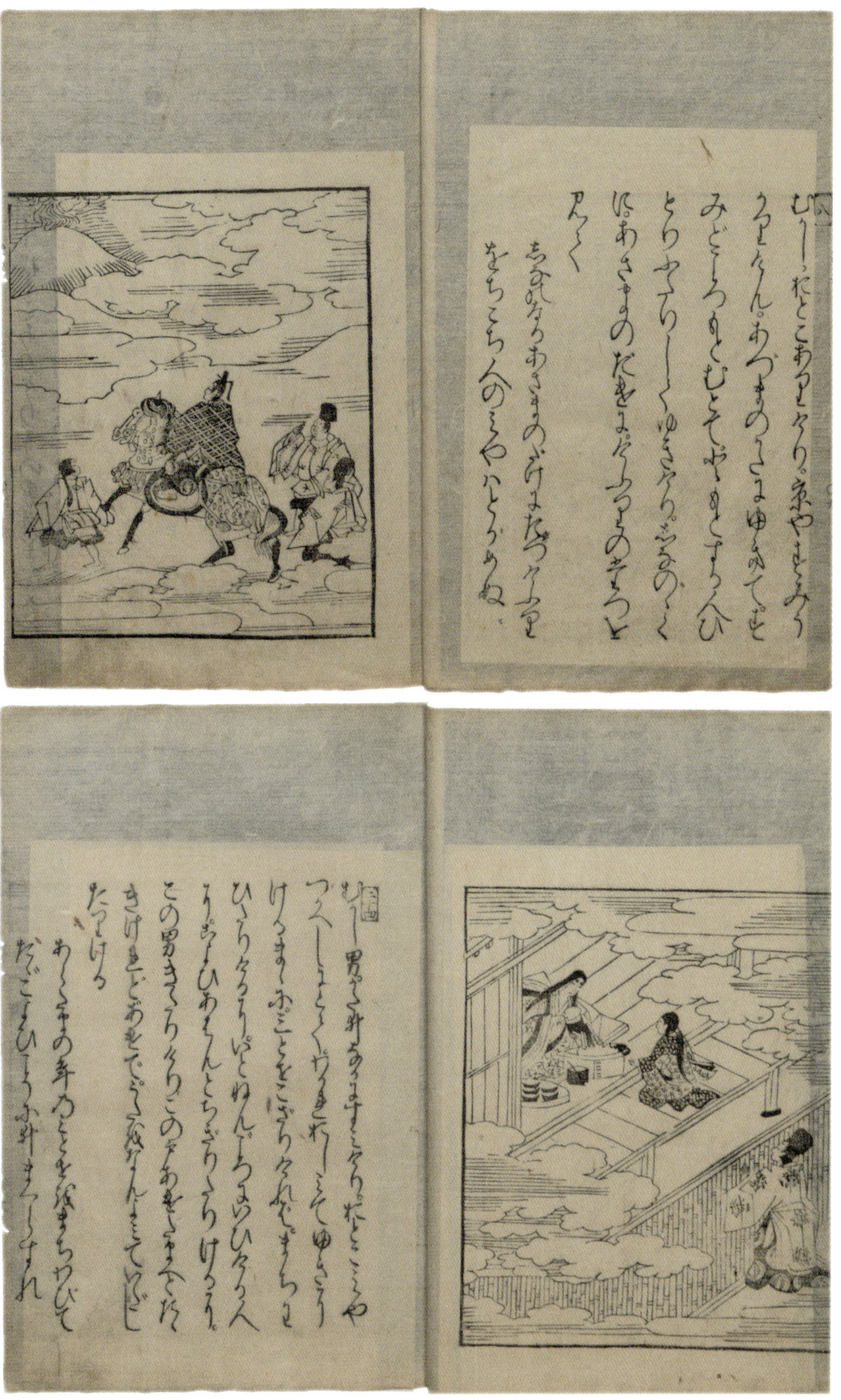

***Ise Monogatari* 伊勢物語, Suminokura Soan 角倉素庵, 1608.**
Courtesy of The Metropolitan Museum of Art, Rogers Fund. Despite having the appearance of running calligraphy, this book was printed with movable type.

Japan's opening to foreign trade was rocky for much of the 1860s, resulting in massive economic instability, inflation, and high unemployment. Economic woes were accompanied by the introduction of cholera by foreigner visitors and famine caused by poor crops, resulting in thousands of Japanese deaths. Anti-foreigner sentiment was strong, though the influence of foreign culture would prove to be a boon to the development of Japanese graphic design.

MODERN MOVABLE TYPE

After two centuries of woodblock printing's dominance, movable type made a resurgence in Japan with the introduction of new technologies from abroad. Motogi Shōzō 本木昌造, often called "Japan's Gutenberg," was born in 1824 and adopted by one of Nagasaki's last Dutch interpreter families. Versed in foreign studies and educated in chemistry and physics, Motogi had a long-standing relationship with metal. He studied at the Nagasaki Naval Center and later worked in the steel industry. His understanding of metallurgy was essential to his later interest in printing and typography.

In 1848 he and three translators, all employed by the shogunate, bought a "movable type and printing machine brought to Nagasaki aboard a Dutch vessel, and three or four years later they began producing cast lead movable type of their own for Japanese."[2] Their collective purchase included a Stanhope hand press and a case of Dutch-produced type. The quartet managed to cast a rough set of katakana type and produced a Japanese/Dutch dictionary called the *Ranwa Tsūben* 蘭和通弁 in 1851 and 1852.

Motogi was incredibly committed to typography and the creation and dissemination of printed matter, and this was evident to the Nagasaki government. The press was purchased by the Nagasaki city commissioner, and a printing office was established under Motogi's direction, giving Motogi the backing to print and disseminate new books at a time when Japan wanted to confront the specter of American colonization. The office acquired additional equipment from Holland between 1856 and 1859 and printed a number of books in Dutch on naval navigation, military science, medicine, and a host of other fields introducing theories from the West. These books were bound in the Western style and are considered the first modern books produced in Japan. Another press arrived in 1857 and a number of other publications were created, including an almanac, a printed version of the treaty between Japan and the Netherlands, military training manuals, and a few other works.

In 1869, Motogi dispatched an employee to the American Presbyterian Press in Shanghai, who noted the speed and capacity with which the press was able to produce Chinese type. This was largely due to the efforts of William Gamble, an Irish-American immigrant who had previously worked in publishing houses in Philadelphia and New York then moved to Shanghai. Gamble had been appointed as a missionary to China by the Presbyterian Church in the U.S. in 1858. The same year, he moved to Ningbo (then Ningpo), where he remained until 1862 operating the The American Presbyterian Mission Press. After moving the press to Shanghai, he supervised publishing work there for another seven years before deciding to return to the United States, right around the time that the individual in Motogi's employ encountered Gamble's contribution to Chinese type production.

Gamble developed sophisticated, labor-saving technologies to improve Chinese movable type casting and printing—systems that stood in opposition to traditional Western means of founding type. Then-state-of-the-art Western typeface production was predicated on punch-cutting and working wholly in metal from start to finish. Gamble's methods were radically different. First, a calligrapher would draw a character on soft poplar wood, and then a dedicated type cutter would carve the character out. The character would be pressed into wax, which was then coated with a layer of graphite in order to make it electrically conductive, and then a thin layer of copper was applied to create the matrix, or base, for the casting of actual type. Whereas Western type design involved punching and carving metal forms in order to produce the mold into which molten metal would be poured, Gamble's process involved carving characters directly out of wood, speeding up the methods of casting type immensely.

Using this method, Gamble and the Press created a series of seven different standardized sizes of typefaces based on a book printing style from the Ming Dynasty. He then made matrices by the hundreds, instead of singly, as in the Western method. Characters produced by the new process, known as "Gamble's Characters," were clearer and also retained more of the original calligraphic effect than the rough-cut Western types. This fidelity of reproduction made it possible to reduce the size of the face of the type without loss of readability, and

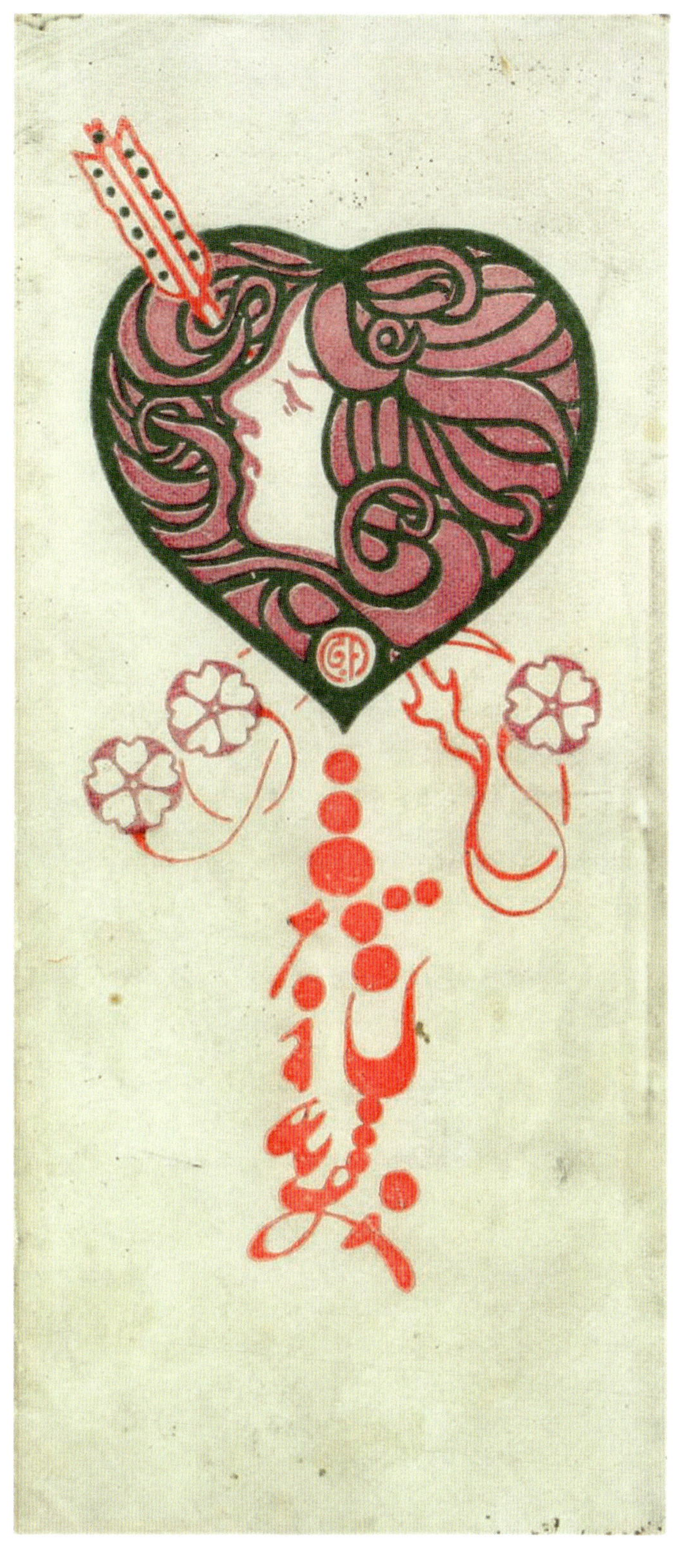

***Tangled Hair* みだれ髪, Yosano (Otori) Akiko 与謝野晶子, 1901,** designed by Fujishima Takeji 藤島武二. A diary-book of 399 tanka poems that were written as a diary of the imagery and inner workings of Yosano's life during the time of her sexual awakening and courtship with the man who would eventually become her husband. The cover mixes Art Nouveau illustration with expressive lettering, substituting the hiragana "み" with a synonym—the character "三"—to help emphasize the symmetry of the design.

2 Joshua A. Fogel, *Articulating the Sinosphere: Sino-Japanese Relations in Space and Time*, (Cambridge, MA: Harvard University Press, 2009), 96.

this small type made it feasible to print the whole Bible in Chinese within one volume. The Presbyterian Mission Press became the most widely known and respected printing establishment in China, supplying typefaces to publishers and newspaper companies nationally.

In addition, Gamble created a system of type case assembly and character organization based on the radical (primary stroke type) of Chinese used in the *Kangxi Dictionary*, the definitive Chinese dictionary at the time, so that typesetting could be enacted with more speed and precision. Gamble conducted the "first systematic frequency counts of Chinese characters and ascertained that only 5,150 different characters were needed for most purposes," a far smaller number of characters than had been previously considered.[3]

Gamble's renown was wide-ranging, both in China and abroad—so much so that it caught the attention of Motogi, who had formed the Typography Workshop 活版伝習所 in Nagasaki in 1869—Japan's first typography school, housed within the steel company he directed at that time. Motogi requested that Gamble come teach at his school in order to share his technological innovations. Having recently decided to return to America, Gamble agreed to work at the school for four months, during which he shared his electrotype plating system to make the production of Japanese type commercially viable.

Within a year, Motogi—alongside his student Hirano Tomiji 平野富二— founded the Nagasaki Shinmachi Type Foundry 長崎新町活版所, one of the first commercial type foundries in Japan. The foundry was able to produce type in unprecedented amounts, though at an incredible cost in time and labor during the first year and a half. In 1871, Motogi asked Hirano, a budding industrialist and steel magnate, to reduce costs by streamlining the foundry's operations. In order to make the business profitable, Hirano "discharged superfluous workers, cut the wages of those who did not produce, and adjusted wages to performance."[4] Hirano then instituted a division of labor in the production process, appointed foremen, and drew up a set of production standards. Finally, he inaugurated a system of fixed working hours and eliminated the after-lunch siesta.

Having made the production process more economical, Hirano opened a second typefounding operation in Tokyo's Kanda district in 1872, where he oversaw the increasingly rapid production of type. The foundry published a number of advertisements that year announcing typesetting services on offer, in addition to the business being open to new custom type designs. This economy of operations allowed the business to open new divisions in Osaka, Kobe, Yokohama, and Tokyo.

Motogi died in Nagasaki in 1875, leaving management of the business to Hirano. The Tokyo division of the foundry was incredibly successful and outgrew its initial commercial space in Kanda, resettling in the Tsukiji area and taking on the name The Tokyo Tsukiji Type Foundry 東京築地活版製造所 in 1885.

These businesses were Japan's first commercially successful type foundries. They were innovators in creating multiple sets of type and introducing movable Latin type into the Japanese printing industry. The first Japanese newspaper typeset using movable lead type, the *Tōkyō Nichi Nichi Shinbun* 東京日日新聞, was set, printed, and published by Motogi's students using type from the Tsukiji Type Foundry alongside hand-carved wooden type.

However, it should be noted that there were other groups working on similar typographic developments, creating Japanese type based on the Gutenberg model. The Institute for the Investigation of Barbarian Books (later renamed the Institute for the Investigation of Western Books) 蕃書調所 in Tokyo, founded in 1857, was involved in the printing of textbooks until 1867. Woodblock carver Kimura Kahei III 三代木村嘉平 also attempted to develop an indigenous system of typesetting from 1854 to 1864. Despite this competition, Motogi and his disciple Hirano were the first to the mass market—they were able to produce higher-quality detailed type at a quarter the cost of type offered by their competitors.

Motogi and Hirano utilized a number of different approaches to type design and production, including a modified form of Gamble's electroplating method, xylography, and lead typecasting. In addition, Motogi and Hirano pulled from many different models of character design, including Gamble's Ming types, Chinese characters from France's official printing works, the *Imprimerie Nationale*, and original designs for hiragana and katakana that the two designed alongside their compatriots at the school and the two type foundries.

3 Endymion Wilkinson, *Chinese History: A Manual*, (Cambridge, MA: Harvard University Press, 2000), 452.

4 Edward Thomas Mack, *Manufacturing Modern Japanese Literature: Publishing, Prizes, and the Ascription of Literary Value*, (Durham, NC: Duke University Press, 2010): 26.

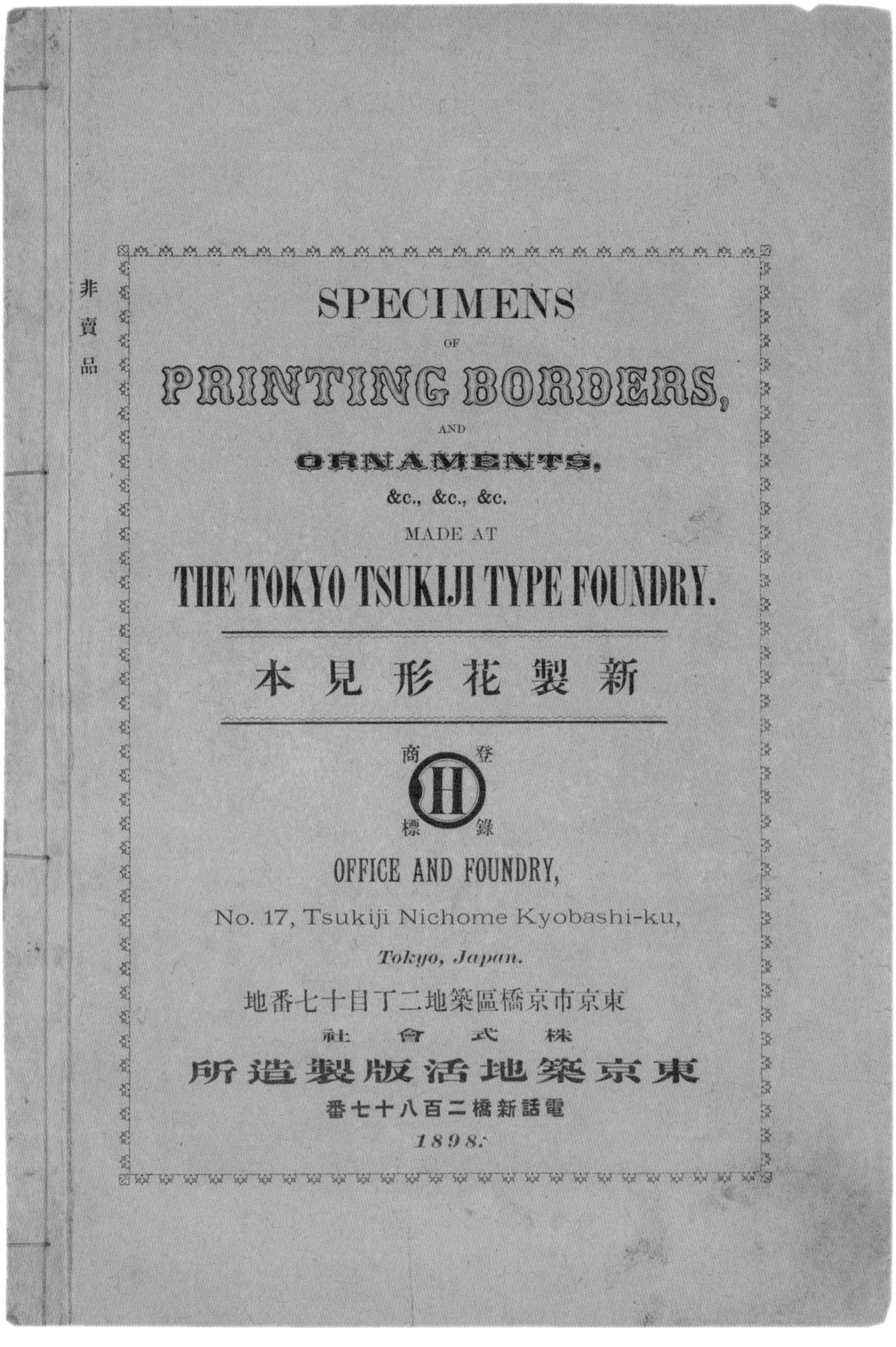

非賣品

SPECIMENS

OF

PRINTING BORDERS,

AND

ORNAMENTS,

&c., &c., &c.

MADE AT

THE TOKYO TSUKIJI TYPE FOUNDRY.

新製花形見本

登録商標

H

OFFICE AND FOUNDRY,

No. 17, Tsukiji Nichome Kyobashi-ku,

Tokyo, Japan.

東京市京橋區築地二丁目十七番地

株式會社

東京築地活版製造所

電話新橋二百八十七番

1898.

Specimen of Printing Borders and Ornaments (Tokyo: Tokyo Tsukiji Type Foundry 東京築地活版製造所, 1898).
A 146-page booklet of assorted typographic ornamentation utilizing both ornaments made at the Tokyo Tsukiji Type Foundry and from assorted other foundries globally. Of note is that the specimen also displays type set in all three orthographic directions alongside illustration cuts, dashes, rules, and borders.

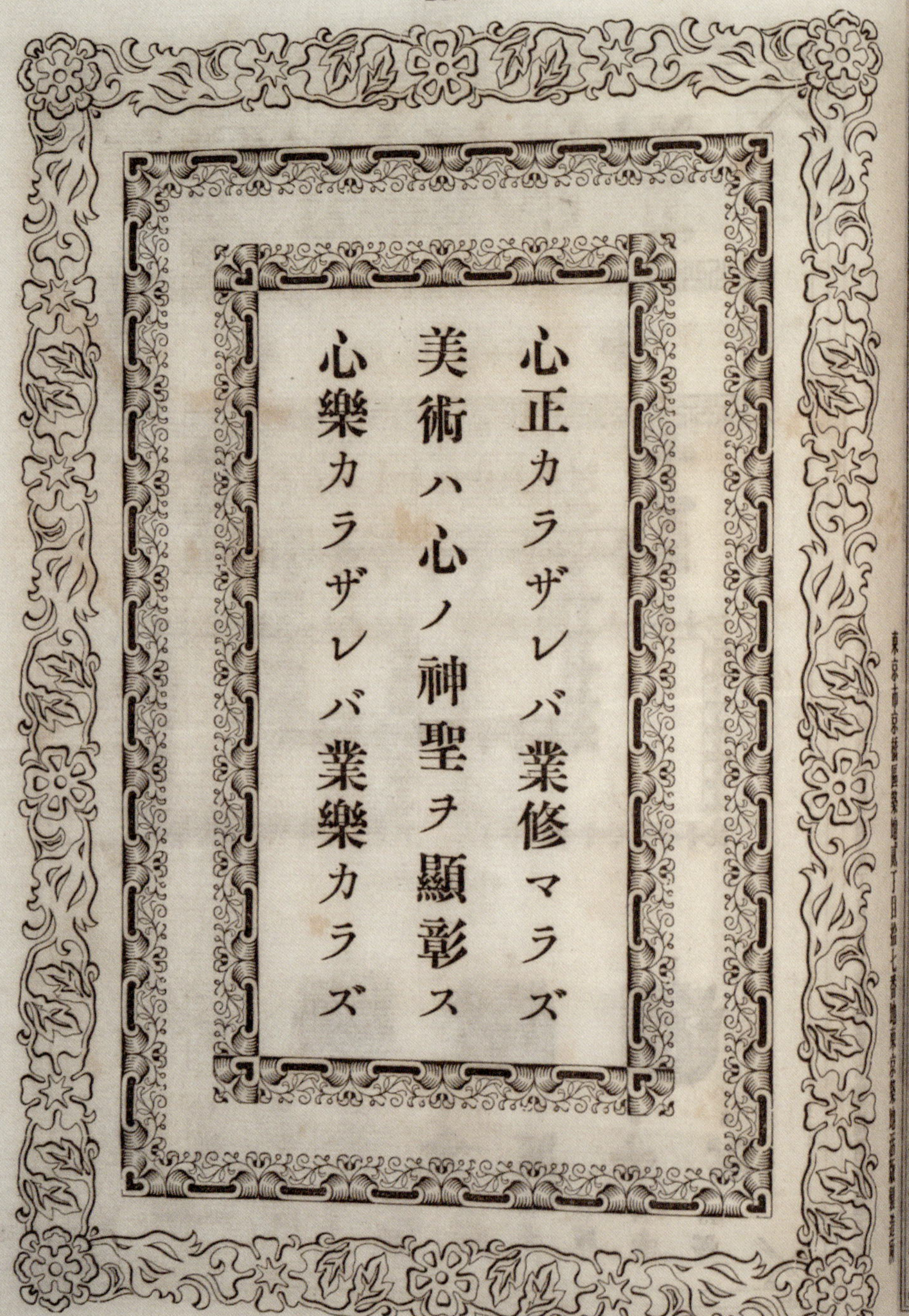
心正カラザレバ業修マラズ
美術ハ心ノ神聖ヲ顯彰ス
心樂カラザレバ業樂カラズ

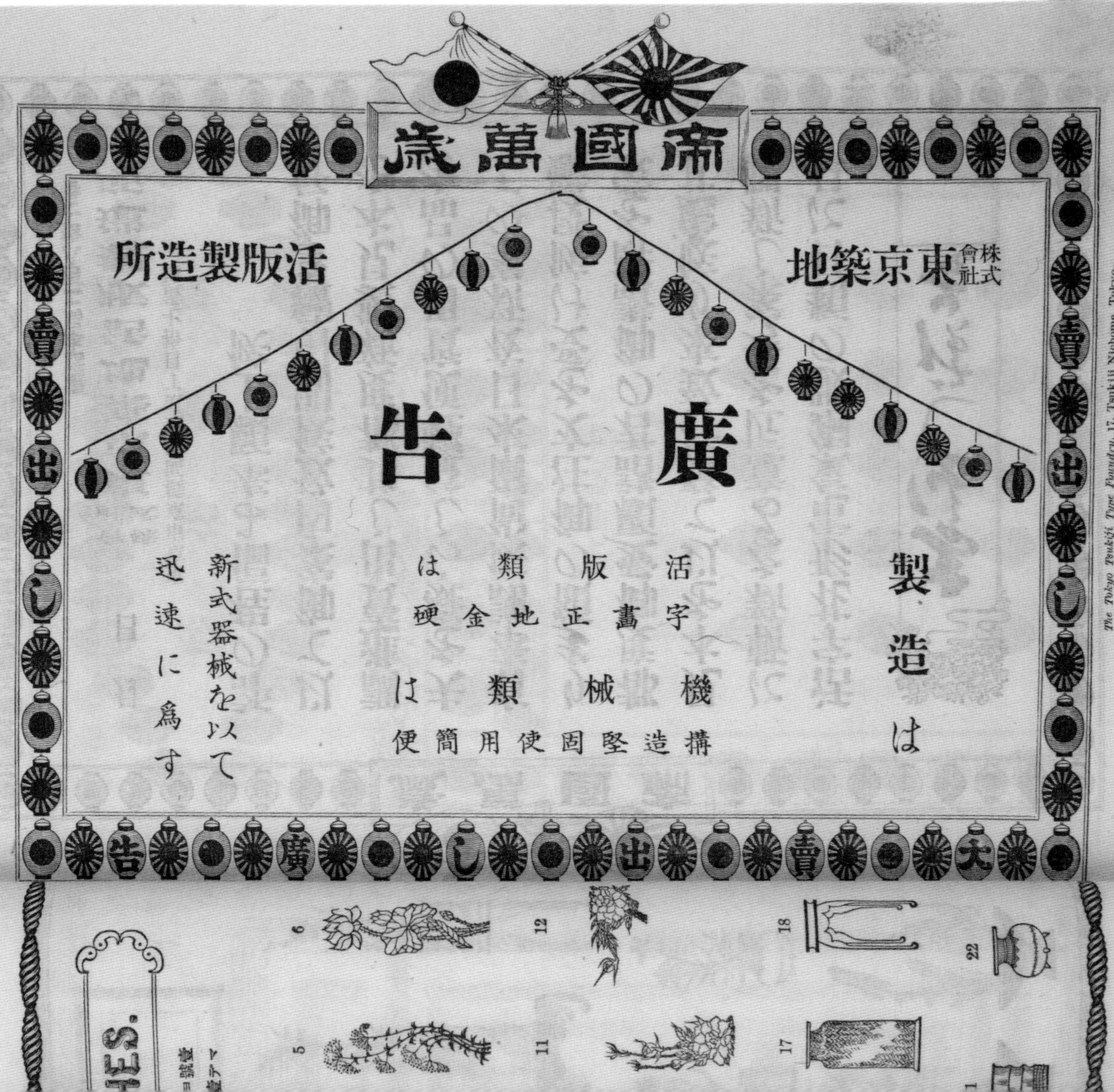
帝國萬歳
株式會社東京築地
活版製造所
廣告
製造は
活版類は
字畫正地金硬
機械類は
構造堅固使用簡便
新式器械を以て
迅速に為す

The birth of mass-produced typography in Japan occurred two years after the modern Japanese military was created and just one year after Japan opened via the Meiji Restoration—a moment in history when the country's rulers insisted that the nation industrialize as rapidly as possible. It was an incredible time: Japan had been closed to most foreigners and their influence for over 200 years, and such a fast reversal of public policy and the opening of the country to trade and globalism must have been staggering to the Japanese populace.

IMAGERY

The Tsukiji Type Foundry transformed into a full-service printing business with the incorporation of image reproduction and printing services offered under the auspices of affiliate Ogawa Kazumasa 小川一眞.

Ogawa was born in 1860 to a samurai family and was introduced to photography at the age of thirteen. He opened his first photo studio in Gunma in 1877, later moving to Yokohama where he worked as an English interpreter before heading to the United States to study the latest photography and photomechanical reproduction processes. In Boston, Ogawa studied collotype printing and typefounding at the Albert Type Company. Ogawa next moved to Philadelphia where he studied dry-plate manufacturing under the inventor of that technology, John Carbutt.

He returned to Japan in 1885 and immediately opened a portrait photography studio. He followed this business with the Ogawa Kazumasa Photographic Copperplate Engraving Studio in 1889, winning contracts with the Japanese army to reproduce photographic materials over the subsequent two decades. Ogawa also pursued a number of entrepreneurial ventures, selling photographic reproductions of portraiture, nature scenes, and cultural scenes, and also had a lively business selling his photographs to newspapers.

Ogawa traveled to the United States again in 1893 as Japan's representative at the Congress of Photographers held at the Chicago World's Fair, where he was introduced to the more economical halftone-based printing process. Ogawa purchased halftone reproduction equipment for import to Japan, which he would use to enhance his assorted businesses, providing photographic printing plates to newspapers and publishers alike.

Ogawa eventually opened the Tsukiji Dry Plate Manufacturing Company 築地乾板製造所, a venture financed by affluent fellow photographer Kajima Seibei 鹿島清兵衛 which supplied photographic materials to other photographers, produced halftone plates, and offered collotype printing, a gelatin-based photographic printing process. Ogawa was an innovator in combining text and image in the printing process, incorporating copper type printing with both collotype and halftone processes, allowing him to print photography and typography in one pass on the press.

Ogawa was an editor of the *Shashin Shimpō* 写真新報, East Asia's first and Japan's only photographic journal at the time, printed in collaboration with Tsukiji Type Foundry. The magazine was a successful mainstream photography magazine aimed at budding photo hobbyists.

In sum, Ogawa was a wide-ranging publisher and printer whose work exposed Japan and the West to photographic documentation of Japan in the Meiji period.

SYNTHESIS

As service providers able to offer image reproduction, typographic composition, and access to Japanese typefaces to their clients, Ogawa and Tsukiji Type Foundry enabled wide distribution of various materials which helped imbue the newly opened nation-state with a collective cultural identity. By 1872, Ogawa and Tsukiji Type Foundry were at times acting as type foundry, printer, editor, and publisher across their various ventures, greatly expanding their means of influence.

The Tsukiji Type Foundry both printed and published a wide range of educational materials, including many for foreign-language learning. By delineating the differences between languages in print, these materials further defined the Japanese visual and verbal language as something inherent and indigenous to the country.

The foundry also designed and printed *The Kokka* 国華, Japan's first mass-produced art journal aimed at foreign audiences, starting in 1889. *The Kokka* was initiated by critic, writer, and educator Okakura Tenshin 岡倉天心 and journalist Takahashi Kenzō 高橋健三 and sought to challenge the preeminence of Western art during the Meiji period. The name "kokka" means "flower of the nation" and refers to the essence of an idealized Japanese nation-state. The art presented

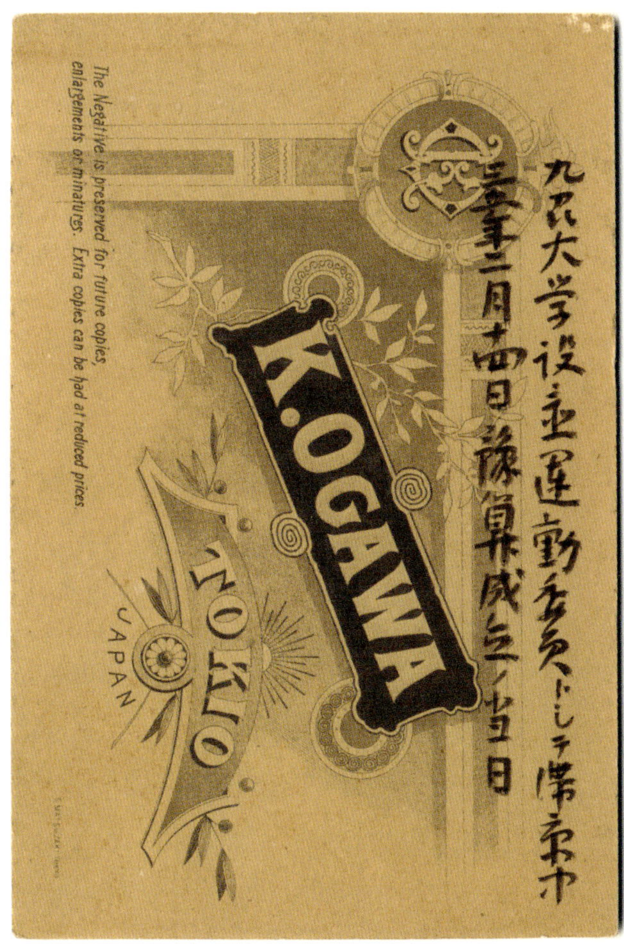

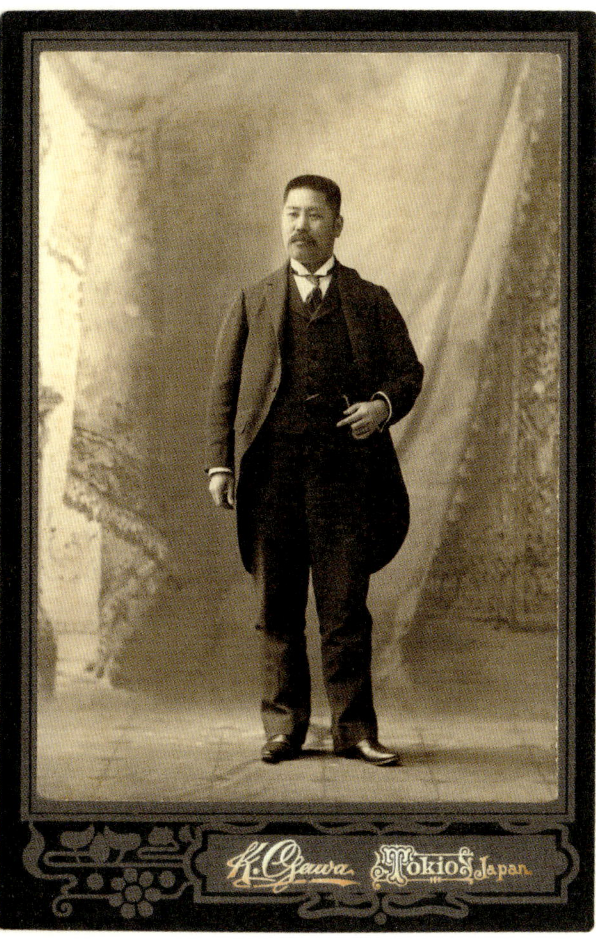

Front and back of a "cabinet card" photograph of Fukuoka Prefectural Assembly member Tomiyasu Yasutaro 富安保太郎 by Ogawa Kazumasa 小川一眞, 1902.

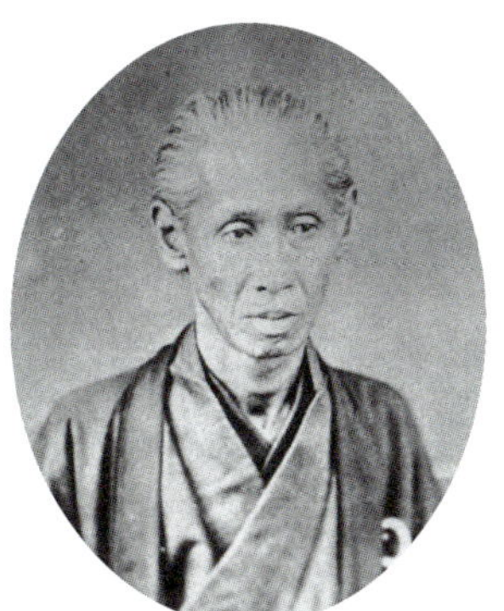

Motogi Shōzō 本木昌造

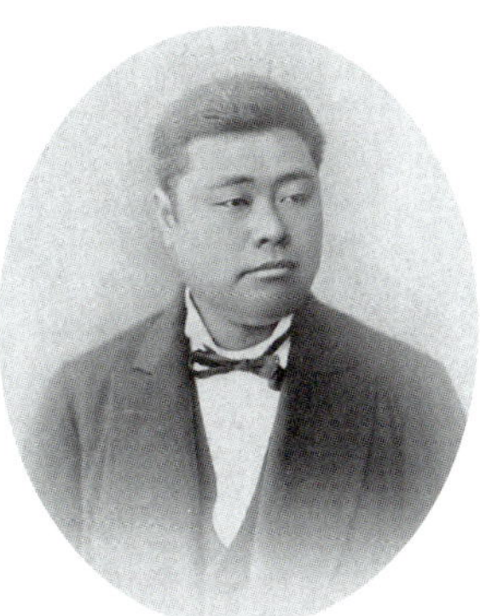

Hirano Tomiji 平野富二

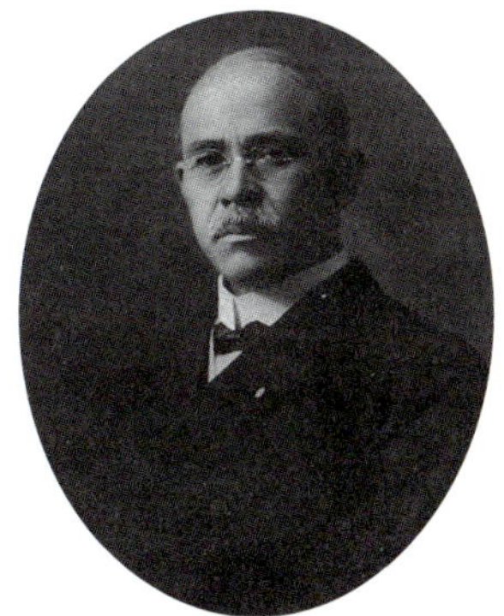

Ogawa Kazumasa 小川一眞

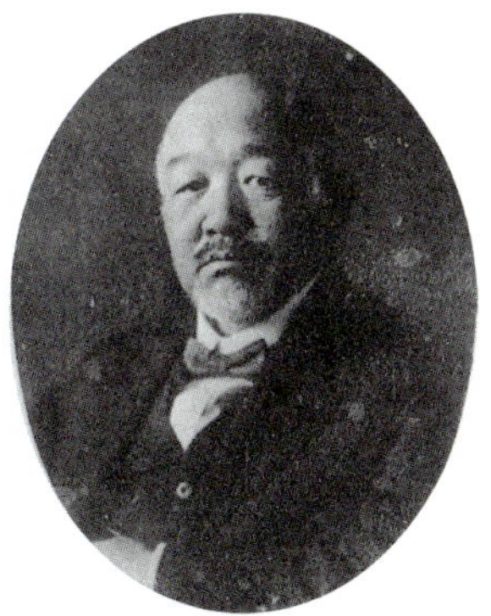

Kuroda Seiki 黒田清輝

within was reproduced using all of the printing technology that Tsukiji Type Foundry and Ogawa Kazumasa's assorted businesses offered, including collotype printing.

Others saw the appeal of offering hybrid graphic design, printing, and publishing services, and the few years following the formation of the Tsukiji Type Foundry saw similar businesses start, including Shueisha 秀英舎 (now Dainippon Printing 大日本印刷株式会社) in 1876 and Toppan Printing 凸版印刷 in 1900. Today, these two wildly profitable businesses dominate the Japanese printing industry. Their divergent ventures span photographic services, software development, publishing, technology patents, and much, much more—from cutting-edge digital displays and monitors to the passport photo machines which are omnipresent outside of Japan's convenience stores.

The rise of Tsukiji's operations neatly mirrored the rapid industrialization of Japan at that time—the business grew as Japan's economy stabilized and turned toward heavy industry while the government established a modern military. Both the private and public sectors had a great need for economical printed communications, and as one of the leading design and printing businesses of the late nineteenth and early twentieth centuries, the Tsukiji Type Foundry was involved in the production of a wide range of books including titles on education, state planning, railways, engineering, silk, economics, foreign policy, cartography and a host of other subjects.

Hirano Tomiji resigned as president of the foundry in 1889 and was replaced by Motogi Kotarō 本木小太郎, the son of Motogi Shōzō, the first of nine subsequent presidents in the foundry's lifetime. The Tsukiji Type Foundry's main buildings were destroyed in the Great Kanto Earthquake of 1923, with the majority of the machinery consumed by fire.

Tokyo's publishing and design industries were rocked by the Great Kanto Earthquake, and it took a number of years for them to fully recover. An untold number of lives were lost, businesses destroyed, and supply chains split asunder due the disaster. For a few years while Tokyo was being rebuilt after the quake, Kansai became the center of print culture in Japan.

The rapid modernization of the Taishō era (1912–1926) was in full swing when the giant earthquake hit, rocking the greater Tokyo area, surrounding environs, and the nearby port metropolis of Yokohama. The scale of the quake cannot be overestimated—in a span of time between four and ten minutes, Tokyo was leveled. Over 142,800 people died in the quake, the firestorms that raged through the wooden city (the earthquake arrived at lunch time when many citizens were cooking), and a fire tornado that alone claimed the lives of 38,000 Japanese within minutes due to a typhoon off the coast that same day. The government declared martial law, and enraged citizens formed mobs which hunted and killed hundreds of Korean and Chinese individuals living in Japan, after rumors spread that Koreans were poisoning Tokyo's water supplies.

These rumors and the resultant killings were largely due to the tideswell of Japanese nationalism that had begun in 1867 with the formation of the modern Japanese military and the beginnings of the Japanese interwar period. Prior to the earthquake, Japan's military had participated in multiple campaigns geared toward aggressive expansion of its empire, having annexed large parts of Korea, invaded Taiwan and Sakhalin, and defeated part of the Russian Navy, all in a lead-up to its participation in World War I. The growing sense of regional superiority and nationalism exhibited by the government and military of interwar Japan kept the ball rolling toward the cataclysmic results of the forthcoming World War a few decades later.

As for the Tsukiji Type Foundry, the business rebuilt and recovered within a year after the Great Kanto Earthquake and remained in business until it went into bankruptcy in 1938, the result of a decline in productivity combined with financial mismanagement. Despite dominating type design, typography, design integrated with photography and illustration, and printing in Japan for the better part of the foundry's sixty-six-year existence, the Tsukiji Type Foundry petered out with a whimper.

BECOMING MODERN: KURODA SEIKI 黒田清輝

The legacy of graphic design in Japan is also largely indebted to artist and educator Kuroda Seiki 黒田清輝 (1866–1924), under whom many of Japan's early modern commercial artists studied. Kuroda was born into a samurai family—an elevated position in Japanese class hierarchy—and was adopted and raised by an uncle who worked in the imperial government in Tokyo. Growing up, Kuroda was exposed to many new "modern" ideas of that time, due to his uncle's position in the government, and he followed them implicitly.

10

(b)

1. Is this a pear?

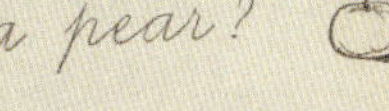

2. Is this a cow?

3. Is this a horse?

4. Is this an inkstand?

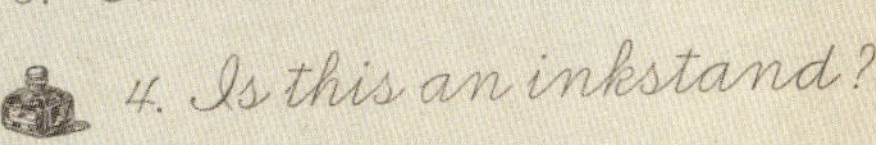

5. Is this your ink-bottle?

LESSON IV.

1.

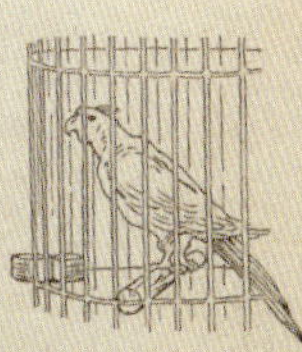

What is **this bird** ?
It is a parrot.
Where is **the** parrot ?
It is in a cage.

bĭrd	păr'rot	whêre
the [thĕ, thē]	ĭn	cāge

11

2.

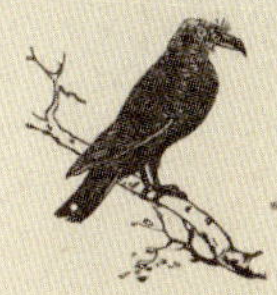

What bird is this ?
It is a crow.
Where is the crow ?
It is on a tree.

1. ***Where is* the** parrot ?

Where is —? にて文を起す場合には,名詞に a 或は an を附せずして the を附すべし。

the は「この」「その」「あの」の意なれど,邦語にては通例これに對する語をいひ表さず。

the を定冠詞と稱し,a (an) を不定冠詞といふ。

2. What is **this bird** ?
What bird is this ?

crōw	ŏn	trēe

Elementary English Course, William E. Laxton Sweet & Kaiseikan Editing Office 開成館編集所 (Tokyo: Kaiseikan 開成館, 1910).
An example of instructional multilingual multiplex typography with integrated illustration cuts designed, composed, and printed by the Tokyo Tsukiji Type Foundry.

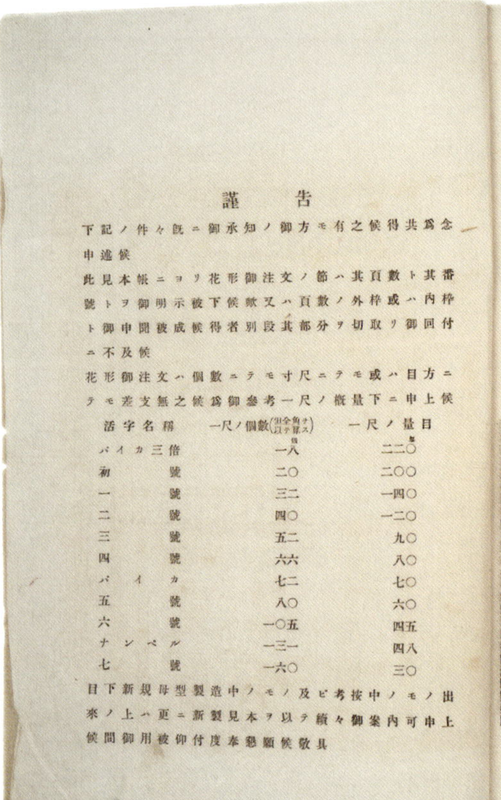

謹告

下記ノ件々既ニ御承知ノ御方モ有之候得共爲念申進候

此見本帳ニヨリ花形御注文ノ節ハ其頁數ト其番號トヲ御明示被下候歟又ハ頁數ノ外枠或ハ内枠ト御申聞被成候得者別段其部分ヲ切取リ御回付ニ不及候

花形御注文ハ個數ニテモ寸尺ニテモ或ハ目方ニテモ差支無之候爲御參考一尺ノ槪量下ニ申上候

活字名稱	一尺ノ個數(但全角ヲ以テ算ス)	一尺ノ量目
バイカ三倍	一八個	二二〇匁
初號	二〇	二〇〇
一號	三二	一四〇
二號	四〇	一二〇
三號	五二	九〇
四號	六六	八〇
バイカ	七二	七〇
五號	八〇	六〇
六號	一〇五	四五
ナンペル	一三一	四八
七號	一六〇	三〇

目下新規母型製造中ノモノ及ビ考按中ノモノ出來ノ上ハ更ニ新製見本ヲ以テ續々御案内可申上候間御用被仰付度奉懇願候敬具

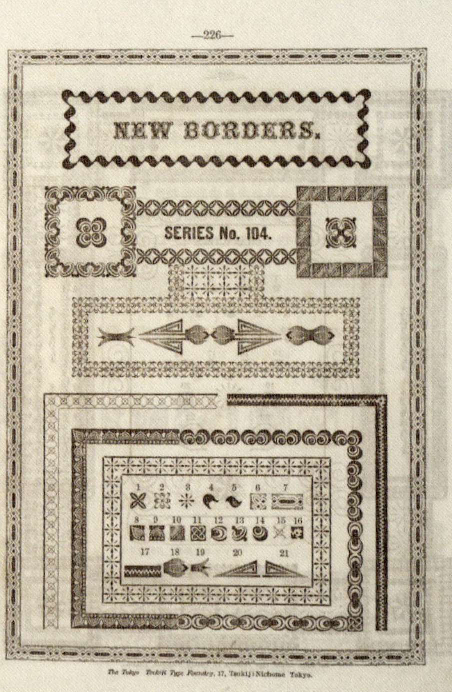

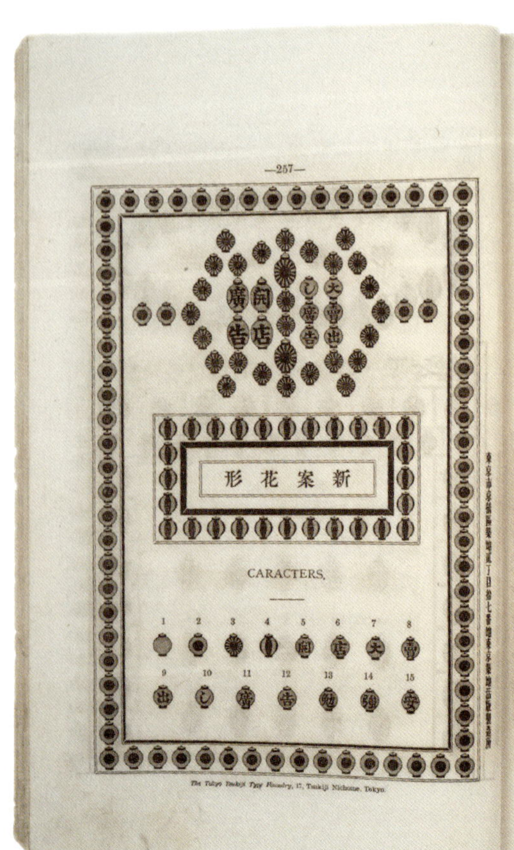

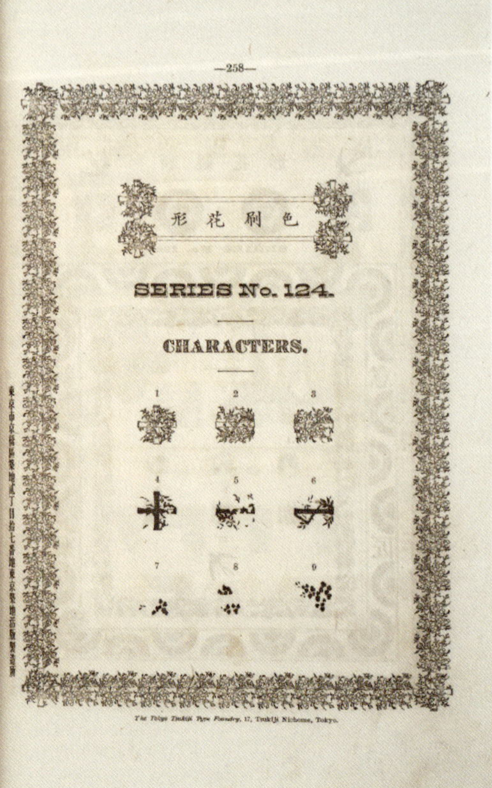

Specimen of Printing Borders and Ornaments (Tokyo: Tokyo Tsukiji Type Foundry 東京築地活版製造所, 1898).

A 146-page booklet of assorted typographic ornamentation utilizing both ornaments made at the Tokyo Tsukiji Type Foundry and from assorted other foundries globally. Of note is that the specimen also displays type set in all three orthographic directions alongside illustration cuts, dashes, rules, and borders.

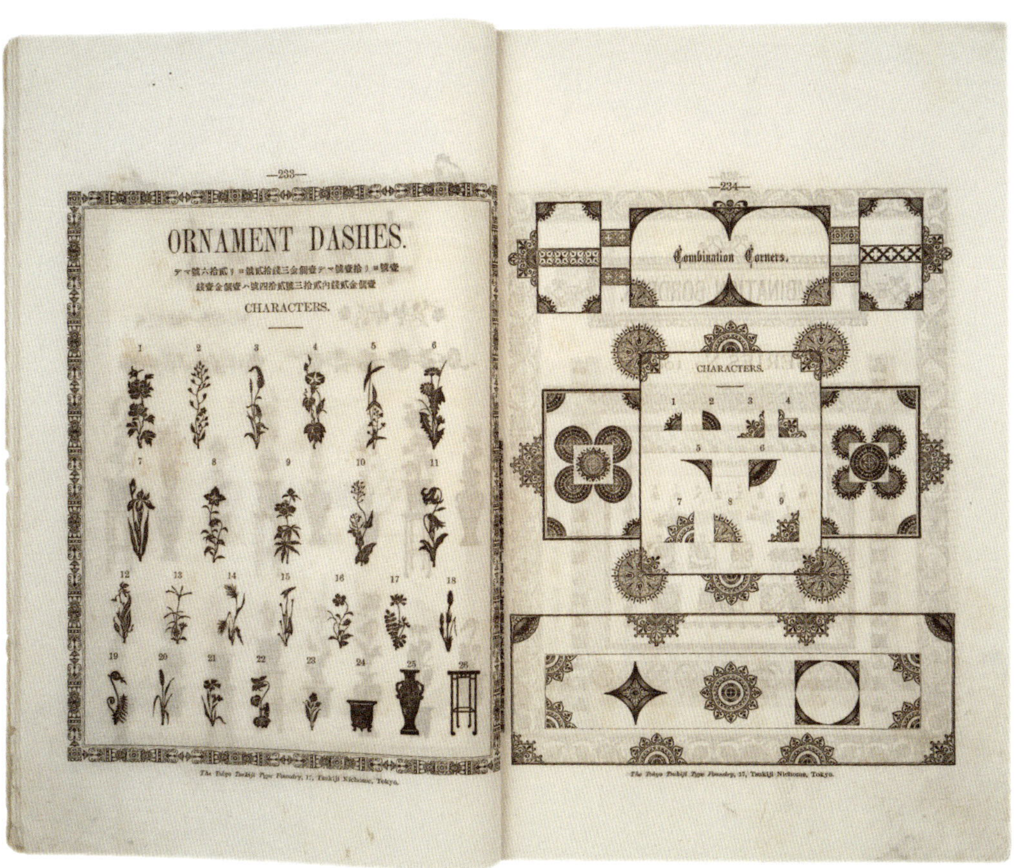
—233—
ORNAMENT DASHES.
CHARACTERS.
The Tokyo Tsukiji Type Foundry, 17, Tsukiji Nichome, Tokyo.
—234—
Combination Corners.
CHARACTERS.
The Tokyo Tsukiji Type Foundry, 17, Tsukiji Nichome, Tokyo.

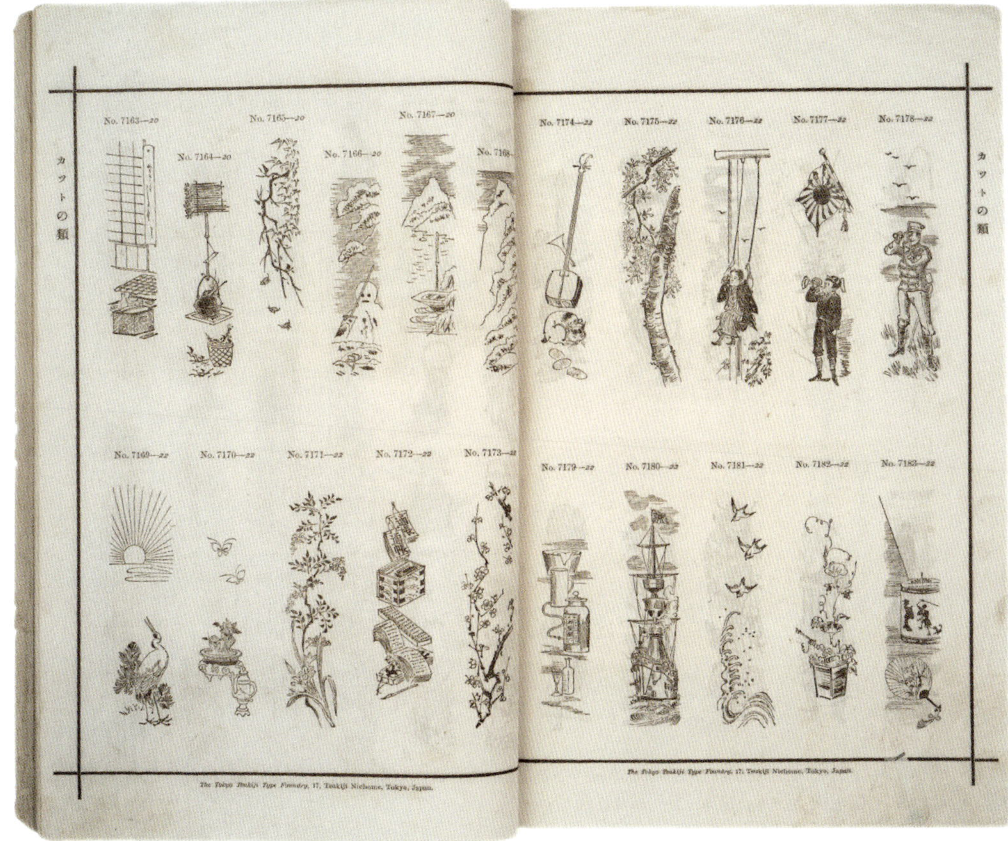
カットの類
No. 7163—20
No. 7164—20
No. 7165—20
No. 7166—20
No. 7167—20
No. 7169—22
No. 7170—22
No. 7171—22
No. 7172—22
No. 7173—22
The Tokyo Tsukiji Type Foundry, 17, Tsukiji Nichome, Tokyo, Japan.
No. 7174—22
No. 7175—22
No. 7176—22
No. 7177—22
No. 7178—22
No. 7179—22
No. 7180—22
No. 7181—22
No. 7182—22
No. 7183—22
カットの類
The Tokyo Tsukiji Type Foundry, 17, Tsukiji Nichome, Tokyo, Japan.

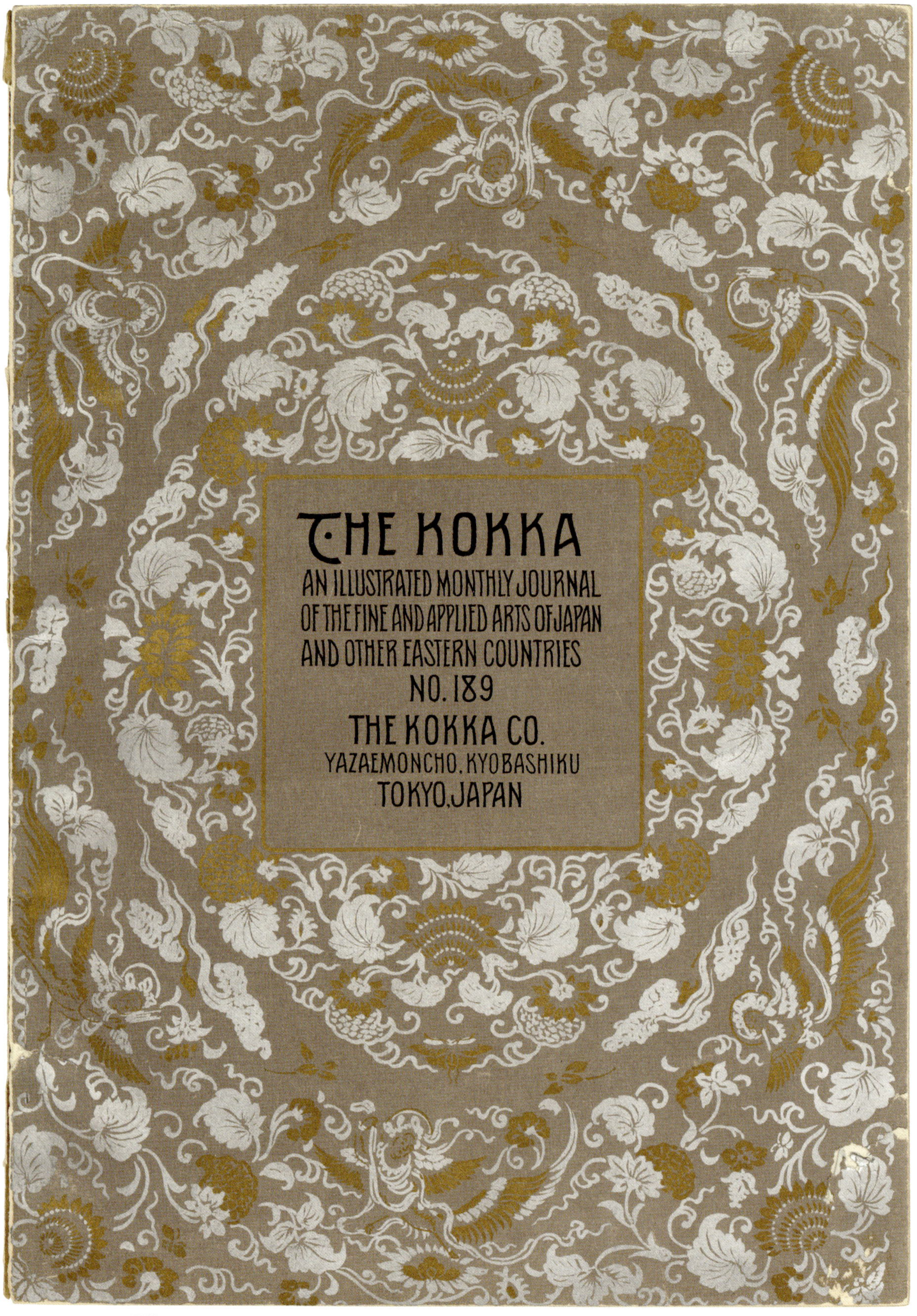

The Kokka No. 189 國華 189 (Tokyo: Kokkasha 國華社, 1906).
Japan's first mass-produced art journal aimed at foreign audiences.

In 1886, Kuroda moved to Paris to study law, but he soon abandoned his legal studies to pursue painting, mastering multiple styles of painting and returning to Japan in 1893, where he began to teach art alongside Yamamoto Hōsui 山本芳翠 at the Tenshin Dojo. In 1912, Kuroda formed the artists' society Hakubakai 白馬会 (named after a kind of unfiltered saké), a group whose intention was to exhibit and promote the works of its members without constraints regarding style.

Instrumental to Kuroda's life and career were two critics and educators—the American Ernest Fenollosa and his former student Okakura Tenshin 岡倉天心—both of whom were influential in emphasizing the importance, inherent beauty, and singularity of native Japanese arts and crafts. After a survey trip to Europe to study art education institutions, Fenollosa and Okakura helped to co-found the Tokyo School of Fine Arts 東京美術学校 with the support of the Japanese government's Ministry of Education. Fenollosa was deeply absorbed with Japanese art and considered it superior to Western approaches. He undertook a lifelong project to recategorize historical forms and movements of Japanese art. Okakura later joined Fenollosa to revive and reinvigorate traditional forms of Japanese painting. Fenollosa and Okakura's project to highlight and elevate the role of traditional Japanese painting helped lay the foundation for Kuroda's investigation of Western forms of painting and representation. These educators' divergent aims informed many of the aesthetics that underlay nascent Japanese commercial art and, later, graphic design.

Kuroda became the head of the Western Painting department at the Tokyo School of Fine Arts (one of the foundations for Tokyo University of the Arts 東京藝術大学), originally founded in 1887 by the government's Ministry of Education. Kuroda's imprint on arts education in Japan is indelible—he was a great promoter of Western-style painting, or *yōga*, and believed that it was a more accurate and realistic representation of natural experience, as opposed to traditional Japanese painting, or *nihonga*. A large number of Japan's early commercial artists were trained either by Kuroda directly or in institutions under his direction, particularly Tokyo University of the Arts and the Hakubakai.

In 1907, the Ministry of Education began a series of annual art exhibitions known as the Monbushō Bijutusu Tenrankai 文部省美術展覧会, or colloquially as the Bunten 文展, in the vein of French salon exhibitions. If one were to be included in a Bunten exhibition, it meant that the individual would be a legally recognized artist and might attempt to sustain a livelihood via art-making and governmental patronage, yet at a time when no private art market had fully developed. A number of other arts groups began to oppose the Bunten system, including the Nikakai 二科会, literally translated as "The Second Division Society," but which is largely translated into English as "Society for Progressive Japanese Artists," a 1914 group dedicated to creating artwork in the European fashion of the day. These groups, both sanctioned and non-sanctioned, helped to rapidly regularize art-making, which spurred markets for fine art and commercial art alike.

In exploring and promoting varied approaches to image-making through education, Kuroda helped to evolve Japan's pictorial legacy, particularly via those who studied under him. Kuroda passed away in 1924 amid Tokyo's reconstruction efforts after the quake and would not see the massive aesthetic shifts that his former students would enact.

Tokyo in 1923 could be considered the origin point of Modernism in Japan. The capital city of Japan largely needed to be rebuilt, as a result, shedding much of its traditional Japanese architecture, objects, tools, and ultimately its graphic design, replacing them with modern versions. The word "modern," or more appropriately the katakana-ized "modan" モダン, was in the air prior to the Great Kanto Earthquake, but the next decade would be the era during which modernity in Japan would become far more realized.

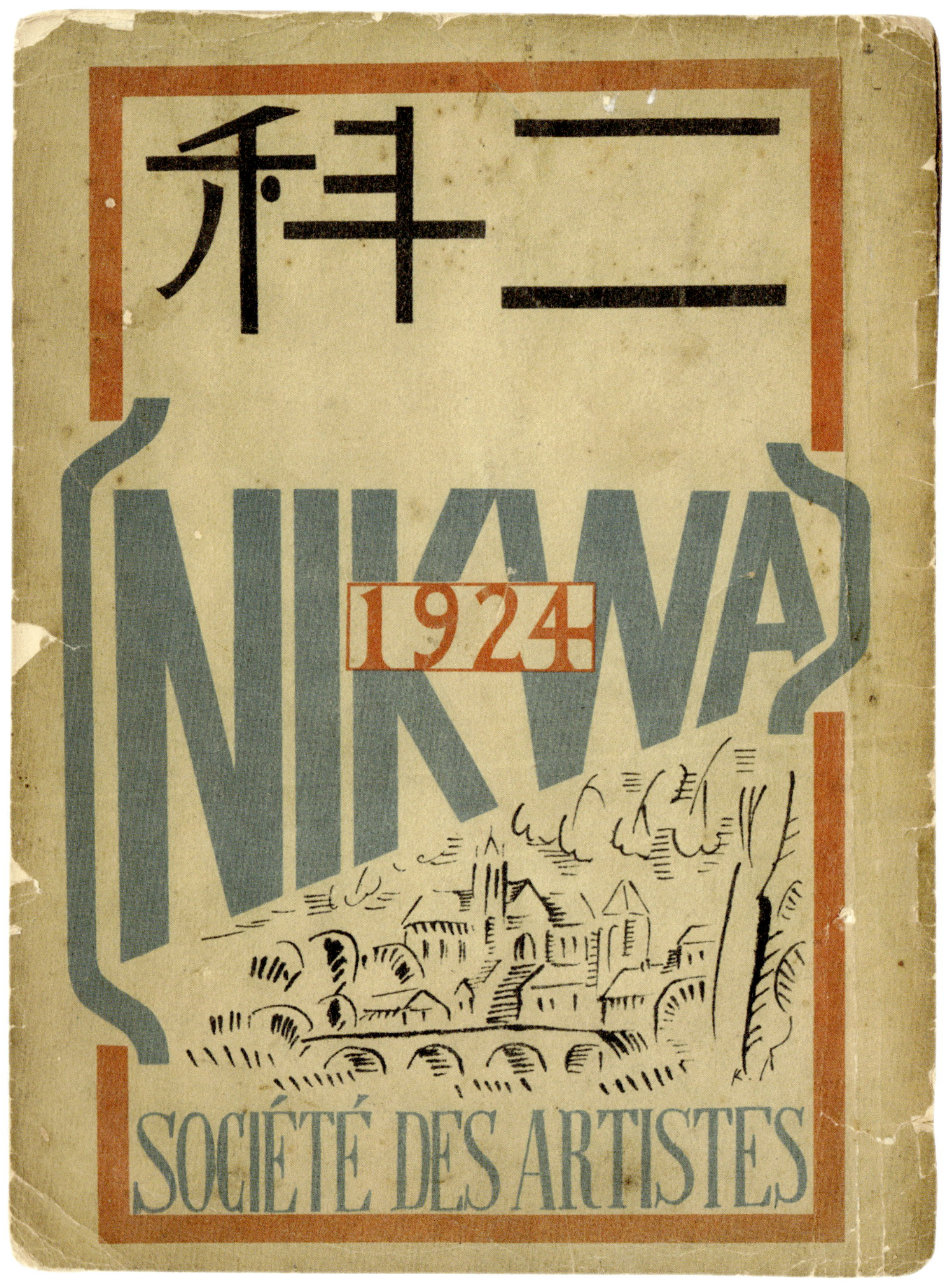

Three-color cover of 1924 ***Nikakai*** **二科会** annual catalog designed using hand lettering and illustration. (Tokyo: Asahi Shimbun 朝日新聞社, 1924).

Fire insurance advertising flyer for Mitsubishi Kaijo Kasai Hoken Kabushiki Kaisha 三菱海上火災保険株式会社, undated. Designer unknown.

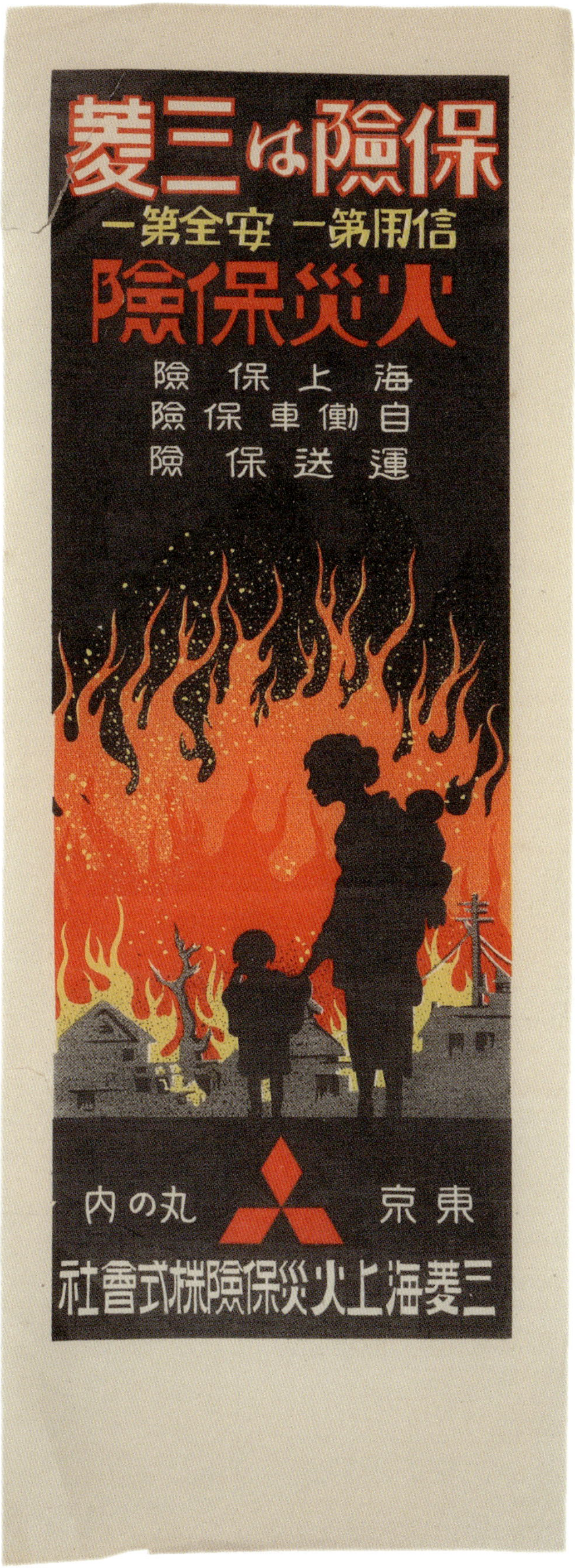

References:

Baxley, George C. "Kazumasa Ogawa Japanese Photographer." Baxley Stamps. Baxley Stamps, 1999. http://www.baxleystamps.com/.

Fogel, Joshua A. *Articulating the Sinosphere: Sino-Japanese Relations in Space and Time*. Cambridge, MA: Harvard University Press, 2009.

Kornicki, Peter F. *The Book in Japan: A Cultural History from the Beginnings to the Nineteenth Century*. Honolulu: University of Hawai'i Press, 2001.

Kuroda, Seiki. *Kuroda Seiki, Nihon Kindai Kaiga No kyoshō, Seitan 150-Nen = Kuroda Seiki, Master of Modern Japanese Painting: the 150th Anniversary of His Birth*. Tokyo: Bijutsu Shuppansha, 2016.

Mack, Edward Thomas. *Manufacturing Modern Japanese Literature: Publishing, Prizes, and the Ascription of Literary Value*. Durham, NC: Duke University Press, 2010.

McCormick, Kelly M. "Ogawa Kazumasa and the Halftone Photograph: Japanese War Albums at the Turn of the Twentieth Century." *The Trans-Asia Photography Review*. Michigan Publishing, University of Michigan Library, April 28, 2017. https://quod.lib.umich.edu/t/tap/7977573.0007.201.

Weisenfeld, Gennifer. "Japanese Modernism and Consumerism: Forging the New Artistic Field of 'Shogyo Bijutsu' (Commercial Art)." In *Being Modern in Japan: Culture and Society from the 1910s to the 1930s*, edited by Elise K. Tipton and John Clark, 75–96. Honolulu: University of Hawai'i Press, 2000.

Wilkinson, Endymion. *Chinese History: A Manual*. Cambridge, MA: Harvard University Press, 2000.

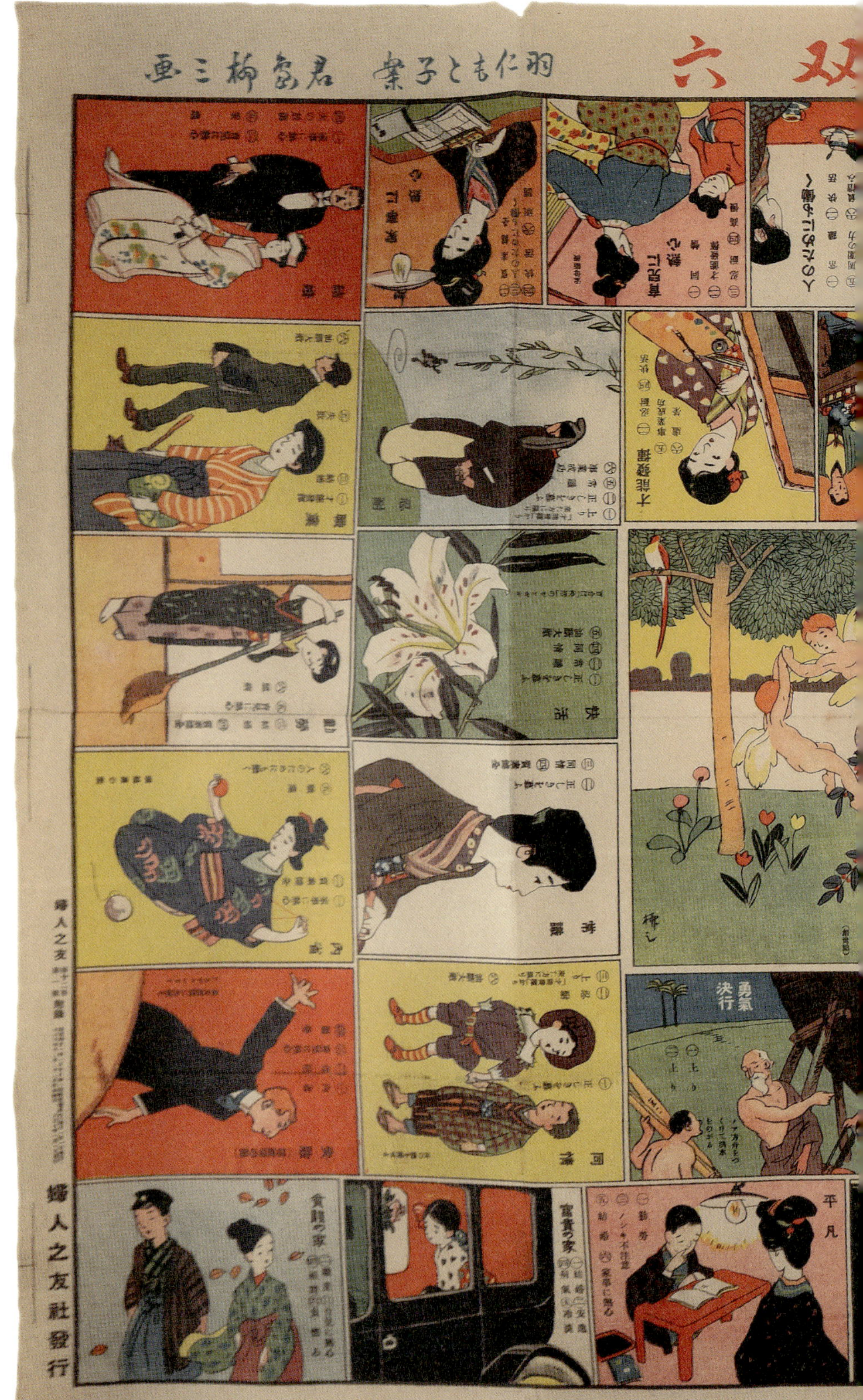

A Family's Good Luck **家庭開運双六, creative direction by Hani Motoko 羽仁もと子, design/illustration by Kishida Ryusei 岸田劉生 (Tokyo: Fujinnotomofuroku 婦人之友附録, 1932).**
A printed board game known as a *sugoroku* 雙六 (or 双六). The game's players would roll dice to race toward the center, confronting marital woes, illness, financial difficulties, loneliness, and interactions with foreigners to see who might make it first to the goal at the center of the broadsheet: domestic bliss, replete with fluttering angels.

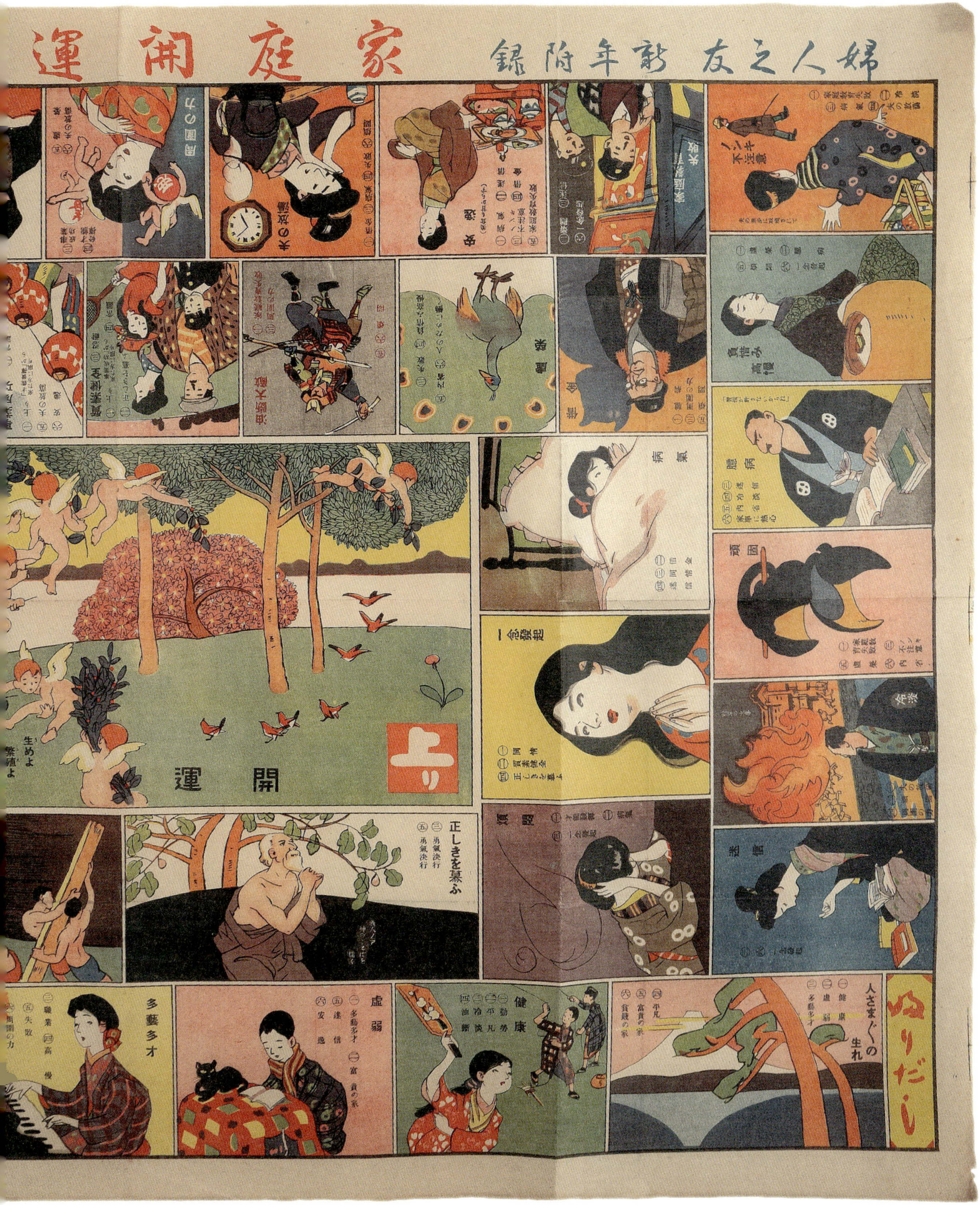

婦人之友新年附録　家庭開運

ふりだし

人さまぐの生れ
㈠健康
㈡虚弱
㈢多藝多才
㈣平凡
㈤富貴の家
㈥貧賤の家

健康
㈠勤勞
㈡平凡
㈢冷淡
㈣油斷

虚弱
㈠多藝多才
㈡富貴の家
㈤迷信
㈥安逸

多藝多才
㈢職業
㈣高慢
㈤失敗
㈥周圍の力

正しきを慕ふ
㈢勇氣決行
㈤勇氣決行

迷信

一念發起

開運

上り

生めよ
繁殖よ

HANI MOTOKO 羽仁もと子

1873–1957

Matsuoka Motoko 松岡もと子 was born into a samurai family in Aomori Prefecture. She studied at Tokyo Women's High School (now Tokyo Metropolitan Hakuō Senior High School) and then at Christian Meiji Girls' School, working as a teacher immediately afterward in Hachinohe, Aomori, and Morioka, Iwate. She married in 1892, though she divorced shortly thereafter and moved to Tokyo in 1895. Despite an elite education and higher socioeconomic background than many, few professional jobs were available to women in the Meiji period, and so Hani worked for two years as a maid to a doctor before securing an editorial position with the staff of the newspaper *Hochi Shimbun* 報知新聞 in 1897.

At the newspaper, she initially worked as a copy editor but quickly began writing editorials, becoming Japan's first female newspaper journalist. She married again in 1897, this time to a coworker named Hani Yoshikazu 羽仁吉一. Together, the couple founded the magazine *Fujin no Tomo* 婦人之友 (literally *Woman's Friend*) in 1908—one of the first mass consumer magazines oriented toward a female readership.

They released a number of other titles geared toward women and children, including *Kodomo no Tomo* 子供之友, a magazine for children that featured the work of pioneering designers and artists such as Takehisa Yumeji 竹久夢二 and Murayama Tomoyoshi 村山知義. Through their publishing company Fujin no Tomosha 婦人之友社, Hani Motoko acted as de facto creative director and art director for innumerable publishing projects, including household accounting texts, games, books, and magazines. By operating as curatorial tastemaker, Hani steered the aesthetic direction of commonplace items in Japanese homes, implicitly instilling aesthetic preferences in the masses.

In 1921, the Hanis set up the pioneering school Jiyū Gakuen 自由学園, which spans different divisions from kindergarten through university, and is still in operation today. Named after the New Testament motto "The truth will set you free" (John 8:32), the students of the assorted divisions of the school were responsible for the majority of the physical maintenance of the Frank Lloyd Wright-designed school itself, encouraging students to learn self-governance. Hani Motoko was the first director of the school, her Christian ideologies helping to mold the direction that the school has undertaken to the contemporary moment.

References:
Shuri, Yuki, and Shinju Onuki. *Kakimoji no Dezain*. Tokyo: Graphic-sha, 2017.

FUJISHIMA TAKEJI 藤島武二

1867–1943

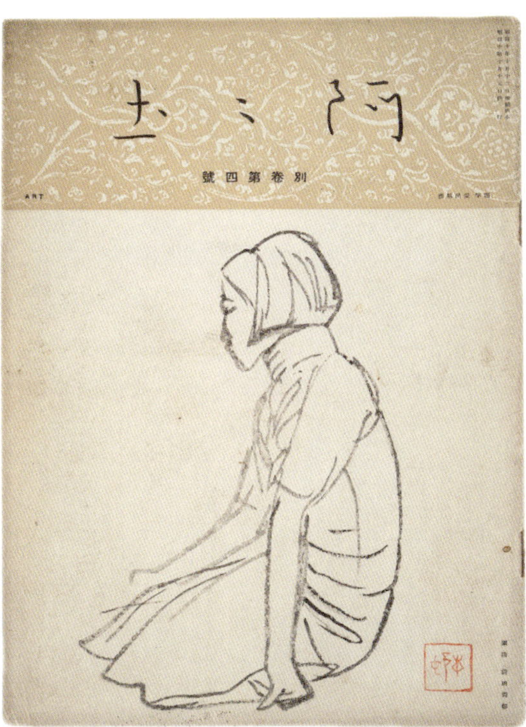

Aado Vol. 4 "Trends in Bird-and-Flower Paintings" 阿々土 別巻4号「花鳥画の動向について」(Tokyo: Aadosha 阿々土社, 1935). Cover design by Fujishima Takeji.

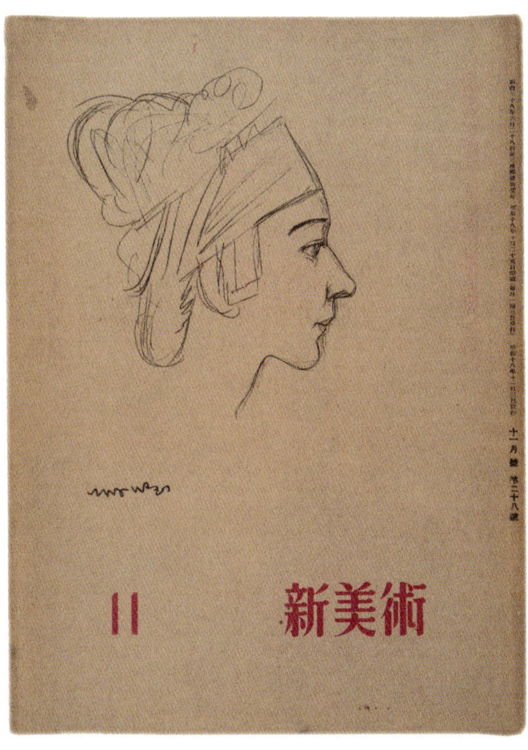

New Art No. 28 新美術 第28号, Fujishima Takeji Special Issue 藤島武二特集号 (Tokyo: Harutorikai 春鳥会, November 1941). An issue of one of Japan's most popular prewar art magazines focusing on Fujishima Takeji..

Fujishima Takeji was a leading artist, illustrator, and designer in the period after Japanese isolation. He was born in Kagoshima Prefecture to a family of former samurai. He studied both *nihonga*, or Japanese-style painting, and *yōga*, or Western-style painting with assorted painters including Kawabata Gyokusho 川端玉章 and Yamamoto Hōsui 山本芳翠. Fujishima became an assistant professor of art at the Tokyo School of Fine Arts in 1896, having been recommended by faculty member Kuroda Seiki, whose Hakubakai group Fujishima would eventually join. His studies led to him adopting the Art Nouveau style, which he would use to great effect in the cover design for the book *Tangled Hair* みだれ髪, the debut collection of classical *tanka* 短歌 poetry by Yosano Akiko 与謝野晶子 in 1901. The book became a runaway bestseller due to its expressions of desire and sexuality, in a time when Japanese society focused on pre-modern women's roles as mothers, daughters, and wives. The same year, Fujishima became the cover designer and illustrator for the magazine *Myōjō* 明星.

In 1905, the Ministry of Education sent Fujishima to Europe, where he studied painting in France at the École Nationale Supérieure des Beaux-Arts and in Rome at the French Academy. Upon his return in 1910, he was appointed a full professor at the Tokyo School of Fine Arts and was made a member of the Imperial Arts Academy and a jury member for the organization's annual exhibitions.

Fujishima is most remembered as a painter and educator, but his importance as an early graphic designer is unequivocal for translating Art Nouveau into graphic form for mass audiences in Japan.

References:

Fujishima, Takeji. *Geijutsu no Esupuri*. Tokyo: Chūō Kōron Bijutsu Shuppan, 2004.

Kobayashi, Mari. *Gaka No Bukku Dezain: sōtei to sōga Kara Miru Nihon no Honzukuri No rūtsu*. Tokyo: Seibundō Shinkōsha, 2018.

Shuri, Yuki, and Shinju Onuki. *Kakimoji no Dezain*. Tokyo: Graphic-sha, 2017.

Match labels

Matches were first produced and sold commercially en masse in Japan in 1876 by the Tokyo-based company Shinsuisha 新燧社, founded by Shimizu Makoto 清水誠. The very first matchbox labels bore red printing on a yellow ground adorned with cherry blossoms. During the first part of the nineteenth century, Japan became the world's third-largest manufacturer and exporter of matches after the United States and Sweden. Assorted motifs came to prominence on early Japanese matchbox labels: crouching lions copied from a Swedish design, tengu folk spirits, chickens, horses, cranes, swallows, elephants, giraffes, and assorted typographic treatments. Numerous other match-manufacturing companies cropped up shortly thereafter, providing matchboxes with customized labels for assorted domestic and foreign businesses, particularly in China and India. Daido Match Co., Incorporated 株式会社ダイドー was established in Japan by the Sweden Match Trust in 1927 via the reorganization of the companies Toyo Match 東洋燐寸株式會社 and Koekisha 株式会社公益社, a part-Japanese, part-Swedish venture that innovated thinner matches in 1900. One of the most enduring match label designs would be the "Momotaro" peach design created by Nittosha Incorporated 株式会社日東社 in 1923 and still available in convenience stores, supermarkets, and home centers across Japan today, no doubt encouraged by Yokoo Tadanori's 横尾忠則 inclusion of the legendary peach motif in his 1966 *Koshimaki-osen* 腰巻お仙 poster for the Situation Theater Group 劇団状況劇場.

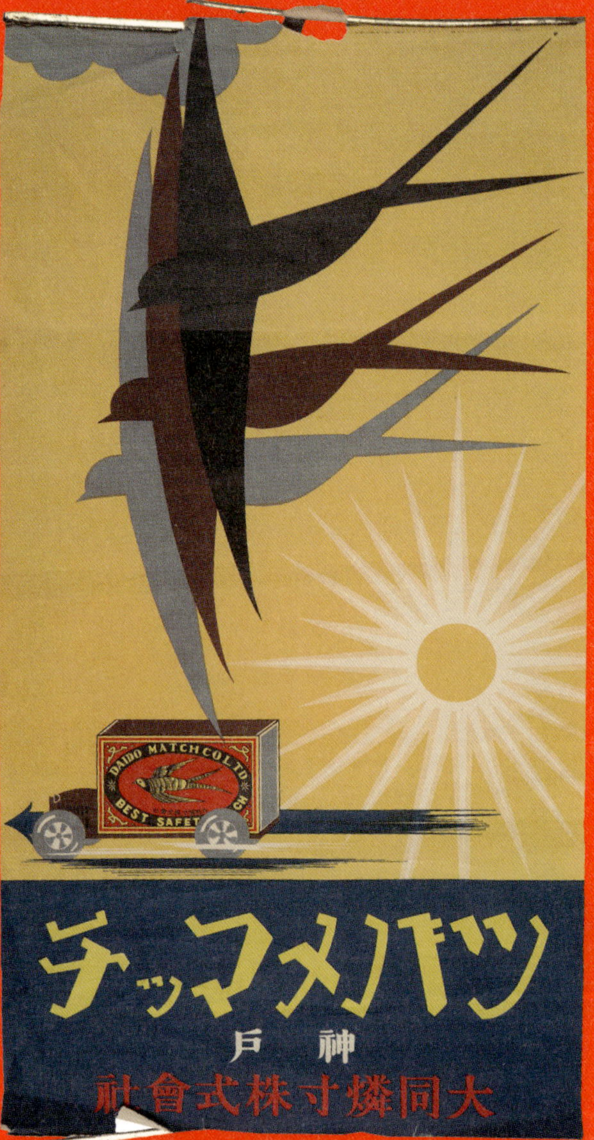

Tsubame Match ツバメマッチ poster for Daido Match Company, designer unknown, early 1920s.
A poster for Tsubame (Swallow) brand matches depicting swallows in flight, and a Tsubame matchbox as an automobile—a symbol of modernity.

Right: Assorted match labels printed in *Gendai Shogyo Bijutsu Zenshu (The Complete Commercial Artist)* 現代商業美術全集 Vol. 12 Wrapping Paper and Package Design 包紙·容器意匠図案集, 1929.

I

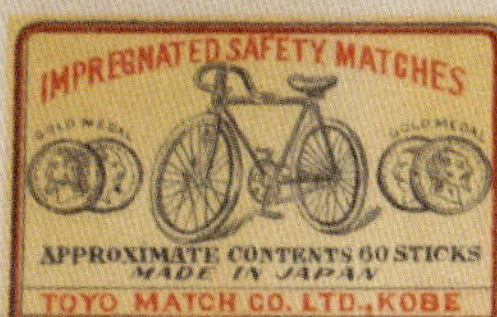

E

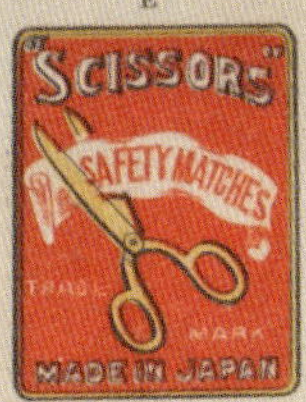

D

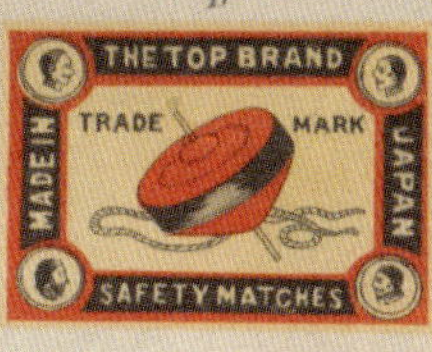

A

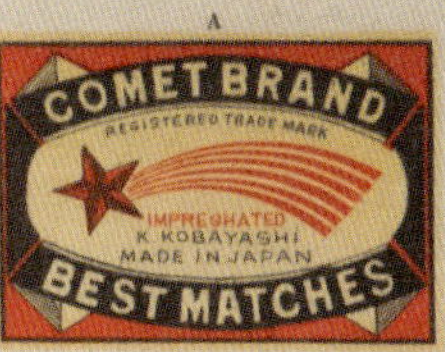

J

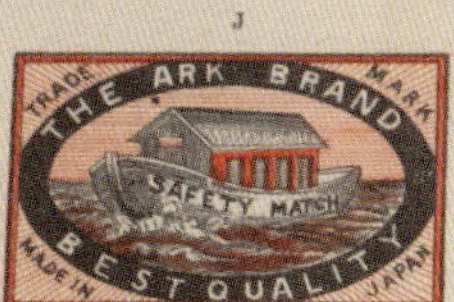

G

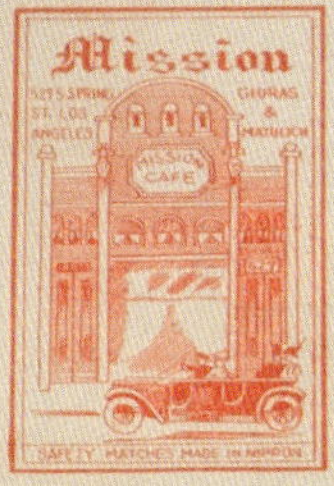

F

B

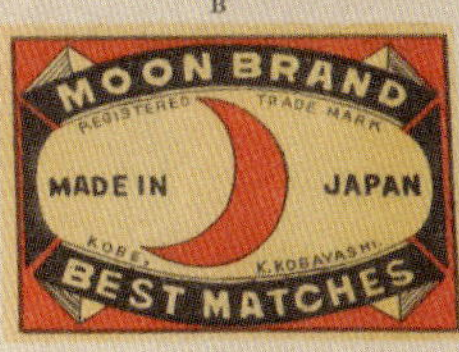

K

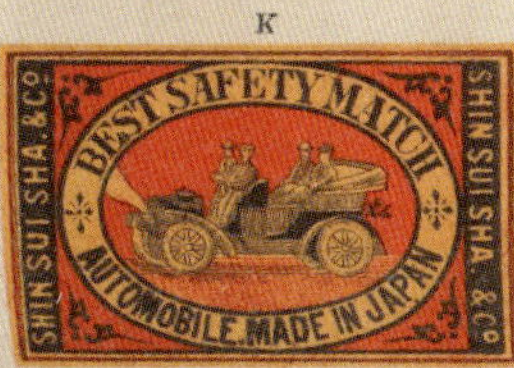

H

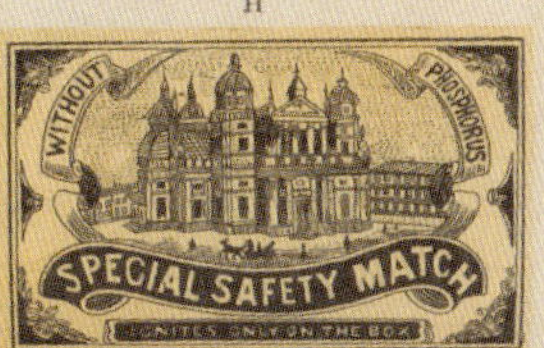

C

G

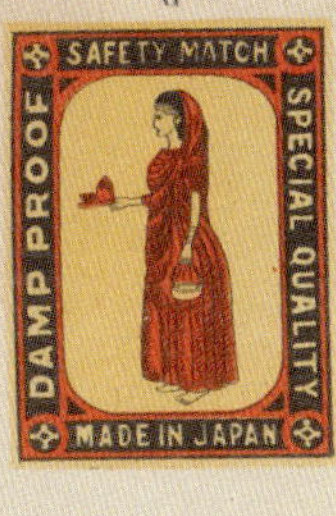

C

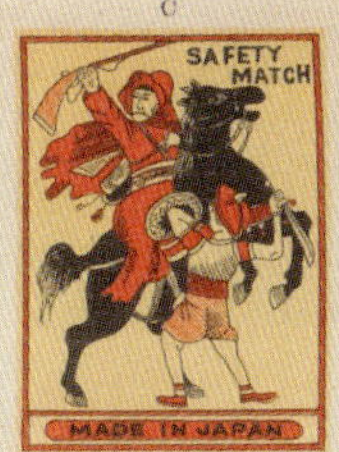

I

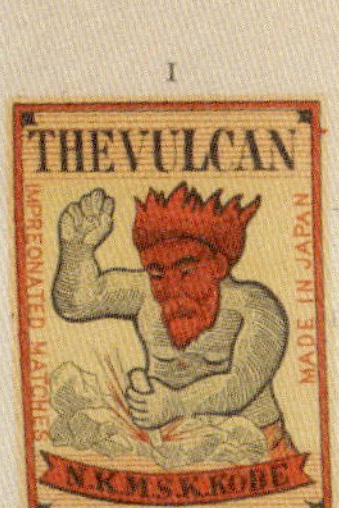

E

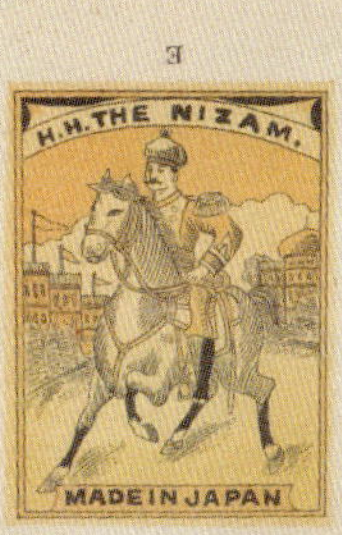

A

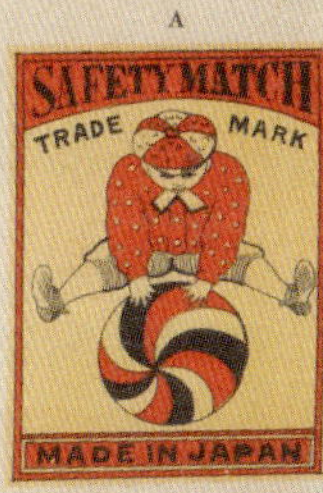

H

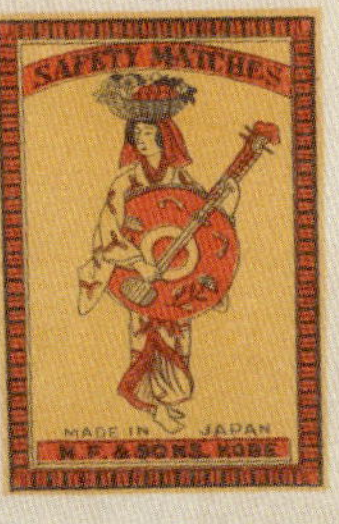

D

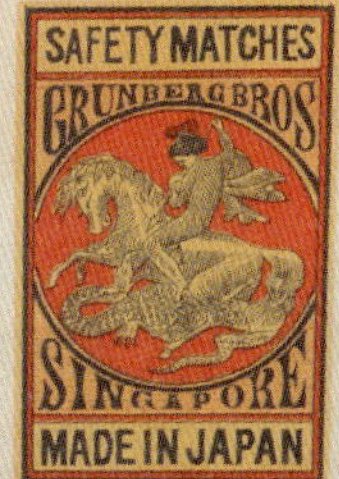

J

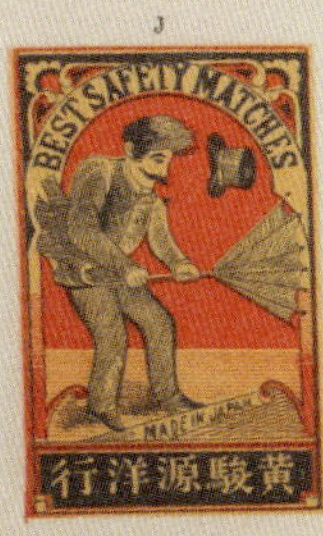

F

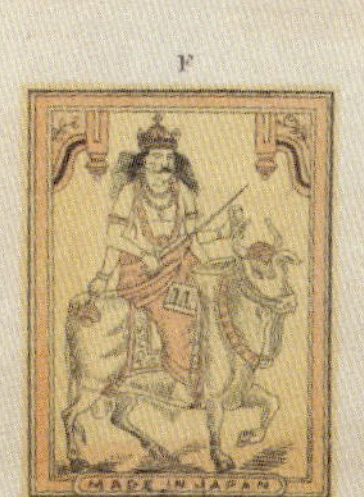

B

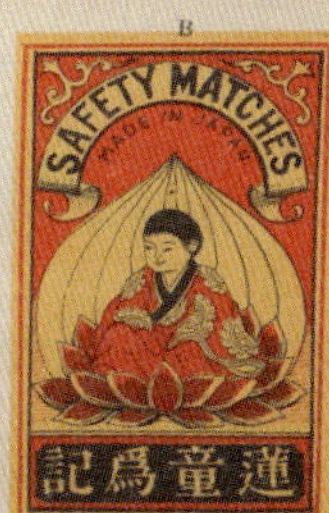

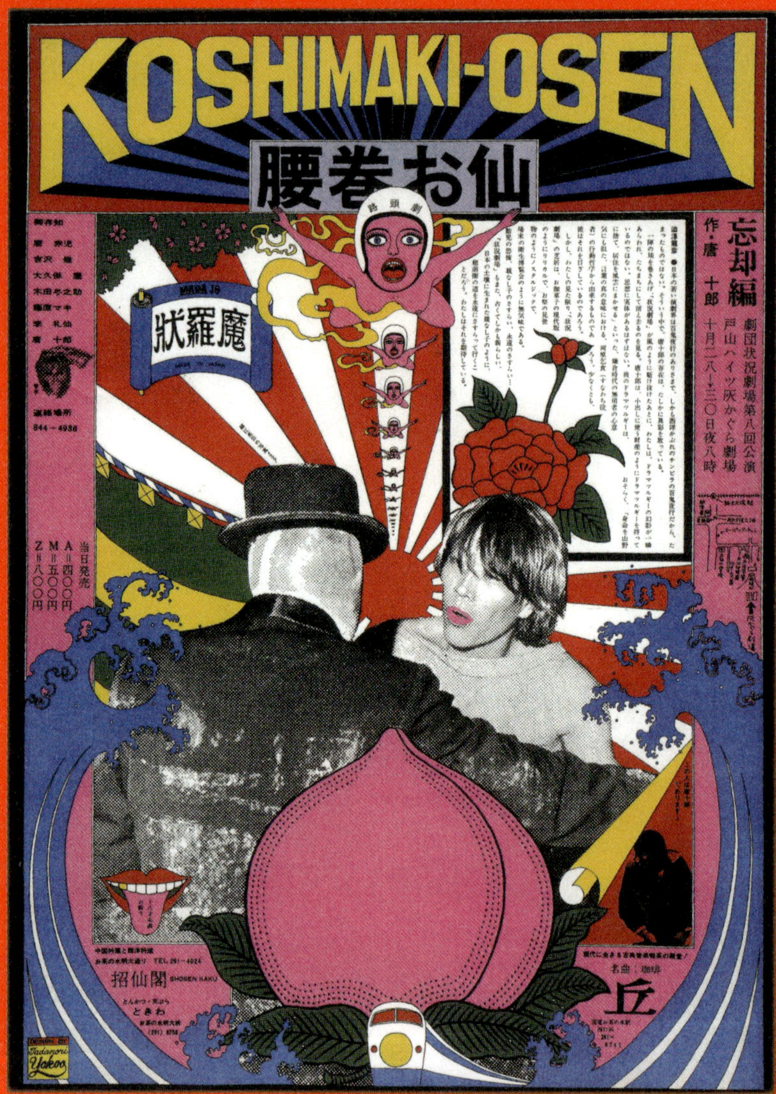

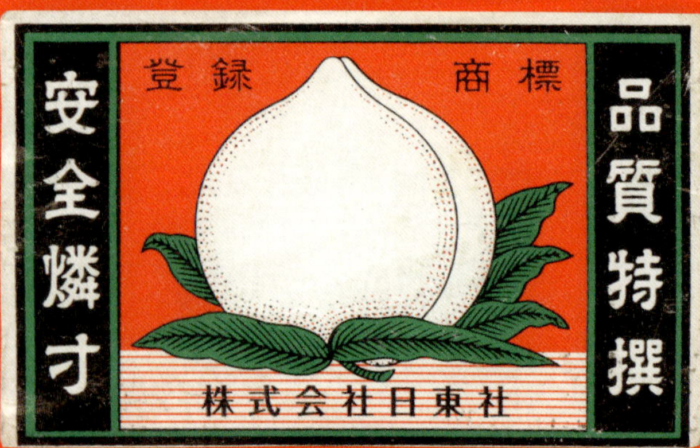

Above: ***Koshimaki-osen*** 腰巻お仙 poster for the Gekidan Jokyo Gekijo 劇団状況劇場 (Situation Theater Group) designed by Yokoo Tadanori 横尾忠則 in 1966. Below: **Nittosha Incorporated 株式会社日東社** matchbox, original design circa 1923. Yokoo utilized the peach motif from historic Nittosha matchboxes in his iconic poster for the 1966 Angura stage production above.

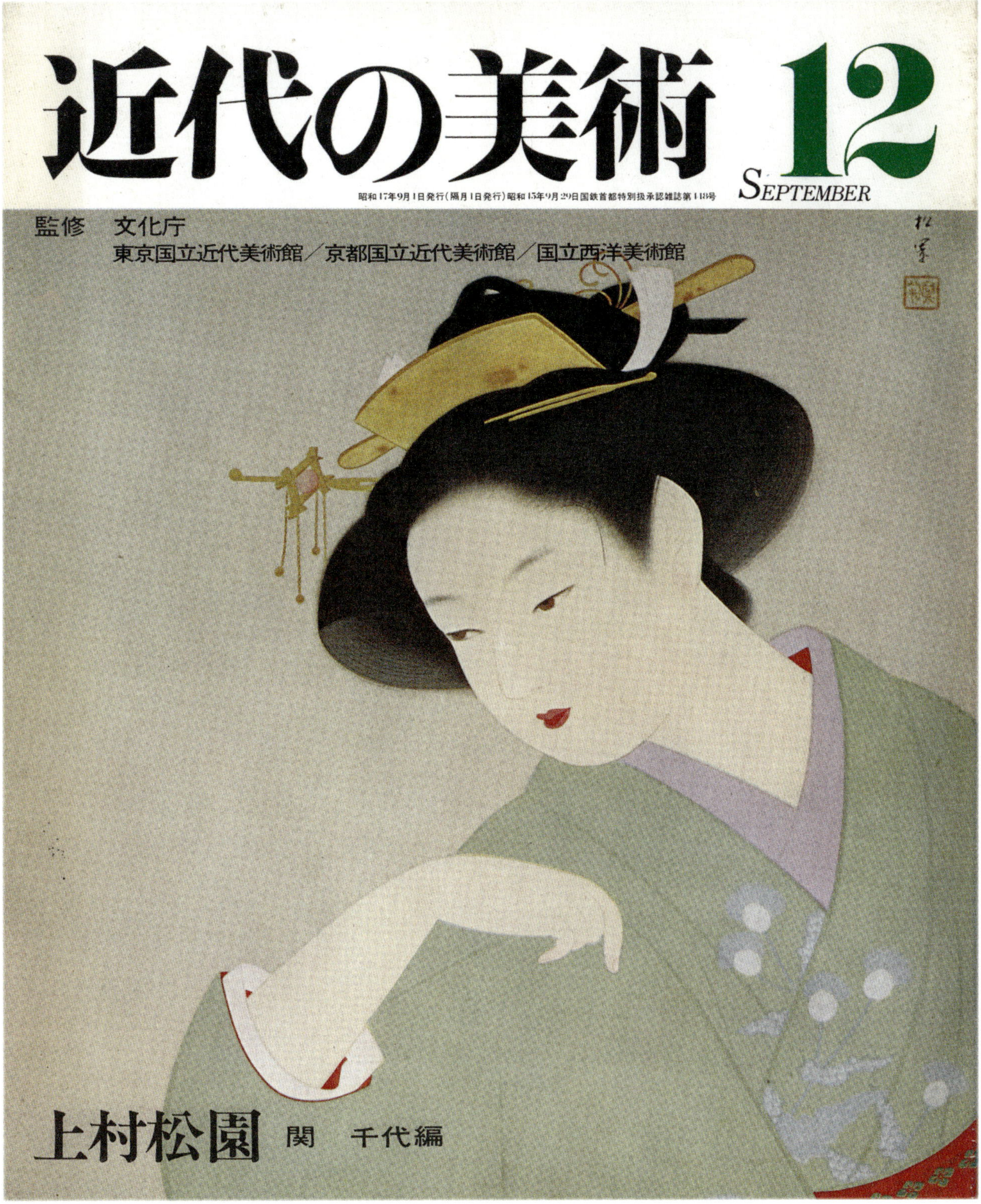

近代の美術 12

SEPTEMBER

昭和17年9月1日発行(隔月1日発行)昭和45年9月29日国鉄首都特別扱承認雑誌第118号

監修　文化庁
東京国立近代美術館／京都国立近代美術館／国立西洋美術館

上村松園　関　千代編

Kindai no bijutsu 12 近代の美術 12 (Tokyo: Shibundo 至文堂, 1972).
Cover of a special issue of *Kindai no bijutsu* (*Modern Art*) magazine focusing on the work of Uemura Shōen.

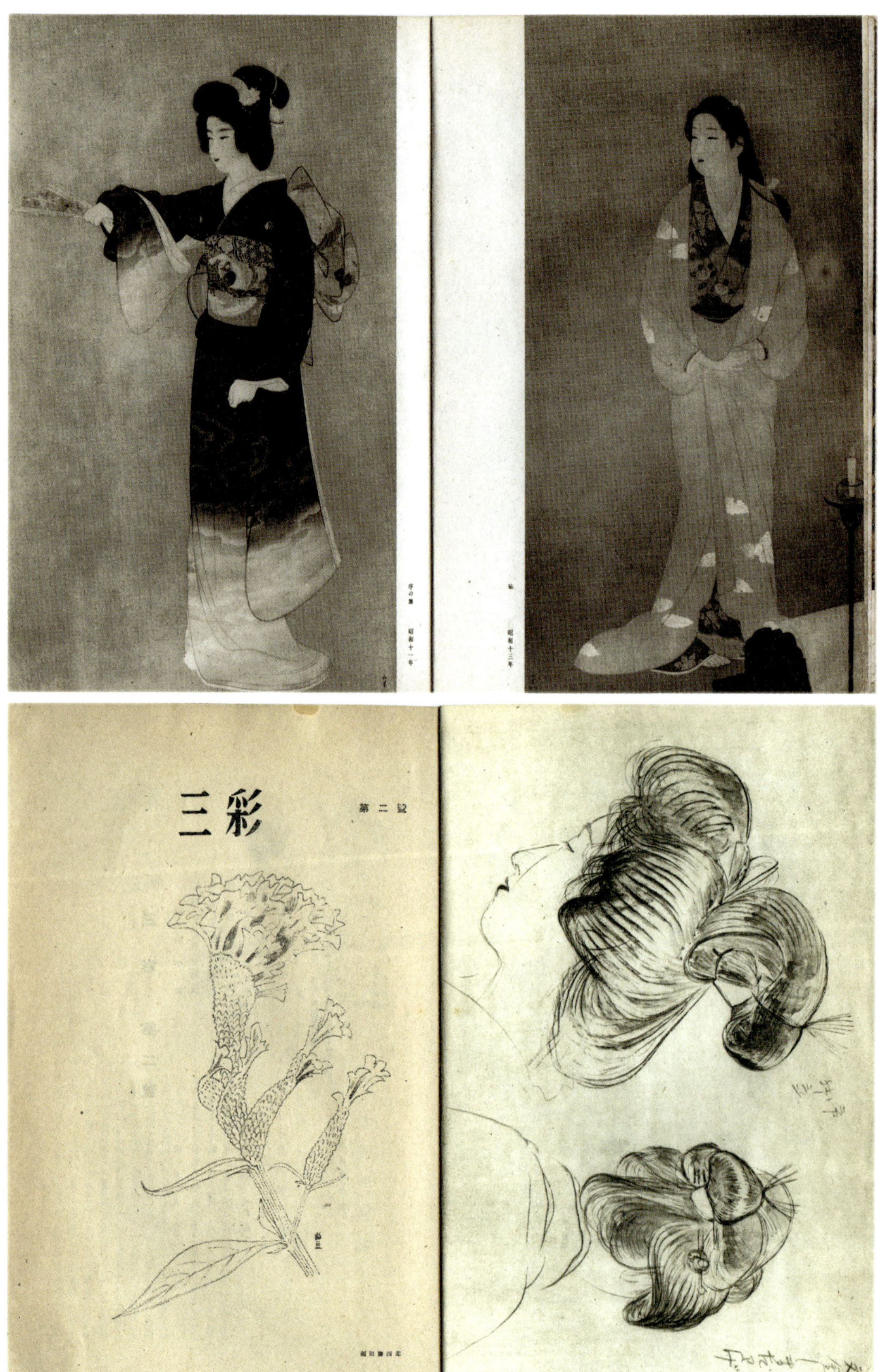

Title page and spreads from ***Sansai*** **No. 2, 三彩 第2号 (Tokyo: Nihon bijutsu shuppan 日本美術出版, October 1946).** One of the last features in a Japanese art publication on the life-work of Uemura Shōen before her death in 1949. The title page includes a floral illustration created by Uemura specifically for this issue of *Sansai*.

UEMURA SHŌEN 上村松園

1875–1949

Uemura Shōen was born Uemura Tsune 上村津禰 in Kyoto to a tea merchant family. Her father passed away two months before she was born, so she was raised in an all-female household, and her mother encouraged her study of art despite criticism from other family members. Sewing lessons were considered more appropriate than studying art for a young woman at that time. Uemura enrolled in the Kyoto Prefectural School of Painting 京都府画学校 in 1887 at the age of thirteen, where she studied under nihonga landscape painter Suzuki Shōnen 鈴木松年, who bestowed upon her the first kanji of her artist name "Shōen," which means "pine."

Suzuki resigned from the school the following year, and Uemura followed him as a private student. Uemura exhibited her painting "Women of the Four Seasons" at the Third Industrial Exposition held in Tokyo in 1890, winning an award. The painting was purchased by a visiting British prince, making Uemura a celebrity in the Japanese art world at the age of fifteen. She left Suzuki's tutelage in 1893 to study under Kōno Bairei 幸野楳嶺 for two years and then began studying under Takeuchi Seihō 竹内栖鳳 in 1895 after Kōno's death, at which time she established herself as a professional painter. She emerged as one of the earliest female painters of the Meiji era who came from a non-elite family and chose to specialize in figurative painting and artwork. Her paintings combined technical mastery with a romanticized reverence for her medium: bijinga 美人画, paintings of idealized beautiful women.

Uemura gave birth to a son, Uemura Shōkō 上村松篁, out of wedlock in 1901, the result of an extramarital relationship with her former teacher Suzuki. The perception of unmarried mothers in greater Kyoto society at that time would normally have led to some social ostracization, yet Uemura's decision to pursue the life of an artist, at a time when it was rare for non-aristocratic women to do so, allowed her to raise her son in what would otherwise be an untenable cultural situation. Uemura and her mother closed their tea shop in 1903 and made their living solely on the income provided by Uemura's painting commissions and sales and her private teaching of a large number of female students. The magazine *Chūō Bijutsu* 中央美術 recognized that she was the wealthiest female painter in Japan in 1916, having built a sizable private home containing her studio two years prior. Uemura was invited to participate in the state-sponsored Bunten exhibition and was bid to demonstrate her painting prowess in front of the empress at the 1916 exhibition.

Primarily remembered as a painter, Uemura designed the covers of periodicals as well, integrating more bold and graphic illustration work depicting her preferred idealized female subjects with a masterful approach to lettering. Her choice to depict women who were fulfilled in their traditional roles as wives and mothers stood in direct opposition to her own circumstances. In her own words, "My paintings are not simply faithful portrayals of beautiful women in reality. Rather, I try to express my own ideal of feminine beauty and womanhood while paying attention to realistic representation." [1]

Uemura received the Cultural Decoration, the highest honor bestowed upon an artist in Japan at that time, in 1948, making her the very first woman to receive it.

1 Morioka Michiyo, *Changing Images of Women: Taishō Period Paintings by Uemura Shoen (1875–1949), Ito Shoha (1877–1968)*, and Kajiwara Hisako (1896–1988) (Seattle: University of Washington Press, 1990), 52.

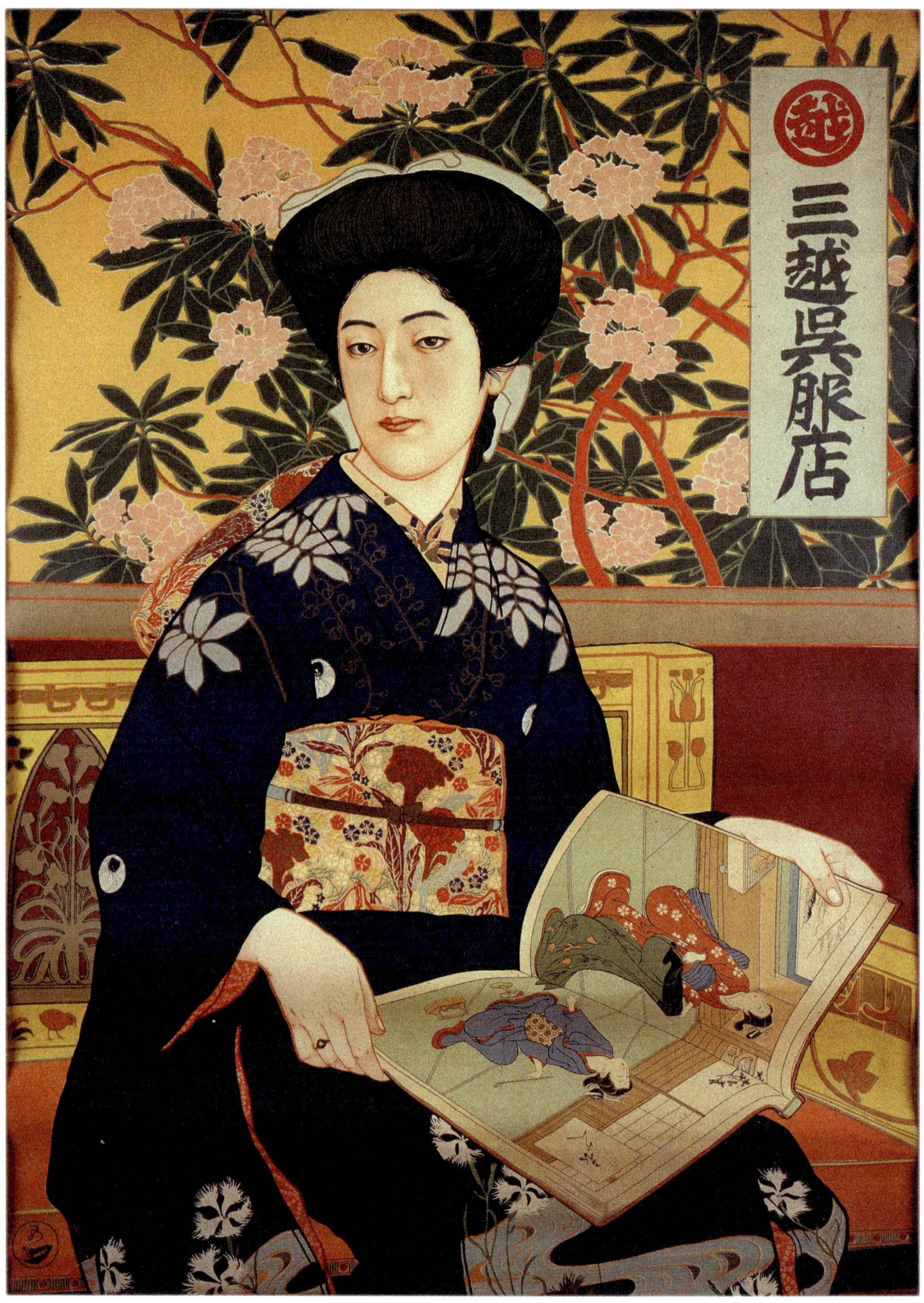

***Mitsukoshi Department Store* poster by Hashiguchi Goyō 橋口五葉, Tokyo: 1911.** This Hashiguchi poster is significant for the mix of Western and Japanese aesthetics, deft use of figure/ground relations, and decorative wallpaper patterning in the background.

HASHIGUCHI GOYŌ 橋口五葉

1880–1921

Hashiguchi Goyō was born under the name Hashiguchi Kiyoshi 橋口清 in Kagoshima Prefecture, on the island of Kyushu. His father was a samurai and a traditional painter. He encouraged his son to pursue art, enrolling the young Kiyoshi in classes with a teacher from the Kano school at ten years old. Kiyoshi later moved to Tokyo and studied at the Hakubakai under Kuroda Seiki before attending the Tokyo School of Fine Arts in the yōga section of the school. Hashiguchi graduated at the top of his class in 1905 and began working under the name Hashiguchi Goyō around that time, "goyō" being the name of a particular five-needle pine tree (*goyō matsu*) that was in his father's garden.

Shortly after Hashiguchi graduated he began doing design work, starting with a commission for the book design and illustration work for author Natsume Sōseki's *I Am a Cat* 吾輩は猫である in 1905. An examination of middle-class Japanese life and criticism of Westernization narrated by a house cat, the story was originally serialized in the literary journal *Hototogisu* ホトトギス. In book form, it became a bestseller and led to numerous further design and illustration commissions for Hashiguchi from authors such as Futabatei Shimei 二葉亭四迷, Uchida Roan 内田魯庵, Morita Sōhei 森田草平, Nagai Kafū 永井荷風, and Izumi Kyōka 泉鏡花. Hashiguchi also designed the English-language translation of Sōseki's *I Am a Cat* in 1906.

Hashiguchi exhibited an oil painting in the first Bunten exhibition in 1907, but he became frustrated at the public's lack of interest in his fine art work afterward. He continued designing commercially, entering a poster competition held by the Mitsukoshi department store in 1911 and winning out over 300 other entrants, earning 1,000 yen in prize money. The poster, a lavish painting of a woman in a formal kimono lounging on a decorative Art Nouveau chaise lounge and perusing a book of ukiyo-e prints, was widely distributed and brought further attention to Hashiguchi. The poster is important for Hashiguchi's use of the *bijinga* theme, literally showing bijinga ukiyo-e prints in the poster's subject's hands with the "bijin," or beautiful woman, rendered in the Western tradition of painting, honoring Japanese historical aesthetics as much as combining it with Western painting. Hashiguchi's deft depiction of the evolution of tradition brought him much acclaim.

Hashiguchi continued designing books and produced a number of print advertisements, posters, and calendars for the Japanese postal steamship company Nippon Yūsen Kaisha 日本郵船会社 throughout the 1910s. He also began writing about ukiyo-e for assorted publications, garnering the attention of Watanabe Shōzaburō 渡辺庄三郎, a publisher of popular prints and a leader in promoting the *shin-hanga* 新版画 (new printmaking) movement. In 1915, Watanabe asked Hashiguchi to create a new painting for his business, to be carved and printed by the Watanabe workshop carvers and printers in the style of older ukiyo-e prints. The resulting bathing-themed print, *Yuami* 湯浴み, gained relative popularity in Japan, along with a large proportion of the print run being sold for export to Europe. This print is notable for largely kicking off the popularity and public interest in the shin-hanga printmaking movement.

In 1916 and 1917, Hashiguchi supervised the twelve-volume collection *Japanese Brocade Prints in the Ukiyo-e Genre Style* 浮世風俗やまと錦絵. Each oversized book contained twenty woodblock-printed reproductions of early ukiyo-e prints from 1600–1800 including works by masters of ukiyo-e such as Utamaro, Sharaku, Toyokuni, Harunobu, Koryusai, Hiroshige, and Hokusai.

Hashiguchi returned to printmaking in 1918, choosing to coordinate the designing, carving, printing, and distribution of his works himself rather than working with Watanabe Shōzaburō's venture, thereby retaining quality control. His prints were of exquisite quality and were produced in small editions which garnered high prices on the art market of the day, further enhancing his reputation. Hashiguchi produced thirteen more prints before succumbing to beriberi-induced meningitis, dying in 1921 at the age of forty-one.

Hashiguchi's family produced seven of his unfinished printmaking works after his death, before the family printmaking studio and many of the woodblocks were destroyed in the Great Kanto Earthquake of 1923, making the surviving Hashiguchi prints incredibly rare and expensive.

Hashiguchi straddled yōga and nihonga aesthetics, a divisive move at that time. His command of multiple forms of artistic production—printmaking, graphic design, publishing, and painting—enabled him to work in the multiple styles of the day and furnished him a decent income. Hashiguchi designed over seventy books and was a lasting influence on European artists during his lifetime.

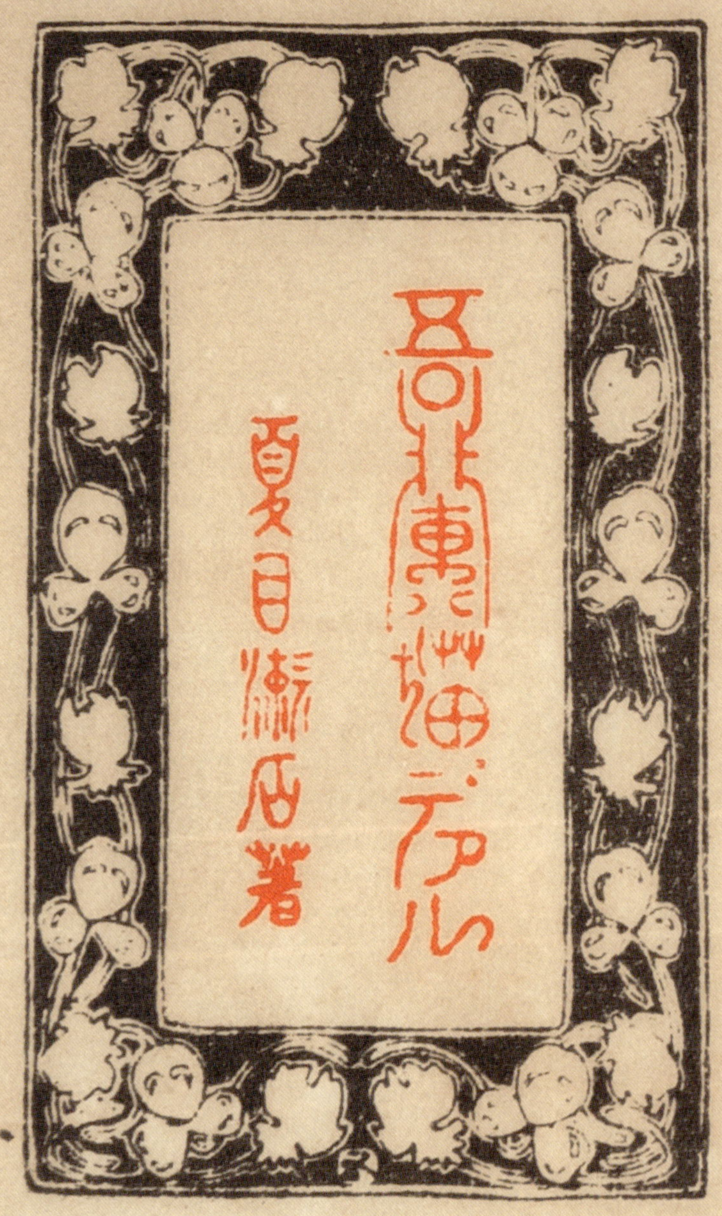
吾輩ハ猫デアル
夏目漱石著

Cover and title page design of ***I Am a Cat* 吾輩ハ猫デアル (吾輩は猫である), Natsume Sōseki 夏目漱石** (Tokyo: **Hattori Shoten 服部書店 & Ōkura Shoten 大倉書店, 1905), design & illustration by Hashiguchi Goyō 橋口五葉, calligraphy by Nakamura Fusetsu 中村不折.**
The cover features Hashiguchi's gold-embossed illustration of a cat playing in a patch of flowers, surrounded with reversed-out motifs that the audience might assume a cat would be preoccupied with, notably mice and fish. The flower-patch theme is carried over into the decorative border framing historic tensho script calligraphy by Nakamura Fusetsu 中村不折.

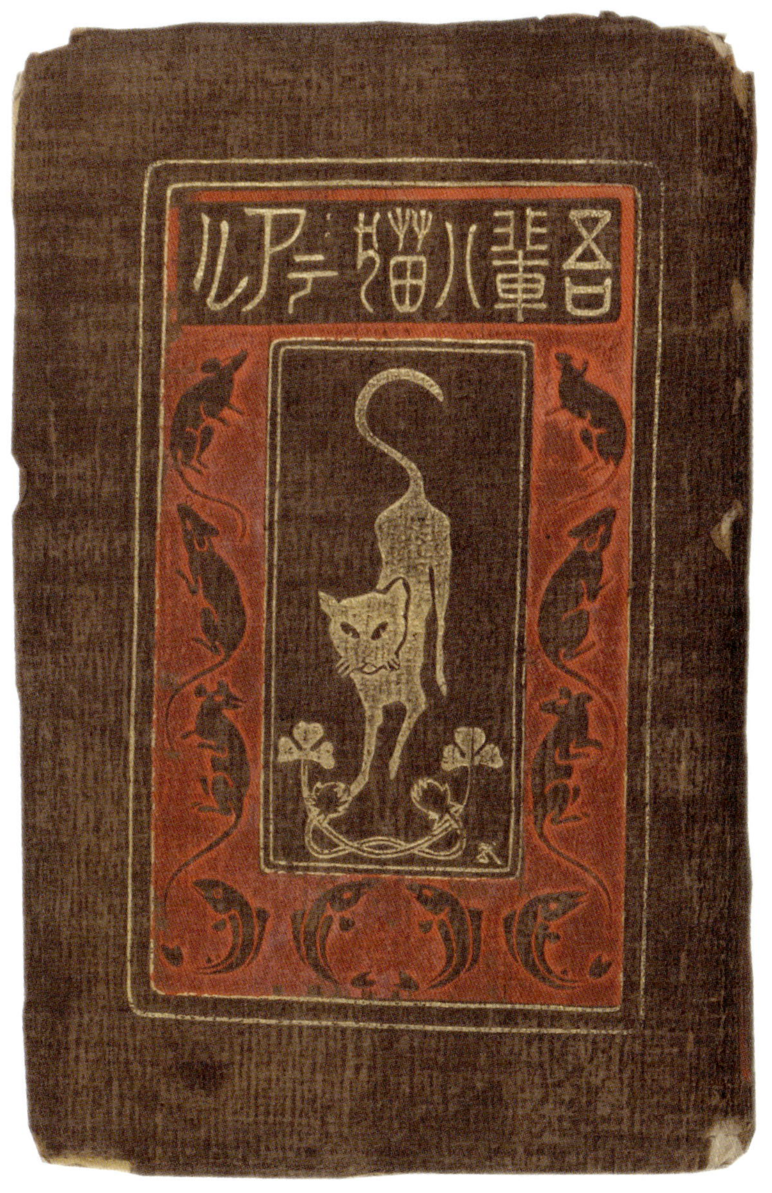

References:

Kobayashi, Mari. *Gaka No Bukku Dezain: sōtei to sōga Kara Miru Nihon no Honzukuri no rūtsu*. Tokyo: Seibundō Shinkōsha, 2018.

Nishiyama, Junko, and Hashiguchi Goyō. *Hashiguchi Goyō: sōshoku-e no jōnetsu*. Tokyo: Tokyo Bijutsu, 2015.

Shuri, Yuki, and Shinju Onuki. *Kakimoji no Dezain*. Tokyo: Graphic-sha, 2017.

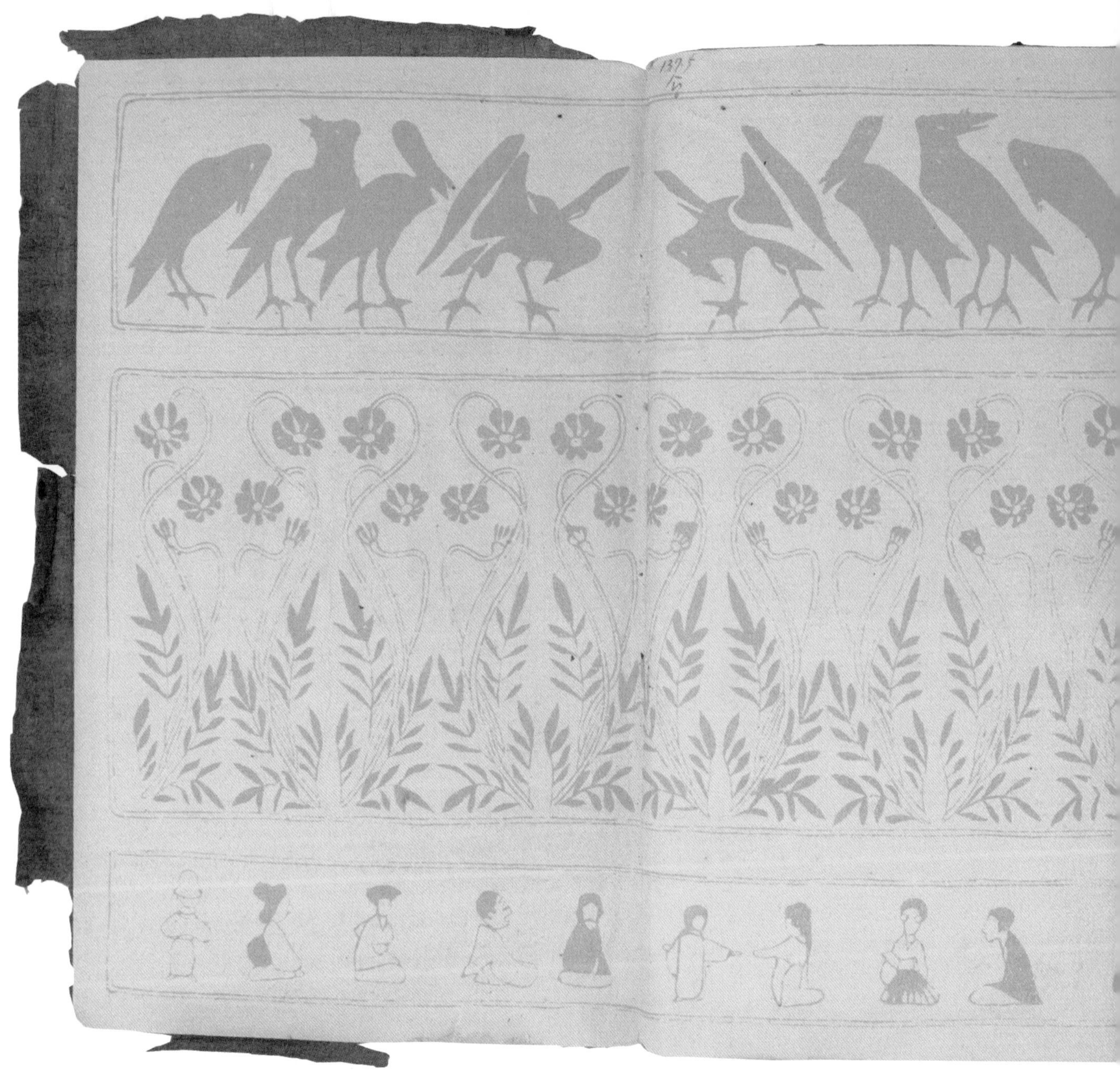

Endpapers of ***I Am a Cat* 吾輩ハ猫デアル (吾輩は猫である), Natsume Sōseki 夏目 漱石** (Tokyo: Hattori Shoten 服部書店 & Ōkura Shoten 大倉書店, 1905), design & illustration by Hashiguchi Goyō 橋口五葉.
The endpapers of the book are a mix of Art Nouveau-inspired flowers, birds, and human forms encapsulated in delicate borders rendered by Hashiguchi.

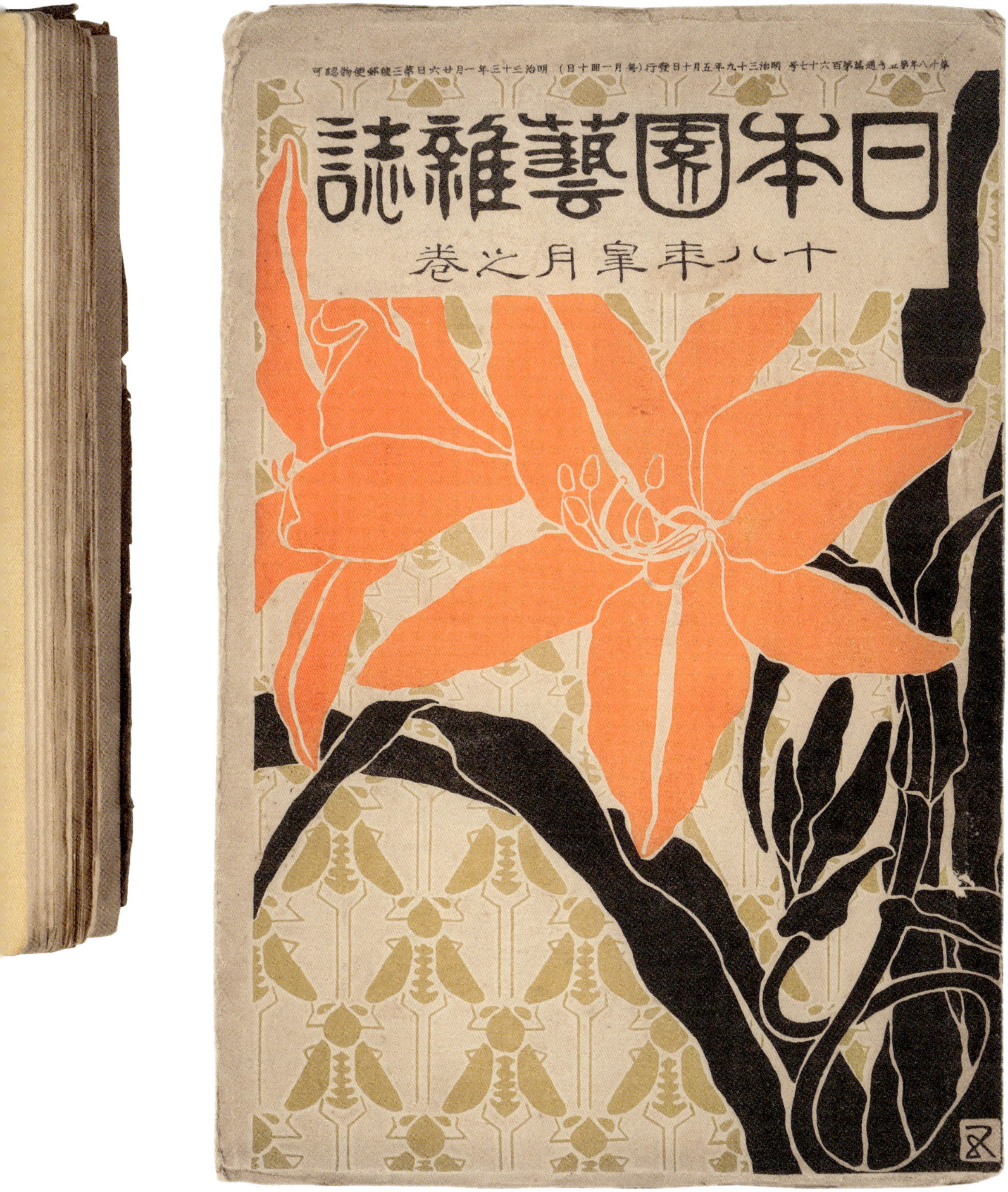

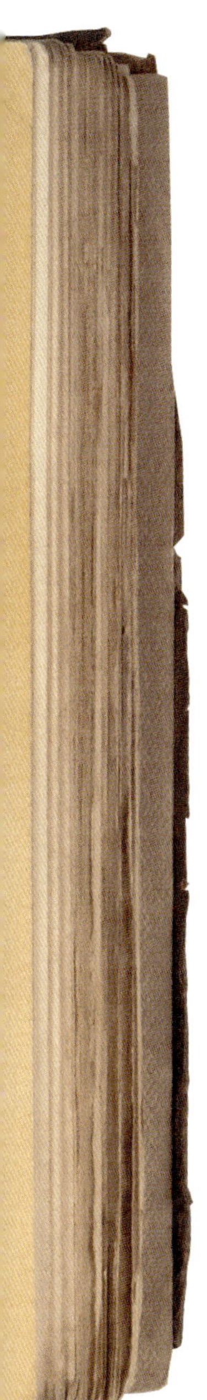

Japanese Horticulture **18th Edition, No. 167 日本園芸雑誌　第18年皐月之巻 第167号, cover by Hashiguchi Goyō 橋口五葉 (Tokyo: Japanese Horticultural Society 日本園芸会, 1906).** This magazine cover by Hashiguchi mixes rigid patterning of a bee motif overlaid with the dominant organic flower illustration. The stroke crowding and the rounded open forms of the masthead lettering mimic and localize Art Nouveau lettering in a Japanese context.

Tōkai yūshigin (East Asian Nomadic Poetry) **東海遊子吟,** Bansui Doi 土井晩翠著 (Tokyo: Dainihontosho 大日本図書, 1906). Designed by Nakamura Fusetsu 中村不折. Image courtesy of Waseda University.

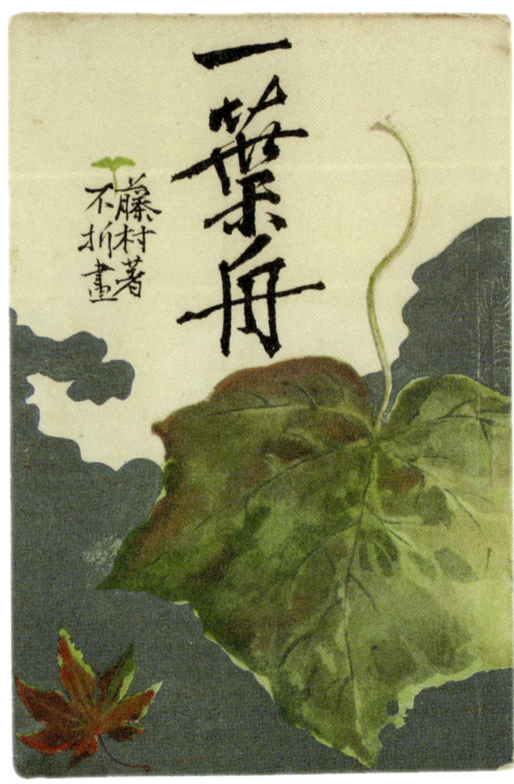

Hitohabune (Pontoon) **一葉舟,** Shimazaki Tōson 島崎藤村著, (Tokyo: Shunyōdō 春陽堂, 1898). Designed by Nakamura Fusetsu 中村不折. Image courtesy of Waseda University.

NAKAMURA FUSETSU 中村不折

1866–1943

Nakamura Fusetsu was born in Ēdo (now Tokyo) and is known for his work as both a painter and a calligrapher. Nakamura's family moved to Nagano prefecture when he was a child, though Nakamura would return to Tokyo in 1887 to study at the school Jūichikai Kenkyūjo 十一会研究所 under the painter Koyama Shōtaro 小山正太郎. Nakamura began working as one of Japan's first newspaper illustrators for the women- and children-oriented newspaper *Sho Nihon* 小日本 in 1894, and he went on to work for another publisher, Nippon Shinbunsha 日本新聞社, in their illustration department.

Nakamura's painting work was exhibited in both the second and fifth Meiji Art Exhibitions, and he traveled to France and stayed there from 1901 to 1905. Nakamura studied under Raphaël Collin at the Académie Colarossi in Paris, then he transferred to the Académie Julian and studied under Jean-Paul Laurens. He also studied with Alphonse Mucha, Henri Royer, and Gabriel Ferrier for short periods. Nakamura returned to Japan in 1905 and continued his work as a painter, illustrator, and designer.

Nakamura was renowned as a lettering artist well versed in a variety of historical lettering styles. In 1906, Nakamura designed the calligraphic lettering for Sōseki Natsume's novel *I Am a Cat* 吾輩は猫である. He also provided editorial design and illustration to Hototogisu ホトトギス, the literary journal which published many of Sōseki's early serialized literary works. Nakamura designed a number of books for the poet and author Shimazaki Tōson 島崎藤村, including his collection *Wakanashu* 若菜集. Nakamura was an avid student of Chinese calligraphy and introduced certain classical forms of calligraphy to Japanese audiences. A collector of related ephemera, Nakamura opened a calligraphy museum called Shodō Hakubutsukan in 1936 (now operated by the local ward as Taitō City Calligraphy Museum 台東区立書道博物館), where he regularly exhibited items from his collection.

References:

Kobayashi, Mari. *Gaka No Bukku Dezain: sōtei to sōga Kara Miru Nihon no Honzukuri No rūtsu*. Tokyo: Seibundō Shinkōsha, 2018.

Ohiro, Noriko. "正岡子規と中村不折--俳句革新運動と「美術」= Masaoka Shiki and Nakamura Fusetsu: On the Modernization of *Haiku* and *Sho* in the Meiji Era" *Machikaneyama Ronso, Graduate School of Letters, Osaka University* 40 (December 2006): 29–44.

Shuri, Yuki, and Shinju Onuki. *Kakimoji no Dezain*. Tokyo: Graphic-sha, 2017.

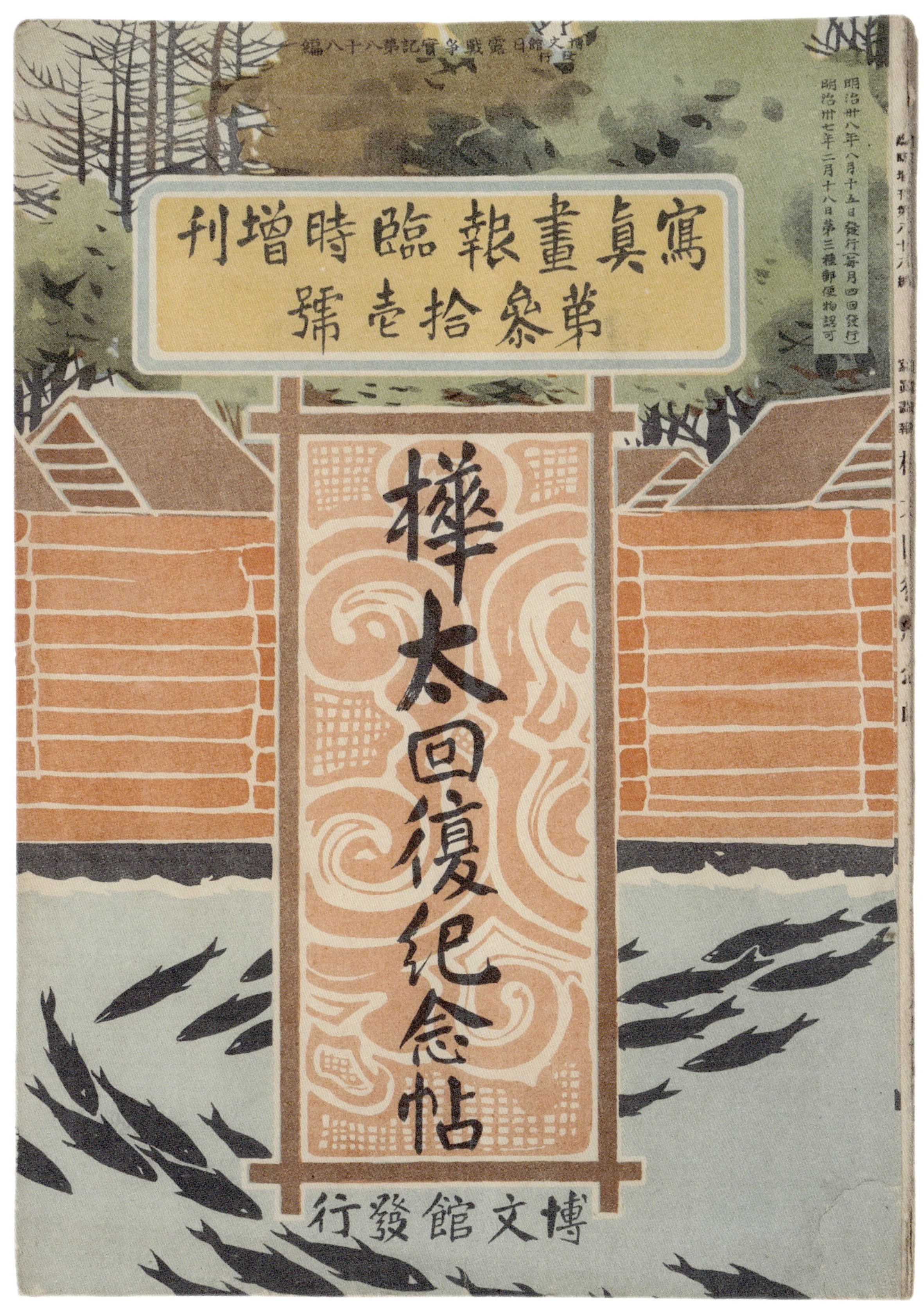

Sakhalin Recovery Calendar 樺太回復紀年帖 (Tokyo: Hakubunkan 博文館, 1905). An example of Nakamura Fusetsu's illustration mixed with his agile calligraphic forms.

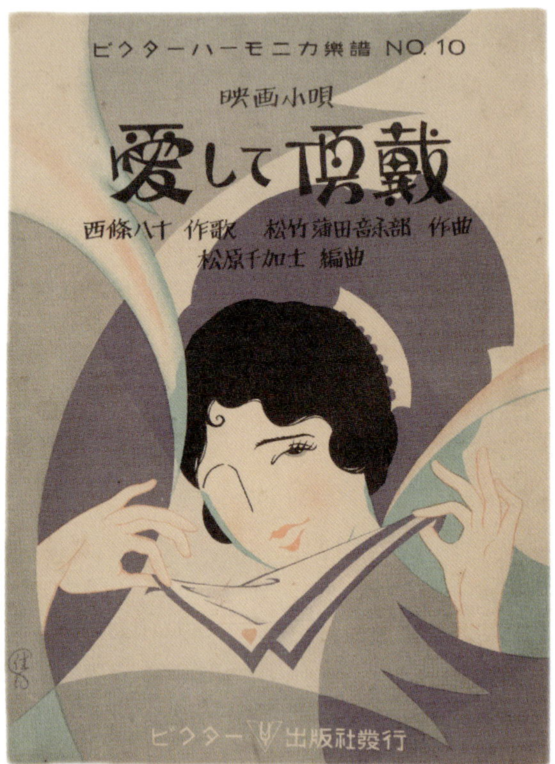

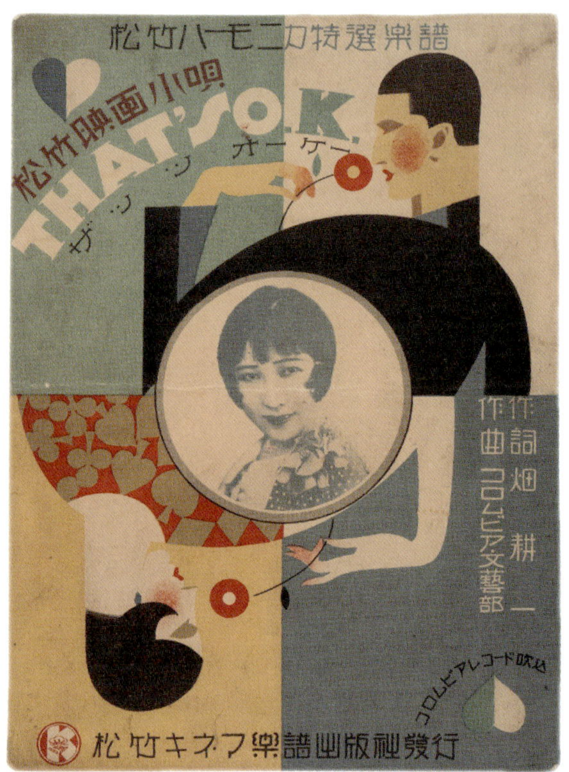

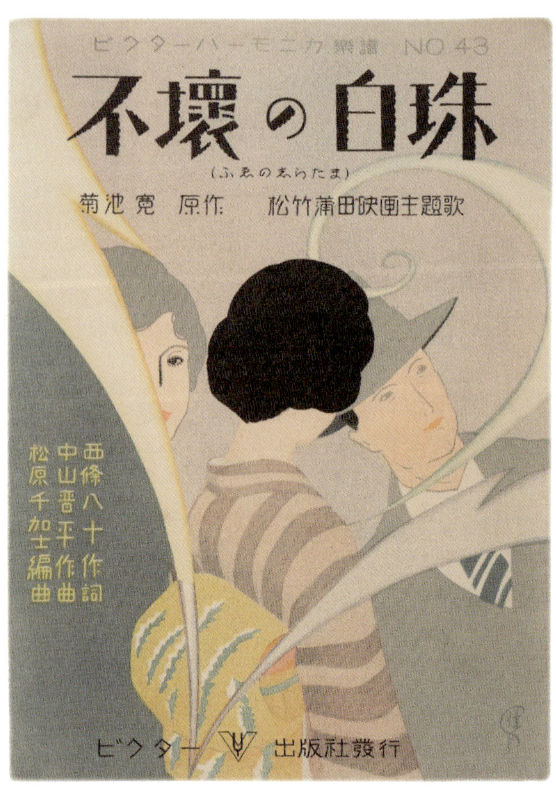

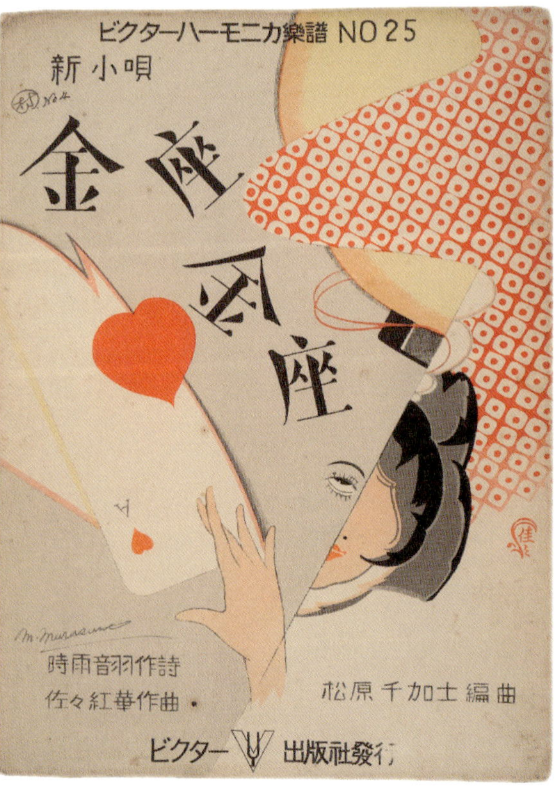

Clockwise from top left: **"Please Love Me" 愛して頂戴** (Tokyo: Victor Publishing ビクター出版社, 1930); **"That's O.K./Miss Nippon's Song" ザッツオーケー ミス・ニッポンの歌** (Tokyo: Victor Publishing ビクター出版社, 1930); **"Kinza Kinza" 金座金座** (Tokyo: Victor Publishing ビクター出版社, 1929); **"Eternal Pearls" 不壊の白珠** (Tokyo: Victor Publishing ビクター出版社, 1930). An assortment of musical score cover designs by Saito Kazo 斎藤佳三 that depict his multiple approaches to composition, cropping, perspective, mixing photographic and illustrative representation, and dissecting the picture plane. At the core of most of these compositions are representations of modern women and modernity rich with symbols of romance, danger, seduction, renewal, and metropolitan living.

SAITŌ KAZŌ 斎藤佳三

1887–1955

Saitō Kazō was born in Yajima-cho in Akita Prefecture. Saitō originally aspired to be a musician, first studying at the Tokyo School of Music and later going to school for design at the Tokyo School of Art. After graduating, Saitō spent time in Berlin, where he became fascinated with German Expressionism, in particular the work of Wassily Kandinsky. Upon his return to Japan, Saitō organized a 1923 exhibition of woodcut prints by German Expressionists at the Hibiya Museum of Art which greatly affected many of his contemporaries, including Onchi Kōshirō and Tōgō Seiji.

Saitō became deeply involved in stage and costume design, reflecting his interest in the integration of art and life, as well as his passion for music. He designed *omoshirogara* 面白柄 novelty patterned fabrics for yukata and kimono and was the cover designer for a large number of musical score booklets released by Victor Publishing and JVC Publishing. His sheet music cover designs in the 1920s and 1930s were influential in both their compositional approaches and their use of connotative and idiosyncratic display lettering. Saito also worked as design director for Yamaha, creating their logo consisting of three crossed tuning forks.

He lectured at Tokyo School of Art from 1919 to 1944, teaching dressmaking and design and taking on the role of director of the school from 1920 onward. Saitō traveled to Europe again in 1922, commissioned by the Ministry of Agriculture and Commerce to research design, patent law, and design education. While in Germany, Saitō visited the Bauhaus in the Weimar Republic and other influential art institutions.

During this time, he became the art director for the film production company Shochiku Kinema 松竹キネマ and was involved in multiple interior design projects, furthering his interests in the integration of art, design, and the everyday.

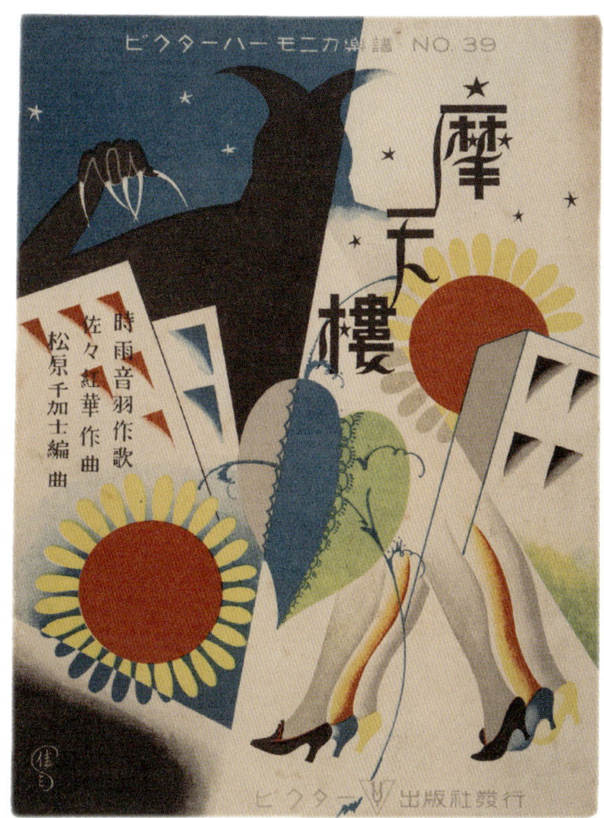

"Skyscrapers" 摩天樓, music score cover (Tokyo: Victor Publishing ビクター出版社, 1929).

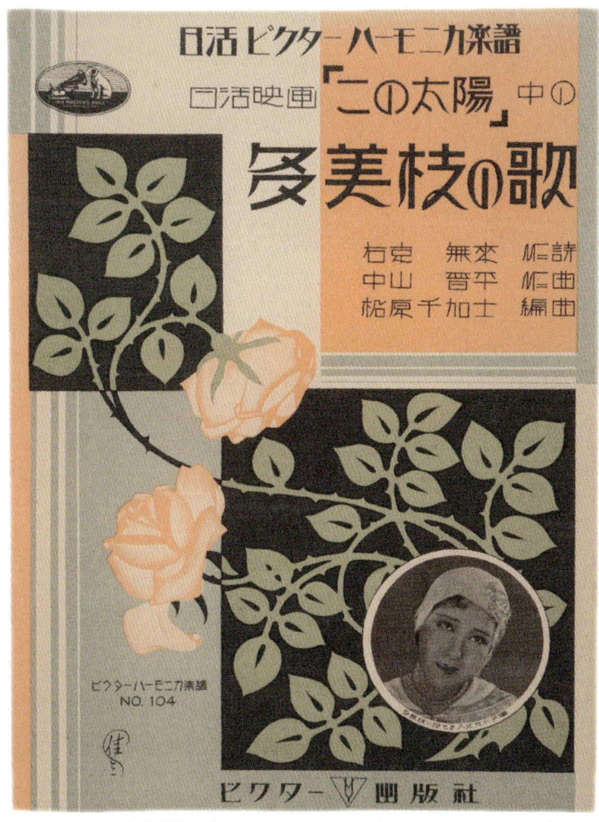

"Tamie's Song" 多美枝の歌 music score cover (Tokyo: Victor Publishing ビクター出版社, 1930).

References:

Koshikakezawa, Mai. "'Senow Gakfu' and the Reception of Western Music in Japan during the Taishō Period." *Bulletin, Faculty of Music, Tokyo National University of Fine Arts & Music* 13, no. 62 (March 13, 1988): 29–98.

Weisenfeld, Gennifer S. *Mavo: Japanese Artists and the Avant-Garde, 1905-1931*. Berkeley: University of California Press, 2010.

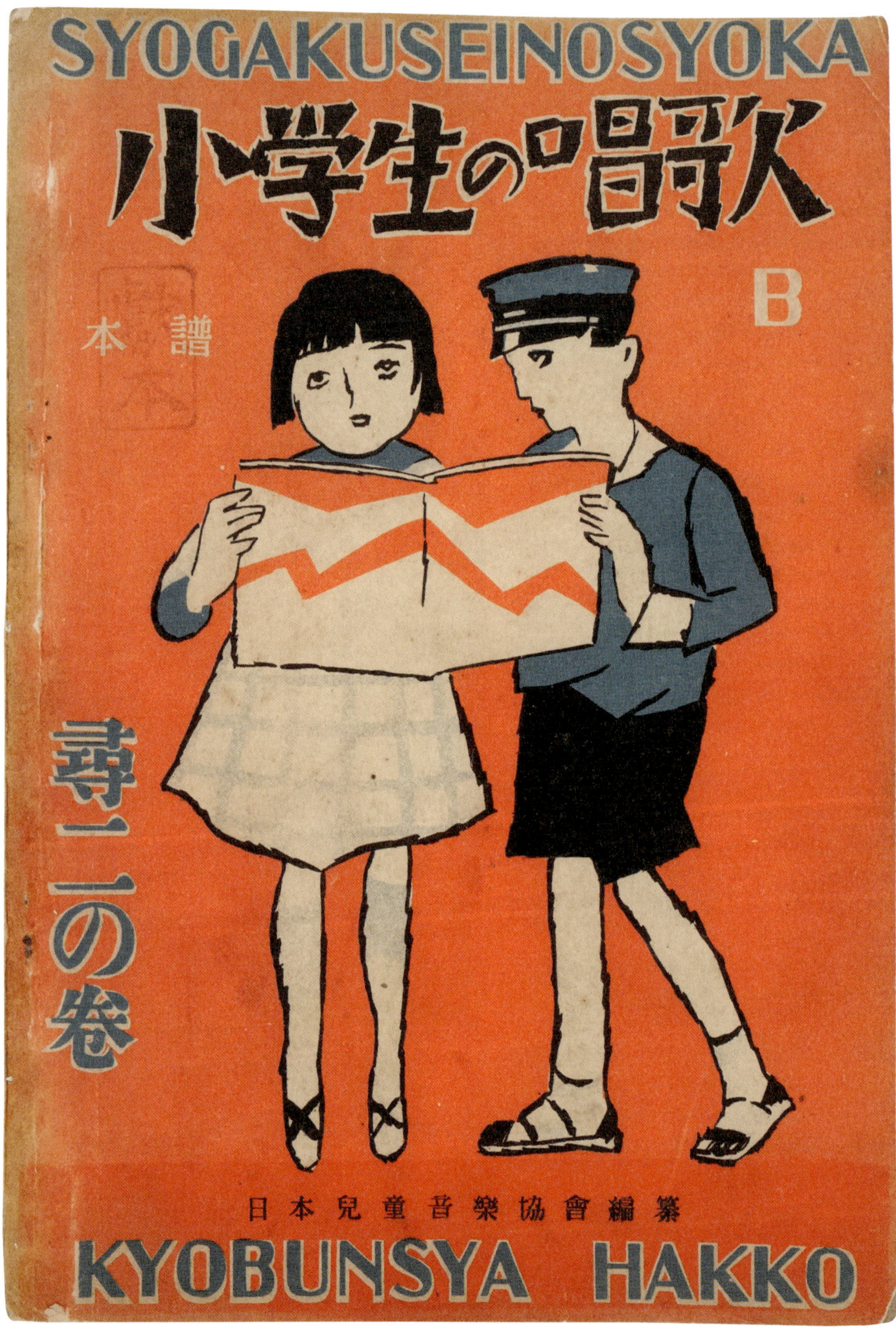

Front cover of ***The Elementary School Songbook* 小学生の唱歌** (Tokyo: Kōbunsha 光文社, 1927). The cover depicts two schoolchildren utilizing the book, with the girl singing and the boy looking on adoringly. Of note is the way that Yumeji has depicted the children's eyes—as with most of his pictorial work, the eyes appear wan and doleful.

1 Takehisa Yumeji and Tomoko Taniguchi, *Takehisa Yumeji: Taishō Modan Dezain Bukku* (Tokyo: Kawade Shobō Shuppansha, 2003), 33.

TAKEHISA YUMEJI 竹久夢二

1884–1934

Takehisa Yumeji was born in Okayama as Takehisa Mojirō 竹久茂次郎, later giving himself the artist name Takehisa Yumeji, and he is largely referred to as "Yumeji" in Japanese popular culture today. As a youth, Yumeji intended to become a poet but shifted toward a career in art, illustration, printmaking, and design in order to make a living. His poetic tendencies would resurface years later through his songwriting. Yumeji did not study art formally, having studied business at Waseda University in Tokyo, where he joined circles of Christians and leftists. He worked at a brush-making business on the side, where he practiced art. While a student, he submitted numerous illustration samples to magazines in the hope of getting published, and he soon began making a living from resultant commissions.

In 1905, Yumeji abandoned his studies and devoted his life to the production of art and illustration. Yumeji created illustration works for the socialist newspaper *Chokugen* 直言 and, using a pseudonym, contributed illustrations to the socialist publications *Hikari* 光 and *Heimin Shimbun* 平民新聞. Yumeji's political beliefs were mirrored in his perspectives on creative work—he opposed contemporary conceptions of "artists," believing the culture of art to be pretentious and classist.

In 1907, Yumeji married Kishi Tamaki 岸たまき, the proprietor of a Tokyo postcard shop for which he then produced printed postcards. Their turbulent marriage ended in divorce just two years later, though they would continue a working and romantic relationship on and off for years afterward. Through his printed projects for the shop and his illustration work published in books and magazines, Yumeji's output slowly grew in popularity.

In 1909, he released his first book of drawings and poems, *Takehisa Yumeji Picture Collection – Spring Volume* 夢二画集春の巻, of which he said, "I am going to write a poem using pictures instead of words."[1]

Yumeji held his first solo exhibition in 1910. His work was filled with renderings of wanly beautiful, large-eyed, melancholic, and sylphlike Japanese women who evoked nostalgia in audiences for the lost floating world of old Ēdo. The women depicted in his illustrations and prints were largely based on Kishi and other lovers he consorted with over the years. Through his obsessive renderings of women, Yumeji became an icon in the Taishō Romanticism movement which combined Western romanticism with indigenous approaches to form and craft. Yumeji's audience was composed of men and women alike, and the affordable nature of his printmaking works led to his popularity. Yumeji was influenced by the Jugendstil school of Art Nouveau, while Jugendstil itself had been informed by Japanese aesthetics. He was an avid reader of the Jugendstil journals *Simplicissimus* and *Jugend* and a fan of German painter Heinrich Vogeler and Japanese painter Fujishima Takeji, both known for their detailed renderings of subjects' eyes, which no doubt influenced Yumeji.

Yumeji struck up a lasting friendship with the artist, designer, and printmaker Onchi Kōshirō 恩地孝四郎 while Onchi was a student. The pair would work together for many years on an assortment of book projects, beginning with *Dontaku* どんたく, a collection of Yumeji's poetry published in 1913. Five years later, one of its poems, "Evening Primrose" 宵待ち草, would be set to music and become a smash hit.

I wait even though I know she will not return.
My heart sinks in melancholy like the evening primrose.
It seems that the moon will not appear tonight

From 1916 until 1929, Yumeji began designing and illustrating the covers for musical scores from the publisher Senoo Ongaku Shuppansha セノオ音楽出版社, resulting in over 280 cover designs. The company was run by Senoo Kōjirō 妹尾幸次郎, a promoter and local manager for Western musicians performing in Japan. Senoo was incredibly influential, as he was the founder and president of The Association for the Study of Occidental Music. During his time working for Senoo, Yumeji became widely known to the public. Many of the scores were purchased by people who neither played nor read music, but who simply appreciated Yumeji's visual output.

Yumeji started collaborating with the successful feminist lesbian novelist Yoshiya Nobuko 吉屋信子 in 1915, the same year Yoshiya began to publicly diverge from gender expectations with her move to Tokyo and adoption of a more androgynous appearance. Her serialized novels were published in girls' and women's magazines and became incredibly popular with young women, and Yumeji provided the accompanying illustrations. Yoshiya introduced the genre of "shōjo fiction,"

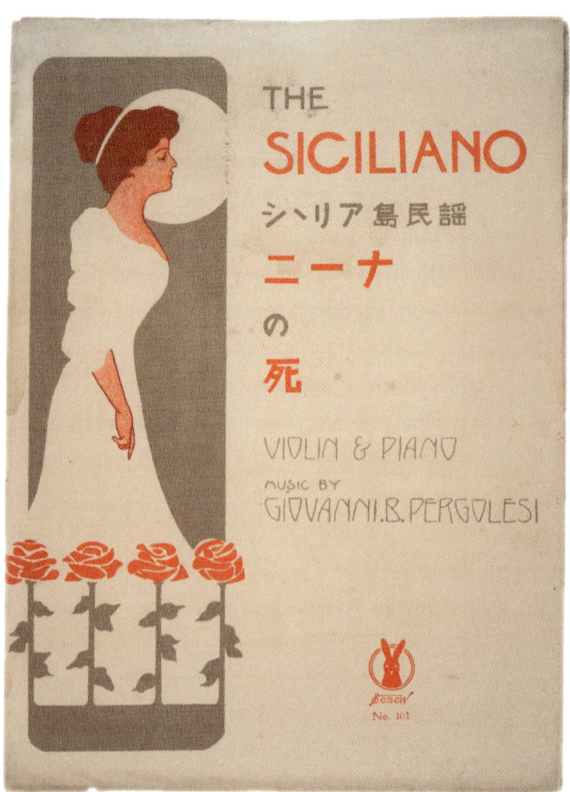

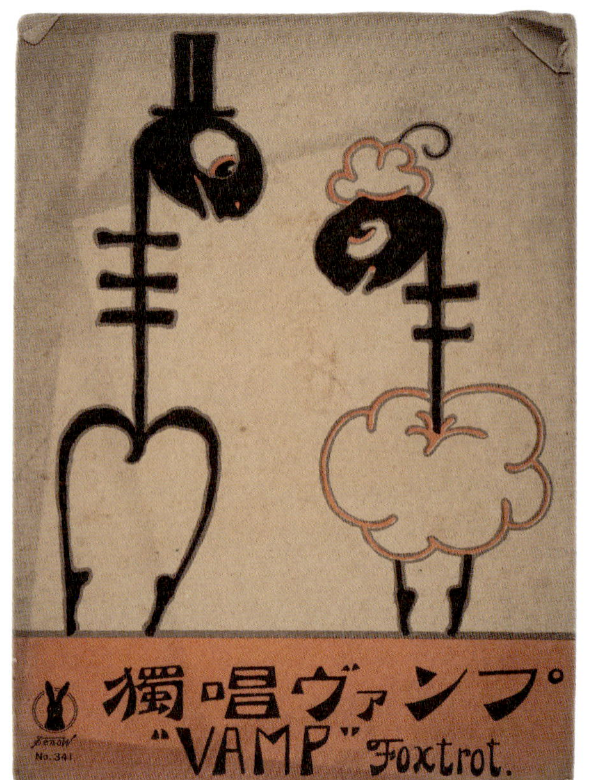

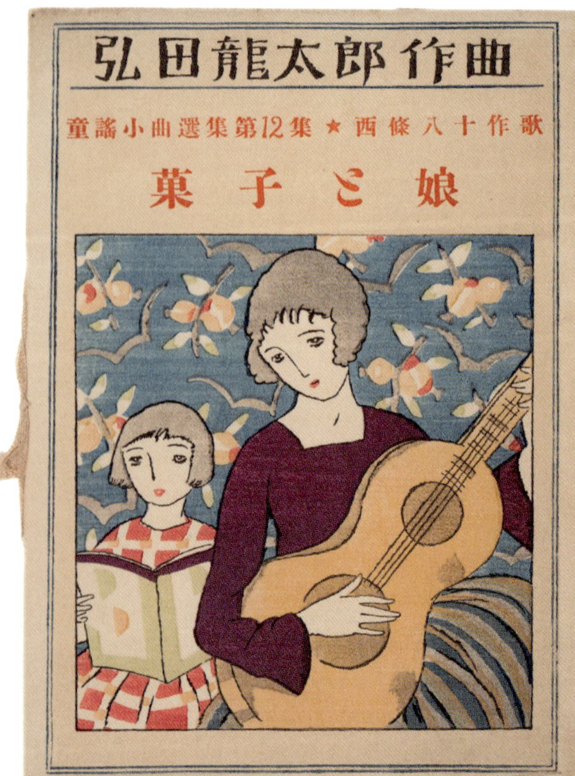

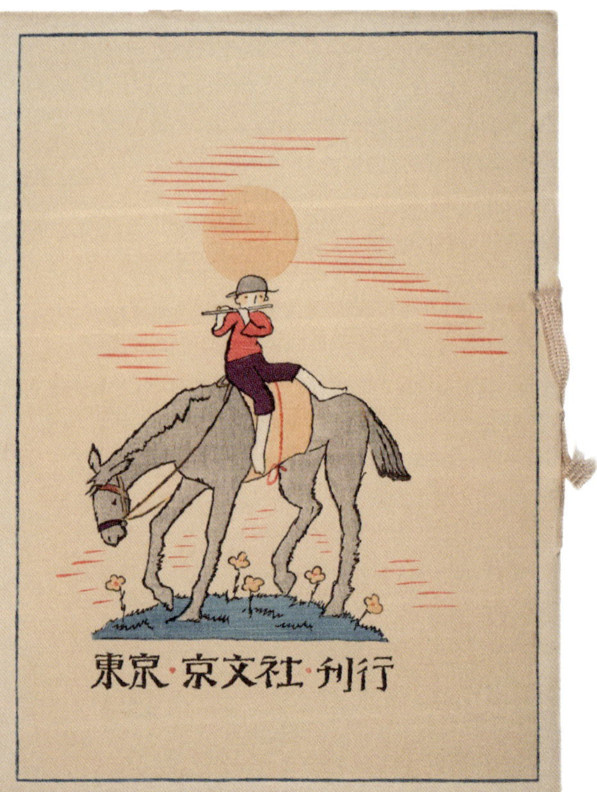

Clockwise from top left: **"The Death of Nina (The Siciliano)" シシリア島民謡ニーナの死** music score (Tokyo: Senoo Ongaku Shuppansha セノオ音楽出版社, 1929); **"Vamp"** (Tokyo: Senoo Ongaku Shuppansha セノオ音楽出版社, 1924); multicolored woodblock-printed front and back cover designs for ***Nursery Rhyme Short Song Selection No. 12, "Sweets and Daughter"*** **弘田龍太郎作曲童謡小曲選集第*12*集「菓子と娘」** (Tokyo: Kōbunsha 光文社, 1931). All designed by Takehisa Yumeji 竹久夢二.

2 Lavenberg, Irwin. "Takehisa Yumeji (1884-1934)." The Lavenberg Collection of Japanese Prints. Irwin Lavenberg, 2017. http://www.myjapanesehanga.com/home/artists/takehisa-yumeji-1884-1934.

alternately known as "Class S" fiction—stories about young women that defied traditional romantic roles. Shōjo 少女, as defined in Suzuki Michiko's book *Becoming Modern Women*, is a classification of young women who might be defined as a "virgin" or a "maiden"—individuals who are older than "girls" but whose heterosexual virginity is still intact.

Yoshiya's writing introduced mutual sexual attraction between young women into popular literature at that time—writing in which strong emotional bonds were formed between young women and resulted in same-gender romantic love. Shōjo fiction helped normalize public attitudes toward same-gender relationships in the late 1910s through the mid-1930s, especially between those in adolescence. Same-gender sexuality was depicted regularly in earlier erotic shunga 春画 ukiyo-e, though woman-on-woman imagery was far less common than man-on-man depictions. Yoshiya's literature extended same-gender female relationships from being voyeuristic to viable, with her own life and lifestyle as example.

Due to the popularity of Yoshiya and Yumeji's collaborative works, in 1916 Yumeji was invited to become the chief illustrator for the magazine *Shin-shōjo* 新少女, a sister publication to Japan's oldest women's magazine, *Fujin no Tomo* 婦人之友. Publications for women of all ages were booming at the time, as publishers and advertisers recognized the economic power that women consumers held in urbanized early-twentieth-century Japan. Because of national educational reforms beginning in 1870, female literacy rates had increased exponentially, helping to make literature aimed at the female populace both profitable.

In particular, the shōjo, the time in women's lives between puberty and marriage which was unregulated by convention, emerged in the public consciousness. As Japan's urban centers rapidly industrialized, liminal roles for women other than loyal daughter, obedient wife, or wise mother were recognized in both popular culture and society. Yumeji's illustrative work became the pictorial analogue in printed media, showing a variety of women who did not conform to these prior archetypes. His celebrity as an image-maker was bolstered by his feats of poetry and songwriting, along with the widely known tales of his romantic exploits.

Despite Yumeji's visibility for his artwork and writing, his talents were ignored by established arts organizations and literary circles due to his bohemian lifestyle. Upset by the rising militarism in Japan, Yumeji traveled to the US in 1931 and then went on to Berlin. There, he lectured at the private art school being run by former Bauhaus faculty member and color theorist Johannes Itten.

While in Berlin, Yumeji witnessed the Nazi persecution of Berlin's Jewish population, including the young Jewish students that he was working with. Yumeji left Germany in 1933, helping a handful of his students to escape through an underground network of sympathetic Christians. He returned to Japan to find the nationalist sentiments he had attempted to escape exponentially amplified.

Yumeji checked into a Nagano sanitarium shortly after his return and died there in 1934 at the age of 49. Yumeji's work would fall from popularity by 1940, and his work would be largely forgotten until a resurgence of interest in the 1970s which continues today. He is considered an icon of the Taishō Era and the liberal attitudes of that time. In his lifetime, he created thousands of covers for assorted magazines and books. Yumeji was one of Japan's earliest popular graphic designers, yet he has been often glossed over in the history of graphic design in Japan.

References:

Ishikawa, Keiko, and Yumeji Takehisa. *Takehisa Yumeji "Dezain": Modan gyaru no Takarabako*. Tokyo: Kabushiki Kaisha Kōdansha, 2012.

Kusaka Shirō, Yumeji Takehisa, Masayuki Okabe, and Udō Yoshihiko. *Takehisa Yumeji: Ai to Kanashimi no Shijin Gaka*. Tokyo: Gakushū Kenkyūsha, 1995.

Kobayashi, Mari. *Gaka no Bukku Dezain: sōtei to sōga Kara Miru Nihon no Honzukuri no rūtsu*. Tokyo: Seibundō Shinkōsha, 2018.

Koshikakezawa, Mai. "'Senow Gakfu' and the Reception of Western Music in Japan during the Taishō Period." *Bulletin, Faculty of Music, Tokyo National University of Fine Arts & Music* 13, no. 62 (March 13, 1988): 29–98.

Lavenberg, Irwin. "Takehisa Yumeji (1884–1934)." The Lavenberg Collection of Japanese Prints. Irwin Lavenberg, 2017. http://www.myjapanesehanga.com/home/artists/takehisa-yumeji-1884-1934.

Ogawa, Akiko. *Motto Shiritai Takehisa Yumeji: shōgai to Sakuhin*. Tokyo: Tokyo Bijutsu, 2009.

Shuri, Yuki, and Shinju Onuki. *Kakimoji no Dezain*. Tokyo: Graphic-sha, 2017.

Takehisa, Yumeji, and Kan Yazawa. *Yoimachigusa: Takehisa Yumeji Uta no Ehon*. Tokyo: Ōtsuki Shoten, 1992.

Takehisa, Yumeji, and Tomoko Taniguchi. *Takehisa Yumeji: Taishō Modan Dezain Bukku*. Tokyo: Kawade Shobō, 2003.

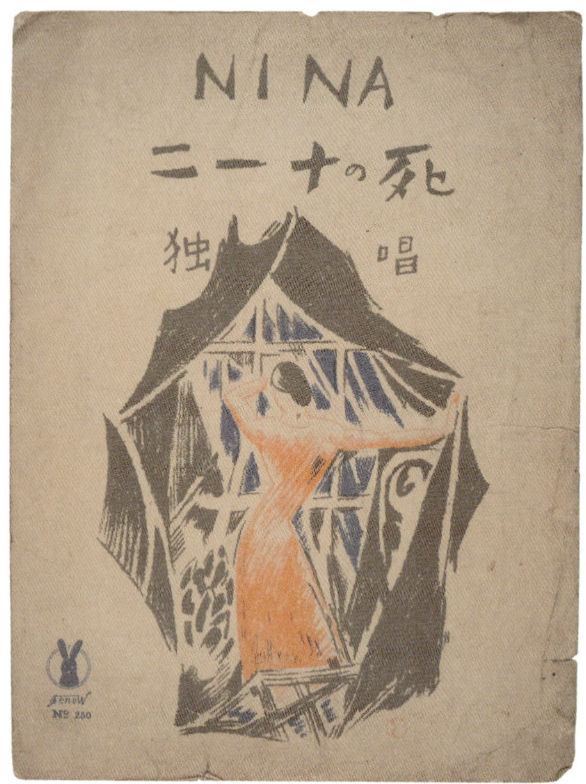

"The Death of Nina" **ニーナの死** music score, (Tokyo: Senoo Ongaku Shuppansha セノオ音楽出版社, 1921).

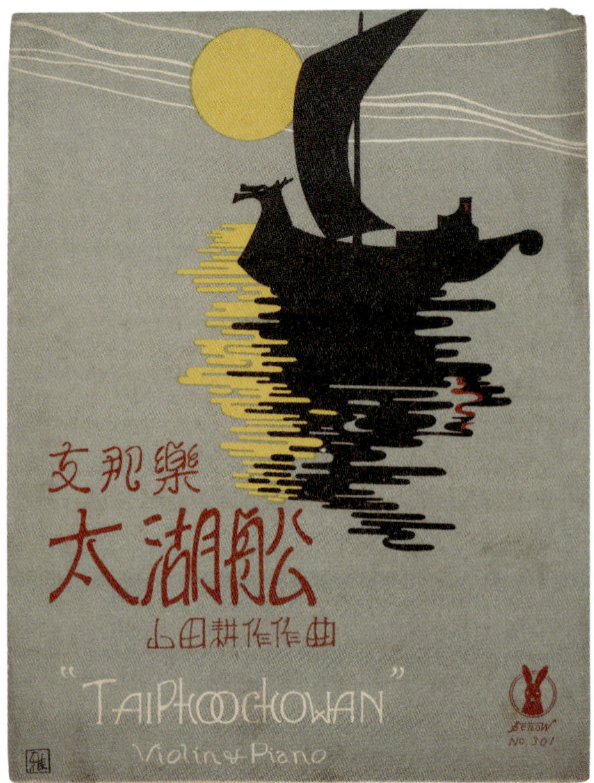

"**Taiphoochowan**" **太湖船** music score (Tokyo: Senoo Ongaku Shuppansha セノオ音楽出版社, 1921).

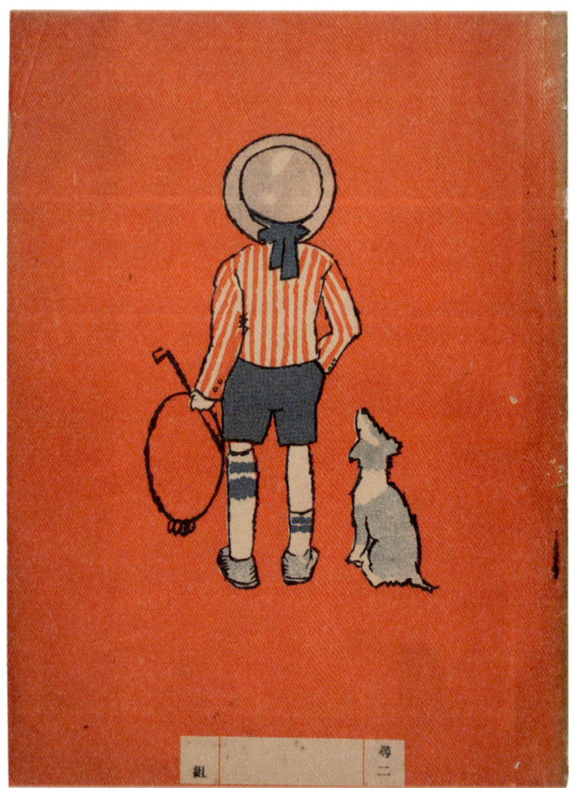

Back cover of ***The Elementary School Songbook* 小学生の唱歌** (Tokyo: Kōbunsha 光文社, 1927). The back cover of the book shows a boy and his dog listening intently to the songs contained within. The lack of figure/ground relations heightens the visual appeal of this composition.

KOIDE NARASHIGE 小出楢重

1887–1931

Koide Narashige was born in Osaka and is primarily known as a painter working in yōga portraiture. He studied at Tokyo School of Fine Arts, initially studying nihonga painting before switching to the yōga department. After graduating in 1914, he returned to Osaka and continued to paint. He won the Chōgyū Prize in the sixth Nikakai arts society exhibition in 1919 and won the Nika Prize the following year, paving the way for both fine art and illustration/design commissions.

Koide traveled throughout Europe in 1921 and 1922 studying painting, as many aspirational Japanese artists did during that time. After returning to Japan, Koide opened his own atelier in Osaka in 1924.

Koide designed a number of books in the 1930s, creating a unified approach to the covers, title pages, and figures that mixed connotative lettering and playful illustration work. Koide illustrated the serial form of Tanizaki Junichiro's 谷崎潤一郎 novel *Some Prefer Nettles* 蓼喰う虫 when it was initially published in the Asahi Shimbun in 1928. He also designed covers for the magazine *Chūō Bijutsu* 中央美術 in 1928, integrating lettering, typography, and abstract figurative illustration.

Koide is primarily noted as a painter in Japanese art history, yet he made important contributions in the field of book design due to his deft mix of typographic and pictorial form, choice of papers, and approaches to printing.

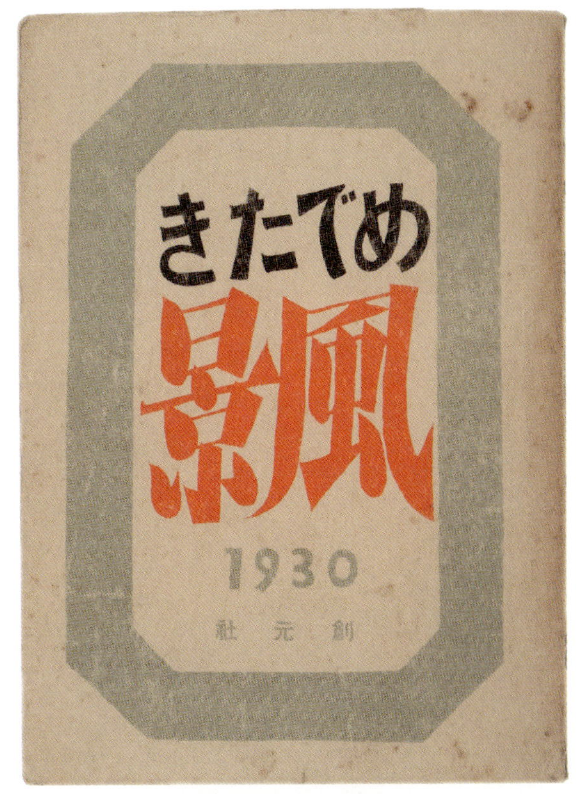

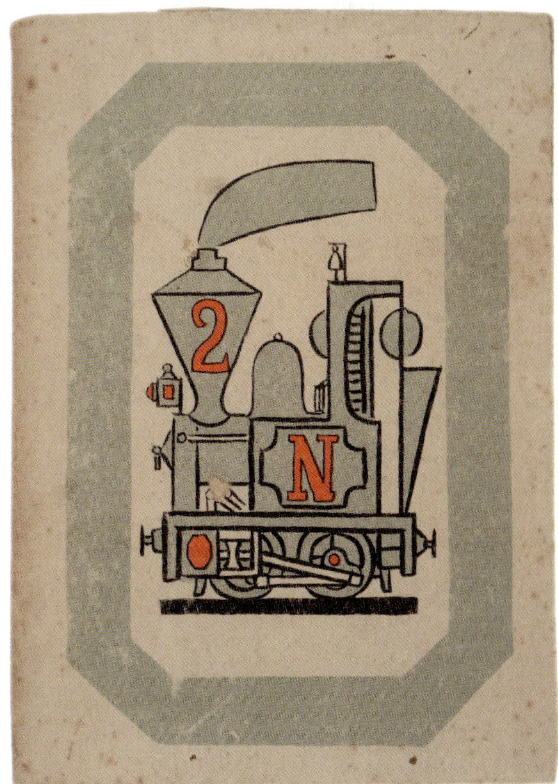

Front and back cover of ***Happy Landscape* めでたき風景**, Koide Narashige 小出楢重, (Tokyo: Sogensha 創元社, 1930). *Happy Landscape* is a collection of writings by Koide Narashige reflecting on art, life, and observations on assorted topics, published a year before his death. The front and back covers feature a lively three-color illustration and hand lettering by Koide contained within a decorative frame.

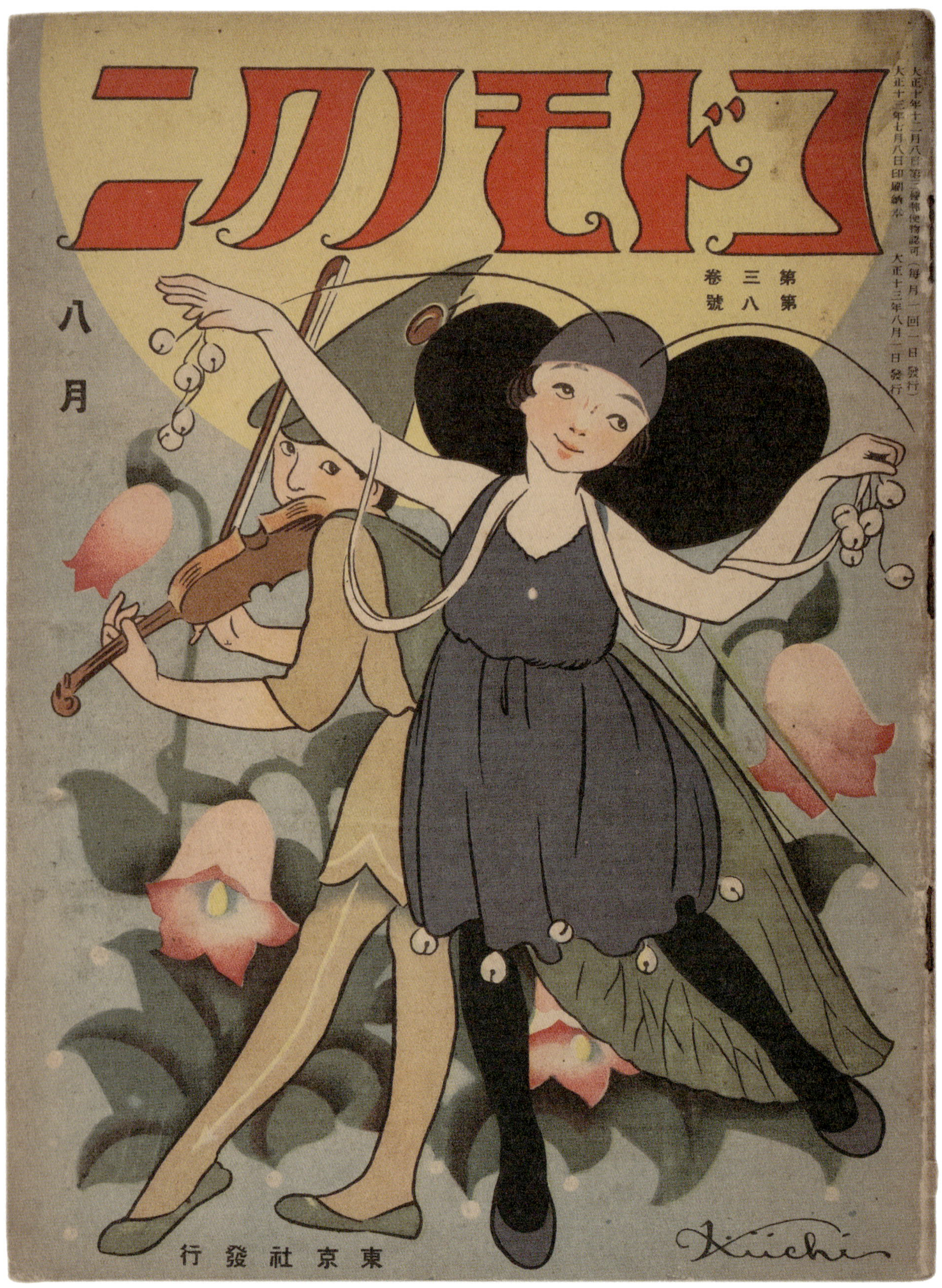

Cover design for ***Kodomo no kuni*** コドモノクニ by Okamoto Kiichi (Tokyo: Tokyosha 東京社, 1923). The illustration is notable for the use of outlines on the figures and masthead and the lack of outlines on the flora in the composition's background.

OKAMOTO KIICHI 岡本歸一

1888–1930

Okamoto Kiichi was born on the island of Awajishima in Hyōgo Prefecture but was raised in Tokyo from the age of four. As an elementary school student, he became enamored with hand-painted fans and decided to study art. At age eighteen, Okamoto began to apprentice and study Western painting under Kuroda Seiki, alongside other students such as Kishida Ryūsei in the Western painting school affiliated with Kuroda's Hakubakai society of artists.

Okamoto and Kishida became enthralled with Post-Impressionist painting, especially the works of Van Gogh and Cezanne, and formed the Post-Impressionist Hyūsain Group ヒュウザン会, holding an exhibition in 1912. The exhibition challenged then-contemporary notions of acceptable visual expression and led to an ideological split between Okamoto and his teacher Kuroda.

Okamoto was drawn to arts initiatives that stressed pushing boundaries, including the *sōsaku hanga* movement, which emphasized the role of the artist as the sole creator motivated by a desire for self-expression. It advocated principles of art that is "self-drawn" 自画, "self-carved" 自刻, and "self-printed" 自刷, in contrast with ukiyo-e and shin hanga, which were collaborative commercial printmaking ventures controlled by a publisher. The ethos of sōsaku hanga is echoed in Sōseki Natsume's statement that art begins and ends with the expression of the self.

In 1915, Okamoto began illustrating and designing the *Model Family Library* 模範家庭文庫 series of books for the publisher Fuzanbo. He crafted illustrations for the children's magazine *Kin no fune* 金の船 and in 1920 was responsible for the production design of Maurice Maeterlinck's play *The Blue Bird* at the Yurakuza Theater in Ginza. Okamoto became the chief illustrator and designer for the high-end children's magazine *Kodomo no Kuni* コドモノクニ in 1922, which increased his public stature and resulted in further commissions from *Shōjo Kurabu* 少女倶楽部 in 1923 and *Kodomo Asahi* コドモアサヒ in 1924. Throughout the 1920s, Okamoto was the nation's most popular illustrator of children's literature. In 1927, Okamoto became one of the co-founders of the Nihon Douga Kyōkai (Japan Association of Illustrators for Children) 日本童画家協会.

Okamoto was recognized for his ability to capture facial expressions and for the bold, detailed lettering and invitingly organic ornamentation he created for the assorted titles that he designed and illustrated.

References:

Kobayashi, Mari. *Gaka No Bukku Dezain: sōtei to sōga Kara Miru Nihon no Honzukuri no rūtsu*. Tokyo: Seibundō Shinkōsha, 2018.

Shuri, Yuki, and Shinju Onuki. *Kakimoji no Dezain*. Tokyo: Graphic-sha, 2017.

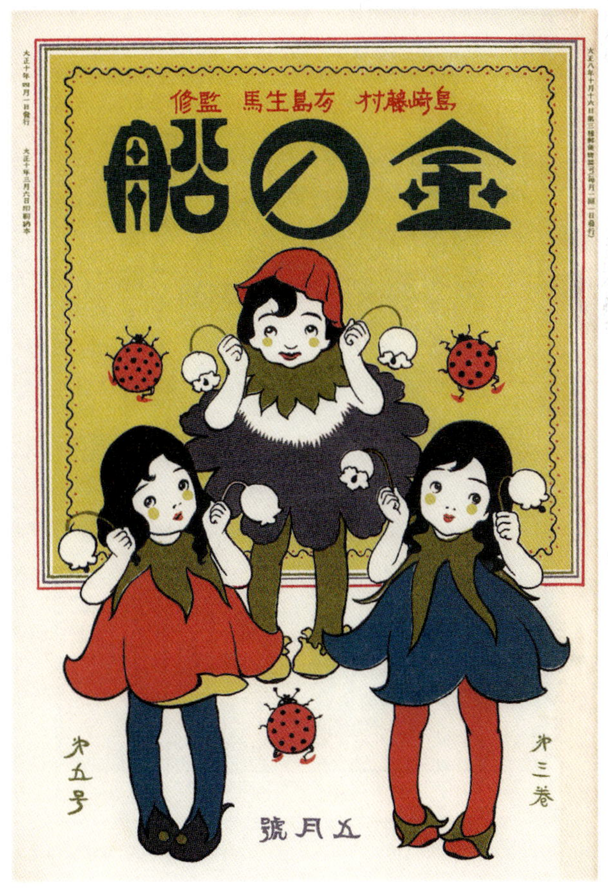

Cover design of ***Kin no fune* 金の船** (Tokyo: Kinnohoshi-sha 金の星社, May 1921).

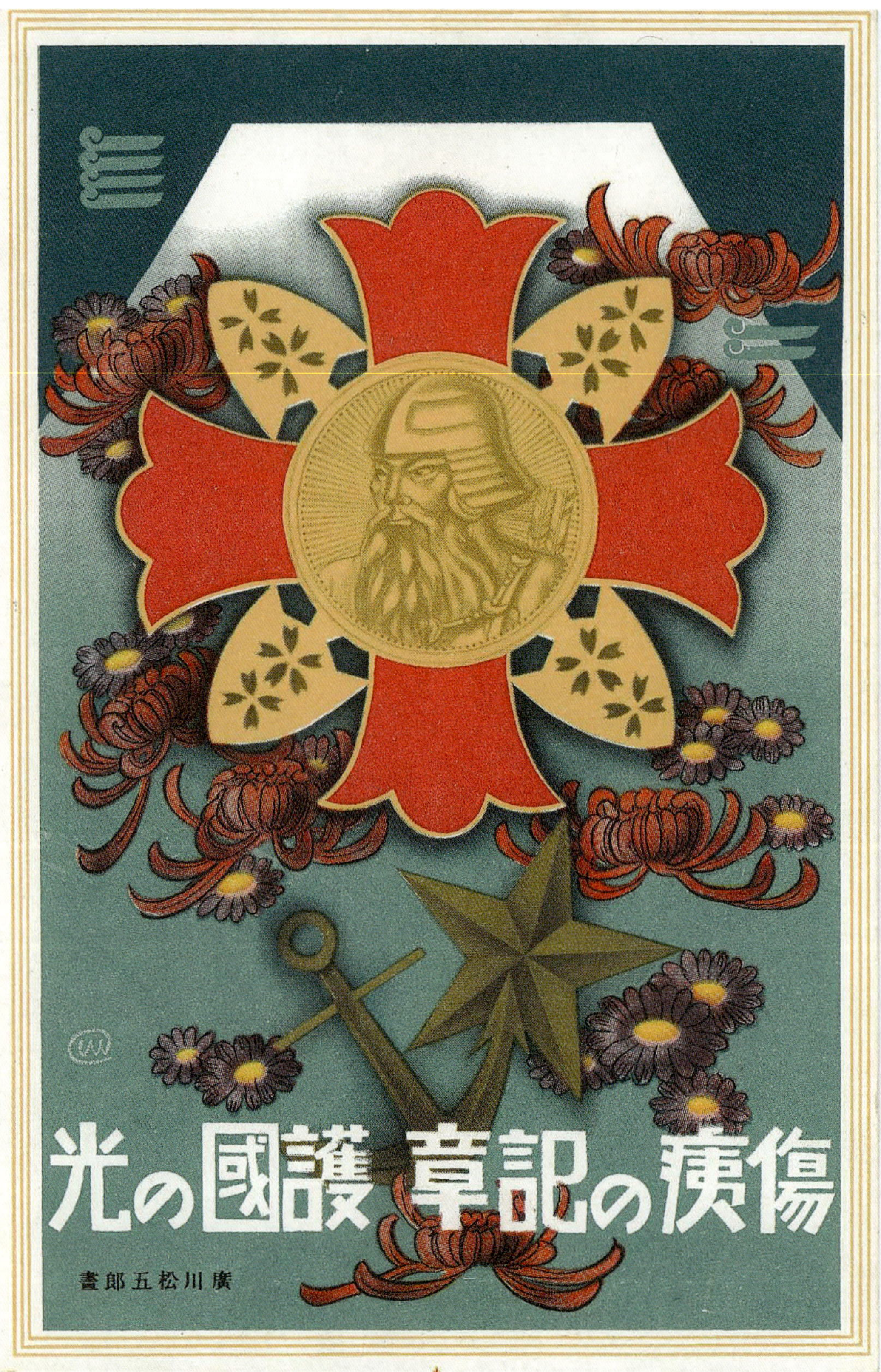

Symbol of the Blessed, Light Protecting the Nation **傷痍の記章護國の光**, Hirokawa Matsugoro 広川松五郎 (Tokyo: Disabled Veteran Conservation Center 傷兵保護院, 1938). A promotional postcard celebrating disabled veterans, designed by Hirokawa Matsugoro, himself a disabled veteran. The mythic veteran pictured wears historical battle garb and has a long beard, signifying time spent abroad. The star and anchor represent the Japanese Army and Navy, while a gradated Mount Fuji looms in the background.

HIROKAWA MATSUGORO 広川松五郎

1889–1952

Hirokawa Matsugoro was born in Sanjo in Niigata Prefecture. He attended Tokyo School of Fine Arts and was associated with the sōsaku hanga printmakers, who would become recognized internationally the year of Hirokawa's death. He was one of the leading contributors to the arts and literature magazine *Kamen* 仮面 between 1913 and 1915, through which he and others would publish their own woodblock prints.

Hirokawa was a prolific book designer and textile designer, as well as a printmaker. He was one of ten members of the *Decorative Artists' Society* 装飾美術家協会, alongside painter, printmaker, and educator Okada Saburōnosuke 岡田三郎助; artist, graphic designer, illustrator, manga artist, and educator Nagahara Kōtarō 長原孝太郎; arts, crafts, and design historian and educator Watanabe Soshū 渡辺素舟; metalwork craftsman Nishimura Toshihiko 西村敏彦; writer and poet Hara Saburō 原三郎; craftsman and printmaker Fujii Tatsukichi 藤井達吉; architect, designer, writer, and researcher Kon Wajirō 今和次郎; graphic designer Saitō Kazō 斎藤佳三; and sculptor Takamura Toyochika 高村豊周. The group's goals, according to scholar Kobayashi Mari, were to "raise the dignity of so-called 'craft art' objects and indicate their ultimate nature, by creating and exhibiting works of art." Members helped publicize one another's works and regularly wrote and lectured about other members' contributions to elevating the status of both craft objects and works of design. The assorted members were among the most established in each of their fields, lending the group an air of both sophistication and progressiveness.

In 1926, Hirokawa began publishing the magazine *Kōgei Jidai* 工芸時代 dedicated to the Mingei 民芸 movement of that time. In 1930, Hirokawa was one of the twenty-eight designers who submitted a proposal for the redesign of Kao soap, though his proposal was rejected.

Hirokawa taught at Tokyo School of Fine Arts and Tokyo University of the Arts for over thirty years.

References:

Kobayashi, Mari. *Gaka No Bukku Dezain: sōtei to sōga Kara Miru Nihon no Honzukuri no rūtsu*. Tokyo: Seibundō Shinkōsha, 2018.

Shuri, Yuki, and Shinju Onuki. *Kakimoji No Dezain*. Tokyo: Graphic-sha, 2017.

Tokyo National Research Institute for Cultural Properties, Independent Administrative Institution National Institutes for Cultural Heritage. *Hirokawa Matsugoro*. Independent Administrative Institution National Institutes for Cultural Heritage Tokyo National Research Institute for Cultural Properties, June 6, 2019. https://www.tobunken.go.jp/materials/bukko/8777.html.

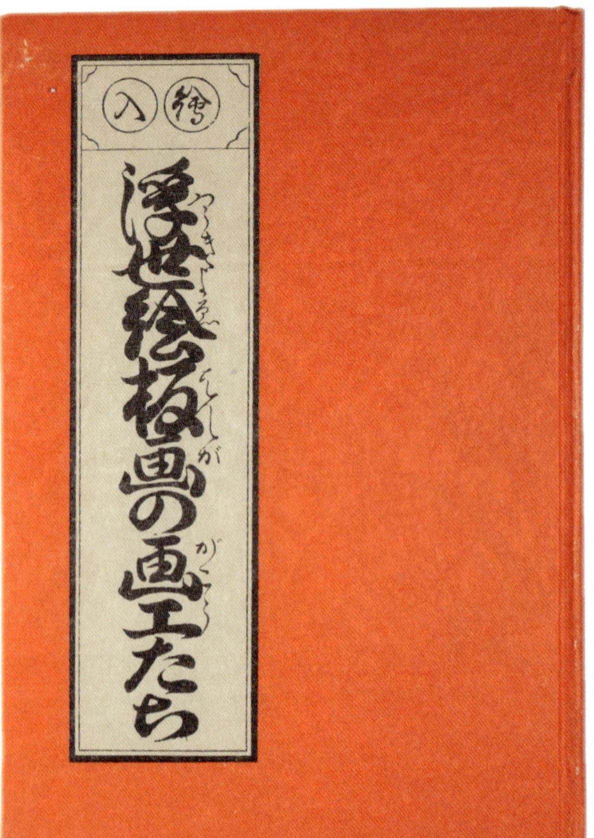

This page and facing page: Jacket and cover design for ***Ukiyo-e Printmakers* 浮世絵板画の画工たち**, Kishida Ryusei 岸田劉生 (Tokyo: Kōfūsha Shoten 光風社書店, 1970). This minimalist yet highly integrated book design reveals Kishida's mastery of both calligraphy and subtle ornamentation.

KISHIDA RYŪSEI 岸田劉生

1891–1929

While remembered most as one of Japan's leading early Modern painters dedicated to portraiture, Kishida Ryūsei sporadically worked as a book jacket designer using illustration and hand lettering. Kishida was born in Tokyo. His father had worked alongside James Curtis Hepburn on Japanese/English dictionaries using what would become the most widely used system of romanization for the Japanese language. Kishida studied painting under Kuroda Seiki and mingled with both the Hakubakai and Shirakaba painting associations before forming his own, the Hyūsain Group ヒュウザン会 in 1912 and another, the Sōdosha 草土社 in 1915. The members of the Sōdosha were involved in elementary art education from 1915 to 1922, insisting that young art students learn by copying both preexisting great works of art and nature scenes.

Kishida's paintings explored a myriad of themes, from portraiture to abstraction to the supernatural, and stand as some of the most valuable early Modern Japanese paintings in the contemporary art market. He collected images of art and practiced photography, as well. Kishida was an influential early Modern Art critic invested in analyzing the values of modernity through the lens of Christianity, as he was highly influenced by the *Bible*'s book of Genesis.

References:
Kishida Ryūsei, and Noriaki Kitazawa. *Kishida Ryūsei Uchinaru Bi: Aru to yū Koto no Shinpi*. Tokyo: Erxuan Society, 1997.

Kishida Ryūsei, and Tadayasu Sakai. *Kishida Ryūsei zuihitsushū*. Tokyo: Iwanami Shoten, 1996.

Sakai, Tadayasu. *Kishida Ryūsei*. Tokyo: Shinchōsha, 1998.

Shuri, Yuki, and Shinju Onuki. *Kakimoji No Dezain*. Tokyo: Graphic-sha, 2017.

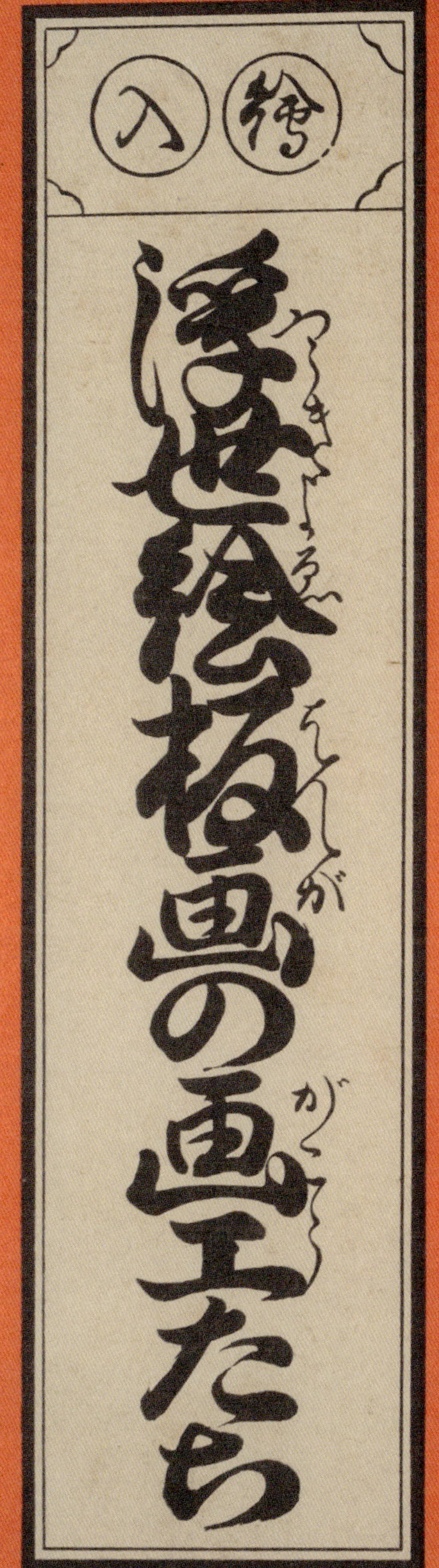

畫工 岸田劉生 著

出版元 光風社書店

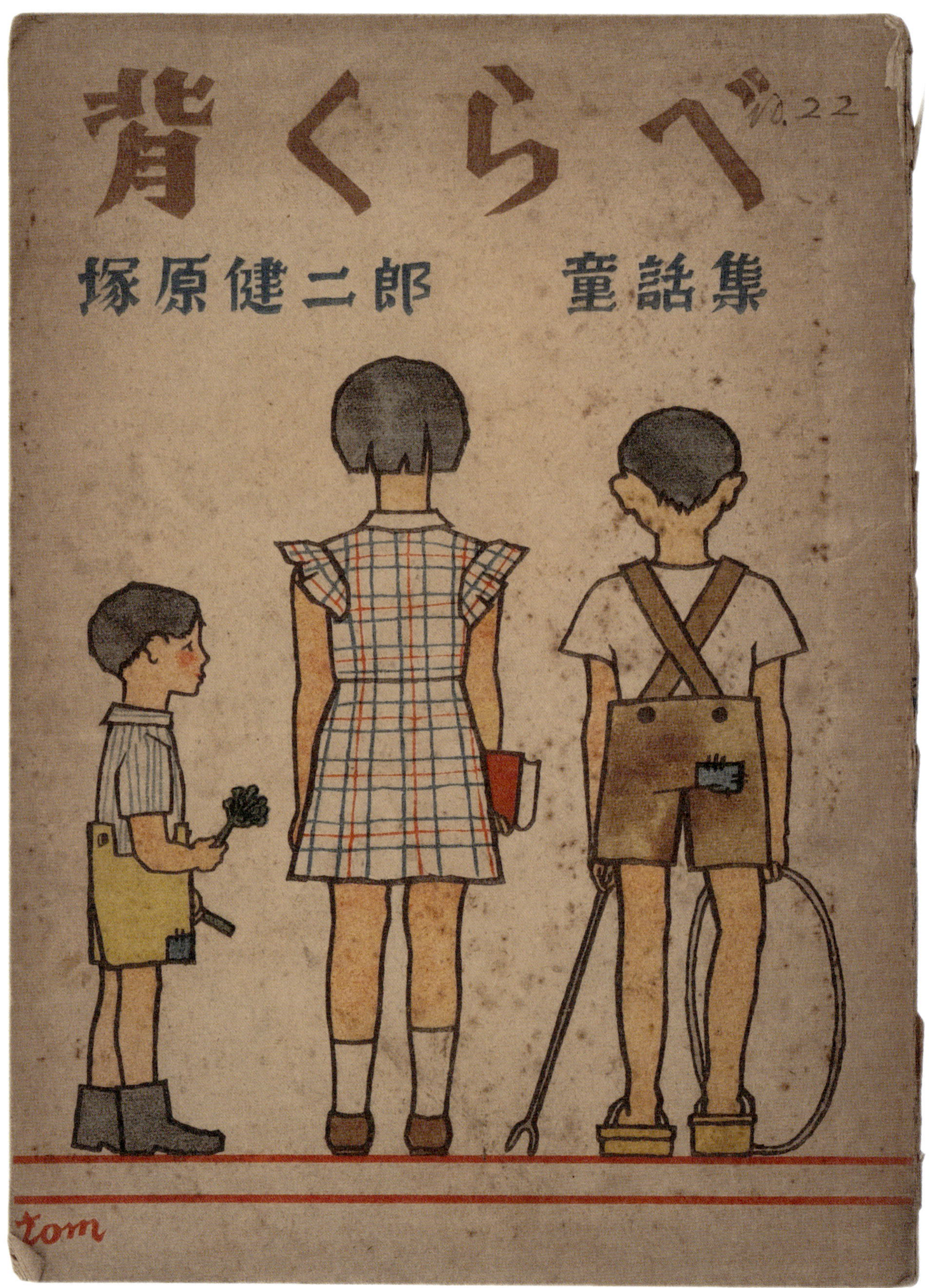

This page and facing page: ***Seikurabe* 背くらべ, Tsukahara Kenjirō 塚原健二郎 (Tokyo: Sakurai Shoten 櫻井書店, 1947).** Front and back cover by Murayama Tomoyoshi 村山知義. A book of fairy tales. Of note is Murayama's use of the abbreviation "tom" to sign his illustration and design work.

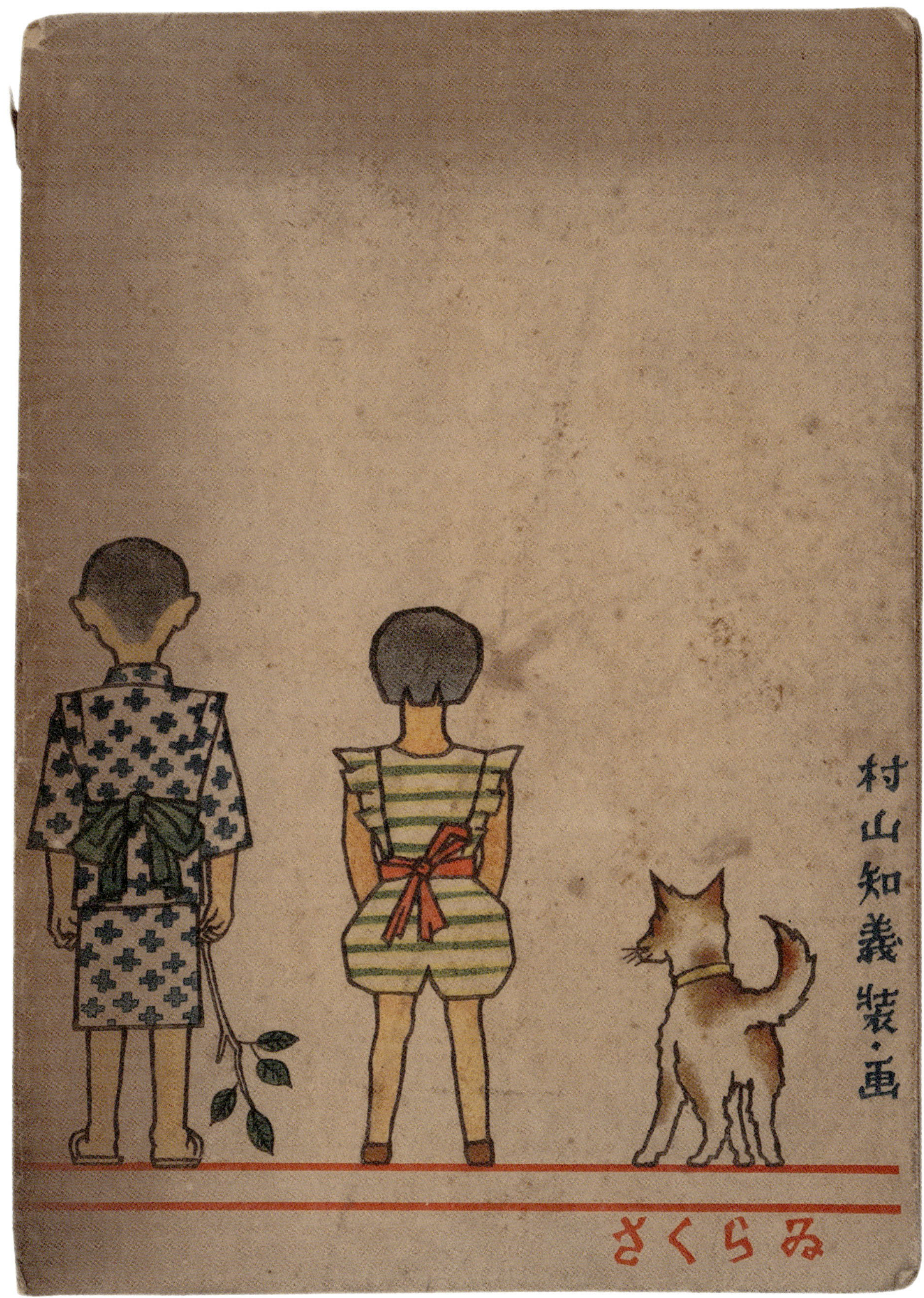
村山知義装・画
みらくさ

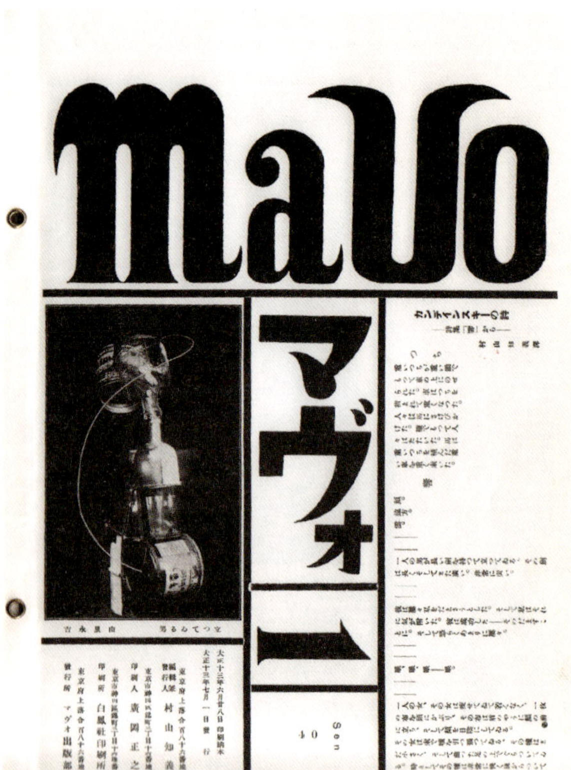

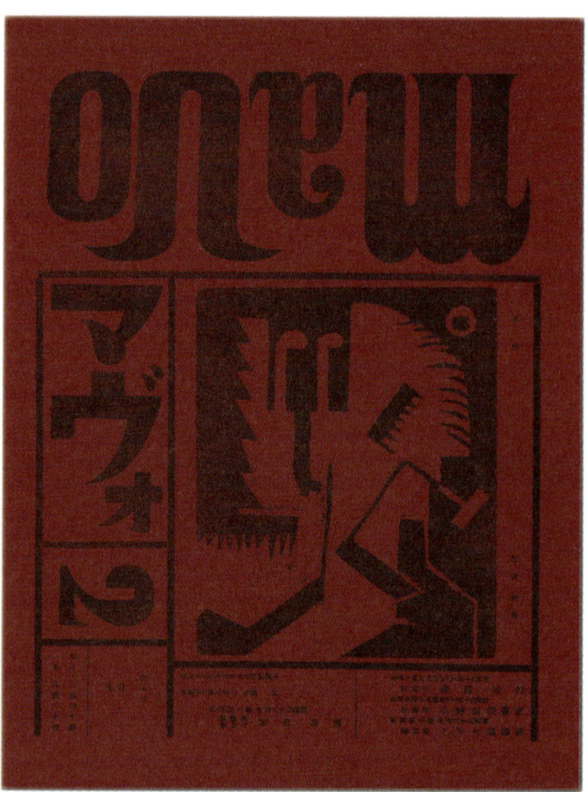

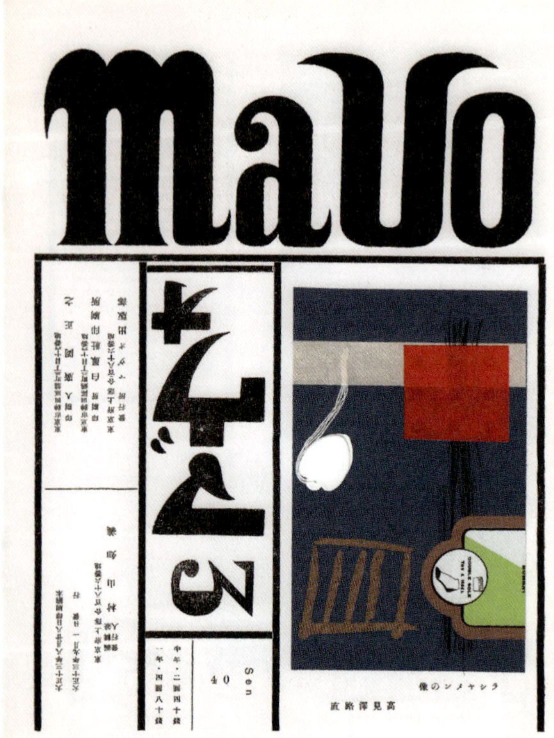

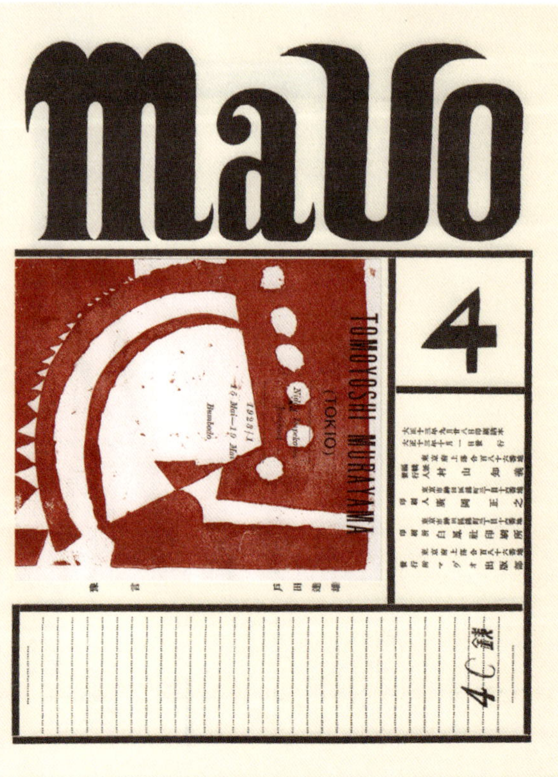

Clockwise from top left: ***Mavo* No. 1** (Tokyo: Mavo マヴォ, July 1924); ***Mavo* No. 2** (Tokyo: Mavo マヴォ, August 1924); ***Mavo* No. 3** (Tokyo: Mavo マヴォ, September 1924); ***Mavo* No. 4** (Tokyo: Mavo マヴォ, October 1924). *Mavo* No. 3 featured a collage that mixed found labels of ankle socks, blank heart-shaped price tags, the hair of a Mavo member glued under a patch of red paper, and metallic printmaking. The inclusion of this mixed-media collage turns this issue of the magazine into a piece of art as well as a designed publication. The fourth issue included a woodblock print glued onto the cover and overprinted with Murayama Tomoyoshi's name in Latin letterforms, again turning the periodical into a piece of printmaking.

MURAYAMA TOMOYOSHI 村山知義 & MAVO マヴォ

1901–1977

Murayama Tomoyoshi was born in the Kanda district of Tokyo. He was a designer, artist, playwright, novelist, and theater producer. Murayama was a Christian and a pacifist, largely due to the influence of his mother, a follower of the iconoclastic American-trained Christian philosopher Uchimura Kanzō 内村鑑三, the founder of the Non-church Movement in Japan. Initially interested in philosophy, Murayama began his studies in 1921 at Tokyo Imperial University then transferred to Germany to study at the Humboldt University of Berlin the following year. Upon arriving in Berlin, Murayama was denied admittance from studying philosophy there due to his inability to read Latin.

Murayama turned to art despite limited formal training, and he began studying under the tutelage of German Expressionist and word artist Herwarth Walden, founder of the magazine *Der Sturm*. In 1922, Murayama exhibited a painting in the group show *The Great Futurist Exhibition* at the Neumann Gallery in Berlin and, along with Walden, participated in the Congress of International Progressive Artists in Dusseldorf, mingling with Futurists and Constructivists alike. At the Congress, Murayama witnessed the formation of The International Faction of Constructivists, organized by Theo Van Doesburg, Hans Richter, and El Lissitzky. Murayama also met the Futurist leader Filippo Tommaso Marinetti and obtained a copy of Marinetti's *Manifesto of Tactilism*, which Murayama would later translate into Japanese and publish in Japan. Murayama's participation in the Congress had a lasting impact on his career by putting him in the company of a number of avant-garde artists and ideas. This can be seen in his adoption of socialist political views and in his Constructivism-influenced mixed-media painting and assemblage.

After eleven months in Europe, Murayama returned to Japan and was the pivotal figure in the formation of the art and design group Mavo マヴォ in Tokyo in 1923. Murayama acted as the bridge between the European avant-garde art movements he had experienced and the previously established Japanese variant of Futurism. During his time with Mavo, Murayama created a localized variant of Constructivism alongside Tokyo-based Russian emigre and educator, artist, printmaker, and designer Varvara Bubnova. Mavo's other founding members included Yanase Masamu 柳瀬正夢, Ogata Kamenosuke 尾形亀之助, Ōura Shūzo 大浦周蔵, and Kadowaki Shinrō 門脇晋郎, though their ranks would swell when Takamizawa Nakatarō 高見澤仲太郎, Toda Tatsuo 戸田達雄, Maki Hisao 牧寿雄, Okada Tatsuo 岡田竜夫, Hagiwara Kyōjirō 萩原恭次郎, Varvara Bubnova, and a handful of others joined shortly after the group formed. According to Mavo ally Kitasono Katué 北園克衛, they came up with the name by writing the Latin letter which represented the sound of the first character of each of the members' last names and throwing them up in the air.

Murayama's exposure to the explosion of activity in Europe lent him an aura of leadership among the group, though Mavo members were not unified by a single ideology. Mavo was a group of individually-minded artists with a panoply of agendas, methods of expression, and subjective aesthetics. The group espoused the notion of "Conscious Constructivism," and its 1923 manifesto sought to connect artistic practice with everyday life. Forgoing a singular group aesthetic or area of activity, Mavo members were active in the expansion of avant-garde aesthetics and performance, spanning art, printmaking, literature, poetry, drama, dance, and graphic design.

Mavo was socially oriented, with members organizing exhibitions, hybrid protest-exhibitions, and performances. They were active in anarchist, socialist, and Marxist politics, and the Great Kanto Earthquake of 1923 presented an opportunity to combine their visual tendencies with their desire for social upheaval and reform: the group helped construct and decorate temporary structures for both living and commerce post-quake. Mavo embraced the oppositional and deconstructive tendencies of anarchic Futurism while simultaneously striving for utopian social renewal in ways akin to the Constructivists.

Mavo members published seven issues of their eponymous journal from 1924 through 1925 that mixed printmaking, collage, poetry, design, social commentary, theater, and illustration. Covers featured collaged elements, a mix of offset printing and printmaking, tipped-in illustrations, and unconventional typography. The group's approach to typographic and orthographic experimentation culminated in a number of small-run artists' books, most strikingly Hagiwara Kyōjirō's *Shikeisenkoku* 死刑宣告 *(Death Sentence)*—an aesthetically experimental book collectively designed and illustrated that highlights the group's diversity as much as their efforts to expound Hagiwara's anarchist ideology. Its text runs amok, with printed arrows leading the readers through compositions of text exhorting "Call the police! To the grave!," onomatopoeic

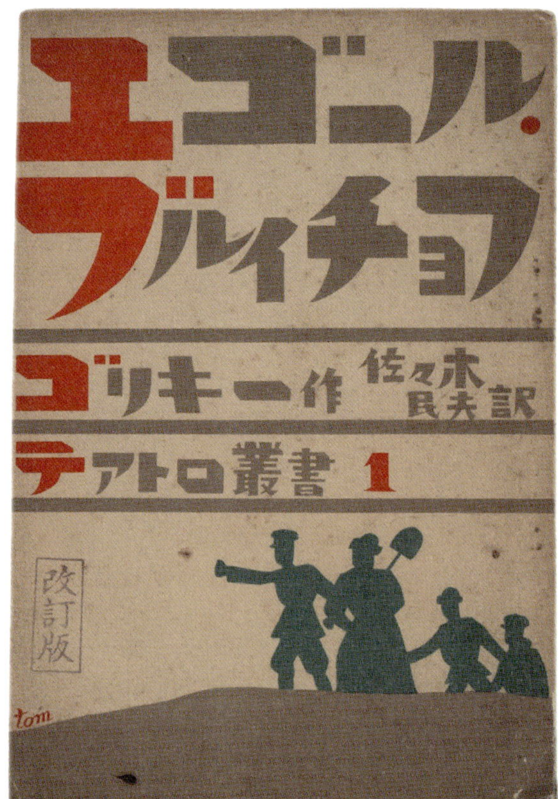

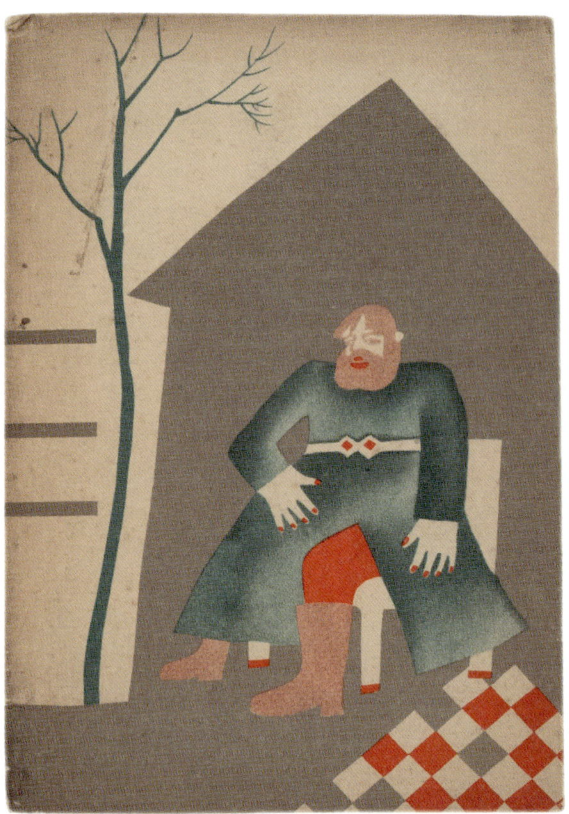

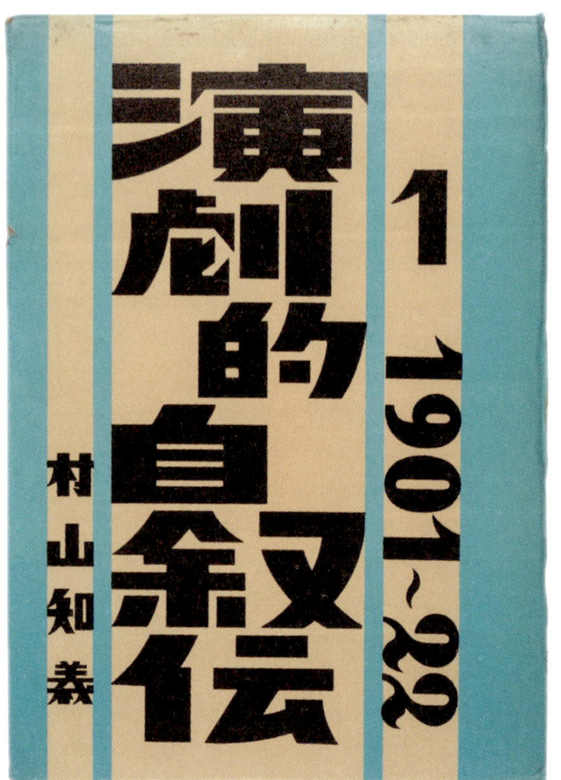

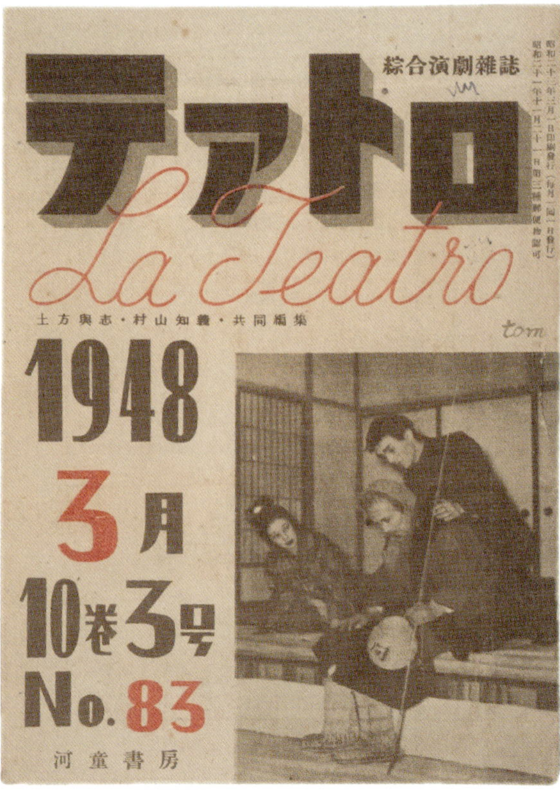

Clockwise from top left: ***Gorky*** **ゴリキー, Egor Bulychov エゴール・ブルイチョフ, Teatro Series 1 テァトロ叢書 1 (Tokyo: Teatro-sha テァトロ社 1934);** ***La Teatro*** **No. 83 テァトロ No. 83 (Tokyo: Kawado Shobo 河童書房, June 1948)**, theater magazine designed by Murayama Tomoyoshi (cover) and Yoshida Kenkichi; ***Theatrical Autobiography 1*** **演劇的自叙伝 1**, **Murayama Tomoyoshi 村山知義 (Tokyo: Tōhō Shuppansha 東邦出版社, 1971).** An assortment of publication covers designed by Murayama Tomoyoshi that reveal his predilection for massive display lettering and mixed orthographic directions.

explosions rendered in expressive typographic constructions, and seemingly random deployment of Latin characters.

Murayama left the group in 1925 to explore new directions in leftist theater, and, despite members' attempts to keep the group alive, Mavo quietly disassembled the following year. The two years they were active produced a flurry of projects, thoroughly documented and researched in Gennifer Weisenfeld's 2002 book *Mavo: Japanese Artists and the Avant-Garde, 1905–1931*.

Mavo's members, particularly Murayama and Yanase, were active in the field of graphic design, both during the group's heyday and well after. Murayama and Okada Tatsu designed covers for a number of periodicals, including the literary journal *Bungei Jidai* 文藝時代 and the film magazine *Aoi Weekly*, a long-running weekly magazine produced by the Aoikan 葵館, a film theater in the Akasaka district of Tokyo. Murayama also designed the interiors for the theater and was active as an illustrator for children's books.

Murayama would go on to be a central figure in leftist theater in Japan, writing the radical plays *Nero in a Skirt* スカートをはいたネロ (1927) and *Record of a Gang of Thugs* 暴力団記 (1929), both of which greatly offended the government. Murayama's political engagement through the theater, outspoken opposition to Japan's imperialist agenda, and increased nationalism in the interwar period would lead to intermittent incarceration and torture throughout the 1930s.

Murayama went to occupied Korea and Manchuria in 1945 following bouts of imprisonment in Japan, returning at the end of the year. He remained active in the theater world, writing for the stage and designing stage sets and publications, including the theater journal *La Teatro* テアトロ. His work in theater after the war culminated in the Tokyo Art Troupe 東京芸術座 which continues today in the Nerima ward of Tokyo.

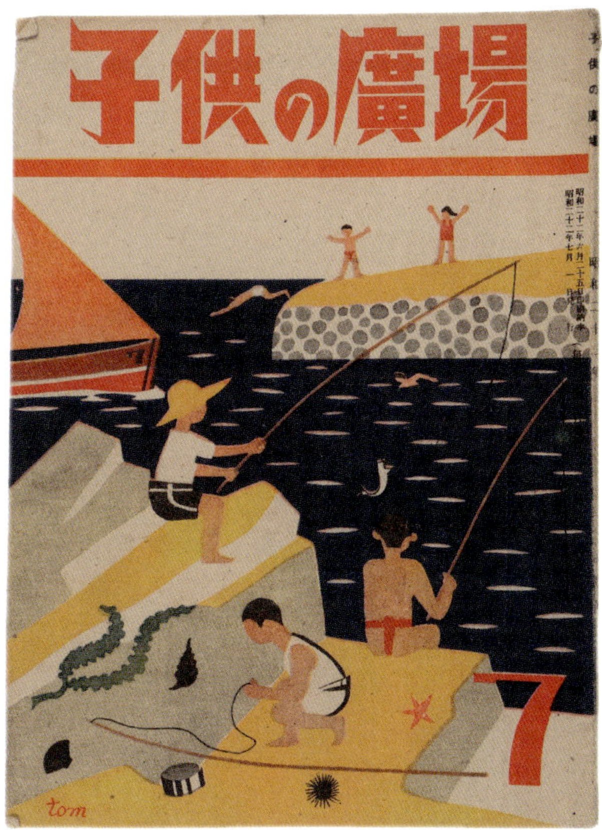

Kodomo no hiroba 子供の廣場 (Tokyo: Shinsekaisha 新世界社, July 1947). Cover design by Murayama Tomoyoshi 村山知義.

References:

Kitasono, Katué, Wajirō Kon, Murayama Tomoyoshi, and Yūsaku Kamekura. *Nihon Dezain Shōshi*. Tokyo: David, 1970.

Omuka, Toshiharu, Tomoyoshi Murayama, and Takizawa Kyōji. *Murayama Tomoyoshi: Bijutsu hihyō to handō 1*. Tokyo: Yumanishobō, 2013.

Weisenfeld, Gennifer. "Japanese Modernism and Consumerism: Forging the New Artistic Field of 'Shogyo Bijutsu' (Commercial Art)." In *Being Modern in Japan: Culture and Society from the 1910s to the 1930s*, edited by Elise K. Tipton and John Clark, 75–96. Honolulu: University of Hawai'i Press, 2000.

Weisenfeld, Gennifer. *Imaging Disaster: Tokyo and the Visual Culture of Japan's Great Earthquake of 1923*. Berkeley: University of California Press, 2012.

Weisenfeld, Gennifer S. *Mavo: Japanese Artists and the Avant-Garde, 1905–1931*. Berkeley: University of California Press, 2010.

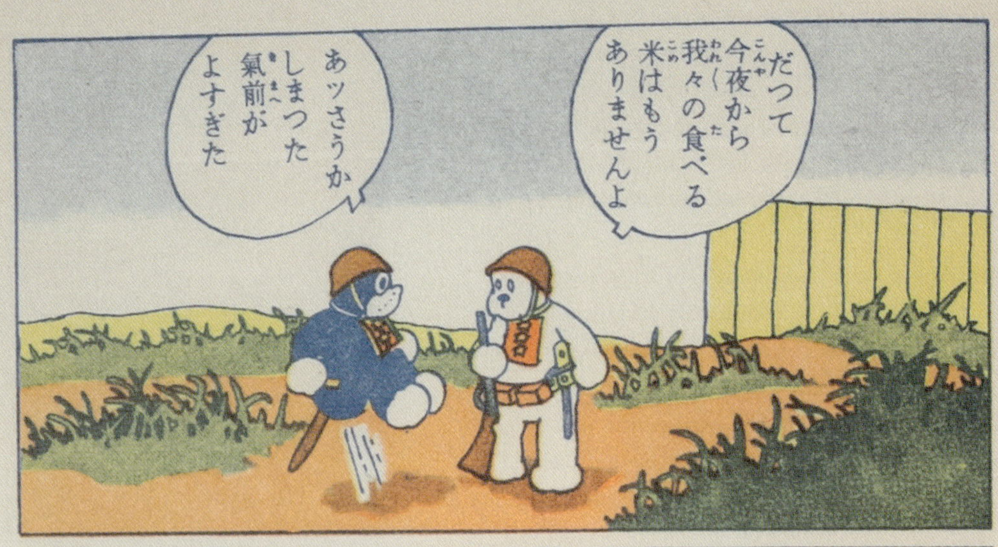

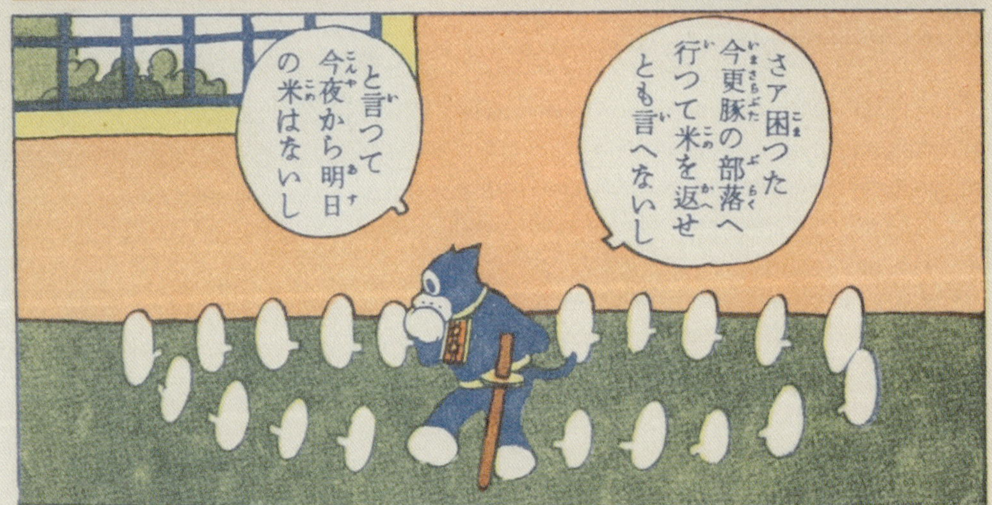

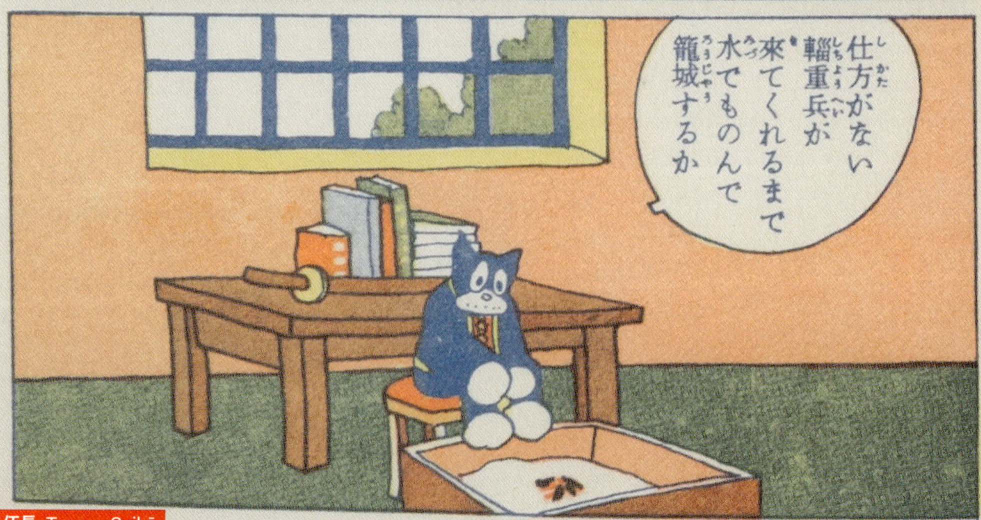

***Corporal Norakuro* のらくろ伍長,** Tagawa Suihō 田河水泡 (Tokyo: Kōdansha 講談社, 1969). Reprinted collection of Norakuro manga.

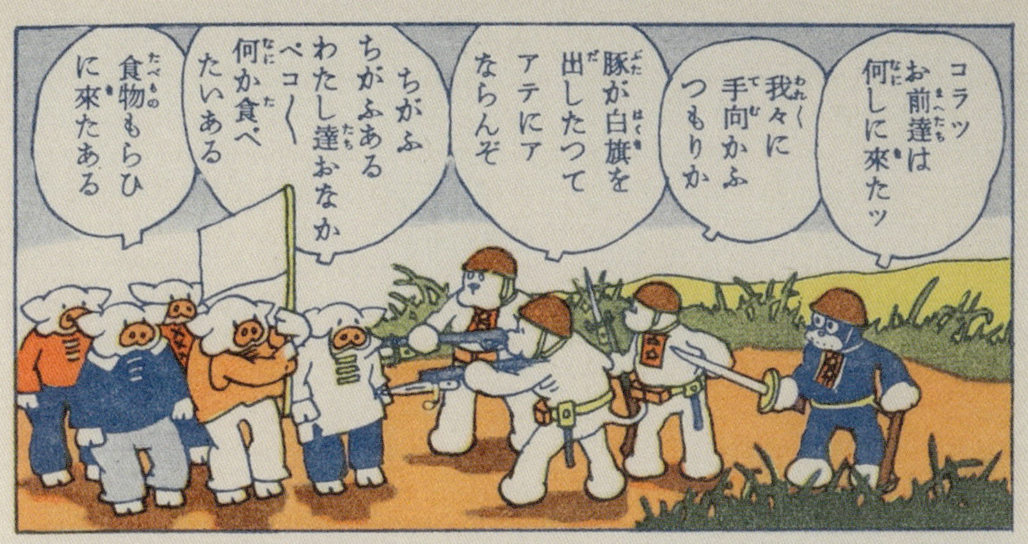
コラッお前達は何しに來たッ
我々に手向かふつもりか
豚が白旗を出したつてアテにアならんぞ
ちがふちがふあるわたし達おなかペコ〳〵何か食べたいある
食物もらひに來たある

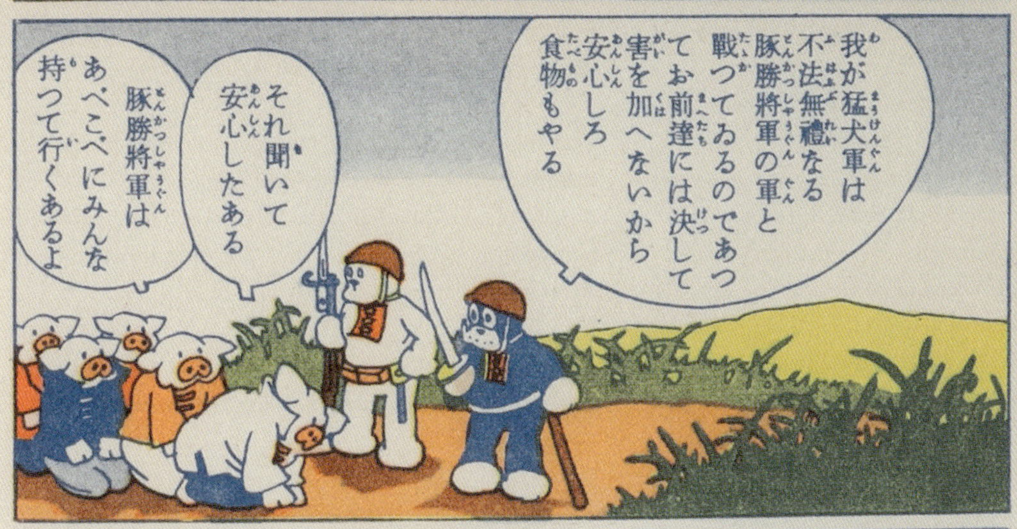
我が猛犬軍は不法無禮なる豚勝将軍の軍と戰つてゐるのであつてお前達には決して害を加へないから安心しろ食物もやる
それ聞いて安心したある
豚勝将軍はあべこべにみんな持つて行くあるよ

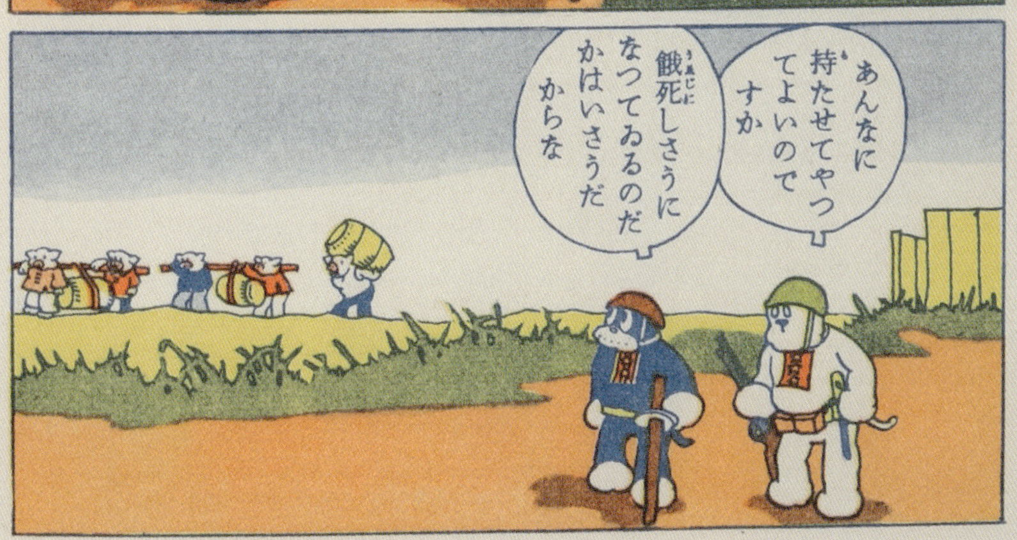
あんなに持たせてやつてよいのですか
餓死しさうになつてゐるのだかはいさうだからな

TAGAWA SUIHŌ 田河水泡

1899–1989

Tagawa Suihō was born Takamizawa Nakatarō 高見澤仲太郎 in Tokyo. His mother died during childbirth, his father remarried, and he was raised by his aunt and uncle. He graduated from elementary school in 1911 and had a keen interest in art. He was conscripted into the Japanese Army in 1919 at age 20, served in Manchuria and Korea, and left the military in 1922.

Returning to Tokyo, Takamizawa adopted the artist name Takamizawa Michinao 高見沢路直 and attended the Japan School of Art 日本美術専門学校 with the intent of studying under Sugiura Hisui, but instead he ended up taking the classes of Imai Kenji 今井兼次, a professor of architecture and crafts from Waseda University.

Takamizawa joined the radical art group Mavo at the beginning of 1923, participating from Mavo's second exhibition onward. Having adopted a radical anarchist political belief system, Takamizawa participated in violent protest-performances with the group, attracting both publicity and notoriety along the way. With other members, Takamizawa explored a wide variety of expressive approaches to creative practices, from architecture-inspired, monumental sculpture building, to avant-garde dance performance, to painting. Perhaps his oddest action was paying to have his photograph published in the newspaper, advertising that he was single and seeking a partner, while also emphasizing his idiosyncratic hairstyle and penchant for Russian-inspired fashion.

After the Great Kanto Earthquake of 1923, Takamizawa joined other Mavo members in the decoration of temporary commercial structures cobbled together from the wreckage. They also exhibited regularly post-quake, and their work from this period is representative of their ideologically anarchistic tendencies: highlighting and embracing the chaos caused by the natural disaster for the purpose of visual expression.

Takamizawa also participated in the creation of the group's eponymous journal and the book *Shikeisenkoku* 死刑宣告 *(Death Sentence)* by Hagiwara Kyōjirō.

After Mavo's dissolution in 1926, Takamizawa worked in the comic storytelling art of *rakugo* as an author and performer shortly thereafter. A knack for comedic narratives led Takamizawa to find work as a manga artist, initially under the pen name Tagawa Suihō, meaning "Water Bubble of the River." Under this name, he began writing and drawing the manga *Norakuro* のらくろ in 1931, first serialized in the children's comic *Shōnen Kurabu* 少年倶楽部. The comic featured a small black feral dog fighting alongside "The Fierce Dogs Fighting Brigade" (a stand-in for the Japanese Kwantung Army) and warring against anthropomorphic pigs (another stand-in for the Chinese military and populace).

Norakuro is recognized as a pioneering body of work in Japanese manga, utilizing consistent framing and word bubbles to clarify the comic's continuity. It was immensely popular and was collated into standalone volumes designed by Takamizawa which feature stunning vernacular motifs and expressive lettering. The comic was popular with children and adults alike, and an immense amount of Norakuro-related memorabilia was produced, including records, toys, plates, and a wide variety of both official and bootlegged fabric patterns for children's kimono.

Despite being the ultimate signifier of wartime propaganda marketed to children, Norakuro's publication was forcibly prohibited from 1941 until the end of the war, but it reappeared postwar in manga and anime forms. The Norakuro anthologies were reprinted in the 1970s.

Takamizawa's work was widely influential on the postwar generation of manga artists, including the legendary Tezuka Osamu 手塚治虫.

References:

Tagawa, Suihō. *Kokkei no kenkyū*. Tokyo: Kōdansha, 2016.

Tagawa, Suihō, and Junko Takamizawa. *Tagawa Suihō: Norakuro Ichidaiki*. Tokyo: Nihon Tosho Sentā, 2010.

Weisenfeld, Gennifer. "Japanese Modernism and Consumerism: Forging the New Artistic Field of 'Shogyo Bijutsu' (Commercial Art)." In *Being Modern in Japan: Culture and Society from the 1910s to the 1930s*, edited by Elise K. Tipton and John Clark, 75–96. Honolulu: University of Hawai'i Press, 2000.

Weisenfeld, Gennifer. *Imaging Disaster Tokyo and the Visual Culture of Japan's Great Earthquake of 1923*. Berkeley: University of California Press, 2012.

Weisenfeld, Gennifer S. *Mavo: Japanese Artists and the Avant-Garde, 1905–1931*. Berkeley: University of California Press, 2010.

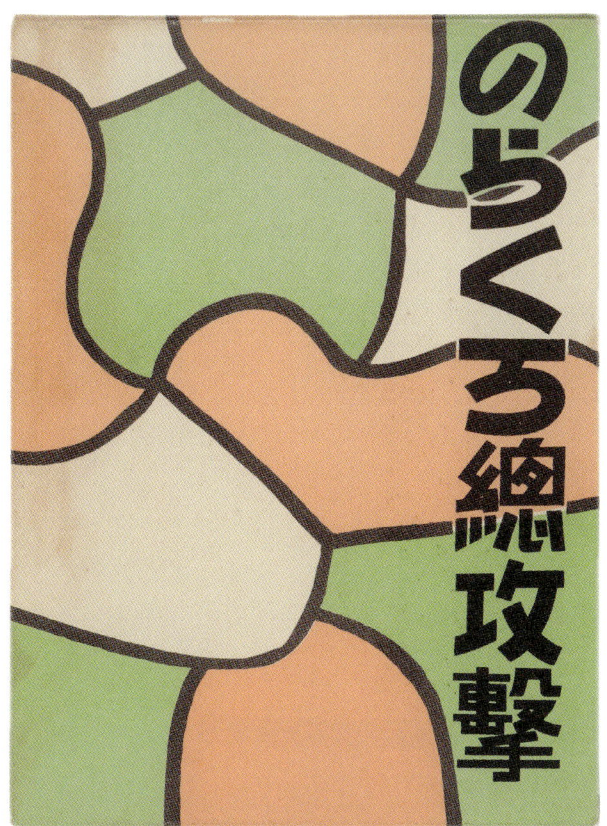

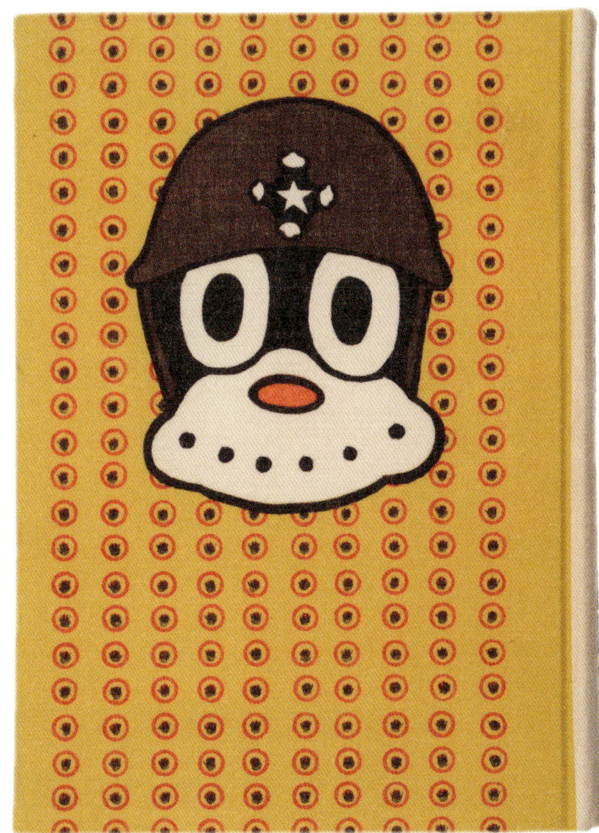

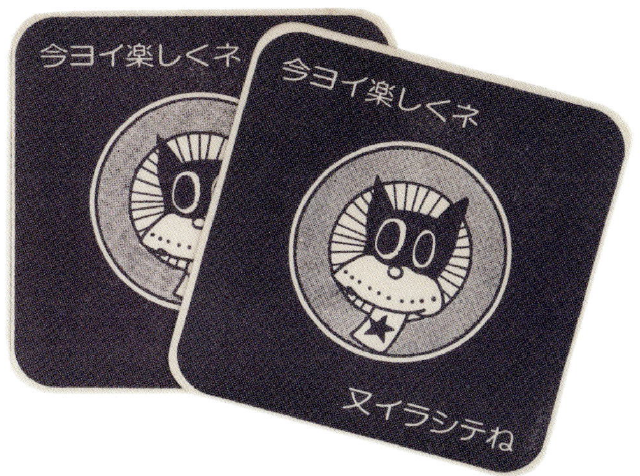

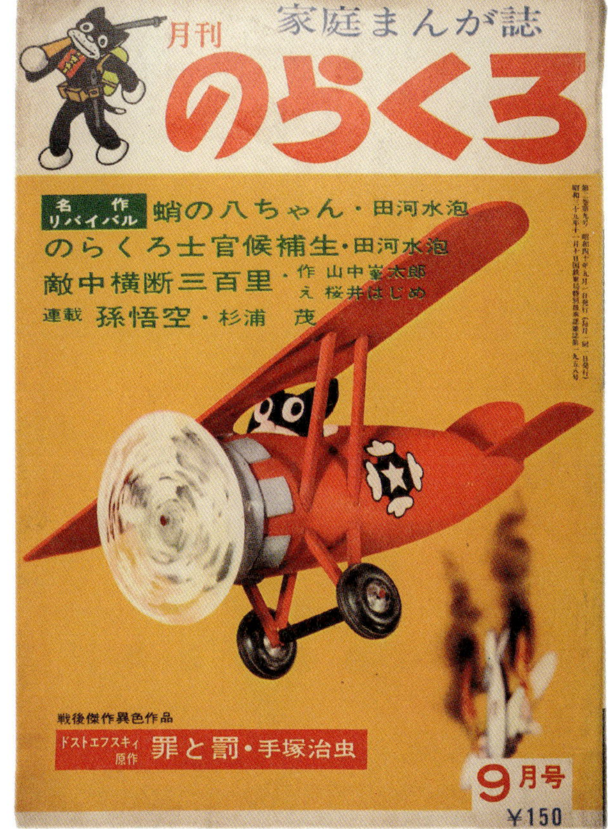

Clockwise from top left: ***Norakuro General Strike* のらくろ総攻撃**, Tagawa Suihō 田河水泡 (Tokyo: Kōdansha 講談社, 1969) reprinted 1934 collection of Norakuro manga, slipcover and cover; ***Monthly Norakuro* 月刊のらくろ**, Tagawa Suihō 田河水泡 (Fukuoka: Roman Shobo ろまん書房, 1964); bootleg Norakuro coasters, date unknown.

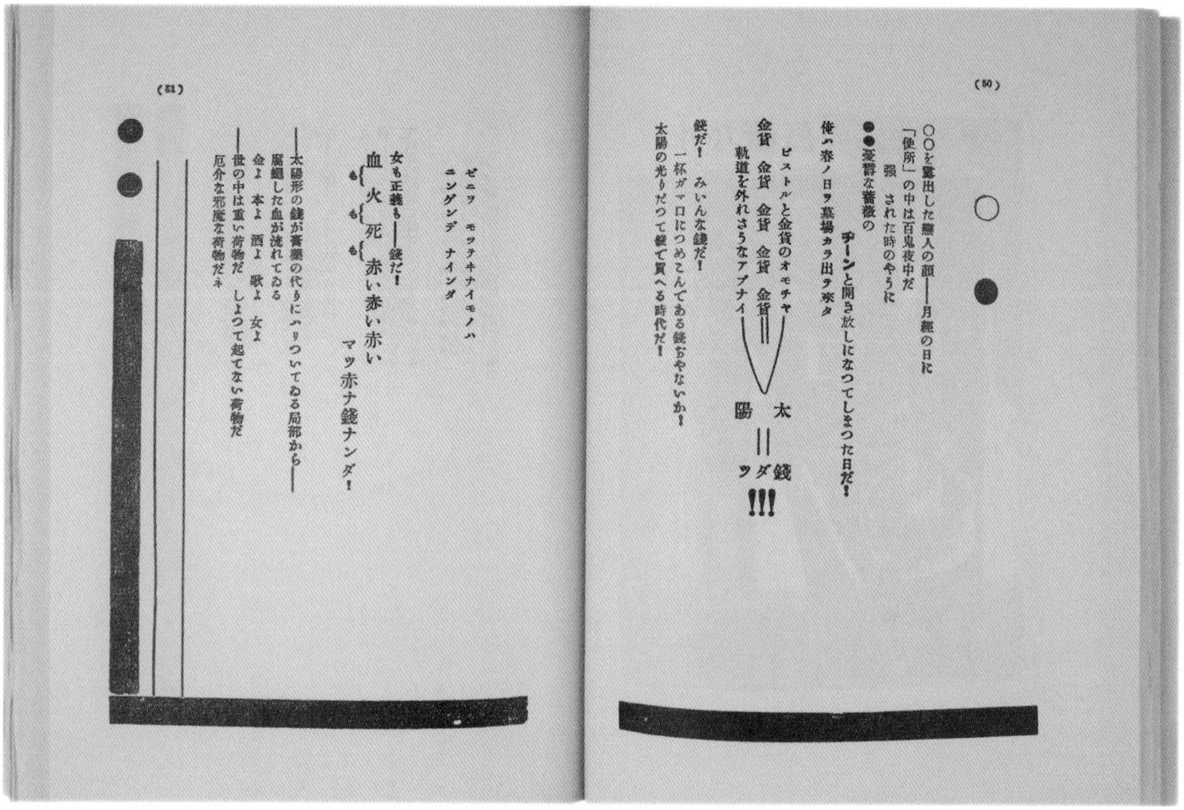

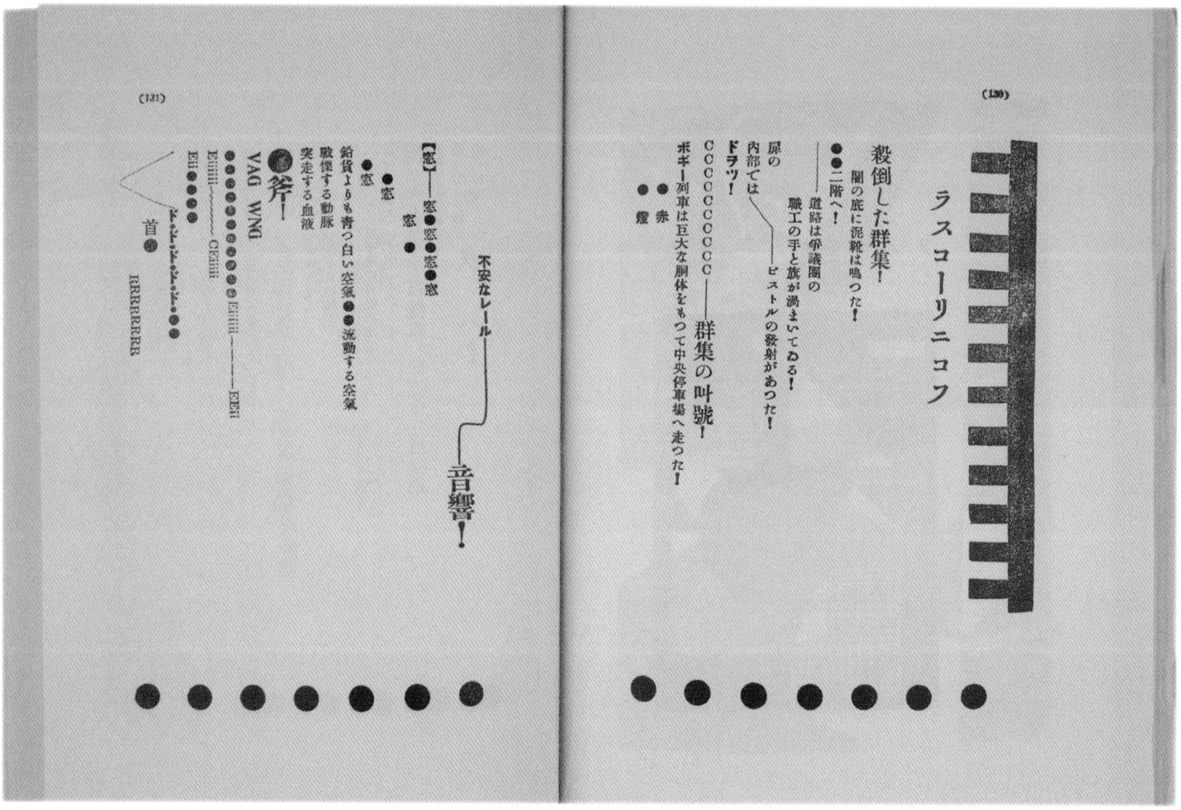

Spreads from ***Shikeisenkoku* 死刑宣告 *(Death Sentence)***, Hagiwara Kyōjirō 萩原恭次郎 (Tokyo: Kabushikigaisha Horupu Shuppan 株式会社ほるぷ出版, 1925). Design by Mavo. These spreads show the Mavo group's eclectic approach to connotative typography that mixed type styles, scales, decorative rules, and abstract forms. Note the three lines of vertical type that converge on the top right-hand page.

HAGIWARA KYŌJIRŌ 萩原恭次郎

1899–1938

Hagiwara Kyōjirō was born in Maebashi in Gunma Prefecture. His early writing consisted of traditional *waka* and *tanka* poetry, but Hagiwara shifted toward modern poetry during the late 1910s, evolving into expressive Dadaist anarchist free verse riddled with onomatopoeia. Hagiwara worked as a banker in Gunma and then moved to Tokyo in 1921, where he began working at another financial institution. In Tokyo, he became increasingly politicized after reading the writings of Kropotkin and engaging in protests and political direct action.

Hagiwara contracted tuberculosis, and his chronic condition informed the radical nature of his writing, design, art-making, and poetry critiquing the equation of modernity with progress. In 1923, he co-founded the anarchist Dada poetry journal *Aka to Kuro* 赤と黒 (*Red & Black*) alongside fellow poet Tsuboi Shigeji 壺井繁治. The duo printed four issues that year, and within those pages they advocated the destruction of historical poetic forms and an embrace of the erotic. They printed their manifesto on the cover of the first issue, calling for poems to be thrown like explosives to tear down the Japanese prison system:

> "What is poetry? What are poets? Discarding all concepts of the past, we boldly proclaim, 'Poetry is a bomb! Poets are dark criminals hurling bombs at the hard walls and doors of prisons!'"

Hagiwara was a member of Mavo and an integral contributor to their eponymous magazine, poignantly expressing the desire for individual expression through his writing for the periodical. Midway through the run of the magazine, Hagiwara published *Shikei Senkoku* 死刑宣告 (*Death Sentence*), a book-length poem typeset in highly articulated expressive typography, collectively designed by the Mavo members. They used shifts in typefaces, cuts, and weights and ranged the starting point of the text from the right, to left, to top, to bottom of different compositions to make readers more fully engage with the text and the book itself. Lines of text converged upon ornamental devices that emphasized critiques of capitalism, accentuated with oversized, bold exclamation points and assorted analphabetic characters. Hagiwara had recently resigned from his bank job and begun drinking heavily, and *Shikei Senkoku* was a radically dark expression of lost faith in modernity, filled with textual images of rioters, looters, expansive violence, and lime-sprinkled mass graves.

After the dissolution of Mavo in 1925, Hagiwara continued to publish widely, though sporadically. He moved to Sendai in 1927, contributing to assorted anarchist poetry magazines and collections over the next few years. He published the journal A *Study of Art Centered on Kropotkin* クロポトキンを中心とした芸術の研究 from 1932 until his death from tuberculosis in 1938.

References:

Hagiwara, Kyōjirō, Shōkichi Negishi, Yōji Arakawa, and Kazurō Koyama. *Hagiwara Kyōjirō*. Gunma-ken, Gunma-gun, Gunma-machi: Gunma Kenritsu Tsuchiya Bunmei Kinen Bungakkan, 1999.

Hagiwara, Kyōjirō. *Shikei Senkoku*. Tokyo: Nihon Tosho Sentā, 2004.

Weisenfeld, Gennifer S. *Mavo: Japanese Artists and the Avant-Garde, 1905–1931*. Berkeley: University of California Press, 2010.

心臓が壓された

行け！ 速時
第三の場所
十字街へ

——あの●●●●●●
——あの●●●●●●●

巻き起された
黄色の砂煙を追ひ

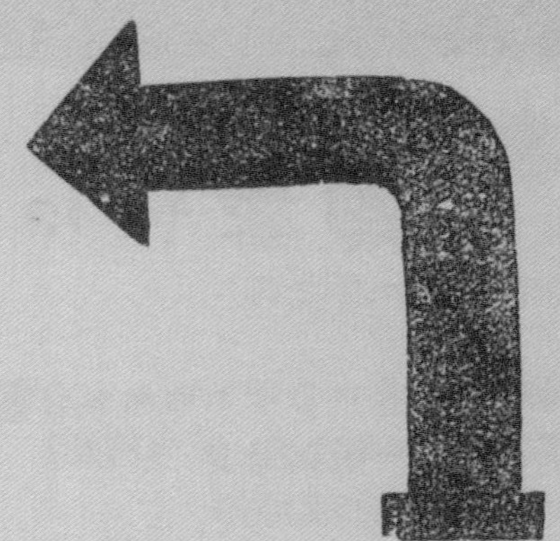

飢ゑた胃
　一度に苦い憎悪
爆裂の　急激な　焦燥の
十倍に
　百倍に
　歩行を進ませよ
笑ひや涙の乾いた街巷を
硝煙臭い突走
走つて
　走つて
　　走つて
　　　走る本能の激怒
——あの××××××
——あの×××××××××××

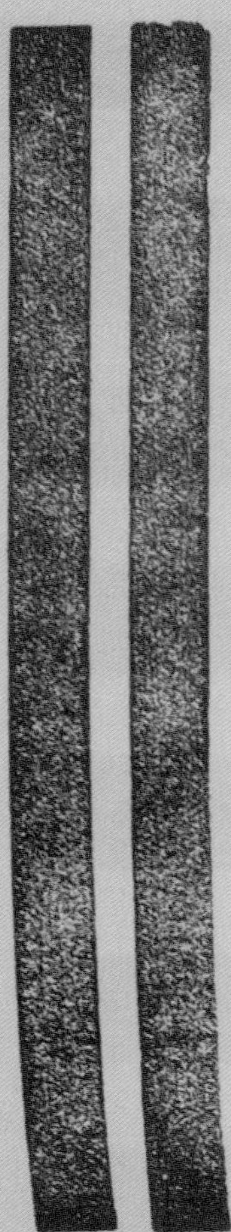

無題

女と若者が
廣場で
秋だ
煙火の遊戯をしてゐる

俺は饑ゑた
坂を匍ひ上つて来た
固い眼で
無神經のやうに

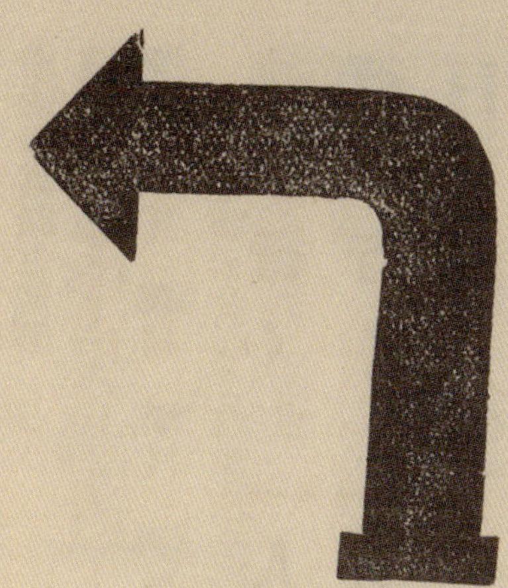

しまつた！
街角を
灰色の自動車は曲つた
罪人のやうな速さで

俺は　神經を
螺旋のやうに廻轉した
小さい眼を――もつと固く
身が前へ　こごむやうに

Spread from ***Shikeisenkoku* 死刑宣告 *(Death Sentence)*,** Hagiwara Kyōjirō 萩原恭次郎 (Tokyo: Kabushikigaisha Horupu Shuppan 株式会社ほるぷ出版, 1925). Design by Mavo. This spread mixes reading direction, type sizes, and type styles to encourage readers to interact with the book with a maximum of physicality.

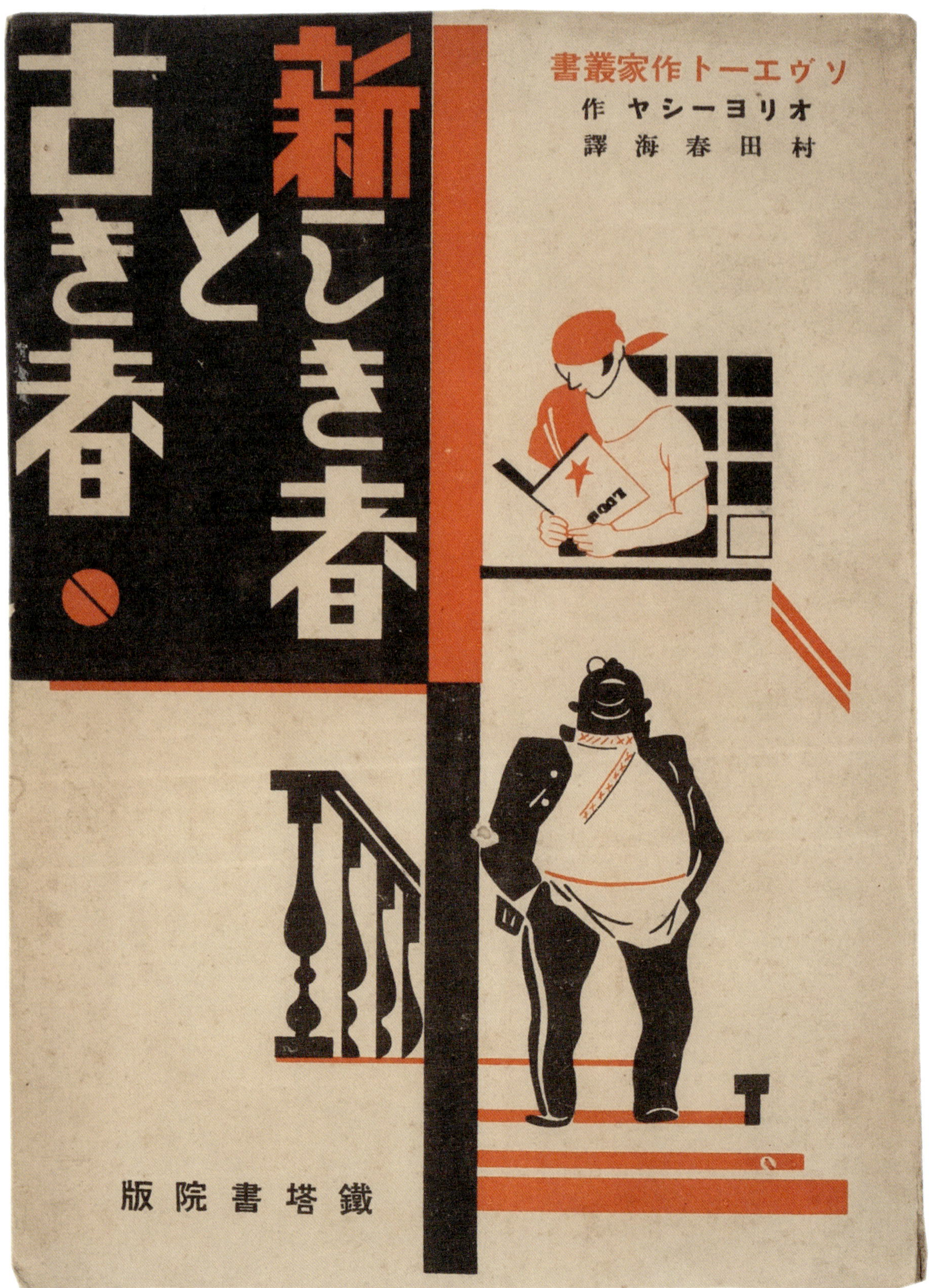

***A New Spring and An Old Spring* 新しき者と古き者**, Oriyoshiya オリヨーシヤ作, **translated by Murata Harumi** 村田春海訳 (Tokyo: Tetsuto Shoin Soviet Writer Series 鉄塔書院 ソヴエート作家叢書, 1929). Design by Yanase Masamu 柳瀬正夢. The cover illustration depicts a slim proletarian worker educating themselves about communism while an overweight capitalist wearing a monocle observes from below.

YANASE MASAMU 柳瀬正夢

1900–1945

Yanase Masamu was born in Matsuyama in Shikoku. He began formally studying art at age fourteen, holding his first solo exhibition of paintings the same year. By the time he was twenty years old, Yanase had moved to Tokyo and incorporated avant-garde approaches into his painting. He was involved with the Futurist Art Association (FAA) and wrote for leftist literary journals. He supported himself by designing books for liberal journalist and critic Hasegawa Nyozekan 長谷川如是閑 and taking on illustration work for assorted magazines, often utilizing leftist symbols in his work.

Yanase also worked as a cartoonist for the newspaper *Yomiuri Shimbun* 読売新聞, creating angular political caricatures that became his signature. The FAA disbanded in 1923, and Yanase joined the Mavo group of experimental artists and designers, with whom he was actively engaged in painting, collage, photomontage, barrack decoration after the Great Kanto Earthquake, and other assorted artistic and activist activities.

In 1925, Yanase completely abandoned fine art and focused his energies on designing books and editorial projects for the proletarian workers' movement. He designed book covers for Hosoi Wakizō 細井和喜蔵 and for a number of journals, employing a mix of abstraction, expressive lettering and typography, leftist symbols such as hammers and broken chains, and Social Realist illustration. Yanase's political views and membership in the Japanese Communist Party resulted in two years of imprisonment and torture starting in 1931. When he was released in 1933, he shifted his career to commercial illustration for various cultural, literary, and children's magazines while also returning to oil painting and pursuing photography. Yanase died in the 1945 firebombing of Tokyo's Shinjuku Station by American warplanes.

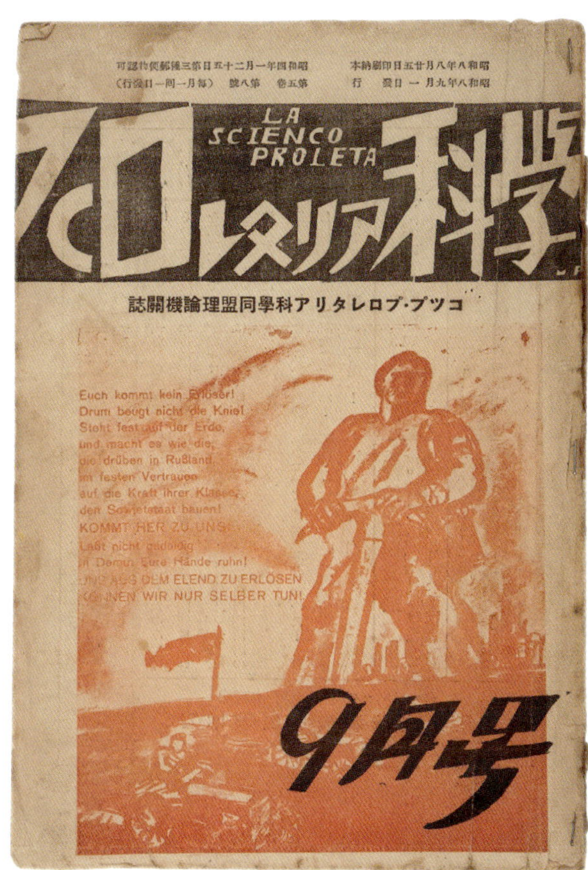

Proletariat Science Vol. 5, No. 8「プロレタリア科学」第5巻8号 (Tokyo: Japan Proletariat Science Alliance 日本プロレタリア科学同盟, 1933). This Yanase Masamu cover features a heroic image of a giant farm worker holding a pickaxe while another farmer driving a tractor toils in the foreground. The masthead reads "La Scienco Proleta" (or "Proletariat Science" in Esperanto), while the image is overprinted with an encouraging appeal in German for readers to join the Communist state.

References:

Sachi, Kaneda. "The Imaging Strategy of Shiseido in the 1930s: Analyzing Visual Magazines that Represented Corporate Identity." *Design History*, no. 14 (2016): [5–27].

Toda, Keita. Tokyo monokurōmu: *Toda Tatsuo, Mavo no Koro*. Tokyo: Bunsei Shoin, 2016.

Weisenfeld, Gennifer S. *Mavo: Japanese Artists and the Avant-Garde, 1905–1931*. Berkeley: University of California Press, 2010.

Yanase, Masamu. *Yanase Masamu zenshū*. Kyōto-shi: Sanninsha, 2013.

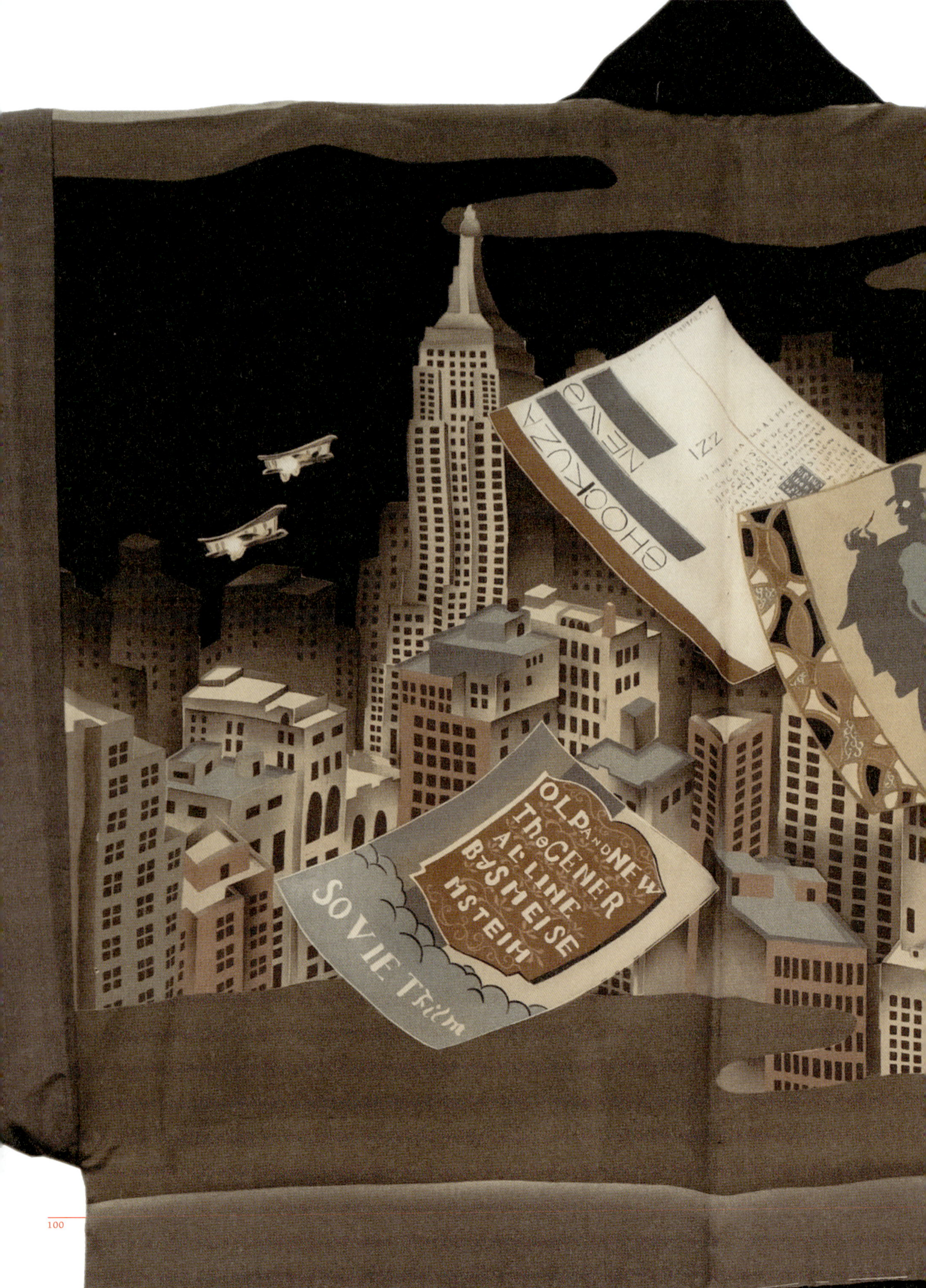
OLP AND NEW
The GENER
AL LINE
MSTEIH
SOVIE TRILM

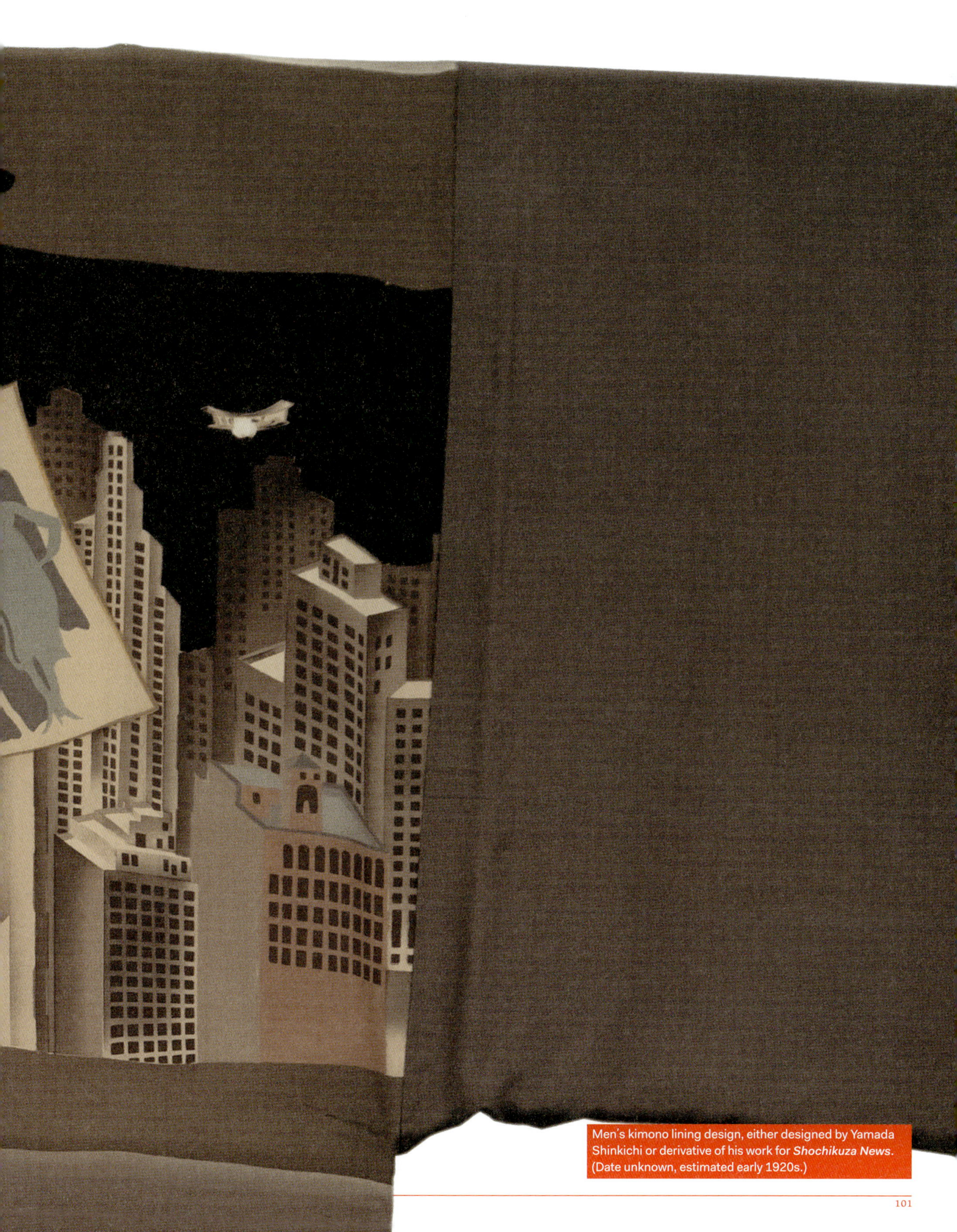

Men's kimono lining design, either designed by Yamada Shinkichi or derivative of his work for ***Shochikuza News***. (Date unknown, estimated early 1920s.)

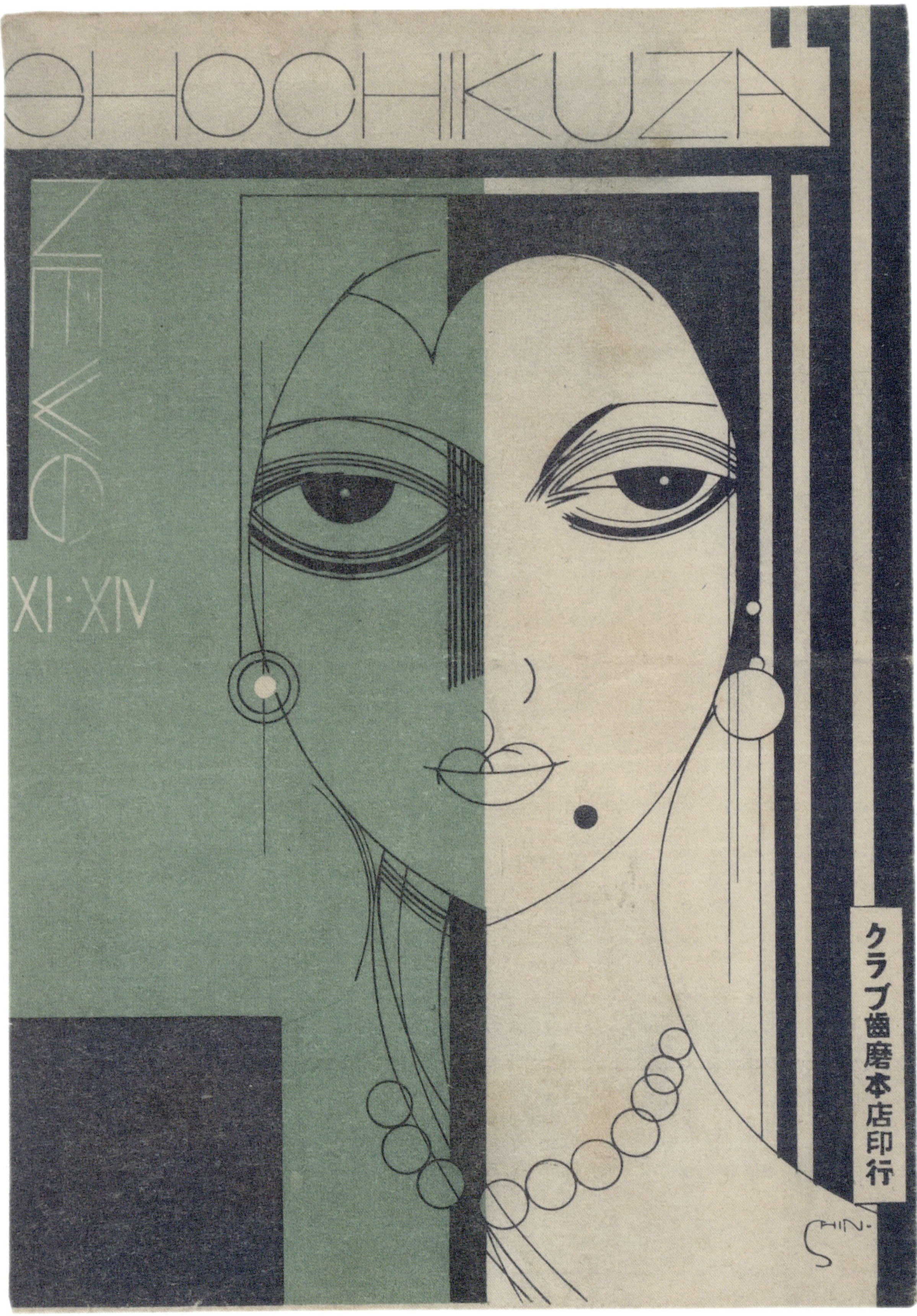

Cover for ***Shochikuza News*** Volume 11 No. 14, designed by Yamada Shinkichi 山田伸吉.

YAMADA SHINKICHI 山田伸吉 & ZUAN MOJI 図案文字

1901/1903–1981

Yamada Shinkichi (born 山田真吉, the kanji he used professionally—山田伸吉—was his artist's name) was born in either 1901 or 1903 in Osaka. (Official records differ as to the year of his birth.) His father, Yamada Toshiyuki, was an architect working in the Kansai region.

In 1922, Yamada joined Shochikuza Theaters' public relations department and was put in charge of designing the posters for movies and stage productions at their Osaka and Kyoto theaters and the covers for the theaters' magazine, *The Shochikuza News* 松竹座ニュース. The Shochikuza were a bastion of modern culture in Osaka and Kyoto at that time, bringing foreign films to the Kansai region for the first time and elevating Osaka's cosmopolitan status.

Yamada's salary was not enough to cover his expenses, and he wanted to move to Tokyo to study art in earnest, yet whenever he would threaten to quit he would immediately be given a raise, which he deemed to be a decent deal despite the intense hours involved in the work. Yamada designed the front cover of the *Shochikuza News* from 1924 to 1930, bringing aspects of ukiyo-e, portraiture, Art Nouveau, and Art Deco to the two-color magazine covers.

Yamada was a key figure in the evolution of "design lettering" or *zuan moji* 図案文字. More particularly, he was a leading designer of the zuan moji subset "cinema lettering" or *kinema moji* キネマ文字: high-contrast display characters for posters and magazine covers within the theater industry. Both zuan moji and kinema moji were visually arresting exemplars of avant-garde lettering of that era—from massive, geometric, and sparse at one end of the visual spectrum to lithe, baroque, and decorative at the other.

The 1910s and 1920s saw an explosion of interest in these forms of modern lettering. The sheer volume of characters involved in the production of Japanese typefaces meant that type was relegated to body copy and that display lettering would be rendered by hand, a trend that continues to the present day. Numerous lettering manuals were published from 1911 through the 1930s, including style charts in instructional art books and booklets. Yamada's work was in step with others who were pushing the boundaries of lettering expression at that time, as cataloged in features in the commercial art magazine *Gendai Shōgyō Bijutsu Zenshū* 現代商業美術全集 (*The Complete Commercial Artist*) issues 15 and 18 and in poster designer Yajima Shūichi's 1926 book *General Survey of Design Letters* 図案文字大観. Much of Yamada's work neatly mirrored his Kanto-based contemporary Murayama Tomoyoshi's work for the Mavo and for theaters in Tokyo.

From 1937 to 1944, Yamada worked for the Kyoto Takarazuka Theater, as well, though the Shochikuza remained the base of his activities. In 1944, Yamada was evacuated to Shiga Prefecture until the end of the war. He worked in the woodworking industry in Kyoto immediately following the war but returned to working for the stage shortly thereafter. His last known project was the stage design for the Osaka Shin Kabukiza in 1959.

Yamada designed a number of book covers for novelist and playwright Hasegawa Yukinori 長谷川幸延 from the 1920s through the 1950s, as well as the stage sets for a play of Hasegawa's that was performed in Tokyo in 1951.

Throughout the 1970s, Yamada illustrated and designed numerous book covers for historic texts, as well as Osaka-themed calendars. He had a thriving business painting imaginary and historic theater scenes and, in 1974, left Japan for the first time to help in the planning of a fully authentic Japanese restaurant in the style of a Japanese theater for Hilton Hotels in Las Vegas. While the restaurant was never realized, a series of sketches of the Las Vegas Strip by Yamada remains in Osaka.

References:

Hase, Yoichi, and Jun Sakuragi. *The World of Shinkichi Yamada, Theatrical Artist*. Edited by Yoichi Hase. Vol. 1. Senriyama: The Ministry of Education, Culture, Sports, Science and Technology's Project to Support the Formation of a Strategic Research Foundation for Private Universities, 2012.

Wiesenfeld, Gennifer. "Japanese Typographic Design." In *Bridges to Heaven: Essays on East Asian Art in Honor of Professor Wen C. Fong* 1, edited by Wen Fong and Jerome Silbergeld, 1:827–48. Princeton, NJ: P.Y. and Kinmay W. Tang Center for East Asian Art, Dept. of Art and Archeology, Princeton University, 2011.

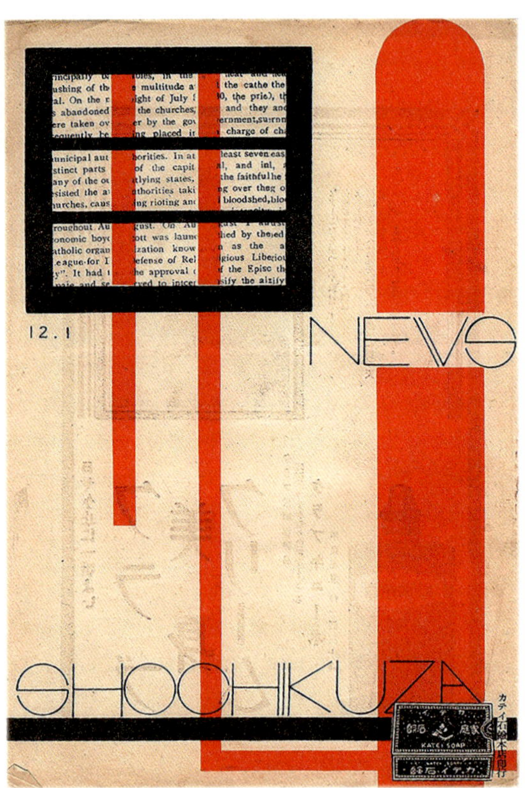

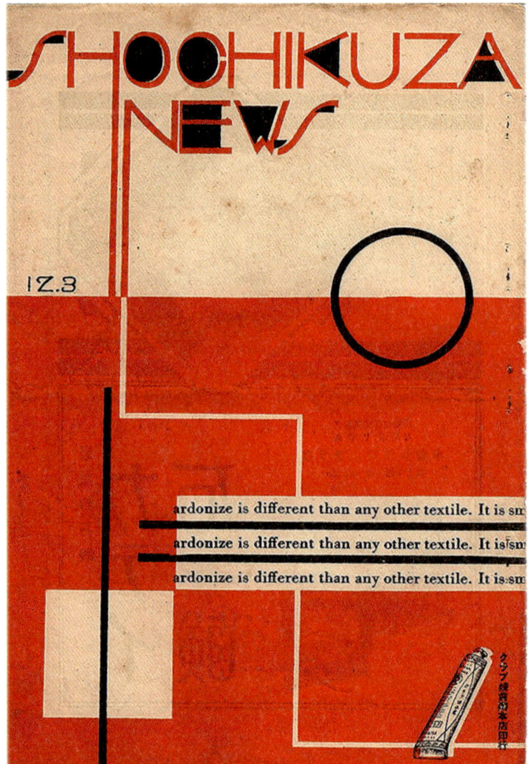

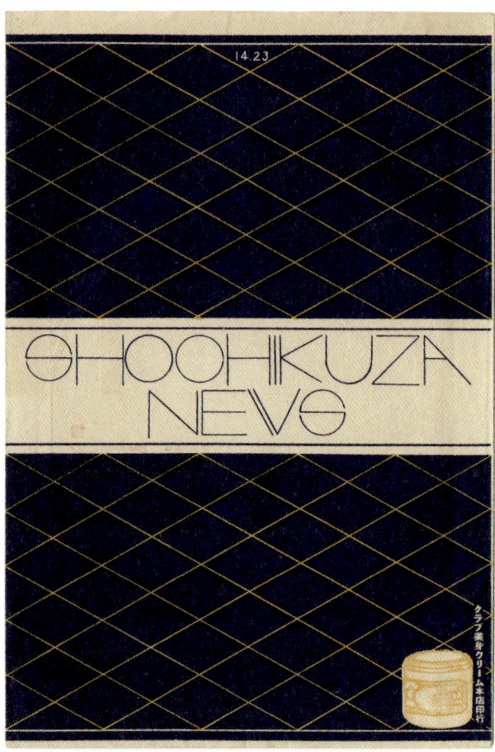

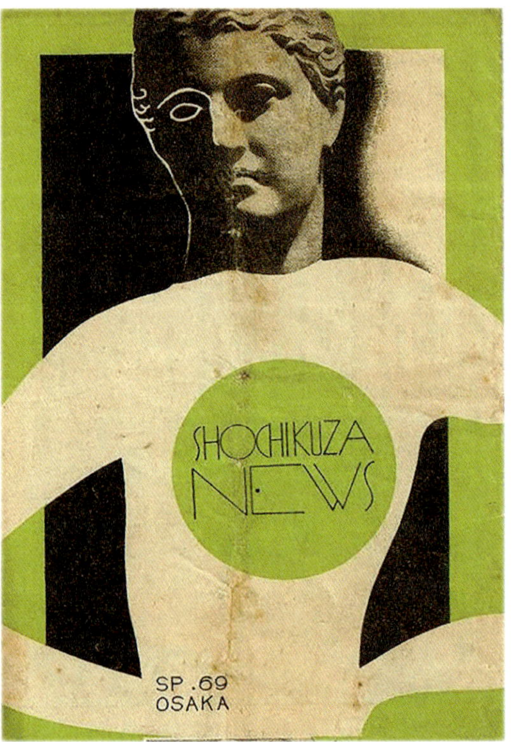

An assortment of covers of ***Shochikuza News*** designed by Yamada Shinkichi 山田伸吉.

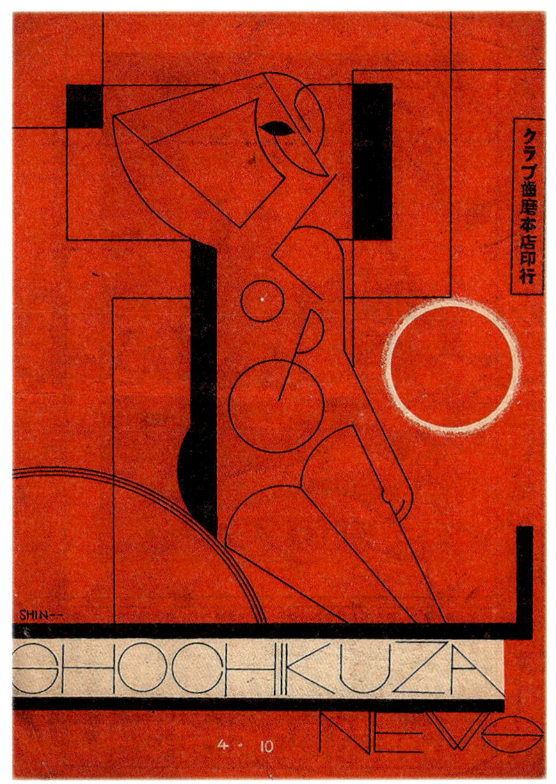
クラブ歯磨本店印行
SHIN—
SHOCHIKUZA
NEWS
4・10

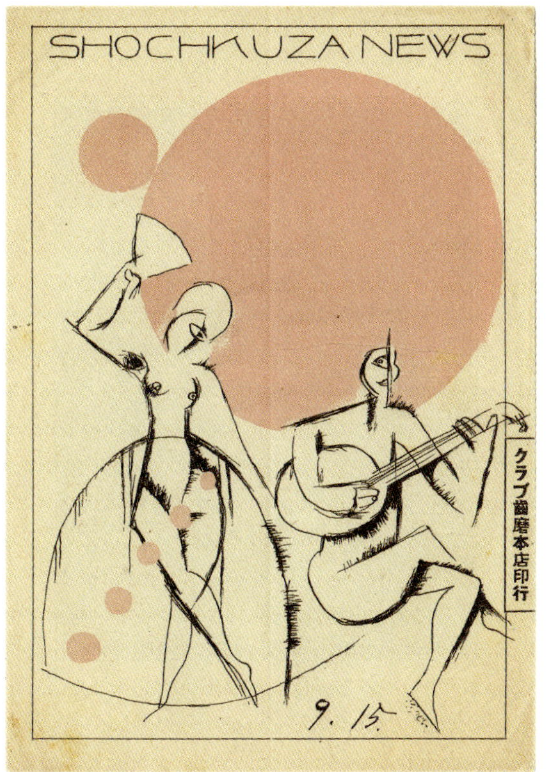
SHOCHIKUZA NEWS
クラブ歯磨本店印行
9. 15.

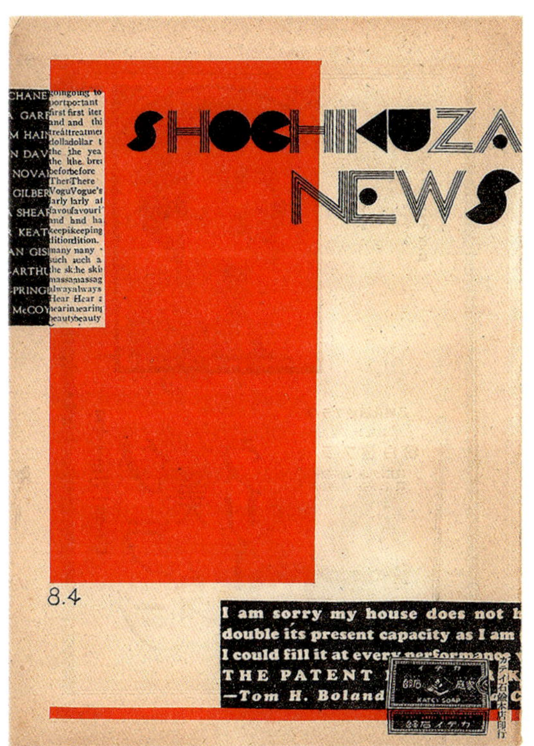
SHOCHIKUZA
NEWS
8.4
I am sorry my house does not
double its present capacity as I am
I could fill it at every performance
THE PATENT
—Tom H. Boland
KATEI SOAP

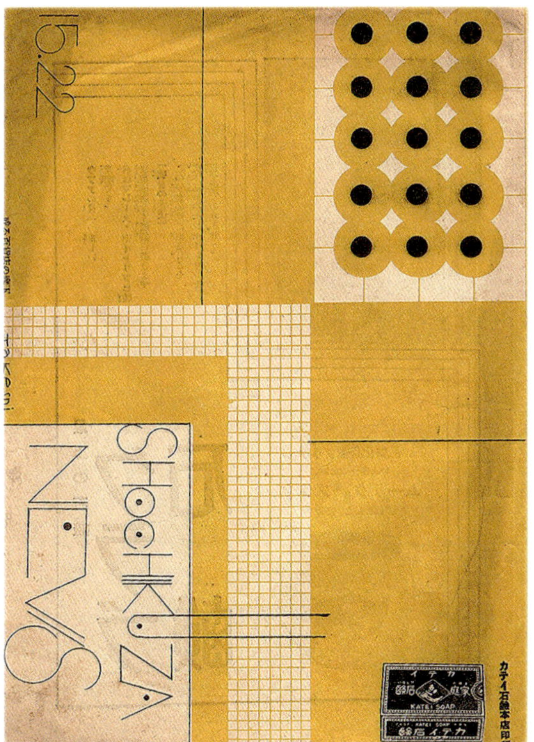
15.22
SHOCHIKUZA
NEWS
KATEI SOAP
カテイ石鹸本店印行

KON WAJIRŌ 今和次郎

1888–1973

"I think the work of decoration is to express the real and practical ways of people's lives."
- Kon Wajirō

Kon Wajirō was born in Hirosaki in Aomori Prefecture. He studied design, textiles, and interior design at Tokyo University of the Arts, graduating in 1912. Immediately afterward, Kon went to work as an assistant professor of architecture at Waseda University, where he would continue as a lecturer and eventually full professor. He contributed greatly to graphic design, architecture, fashion studies, and many other areas of cultural production over his lifetime.

In 1917, Kon began studying traditional Japanese *minka* 民家 farmhouses, and would travel extensively throughout Japan and its then-colonies to study and sketch minka and the effects of urbanization on the countryside. He compiled his research in the 1922 book *Nihon no Minka* 日本の民家. Kon was a member of two notable associations before 1920: the Association of Decorative Artists, a group dedicated to elevating the status of crafts, and the Hakubōkai, a research group led by Japanese folklore scholar Yanagita Kunio 柳田國男 and committed to the studies of rural society, culture, nature, and the rural built environment.

The Great Kanto Earthquake of 1923 was a formative moment for Kon—he realized that this terrible disaster, which had claimed the lives of 142,800 people and reduced much of greater Tokyo and Yokohama to rubble, would force Kanto to rebuild and, in doing so, modernize. In the aftermath of the quake and the resulting wildfires, the denizens of the Kanto region were forced to create makeshift homes and businesses, called *barakku* or "barracks," from what they could salvage in the wreckage. Fascinated with these structures, Kon and graphic designer/stage designer Yoshida Kenkichi 吉田謙吉 founded the Barakku Soshoku-sha バラック装飾社 (Barrack Decoration Group), helping to decorate the structures' interiors and exteriors—a reflection of Kon's interest in ornamentation, which ran contrary to his modernist architect contemporaries.

In 1925, together with his students at Waseda and his friend Yoshida, Kon founded Modernology, an initiative and method of study in which they observed, recorded, and analyzed the massive changes occurring in Tokyo before their eyes. Modernology was also known as "Kōgengaku" 考現学 or "archeology of the present day" and "Modernologio"—Esperanto for Modernology.

Over the span of a few days, Kon and his friends, sometimes assisted by scores of volunteers from various walks of life, would mobilize to different parts of Tokyo's Ginza district, record their observations as drawings and handwritten notes on small survey-based cards that Kon provided, then analyze the data. Kon and his team compiled information on material possessions, styles of dress, architecture, class backgrounds, and behavior, capturing outdoor social life in Ginza in stunning detail. At the same time, their research methods were idiosyncratic and based on short-term group work, and they stand in stark contrast to contemporary methods of immersive ethnography and anthropology.

The 1925 study found that sixty-seven percent of men in the Ginza district wore Western clothing while thirty-three percent wore traditional Japanese clothing, whereas the numbers were staggeringly flipped for women—ninety-nine percent wore traditional Japanese clothing and a mere one percent wore Western-style clothing. Kon's stylishly executed visual taxonomies give us a realistic and robust understanding of what the citizens of 1920s Ginza actually looked like and how the objects in their lives helped to shape their experiences. Kon's use of drawing as a documentarian tool was born out of his study of minka and how tools, craft, farming, and farmers' lives were deeply connected.

Kon's studies cut a wide path through peoples' daily lives post-quake. He examined how clothing affected human physiology; how people read books, moved through space, and constructed their living spaces; what they purchased, what they desired, how their clothing was damaged, and how living spaces were arranged by the people who lived in them. Another of Kon's taxonomies from 1925 analyzed the entire belongings of a newly married couple from the Fukagawa district of Tokyo. In two separate illustrations, Kon breaks down every implement owned by the husband and wife, including each object's value.

Kon's Modernology work is as much ethnographic as it is designed—the mix of imagery, lettering, and accompanying typography highlights humans' ability to restructure the material world in ways that are as economic as they are practical. In the description of "Examination of the Household of a Newly Married Couple" in Yoshida's and his book *Modernologio* (1930),

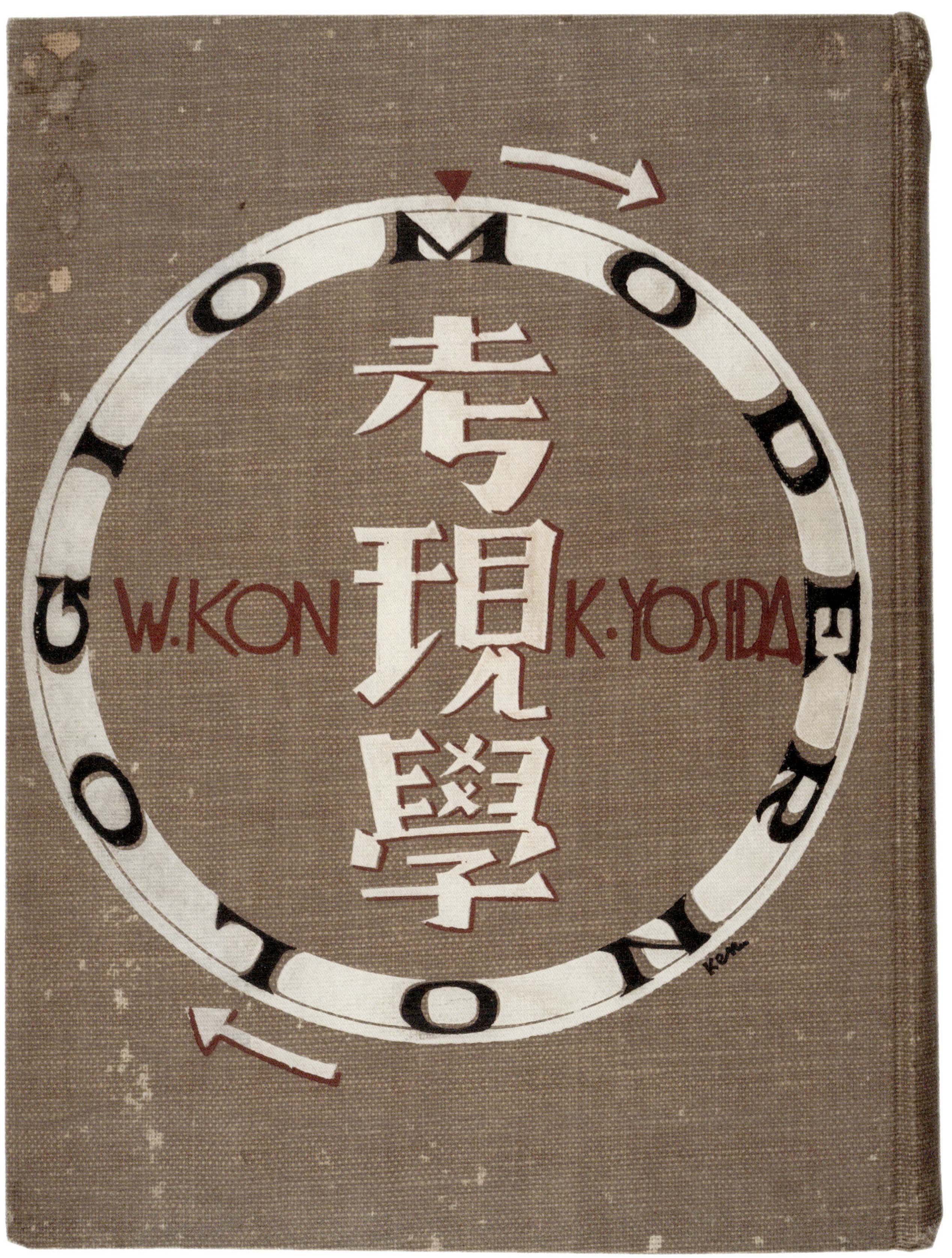

Cover of ***Modernologio* 考現学**, Kon Wajiro 今和次郎 & Yoshida Kenkichi 吉田謙吉 (Tokyo: Shunyōdō 春陽堂, 1930).

第二圖　本所深川の商店に見らるゝ品物及値段

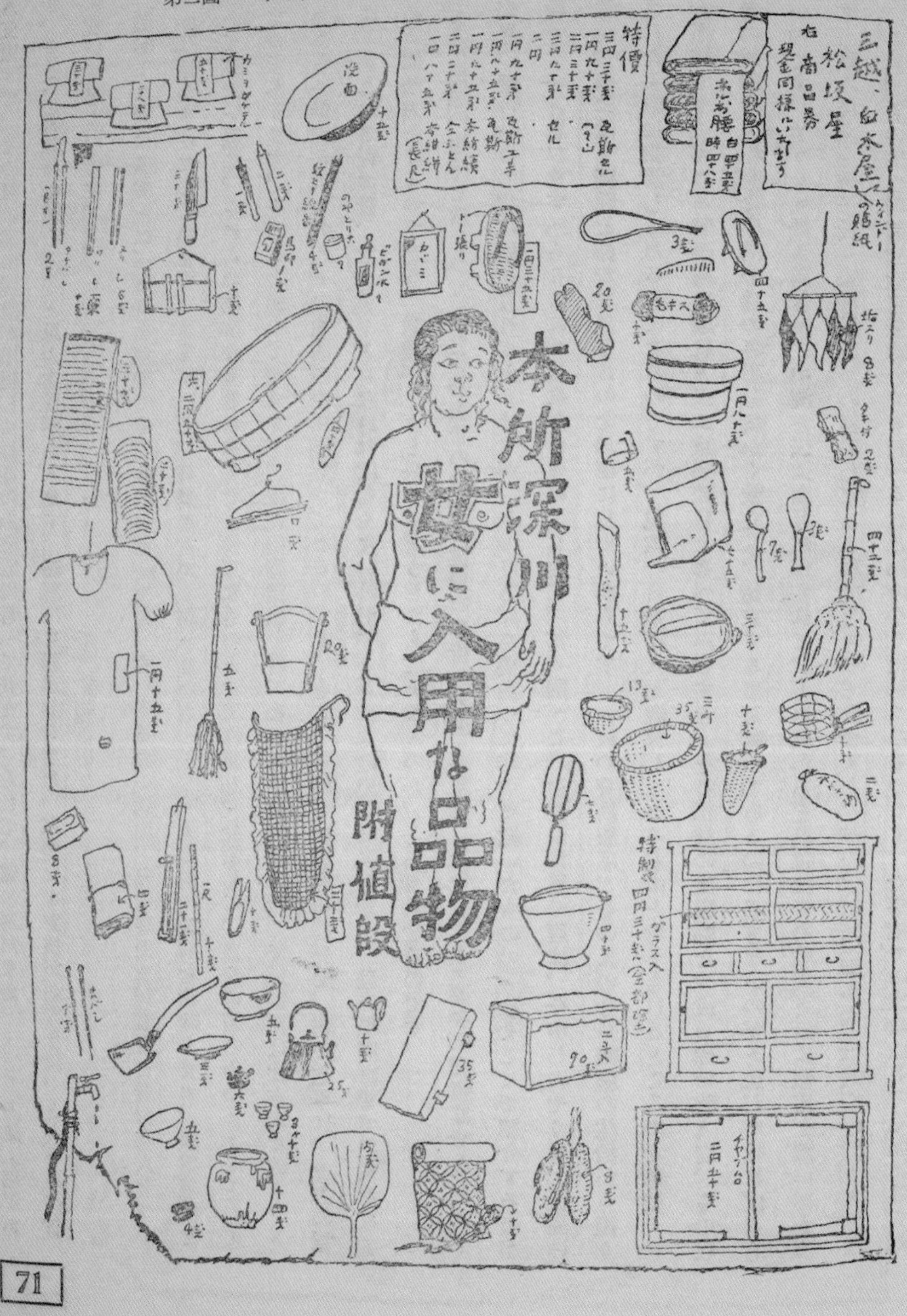

71

第一圖　本所深川の商店に見らるゝ物品及値段

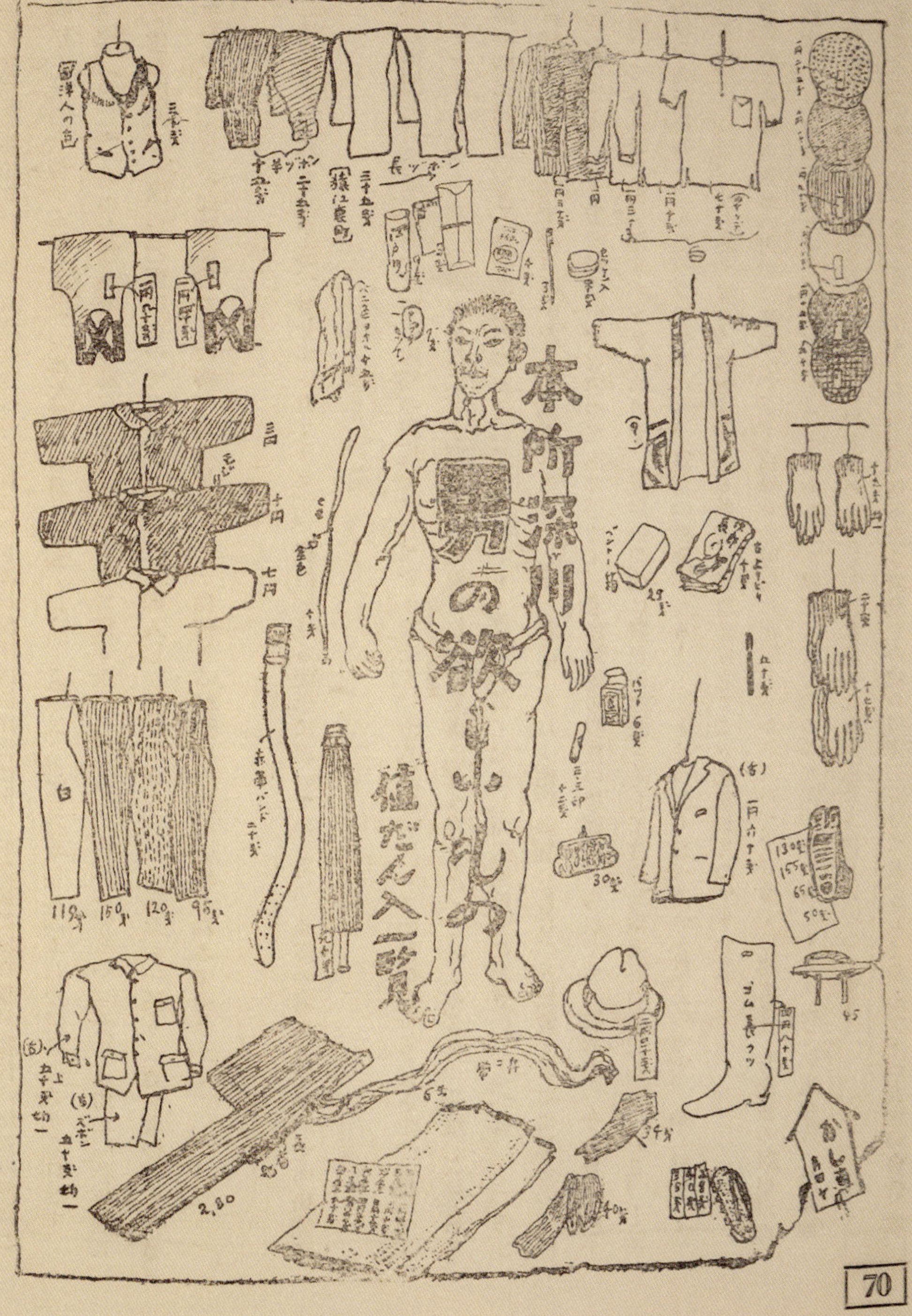

Spread from *Modernologio* **考現学** showing the entire household possessions of a married couple in Fukugawa Ward in Tokyo.

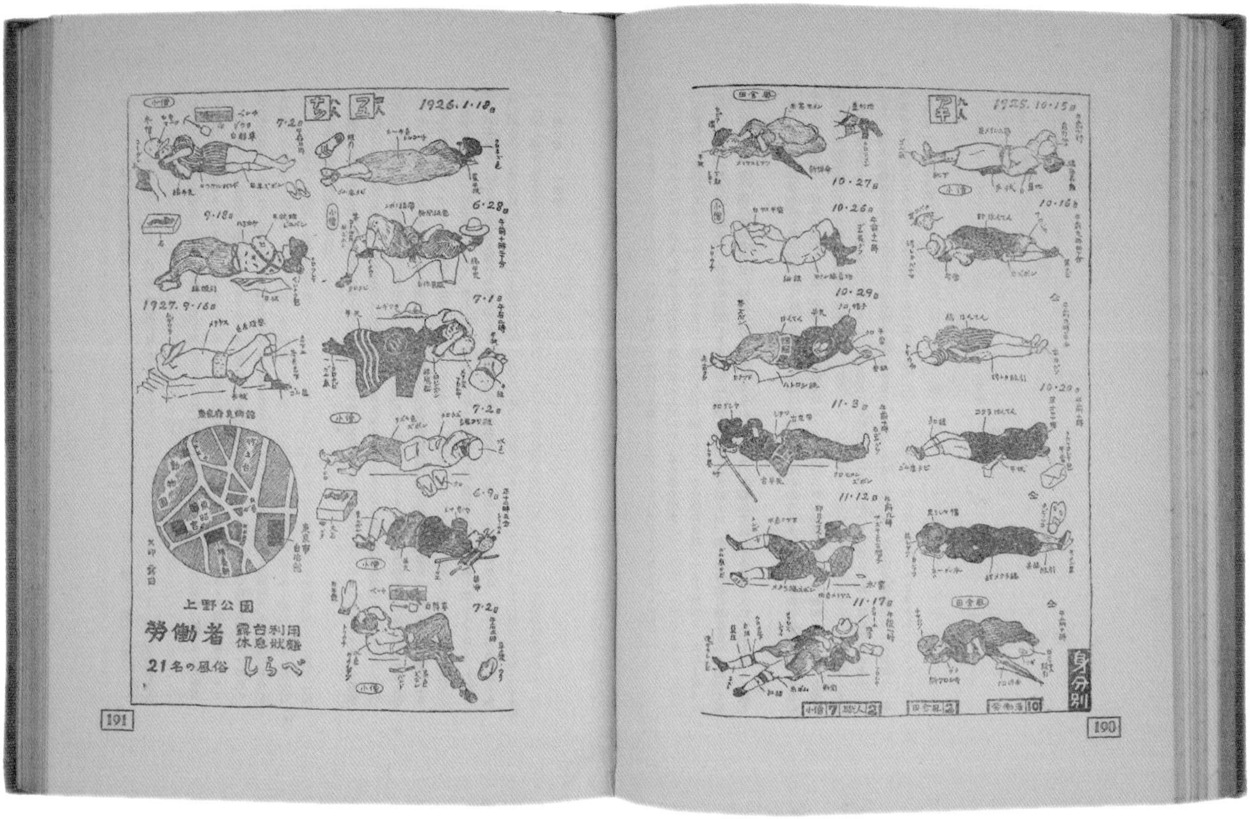

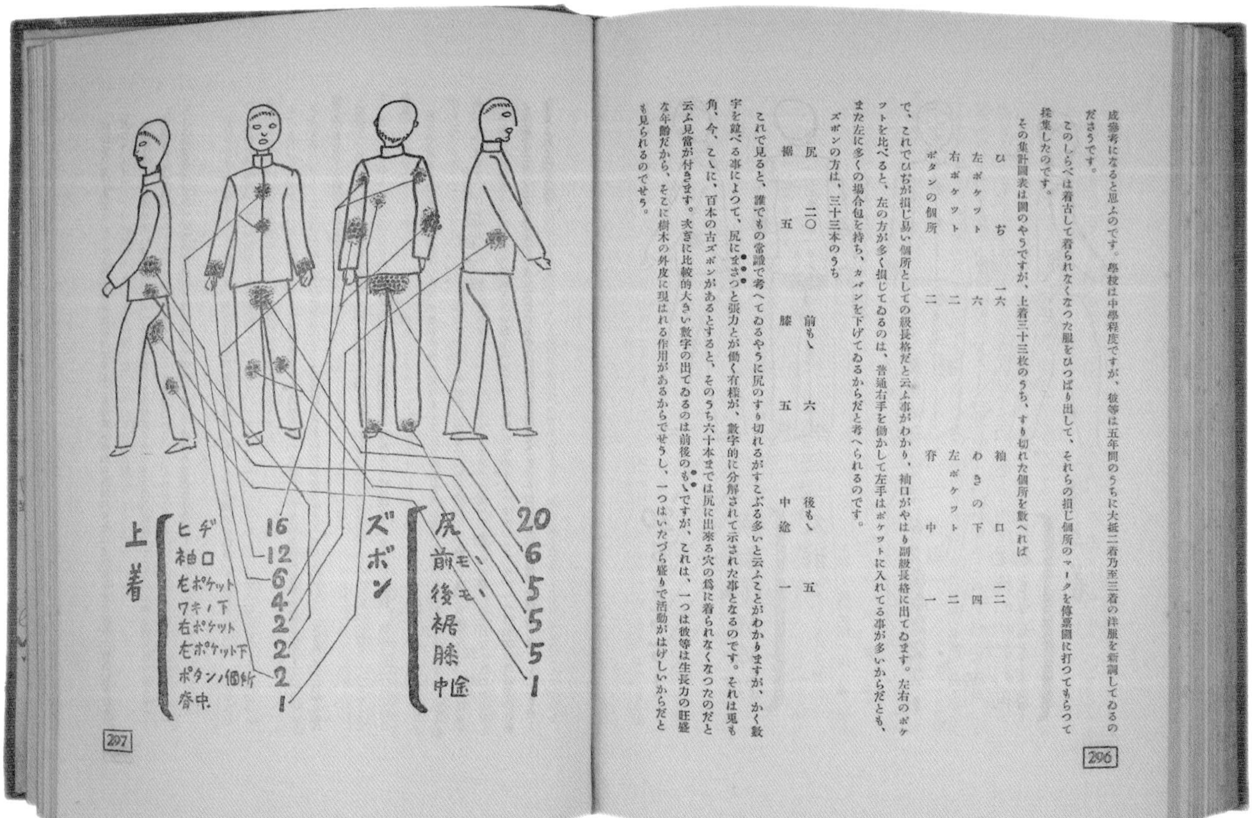

Spreads from ***Modernologio* 考現学** depicting the positions of individuals sleeping on the streets and the focal points of wear and tear on children's school uniforms.

Kon wrote, "In this work I am trying to further develop an anthropological method in order to record and examine comparatively our contemporary material culture."

Kon's work with Modernology gives us a unique perspective on Tokyo life in the early Shōwa period (1926–1989), largely through the effects that objects had on citizens' lives rather than the spaces they inhabited. His taxonomies of firefighters' decorative poles and vernacular street signage were published in the debut issue of *Affiches* magazine in 1927 and other illustrations in subsequent issues. Kon also served as an advisor to the design journal *Shōgyō Design Zenshū* 商業デザイン全集 (*The World's Commercial Design*) from 1953–1954.

Modernology became relatively popular in Tokyo in 1927 due to a well-attended exhibition of Kon's research held at Kinokuniya Books and the later publication of Yoshida's and his bestselling 1930 and 1931 books on the topic. By studying and documenting aspects of peoples' lives, Kon attempted to explain how Tokyo became a "modern" city.

Kon's life was driven by his observations of common people—how they related to society, objects, and social spaces. His taxonomic approach to design was tempered by the influence of the utopian writings of John Ruskin and William Morris, and by the profound influence that he drew from the writings and visual works of Owen Jones, author of *The Grammar of Ornament*. Through his visual documentation, it is clear that Kon desired a life that made sense for the denizens of Tokyo, yet Kon was a shy man who never included any commentary from the people he studied in his pursuit of the archeology of the present day.

Kon passed away in 1973. He had dedicated his life to his pursuits and was to the very end the bearer of an infectious smile and keen, searching eyes, hidden behind thick eyeglasses.

References:

Kawazoe, Noboru. *Kon Wajirō*. Tokyo: Chikuma Shobo, 2004.

Kon, Wajirō, and Kenkichi Yoshida. *Kōgengaku saishū: Moderunorojio*. Tokyo: Gakuyō Shobō, 1986.

Takeuchi, Yukie. *Kaifu Sengo Nihon no Insatsu Kokoku: Puresuaruto Dokon Kokoku Kessakusen Senkyuhyakuyonjukyu Senkyuhyakunanajunana*. Osaka: Sogensha, 2020.

Sugiura, Hisui. *Afisshu: Zuan kenkyū Zasshi 3–7*. Tokyo: Kokusho Kankōkai, 2009.

YOSHIDA KENKICHI 吉田謙吉

1897–1982

Yoshida Kenkichi was born in Tokyo and studied design at Tokyo University of the Arts. Yoshida was involved with design and direction for cinema and theater. He worked with Kon Wajiro in creating Modernologio, the study of Tokyo's modernization after the Great Kanto Earthquake of 1923, and the duo wrote and designed two books on the subject: *Modernologio: Kōgengaku* 考現学, published by Shunyōdō 春陽堂 in 1930, and *Kōgengaku saishū: Modernologio* 考現学採集: モデルノロヂオ, published by Kensetsusha in 1931.

Yoshida was a co-founder of the radical leftist arts group Third Section Plastic Arts Association 三科造形美術協会, which was referred to by the abbreviation Sanka 三科, alongside Mavo members Murayama Tomoyoshi, Yanase Masamu, and others. The group held its first annual exhibition in 1925, to which Yoshida contributed five different typographic *kanban* 看板 sign designs and a Constructivist-oriented assemblage devoted to then-current notions of the modern girl. Sanka only existed for two years and only held two of its planned annual exhibitions before splintering due to ideological conflicts between member factions. Yoshida was also a member of the Sanka-associated arts groups Action and Zōkei.

He was a founder, alongside Murayama and designer Maki Hisao, of the Union of Woven and Dyed Art 織染芸術連盟, a group that worked with textile designers in Kyoto to study and produce textiles with contemporary avant-garde aesthetics. They held exhibitions at department stores across Kansai and then traveled to Nagoya and Tokyo's Mitsukoshi department store in 1926. The exhibitions featured both abstract and pictorial kimono and obi designs and was featured in a number of publications.

Yoshida's work was regularly included in the commercial art journal *Gendai Shōgyō Bijutsu Zenshū* 現代商業美術全集 *(The Complete Commercial Artist)* throughout the course of its publication, and he was a contributor to the Japanese design journal *Desegno* デセグノ. He designed a number of books, including providing the total design and illustration for *Three Fairy Tales* 三つの願ひ by Koyamauchi Kaoru 小山内薫 in 1925. Yoshida was also responsible for designing the identities and interiors of a handful of retail establishments, including in 1934 the Locomotive Bar 機関車 in Ginza, whose interior he clad entirely in metal to make it resemble a train.

After the Great Kanto Earthquake, Yoshida became involved in the leftist Tsukiji Small Theater as its principal designer, designing twenty-two posters in the first year alone using an eclectic mix of display lettering, illustration, and compositional strategies. Beyond his design work for the theater, he wrote the play *Button: Opening Play of Oppositions Between White and Red* which was performed in the collaborative revue *Sanka in the Theater* held by members of Sanka and Mavo. The performance involved a caged monkey, the projection of an abstract film, a motorcycle being driven down the aisle of the theater, and the audience being pelted with food waste.

Yoshida was involved in stage and costume design for most of his life, working between Tokyo and Kyoto. He was one of the designers for the magazine *La Teatro* テァトロ alongside close friend Murayama Tomoyoshi, with whom he collaborated often in the proletarian theater movement. Yoshida participated in a group exhibition alongside Murayama and others at the Shirokiya department store in 1925. He codified his ideas for the design of expressive theatrical productions and promotional materials in the book *A Stage Designer's Handbook* 舞台装置者の手帖, published in 1930. Yoshida also worked as art director for a number of films released by Toho Studios.

Yoshida traveled to Manchuria as a foreign correspondent in 1934 and photographed the everyday lives of Manchurian people. He worked in China as a stage designer for the Japanese navy starting in 1939, publishing the book *Southern Chinese Culture* 南支風土記 that same year. Yoshida taught theater in Mongolia in 1944 and remained there through the end of the war, spending time imprisoned in an internment camp before being repatriated to Japan in 1946.

Yoshida went on to publish a number of other books about stage design and a history of the Tsukiji Small Theater. He formed the Yoshida Kenkichi Stage Art Research Institute 吉田謙吉舞台美術研究所 in 1945 and taught on and off at Nihon University and Tama Art University, whose auditorium he designed.

References:

Kon, Wajirō, and Kenkichi Yoshida. *Kōgengaku saishū: Moderunorojio*. Tokyo: Gakuyō Shobō, 1986.

Yoshida, Kenkichi. *Butai sōchisha no techō*. Tokyo: Shiroku Shoin, 1930.

Sugiura, Hisui. *Afisshu: Zuan kenkyū Zasshi 3–7*. Tokyo: Kokusho Kankōkai, 2009.

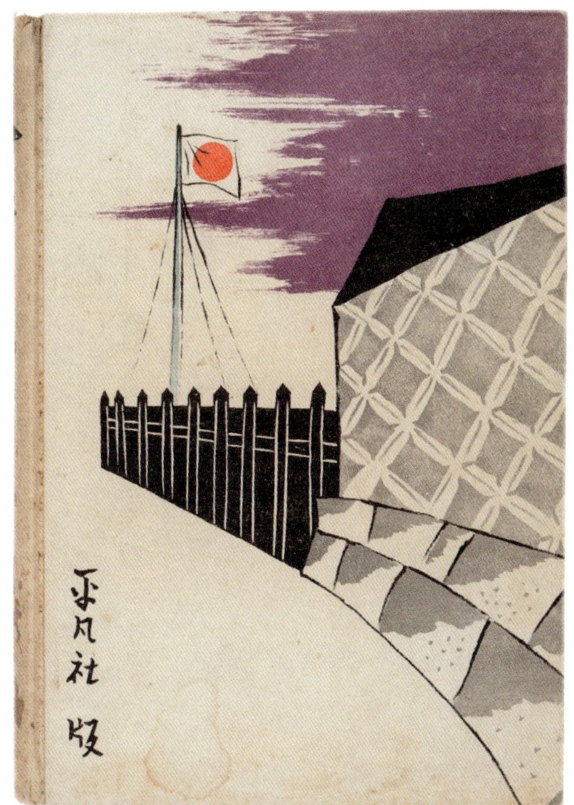

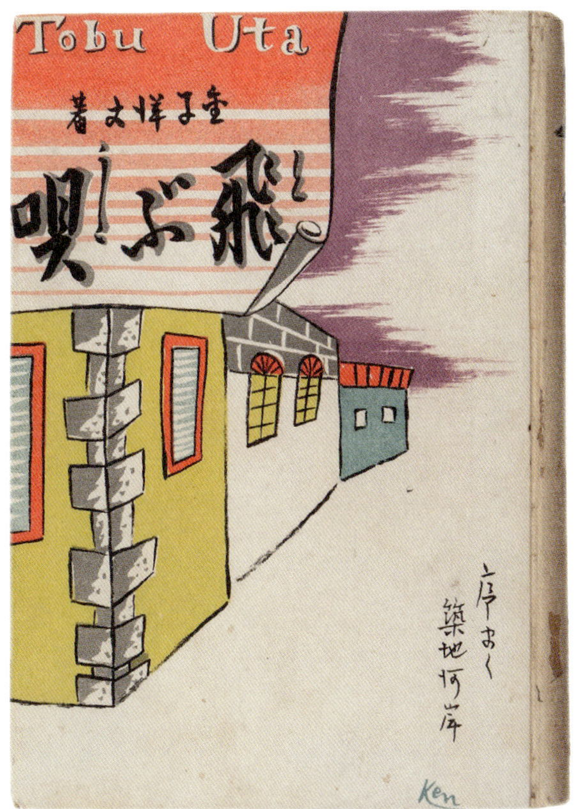

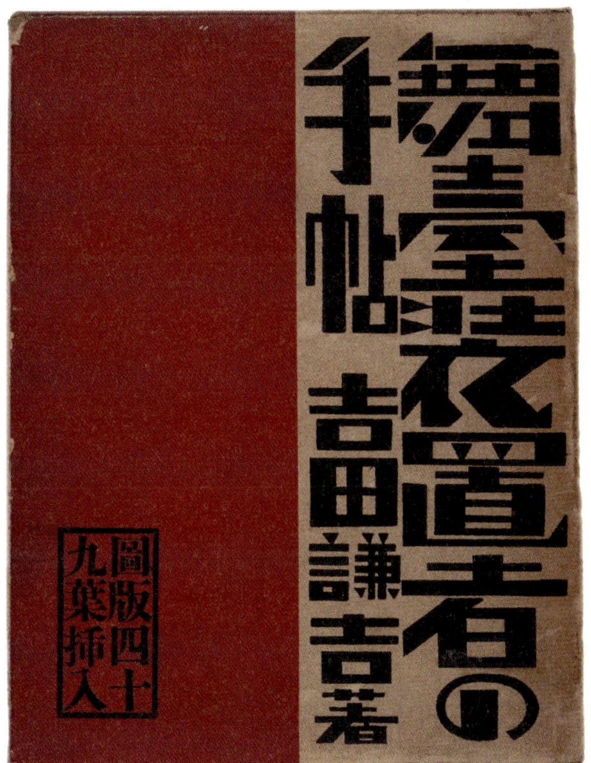

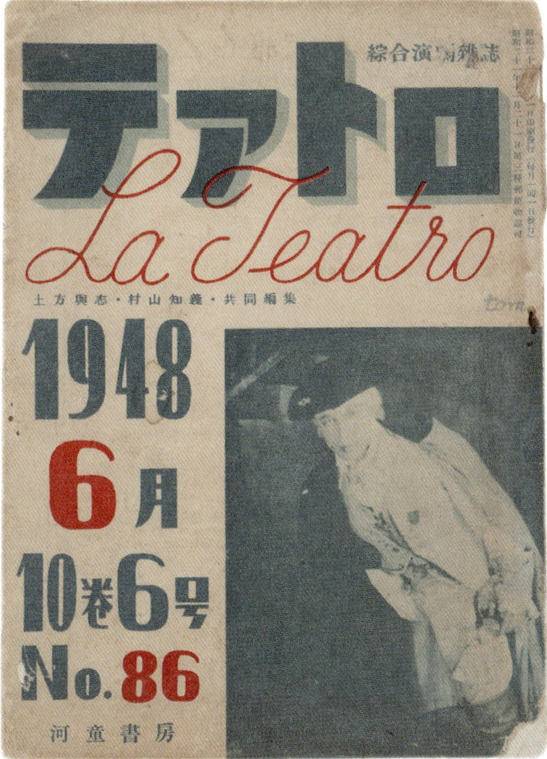

Clockwise from top left: Back and front cover of ***Flying Song* 飛ぶ唄**, Kaneko Yōbun 金子洋文 (Tokyo: Heibonsha 平凡社, 1929) cover by Yoshida Kenkichi 吉田謙吉; ***La Teatro* No. 86 テアトロ 86** (Tokyo: Kawado Shobō 河童書房, June 1948) theater magazine designed by Murayama Tomoyoshi and Yoshida Kenkichi; ***Guide to Stage Design* 舞台装置者の手帖**, Yoshida Kenkichi 吉田謙吉 (Tokyo: Yonjurokushoin 四六書院, 1930).

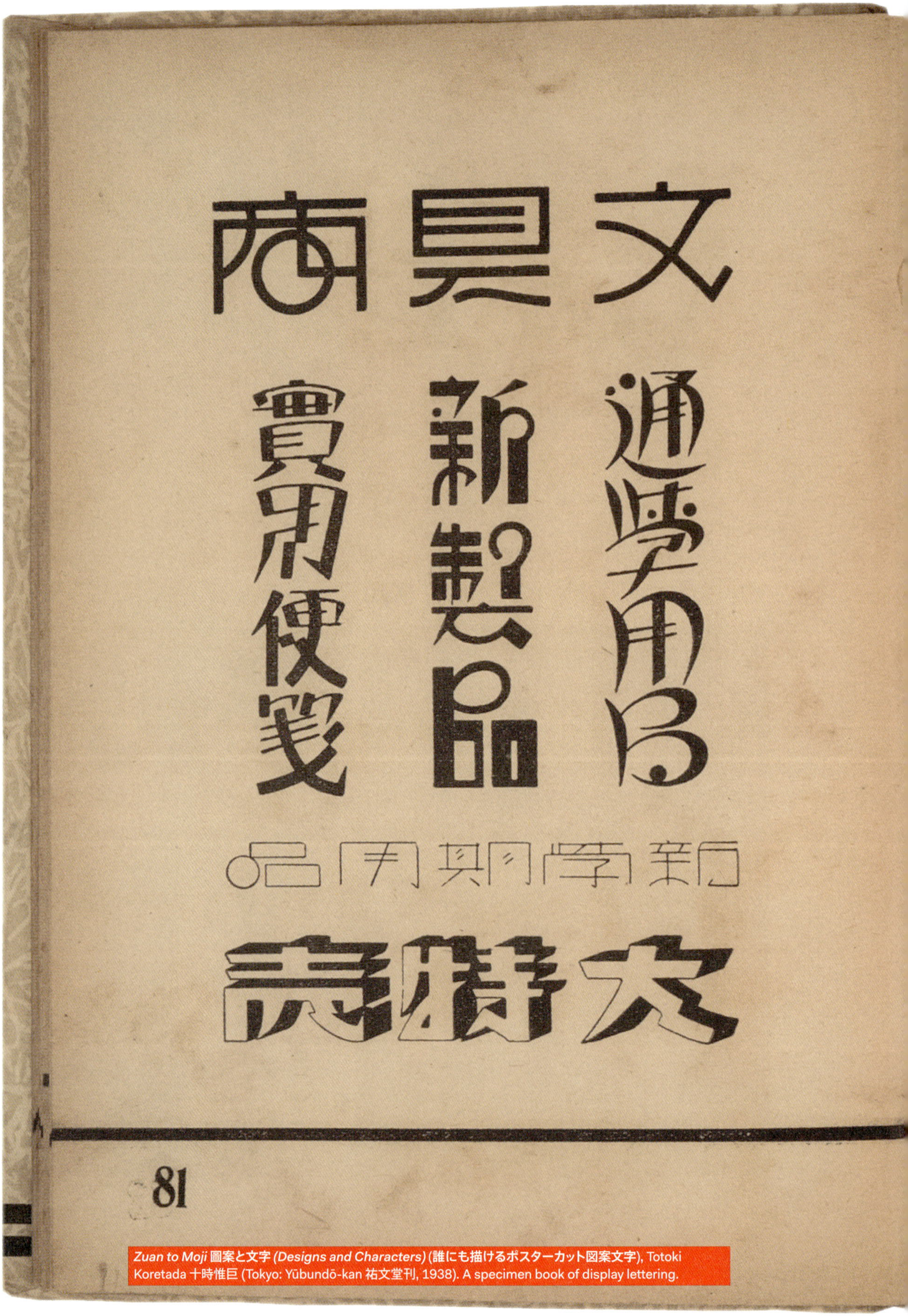

文具商

通學用品

新製品

實用便箋

新學期用品

大特売

81

Zuan to Moji 圖案と文字 *(Designs and Characters)* (誰にも描けるポスターカット図案文字), Totoki Koretada 十時惟巨 (Tokyo: Yūbundō-kan 祐文堂刊, 1938). A specimen book of display lettering.

スポーツ

野球庭球

陸上競技大会

運動具店

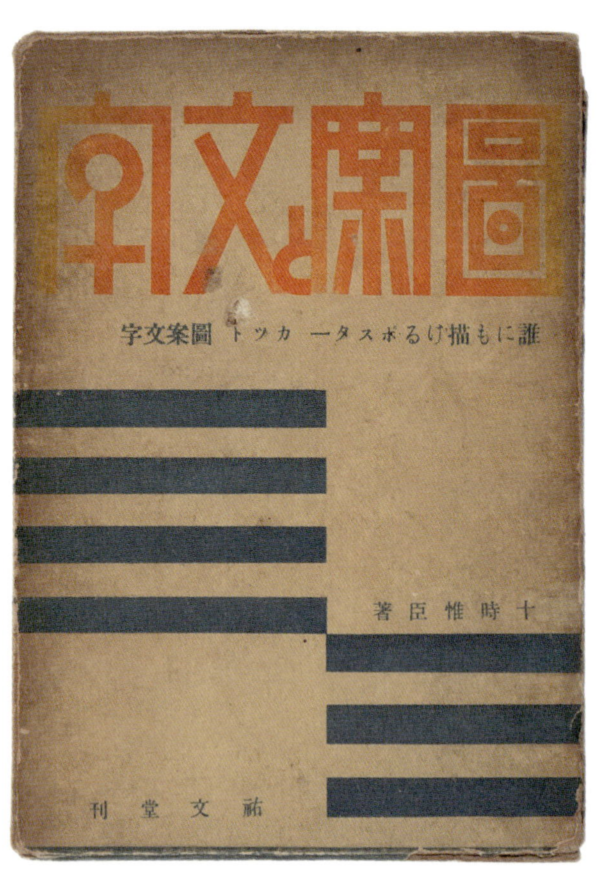

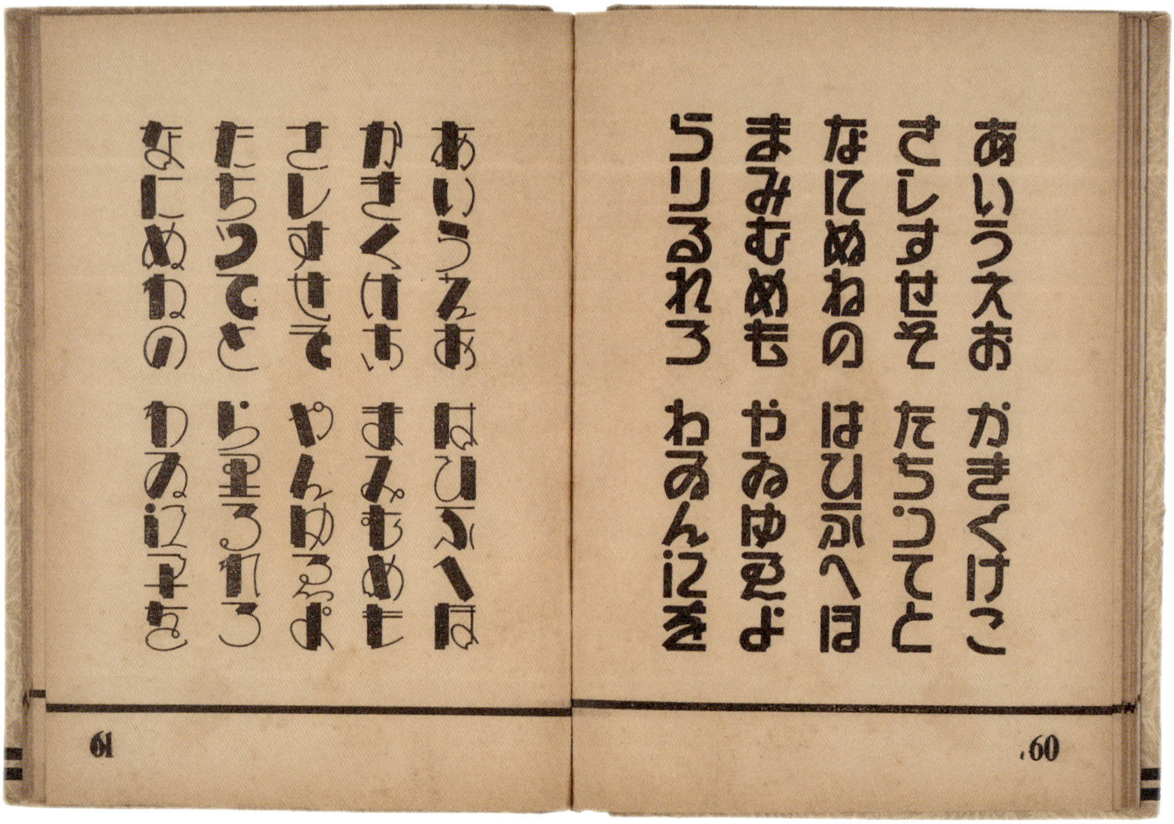

Zuan to Moji 圖案と文字 *(Designs and Characters)* (誰にも描けるポスターカット図案文字), Totoki Koretada 十時惟巨 (Tokyo: Yūbundō-kan 祐文堂刊, 1938). A specimen book of display lettering.

PL.44

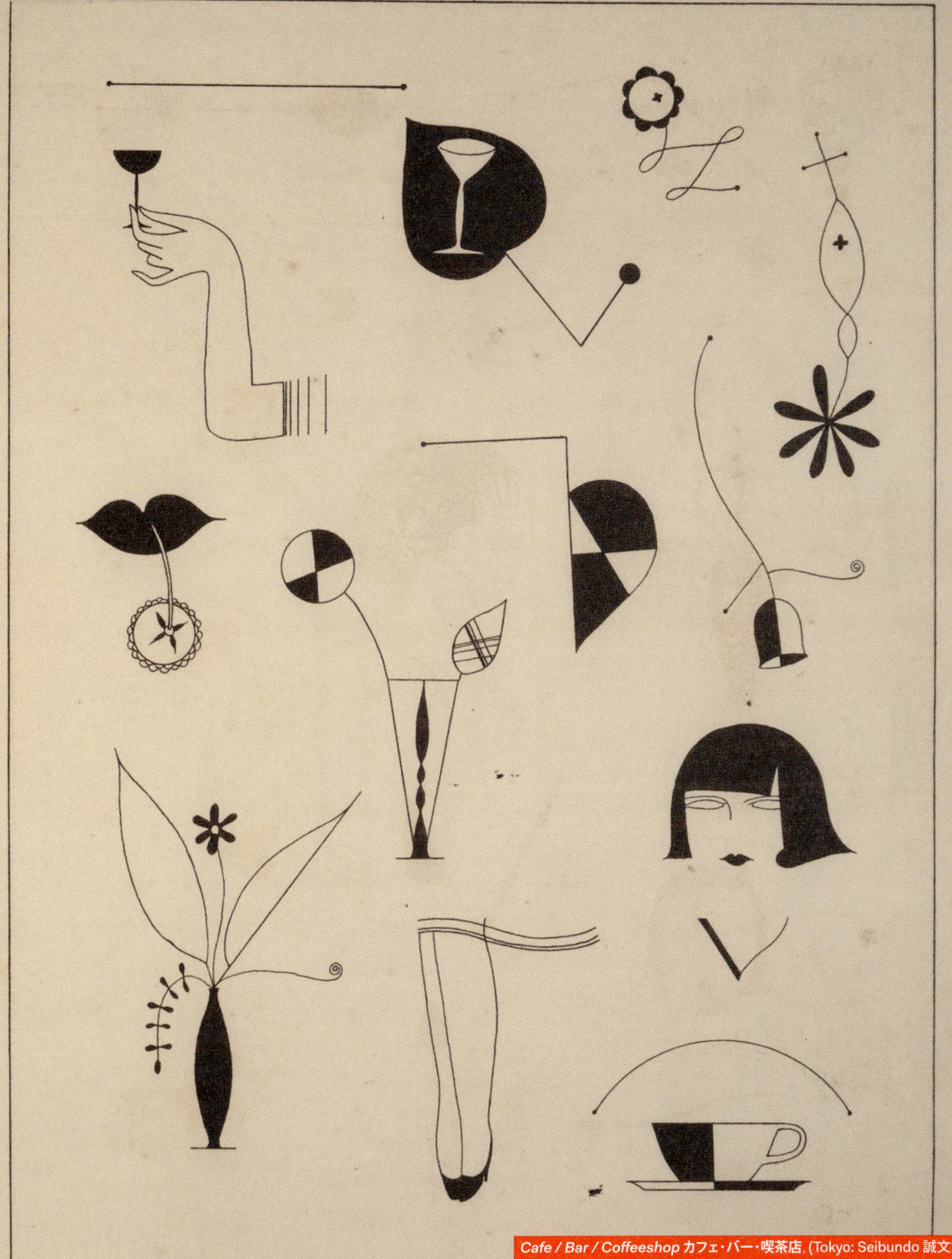

Cafe / Bar / Coffeeshop カフェ・バー・喫茶店, (Tokyo: Seibundo 誠文堂発, 1930). One of the series of twelve books published by Seibundo about specialized advertising and graphic design. Designed and authored by Yamana Ayao 山名文夫.

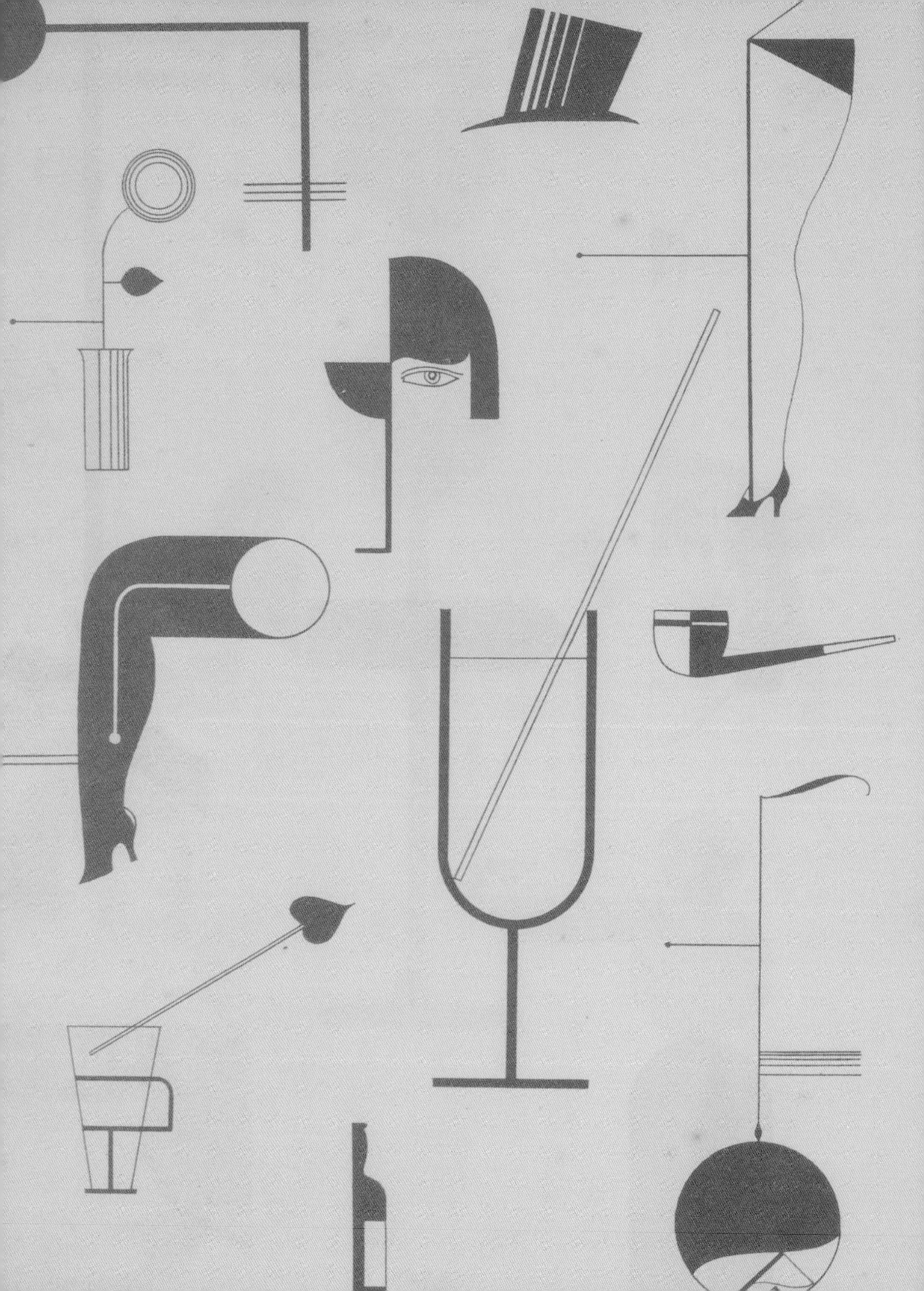

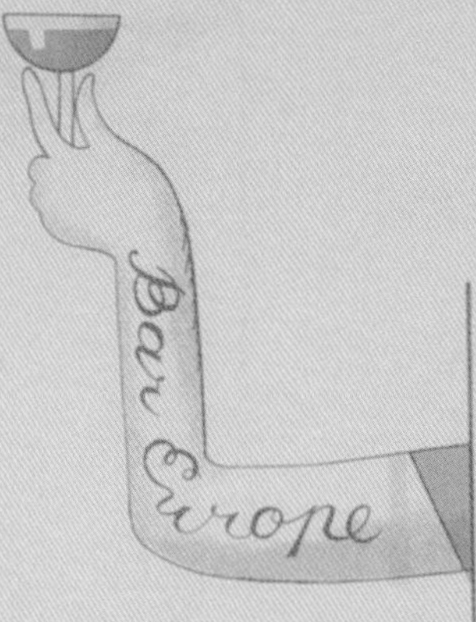

the double-edged mirror

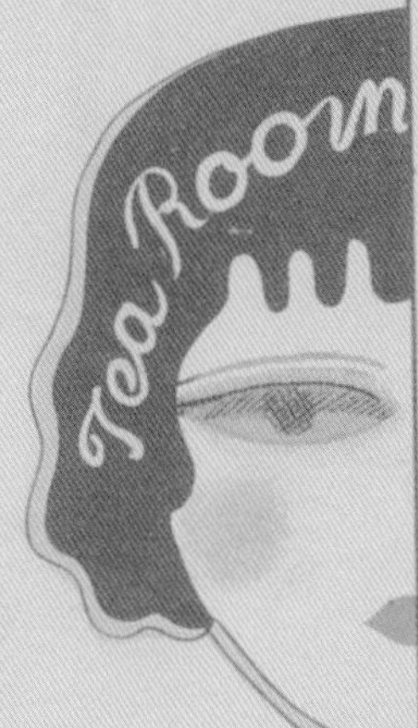

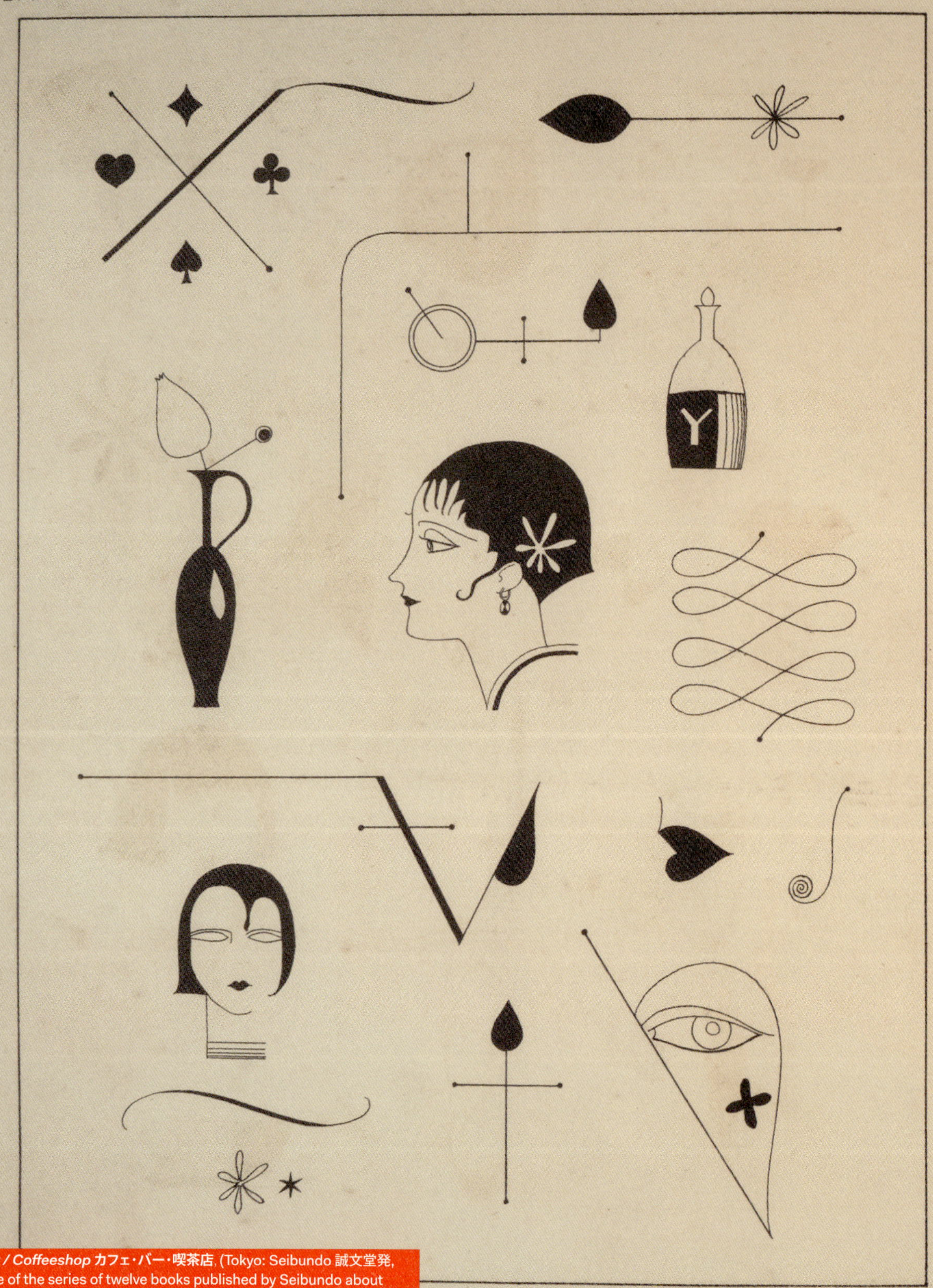

Cafe / Bar / Coffeeshop カフェ・バー・喫茶店, (Tokyo: Seibundo 誠文堂発, 1930). One of the series of twelve books published by Seibundo about specialized advertising and graphic design. Designed and authored by Yamana Ayao 山名文夫.

The Double-Edged Mirror: Making the Modern Japanese Woman

The 1920s were an important era in Japanese history, as the country was in the throes of constructing an energetic, cosmopolitan, and relatively affluent modern society. It was a time of great change for all of Tokyo's citizens, but especially for Japanese women. The waning years of the Taishō Era (1912–1926) were a time of incredible liberation and new-found self-expression and cultural engagement for women.

For this to happen, something had to give in the capital, and it did on September 21, 1923, when the Great Kanto Earthquake struck, rocking the greater Tokyo area, surrounding environs, and the nearby port metropolis of Yokohama. Over 142,800 people died between the quake, freak firestorms that raged through the city, and a fire tornado that further claimed the lives of 38,000 inhabitants within minutes due to a typhoon off the coast that same day.

When the unrest quieted down, the people of the Kanto region were forced to create makeshift homes and businesses from what they could salvage in the wreckage. Thousands lost everything in the fires, and the ensuing years would see the mass adoption of more modern clothing—both Western-style clothing, or *yōfuku* 洋服, as well as newer Japanese fashions, or *wafuku* 和服. Technological advances in weaving and dyeing made more modern-style clothing abundant and affordable. With these advances came changes in the lives of women in Japan as consumers and as citizens.

NEW WOMEN—CLOTHING & PUBLISHING

Since the decline of the *Ritsuryō* 律令 system between 1100–1600, when matrilocal marriages gave way to patrilocal marriages, women's lives in Japan were bound by a series of "submissions": daughters were to follow the lead of their fathers, wives were to comply with the wishes of their husbands, and elderly women were to accede to the leadership of their sons. As historian Yasutake Rumi explains, roles for women were generalized—they were either, or simultaneously, the loyal daughter, the obedient wife, or the devoted mother. The right to state-ordered compulsory basic education in 1871 paved the way for the *jogakusei* 女学生, or female student, as a new social force. The 1898 Civil Code placed women under the authority of men in their families, yet even with this legal subjugation radical changes and growth occurred within the female Japanese populace. Meanwhile, this designation led to the widespread recognition of the role of the housewife or *shufu* 主婦 as a legitimate laborer within the household, not merely to be taken for granted. These changes to women's positions created demand for new mass publications with new forms of visual representation and communication, often designed by women.

This plurality of roles for women was mirrored in the formation of early feminist groups such as the Seitōsha 青鞜社, or Blue Stocking Society, in 1912. The group, consisting of highly educated and largely middle-class women, was led by activist Hiratsuka Raichō 平塚らいちょう (らいてう). Its name is derived from the English Bluestocking Society, the group credited with kickstarting first-wave feminism in the West, though the term "bluestocking" would go on to be associated with feminist movements globally. The Seitōsha published the literary magazine *Seitō* 青鞜—or Bluestocking—which, over the course of fifty-two issues, brought women's rights to the fore, with these issues becoming part of the national discourse and debate. Hiratsuka emphasized the need for women's inner development and growth in the face of political oppression. *Seitō* was largely designed by visual artist Naganuma Chieko 高村智恵子, with the cover of the first issue bearing a heroic illustration of a woman gazing at the sky in an elongated vertical strip, with the two kanji making up the name of the publication flanking the top quadrants on the illustration's ground, creating an abstract kimono.

Even more divergent roles for women began to appear in the late 1920s, accompanying the arrival of the Shōwa period from the end of 1926 onward. The mobilization of Japanese populations to urban centers helped create new roles for women in the workforce, as the boom in clerical and secretarial work cast many women as the *shokugyō fujin* 職業婦人, or working woman.

The Education System Ordinance, crafted in 1871 and fully realized by 1910, triggered a marked increase in literacy for men and women, which in turn fueled massive growth in the publishing industry by 1920. By 1930, over ninety percent of the Japanese populace had received compulsory education. This, combined with rapid developments in printing technology led to a sharply increased demand for literature-as-entertainment among the Japanese populace.

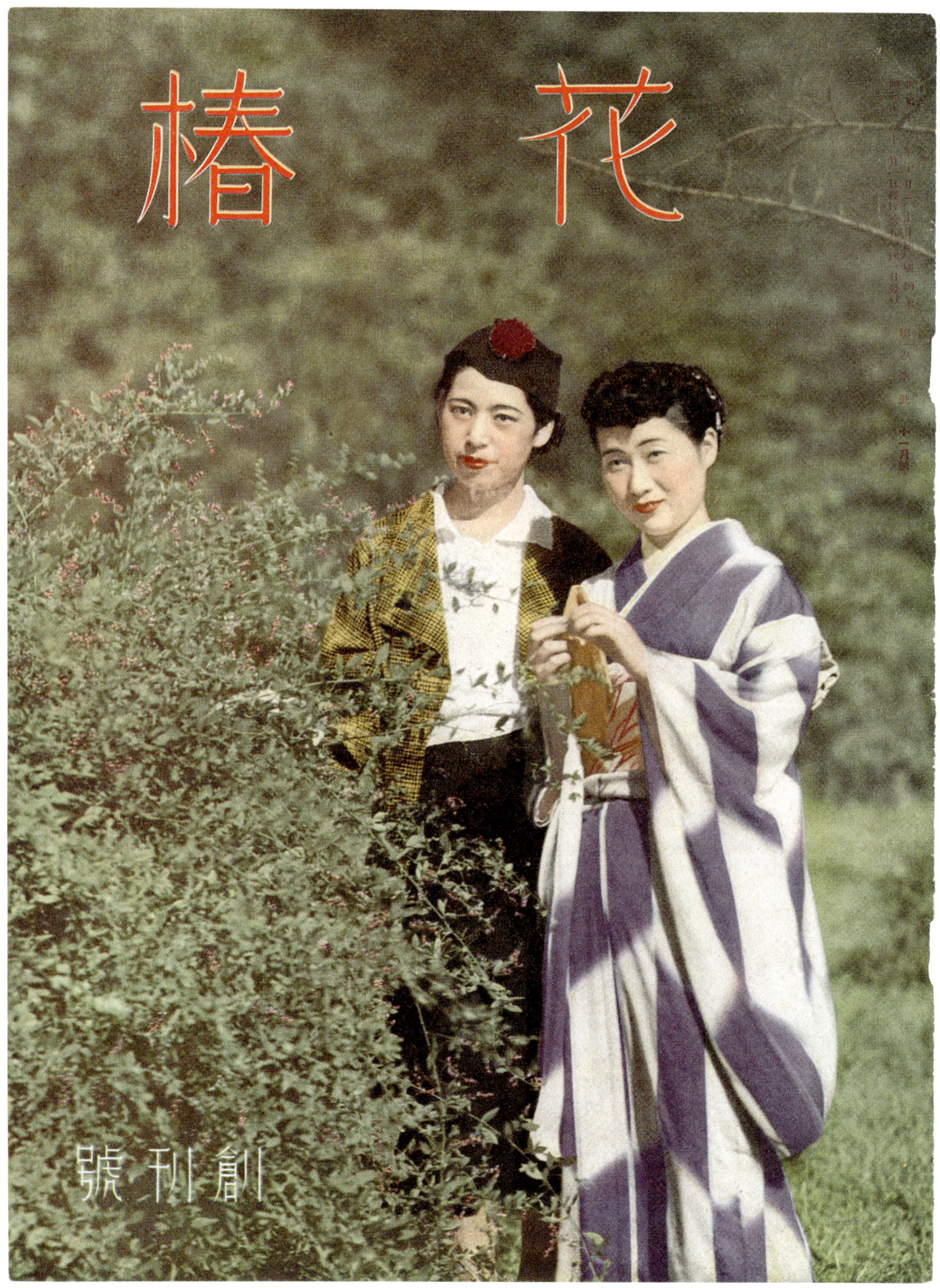

Cover of ***Hanatsubaki* 花椿** (Tokyo: Kabushikigaisha Shiseido 株式会社資生堂, October 1937), depicting women in both kimono and western clothing.

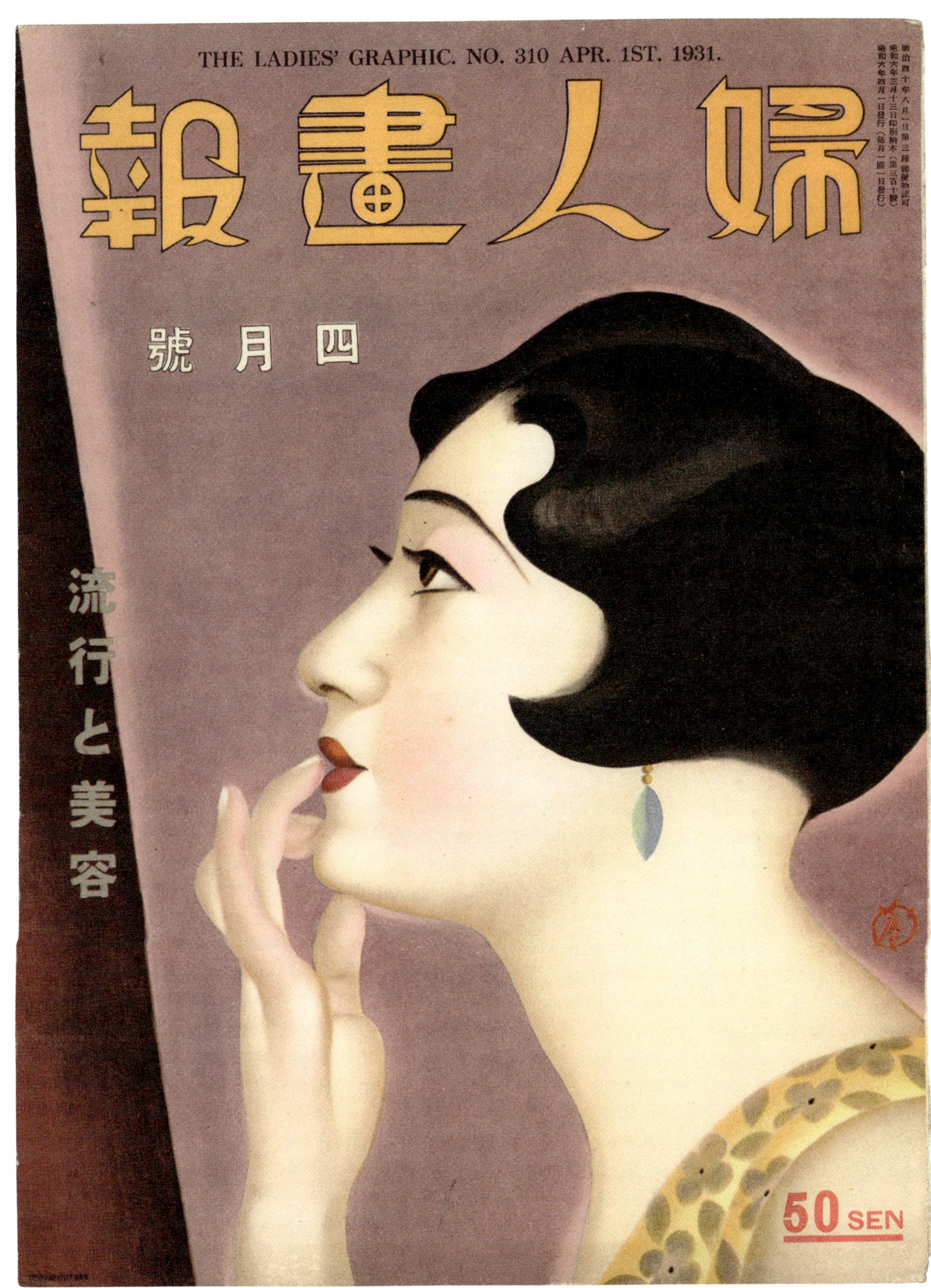

Fujin Gaho No. 310 婦人画報 310 (Tokyo: Fujingahōsha 婦人画報社, April 1931).

There was a massive boom in the publication of newspapers and magazines from 1918 to 1932, accompanied by an increased use of photography, most notably the major newspaper *Asahi Shimbun*'s 朝日新聞 1923 launch of their weekly news magazine, *Asahi Graph* アサヒグラフ, a large-scale publication which integrated typography, photography, and illustration. Mass-distributed magazines with apolitical content targeted specifically at women appeared shortly thereafter, including *Fujin Gahō* 婦人画報 and *Fujin Graph* 婦人グラフ. These publications were laden with advertising that appealed directly to women as consumers, including ads from cosmetics companies such as Shiseido, Kanebo, and Club Cosmetics. Publications for women helped their readerships gain a more variegated sense of their roles in society, while helping to define "the new woman" intellectually and aesthetically.

Both the most romanticized and threatening new female archetype to emerge in the late Taishō and early Shōwa eras was the *moga* モガ, the neologism serving as shorthand for the "modern girl." The stereotypical moga wore bobbed hair akin to Hollywood "it girl" Clara Bow (often permed or curled, as curling machines became readily available in the 1920s), was a city dweller who occupied public spaces, was viewed as sexually promiscuous due to her deliberate use of makeup and cosmetics, and wore Western-inspired "pajama clothing."

Both the allure and the perceived threat of the moga lay in their ability to think and act freely—merely to exist as autonomous individuals in opposition to the filial and feudal roles of the submissive daughter/wife/mother from preceding eras. Perhaps the ultimate archetype of the modern girl was the character Naomi from Tanizaki Junichiro's serialized book *A Fool's Love* 痴人の愛, published simply as *Naomi* in the West. The eponymous character stands in opposition to her husband, the book's protagonist Jōji—she is sexually aggressive, manipulative, and an insatiable consumer. Over the course of the novel's installments in the *Osaka Morning Press* starting in 1924, Naomi shifts from being a subservient, Eurasian-complected, fifteen-year-old cafe waitress to becoming the dominant force in their household, with her husband sleeping in a separate room, both tormented and simultaneously in the sexual thrall of Naomi.

The story of Naomi shocked older readers and titillated younger audiences while also presenting a role model for young Japanese women seeking autonomy. It is notable that Naomi occupies the role of cafe waitress, or *jokyū* 女給, in the beginning of the book, as cafes—some of Japan's first liminal public/private spaces—served as sites of sexual, political, and cultural expression. The cafe was rivaled by the dance-hall, the cinema, and the department store as specific locales where the modern Japanese citizenry reveled in consumption while forging new modes of thinking about gender, labor, and individuality.

Most metropolitan women were not Naomi—they did not fall into simple definable categories of being "traditional" or "modern" but instead represented and embodied a complex and heady mix of traditional values alongside cosmopolitan desires. Design ethnographers and co-founders of Modernology Kon Wajirō and Yoshida Kenkichi, in their 1925 survey of the Ginza district—Tokyo's most popular shopping area—showed that, two years after the Great Earthquake, a mere one percent of women wore Western-style clothing, as opposed to sixty-seven percent of males wearing Western garb. Neither tradition nor modernity were positions that were set in stone in the 1920s; the design of nationalist propaganda was considered "modern," while Yanagi Sōetsu's founding of the Mingei movement was inspired by the traditional vernacular pottery of Japan's occupied territories.

Despite the efforts of the Blue Stocking Society, other early feminist groups in Japan, and the advent of mass-publishing for female readerships, it was not until after the end of World War II that women would receive the right to vote in national elections, with the creation of a new constitution under the occupation government in 1946. Nonetheless, representations of women became more culturally pervasive in the Taishō and Shōwa periods. While the majority were depictions of women cast by men, women such as Uemura Shōen 上村松園, Hani Motoko 羽仁もと子, and Hirose Chika 廣瀬千香 created vibrant careers in art, illustration, design, and publishing.

THE RISE OF THE DEPARTMENT STORE

The modern woman wore a mix of Western clothing and kimono and was as modest as she was objectified in popular literature, cinema, and stage at that time. The cut of kimono had remained unchanged from the late Ēdo period, yet the patterns applied to the cloth they were sewn from employed more expressive variation due to the popularity of synthetic dyes. Patterns ranged from traditional abstract and organic themes to the whiplash line of Art Nouveau to geometric Art

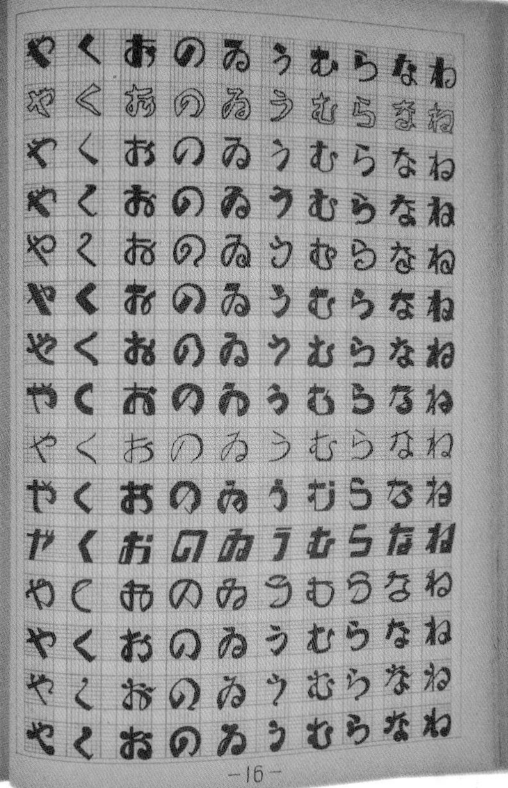

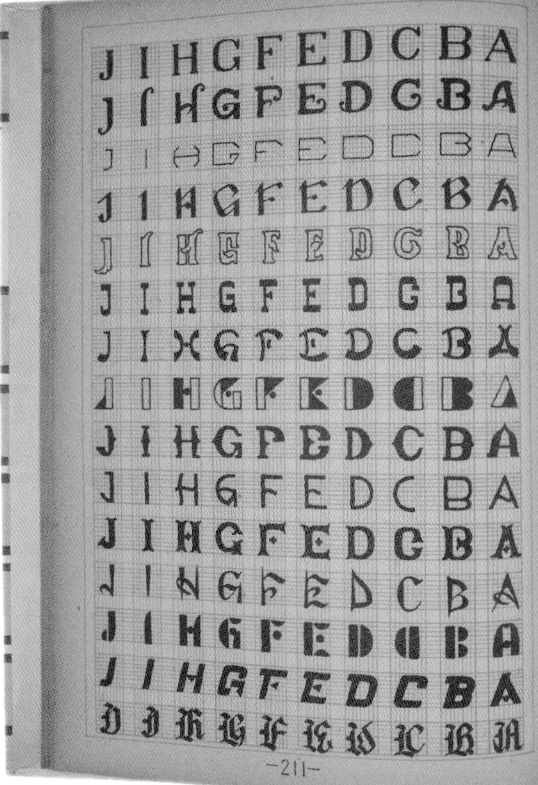

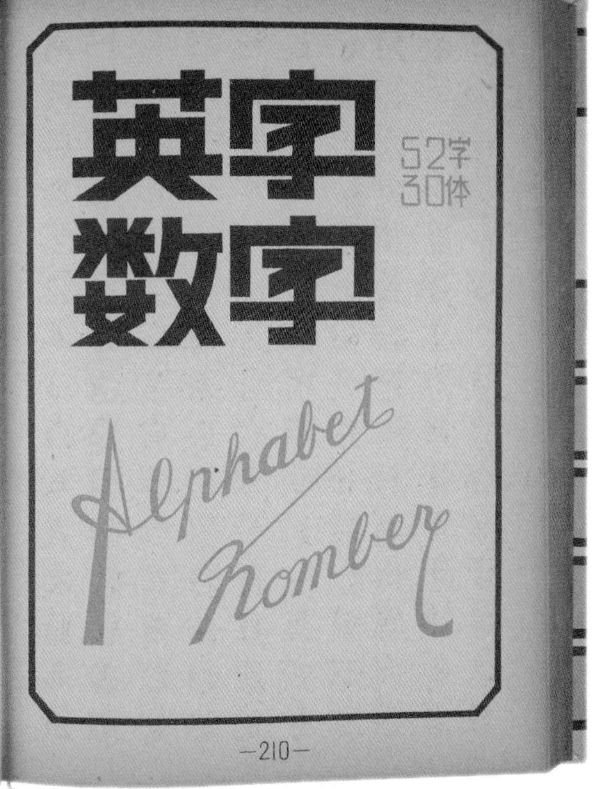

Zuan Moji Taikan 図案文字大観, Yajima Shuichi 矢島周一 (Tokyo: Shobunkan, 1926).
One of the premiere guides to display lettering during the very early Shōwa period.

Through the Looking Glass

The magazine *The Show Window* ウヰンド画報 was launched in 1915 by the publisher Semi Kenji 瀬味建二 (founder and owner of the printing company Semi Shōten 瀬味商店) and helmed by a revolving cast of editors including Masuda Heikichi 増田平吉, Sasaki Juku 佐々木十九, and Akiyama Kōnosuke 秋山紅之助. The debut issue highlighted approaches to window display, sign-painting techniques, associated poster advertising, and novelty design formats such as "poster stamps," small-scale multicolored promotional stamps.

The magazine, Japan's first dedicated to design and advertising, featured photos of award-winning department stores and specialty store window displays from cities all over Japan, not just the nation's capital, Tokyo. The imagery was accompanied by bilingual Japanese and English captions, alongside interviews with commercial artists and individuals working in advertising. *The Show Window* functioned as a chronicle of new approaches to retail display advertising, as well as the psychological effects of advertising on Japanese consumers.

The editorial staff presented conceptual approaches to advertising that considered representation, abstraction, composition, and negative space and offered design criticism: for example, the second issue includes an evaluation of the work of Japanese artist and designer Hashiguchi Goyo as compared to the work of British illustrator Aubrey Beardsley.

Each issue featured a multicolored woodblock-printed cover. The majority of the body of the magazine was printed with offset lithography, but tipped-in throughout were multicolored woodblock prints and assorted inserts, such as posters printed using a variety of processes. It was a golden era for print plurality in Japan, as multiple commercially viable, full-color, lithographic printing processes, single-color halftone, and collotype printing were available alongside commercial woodblock printing. All of these different forms were folded into *The Show Window*.

Photographs of the retail displays within were accompanied by expressive typography and whimsical illustrations. The magazine included progressive approaches to the lettering and typography of the time, considering the typographic arrangement of characters to be just as important as the quality of characters' design. *The Show Window*'s content was outward-looking, featuring illustrated essays on poster art from England and Germany.

The magazine was renamed *The Window Times* ウヰンドータイムス in 1917. Over the twenty-four issues of the magazine that were published from 1915 to 1918, *The Show Window/The Window Times* presented cutting-edge approaches to advertising and analyzed stylistic trends.

References:

Takeuchi, Yukie. "Emergence of Modern Advertisement Designs in Taishō Era Seen in 'Window Gaho' and 'Window Times.'" *Design Society* 71, no. 1 (January 15, 2018): 1–14.

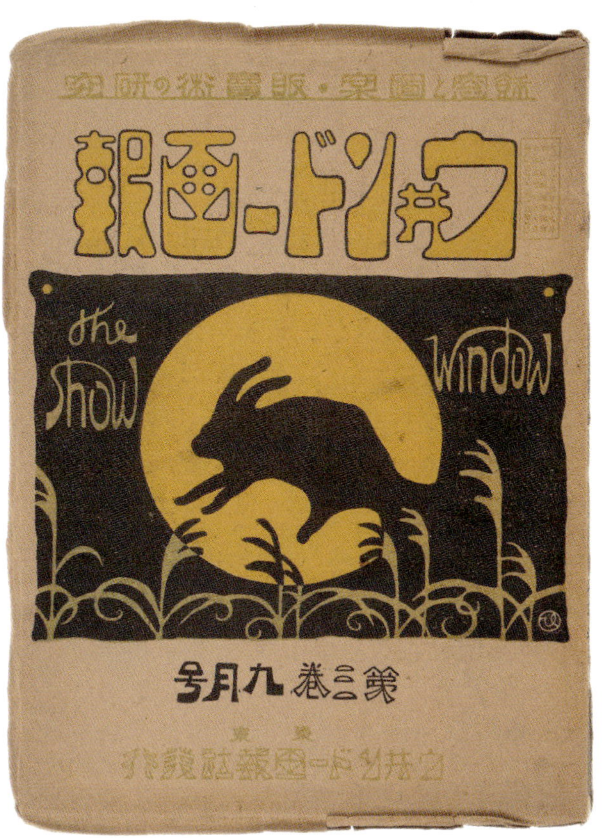

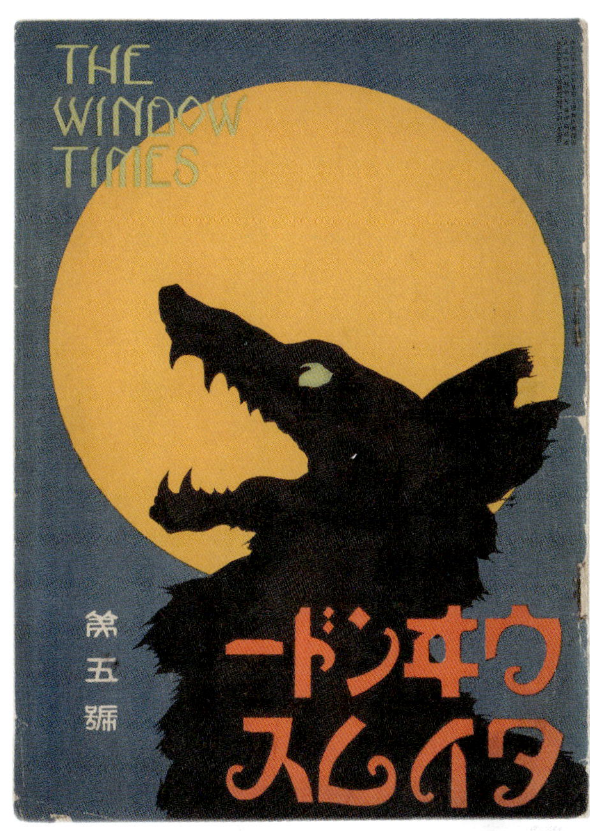

Above left: ***The Show Window* ウヰンドー画報 Volume 1** (Tokyo: Window Gaho-sha ウヰンドー画報社, January 1918). The debut issue of *The Show Window*. Above right: ***The Window Times* ウヰンドータイムス Volume 6** (Tokyo: Window Times-sha ウヰンドータイムス社, November 1918). Below: Spread from ***The Show Window*ウヰンドー画報 Volume 1** (Tokyo: Window Gaho-sha ウヰンドー画報社, January 1918) showing a tipped-in poster stamp.

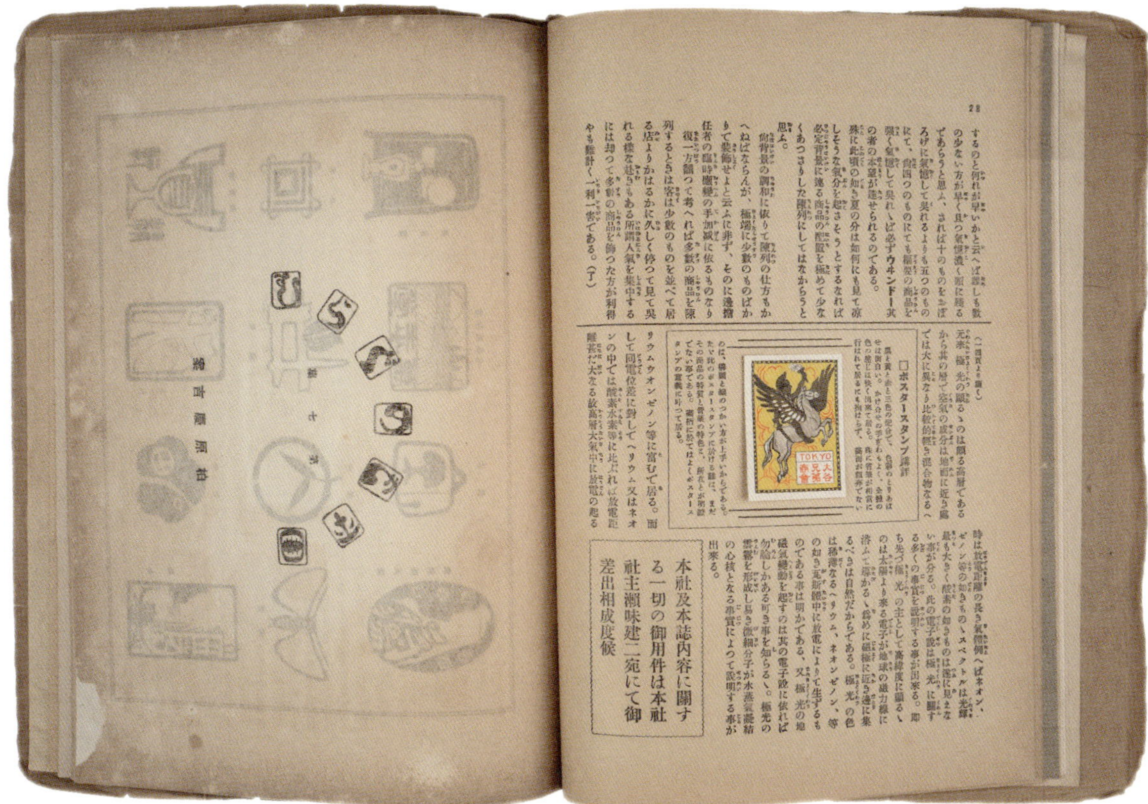

Deco patterns and graphics. Some of the most expressive are termed *omoshirogara* 面白柄, or "novelty patterns," many of which featured illustrations contrasting modern girls and traditional women—the difference between the two delineated on silk to adorn the wearer and catch her in a visual feedback loop. Department stores such as Mitsukoshi offered catalogs wrapped in sumptuous cover designs with sample fabric swatches for shoppers both in cities and in rural areas.

Mitsukoshi Ltd. 株式会社三越 was a Tokyo kimono retailer turned department store and a leading force in early female-oriented marketing and consumer product development. The company's strategy was tripartite: to accumulate many types of appealing products under one roof, to openly display them, and to engage in outward-facing cultural activities in order to appeal to the buying public.

Mitsukoshi sells a mix of both domestic and foreign products and was one of the first Japanese businesses to feature glass-fronted showcases to highlight their wares, adding glass windows to the facades of their shops to further promote their stock in 1903. (The very first, however, was the Kyoto branch of Takashimaya department stores, which unveiled a glass facade in 1896.) While seemingly simple, these actions invited the gaze of potential customers and led to staggering sales figures.

Mitsukoshi offered its own lines of seasonal kimono fabrics starting in 1895, with designs created by both hired artists and in-house staff, creating a demand for clothing designed by the company rather than the manufacturers they stocked. Mitsukoshi launched its own public relations magazine in 1899 to further attract attention and was the owner of Japan's very first delivery van emblazoned with a corporate logo in 1903. Mitsukoshi's management sought constant iteration and expansion—by 1922 the main store boasted fifty different departments over six floors with a rooftop Sky Garden "replete with pond, fountain, shrubs, and bonsai plants."

The company's strategic marketing and public relations activities stood out in the nascent design industry at the start of the century—from Mitsukoshi's posters to editorial design and billboards. Led by Japan's first graphic design superstar, Sugiura Hisui, hired in 1910, the promotions department at Mitsukoshi used a wide array of advertising methods to attract consumers of all stripes to buy affordable ready-made kimono, and it rewarded them with lavish experiences at Mitsukoshi locations that largely can still be enjoyed today. Department stores in Japan include a mix of fine dining, cafes, semi-public areas, exhibition spaces, and retail shops.

Mitsukoshi accumulated further cultural capital by setting up galleries within their retail environs, displaying and selling works by leading artists at that time, hybridizing department stores as palaces of culture as much as buying and selling. When Mitsukoshi installed the first escalator in Japan in their Nihonbashi location in 1914, the company's adoption of the latest foreign technologies consolidated the department store's cultural, social, and aesthetic authority.

Sugiura's work for Mitsukoshi was incredibly popular, including advertising posters that updated the ukiyo-e woodblock printing theme of the bijinga, or "depictions of beautiful women." One of Sugiura's best-known posters from 1914 depicts a beautiful woman perusing Mitsukoshi's own Sugiura-designed *Mitsukoshi Times* 三越タイムズ promotional magazine, clad in sumptuous decorative kimono and juxtaposed with then-contemporary Art Nouveau interiors.

Sugiura's posters, advertisements, and advertorial magazines for Mitsukoshi, as well as his kimono fabric designs, targeted male and female consumers alike through Art Deco-infused illustration work, expressive lettering, and aspirational imagery that suggested the creation of a light-filled, de la mode dream world, achievable through consumption of Mitsukoshi products.

Mitsukoshi and its many imitators are one example of how cosmopolitan material culture shaped middle-class consumer aspirations and conceptions of women in bourgeois society. Yet, it must be noted that department stores were equally important to men. Cultural researcher Kon Wajirō undertook studies of Tokyo department stores in the 1920s and 1930s and found that up to fifty percent of shoppers at Mitsubishi in Ginza in 1928 were male. There is little doubt that the display of commodities in department stores was just as important in shaping cultural notions of the modern man as the modern woman.

BEAUTY & LETTERS

The 1920s and 1930s saw a staggering rise in publications specifically for women, with industries sprouting up to advertise to women and manufacture products for them. It was no coincidence that Yamana Ayao 山名文夫, Japan's second graphic design superstar, started his career working as de-

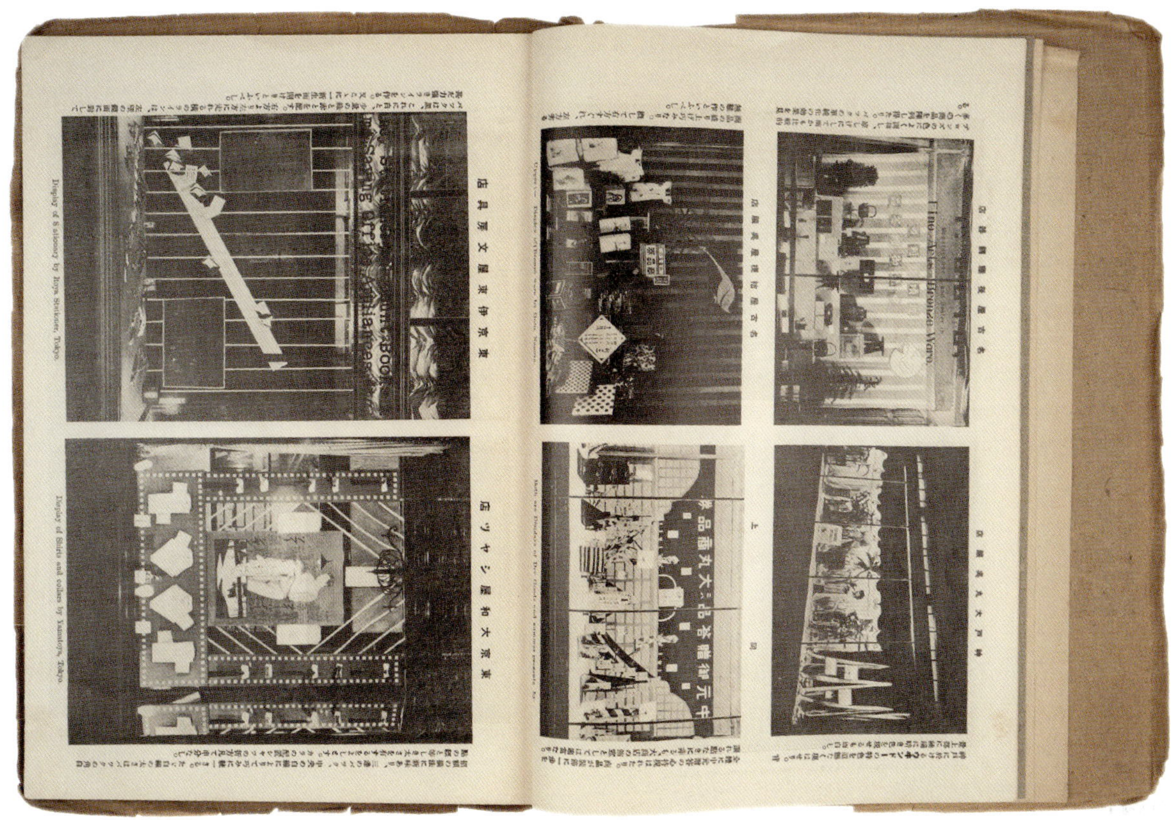

Spread from ***The Show Window* ウヰンドー画報 Volume 1** (Tokyo: Window Gaho-sha ウヰンドー画報社, January 1918). The debut issue of *The Show Window* depicting assorted window displays with captions in English and Japanese.

signer and illustrator for the women-oriented magazines *Josei* 女性 and *Kuraku* 苦楽 (released by Club Cosmetics' newly created publishing division, Platon-sha) before going on to work at Shiseido, Japan's leading manufacturer of cosmetics. His popularity was due to the graphic work that he had done for female audiences and consumers.

Shiseido's advertising, promotions, and product design represented women in new social roles as Japanese society adopted new notions of public and private beauty. The company's founder, Fukuhara Shinzo 福原信三, had spent years studying in Europe and the United States and was dedicated to maintaining an internationalist approach to cosmetics at his company. A painter and photographer, Fukuhara understood that, in order to effectively promote products that aestheticize women, the products themselves would have to be aesthetic and promoted as thoroughly as possible. He contributed artwork to Shiseido promotional materials and hired the best design talent possible at Shiseido's PR department.

Shiseido positioned itself as a luxury goods manufacturer, much more expensive than competitors. Specific attention was paid to Shiseido's packaging and print promotions, each intimating luxury and beauty through the use of contemporary trends in lettering and illustration and via the representations of beautiful women featured on bottles, in ads, and on boxes.

The company conspicuously utilized a mix of Latin lettering alongside Japanese characters to impart a sense of international luxury on all aspects of communication. Shiseido's designers Yabe Sue 矢部季, Maeda Mitsugu 前田貢, and Yamana Ayao were all adept at lettering and illustration and created bilingual packaging designs that tastefully integrated connotative approaches to typography, with Maeda integrating arabesque patterning into ads and packages alike—a trope that Ayao would take to dizzying heights of expression over the following decades.

Japanese graphic design cycled through modes of stylistic expression during this time, shifting from the curvilinear forms of Art Nouveau to Art Deco to more constructed, Futurist/Bauhaus/Constructivist-influenced approaches to composition. It was during this time that gothic (sans serif) lettering came to prominence, alongside other, more decorative approaches to lettering and typography.

A wide variety of lettering books featuring zuan moji were published at the time showing the possibilities of expression using kanji, katakana, and hiragana. The range of lettering exemplars was wide—extending from self-contained lettering guidebooks, to lettering included in trade publications, to academically oriented art-education books. There were entire compendia of popular kana, kanji, and Latin characters, and slogan-based samples of eye-catching lettering. Both horizontal and vertical orthography was accommodated, and a range of styles emerged, from Tuscan-terminaled display lettering, to Didone-inspired high-contrast lettering, to solid Broadway-style gothics.

The design surrounding and emblazoned on Shiseido's products suggested what feminine beauty might be to consumers—Yabe Sue's advertisements for Eudermine オイデルミン, a toning lotion which was one of Shiseido's leading products, mixed the ornamental and baroque with the restrained and put the focus on the product and the atmosphere of luxury it conveyed. Other advertisements designed by Yabe put the focus on the female form instead, with the subject most often surveying herself in the mirror and evaluating the change brought on through the use of Shiseido products.

References:

Akiyama, Kuniharu, Kotaro Iizawa, Hiroyuki Suzuki, Koji Taki, Masaru Ichikawa, Hidetsugu Yamano, Tokuhiro Nakajima, Naoyuki Kinoshita, Kenichi Nagata, and Hiroshi Kashiwagi. *1920-Nendai Nihon Ten: Toshi to zōkei no montyaju; The 1920s in Japan*. Tokyo: Asahi Shinbunsha, 1988.

Atkins, Jacqueline M., and John W. Dower. *Wearing Propaganda: Textiles on the Home Front in Japan, Britain, and the United States, 1931–1945*. New Haven, CT: Yale University Press, 2005.

Dower, John W., Anne Nishimura Morse, Jacqueline M. Atkins, and Frederic A. Sharf. *The Brittle Decade: Visualizing Japan in the 1930s*. Boston, MA: MFA Publications, 2012.

Kon, Wajirō, and Kenkichi Yoshida. *Kōgengaku saishū: Moderunorojio*. Tokyo: Gakuyō Shobō, 1986.

Molony, Barbara. "Feminism in Japan." Oxford Research Encyclopedia of Asian History. Oxford University Press, January 24, 2018. https://doi.org/10.1093/acrefore/9780190277727.013.194.

Sano, Hiroaki. Rōman Zuan: Meiji, Taishō, *Shōwa no shōgyō Dezain*. Kyōto-shi: Mitsumura Suiko Shoin, 2010.

Shizume, Masato. "The Japanese Economy during the Interwar Period." *Bank of Japan Review* 2009, no. 2 (May 2009): 1–10.

Takeuchi, Yukie. "The World of Kokoku-Kai." *Idea* 1, no. 360 (September 2013): 112–27.

Tanaka, Keiko. "Japanese Women's Magazines: The Language of Aspiration." In *The Worlds of Japanese Popular Culture: Gender, Shifting Boundaries and Global Cultures*, edited by D. P. Martinez, 120–22. Cambridge: Cambridge University Press, 1998.

Treat, John Whittier, and Karatani Kojin. "Origins of Modern Japanese Literature." *Journal of Japanese Studies* 21, no. 2 (1995): 440. https://doi.org/10.2307/133018.

Weisenfeld, Gennifer. "Japanese Modernism and Consumerism: Forging the New Artistic Field of 'Shogyo Bijutsu' (Commercial Art)." In *Being Modern in Japan: Culture and Society from the 1910s to the 1930s*, edited by Elise K. Tipton and John Clark, 75–96. Honolulu: University of Hawai'i Press, 2000.

Weisenfeld, Gennifer. "'From Baby's First Bath': Kao Soap and Modern Japanese Commercial Design." *The Art Bulletin* 86, no. 3 (2004): 573. https://doi.org/10.2307/4134447.

Yasutake, Rumi. *Transnational Women's Activism: The United States, Japan, and Japanese Immigrant Communities in California, 1859–1920*. New York, NY: New York University Press, 2004.

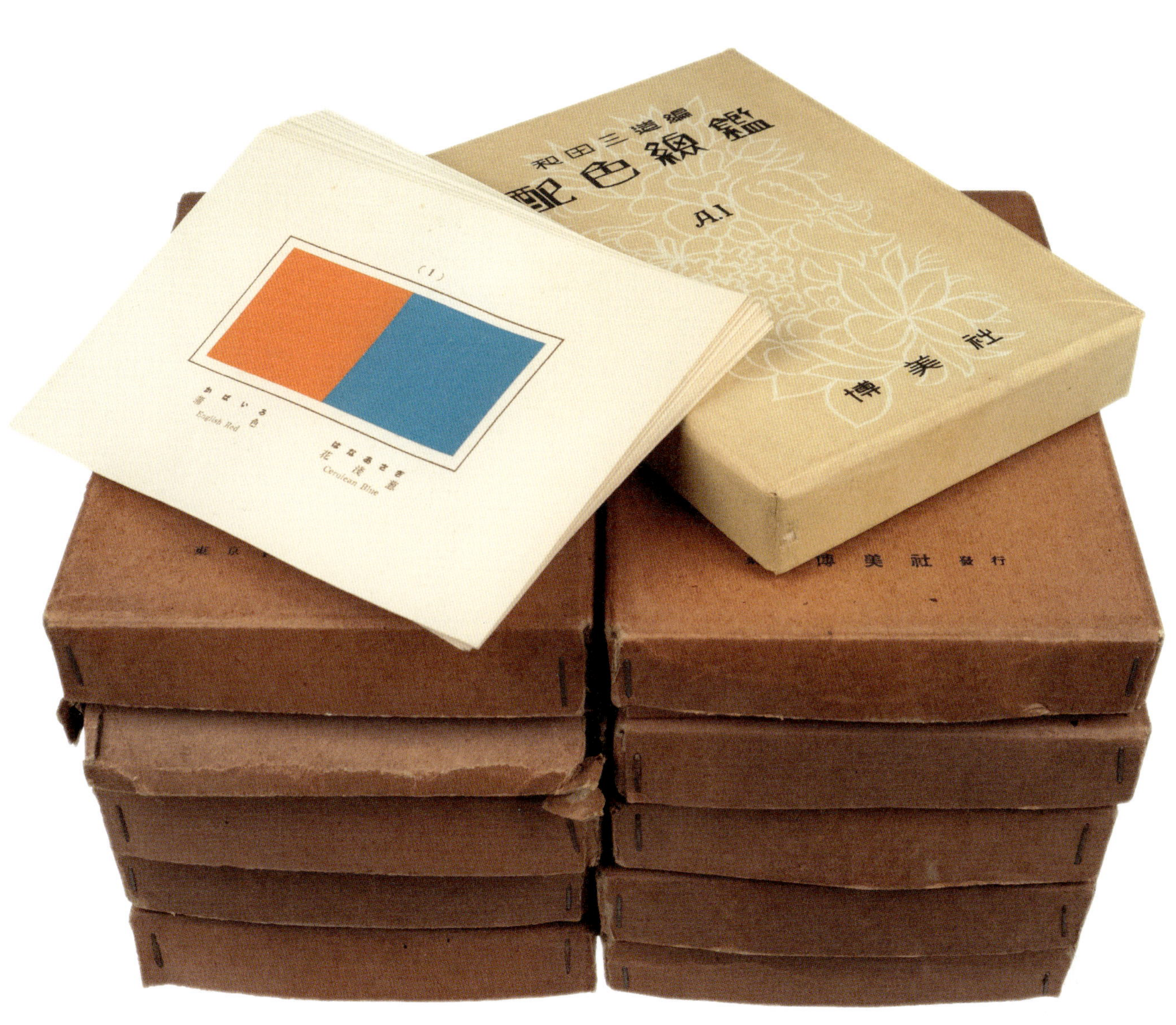

Haishokusōkan A (Color Schemes A) 配色総鑑 *A*, Wada Sanzō 和田三造 (Tokyo: Hiromi-sha 博美社, 1934). Wada's twelve-volume boxed series of assorted comparative color studies.

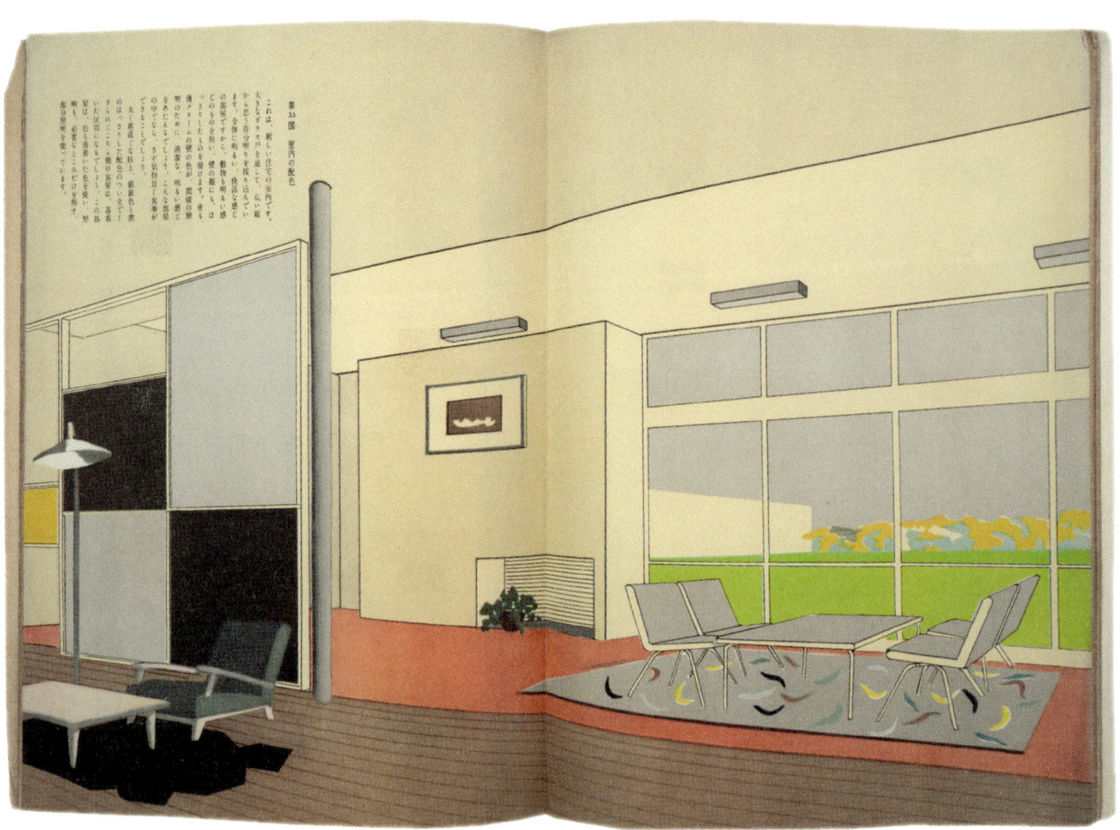
第33図　室内の配色

これは、新しい住宅の室内です。

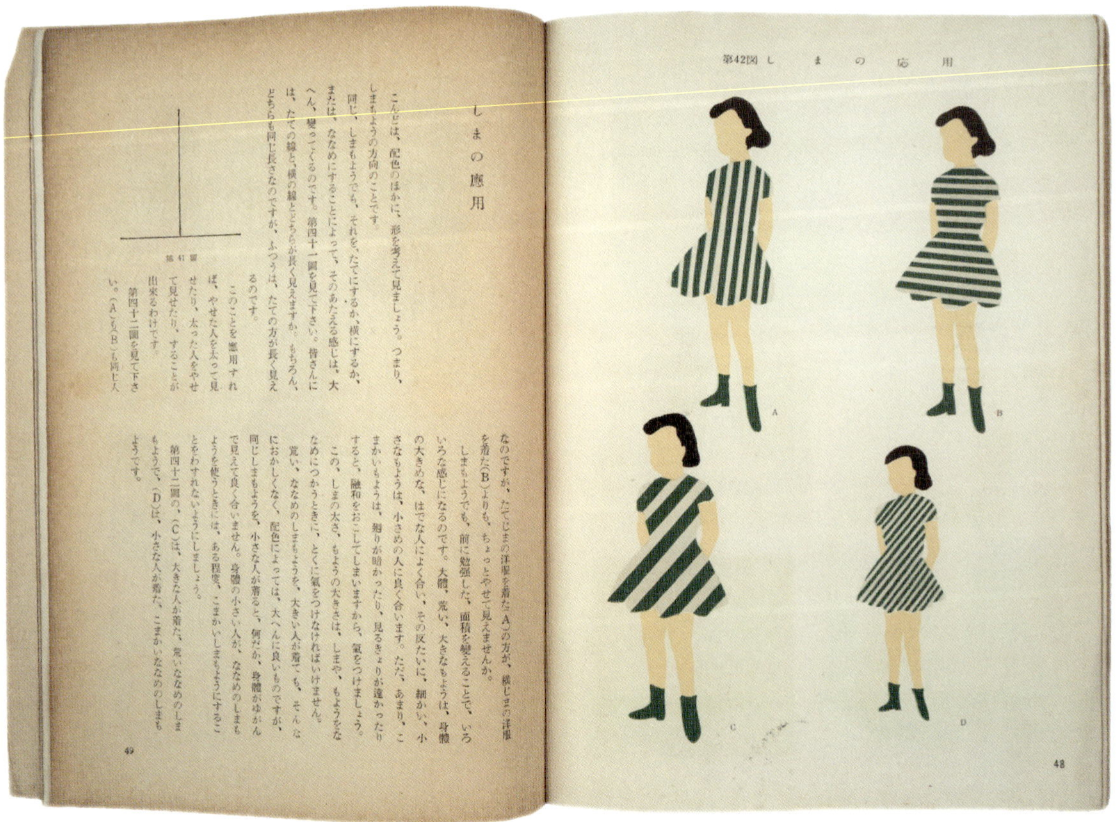
しまの應用

こんどは、配色のほかに、形を考えて見ましょう。つまり、しまもようの方向のことです。

同じ、しまもようでも、それを、たてにするか、横にするか、または、ななめにすることによって、そのあたえる感じは、大へん、變ってくるのです。第四十一圖を見て下さい。皆さんには、たての線と、横の線とどちらが長く見えますか。もちろん、どちらも同じ長さなのですが、ふつうは、たての方が長く見えるのです。

このことを應用すれば、やせた人を太って見せたり、太った人をやせて見せたり、することが出来るわけです。

第四十二圖を見て下さい。(A)も(B)も同じ人なのですが、たてじまの洋服を着た(A)の方が、横じまの洋服を着た(B)よりも、ちょっとやせて見えませんか。

しまもようでも、前に勉強した、面積を變えることで、いろいろな感じになるのです。大體、荒い、大きなもようは、身體の大きめな、はでな人によく合い、その反たいに、細かい、小さなもようは、小さめの人に良く合います。ただ、あまり、こまかいもようは、廻りが暗かったり、見るきょりが遠かったりすると、融和をおこしてしまいますから、氣をつけましょう。

この、しまの太さ、もようの大きさは、しまや、もようをななめにつかうときに、とくに氣をつけなければいけません。

荒い、ななめのしまもようを、大きい人が着ても、そんなにおかしくなく、配色によっては、大へんに良いものですが、同じしまもようを、小さな人が着ると、何だか、身體がゆがんで見えて良く合いません。身體の小さい人が、ななめのしまもようを使うときには、ある程度、こまかいしまもようにすることをわすれないようにしましょう。

第四十二圖の、(C)は、大きな人が着た、荒いななめのしまもようで、(D)は、小さな人が着た、こまかいななめのしまもようです。

第41圖

49

第42図　しまの応用

A

B

C

D

48

Shikisai no hanashi (The Story of Color) **色彩の話**, Wada Sanzō 和田三造, (Tokyo: Bijutsu Shuppansha 美術出版社, 1957). A study of color and perception.

WADA SANZŌ 和田三造

1883–1967

Wada Sanzō was born in Hyogo Prefecture, moved to Fukuoka with his family at age thirteen, and moved again to Tokyo at age sixteen with the intention of becoming a painter. In Tokyo, Wada studied under Kuroda Seiki both privately and at the Tokyo School of Fine Arts. He was a member of the Hakubakai artists' society, with whom he exhibited his works. Wada was sent to France by the Ministry of Education to study art in 1909 and stayed in Europe until 1914, returning to Japan in 1915 after a year-long stay in India and Burma (now Myanmar) studying the arts of those cultures.

Wada became a faculty member of the Imperial Art Institute 日本芸術院 and founded the Japan Standard Color Association 日本標準色協会 in 1927. In 1932 he was appointed professor at the Design Department of Tokyo School of Fine Arts, where he served until 1944. Wada was a leading color theorist and created one of the first holistic systematic approaches to color in Japan. He published the twelve-volume boxed series *Color Schemes A* 配色総鑑 A in 1934 and his monthly follow-up series, *Color Schemes B* 配色総鑑 B in 1934 and 1935. The two series were the first mass-produced in-depth analyses of color pairings and combinations in Japan, laying the groundwork for modern color studies that accommodated both traditional Japanese color schemes and imported Western colors. Each box contained another immaculately bound, two-color printed, gatefold box that held a series of thirty postcard-sized pieces of cardstock. The cards were precisely printed with die-cut squares of color combinations glued on top of bilingual English, kanji, and hiragana letterpress-printed descriptions of each color dyad, triad, or tetrad. The collection is a tour de force of both print production and consideration of the impact of color.

In 1945, Wada co-edited and designed the book *Standard Designed Imagery* 標準圖画 with painter, printmaker, art educator, and art luminary Isshi Hakutei 石井柏亭. The slim book is a collection of work by assorted designers, including Satomi Munetsugu.

Wada reorganized the Japan Standard Color Association into the Japan Color Research Laboratory in 1945 and served as its president. He was also an award-winning designer—his poster for the ill-fated 1940 Tokyo Olympics won out against other competitors in the late 1930s. Wada also won the Costume Design Award at the twenty-seventh Academy Awards in 1954 for his work on the movie *Hell's Gate* 地獄門. Wada was prolific in his output, designing postcards, painting, pursuing printmaking, and creating illustration work.

His book *The Story of Color* 色彩の話 was published in 1952 and reprinted in 1957. Wada's work is the foundation of the Japan Industrial System's JIS Standard Color Chart, the official national guidelines for color usage in Japan.

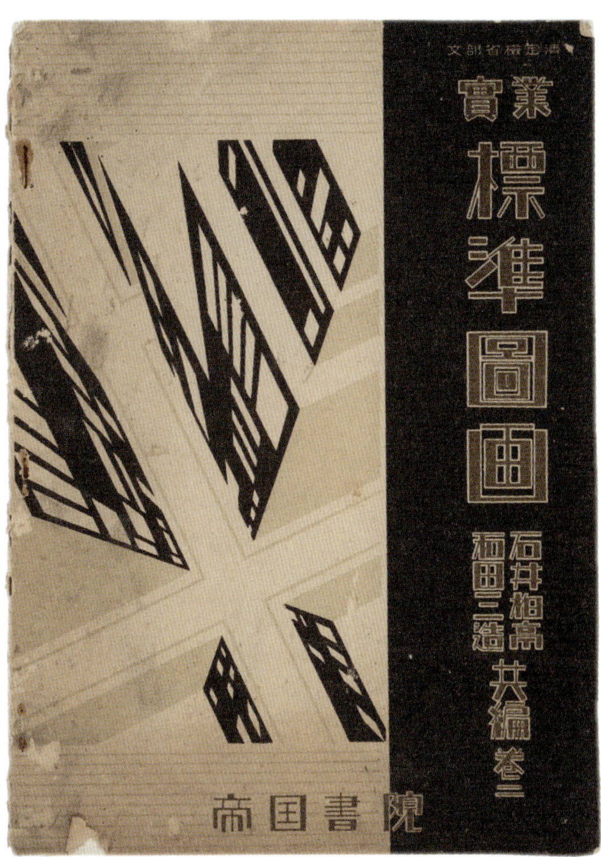

***Hyōjun Zuga (Standard Designed Imagery)* 標準圖画**, co-edited by Wada Sanzō 和田三造 with painter, printmaker, art educator, and art luminary Ishii Hakutei 石井柏亭 (Tokyo: Teikoku Shoin 帝国書院, 1945).
A compendium of notable design work from Japan.

References:

Hamada, Masuji, ed. *Gendai shōgyō Bijutsu zenshū*. 1st ed. 12 vols. Tokyo: ARS, 1930.

Kamekura, Yūsaku, and Ayao Yamana. *Gurafikku Dezain no Seiki: Bunshō to Danwa to Sakuhin De kōsei: Meiji Sedai Yamana Ayao Sugiura Hisui Kara shōwa Sedai Made*. Tokyo: Bijutsu Shuppansha, 2008.

Sanzō, Wada. *Haishoku Jiten = A Dictionary of Color Combinations: Taishō shōwa no Shikisai nōto*. Kyōto: Seigensha, 2010.

Sugiura, Hisui. *Afisshu: Zuan kenkyū Zasshi 3–7*. Tokyo: Kokusho Kankōkai, 2009.

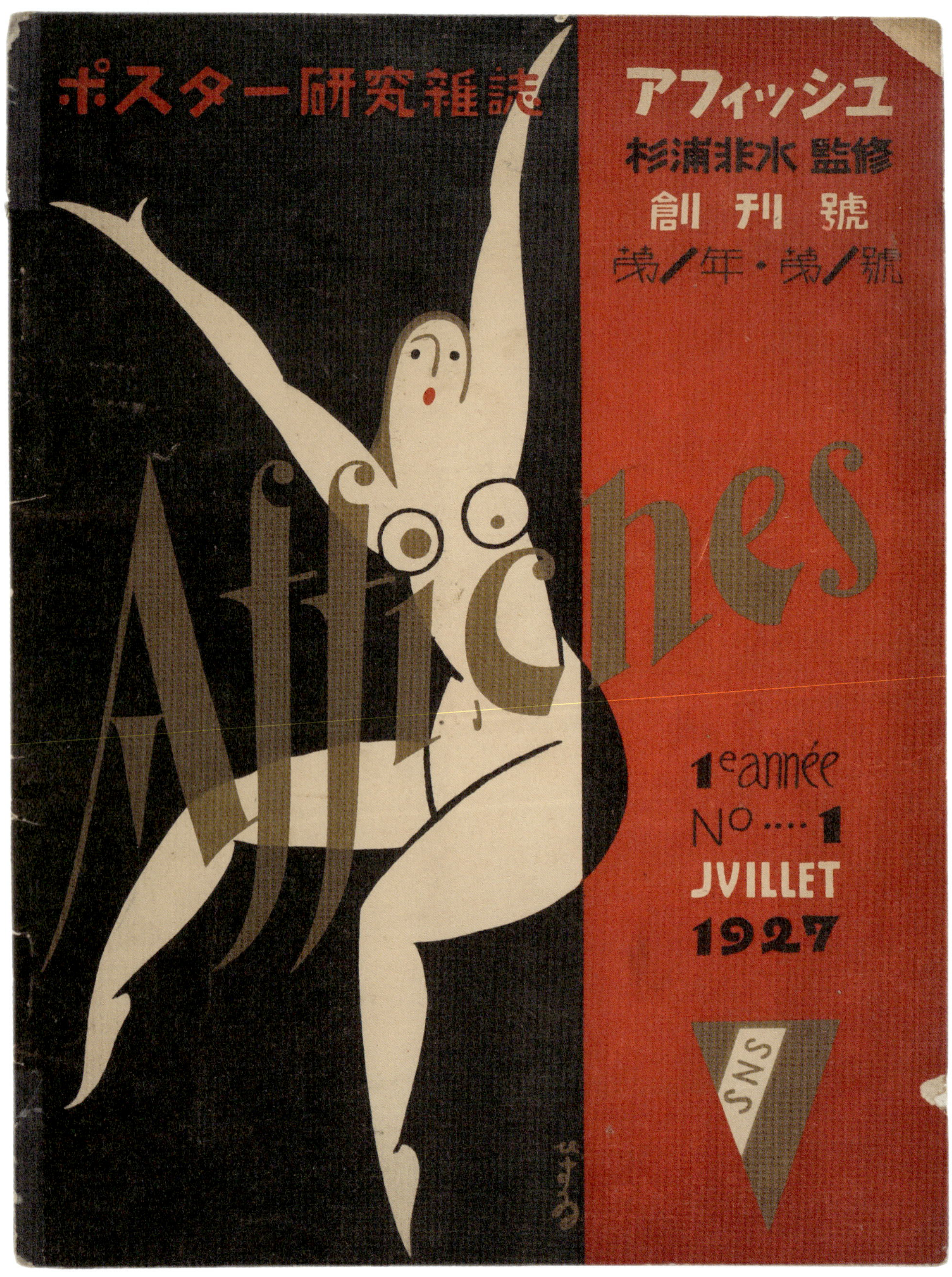

Affiches アフィッシュ, Vol. 1 (Tokyo: Shichininsha 七人社, 1927). Cover design by Sugiura Hisui 杉浦非水.

SUGIURA HISUI 杉浦非水

1876–1965

"Today, design does not signify anything other than practicality.... Modern people must create living forms of design that transcend modern utilitarianism."
- Sugiura Hisui, "Design Review"

Design departments at the Mitsukoshi 株式会社三越 and Takashimaya 株式会社髙島屋 department stores opened in 1909 and 1912 respectively. Each provided advertising with streamlined visual messaging that showed an economy of form and directness in consumer appeal. The department stores' promotions can be described as modern—largely free from visual frippery, the excess ornament of earlier times, instead utilizing direct, to-the-point advertising copy.

It was in these design departments that Japan's first "design stars" were born, including Sugiura Hisui, lead designer at Mitsukoshi (then Mitsukoshi Dry Goods 三越呉服店). Hisui was a prolific designer of promotional travel material, one of the leaders of Japan's early modern design publishing ventures, and an influential early Japanese design educator. The impact of his designs for Mitsukoshi were so powerful to the public that the department store was said to be "Hisui's Mitsukoshi" and the designer "Mitsukoshi's Hisui." (Sugiura preferred being referred to by his given name, Hisui, and this biography reflects the preferred usage of the time, as much as how he is referred to in contemporary Japanese parlance.)

Hisui was born in Matsuyama City, Ehime Prefecture, in 1876, and moved to Tokyo in 1897. He graduated from Tokyo School of Fine Arts in 1901, having studied nihonga, or the Japanese style of painting, alongside yoga, or Western-style painting. Hisui was a favored pupil of painter Kuroda Seiki, and Hisui was enraptured with Kuroda's collection of European ephemera collected during a trip in 1900. Hisui himself would become an obsessive collector of visual material, amassing scores of reference books and self-created thematic scrapbooks dedicated to animals, insects, nature, and lettering. After graduation, he worked briefly as a designer for a printing business in Osaka, tried his hand at teaching junior high school in Shimane Prefecture, and then returned to Tokyo to work as a designer for the newspaper *Tokyo Chūō Shimbun* 東京中央新聞.

Hisui's relationship with Mitsukoshi began in 1908, when he was hired as a freelance designer by Executive Director and Senior Managing Director Hibi Ousuke 日比翁助 to design and illustrate hybrid magazine/catalog covers for the nascent department store's *Mitsukoshi Times* 三越タイムズ. Formerly a kimono shop that catered to the affluent and powerful, under Hibi's guidance Mitsukoshi became one of Tokyo's leading department stores, serving Tokyo's upper crust alongside the upper-middle class that emerged during the early Meiji era. Working under Hibi, Hisui was elevated to the position of Chief Manager of the newly-formed Mitsukoshi Design Department in 1910. His monthly duties expanded in 1911 to include designing and illustrating the covers of Mitsukoshi's eponymous magazine, as well.

Hisui held his exhibition *Publication Book Magazine Cover Design Exhibition* 雑誌表紙図案展覧会 at the Hibiya Library in 1912, showing off over 200 examples of his publication design works spanning catalogs, magazines, and books. The works featured printing techniques that were atypical for that time in Japan, including printing on cotton book board, the use of metallic foils, and the use of lacquers. Hung salon-style, with framed individual cover designs mixed with looming overhead boards pasted over with multiple designs, the exhibition was offset by a glass-faced display case showcasing his more upmarket works, accompanied by a plain table heaped with Hisui-designed publications.

Hisui was also a prolific designer of posters for Mitsukoshi and later clients such as the Calpis Corporation カルピス株式会社, manufacturer of yogurt-based soft drinks. Hisui designed red and blue variants of wrapping paper for Calpis's large-size bottles in the 1920s, decorated with dot patterns representing the fizzy carbonation of the beverages. Calpis is still sold with dotted wrapping paper in Japan's department stores today. Additionally, Calpis's standard retail packaging in supermarkets and convenience stores still includes the dot patterns—an echo of Hisui's design decisions in the 1920s.

Hisui utilized both illustration and photo-collage when necessary to connect viewers with the appropriate visual message for a client, often returning to themes of the feminine and of nature.

These themes would extend into designs for tourism—starting in 1913, Hisui designed *The Tourist*, a promotional English-language travel magazine for the Japan Tourist Bureau (JTB).

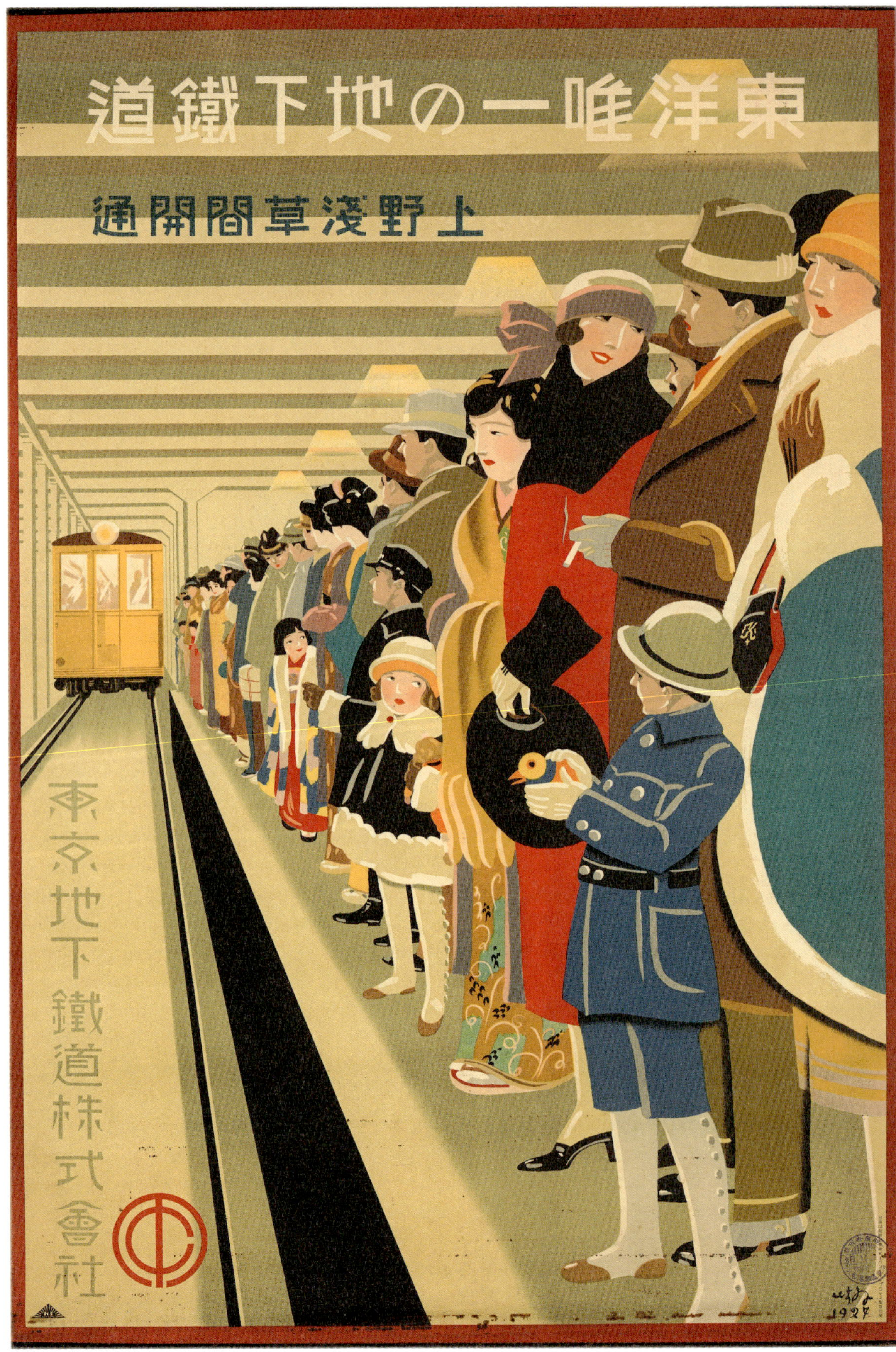
東洋唯一の地下鐵道
上野淺草間開通
東京地下鐵道株式會社
1927

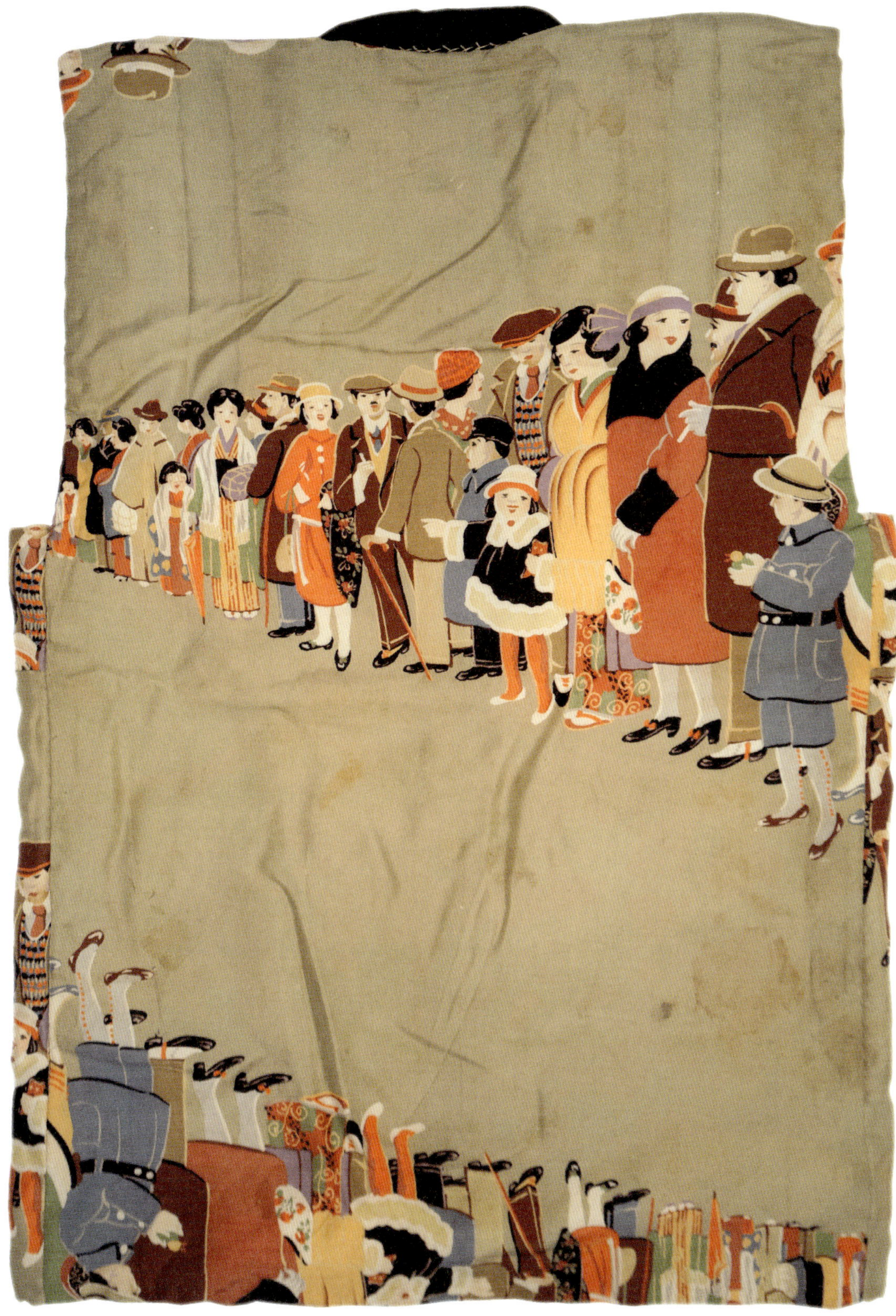

Facing page: ***Tōyō yuiitsu no chikatetsu-dō* (The Only Subway in the East) 東洋唯一の地下鐵道, Sugiura Hisui 杉浦非水, color lithograph, offset 91.0 x 62.0 cm, 1927.** Poster advertising the opening of Tokyo's Ginza subway line in 1927. (Image courtesy of National Gallery of Victoria, Melbourne. Purchased NGV Foundation, 2018 © Estate of Hisui Sugiura) This page: **Rear of child's kimono, Sugiura Hisui 杉浦非水, date unknown.** A depiction of the same scene from Sugiura's iconic poster, with the perspective foreshortened, printed on a child's kimono.

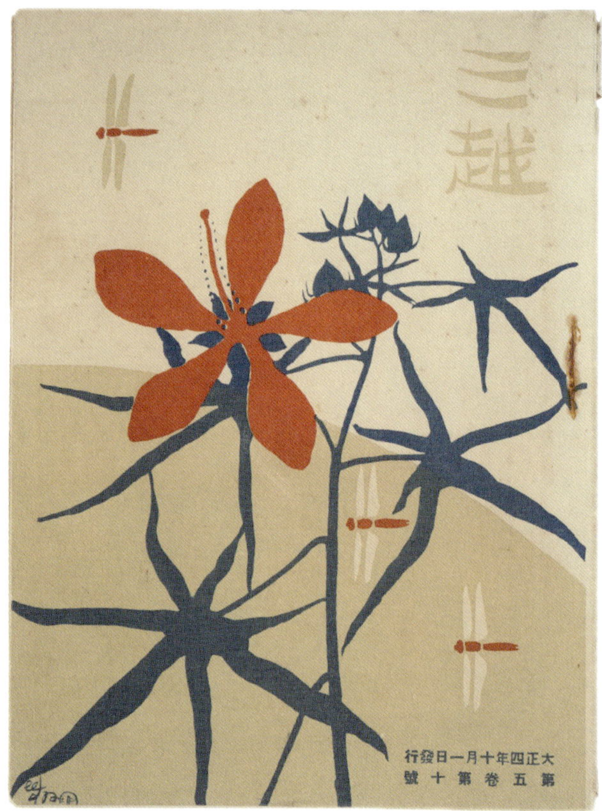

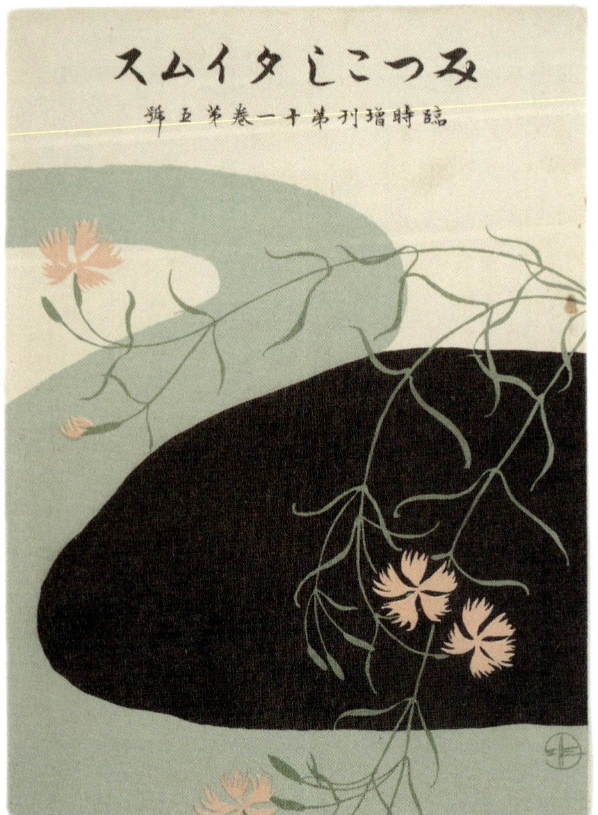

This page and second page after: Three covers for ***Mitsukoshi Times* 三越タイムス** (Tokyo: Mitsukoshi 三越, 1920s).

He also designed a wide range of promotional postcard designs, form-rich posters, and books targeting foreign tourists for JTB.

In 1921, Hisui became a lecturer in the Tokyo School of Art's *zuan* department[1] and, starting in 1922, traveled throughout Western Europe for two years, collecting materials for inspiration and taking in the European aesthetic sensibilities of the day. Before and after his sojourn, Hisui's resonant designs incorporated elements of European Art Deco and Secessionist influence, while also drawing on the Japanese legacy of printmaking. Upon his return in 1925, he formed the design study group Shichininsha 七人社, or "Group of Seven" (also abbreviated as "SNS"), with Arai Izumi 新井泉, Kubo Yoshihiro 久保吉朗, Suyama Hiroshi 須山浩, Koike Iwao 小池巌, Hara Mansuke 原万助, Kishi Hideo 岸秀雄, and Nomura Noboru 野村昇. Hisui and his colleagues' interests in critically studying design would help define the rest of his career—as a designer, design writer, critic, publisher, and educator.

Avant-garde art and design books from outside of Japan were easily available in Tokyo from the early 1920s through 1938 from Kaiser, a German bookstore in Kanda, and the nearby book retailer Sanseido Shoten 三省堂書店. Each stocked the renowned German design periodical *Gebrauschgrafik* alongside a wide array of exhibition catalogs and photography annuals from around the world. Soviet art and design publications were available from Nauka ナウカ, a bookshop in Tokyo's popular book-selling district, Jimbōchō, that still exists today.

The influence of European and Russian design publications on Hisui was immense and helped him to craft a practice that combined design research and design education with his commercial practice. Hisui contributed regularly to Hamada

1 The term zuan 図案 was more commonly used at that time when referring to what we now know as "graphic design." Before the widespread adoption of the loan word "design" デザイン, the Japanese language had two earlier terms for the processes that map to a western idea of design: "zuan" 図案, the physical execution of a design (imagine pencils hitting paper with the use of rulers and geometric aids to create lettering and patterns), and "kōan" 考案, the mental and intellectual articulation of a concept to be executed. Due to the time period in which "zuan" 図案 was popularized, many historians conflate the term with early Japanese commercial arts that integrated an Art Nouveau aesthetic, though the term in use went far beyond period aesthetics.

2 The title of the journal heralded an etymological shift in what the practice that we now call "graphic design" would come to be called by practitioners and the general public alike. The coining of the term "shōgyō bijutsu" 商業美術 (quite literally, "commercial art") would be the next step in how practitioners and the public might define this sector of cultural production. This term was in popular usage until the early 1950s, when the term "shōgyō dezain" 商業デザイン (commercial design) was popularized, followed the widespread adoption of "gurafikku dezain" グラフィックデザイン (graphic design) in the mid-1950s through today.

Masuji's journal *Gendai Shōgyō Bijutsu Zenshū* 現代商業美術全集 (*The Complete Commercial Artist*)[2] released by Tokyo publishing house ARS, beginning in 1927.

Hisui's commercial practice continued to flourish through the late 1920s. He designed the poster *The Only Subway in the East* celebrating the opening of the Tokyo Metro Ginza Line in 1927, took on an astounding number of book design projects, and continued his work for Mitsukoshi. His association with Mitsukoshi also gave him the opportunity to design *omoshirogara* 面白柄 novelty kimono fabrics and a large number of decorative *obi* 帯 kimono sash designs. Many of the graphic themes in Hisui's posters would be echoed, redrawn, or adapted in these surface designs, and the fabrics are highly collectible today.

Hisui founded the oversized journal *Affiches* アフィッシュ and pursued associated exhibitions with the other members of the Shichininsha from 1927 through 1930. The debut issue of *Affiches* featured a statement of intent/working manifesto highlighting the importance of commercial art and the group's desire to explore the subject matter intentionally. It also included taxonomies of commercial signage and decorative firefighter's pole headers by Hisui's colleague Kon Wajirō, reproductions of work from abroad, and one perforated page featuring multicolored *Affiches* poster stamp designs. The magazine ran from 1927 to 1930, extending across three volumes, each with a number of editions.

Hisui designed the covers for the Tokyo Central Telephone Directory in 1933 and 1934 and for neighboring Yokohama's telephone directory in 1934. He was a prolific designer of magazine covers, creating hundreds of covers for assorted publications, as well as a few dozen book covers and spine designs. Hisui also designed a large number of packaging designs, including sleeve designs for the cigarette brands Hibiki, Hikari, Minori, Momoyama, and Fuso and label designs for lacquer, varnish, and paint compounds manufactured by Hitachi Chemical.

Hisui was invited to become head of the Craft Pattern Faculty at the Imperial Art School in 1929 and stayed through 1935, when he resigned after locking horns with the school's administration. The previous year, he had also resigned from Mitsukoshi. With his time freed up, Hisui co-founded Tama Imperial Art School—today's Tama Art University—in 1935, bringing a variety of established educators on board including Arai Izumi and Koike Iwao from Shichininsha. The faculty held its first exhibition the following year and launched a group publication called *Desegno* デセグノ, the Esperanto word for "design." *Desegno* was a journal of design theory published from 1936 until 1939, at which time the journal was absorbed into the university's house magazine, *Tama Art*.

It is interesting to note that one of the premier art universities in Japan was co-founded by a graphic designer, not a fine artist. While continuing to work as a faculty member, Hisui became first the president and later chairman of the Board of Trustees, holding the latter position until 1963. Those around Hisui exhibited an exceptional sense of solidarity, especially faculty members Satomi Munetsugu and Yamana Ayao, who would lead the design faculty after the end of World War II. Hisui was a rigorous teacher, demanding that his students draw a minimum of one hundred botanical sketches with a high level of detail over their summer holidays.

Hisui published a handful of books during his career, including *Complete Practical Design Materials* 実用図案資料大成 in 1933, *The Aesthetics of Design* 図案の美学 in 1950, and *Compilation of World Design Materials* 世界動物図案資料集成 with colleague Watanabe Soshu 渡辺素舟 in 1952.

References:

Kamekura, Yūsaku, and Ayao Yamana. *Gurafikku Dezain No Seiki: Bunshō to Danwa to Sakuhin De kōsei: Meiji Sedai Yamana Ayao Sugiura Hisui Kara shōwa Sedai Made*. Tokyo: Bijutsu Shuppansha, 2008.

Kiyasu, Rei, and Hisui Sugiura. *Seitan 140-Nen, Sugiura Hisui: Kaikasuru Modan Dezain: A Retrospective*. Japan: Sugiura Hisuiten Jikkō Iinkai, 2017.

Hamada, Masuji, ed. *Gendai shōgyō Bijutsu zenshū*. 1st ed. 12 vols. Tokyo: ARS, 1930.

Sugiura, Hisui, Yui Nakao, and Sakura Nomiyama. *Imēji korekutā Sugiura Hisui Ten = Sugiura Hisui: Image Collector*. Tokyo: Tokyo Kokuritsu Kindai Bijutsukan, 2019.

Sugiura, Hisui. *Afisshu: Zuan kenkyū Zasshi 3–7*. Tokyo: Kokusho Kankōkai, 2009.

Sugiura, Hisui. *Sugiura Hisui no Dezain: Hisui Sugiura*. Japan: PIE Books, 2014.

Sugiura, Hisui. "Design Review." In *New Design Techniques Course*, Volume 1: Basic Design Method, 3–15. Tokyo: Atelier Publishers, 1932.

Weisenfeld, Gennifer. "Japanese Modernism and Consumerism: Forging the New Artistic Field of 'Shogyo Bijutsu' (Commercial Art)." In *Being Modern in Japan: Culture and Society from the 1910s to the 1930s*, edited by Elise K. Tipton and John Clark, 75–96. Honolulu: University of Hawai'i Press, 2000.

Weisenfeld, Gennifer S. *Imaging Disaster: Tokyo and the Visual Culture of Japan's Great Earthquake of 1923*. Berkeley: University of California Press, 2012.

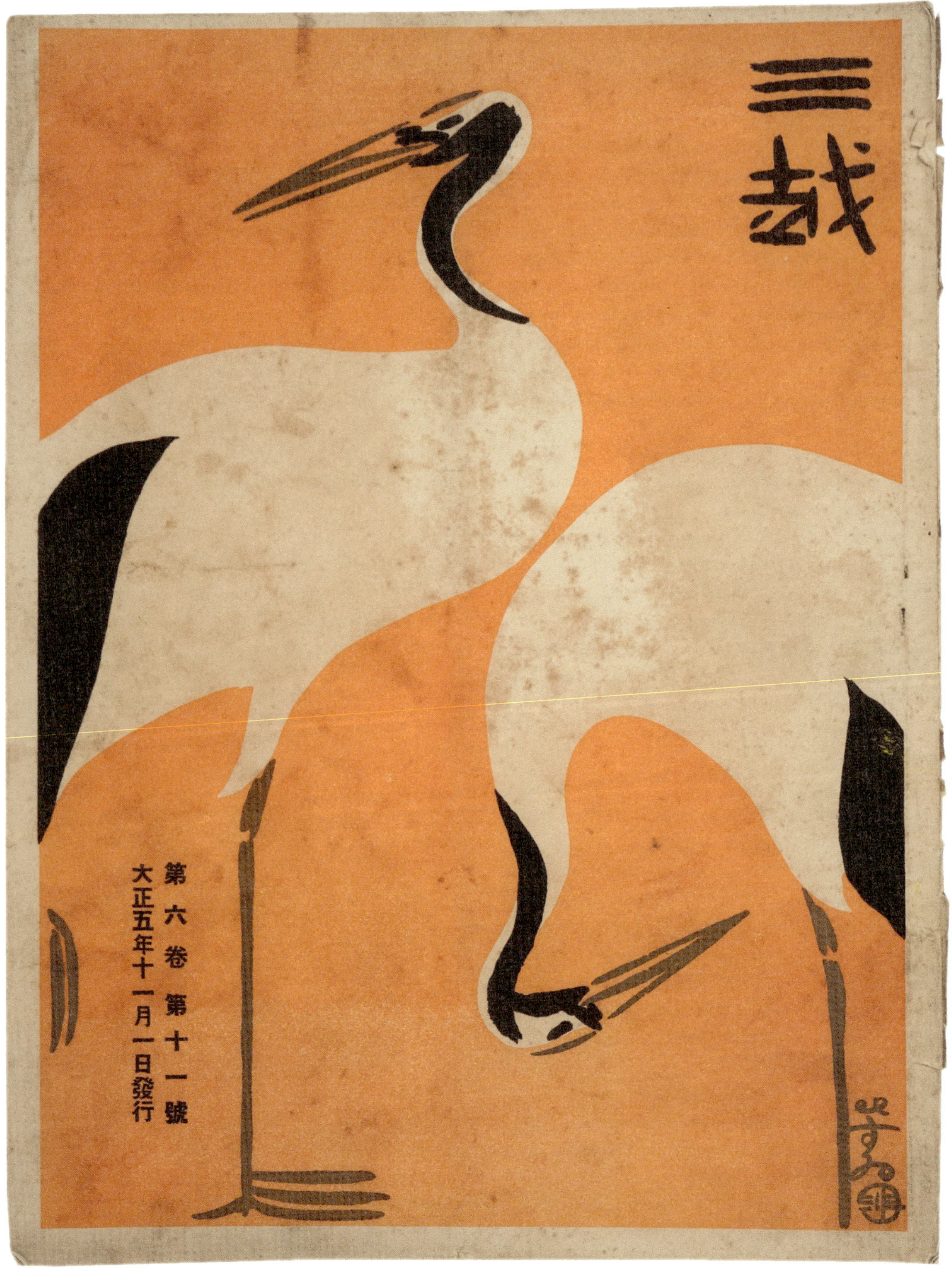
三越
第六巻第十一號
大正五年十一月一日發行

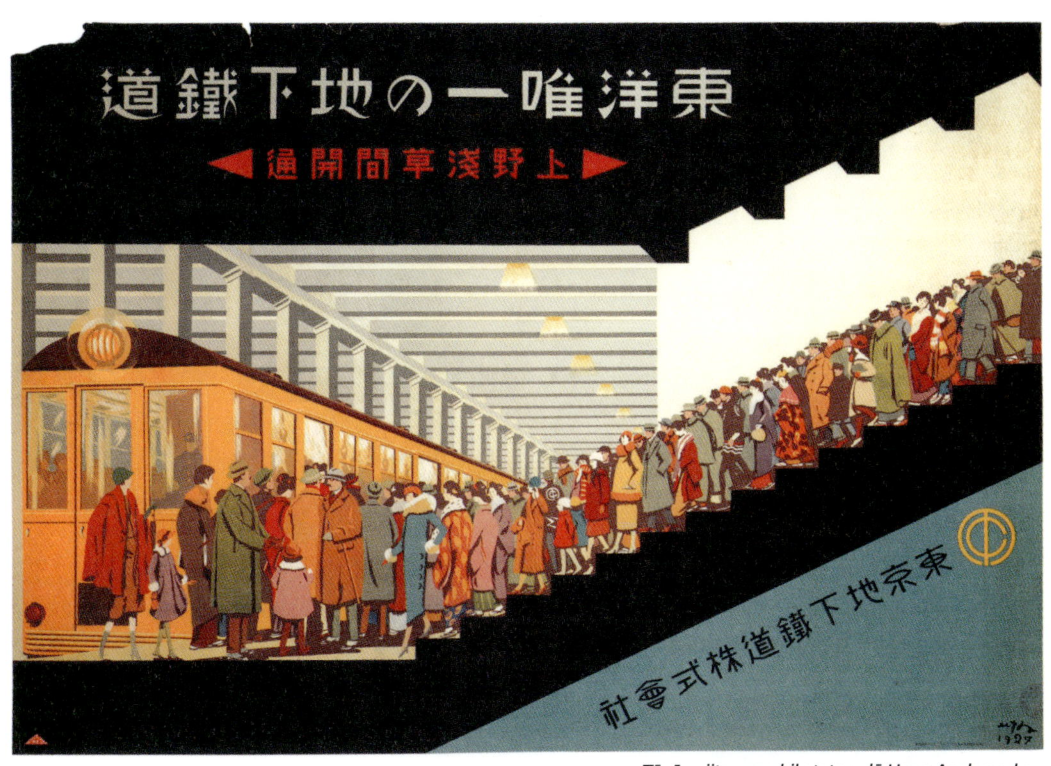

Tōyō yuiitsu no chikatetsu-dō Ueno Asakusa-kan
(The only subway in Asia's service between Ueno and Asakusa has begun)
東洋唯一の地下鉄道 上野浅草間開通 poster, 1927.

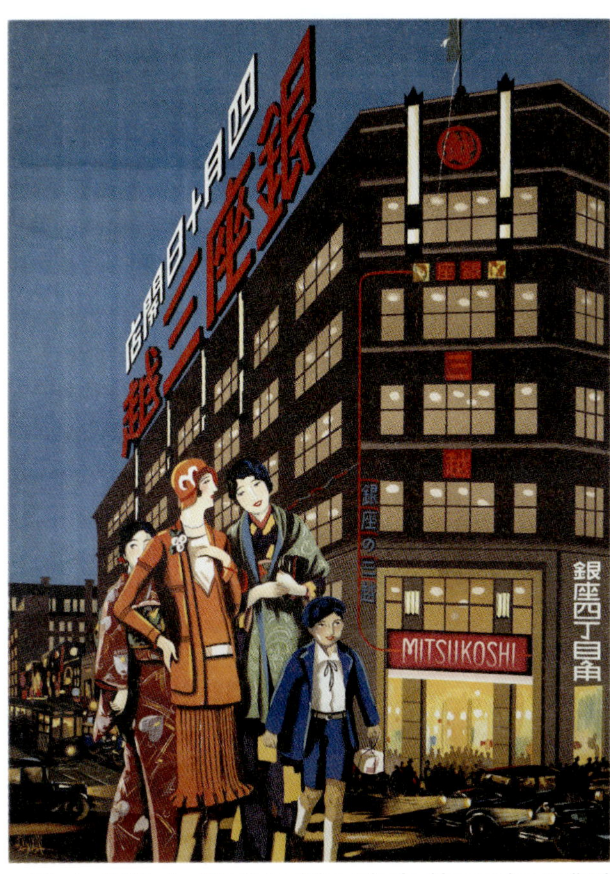

Ginza Mitsukoshi Shigatsu Tōka Kaiten (Ginza Mitsukoshi opened on April 10)
銀座三越四月十日開店 poster, 1930.

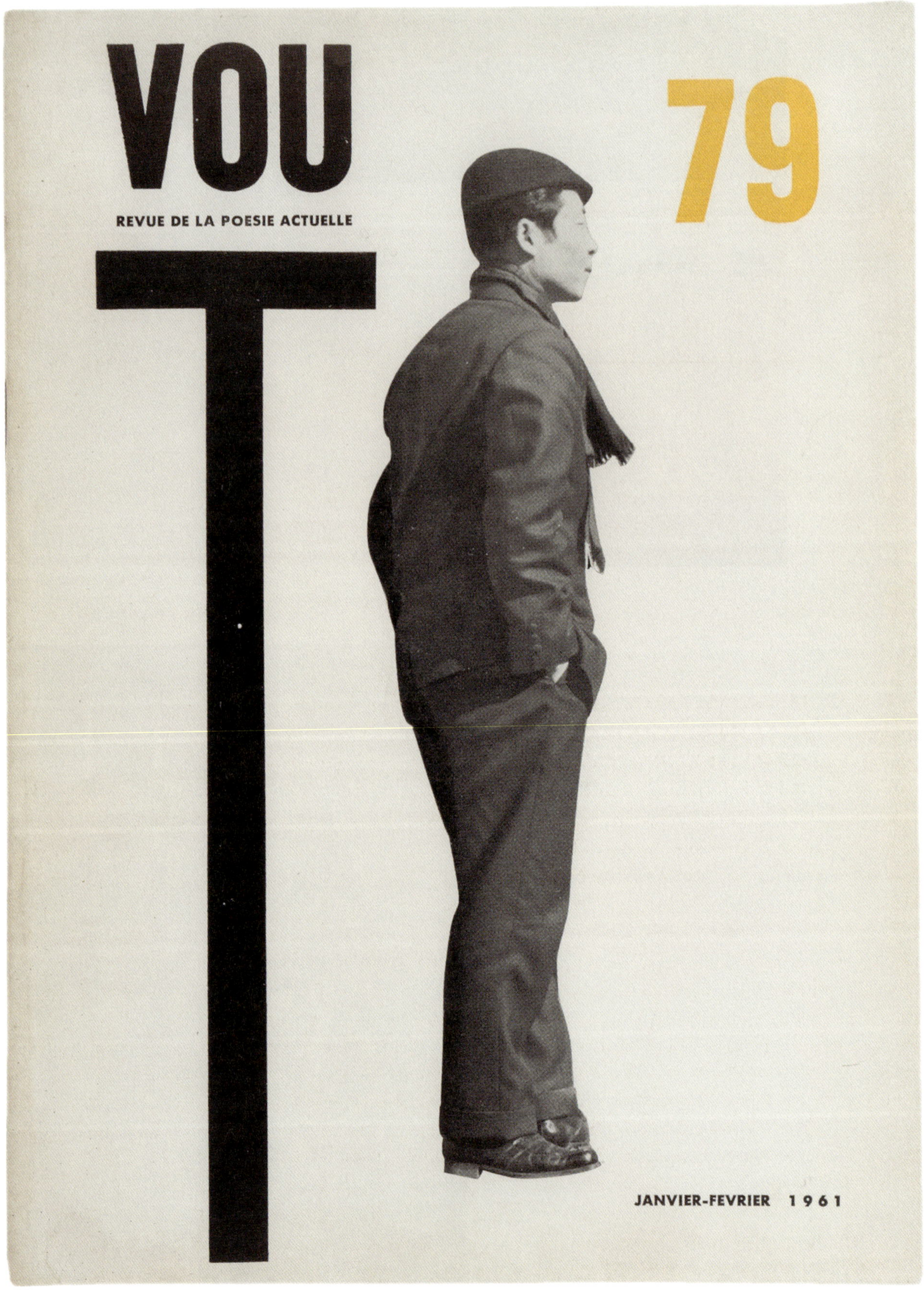

Cover of ***VOU* Vol. 79 (Tokyo: VOU Club, 1961)**, design by Kitasono Katué 北園克衛.

KITASONO KATUÉ 北園克衛

1902–1978

Pronounced Kitazono Katsue, Kitasono Katué was the pen name of Hashimoto Kenkichi 橋本健吉, a poet, prose writer, photographer, artist, translator, and graphic designer born in the village of Asama in Mie Prefecture. Having moved to Tokyo at age nineteen, he studied economics at Chūō University with the intent of becoming a newspaper reporter, though he never graduated. Briefly infatuated with socialism, Kitasono became a prolific poet and artist in the early 1920s after the disruption of the Great Kanto Earthquake and a months-long stay back in his hometown.

Returning to Tokyo in 1924, Kitasono was introduced to a new poetry journal called *Ge.Gjmgjgam.Prrr.Gjmgem* ゲエ·ギムギガム·プルルル·ギムゲム (abbreviated *GGPG*),), edited by the Tokyo poet Nogawa Takashi 野川隆, which mirrored the abstruse approaches to language, meaning, and form in poetry that had been taken up by the European Dada movement. *GGPG* was a hotbed of poetic experimentation and would feature the work of a number of writers over the course of ten issues, including the writing of Mavo leader Murayama Tomoyoshi. Kitasono became the editor of subsequent issues before the magazine folded in 1926. *GGPG* and *Mavo* each advertised in the other's pages, with Kitasono contributing writing to *Mavo*, as well.

After the collapse of *GGPG*, Kitasono contributed poems to a number of small literary journals before being invited to edit and creatively overhaul a small literary magazine called *Retsu* 列. Kitasono renamed the magazine *Shōbi Majutsu Gakusetsu* 薔薇魔術学説 (subtitled as *Rose Magic Theory* in English) and refashioned it as the first magazine dedicated wholly to the interpretation of surrealist poetry in Japan. In 1929, Kitasono released his first book of poetry, *Shiro no Arubamu* 白のアルバム, featuring a stunning mix of expressive typography and simplistic illustration on a cover designed by the author himself. The book included a mix of different poetic approaches set in connotative typography, often relying on typographic ornaments and rules to give the compositions visual impact. Kitasono began publishing the poetry magazine *Hakushi* 白紙 in 1930—renamed *Madame Blanche* マダムブランシュ in 1932. A club of young poets organized by Kitasono funded the printing and publishing through their membership dues until the magazine folded in 1935.

Kitasono continued to use this method of establishing a club to both contribute to and financially support a publication, establishing the VOU Club and their associated publication, *VOU*, in 1935. The three letters meant nothing other than a desire to fill them with new meaning in the context of Japanese poetry. The following year, Kitasono began a lively correspondence and friendship with American poet Ezra Pound (who nicknamed him "Kit Kat" in their letters). The typographically expressive *VOU* journal began publishing poetry by American and European poets alongside the poetry written by club members. Pound actively campaigned for the group in European and American literary journals, giving their work and publication international stature.

Kitasono's internationalism came under the scrutiny of censors and government police forces in 1940, and he was arrested and interrogated. Subsequently, the thirtieth issue of *VOU* included a manifesto-style note announcing that the publication would double down on Japanese-oriented cultural production and that the prior incorporation of Western influence was merely to glorify and uplift cultural production from Japan. The note was signed by "the members of the VOU Club," though no other members had vetted the statement.

The journal's name was promptly changed to *Shin Gijutsu* 新技術 (*New Technology*). A hasty disavowal and removal of the use of Latin letterforms allowed Kitasono to keep the journal in print. *Shin Gijutsu* was printed at a reduced size and page count, adopted nationalistic terminology, and did not include any imagery that appeared to be of foreign influence. *Shin Gijutsu* initiated publication at issue #31, shortly after *VOU* #30 had been released, continuing the legacy of *VOU*, though with increasingly detailed lists of what was not to be included in submissions in order to appease government censors.

Kitasono kept *Shin Gijutsu* in business until wartime paper shortages ceased publication. Kitasono continued working on other publications during the later war years, tackling a number of freelance editorial design projects and continuing his work as the librarian of a dental college while publishing a number of books of poetry. Many of these poems featured as their locus both the nostalgic idea of one's hometown and the concept of Japan-as-nation.

Kitasono began publishing *VOU* again in 1949 as the postwar environment in Japan began to stabilize. He was a regular contributor to the fine art publications *Bijutsu Techō* 美術手帖 and *Atelier* アトリエ and a contributor to Onchi Kōshirō's journal on book

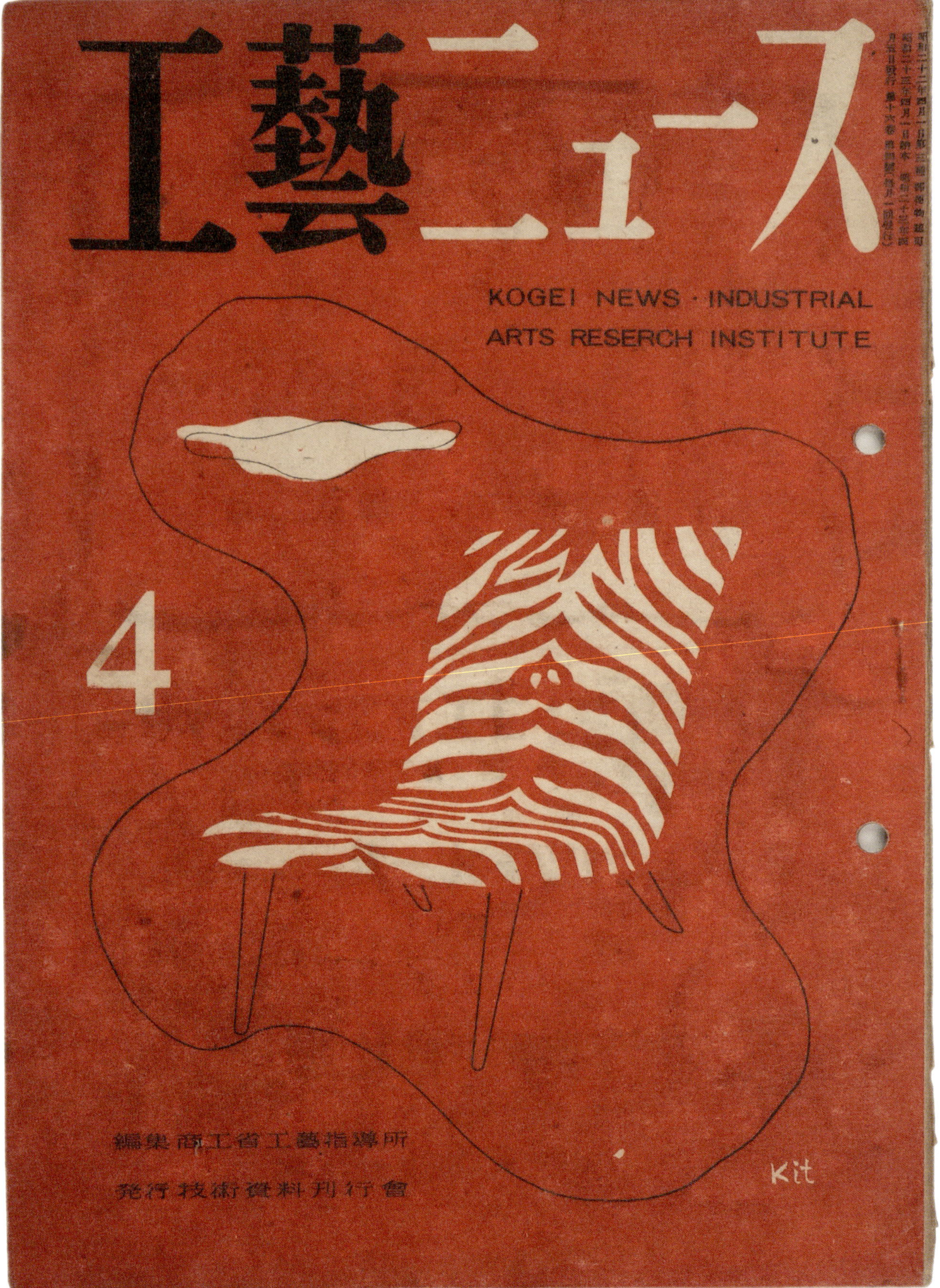
工藝ニュース
KOGEI NEWS · INDUSTRIAL
ARTS RESERCH INSTITUTE
4
編集 商工省工藝指導所
発行 技術資料刊行會
Kit

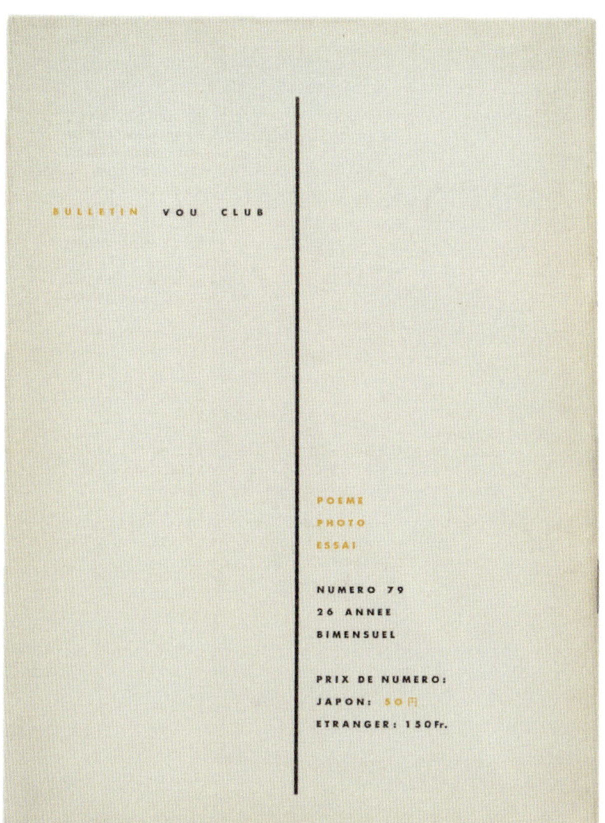

design and typography, *Shosō* 書窓.

In a 1975 interview with Matsuoka Seigō 松岡正剛 and Sugiura Kōhei for the magazine *Yū* 遊, Kitasono stated that "the fundamental consciousness that cultivated my sensibility about objects was the introduction of the Bauhaus to Japan." Within the interview, he also discussed his preference for cleanliness and order in his editorial designs and a desire to balance visual and typographic form with abundant negative space. After the war, Kitasono regularly contributed staged photographs of everyday objects—which he called "plastic poems"—to international journals. Numerous postwar issues of *VOU* featured Kitasono's plastic poem photography on the covers.

Before his death in 1978, he would publish numerous books of poetry and would design a number of them, playing with typographic orthography to both confound and inspire readers.

References:

Kato, Jin. "Kitasono and Poetry Journals in the Pre-War Period." *Idea* 1, no. 364 (May 2014): 82–88.

Solt, John. *Shredding the Tapestry of Meaning: The Poetry and Poetics of Kitasono Katué (1902–1978)*. Cambridge, MA: Harvard University Press, 2011.

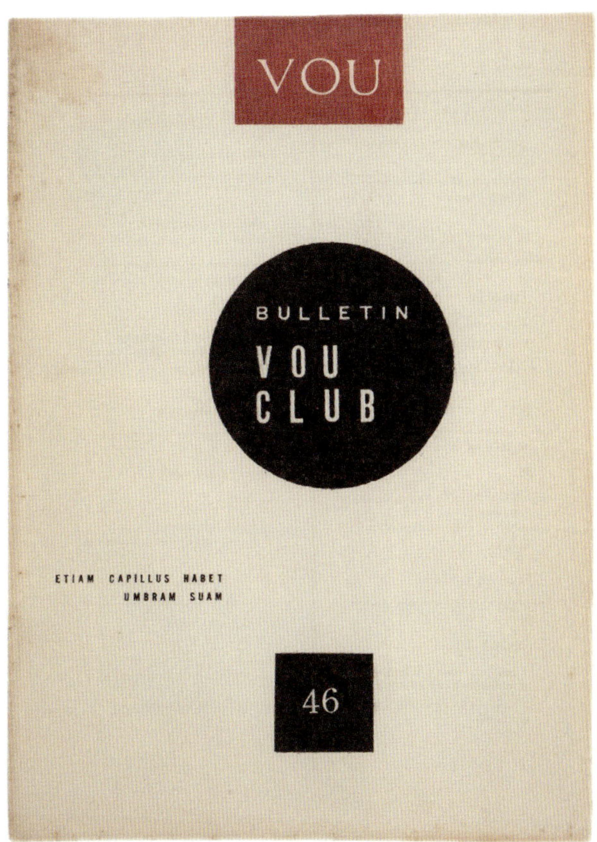

Facing page: ***Industrial Arts News* 工芸ニュース** (Tokyo: Ministry of Commerce and Industry Craft Guidance Center 商工 省工芸指導所, 1948). Above: back cover of ***VOU* Vol. 79** (Tokyo: VOU Club, 1961). Below: front cover of ***VOU* Vol. 46** (Tokyo: VOU Club, 1955); all designed by Kitasono Katué 北園克衛.

JAPAN
JAPANESE GOVERNMENT RAILWAYS
SATOMI 37
BOARD OF TOURIST INDUSTRY

Japan poster, Satomi Munetsugu 里見宗次, Japan Government Railways, 1937.

References:

Satomi, Munetsugu. *Satomi Munetsugu Posutā-Ten Zai Futsu 70 Nenkinen*. Osaka: Shinsaibashi Sogō, 1990.

Satomi, Pierre. "Satomi Munetsugu Satomi." Munetsugu Satomi - 里見宗次. Pierre Satomi, June 2019. https://www.munetsugusatomi.com/.

Segi, Shin'ichi, Tanaka Ikkō, and Hiroshi Sano. *Nissenbi No Jidai = The Epoch of the Japan Advertising Artists Club: Nihon No Gurafikku Dezain 1951–70*. Tokyo: Toransuāto, 2000.

SATOMI MUNETSUGU 里見宗次

1904–1996

Satomi Munetsugu was born in Osaka. In 1922, he moved to Paris and enrolled in the École des Beaux-Arts while also studying French at the Sorbonne. He met Marioara Rasuceanu at the Sorbonne, and they married in 1925. After his father passed away two years later, Satomi shifted from fine art toward design as a vocation in order to make a living for his new family. He joined an advertising agency as their studio director in 1928, working under the Westernized name Satomi Mounet. He won a design contest for Gauloises that same year, the results of which traveled globally. The early 1930s brought a number of commercial projects and international recognition, notably for the catalog cover design for Les Galeries Lafayettes department store and posters for La Foire de Paris and the Vel D'hiv six-days/nights bicycle race.

In 1933, Satomi went freelance, creating commercial design work for the airline KLM and other large companies. While in France, Satomi cultivated lasting friendships with fellow artists and designers like AM Cassandre Man Ray, and Jean Carlu.

In 1936, Satomi returned home to Japan for the first time in fourteen years. During his time in Japan, he designed posters for the Japan Railways, Mikimoto Pearls, and Nippon Yūsen Kaisha, one of the oldest and largest shipping companies in the world, which provided military transport and hospital ships for the Imperial Japanese Army and Navy during World War II. In particular, Satomi's 1937 poster for Japan Railways received attention due to its depiction of a blurred, abstracted Japanese landscape dotted with telephone poles—a portrait of speed and modernity in absorbing color.

He returned to Europe, but he and his family were forced back to Japan in 1939 due to the war in Europe, taking up residence in Tokyo's Aoyama district. Satomi ventured to the United States in 1940, handling the decoration of the Japanese Pavilion at the New York World's Fair. While in the USA, he designed a well-received poster for the American Locomotive Company.

In July 1941, the Japanese-led Thai/French Indochina Border Demarcation Committee sent him to Saigon to design a series of pro-government propaganda posters. He opened a design studio in that city and produced bilingual French and Japanese posters, while continuing his freelance poster work for Nippon Yūsen Kaisha. From 1943 to 1945 he was assigned to Bangkok, where he was in charge of national design campaigns for Thailand. At the end of the war, Satomi and his family were sent to a POW camp just outside Bangkok, and the Thai police confiscated and destroyed all of the posters found in Satomi's house.

Japanese prisoners of war in Thailand were released throughout 1946, but Satomi followed the suggestion of the former Thai foreign minister, Phichit Kriangsakphichit, and decided to stay on in Bangkok. This decision caused the Thai government to hold the family's passports to ensure their mutual commitment to Thai restoration. Satomi designed a number of posters for clients like the Bangkok Post and Siamese Airways and was appointed Thailand Art School advisor in 1948. In this position, he created the first Thailand Art Competition.

In 1952, the Satomi family's passports were returned and they boarded a Norwegian ship to France, arriving in Paris in October after thirteen years away. Satomi purchased an apartment in Paris's 14th Arrondissement near his artist friend Tsuguharu "Leonard" Foujita, another noted producer of Japanese imperial propaganda during the war. Satomi cultivated a thriving commercial practice throughout the remainder of the 1950s and 1960s, designing works for the Salon International de l'Alimentation, Esso, Shell Oil, and Concorde.

In 1973, Satomi returned to Japan for the first time in thirty-two years to hold an exhibition of his work at the Matsuya department store in Ginza, for which he recreated sixty pieces of artwork that had been destroyed during the war. The following year, Satomi was awarded the Order of the Sacred Treasure 瑞宝章, a Japanese national award given to those who have made distinguished achievements in culture, business, or social work. In 1981, Satomi held a large-scale retrospective exhibition featuring 300 pieces of artwork at Matsuzakaya department store in Tokyo, celebrating the sixtieth anniversary of his arrival in France. Throughout the 1980s and 1990s, he had a variety of other exhibitions at Matsuya Ginza in Tokyo, Sogo Shinsaibashi in Osaka, and Kyoto Institute of Technical Arts and Crafts Museum.

In August 1991, Satomi published his biography, *J'ai deux amours, Le Paris de Munetsugu Satomi* 二つの愛ムネ・サトミのパリ, returned to Japan for good in 1993 and died in 1996 at ninety-two years old.

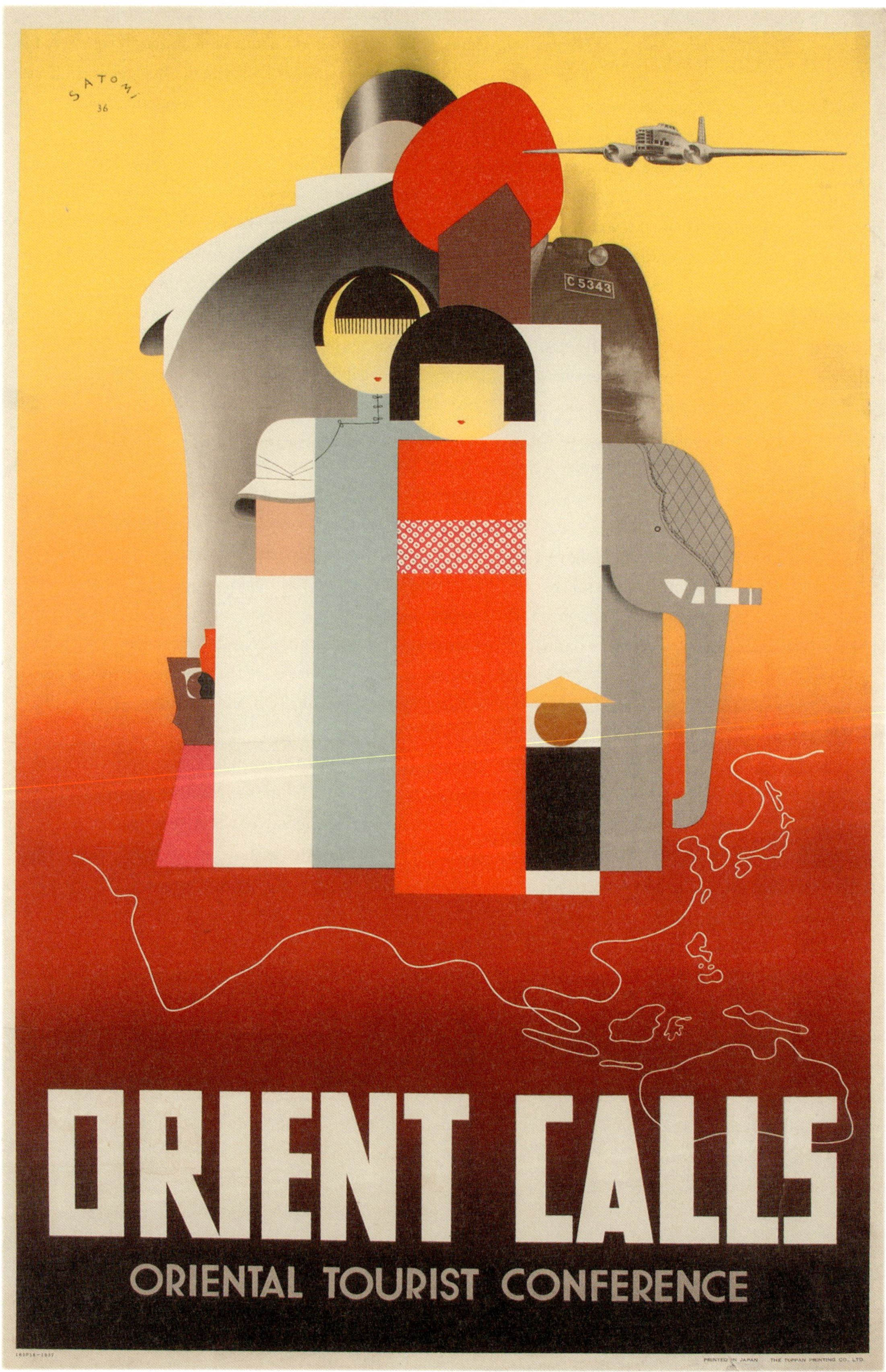

Orient Calls poster designed for the Oriental Tourist Conference, Satomi Munetsugu 里見宗次, 1936.

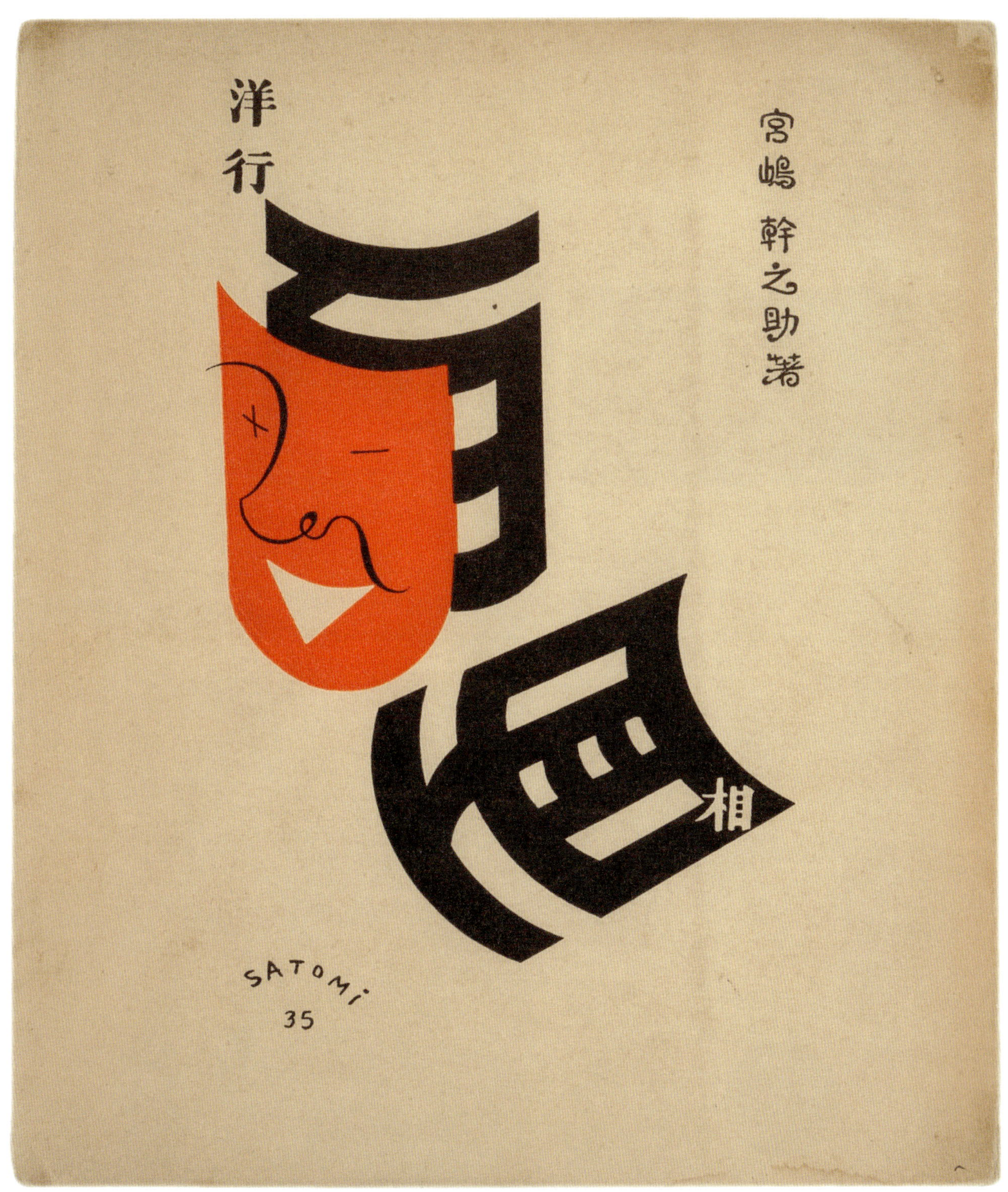

The 100 Faces of Western Travel 洋行百面相, Miyajima Mikinosuke 宮嶋幹之助 (Tokyo: Somasabō 双雅房, 1936). Book design by Satomi Munetsugu 里見宗次.

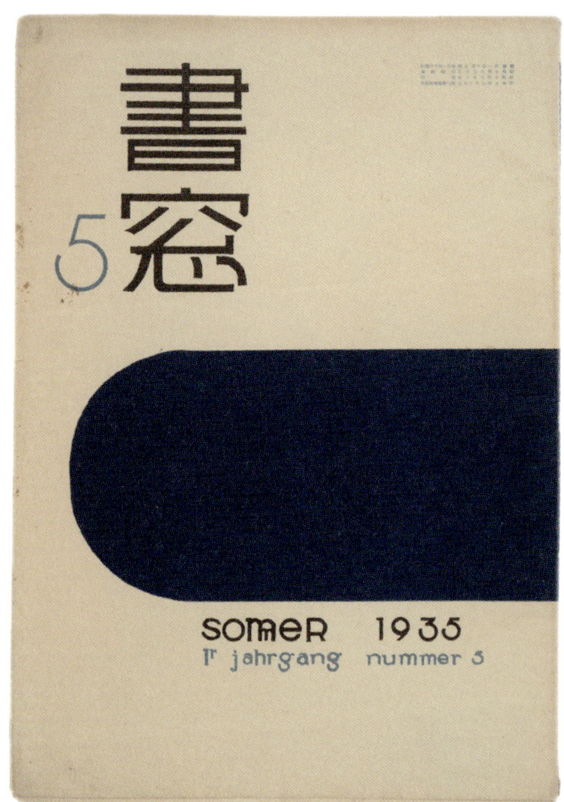

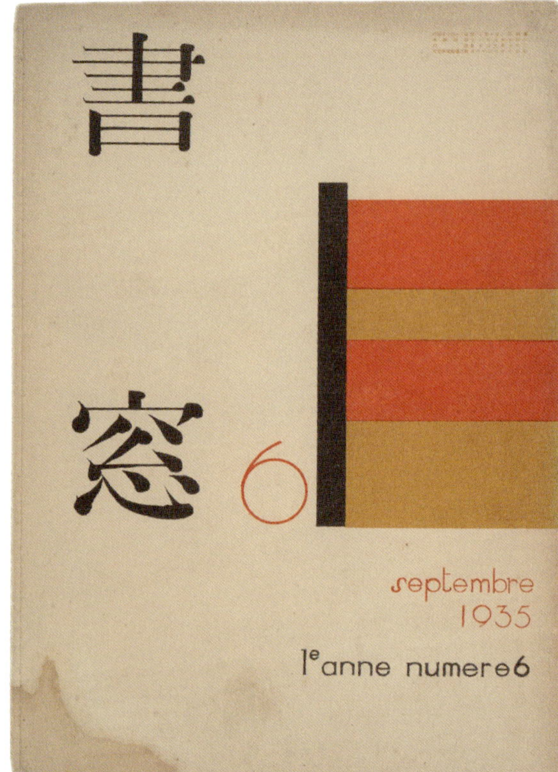

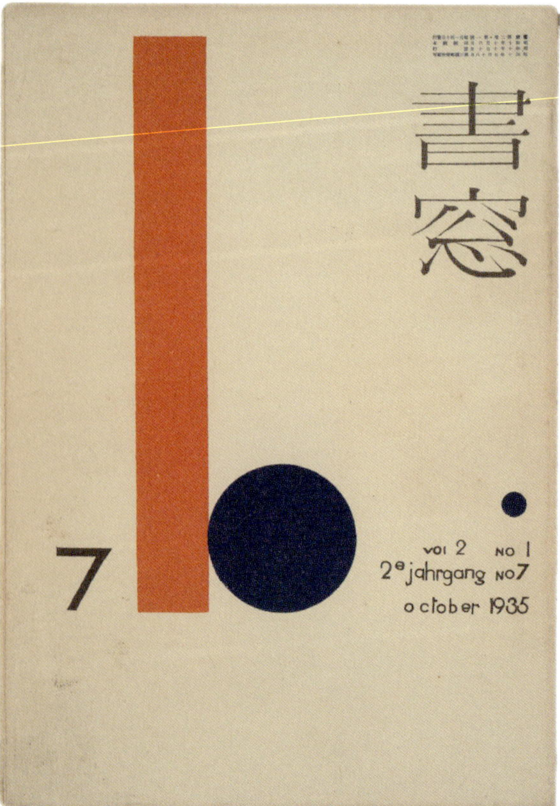

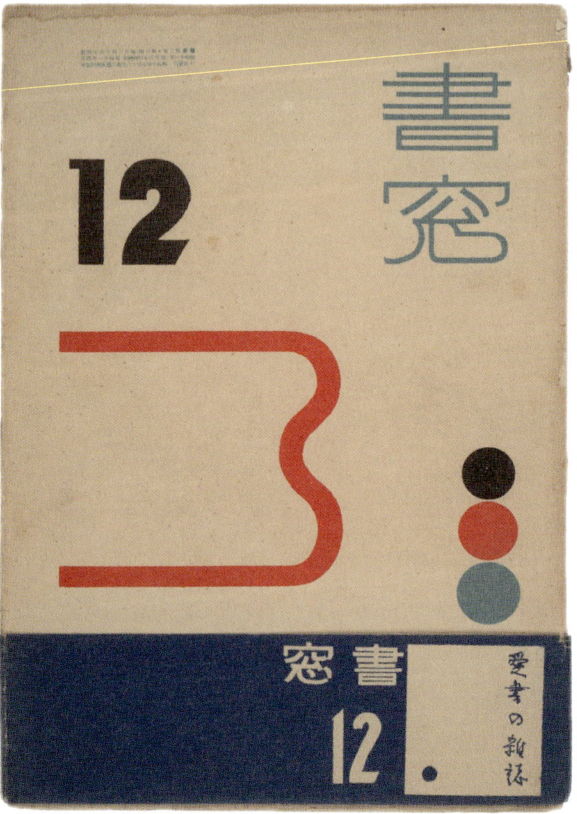

Assorted covers from ***Shōso* 書窓**, published by Aoi Shobō アオイ書房 in Tokyo in the 1930s. Design by Onchi Kōshirō 恩地孝四郎. The covers of *Shosō* were thematically quite similar—an exploration of simplified form and nuanced modern lettering with a generous amount of negative space to help activate the relationships between the form and lettering.

ONCHI KŌSHIRŌ 恩地孝四郎

1891–1955

Onchi Kōshirō was born in Tokyo to a wealthy and respected family. His father worked in a variety of evolving roles in the Imperial household and was responsible for the education of royal youth who were to marry into the Imperial family. Onchi was educated in the classical style, was highly literate in historical kanji, and was also able to read and write German. He attended the Hakubakai Society school in Akasaka, studying their interpretation of French Impressionism under the Western-style painter and arts educator Kuroda Seiki.

While a student, Onchi contacted the painter, illustrator, and designer Takehisa Yumeji, offering well-received feedback on a publication of Yumeji's. The two struck up a fast friendship, with Takehisa introducing the young Onchi to Jugendstil and German Impressionism. Onchi went on to study oil painting and sculpture at the Tokyo School of Fine Arts 東京美術学校 in 1910, though he dropped out in his second year of study due to his discontentment with the quality of education. During Onchi's time at the Tokyo School of Fine Arts, Yumeji offered Onchi his first professional project working on one of Yumeji's books for the publisher Rakuyōdō Kawamoto 洛陽堂, from whom Onchi would receive further commissions.

Onchi returned to school in 1912 but was in constant conflict with his teachers, often turning to Yumeji for advice. Onchi was eventually kicked out of the institution, but not before founding the small art and poetry magazine *Tsukuhae* 月映 with his classmates Fujimori Shizuo 藤森静雄 and Tanaka Kyokichi 田中恭吉 in 1913. Hand-printed by the trio and published by Rakuyōdō, *Tsukuhae* ran for six issues with a print run of 300 copies, each saturated with lushly poetic verses about urbanity, sexuality, and pathos. Woodblock-printed illustrations by Onchi, Fujimori and Tanaka accompanied the poems until Tanaka died of tuberculosis at age twenty-three.

Yumeji invited Onchi to exhibit his prints from *Tsukuhae* at his gallery Minato-ya みなとや, which led to further commissions for both his printmaking and commercial design work. Onchi married in 1916 and began raising a family, remaining deeply involved in book design in order to support them. Other early projects included the total design of the art magazines *Naizai* 内在, *Shi to Ongaku* 詩と音楽, and *Shi to Hanga* 詩と版画, and he was active in the various burgeoning creative-print coteries and critique groups across Tokyo.

Throughout his early career, Onchi refined his sense of visual composition, exercising "a careful placement, a rigid control of space on the paper surface and an acute sensitivity to the structural tensions created by the relationships between the edges of the surface and the lines and the shapes and placed on it," according to biographer Elizabeth de Sabato Swinton. Onchi's interest in literature and poetry paved the way for important connections. His friendship with influential poet Kitahara Hakushū 北原白秋 led to a subsequent friendship with Kitahara's brother Tetsuo 北原鉄雄, head of the independent publishing company ARS—a leading publisher of art, commercial art, and photography magazines and books. Onchi's unified approach to the design of books for ARS—from paper choice to illustration to typographic nuance—catapulted him into the role of Japan's best-known book designer. His titles for ARS spanned mathematics textbooks, children's literature, fine art books, and graphic design books and journals.

Onchi's ARS children's book designs featured matching front and back covers with idyllic, full-color scenic paintings or illustrations of naturalistic archeological findings, each contained within decorative framing. Spines were designed using a mix of modern Mincho display lettering and arabesque and baroque visual elements and were produced using gold foil stamping on maroon book cloth. These books were housed in durable chipboard sleeves printed with the series title and associated volumes in one color. Each featured lavish two-color title page designs and one-color, full-bleed endpapers printed with assorted patterns; one pattern that mixed organic arabesque tendrils with half-cloud forms was used repeatedly. Later titles featured geometric single-color compositions for the endpapers and much more modern typographic compositions for the title pages. The interior typography was primarily typeset either fully vertically or horizontally in Mincho typefaces with generous letterspacing and leading.

Onchi was the co-designer of the highly influential commercial art journal *Gendai Shōgyō Bijutsu Zenshū* 商業美術全集 (The Complete Commercial Artist) alongside editor Hamada Masuji 浜田増治. Onchi's unified designs for the journal helped define public conceptions of nascent graphic design. Hamada was also a graduate of the Hakubakai, and his and Onchi's

1 Swinton, Elizabeth de Sabato. *The Graphic Art of Onchi Koshiro: Innovation and Tradition*. New York: Garland, 1986.

intellectual and methodological approaches to commercial art were in lock-step with each other. *Gendai Shōgyō Bijutsu Zenshū* promoted a scientific approach to design, emphasizing proper form, rationality, clarity, and precision.

Onchi created a number of influential books for other presses throughout the 1920s and 1930s, including his books *Umi no Dōwa* 海の童話 and *Hikō Kannō* 飛行官能 in 1934. Both books featured highly articulated compositions of Onchi's poetry using typography, photographs, and printmaking, in a style akin to the Bauhaus method called "typofoto": a consummate approach to graphic design, perhaps most famously expressed in the work of Bauhausler Laszlo Moholy-Nagy, as well as that of Constructivist El Lissitzky. There is little doubt that Onchi had seen work by these designers; Japan had a healthy book trade importing foreign design and art publications after the country opened. There was a high amount of interest—for example, Filippo Tommaso Marinetti's *Futurist Manifesto* was translated into Japanese in 1910, just one year after it was published.

From 1935 to 1944, Onchi published a monthly journal called *Shosō* 書窓 with his friend Shimo Taro 志茂太郎 through their publishing imprint Aoi Shobo アオイ書房. *Shosō* explored book design and the practice's component forms, with issues covering illustration, Western typography, Japanese typography, lettering design, book design, approaches to layout, materials, and a host of other topics. The journal was printed using a mix of letterpress, photogravure, and lithographic printing, with specific methods being suited to that particular issue's content. One of the most notable issues is Volume 4, Number 20, published in 1937—a career survey of the work of Onchi's longtime friend and mentor, Takehisa Yumeji.

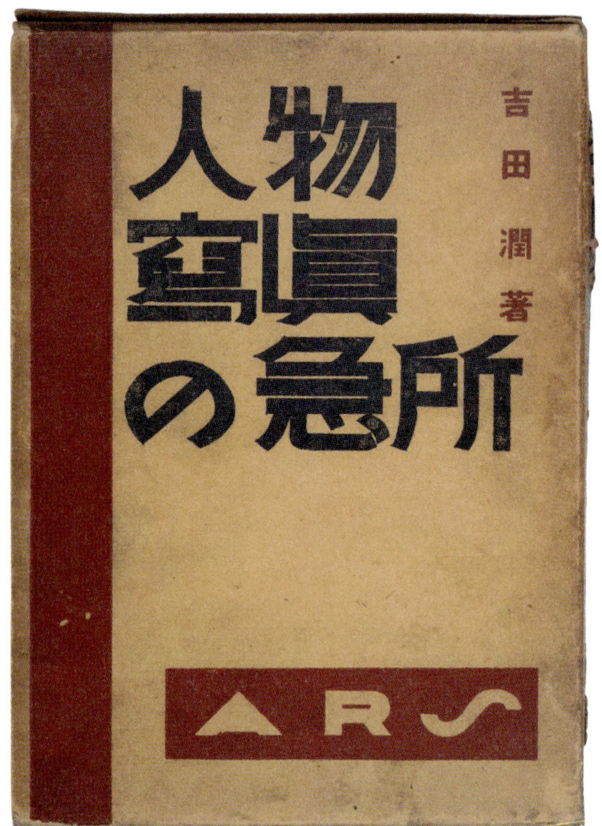

***Key Points of Portrait Photography* 人物写真の急所**, Yoshida Jun 吉田潤 (Tokyo: Kabushikigaisha ARS 株式会社アルス, 1936). One of countless book slipcover designs for ARS by Onchi Kōshirō 恩地孝四郎.

References:

Kobayashi, Mari. *Gaka no Bukku Dezain: Sōtei to Sōga Kara Miru Nihon no Honzukuri no rūtsu*. Tokyo: Seibundō Shinkōsha, 2018.

Miki, Tetsuo, Koichi Wada, Keiko Kano, and Yoshiko Inoue. *Onchi Kōshirō: Iro to Katachi no Shijin*. Tokyo: Yomiuri Shinbunsha, 1994.

Swinton, Elizabeth de Sabato. *The Graphic Art of Onchi Kōshirō: Innovation and Tradition*. New York, NY: Garland, 1986.

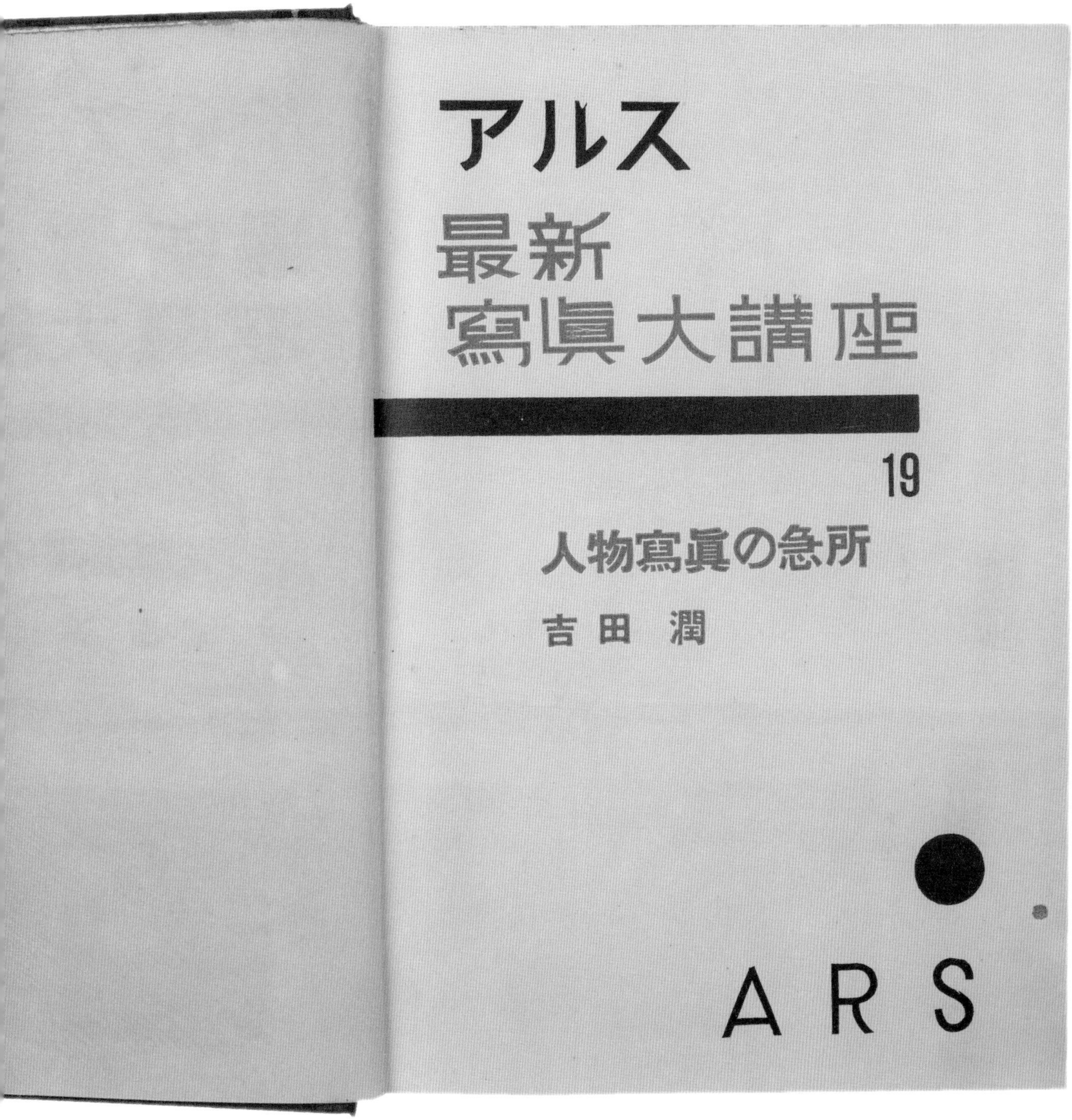

アルス

最新
寫眞大講座

19

人物寫眞の急所

吉田 潤

ARS

Title page design of ***Key Points of Portrait Photography* 人物写真の急所**, Yoshida Jun 吉田潤 (Tokyo: Kabushikigaisha ARS 株式会社アルス, 1936). Designed by Onchi Kōshirō 恩地孝四郎.

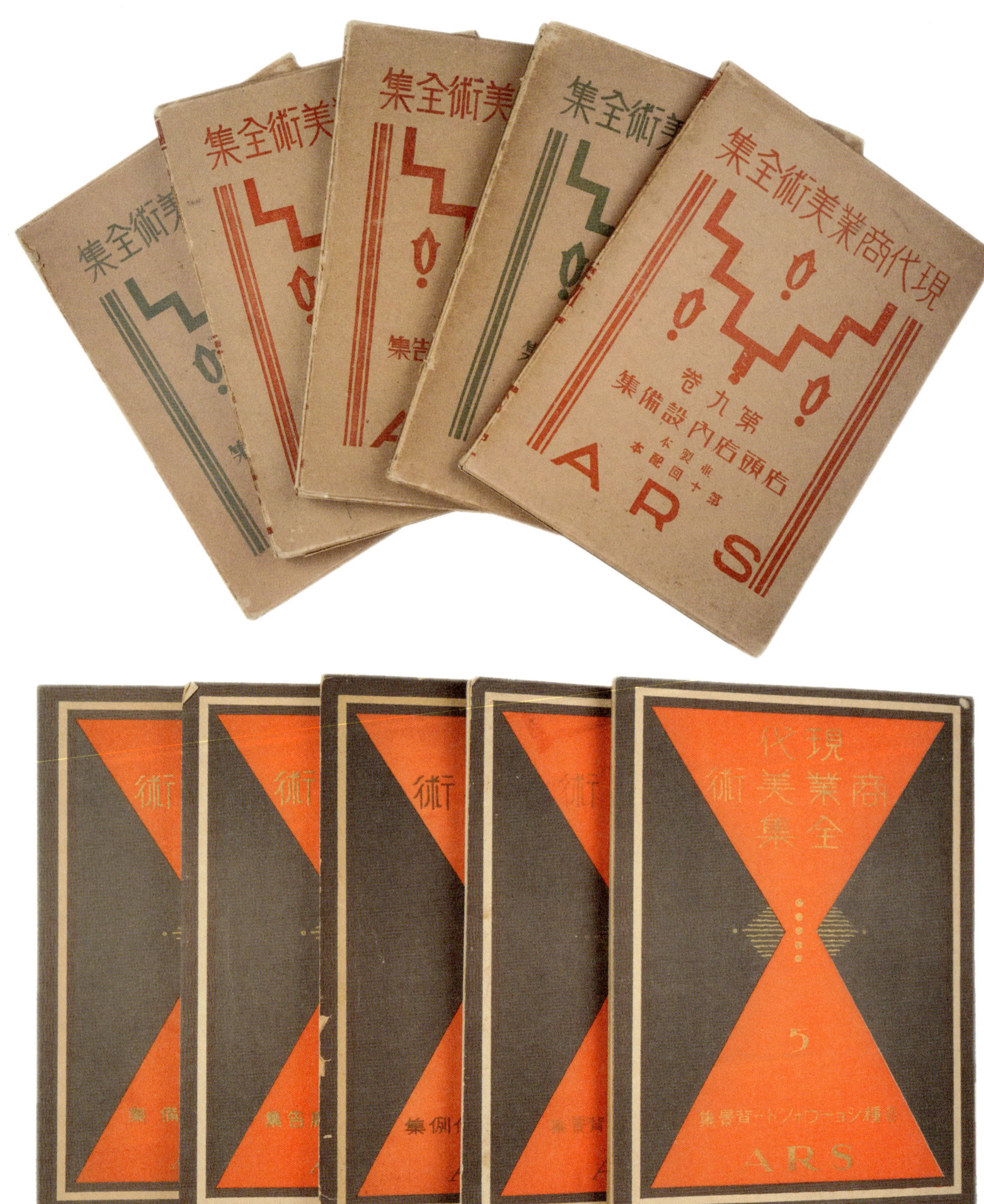

Slipcovers and softcover versions of ***Gendai Shōgyō Bijutsu Zenshū (The Complete Commercial Artist)* 現代商業美術全集** Vol. 1–24, edited by Hamada Masuji 濱田増治 and Kitahara Yoshio 北原義雄 (Tokyo: Kabushikigaisha ARS 株式会社アルス, 1928–1930). Design by Onchi Kōshirō 恩地孝四郎.

HAMADA MASUJI AND GENDAI SHŌGYŌ BIJUTSU ZENSHŪ
濱田増治と現代商業美術全集

1892–1938

The *Gendai Shōgyō Bijutsu Zenshū* 現代商業美術全集 (The Complete Commercial Artist) was one of the most important early journals of Japanese commercial art. Founded by design theorist and critic Hamada Masuji 濱田増治, the title spanned twenty-four volumes and helped to define the pre-"graphic design" (グラフィクデザイン) term "commercial art," or "shōgyō bijutsu" (商業美術) in the Japanese context. Prior to the popularization of the term "shōgyō bijutsu," the term "zuan" (図案) was more commonly used when referring to what we now know as "graphic design."

Hamada was born in 1892 and trained in Western-style yōga painting at the Hakubakai under Kuroda Seiki and later at the Pacific Painting Society studio before entering the Tokyo School of Fine Arts, where he studied sculpture. While studying, Hamada began freelancing in the commercial art sector. After graduating, he worked as an editor in children's literature magazines and formed the Commercial Art Association 商業美術協会 in 1926. The Association curated annual exhibitions of commercial art and opened up associated chapters in Osaka, Nagasaki, Sendai, Iwate, and Hiroshima. Hamada began editing the journal *Gendai Shōgyō Bijutsu Zenshū* two years later, in association with the publishing house ARS.

The B5-size *Gendai Shōgyō Bijutsu Zenshū* was available strictly by subscription, and subscribers included individuals, corporations, and retailers seeking to keep up with the latest trends in advertising. Each issue was replete with theoretical writings on the topic of design, the function of design in the marketplace, and design news, and included color plates showing the latest commercial artwork in Japan and from abroad.

The *Gendai Shōgyō Bijutsu Zenshū* was one of the most influential guidebooks on persuasive packaging, advertising, and visual form during its publication run from 1928 through 1930. Hamada's six-member editorial committee included designer Sugiura Hisui—Japan's first commercial art superstar and designer for the Mitsukoshi chain of department stores—and Tada Hokuu, the poster designer for the Kirin Brewing Company. As designers widely recognized by the public despite the anonymous nature of the profession, Hisui's and Tada's involvement brought the *Gendai Shōgyō Bijutsu Zenshū* clout that it would not have had otherwise.

Each issue of *Gendai Shōgyō Bijutsu Zenshū* was devoted to a specific topic such as poster design, advertising, package design, shop signs, billboards, flyers and broadsides, page layout and design, or typography and lettering.

One of the key features of the journal was the juxtaposition of commercial art from the Americas and Europe and work created in Japan. Subscribers could follow the rapid and globally competitive development of commercial art in Japan in contrast and competition with the West, inserting themselves and Japanese commercial art into a global context. This side-by-side comparison was incredibly important for Japanese designers, as it provided them with an increased visual vocabulary as well as a sense of pride and value in their work.

The *Gendai Shōgyō Bijutsu Zenshū* provided its readership with more than a mere trade journal—it included prototypes for potential work in addition to documentation of what had come before. The publisher included prototype sketches for vehicular advertising and speculative, hyper-baroque architectural ornament, proposals for sales kiosks, blueprints for advertisements, and examples for the design of signage. The journal did not just offer the mundane present—it sold subscribers *the future*.

The *Gendai Shōgyō Bijutsu Zenshū* was sold in both softcover and hardcover editions. The softcover issues' covers were printed in red and orange on white cardstock, and the hardcover editions were housed in maroon bookbinding cloth stamped in gold foil.

The final issue, No. 24, was devoted to Hamada's theory of commercial art—that it should be a practice that transcends clients, should be worthy of love, and should have a reason for existing beyond mere aesthetics. In short, it should be "art with a purpose."[1]

Following the end of the journal's publication, Hamada opened the Institute of Commercial Art, a three-year certification course. Hamada wrote and published a wide array of books on commercial art, including *Practical Commercial Art for Salesmen* 商人常識商業美術読本 in 1934, *Composition Principles*

1 Hamada Masuji, *Shogyo Bijutsu Kyōhon Nyumon'yō Kaisetsu* (Tokyo: Fuzanbo, 1938), 45.

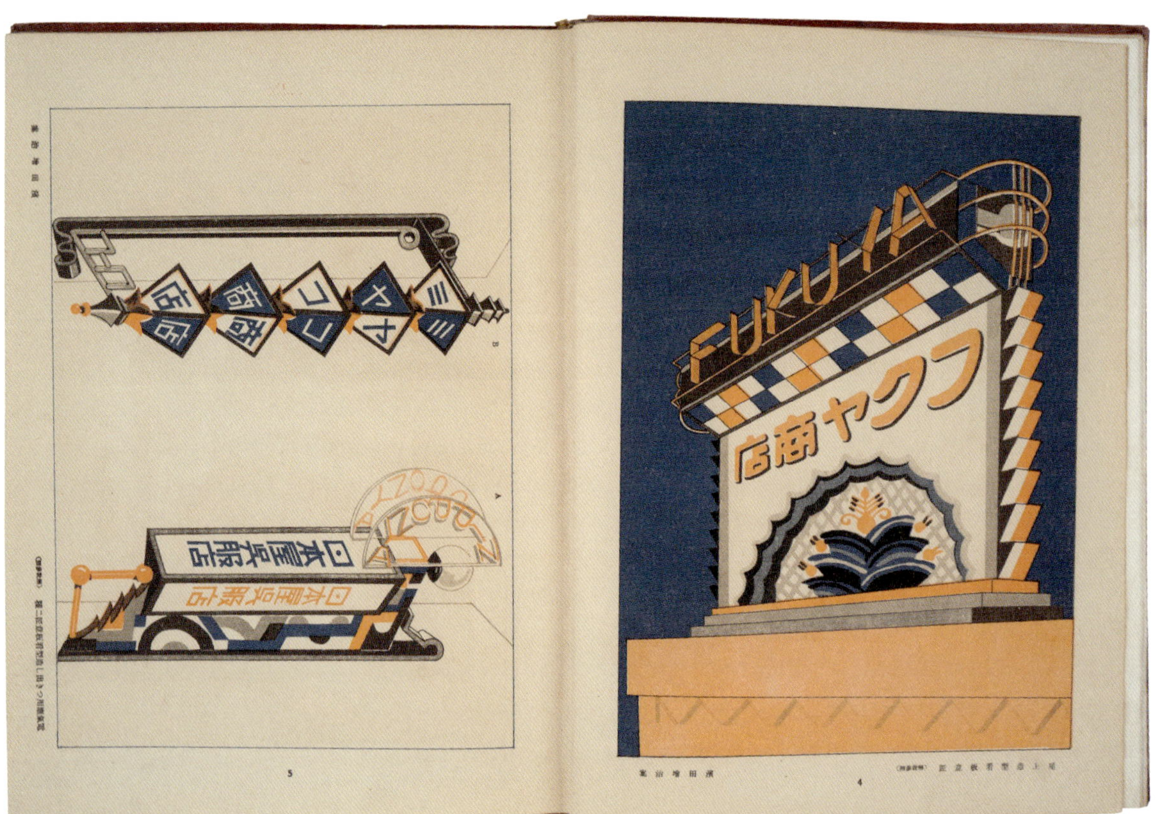

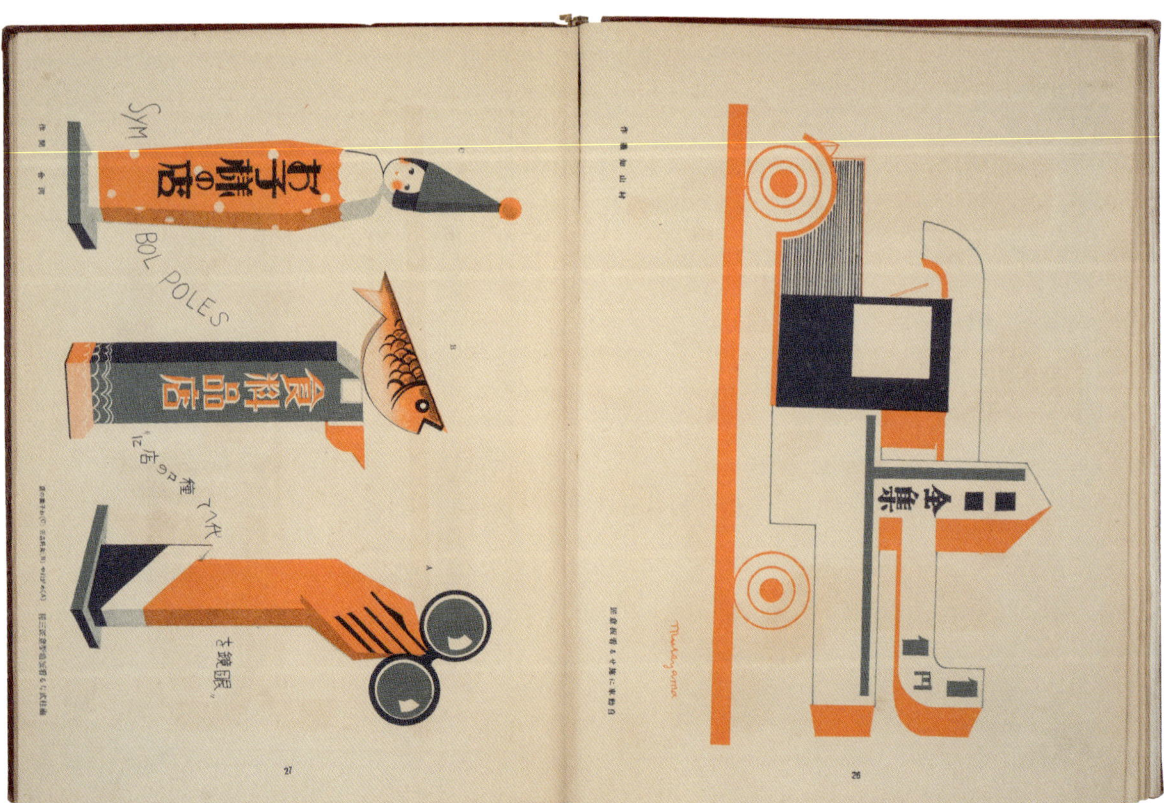

Spreads from ***Gendai Shōgyō Bijutsu Zenshū* 現代商業美術全集 *(The Complete Commercial Artist)*** **Vol. 1–24, edited by Hamada Masuji 濱田増治 and Kitahara Yoshio 北原義雄 (Tokyo: Kabushikigaisha ARS 株式会社アルス, 1928–1930).** These spreads show architectural signage and window display concepts.

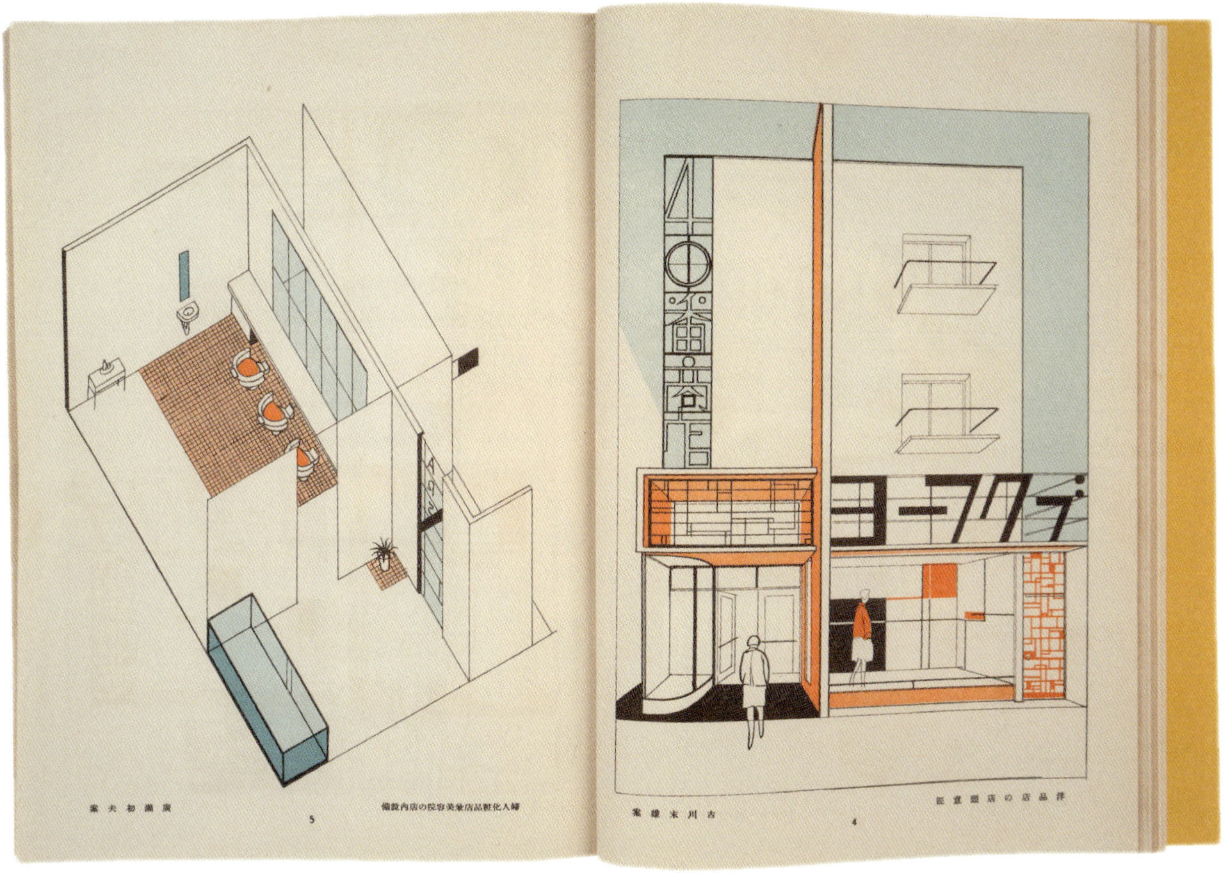

廣瀬初夫案

5

婦人化粧品店兼美容院の店内設備

古川末雄案

4

洋品店の店頭意匠

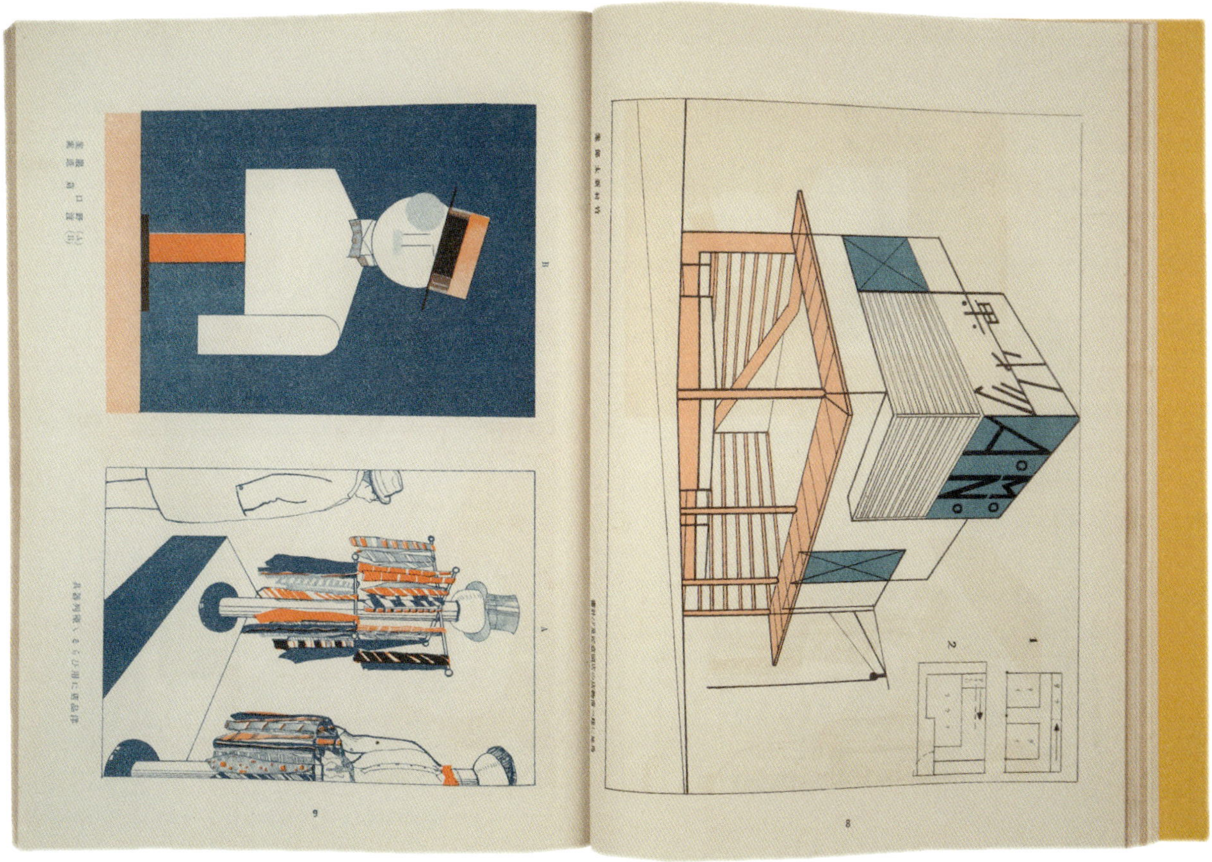

9

8

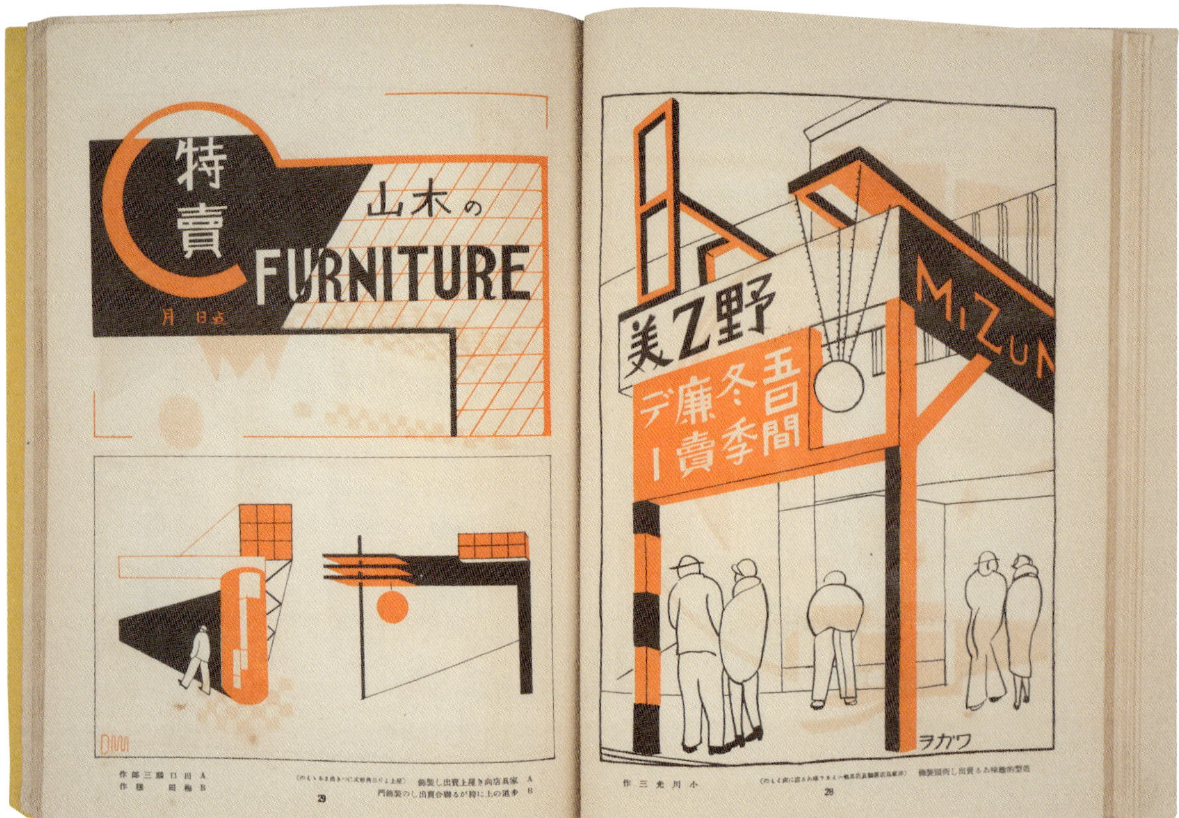

of Commercial Art 商業美術構成原理 in 1935, *Commercial Art for Advanced Use* 商業美術教本 上級用 in 1936, *Commercial Art for Beginners* 商業美術教本 入門用 in 1936, *Lectures on Commercial Art, Volume 1–5* 商業美術講座. 第1-5巻 in 1937, and 1938 and *Commentary on Commercial Art* 商業美術教本入門用解説 in 1938. Throughout, Hamada expanded on his ideas about the elevation and integration of art for commerce.

Throughout his publishing and educational endeavors, Hamada found inspiration in the work of early avant-garde movements, particularly De Stijl and the Bauhaus. *Gendai Shōgyō Bijutsu Zenshū* featured architectural and spatial design plans and illustrations as well as flat graphic design, no doubt inspired by Hamada's training in sculpture.

Hamada died at age forty-seven in 1938 due to a cerebral hemorrhage. He was a pioneer in Japanese discourse around commercial art and graphic design.

References:

Hamada, Masuji, ed. *Gendai shōgyō Bijutsu zenshū*. 1st ed. 12 vols. Tokyo: ARS, 1930

Hamada, Masuji. *Shōgyō Bijutsu Kyōhon Nyumon'yō Kaisetsu*. Tokyo: Fuzanbo, 1938.

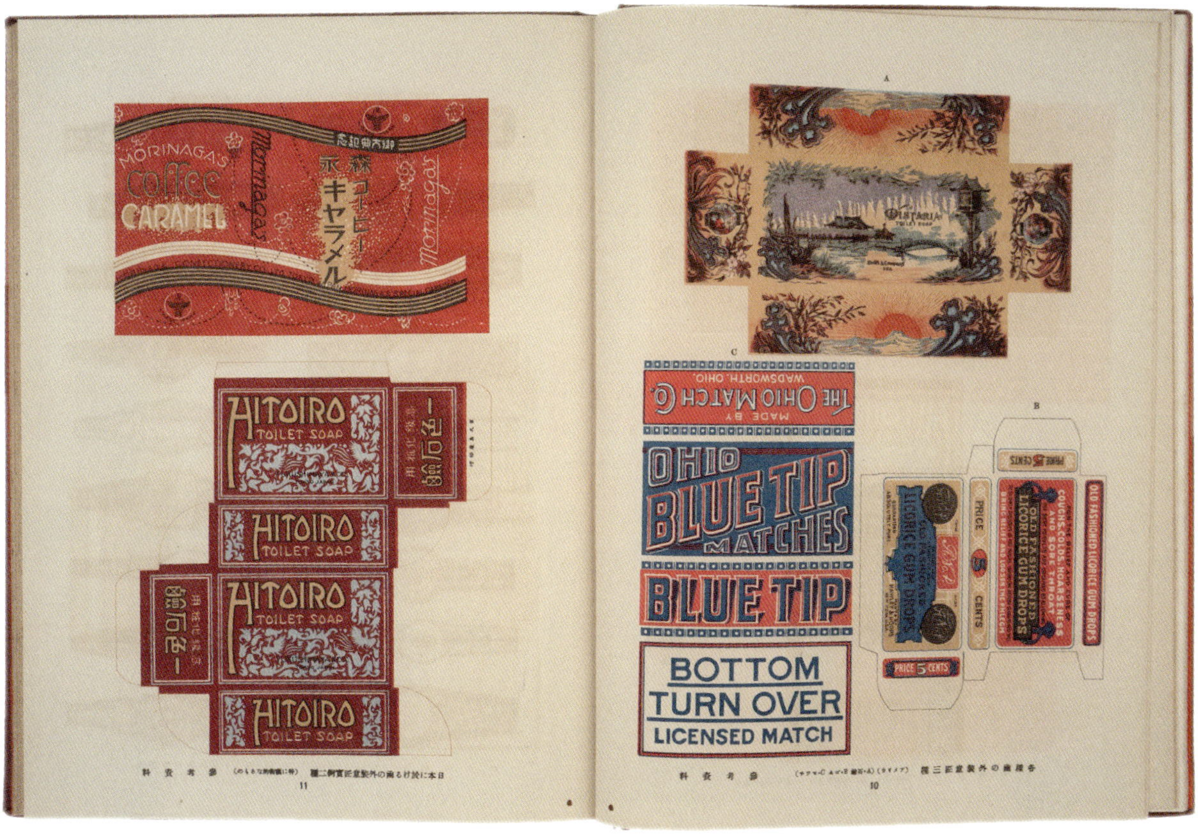

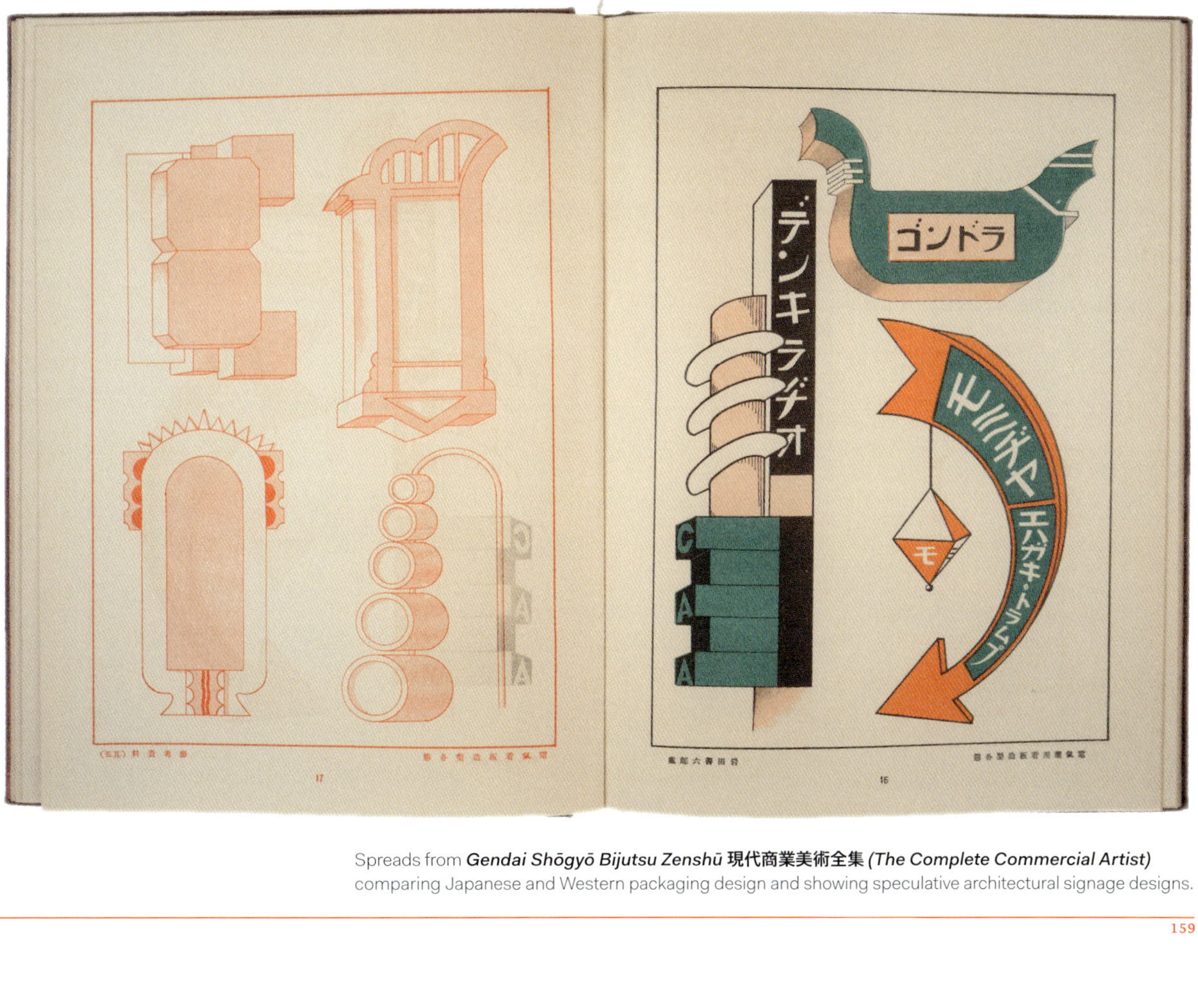

Spreads from ***Gendai Shōgyō Bijutsu Zenshū* 現代商業美術全集 *(The Complete Commercial Artist)*** comparing Japanese and Western packaging design and showing speculative architectural signage designs.

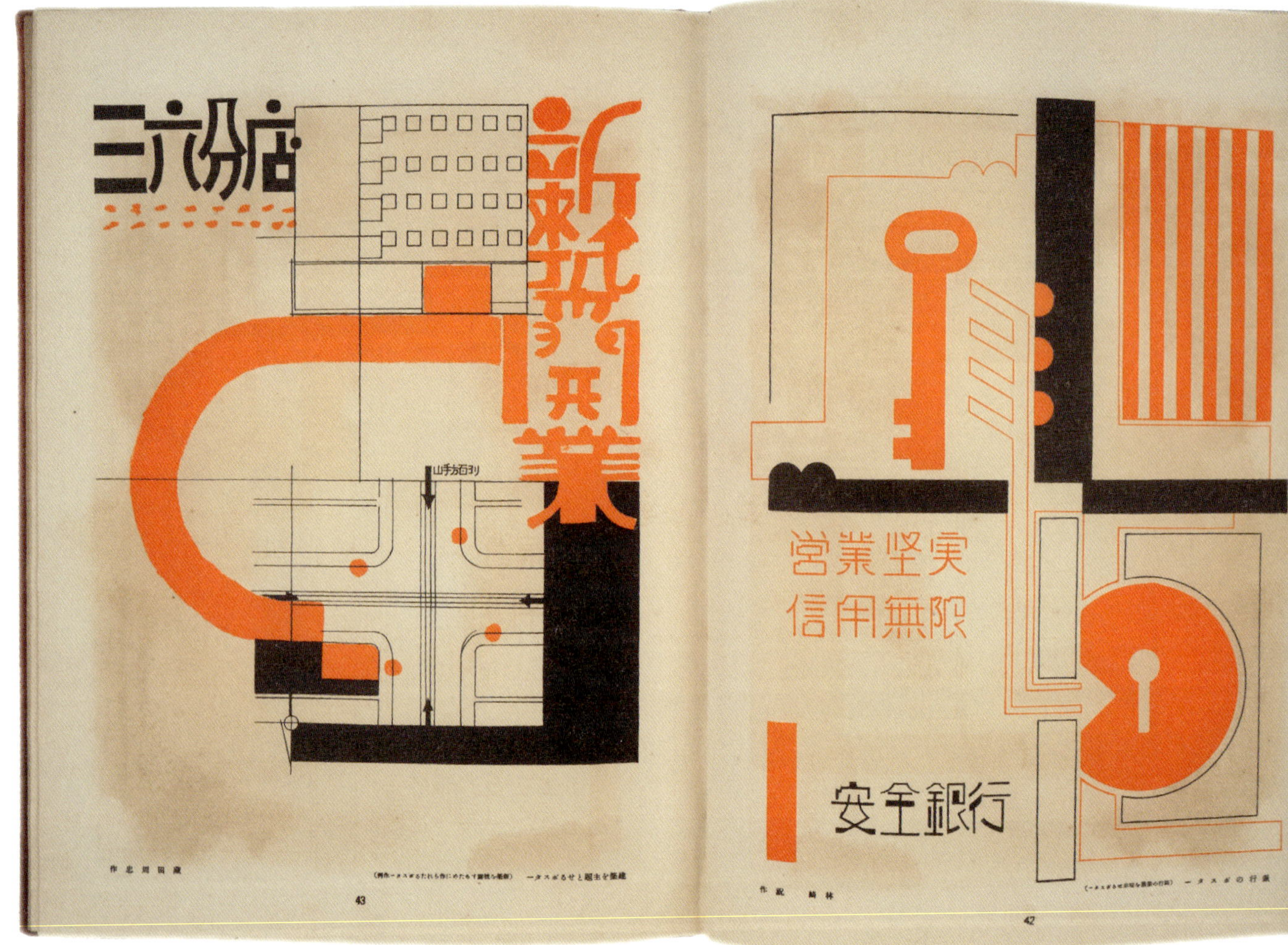

Gendai Shōgyō Bijutsu Zenshū (The Complete Commercial Artist) 現代商業美術全集 Vol. 1–24, edited by Hamada Masuji 濱田増治 and Kitahara Yoshio 北原義雄 (Tokyo: Kabushikigaisha ARS 株式会社アルス, 1928–1930).

An overview of the topics covered in the journal:

Vol. 1 .... Posters from around the world 世界各国ポスター集
Vol. 2 .... Practical poster designs 実用ポスター図案集
Vol. 3 .... Global show window retail display designs 世界模範ショーウヰンドー集
Vol. 4 .... Show window equipment 各種ショーウヰンドー装置集
Vol. 5 .... Show window background collection 各種ショーウィンドー背景集
Vol. 6 .... Signs from around the world 世界各国看板集
Vol. 7 .... Practical sign design 実用看板意匠集
Vol. 8 .... Applied electrical advertising 電気応用広告集
Vol. 9 .... Retail facilities 店頭店内設備集
Vol. 10 .... Street decoration and display 賣出し街頭装飾集
Vol. 11 .... Exhibition display and decoration 出品陳列装飾集
Vol. 12 .... Wrapping paper and package design 包紙·容器意匠図案集
Vol. 13 .... Collected samples of newspaper and magazine advertisements 新聞雑誌広告作例集
Vol. 14 .... Comics and photographs 寫眞及漫畫應用廣告集
Vol. 15 .... Display lettering 図案文字
Vol. 16 .... Practical illustration designs 実用カット図案集
Vol. 17 .... Typographic arrangement, display Lettering and copywriting 文字の配列と文案集
Vol. 18 .... Flyers and labels チラシ·レッテル図案集
Vol. 19 .... New trademarks and monograms 新案商標·モノグラム集
Vol. 20 .... Wrapping paper and package design 包紙·容器意匠図案集
Vol. 21 .... Catalog and pamphlet cover design カタログ·パンフレット表紙図案集
Vol. 22 .... Hobby advertising in Japan 日本趣味広告物集
Vol. 23 .... Latest trends in advertising 最新傾向広告集
Vol. 24 .... Commercial Art Theory 商業美術總論

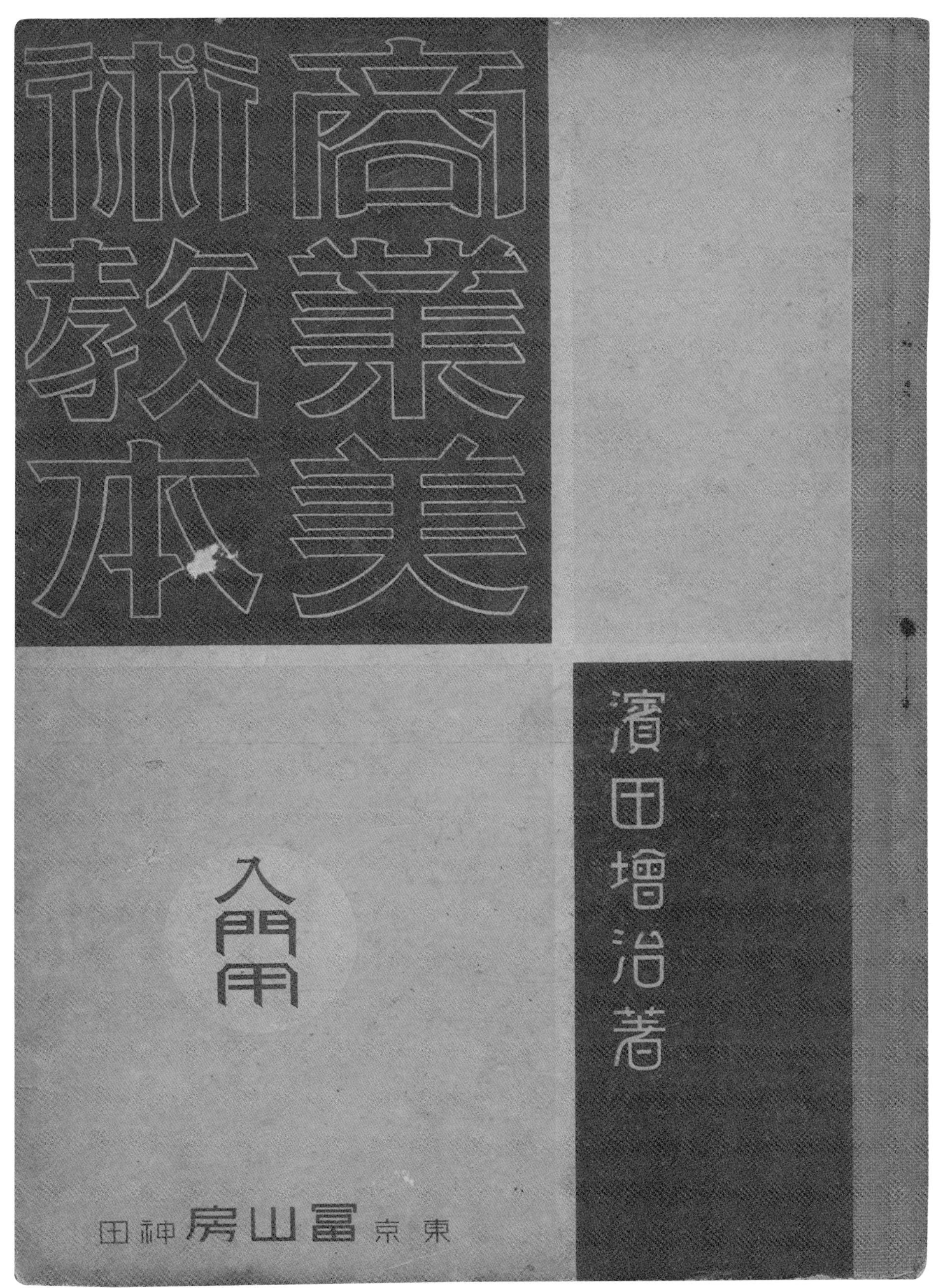

Commercial Art for Advanced Use **商業美術教本**, Hamada Masuji 濱田增治 (Tokyo: Fuzambo 冨山房, 1936).

HIROSE CHIKA 廣瀬千香

1897–1995

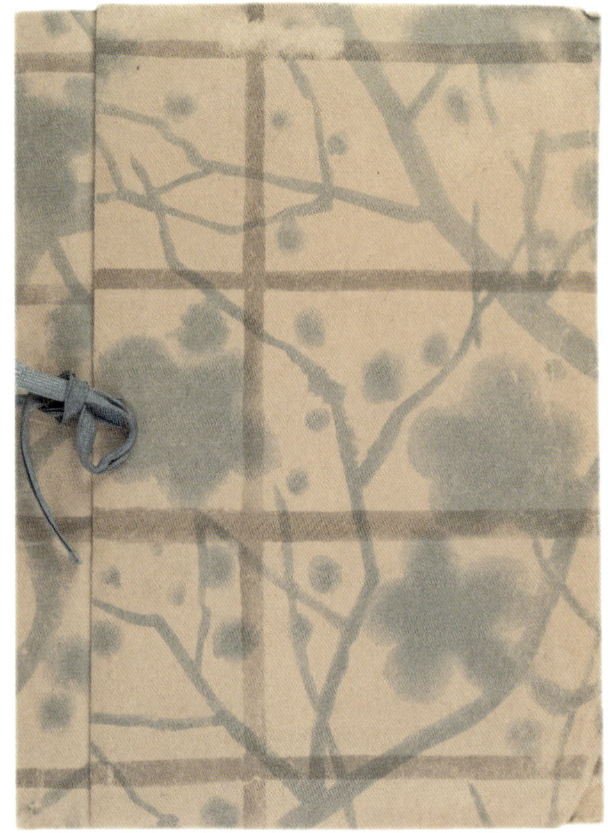

Hirose Chika was born in Yamanashi Prefecture to a family of raw-silk wholesalers. She married sexologist and researcher Kitano Hiromi 北野博美 in 1916. The couple moved to Tokyo and raised three children there for a decade, but they divorced in 1926. Afterward, Hirose moved to Omori and began working as a freelance writer and editor.

In 1931, she co-published the first volume of *Shomotsu Tenbō* 書物展望, a journal dedicated to book design and print culture, with Saitō Shozō 斎藤昌三, who would continue publishing the journal for a number of years. Three years later, she founded her own publishing imprint, Seitonsha 青燈社, publishing a number of memoirs that combined illustration and text.

Hirose also designed a number of book covers for assorted publishers, including the cover of the Japanese translation of Yolande d'Ormesson Arsène-Henry's *Histoire d'Enfants* and *Kokunitei Kokyokushū* 此君亭小曲集：自作肉筆版 色彩入愛蔵本 by Ito Shinsui 伊東深水.

References:
Khori, Junichiro. "An Alternative History of Publishing in Japan 1923–1945: Books Beautiful Truly." *Idea* 60, no. 354 (September 2012): 100–103.

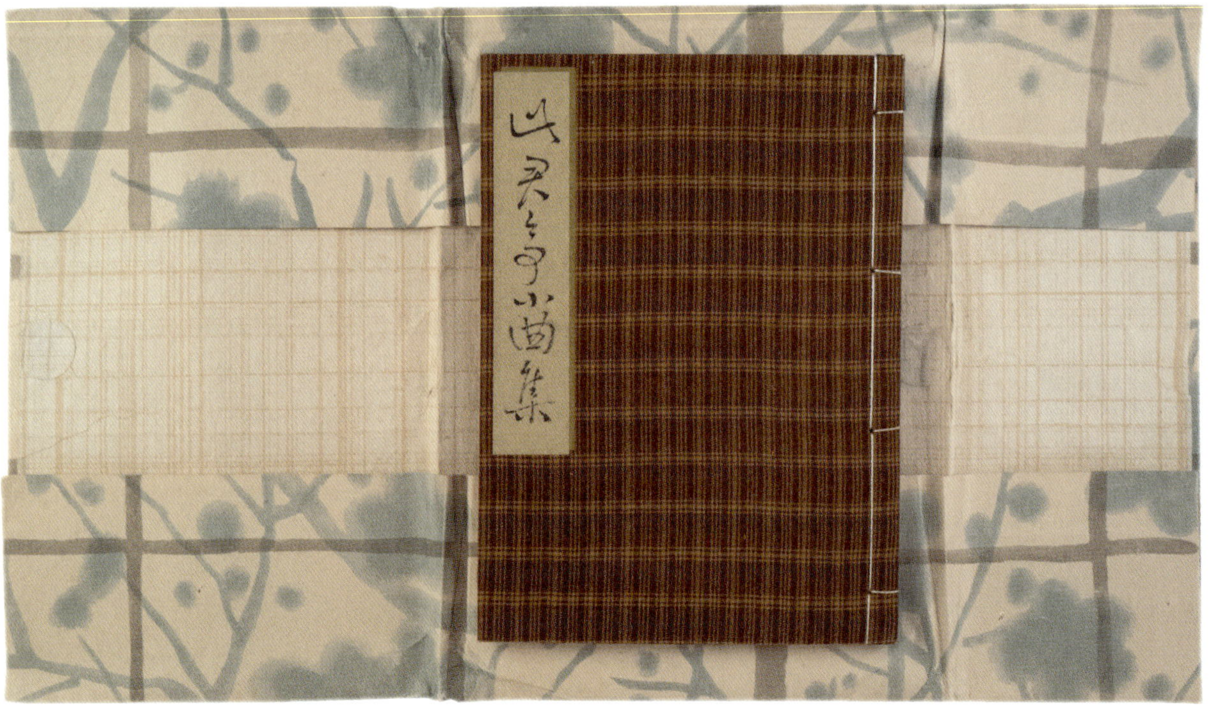

This page and adjacent: ***A Collection of Short Verse* 此君亭小曲集**, Itō Shinsui 伊東深水 著 (Tokyo: Seitonsha 青燈社, 1940).
A beautifully produced, limited-edition book of verse accompanied by illustrations and wrapped in a jacket featuring a flowering plum tree motif filtered through traditional latticed Japanese *shoji* paper screens.

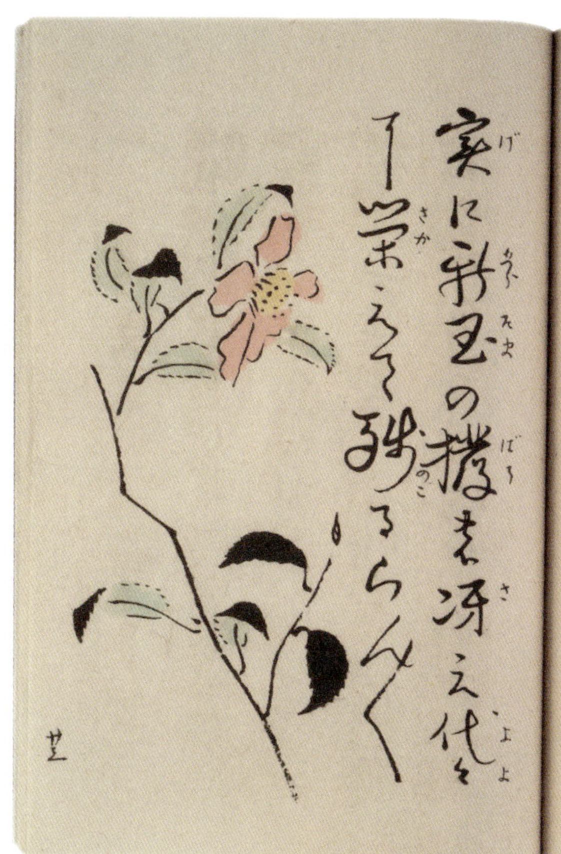

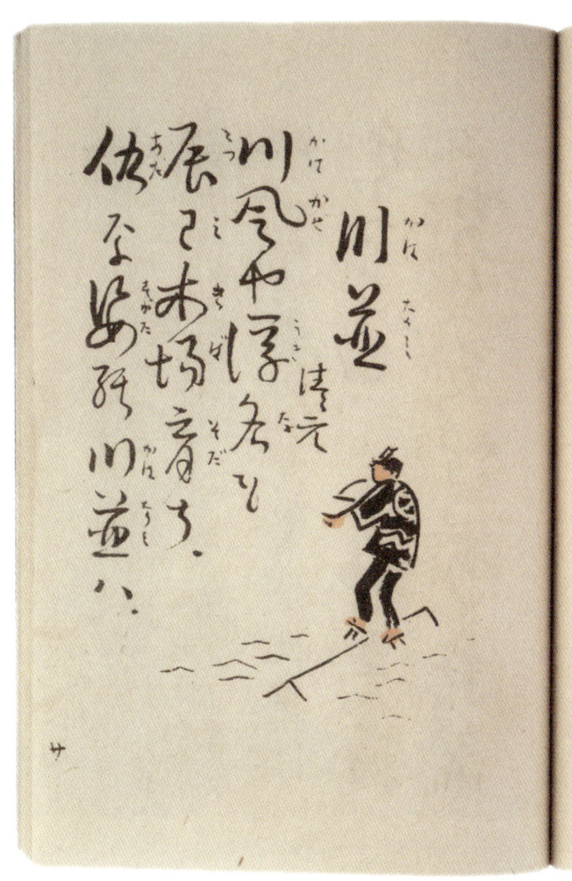

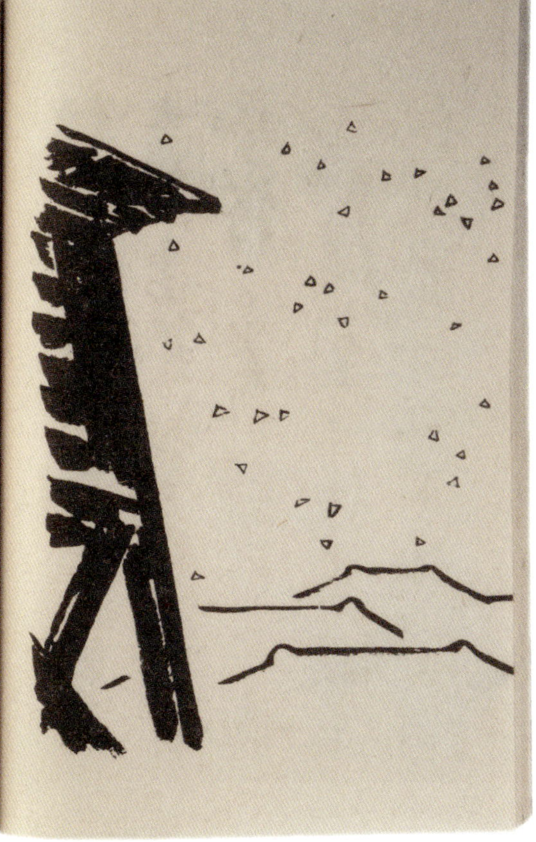

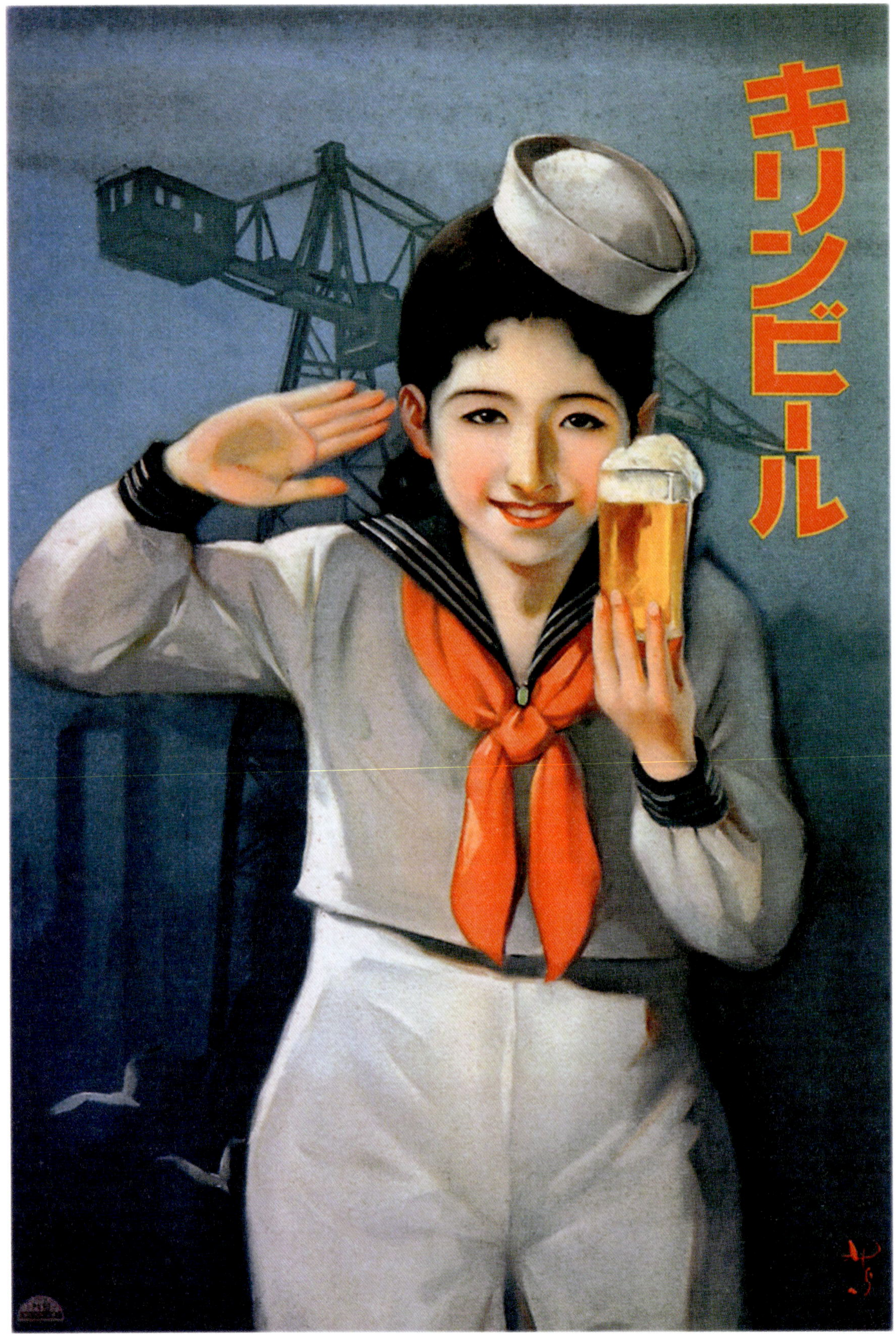

Kirin Beer キリンビール poster, Tada Hokuu 多田北烏 (Tokyo: Kirin Brewery Company 麒麟麦酒株式会社, 1939). Tada's posters for Kirin often incorporated militaristic themes, aligning consumption with militarism.

TADA HOKUU 多田北烏

1889–1948

Tada Hokuu was a prominent poster designer and illustrator who was active throughout much of the Taishō and Shōwa periods. Tada was born in Matsumoto in Nagoya Prefecture and developed a keen interest in painting as a child, studying nihonga as an adolescent. He moved to Tokyo to study painting at age thirteen.

Tada enrolled in the vocational training institution Tokyo High School of Industrial Arts 東京高等工芸学校 at age nineteen and stayed for one term before transferring to the Kawabata Art School 川端美術学校, where he studied Western-style painting under Fujishima Takeji. Tada developed an interest in poster design and joined the Kirin Brewing Company as a poster designer in 1920. For Kirin, Tada primarily designed posters featuring romantic, Western-style depictions of young, attractive women serving or enjoying Kirin Beer, the company's flagship product. Tada's work largely fits into the context of *bijinga*, pictorial representations of beautiful women. The products advertised in his poster designs resonated widely with Japanese consumers, and his design work connected these products to notions of youth and beauty.

Tada Hokuu's posters reflected the aesthetics and fashions of the Showa period, ranging from his bijinga designs to compositions that depicted families, coworkers, and lively parties, all using a shallow depth of field to highlight the product advertised and imbuing Kirin Beer with a atmosphere of desire. Many of his Kirin posters utilized a hazy, French-Impressionist approach to rendering human subjects, with the images of products being much more sharply defined in contrast.

In 1922, Tada established a pioneering commercial art studio called Sun Studio サン·スタジオ and began taking on commissions. The following year, Tada began designing and illustrating the covers for the incredibly popular women's magazine *Shufu no Tomo* 主婦の友. *Shufu no Tomo*'s editors upheld a conservative aesthetic stance toward their lower-middle-class female readership for a number of years. Tada was encouraged to create covers featuring women clad in traditional Japanese dress until 1927, when he was allowed to render women dressed in Western clothing, reflecting Japan's modernization and widespread adoption of Western fashion.

Tada established the Commercial Art Association alongside Hamada Masuji, Sugiura Hisui, and others in 1926. Together, the group published the *Gendai Shōgyō Bijutsu Zenshū* 現代商業美術全集 *(The Complete Commercial Artist)* and led popular conceptions of commercial art in the late 1920s. Tada contributed masterful studies of poster design and illustration to the journal, examining global notions of contemporary design at that time.

Tada was also the co-founder of both the Domestic Printing Art Association 実用版画美術協会 and the National Commercial Art Association 全日本商業美術連盟, in which he was the leader of a design research group called the Japan Poster Association 日本ポスター作家協会.

In the lead-up to and during World War II, Tada worked as an illustrator and designer for children's books alongside his continued work for women's magazines, creating a wide variety of illustrated stories promoting the alliance of Germany and Japan and their occupied territories, battle victories, and Japan's annexation of Manchuria.

In 1948, Tada died at the age of fifty-nine in Numazu in Shizuoka Prefecture due to gastrointestinal illness. His work continues to be popular in Japan, with the Kirin Brewing Company reprinting his poster designs to evoke nostalgia for the Showa period. Tada Hokuu's posters can be found in bars and *izakaya* (Japanese-style pubs) across Japan today.

References:

Hamada, Masuji, ed. *Gendai shōgyō Bijutsu zenshū*. 1st ed. 12 vols. Tokyo: ARS, 1930.

Hamada, Masuji. *Shōgyō Bijutsu Kyohon Nyumon'yo Kaisetsu*. Tokyo: Fuzanbo, 1938.

Itoi, Shigesato. "Horiuchi-san." Hobo Nikkan Itoi Shinbun, January 4, 2017. https://www.1101.com/horiuchi.

Takehara, Akiko, and Akiko Moriyama. *Nihon Dezainshi: karāban*. Tokyo: Bijutsu Shuppansha, 2003.

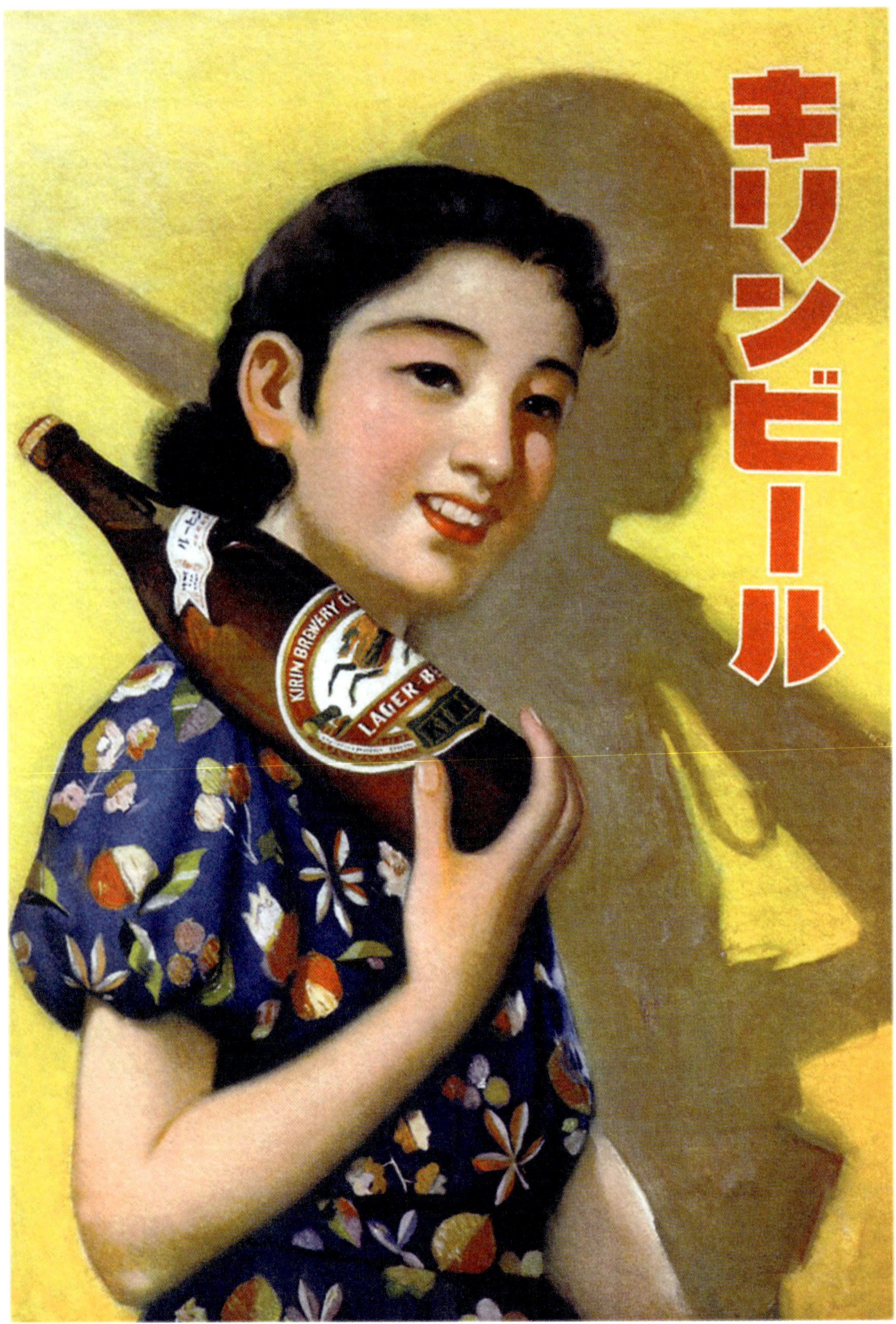

Kirin Beer キリンビール poster, Tada Hokuu 多田北烏 (Tokyo: Kirin Brewery Company 麒麟麦酒株式会社, 1939). Another of Tada's militaristic promotional posters for Kirin—the shadow cast by the young woman resting a bottle of Kirin on her shoulder is of a soldier bearing a rifle.

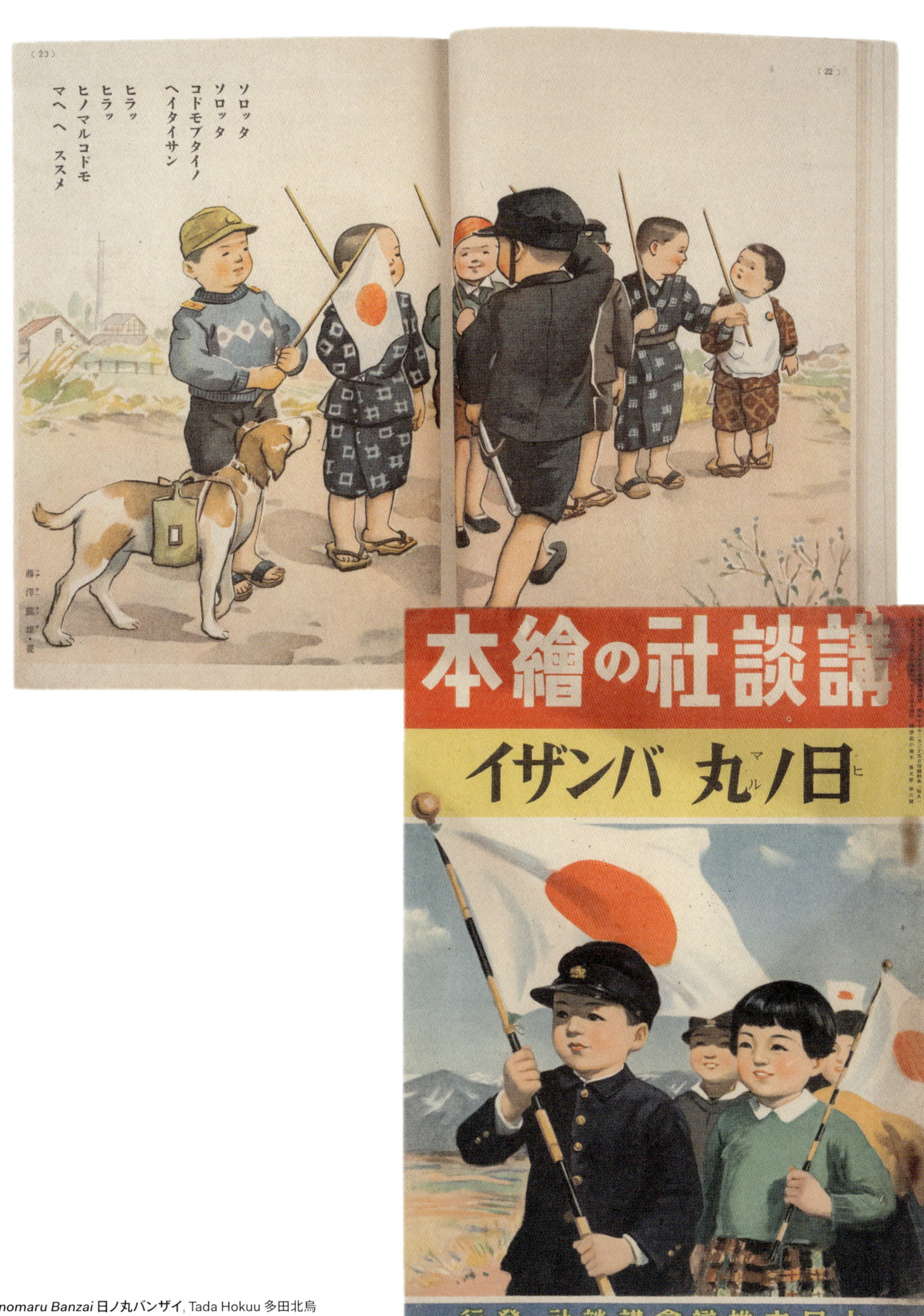

Hinomaru Banzai 日ノ丸バンザイ, Tada Hokuu 多田北烏 (Tokyo: Kodansha 講談社, 1942). A children's propaganda book encouraging patriotism and discipline.

コドモノクニ

秋ノ増刊

武井武雄

童画集

第1輯

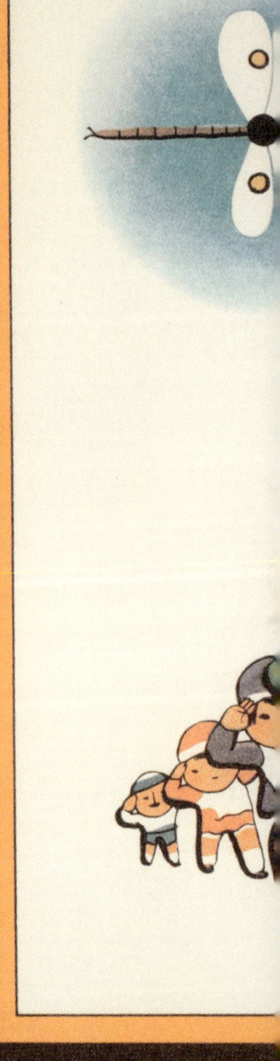

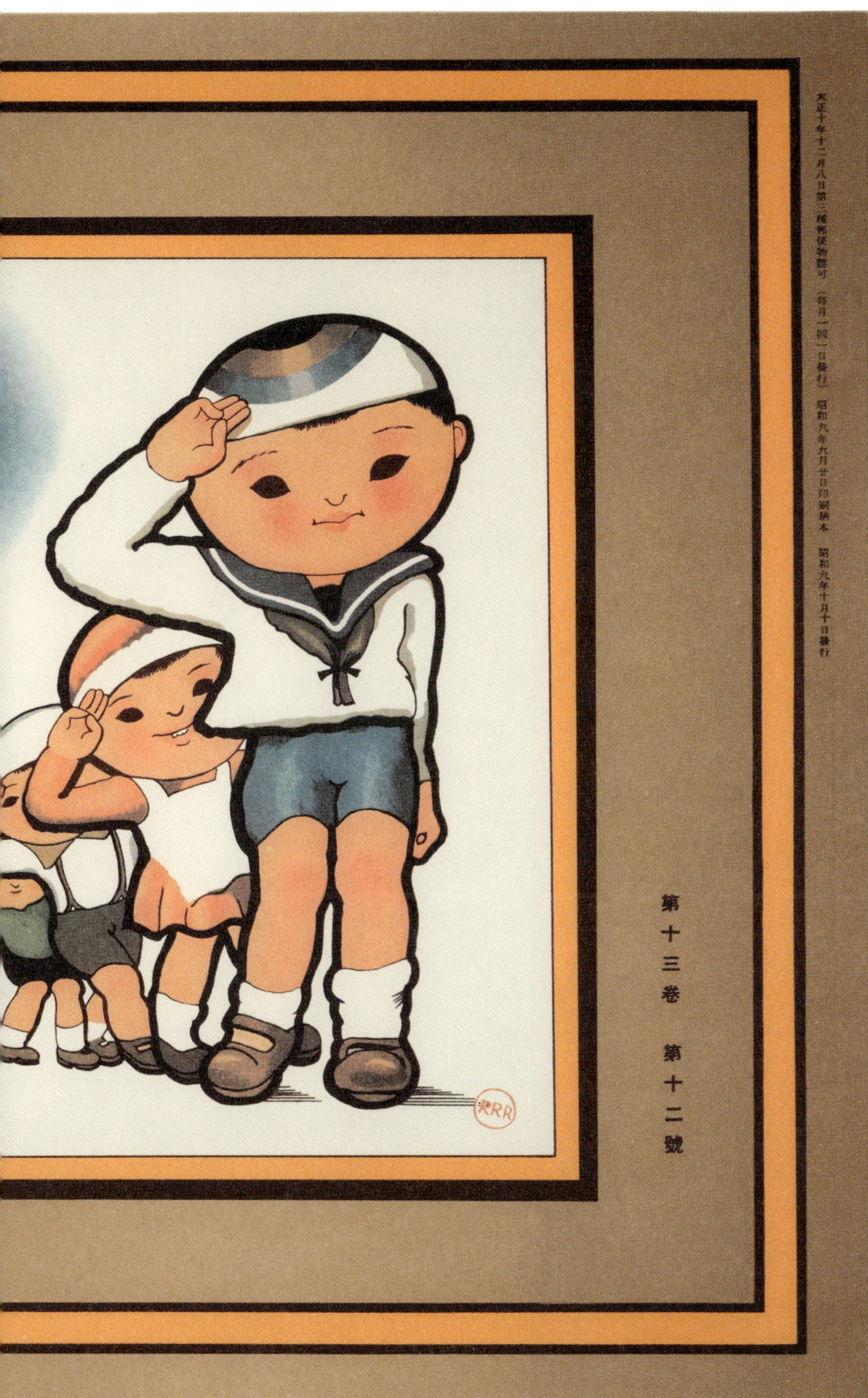

Takeo Takei cover design for *Kodomo no kuni* コドモノクニ published by Tokyosha 東京社 in Tokyo. Of note are the multiple forms of display lettering in use on the cover of this children's magazine.

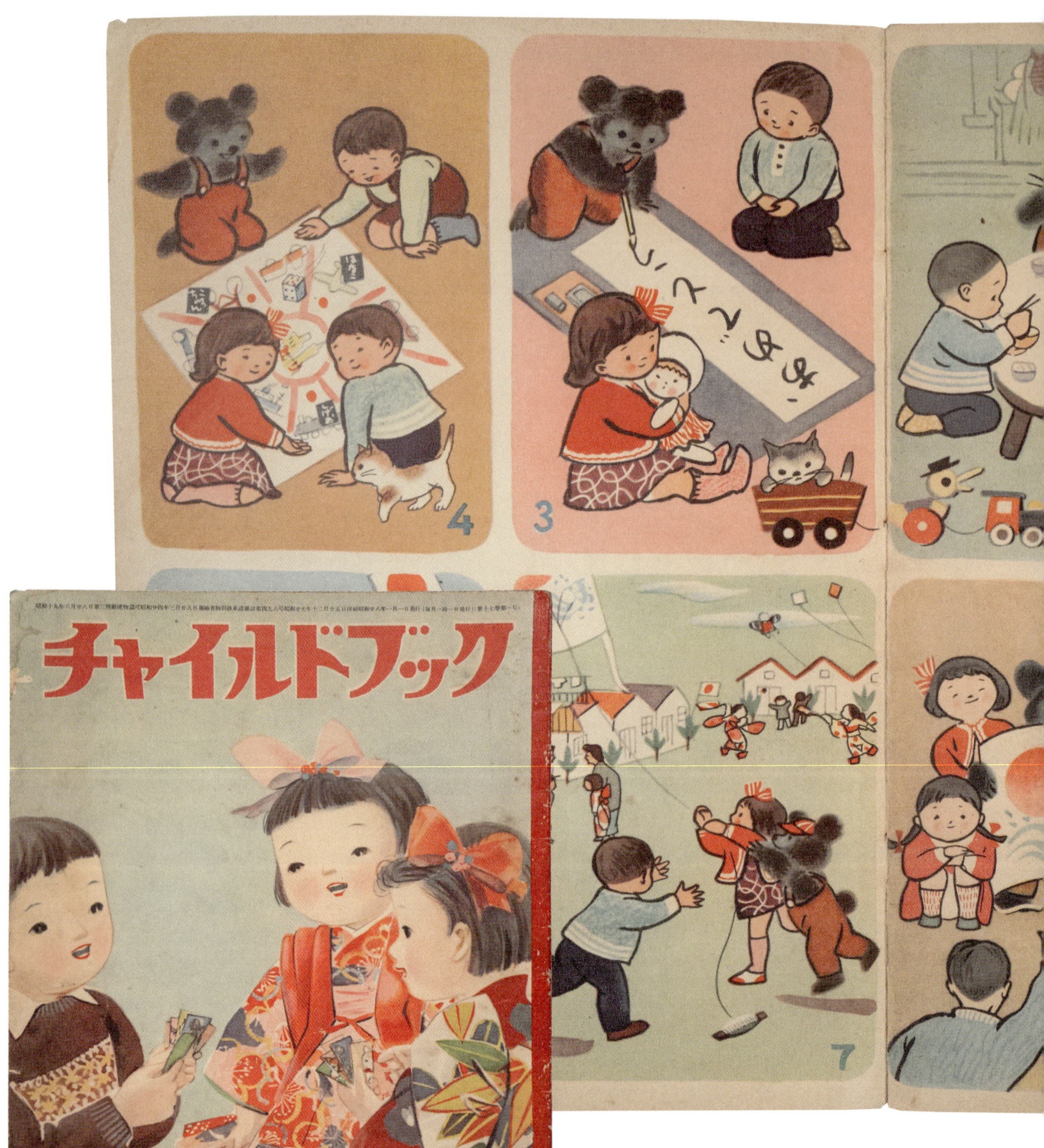

Child Book Vol. 17, No. 1 チャイルドブック 第17巻第1号, Kokumin Toshokankōkai 国民図書刊行会, Takei Takeo 武井武雄 (Tokyo: Kokumin toshokankōkai 国民図書刊行会, 1953).

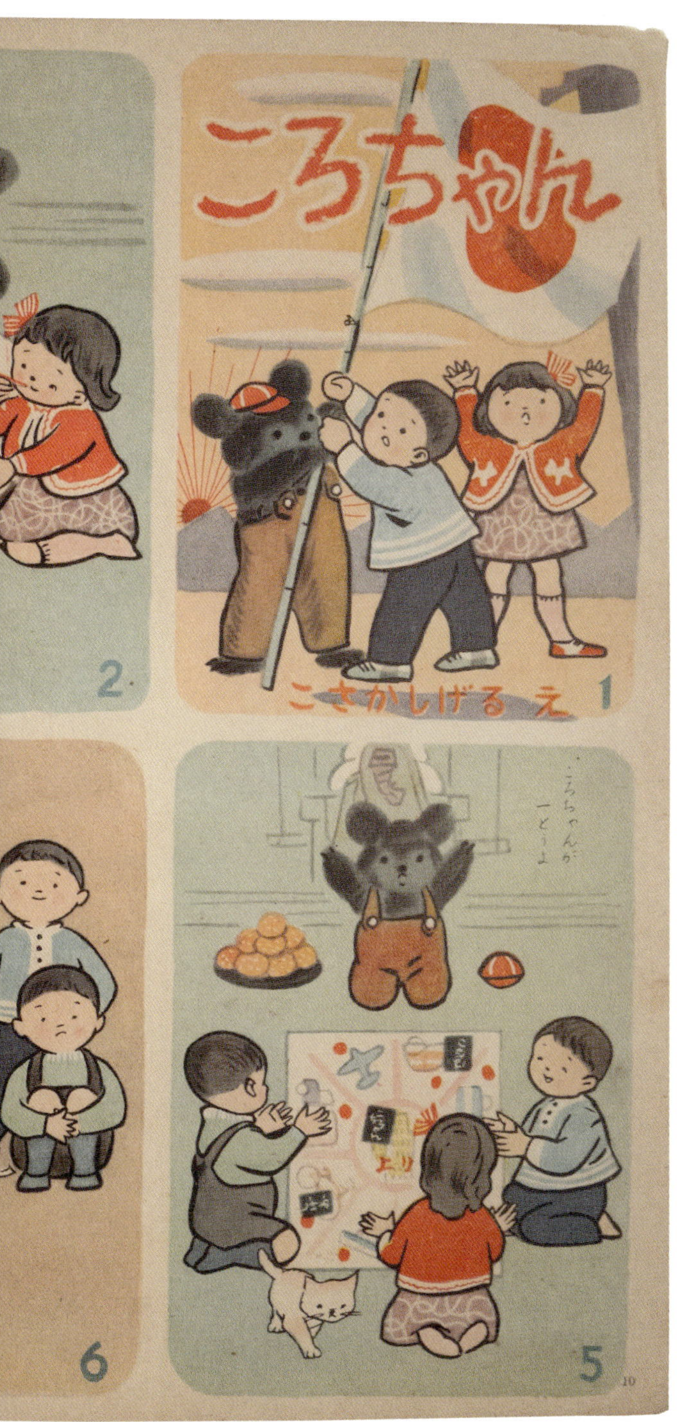

TAKEI TAKEO 武井武雄

1894–1983

Takei Takeo was born in Nagano Prefecture and studied Western painting at Tokyo Art School (now Tokyo University of the Arts). He was the cover illustrator, lettering artist, and designer for the magazine *Kodomo no Kuni* コドモノクニ from its inception in 1922. Takei created the neologism *dōga* 童画 ("pictures of children") in 1925 to help explain painting and illustration for children in their formative years, especially through fairy tales and children's literature.

Takei worked on numerous freelance projects across illustration, graphic design, and editorial design throughout his lengthy career. He both wrote and illustrated his own stories, historic Japanese folktales, and other original fairy tales by Japanese writers such as Miyazawa Kenji 宮沢賢治. Takei co-founded and led the Japan Association of Illustration for Children 日本動画協会 (Nihon Dōga Kyōkai) in 1927 until it dissolved in 1941 due to the war, then reestablished the organization in 1962.

From 1935 until his death in 1983, Takei had both designed and coordinated over 139 book projects, overseeing the printing, paper selection, and editing, and heralding each design into print. His oeuvre included an amazing range of book designs including books housed in transparent sleeves, books housed in electroplated boxes with brass ornamentation, and everyday books. He was both a masterful illustrator and lettering artist.

References:

ILF Douga Museum. *Takei Takeo no Hon: dōga to Gurafikku no ōsama*. Tokyo: Heibonsha, 2014.

Kobayashi, Mari. *Gaka No Bukku Dezain: sōtei to sōga Kara Miru Nihon no Honzukuri no rūtsu*. Tokyo: Seibundō Shinkōsha, 2018.

Shuri, Yuki, and Shinju Onuki. *Kakimoji no Dezain*. Tokyo: Graphic-sha, 2017.

Takei, Takeo. *Hon to Sono Shuhen*. Tokyo: Chūōkoronshuppansha, 1960.

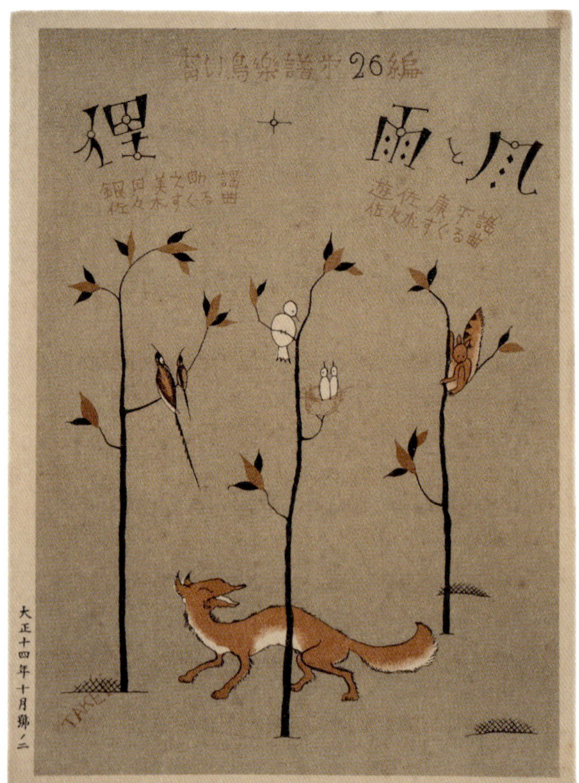

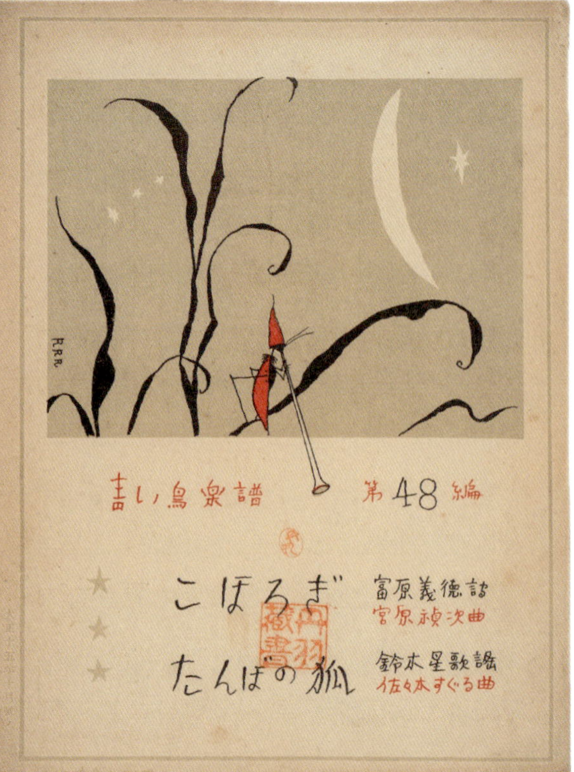

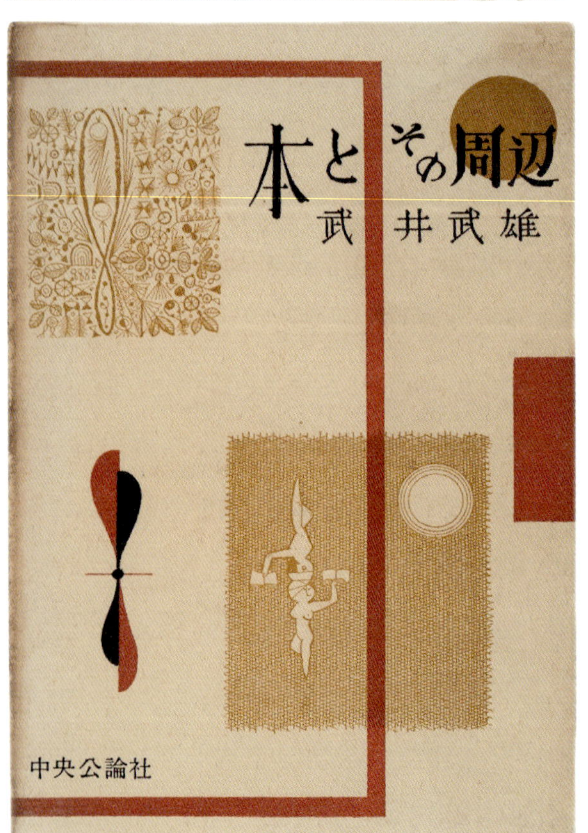

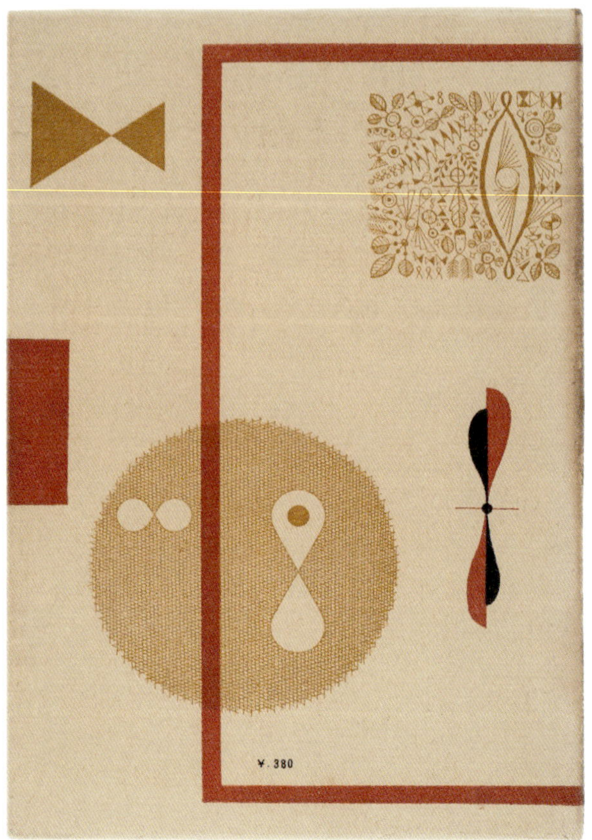

Top: front and back covers of ***Blue Bird Sheet Music Vol. 48, "Kohorogi Tambo no Kitsune" (The Fox in the Rice Field)* 青い鳥楽譜 第48篇 こほろぎ たんぼの狐**, Sasaki Hide 佐々木英編, Tokyo: Sasaki Suguru 佐々木すぐる, 1926). Designed by Takei Takeo 武井武雄. Bottom: front and back covers of ***Books and Their Surroundings* 武井武雄 本とその周辺**, Takei Takeo 武井武雄, (Tokyo: Chuokoron-sha 中央公論社, 1950).

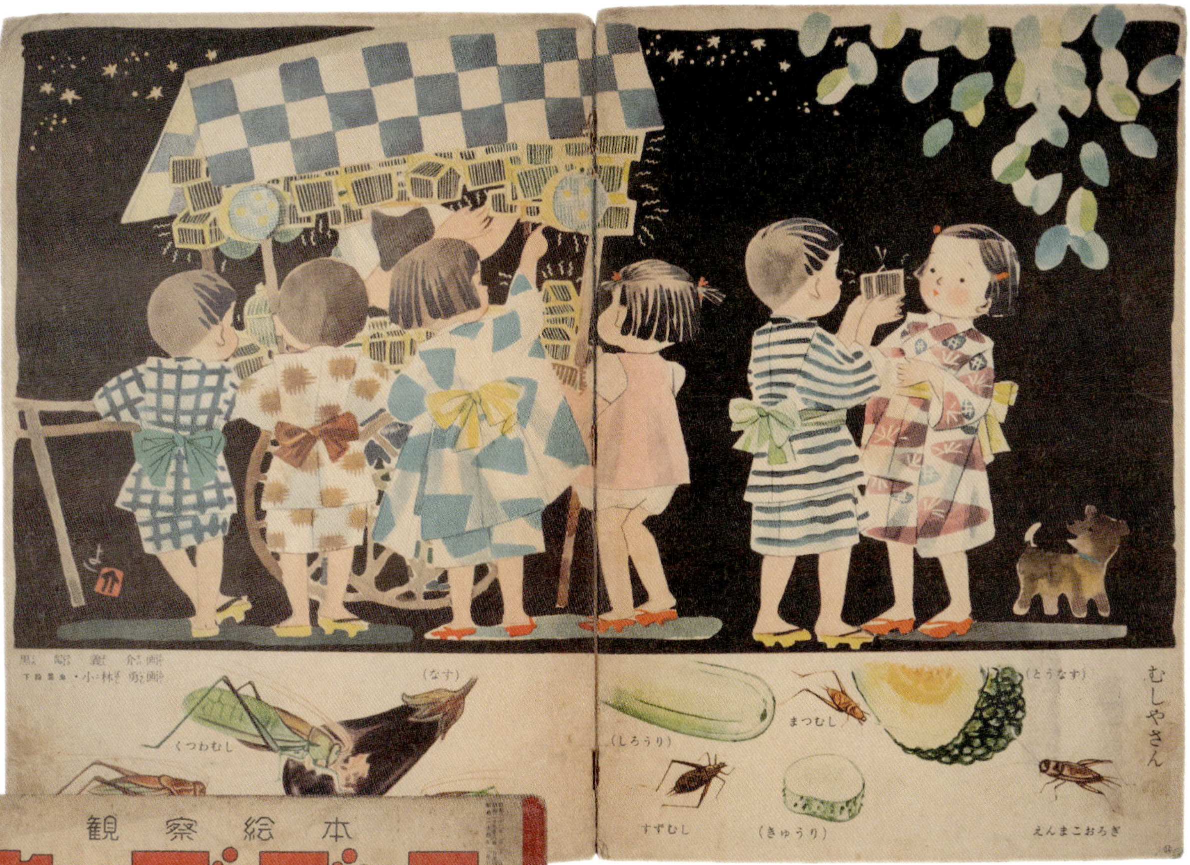

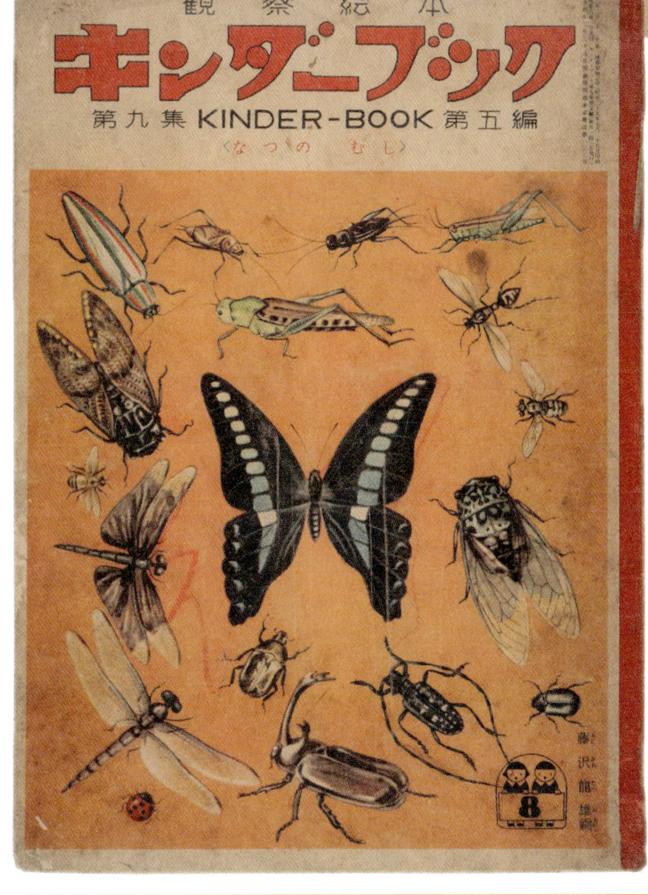

Kinder Book (Natsumushi) **キンダーブック (なつのむし)**, Takei Takeo 武井武雄 (Tokyo: Froebel-kanフレーベル館, August 1954). Designed by Takei Takeo 武井武雄.

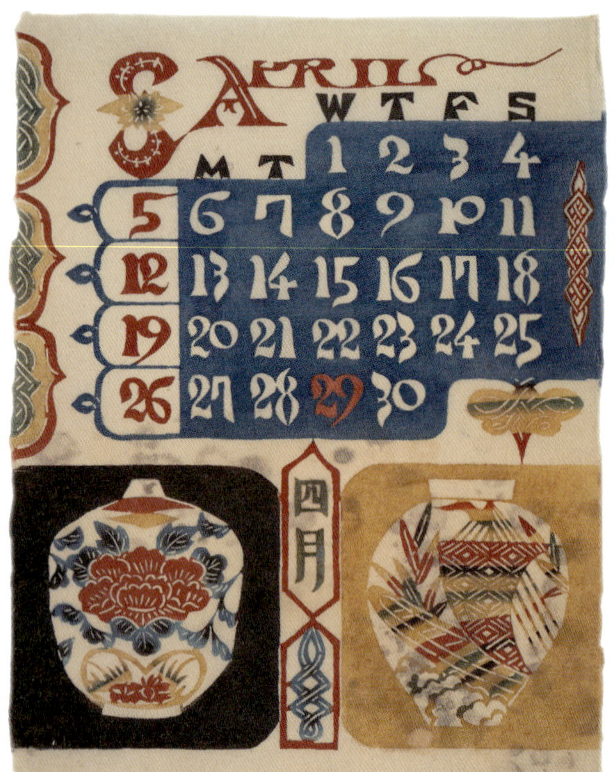

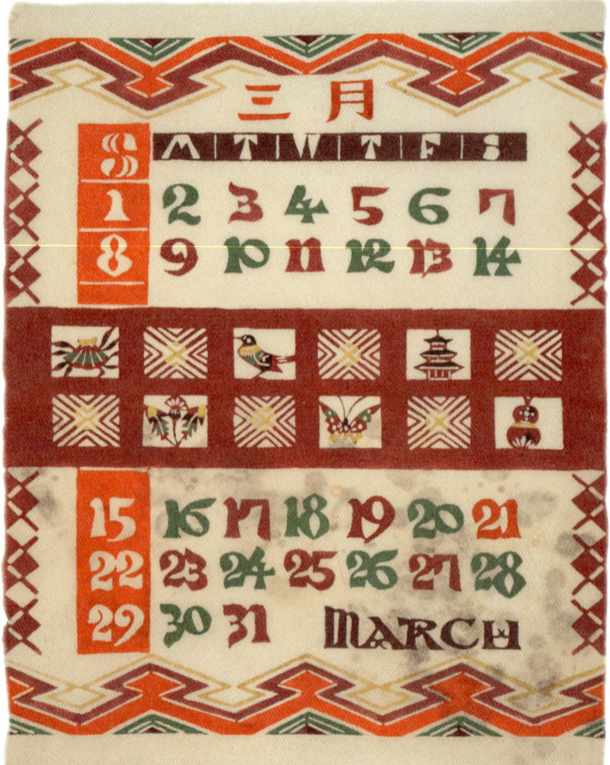

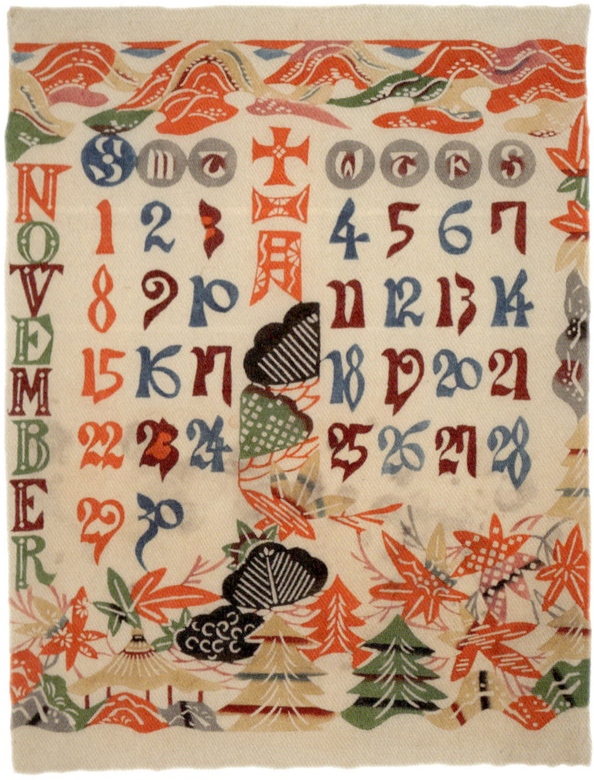

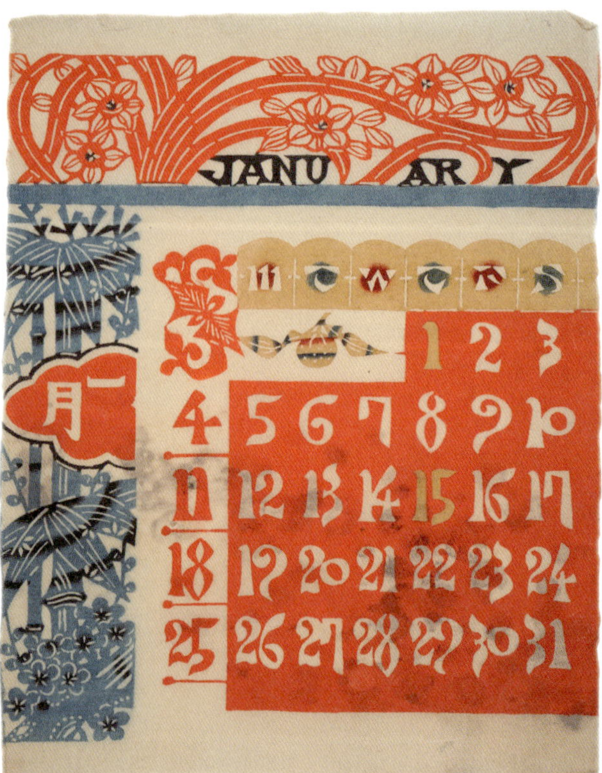

Katazome-dyed 1959 calendar* 芹沢銈介型染カレンダー *1959, **Serizawa Keisuke 芹澤銈介 (Shizuoka: Serizawa Paper Dyeing Institute 芹沢染紙研究所, 1959).** One of Serizawa's celebrated multicolor annual calendar designs printed using *katazome*, a method of dyeing papers (and fabrics, traditionally) using a resist paste applied through a stencil, similar to screenprinting. The calendar is printed on relatively thick *washi* paper.

Kōgei (Craft) 工芸 No. 116: Dyeing and paper pattern, 工藝 百十六号 染絵と型紙, 芹澤銈介, Yasushibunsha 靖文社 Tokyo: 1947.
Cover design by Serizawa Keisuke 芹澤銈介 printed using the *katazome* resist dyeing technique.

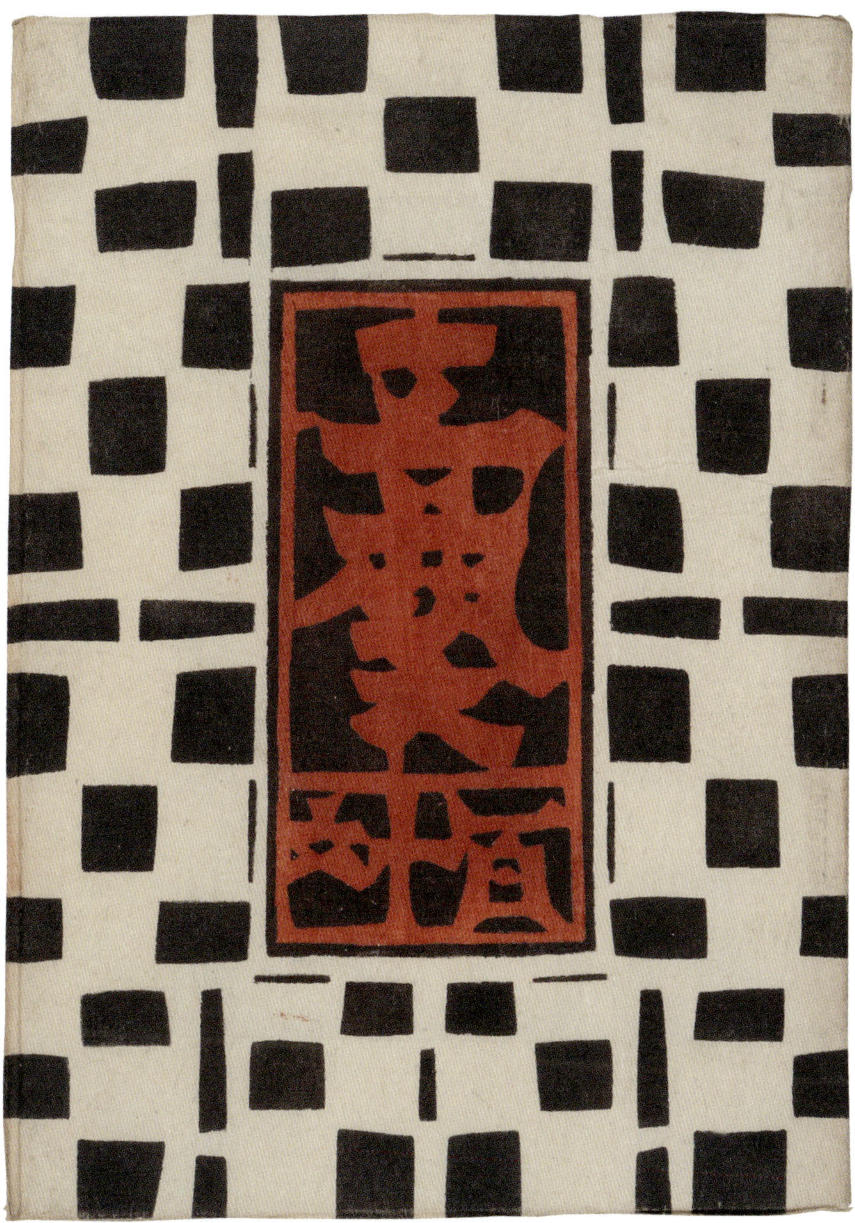

SERIZAWA KEISUKE 芹沢銈介

1895–1984

Serizawa Keisuke was born in 1895 in Shizuoka. In 1956, he was designated as a Living National Treasure by the Japanese government due to his skill at assorted forms of fabric dyeing. Serizawa was a prominent figure in the Mingei 民芸 Japanese folk crafts movement, which he joined in 1927 after meeting Mingei co-founder Yanagi Sōetsu.

Serizawa is best known for his fabric-dyeing works, including book covers and fabric wall hangings that he created using a glue-resist method of dyeing, though he worked designing books, illustrations, and posters using more traditional design methods, as well. Serizawa developed his own technique of resist dyeing for both designing and printing books, integrating the design and production process. His hand-cut stencil works utilize dramatically serifed letterforms, arabesque numerals, and ornamentation that is integral to the compositional structure. He exhibited internationally, briefly taught in San Diego, and has a museum dedicated to his work in Shizuoka.

References:

Kobayashi, Mari. *Gaka no Bukku Dezain: sōtei to sōga Kara Miru Nihon no Honzukuri no rūtsu*. Tokyo: Seibundō Shinkōsha, 2018.

Shuri, Yuki, and Shinju Onuki. *Kakimoji no Dezain*. Tokyo: Graphic-sha, 2017.

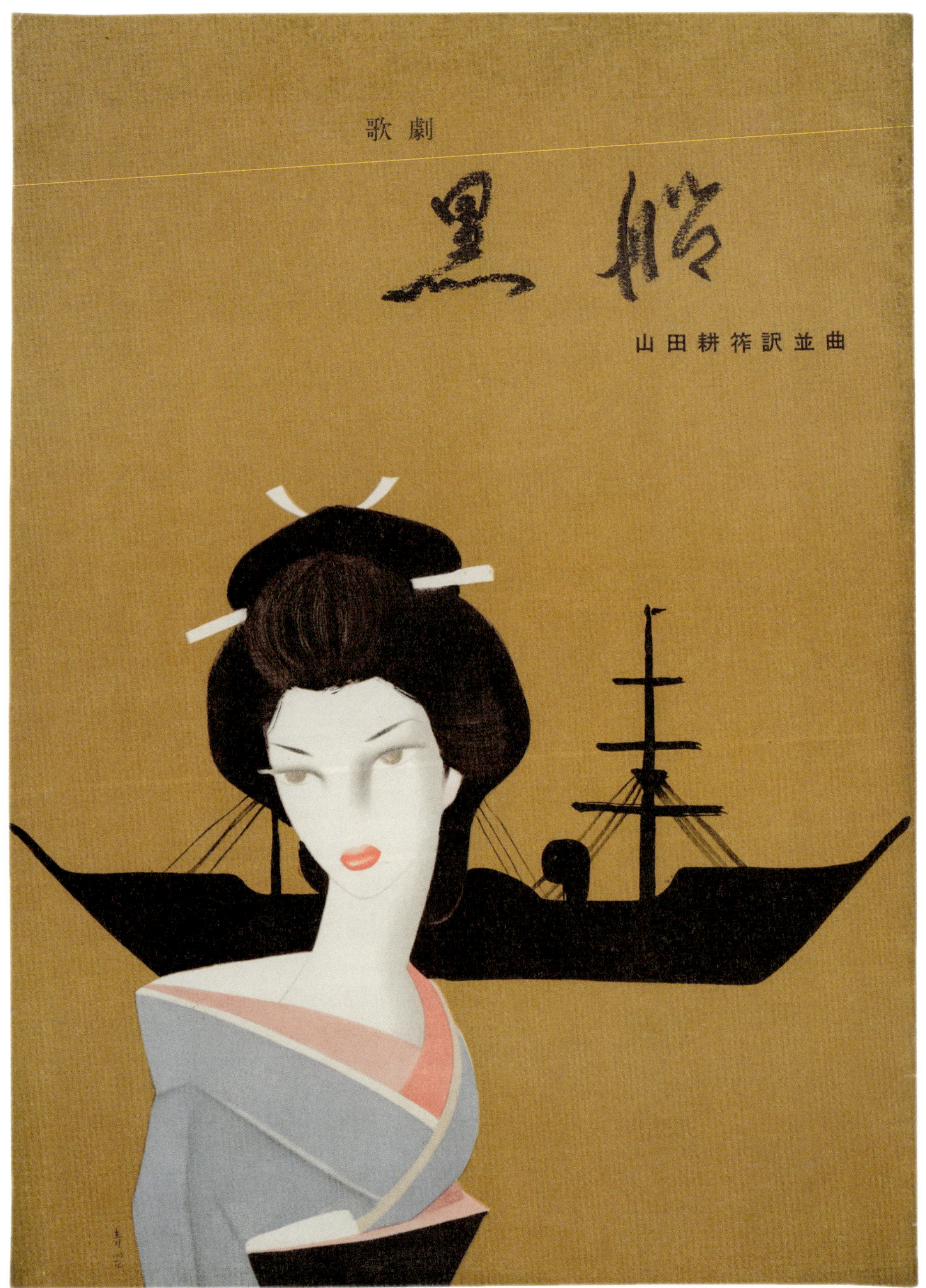

Opera Kurofune Japan Music Drama Association 10th Performance **歌劇 黒船 日本楽劇協会第十回公演 日比谷公会堂** (Tokyo: Hibiya Public Hall, 1954). Cover design by Tōgō Seiji 東郷青児, who often utilized a variety of gradation techniques to render his subjects.

TŌGŌ SEIJI 東郷青児

1897–1978

Tōgō Seiji (born Tōgō Tetsuharu 東郷鉄春) was a Japanese painter, illustrator, and occasional designer known for his abstract depictions of women. Born in Kagoshima Prefecture, he studied at Aoyama Gakuin University and became a frequent visitor to Takehisa Yumeji's Minato-ya shop, seeking guidance and mentorship for his artwork. The mentorship would sour when the seventeen-year-old Tōgō fell in love with Yumeji's ex-wife, Kishi Tamaki, fifteen years his senior. An enraged Yumeji, knife in hand, would threaten them sufficiently to end Tōgō and Kishi's relationship. Romantic dissonance became a hallmark of Tōgō's career—his reputation as a veritable lothario was just as popular as his stunning visual work.

Tōgō exhibited his first solo show at Hibiya Art Museum in 1915 at the age of eighteen. The following year, he won the Nika Award for a painting in the 3rd Nika Exhibition, the first of many awards he would win from the organization. Tōgō married heiress Nagano Akiyo 永野明代 in 1920, and the couple moved to France in 1921 so that he might study at the École des Beaux-Arts. In 1924, Tōgō worked as a designer of decorative arts at the Galeries Lafayette department store in Paris and its branch in Nice. While in Europe, Tōgō spent time with the Dadaists Tristan Tzara and Philippe Soupault and with Futurist leader Filippo Tommaso Marinetti.

Upon his return to Japan in 1928, Tōgō worked as a freelance designer and artist. He began an extramarital love affair with Nishizaki Mitsuko 西崎みつ子, which ended in a failed double-suicide attempt. Afterward, he would participate in a marriage ceremony with another heiress, Nakamura Shuko 中村修子, despite not being divorced from his previous wife, and the new relationship ended abruptly as a result.

Tōgō's fatalistic romantic exploits attracted another suitor, publisher Uno Chiyo 宇野千代, founder of the magazine *Style* スタイル, for which Tōgō would create numerous cover designs. Uno wrote a fictionalized account of Tōgō's torrid past in her book *Confessions of Love* 色ざんげ, though she would also marry him afterward and they would stay together for a handful of years. Tōgō later married Nishizaki Mitsuko 西崎みつ子, the woman he'd attempted suicide with years earlier, to whom he would remain married until his death.

Throughout the 1930s, Tōgō worked on book cover designs, magazine illustration, and fine art projects, particularly mural painting, which would become one of his primary focuses. His romanticized images of women are still used on a number of Tokyo confectionery companies' packaging today, including Takase, Mont-Blanc, and Flammarion, ghosts of the scores of projects that he designed for sweets companies while alive, including wrapping paper designs for assorted bakeries.

Like Yumeji, leading artist and bohemian of the Taishō era, Tōgō kept visual romanticism alive well into the Shōwa era—his renderings of women focused on the eyes just as much as those of his early hero.

References:

Kobayashi, Mari. *Gaka no Bukku Dezain: sōtei to sōga Kara Miru Nihon no Honzukuri no rūtsu*. Tokyo: Seibundō Shinkōsha, 2018.

Nozaki, Izumi. *Tōgō Seiji: Ao no Shi Eien No Otometachi*. Tokyo: Kawadeshobōshuppansha, 2009.

Tanaka, Jō. *Kokoro Sabishiki Kyojin Tōgō Seiji*. Tokyo: Shinchōsha, 1983.

Togo, Seiji, and Izumi Nozaki. *Ren'aitan: Togo Seiji Bunpitsu Senshu*. Tokyo: Sogensha, 2018.

Tōgō, Seiji. *Tōgō Seiji: Tagon muyō*. Tokyo: Nihon Tosho Sentā, 1999.

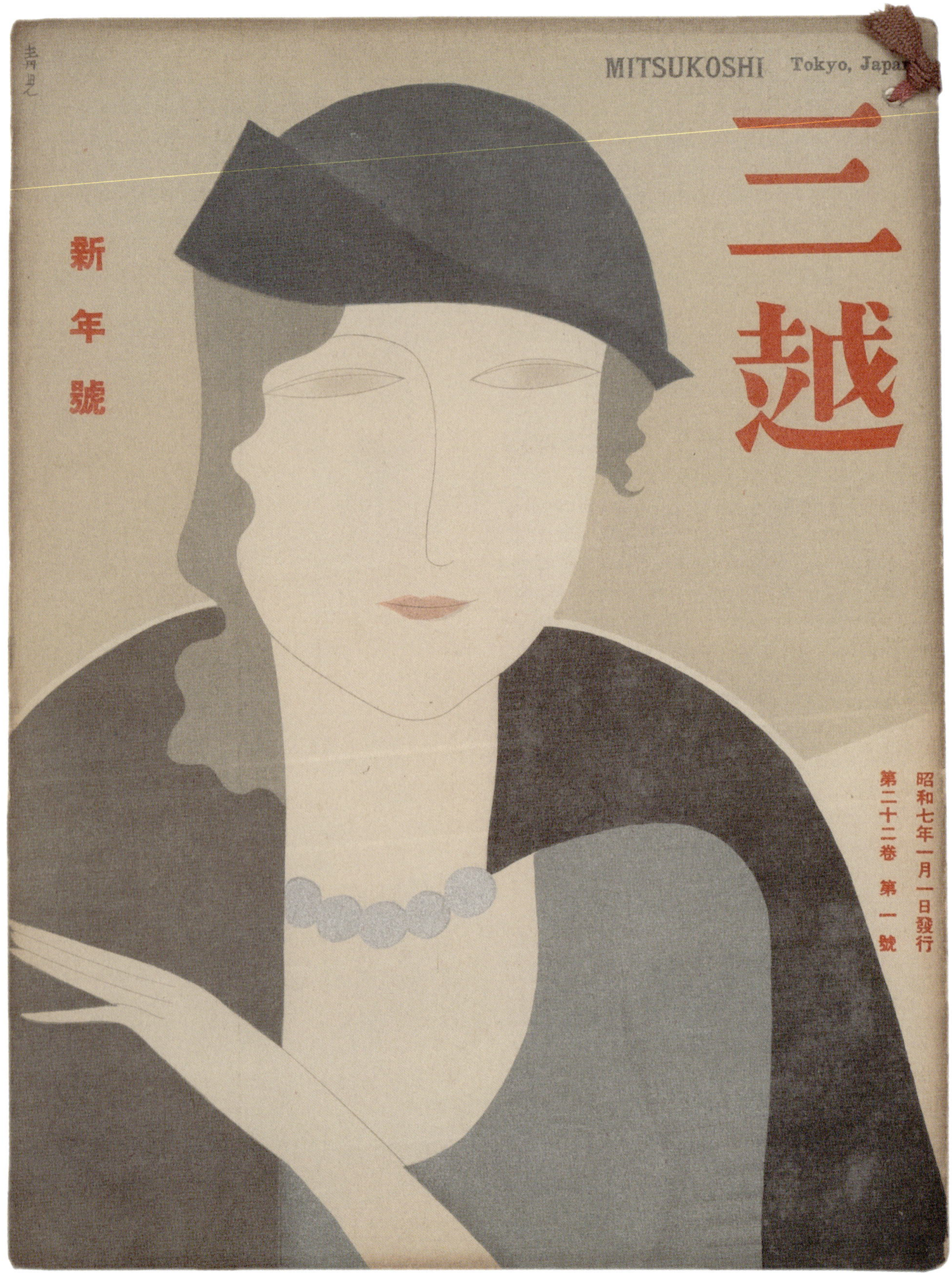

Mitsukoshi 三越 cover (Tokyo: Mitsukoshi 三越, 1932). Cover design by Tōgō Seiji 東郷青児.

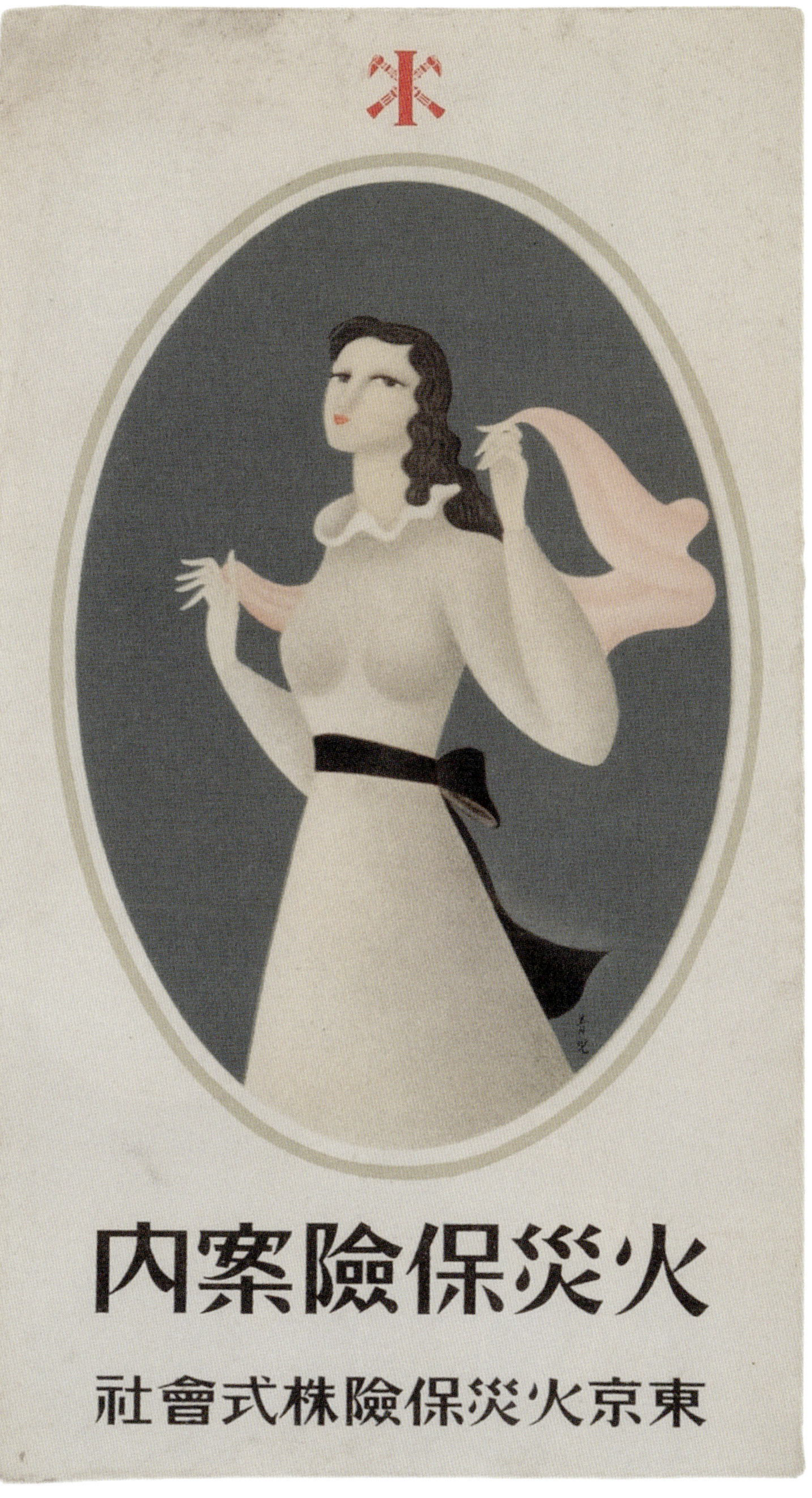

Fire insurance information pamphlet **火災保険案内**, Tokyo Fire Insurance Company 東京火災保険株式会社, undated. Cover design by Tōgō Seiji 東郷青児.

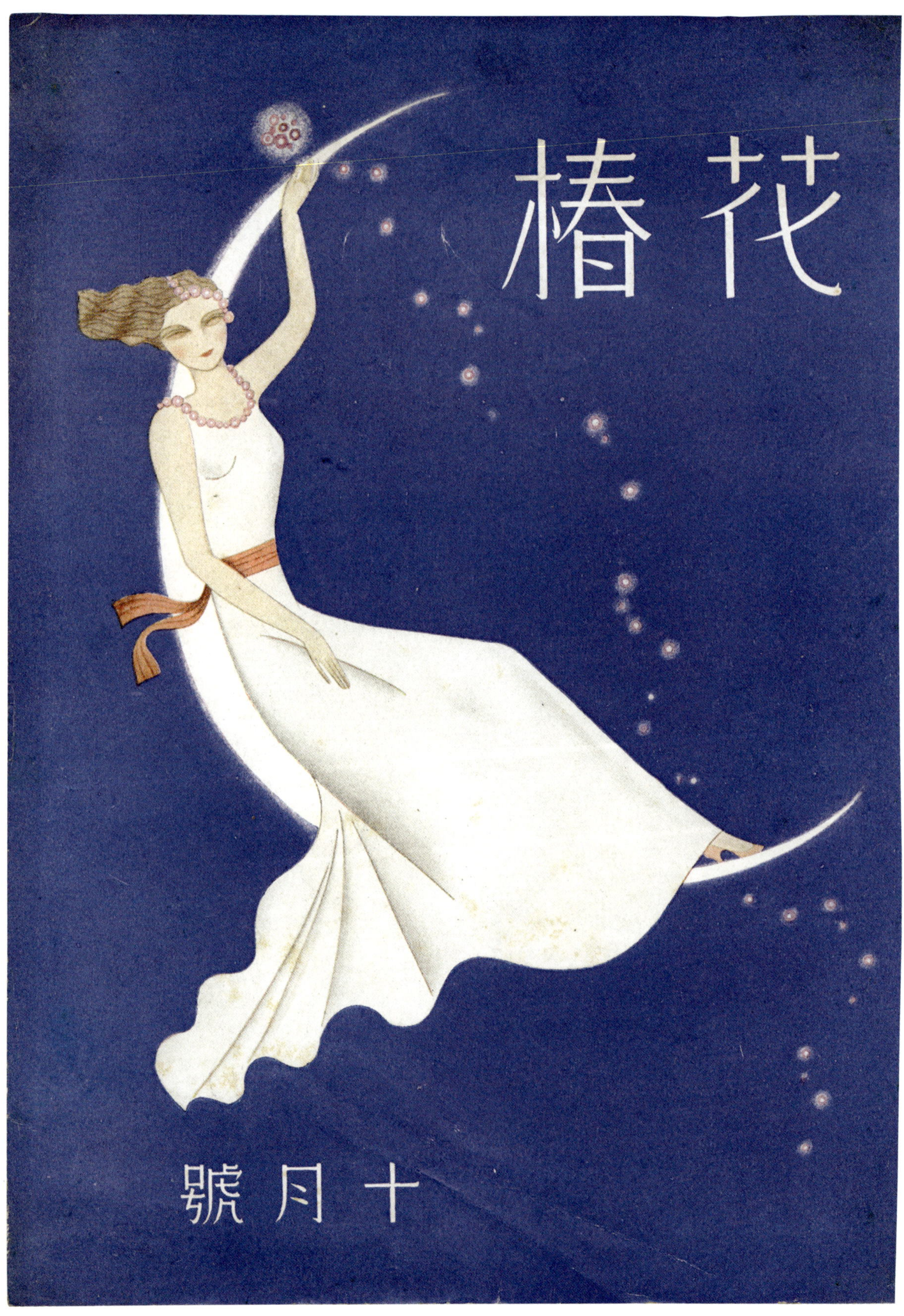

Cover of ***Hanatsubaki* 花椿** (Tokyo: Kabushikigaisha Shiseido 株式会社資生堂, October, 1938), designed by Yamana Ayao 山名文夫.

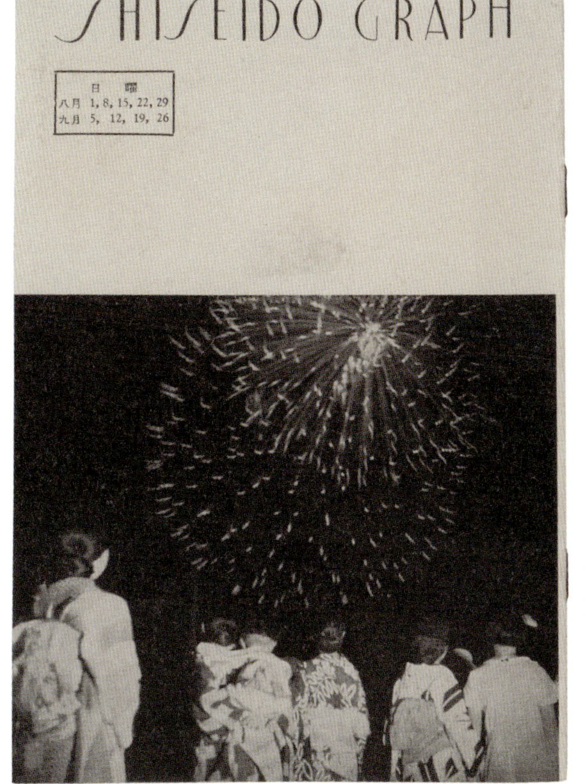

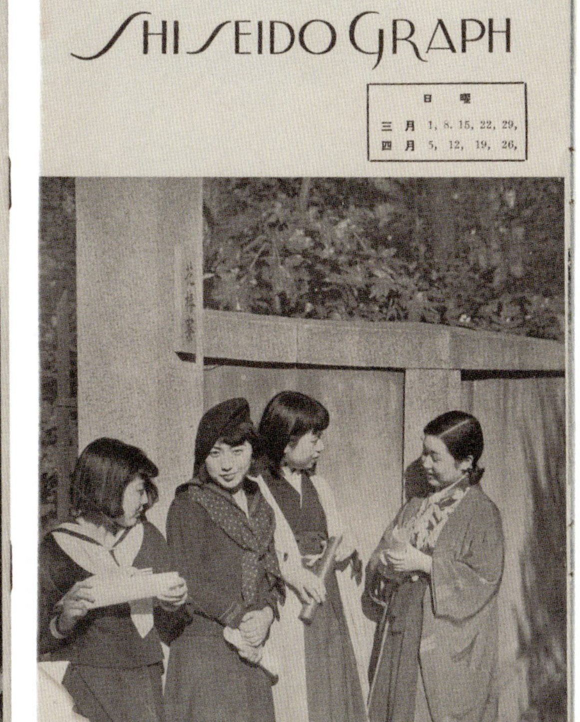

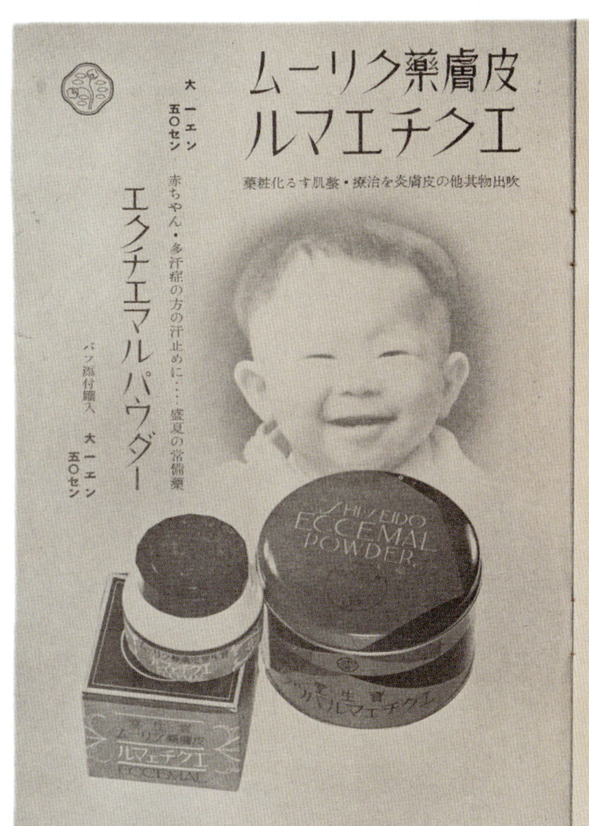

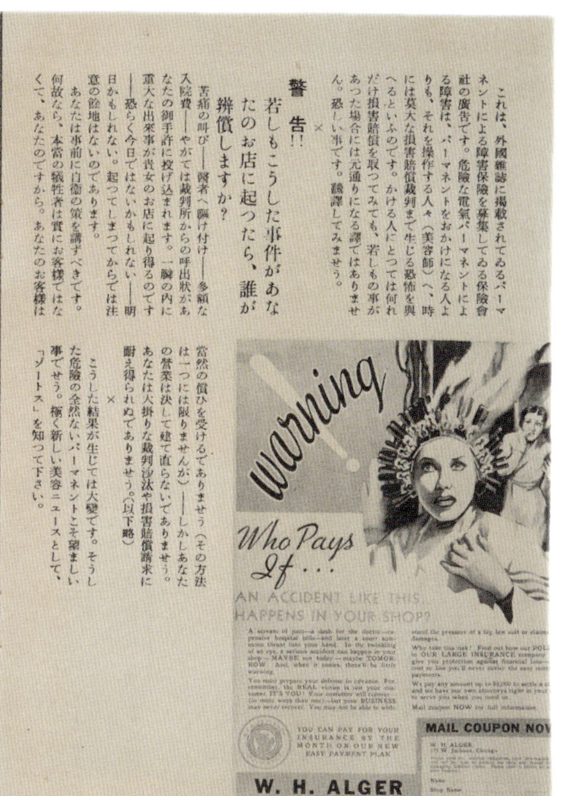

これは、外國雜誌に掲載されてゐるパーマネントによる障害保險を募集してゐる保險會社の廣告です。危險な電氣パーマネントによる障害は、パーマネントをおかけになる人よりも、それを操作する人々（美容師）へ、時には莫大な損害賠償裁判まで生じる恐怖を與へるといふのです。かける人にとつては何れだけ損害賠償を取つてみても、若しもの事があつた場合には元通りになる譯ではありません。恐しい事です。飜譯してみませう。

×

警告!!

若しもこうした事件があなたのお店に起つたら、誰が辨償しますか？

苦痛の叫び——醫者へ驅け付け——多額な入院費——やがては裁判所からの呼出狀があなたの御手許に投げ込まれます。一瞬の内に重大な出來事が貴女のお店に起り得るのです——恐らく今日ではないかもしれない——明日かもしれない。起つてしまつてからでは注意の餘地はないのであります。

あなたは事前に自衛の策を講ずべきです。何故なら、本當の犧牲者は實にお客樣ではなくて、あなたのですから。あなたのお客樣は當然の償ひを受けるでありませう（その方法は一つには限りませんが）——しかしあなたの營業は決して建て直らないでありませう。あなたは大掛りな裁判沙汰や損害賠償請求に耐え得られぬでありませう。（以下略）

×

こうした結果が生じては大變です。そうした危險の全然ないパーマネントこそ望ましい事でせう。極く新しい美容ニュースとして、「ゾートス」を知つて下さい。

Covers and spreads of 1937 and 1938 issues of ***Shiseido Graph***
with calligraphic titling by Yamana Ayao 山名文夫
(Tokyo: Kabushikigaisha Shiseido 株式会社資生堂).

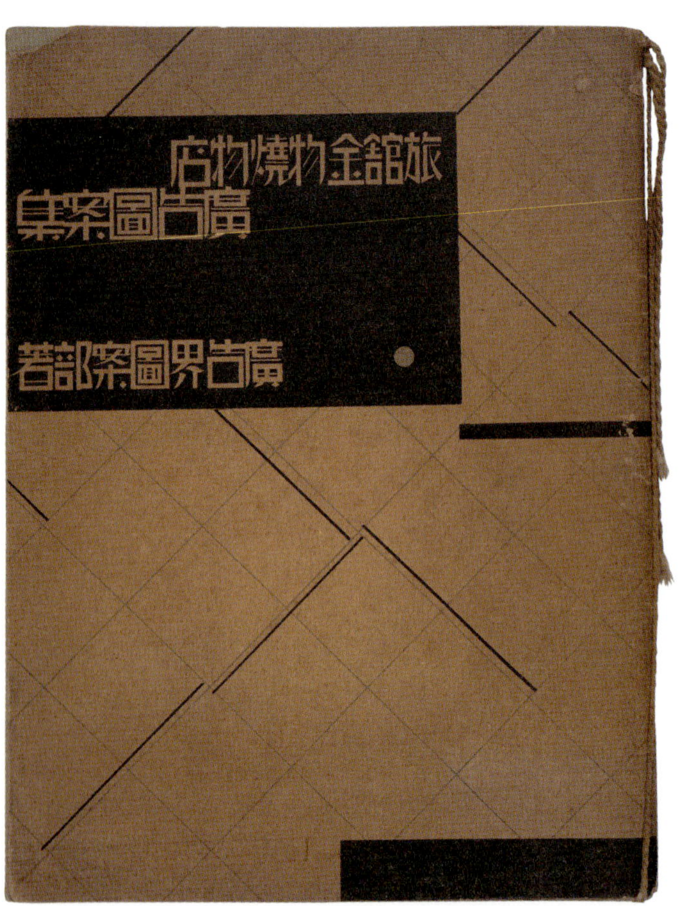

Ryokan / Hardware Store / Pottery Shop: Collection of Advertisements **旅館金物焼物店 - 廣告圖案集** (Tokyo: Seibundo Shinkosha 誠文堂発行, 1930). One of a series of twelve books published by Seibundo Shinkosha about specialized advertising and graphic design. Designed by Yamana Ayao 山名文夫.

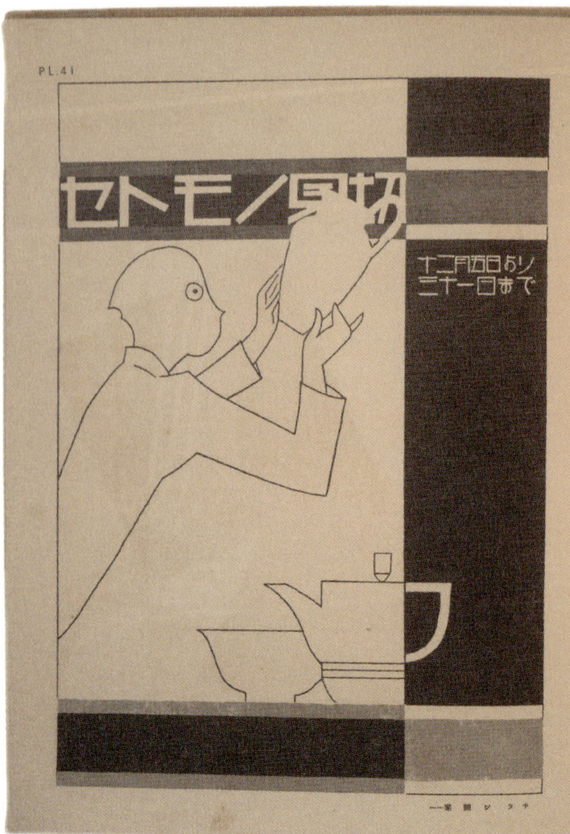

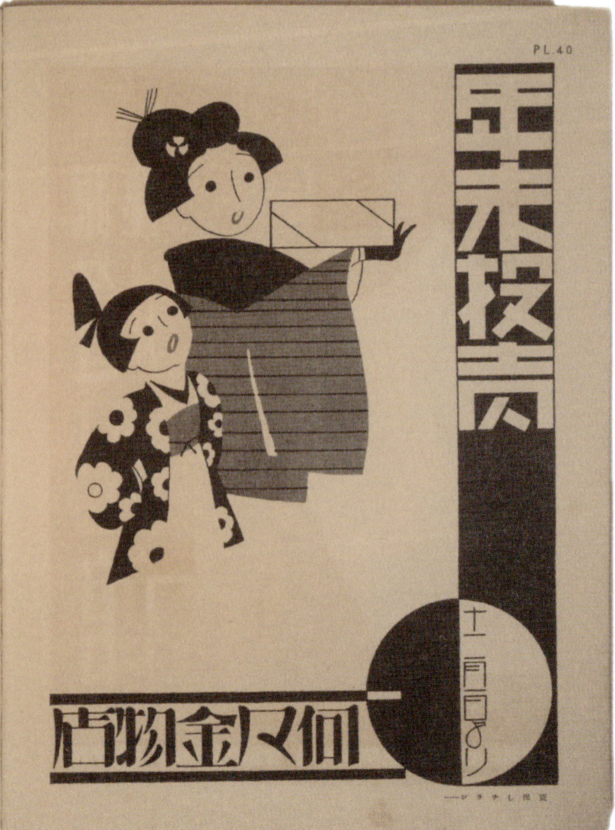

YAMANA AYAO 山名文夫

1897–1980

Yamana Ayao was born in 1897 in Hiroshima Prefecture. In 1916, he enrolled at the Osaka atelier of painter, newspaper cartoonist, and art educator Akamatsu Rinsaku 赤松麟作, where he studied Western art techniques. Yamana was strongly influenced by Japanese artist Takehisa Yumeji, French Art Deco, and the work of British illustrator Aubrey Beardsley (whose own elongated female forms were in turn influenced by Japanese *ukiyo-e* printmaking). In 1917, at age 20, Yamana would directly incorporate their works into a student-produced magazine called *Chocolate* チョコレート and would reference aspects of his inspirations throughout his fifty-year career. His published work in *Chocolate* would include paeans to his collaborator, poet Kumada Seika 熊田精華, a figure Yamana adored, admired, and idolized for his visual form-giving and writing.

In his early twenties, Yamana spent time in occupied Korea alongside his family, working to promote the Manchurian Railroad. While there, he would contract malaria and beriberi and return home emaciated, needing months to recuperate.

In 1923, Yamana joined the publishing company Platon-sha プラトン社, a subsidiary of Club Cosmetics 株式会社クラブコスメチックス, where he worked as both illustrator and designer for their magazines *Josei* 女性 and *Kuraku* 苦楽. While the Great Kanto Earthquake caused major setbacks to most in the publishing industry, Platon-sha was spared the worst of it due to their editorial offices being located to the south in Osaka. Yamana worked at Platon-sha as an editor as well as a designer, providing writing alongside his design and illustration work.

Platon-sha marketed to emerging female consumers en masse, and Yamana's covers for the magazines became incredibly popular. With the expansion of Platon-sha to new offices in Tokyo in 1926, Yamana gained wider attention. His first book, *Josei no Katto* 女性のカット (*Illustration Cuts of Women*), a collaboration with his Platon-sha colleague Yama Rokurō 山六郎, was published in 1928. He exhibited work at the short-lived Ginza branch of the Marubishi department store, but Platon-sha's business dissolved shortly thereafter, leaving Yamana to return to Osaka crestfallen, though not for long.

Yamana's experience and notoriety soon earned him a new position in Tokyo at Shiseido 資生堂, Japan's largest cosmetics company, in 1929. Working alongside hybrid designers/illustrators Maeda Mitsugu 前田貢 and Yabe Sue 矢部季, Yamana would help define Shiseido's house style—a visual mix of arabesque ornament, reductive-yet-modern gothic display lettering for much of the English copy, Mincho lettering for the Japanese lettering, and wide-eyed, poignant, and evocative illustrations of women, often using Shiseido products.

In 1929, Yamana was featured as a rising star in *Kōkokukai* 広告界 (subtitled in English as *Advertising World*), the predecessor to the contemporary Japanese graphic design magazine *Idea*, giving the young designer a much-needed PR boost and ensuring his employability for years to come.

Yamana worked on an array of projects at Shiseido during his on-again, off-again tenure—from baroque newspaper and magazine advertisements to promotional fans, flourished calendars, pamphlets, store displays, matchbox labels, bags, and miscellaneous packaging. Yamana would depart the corporation intermittently throughout the entirety of his career, yet he would always return to work for Shiseido in one form or another. His groundbreaking designs for Shiseido's trio of magazines *Shiseido Graph* 資生堂グラフ, *Hanatsubaki* 花椿, and *Chainstore* (later renamed *The Chainstore Research*) were stylistic precursors to the modern Japanese magazine as it would develop in the interwar period.

Within two scant years of joining Shiseido, Yamana became Japan's second full-fledged graphic design superstar. A 1929 issue of *Kōkokukai* stated, "Yamana has been so lionized that we can almost believe that there are young ladies out there who believe that they will become 'modern girls' if they simply write out the letters 'A-Y-A-O' from Yamana Ayao's name on paper and swallow it." Yamana's work had become so popular that "people would say that there was no telling whether he represented Shiseido or Shiseido represented him."

Yamana published the book *The Collected Works of Drawings for Advertisements for Cafes, Bars, and Tearooms* カフェ・バー・喫茶店広告図案集 in 1930, and he also began freelancing for the publishing companies Chūōkōron-sha 株式会社中央公論社 and Shinchōsha 株式会社新潮社. The next few years were a flurry of activity—quitting Shiseido, opening and shuttering his own studio, and getting married.

In 1933, Yamana joined Natori Yōnosuke's 名取洋之助 propaganda publishing house, Nippon Kōbō 日本工房, where he worked on their flagship magazine, *Nippon*, becoming billed as Japan's

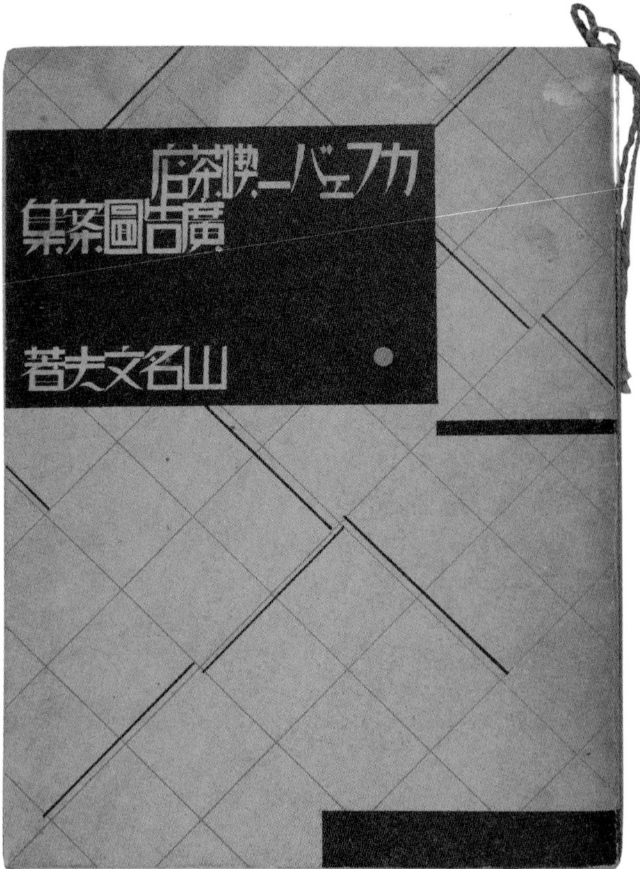

This spread and following page: ***Cafe / Bar / Coffeeshop* カフェ・バー・喫茶店** (Tokyo: Seibundo Shinkosha 誠文堂, 1930). Another of the series of twelve books published by Seibundo about specialized advertising and graphic design. Designed and authored by Yamana Ayao 山名文夫.

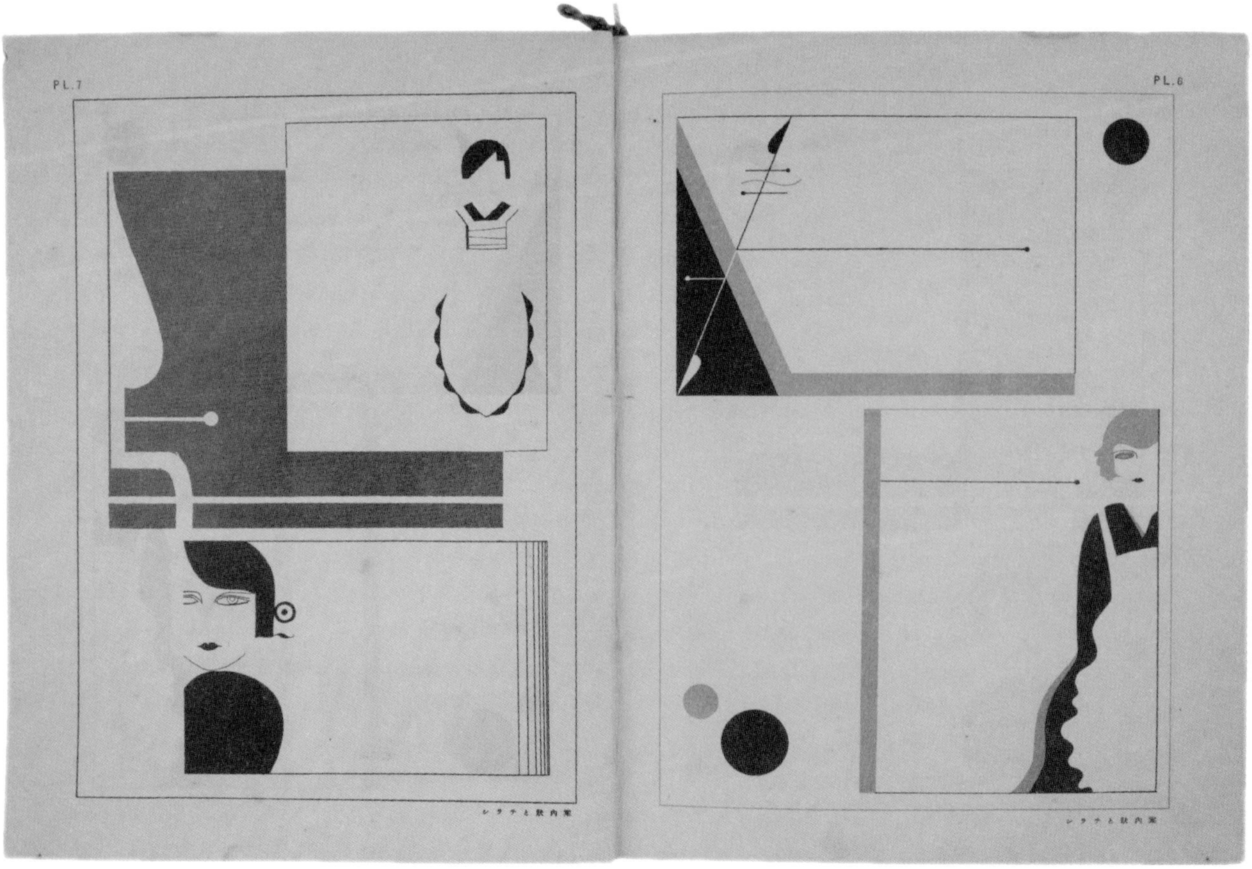

PL.7

案内状とチラシ

PL.6

案内状とチラシ

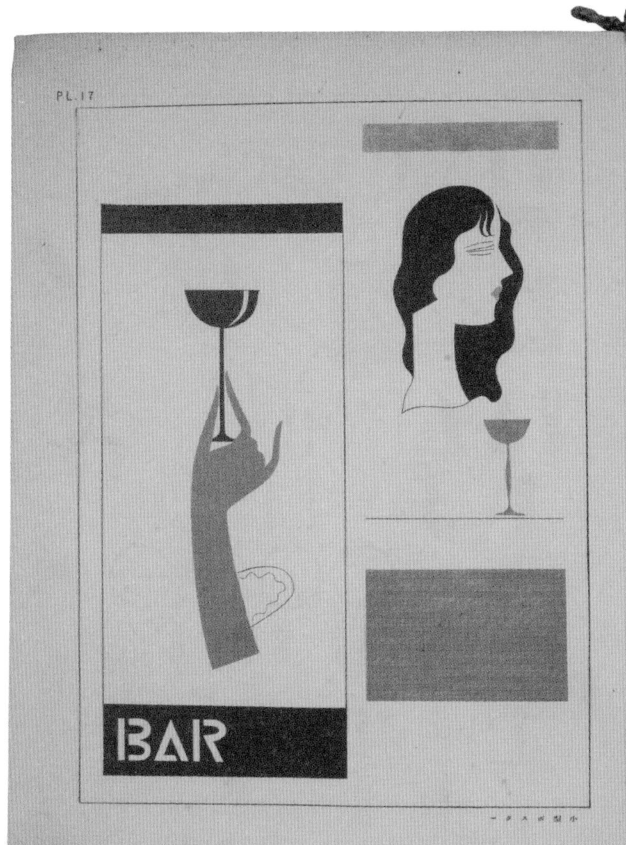
PL.17
BAR
小型ポスター

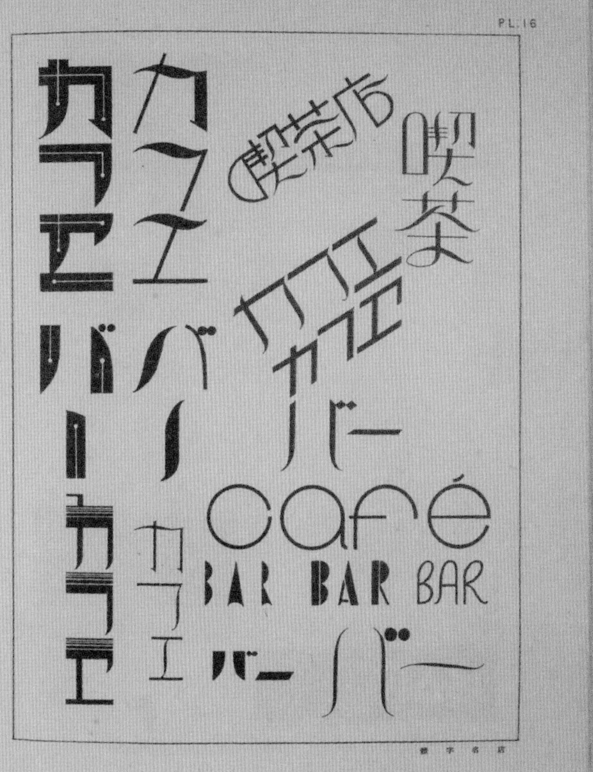
PL.16
喫茶
喫茶店
カフエ
カフエ
バー
café
BAR BAR BAR
バー バー
カフエ
カフエ
バー
カフエ
バー
カフエ
店名字體

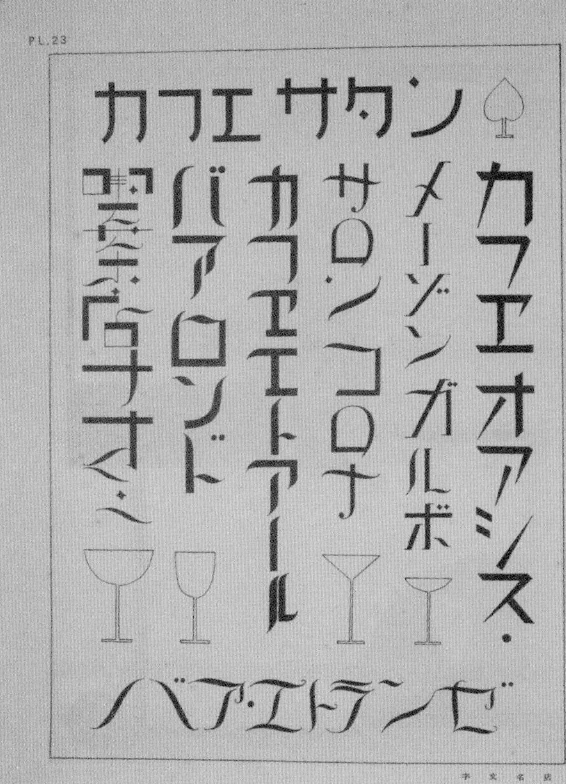
PL.23
カフエサタン
カフエオアシス・
メーゾンガルボ
サロンコロナ
カフエエトアール
バアロンド
バア・エトランゼ
店名文字

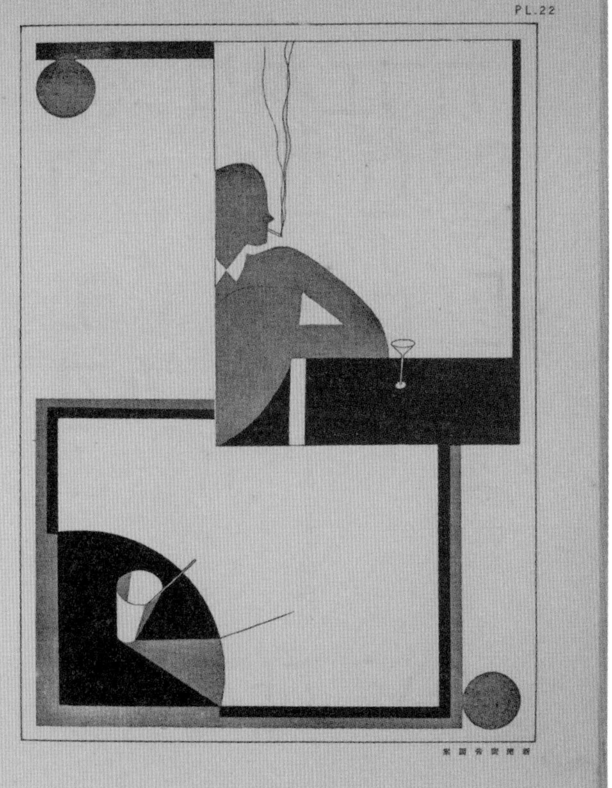
PL.22
新聞廣告圖案

PL.49

NIPON HOTEL

TOKYO HOTEL

ABC KAN

HANAYA

HOTEL

UMINO HOTEL

YAMANO HOTEL

廣告文字集——

PL.48

年末贈答用品揃

家庭用金物

趣味的陶器具

年の市見切品

店内全部

正札値段

歳末売出シ

廣告文字集——

PL.47

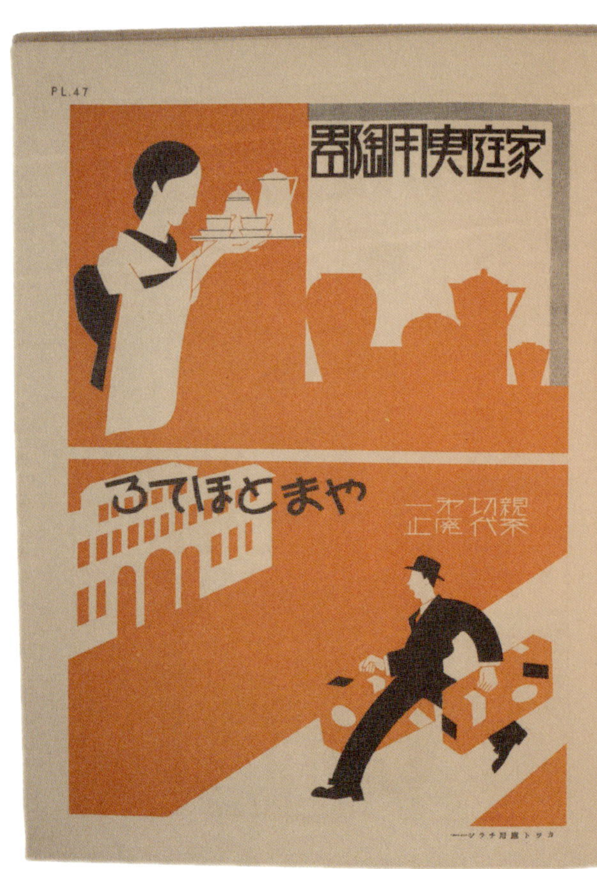

PL.46

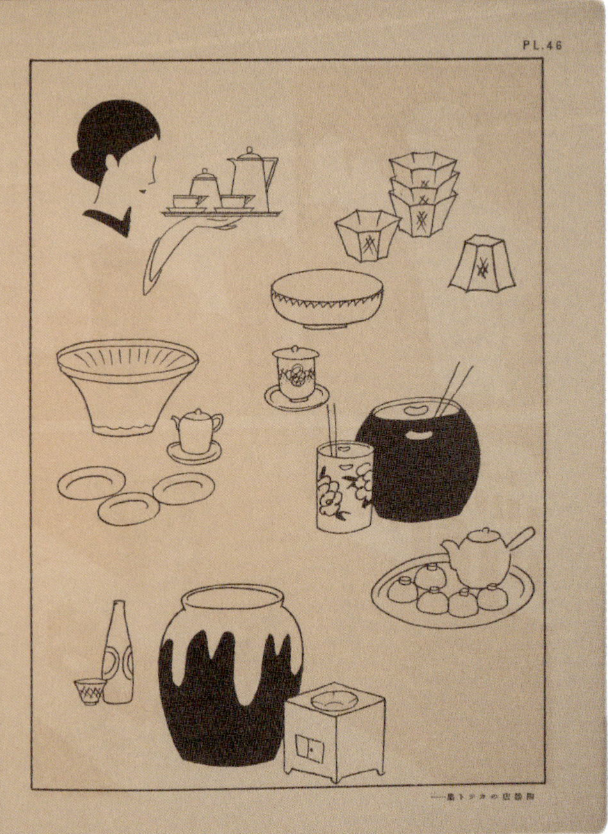

first Art Director. During his time at Nippon Kōbō, Yamana would create some of the most iconic covers and layouts for *Nippon*, often featuring his hand-wrought redesign of Paul Renner's typeface Futura both for the magazine's masthead and within the magazine's interiors. (Yamana would later publish his typeface redesign in an issue of *Kōkokukai*.) The cover of the second issue of *Nippon* features a haunting collage of one of Yamana's female forms set against a photographic interior of a traditional Japanese tatami room, yet the garb of the woman is a kimono, in lieu of his illustrated women's usual Western dress.

During the 1930s, inspired by Sugiura Hisui's design study group Shichininsha, Yamana would initiate first the Shiseido Society for the Study of Advertising Art 資生堂広告美術研究会, then the Tokyo Advertising Arts Society 東京広告美術協会, which later morphed into the Tokyo Advertising Artists Club 東京広告美術家クラブ.

Yamana would return to Shiseido's employ in 1936, working there until 1943.

In 1940, Yamana joined and became Chairman of the Society for the Study of Media Technique 報道技術研究会, a cooperative corporate/government-sponsored committee devoted to the development and dissemination of propaganda. Yamana worked on a wide range of war-effort posters and publications promoting the recycling of materials for use in war machines, national savings and bonds efforts, and evacuation procedures.

After the end of the war, Yamana was hired by his childhood hero Sugiura Hisui to become faculty at the Tama Art University, re-formed after the school's campus had been lost during the war. Prior, Yamana had worked at what would become Musashino Art University and for a splinter group at the advertising agency Dentsu. While educational material was hard to come by in the immediate postwar period, Yamana would scour secondhand bookshops and clip advertisements from foreign publications to share with his students. He worked at Tama Art University from 1947 to 1966, first as faculty and later as head of its Graphic Design department.

Yamana was one of the founders of the Japan Advertising Artists Club 日本宣伝美術会 in 1951 and would be its first Chairman. He went on to set up the vocational trade school Nihon Dezaina Gakuin 日本デザイナー学院 (Japan Designer College) in 1965. Yamana was a prolific writer throughout his career, writing about design first for *Affiches* in 1930, then for *Press Art* in 1938, advising *Shōgyo Design Zenshū* 商業デザイン全集 (*The World's Commercial Design*) from 1953 to 1954, and publishing sporadically in *Idea* afterward.

In 1976, Yamana published *Design History as Experience* 体験的デザイン史, a memoir of his immersion in design culture from the formation of commercial art through his involvement in the Japan Advertising Artists Club, replete with a timeline and black-and-white illustrations.

Yamana died in 1980, aged 82. While known primarily for his work for Shiseido, Yamana was also an ardent letteirng and type designer, having completed the hiragana typeface Aya in 1950. His designs are still seen throughout Japan today.

References:

Germer, Andrea. "Visual Propaganda in Wartime East Asia – The Case of Natori Yōnosuke." *The Asia-Pacific Journal: Japan Focus*. Asia-Pacific Journal, May 9, 2011. https://apjjf.org/2011/9/20/Andrea-Germer/3530/article.html.

Kamekura, Yūsaku, and Ayao Yamana. *Gurafikku Dezain no Seiki: Bunshō to Danwa to Sakuhin De kōsei: Meiji Sedai Yamana Ayao Sugiura Hisui Kara shōwa Sedai Made*. Tokyo: Bijutsu Shuppansha, 2008.

Muroga, Kiyonori, and Makie Kubo. "Contribution to Republishing Yamana Ayao 'The Experiential History of Design.'" *Idea* 83, no. 369 (April 2015): 142–43.

Natori, Yōnosuke, Mari Shirayama, and Yoshio Hori. *Natori Yōnosuke to Nihon Kōbō: 1931–45*. Tokyo: Iwanami shoten, 2006.

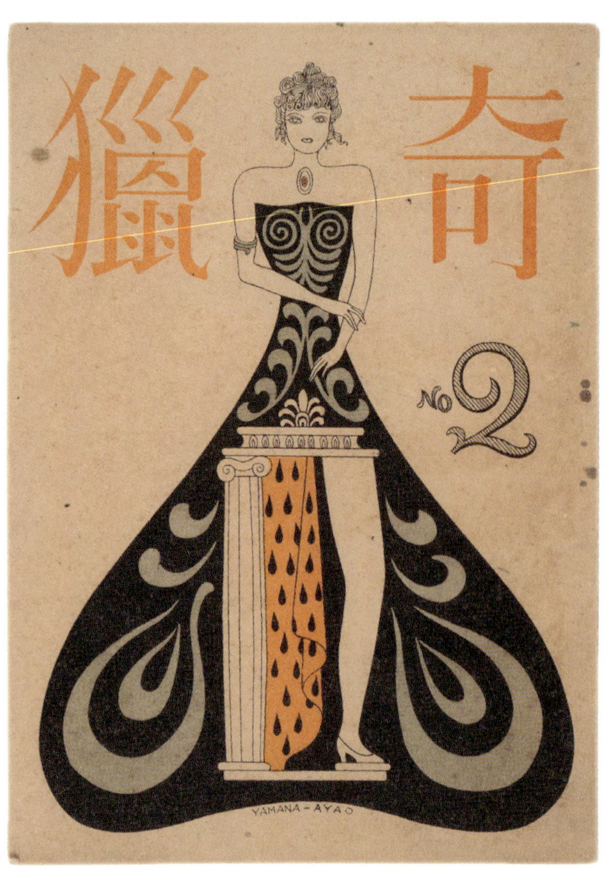

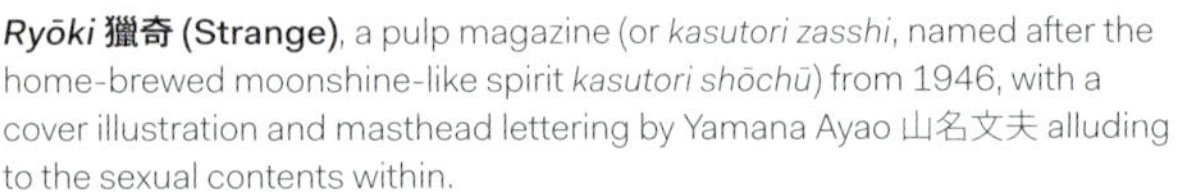

Ryōki **獵奇 (Strange)**, a pulp magazine (or *kasutori zasshi*, named after the home-brewed moonshine-like spirit *kasutori shōchū*) from 1946, with a cover illustration and masthead lettering by Yamana Ayao 山名文夫 alluding to the sexual contents within.

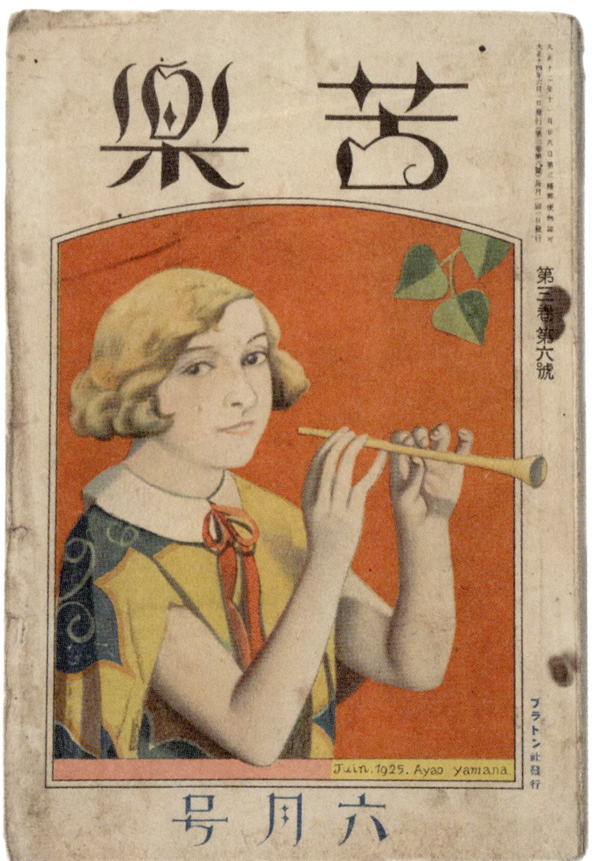

Kuraku **苦楽 *(Joys and Sorrows)*, Vol. 3 No. 10 (Osaka: Platon-sha プラトン社, June 1914).** Cover by Yamana Ayao 山名文夫.

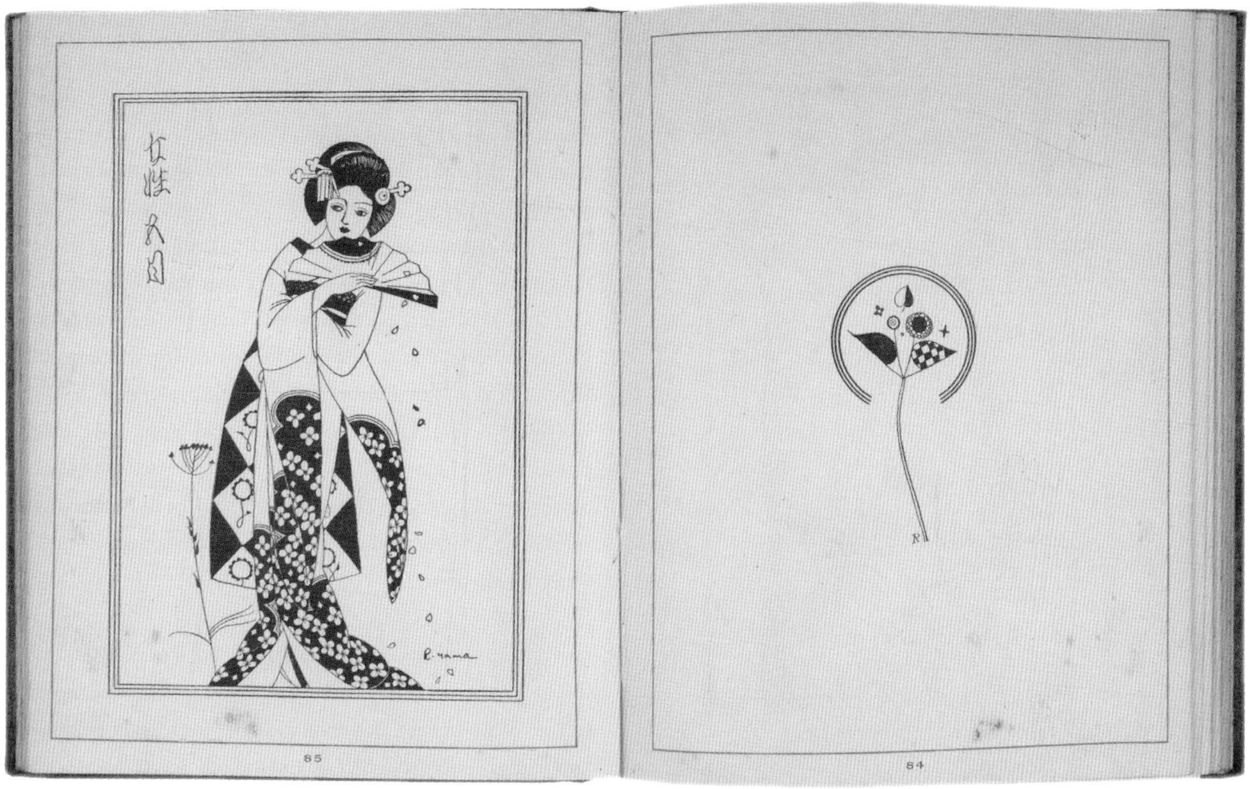

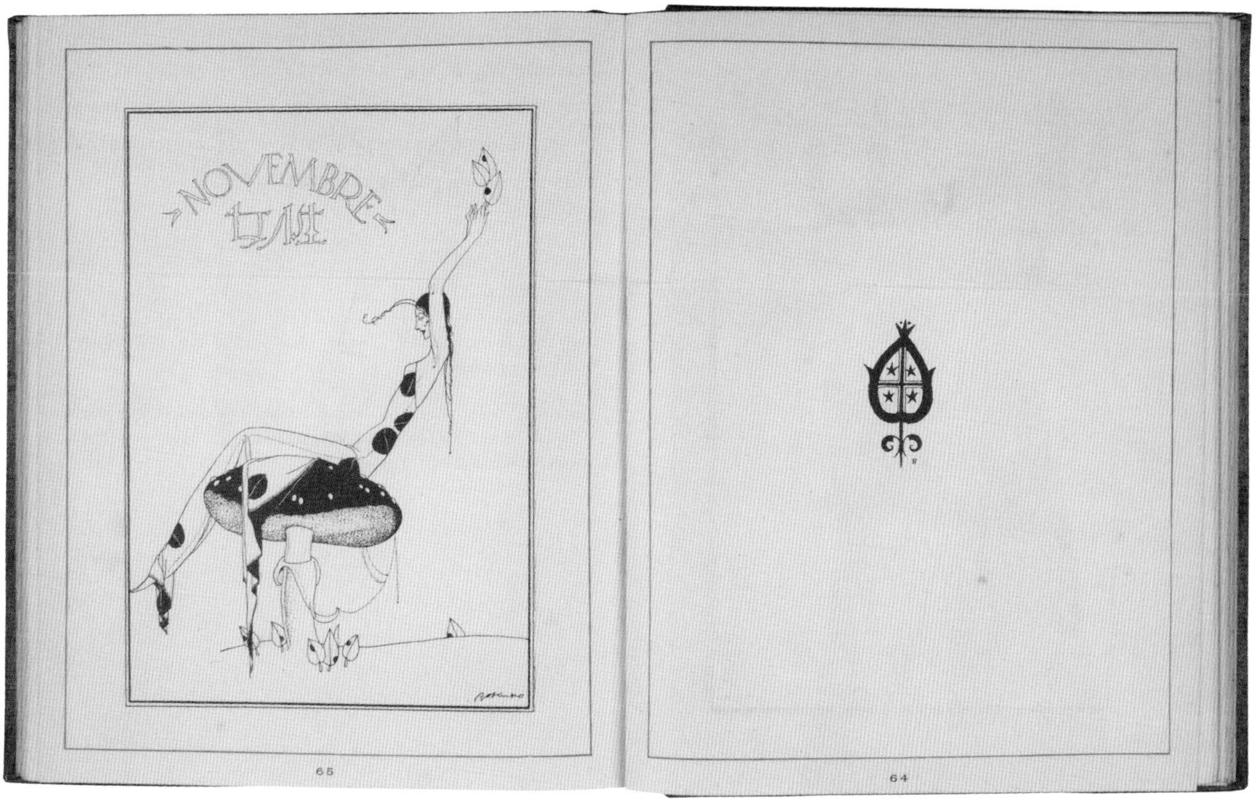

Illustrations from ***Josei no Katto* 女性のカット *(Illustration Cuts of Women)*** by Yamana Ayao 山名文夫 and Yama Rokurō 山六郎, a box-sleeved collection of illustration cuts by colleagues Yamana and Yama from the pages of *Josei* magazine, published in 1928 by Platon-sha プラトン社.

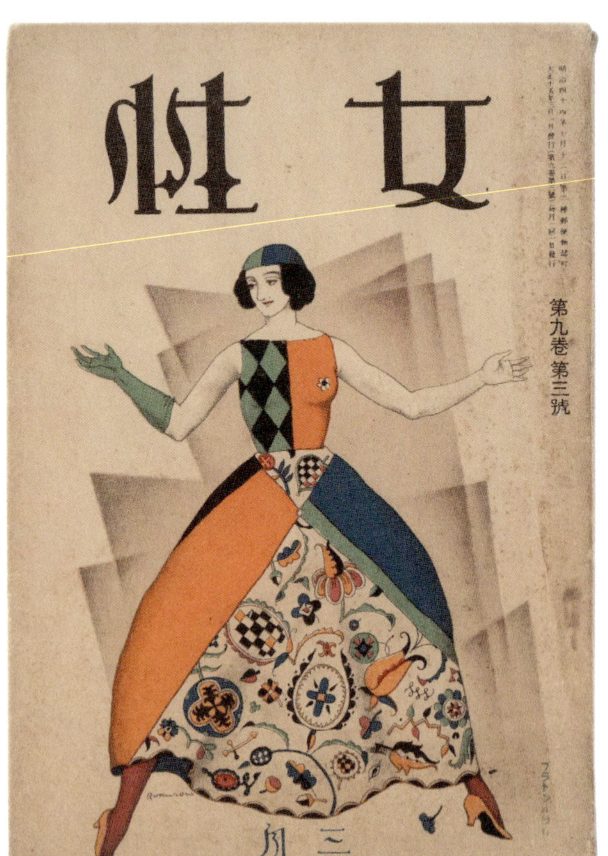

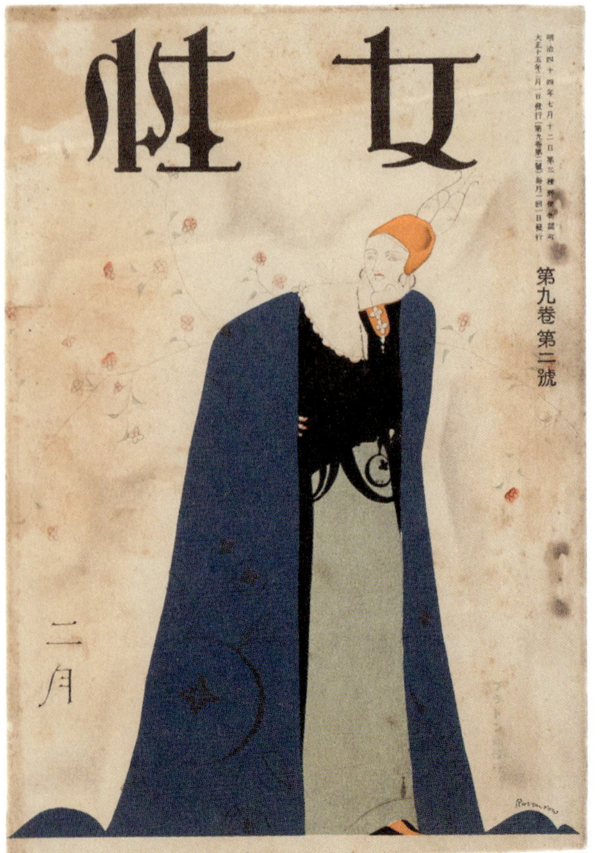

YAMA ROKURŌ 山六郎

1897– 1982

Yama Rokurō was born in Kochi Prefecture. After graduating from Kyoto High School of Art and Chemistry, he became employed at Club Cosmetics クラブコスメチックス, which created the internal house publicity publishing group Platon-sha in 1922. Yama designed the masthead for their debut magazine, *Josei* 女性. The following year, he was joined by fellow designer Yamana Ayao at Platon-sha. The duo worked on the magazine *Kuraku* 苦楽 and on Platon-sha's *Theater·Movie* 演劇·映画, which ran for eight issues in 1925 and 1926. Yama and Yamana published the book *Josei no Katto* 女性のカット *(Illustration Cuts of Women)* in 1928 with Platon-sha—a book of illustrations of women adorned with the type of deft lettering that the pair was renowned for.

Josei and *Kuraku* continued publication until 1928, when Platon-sha went out of business. With the closure, Yama moved to Tokyo and worked as a book designer for the publishing companies Heibonsha 平凡社 and Shinchōsha 株式会社新潮社. Yama designed a number of covers for assorted books across popular literature, including mystery novels and detective novels. He returned to Kochi in 1945 at the end of the war and was active in art education there for the remainder of his life, occasionally exhibiting while continuing to design numerous book packaging projects.

References:

Aramata, Hiroshi. *Ryūsenkei No Megami: aaru Deko Sashiebon No Sekai Covers*. Tokyo: Ushiwakamaru, 1998.

Kamekura, Yūsaku, and Ayao Yamana. *Gurafikku Dezain no Seiki: Bunshō to Danwa to Sakuhin De kōsei: Meiji Sedai Yamana Ayao Sugiura Hisui Kara Shōwa Sedai Made*. Tokyo: Bijutsu Shuppansha, 2008.

Top: ***Josei* (Women) 女性**, Vol. 9 No. 3 (Osaka: Platon-sha プラトン社, March 1926). Bottom: ***Josei* (Women) 女性**, Vol. 9 No. 2 (Osaka: Platon-sha プラトン社, February 1926). Both cover designs by Yama Rokuro 山六郎.

HIROTA TATSU 広田多津

1904–1990

Hirota Tatsu was born in Kyoto to an impoverished family, yet she went on to study art under the teachers Kainosho Kusune 甲斐荘楠音, Takeuchi Seihō 竹内栖鳳, and Nishiyama Suishō 西山翠嶂. Her paintings tended to focus on female subjects, with decades of her career dedicated to painting *maiko* 舞妓 (apprentice *geisha* 芸者) and to popularizing the nude in portraiture.

Her paintings won some of the top awards in Japan, including prizes at both the Nitten and Shin-Bunten national exhibitions. While remembered primarily as a painter, Hirota also contributed cover designs to various publications sporadically over her career, including *The Sunday Mainichi* サンデー毎日 and *Weekly Asahi* 週刊朝日.

In addition to her accolades, Hirota Tatsu is also credited for being a founding member of the Creative Art Society 創造美術協会, a prominent feature of postwar traditional Japanese painting starting in 1948. She became more closely associated with art in the academic field in 1952 when she later became principal of Kyoto Nihonga College 京都日本画専門学校, where she received the Cultural Merit Award from Kyoto Prefecture and Kyoto City in 1953.

References:

Tokyo National Institute of Cultural Properties. “Hirota Tatsu.” In *Nihon Bijutsu Nenkan*, 325–26. Tokyo: Ministry of Finance Printing Bureau, 1992.

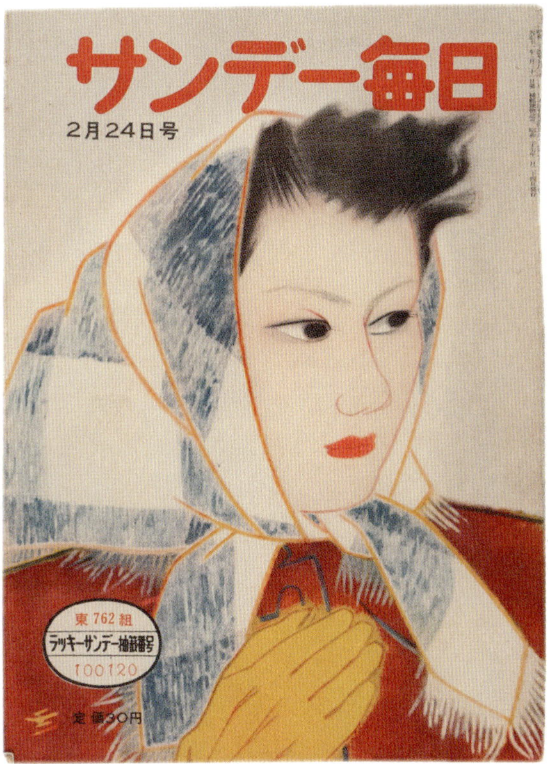

***The Sunday Mainichi* サンデー毎日,** “Spring Cold” (Tokyo: Mainichi Shimbun Kabushikigaisha 毎日新聞出版株式会社, February 24, 1952). Cover by Hirota Tatsu 広田多津.

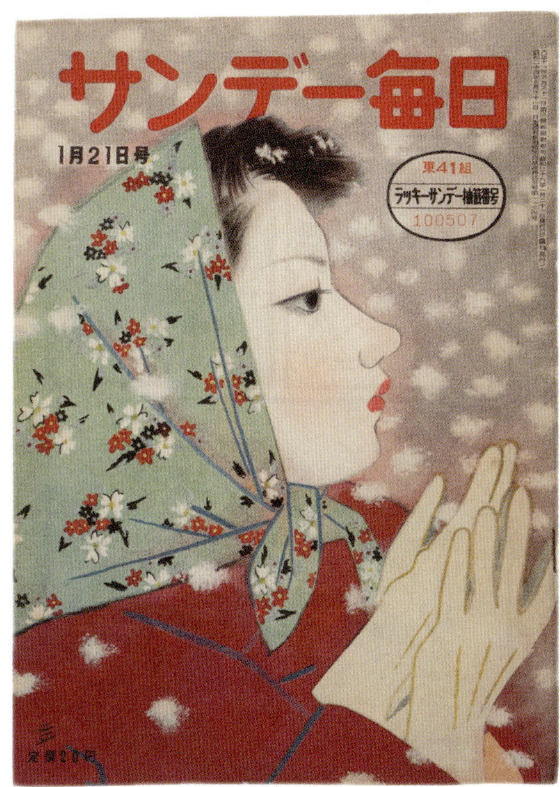

***The Sunday Mainichi* サンデー毎日,** “Snow” (Tokyo: Mainichi Shimbun Kabushikigaisha 毎日新聞出版株式会社, January 21, 1951). Cover by Hirota Tatsu 広田多津.

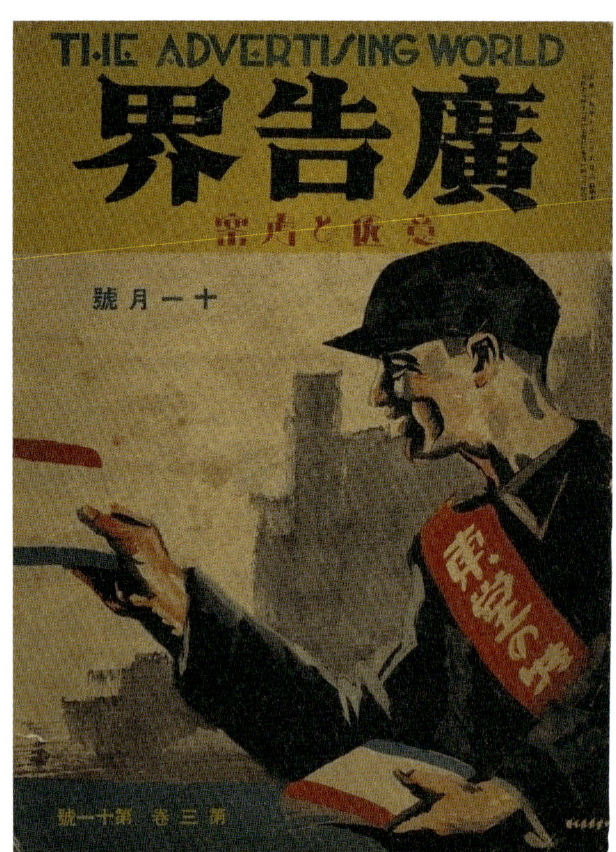

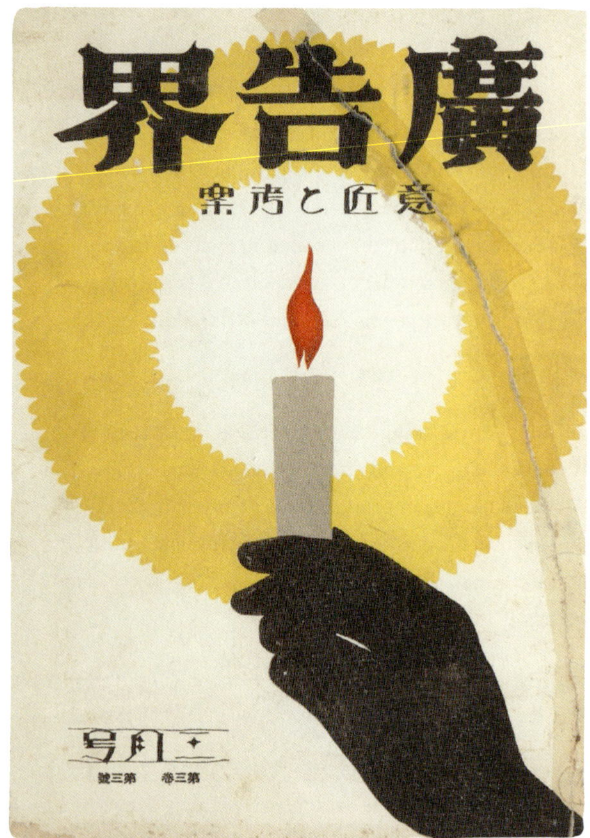

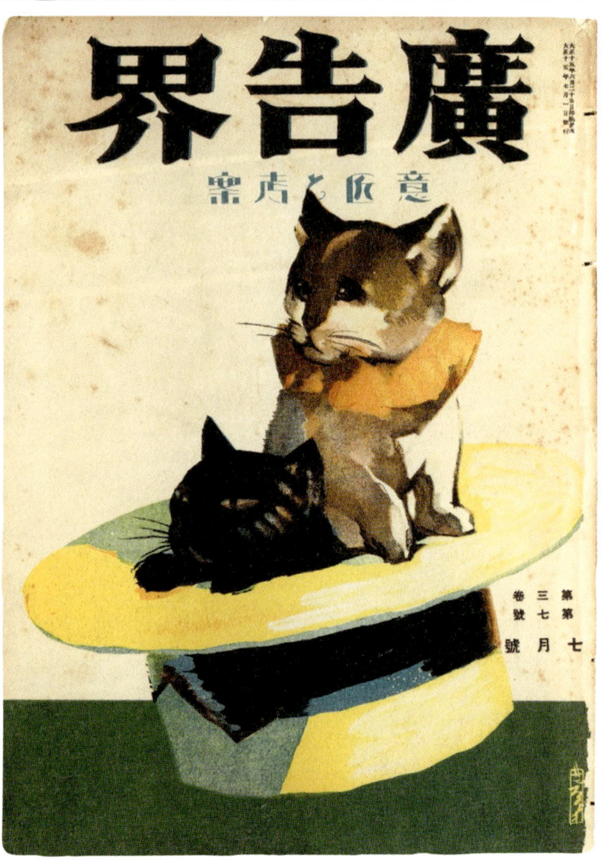

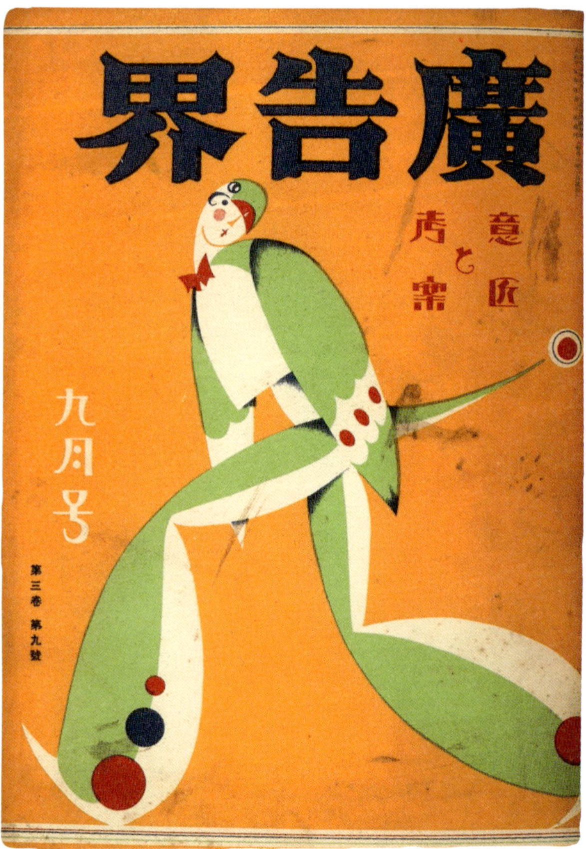

Covers from 1926, the first year that ***Kōkokukai*** **広告界** was published by **Seibundo 誠文堂**.

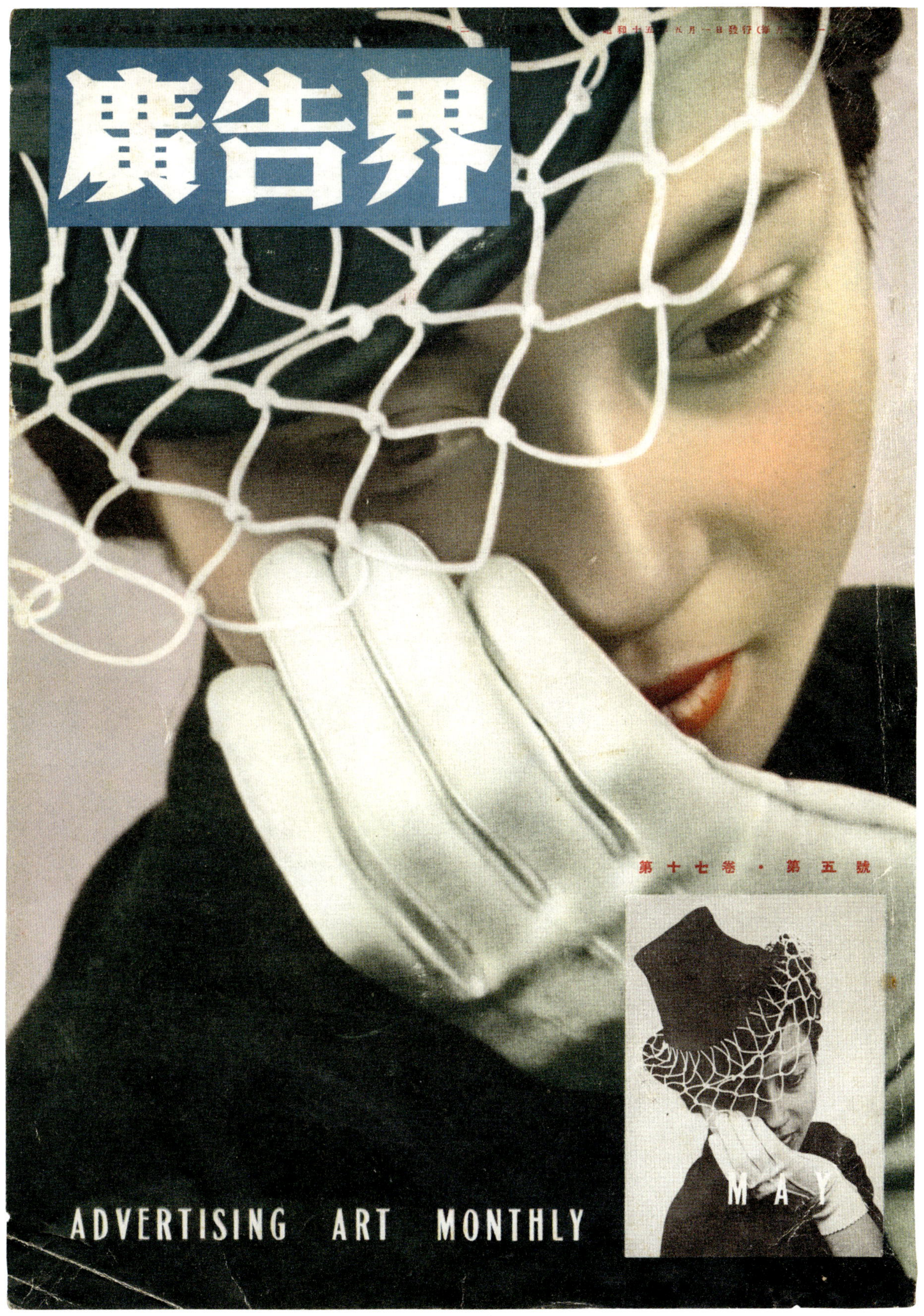

Cover of *Kōkokukai* 広告界 (Tokyo: Seibundo 誠文堂, May 1940).

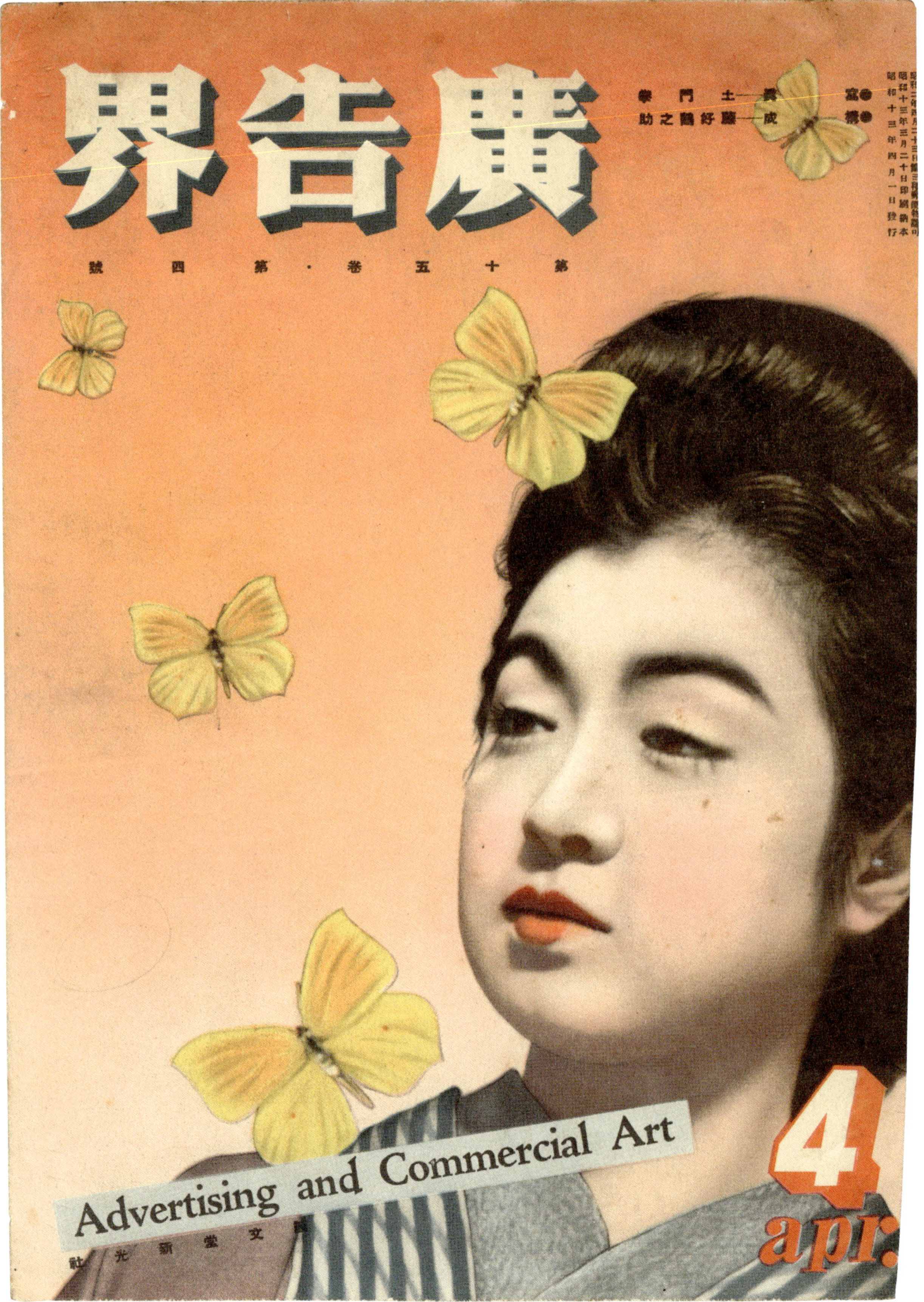

廣告界
●寫眞——土門拳
●構成——藤好鶴之助
昭和三年四月二十三日第三種郵便物認可
昭和十三年三月二十日印刷納本
昭和十三年四月一日發行
第十五巻・第四號
Advertising and Commercial Art
4
apr.
誠文堂新光社

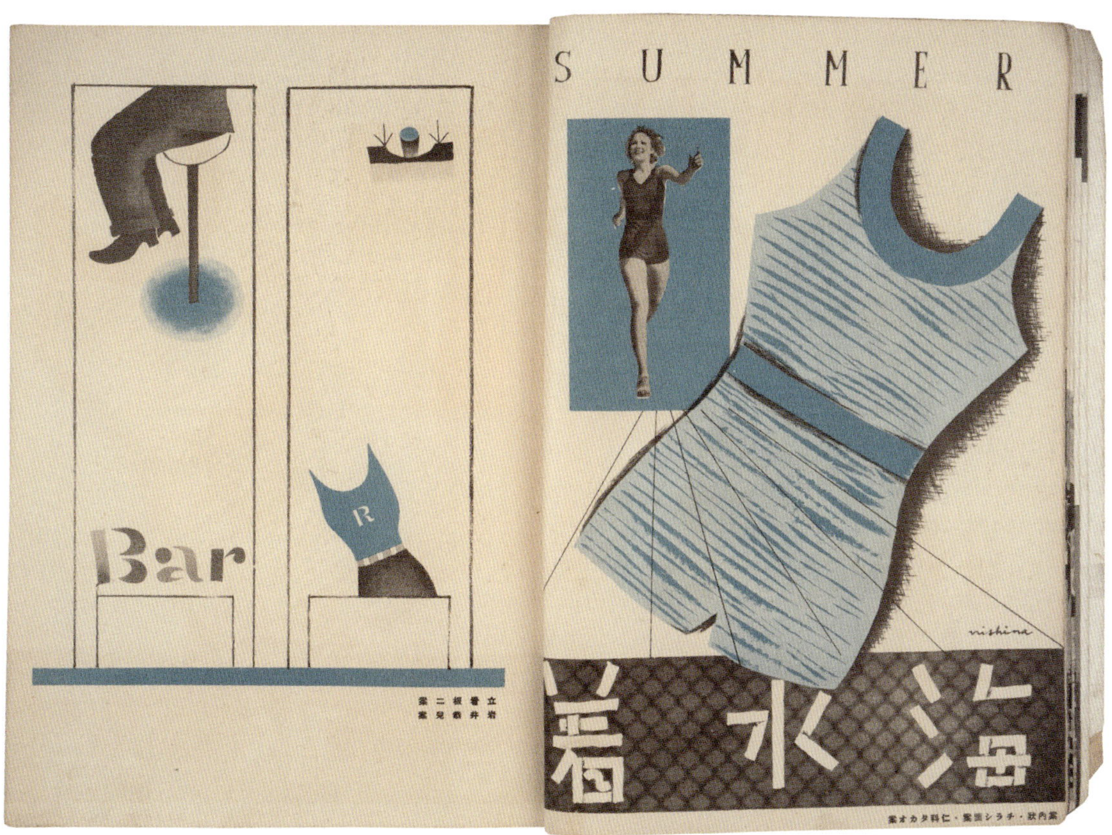

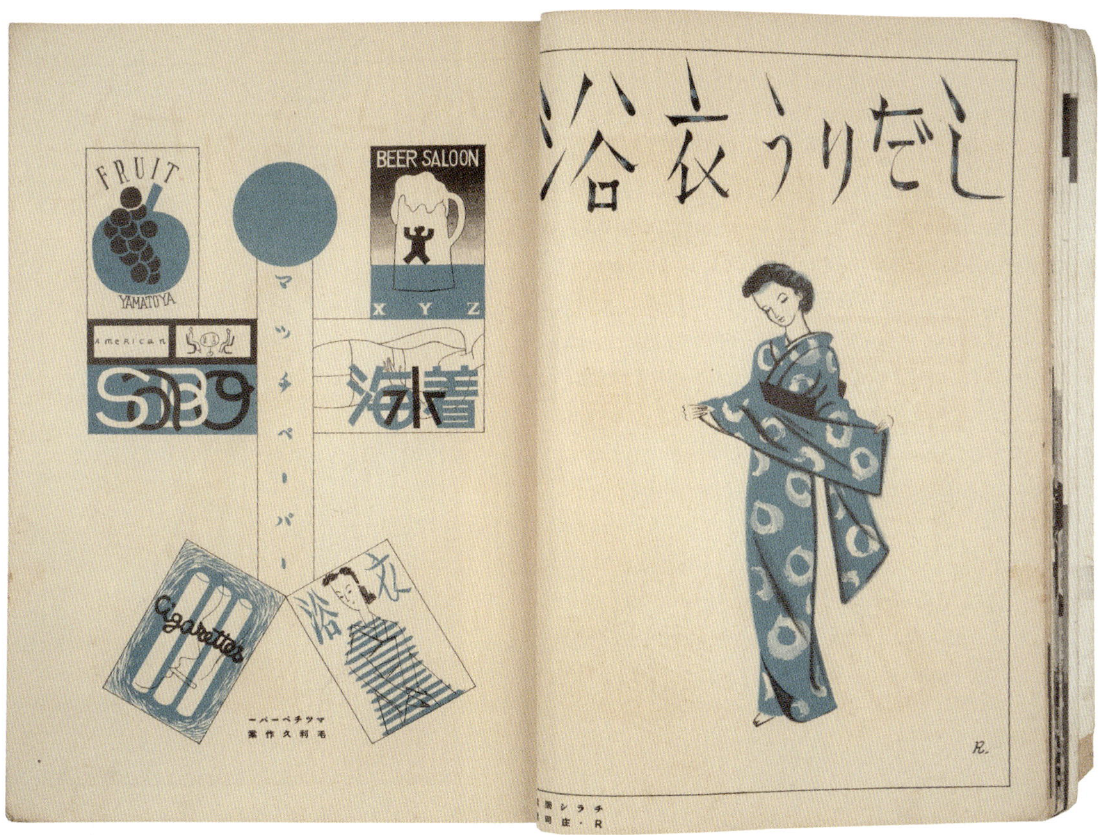

This page and opposite: Covers and spreads from ***Kōkokukai* 広告界** from the 1930s and 1940s published by **Seibundo 誠文堂** in Tokyo.

KŌKOKUKAI 広告界

Kōkokukai was a trade journal published by Seibundo 誠文堂 (now Seibundo Shinkosha 誠文堂新光社) from 1926 to 1941. Established in 1912, Seibundo is a publisher of magazines and books on assorted titles from astronomy to geography, to ham radio, to house pets, to graphic design.

Kōkokukai was a diverse commercial art journal that mixed dynamic multicolored illustrations of lettering, page layouts, signage, and proposed kiosk designs with halftoned imagery of graphic design, interior design, and architecture from abroad. The first editor-in-chief was Murota Kurazō 室田庫造, a designer and writer who initiated early investigations into the appeal of "layout"—considered compositions in graphic design. In 1935, Murota was succeeded as editor-in-chief by Miyayama Takashi 宮山峻, who would steer the direction of *Kōkokukai* and subsequent Seibundo design publications. Contributors included a who's who of graphic designers from the interwar period.

Kōkokukai went through a veritable barrage of translated English titles throughout the print run of the magazine. It was initially titled in English *The Advertising World*, then *The Publicity World* for the final two issues of 1927, with that title lasting through 1931. *Kōkokukai* was re-titled *Advertising, Commercial Art, Show Window*, then just *Publicity* in 1932, lost the English subtitle in 1934 for four years, then was re-titled *Advertising and Commercial Art* in English in 1938. The magazine was renamed *Advertising Art Monthly* in English in 1940 until the September issue of that year, when it settled for the name *Industrial Art and Propaganda* until the magazine's demise the following year. This final English title was perhaps the best indicator of the shift in interwar Japanese culture away from the greater trend of liberal modernization and its veer toward wartime industrialization and the departure from market-based capitalism to state-driven capitalism.

The magazine ceased publication due to wartime paper shortages. It would reemerge postwar as *New Kōkokukai* in 1949 through 1950, then it finally would be renamed *Idea* in 1953. Today, *Idea* stands as Japan's longest-running graphic design publication.

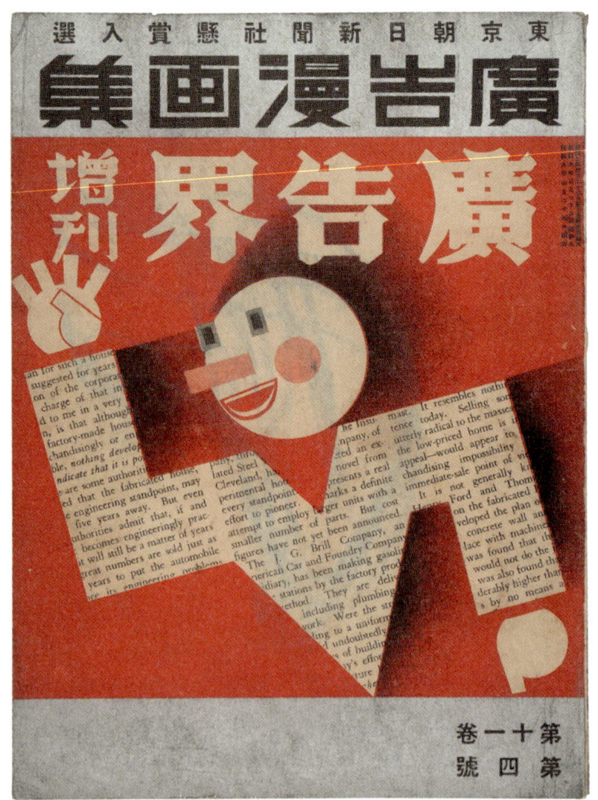

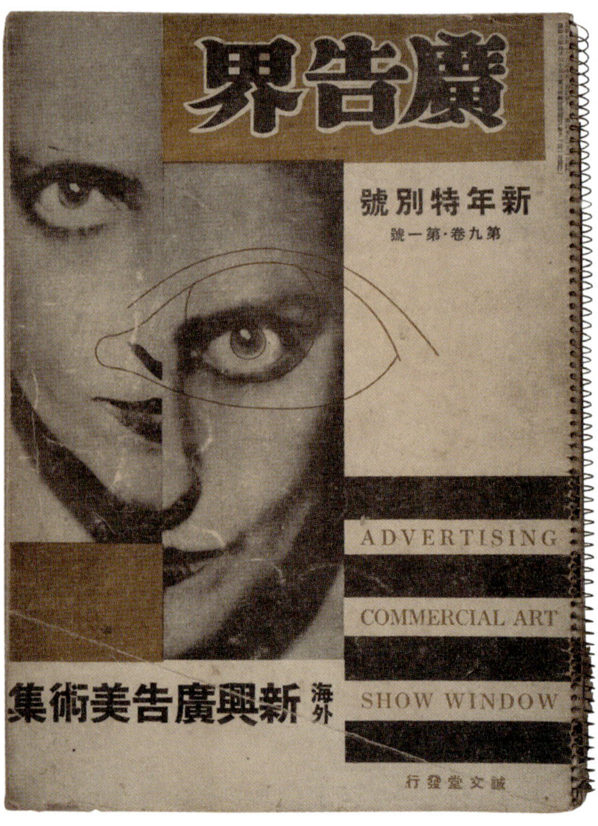

This page: 1930s covers of ***Kōkokukai* 広告界** published by Seibundo 誠文堂 in Tokyo.

References:
Takeuchi, Yukie. "The World of Kokokukai." *Idea* 1, no. 360 (September 2013): 112–27.

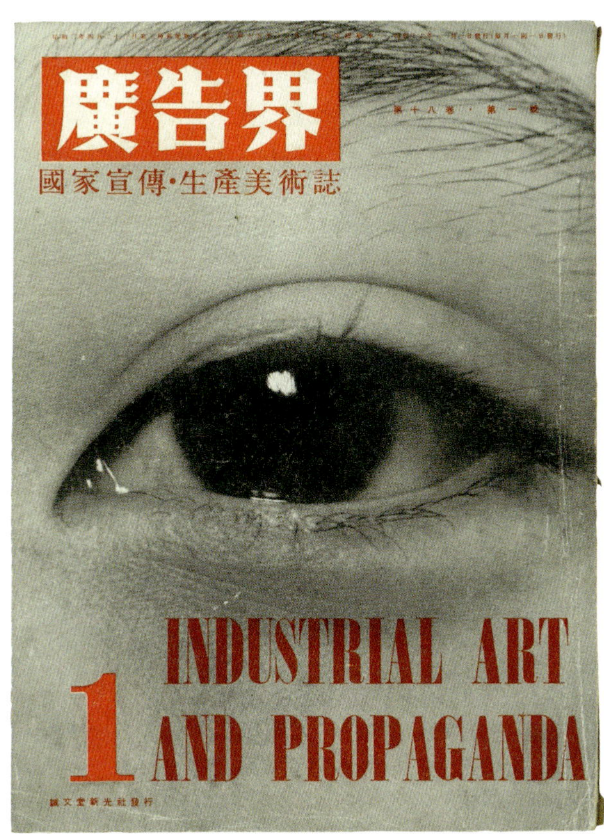

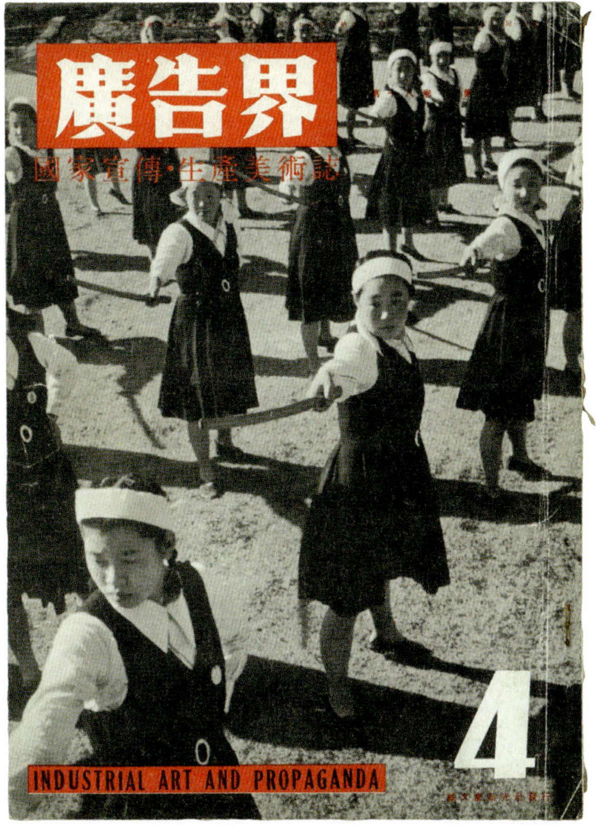

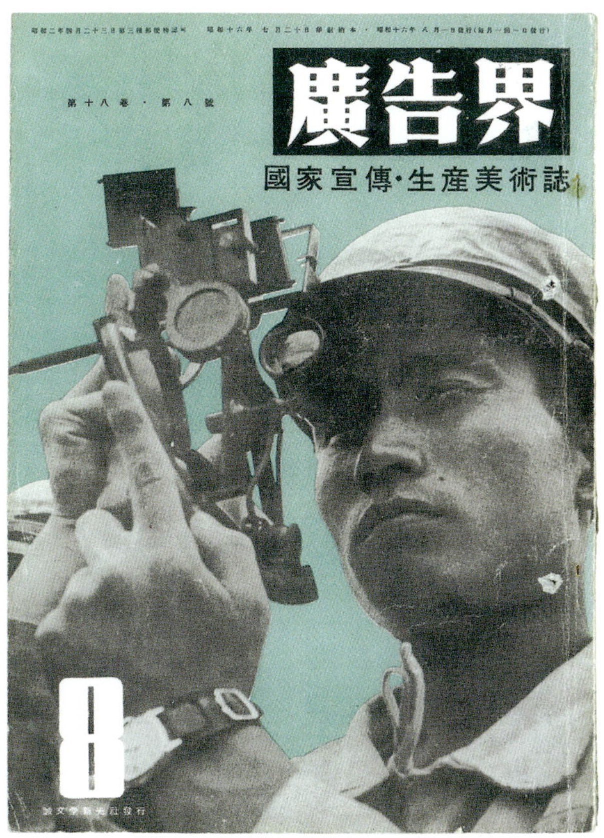

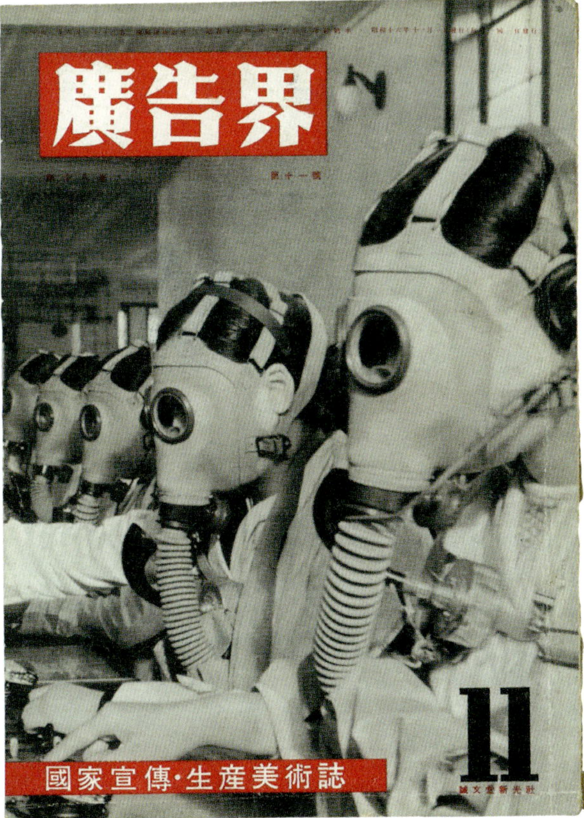

This page: Covers of ***Kōkokukai* 広告界** from 1941, the last year of the magazine's production.

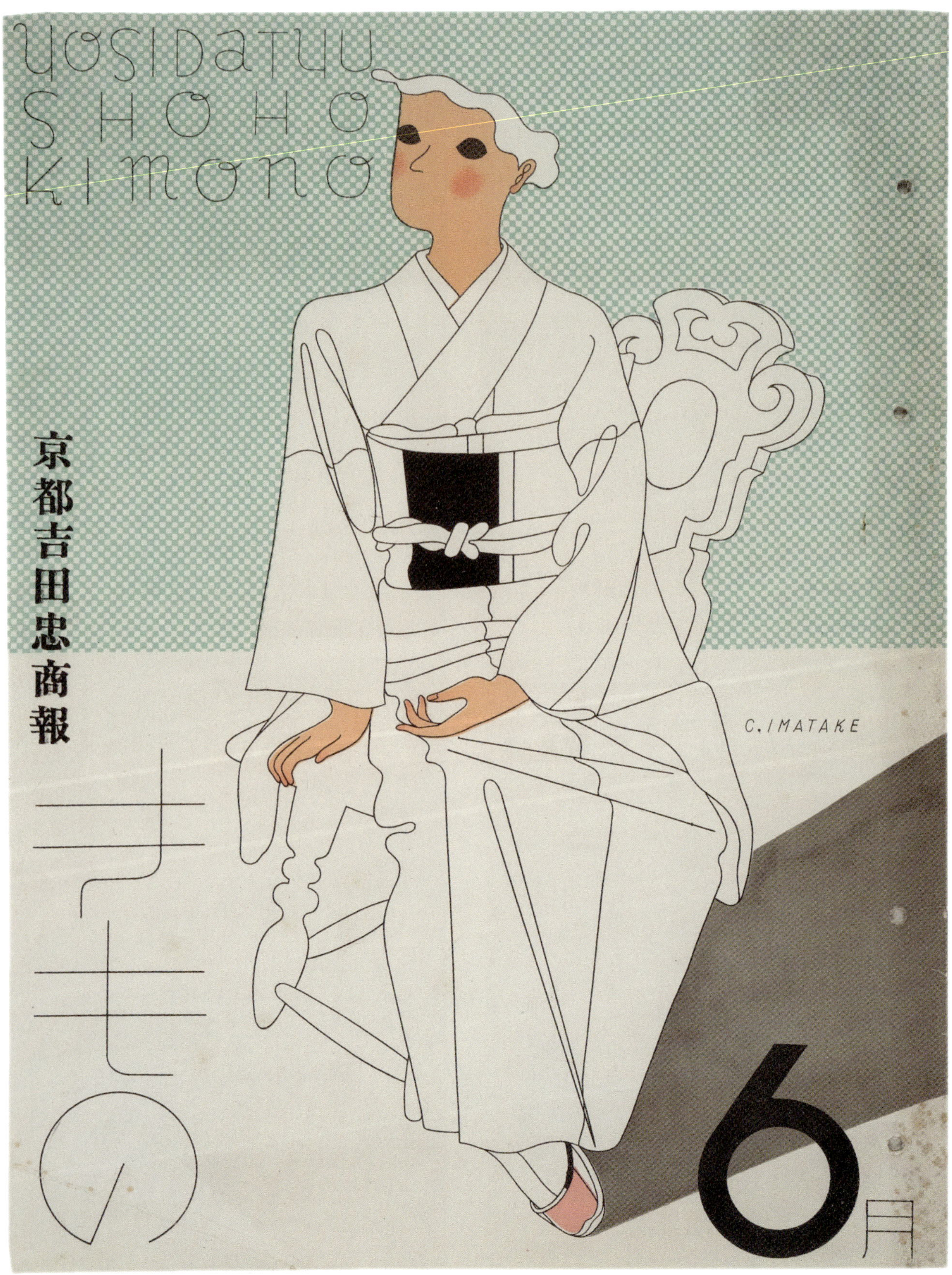

Kimono shop advertising booklet from 1939 designed by Imatake Shichiro 今竹七郎.

IMATAKE SHICHIRŌ 今竹七郎

1905–2000

Imatake Shichirō was one of the leading figures in the very early stage of Japanese design. He was renowned for his masterful use of color, his playful style of illustration, and the high quality of finish of his works.

He was born in Kobe, where his family owned a fine toilet soap manufacturing and distribution company with a section of their business devoted to imported glassware. As a child, Imatake studied English, though his parents were reticent to let him study art and design. Imatake's father compared the roles of artists to those of beggars and attempted to pull young Imatake out of school. Imatake's mother died in 1916 and his bereft father abandoned his previous businesses, opening a shop that applied traditional decorative papers to dooring and windows based on his business connections in the government. The following year, the father forced the son to take over the family business—a task that the young Imatake was uninterested in, yet feigned ready acceptance.

Over the next decade, young Imatake would steep himself in the culture of the day, frequenting cinema houses, exploring filmmaking independently, and eventually settling on design and illustration. His initial influences were Takehisa Yumeji, the Italian painter Massimo Campigli, and early Bauhaus designers. Imatake worked on a number of small-scale projects in his late teens: painting and self-publishing *dōjinshi* 同人誌 (mini-comics).

In 1926, Imatake assisted editor Hayashi Toshiko 林俊子 to design and illustrate the interiors of Hayashi's monthly literary magazine for young women called *Garden of Maidens* 乙女の園. Imatake's father became increasingly incensed by his son's commitment to art- and design-making, forbidding his son to continue to pursue design and illustration. As a result, Imatake wound up moving in with Hayashi for a time before his editor, a high school teacher, could convince Imatake's father to reconcile with his son's ambitions. The amends would be short-lived, as Imatake would sever all ties with his father when he turned 22 one year later, abandoning the family papering business that his father had forced on him a decade earlier.

In 1927, Imatake entered the advertising and public relations division of Daimaru's Kobe department store, having decided to pursue advertising design. There, he undertook the design of store displays, window displays, and printed advertisements. The same year, he took his physical exam for national military service and was refused due to having extreme myopia. At Daimaru, Imatake worked as the lone designer on a small team, designing bilingual advertising and publicity materials in Japanese and English in order to target local foreign-expat customers and tourists, and to lend Daimaru an air of international sophistication. At Daimaru, Imatake was exposed to a wide spectrum of foreign and domestic design publications like *Gebrauchsgrafik*, *Commercial Art*, and *Modern Publicity*.

At age 27, Imatake moved to Osaka and the advertising division of Takashimaya department stores for a higher wage, having been scouted due to his exceptional talents. Around this time, Imatake studied under the Japanese Impressionist painter Hayashi Shigeyoshi 林重義 in the evenings and was also influenced by the dynamic lettering work of Shochikuza Theatre's designer Yamada Shinkichi 山田伸吉, arguably the originator of "kinema characters," a form of high-contrast display lettering used on movie posters.

In 1929, Imatake and photographer Nakayama Iwata 中山岩太 started the Kobe Commercial Art Study Group 神戸商業美術研究会, a private group devoted to researching the nascent field of graphic design. Imatake was a member of Kansai-based Press Art Study Group プレスアルト研究会, publishers of *Press Art* プレスアルト, and in 1937 Imatake contributed an essay titled "The Climate of Printing and Design" to the influential advertising art portfolio/journal. The essay sparked a lively critical debate between himself and fellow Kansai designer Sakae Kawata 川田栄 about the purposes of design, which ranged across a few issues of *Press Art*.

Imatake was a regular contributor to *Kōkokukai*, writing a series called "Dessin Class" on the contributions of surrealism to commercial art, the influence of deformation, and practical design articles in 1939 and 1940. He thought "Dessin Class" would be a one-off piece, but it turned into a series on emerging graphic design theory in that publication.

Imatake founded his private design studio in 1946, initially naming it Nippon Design 日本デザイン, but then reorganized it into a limited liability corporation with seven employees in 1948—the first in Japan to do so—rechristening it Imatake Design Associates, Inc 今竹造型美術研究室. The creation of the studio at the epicenter of Osaka was reliant upon Takashimaya's underwriting.

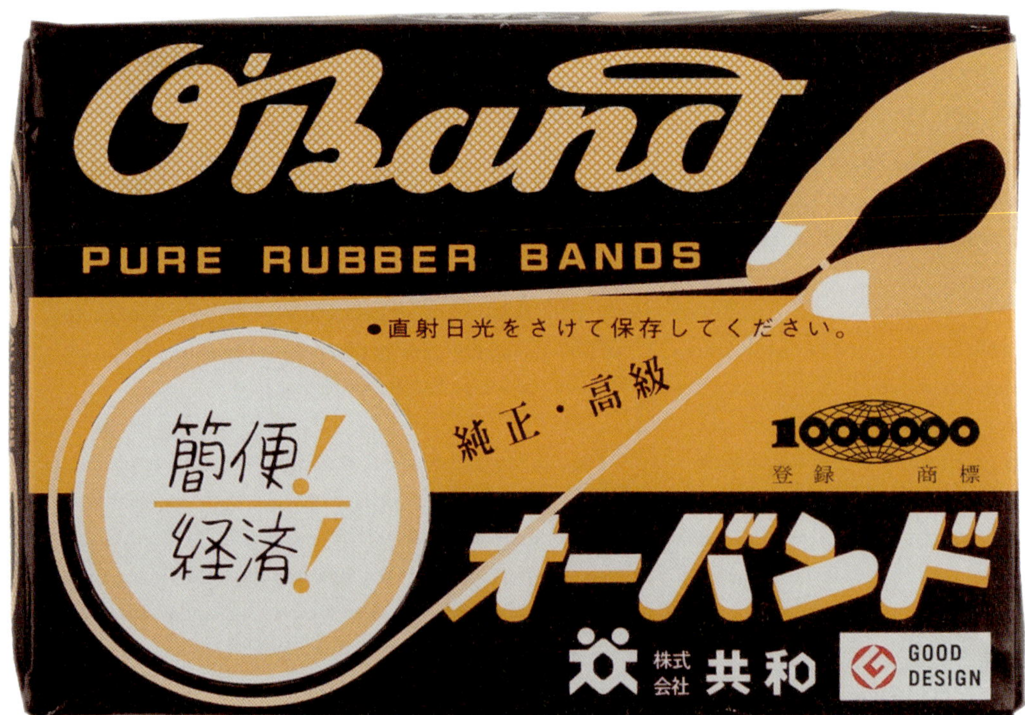

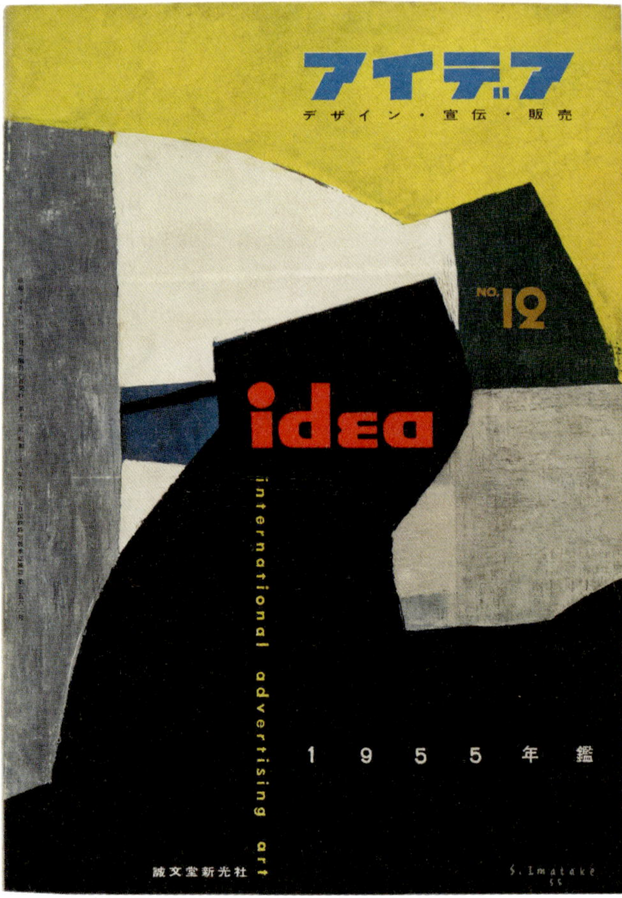

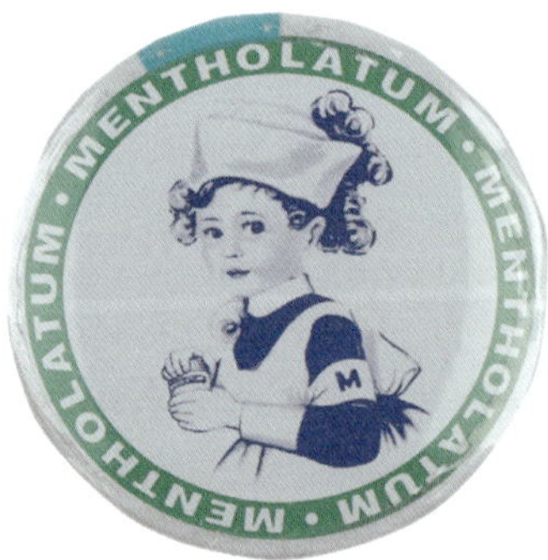

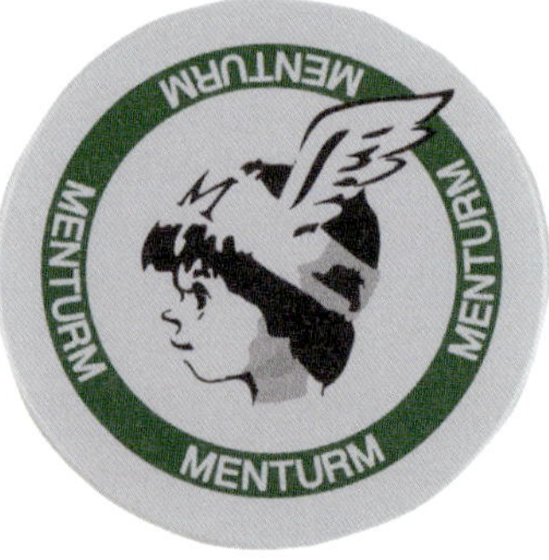

Top: **O' Band rubber bands** (Osaka: Kyowa Limited, 2021)—the contemporary design still uses Imatake's 1951 layout with the addition of slight contemporary typographic elements. Bottom left: Cover design by Imatake Shichiro 今竹七郎 for ***IDEA* アイデア No. 12**, (Tokyo: Seibundo Shinkosha 誠文堂新光社, 1955). Bottom right: Packaging for **Mentholatum** and **Menturm**, both designed by Imatake in 1974.

Regarding the formation of his studio, Imatake recounted, "I opened my own studio by special arrangement with Takashimaya, as I needed to continue being an employee for stability, yet was contacted by Sumitomo Bank to act as advertising advisor."[1] Despite having gigantic clients, Imatake was in the precarious situation of attempting to open a corporate design consultancy at a time when there were no antecedent models. He wrote that "there was no established definition of graphic design in Japan" and that graphic design was akin to a "gaseous object" not yet given form in Japanese culture.[2]

He would engineer Japan's first printed—not painted—billboard in 1951 and was one of the key founding members of the Japan Advertising Artists Club that same year. Imatake's intimate relationship with Takashimaya paved the way for design-centric activities at the department store's branches, prominently the *Graphic '55* exhibition held at Takashimaya's Tokyo branch in 1955. While not a participant, it was Imatake who helped organize the exhibition.

Imatake created a number of packaging designs that are iconic in the Japanese product landscape, markedly his illustration of "the little nurse" used for Mentholatum products in 1950, his 1953 logo and box for O'Band rubber bands, and later designs for Menturm lip balm. He also designed the logos for the Nankai Hawks 南海ホークス baseball team and the Kansai Electric Power Company 関西電力株式会社, among many other designs that would help define the local Kansai aesthetic.

Imatake was a key contributor to Idea magazine from its founding in 1953. He designed the cover of issue six and frequently wrote on design theory and history for the magazine through the 1970s.

Imatake passed away in 2000. His design work for consumer packaging helped to define aesthetic notions in Japan. While many of his contemporaries relocated to Tokyo, Imatake decided to remain in the Kansai region for nearly the entirety of his life—he opened a branch office of his design studio in 1955, but Imatake always maintained that he was more of a visitor than a resident of Tokyo.

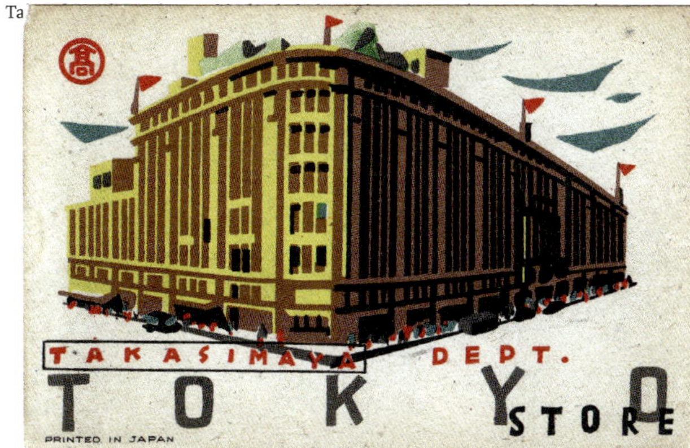

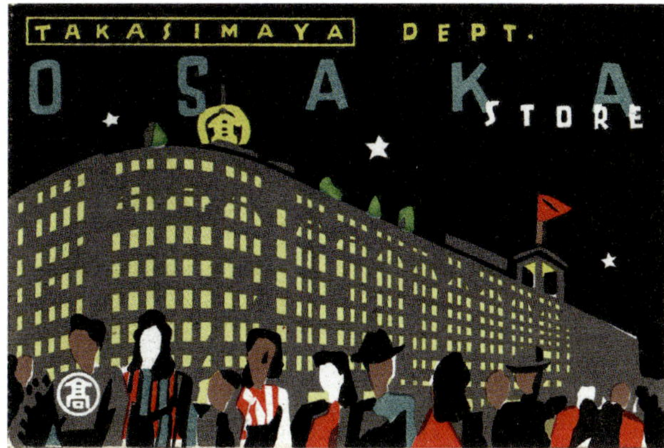

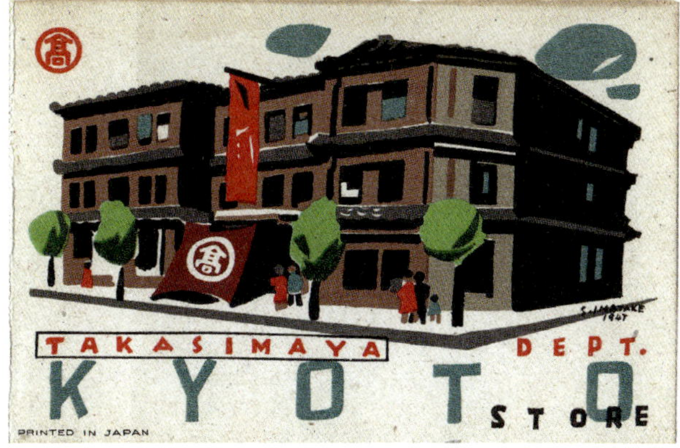

Postcards for **Takashimaya** department stores in Tokyo, Osaka, and Kyoto designed by Imatake in 1947.

References:

Imatake, Shichiro. *Imatake Shichirō to Sono Jidai: Gurafikku Dezain, Modan Kaiga no Senkusha = Shichiro Imatake, Life and Times 1905–2000*. Tokyo: Seibundō Shinkōsha, 2003.

Imatake, Shichiro. *Modernism in Japan: The world of Shichirō Imatake*. Osaka: Imatake & Associates, Inc., 1989.

1 Imatake Shichirō, *Imatake Shichirō to Sono Jidai: Gurafikku Dezain, Modan Kaiga No Senkusha = Shichiro Imatake, Life and Times 1905–2000* (Tokyo: Seibundō Shinkōsha, 2003), 34.

2 Ibid.

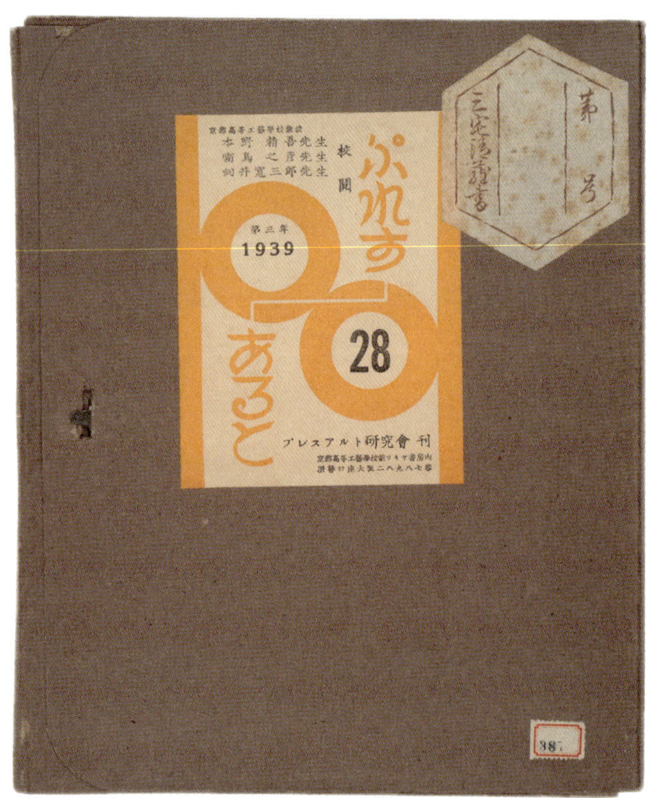

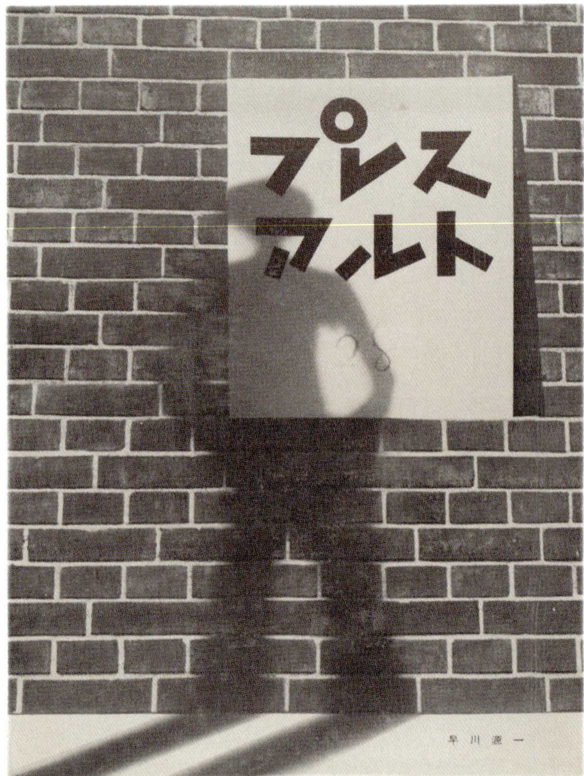

This spread: Portfolio cover, short-form magazine, and advertising brochures placed in die-cut chipboard sample sheets from *Press Art* プレスアルト, No. 28,(Kyoto: Press Art Study Group プレスアルト研究会, 1939).

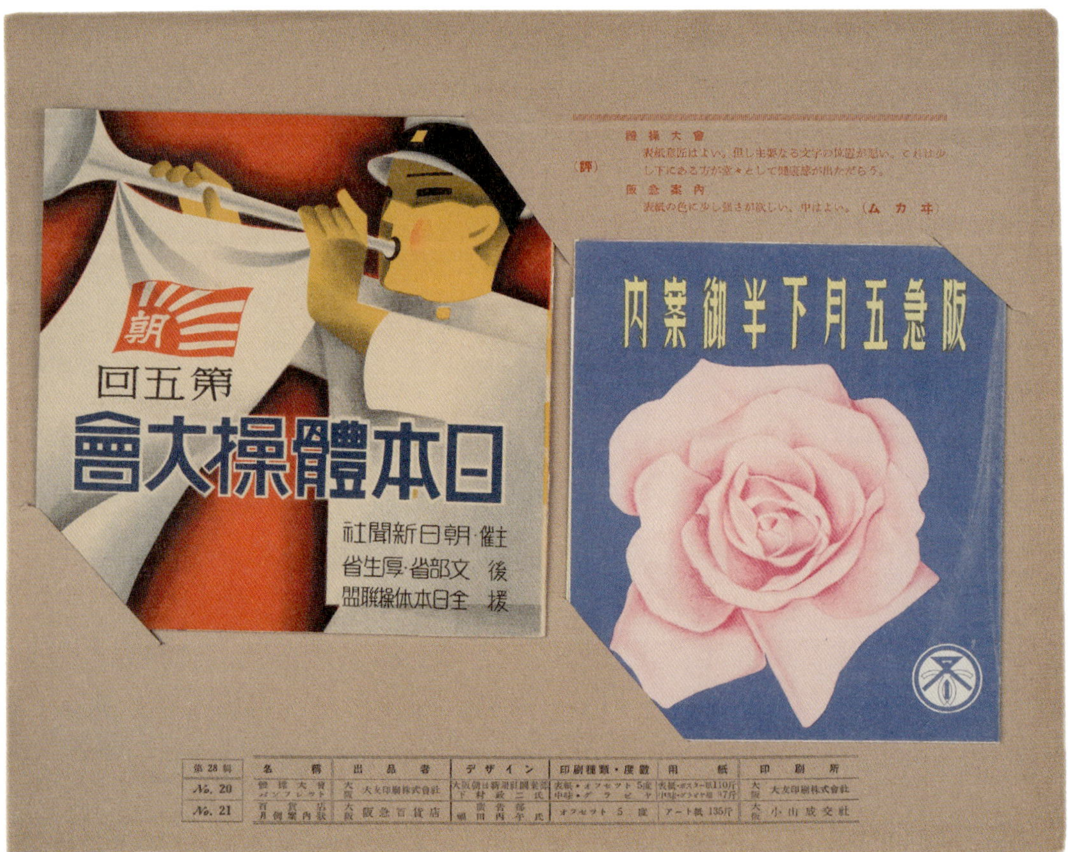

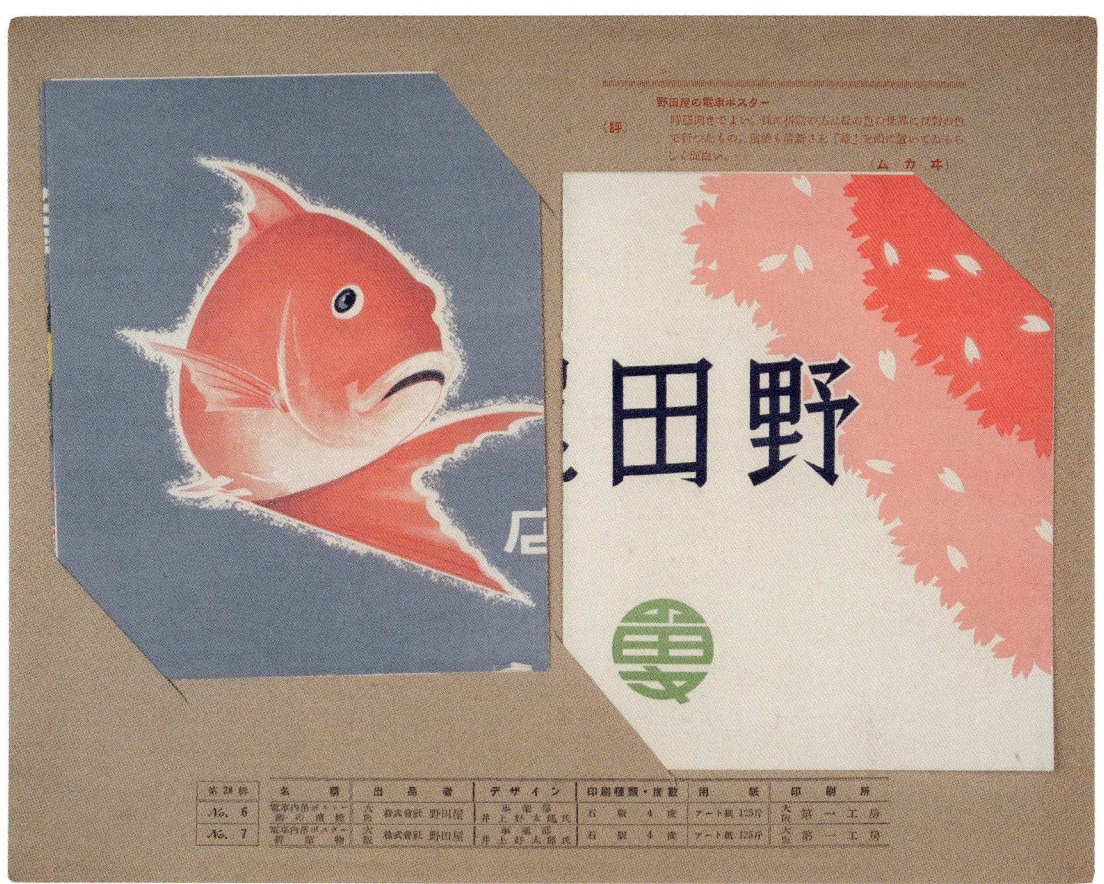

PRESS ART プレスアルト

Puresu Alto, katakanized Esperanto for "Printing Art" or "Press Art" in English, was a long-running design publication from the Kansai area. The format of the publication was rather unusual—as opposed to a bound journal printed with reproductions of design work, issues of *Press Art* were composed of original individual posters, flyers, and advertisements which were inserted into die-cut sheets of carefully printed cardstock which held information about the designer, client, printing company, printing method, paper stock, and other details about each work. The size of the sheets changed form issue-to-issue, but each issue of *Press Art* also included a folded and stapled offset-printed journal documenting trends in design and printing of that time,

As *Press Art* had a limited, subscription-based audience and the journal was not sold in bookstores, the print run of each issue varied from 100 copies at the start to 300 copies from the second issue onward. Each issue included additional support materials, from newsletter broadsheets to booklets featuring design criticism, news, and history.

Press Art was instigated by The Press Art Study Group プレスアルト研究会, whose meetings were held in the secondhand book store Wakiya Shobō ワキヤ書房 run by founder Waki Seikichi 脇清吉, and whose initial members comprised of Department of Design at Kyoto High School of Industrial Arts faculty members Motono Seigo 本野精吾 and Shimotori Yukihiko 霜鳥之彦 alongside Kotani Shoichi 小谷正一 of the newspaper publisher *The Mainichi Shimbun* 毎日新聞. From 1937 to 1944, then again from 1949 to 1966, each of the seventy-three volumes was hand-assembled by Waki, though local designers such as Imatake Shichirō and Tanaka Ikkō offered financial, material, and research support to the group. Tokyo-based designers like Yamana Ayao also offered support, with Yamana briefly entertaining the notion of publishing a Kantō version of *Press Art*. Waki passed away in 1966, yet the Study Group continued publishing *Press Art* regularly until the 335th issue in 1977 under the direction of Waki's son Waki Tōho 脇とうほ. A one-off special issue was published in 1986, celebrating a decade since the last issue of the journal.

Each issue feels like a time capsule and a labor of love through research—the entire print run of *Press Art* included over 6,000 examples of contemporary printed design pieces from that time.

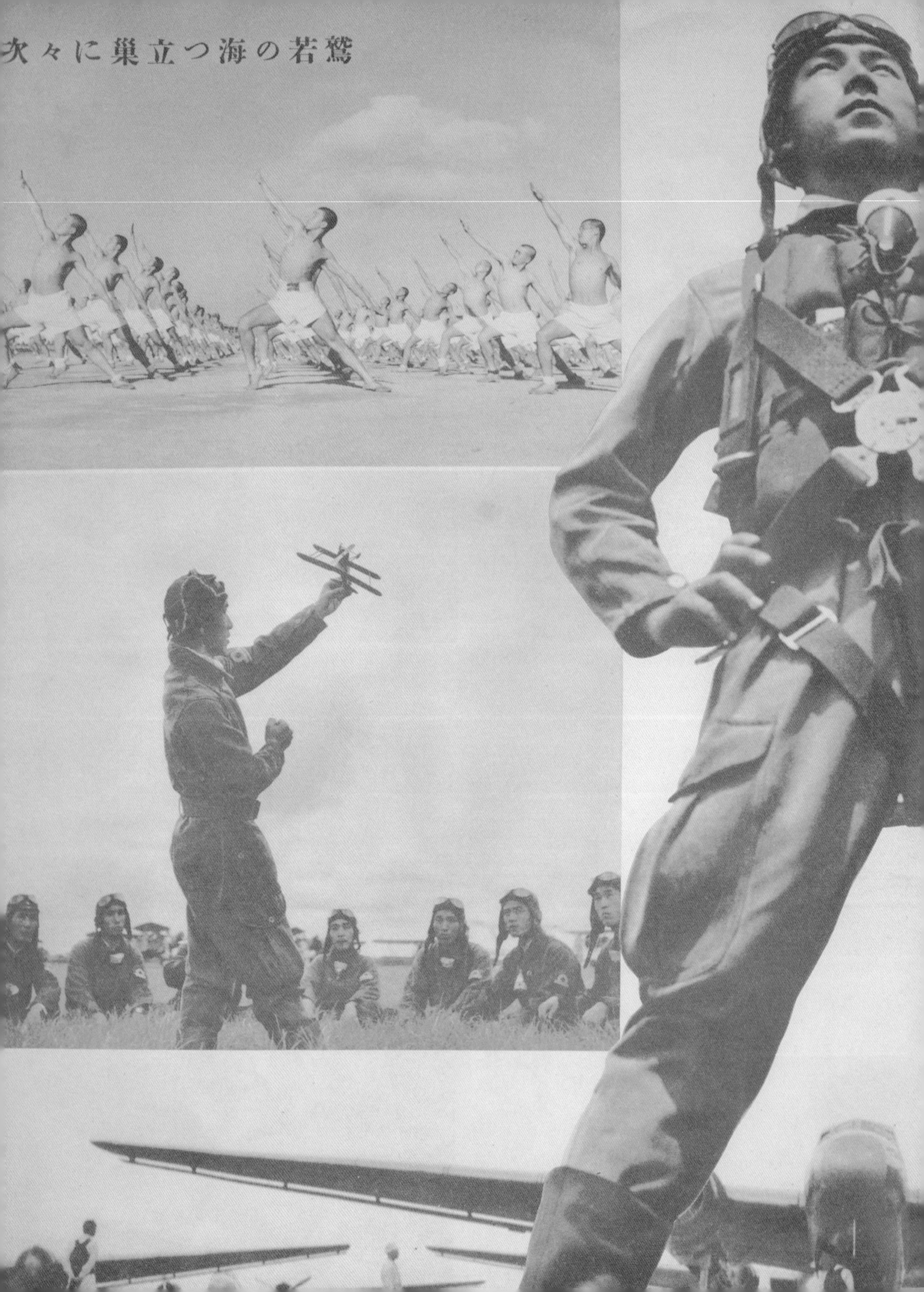
次々に巣立つ海の若鷲

海軍航空隊の訓練

propaganda in print

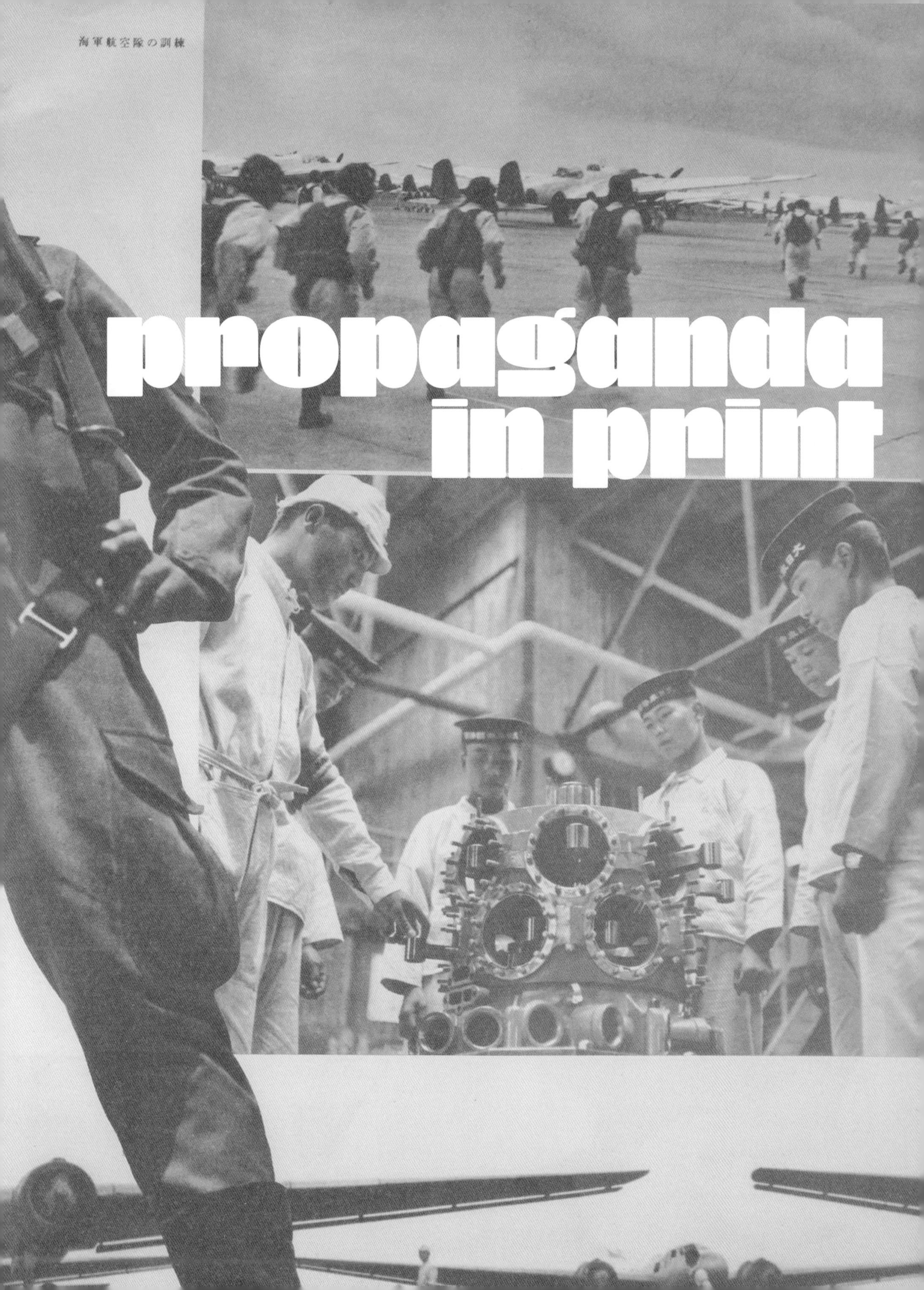

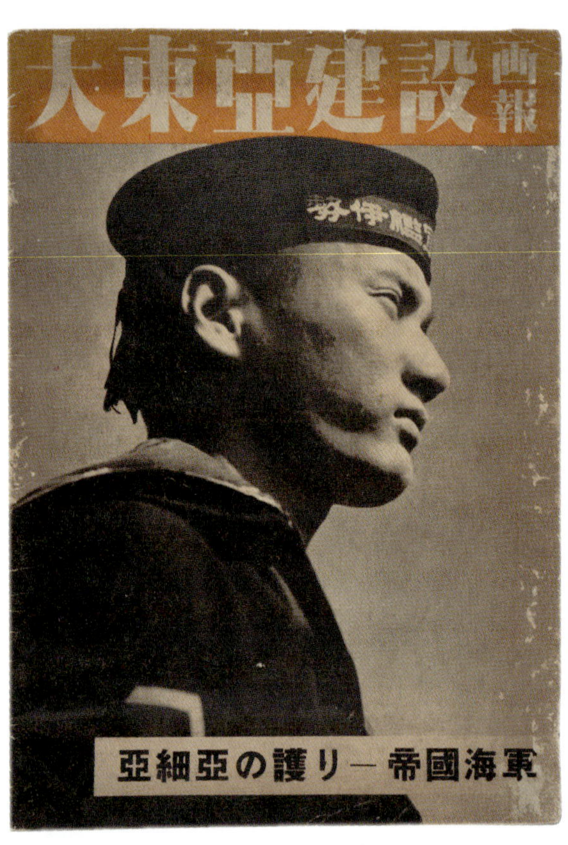

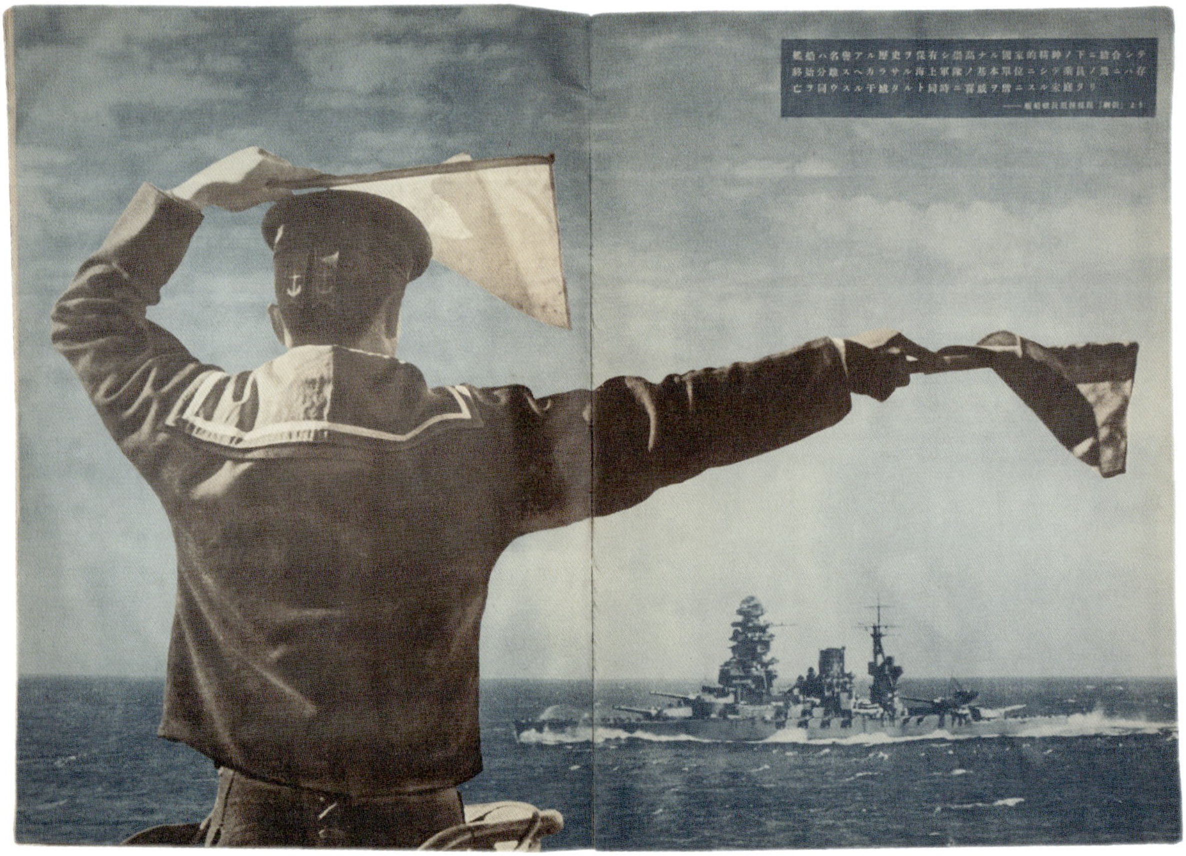

Debut issue of **大東亜建設画報**, the Japanese language version of ***FRONT*** (Tokyo: Chuo Kōbo 中央工房, 1942), designed by Hara Hiromu 原弘 with photography by Kimura Ihei 木村伊兵衛.

Propaganda in Print: The Inter-War Period

Japan's history of imperialism and colonial projects stretches back to the beginning of the nineteenth century, with a mounting number of military victories, alliances, annexations, and colonizations that would continue unabated until the end of World War II. This aspect of Japan's history set the stage for the country's involvement in that war, but it also helps to explain the culture of patriotic fervor within which Japanese graphic design would develop, amongst other forms of applied arts.

The First Sino-Japanese War was waged in 1895 between the Qing Empire of China and the Empire of Japan. Both nations were fighting over the right to enact trade and governance in Korea, though China's resounding defeat resulted in Korean independence and Japan's annexation of Taiwan (then Formosa), as well as the archipelago of Penghu and the Senkaku Islands.

This war was followed by the Russo-Japanese War in 1904 and 1905 when the Japanese government perceived Russia as a threat to Asian expansionism and initiate a naval attack on the Russian Eastern Fleet docked at a rented port in Port Arthur, China. Despite the optimism of Russia's Tsar Nicholas II, Japan success in a number of naval battles heralded Japan's entry under the world stage; this was the first time that an Asian power had defeated a western one. The Empire of Japan attempted to formalize its control over Korea in 1905, as Russia had formerly had military predominance there, and Korea became a Japanese protectorate. After a number of treaties, Japan annexed Korea completely in 1910, with the Korean emperor conceding the nation's sovereignty to Japan's emperor and the Japanese military police forces taking control over Korea's legislative bodies and media.

From 1914 to 1918, Japan fought in alliance with France, the United Kingdom, and Russia in World War I, securing the sea lanes from the Imperial German Navy. Their participation in the war yielded them the Palau, Caroline, Northern Mariana, and Marshall Islands, as dictated by the Treaty of Versailles in 1918. The expansion of the Japanese Empire and Japan's involvement in this successful series of incursions and wars led to widespread adoption of ultra-nationalist ideologies in the post-quake 1920s, with an insistence upon expansionist rhetoric.

Japan invaded the Chinese province of Manchuria in 1931 believing that Manchurian resources would help Japan emerge successfully from its economic struggles. A chronic financial recession had plagued Japan in the 1920s following the economic boom of World War I, and then the global economic collapse of the Great Depression resulted in the Showa Depression of 1930–1931. Japan's invasion of Manchuria was incredibly popular, as government- and industry-spread propaganda decreed that Manchuria's vast natural resources were the "lifeline" Japan needed. By 1932, Japan had installed Manchuria as a puppet state under the romanized name Manchukuo 満州国 ("Manshūkoku" in Japanese), and mass immigration from Japan to Manchukuo followed as the new nation underwent a period of rapid industrialization directed by the Japanese military.

During the 1930s, propaganda reached a fever pitch in Japan, with images of Japanese dominance omnipresent in the public sphere. The *omoshirogara* patterns used for kimono morphed into *sensōgara* 戦争柄 (literally "war patterns"), which were emblazoned on the interiors of male kimono jacket linings and on underlinings. Kimono for men have traditionally been reserved in the expression of pattern, but inside and underneath there is a rich history of self-expression, just barely hidden from view.

Similar patterns were used on children's kimono, mixing imagery of childhood, toys, animals, and cartoons with warplanes, battleships, zeppelins, and tanks. Some bore imagery of child soldiers blaring bugles and straddling the globe, with Japan's territories carefully picked out in bright colors, though usually red. Others incorporated popular propaganda imagery such as Norakuro のらくろ, the cartoon dog, and member of "The Fierce Dogs Fighting Brigade" created by former Mavo member Tagawa Suiho. Sensōgara patterns include illustrations of then-recent historical battle scenes, military technology and vehicles, daring scenes of aerial combat, bold interpretations of Japan's navy, and many other signs and symbols of Japanese militarism, patriotism, and nationalism.

For children, the inclusion of drawings of toys and playthings alongside weapons, zeppelins, fighter planes, and musical instruments normalized concepts of war, instilling early preparedness and a semiotic cognizance that a drum was created to provide the rhythm of both the playground and the battlefield. Sensōgara often pair propaganda with the transmissive media: zeppelins, hot air balloons, tanks, trains, planes, battleships, and automobiles feature as widely as radio, telegraph, and post. Children cheer, and Norakuro salutes his brave dog army from

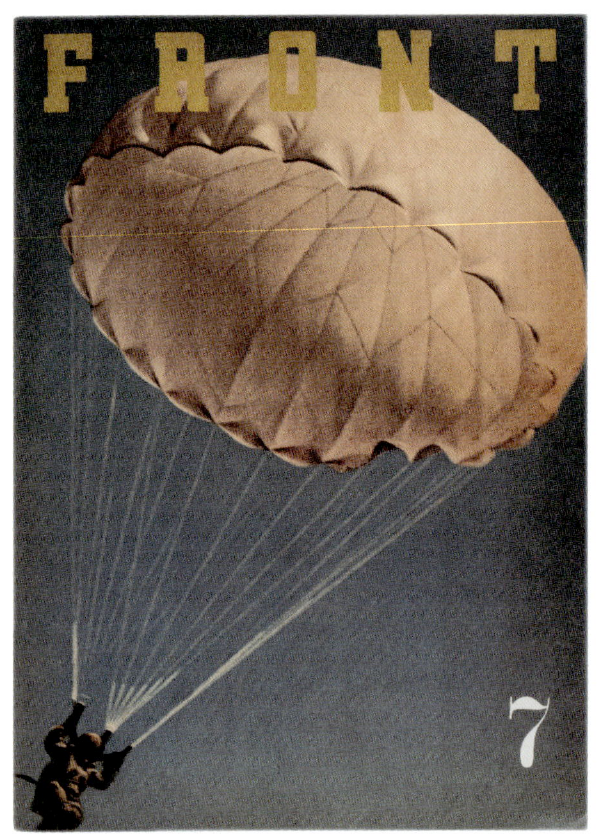
FRONT
7

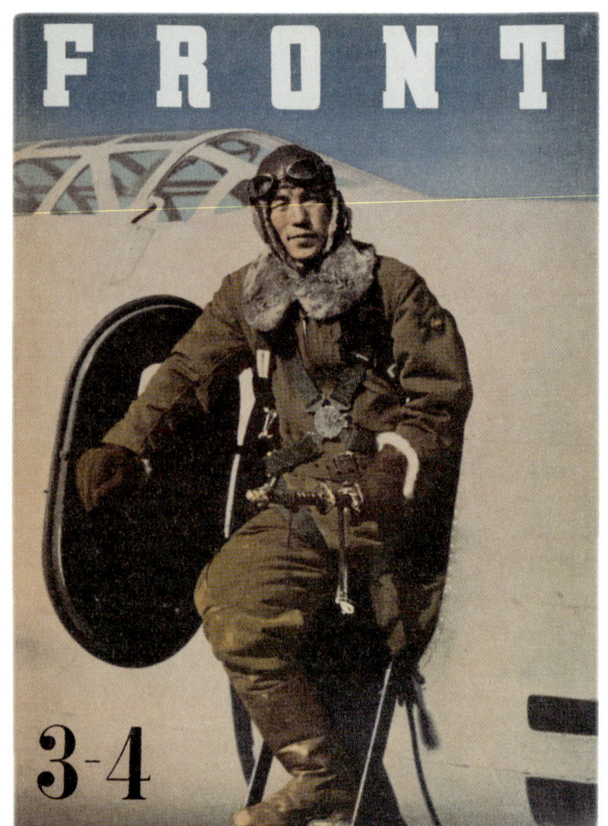
FRONT
3-4

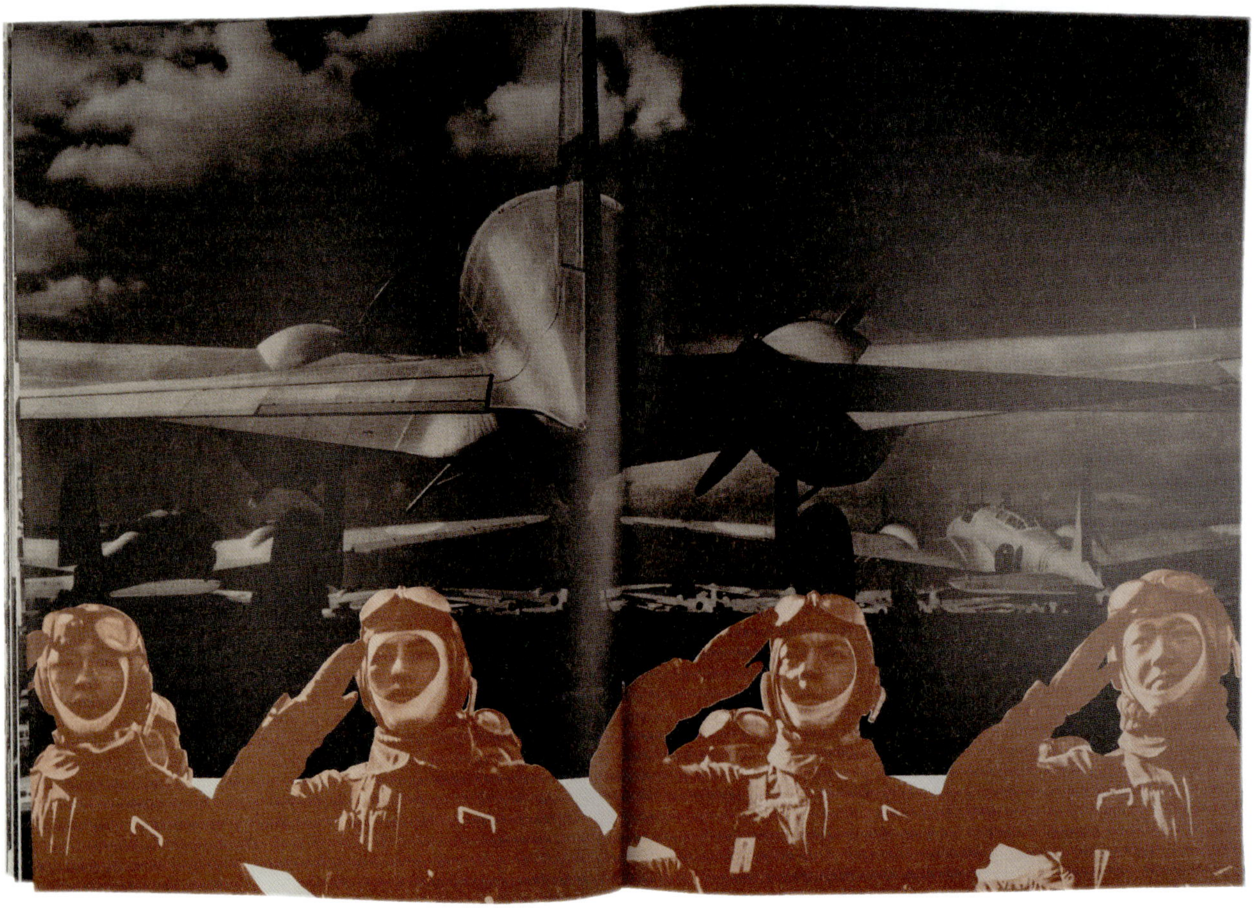

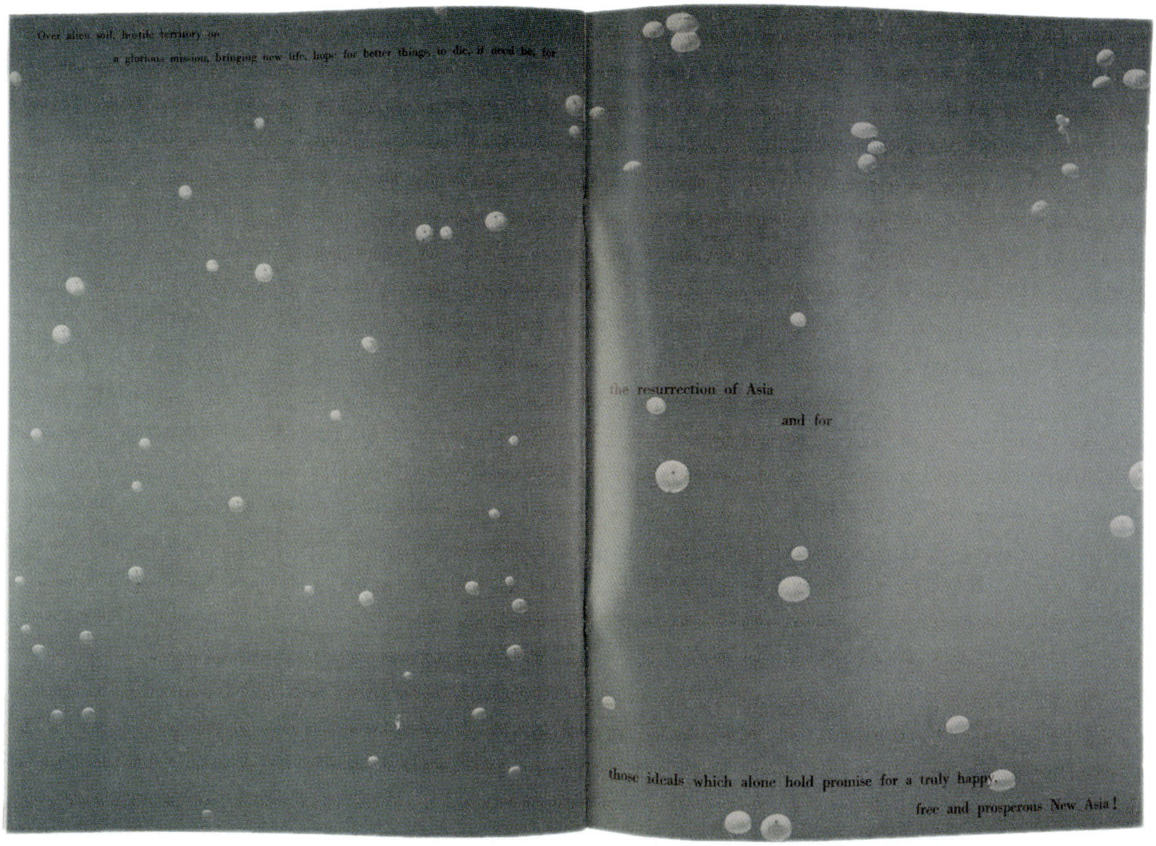

Over alien soil, hostile territory on

a glorious mission, bringing new life, hope for better things, to die, if need be, for

the resurrection of Asia

and for

those ideals which alone hold promise for a truly happy,

free and prosperous New Asia!

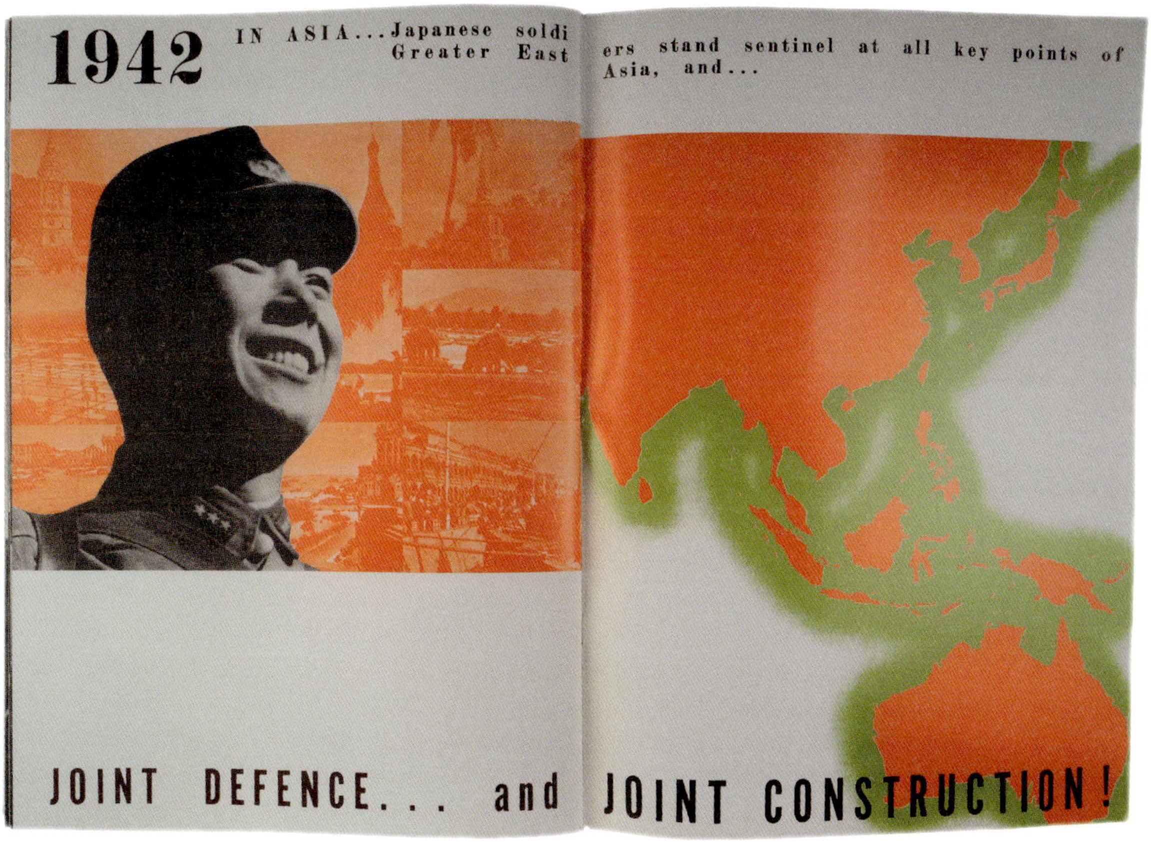

1942 IN ASIA... Japanese soldiers stand sentinel at all key points of Greater East Asia, and...

JOINT DEFENCE... and JOINT CONSTRUCTION!

Assorted covers and spreads from ***FRONT***.

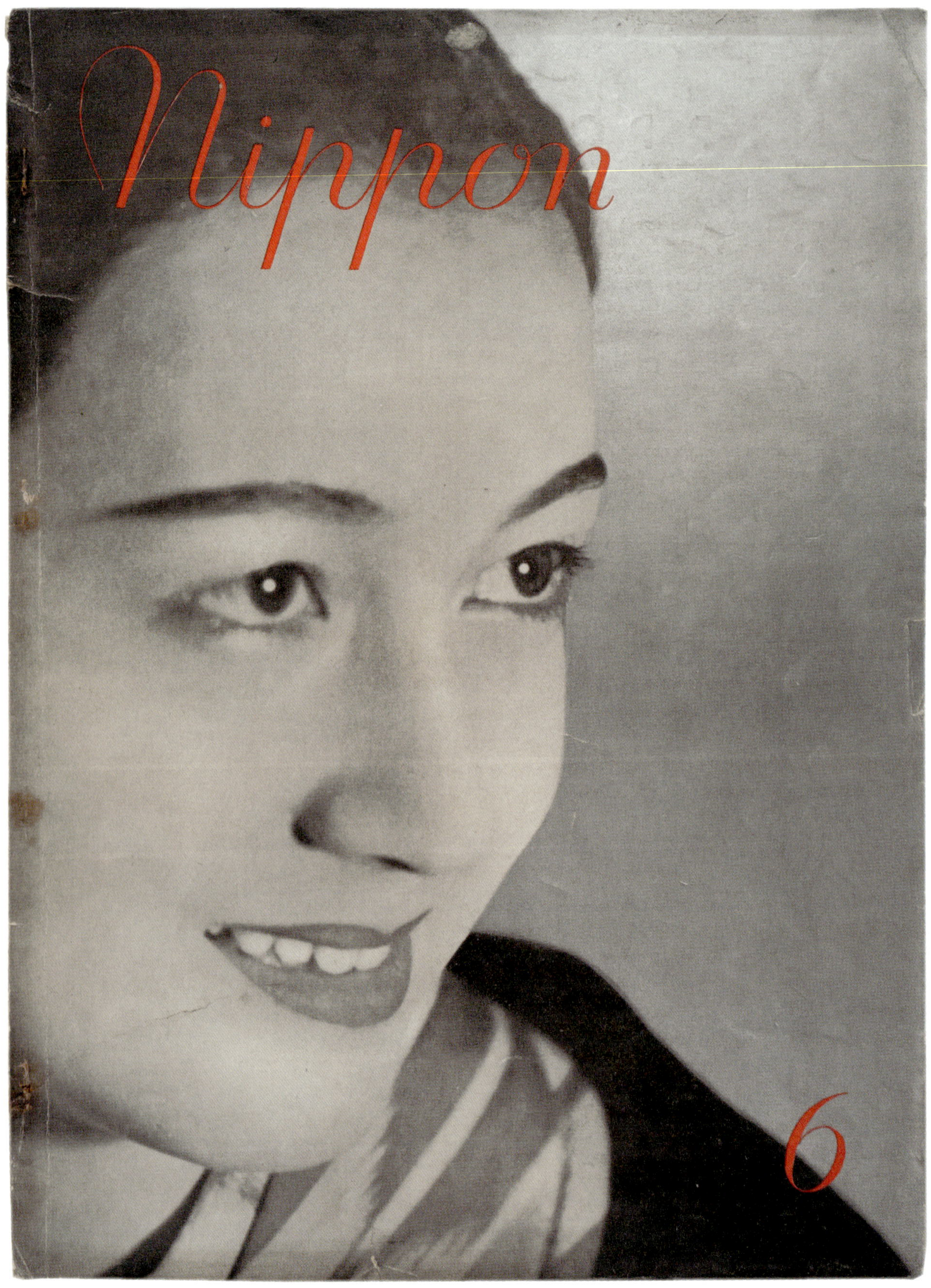

This page and following two spreads: Assorted covers from ***Nippon*** (Tokyo: Nippon Kōbo 日本工房, 1934–1944).

his position guarding the doghouse as a bulldog fiercely drives by in a tank.

In one fabric pattern design, a mix of scenes from both a *kamishibai* 紙芝居 street performer and a film projector recount the silhouettes of child soldiers prancing in victory dances in foreign jungles, while a child spy with his rabbit and black squirrel pals navigate the high seas by boat. That image is overlapped by a framed illustrated scene of a tank in front of razor wire and the rolling smoke of the battlefield. In too many others, the Japanese flag stands prominently in the foreground with the flags of Manchukuo and occupied Korea waving behind it, examples of soft propaganda that might be worn by man, woman, and child alike.

Throughout the 1930s, Japanese self-perception was that of a modern nation, with these materials embodying an increasingly militarized approach to Modernism—"the modern" of the 1930s was power, domination, and occupation as much as domestic cosmopolitanism. These patterns capture a slice in time just prior to what Japanese expansion would become—by the early 1940s, mass-produced textiles were in short supply due to wartime shortages and the country's production intensification for the military.

During the 1930s and 1940s, a number of propaganda magazines 宣伝雑誌 (*senden zasshi*) and publications emerged that were aimed at both the domestic populace and the promotion of Japan abroad. The two major magazines designed to convey Japan's public relations and propaganda messaging overseas, *Nippon* and *Front*, were hybrid public/private concerns with a singular starting point: the controversial figure Natori Yōnosuke 名取洋之助.

Natori was born in 1910 to a wealthy family and attended high school in Japan, though he insisted on being sent to Germany for further education at age eighteen. In Munich, he studied design and photography and married a German woman named Erna Mecklenburg, and he began freelancing as a photographer for various publications afterward. Working for the publisher Ullstein Press, Natori was sent on photographic assignments first to Japan in 1932 and then to Manchukuo in 1933. His photography was widely published in Germany, which earned him a substantial income and established him as an internationally recognized photographer—so much so that he and Mecklenburg decided to create a company in Japan in 1933 that might function as a news agency and publishing entity. This company was called Nippon Kōbō 日本工房 and was co-founded with photographer Kimura Ihei 木村伊兵衛, designer Hara Hiromu 原弘, critic Ina Nobuo 伊奈信男, and the multi-talented and powerful producer and photographer Okada Sōzō 岡田桑三. The fledgling group would dissolve within a year due to financial and interpersonal difficulties, but not before they held two successful exhibitions in Leipzig and Berlin. Kimura, Hara, and Ina would go on to form Chūō Kōbō 中央工房, a rival organization which would evolve to later produce the propaganda magazine *Front*.

Natori and Mecklenburg regrouped quickly and recruited graphic designer Kōno Takashi 河野鷹思 and German editor Albert Theile to create a mockup of what would become Nippon, a Japanese magazine aimed at foreign audiences that promoted Japan as a modern nation-state, as well as promoting Japanese products and tourism.

When Japan seceded from the League of Nations in 1933 due to its invasion of Manchuria, it tarnished the country's reputation internationally. *Nippon* was a public relations vessel designed to help restore national dignity abroad. Natori obtained corporate sponsorship through the cosmetics company Kanebo カネボウ株式会社 for the first issue and was quickly able to bring on other advertisers, notably the corporations Mitsubishi 三菱財閥 and Mitsui 三井財閥, and obtain state sponsorship through the Press Unit of the Army Ministry.

Forty-one issues of *Nippon* were published in English, French, German, and Spanish, including five Japanese-language editions, all between 1934 and 1944. The debut issue included a photographic editorial piece that featured foreign ambassadors and their wives enjoying themselves at assorted tourist locations. According to academic Andrea Germer, the piece suggests that, "by visually inviting foreign readers to join Western diplomats and their spouses on their joyful and relaxed trips to scenic spots of the country, it cleverly combined 'semi-official' representation with a private, personal, cultural and peaceful context, displaying a community of friends hosted by the Japanese."[1]

Nippon's visual design reflected the modern aesthetics of the Bauhaus. Its content proposed a version of Japan that was more lifestyle-oriented, while simultaneously examining the

1 Andrea Germer, "Visual Propaganda in Wartime East Asia – The Case of Natori Yōnosuke," *The Asia-Pacific Journal: Japan Focus*, (May 9, 2011): https://apjjf.org/2011/9/20/Andrea-Germer/3530/article.html.

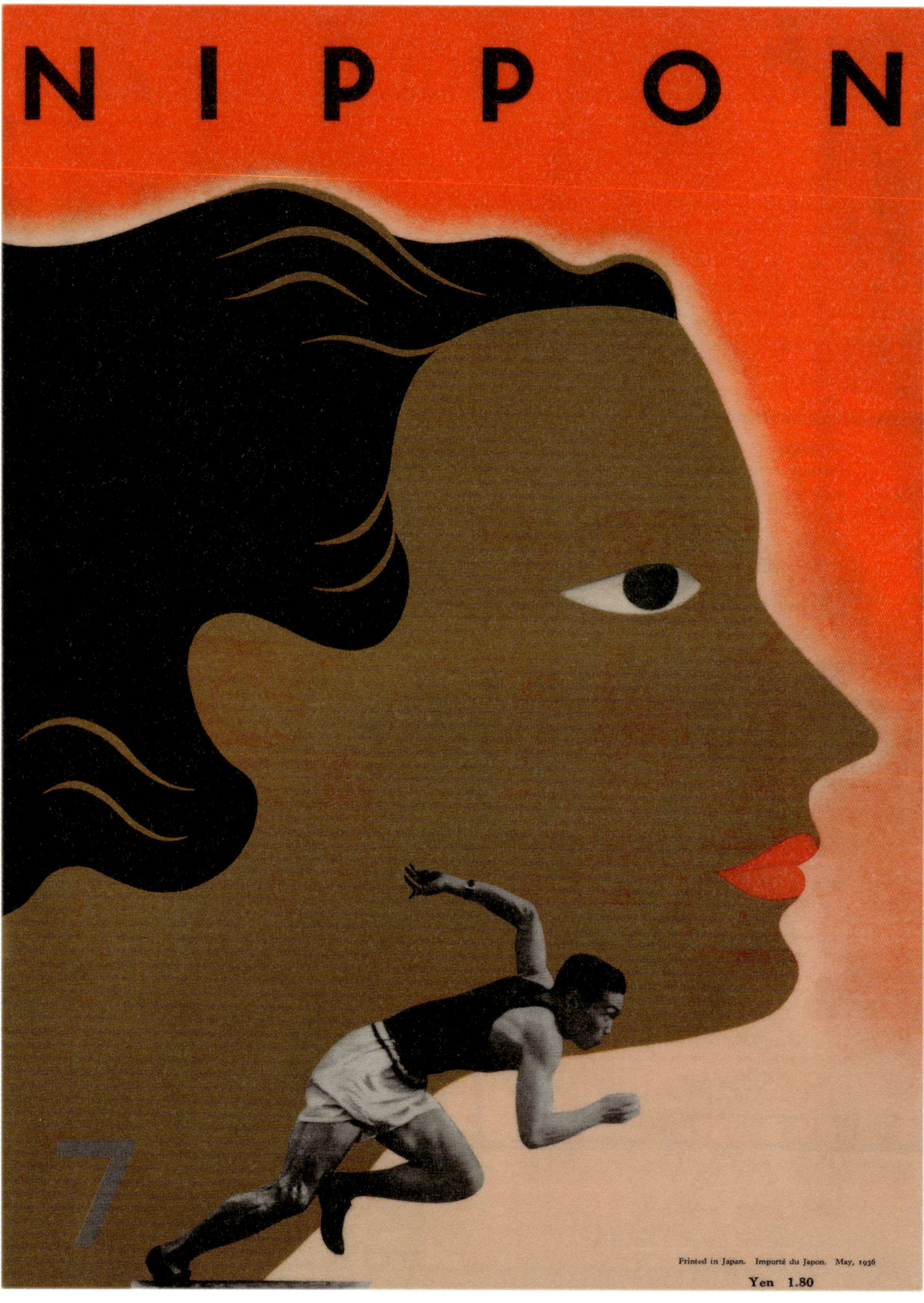
NIPPON
7
Printed in Japan. Importé du Japon. May, 1936
Yen 1.80

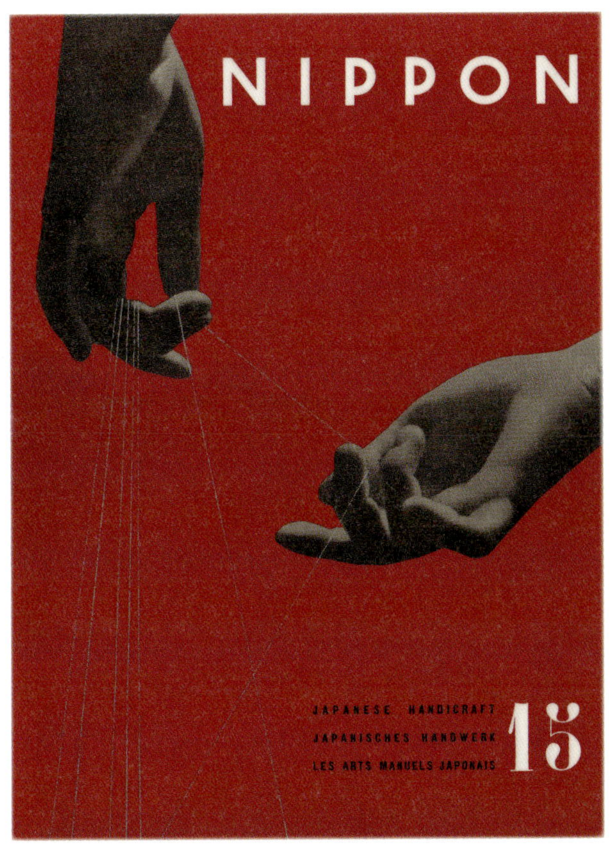
NIPPON
JAPANESE HANDICRAFT
JAPANISCHES HANDWERK
LES ARTS MANUELS JAPONAIS
15

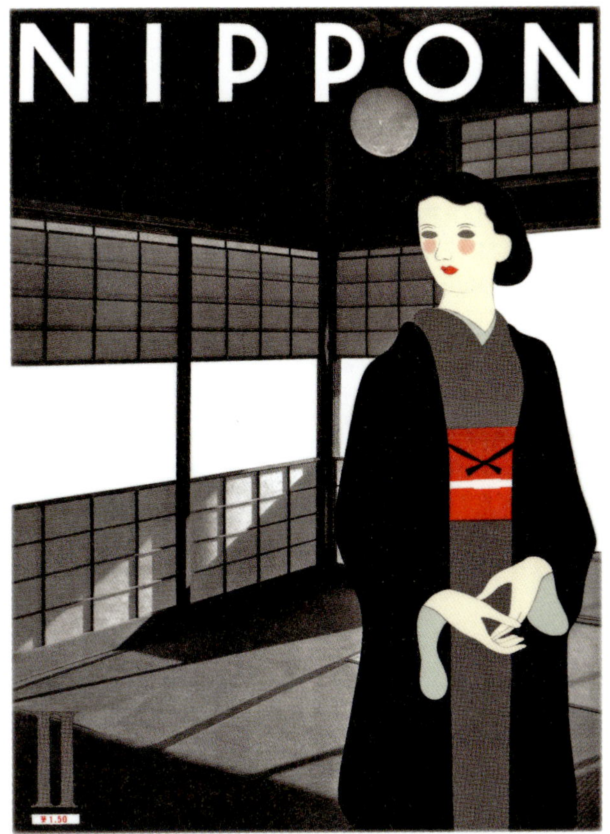
NIPPON
11
¥1.50

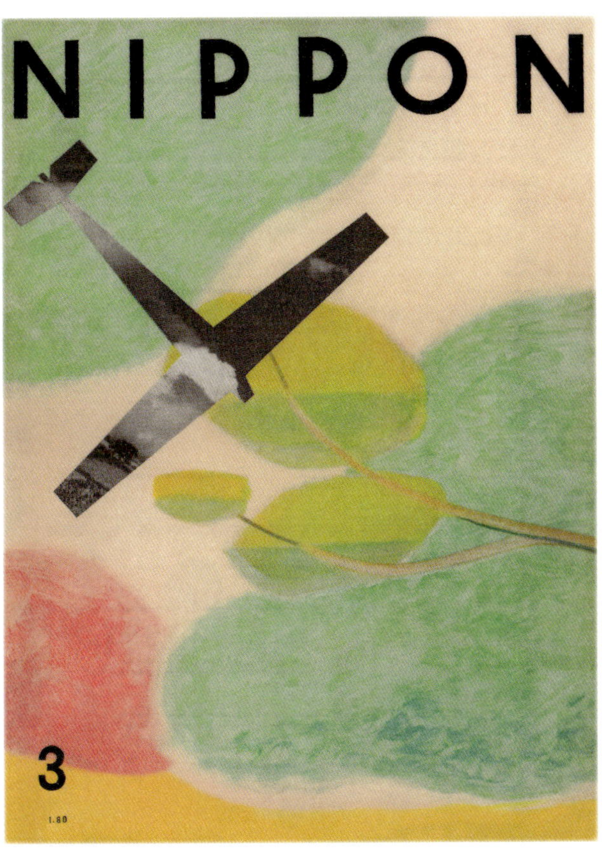
NIPPON
3
1.80

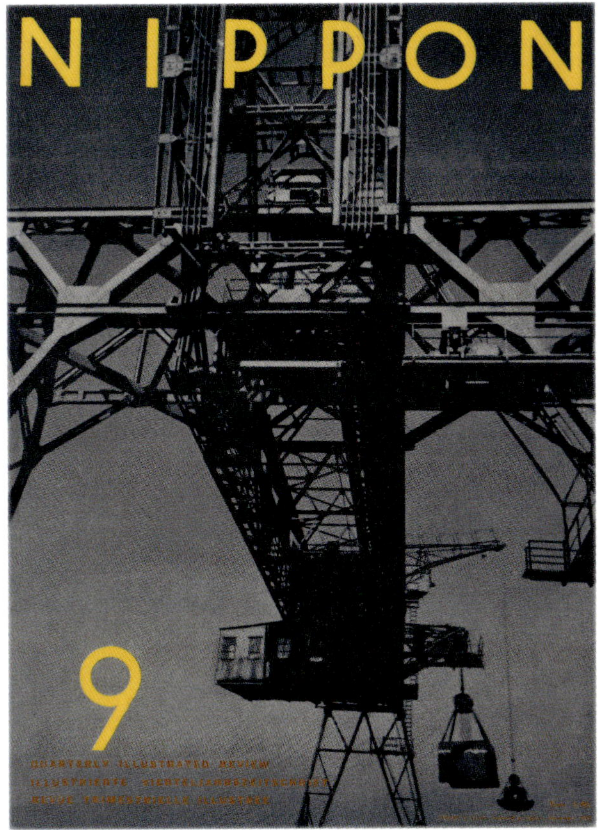
NIPPON
9
QUARTERLY ILLUSTRATED REVIEW

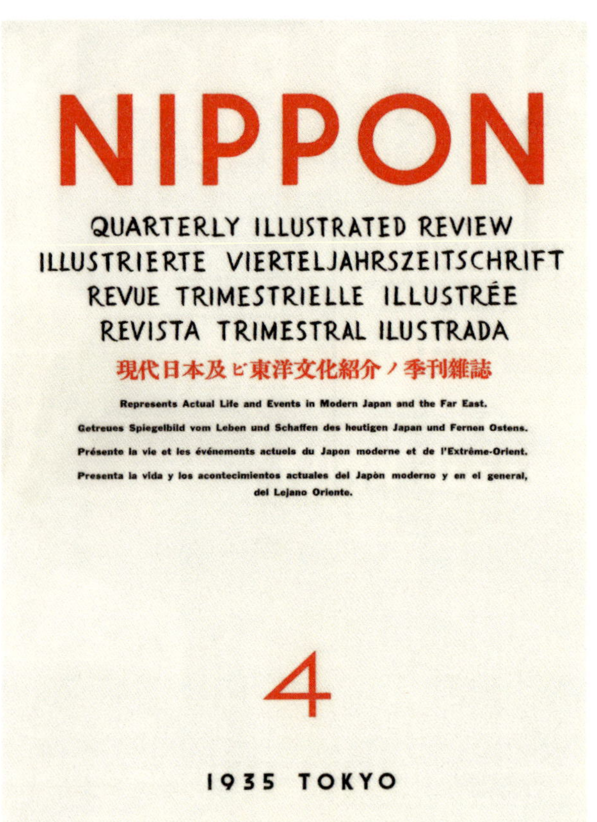
NIPPON
QUARTERLY ILLUSTRATED REVIEW
ILLUSTRIERTE VIERTELJAHRSZEITSCHRIFT
REVUE TRIMESTRIELLE ILLUSTRÉE
REVISTA TRIMESTRAL ILUSTRADA
現代日本及ビ東洋文化紹介ノ季刊雑誌
Represents Actual Life and Events in Modern Japan and the Far East.
Getreues Spiegelbild vom Leben und Schaffen des heutigen Japan und Fernen Ostens.
Présente la vie et les événements actuels du Japon moderne et de l'Extrême-Orient.
Presenta la vida y los acontecimientos actuales del Japòn moderno y en el general, del Lejano Oriente.
4
1935 TOKYO

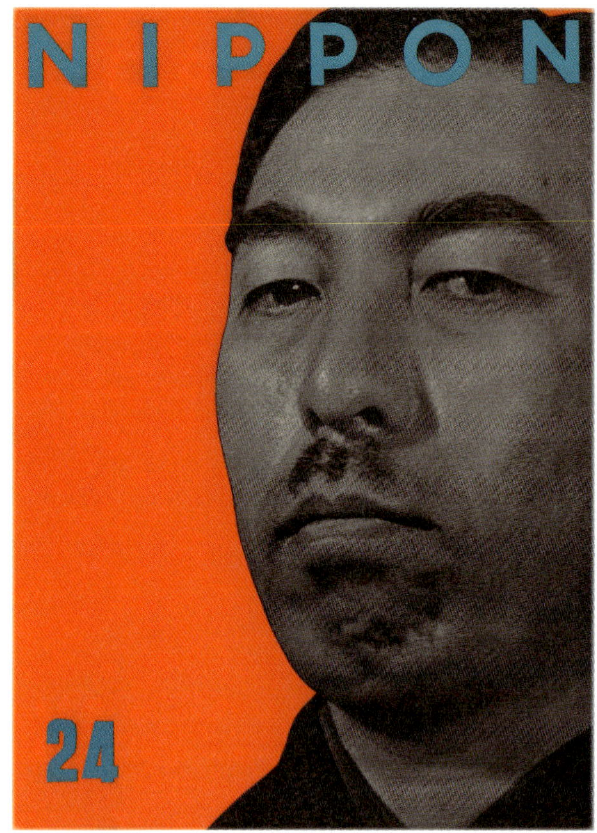
NIPPON
24

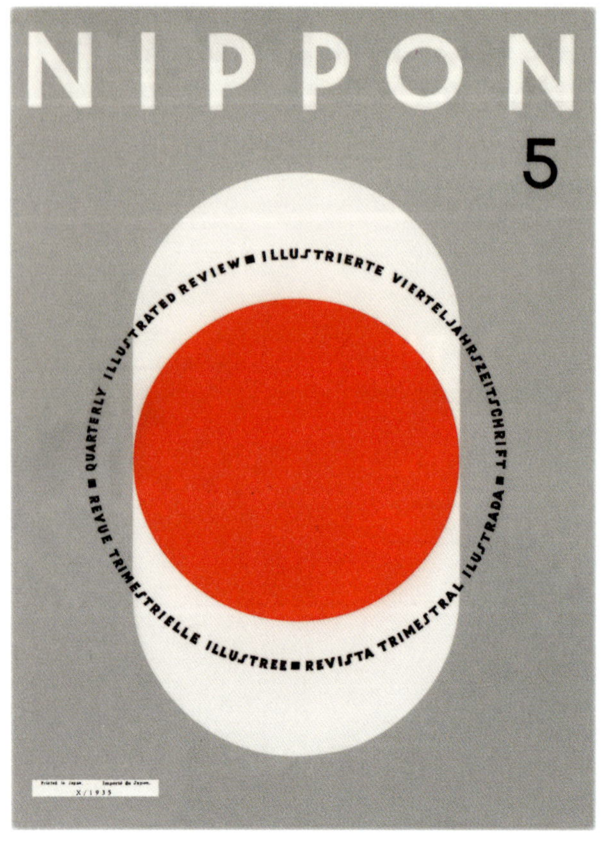
NIPPON
5
QUARTERLY ILLUSTRATED REVIEW ■ ILLUSTRIERTE VIERTELJAHRSZEITSCHRIFT ■ REVISTA TRIMESTRAL ILUSTRADA ■ REVUE TRIMESTRIELLE ILLUSTREE ■

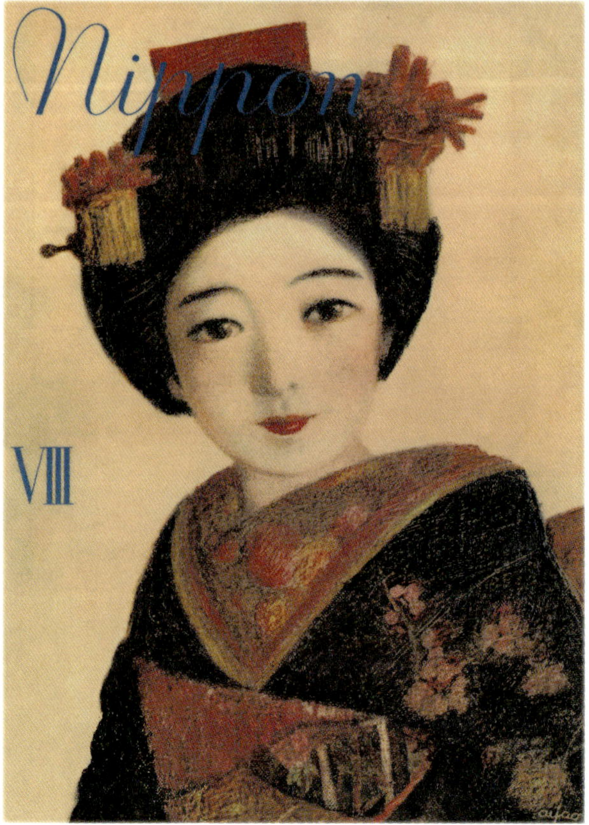
Nippon
VIII

country's deep historical traditions. The magazine consistently promoted Japan as being in-step with the West's developments in industry and culture, while also propping up the Shinto religion and a family-oriented worldview. Natori was able to attract some of Japan's finest graphic design talent, including veteran designer Yamana Ayao and a young Kamekura Yūsaku, both of whom acted as designers and art directors for assorted Nippon Kōbō publications.

Natori became an attaché to the Japanese government, and Nippon Kōbō began producing other propaganda magazines such as *Shanghai*, an army-sponsored magazine that posed as a Chinese publication but was actually produced in Tokyo. He also founded the magazines *Canton* and *South China Graphic* in 1939, *Manchukuo* and *Eastern Asia* in 1940, and a host of others that were localized for specific regions and languages. His activities in propaganda-making extended from running printing companies in Tokyo to running propaganda offices throughout Asia.

Nippon Kōbō's rival studio Chūō Kōbō went out of business in 1941 when member Okada Sōzō started the company Tōhōsha 東方社 and quickly absorbed many of Chūō Kōbō's staff, including graphic designer Hara Hiromu and photographer Kimura Ihei, who went on to create the magazine *Front*.

Front was a large-format A3-size magazine that focused on stylized graphic and photographic depictions that dramatized and celebrated Japanese nationalism, militarism, and expansion. It was published in up to fifteen languages per issue with a minimum of text, though what text was included was pointedly anti-Western and promoted the expansion of the Japanese Empire, known as the Greater East Asia Co-Prosperity Sphere, a term coined in 1940. Front was funded by the Japanese government with supplementary finances from Okada Sōzō. As with Nippon, the Mitsui, Mitsubishi, and Sumitomo conglomerates also advertised within.

Front's aesthetic was closely modeled on the Soviet magazine *USSR in Construction (SSR Na Stroike)*, designed largely by Soviet Constructivist artists/designers Alexander Rodchenko and Varvara Stepanova. Tōhōsha's offices were bombed in 1945, and the proofs of the final issue—a special on "war art"—were destroyed prior to publication.

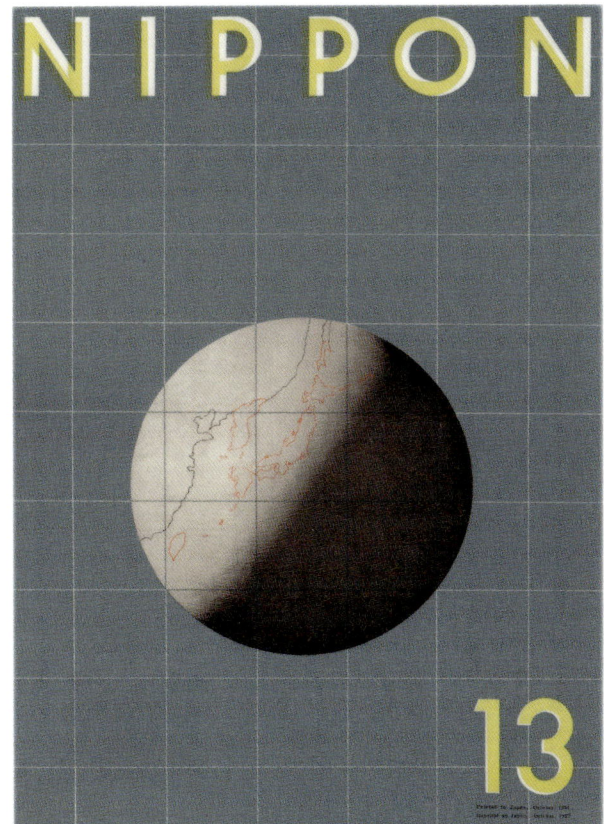

The ways in which Japanese propaganda was both created and disseminated were multivarious—from the "'soft" propaganda patterns on clothing intended for Imperial subjects to the more concrete propaganda published in assorted public relations magazines that espoused a clearly delineated worldview supported by private and public concerns alike.

References:

Germer, Andrea. "Shared Origins, Shared Outcomes?" *Eurasian Encounters*, 2016, 231–56. https://doi.org/10.1515/9789048527472-010.

Germer, Andrea. "Artists and Wartime Politics: Natori Yōnosuke – a Japanese Riefenstahl?" *Contemporary Japan* 24, no. 1 (2012): 21–50. https://doi.org/10.1515/cj-2012-0002.

Germer, Andrea. "Visual Propaganda in Wartime East Asia – The Case of Natori Yōnosuke." *The Asia-Pacific Journal: Japan Focus. Asia-Pacific Journal*, May 9, 2011. https://apjjf.org/2011/9/20/Andrea-Germer/3530/article.html.

Natori, Yōnosuke, Mari Shirayama, and Yoshio Hori. *Natori Yōnosuke to Nihon Kōbō: 1931–45*. Tokyo: Iwanami shoten, 2006.

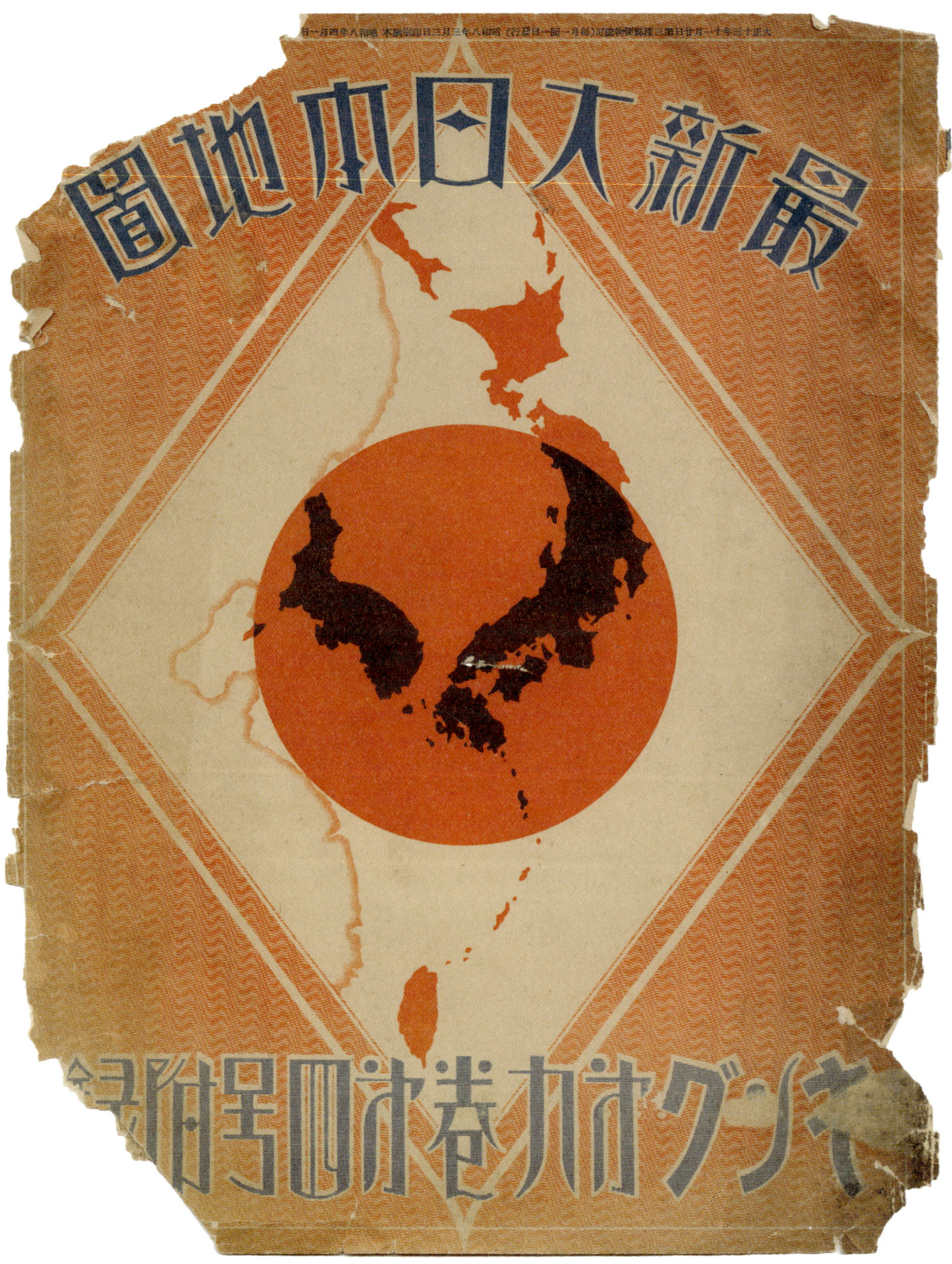

Latest Map of Japan 最新大日本地圖, 1933 depicting Japan and occupied territories.

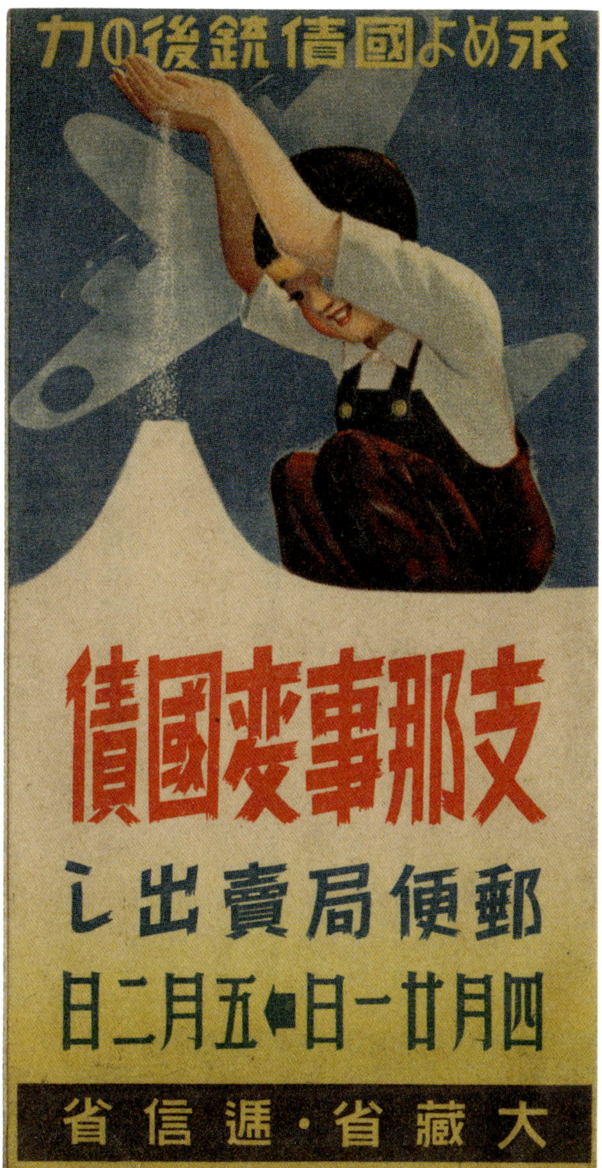

China Incident National Bonds 支那事変國債 郵便局売出し (Tokyo: Ministry of Finance, Division of Posts and Telecommunication 大蔵省 逓信省, 1937). An advertisement depicting a child building a sand castle as a visual metaphor for the national symbol of Mount Fuji and further expansion of the Japanese Empire.

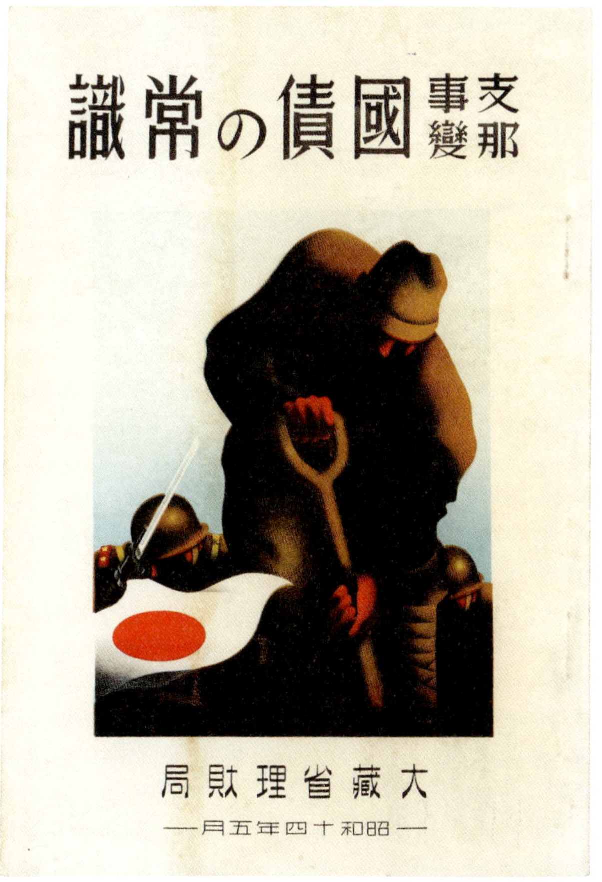

China Incident National Bonds for Sale at Post Offices 支那事変国債の常識 (Tokyo: Ministry of Finance, Division of Posts and Telecommunication 大蔵省 理財局, 1937). Postcard showing a soldier digging in the frontlines in China, intimating death as much as construction.

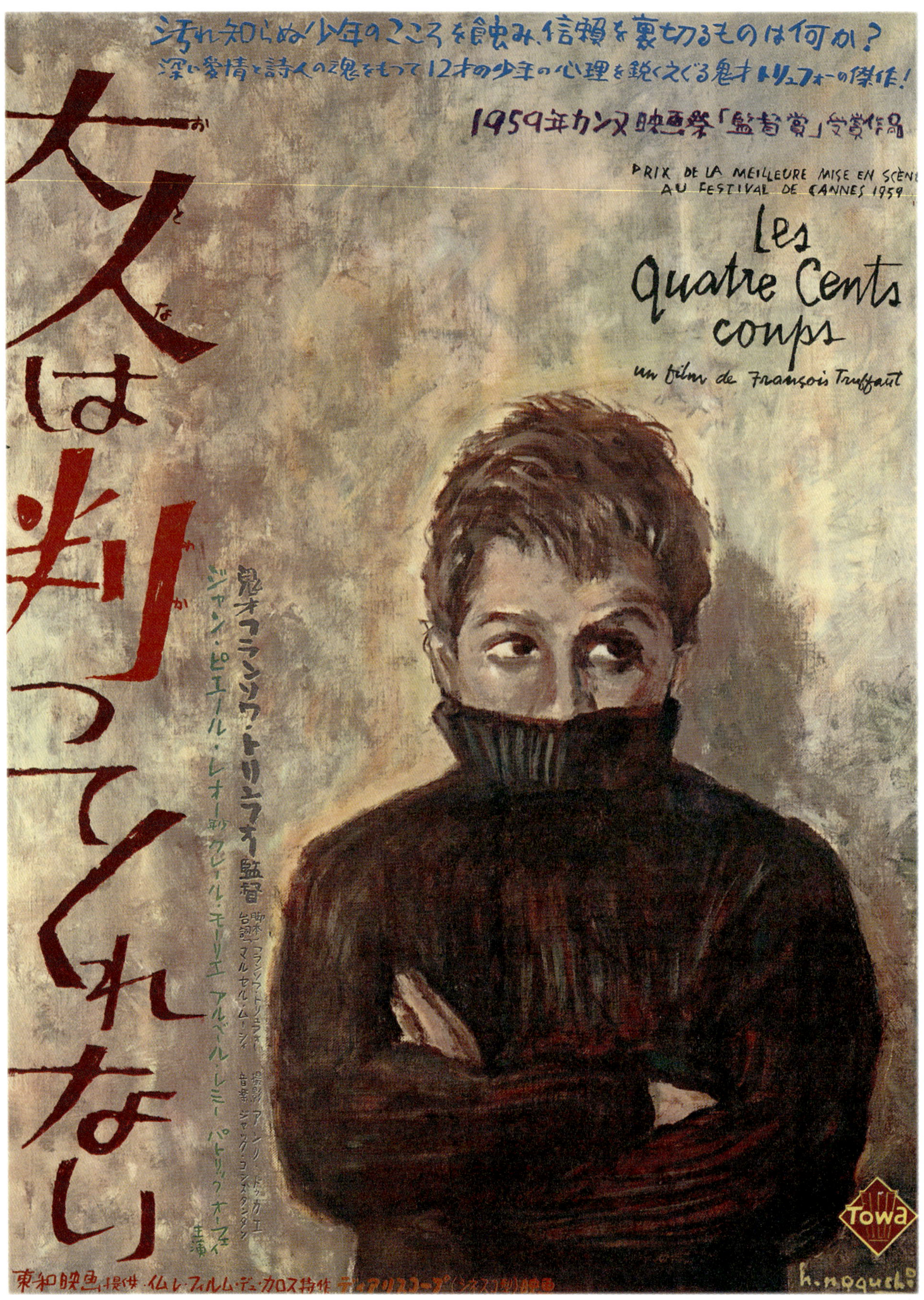

Poster for François Truffaut's film ***1,000 Blows*** (**大人は判ってくれない**) designed in 1960 by Noguchi Hisamitsu 野口久光.

NOGUCHI HISAMITSU 野口久光

1909–1994

Noguchi Hisamitsu was born in Tochigi Prefecture. He studied western painting at Tokyo School of Fine Arts (now Tokyo National University of the Arts), graduating in 1933. He studied film and design, instigating independent film projects and designing the posters for the films. Noguchi was inspired by European film posters, and his final project before graduation was the design of a number of posters for foreign films, all of which were purchased by the school before he graduated. After graduation, Noguchi joined the film and film distribution company Tōwa, where he worked on hundreds of poster designs over the following decade. His poster designs tended toward the lyrical and expressive, combining expertly rendered painting and illustration with detailed lettering and typography.

Tōwa was dissolved in 1942 due to the war, and Noguchi traveled to Shanghai, where he worked organizing music recitals while continuing to design posters for assorted clients. He returned to Tokyo in 1946 and joined the film company Shin Tōhō, working as a film producer for the next five years. In 1951, he left Shin Tōhō and joined the newly reformed Tōwa Studios, working in their advertising division. There, Noguchi worked on the posters for many foreign films, including postwar European cinematic masterpieces such as *The Third Man* and *400 Blows*. Noguchi's work won him masses of fans both in Japan and abroad, including French New Wave director Francois Truffaut, who struck up a friendship with Noguchi and kept Noguchi's poster for *400 Blows* in a prized place in his office until his death in 1984.

Noguchi produced over 1,000 posters in his lifetime. In the 1950s, he shifted his focus from graphic design toward music and film criticism, publishing widely. He received the Purple Ribbon from the Imperial government in 1973 for his decades of cultural contributions and was made an honorary citizen of New Orleans for his jazz writing, criticism, and analysis. Noguchi passed away in 1994 at eighty-four years old.

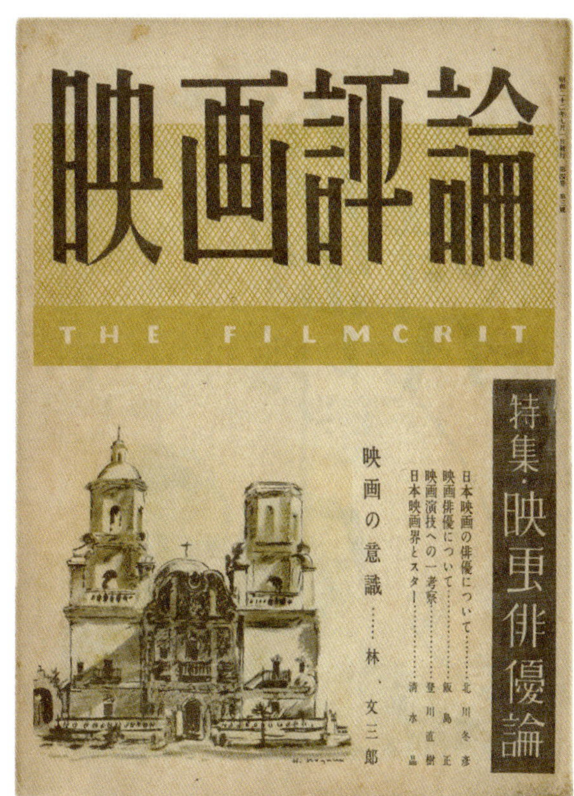

Film Criticism Vol. 4, 映画評論　第4巻3号 (Tokyo: Nihon Eiga Shuppan 日本映画出版, July 1947). Cover by Noguchi Hisamitsu 野口久光.

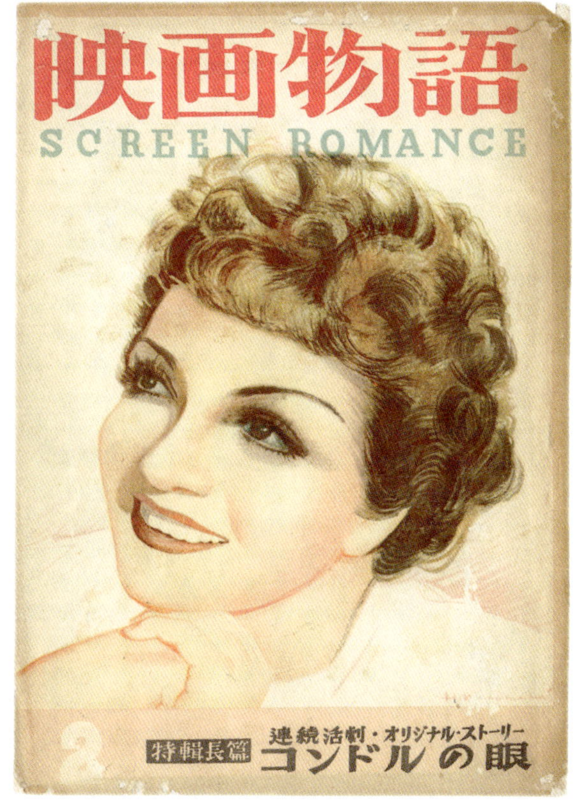

Screen Romance Vol. 1 No. 2 映画物語 第2号 (Tokyo: Saneisha 三英社, 1946). Cover by Noguchi Hisamitsu 野口久光.

References:

Shuri, Yuki, and Shinju Onuki. *Kakimoji no Dezain*. Tokyo: Graphic-sha, 2017.

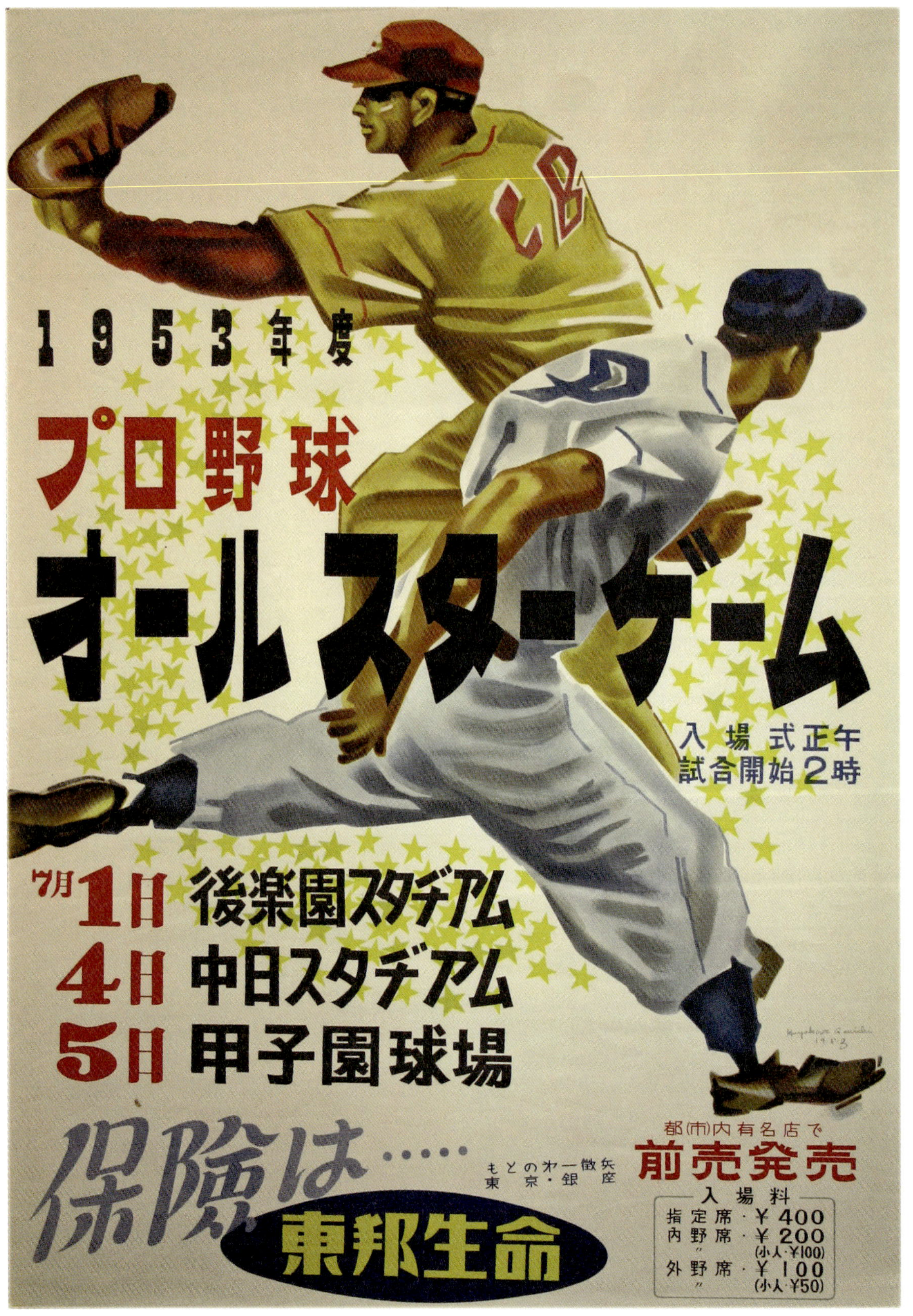

Poster for all-star baseball game series from 1953 designed by Hayakawa Genichi 早川源一.

HAYAKAWA GENICHI 早川源一

1906–1976

Hayakawa Genichi was born in Kansai. He studied design at Kyoto Industrial Arts Technical College 京都工芸繊維大学. After graduating, he became a full-time designer at Hanshin Electric Railway, where he was involved in the design of posters, advertisements, and signs for the railroad company.

Hayakawa is most noted for the original logo that he designed for the company's baseball team, the Hanshin Tigers. Prior to the team's formation, Hayakawa was heavily involved in the design of posters for sporting events, and the corporate-sponsored team provided him with nearly endless design work to promote the Tigers. He designed decades' worth of advertisements, game posters, and assorted ephemera for the team, often placing the logo against a field of yellow-and-black stripes based on the original flag Hayakawa had designed for the team.

Most contemporary baseball fans would be surprised to learn that a junior division of the team was imagined and branded by Hayakawa in 1954—the Hanshin Jaguars—and that a fleet of uniforms bearing a completely different logo and naming convention were completed, yet went unused.

Hayakawa also was involved with *Press Art* プレスアルト, the Kansai graphic design and commercial art journal.

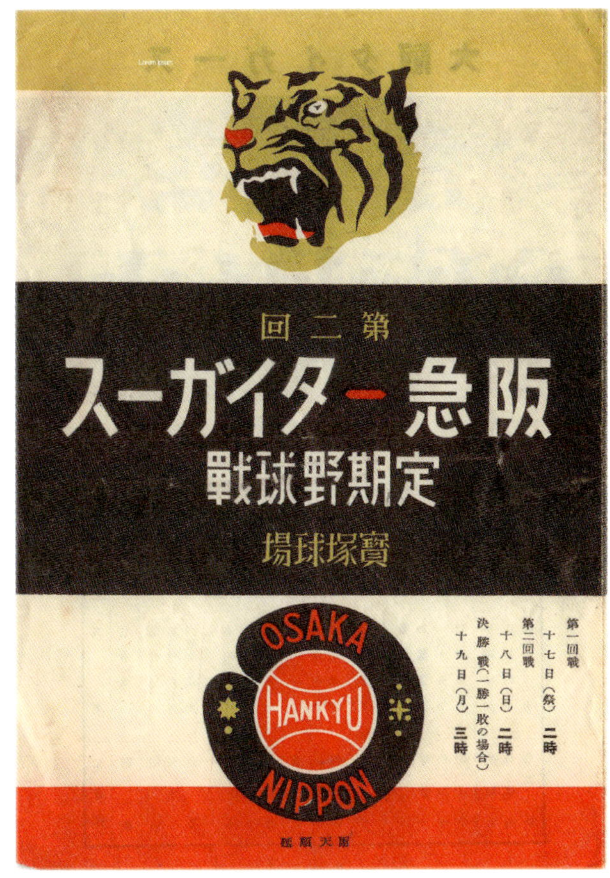

Promotional flyer for the Hanshin Tigers from 1945 designed by Hayakawa Genichi 早川源一.

References:

Editorial, Hanshin Tigers. "Tsunashima ritomo no yunifōmu monogatari." Hanshin Tigers, March 2015. https://hanshintigers.jp/data/uniform/design.html.

Shuri, Yuki, and Shinju Onuki. *Kakimoji no Dezain*. Tokyo: Graphic-sha, 2017.

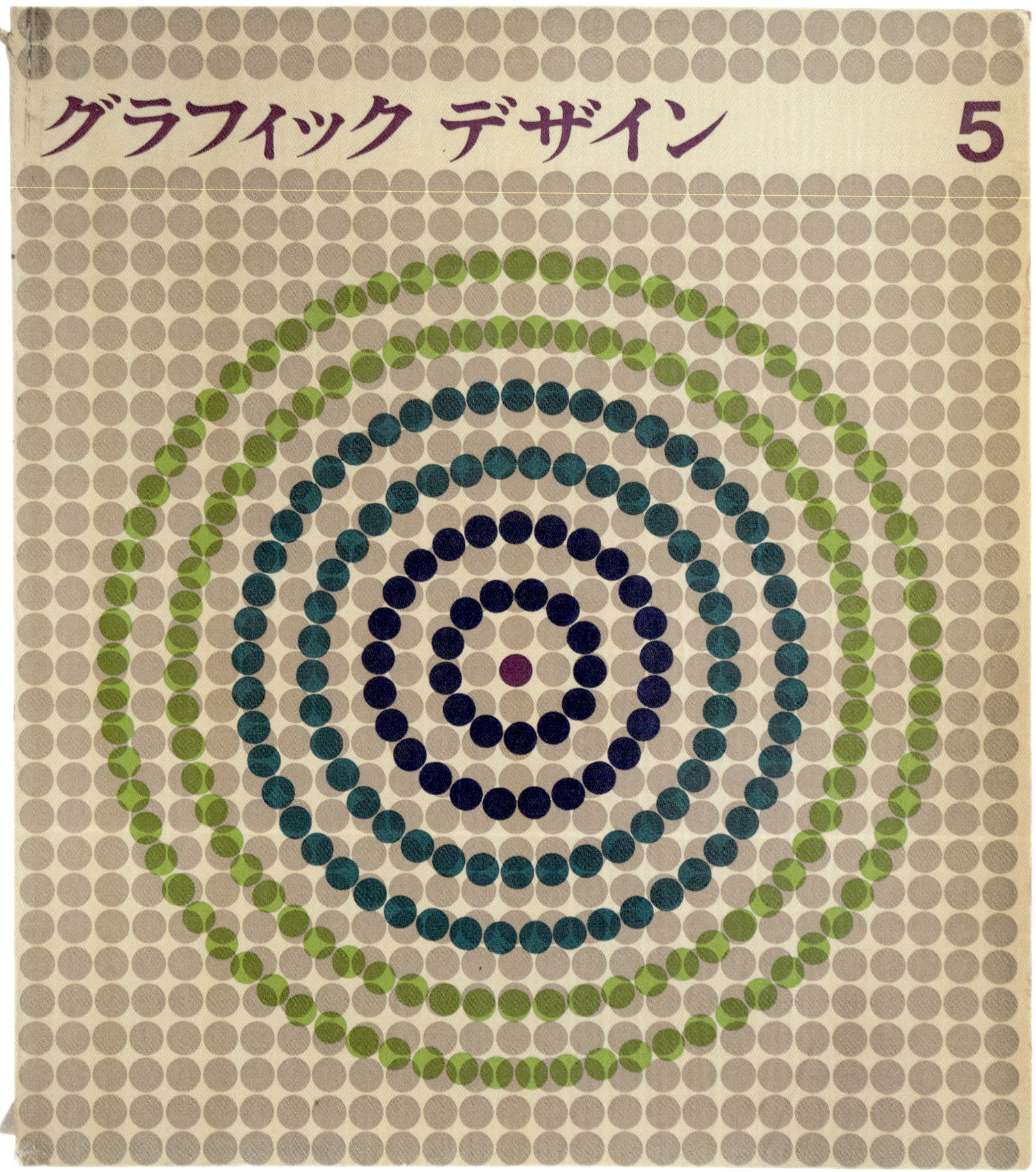

Cover of ***Graphic Design* グラフィックデザイン No. 6** (Tokyo: **Geibi Shuppansha 芸美出版社, 1961**). Design by Kamekura Yūsaku 亀倉雄策.

KATSUMI MASARU 勝見勝

1909–1983

Katsumi Masaru (though often referred to in print using the unconventional spelling "Katzumie" during his lifetime, as he preferred) was the leading design critic of the postwar period and was a relentless booster and organizer of design-related events, publications, and infrastructure throughout his lifetime.

Born in Tokyo, he attended Tokyo Teikoku University 東京帝国大学, where he studied Aesthetics and Art History for both his undergraduate and graduate education. Katsumi taught at Yokohama University from 1934 to 1939 and became involved in translation projects for *Kōkokukai* in 1939. His involvement with design deepened beginning in 1941 when he began working with the Japanese Ministry of Commerce and Industry's Craft Guidance Center, working under the Bauhaus-educated Yamawaki Iwao 山脇巌 after finishing his mandatory military service. He served as an editorial advisor to the magazine *Kogei News* 工芸ニュース (*Industrial Art News*) and edited *Aesthetics of Design*, the first volume of the journal series *Shōgyo Design Zenshū* 商業デザイン全集 (*The World's Commercial Design*), both in 1951. These early forays set the course for Katsumi's constant editorial involvement with assorted design publications, from books to magazines. He co-translated Sir Herbert Edward Read's 1934 book *Art and Industry: The Principles of Industrial Design* into Japanese alongside Maeda Yasuji 前田泰次 in 1957.

He worked as an exhibition advisor to the World Graphic Design Exhibitions that were held by Tokyo's Metropolitan Government from 1951 through 1960. Katsumi was one of the founders of the Japan Design Committee 日本デザイン学会 in 1953, as well as on the board of directors of the Kuwasawa Design School from 1962 to 1965. He was a co-founder of Tokyo Zokei University in 1966 and served as a professor there. Katsumi also worked as advisor to the Tokyo National Museum of Art on design-oriented exhibitions revolving around the Bauhaus and 20th Century Design in 1954 and 1957, respectively.

Katsumi's influence on the culture of Japanese graphic design is inestimable—as a critic, educator, advisor, writer, and tastemaker, he wielded huge influence. He was involved in all of the prevalent postwar design organizations, including the Japan Advertising Artists Club, the Tokyo Art Directors Club, the Japan Design Committee, and the Japan Graphic Design Association.

Katsumi served in dual roles as both design coordinator and art director for the visual design of the 1964 Tokyo Olympics, having created the Olympic Design Colloquium and two later Olympic design departments: the Olympic Design Communication Association and the Olympic Design Studio. Katsumi recruited Japan's top designers at the time, including Kamekura Yūsaku, Kōno Takashi, and Hara Hiromu, alongside younger designers such as Tanaka Ikkō 田中一光 and Yokoo Tadanori. The teams worked to create a programmatic approach to the design of the Olympics so that each aspect was uniform and related—including emblems, symbols, colors, and typography—all unified in a design manual. Kōno approached the color aspects and Hara supervised the design of pictograms and symbols—a first for the Olympics, with the actual design work largely falling upon Yamashita Yoshirō 山下芳郎 and Yokoo Tadanori, amongst others. All aspects of the identity program were overseen by Katsumi as chief decision-maker.

Katsumi had engineered a private logo competition for the Olympics with Inagaki Kōichiro 稲垣行一郎, Kamekura Yūsaku, Kōno Takashi, Nagai Kazumasa 永井一正, Sugiura Kōhei, and Tanaka Ikkō pitted against one another. Kamekura's modern logo design was the winner—a stacked composition with a red circle at the top, the Olympic Rings rendered in gold in the center, and bold, condensed characters reading "Tokyo 1964" at the bottom, also in gold. It was undoubtedly helpful that Kamekura enlisted the help of his mentor Hara Hiromu in approaching the compositional and lettering aspects of the logo, though Hara's contribution has been downplayed in published histories.

Katsumi's success with the design of the 1964 Olympics led to him being chosen to lead the visual design for the 1970 Osaka World Expo, the 1975 World's Fair/World Expo in Okinawa, the 1972 Sapporo Olympics, and a seemingly endless number of other globally oriented events in Japan.

Other influential publications that Katsumi contributed to were the five-volume *Guide to Graphic Design* グラフィックデザイン大系 published in 1960 and 1961 and the seven-volume *Graphic Design of the World* 現代のグラフィックデザイン book series. Both series' volumes analyzed graphic design from both theoretical and applied perspectives in a highly graphic manner.

和文書体 競技場名

和文書体

国立競技場

屋内総合競技場

駒沢陸上競技場

東京体育館

所沢クレー射撃場

駒沢バレーボール場

横浜文化体育館

相模湖　　戸田漕艇場

東京体育館屋内水泳場

後楽園アイスパレス

八王子自転車競技場

ロードレースコース

早稲田大学記念会堂

秩父宮ラグビー場

三ツ沢蹴球場

大宮蹴球場

渋谷公会堂

駒沢第一　第二　第三

ホッケー場

神宮野球場

馬事公苑　日本武道館

駒沢体育館

朝霞射撃場

東大検見川総合運動場

屋内総合競技場本館

朝霞根津パーク

軽井沢総合馬術競技場

E－2 | TOKYO OLYMPIC 1964 / DESIGN GUIDE SHEET

和文・欧文併用例

和文・欧文併用例

第18回オリンピック競技大会

GAMES OF THE XVIII OLYMPIAD

LES JEUX DE LA XVIII OLYMPIADE

国際オリンピック組織委員会

THE INTERNATIONAL OLYMPIC COMMITTEE

LE COMITE ORGANISATEUR DES JUEX DE LA

明治公園

MEIJI OLYMPIC PARK

PARC OLYMPIQUE DE MEIJI

陸上競技

ATHLETICS

ATHLETISME

国立競技場

NATIONAL STADIUM

STADE NATIONAL

選手村

OLYMPIC VILLAGE

VILLAGE OLYMPIQUE

E－4 | TOKYO OLYMPIC 1964 / DESIGN GUIDE SHEET

Design Guide Sheet 18th Olympic Games Tokyo 1964 デザインガイド シート 第18回オリンピック東京大会 (Tokyo: Olympic Organizing Committee オリンピック東京大会組織委員会, 1964) Planning by Katsumi Masaru 勝見勝; design by Awazu Kiyoshi 粟津潔 (Latin typography), Katsui Mitsuo 勝井三雄 (Japanese typography), and Michiyoshi Takeshi 道吉剛 (production design).

Katsumi published and edited the influential quarterly magazine *Graphic Design* グラフィックデザイン from 1959 until his death in 1983. Katsumi's editorial policy for the magazine was a mix of historical evaluation of forms of Japanese design, art, and folk arts as much as a compendium of rational, non-subjective approaches to graphic design. His interest was in the disseminative and communicative aspects of graphic design for commerce and culture. The magazine continued publication for three years afterward, with the ninety-fourth issue being the final in 1986.

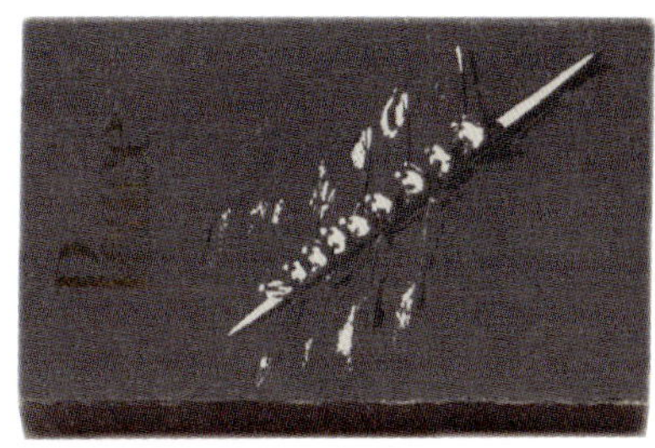

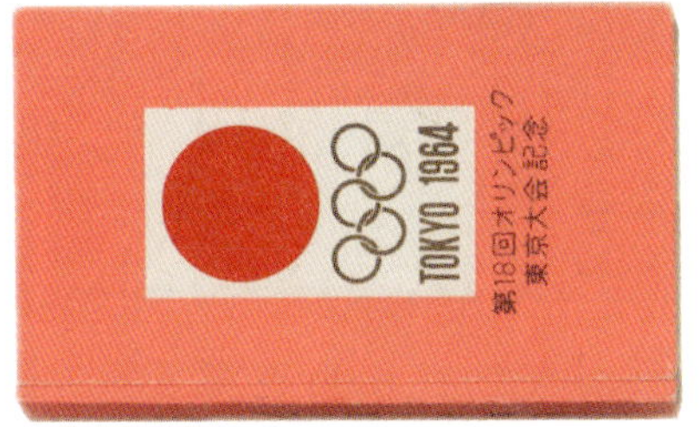

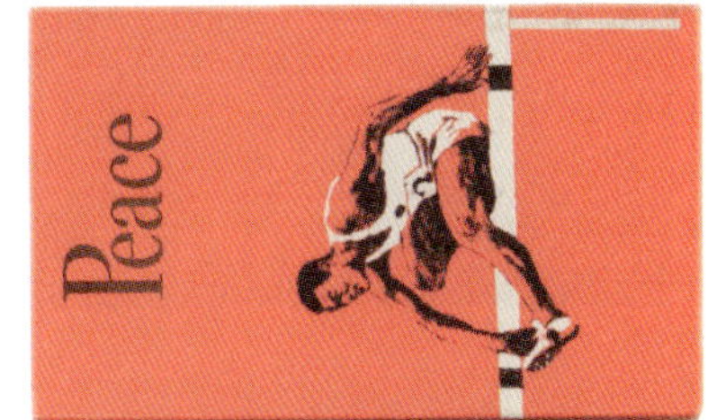

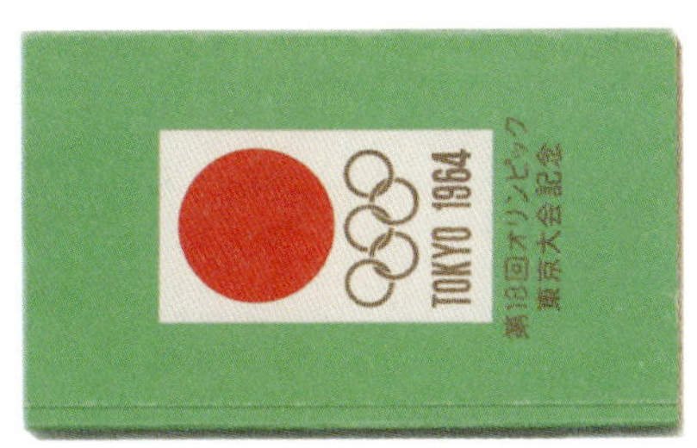

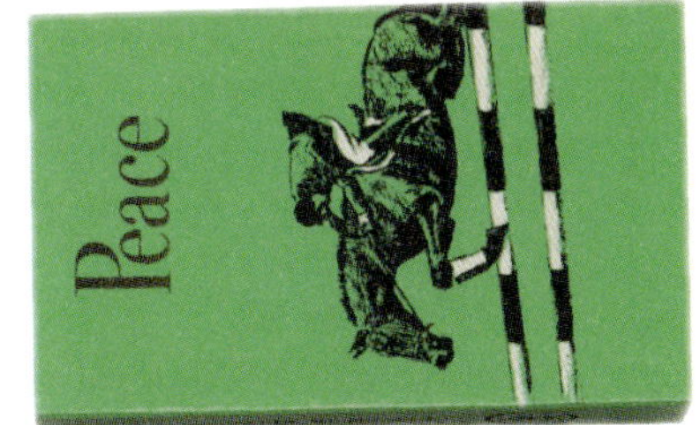

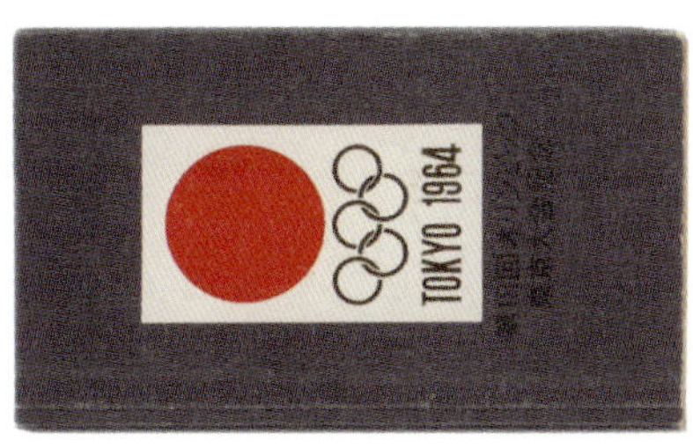

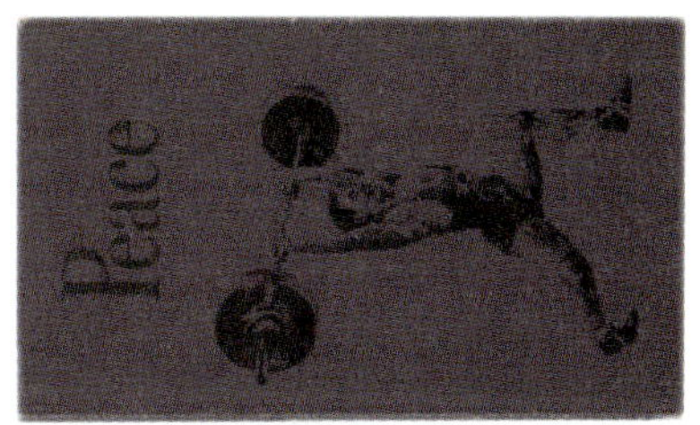

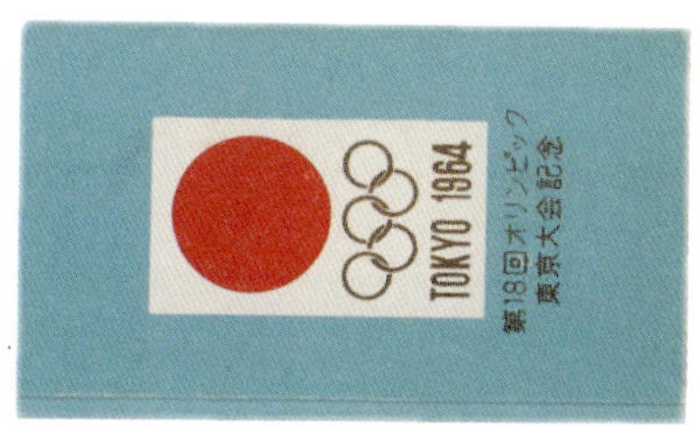

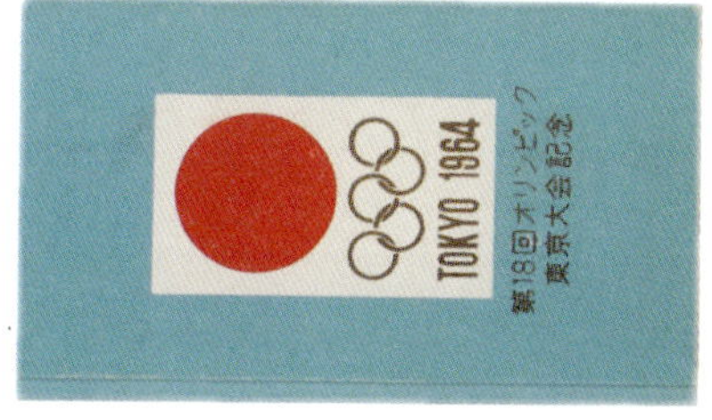

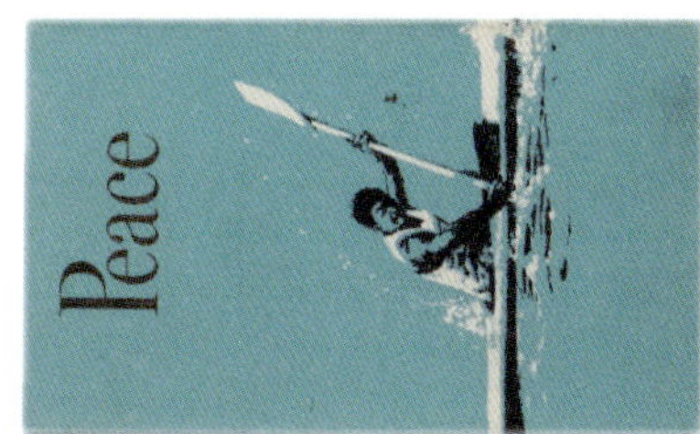

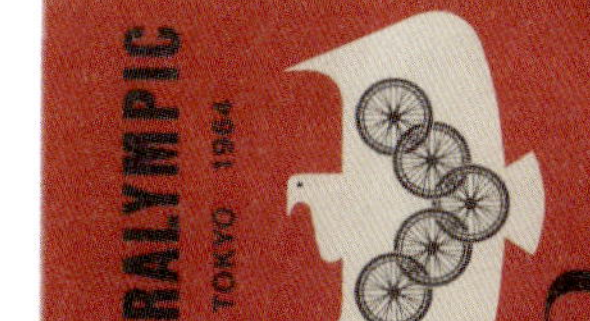

Olympic-themed **Peace** cigarette packaging circa 1963.

References:

Kamekura, Yūsaku, and Ayao Yamana. *Gurafikku Dezain No Seiki: Bunshō to Danwa to Sakuhin De kōsei: Meiji Sedai Yamana Ayao Sugiura Hisui Kara shōwa Sedai Made*. Tokyo: Bijutsu Shuppansha, 2008.

Kashiwagi, Hiroshi. "Implementer of Design Fundamentals." *Approach*, January 1, 2015, 4–9.

Katsumi, Masaru. *The Masaru Katsumi Collection*. Vol. 1-5. Tokyo: Kōdansha, 1986.

Segi, Shin'ichi, Tanaka Ikkō, and Hiroshi Sano. *Nissenbi No Jidai = The Epoch of the Japan Advertising Artists Club: Nihon no Gurafikku Dezain 1951–70*. Tokyo: Toransuāto, 2000.

Sugiura, Kōhei. "Masaru Katzumie: A Pointillist Landscape of the Universe" *Approach*, January 1, 2015, 10–11.

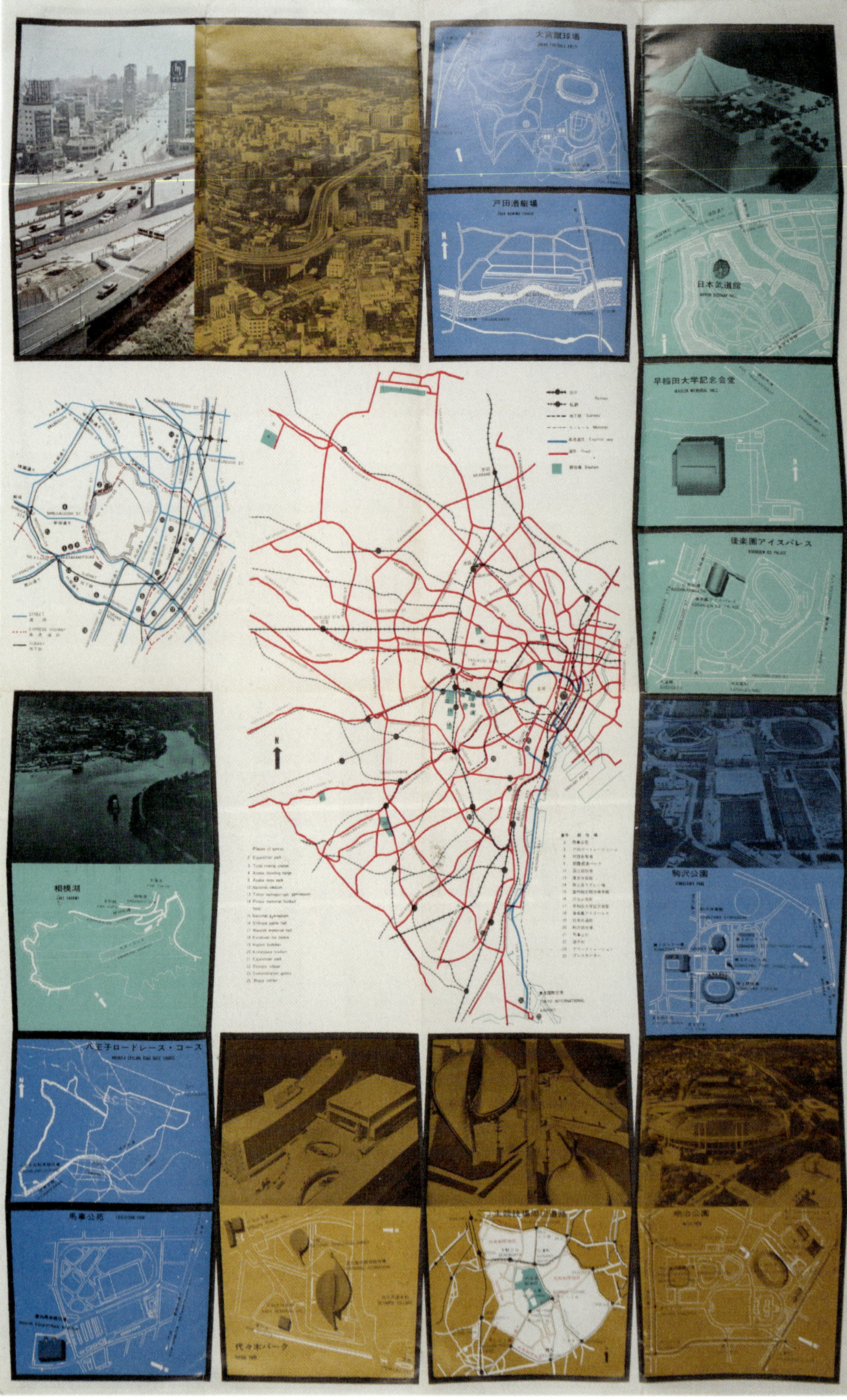

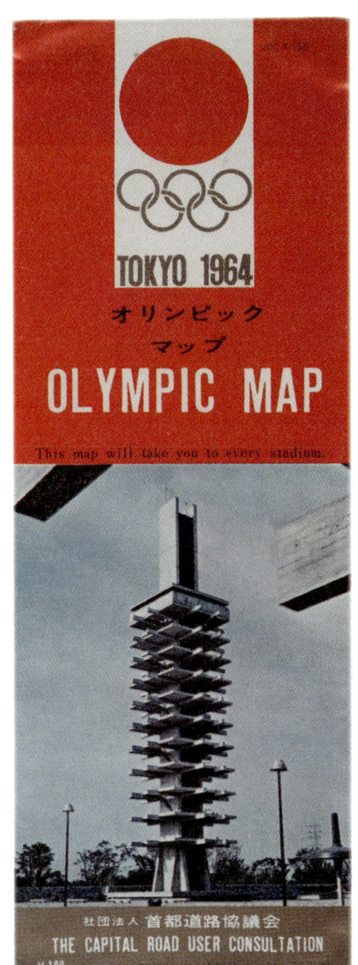

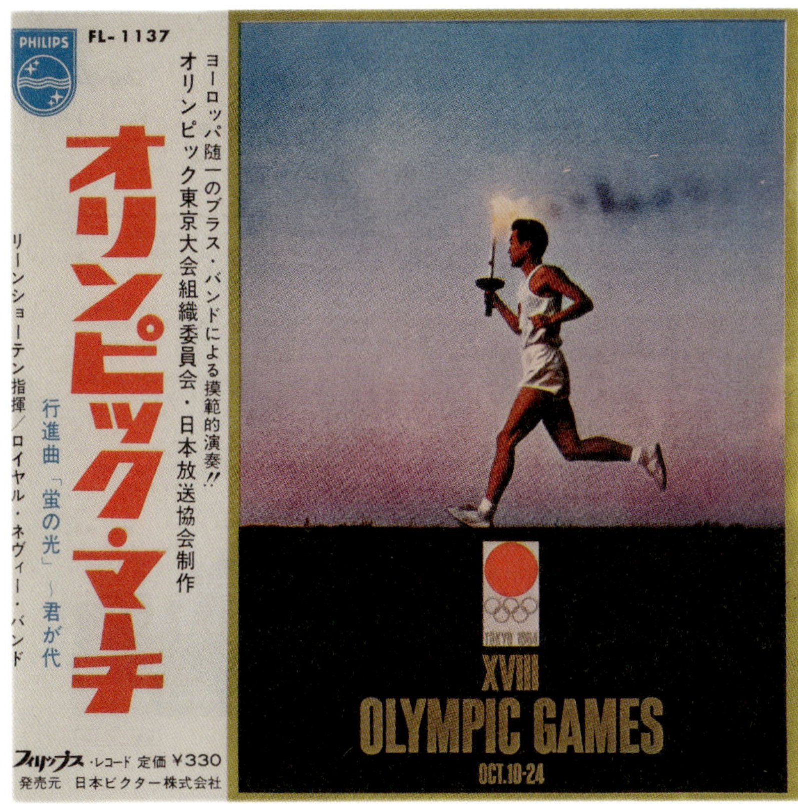

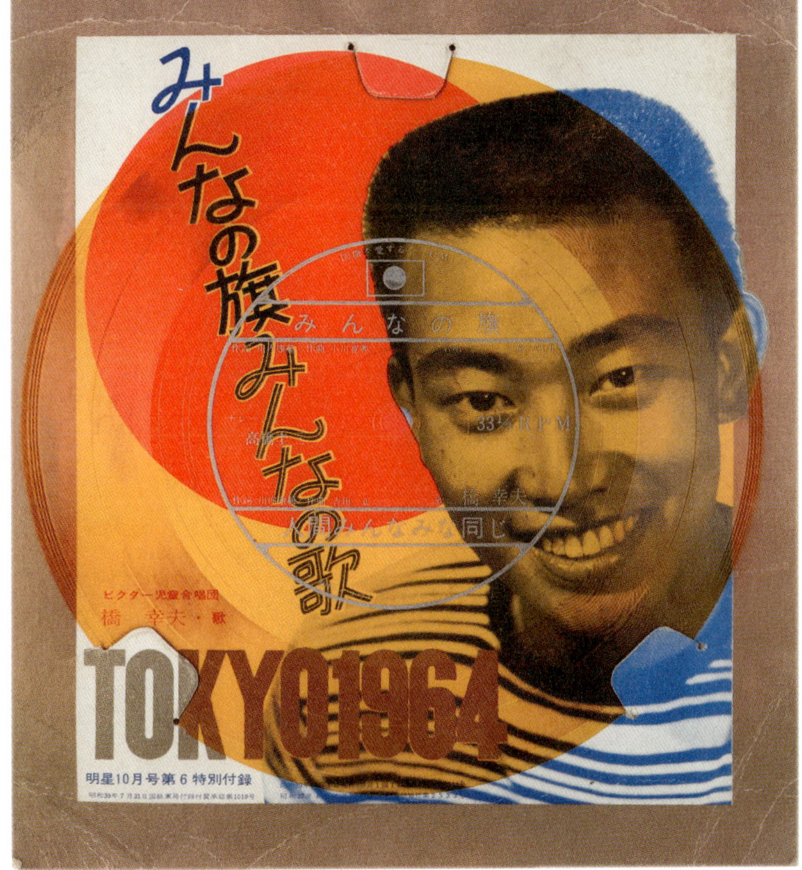

Above and facing page: *Olympic Map* produced by the Mitsubishi Exhibition Center in Tokyo. Top right: ***Olympic March* オリンピック・マーチ** 7" flexidisc phonograph record **(Tokyo: Philips, 1964)**. Below: ***"Everyone's Flag / Humanity's Flag-Loving Party"* みんなの旗／人間みんなみな同じ**, a 7" translucent orange flexidisc phonograph record by Hashi Yukio 橋幸夫 bearing Hara Hiromu's 1964 Olympic logo lettering **(Tokyo: Victor, 1964)**.

工芸ニュース

INDUSTRIAL ART NEWS

TK

4

編集・工業技術院産業工芸試験所
発行・丸善出版株式会社

VOL. 21

Cover design by Kōno Takashi 河野鷹思 for ***Kogei News (Industrial Art News)* 工芸ニュース**
Volume 21 No. 4, 1953.

KŌNO TAKASHI 河野鷹思

1906–1999

Kōno Takashi was a Japanese graphic designer who worked across illustration, photo-collage, lettering design, editorial design, packaging, and broadcast.

Kōno was born in Tokyo. While in high school, he published a number of political cartoons in English in the *Tokyo Nichi Nichi Shimbun* 東京日日新聞, Tokyo's leading newspaper at that time. He studied art and design at Tokyo University of the Arts, graduating in 1929. The same year, he entered the publicity department of Shochiku Kinema, a production company devoted to kabuki, theater, and filmmaking. There, he worked for seven years creating movie posters, magazine ads, and stage designs. His poster work at that time mixed Bauhaus-influenced typographic/photographic collage, a foreshortened use of abstraction, and a dazzling sense of color.

Simultaneously, Kōno was working in a much more reductive yet highly expressive mannerthrough his illustration and lettering. His display lettering used a playful, constructive approach that exaggerated the thicks and thins of Japanese characters in a seemingly naïve yet highly controlled manner. His illustration became more reductive, balancing the connotational and denotational aspects of depiction, and occasionally dissolving his illustrative forms halfway, making the audience work to put together the meaning.

Aside from his work at Shochiku, Kōno created advertisements that ran in assorted newspapers, particularly for the gourd-derived skincare product Hechima Cream in the early 1930s. He also designed magazine covers for the women's publication *A La Mode* アラモード in the 1930s. In 1936 he became independent, continuing to work across poster design, newspaper advertisement design, and editorial design.

At age thirty-four, Kōno joined the propaganda publishing group Nippon Kōbō, working under Natori Yōnosuke on the publications *Nippon*, *Shanghai*, and *Commerce Japan*, while also designing many of the advertisements within, for corporations like Kanebo and Mitsubishi. At Nippon Kōbō, Kōno worked alongside German designer and bookmaker Erna Mecklenburg (Natori's wife) and designers Ayao Yamana and Kamekura Yūsaku. Kōno's contributions to Nippon Kōbō publications were largely influenced by Soviet Realism. He collaged illustration, abstract form, typography, and photography into a highly integrated melange in all of the magazines he worked on.

In 1940, Kōno became the head editor and cover designer for the Indonesia-based Nihon Shashin Kougeisha 日本写真工芸社, another Japanese propaganda publisher which produced the magazines *VAN* and *NDI* (*Nippon Deutschland Italia*). Kōno was responsible for creating an extensive array of propaganda advertising and poster work while stationed in Indonesia. He was officially conscripted into the Japanese military in 1941 and fought in the war.

After being imprisoned in a POW camp at the end of the war, Kōno returned to Japan and started his career anew, designing the relaunched *VAN*, now a satirical cultural magazine for domestic audiences, and creating work for a variety of freelance clients including companies in the photography, beverage, and textile industries.

Kōno was a key founding member of the Japan Advertising Artists Club and participated in the *Graphic '55* exhibition at the Takashimaya department store in 1955.

One of Kōno's signature works was created during this period, the 1953 poster *Sheltered Weaklings: Japan*. The poster depicts Japan as a school of small, passive fish following a massive, stars-and-stripes-decorated American fish with giant teeth and an abject, hungry stare. In the background lurk two red fish with insidious yellow eyes, alluding to Cold War tensions with the Soviet Union and China. Kōno would continue to create politically charged work for the rest of his life; his experiences in wartime profoundly influenced his perspective on the world.

In 1959, Kōno established the multidisciplinary design company Deska デスカ (DESigners Kono Associates) in Tokyo's Omotesando area, for which he and his staff worked across editorial design, packaging, advertising, stage design, and textiles. Kōno participated in the World Design Conference in 1960, designing the logo for the conference itself.

Kōno contributed two separate designs to the 1964 Tokyo Olympics logo competition—one bearing an abstracted Mount Fuji motif and the other a decorative fan capping the five Olympic rings. He would participate as one of the team members who designed the 1964 Olympic identity, a role he would later reprise as one of the designers who worked on materials for the 1972 Sapporo Olympics.

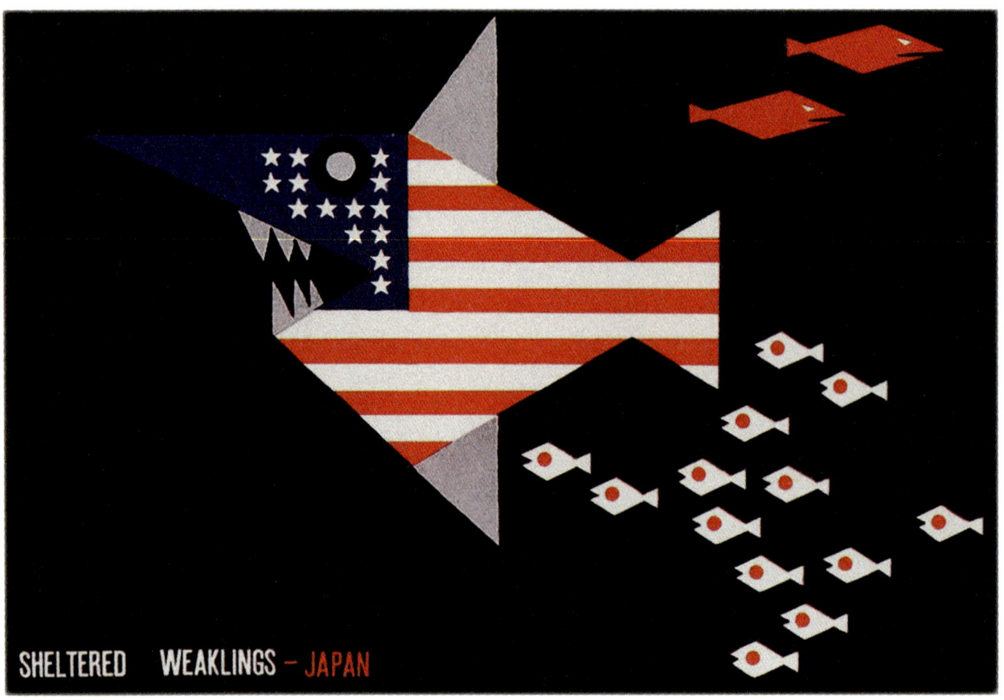

Above: ***Sheletered Weaklings - Japan*** (1953). Below: Spread from ***Kōno Takashi no Dezain (The Design of Takashi Kōno)*** **河野鷹思のデザイン** (Tokyo: Meijishobō/Nishikawashoten 明治書房/西川書店, 1957).

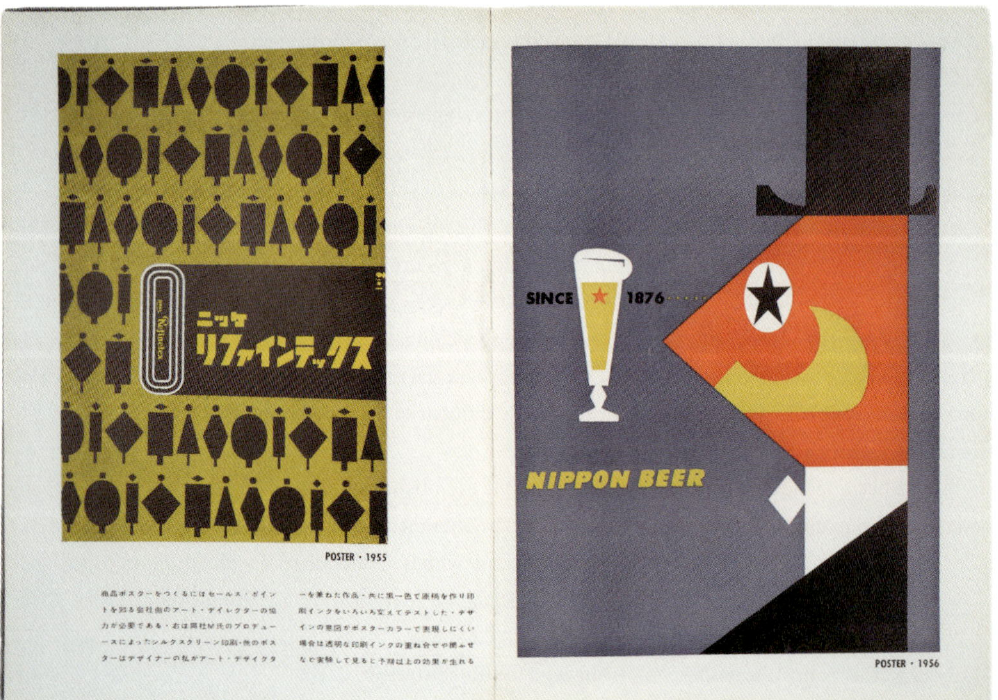

References:
Kawahata, Naomichi. "The Books and Magazines of Takashi Kono." *Idea* 56, no. 326 (January 2008): 21–99.

Nakajo, Masayoshi, Gan Hosoya, Hanmo Sugiura, and Michiaki Matsuyama. "Recollection of Takashi Kono." *Idea* 56, no. 326 (January 2008): 100–104.

Natori, Yōnosuke, Mari Shirayama, and Yoshio Hori. *Natori Yōnosuke to Nihon Kōbō: 1931–45*. Tokyo: Iwanami shoten, 2006.

Kōno taught design at Musashino University, Tokyo National University of Fine Arts and Music, Joshibi University of Art and Design, and Aichi Prefectural University of Fine Arts and Music, where he later served as president. He published two books, *Package Design* 河野鷹思のデザイン in 1956 and *Takashi Kōno: My Momentum* マイデザイン·河野鷹思 in 1983.

Kōno held two solo exhibitions in his lifetime, one in 1941 and another in 1967. A posthumous career-survey exhibition was mounted first at Tokyo's Ginza Graphic Gallery in 2003 and later at The National Museum of Modern Art, Tokyo, in 2005.

赤と黒

昭和二十一年十二月一日印刷納本第一卷第三號　毎月一回五日發行　昭和二十一年十二月五日發行

耽奇尖端特輯號

Cover design for the *kasutori zasshi* magazine ***Red & Black*** **赤と黒** designed by Minegishi Yoshikazu 峯岸義一, 1946.

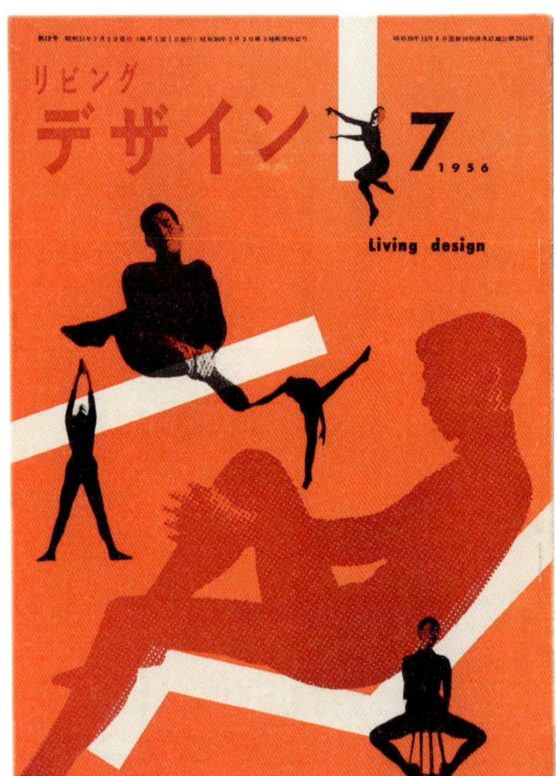

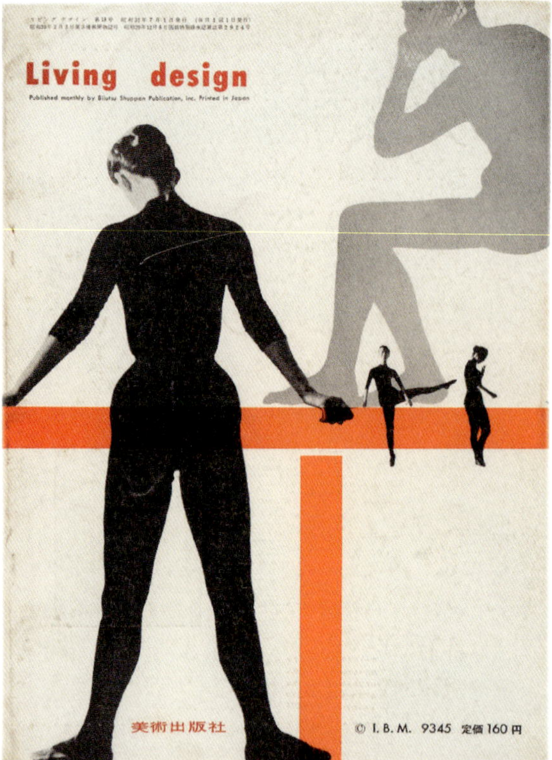

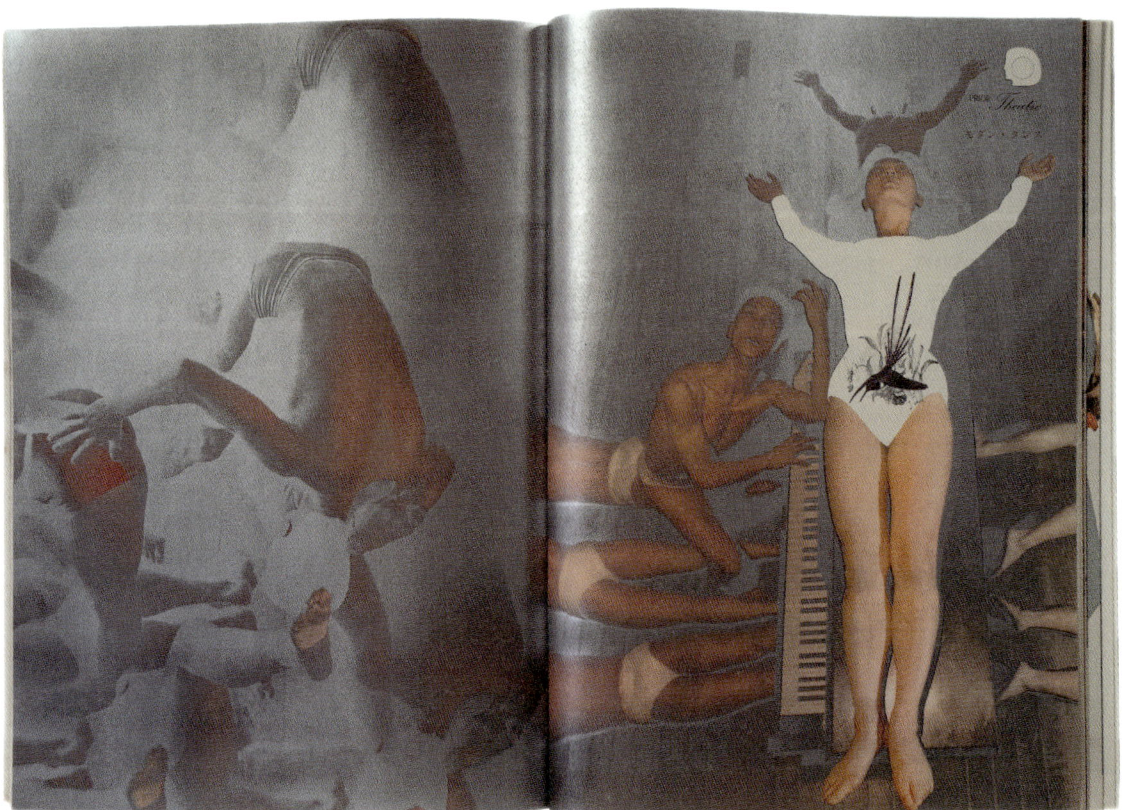

Clockwise from top left: front and back cover of ***Kogei News* 工芸ニュース Vol. 21 No. 4**, **edited by Industrial Arts Institute (IAI), Tokyo, Japan; published by Maruzen Co., Ltd., Tokyo (Tokyo: Maruzen, 1953)**, designed by Kōno Takashi; spread from ***Prior***, a 1965 promotional catalogue for **Shiseido** art directed by Kōno Takashi including photography by Hosoe Eikoh and printed utilizing a mix of process, monochrome, spot color, and metallic spot color printing.

HARA HIROMU 原弘

1903–1986

"This may be presumptuous but Hiromu Hara was a very clumsy designer. That clumsiness and his silence was his strength as a designer." [1]
- Hara Kenya

Hara Hiromu created work that would help define the modern Japanese aesthetic in the 1920s and 1930s. The supposed "clumsiness" of his work most likely comes from Hara Hiromu being the first designer in Japan to wholeheartedly embrace notions of what would come to be called "total design": being the first means that everything is new and that refinement comes later, especially when Hara incorporated new, streamlined, European aesthetic sensibilities and localized them in Japanese culture and society for the first time.

Hara was born into a family of printers in 1903 in the town of Iida in Nagano Prefecture. He relocated to Tokyo solo when he was fifteen and enrolled in the Printing Department of the Tokyo Prefectural School of Technology. Hara was in contact with Murayama Tomoyoshi and other early modern designers during his studies. He stayed on at the school as an assistant after graduation and taught there from 1922 to 1941.

In the 1920s, Hara discovered the European New Typography movement through printing trade journals and publications, markedly the work of El Lisstizky in a copy of the American printing magazine *The Inland Printer*. This work would be incredibly influential to the young designer and would help inform many of his aesthetic decisions over the course of his career.

Hara wrote an essay called "New Trends in Typographic Designs in Europe" in 1929, largely agreeing with the ideas proposed by German typographer and theorist Jan Tschichold. Hara went on to write his own manifesto for Japanese typography in 1931, mirroring Tschichold's sensibilities with regard to modern expression, but calling for the continued use of Mincho type (the Japanese equivalent to serif typefaces) so that Japanese typographic expression might feel culturally appropriate. Hara also wrote about the importance of photography in relation to typography, similar to Bauhaus notions of "typofoto." Hara would go on to reiterate these ideas elsewhere in print over the 1930s and incorporate these aesthetics into his work in Japan—in many cases this was the first time such highly integrated work appeared. Hara's ideas, expressed through his writing, endeared him to photographer Kimura Ihei, with whom he would collaborate frequently throughout the rest of his career.

Hara's giant commercial break came in 1930 when he won an invitational design competition held by Kao Soap as part of a total rebrand. The stylized script lettering against a red background was a massive departure from the company's previously baroque packaging and captured the nation's interest with its friendliness and symbolic cleanliness. The bold redesign by the relatively unknown Hara won out over paid submissions by design heavyweights of that time such as Sugiura Hisui and Murayama Tomoyoshi and launched Hara into the upper echelon of working designers. The new Kao logo would be presented in a unified manner throughout all of the company's printed communications, including sales staff uniforms, banners, and print advertising.

Hara was keenly interested in graphic design as a unifying force incorporating proper planning, methodological awareness, and mastery of design methods and production.

He wrote a serialized essay called "Picture—Photograph, Letter—Type, and Typofoto" 絵ー写真、文字ー活字、そしてタイポフォト for the photography magazine *Kōga* 光画 in 1932, published by Nojima Yasuzō 野島康三 and Hara's collaborator Kimura Ihei. Over three issues, from the second issue through the fifth issue of the magazine, Hara espoused the combination of photography and typography as being essential for modern design. The fifth issue, also featured the essay "Movement 移す" by film theorist Nakai Masakazu 中井正一, a multivarious examination of photography that explored the power of the medium beyond mere representation and opened the floodgates for modernist interpretations of photography as a medium and a process. That Hara's and Nakai's writings were published side-by-side helped reify each author's work and exemplify the importance of modern photography and modern typography.

Hara was a founding member of the first Nippon Kōbō in 1933, together with director Natori Yōnosuke, producer Okada Sōzō, photographer Kimura Ihei, and critic Ina Nobuo. The group would break within a year's time, and most of the members aside from Natori would form the rival publishing group Chūō Kōbō 中央工房. Hara began working for the Chūō Kōbō sub-group Japan Photo Service (JPS) in 1933, designing

1 Hara Kenya and Naomichi Kawahata, "GGG The 181th / Kenya Hara / Naomichi Kawahata," *Typography of Hiromu Hara* Exhibition (gallery talk, DAI Nippon Printing Co., Ltd., 2003), http://www.dnp.co.jp/gallery/gallerytalk/ggg/gt181/gt181_e.html.

assorted magazines, publications, flyers, and leaflets for the Japan Government Railways. He was tasked with creating large-scale works such as a photo mural for the Japanese pavilion at the Paris Expo of 1937.

Chūō Kōbō member Okada Sōzō created the company Tōhōsha, helped by his government connections as a famous actor, director, and producer, and Tōhōsha took in Chūō Kōbō's members into this new organization. Tōhōsha had the distinct mission of publishing propaganda aimed at foreign audiences akin to Natori Yōnosuke's reformed Nippon Kōbō. Tōhōsha's flagship publication was the illustrated propaganda magazine *Front*—a large-format, full-color magazine that was co-financed by the Japanese Army and major state-aligned corporations such as Mitsui, Mitsubishi, and Sumitomo.

Hara's design work for *Front* was heavily inspired by Russian Constructivist designers Alexander Rodchenko and Varvara Stepanova, with many layouts being nearly identical to the magazine that they designed, *USSR in Construction* (*SSSR na stroike*). All eleven issues of Front were themed, individually focusing on the Japanese Marines, the Army, the occupied state of Manchuria, parachutes, the Japanese Air Force, iron, North China, the Philippines, India, and wartime Tokyo. The final issue was devoted to the theme of wartime art but was never printed, as the plates and the printing factory producing the issue were destroyed in an American air raid. Despite their stylistic imitation, Front helped to define the standards of pictorial composition and integration for modern Japanese graphic design.

Hara created a range of design work for the 1940 Olympics (planned for Tokyo but eventually canceled due to the escalating war in Europe), notably the covers of the magazine *Travel in Japan* for Volume 2, Number 3, in 1936 and Volume 2, Number 4, in 1937.

After the war, Hara joined a publishing company called Bunkasha 文化社, but the company went out of business quickly due to postwar economic inflation, and he found himself a freelance designer. Hara quickly took up book design as one of the main aspects of his post-war profession, beginning with the redesign of the collected books *The Secret History of the Lord of Musashi* and *Arrowroot* 武州公秘話 吉野葛 by Tanizaki Junichirō, published by Chūō Kōron 中央公論 in 1946.

Throughout the 1950s, Hara worked from his home, an apartment conveniently located in Edogawabashi, one of Tokyo's centers for the printing industry. By 1960, Hara had designed over 1,000 books for assorted publishers and helped raise the value and quality of book design in Japan to unprecedented levels.

Hara would go on to help found the Japan Advertising Artists Club in 1951 alongside Kamekura Yūsaku, Kinkichi Takahashi, and other designers interested in uplifting the role of design and designers. One of Hara's most notable clients was the National Museum of Modern Art, Tokyo (MOMAT), which was created in 1952 and for whom Hara designed more than 200 exhibition posters over twenty-three years.

Hara stated that "design is an anonymous art"[2] and felt that his role as a designer was to uplift visual communications for clients and collaborators in lieu of working as an artist engaged in self-glorification.

Hara was invited to exhibit in the *Graphic '55* exhibition and would go on to participate in the World Design Conference. He helped form the Nippon Design Center 日本デザインセンター, becoming president in 1969 and later CEO.

Hara's earlier work designing promotional materials for the 1940 Olympics would have a direct influence on the design of the identity for the 1964 Olympics—an identity that was consummately reductive, poised, and modern. Hara acted as typographic/lettering consultant and collaborator for Kamekura Yūsaku's logo for the Olympics, oversaw the Olympic typographic guidelines (a first for the Olympics), and designed the tickets and invitations for the event.

At the Nippon Design Center, Hara continued working for MOMAT, Takeo Paper, and other corporations. Hara designed multiple iconic covers for the design magazines *Graphic Design* and *Idea*, as well. Hara taught at a variety of schools, including the Aichi Prefectural School of Art, Musashino Art University, and Kyushu Art Institute of Technology. In 1971, he was awarded the Purple Ribbon by the Japanese government for his multiple achievements and his contributions to Japanese visual culture.

Hara became ill in 1975 on a trip to Malaysia, suffering from a cerebral blood clot that impaired his ability to design. He

2 Hara Hiromu, *Tokubetsuten Hara Hiromu: Kindai Guraffiku Dezain No Yoake* (Nagano-ken Iida-shi: Iida-shi Bijutsu Hakubutsukan, 1996), 19.

subsequently resigned from his position as visiting lecturer at the Aichi Prefectural School of Art and his directorship at the Nippon Design Center, shifting to an advisory role.

Hara published a number of books over the course of his career, including *Graphic Design Systems Volumes 1–5* グラフィックデザイン大系 第1巻〜第5巻 in the early 1960s, *Graphic Design in the World 2* 世界のグラフィックデザイン2 in 1974, the monograph *Hara Hiromu: The Origins of Graphic Design* 原弘 グラフィック·デザインの源流 in 1985, and *Contemporary Japanese Book Design from 1975 to 1984* 現代日本のブックデザイン 1975〜1984 in 1986.

Called "the emperor of book design" by critic and design organizer Katsumi Masaru and "a god of book design" by designer Tanaka Ikkō, Hara died in 1986.

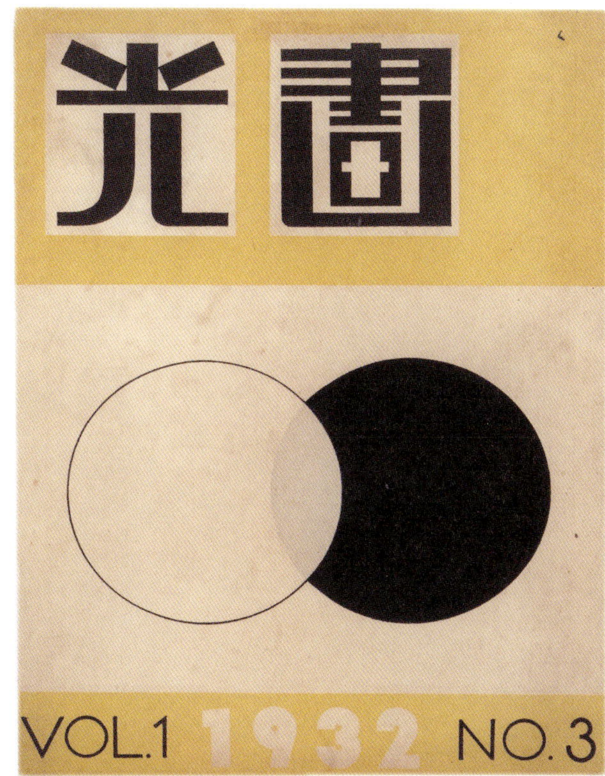

***Kōga* 光画** Vol. 1 No. 3., 1932.

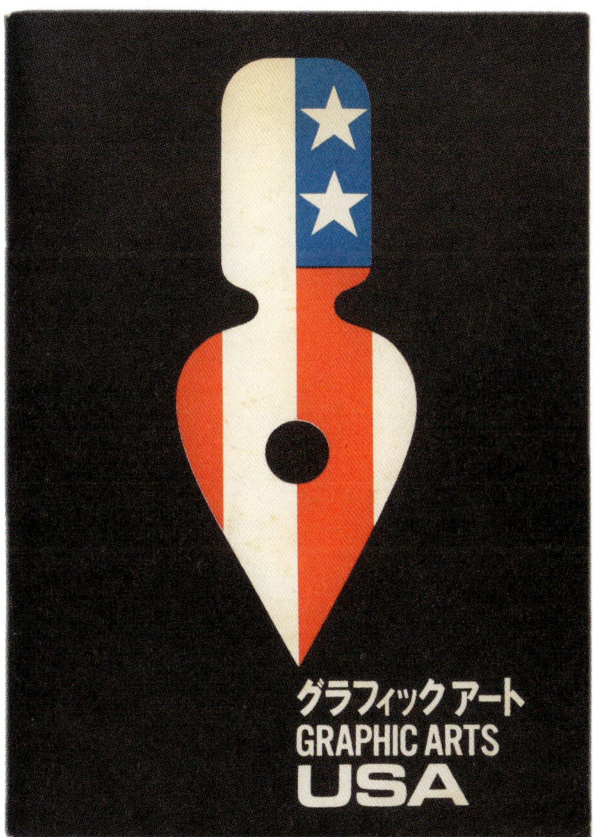

Graphic Arts USA exhibition catalog with Ivan Chermayeff's artwork redrawn and localized by Hara Hiromu (Tokyo: National Museum of Modern Art 国立近代美術館, 1967).

References:

Natori, Yōnosuke, Mari Shirayama, and Yoshio Hori. *Natori Yōnosuke to Nihon Kōbō: 1931–45*. Tokyo: Iwanami shoten, 2006.

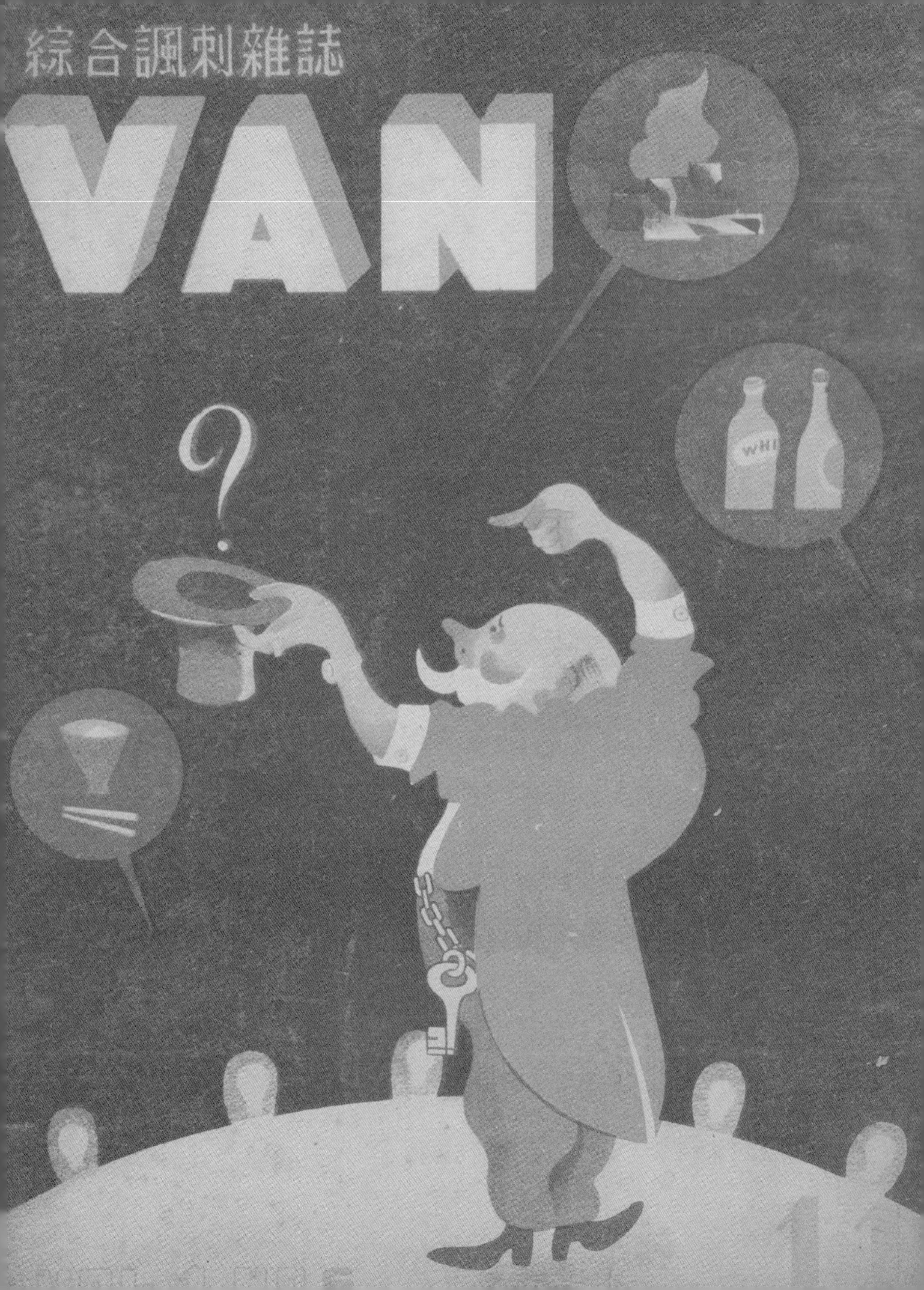

綜合諷刺雜誌

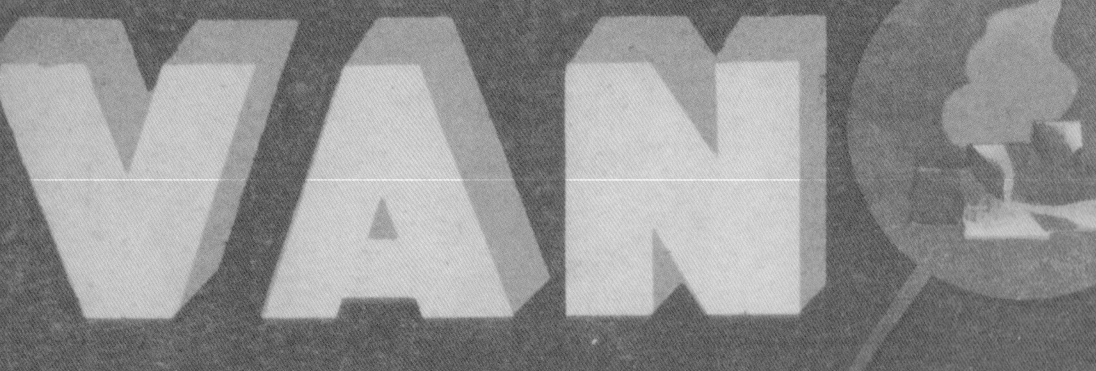

昭和21年6月20日 印刷納本 ★ 昭和21年7月1日 發 行

綜合諷刺雜誌

VAN

multiple modernisms/ the case of the disappearing olympics

Multiple Modernisms

When we approach the topic of Modernism, it's important to specify exactly which Modernism or Modernisms we are talking about.

There are innumerable strains associated with different cultures (e.g., Swiss Typographic Modernism) and sectors of cultural production (e.g., Modern British Literature). Each is culturally relative, entangled in differing chronologies, and informed by great cultural shifts. Different countries and regions have divergent histories and legacies of cultural development. History does not perform for us in neat phases.

Japanese graphic design informed and was informed by multiple strains of Modernism—global, regional, and national—expressed across multiple concurrent shifts in policy, cultural production, and lifestyle spanning a century and counting.

Global Modernism as a Social Project is a utopian ideal that we as a global society are still undertaking. Global Modernism is the search for basic human rights and basic human needs such as access to health care, clean water, and food. As these issues are still prevalent in many nations, Global Modernism is a project as yet *unfulfilled*. Critics of Modernism argue that it is a logocentric idea of all human life as being relatively similar and a belief that citizens of societies across the globe should be made subservient to autocratic/technocratic central planning, modeled on Western European and North American nation-states. Global Modernism as a Social Project began around 1900 and still continues today.

Modernization in Japanese design was different than in Europe and North America, as it was functional but largely state-driven. The Meiji period (1868–1912) is most often considered the advent of "Modern Japan," with the Emperor being restored to nominal power, the government abolishing the Neo-Confucian class structure of Japanese society, rapid urbanization, and widespread Westernization.

The 1920s saw a fusion between Japanese and Western styles of visual arts, music, architecture, and design that was described in Japan as *modan*, the katakana transliteration of "modern." This blending of aesthetics that largely flourished in metropolitan areas would reach its peak during the early Shōwa period (and often referred to as *Shōwa modan*), then faded in the mid-1930s with the rise of militarism, the termination of party politics, and the escalation of the Sino-Japanese War of 1937. Modan as a term used by residents of Japan is a highly evocative word that evokes nostalgia for the 1920s and early 1930s, yet does not relate to the Global Project of Modernism as a universal utopian initiative.

Throughout the 1930s, Japanese self-perception was that of a "modern" nation coupled with an increasingly militarized approach to Modernism—"the modern" of the 1930s was power, domination, and occupation hand-in-hand with domestic cosmopolitanism. Modernism in Japanese design in the early twentieth century was characterized by a pluralistic mix of aesthetics that spanned minimalist and function-oriented approaches alongside processes that were decorative and ornate.

Modern Japanese approaches to typographic composition in the 1920s were not driven by the universalist ideological approaches exemplified by work from the Bauhaus, such as László Moholy-Nagy's reductive typography and Josef Albers' attempts at the reform of typeface design. Reductive approaches to the design of *zuan moji* as created by Yamada Shinkichi and others in the 1920s tended to be born out of stylistic rather than utopian ideologies. Additionally, Hara Hiromu's writing about typography in the late 1920s exemplified an invigorated approach to typographic reform, yet he did not call to throw out historically classical forms of typefaces such as mincho types.

Ideologically, some pre-World War II Japanese modern aesthetics were driven by utopian notions held by designers associated with the left (e.g., Murayama Tomoyoshi and Kon Wajirō). At the same time, some aesthetics drew from the expansionist imperialist agendas of the Japanese government, which many designers were ideologically allied with or at least worked under (e.g., Natori Yōnosuke, Kamekura Yūsaku, and Yamana Ayao). While all of these works included rich visual expression, the ideological underpinnings diverged.

For the designers allied with authoritarian regimes, "utopia" as they saw it during the interwar period was a world, or at the very least an Asia, as a whole incorporated into the Japanese Empire, as mandated by the Japanese government. In this way, the ideologies behind Japanese Modern graphic design were simultaneously utopian *and* authoritarian.

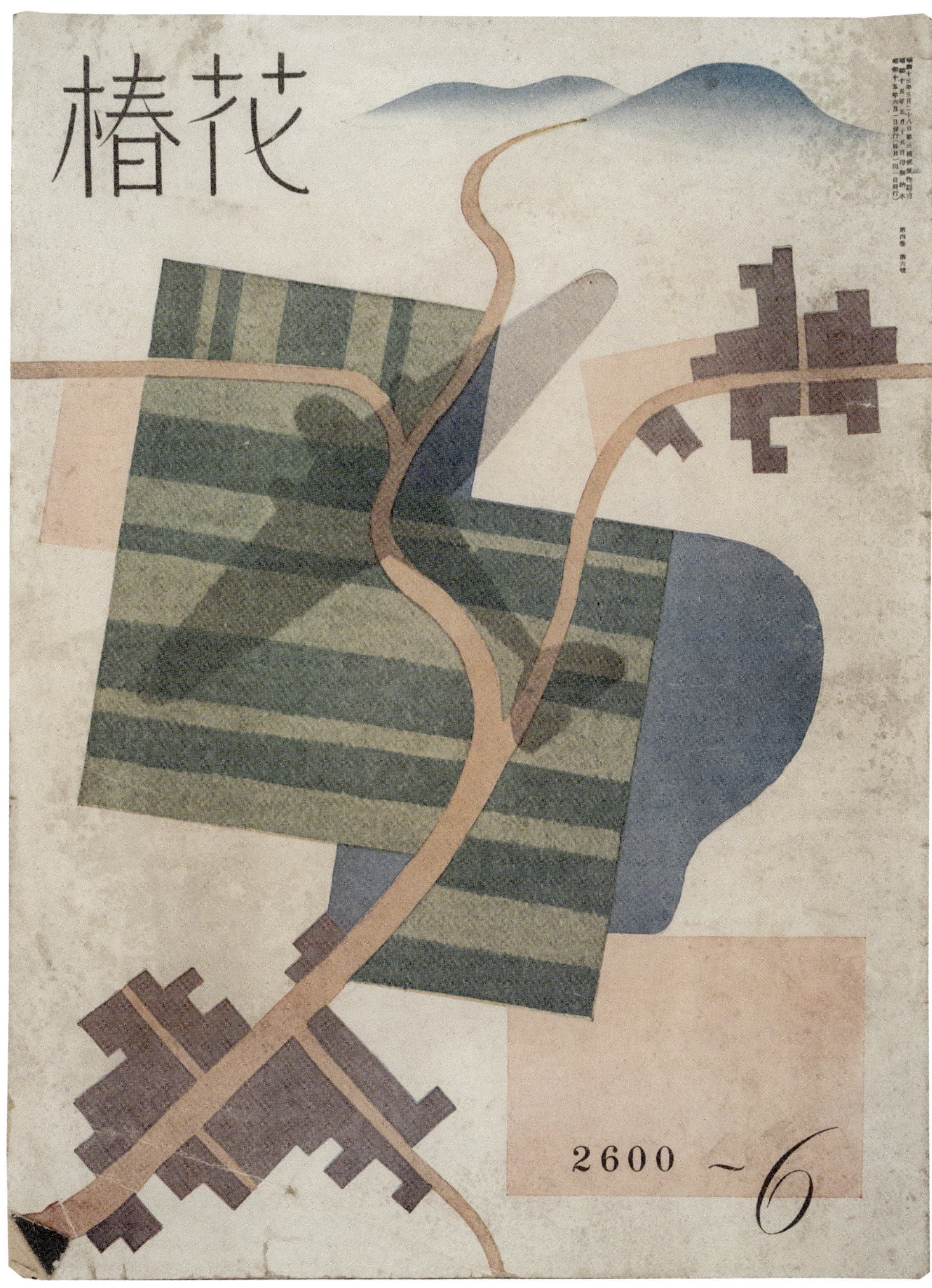

Cover design for 1938 issue Shiseido's in-house magazine, ***Hanatsubaki* 花椿**, by Yamana Ayao 山名文夫 depicting planned fertile fields and towns with the shadow of protection from a warplane overhead. The composition is embellished with delicate lettering and letterspaced typography, adding a feminine touch to the propaganda image **(Tokyo: Kabushikigaisha Shiseido 株式会社資生堂, 1938)**.

1940 Olympic poster design by Wada Sanzō 和田三造, reproduced here in *Industrial Art* 産業美術 by Satomi Munetsugu 里見宗次 (Tokyo: Japan Advertising Club 日本広告俱楽部, 1940).

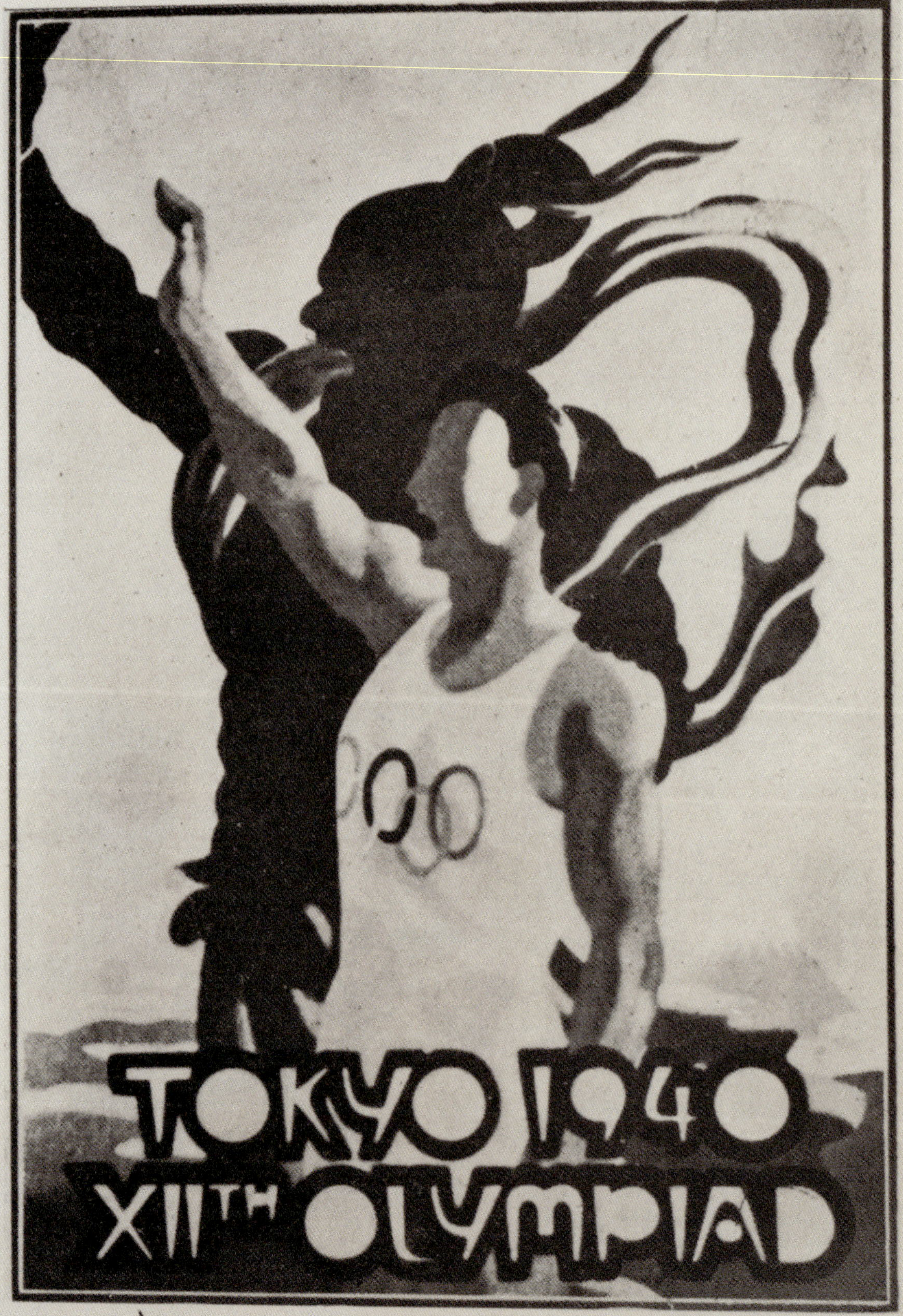

和田三造氏作

The Case of the Disappearing Olympics

The 1940 Olympics, officially known as the XII Olympiad, was designed to be an event of both domestic and international interest. The Japanese government and International Olympic Committee promoted the Games within Japan as being held on the 2,600th anniversary of Japan. The 1940 Olympics were to be a celebration of the mythic rise to power of Emperor Jimmu 神武天皇, Japan's first emperor. Additionally, holding the Olympics in Tokyo would solidify international recognition of Japan as a world power as well help mitigate Japan's 1933 withdrawal from the League of Nations. Simultaneously, official sanctioning of Tokyo as the site for such a prestigious international event would tacitly justify, acknowledge, and approve of Japan's continued course of imperialism and colonialism.

Tokyo entered into the competition to host the games in 1932, vying against a host of European cities. Japanese athletes had begun participating in the Olympic Games in 1912, with the first gold medals won by Japanese athletes in Amsterdam in 1928. The introduction of physical education and sports during the Meiji Restoration helped modernize the Japanese educational system, as well. Sports also functioned symbolically for the government: keeping oneself fit was a stand-in for the health of the aggregate nation-state and its interests.

Japanese members of the International Olympic Committee, including Ambassador Sugimura Yōtarō 杉村陽太郎, met behind the scenes with other IOC representatives to engineer deals to help secure Tokyo's candidacy throughout the early 1930s, resulting in Tokyo's selection as the site of the 1940 Olympics in 1936. Sapporo was simultaneously chosen as the site for the fifth Winter Olympics that same year. Planning had already begun in earnest for programming, organization, sites, transportation, and promotion of the Games. The Publicity Section of the Olympic Committee published a monthly magazine called Olympic News in a variety of languages and distributed it globally via Japanese embassies, tourism organizations, and assorted publishing companies and literary distribution concerns, in an effort to help promote the Tokyo Olympics.

Foreign-language pamphlets with the cover messages "We Call the Youth of the World" and "Way to Olympic Japan" with cover art by commercial artists Adachi Genichirō 足立源一郎 and Yūki Somei 結城素明 were produced in collaboration with the Japanese Board of Tourist Industry and distributed globally, as well.

Prior to 1938, myriad other publications were planned under the titles *Olympic Information*, *Sports in Japan*, *The Olympic Guide Book*, *The History and Spirit of the Olympic Games*, *The Olympic Games and Public Morality*, *The Children's Olympic Reader*, and *The People's Olympic Reader*, as well as a host of postcards, posters, seals, and leaflets.

The Olympic Publicity Section decided to hold competitions for the visual design of the official poster and mark of the XII Olympiad. The competition for the Olympic mark, or logo, drew 102,113 separate submissions from the public. The winning submission was designed by Hiromoto Taiji 廣本泰史—an ovoid composition with concentric rings surrounding it, akin to a track or stadium with the Olympic rings, the Japanese flag, and the text "XII OLYMPIAD TOKYO 1940" contained within. The Olympic poster public design competition received 1,992 submissions, with Kyoto artist Kuroda Norio's 黒田典夫 design depicting Emperor Jimmu prevailing.

The Publicity Section took issue with Kuroda's depiction of Japan's mythical founding emperor and commissioned art and design educator Wada Sanzō of the Tokyo Art School to design the final poster for the Olympiad. Wada's poster featured a saluting athlete with Niō, one of the muscular guardians of the Buddha, behind the human figure—a paean to physicality and spirituality, as much as a symbol of East Asian Buddhist tradition.

Painter Ihara Usaburo 伊原宇三郎 was commissioned to design the poster for the fifth Winter Olympics to be held in Sapporo. He rendered a cheering crowd with a snowy backdrop emerging from a wavy decorative frame bracketed by assorted styles of sans serif display lettering.

A number of other promotional publications were released in the lead-up to the Olympics, including the quarterly Board of Tourist Industry of Japanese Government Railways magazine, *Travel in Japan*. The cover of the fourth issue of the second volume was designed by Hara Hiromu, who adopted many European avant-garde aesthetics, evident in the large amount of white space, sans serif lettering, and a reductive, stylized depiction of Mount Fuji taking center stage. Hara's design for *Travel in Japan* directly prefigured the design of the 1964 Olympics, informing the continuation of the domestic development of Japanese Modern Graphic Design as a stylistic approach. The influence of professional networks in the design industry secured a spot for Hara's Nippon Kōbō colleague Kamekura

Yūsaku in the 1964 Olympic logo design team, as well as leading to Hara's reappointment for the 1964 Olympics.

Japan's involvement in the second Sino-Japanese War in 1937 put an incredible economic strain on the country, just as Japan was ramping up preparations for the Games. After insisting for a year that the Games could still be held, the government finally bowed out. The International Olympic Committee designated Helsinki, Finland, to replace Tokyo, though the 1939 outbreak of World War II meant that the 1940 Olympics would never come to pass.

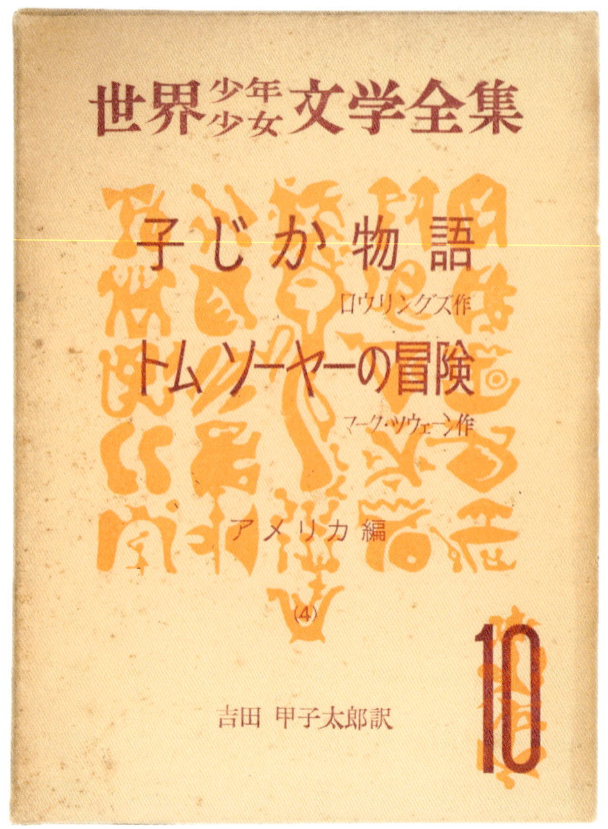

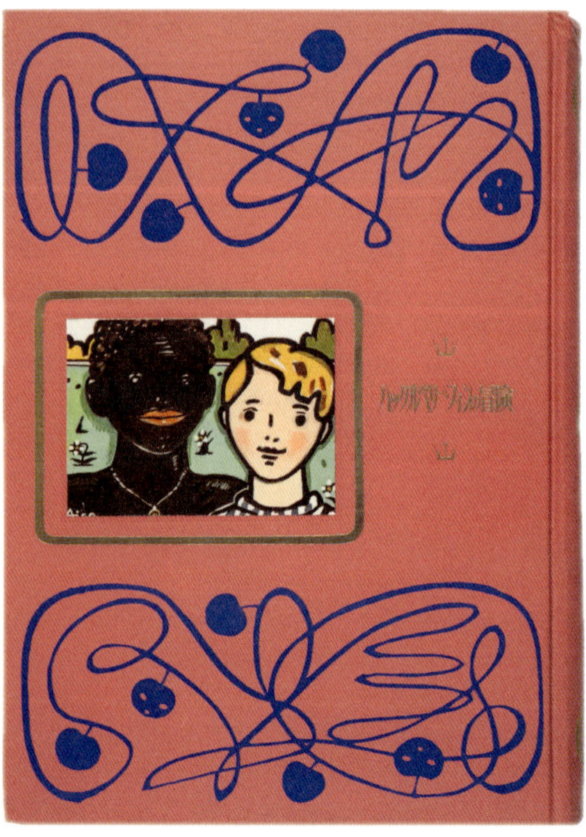

World Boys and Girls Literature Complete Works, Vol. 10 No. 4, "*The Adventures of Tom Sawyer*" 世界少年少女文学全集·10巻 アメリカ編·4 子じか物語/トム·ソーヤーの冒険 (Tokyo: Sogensha 創元社, 1954). Slipcover and book cover design by Hatsuyama Shigeru 初山滋.

HATSUYAMA SHIGERU 初山滋

1897–1973

Hatsuyama Shigeru was born in Tokyo. He studied painting from the age of eight and was recognized as a child prodigy. He left school at age nine to apprentice first under a goldsmith and then under a fabric dyer the following year. Hatsuyama's second apprenticeship only lasted five years, just half of his expected tenure. From there, he apprenticed under illustrator, painter, and artist Igawa Sengai 井川洗厓, creating pencil sketches for Igawa to finish up. During this time, he joined a study group of Japanese-style painters which included the famous *shin hanga* artist Ito Shinsui 伊東深水.

In 1916, he left Igawa's employ, working initially for a kabuki actor and then returning to the dyeing shop. Hatsuyama submitted his illustration work to assorted publications and was consistently turned down until 1919, when his work was published in the newly founded magazine *Otogi No Sekai* おとぎの世界. He was a regular contributor until the magazine closed in 1923. Hatsuyama became a regular contributor to the printmaking journal *Han Geijutsu* 版芸術 and created illustrated stories for the newspaper *Asahi Shimbun*. He was a member of Onchi Kōshirō's Ichimokukai 一木会, a wartime and postwar group which helped to keep *sōsaku hanga* printmaking alive during the years of censorship and lack of resources. Hatsuyama was very active in the design and printmaking community in addition to his illustration work.

In the 1940s, Hatsuyama was a regular contributor to the children's magazine *Kodomo no Kuni*, for which he provided both illustration work and cover designs employing expressive lettering and typography.

References:
Shuri, Yuki, and Shinju Onuki. *Kakimoji no Dezain*. Tokyo: Graphic-sha, 2017.

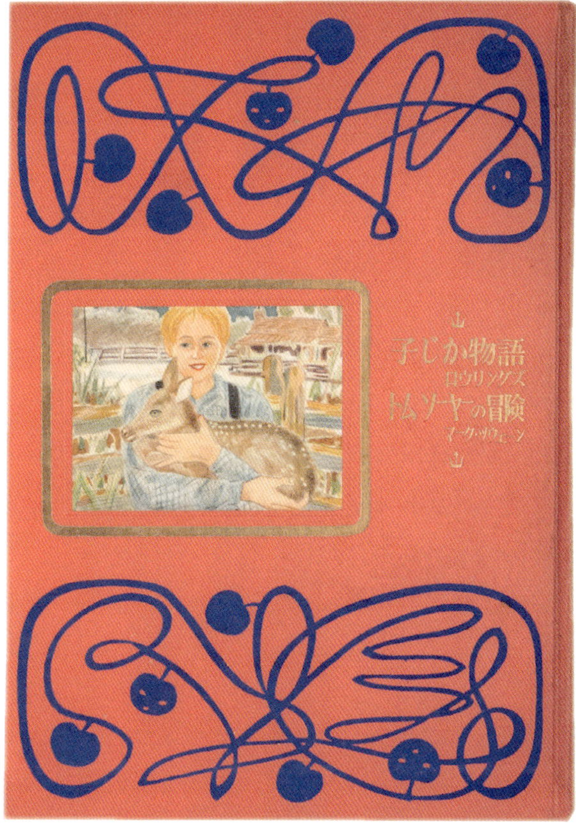

World Boys and Girls Literature Complete Works, Vol. 35 No. 5, "*Huckleberry Finn's Adventure*" (Mark Twain) 世界少年少女文学全集・35巻 アメリカ編・5 ハックルベリー・フィンの冒険（マーク・ツウェーン）(Tokyo: Sogensha 創元社, 1956). Slipcover and book cover design by Hatsuyama Shigeru 初山滋.

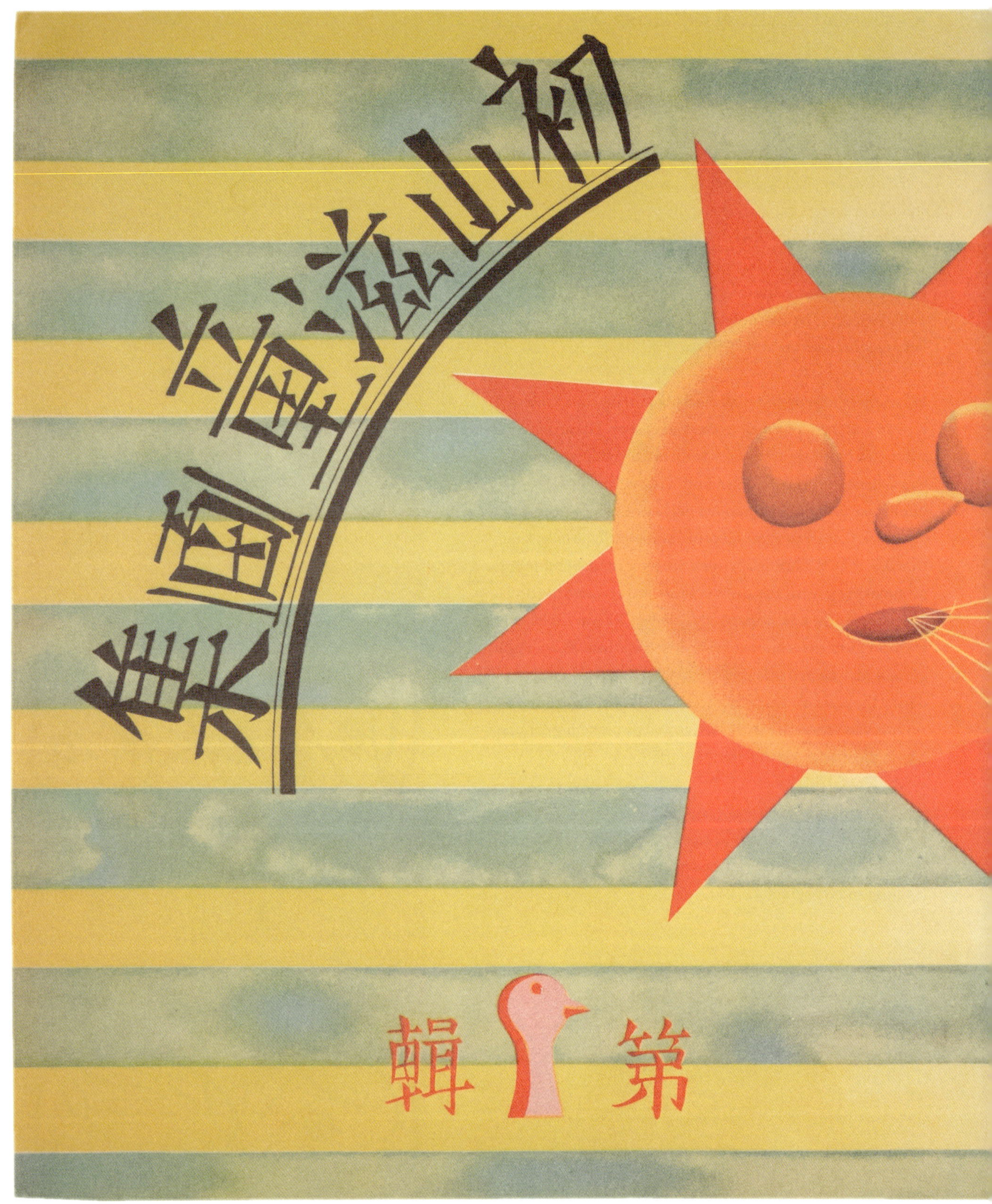
初山滋童畫集
第 輯

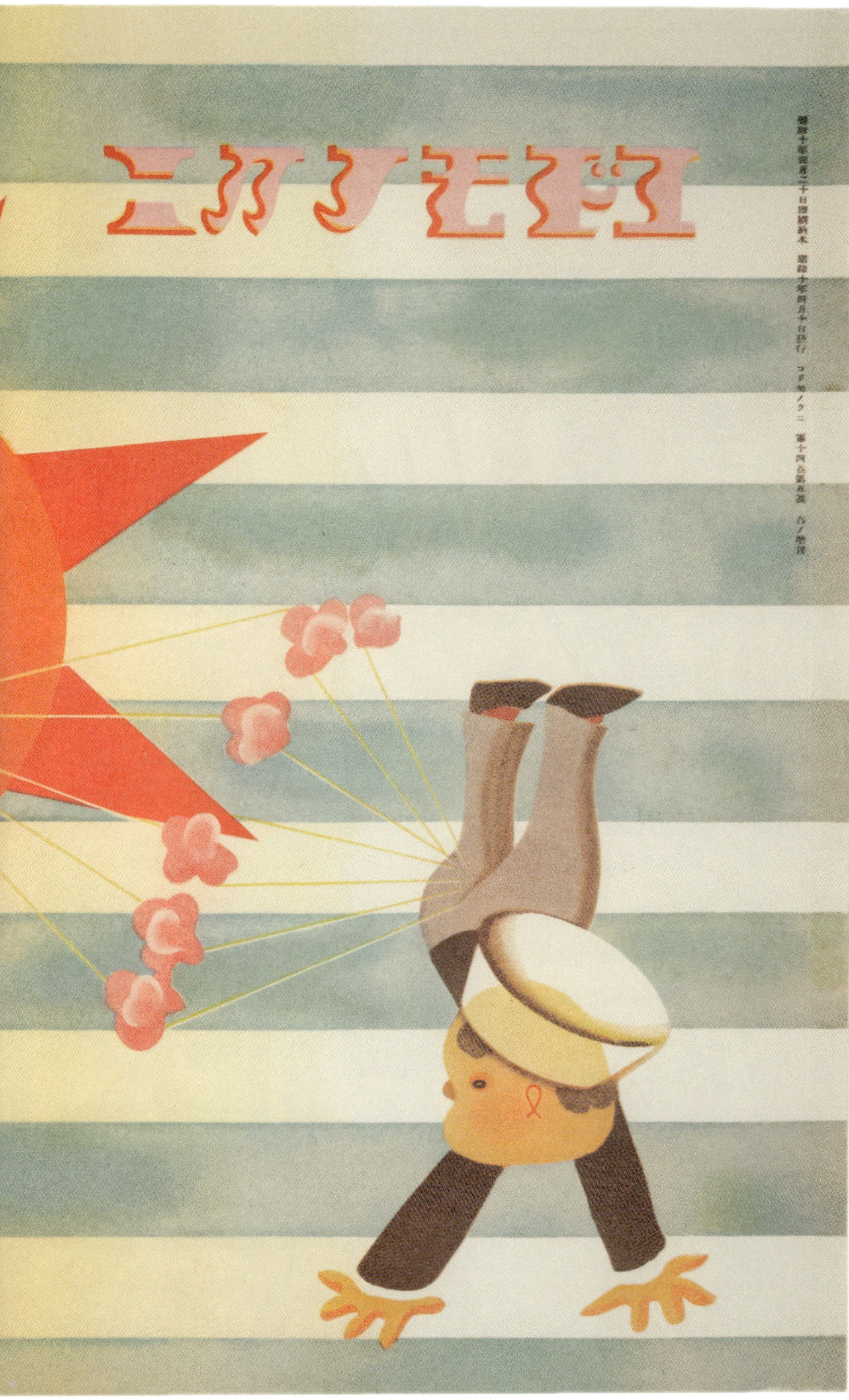

Hatsuyama Shigeru 初山滋 cover design for ***Kodomo no kuni*** **コドモノクニ** published by **Tokyosha 東京社** in Tokyo. An extraordinarily playful cover design showing the sun blowing away a young boy's flatulence as a pink bird looks on.

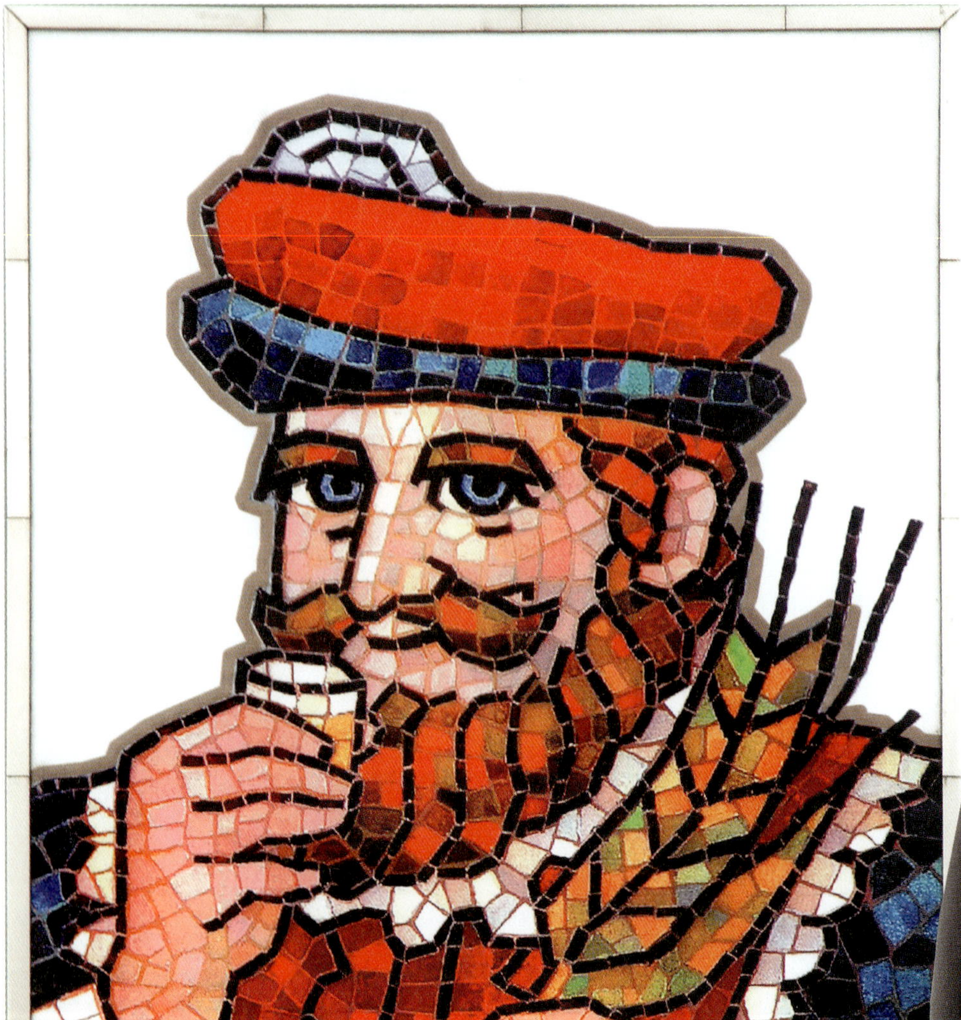

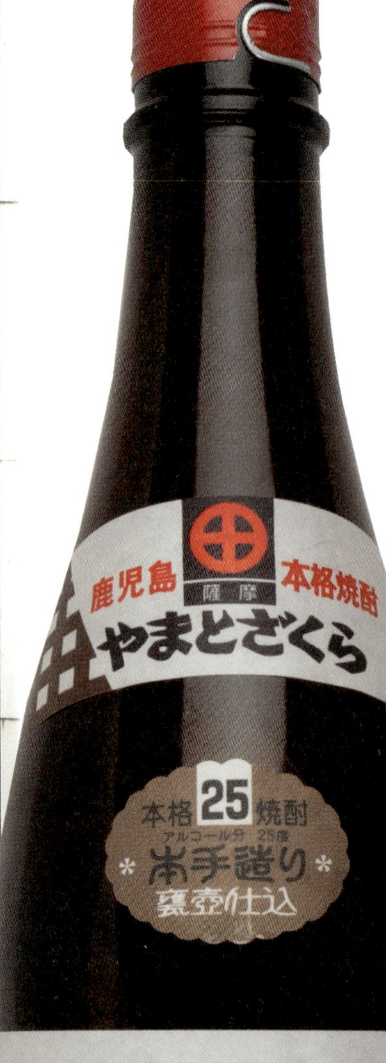

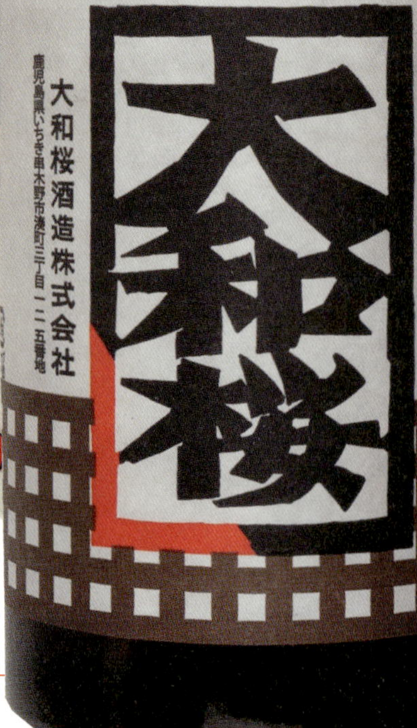

Left: Design for the bearded **Nikka Whisky** mascot, and accompanying lettering by Okuyama Gihachiro 奥山儀八郎 and Otaka Shigeji 大高重治.
Right: ***Yamatosakura* 大和桜** shōchū label design by Ōtaka Shigeji 大高重治.

ŌTAKA SHIGEJI 大高重治

1908–2002

Ōtaka Shigeji was born in Tokyo. After graduating from elementary school, Ōtaka was sent to work at his uncle's commercial printing business, where he learned plate-making, print production processes, and design. Throughout the 1930s, Ōtaka found regular design work for Dai-Nippon Kaju Co. Ltd 大日本果汁, a juice company based in Hokkaido.

In 1940, he was tasked with designing a poster for Nikka Whisky, a new brand of whiskey that the company was developing (the name "Nikka" is a conflation of the "ni" sound of Nippon 日本 and "ka" of *kaju* 果汁, or "fruit juice" in Japanese). The company's founder was a Scotland-trained whiskey-distillation expert who had worked previously for Suntory's predecessor, Kotobukiya. The company was pleased with his design, and Ōtaka was hired to design all of the Nikka Whisky labels and promotional materials for decades, alongside fellow designer Okuyama Gihachirō. His labels for Black Nikka, the lowest-priced nationally distributed whiskey, became pervasive on the shelves of Japan's corner and convenience stores.

In addition to his work for Nikka Whisky, Ōtaka created numerous designs for assorted companies' posters, packaging, and book covers.

After converting to Christianity at age sixty-seven, he sought out fellow Christian clients and designed materials for his local church in Kokubunji and for associated Christian publishers.

OKUYAMA GIHACHIRO 奥山儀八郎

1907–1981

Okuyama Gihachirō was born in Yamagata Prefecture to a family of shoemakers. After finishing elementary school, he moved to Tokyo to pursue a career in art. In 1928, he was a winner in the eighth Japan Sōsaku Hanga Association Exhibition 8回日本創作版画協会展 and as a result obtained employment from the fabric and clothing manufacturer Nikke ニッケ, for whom he both designed and printed a variety of posters over the subsequent decade. He signed his bold, colorful designs with creative takes on his own name, such as ギ8 (gi-hachi).

Okuyama went on to open his own printmaking studio in the 1950s and was actively involved in printmaking until his death in 1981. He was an avid coffee drinker and an amateur historian who focused on the spread of coffee and coffee culture in Japan. Okuyama worked for a number of other clients including Nikka Whisky, Nippon Breweries, and assorted publishing companies, designing book covers, posters, and packaging.

References:
Shuri, Yuki, and Shinju Onuki. *Kakimoji no Dezain*. Tokyo: Graphic-sha, 2017.

Asacoco. "Asacoco." Atarashī raifusutairu' o hasshin. Asacoco Kabushikigaisha, November 6, 2014. http://asacoco.jp/topnews/otaka/.

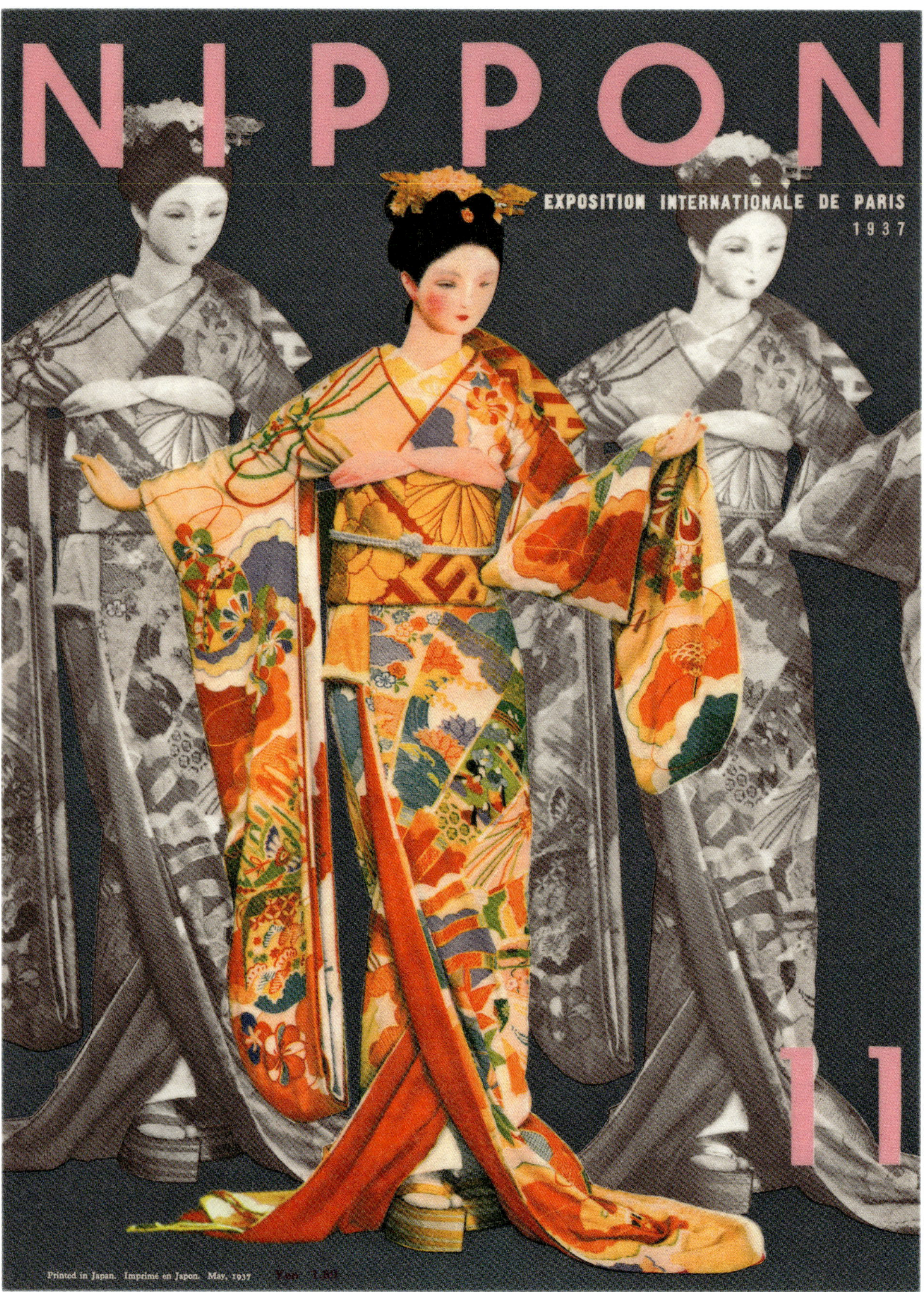

Cover of ***Nippon No. 11*** (Tokyo: Nippon Kōbō, 1937). Designed by Kumada Goro 熊田五郎.

KUMADA GORŌ 熊田五郎

1911–2009

Kumada Gorō was born in Yokohama. He studied design at Kanagawa Prefectural Industrial Arts Academy 神奈川県立工業学校, alongside fellow student Takahashi Kinkichi, and later at Tokyo School of Fine Arts. In 1933, he began apprenticing under Yamana Ayao, having been introduced by his elder brother, a close friend of Yamana's. With Yamana, Kumada worked on projects for Shiseido and on a number of issues of the propaganda magazine *Nippon* for Nippon Kōbō, under the direction of publisher Natori Yōnosuke, designing both the interior layouts and the cover of issue 11 in 1937. Kumada left Nippon Kōbō in 1939 and began working for Nippon Photographic Industrial Arts 日本写真工芸社 in 1943 alongside his old classmate Takahashi Kinkichi.

Postwar, Kumada worked for Kanebo Cosmetics for a number of years before turning to freelance illustration and writing/drawing children's books under the pen name Kumada Chikabo 熊田千佳慕.

King's Cream 王さまのクリーム, Mitsuyoshi Natsuya 光吉夏彌 (Tokyo: Sakurai Shoten 櫻井書店, 1948). Cover design by Kumada Goro 熊田五郎.

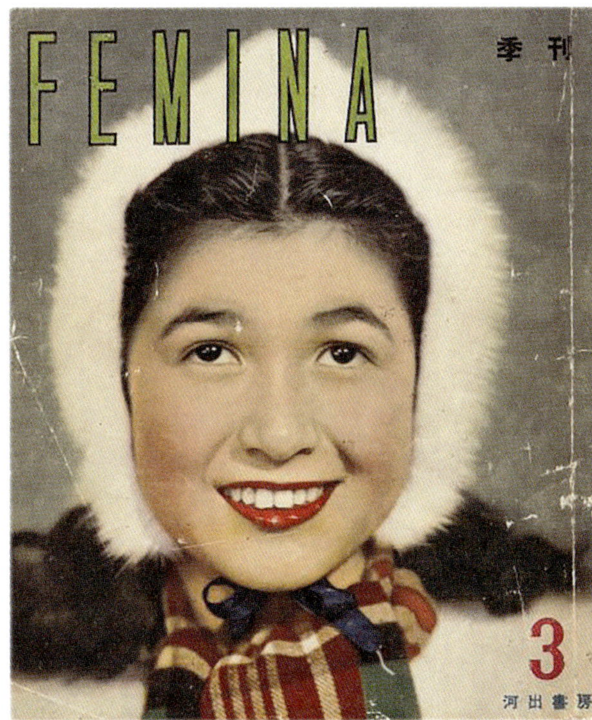

Quarterly Femina No. 3 季刊FEMINA 3号 (Tokyo: Kawade Shobo 河出書房, 1948). Cover design by Kumada Goro 熊田五郎.

References:

Natori, Yōnosuke, Mari Shirayama, and Yoshio Hori. *Natori Yōnosuke to Nihon Kōbō: 1931–45*. Tokyo: Iwanami shoten, 2006.

Shuri, Yuki, and Shinju Onuki. *Kakimoji no Dezain*. Tokyo: Graphic-sha, 2017.

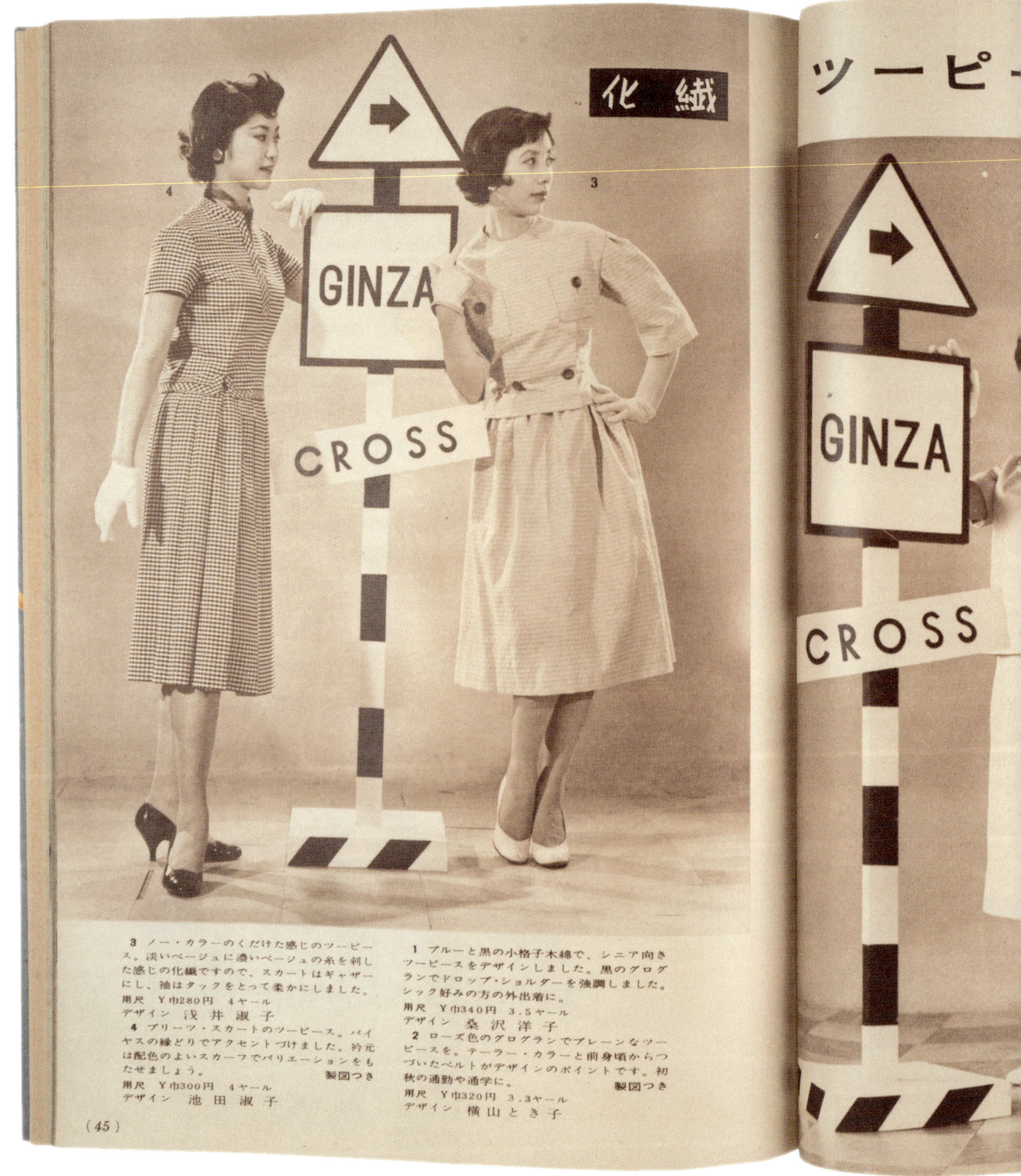

3 ノー・カラーのくだけた感じのツーピース。淡いベージュに濃いベージュの糸を刺した感じの化繊ですので、スカートはギャザーにし、袖はタックをとって柔かにしました。
用尺　Y巾280円　4ヤール
デザイン　浅 井 淑 子

4 プリーツ・スカートのツーピース。バイヤスの縁どりでアクセントづけました。衿元は配色のよいスカーフでバリエーションをもたせましょう。
製図つき
用尺　Y巾300円　4ヤール
デザイン　池 田 淑 子

1 ブルーと黒の小格子木綿で、シニア向きツーピースをデザインしました。黒のグログランでドロップ・ショルダーを強調しました。シック好みの方の外出着に。
用尺　Y巾340円　3.5ヤール
デザイン　桑 沢 洋 子

2 ローズ色のグログランでプレーンなツーピースを。テーラー・カラーと前身頃からつづいたベルトがデザインのポイントです。初秋の通勤や通学に。
製図つき
用尺　Y巾320円　3.3ヤール
デザイン　横 山 と き 子

(45)

The Style of Autumn 秋のスタイルブック (Tokyo: Nihon Yūbenkai Kodansha 日本雄弁会講談社, 1957).

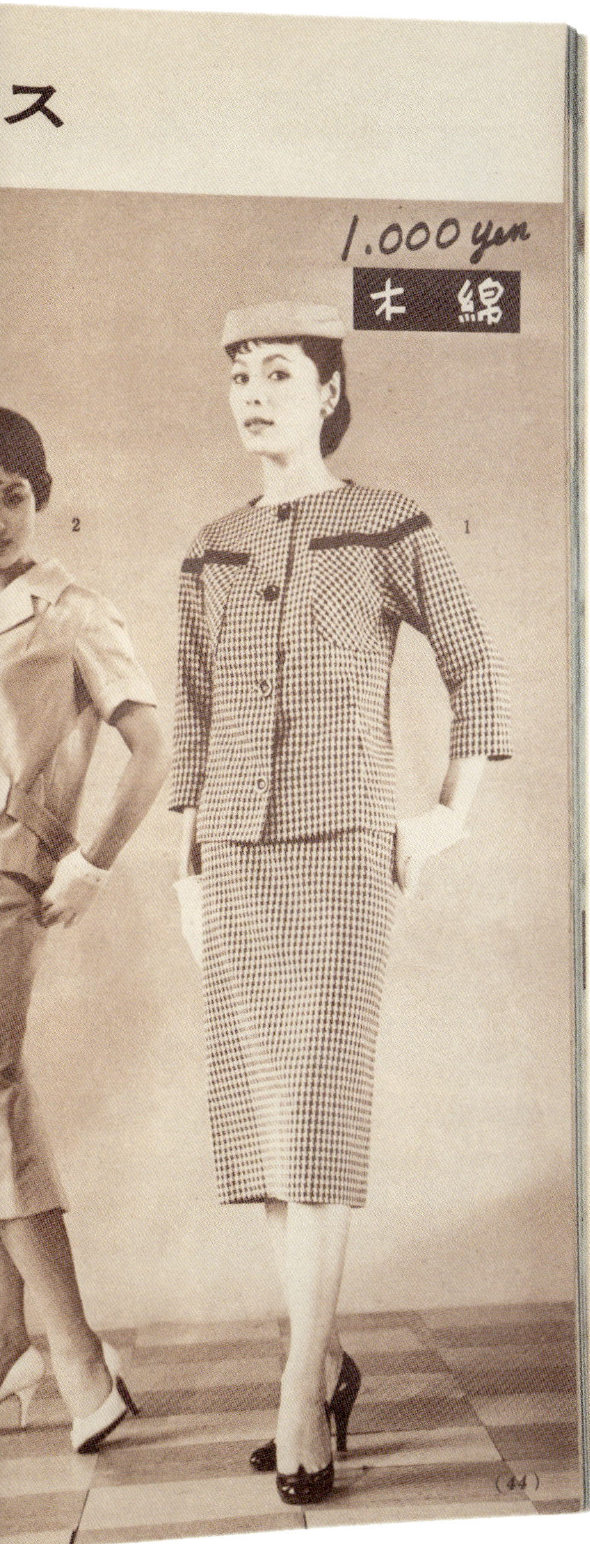

KUWASAWA YŌKO 桑沢洋子

1910–1977

Kuwasawa Yōko was born in Tokyo and studied at Women's Academy of Fine Arts (WAFA) 女子美術専門学校 and at School of New Architecture and Design 新建築工芸学院, where she was introduced to aspects of Bauhaus pedagogy by founder Kawakita Renshichirō 川喜田煉七郎. She joined the editorial staff of the magazine *Fujin Gahō* 婦人画報 in 1937, working on projects related to professional clothing for women and the advancement of women in Japanese society. In 1942, she started her own fashion design studio, focusing on industrially produced, functional clothing for women. She became a regular columnist for *Fujin Gahō* in 1945 and helped to establish the Japan Designers' Club 日本デザイナークラブ in 1948.

She became a lecturer at her alma mater, Joshibi University of Art and Design, before founding her own "pure" design school, Kuwasawa Design School 桑沢デザイン研究所, situated first in Aoyama in 1954 before moving to its present location in Shibuya in 1958. Steeped in Bauhaus pedagogical practices, the vocational school offered (and offers) a wide range of design-oriented educational paths in fashion, architecture, industrial design, and graphic design. The same year the school opened, Kuwasawa invited Bauhaus founder Walter Gropius to lecture there, the first of many European modernists who would guest lecture over subsequent decades. In 1966, Kuwasawa also founded the private university Tokyo Zōkei University 東京造形大学, which offers bachelor's and master's degrees in a wide range of art- and design-related fields. She held the role of president of the university for many years.

Until her death in 1977, Kuwasawa remained one of Japan's leading design educators. She emphasized the need for students to "break concepts" 概念砕き[1] demanding that students dismantle their preconceptions and view design projects through a renewed perspective and methodological approach. Kuwasawa designed the uniforms for the 1964 Tokyo Olympic team and event staff and wrote widely on design, publishing several books on fashion design.

References:

Barbora. "History of Design Education in Japan." *Idea* 61, no. 359 (July 2013): 5–8.

Ikegami, Hidehiro. "Kosei and Zokei Education: Bauhaus and the Formation of Kuwasawa Design School." *Asian Conference of Design History and Theory Journal* 1, no. 1 (March 2016): 85–94.

1 "デザイン教育の先駆者〈桑沢〉の歴史と理念·所長あいさつ." 専門学校 桑沢デザイン研究所. Kuwasawa Design School (December 1, 2020), https://www.kds.ac.jp/about/.

HANAMORI YASUJI 花森安治

1911–1978

Hanamori was the publisher and editor-in-chief of the magazine *Kurashi no Techō* 暮しの手帖, or *Handbook for Everyday Life*, one of the most influential cultural magazines for women in postwar Japan. For three decades—from 1948 until his death in 1978—Hanamori shaped the magazine's editorial approach, advertising policy, and visual form according to his singular vision, informed by his political views and personal experiences of war.

In 1937, Hanamori was sent to occupied Manchuria as a soldier and was again conscripted during World War II, though was discharged due to a severe case of tuberculosis. Hanamori then worked as a propagandist for the Imperial Rule Assistance Association 大政翼賛會, a propaganda organization which aimed to promote the economic growth and political unification of Japan. Hanamori wrote in 1942, "People who engage in politics must know about advertising techniques, and people who engage in advertising must know about politics."

After the war, Hanamori launched the short-lived fashion magazine *Style Book* スタイルブック in 1946—lasting only five issues—followed by the publication of *Kurashi no Techō* in 1948. *Kurashi no Techō* attended in detail to a wide range of homemakers' desires and interests, cultivating an editorial approach meant to influence both the individual and greater society. Its recipes were designed to be made by homemakers using common ingredients and kitchen implements. Hanamori also produced intensive quarterly issues devoted to investigating the quality of home products, akin to the American magazine *Consumer Reports*.

Hanamori's conception of *kurashi* 暮し or "everyday life" in the postwar period was that the personal was both overtly and implicitly political. He politicized the domestic sphere within the pages of the magazine, especially during the political turmoil of 1960s Japan. In a special issue of *Kurashi no Techō* in 1968, a feature titled "The Records of Wartime Life" included personal accounts of wartime by normal citizens—one of the first articles of its kind. In his editorial statement, Hanamori questioned blind patriotism, stating, "If our life conflicts with the government's policy, we overthrow the government. That is true democracy." Hanamori insisted that readers not forget the hardships they suffered during the war, empowering his readership to speak publicly about their experiences. He sought to be a spokesperson for the nation's "forgotten people," with the hope of empowering readers' autonomy by articulating the power of the everyday.

During Hanamori's tenure, issues of the magazine did not include advertising so as to protect his editorial goals from outside influence.

Hanamori also was the primary designer of *Kurashi no Techō*. He designed the logo, did much of the illustration and lettering work, and steered the creative vision of the magazine, both visually and editorially. He appealed to readers with an approach both intellectual and emotional, combining professional staged photography with often naïve-seeming hand lettering. *Kurashi no Techō* in Hanamori's time was a magazine for the people which bore the traces of being made by a person, singular in its desire to reach many.

References:
Funase, Shunsuke. *Kurashi no Techō o Tsukutta Otoko: Kimi Wa Hanamori Yasuji o Shitte Iruka*. Tokyo: Isutopuresu, 2016.

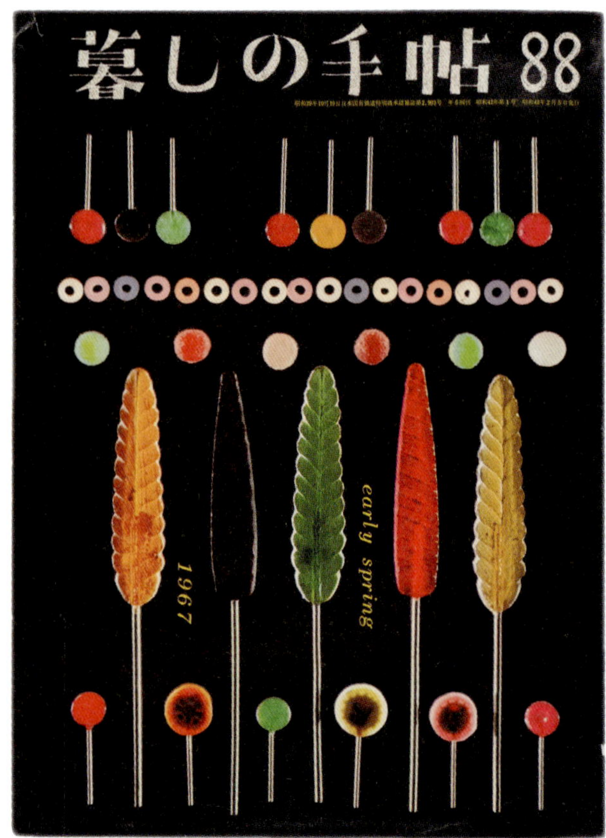

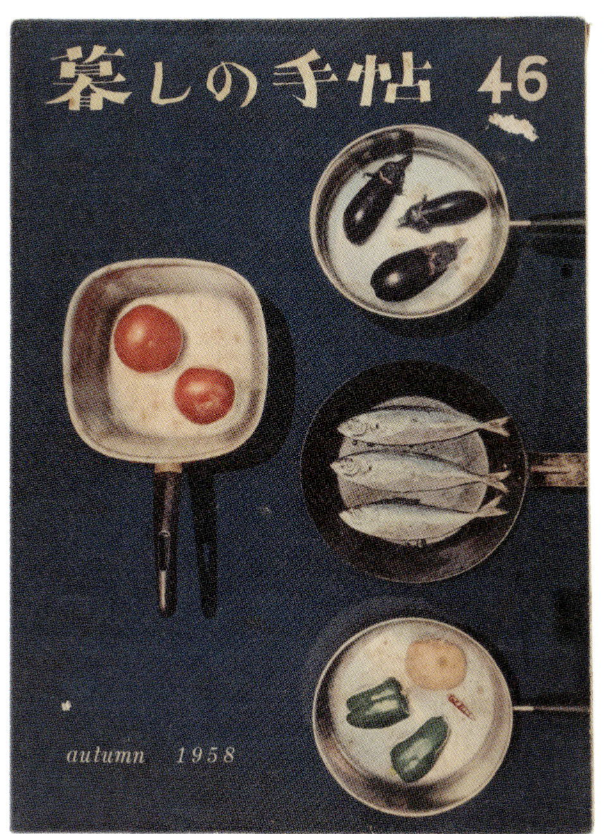

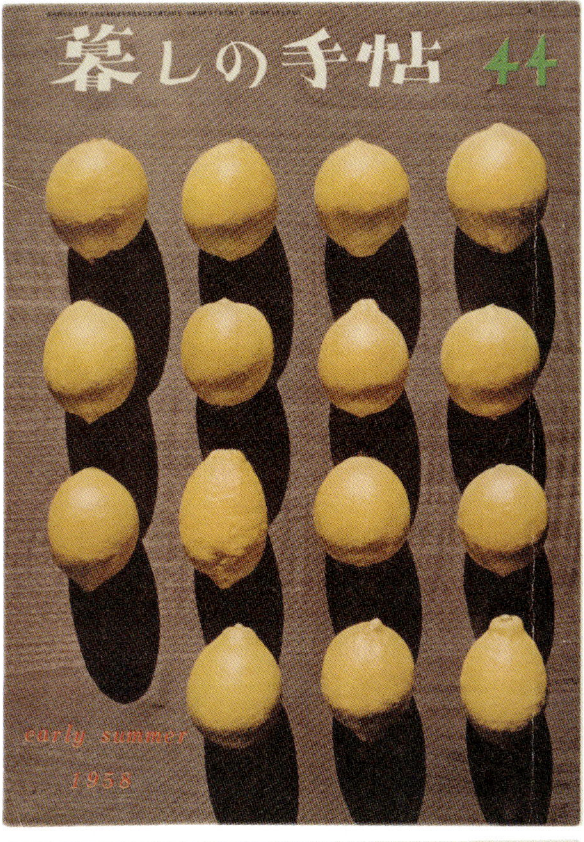

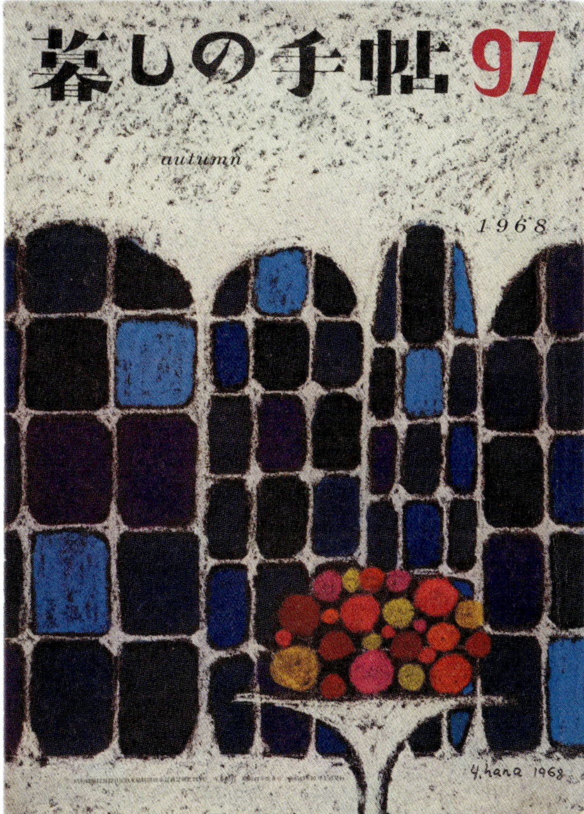

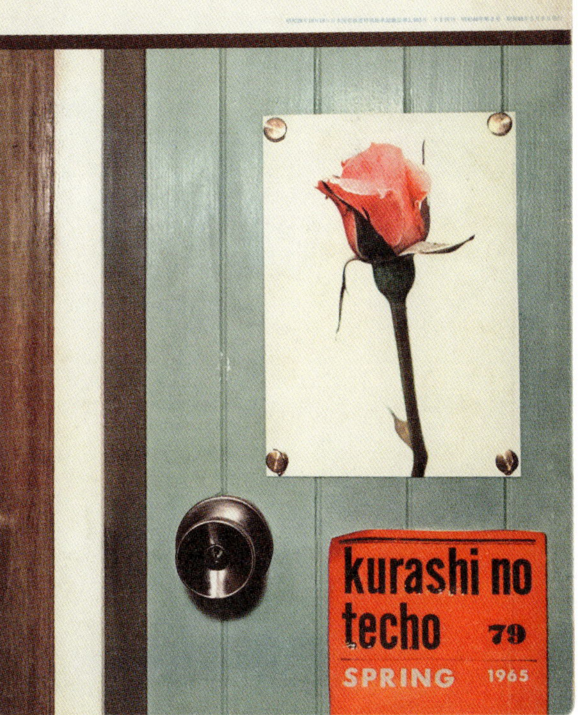

Assorted covers and spreads from ***Kurashi no Techō***
暮しの手帖, or ***Handbook for Everyday Life***.

TAKAHASHI KINKICHI 高橋錦吉

1911–1980

Takahashi Kinkichi was born in 1911 in Tokushima Prefecture. He studied design at Kanagawa Prefectural Industrial Arts Academy 神奈川県立工業学校 and went to work for the department store Sanseido upon graduation, designing their promotional magazine *Echo* エコー.

Takahashi was invited to work for Nippon Photographic Industrial Arts Co., Ltd 日本写真工芸社 by his former classmate Kumada Gorō. There, he worked on a wide variety of projects, including the design of the foreign-audience-oriented graphic propaganda magazine *VAN*. For the debut issue in 1940, Takahashi worked alongside fellow designer Kōno Takashi on the editorial art direction and design, both strongly influenced by *LIFE* magazine.

Postwar, Takahashi was one of the founders of the Japan Advertising Artists Club and went on to publish a number of books about design foundations, editorial design, and lettering.

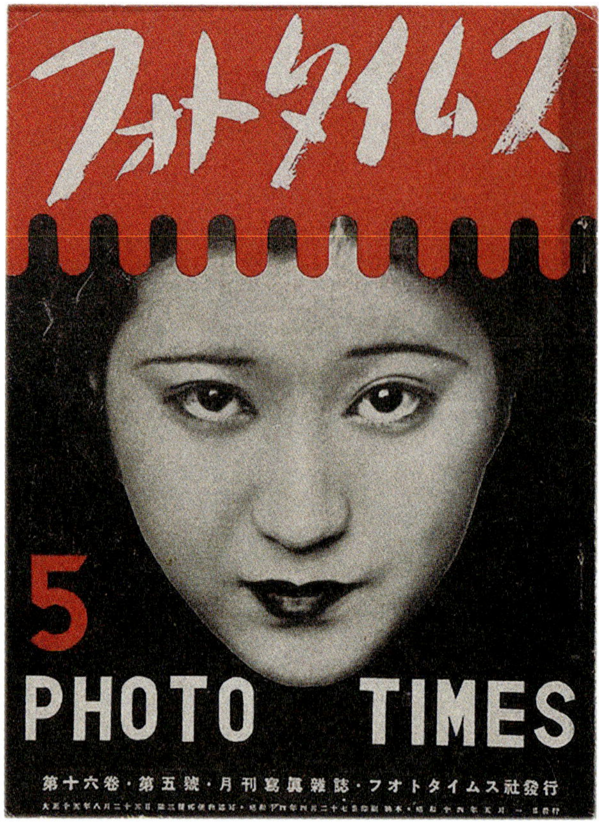

Photo Times フォトタイムス, Vol. 16 No. 5 (Tokyo: Photo Times-sha フォトタイムス社, May 1945). Cover design by Takahashi Kinkichi 高橋錦吉.

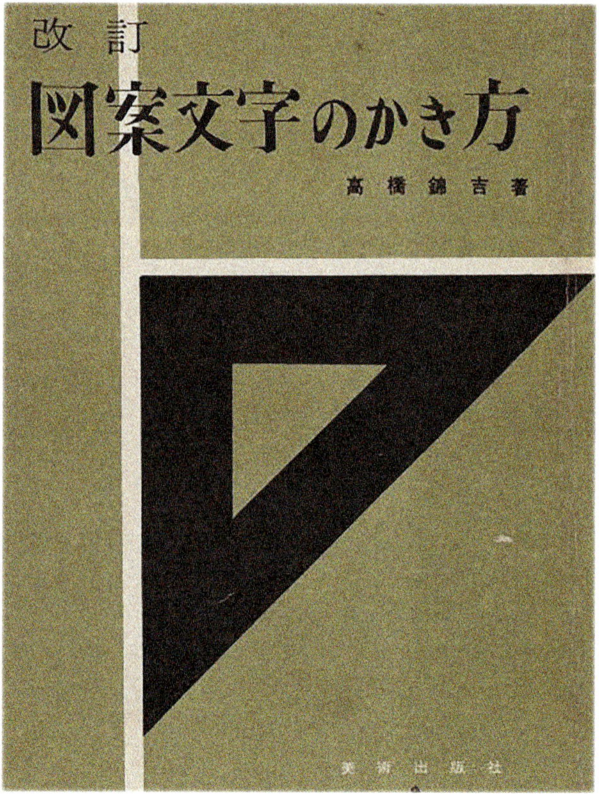

How to Create Design Characters 図案文字のかき方, Takahashi Kinkichi 高橋錦吉 (Tokyo: Bijutsu Shuppansha 美術出版社, 1958).

References:

Kamekura, Yusaku, and Ayao Yamana. *Gurafikku Dezain no Seiki: Bunshō to Danwa to Sakuhin De kōsei: Meiji Sedai Yamana Ayao Sugiura Hisui Kara shōwa Sedai Made*. Tōkyō: Bijutsu Shuppansha, 2008.

Segi, Shin'ichi, Tanaka Ikkō, and Hiroshi Sano. *Nissenbi o Jidai = The Epoch of the Japan Advertising Artists Club: Nihon No Gurafikku Dezain 1951-70*. Tōkyō: Toransuāto, 2000.

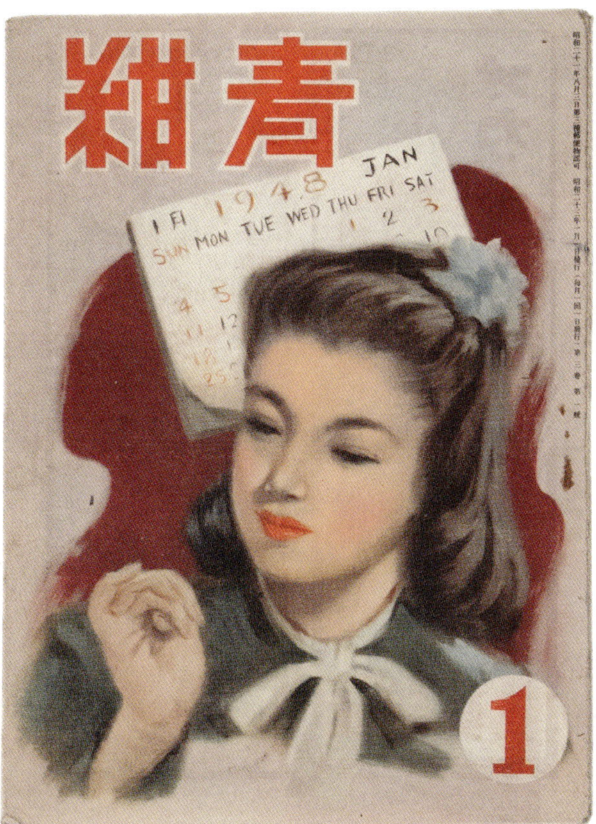

Konjo **紺青 (Tokyo: Ondorisha 雄鶏社, January 1948).** Cover design by Akamatsu Toshiko 赤松俊子 (later Maruki Toshi 丸木俊).

MARUKI TOSHI 丸木俊

1912–2000

Maruki Toshi (née Akamatsu Toshiko 赤松俊子) was born on February 11 in Chippubetsu, Hokkaido, to the family of the head priest of Zenshōji Temple. She studied oil painting at the Women's Academy of Fine Arts in Tokyo, after which she spent time in both Russia and Micronesia.

She worked as a secondary school teacher from 1933 until 1937 and married the artist Maruki Iri 丸木位里 in 1941, though she continued to use her maiden name for commercial projects until the latter half of the 1940s. Maruki designed and illustrated a wide range of covers for children's books and women's magazines before and after the war, including *Hiroshima no Pika* ひろしまのピカ and *Tsutsuji no Musume* つつじのむすめ.

She was a private teacher to the illustrator and painter Iwasaki Chihiro いわさきちひろ. In 1967, she and her husband opened the Maruki Gallery in Higashimatsuyama, Saitama, home to a series of their paintings known as "The Hiroshima Panels," depicting the atrocities of nuclear war. (The couple had done relief work immediately after the bombing of Hiroshima in 1945.)

Maruki was a candidate for the Nobel Peace Prize in 1995.

References:
Sugawara, Noriyoshi. *Will: Fifty Years of Maruki Toshi*. Tokyo: Aoki-shoten, 1996.

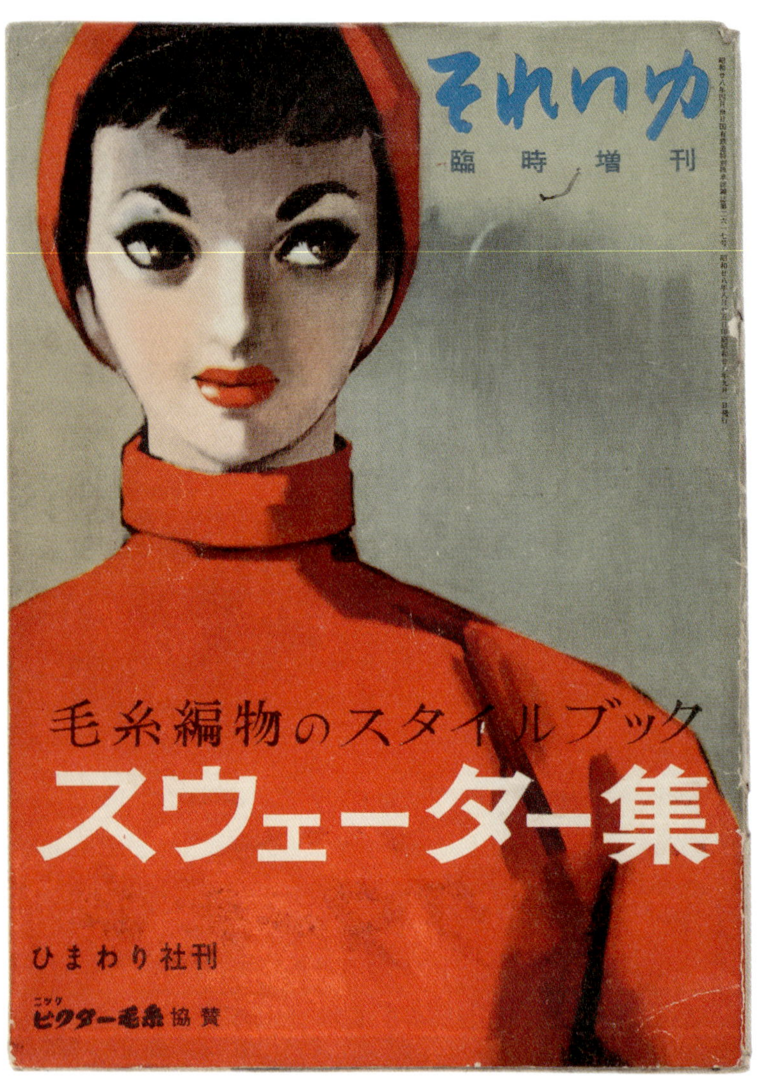

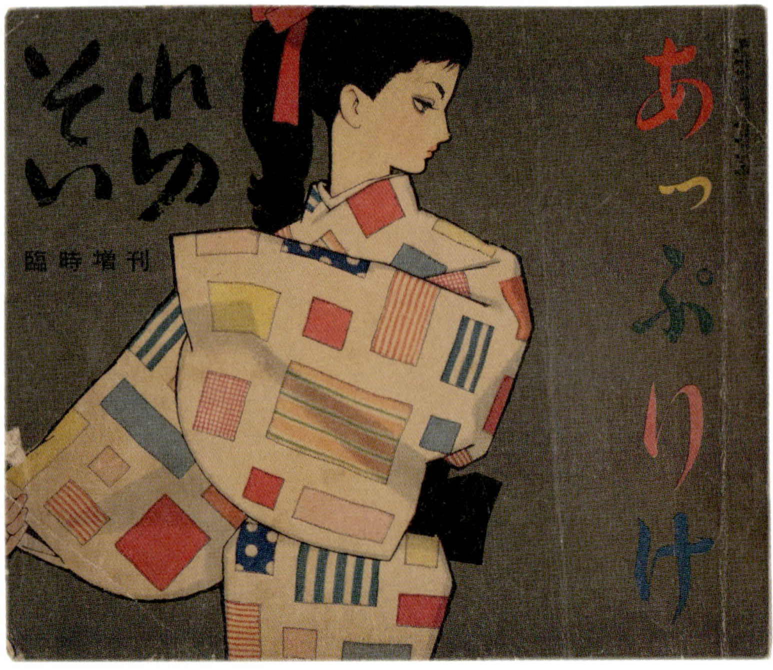

Covers from ***Soreiyu* それいゆ** designed by Nakahara Jun'ichi 中原淳一.

NAKAHARA JUN'ICHI 中原淳一

1913–1983

Nakahara Jun'ichi was born in 1913 in Kagawa Prefecture. Strongly influenced by Takehisa Yumeji, Nakahara worked as a graphic designer, interior designer, illustrator, painter, doll-maker, and fashion designer. His illustrative work emphasized the unfocused, dewy-eyed appeal of female characters and helped canonize the aesthetics of *shōjo manga* 少女漫画 for young women through the 1920s and 1930s through his work on the girls' magazine *Shōjo no Tomo* 少女の友. Nakahara married Ashihara Kuniko 葦原邦子, a Takarazuka Revue star specializing in male roles, who went on to be active in films and television in the postwar era. Ashihara served as the model and inspiration for much of Nakahara's illustration.

Nakahara was a prolific designer of books and magazines who was equally adept at lettering and illustration. His work for *Shojo no Tomo* led to a abundance of cover designs for the girls' magazine *Himawari* ひまわり until 1952. Nakahara began publishing his own girl's magazine, *Junior Soreiyu* ジュニアそれいゆ, two years later, a supplement to the women's magazine *Soreiyu* それいゆ, for which Nakahara was a regular cover designer. Both magazines were discontinued following Nakahara's hospitalization due to a heart attack in 1960.

Nakahara remained in poor health for the bulk of the 1960s. He returned to publishing with the magazine *Onna no Heya* 女の部屋 in 1970, of which only five issues were published due to Nakahara's continued health issues, which plagued him until his death in 1983. Nakahara's family established businesses to license Nakahara's imagery and to market related products after his passing—his illustration work remains very popular today.

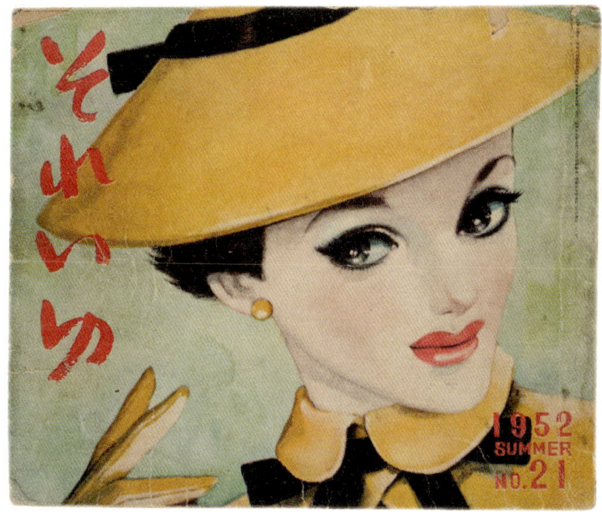

Cover of ***Soreiyu* それいゆ No. 21** designed by Nakahara Jun'ichi 中原淳一 in 1952.

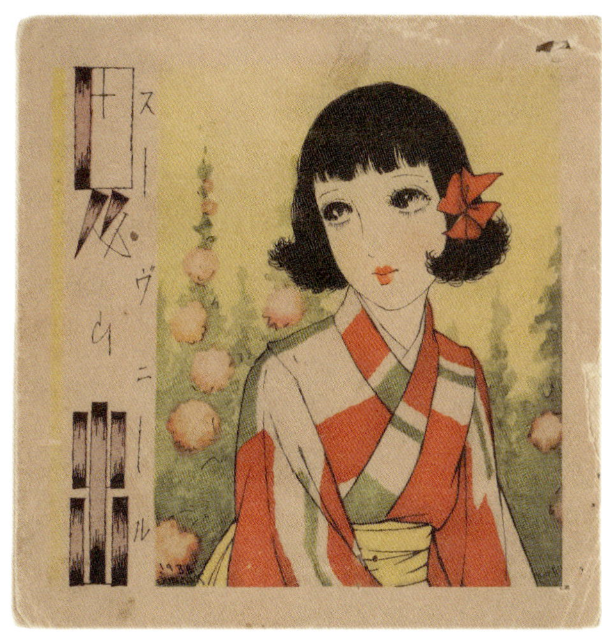

Cover of Nakahara's 1937 illustrated poetry booklet ***Souvenir Memories* スーヴニール 思い出**.

References:
Kamekura, Yūsaku, and Ayao Yamana. *Gurafikku Dezain no Seiki: Bunshō to Danwa to Sakuhin De kōsei: Meiji Sedai Yamana Ayao Sugiura Hisui Kara shōwa Sedai Made*. Tokyo: Bijutsu Shuppansha, 2008.

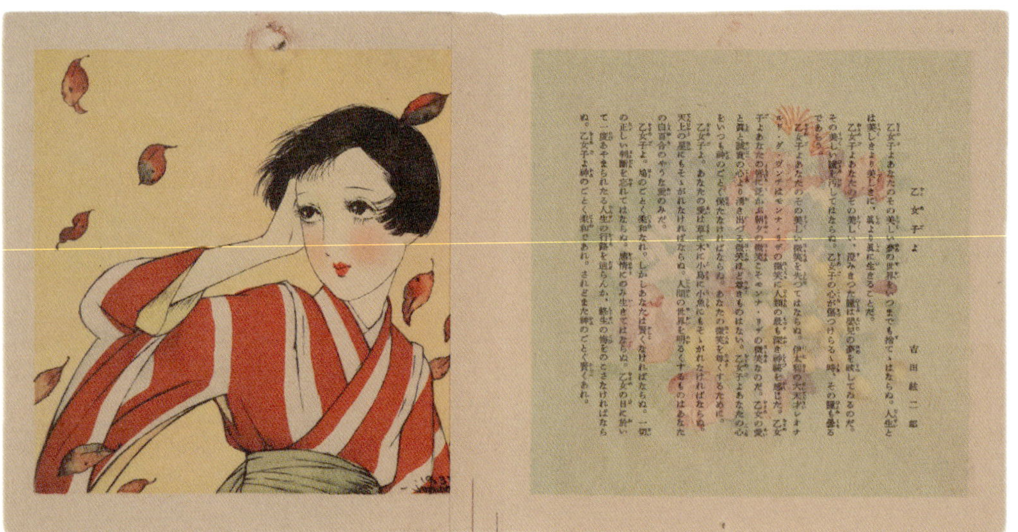

乙女子よ

吉田絃二郎

乙女子よあなたのその美しい夢の世界をいつまでも捨てゝはならぬ。人生とは美しきより美しきに、真より真に生きることだ。

乙女子よあなたのその美しい、澄みきつた瞳は永遠の夢を映してゐるのだ。その美しい瞳を汚してはならぬ。乙女子の心が傷つけらるゝ時、その瞳も曇るであらう。

乙女子よあなたのその美しい微笑を失つてはならぬ。伊太利の大天才レオナルド・ダ・ヴンチはモンナ・リザの微笑に人類の最も深き神秘を感じた。乙女子よあなたの頬に浮かぶ刹那の微笑こそモンナ・リザの微笑なのだ。乙女の愛と真と謙譲の心より湧き出づる微笑ほど尊きものはない。乙女子よあなたの心をいつも神のごとく保たなければならぬ。あなたの微笑を尊くするために。

乙女子よ。あなたの愛は草に木に小鳥に小魚にもそゝがれなければならぬ。天上の星にもそゝがれなければならぬ。人間の世界を明るくするものはあなたの白百合のやうな愛のみだ。

乙女子よ。焔のごとく柔和なれ。しかしあなたは賢くなければならぬ。一切の正しい判断を忘れてはならぬ。感情にのみ生きてはならぬ。乙女の日に於いて一度あやまられたる人生の行路を通らんか、終生の悔をのこさなければならぬ。乙女子よ神のごとく柔和であれ。されどまた神のごとく賢くあれ。

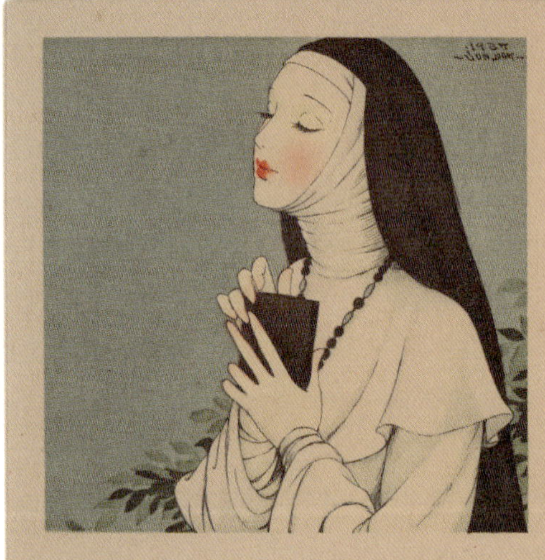

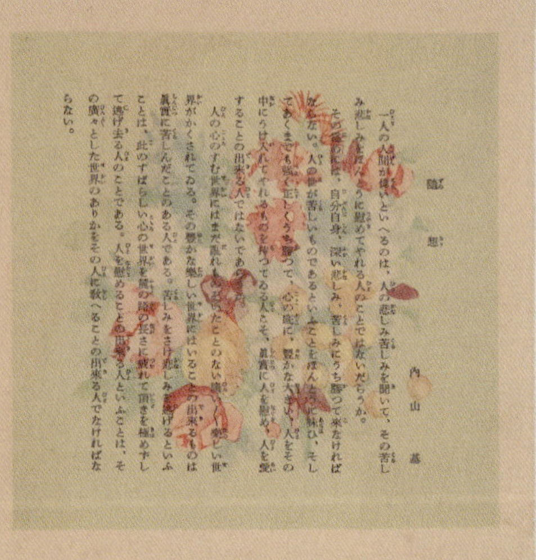

随想

内山基

一人の人間が偉いといへるのは、人の悲しみ苦しみを聞いて、その苦しみ悲しみをほんたうに慰めてやれる人のことではないだらうか。

その為には、自分自身、深い悲しみ、苦しみにうち勝つて来なければならない。人の世が苦しいものであるといふことをほんたうに味ひ、そしてあくまでも強く正しくうち勝つて、心の底に、豊かな大きい、人をその中にうけ入れてやれるものを持つてゐる人こそ、真實に人を慰め、人を愛することの出来る人ではないであらうか。

人の心のすむ世界にはまだ[illegible]たことのない[illegible]しい世界がかくされてゐる。その豊かな美しい世界にはいることの出来るものは真實に苦しんだことのある人である。苦しみをさけ悲しみを避けるといふことは、此のすばらしい心の世界を[illegible]の路の長さに疲れて頂きを極めずして逃げ去る人のことである。人を慰めることの出来る人といふことは、その廣々とした世界のありかをその人に教へることの出来る人でなければならない。

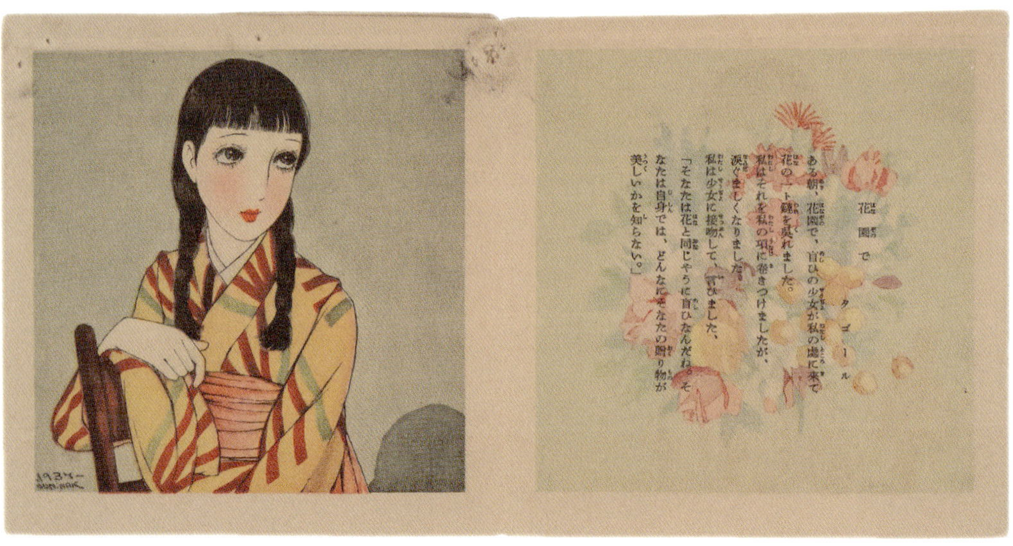

花園で

タゴール

ある朝、花園で、盲ひの少女が私の處に来て
花の一ト鎖を呉れました。
私はそれを私の項に巻きつけましたが、
涙ぐましくなりました。
私は少女に接吻して、言ひました、
「そなたは花と同じやうに盲ひなんだねえ。そ
なたは自身では、どんなにそなたの贈り物が
美しいかを知らない。」

Spreads from Nakahara's 1937 illustrated poetry booklet
***Souvenir Memories* スーヴニール 思い出.**

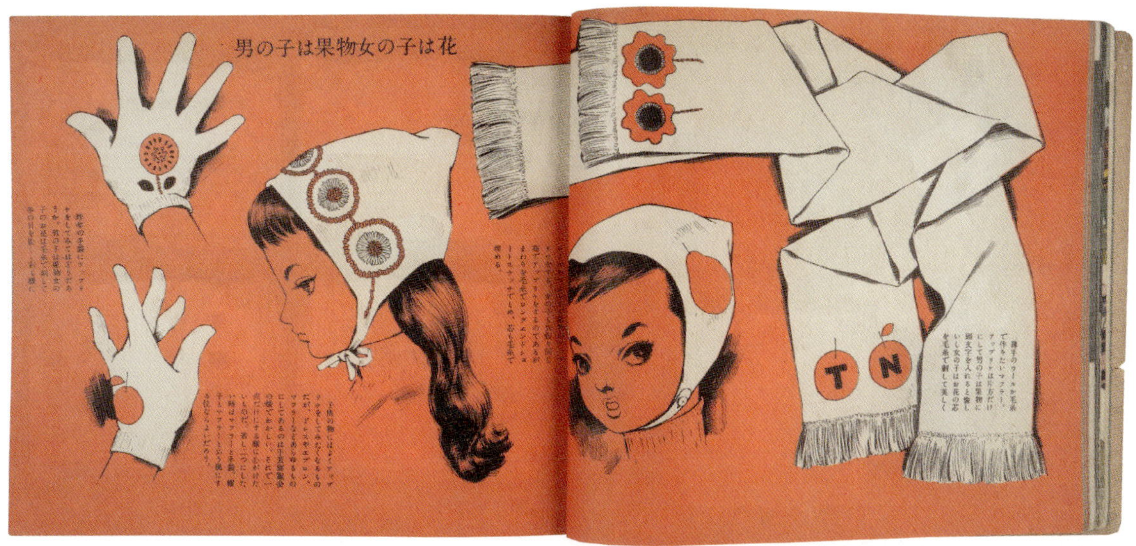

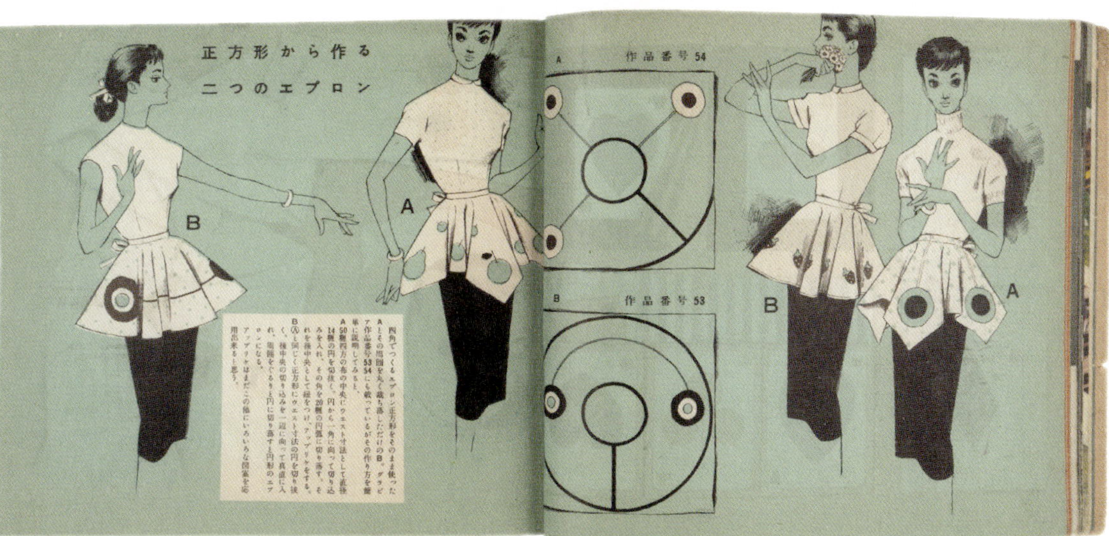

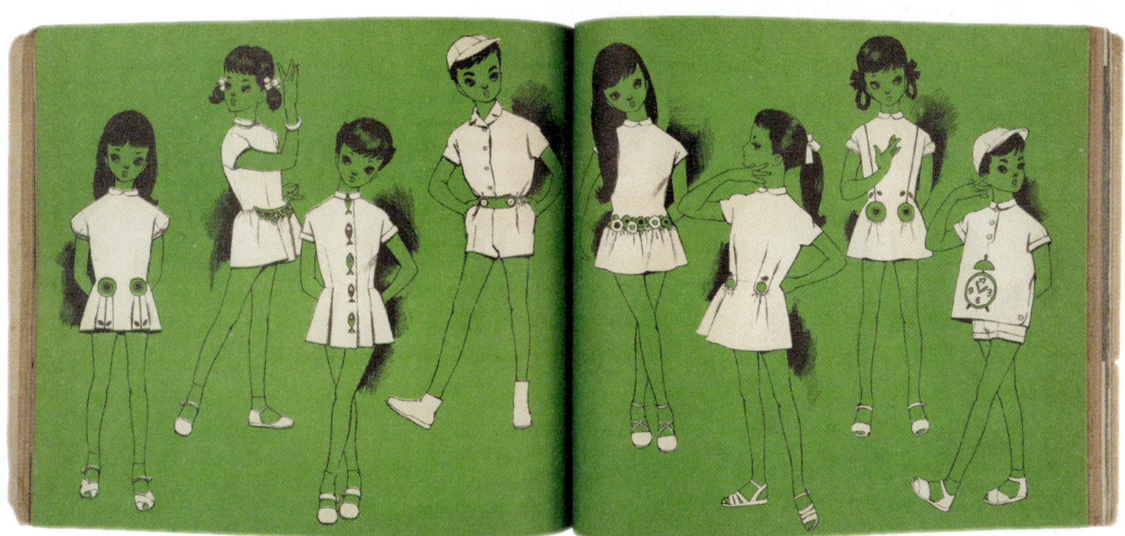

Spreads from ***Soreiyu* それいゆ** designed and illustrated by Nakahara Jun'ichi 中原淳一.

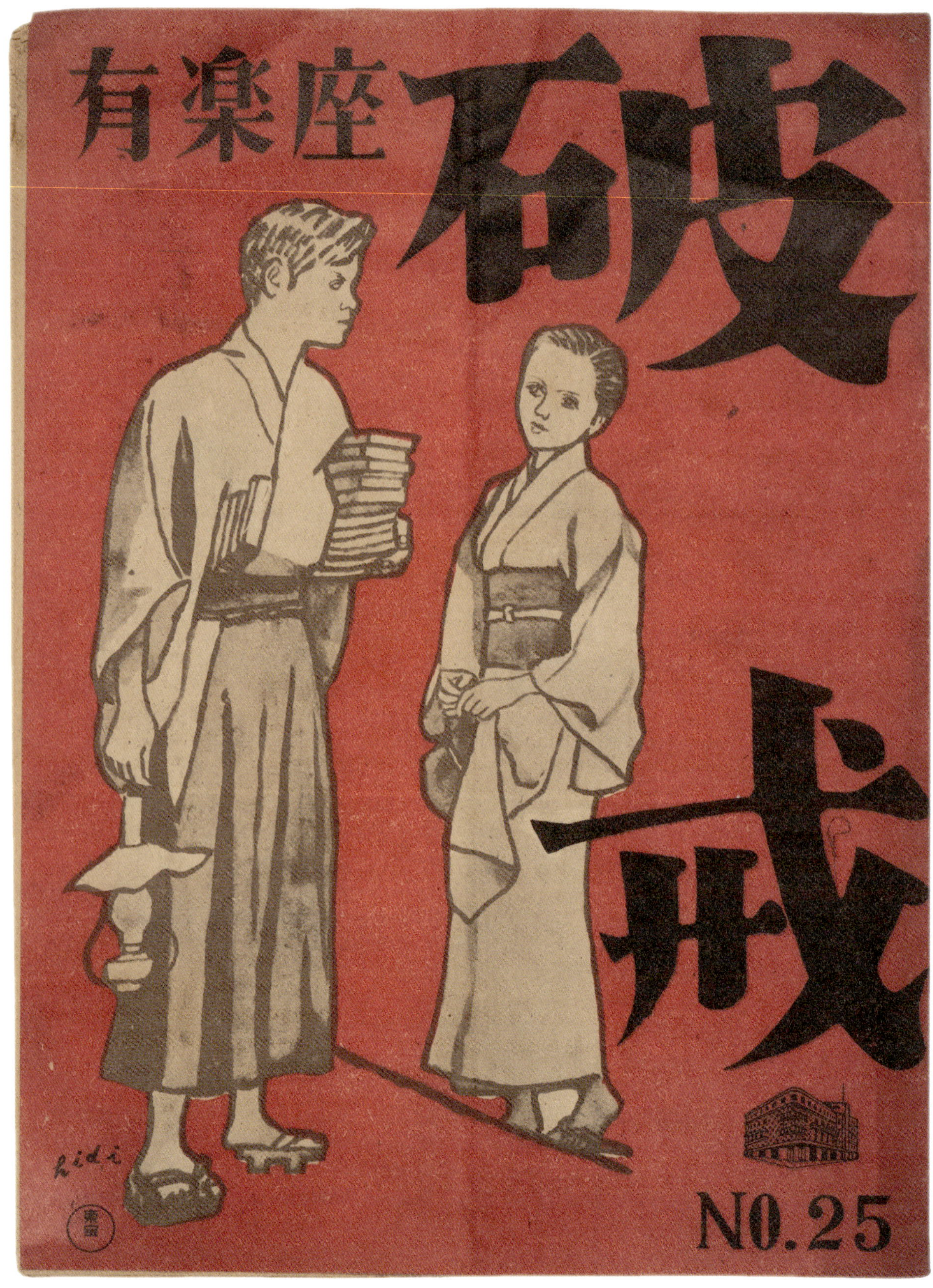

Toho Theater Yūrakuza No.25 東宝有楽座 No.25, (Tokyo: Toho Kabushikigaisha 東宝株式会社, January 2, 1948).
Cover by Hijikata Shigemi 土方重巳.

HIJIKATA SHIGEMI 土方重巳

1915–1986

Hijikata Shigemi was born in Hyogo Prefecture. His father worked for a shipping company, and his family moved often when he was a child. He graduated from Tama Art University in 1938 and immediately began working for Toho Films designing movie posters and assorted advertisements. He was conscripted into the Japanese Marine Corps in 1944.

Postwar, Hijikata again took up employment at Toho for a few years, leaving in 1948 to go freelance. He first focused on illustrating children's picture books, before moving on to designing characters and puppets for children's programs on television, including the three little pigs Boo ブー, Foo フー, and Woo ウー for NHK's show *Okāsan to Issho* おかあさんといっしょ in 1959.

Hijikata designed numerous mascots for assorted corporations, the most popular being Sato-chan サトちゃん and Satoko-chan サトコちゃん, the elephant mascots for Sato Pharmaceutical 佐藤製薬, makers of topical creams. Sato-chan was released in 1962, and his little sister Satoko-chan was released in 1982. Hijikata published a number of books about character design, model-making, and puppet-making.

The Sato-chan Book さとちゃんブック, Iizawa Tadasu 飯澤匡, Hijikata Shigemi 土方重巳, and Nakajima Shōsaku 中島章作 (Tokyo: Sato Pharmaceutical Co. 佐藤製薬, 1960).

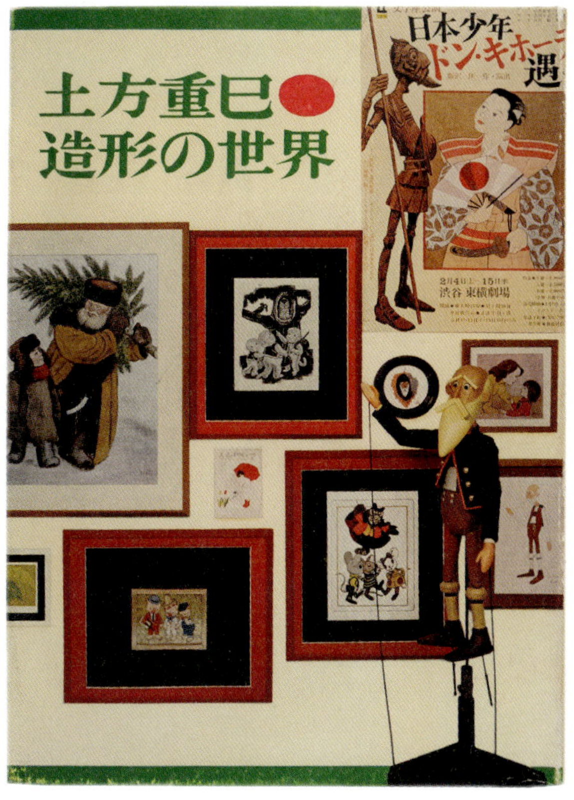

The World of Puppet-making 造形の世界, Hijikata Shigemi 土方重巳 (Tokyo: Zoukeisha 造形社, 1978).

References:
Hijikata, Shigemi. *World of Modeling*. Tokyo: Zoukeisha, 1978.

Nikui, Yasunori. "Satōseiyaku no masukottokyarakutā 'satochan 'wa naze zōna no ka - kōhō-san ni kiite mita." MyNavi News. MyNavi Corporation, June 19, 2013. https://news.mynavi.jp/article/20130619-st/.

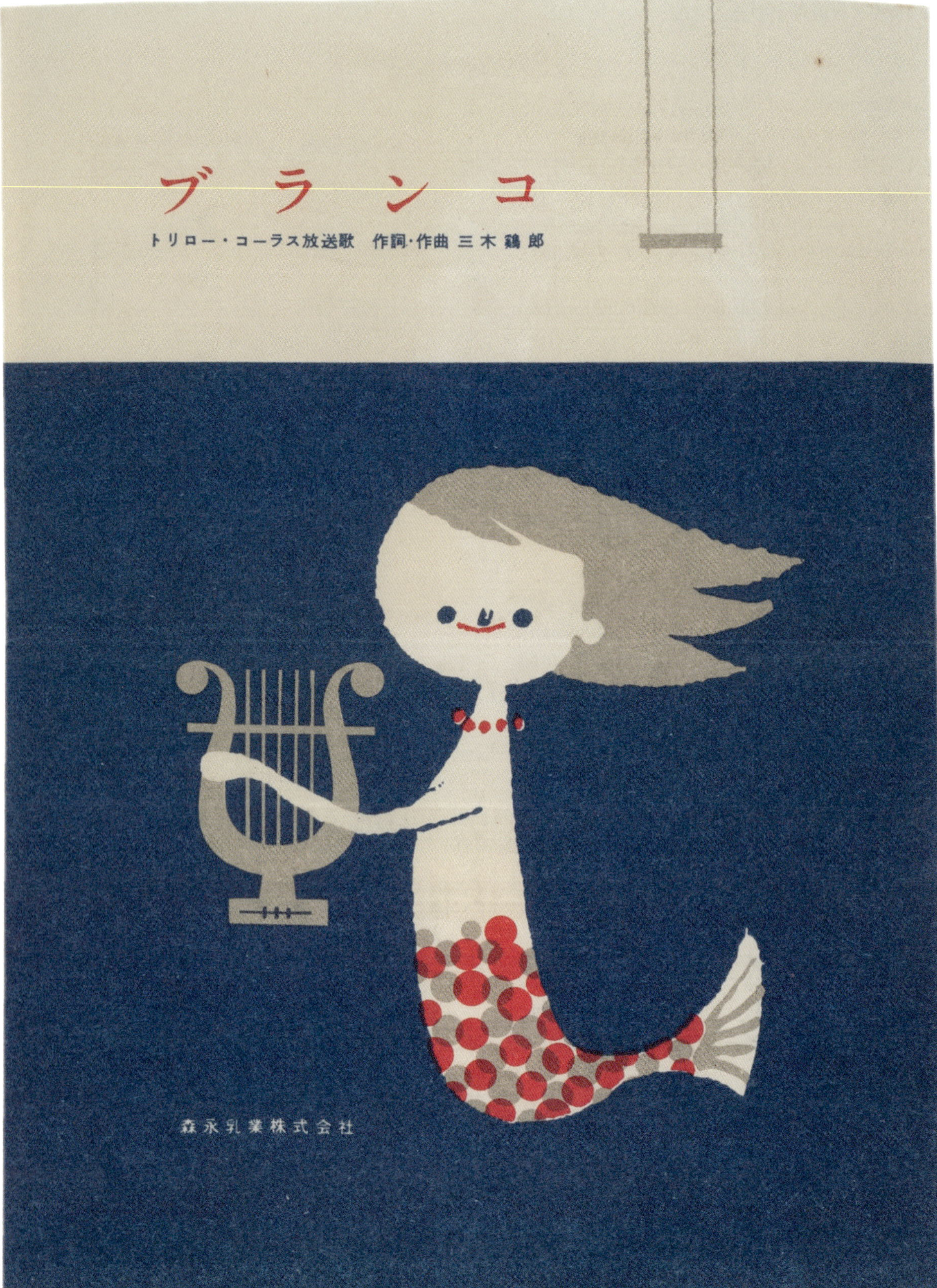

Cover of undated sheet music pamphlet for Tyrolean chorus-themed radio programs broadcast nationally with assorted featured singers sponsored by Morinaga Coffee in the 1960s designed by Ohashi Tadashi 大橋正.

OHASHI TADASHI 大橋正

1916–1998

Ohashi Tadashi was born in Kyoto and graduated from the vocational Tokyo High School of Arts and Crafts in 1937. After graduating, Ohashi worked for the Osaka and Kyoto advertising divisions of the Daimaru department store chain. He moved to Tokyo in 1940 to join the advertising agency Dentsu after winning a newspaper advertisement competition sponsored by the agency. At Dentsu, Ohashi joined the publishing department and art directed the Dentsu PR magazine *Nippon Telegram*.

Ohashi joined the public policy propaganda wing of Dentsu before being conscripted into the 16th Battalion in Kyoto just prior to the end of the war.

After World War II, Ohashi co-founded the Japan Advertising Artists Club and participated in the exhibition *Graphic '55*. Ohashi taught at Chiba University from 1956 to 1960 and at Musashino Art University, first from 1961 to 1967 and then from 1981 to 1985.

Ohashi had a vibrant commercial practice working with corporations like Meiji Confectioners and Kikkoman, for whom he would create decades' worth of promotional work peppered with illustrations of vegetables—what he viewed as the perfect pairing for soy sauce. He also created the character Chicco-chan, Kikkoman's corporate mascot in the early 1950s.

The publishing company Bijutsu Shuppan-sha released Ohashi's bilingual English and Japanese book *Vegetables Through Illustration* ヴェジタブル・イラストレーション in 1992. A former director of the Japan Graphic Design Association, Ohashi was the recipient of numerous design awards throughout his long-ranging career. The Japanese government awarded him the Purple Ribbon Medal in 1984 and the Fourth Order of Merit, Cordon of the Rising Sun, in 1990.

References:

Kabayama, Koichi, Naoyuki Takashima, Hiroshi Kashiwagi, Minako Teramoto, Mutsuko Sakanakura, and Hitoshi Mori. *1950-Nendai Nihon no Gurafikku Dezain: dezainā tanjō = Japanese Graphic Design in the '50s: the Designer Is Born*. Tokyo: Kokusho Kankōkai, 2008.

Kamekura, Yūsaku, and Ayao Yamana. *Gurafikku Dezain no Seiki: Bunshō to Danwa to Sakuhin De kōsei: Meiji Sedai Yamana Ayao Sugiura Hisui Kara shōwa Sedai Made*. Tokyo: Bijutsu Shuppansha, 2008.

Segi, Shin'ichi, Tanaka Ikkō, and Hiroshi Sano. *Nissenbi no Jidai = The Epoch of the Japan Advertising Artists Club: Nihon No Gurafikku Dezain 1951–70*. Tokyo: Toransuāto, 2000.

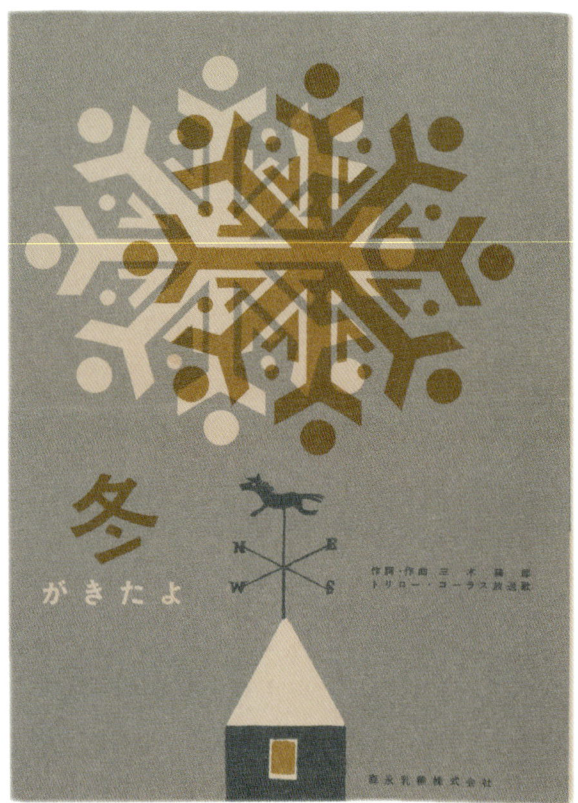

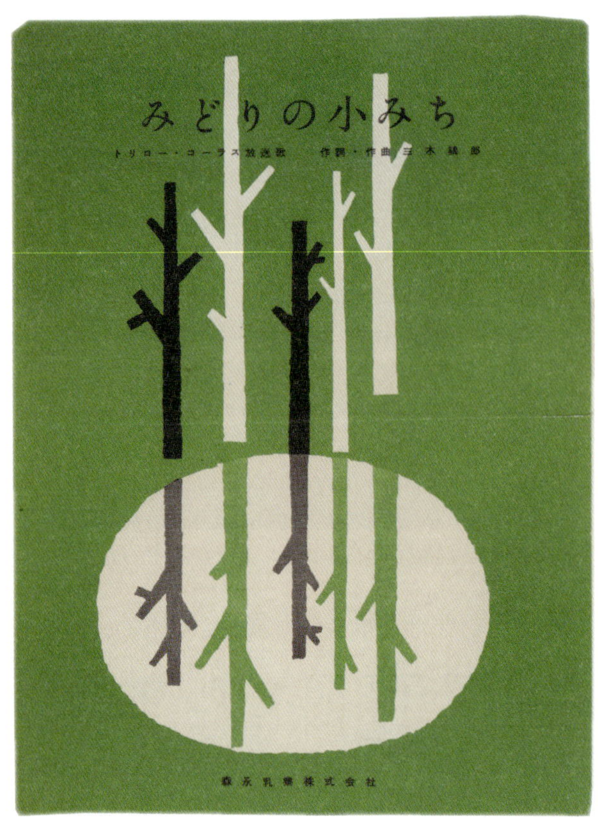

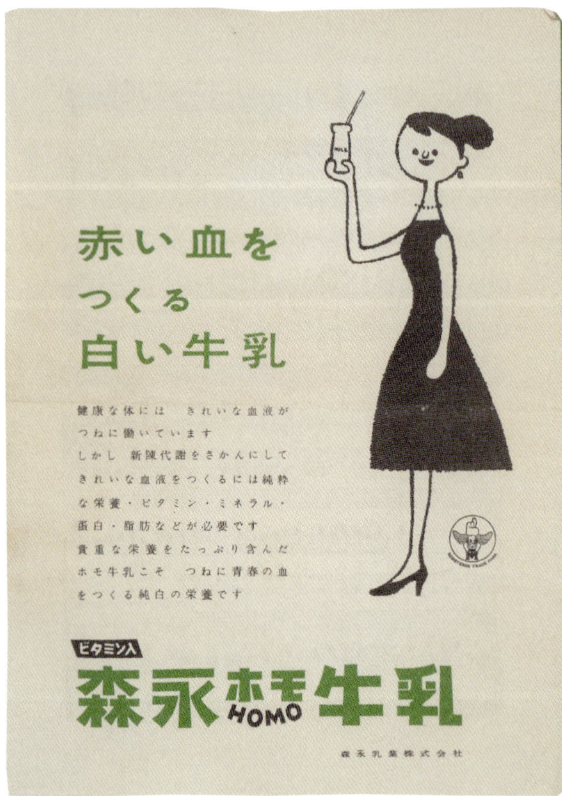

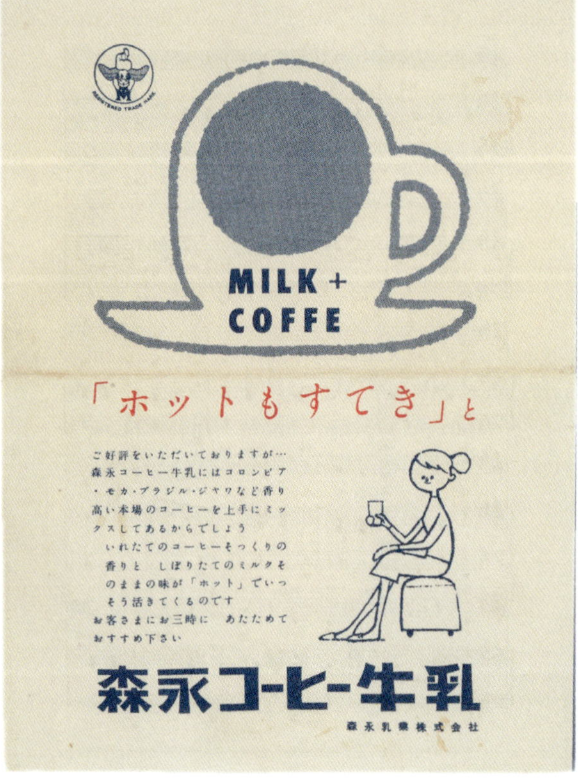

A series of sheet music pamphlets for Tyrolean chorus-themed radio programs broadcast nationally, with assorted featured singers, sponsored by Morinaga Coffee in the 1960s. Design by Ohashi Tadashi 大橋正, undated.

きつねの花嫁

トリロー・コーラス放送歌　作詞・作曲 三木鶏郎

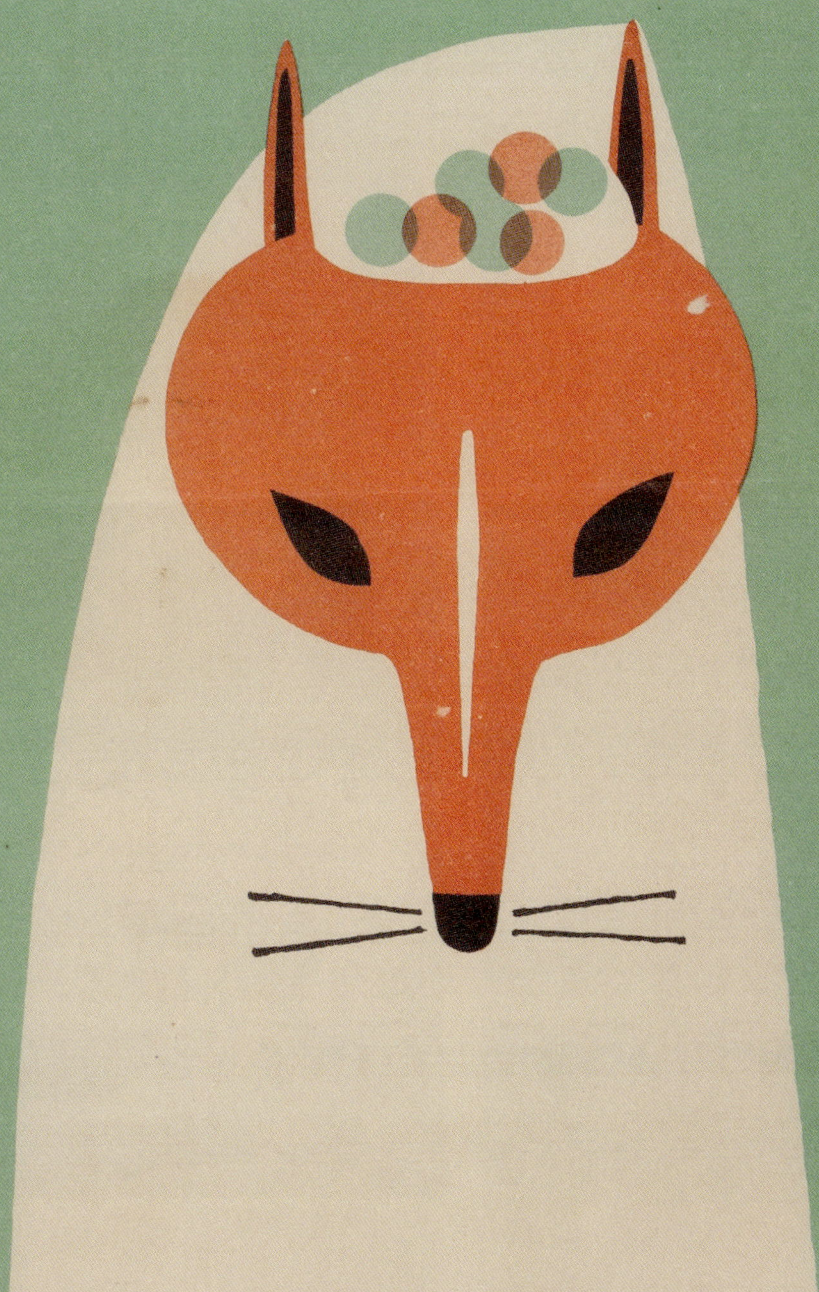

森永乳業株式会社

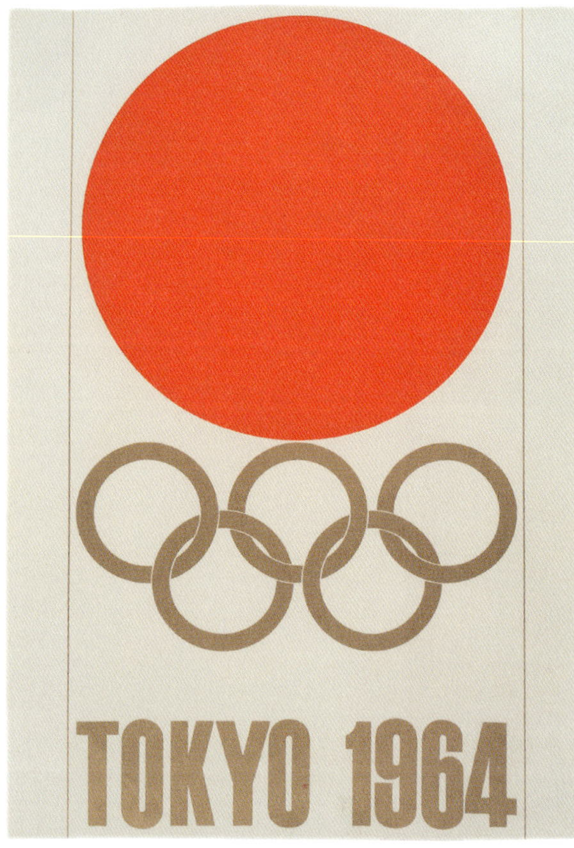

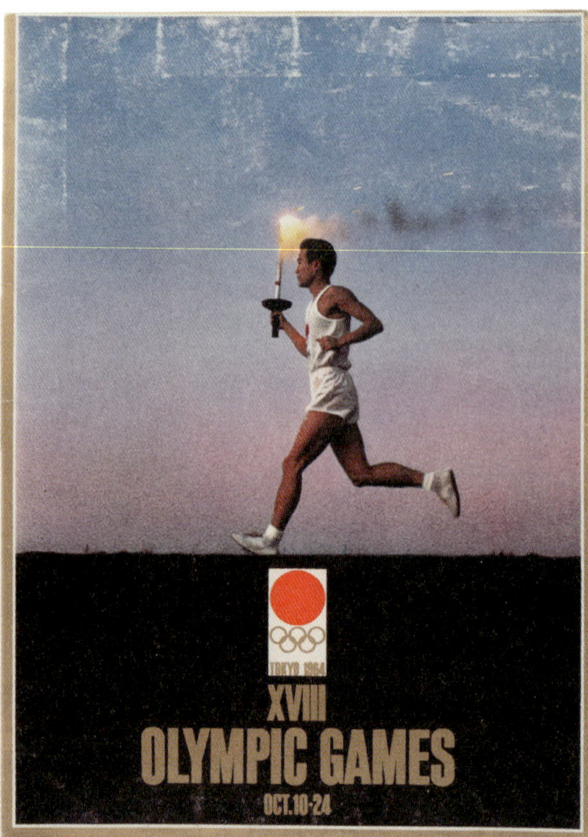

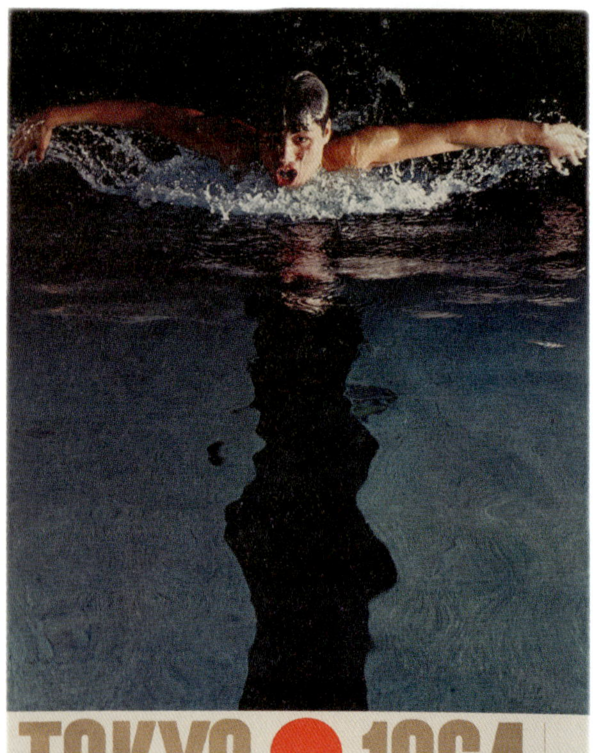

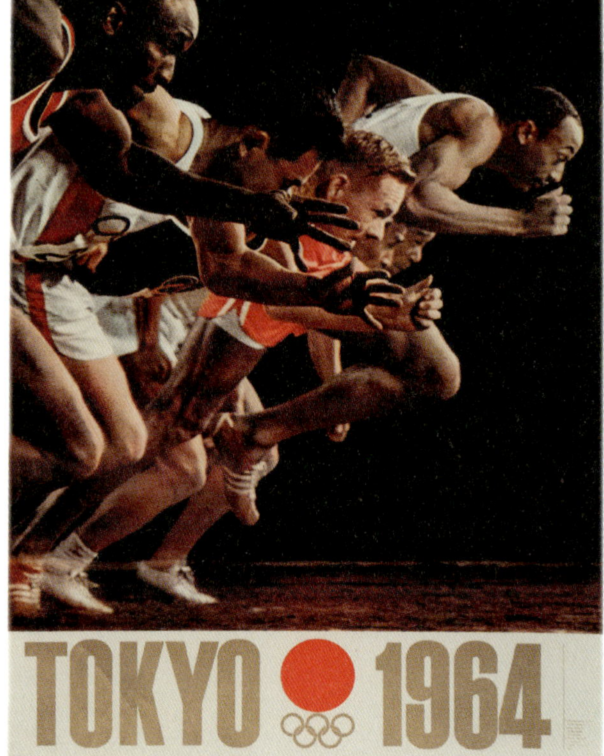

1964 Tokyo Olympics posters designed by Kamekura Yusaku 亀倉雄策.

KAMEKURA YŪSAKU 亀倉雄策

1915–1997

"No matter how much money I am offered, I will not do work that I am not convinced is right. This means that I refuse to do any work for political parties or religious groups because I find that I usually cannot agree with their ideals and purposes. I simply cannot get inspiration to do work that does not seem worthwhile and of interest to me. My work is only valid if I am involved in creating the image for the entire company in terms of logos and poster designs and so forth, and I don't like to leave even a single poster design in an ambivalent stage of development."[1]

-Kamekura Yūsaku

Kamekura Yūsaku's presence looms over the history and development of Japanese graphic design. Profoundly successful commercially and renowned culturally, Kamekura was a key figure in organizing graphic designers and popularizing graphic design as a meaningful and socially relevant activity after World War II, yet he was also a polarizing individual due to his straightforwardness with colleagues and the press. Kamekura's life was fraught with occasional conflict, though those aspects of his life were overshadowed by his leadership and legendary status.

Born in 1915 in Niigata Prefecture, Kamekura Yūsaku graduated from the Institute of New Architecture and Industrial Arts 新建築工芸学院, a pioneering school run by former Bauhaus student Kawakita Renshichirō 川喜田煉七郎. Kamekura then worked under the pioneering art director Ōta Hideshige 太田英茂 and was responsible for popularizing Kao Soap, one of the first breakout cosmetic products in Japan. The connections that Kamekura made under Ōta's oversight would remain incredibly valuable for the rest of his career, particularly his longstanding relationship with fellow designer Hara Hiromu.

In 1938, Kamekura joined Nippon Kōbō, a foreign-audience-oriented propaganda and public relations publishing company operated by photographer and editor Natori Yōnosuke. At Nippon Kōbō, Kamekura worked as art director for the magazine *Commerce Japan*, the propaganda magazines *Canton* and *Shanghai*, and later for Nippon Kōbō's flagship publication, *Nippon*—a propaganda magazine published in English, Simplified Chinese, Traditional Chinese, French, Spanish, Arabic, and Russian.

Kamekura designed numerous iconic magazines while at Nippon Kōbō, with perhaps the standout being *Nippon* issue 19. Published in 1939, this issue, somewhat divergent from Kamekura's above statement on politics, was wholly devoted to Manchukuo, the puppet state established in Manchuria after the Japanese invasion of 1931 and lasting from 1932 to 1945. The issue was dedicated to the promotion of apparent harmony between Manchukuo and Japan: "Cut-out figures from the interior of the magazine that are identifiable by costume as Japanese, Western, Korean, Han-Chinese, Mongolian and Manchurian are superimposed on an orange map of Manchukuo and visualize a variation of the ideology of the 'harmony of the five races' in Manchuria."[2] Kamekura's cover design shows multiple races engaging in harmonious agricultural labor while implicitly ignoring the activities of Japanese initiatives such as Unit 731, a covert biological and chemical warfare research-and-development unit of the Imperial Japanese Army that undertook lethal human experimentation, vivisection, germ warfare testing, and innumerable other atrocities. The design of *Nippon* 19 also depicts one lone figure in Manchukuo uniform, "standing outside the frame of the Manchurian map and pointing to it with great purpose,"[3] none other than *Nippon* publisher Natori Yōnosuke.

While visually striking and pleasing to the eye, the cover of *Nippon* 19 reveals Kamekura's complicity with wartime propaganda and willful misrepresentation of genocide. This is an aspect of his history that has been under-recognized and intimates career similarities with American designer Paul Rand, who was also active in wartime propaganda. Kamekura's active participation as a propagandist has been largely ignored or glossed-over in accounts of his life postwar, though he wrote unabashedly of his propaganda activities in his posthumously published 2006 memoir, *Kamekura Yūsaku 1915–1997*. Kamekura and Rand did much to uplift graphic design as a vocation throughout their postwar careers as organizers, leaders, and educators, yet their involvement in wartime propaganda-making is little known.

In 1949, Kamekura became the art director for the Japanese division of the American National Institutes of Health アメリカ国立衛生研究所. He worked for a variety of corporations

1 Kamekura Yūsaku and Tanaka Ikkō, *Kamekura Yūsaku* (Tokyo: Ginza Graphic Gallery, 1993), 123.

2 Andrea Germer, "Visual Propaganda in Wartime East Asia – The Case of Natori Yōnosuke," *The Asia-Pacific Journal: Japan Focus* (May 9, 2011), https://apjjf.org/2011/9/20/Andrea-Germer/3530/article.html.

3 Ibid.

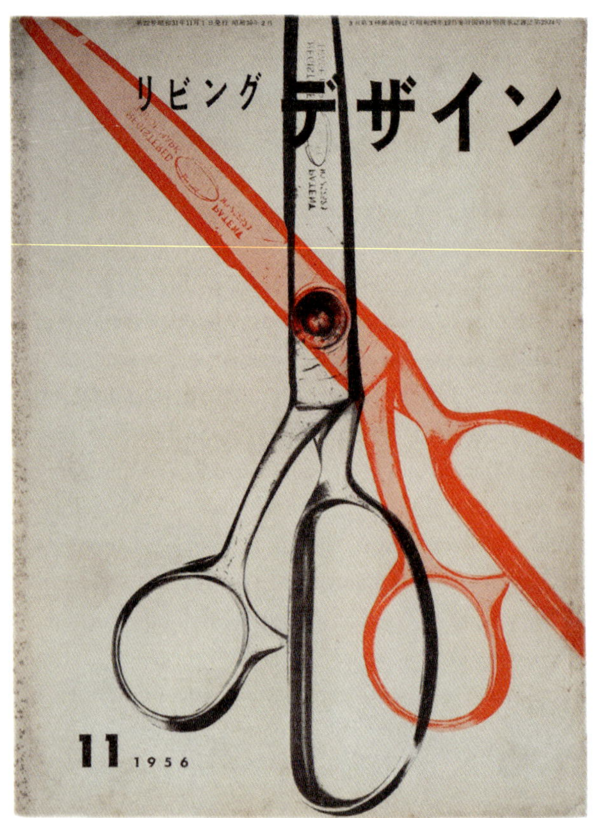

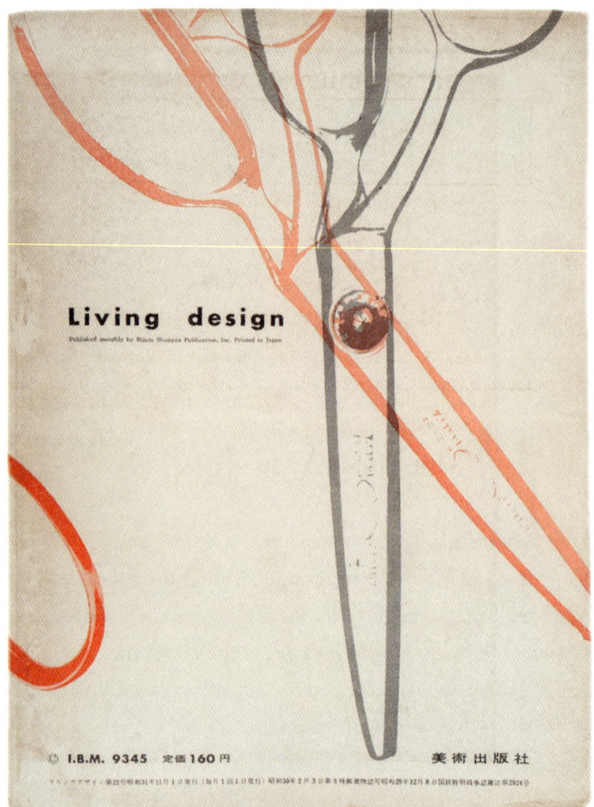

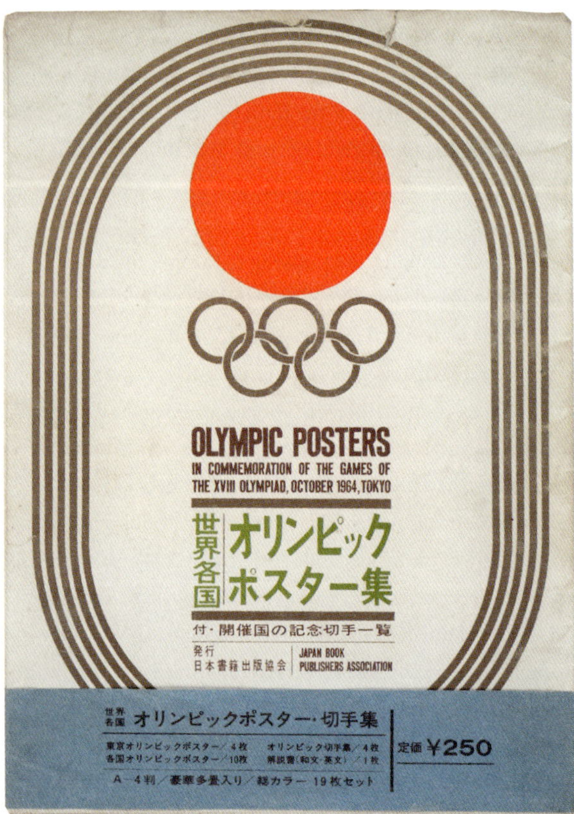

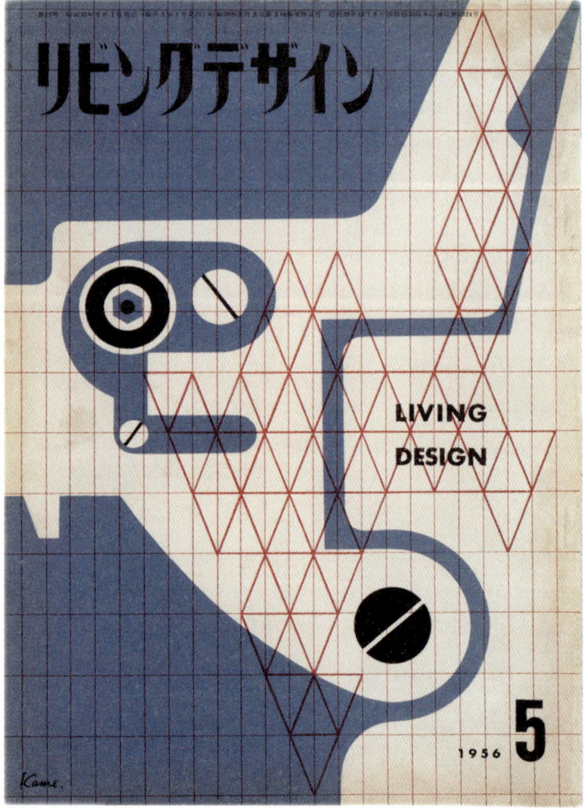

Clockwise from top left: front and back cover designs for ***Living Design* リビングデザイン** No. 11 (Tokyo: Bijutsu Shuppansha 美術出版社, 1956); front cover design for ***Living Design* リビングデザイン** No. 5 (Tokyo: Bijutsu Shuppansha 美術出版社, 1956); ***1964 Tokyo Olympics*** poster set cover (Tokyo: Japan Book Publishers Association, 1964).

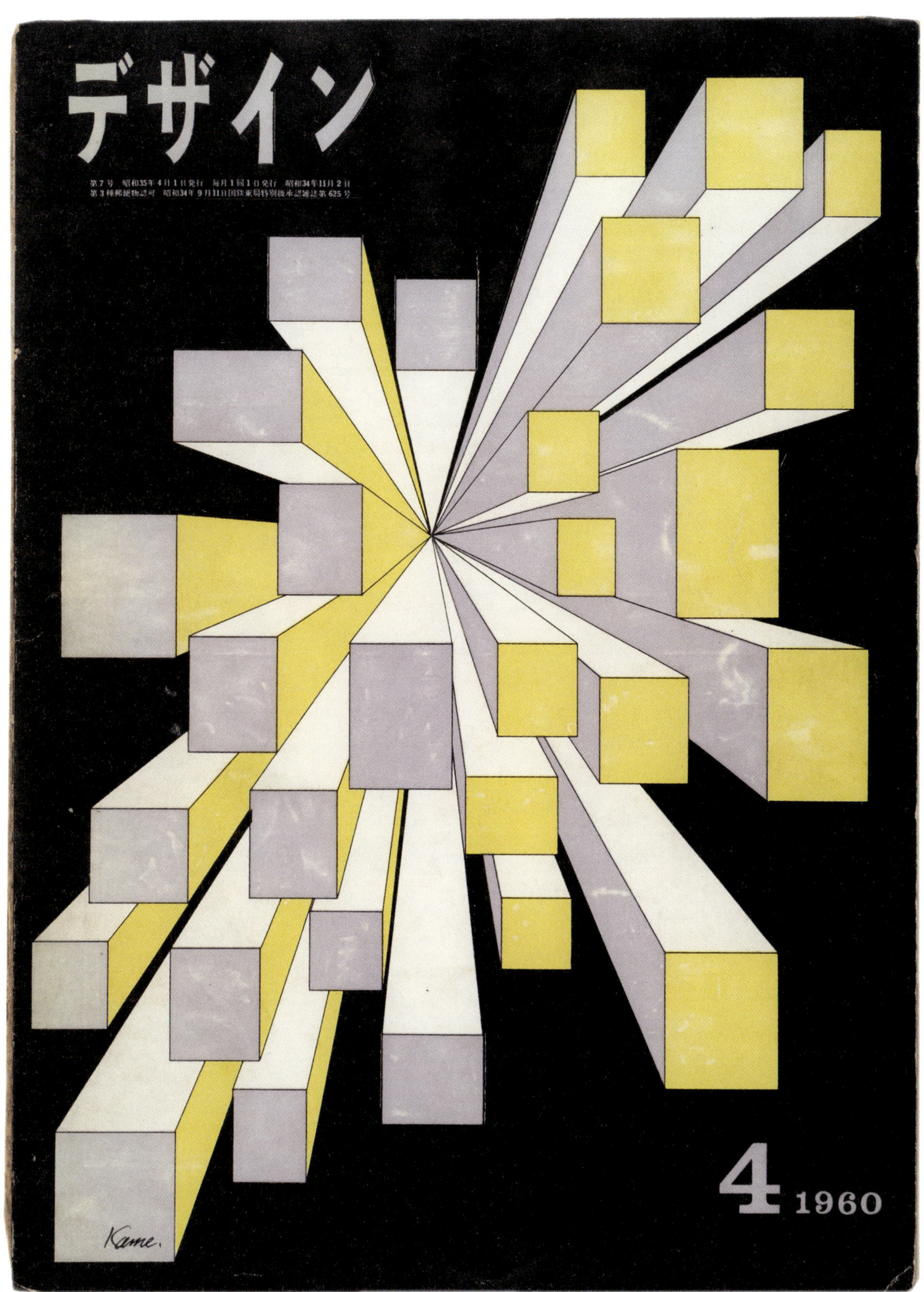

Cover of ***Design*** **デザイン No. 4** (Tokyo: Bijutsu Shuppansha 美術出版社, 1960). Designed by Kamekura Yūsaku 亀倉雄策.

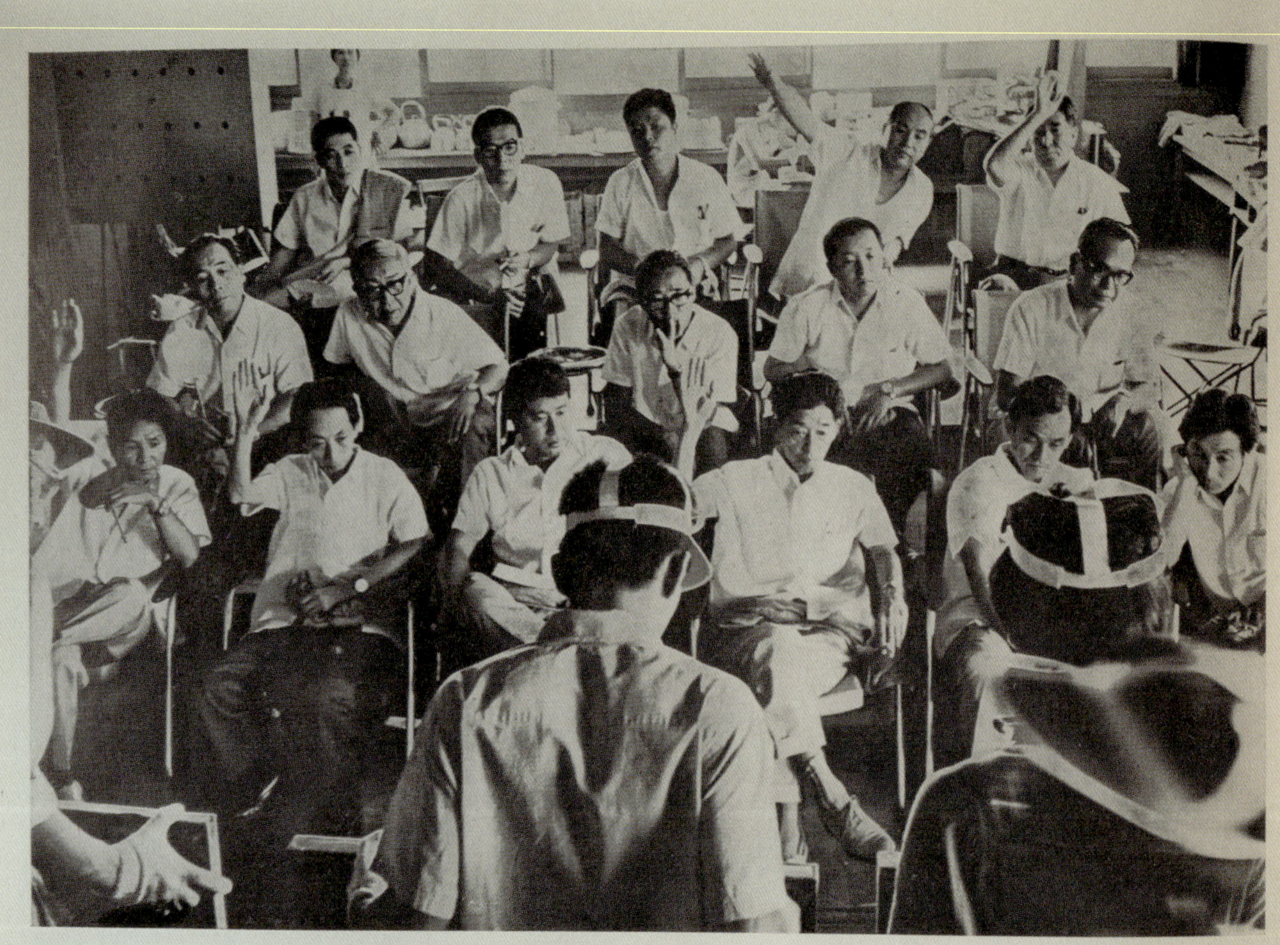

審査風景<7月31日—8月3日>

Image of JAAC members in a meeting from the ***14th JAAC exhibition catalog*** in 1964.

during the American occupation of Japan, including Nikon Cameras, Nippon Broadcasting System, Daido Worsted Mills, and Fuji Television.

Kamekura was instrumental in forming the Japan Advertising Artists Club 日本宣伝美術会 (in Japanese, the Nihon Senden Bijutsukai, or Nissenbi, for short, and abbreviated as the JAAC in English), the nation's first major domestic organizing body for graphic designers, begun in 1951 and publicly kicked-off with a members-only poster exhibition. Kamekura allied with longtime associates Hara Hiromu, Hayakawa Yoshio 早川良雄, Itō Kenji 伊藤憲治, Kōno Takashi, Yamashiro Ryuichi 山城隆一, and Ohashi Tadashi to create a union-like organization that was originally intended to improve the lives of graphic designers. JAAC members were active in the promotion of the organization, running regular exhibitions to promote the group and to encourage new membership.

Meanwhile, Kamekura began writing actively to promote design as a sector of cultural production, as much as an organizing force for the postwar economy. His essay "Japan National Railway and P.R. Design" for the July 1952 issue of the *Kogei News* 工芸ニュースcriticized the fractured state of Japan's National Railway communications and equated "the cultural level of the National Railway" with "the cultural level of Japanese society," intimating that the design of national services should be reflective of the nation's people and culture and should be standardized for ease of use. Kamekura insisted that a unified modern design plan should be implemented, referencing similar European campaigns of the time. Kamekura would write for the graphic design press for the rest of his life, including numerous essays in the newly launched magazines *Idea* (1953–present) and *Graphic Design* (1959–1986).

THE JAAC AND *GRAPHIC '55*

As the postwar economy stabilized and then bloomed into the Japanese "economic miracle"—Japan's record period of economic growth between the post-World War II era to the end of the Cold War—the JAAC's exhibition series was instrumental in establishing the careers of emerging young designers. Designers as wide-ranging as then-college student Wada Makoto 和田誠,[4] Awazu Kiyoshi 粟津潔, Hosoya Gan 細谷巖, Sugiura Kōhei 杉浦康平, and Katsui Mitsuo 勝井三雄. Each would benefit incredibly from their individual placements in JAAC competitions and would go on to lead graphic design as it emerged as a key form of cultural communication in postwar Japan. Each would in turn pay homage to Kamekura, ensuring their continued recognition from the JAAC.

Kamekura participated in the exhibition *Graphic '55*, the first internationally recognized exhibition of Japan's top designers at the time—all of whom were founding members of the JAAC: Kamekura Yūsaku, Hayakawa Yoshio, Hara Hiromu, Itō Kenji, Kōno Takashi, Yamashiro Ryuichi, and Ohashi Tadashi. Paul Rand exhibited alongside the Japanese designers, being the preeminent North American designer for the global business sector at that time.

Kamekura traveled to the United States in 1954 and met Rand there, inviting him to participate in the planned exhibition. Rand gracefully accepted, and his loose, soft-focus, American take on European Modernism would serve as an inspirational touchstone both for the Japanese public who attended the exhibition (largely unfamiliar with his work) and for his fellow exhibitors. Most exhibitors were influenced by the visual template engineered by Rand and his predecessor Raymond Loewy, which coupled geometric abstraction and simplification with simplified typography, an influence that can be seen in their output for the remainder of the decade.

"When we Japanese look at Paul Rand's work and ponder the futility of our struggle to absorb western culture, we are stunned to recognize traditional Japanese styles—styles which we Japanese have long forgotten—running beautifully and refreshingly through them."[5]
-Kamekura Yūsaku

Held at the Takashimaya department store in 1955, the *Graphic '55* exhibition helped introduce the general Japanese populace to "graphic design" as a term and a profession worth pursuing.

Prior to the exhibition, graphic design was a relatively unknown term, and the notion of an independent graphic designer was incredibly rare. One of the very first graphic design studios created in Japan was the Imatake Design Office, founded in 1946 by Imatake Shichiro, who had previously been an in-house designer at Takashimaya, and under whose auspices the *Graphic '55* exhibition was allowed to take place.

The exhibition helped the public associate iconic advertising

4 Wada, who would go on to create an homage poster to Kamekura later in his career showing the later white-maned Kamekura in the foreground of an illustrated dash akin to Kamekura's legendary 1964 Olympic poster.

5 Kamekura Yūsaku, *Creation: International Graphic Design, Art & Illustration*, 1st ed. Vol. 1 (Tokyo: Recruit, 1989), 12.

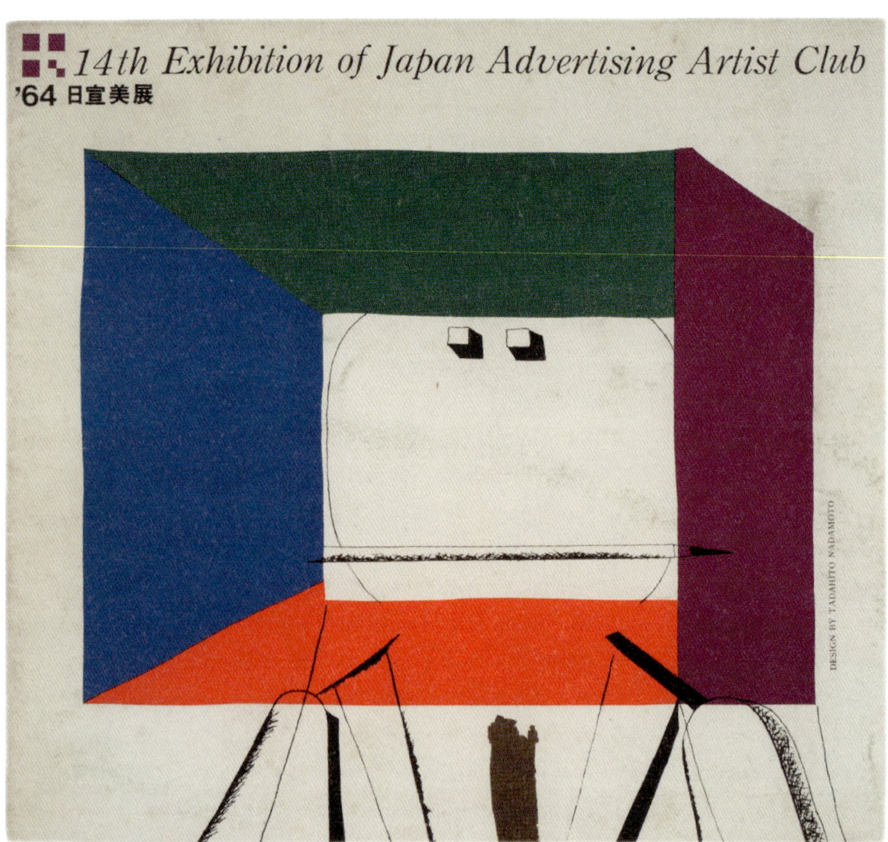

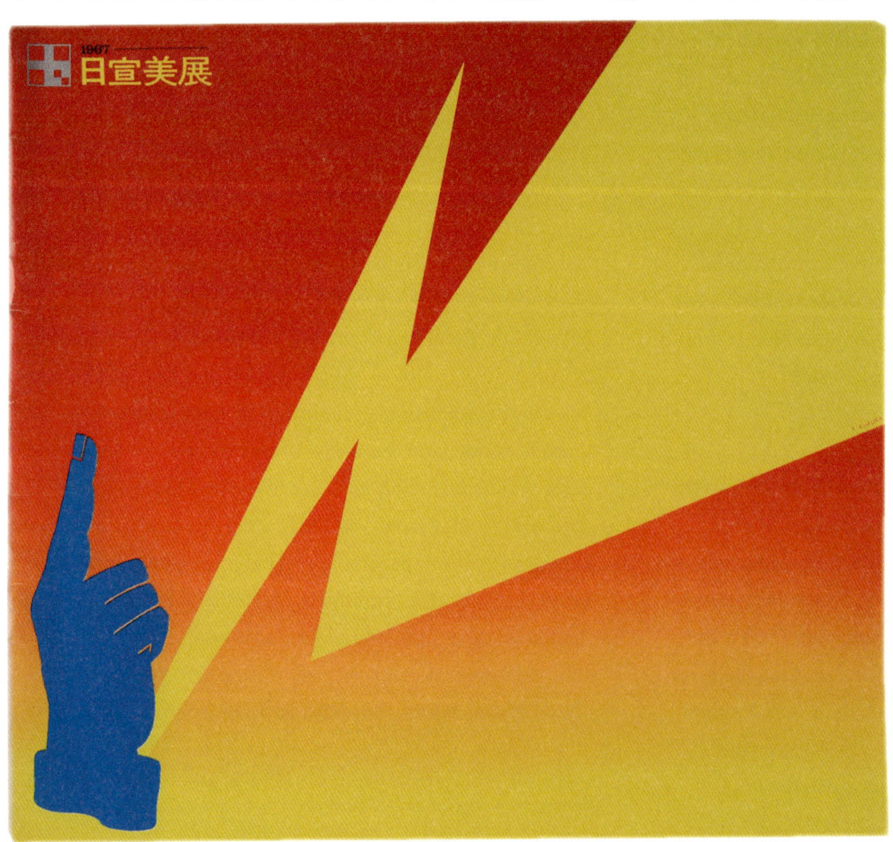

Top: Cover from the ***14th JAAC exhibition catalog*** in 1964. Designed by Nadamoto Tadahito 灘本唯人.
Bottom: Cover from the ***17th JAAC exhibition catalog*** in 1967. Designed by Kimura Tsunehisa 木村恒久.

imagery with individual designers, enhancing their social recognition and allowing the designers involved to incrementally increase design fees. Whereas earlier domestic graphic design exhibitions tended to focus on the sole format of the poster, *Graphic '55* included a range of design project formats and showed the public the range of works that designers could tackle.

The exhibition, originally intended to be held annually, was as much a reaction to the increased attention that graphic design had been receiving in the media and from the public as it was a showcase for the different kinds of projects that graphic designers undertook. Within *Graphic '55*, magazine covers, newspaper advertisements, book designs, packaging, and product design shared the stage with large-scale posters. The exhibition potentially was the first to highlight graphic design as an expanded domestic practice, not merely relegated to the production of poster design, and the first that promoted the output of graphic design in many of its forms.

The popularity of the *Graphic '55* exhibition and the insistence upon showing only produced graphic design projects would have reverberations in the JAAC afterward. Kamekura Yūsaku would only submit professionally printed or, at the very least, screen-printed projects after 1955. His decision inspired the submission of numerous affordable screen-printed projects by others to subsequent JAAC competitions. This resulted in the creation of further divisions within the competition, namely the creation of categories for "printed works" and "original works" (speculative projects that were not printed).

Design began to play a more enhanced and culturally popular role throughout the later 1950s in Japan, particularly when the Good Design Products Selection System, the predecessor to the contemporary Good Design Award グッドデザイン賞, was established by the Ministry of International Trade and Industry in 1957. This private/public competition sought to recognize products that helped enhance society and culture in Japan. The ministry wanted to create a discernable mark that would identify winning products of the competition, and Kamekura was hired to create the corporate identity surrounding the award, known as the "G Mark System," a modular uppercase letter G set diagonally in white against a red circle. The Japanese government's advocacy of design that connected industry and consumer lifestyles became a major initiative that continues today.

WORLD DESIGN CONFERENCE

The International Design Conference in Aspen (IDCA) was organized by Walter Paepcke, president of the Container Corporation of America, in 1951 in Aspen, Colorado, and quickly became the leading design conference internationally. The IDCA's Japanese Committee asked to host the 1958 IDCA meeting in Japan with the intention of elevating the conference to one of international stature with a shifting locale, but this request was rejected by Paepcke and the American organizers.

In response, Japanese architects and designers organized the World Design Conference (WoDeCo) in 1960 with the hope of establishing a permanent and truly international design organization. While only one WoDeCo was held, it was a momentous event involving Japanese graphic designers, architects, and industrial designers along with their counterparts from Europe and the United States and focused on the theme of the "Total Image for the 20th Century."

Over 250 guests from twenty-six countries joined the event to participate in six days of lectures, workshops, panel discussions, and presentations—each hampered by translation issues—broken up by group lunches, one even featuring then-exotic hot dogs. Seventeen satellite exhibitions related to the conference were held in nearby Tokyo department stores, helping to promote further awareness of design in Japan's capital.

The conference themes were Personality, Practicability, and Possibilities. While architecture was a primary focus, European graphic designers like Herbert Bayer, Josef Müller-Brockmann, Max Huber, and Otl Aicher and Americans such as Saul Bass and Walter Landor each gave lectures on visual culture, design education, corporate responsibility, and corporate design. (Incidentally, both Müller-Brockmann and Huber met Japanese women who worked at the conference whom they would later marry, paving the way for Swiss high Modernism to make great inroads in Japan.[6])

The World Design Conference was notable for the debut of the hybrid architecture and graphic design movement Metabolism 新陳代謝, whose members included architect Kurokawa Kishō 黒川紀章 and graphic designer Awazu Kiyoshi. The Metabolists' aims included the exploration of physical, spatial, and graphic megastructures built up through organic biological growth.

6 Yoshikawa Shizuko 吉川静子, one of the translators and organizational workers married Müller-Brockmann after two years of study at Hochschule für Gestaltung in Ulm's Visual Communication Department, while Kōno Aoi 河野葵, daughter of Japanese designer Kōno Takashi, also working as a WoDeCo translator, married Max Huber after briefly studying in Stockholm.

The group released their ninety-page oversized book *Metabolism: The Proposals for New Urbanism* at the WoDeCo. The book opened with the Metabolism Manifesto:

"Metabolism is the name of the group, in which each member proposes further designs of our coming world through his concrete designs and illustrations. We regard human society as a vital process - a continuous development from atom to nebula. The reason why we use such a biological word, metabolism, is that we believe design and technology should be a denotation of human society. We are not going to accept metabolism as a natural process, but try to encourage active metabolic development of our society through our proposals."[7]

The book, designed by Awazu, included speculative works and essays by Kurokawa, Kikutake Kiyonori 菊竹清訓, and Kawazoe Noboru 川添登, organizer of the WoDeCo.

The conference also featured a notable presentation by industrial designer Yanagi Sori 柳宗理 on anonymity in design. This lecture contributed greatly to indigenous design theory in Japan, connecting it with his father Yanagi Sōetsu's 柳宗悦 writings on *Mingei* folk crafts. Yanagi spoke of the power of the use-function of what he termed "Anonymous Design," citing blue jeans, the baseball, and the ice ax as examples of unauthored yet refined considerations of form and functionality.

Kamekura Yūsaku delivered the keynote lecture on Japanese graphic design, entitled "Katachi 形" ("Shape" or "Form"), wherein he explored the challenges of tradition and modernity for graphic designers. An excerpt:

"Tradition is one of the problems Japanese designers must work with. For designers, it is a burden that must be borne, and there is no means of refusing it. It is our duty to break down our tradition into pieces and then reassemble those pieces as a new tradition."[8]

Conspicuously absent from the World Design Conference was the inclusion of apparel design in the conference's proceedings—then-Tama Art University graphic design student Miyake Issey 三宅一生 wrote to the organizers taking issue with the omission of such an important aspect of design.

NIPPON DESIGN CENTER

The World Design Conference was notable largely for the design of the conference materials—all carried out by designers associated with the newly formed Nippon Design Center 日本デザインセンター, including Kōno Takashi, Tanaka Ikkō, Hara Hiromu, Nagai Kazumasa, Sugiura Kōhei, Yamashiro Ryuichi, and Hosoya Gan. The internationalism and United Nations-like setting of the WoDeCo helped launch the Nippon Design Center in the eyes of industry and the public as a purveyor of effective and trusted design.

The Nippon Design Center is an advertising consortium that initially received investment funding from eight major corporations (Asahi Breweries, Asahi Kasei, Nippon Steel, Toshiba, Toyota Motor, Nikon, NKK, Nomura Securities) and which continues to define advertising-oriented design and branding in Japan in the present day. All of the committee members that organized the WoDeCo were Nippon Design Center affiliates, with Kamekura Yūsaku front and center as both the major Japanese representative speaker at the WoDeCo and the founding President of the Nippon Design Center. While the international design conference helped popularize modern Japanese graphic design to influential international peers, the corporate undercurrent was a sign of the times, as the Japanese economy rebounded after World War II and experienced a time of record growth.

"I drew a large red circle on top of the Olympic logo. People may have considered that this large red circle represented the hinomaru[9]*, but my actual intention was to express the sun. I wanted to create a fresh and vivid image through a balance between the large red circle and the five-ring Olympic mark. I thought that it would make the hinomaru look like a modern design."*[10]

- Kamekura Yūsaku

1962 was an auspicious year for Kamekura: abandoning the Nippon Design Center, he founded his own design practice, the Kamekura Design Laboratory, where he worked for a wide range of corporate clients, both old and new, and was the unanimous winner of a private logo design competition for the 1964 Olympics. Pitted against five of his colleagues—Inagaki Kōichiro, Kōno Takashi, Nagai Kazumasa, Sugiura Kōhei, and Tanaka Ikkō—Kamekura supposedly "forgot about the competition" until two days prior to the judging and "dashed off [the design] in a matter of five or six minutes" for the initial

7 Kurokawa Kisho, Kiyoshi Awazu, Kiyonori Kikutake, and Noburo Kawazoe, *Metabolism: the Proposals for a New Urbanism* (Tokyo: Bijutsu Shuppan Sha, 1960), 24.

8 Kamekura Yūsaku and Tanaka Ikkō, *Kamekura Yūsaku = Yūsaku Kamekura*, (Tokyo: Ginza Graphic Gallery, 1993), 181.

9 The hinomaru is the red circle on the Japanese flag.

10 Ibid.

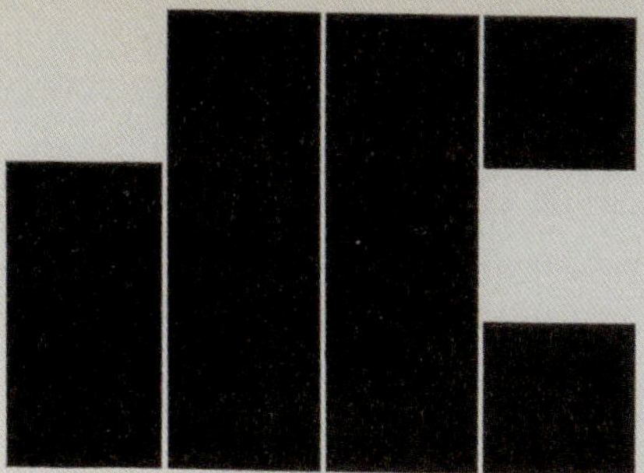
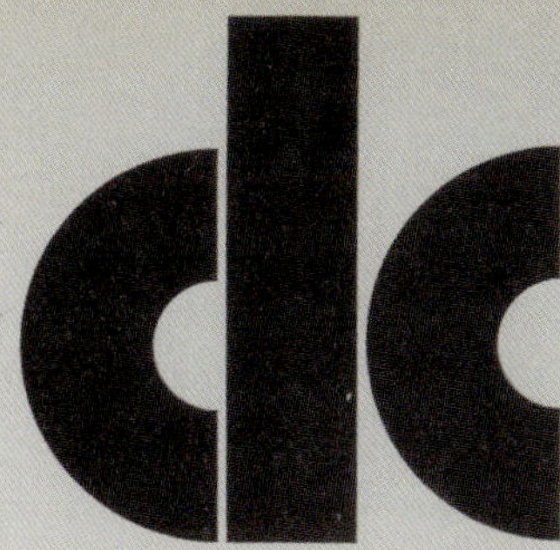
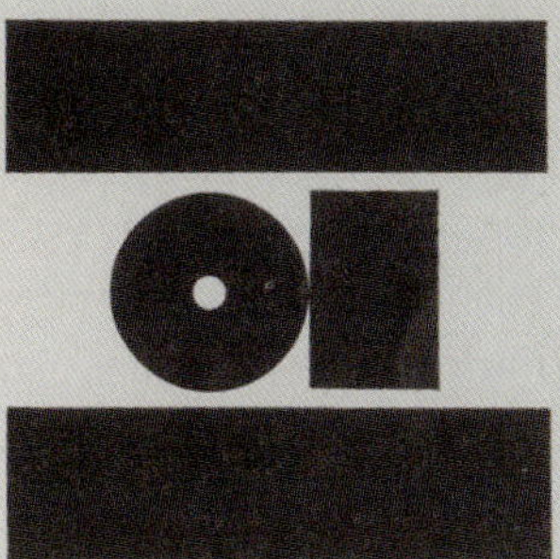
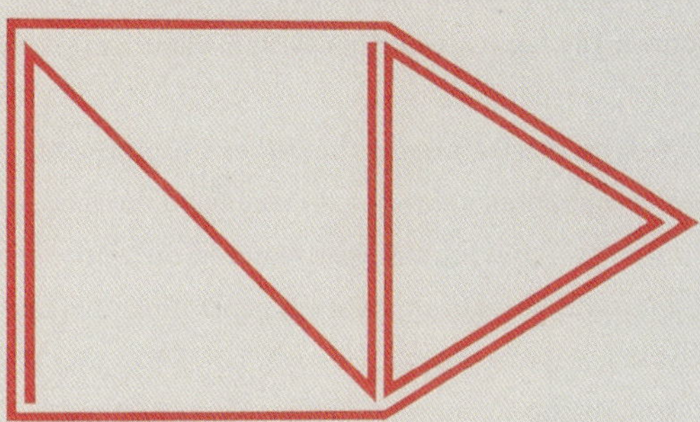
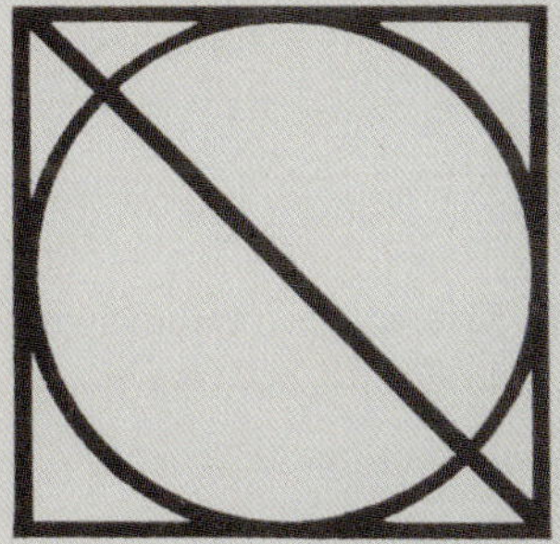
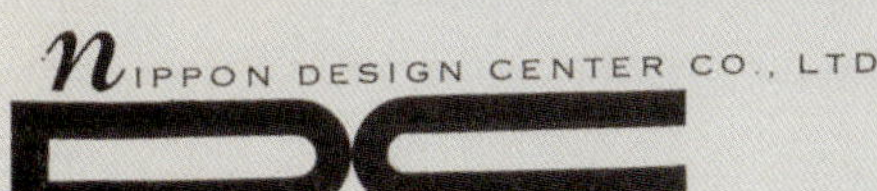

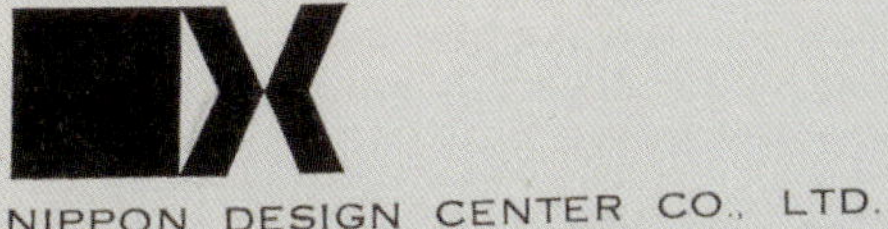

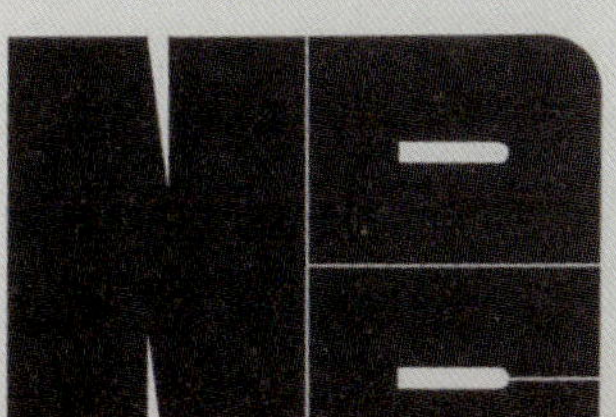

Spread of potential logos for Nippon Design Center designed by Yusaku Kamekura from ***Design* デザイン** issue #4 (Tokyo: Bijutsu Shuppansha 美術出版社, 1960). Final Nippon Design Center logo debut in red.

proposal in 1960.[11] A fact largely unknown today is that the logo design was actually a collaboration, as Kamekura's mentor Hara Hiromu designed the logo's lettering.

Under the direction of design critic, writer, and Olympic Katsumi Masaru, the logo competitors worked with teams of designers to execute each aspect of the Olympic identity and collateral. Kamekura was paid ¥1,250,000 for his four poster designs for the 1964 Olympics (approximately $10,000 in 2022). He had to pay out three-quarters of the commission to photographic director Murakoshi Jo 村越襄 and photographer Hayasaki Osamu 早崎治. Murakoshi and Hayasaki coordinated eighty-plus photographs of runners at the starting line posed in the dark and illuminated by over fifty small flash units. They also had to create similar setups for the photographs of the runner carrying the Olympic torch and the swimmer used on other posters. The budget was used to pay Murakoshi, Hayasaki, additional photographers, and assistants for the shoots. After covering the cost of photography, Kamekura walked away with the equivalent of $2,500 in 2022 for his labors.

Later, other designers would toil for months on the application of the Olympic identity, yet were unpaid. "Fukuda Shigeo 福田繁雄, a member of the 'symbol' sub-committee, related that he had worked for three months without pay, and to make matters worse, was required to sign a document surrendering copyright privileges."[12] Fukuda and the other eleven members of the pictogram design team (including Tanaka Ikkō, Yokoo Tadanori, Uno Akira 宇野亜喜良, Yamashita Yoshirō, Takimoto Tadahito 瀧本唯人, Hirohashi Keiko 広橋桂子, Ejima Hitoshi 江島任, Uematsu Kuniomi 植松国臣, Harada Tsunao 原田維夫, and Kimura Tsunehisa 木村恒久) assigned to the Olympics were paid "in-kind," receiving only tickets to the Olympics in return for thousands of hours of collective labor.

The 1960s were an incredibly tumultuous decade for Japan as it faced reintegration on a global scale, a continued economic upswing, reconciliation of the national identity, and more than the nation's fair share of political tumult. The goal of the Tokyo Games was, as Japanese officials stated, "to show the world that Japan is not just a country of cherry blossoms and geishas [but] to demonstrate that Japan had been rebuilt after the war and [was] willing to connect itself to the western world."[13] The design for the 1964 Olympics eschewed the stereotypical imagery that Japan had been saddled with previously, in favor of a reductive, streamlined, and profoundly modern aesthetic. In many ways, the design for the Olympics was a visual analog for the profound economic changes that were happening in the country.

Being "interested in 'representing Japanese-ness' even though they were 'rejecting nationalism,'"[14] Kamekura and the members of both design teams were in a difficult position when designing the materials for the Japanese Olympics less than two decades after World War II, and seeking to "reintegrate a national consciousness among the Japanese people, to restore continuity with the past and reawaken pride in Japanese culture."[15]

This was the first time that a unified design approach was used in the Olympics, with a set of identity guidelines for the implementation of the Olympic logo, pictograms, colors, and typography that the designers used. Pictograms were applied for the first time in Olympic history. The pictograms were designed by a team led by Yamashita Yoshirō and which included designer Yokoo Tadanori. Inspired by Otto and Marie Neurath's Isotype system, the pictogram design for the 1964 Olympics has been continually reinterpreted in Olympic identities ever since.

Kamekura was featured in the 1965 exhibition *Persona*, Japan's next major graphic design exhibition and the successor to *Graphic '55*. The exhibition also featured the work of emerging graphic designers of the postwar generation, including Awazu Kiyoshi, Fukuda Shigeo, Hosoya Gan, Katayama Toshihiro, Katsui Mitsuo, Kimura Tsunehisa, Nagai Kazumasa, Tanaka Ikkō, Uno Akira, Wada Makoto, and Yokoo Tadanori. Kamekura's work was exhibited separately, as he was graphic design's major figure in Japan at that time, alongside the work of foreigners Paul Davis, Louis Dorfsman, Karl Gerstner, and Jan Lenica. *Persona* was organized by Tanaka Ikkō, Nippon Design Center member and designer of the World Design Conference logo. Tanaka invited his senior Kamekura, alongside Davis, Dorfsman, Gerstner, and Lenica, all of whom he had met while traveling the globe during the first half of the 1960s.

---

11 Ibid.

12 Jilly Traganou, "Tokyo's 1964 Olympic Design as a 'Realm of [Design] Memory,'" *Sport in Society* 14, no. 4 (2011): 466–81, https://doi.org/10.1080/17430437.2011.565925.

13 Sandra Collins, "'Samurai' Politics: Japanese Cultural Identity in Global Sport – The Olympic Games as a Representational Strategy," *The International Journal of the History of Sport* 24 (February 20, 2007): 364, https://doi.org/10.1080/09523360601101345.

14 Jilly Traganou, *Designing the Olympics: Representation, Participation, Contestation*, (London: Routledge, 2017), 264.

15 Ibid.

While only up for one week, *Persona* was incredibly successful—more than 35,000 visitors attended the exhibition held at the Matsuya Ginza department store. One of the key events in the history of Japanese graphic design, *Persona* documented the rise of the new generation of designers born during the late 1920s and 1930s and showed their assertion of individuality in design work. The posters exhibited by Yokoo Tadanori most clearly exemplified the cultural shift from the universal to the subjective and personal, standing in stark contrast with the Bauhaus-inspired geometric simplicity of elder statesman Kamekura's contributions.

Meanwhile, the Japan Advertising Artists Club continued to dominate the culture of graphic design in Japan, yet trouble was on the horizon. Kamekura would later acknowledge the issue:

> "*As the annual event approached the end of its second decade, critics began to castigate the designers' dependency on the exhibition format, saying they were acting precisely as if they were painters. They simultaneously began to suggest that designers should address issues that had greater social relevance. These criticisms were indeed on target. The JAAC by this time had become a mecca for the nation's designers, and it wielded enormous power over them. In fact, in many quarters, this power was viewed as a kind of authoritarianism. This was around 1967, a time when the student activist movement in France and the United States began to spread to Japan. The movement affected both private and national universities alike, with student demonstrations resulting in the widespread suspension of classes and harsh criticism of professorial staff. I can still recall quite vividly how, on August 2, 1969, dozens of helmeted students wearing masks over their faces to conceal their identities stormed into the JAAC committee meeting where judging was underway to select works by nonmembers for the exhibition. The intruders represented a leftwing group intent on crushing the JAAC and its activities. Ongoing debates followed between the JAAC and the students, but no mutually satisfactory outcome was reached. Confusion reigned even within the ranks of the JAAC, and some members began to suggest that the organization would have to give in to prevailing trends. And so, on June 30, 1970, the JAAC ultimately yielded to the pressures of the times and disbanded. One newspaper likened the event to the toppling of a grand old tree.*"[16]
>
> -Kamekura Yūsaku, "Graphics"

The violent demise of the JAAC left a giant hole in the culture of graphic design in Japan, which a number of other smaller professional organizations attempted to fill. None did until the 1978 formation of the Japan Graphic Designers Association (JAGDA), over which Kamekura would preside as president until 1994, three years before his death in 1997. JAGDA would offer freelance graphic designers insurance and health care, the potential for publication, and social functions for what often can be a solitary form of labor.

In 1999, JAGDA established the annual Yūsaku Kamekura Design Award, which "is given to graphic designs that express universality and innovation."[17]

16 Patricia Jane Graham, *Japanese Design: Art, Aesthetics & Culture*, (North Clarendon, VT: Tuttle Publishing, 2014), 41.

17 "Yūsaku Kamekura Design Award," Japan Graphic Designers Association Inc. (2020), https://www.jagda.or.jp/en/awards/kamekura/.

18 Patricia Jane Graham, *Japanese Design: Art, Aesthetics & Culture*, (North Clarendon, VT: Tuttle Publishing, 2014), 40.

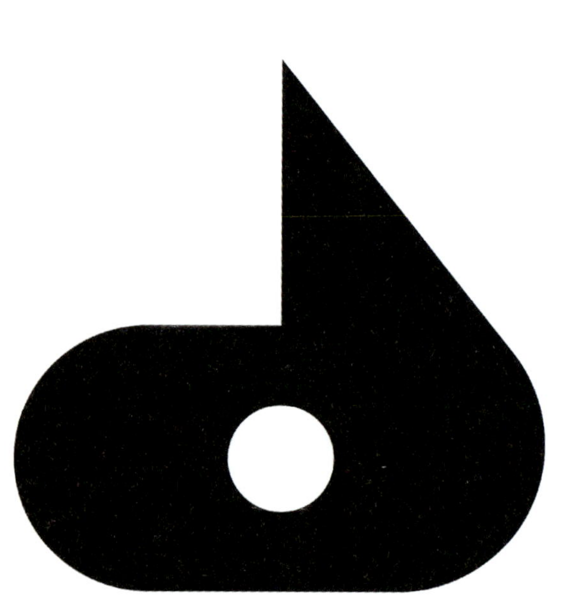

Japan Industrial Designers Association mark, 1953.

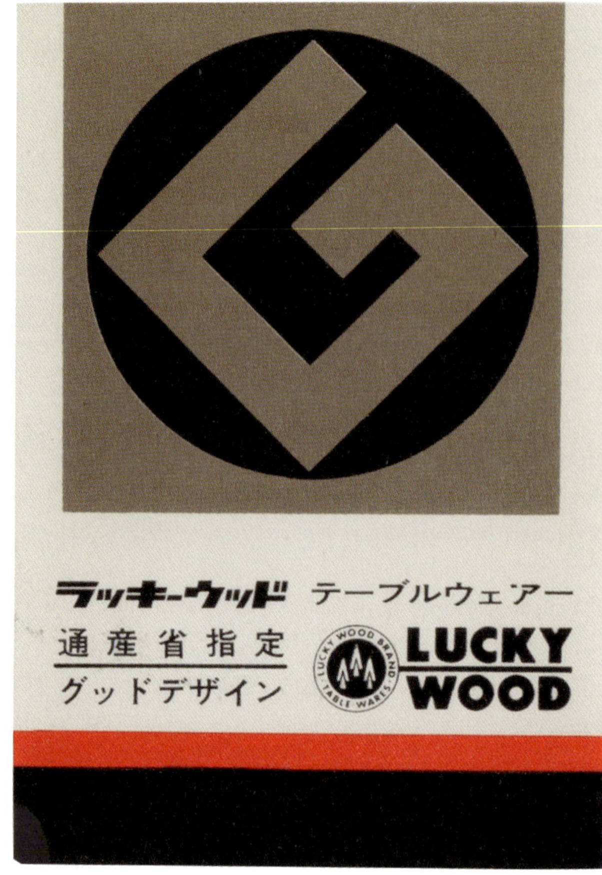

Original Good Design mark, 1957.

"I should like to recount in this connection a most interesting anecdote concerning Walter Gropius and Kamekura Yūsaku. Kamekura was more strongly influenced than any other Japanese graphic designer by the Bauhaus movement, and he is famous for the functionalist style of his work; yet when Gropius happened to visit Japan and see a logo designed by Kamekura, he (Gropius) asked if its shape did not derive from some Japanese folk implement. I would not be surprised if Kamekura was a little upset by this totally unexpected inquiry. Be that as it may, the lesson of this story, in my view, is that a logo that Kamekura designed with no consciousness of his Japanese background should appear in Gropius' eyes to have something Japanese about it." [18]

- Katsumi Masaru, "Japan Style—Yesterday, Today and Tomorrow"

References:

Kabayama, Koichi, Naoyuki Takashima, Hiroshi Kashiwagi, Minako Teramoto, Mutsuko Sakanakura, and Hitoshi Mori. *1950-Nendai Nihon no Gurafikku Dezain: dezainā tanjō = Japanese Graphic Design in the '50s: The Designer Is Born*. Tokyo: Kokusho Kankōkai, 2008.

Kamekura, Yūsaku, and Ayao Yamana. *Gurafikku Dezain no Seiki: Bunshō to Danwa to Sakuhin De kōsei: Meiji Sedai Yamana Ayao Sugiura Hisui Kara shōwa Sedai Made*. Tokyo: Bijutsu Shuppansha, 2008.

Segi, Shin'ichi, Tanaka Ikkō, and Hiroshi Sano. *Nissenbi no Jidai = The Epoch of the Japan Advertising Artists Club: Nihon No Gurafikku Dezain 1951–70*. Tokyo: Toransuāto, 2000.

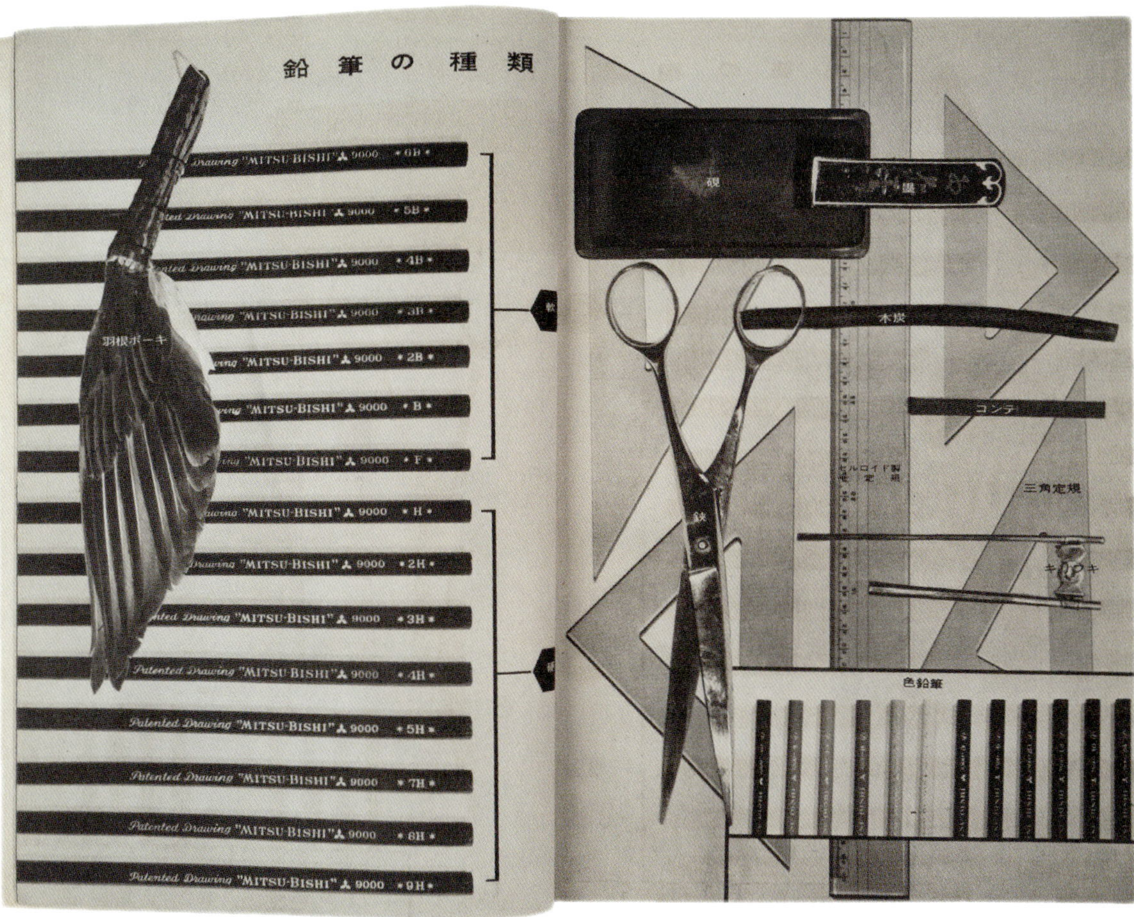

Photographic composition-based feature on design tools in an issue of ***Bessatsu Atelier* 別冊アトリエ No. 28**, the subtitle of which was ***Design Techniques* デザイン技法** (Tokyo: Fujingahōsha 婦人画報社, 1956).

MURAKOSHI JŌ 村越襄

1925–1996

Murakoshi Jō was born in Yokohama. He studied both Western and Japanese forms of painting. At age twenty, he was drafted into the military and was present in Okinawa at the end of the war. In 1946, he began working for the Victor Company of Japan. Five years later, he co-founded Light Publicity Co. Ltd., working as an art director under Natori Yōnosuke, former director of Nippon Kōbō.

Murakoshi was the photography director for the 1964 Olympic poster depicting six runners, designed by Kamekura Yūsaku. Murakoshi had the photographers and runners shoot the scene more than eighty times over the course of three hours in the unfinished Olympic stadium to achieve the desired effect.

Murakoshi left Light Publicity in 1977 and began his own design studio, intermittently working as a model for assorted fashion magazines.

References:

Kabayama, Koichi, Naoyuki Takashima, Hiroshi Kashiwagi, Minako Teramoto, Mutsuko Sakanakura, and Hitoshi Mori. *1950-Nendai Nihon no Gurafikku Dezain: dezainā tanjō = Japanese Graphic Design in the '50s: the Designer Is Born*. Tokyo: Kokusho Kankōkai, 2008.

Murakoshi Jō. *Murakoshi Jō*. Tokyo: DNP Bunka Shinkō Zaidan = Ginza Graphic Gallery, 2013.

Segi, Shin'ichi, Tanaka Ikkō, and Hiroshi Sano. *Nissenbi no Jidai = The Epoch of the Japan Advertising Artists Club: Nihon No Gurafikku Dezain 1951–70*. Tokyo: Toransuāto, 2000.

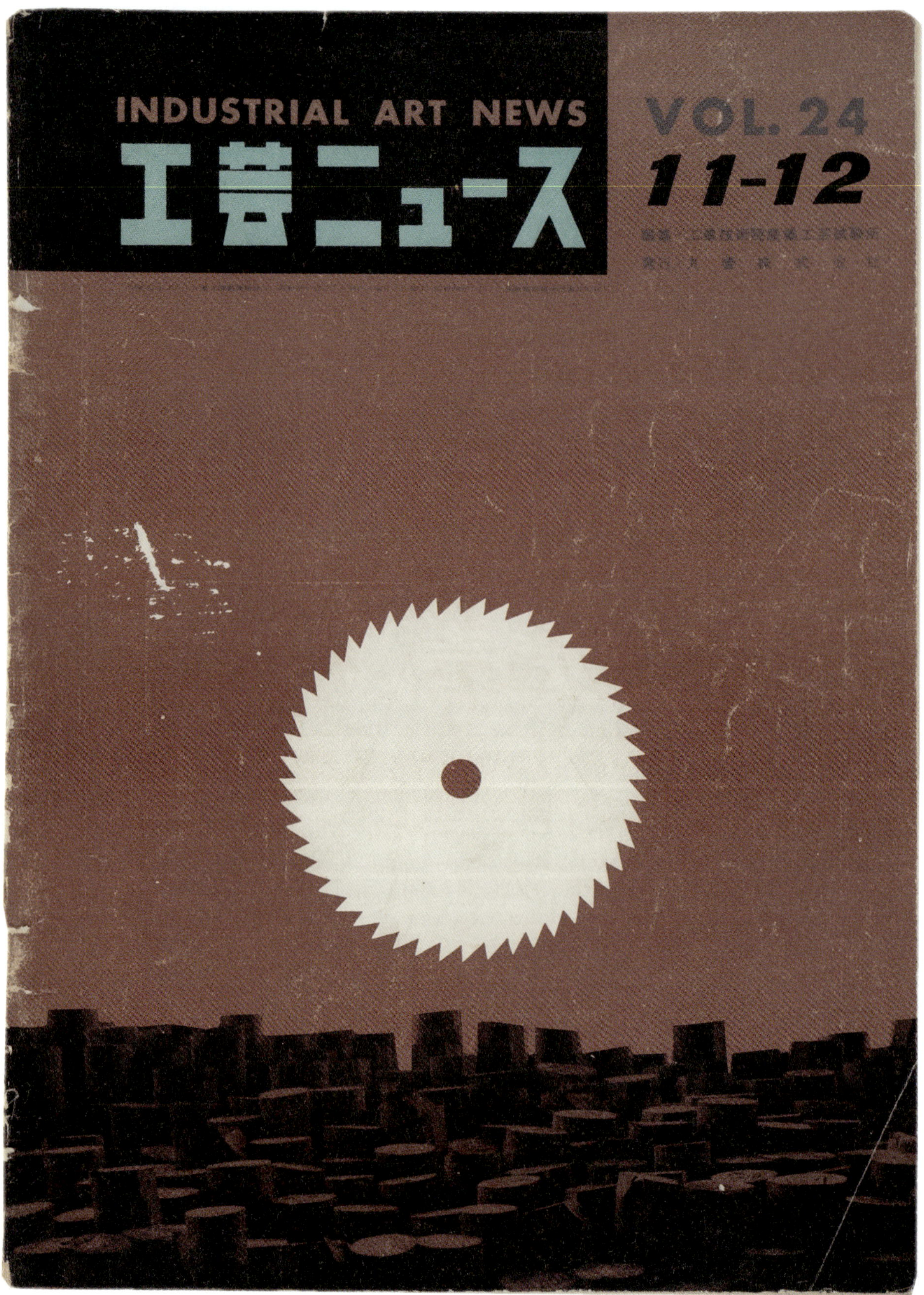

***Kōgei News* 工芸ニュース, Vol. 24, No. 10 (Tokyo: Maruzen, December 1956).** Cover designed by Mukai Ryōkichi 向井良吉, edited by Industrial Arts Institute (IAI), Tokyo.

Shinri no Kuni 眞理の國 *(Country of Truth)*, No. 9 (Tokyo: Mimisha 未見社, 1946). Design & illustration: unknown.

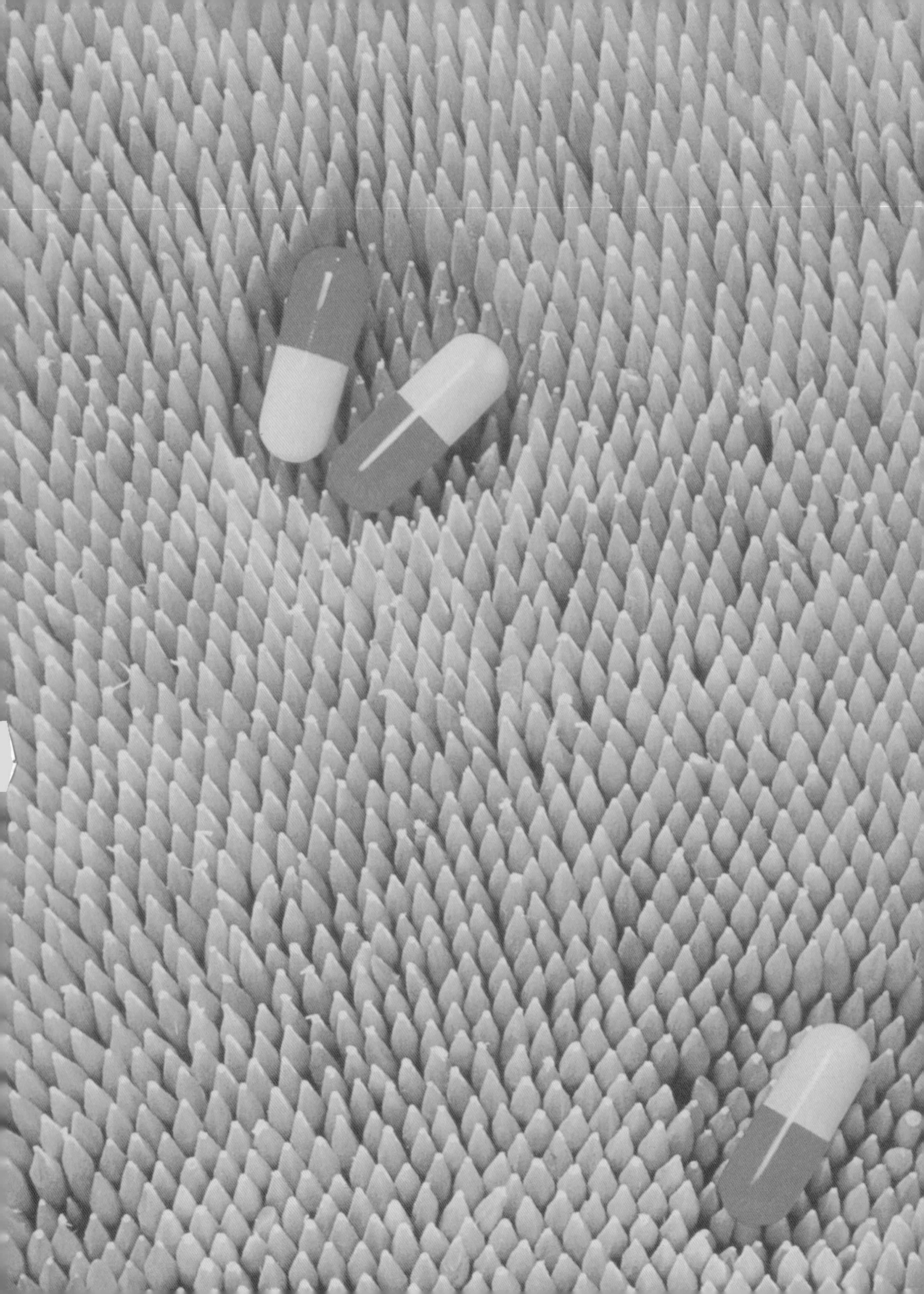

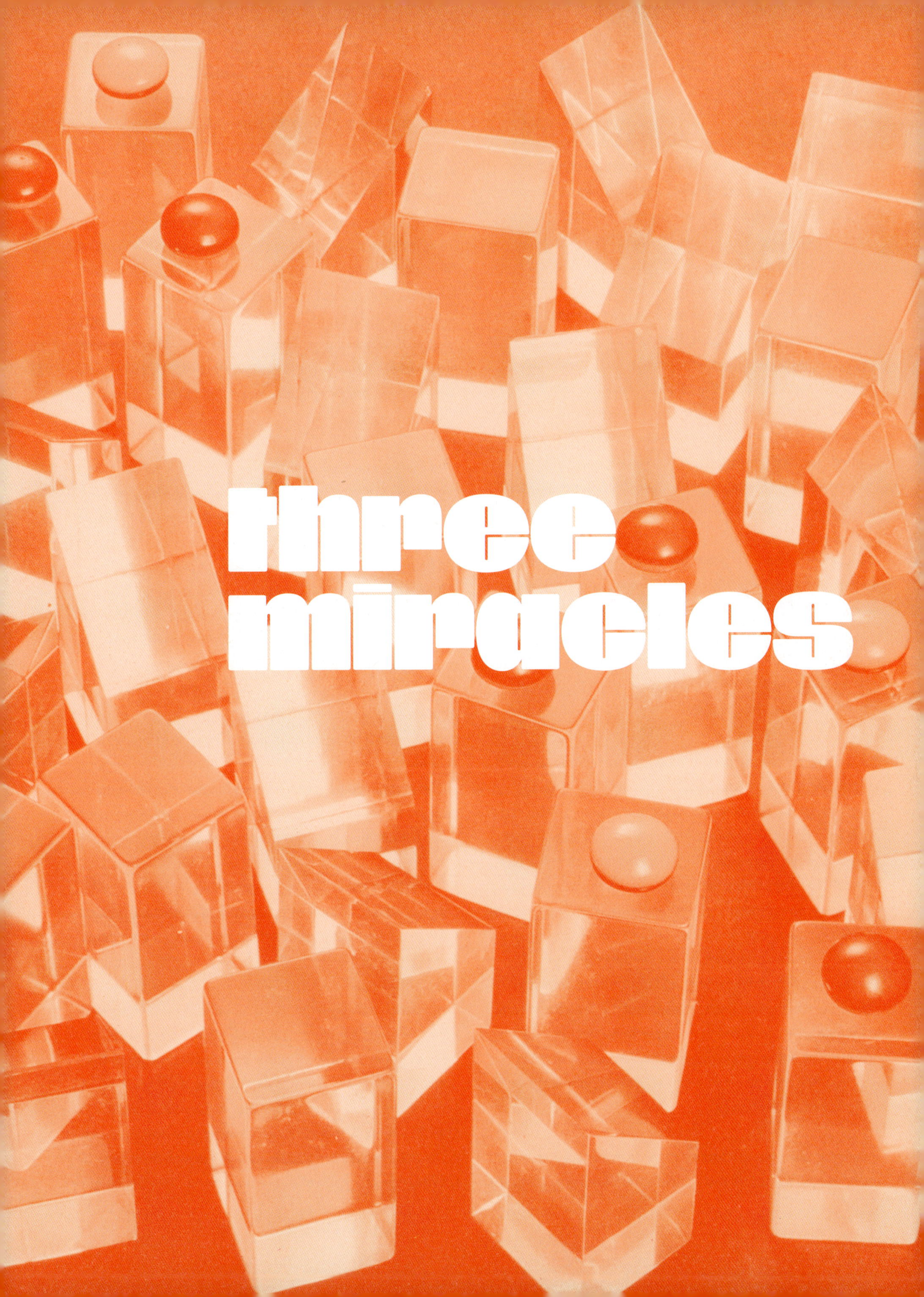
three
miracles

From Postwar to the Three Miracles: The Rise of "Design"

The mid-1950s were a time of incredible transformation for Japanese society outside of graphic design, as well—after General Douglas MacArthur's move to the Korean War front and the 1952 dissolution of the American-led SCAP (Supreme Commander for the Allied Powers) administration, government-run economic reform was paramount to the recovery of the nation. The Japanese government led an all-out effort to focus on the production of raw materials such as coal, steel, and textiles in order to help rebuild the country's economy. Recovery was bolstered by trade agreements with the United States that subsidized Americans' land use in Japan and allowed for massive industrial and manufacturing deals between the two countries. Japan's mobilization of its female workforce, seen as commensurate with women's right to vote (newly established in the postwar constitution), was also a significant contribution to the recovery of the national economy.

Alongside economic recovery, the 1950s also saw design emerge as a popular public conception in Japan. Prior to World War II, the term *shōgyō bijutsu* (commercial art) made headway in the public consciousness, but the postwar period would bring about a more robust public cognizance and valuation of what would come to be known as design, or more accurately transliterated, *dezain*.

It is worth considering the etymology of this foreign loan word as it is used in Japan. *Shōgyō bijutsu* (literally translated, "commercial art") covered the subject somewhat, but bijutsu is the term for art. For example, Hamada Masuji, publisher of *Gendai Shōgyō Bijutsu Zenshū*, perceived commercial art as being more far-reaching than graphic design as we understand it today, encompassing more than image-making and typography. Hamada saw commercial art as being a hybrid of graphic design, copywriting, lettering design, architecture, lighting, display design, and much more, and this broader definition can be seen in the rich illustration work of the Taishō and early Shōwa periods, the attention to shop window design, and the way in which fine artists like Murayama Tomoyoshi and Onchi Kōshirō often created commercial work for department stores and cosmetics companies.

Before the widespread adoption of the loan word *dezain*, the Japanese language had two earlier terms for the processes that map to a Western idea of design: *zuan* 図案, the actual execution of a design, as well as *kōan* 考案, the mental and intellectual articulation of a concept to be executed.

What pushed the popularity of the term dezain forward was the organization and mobilization of multiple design-oriented professional groups, including the Advertising Federation of Japan (AFJ), local Commercial Artists Associations, the Tokyo AD Art Directors Club (founded in 1952 and renamed the Tokyo Art Directors Club in 1961), and, foremost, the Japan Advertising Artists Club (JAAC)—the first national organization devoted to graphic design in Japan. From 1947 to 1953, the AFJ held a national poster exhibition, and in 1951 the JAAC began organizing exhibitions in which the public was invited to send submissions for potential display.

Other groups sprang up during the same time period, though they gained less traction, including the Japan Designers Association (1946), the Japan Advertisement Club (1947), 1953's New Commercial Art Group, the International Design Committee (founded in 1953 and renamed the Japan Design Committee in 1963), and the DAS Designers Association (1956), amongst others. The criticism and discussion-oriented A Club was organized by Katayama Toshihiro, Tanaka Ikkō, Nagai Kazumasa, and Kimura Tsunehisa in the Kansai region.

All of these groups contributed to the popularization of design and the roles that designers played in helping to shape the postwar cultural landscape. The large number of participants in public graphic design competitions helped popularize graphic design as a sector of cultural production and imparted democratic notions that "anyone could be a designer."

The JAAC's mission was "to impart the sociocultural significance of advertising art, to establish and protect the occupational position of advertising artists, to support them mutually and to promote friendship." The organization sought to serve designers but also society at large, not just advertisers. As the organization developed, so did their exhibitions, shifting from being "members-only" to adopting a bifurcated model of exhibiting members' work alongside work submitted by the public in 1953. Early nonmember winners of the lauded JAAC Prize included Uraga Yasuro 宇留河泰呂 in 1953 and Ito Teizo 伊藤貞三 in 1954, though Ito's winning poster design would go on to be heavily criticized in both the design press and the national news for its formal resemblance to a similar poster by the British designer FHK Henrion for the Olivetti corporation. (In 1955, the organization imposed a new rule: that members' works would be judged by their *originality* as much as their quality in the public-facing part of the competition.) Tama University design student Wada Makoto was a prizewinner in the JAAC's seventh exhibition and immediately began picking up contract design work for large clients.

JAAC exhibitions often featured original artwork for speculative designs—a case of necessity for members in the early 1950s due to the Japanese economic recovery, and later a necessity for nonmembers who submitted their work, as the organization did not want to limit potential members due to the expense of having their works printed.

The JAAC had separate classifications for works to be exhibited, including "commercial works" devoted to public relations, advertising, and tourism, and "public-oriented works" reserved for political, cultural, and socially oriented projects. An example of the latter type of work was Awazu Kiyoshi's 1955 JAAC Award-winning environmental activism poster, *Give Back Our Sea*, protesting the pollution of Japanese waters by the American military.

Beyond design organizations' competitions, many corporations, newspapers, and government bureaus also held design competitions for promotional advertising throughout the 1950s. Some, such as the Kyodo Press in collaboration with the Tokyo Metropolitan Government, put on a series of exhibitions that placed wide selections of foreign commercial art and graphic design in front of mass audiences in Tokyo for the first time in 1951, 1952 and 1955. In 1952, the conglomerate Japan Tobacco solicited French-American designer Raymond Loewy to redesign the packaging for Peace Cigarettes. A decade earlier, Loewy had designed the packaging for Lucky Strike, then the world's best-selling cigarette brand. Loewy's redesign increased the sales of Peace Cigarettes exponentially, and he discussed the sizable fee he charged Japan Tobacco in print, as well. Both of these factors were influential in raising the economic value and public recognition of graphic design and graphic designers in Japan.

During the late 1950s, graphic design would continue to receive attention and pick up cultural capital through the formation of the Nippon Design Center consortium, the continued efforts of the JAAC, and many other groups. In 1959, a number of core members of the JAAC would join another group called the "21s," a collection of design professionals from all walks of life who would meet on the twenty-first of each month under the leadership of Kamekura Yūsaku and Yamashiro Ryuichi. Members included Awazu Kiyoshi, Fukuda Shigeo, Gan Hosoya 細谷巖, Nakajo Masayoshi 仲條正義, Sugiura Kōhei, Uno Akira, and more than a dozen others who would go on to help shape the influence of graphic design in Japanese culture after the 1950s.

By 1956, the Japanese Economic Survey decreed that the "postwar" period was over. The government stabilized after years of power struggles amongst various parties with the creation of the Liberal Democratic Party, in actuality a conservative political party which has dominated Japanese politics since.

The mid-1950s also heralded the arrival of the era's "Three Sacred Treasures," the black-and-white television, the washing machine, and the electric refrigerator. The introduction of these goods helped open up possibilities for Japanese women beyond the drudgery of domestic work. The postwar housing crisis was solved through the mass production of apartment buildings throughout the country, and, simultaneously, office buildings were constructed in metropolitan areas to allow for ease of access.

Japan's "economic miracle" would continue relatively unabated for decades, paving the way for the further relevance of graphic design as a form of communication, a viable profession, and a socially significant organizing force. The explosion of new products and consumption meant more companies were in need of new corporate-identity design, packaging design, advertising design, and printed promotional materials. There was more work to be done, more client demand, and more money to pay for it all.

References:

Kabayama, Koichi, Naoyuki Takashima, Hiroshi Kashiwagi, Minako Teramoto, Mutsuko Sakanakura, and Hitoshi Mori. *1950-Nendai Nihon no Gurafikku Dezain: dezaina tanjō = Japanese Graphic Design in the '50s: The Designer Is Born*. Tokyo: Kokusho Kankōkai, 2008.

Kamekura, Yūsaku, and Ayao Yamana. *Gurafikku Dezain No Seiki: Bunshō to Danwa to Sakuhin De kōsei: Meiji Sedai Yamana Ayao Sugiura Hisui Kara shōwa Sedai Made*. Tokyo: Bijutsu Shuppansha, 2008.

Segi, Shin'ichi, Tanaka Ikkō, and Hiroshi Sano. *Nissenbi no Jidai = The Epoch of the Japan Advertising Artists Club: Nihon No Gurafikku Dezain 1951–70*. Tokyo: Toransuāto, 2000.

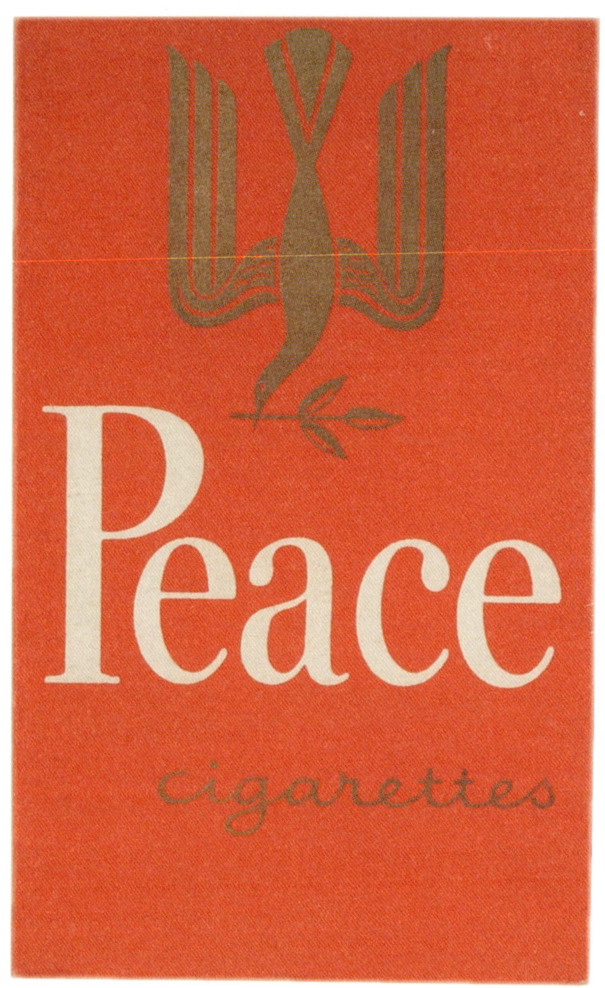

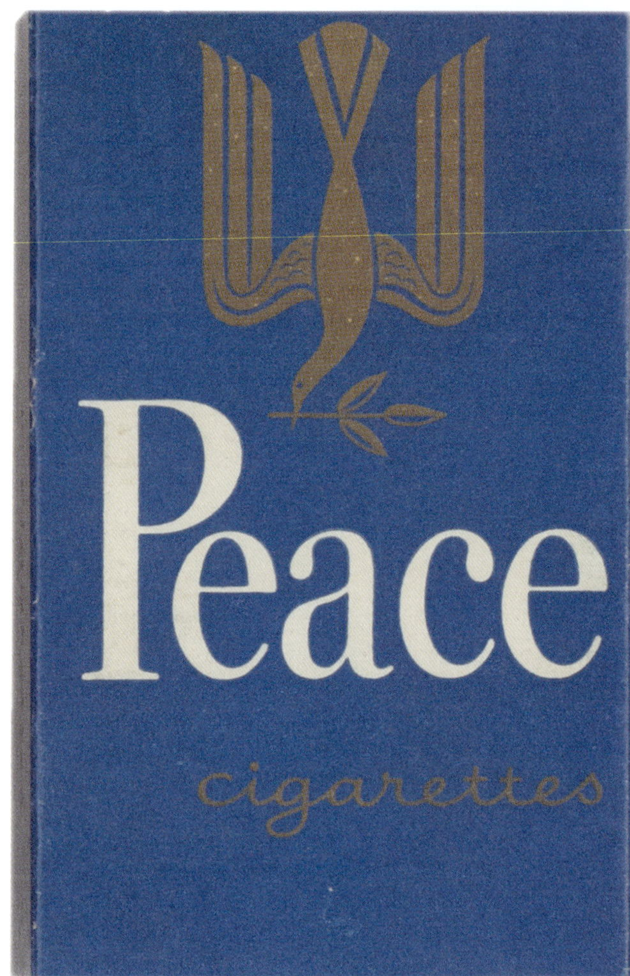

Packaging for **Peace cigarettes** designed by Raymond Loewy in 1952.

Cut Design Idea **カットデザインアイデア by Katsumoto Fujio 勝本富士雄, Kawahara Jun 河原淳, and Namba Junro 難波淳郎**, cover design by Ōmori Tadayuki 大森忠行 (Kagoshima: Edition Iwasaki Art Co., 1966).

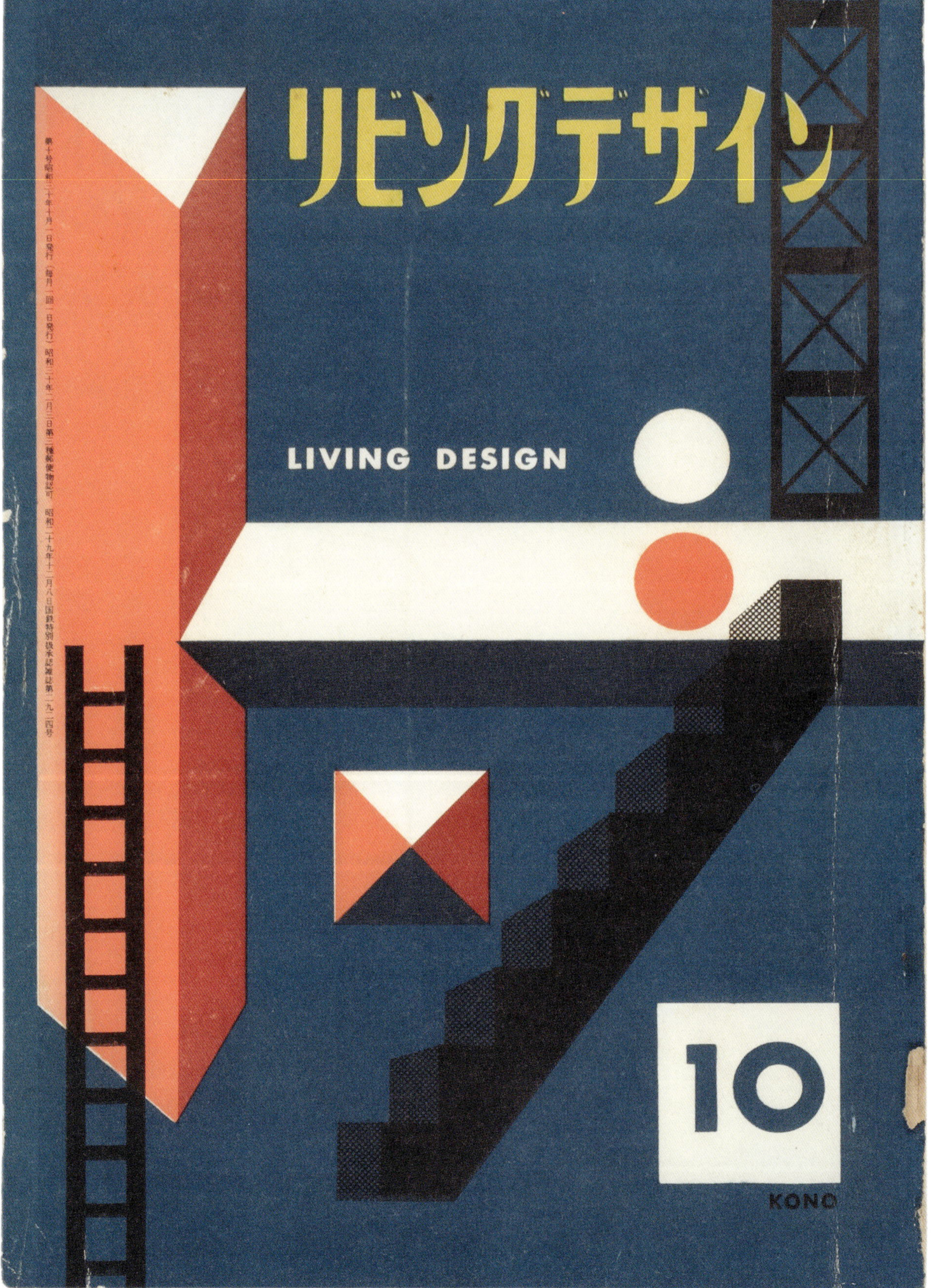

***Living Design* リビングデザイン No. 10 (Tokyo: Bijutsu Shuppansha 美術出版社, 1955).** Cover design by Kōno Takashi 河野鷹思.

LIVING DESIGN リビングデザイン

Living Design リビングデザイン was a monthly magazine launched in 1955 by Bijutsu Shuppansha 美術出版社, publishers of the long-running art magazines *Mizue* みづゑ (1905–1992) and *Bijutsu Techō* 美術手帖 (1948–present).

Throughout the first twelve issues of *Living Design*, Katsumi Masaru 勝見勝 wrote a series of design history essays exploring the Arts & Crafts movement, Art Nouveau, the Deutscher Werkbund, the Bauhaus, British promotional design of the 1930s, and design in the United States in the early 1950s. Katsumi wrote about design's turn away from humanist historical models and toward mechanistic design aesthetics. These historical and theoretical essays were accompanied by analyses of the designs of household products, DIY designs for furniture, consumer goods, and handcrafts. Other features were dedicated to the history of poster design, the emergence of the Good Design Products Selection System, toys, crafts, furniture design, textile design, glassware, and other aspects of both industrial and graphic design.

Over the course of the initial three-year run of the magazine, cover designs were provided by Yamashiro Ryuichi, Itō Kenji, Kono Takashi, and others. In the 1960s, the word "living" (リビング) became diminished in size and was eventually eliminated, resulting in the magazine being quietly renamed merely *Design* デザイン. The magazine ceased publication in 1979.

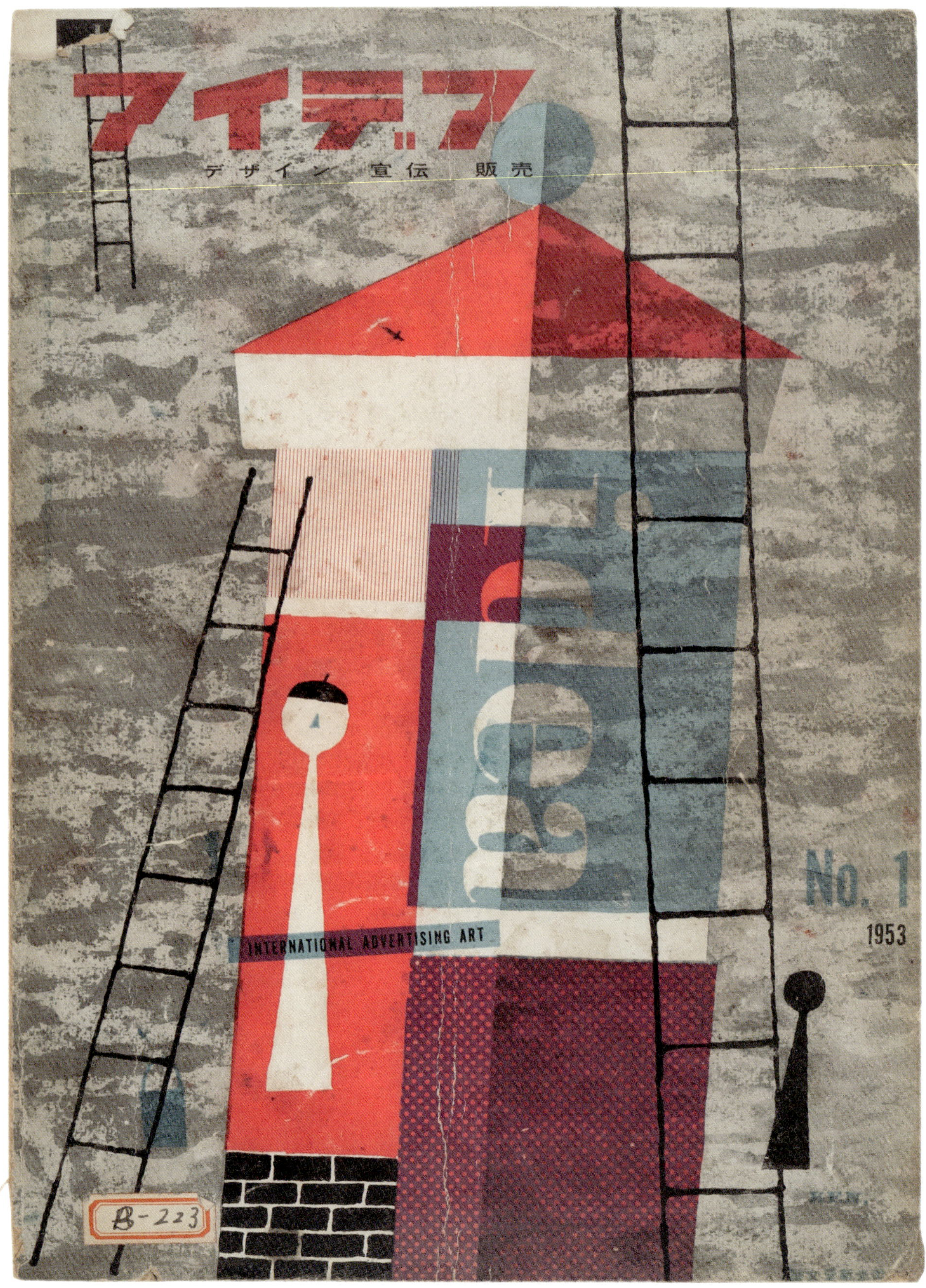

This spread and following two spreads: the first 10 covers of *Idea* アイデア from 1953 through 1954 published by Seibundo Shinkosha 誠文堂新光社, Tokyo. Cover of first issue designed by Itō Kenji 伊藤憲治.

IDEA アイデア

Idea launched in 1953, the continuation of Seibundo's commercial art publications *Kōkokukai* and *New Kōkokukai*. The founding editor-in-chief was Miyayama Takashi 宮山峻, previously the second editor of *Kōkokukai*, and the art director was Ohchi Hiroshi 大智浩. The first issue's cover featured a collaged composition by Itō Kenji depicting a beret-wearing, *kokeshi* doll-like figure preparing to ascend a tilted ladder with another silhouetted figure already ascending a vertical ladder that reached past the border of the composition.

The initial issue of *Idea* introduced the role of the Art Director to Japanese readers, highlighting the careers of foreign designers Raymond Savignac and Paul Rand at the start of the magazine, with texts written by Hara Hiromu and Kamekura Yūsaku respectively. It included one-page features on Japan's leading art directors, such as Yamana Ayao, Yamashiro Ryuichi, Kōno Takashi, Ōhashi Tadashi, Hayakawa Yoshio, Itō Kenji, and Imatake Shichirō. It also contained a feature on abstract art and design by Katsumi Masaru and a bilingual Japanese/English statement of intent highlighting Miyama's goals to introduce graphic design from Europe, the United States, and Japan in *Idea*.

The first four issues would cover the design of specific Japanese companies active in advertising, such as Morinaga Milk Products and Matsuzakaya department store, as well as a feature on posters from around the world with accompanying text by Yamana Ayao, a multi-page feature on the Japan Advertising Artists Club's 1953 exhibition, a profile of the work and life of American designer Alvin Lustig, and a lengthy feature on Italian graphic artists. Writing by Ladislav Sutnar, Kamekura Yūsaku, Kōno Takashi, Imatake Shichirō, and a host of both foreign and Japanese designers and critics was featured in the editorial sections.

The fifth issue was an annual completely dedicated to homegrown Japanese design work, with sections devoted to posters, packaging designs, direct-mail designs, publication cover designs, and advertisement designs, and a spread devoted to symbols and trademarks. The issue features a dizzying amount of work, a testament to the demand for graphic design generated by postwar Japanese economic recovery.

Idea's first decade would largely focus on the development of the JAAC and expose the Japanese design community to a range of work by international designers, as the magazine still does today.

References:

Henrion, FHK, Gene Federico, Helen Federico, Anton Stankowski, Will Van Sambeek, and Yoshihisa Ishihara. "Lifetime Work of the Late Professor Hiroshi Ohchi." *Idea* 23, no. 128 (January 1975): 32–51.

Kamekura, Yūsaku, and Ayao Yamana. *Gurafikku Dezain no Seiki: Bunshō to Danwa to Sakuhin De kōsei: Meiji Sedai Yamana Ayao Sugiura Hisui Kara shōwa Sedai Made.* Tokyo: Bijutsu Shuppansha, 2008

Takeuchi, Yukie. "The World of Kōkoku-Kai." *Idea* 1, no. 360 (September 2013): 112–27.

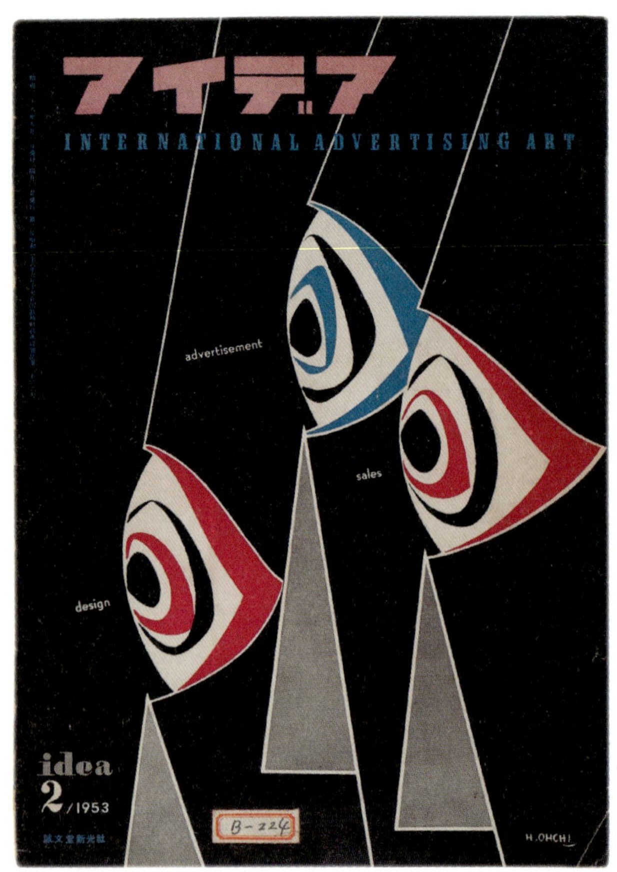
アイデア
INTERNATIONAL ADVERTISING ART
advertisement
sales
design
idea
2/1953
B-224
誠文堂新光社
H.OHCHI

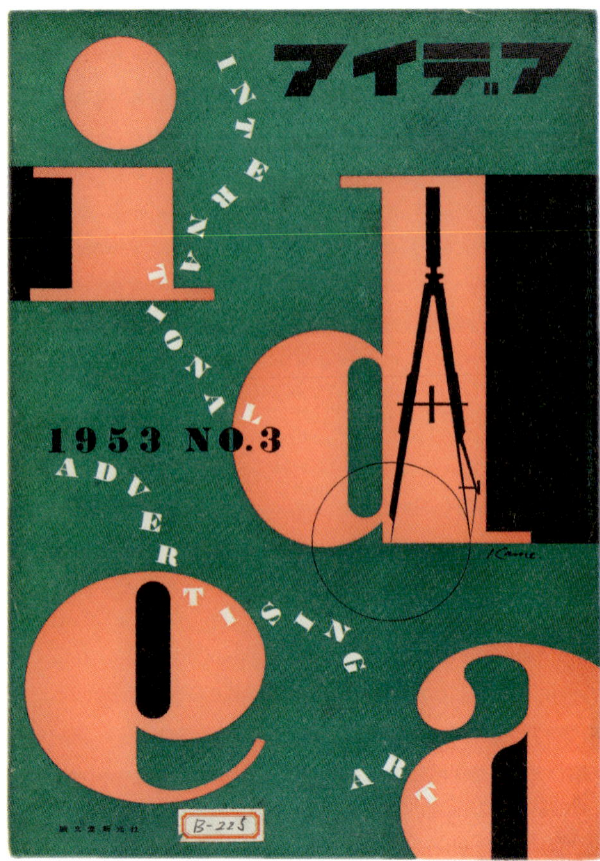
アイデア
INTERNATIONAL ADVERTISING ART
idea
1953 NO.3
誠文堂新光社
B-225

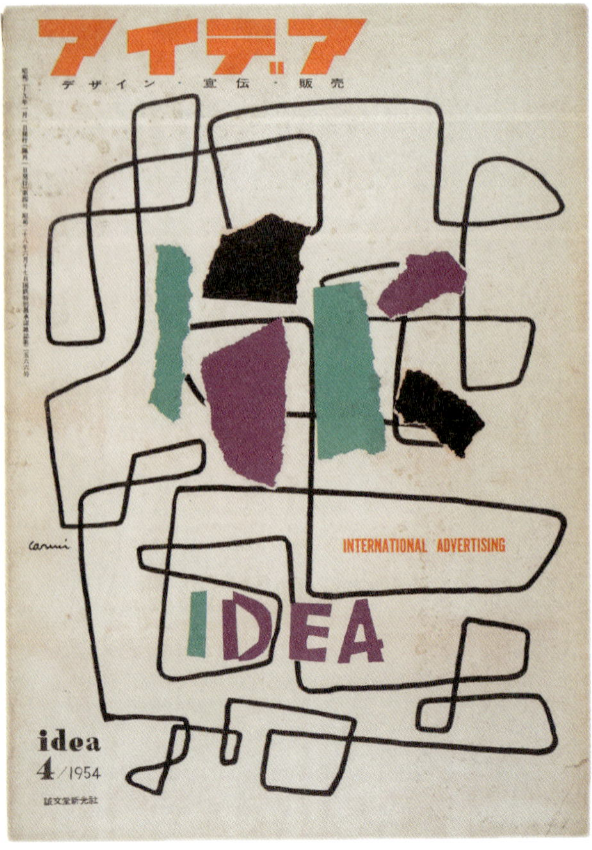
アイデア
デザイン・宣伝・販売
carmi
INTERNATIONAL ADVERTISING
IDEA
idea
4/1954
誠文堂新光社

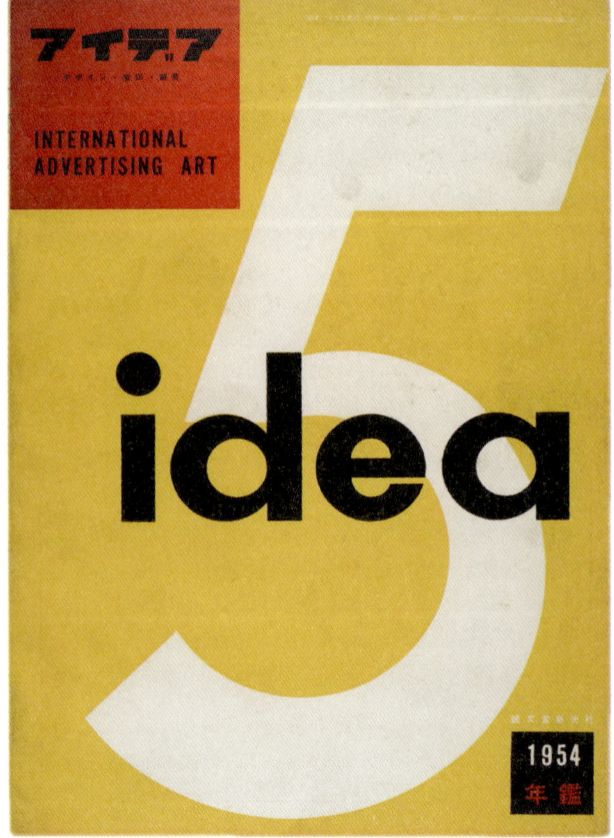
アイデア
INTERNATIONAL
ADVERTISING ART
5
idea
誠文堂新光社
1954
年鑑

OHCHI HIROSHI 大智浩

1908–1974

Ohchi was born in 1908 in Okayama Prefecture and studied electrical engineering at the Nagaoka Higher Industrial School. He turned to design after graduation and returned to school years later, studying in the Design Department of the Tokyo School of Fine Arts, graduating in 1938. He entered the promotions department of the food company Ajinomoto 味の素株式会社 for a time, then moved to the electronics and electrical wire company Riken Densen 理研電線株式会社. Ohchi began writing for both *Kōkokukai* and *Press Art* around this time.

Ohchi was conscripted into the army publicity unit—the first exclusively military design and propaganda division—alongside fellow designer Kōno Takashi. He served in Southeast Asia throughout 1942, then he was placed in a naval research unit until the end of the war. He worked at the Dentsū advertising agency and as a design advisor for the government until 1949, when he established his eponymous design studio. He and his staff worked on print design and corporate identity work for Kirin, Mazda, the Japan Tourist Association, the city of Hiroshima, and Idemitsu, alongside a host of other clients. In addition, Ohchi taught at Kanazawa College of Art and wrote and translated more than thirty books on design.

Ohchi's hybrid practice across design, design education, writing, and translation instigated his friend Miyama Takashi to invite Ohchi on board as *Idea*'s first art director. His name stayed on the masthead from 1953 through 1974, despite the actual design work being handled by his staff members in later years.

Ohchi was the first Japanese member of the elite design organization Alliance Graphique Internationale (AGI), having joined in 1954. Through his connections with the AGI and Gallery 303 in New York City, Ohchi was able to direct much of the editorial content for *Idea*. His relationship with Dr. Robert Leslie, 303's curator, afforded Ohchi the ability to collect and publish examples of work by groups largely underrepresented in graphic design, including African Americans and women.

Meanwhile, Ohchi continued translating and writing books outside of *Idea*, including translations of seminal works by Johannes Itten, Max Ernst, Armin Hoffmann, and others. His original titles focused on design basics, design theory, and both theoretical and practical applications of color. He helped found the design department at the Tokyo University of Education and lectured at a host of universities across Japan.

References:

Henrion, FHK, Gene Federico, Helen Federico, Anton Stankowski, Will Van Sambeek, and Yoshihisa Ishihara. "Lifetime Work of the Late Professor Hiroshi Ohchi." *Idea* 23, no. 128 (January 1975): 32–51.

Kamekura, Yūsaku, and Ayao Yamana. *Gurafikku Dezain no Seiki: Bunshō to Danwa to Sakuhin De kōsei: Meiji Sedai Yamana Ayao Sugiura Hisui Kara shōwa Sedai Made*. Tokyo: Bijutsu Shuppansha, 2008.

Muroga, Kiyonori, and Tomoko Kondo. "Hiroshi Ohchi: Design, Education and Journalism." *Idea* 52, no. 303 (March 2004): 109–34.

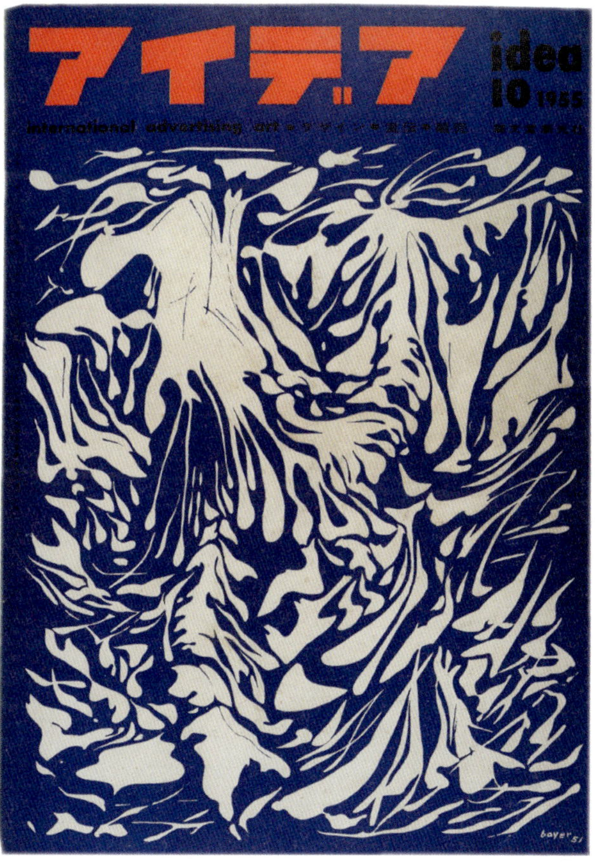

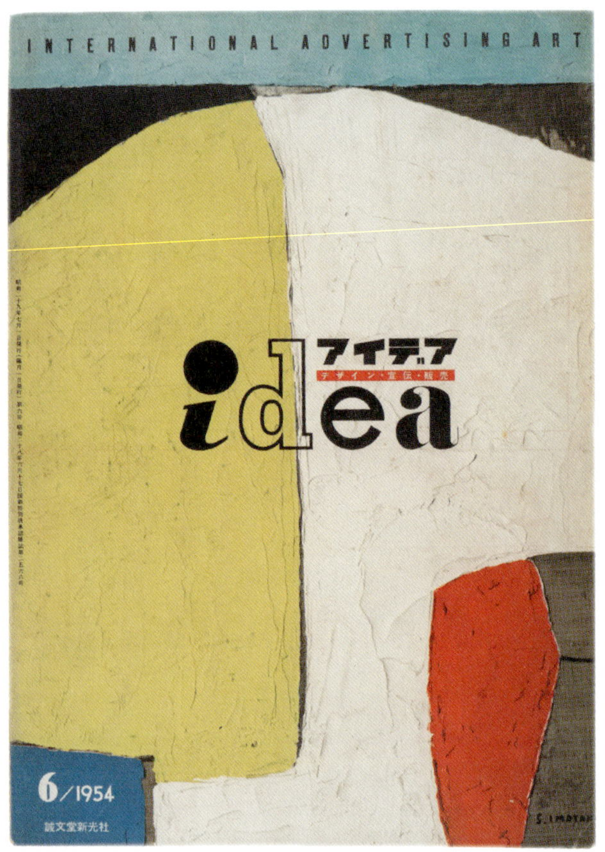
INTERNATIONAL ADVERTISING ART
アイデア
デザイン・宣伝・販売
idea
6/1954
誠文堂新光社

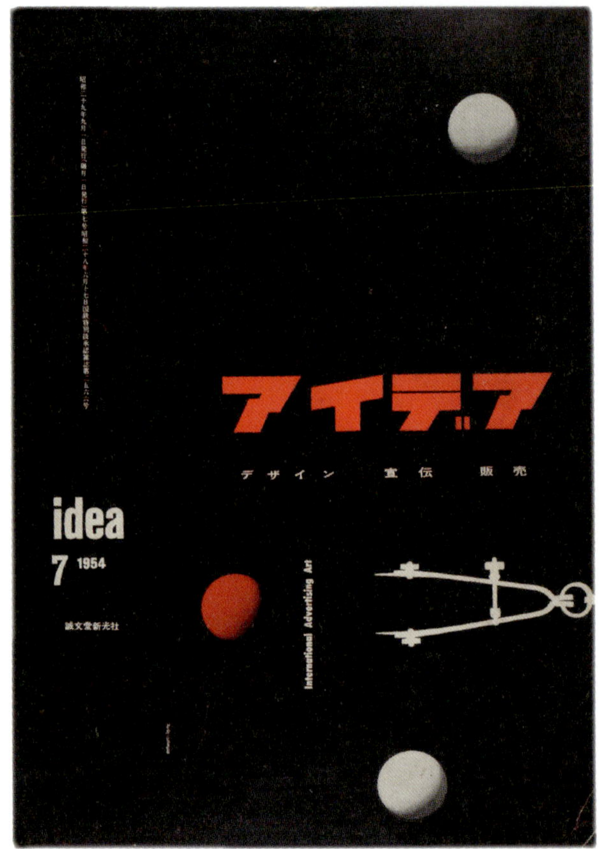
アイデア
デザイン 宣伝 販売
idea
7 1954
誠文堂新光社
International Advertising Art

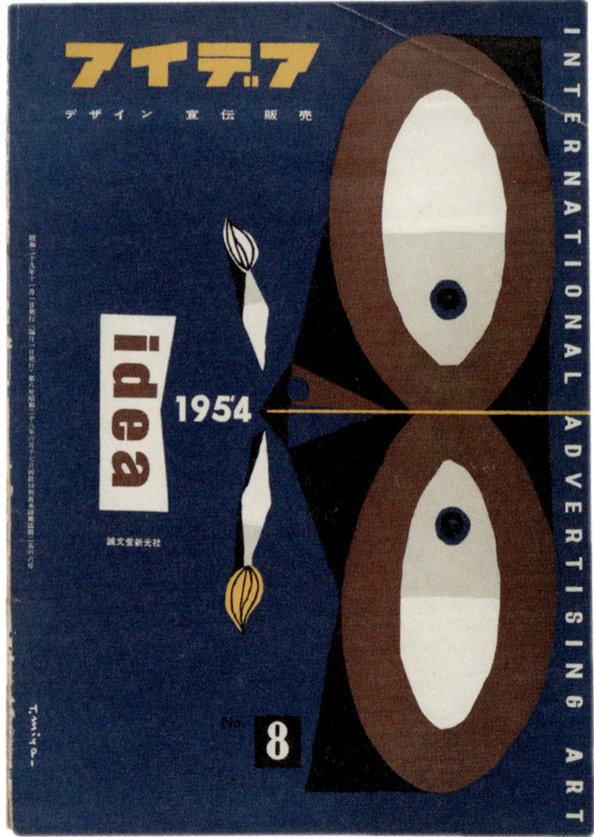
アイデア
デザイン 宣伝 販売
INTERNATIONAL ADVERTISING ART
idea
1954
誠文堂新光社
No. 8

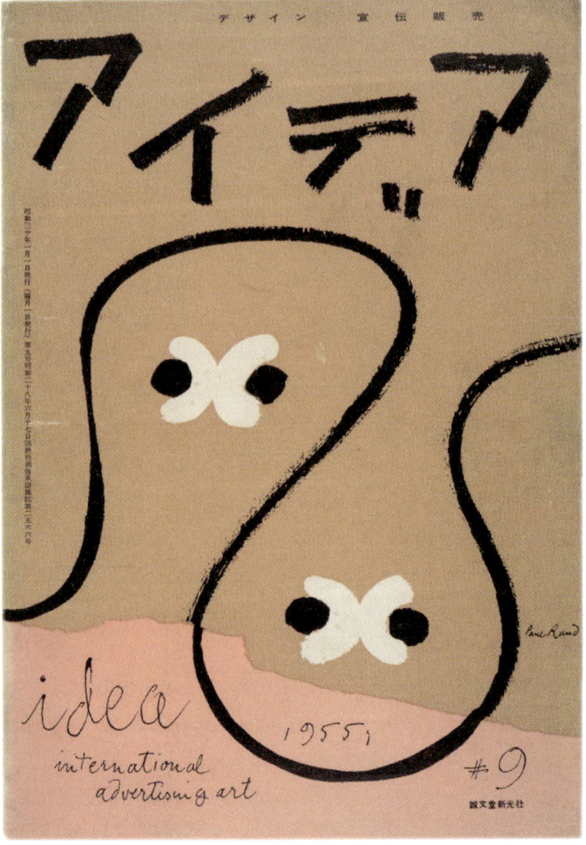
デザイン 宣伝 販売
アイデア
Paul Rand
idea
1955
international advertising art
#9
誠文堂新光社

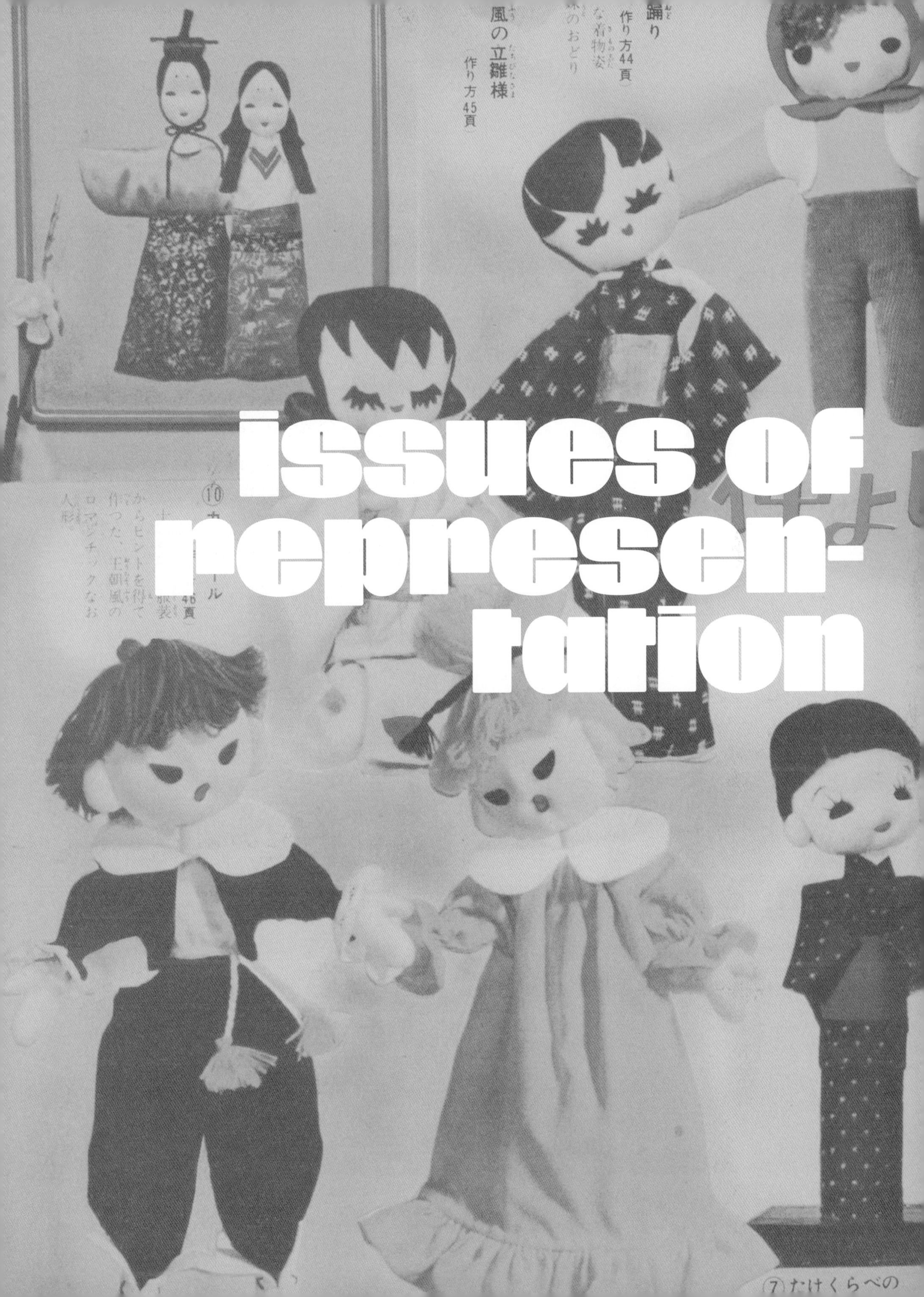

issues of representation

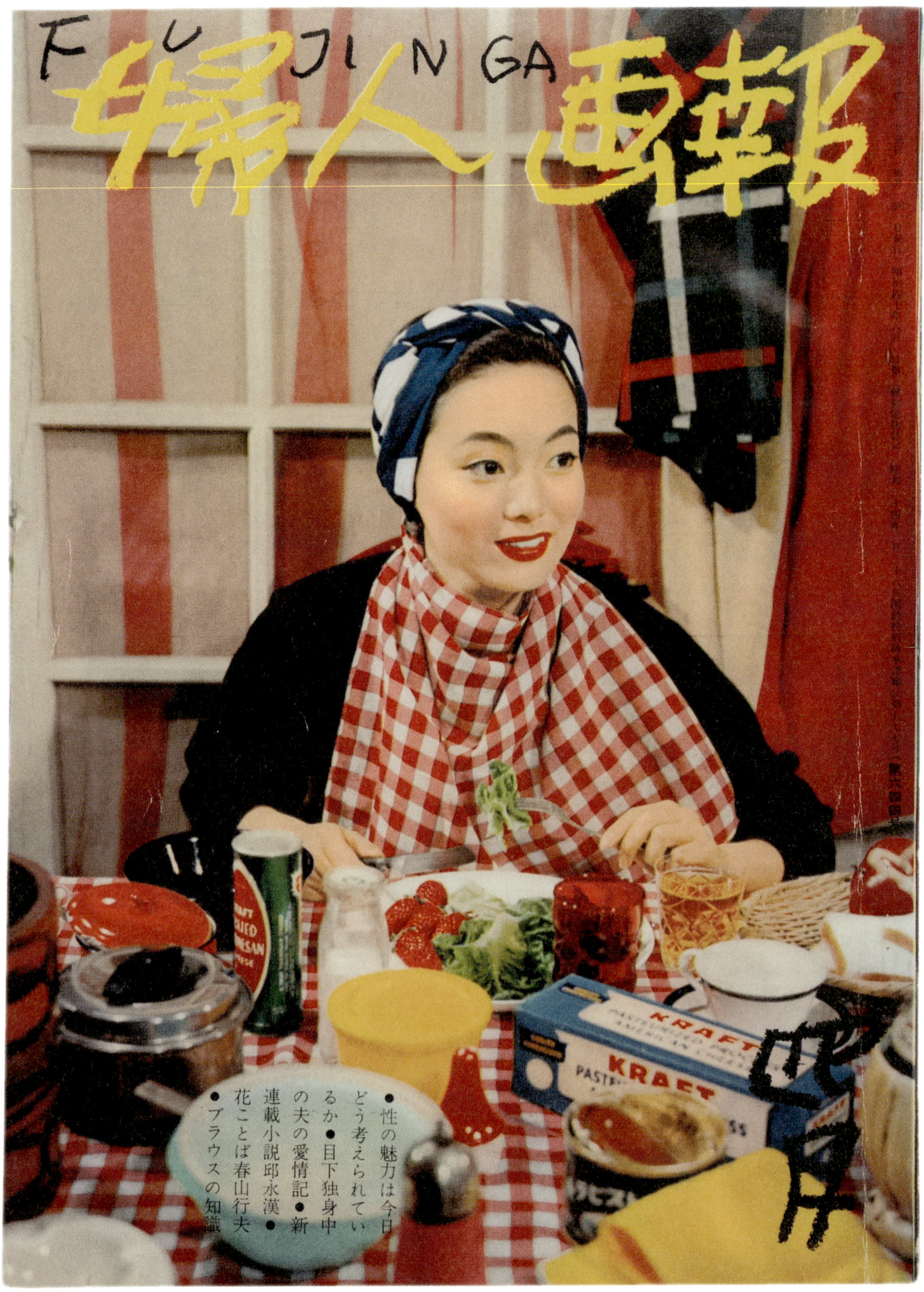

Fujin Gahō **婦人画報** cover art directed by Madame Masako. (Tokyo: Fujin Gahō 婦人画報, 1958).

Issues of Representation: Women in Graphic Design Post-War

Despite being underrepresented in the design press of the time, women were employed in design studios, as evinced by the photograph in the 1957 standalone graphic design-themed issue of *Atelier* 別冊アトリエ subtitled "From idea to completion" 発想から完成まで, showing a nameless female designer working on a layout in Kamekura Yūsaku's studio. A number of well-known male designers employed female designers and assistants, yet few women rose to prominence or were featured regularly in Japanese design publications until the careers of Ishioka Eiko 石岡瑛子 and Yamaguchi Harumi 山口はるみ exploded in the 1970s.

One of the few examples prewar was the French designer Charlotte Perriand, who left Paris upon its invasion in 1940 to work as the official advisor for industrial design to the Japanese Ministry for Trade and Industry. Having previously worked alongside Le Corbusier and Jean Prouvé, Perriand advised the government on raising the standards of design in Japanese industry to develop products for export. In 1941, she held an exhibition of her work titled "Selection, Tradition, Creation" at Tokyo's Takashimaya department store. Industrial designer Yanagi Sōri 柳宗理 worked as her assistant during Perriand's two-year stay in the capital. Perriand's approach to design indelibly informed the development of industrial design in Japan.

The employment ratio of women in urban areas in Japan hovered between 45% to 50% from 1955 to 1985, whereas the employment ratio for men in urban areas fluctuated between 82% to 86% during those same decades.[1] It is hard to interpret these statistics, though, since many households since before the Edo period and into the twentieth century operated family- or neighborhood-run businesses where participation in activities would be divided according to practicality. The proportion of Japanese women with a college education was low compared to women in the United States well through the 1970s.[2] These factors, combined with a corporate culture of overworking and late-night socializing that, compared to family-run workshops, provided no opportunity to combine roles, kept women in the background of corporate graphic design for decades postwar.

It was not until issue 28 of *Idea*, published in 1958, that female designers were featured in a Japanese graphic design magazine. The women represented were all freelance and were lumped together under the name "Shiroi-kai" 白い会, or "White Club." Each designed projects for the Mainichi Shimbun Newspaper Group, and the double-page spread includes twelve magazine cover designs by the eleven female designers: Tachibana Chieko 立花智恵子, Sekiguchi Emiko 関口恵美子, Kaneko Chie 金子智恵, Tanaka Mikiko 田中幹子, Sato Reiko 佐藤玲子, Okuno Reiko 奥野玲子, Akagi Tsurue 赤木都留江, Terashima Kazuko 寺島和子, Yamana Shūko 山名誘子, Kudo Megumi 工藤恵, and Sato Katsuko 佐藤勝子.

Their inclusion in this issue both illustrates and exacerbates issues of representation of women that were endemic to Japanese graphic design at that time. While women were included, they were randomly represented as a collective.

Tachibana Chieko would go on to write books about illustration and author a number of children's books. Kudo Megumi would go on to have a prolific career designing book covers, winning the Ministry of Trade and Industry Design Award for a poster design advertising sunscreen for the pharmaceutical company Taiyo.

A Geidai graduate, Okuno Reiko went on to work as a designer for the petroleum company San-Ai 三愛石油株式会社, crafting interior design projects and window displays. Later, she worked as a book designer, putting together a five-volume collection of books on the work of Takehisa Yumeji. She was an Incentive Award winner in the 1953 JAAC Exhibition and was interviewed in the 1955 first issue of *Living Design* magazine.

If we turn to one of the other notable design publications of that same year, the *1958 Annual of Advertising Art* in Japan, of the twenty-six individuals to receive an award, only one woman, Matsumoto Haruyo 松本春代, won a Bronze Medal for her range of packaging designs for skincare products manufactured by Kobayashi Kosé Cosmetic Co. Ltd.

MADAME MASAKO

One other woman was featured in the *Annual*—the mysteriously named Madame Masako マダムマサコ, art director of

1 Kamiya Hiroo and Eriko Ikeya, "Women's Participation in the Labour Force in Japan: Trends and Regional Patterns," *Geographical Review of Japan*, B, 67, no. 1 (1994): 15–34, https://doi.org/10.4157/grj1984b.67.15.

2 Samuel J. Coleman. "The Development of Japanese Educational Policy," In *Family Planning in Japanese Society: Traditional Birth Control in a Modern Urban Culture* (Princeton, NJ: Princeton University Press, 1983), 309–10.

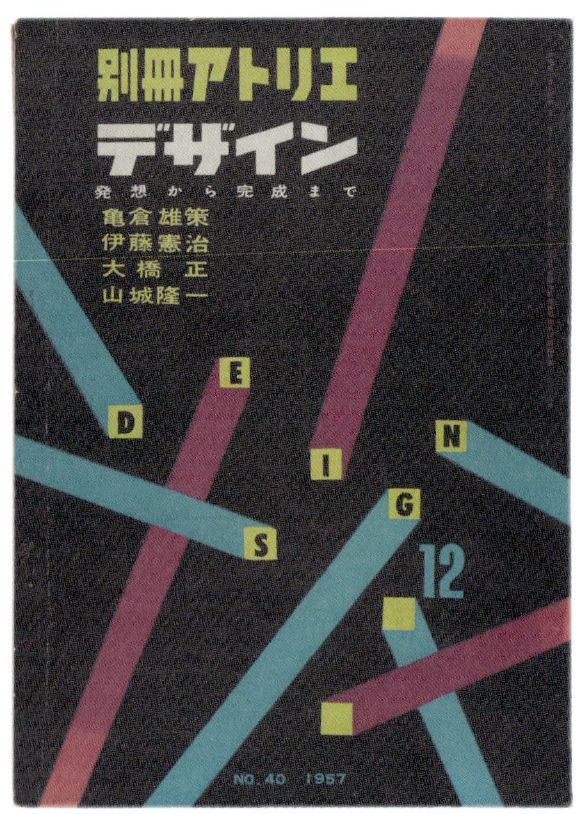

Fujin Gahō 婦人画報, a monthly magazine for women and one of Japan's oldest magazines. Born in 1916 in Horie, Osaka, she studied French literature and wrote for assorted women's magazines. She was a contributor to the fashion magazines *Soen* 装苑 and *Style* スタイル, both founded in 1936. *Style* was a leading fashion magazine founded in 1936 by female publisher Uno Chiyo 宇野千代 and was a tour de force of editorial design in the 1930s. The masthead was drawn by Tōgō Seiji 東郷青児, and each issue featured design and illustration contributions from Léonard Tsuguharu Foujita 藤田嗣治 and a revolving cast of both fine artists and commercial artists. Madame Masako's serialized column for *Style*, "Mode Guide," was collected into a book titled *Mode Guide 1* モード案内・1 in 1950, featuring a cover design by Hans Arp that was art directed by Madame Masako.

Madame Masako had previously opened a retail dressmaking store in Tokyo's Ginza district in the 1940s, with a sign reading "American Francais a la mode Tailor and Dressmaker Couturier Madame Masaco," and her establishment solidified her presence as a fashion tastemaker. She was rumored to

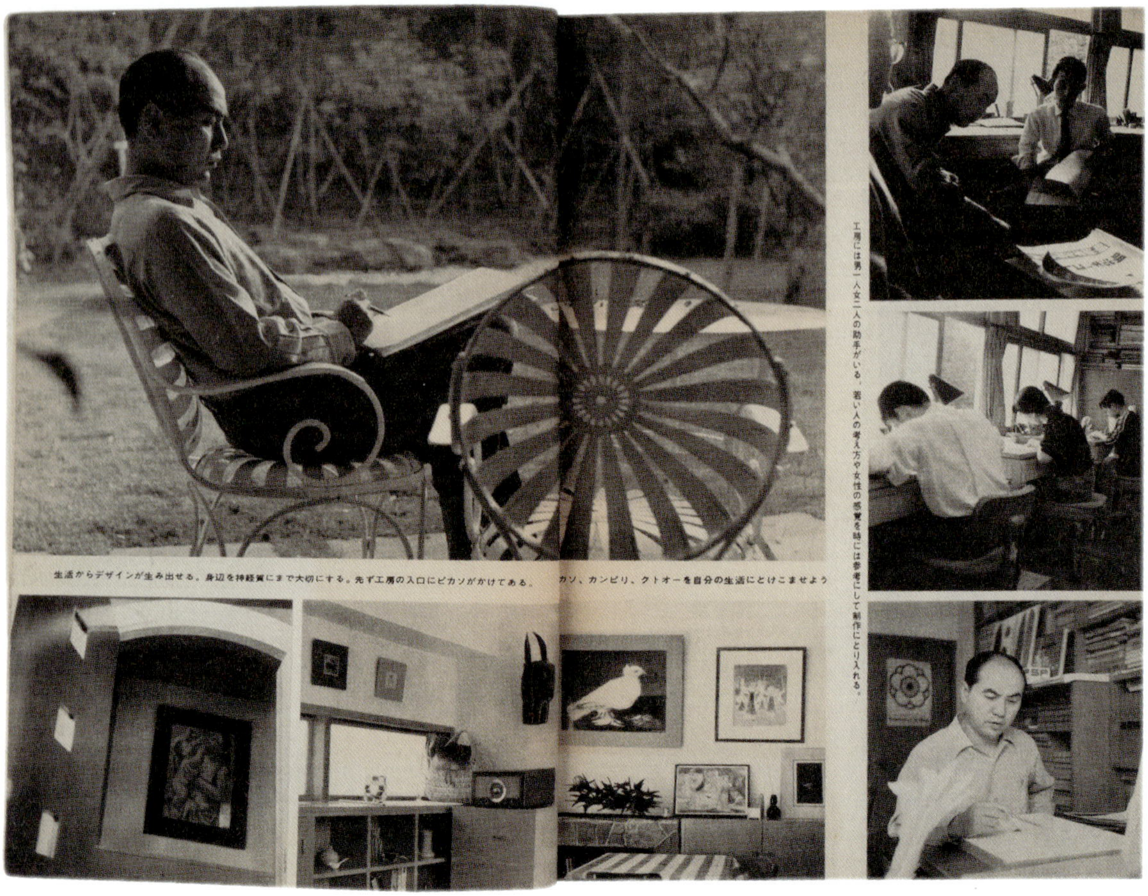

工房には男一人女二人の助手がいる。若い人の考え方や女性の感覚を時には参考にして制作にとり入れる。

生活からデザインが生み出せる。身辺を神経質にまで大切にする。先ず工房の入口にピカソがかけてある。 カソ、カンピリ、クトオーを自分の生活にとけこませよう

Cover and spreads from ***Atelier: From Idea to Completion* 別冊アトリエ 発想から完成まで** (Tokyo: Atelier Publishing アトリエ出版社, 1957).

have legally changed her name to her pen name around this time, as well, having zealously guarded her given name, which began with "T."

In the early 1950s, Madame Masako spent a few years living in Paris, reporting for *Fujin Gahō* on the fashion scene and the French fashion press, including a feature about the editorial offices of *Vogue* magazine. She studied art, design, and couture fashion at Académie Julian, a private atelier art school in Paris, relating her findings in the column "Paris Note" 巴里ノート in *Fujin Gahō*, exploring materials, tools, design directions, and her own analysis of the latest design and fashion trends.

Upon her return to Japan in 1954, she was charged with art directing *Fujin Gahō*'s magazine covers due to her experiences in France and her desire to steer Japanese fashion design toward a more developed expression of elegance. She continued to write for the magazine through the 1960s and was a regular columnist for the magazine *Ginza Hyakuten* 銀座百点. The photographer Domon Ken 土門拳 wrote a brief essay in homage to Madame Masako in his 1974 book *Dying and Living* 死ぬことと生きること illustrated with her portrait.

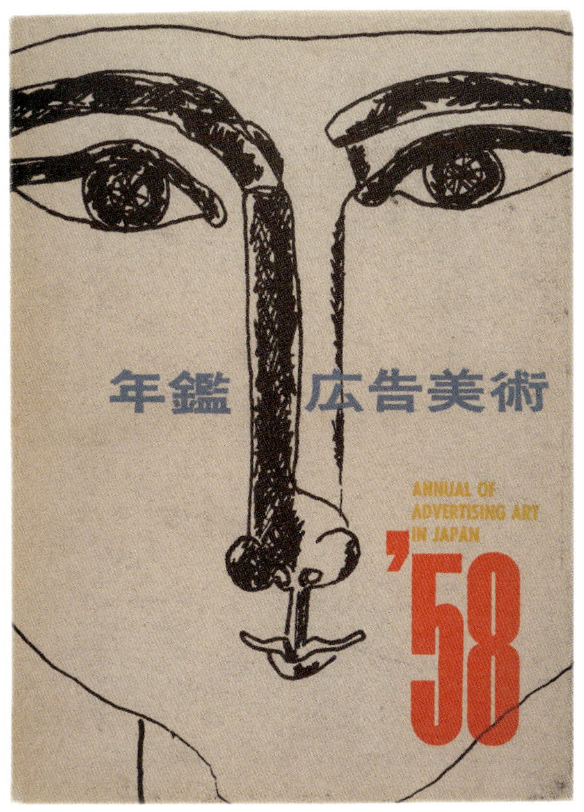

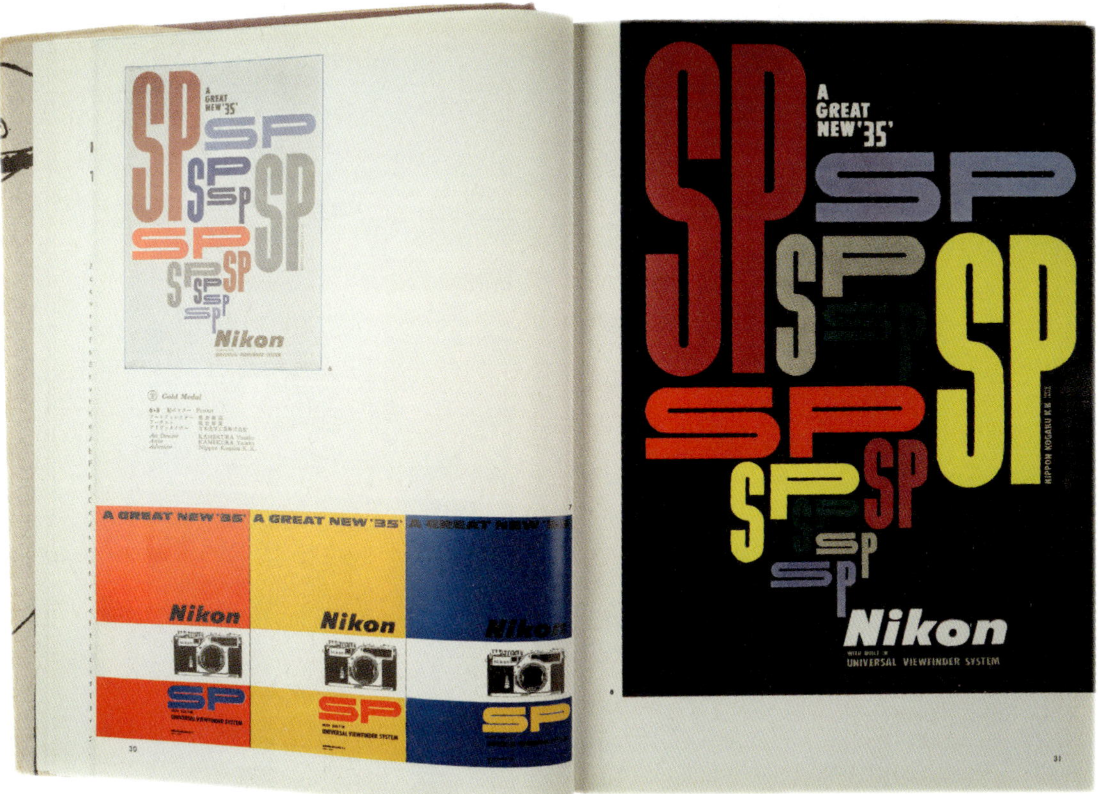

Top: ***Annual of Advertising Art** '58* (Tokyo: Bijutsu Shuppansha 美術出版社, 1959). Cover illustration by Hayakawa Yoshio and layout by Kamekura Yūsaku. Bottom: Kamekura's award-winning works from ***Annual of Advertising Art** '58* (Tokyo: Bijutsu Shuppansha 美術出版社, 1959).

白 い 会
SHIROI KAI

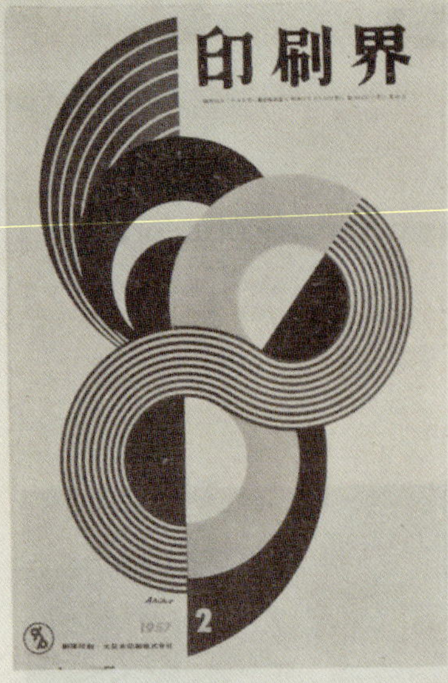

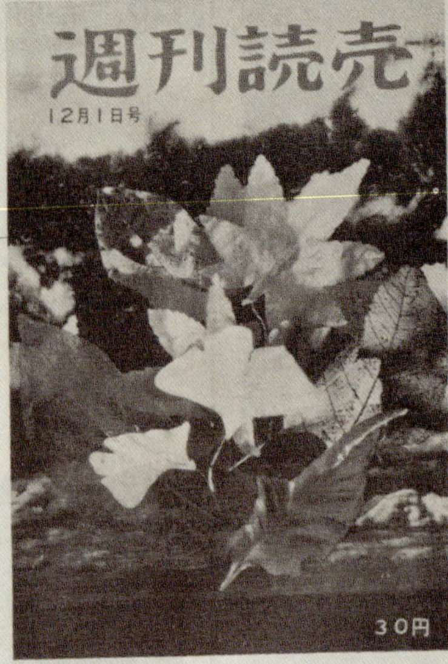

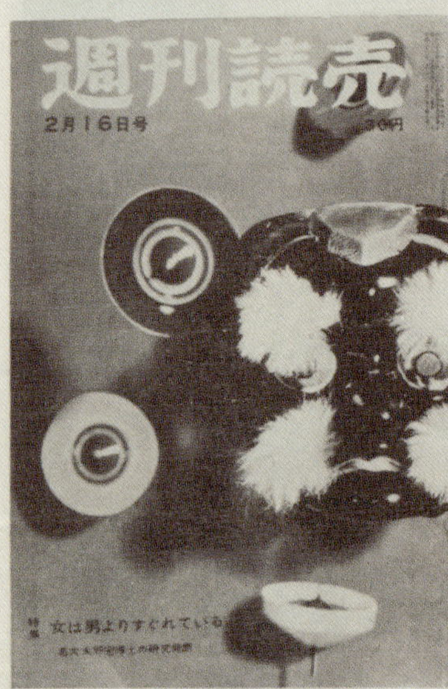

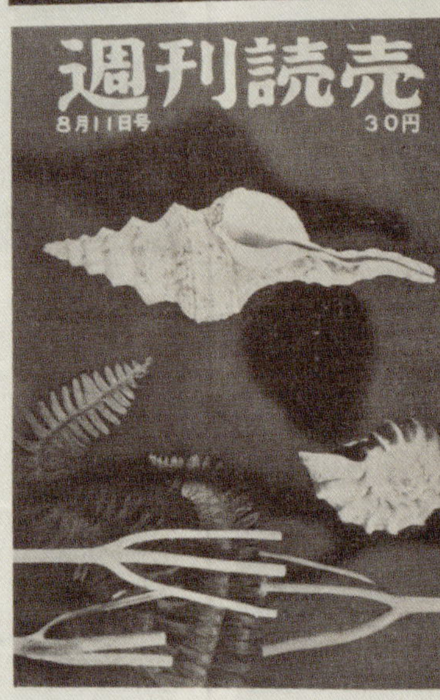

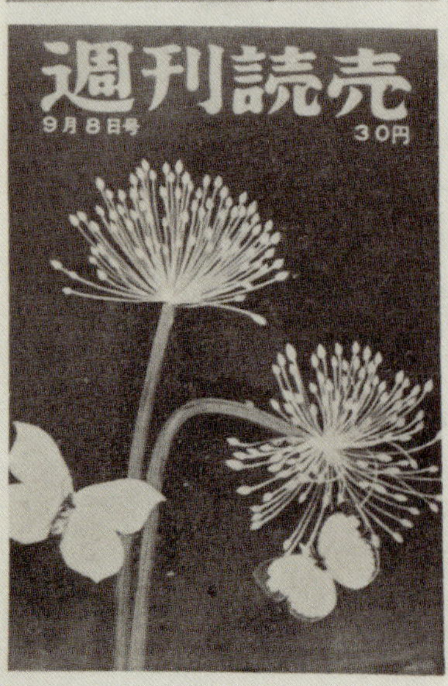

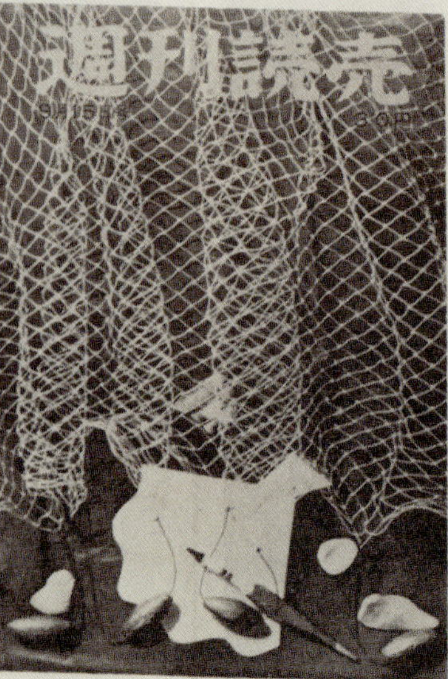

122. 立 花 智 恵 子 (旧姓秋保)
CHIEKO TACHIBANA

1930 年生。
お茶の水 女子大化学科卒後 亀倉雄策氏に師事、現在フリー。
文京区丸山町 6

333 雑誌表紙・日本印刷新聞社

333) Magazine cover for Nihon Printing Newspaper Co., Ltd.

123. 関 口 恵 美 子
EMIKO SEKIGUCHI

早稲田大学工芸美術図案科卒、東京美術学校工芸講習所卒。
現在フリー。
豊島区雑司ヶ谷 3 ノ 527

334 雑誌表紙・読売新聞社

334) Cover of the weekly magazine for Yomiuri Newspaper Co., Ltd.

124. 金 子 智 恵
CHIE KANEKO

文化学院卒。
現在フリー。
世田ヶ谷区松原町 2 ノ 618

335 雑誌表紙・読売新聞社

335) Cover of the weekly magazine for Yomiuri Newspaper Co., Ltd.

125. 田 中 幹 子
MIKIKO TANAKA

山口女子専門学校国語科卒。
花王石鹸株式会社宣伝部勤務。
新宿区柏木 4 ノ 927 柏荘

336 雑誌表紙・読売新聞社

336) Cover of the weekly magazine for Yomiuri Newspaper Co., Ltd.

126. 佐 藤 玲 子
REIKO SATO

文化学院美術科卒。大智浩氏に師事。
杉並区大宮前 6 ノ 353

337 雑誌表紙・読売新聞社

337) Cover of the weekly magazine for Yomiuri Newspaper Co., Ltd.

127. 奥 野 玲 子
REIKO OKUNO

東京美術学校図案科卒。
株式会社三愛宣伝部勤務。
中野区昭和通 1 ノ 25

338 雑誌表紙・読売新聞社

338) Cover of the weekly magazine for Yomiuri Newspaper Co., Ltd.

82

The first female graphic designers featured in *Idea*. ***Idea* アイデア *No.* 28** (Tokyo: Seibundo Shinkosha 誠文堂新光社, 1958).

128. 赤木都留江
TSURUE AKAGI

台北第一高女卒。
ナショナル金銭登録機 K.K. 広告課。
大田区西六郷 1 ノ 1

339 雑誌表紙・読売新聞社

339) Cover of the weekly magazine for Yomiuri Newspaper Co., Ltd.

129. 寺島和子
KAZUKO TERASHIMA

東京都立鷺の宮高校卒業後、宮永岳彦氏に師事。現在に至る。
港区芝高輪西台町 33 梅里荘

340 雑誌表紙・読売新聞社
342 〃 〃

340) Cover of the weekly magazine for Yomiuri Newspaper Co., Ltd.
342) 〃 〃

130. 山名琇子
SHUKO YAMANA

文化学院美術科卒。
桑沢デザイン研究所卒。
亀倉雄策氏に師事、ブリジストンタイヤ、その他を経て、現在フリー。
足立区南宮城町 44

341 雑誌表紙・読売新聞社

341) Cover of the weekly magazine for Yomiuri Newspaper Co., Ltd

333	334
335	336
337	338

339	340
341	342
343	344

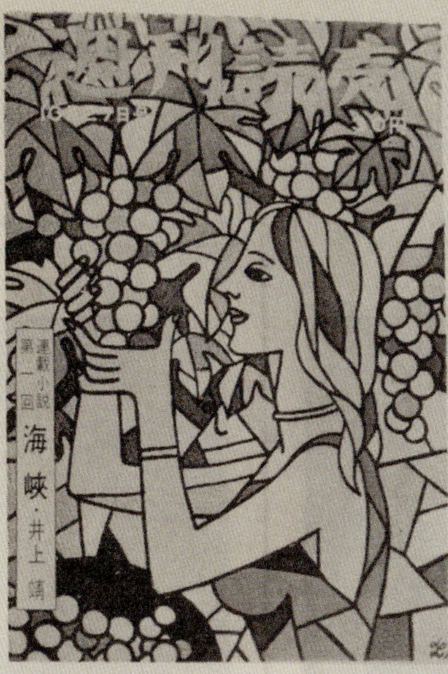

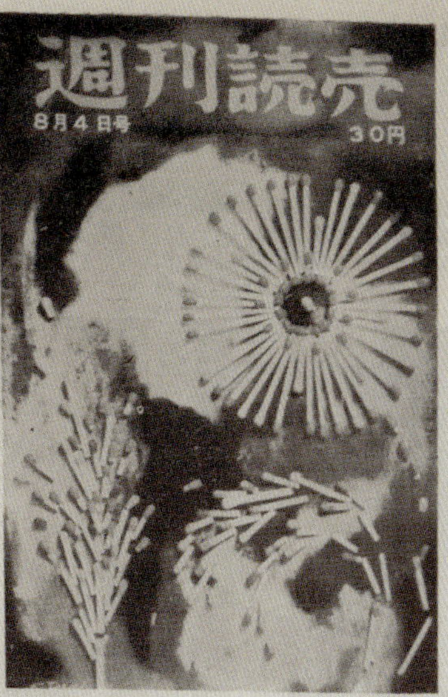

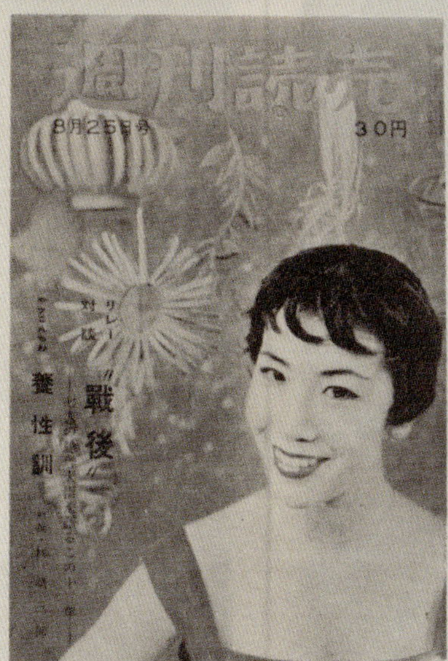

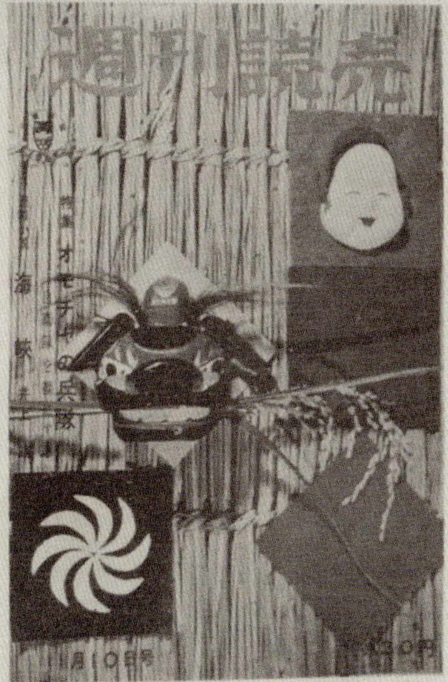

131. 工藤恵
MEGUMI KUDO

東京芸術大学図案科卒。
森永製菓広告部勤務。
新宿区下落合 3 ノ 1417

343 雑誌表紙・読売新聞社

343) Cover of the weekly magazine for Yomiuri Newspaper Co., Ltd

132. 佐藤勝子
KATSUKO SATO

女子美術専門学校卒。
現在フリー。
墨田区厩橋 3 ノ 8

344 雑誌表紙・読売新聞社

344) Cover of the weekly magazine for Yomiuri Newspaper Co., Ltd.

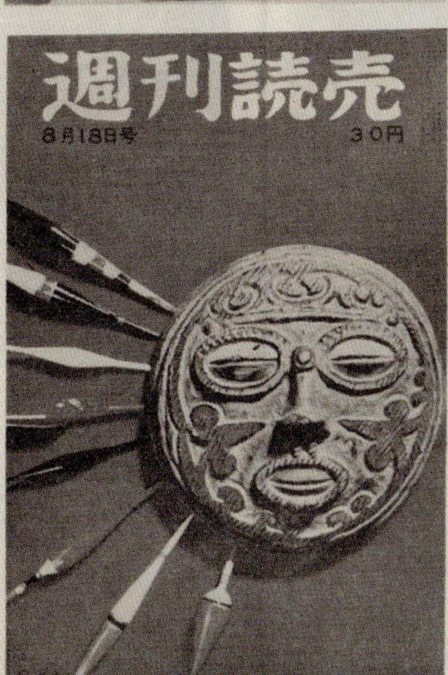

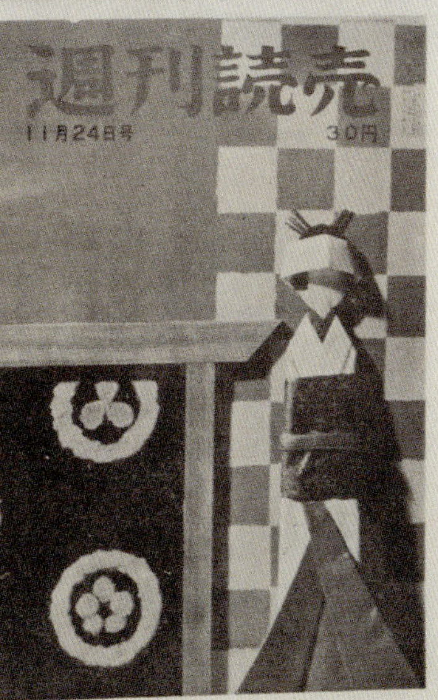

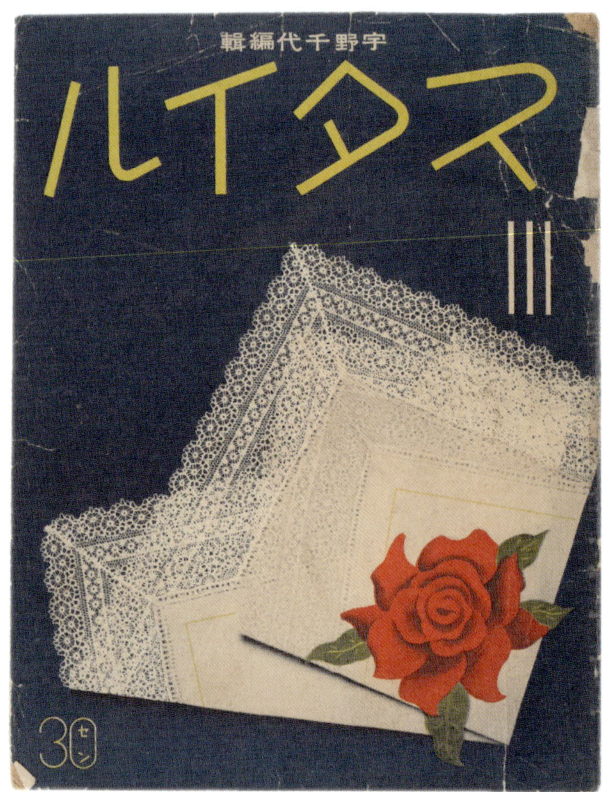

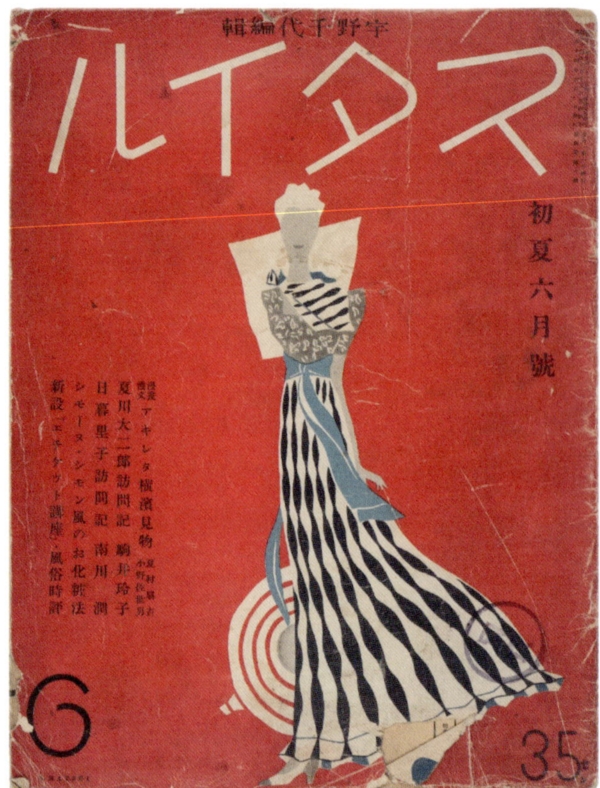

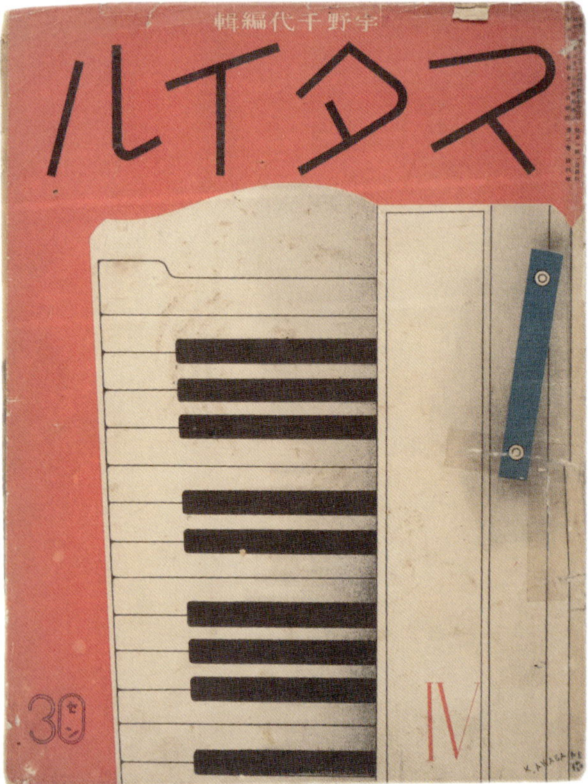

Madame Masako authored over a dozen books on fashion and design throughout the 1950s and 1960s.

Female representation in the mainstream Japanese graphic design press remained nominal throughout the late 1950s and early 1960s. The work of one lone woman, Tahira Haruyo 多比良春代 was included in the *1958 Annual of Advertising Art in Japan*. The *1960 Annual* featured the work of two women, Kusaka Mitsuko 日下光子 and Matsumoto Harumi 松本晴海. (This is her maiden name—Matsumoto became Yamaguchi Harumi 山口はるみ and rose to prominence as an illustrator in the 1970s and 1980s.) It wasn't until 1963 that a woman would be featured in the *Annual* again, with the work of powerhouse calligrapher and artist Shinoda Toko 篠田桃紅.

It took until 1965 for Ishioka Eiko to win the Japan Advertising Artists Club's fifteenth JAAC competition/exhibition—the first time for a woman—and for her winning poster series to be covered widely in the Japanese design press.

Assorted covers of ***Style* スタイル** designed by Ono Saseo 小野佐世男, published by Uno Chiyo 宇野千代 in the mid-1930s.

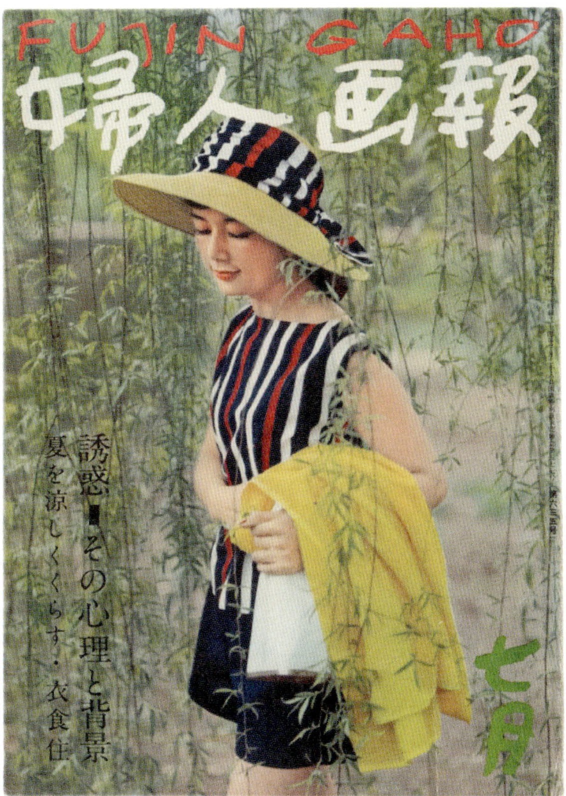

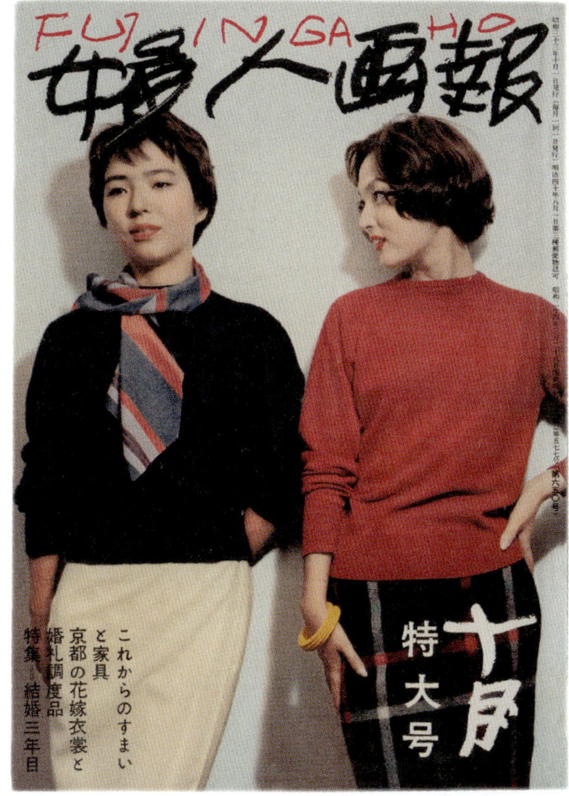

References:

Annual of Advertising Art in Japan '58. Tokyo: Bijutsu Shuppan-Sha, 1958.

Chisho, Chisa. Madamu Masako ga ita jidai, 2019. https://madamemasaco.hatena-diary.com/.

Masako, Madamu. *Oshare Annai: Haikaratoha dō Suru Koto Ka*. Tokyo: Kōbunsha, 1956.

Kon, Wajirō, and Haley Blum. "Roundtable: young women designers speak (1956)." *Review of Japanese Culture and Society*, vol. 28, 2016, p. 128+.

Kon, Wajirō. "Zadankai: wakai josei dezaina wa kataru," Ribingu dezain (*Living Design*), no. 1 (1956): 31–38.

Top: ***Fujin Gahō* 婦人画報** covers art directed by Madame Masako (Tokyo: Fujin Gahō 婦人画報, 1958). Bottom: Cover of ***Fashion Guide Part 2* モード案内〈第2〉**, **Madame Masako マダムマサコ**, cover design by Hans Arp, art direction by Madame Masako (Tokyo: Fujin Gahō 婦人画報, 1952).

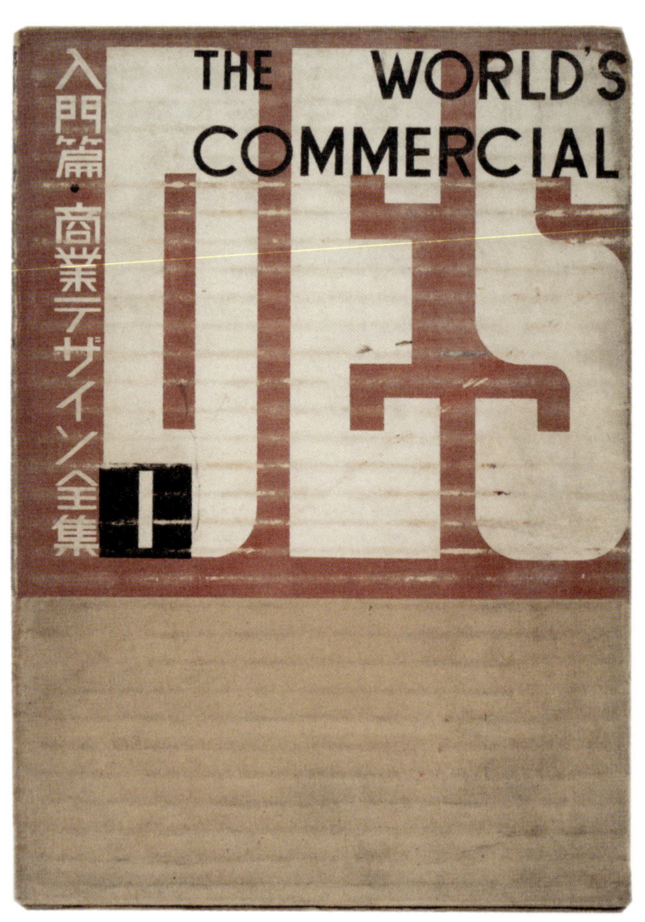

Shōgyō Dezain Zenshū No. 1 (The World's Commercial Design) 商業デザイン全集 (Tokyo: David-sha ダヴィッド社, 1953). Slipcover design by Hara Hiromu 原弘.

SHŌGYŌ DESIGN ZENSHŪ 商業デザイン全集

The next great publication series that emerged postwar was *Shōgyō Design Zenshū*, titled *The World's Commercial Design* in English and published from 1953 to 1954. Five issues were released, each volume housed in a protective cardboard slipcover adorned with a typographic design by Hara Hiromu. Within the slipcover, each volume was bound in a blind-debossed, gold-foil-stamped, and screen-printed hardcover with monochromatic spot color, and four-color process printing on the pages within. It was published by the Evening Star Publishing House イブニングスター社, which released a range of titles devoted to photography and satire.

Within *Shōgyō Design Zenshū*, foreign and domestic design work were placed side by side, creating a literal in-step reference for how Japanese design fit into the global continuum.

Shōgyō Design Zenshū was the vehicle for introducing much contemporary work to Japanese designers, particularly Herbert Matter's work for the Container Corporation of America. Designers such as Paul Rand, AM Cassandre, Raymond Savignac, and many others were featured within.

The editorial committee comprised Arai Sen 新井泉, Hara Hiromu, Hijikata Teiichi 土方定一, Imatake Shichirō, Katsumi Masaru, Kamekura Yūsaku, Kōno Takashi, Koike Shinji 小池新二, Takiguchi Shūzō 滝口修造, and Yamana Ayao. Advisors to the publication were Kon Wajirō, Miyashita Takao 宮下孝雄, Onchi Kōshirō, Sugiura Hisui, and Wada Sanzō.

The bulk of *Shōgyō Design Zenshū* was devoted to graphic design work, while the approximate rear third of each volume was dedicated to critical writings about topics including design and printing processes, public relations, histories of specific designers' legacies, packaging design, the design of retail spaces, approaches to applied pattern, profiles of foreign designers—Paul Rand, Herbert Matter, E. McKnight Kauffer, AM Cassandre, Jean Carlu, and others—and, in the final issue, an essay about the influence of Pablo Picasso on commercial design.

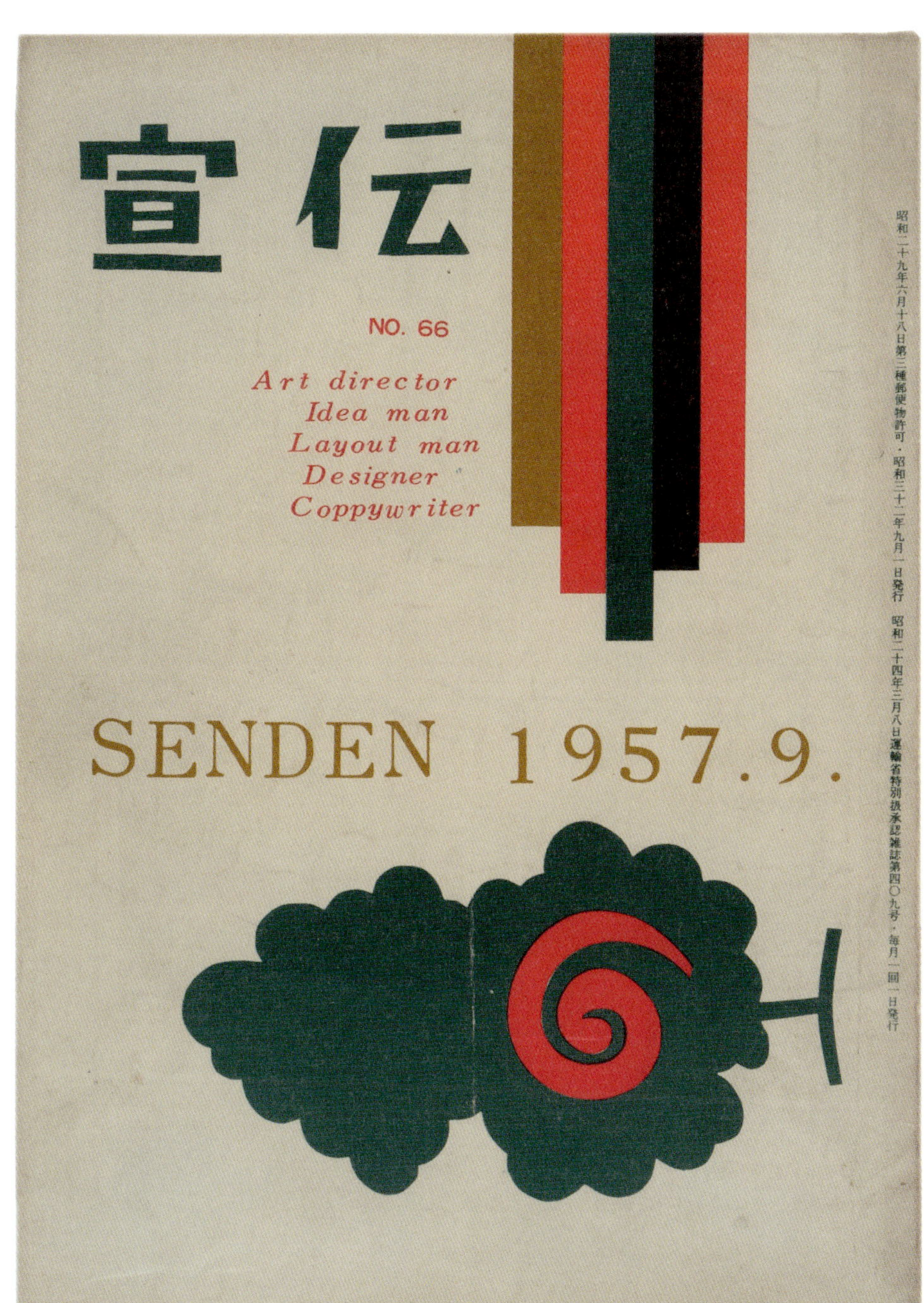

SENDEN 宣伝

1954

The advertising magazine *Senden* 宣伝 was launched in 1954, later renamed *Sendenkaigi* 宣伝会議. *Senden* was wide-ranging in its subject matter, exploring advertising-oriented design, marketing, art direction, conceptual thinking, copywriting, and production design. In contrast, today's version of the magazine is devoted to "brand communication." The magazine was the springboard for the eponymous publishing house which would go on to publish additional titles devoted to various aspects of promotion, public relations, and advertising.

September 1957 issue of ***Senden* 宣伝**.

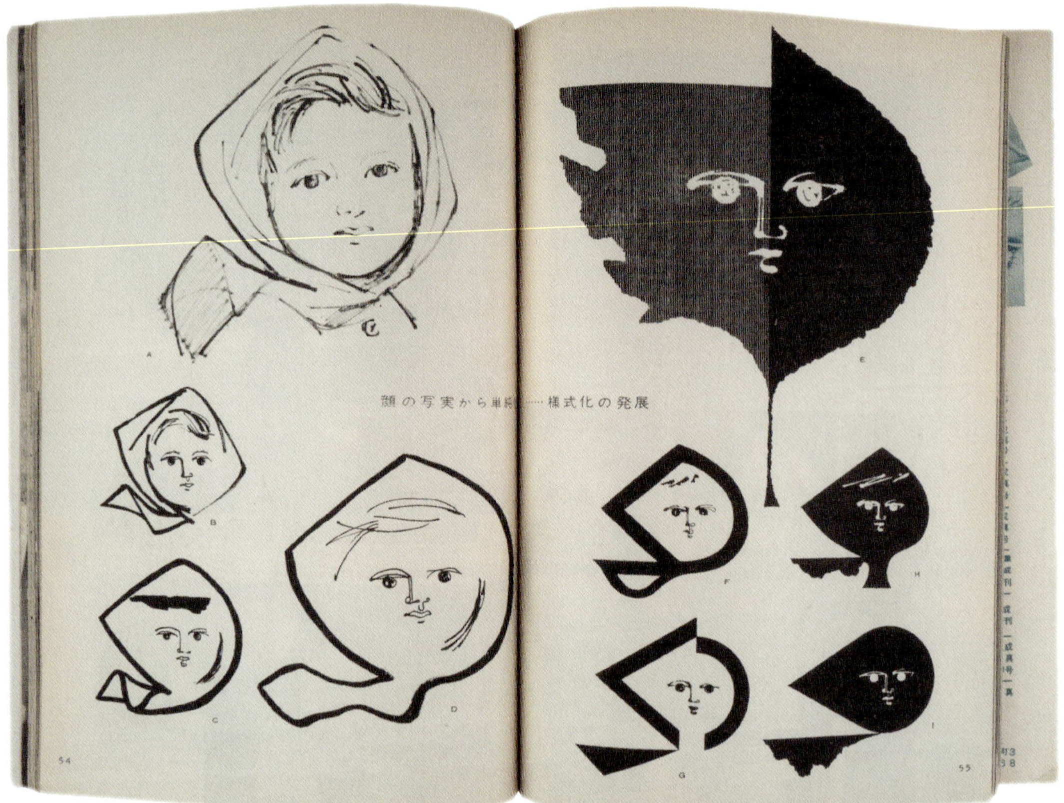

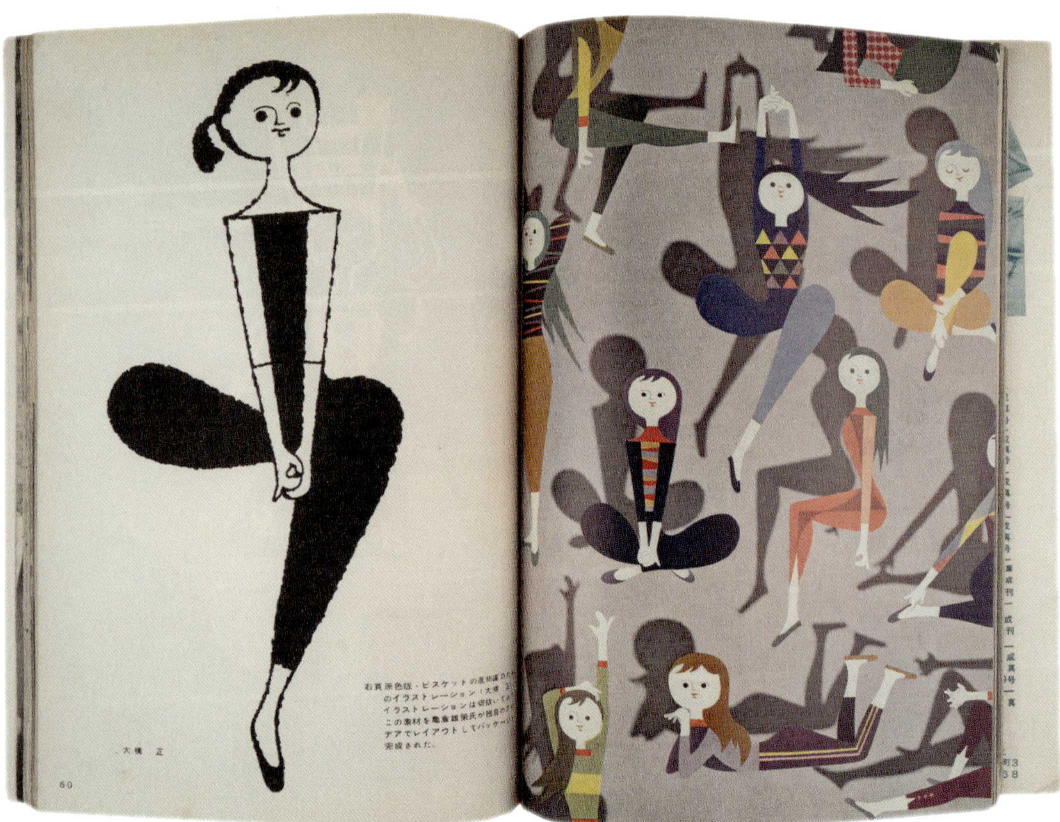

Spreads of illustration work by Hayakawa Yoshio 早川良雄 from ***Bessatsu Atelier: From Idea to Completion* 別冊アトリエ 発想から完成まで** (Tokyo: Atelier Publishing アトリエ出版社, 1957).

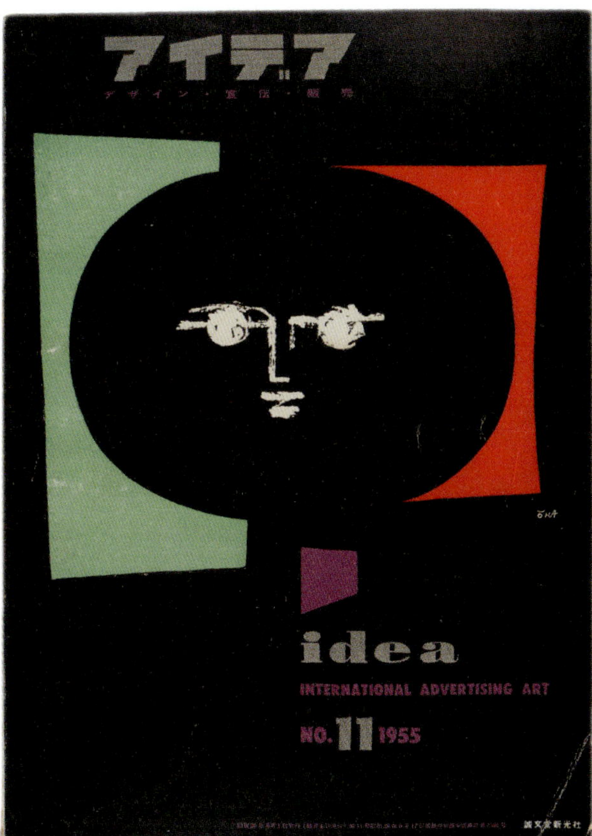

Idea アイデア No. 12 (Tokyo: Seibundo Shinkosha 誠文堂新光社, 1955).
Cover design by Hayakawa Yoshio 早川良雄.

HAYAKAWA YOSHIO 早川良雄

1917–2009

Hayakawa Yoshio was born in Osaka. He enrolled in the Osaka Municipal Crafts and Design Design Department in 1931 and was trained in the then-new Bauhaus methods by Yamaguchi Masaki 山口マサキ. After graduating, Hayakawa joined Mitsukoshi Department Store's Osaka division, where he was put in charge of window display design and spatial arrangement for the stage and interiors.

Hayakawa was conscripted into the army during World War II. He joined the Kintetsu Department Store Advertising Division after a brief stint working for Osaka City Hall upon his return from the front. Shortly thereafter, he married Chihata Ume 千畑梅, designer Imatake Shichirō's longtime assistant.

Hayakawa participated in the Graphic '55 exhibition and the World Design Conference of 1960, and he was a founding member of the Japan Advertising Artists Club. In 1985, the publishing company Kōdansha 株式会社講談社 released a book on Hayakawa's graphic work titled *The World of Hayakawa Yoshio* 早川良雄の世界, and Hayakawa released a book of essays, *Feeling the Edges* 徒然感覚, the following year. He held a career retrospective exhibition at the Ginza Graphic Gallery in Tokyo in 2006.

References:

Hayakawa, Yoshio. *Hayakawa Yoshio no Shigoto to shūhen*. Tokyo: Rikuyōsha, 1999.

Hayakawa, Yoshio. *Yoshio Hayakawa*. Tokyo: Ginza Graphic Gallery, 2003.

Kamekura, Yūsaku, and Ayao Yamana. *Gurafikku Dezain no Seiki: Bunshō to Danwa to Sakuhin De kōsei: Meiji Sedai Yamana Ayao Sugiura Hisui Kara shōwa Sedai Made*. Tokyo: Bijutsu Shuppansha, 2008.

Segi, Shin'ichi, Tanaka Ikkō, and Hiroshi Sano. *Nissenbi no Jidai = The Epoch of the Japan Advertising Artists Club: Nihon No Gurafikku Dezain 1951–70*. Tokyo: Toransuāto, 2000.

Shibukawa, Ikuyoshi, and Ryoichi Enomoto. "Memory of Yoshio Hayakawa." *Idea* 58, no. 340 (May 2010): 205–12.

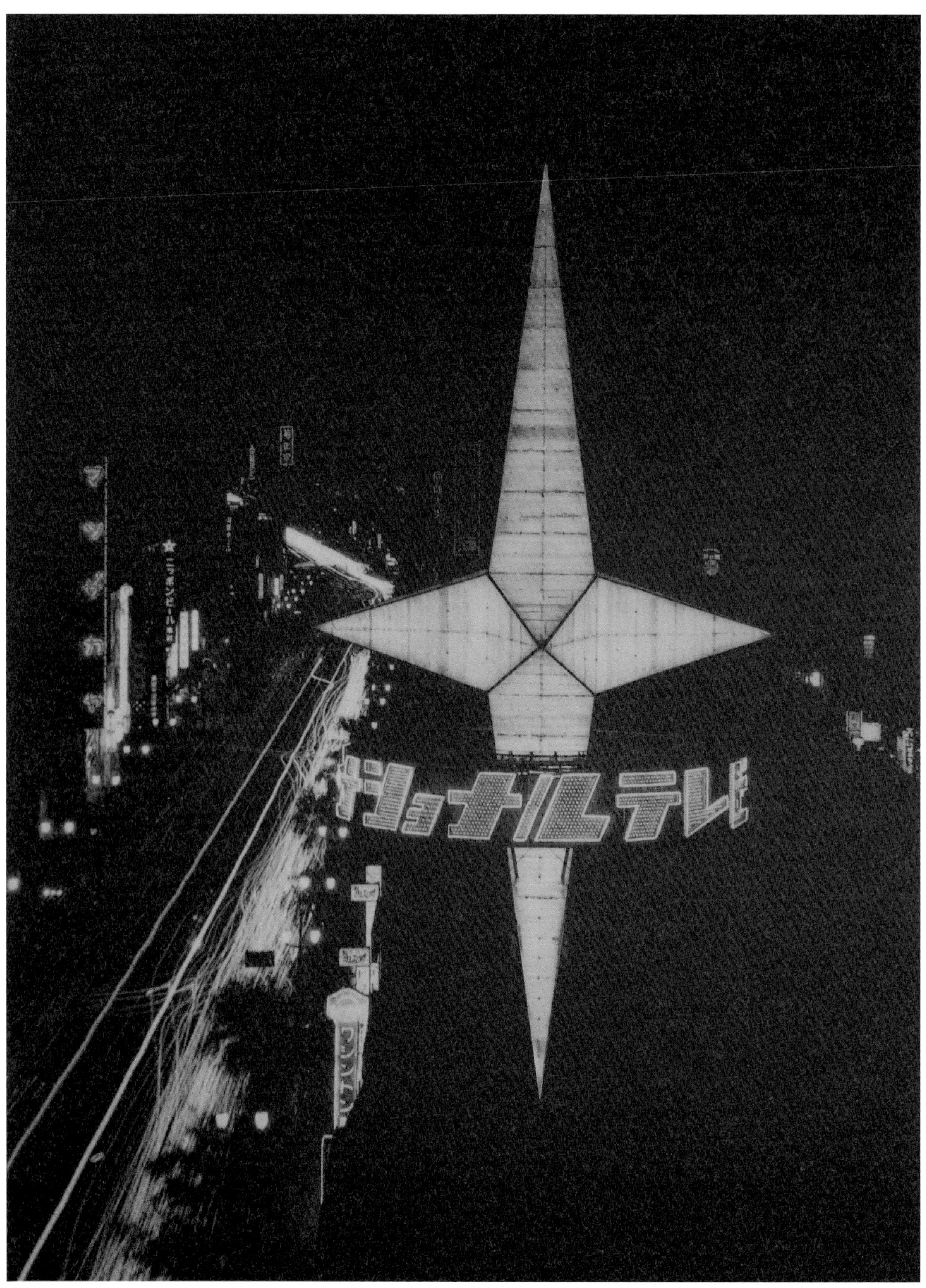

1953 Matsushita Electrical Corporation signage in Ginza from ***Brilliant Color of Design: Works of Kenji Itoh* 伊藤憲治・デザインの華麗多彩** (Tokyo: Rikyusha 六耀社, 1986).

ITŌ KENJI 伊藤憲治

1915–2001

Itō Kenji (spelled "Itoh Kenji" in his lifetime) was born in Tokyo. He graduated from the Tokyo High School of Arts and Crafts, a vocational school where he studied carpentry, and went on to study in the Department of Engineering at Tokyo Industrial Arts College (now Chiba University), from which he graduated in 1935.

Itō worked as a freelance graphic designer from 1935 to 1943, designing magazine covers for *Nutrition and Cooking* 栄養と料理 and *Aviation Japan* 飛行日本, while also creating window display designs for Mitsukoshi department stores. He was drafted into the army and was in active service from 1943 through 1945. After the end of World War II, Itō returned to freelance design work, garnering national attention with his cover designs for the women's magazine *Fujin Asahi* 婦人朝日 from 1950 through 1952.

Itō held a solo exhibition called *The Work of Itoh Kenji* 伊藤憲治作品展 at the Shiseido Gallery in Ginza in 1951, focusing on his magazine cover designs. He joined the nascent Japan Advertising Artists Club that same year. Itō's work was featured in the German graphic design magazine *Gebrauchsgrafik* in 1952.

A technically proficient illustrator, lettering artist, and award-winning photographer, Itō developed a singular approach to hybrid illustration and photomontage informed by the Surrealist sensibilities of French painter Pierre Roy. His work mixed silhouetted illustration, deft airbrush work, and staged photography in a manner that was highly integrated and visually seamless.

Beginning in 1952, he designed posters and advertising materials for the textile manufacturer Daido and window display designs for the retailer Ginza Wako, and he became visiting lecturer at his alma mater for three years.

Itō was a prolific magazine cover designer. He designed many covers for the long-running magazine *Industrial Art News* 工芸ニュース and designed a new cover each month for the pharmaceutical company Sankyo's medical magazine *Stethoscope* for thirty-four years—560 covers in total. He was also the designer of the very first cover for *Idea* magazine when it launched in 1953.

Itō won a design competition for the Matsushita Electrical Corporation in that same year, and his massive four-pointed star design was installed conspicuously atop the tony Ginza neighborhood's 4-chōme corner, one of the most significant symbols of Tokyo's economic reconstruction. The Matsushita sign led to a large number of neon sign design projects that would help define Itō's later career. He designed an incredible number of massive animated neon signs for major Japanese corporations such as Sankyo, Toshiba, Teijin, NSK, and NEC from the 1950s through the 1980s, many pushing the possibilities of design, technology, and engineering in highly innovative ways.

Itō's work largely helped to define the corporate aesthetic of the Japanese postwar camera industry. In 1954, he designed the logo for the Canon camera company—still in use today—alongside a host of promotional posters, print ads, and packaging designs for the company throughout the 1950s and early 1960s. Itō also designed the corporate identity for the camera company Yashica, from their packaging, print advertising, and promotional materials, posters, to the Yashica corporate headquarters' neon sign design.

Projects that Itō designed were found in homes and on the street—from packaging for Nescafé instant coffee, to the logo and packaging for Furuya candies, to packaging for Asahi beer. Itō participated in a wide array of both solo and group exhibitions, including the groundbreaking *Graphic '55* show which helped to make "graphic design" a popular term in Japan. Itō won numerous awards throughout his career—notably the Mainichi Design Award consecutively in 1955 and 1956—and a retrospective monograph called *The Brilliant Color of Design: Works of Kenji Itoh* 伊藤憲治·デザインの華麗多彩 was published in 1986.

An avid golf enthusiast until the end, Itō passed away in 2001.

References:

Itō Kenji. *Itō Kenji Dezain no Karei Tasai*. Tokyo: Rikuyosha, 1986.

Kamekura, Yūsaku, and Ayao Yamana. *Gurafikku Dezain no Seiki: Bunshō to Danwa to Sakuhin De kōsei: Meiji Sedai Yamana Ayao Sugiura Hisui Kara shōwa Sedai Made*. Tokyo: Bijutsu Shuppansha, 2008.

Segi, Shin'ichi, Tanaka Ikkō, and Hiroshi Sano. *Nissenbi no Jidai = The Epoch of the Japan Advertising Artists Club: Nihon No Gurafikku Dezain 1951–70*. Tokyo: Toransuāto, 2000.

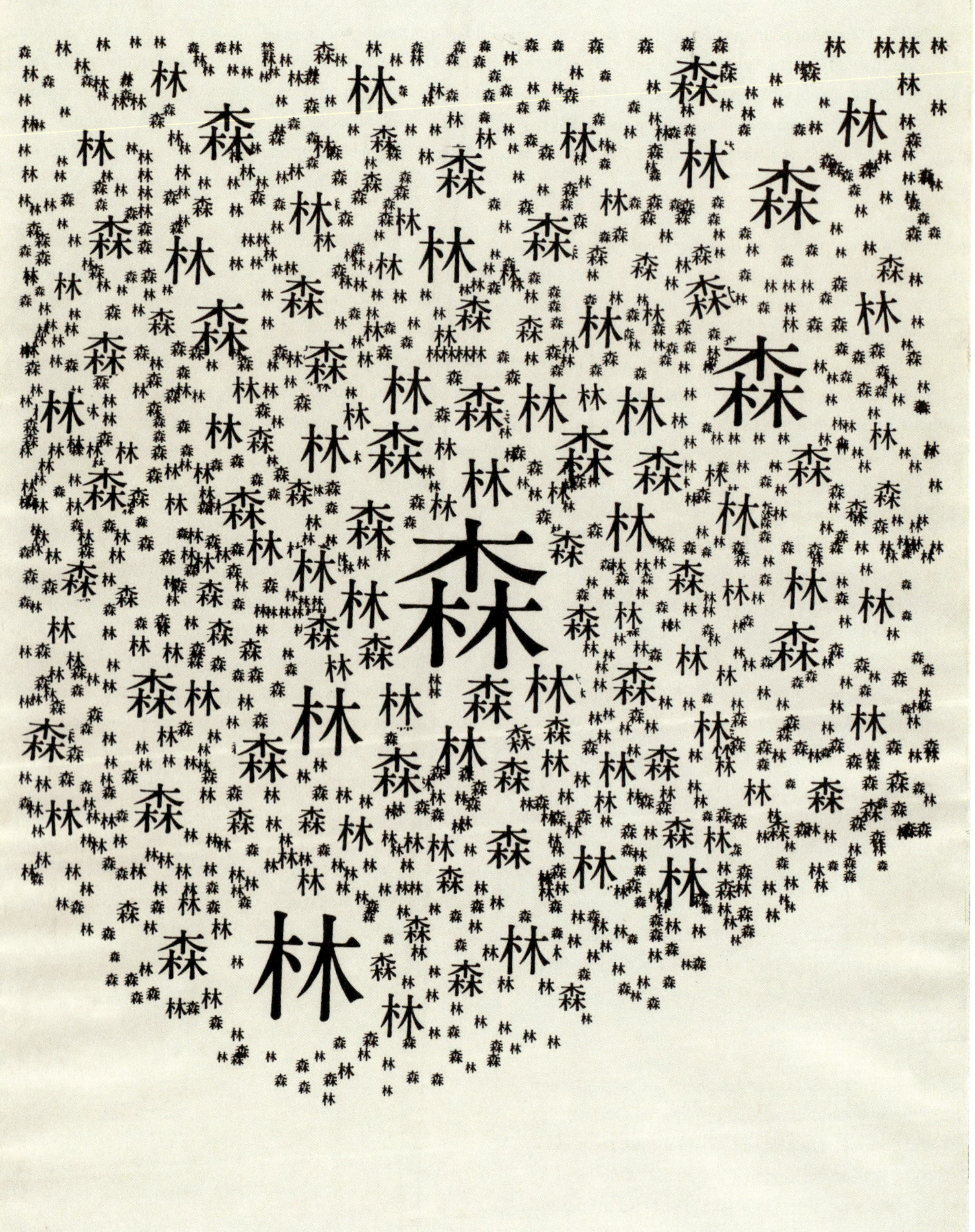

***Forest* 森·林** poster by Yamashiro Ryūichi 山城隆一, 1954.

YAMASHIRO RYŪICHI 山城隆一

1920–1997

Yamashiro Ryūichi was born in 1920 in Osaka. He studied at the Municipal Polytechnic Osaka, graduating in 1938.

He worked for a time for the Hankyu and Takashimaya department stores' advertising divisions and then went freelance in 1952, working for Toshiba Electrical Works, Toyota Automobiles, Fuji Steel Mills, and others. Yamashiro exhibited as one of the members of the *Graphic '55* exhibition in 1955.

Yamashiro was responsible for the exhibition graphics for the Japanese pavilion at Expo 58, the 1958 World's Fair in Brussels. The following year, Yamashiro became one of the founding members of the Nippon Design Center, where he served as design advisor to Asahi Chemical and Toshiba. Yamashiro designed the covers of the *Asahi Journal* for a number of years.

Yamashiro is best remembered for his 1961 tree-planting campaign poster *Hayashi-Mori* 森·林 that was exhibited in *documenta III* in Kassel, Germany. A large portion of his later career was dominated by self-initiated works using a mix of collage, paintings, and illustrations of cats.

Yamashiro is best remembered for his 1961 tree-planting campaign poster *Hayashi-Mori* 森·林 was exhibited in *documenta III* in Kassel, Germany, yet a large portion of his career was dominated by works using collage and with cats as a running theme.

Yamashiro received the Purple Ribbon Medal in 1985 and the Fourth Order of Merit, Cordon of the Rising Sun in 1993 from the Japanese government. He held a solo exhibition, *Ryuichi Yamashiro Solo Exhibition: The Portrait of the Cat*, at Seibu's Shibuya department store the same year.

References:

Kamekura, Yūsaku, and Ayao Yamana. *Gurafikku Dezain no Seiki: Bunshō to Danwa to Sakuhin De kōsei: Meiji Sedai Yamana Ayao Sugiura Hisui Kara shōwa Sedai Made*. Tokyo: Bijutsu Shuppansha, 2008.

Segi, Shin'ichi, Tanaka Ikkō, and Hiroshi Sano. *Nissenbi no Jidai = The Epoch of the Japan Advertising Artists Club: Nihon No Gurafikku Dezain 1951–70*. Tokyo: Toransuāto, 2000.

Yamashiro, Ryūichi. *Ryūichi Yamashiro = Yamashiro Ryūichi*. Tokyo: Ginza Graphic Gallery, 1993.

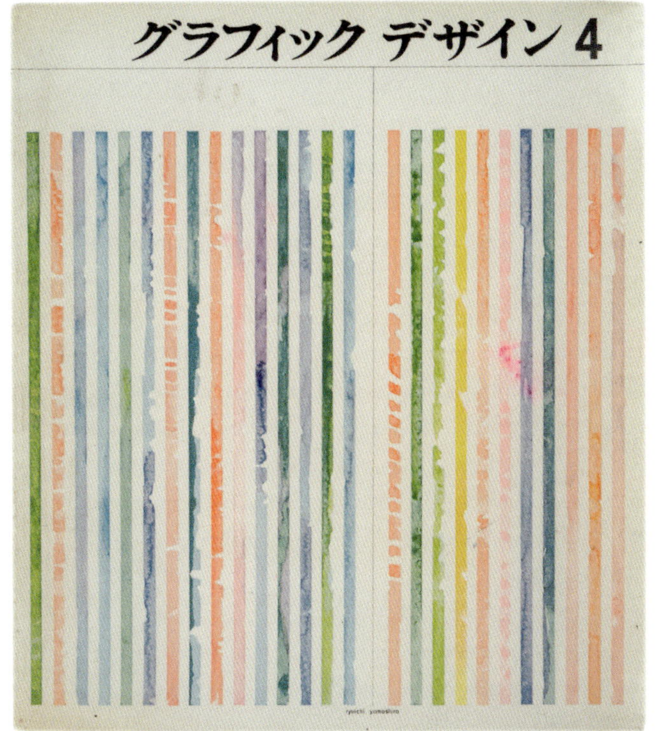

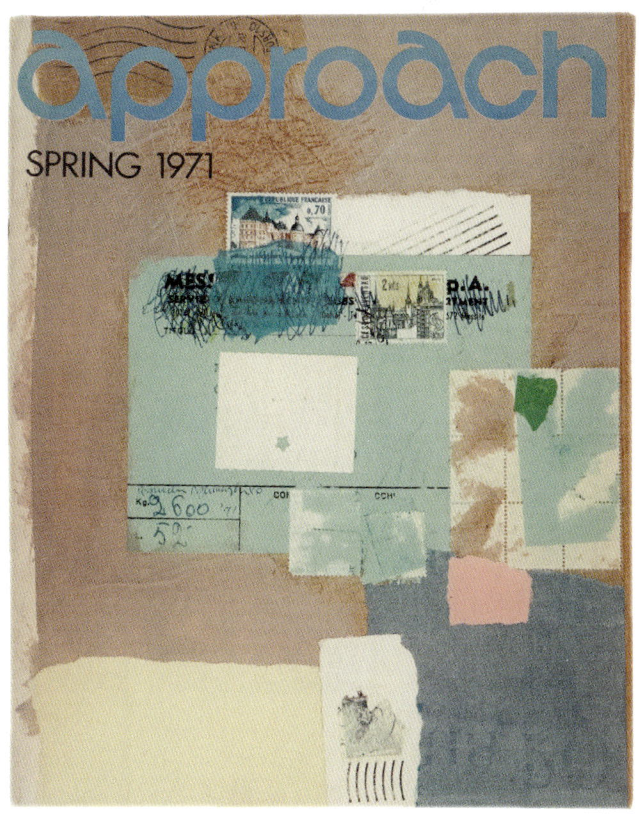

Top: Cover design for ***Graphic Design* #4** (Tokyo: Geibi Shuppansha 芸美出版社, February 1961).
Bottom: Cover design for ***Quarterly Approach* 季刊 Approach** (Tokyo: Takenaka Corporation 竹中工務店, 1970).

SHINOHARA EITA 篠原榮太

1927–

Shinohara Eita was born in Tokyo. He worked as the title designer for the Tokyo Broadcasting System for hundreds of notable television shows, including *Takeshi's Castle*. Shinohara's oeuvre is a dizzying array of calligraphic and structural approaches to Japanese and Latin lettering.

He established the Japan Lettering Designers Association (now called the Japan Typography Association) in 1964 and served as its president and chairman for many years. Shinohara also works in packaging design, illustration, and corporate identity. He has taught at Tama Art University and Tokyo Designer Gakuin and has published eleven books about design, lettering, designing for screens, and book design.

He designed the typefaces Shino-M and Shino-B for Ryobi, among others, including the design for the digital signage typeface at Narita Airport.

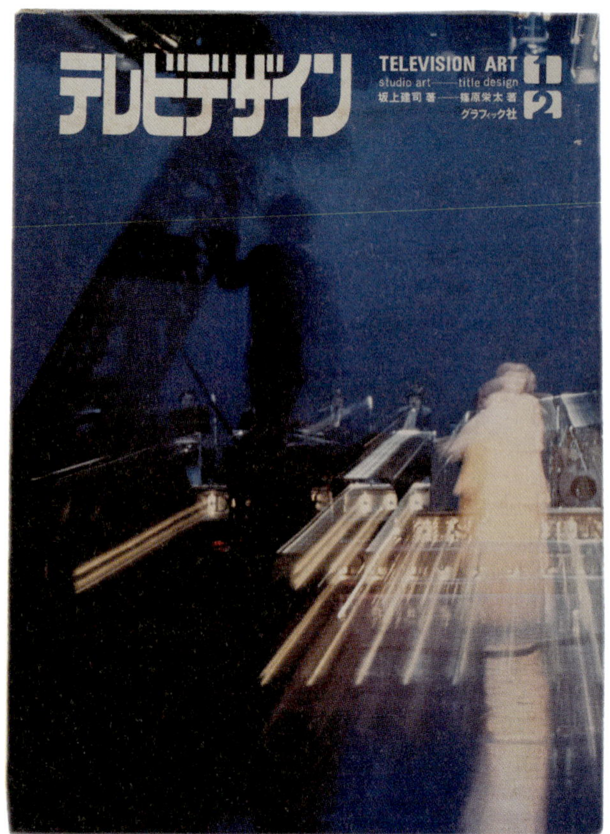

References:

Shinohara, Eita. *Shinohara Eita no Terebi Taitoru Dezain*. Tokyo: Graphic-sha, 2020.

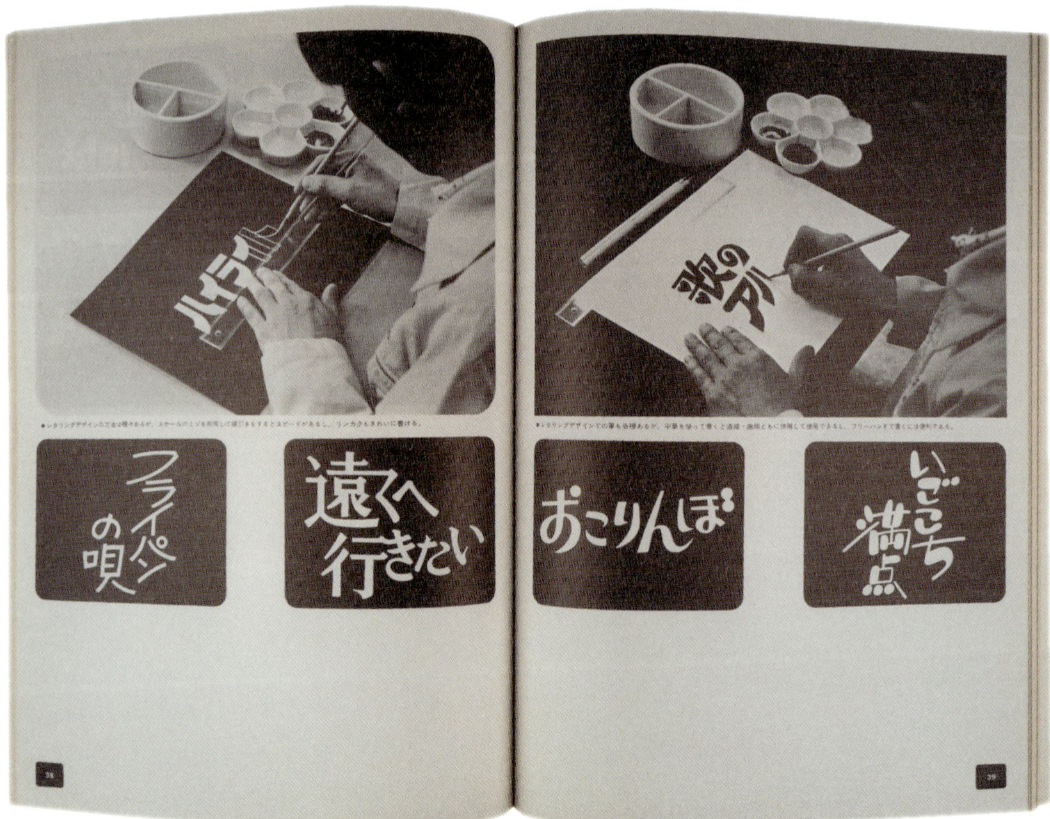

One of two twin volumes dedicated to design for television, ***Television Art* テレビデザイン *Vol. 2: Title Design* タイトルデザイン,** Shinohara Eita 篠原栄太 (Tokyo: Graphic-sha グラフィック社, 1977).

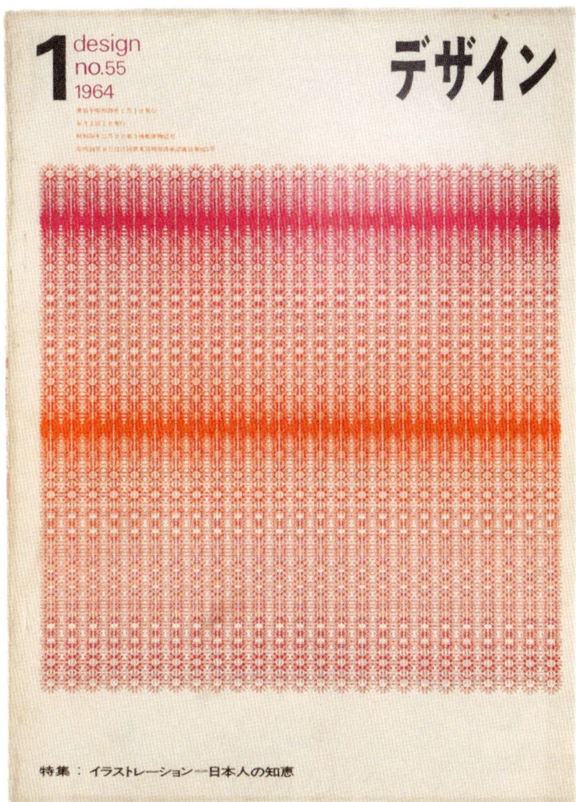

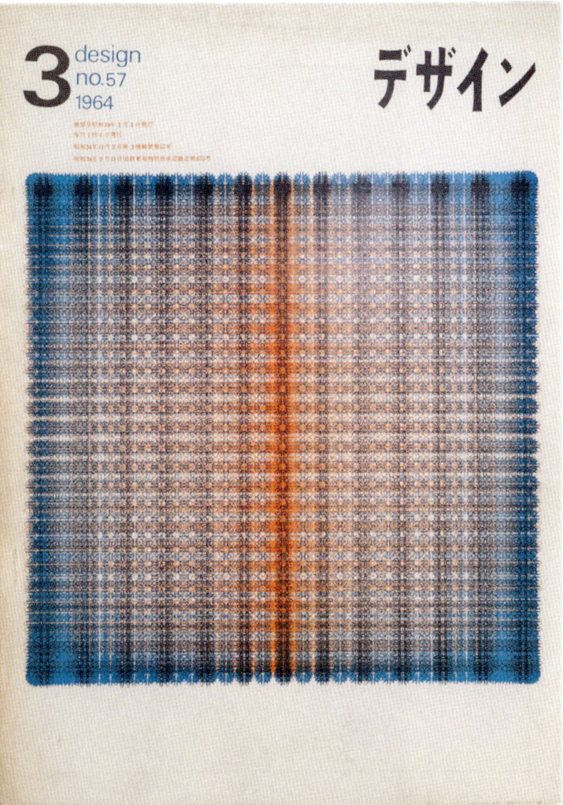

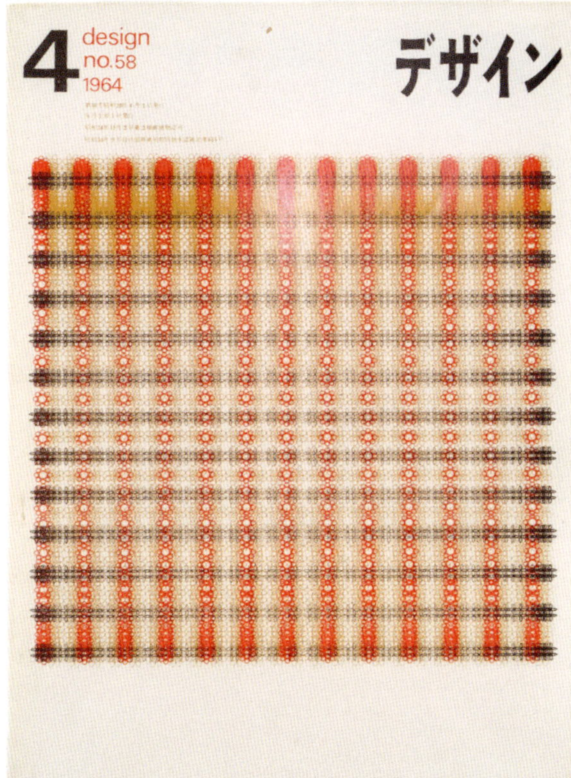

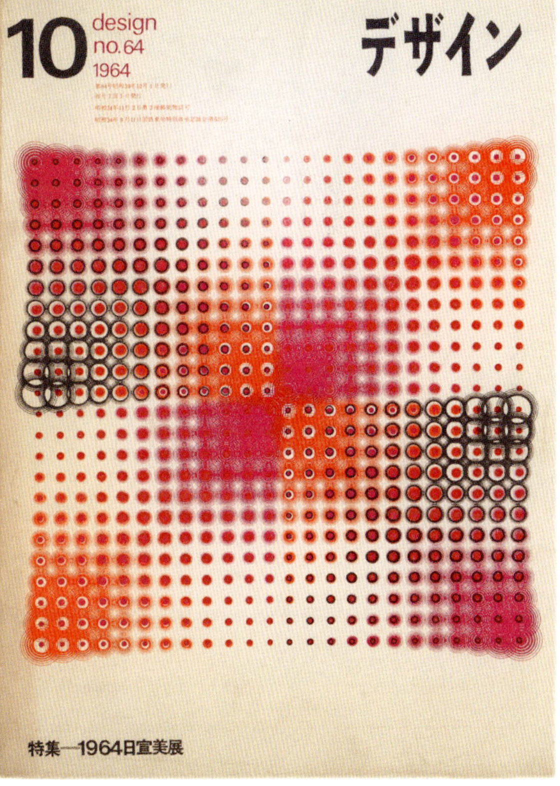

Front cover designs of ***Design* デザイン Nos. 1, 3, 4, and 10** (**Tokyo: Bijutsu Shuppansha 美術出版社, 1964**). These designs show an integrated and architectonic approach to both graphics and typography as practiced by Sugiura that connect the front cover designs to the back cover advertisements by sponsor Nicker Color ニッカー絵具株式会社, a manufacturer of paints and pigments.

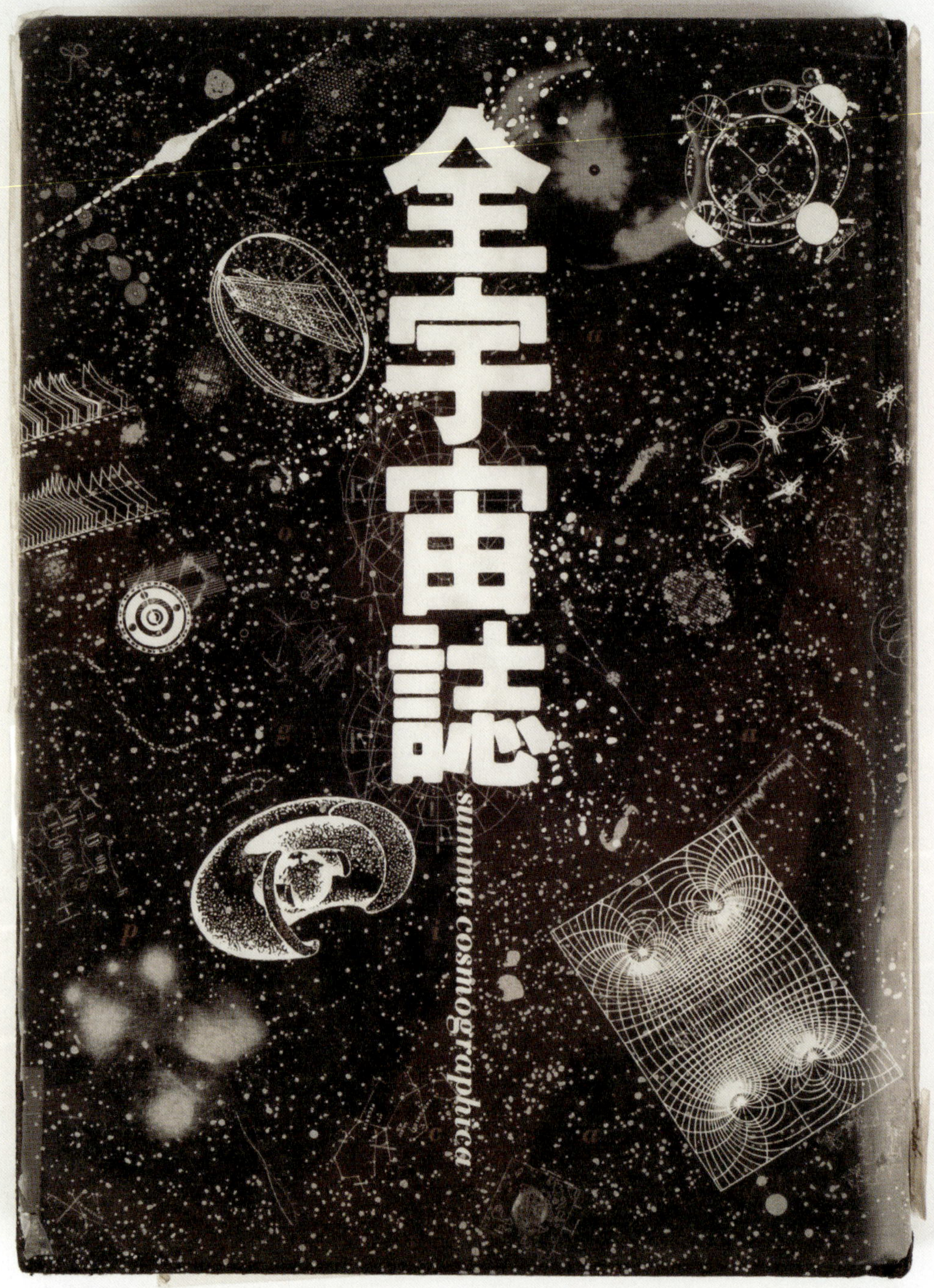

***Summa Cosmographica* 全宇宙誌, edited by Matsuoka Seigo 松岡正剛** (Tokyo: Kōsaku-sha 工作舎, 1980).
A mammoth, 378-page, black-and-white book designed over a period of seven years by Sugiura Kōhei, with design assistance from Toda Tsutomu 戸田ツトム and Harata Heikichi 羽良多平吉. The *Summa Cosmographica* consists of eight thematic sections: the universe as time; the universe as space; the universe as structure; the universe as a radio source; the universe as a phenomenon; the universe as an object; the universe as an idea; and the universe as a substance. All sections are interrelated and speak to the global thinking involved in planning and executing the project. The entire project includes a consummate system that maps and dissects the typographic space of the book, including a review of 151 historic astronomers, as well as meticulous edge printing that displays Andromeda when the pages are fanned from the front, as well as a constellation map when the book's pages are fanned from the back. The *Summa Cosmographica* is wrapped in a screen-printed clear plastic jacket bearing the name of the book, with gatefold opposing endpapers printed in black and silver.

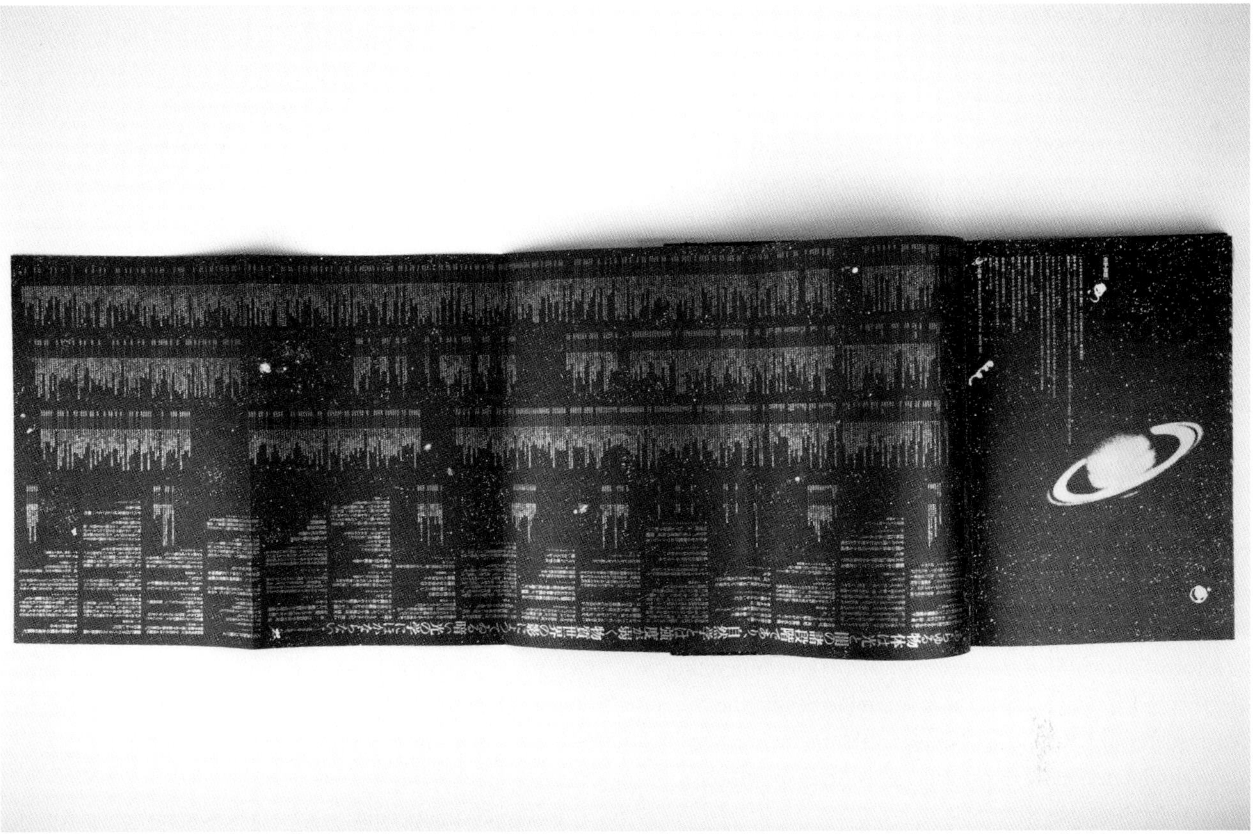

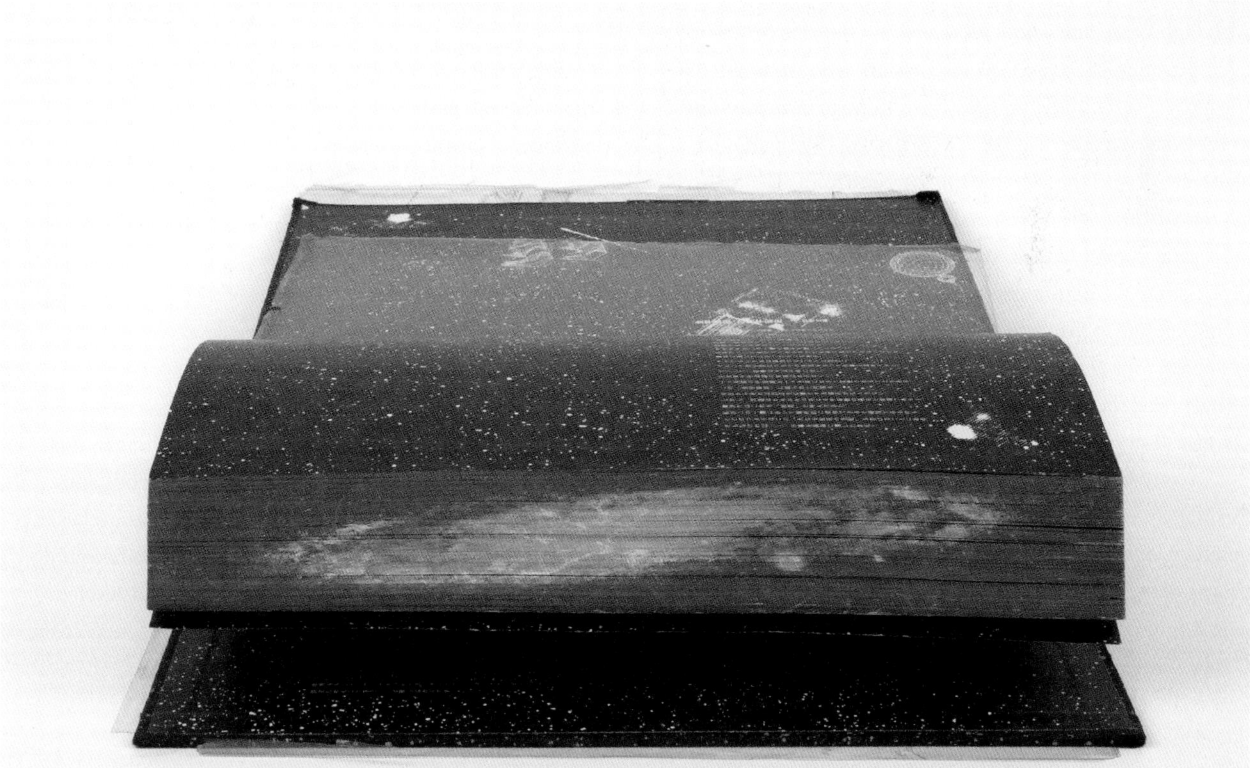

SUGIURA KŌHEI 杉浦康平

1932–

Sugiura Kōhei was born in Tokyo in 1932 and graduated from Tokyo University of the Arts' Architecture Department in 1956. The following year, Sugiura began working in the design and promotions department of Takashimaya department stores. While working at Takashimaya, Sugiura submitted a speculative record jacket design project that won the fifth Japan Advertising Artists Club Award. Winning one of the coveted JAAC Awards paved the way for commercial success and recognition within the realm of graphic design in Japan, greatly improving the possibility for career advancement.

Sugiura's JAAC Award in 1955 led to both. Within six months of receiving his award, he was able to create his own design studio due to the abundance of design commissions offered by assorted clients. Sugiura was recognized as a leading young designer by Katsumi Masaru, the mastermind behind the design planning for the 1964 Olympics. Katsumi invited Sugiura to submit designs to the private competition for the 1964 Olympic logo design.

Although Kamekura's work was chosen as the logo for the 1964 Olympics, Sugiura's two logo submissions were undoubtedly the most futuristic and progressive of the logo options—one of his designs featured a black circle trisected by an angular, abstract "T" with the Olympic rings in miniature and "XVIII Olympiad Tokyo 1964" rendered in slightly letterspaced, all-capital, sans serif type. This submission by Sugiura is a precursor to the high-modernist typographic design that would emerge in the 1970s in Europe, wherein increased use of negative space and abstraction would come to the fore—a visual precursor and aesthetic cousin to Otl Aicher's design for the 1972 Munich Olympics.

Despite not winning the logo competition, Sugiura worked on other aspects of the Olympic identity in 1960 alongside a throng of other young Japanese designers of note. The same year, Sugiura was a panelist and participant in the World Design Conference and began working at the Nippon Design Center. In 1961, Sugiura received the Mainichi Design Award, one of Japan's premier design awards, for a series of concert posters. He was widely recognized by his peers for his programmatic approach to design—a mix of Swiss-inspired structural typography and architectonic modular forms.

Sugiura was invited as guest faculty to teach at Hochschule für Gestaltung Ulm in the last quarter of 1965 and stayed on through 1967. While HfG Ulm only operated from 1953 to 1968, the school implemented progressive approaches to assorted design processes within the departments of Product Design, Visual Communication, Industrialized Building, Information, and Filmmaking. The subjects of sociology, psychology, politics, economics, philosophy, and systems-thinking were integrated with aesthetics and technology. Sugiura quickly came to the realization that the curriculum at HfG Ulm was easily a decade or two ahead of other design schools at that time.

The goal of HfG Ulm's founders was to create a teaching and research institution that would foster a human-centered pedagogical ideal and link creative activity to everyday life. HfG Ulm quickly gained international recognition by emphasizing the holistic, multidisciplinary context of design beyond the Bauhaus's integration of art, craft, and technology. Still, Sugiura sensed a certain rigidity to the German worldview which he felt differed greatly from his Japanese upbringing.

> *"The German way of thinking is the same in today's computerized society, and it is 'Ja oder nein?' In other words, 'yes or no.'"*[1]

He found the culture of Ulm to be incredibly binary, with little room for ambiguity—an incredibly important and inherent attribute of Japanese culture.

> *"There is 'anonymity' at the root of the richness of Asian culture and religion. Supporting Asian beauty is something that people unconsciously created from the depths of the mind and the body, and the Western beauty that claims the existence of 'I' is fundamentally different."*[2]

Sugiura's divergent mode of thinking and teaching in this foreign cultural setting awakened him to a new consciousness of being "Asian," of cultivating different approaches to design practice and theory than what was quickly becoming standardized in the West, and encouraged him to develop his own pan-Asian approach to design over the course of the

1 Nguyen Hung Ky, "Ma: The Realm of Mystery in Sugiura Kohei's 'Asian Grammar of Design,'" In *DS 66-2, Proceedings of the First International Conference on Design Creativity (ICDC 2010)* (Kobe: The Design Society, 2010), 3. https://www.designsociety.org/publication/30278/Ma%3A+The+Realm+of+Mystery+in+Sugiura+Kohei%E2%80%99s+%E2%80%98Asian+Grammar+of+Design%E2%80%99.

2 Megha Rajguru and Yasuko Suga, *Kohei Sugiura and Kirti Trivedi: Capturing Asia as Transnational in Four Dimensions*, (Tokyo: Tsuda University, 2017), 4.

rest of his career. His time at the HfG Ulm gave him a more robust understanding of the logic-based Western modernist approach to design theory and practice, working out aspects of typographic hierarchy and integrated approaches to design and composition.

Simultaneously, Sugiura began to explore aspects of new sciences and pseudosciences that gained critical momentum in the 1960s, incorporating aspects of psychology into his writing and work alongside *proxemics* (the study of partial perception and awareness of the individual and of society) and *chronemics* (the study of the role of time in communication). With regard to chronemics, Sugiura was keenly interested in the subset notion of polychronic time—perceptions and experiences of time when multiple actions can be accomplished simultaneously, in which wider views of time might be exhibited, and when time itself is perceived in large fluid sections.

These theoretical interests led Sugiura to refute certain notions of pure, logical, function-driven Modernism, and his typography began to reflect both experiential and individual viewership, exploring different voices within one text. Sugiura has consistently refuted the idea that his renewed approach to graphic design was in any way philosophically Postmodern, instead insisting that he shifted his thinking and making of design to more accurately reflect a communal Asian perspective.

This rejection of designing from the perspective of the singular allowed Sugiura to not dismiss Modernism, but to shear it and inflect it with a communally oriented direction, both in terms of intent and output. He set out to identify the multiple ways in which Asian culture expresses reflection, ambiguity, and aesthetics, hoping to create a more holistic design theory that was not merely Western Modernism grafted onto Asian philosophies, but one that implicitly and explicitly expressed an Asian worldview.

Upon leaving HfG Ulm in 1967, Sugiura returned to Japan, where he has had an expansive career in graphic design since, particularly in book design. A master of formal and typographic control, Sugiura's body of work encompasses a number of masterpieces, including the nine-year undertaking *Summa Cosmographica* 全宇宙誌, a black-and-white book serving as an expansive study and semantic manifestation of the cosmos wrapped in a screen-printed, clear-vinyl, tubular sleeve, published by Kousakusha in 1979. Nearly the entirety of the *Summa Cosmographica* includes individual star fields printed to bleed from edge to edge of each spread with discrete reversed-out text fields harmoniously nestled in appropriate sectors. The facing edge of the book's pages featured distinct maps of Andromeda and a constellation map when readers shifted the entirety of the book left or right—a technical achievement in the pre-digital age.

Sugiura has also dedicated much time to mapping aspects of the world which are invisible, creating information graphics which chart the world of taste and the hierarchy of time. He has written about how assorted animal species experience the world differently than humans and how the globe can be mapped according to time instead of geography.

Sugiura began teaching at Tokyo Zokei University in 1968 at the invitation of Katsumi Masaru, transferring to Kobe Design University and teaching there from 1989 through 2003. Sugiura designed stamps for the West German government celebrating the Sapporo Olympics in 1972, and he designed the logo for preeminent stereo component manufacturer Audio-Technica. In 1997 Sugiura received the Medal of Honor with Purple Ribbon from the Japanese government for his contributions to art and society. Sugiura is still active today, lecturing about Pan-Asian aesthetics and symbolism at design conferences globally.

"A book embodies the concept of 'one in many' and, at the same time, 'many in one.' The concept of 'many' is reflected not just in the number of pages but also in a book's many characters, many images, its gathering of many elements, many chapters (as in short story collections or anthologies) and many subjects (as in a dictionary). Space and time are folded into multiple layers, creating a universe in the shape of a book. In this concept of 'one in many, many in one,' 'one' and 'many' are of the same rank, in a mutual relationship as equals, forming a circle."[3]

By embracing the expanded visual language of Asian typography, the spiritual ambiguity of Confucian cultures, and an expanded understanding of how both designer and audience experience time and physicality, Sugiura imbues his work with a multiplicity of readings, through both multivalent approaches to typographic and multivarious semantic hierarchy, as much as through material design. The thousands of publications designed by Sugiura's studio force a reader to slow down, speed

3 Sugiura Kohei, *Tashugoteki na Asia* (Tokyo: Kosakusha, 2010), 24.

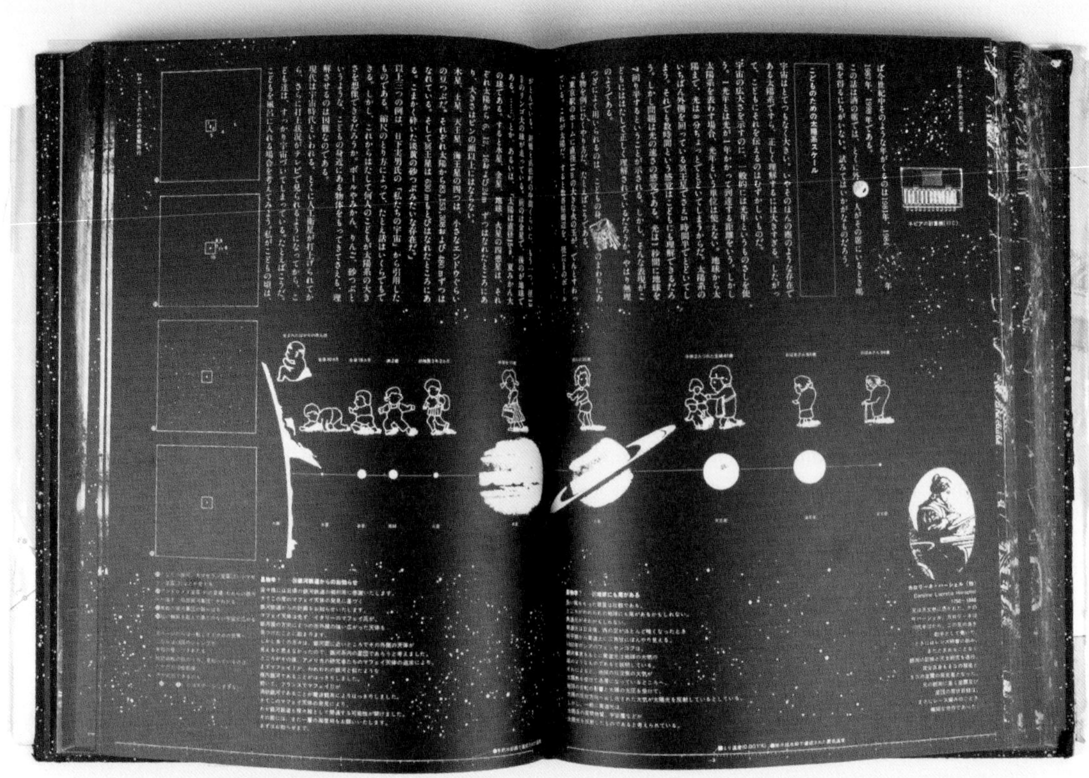

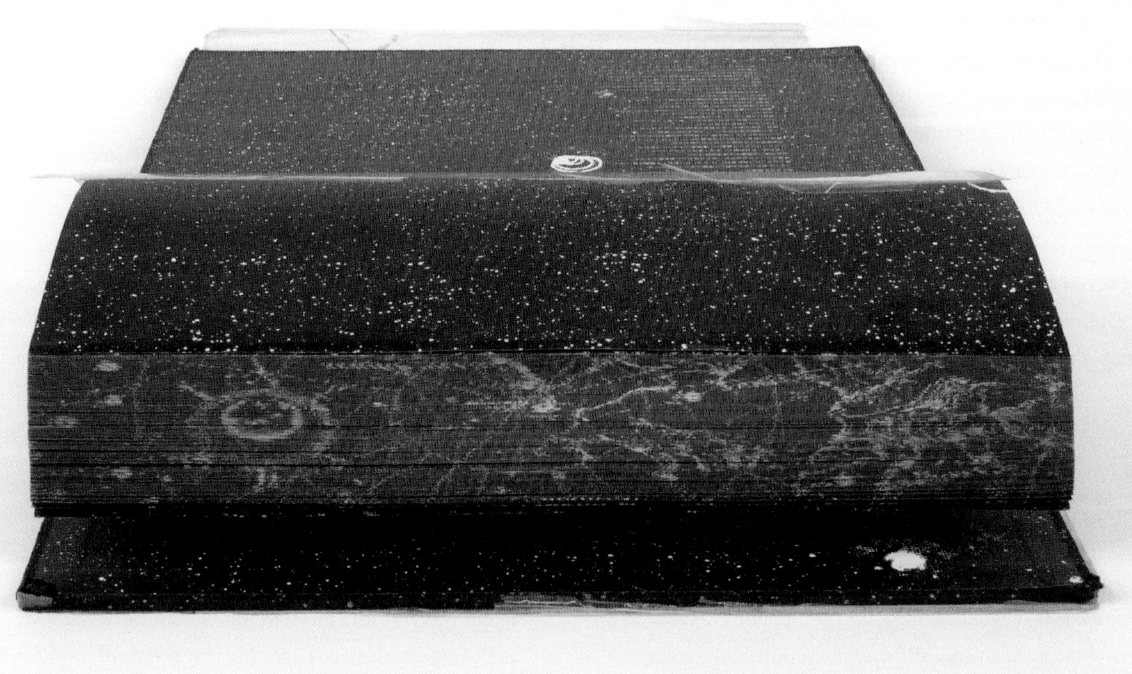

Summa Cosmographica 全宇宙誌, edited by Matsuoka Seigo 松岡正剛 (Tokyo: Kōsaku-sha 工作舎, 1980).

up, be surprised, and appreciate the delicacy with which typography is handled, materials are considered, and how every aspect of the printing, binding, and packaging of a book might be examined, broken, disassembled, and reassembled.

Sugiura's Pan-Asian approach is underpinned by a critical evaluation of Western Modernism as being largely materialist and functionalist at its core, with Asian aesthetic approaches reading as the spiritual and emotional opposite of these values. He places emphasis on the history of material and cultural communication shared between Asian cultures and societies prior to the pre-World War II rise of the Japanese empire and the adjacent rise of Japanese Orientalism.

Sugiura's work as a designer and educator is deeply informed by the duality he perceives between the "rational" West and the "non-rational" East. An equally important influence is the accretion of experiences whereby he, as well as other Asians, comprehend time in a more expansive way than many of us outside of the Asian mindset might be used to.

During his time at Ulm, Sugiura's colleagues graced him with the German nickname "Vielleicht," meaning "perhaps," due to his inability to constrain himself to absolute judgments such as "good" or "bad".

Of the many educators who contributed to the pedagogy of Hochschule für Gestaltung Ulm, few have had such influential legacies as Sugiura Kōhei. Simultaneously, few of the educators working at the HfG Ulm have had their careers glossed over in Western design history as much as Sugiura's. One of Japan's foremost designers, design thinkers, critics, and educators, Sugiura's body of work went mostly unmentioned in the HfG Ulm's in-house journal and in Western history books. Yet, in Japan, his name is synonymous with the HfG Ulm as an academic institution and with graphic design as a sector of cultural production.

References:

Kamekura, Yūsaku, and Ayao Yamana. *Gurafikku Dezain no Seiki: Bunshō to Danwa to Sakuhin De kōsei: Meiji Sedai Yamana Ayao Sugiura Hisui Kara shōwa Sedai Made*. Tokyo: Bijutsu Shuppansha, 2008.

Trivedi, Kirti, and Kohei Sugiura. *Graphic Design Methodology and Philosophy*. Mumbai: Asian Design and Art Research Group, 2015.

Sugiura, Kōhei. "Design Thinking," *Moderne Design*. Tokyo: Musashino University Press, 1999.

Segi, Shin'ichi, Tanaka Ikkō, and Hiroshi Sano. *Nissenbi no Jidai = The Epoch of the Japan Advertising Artists Club: Nihon No Gurafikku Dezain 1951–70*. Tokyo: Toransuāto, 2000.

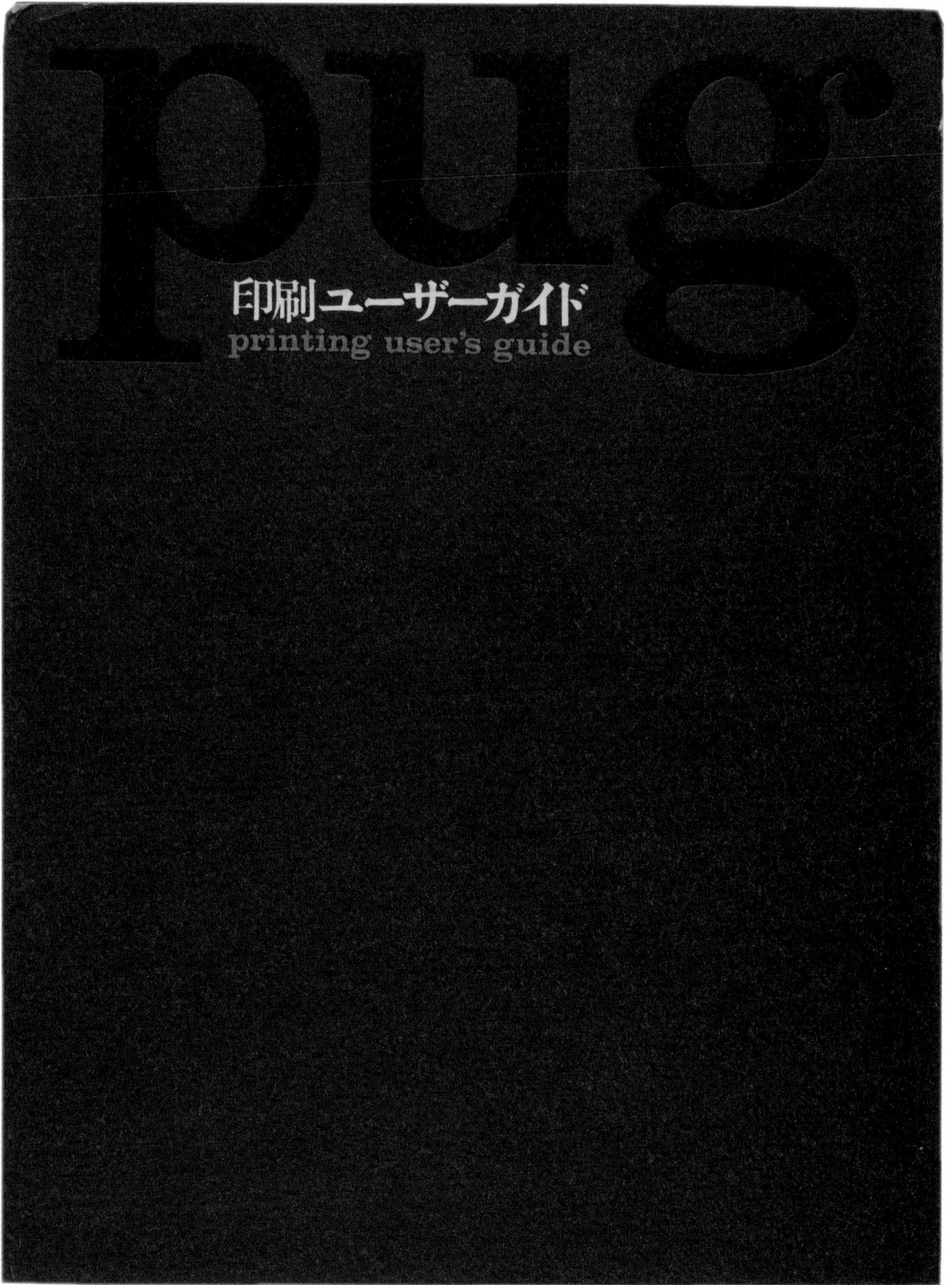

Printing User's Guide **印刷ユーザガイド***, a trade manual of printing processes, techniques, papers, finishes, and embellishments for smaller publishers and businesses* **(Tokyo: Printing Society Publishing Department 印刷学会出版部, 1965).** Co-designed with Nakagaki Nobuo 中垣信夫, this book features a wide variety of tipped-in printing, paper, and finishing examples.

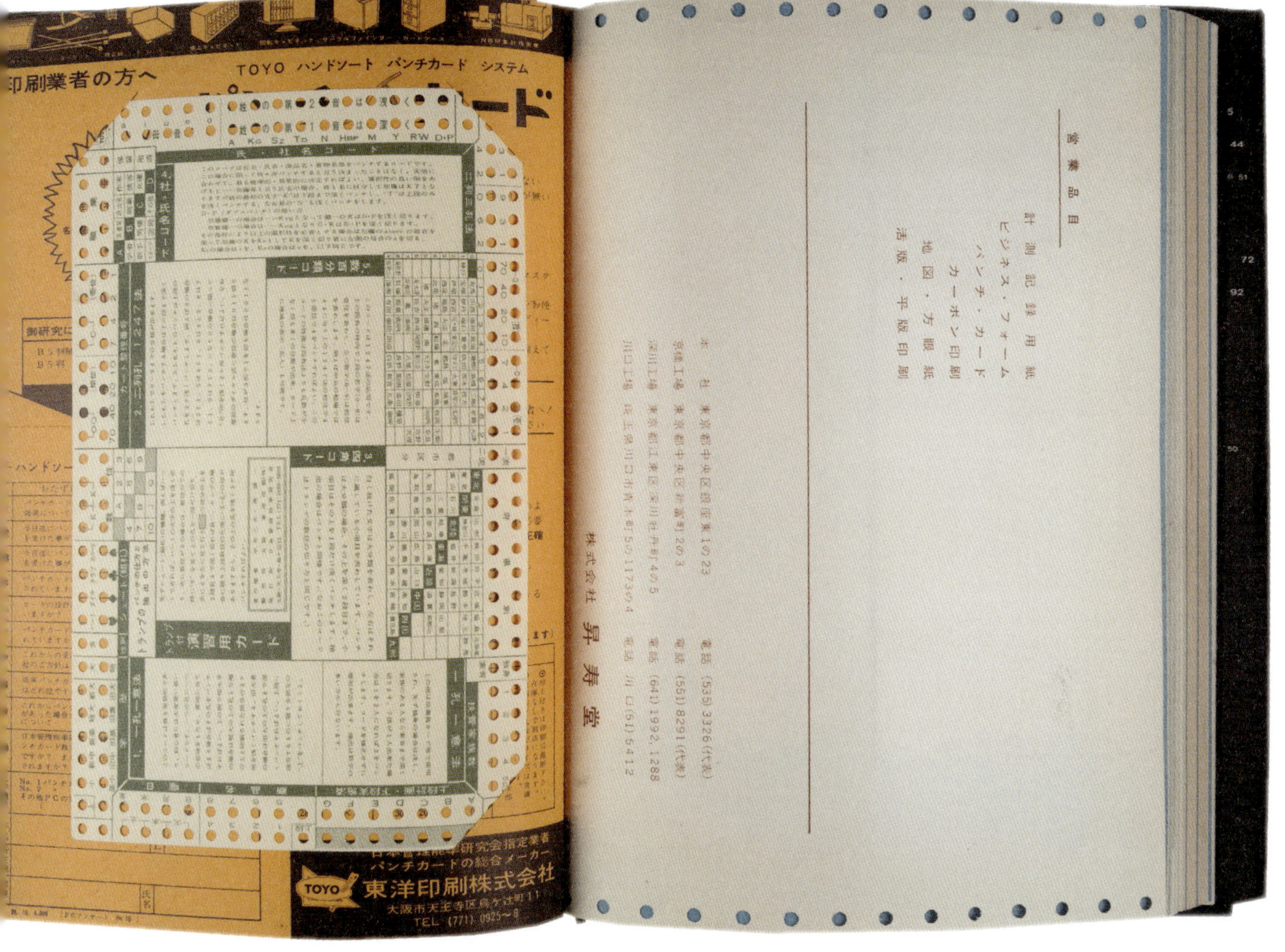
印刷業者の方へ
TOYO ハンドソート パンチカード システム
パンチカードの総合メーカー
TOYO
東洋印刷株式会社
大阪市天王寺区烏ヶ辻町11
TEL (771) 0925～8
営業品目
計測記録用紙
ビジネス・フォーム
パンチ・カード
カーボン印刷
地図・方眼紙
活版・平版印刷
本社 東京都中央区銀座東1の23 電話(535)3326(代表)
京橋工場 東京都中央区新富町2の3 電話(551)8291(代表)
深川工場 東京都江東区深川牡丹町4の5 電話(641)1992, 1288
川口工場 埼玉県川口市青木町5の1173の4 電話 川口(51)5412
株式会社 昇寿堂

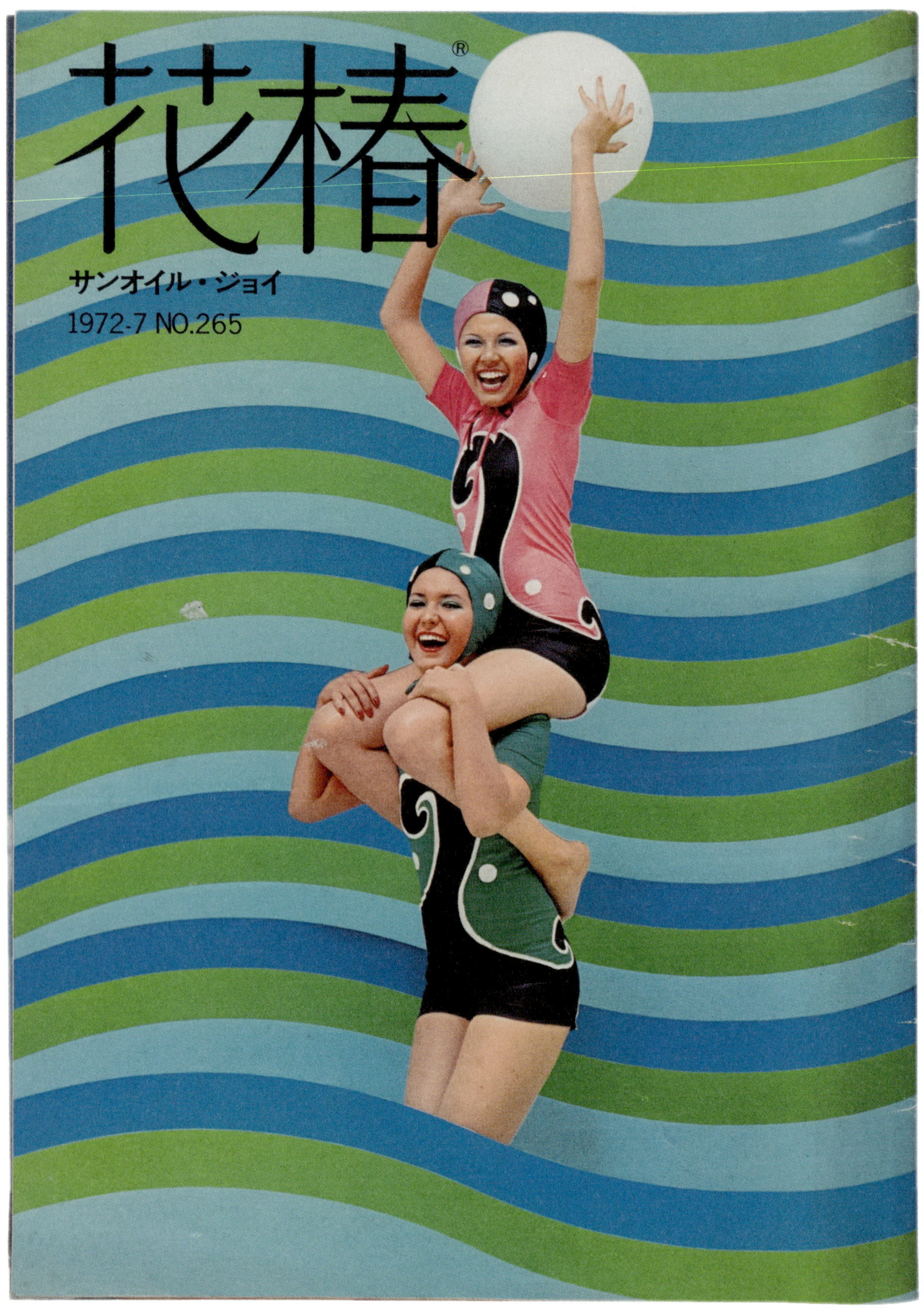

This spread and next: A sampling of covers and spreads from Shiseido's monthly magazine, ***Hanatsubaki* 花椿**, from the 1960s and 1970s that demonstrate Nakajō Masayoshi's 仲條正義 dynamic approach to art direction, photographic direction, design, and typography.

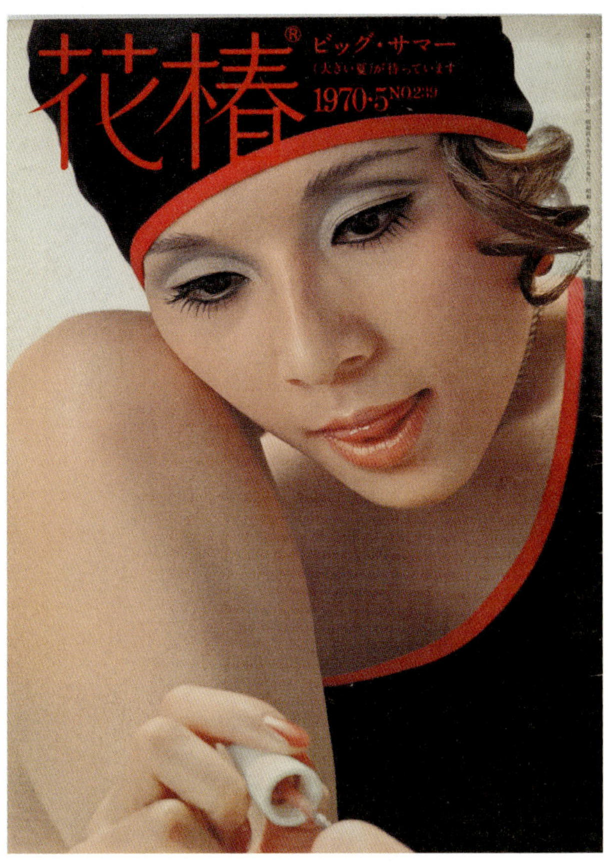

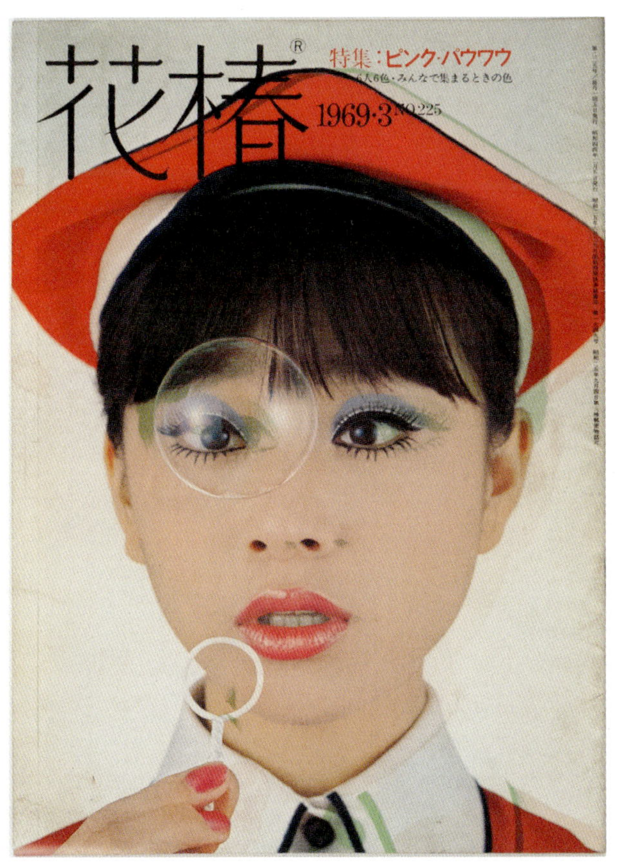

NAKAJŌ MASAYOSHI 仲條正義

1933–

Nakajō Masayoshi was born in Tokyo. After graduating from high school in Chiba, he attended the Tokyo National University of Fine Arts and Music, studying in the Department of Design. After graduation, he began working in Shiseido's advertising department and Kōno Takashi's design studio, Deska, before starting his own design practice, Nakajō Design Office, in 1961.

Nakajō was the art director of Shiseido's influential promotional magazine, *Hanatsubaki* 花椿, from 1968 to 2011. Under Nakajō's visual direction, *Hanatsubaki* was a dynamic public relations tool which also highlighted various approaches to composition, layout, lettering, and typography spanning the analog to digital design eras.

Nakajō has designed innumerable other projects including the logo for Chiba Prefecture, two redesigns of the suite of nostalgic packaging designs for Shiseido Parlor, the identity designs for the Tokyo Ginza Shiseido Building, Matsuya Ginza Department Store, Wacoal Spiral Building, Museum of Contemporary Art Tokyo, and the Hosomi Museum.

He has been awarded the Membership Grand Prize of the Tokyo Art Directors Club, the Members Gold Prize of the Tokyo Type Directors Club, the Yūsaku Kamekura Design Award of the Japan Graphic Designers Association, the Mainichi Design Award, and the Japan Advertising Awards Yamana Prize, and he received the Medal with Purple Ribbon and the Order of the Rising Sun, Gold Rays with Rosette, from the Government of Japan.

Nakajō held three solo exhibitions at Tokyo's Ginza Graphic Gallery, an eponymous retrospective in 1988, ○○○ in 1997, and *In & Out*, あるいは飲&嘔吐 *In & Out*, or *Imbibing and Vomiting* in 2017. His book *Thirty-Six Views of Mount Fuji*, a Brutalist homage to Hokusai's bound series of landscape prints of the same title from 1830–1832, was published in 2002.

References:

Gotō, Shigeo. *Hanatsubaki and Nakajō: Hanatsubaki 1968–2008*. Tokyo: PIE Books, 2009.

Muroga, Kiyonori, and Makie Kubo. "Interview with Masayoshi Nakajō." Idea 60, no. 350 (January 2012): 99–104.

Nakajō, Masayoshi. *Nakajō Masayoshi*. Tokyo: Ginza Graphic Gallery, 1994.

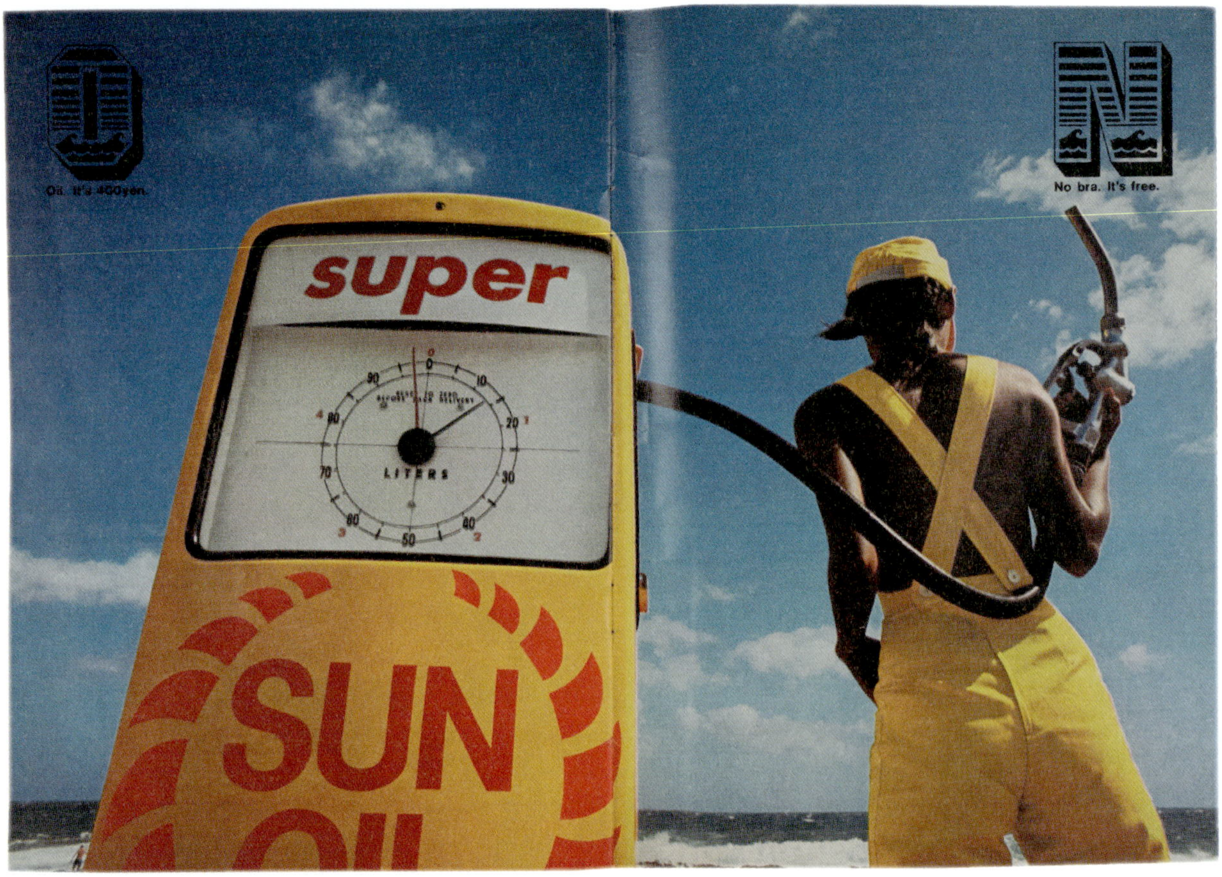

O
Oil. It's 400yen.
super
LITERS
SUN
OIL
N
No bra. It's free. 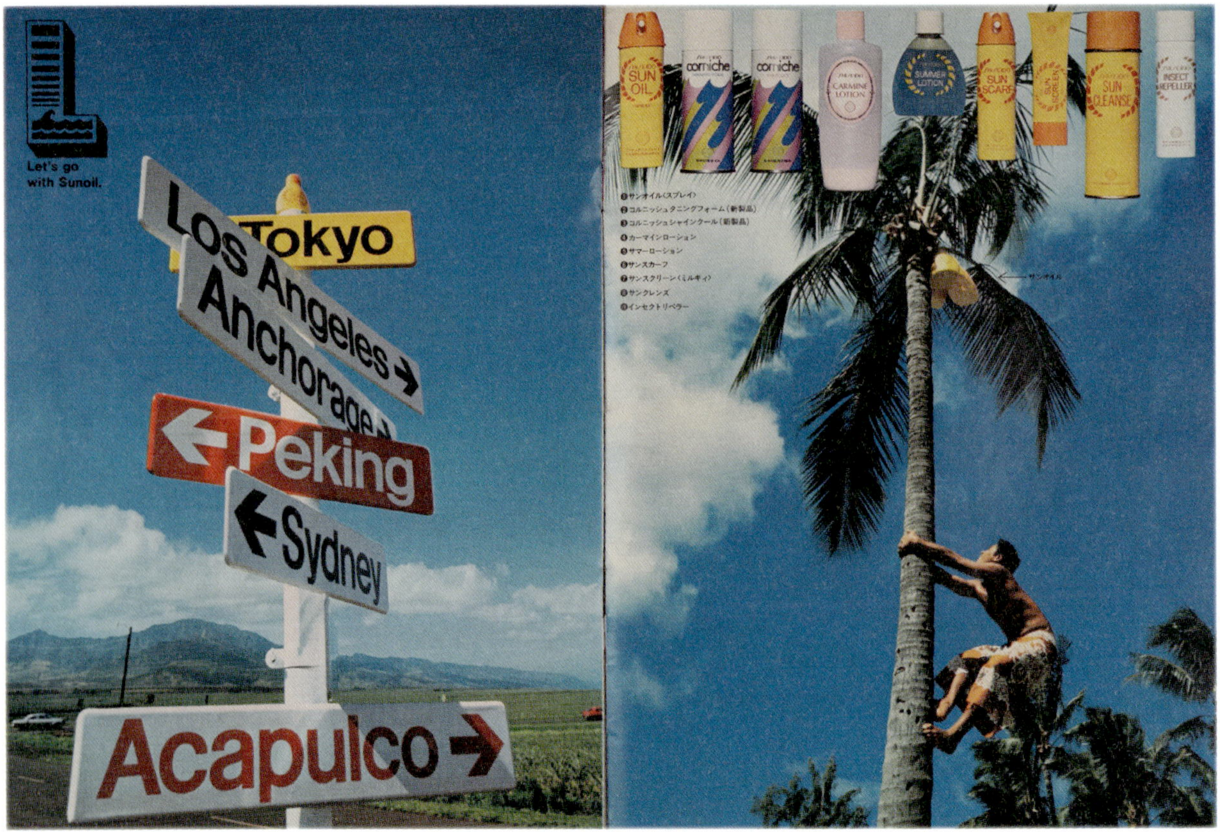
L
Let's go
with Sunoil.
Tokyo
Los Angeles
Anchorage
Peking
Sydney
Acapulco
SUN OIL
corniche
corniche
CARMINE LOTION
SUMMER LOTION
SUN SCARF
SUN SCREEN
SUN CLEANSE
INSECT REPELLER
❶サンオイル〈スプレイ〉
❷コルニッシュタニングフォーム（新製品）
❸コルニッシュシャインクール（新製品）
❹カーマインローション
❺サマーローション
❻サンスカーフ
❼サンスクリーン〈ミルキィ〉
❽サンクレンズ
❾インセクトリペラー

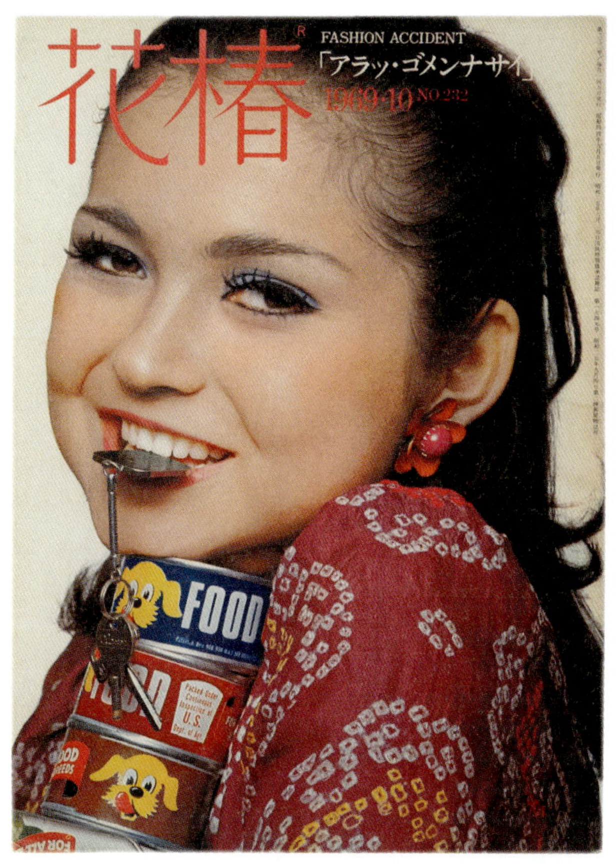
花椿®
FASHION ACCIDENT
「アラッ・ゴメンナサイ」
1969·10 NO.232
FOOD

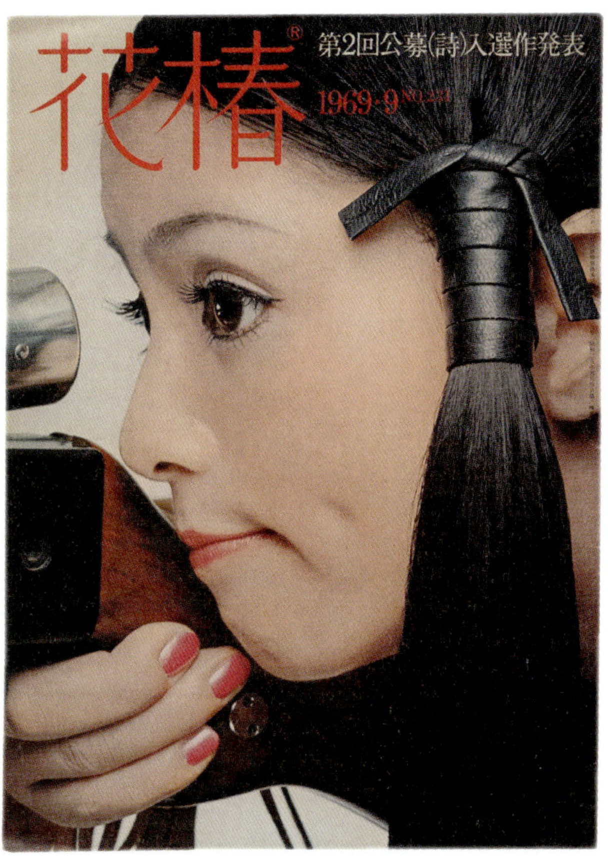
花椿®
第2回公募(詩)入選作発表
1969·9

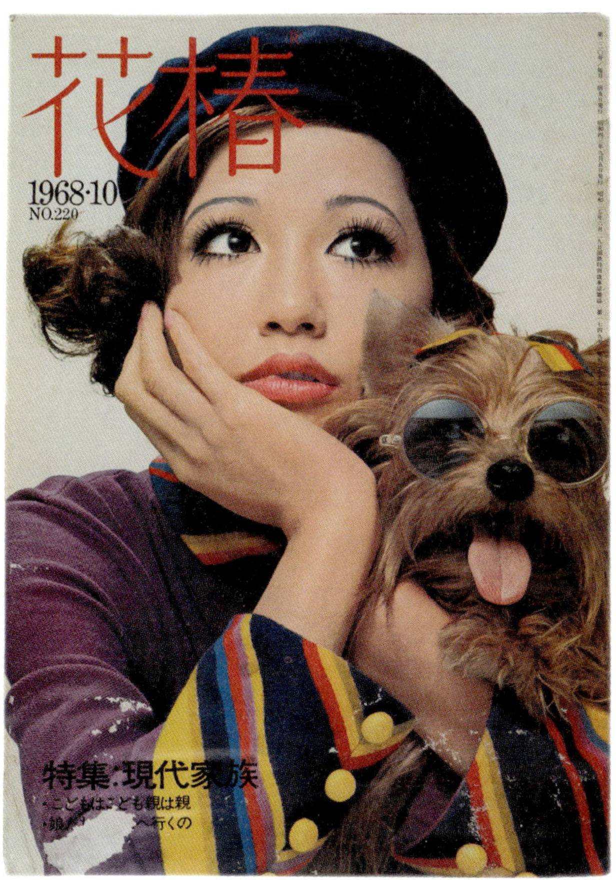
花椿®
1968·10
NO.220
特集:現代家族

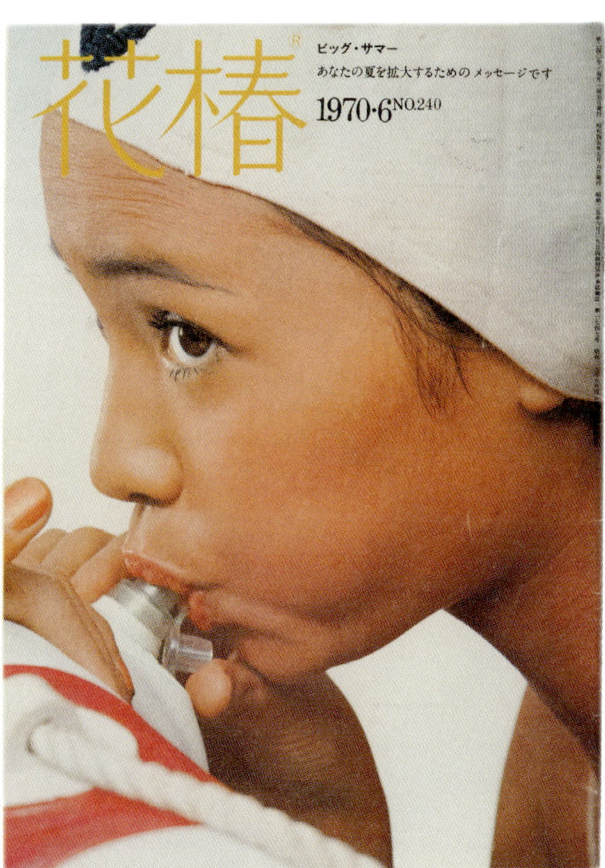
花椿®
ビッグ・サマー
あなたの夏を拡大するための メッセージです
1970·6 NO.240

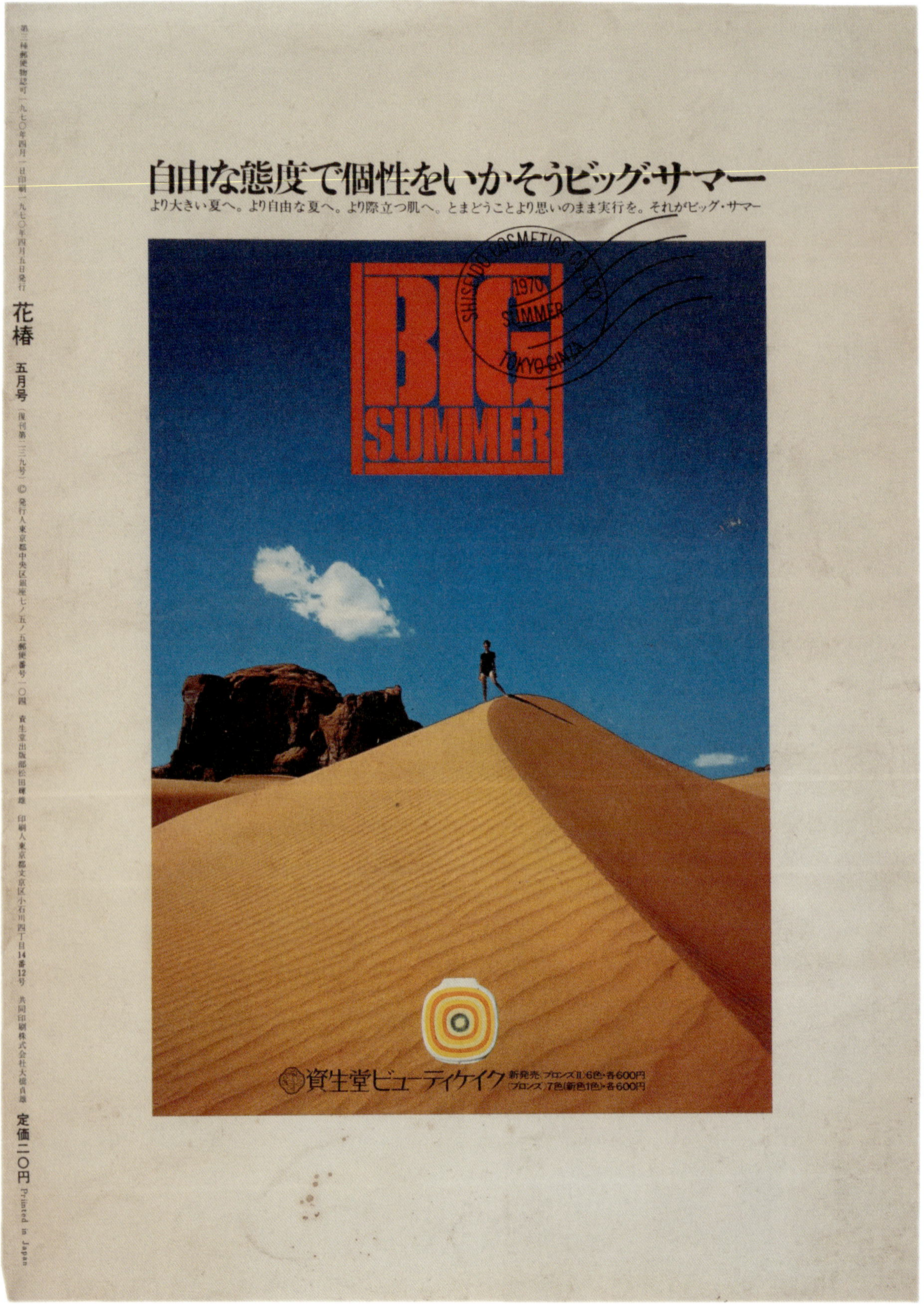

Back cover advertisement from 1970 summer issue of Shiseido Cosmetics' house magazine ***Hanatsubaki* 花椿** depicting the desert as a stand-in for the beach, art directed by Nakamura Makoto 中村誠.

NAKAMURA MAKOTO 中村誠

1926–2013

Nakamura Makoto was born in Iwate Prefecture and attended Tokyo National University of Fine Arts and Music. While a student, Nakamura worked freelance for the Shiseido cosmetics company, joining Shiseido's advertising, design, and public relations department full time upon his graduation in 1949. Nakamura worked in many roles at Shiseido, moving up from Designer, to Art Director, to Production Office Manager of the company's Advertising Department, then to the Director of Advertising. After 1987, he worked as Special Advisor to the company—a post-retirement position hand-crafted for him. Throughout his tenure at Shiseido, Nakamura kept up to date with the changing roles and methods of advertising and largely led the company toward promotions that were rich with photographic expression, abandoning the legacy of illustration-driven advertising that Shiseido had produced prewar.

Nakamura used a dizzying variety of techniques to push the technical and aesthetic qualities of Shiseido's advertising, including radical approaches to composition, abstraction, experimentation with depth of focus, and photo manipulation. These approaches helped to define Shiseido's house style from the 1950s through the 1980s, as well as Nakamura's own. Nakamura worked heavily with top fashion model Yamaguchi Sayoko 山口小夜子, once commenting,"Her beauty is not in the adornment on her face, but in the adornment from her spirit."[1] Many of Nakamura's posters that featured Yamaguchi as a model utilized extreme cropping and macro-photography, infusing them with rich detail.

Nakamura's expressive work exemplified the visual tendency toward ambiguity in 1970s and 1980s advertising, summoning up an atmosphere of glamor, luxury, and beauty through visual connotation rather than product-focused denotation. Nakamura was quoted as saying, "I try to capture the emotions, moods, and feelings that defy quantifiable expression, what you might even call a 'sense of human presence and spirit." He continued, "It's not about form, ... it's about letting the personality and character of the company come through."[2]

Nakamura was a member of the Alliance Graphique Internationale (AGI), a committee member for the Tokyo Art Directors Club, and a director of the Japan Graphic Designers Association Inc. He was awarded the Medal with Purple Ribbon by the Japanese government in 1993.

1 Bi to Chi No mīmu Shiseidō, Shiseido Meme Katarogu = Shiseido 1872-1998. Tōkyō: Shiseidō, 1998.

2 Ibid.

References:

Kamekura, Yūsaku, and Ayao Yamana. *Gurafikku Dezain no Seiki: Bunshō to Danwa to Sakuhin De kōsei: Meiji Sedai Yamana Ayao Sugiura Hisui Kara shōwa Sedai Made*. Tokyo: Bijutsu Shuppansha, 2008.

Muroga, Kiyonori, and Makie Kubo. "Obituary: Makoto Nakamura." Idea 61, no. 361 (November 2013): 199–201.

Sachi, Kaneda. "The Imaging Strategy of Shiseido in the 1930s: Analyzing Visual Magazines That Represented Corporate Identity." *Design History* 1, no. 14 (2016), 12–14.

Segi, Shin'ichi, Tanaka Ikkō, and Hiroshi Sano. *Nissenbi no Jidai = The Epoch of the Japan Advertising Artists Club: Nihon No Gurafikku Dezain 1951–70*. Tokyo: Toransuāto, 2000.

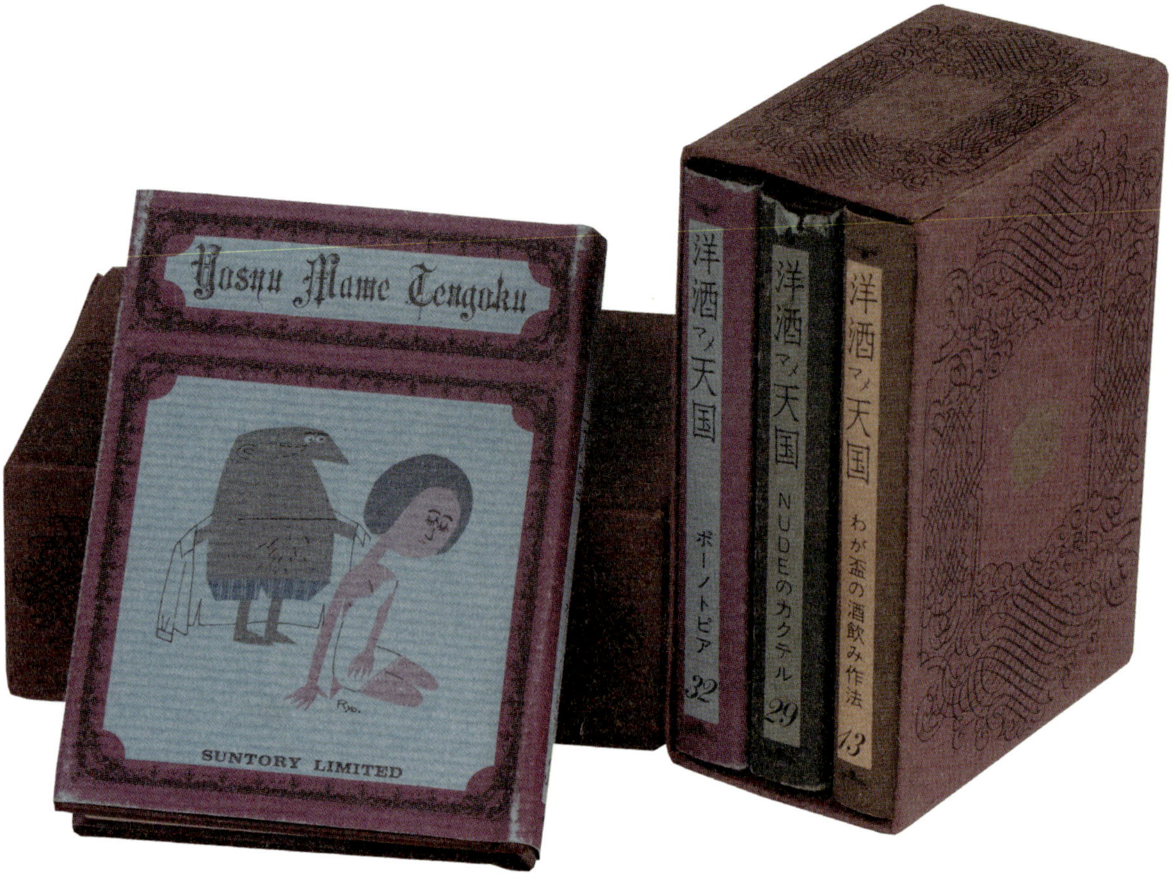

Yōshu Mame Tengoku 洋酒マメ天国, Yaguchi Jun 矢口純, (Osaka: Kabushikigaisha Suntory 株式会社サントリー, 1968–1969). A series of small promotional books whose name translates to "A Small Piece of Liquor Heaven," produced by Suntory to promote their assorted brands of alcohol, each designed by Yanagihara Ryōhei. The books feature artwork by assorted designers and illustrators including Yokoo Tadanori and photographers like Hosoe Eikoh 細江英公 to accompany writing by popular authors of the day. The books were edited by Suntory's in-house advertising agency, SUN-AD Co. 株式会社 サン・アド.

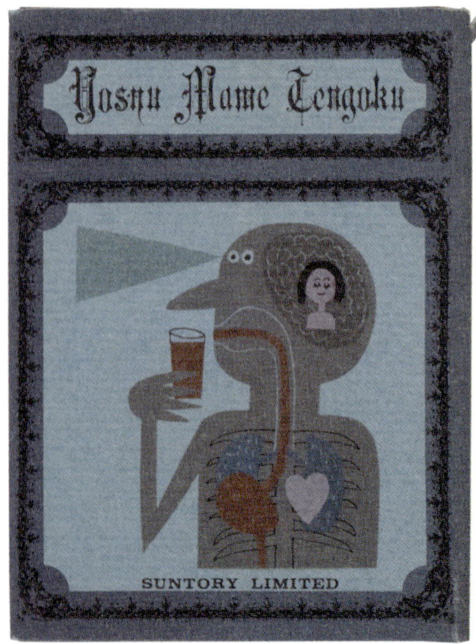

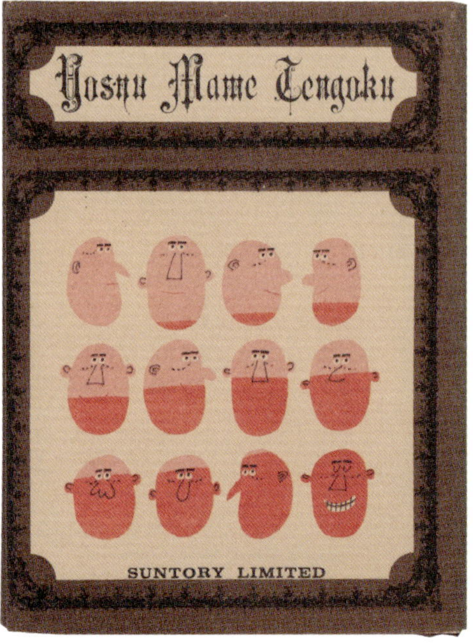

YANAGIHARA RYOHEI 柳原良平

1931–2015

Yanagihara Ryōhei was born in 1931 in Tokyo. He studied commercial design at Kyoto University's Department of Craft and Design. After graduating, Yanagihara took up a position at Kotobukiya Limited, the predecessor to Suntory, where he worked until 1959. While there, he created the mascot character Uncle Torys アンクルトリス for Torys Whisky, which featured prominently in both Torys and Suntory Whisky ads in the 1950s and 1960s and was revived in the early 2000s for a number of promotional campaigns that spurred Japan's highball boom. In 2008, Suntory Global made new commercials utilizing Yanagihara-style characters and mimicking his original animation style.

Uncle Torys—a diminutive, sexually promiscuous character with a penchant for whisky—appeared across innumerable pieces of print and broadcast advertising, but he was most visible in *Yōshu Mame Tengoku* 洋酒まめ天国 (*A Piece of Liquor Heaven*), Suntory's house "style guide" for the swinging gentleman of the 1950s and 1960s. Yanagihara's cover designs for *Yōshu Mame Tengoku* featured tawdry illustrations contained within baroque borders. The small journal contained racy nudes by some of Japan's top photographers and sexually explicit illustration work by Yokoo Tadanori and others, including Yanagihara himself. The palm-sized, book-like magazines were read at assorted bars throughout Japan.

Uncle Torys's pink visage also appeared in countless promotional items, from posters to figurines to assorted accoutrements, helping to sear the horny caricature onto Japan's national consciousness. Unknown to many Japanese consumers at that time was that Yanagihara's character's skin-color change upon drinking Suntory products was a fairly direct lift of French designer AM Cassandre's series of posters for the wine company Dubonnet in the 1930s.

In 1959, Yanagihara's work for Suntory vaulted him into a freelance career designing innumerable book covers for various publishers including Kogumasha and Gakken, making record jackets for Toshiba-EMI, and creating thousands of illustrations for assorted shipping companies. Yanagihara's work for clients like Mitsui OSK lines, Sado Steam Ship Co., Taiheiyō Ferry Co., and Tōkai Kisen Co. gave him the opportunity to fully express his love for the sea and for marine transport—Yanagihara moved to Yokohama in the 1960s to be closer to the ocean. Over the years, he was awarded the title of "Honorary Captain" for each of these maritime companies—a first for an illustrator anywhere in the world.

Yanagihara worked in animation as well as illustration. He formed the three-member experimental animation and production company Animation Sannin no Kai 三人の会 with Kuri Yōji 久里洋二 and Manabe Hiroshi 真鍋博 in 1960, and they created a number of stop-motion works that were played at Sōgetsu Hall in Akasaka.

Yanagihara explored sequential art in manga form, as well—drawing the manga strip *Kyō mo Ichinichi* 今日も一日 for the evening edition of the *Yomiuri Shimbun* from 1962 through 1966.

Perhaps the most iconic extant image of Yanagihara shows him with a highball raised, surrounded by models of ships—an image of a Yokohama man happy with his work.

References:

Lynam, Ian. "Obituary: Yanagihara Ryohei." Néojaponisme. Néojaponisme, August 24, 2015. https://neojaponisme.com/2015/08/24/obituary-yanagihara-ryohei/.

Yanagihara, Ryōhei. *Ryohei Yanagihara*. Tokyo: DAN, 2003.

Yanagihara, Ryōhei. *Yanagihara ryōhei No Waga Jinsei*. Tokyo: Kisaragishuppan, 2017.

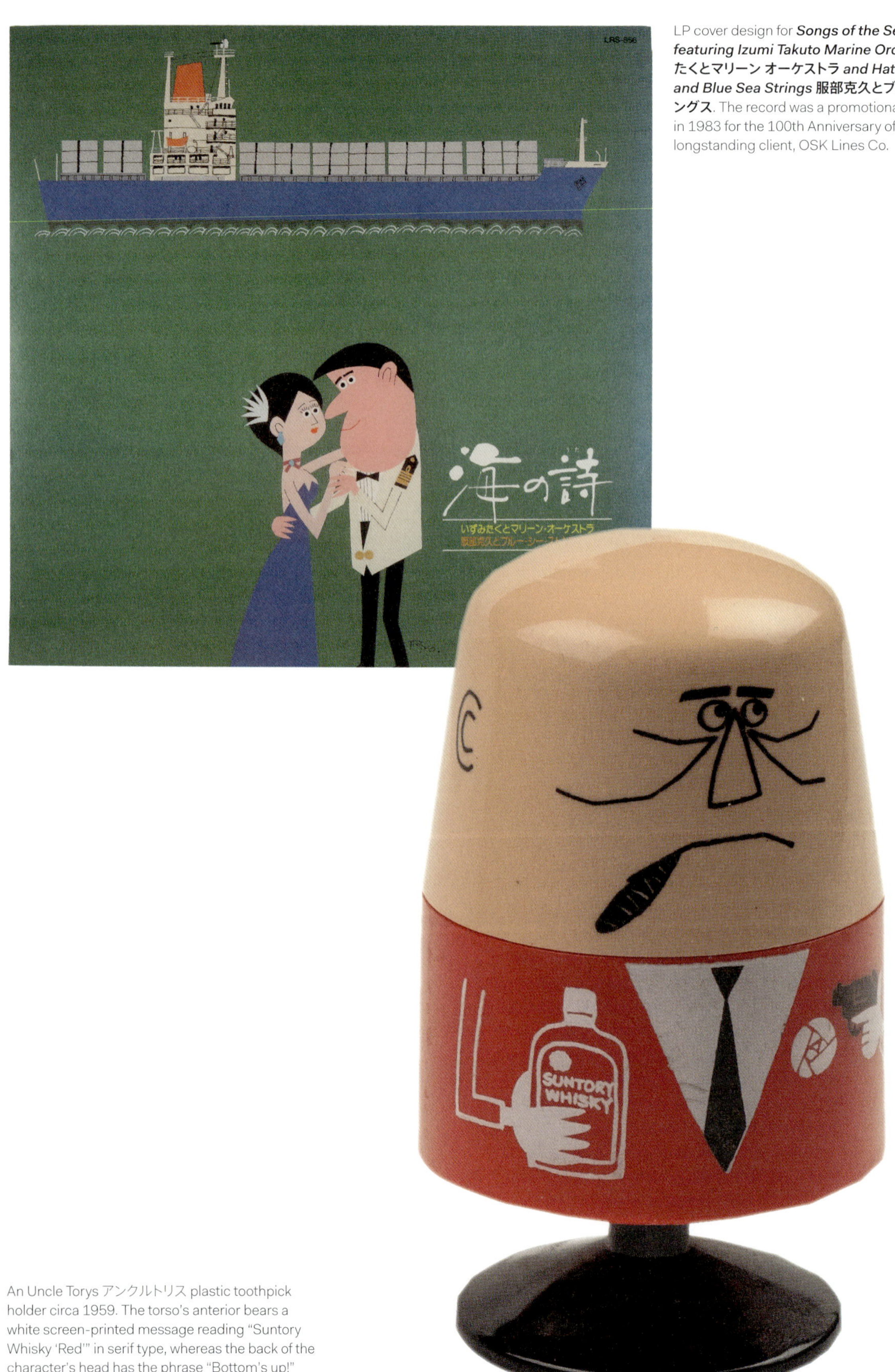

LP cover design for ***Songs of the Sea* 海の詩 *featuring Izumi Takuto Marine Orchestra* いずみたくとマリーン オーケストラ *and Hattori Katsuhisa and Blue Sea Strings* 服部克久とブルー シー ストリングス**. The record was a promotional item produced in 1983 for the 100th Anniversary of Yanagihara's longstanding client, OSK Lines Co.

An Uncle Torys アンクルトリス plastic toothpick holder circa 1959. The torso's anterior bears a white screen-printed message reading "Suntory Whisky 'Red'" in serif type, whereas the back of the character's head has the phrase "Bottom's up!" printed in script lettering ensnared within a dotted-line word bubble.

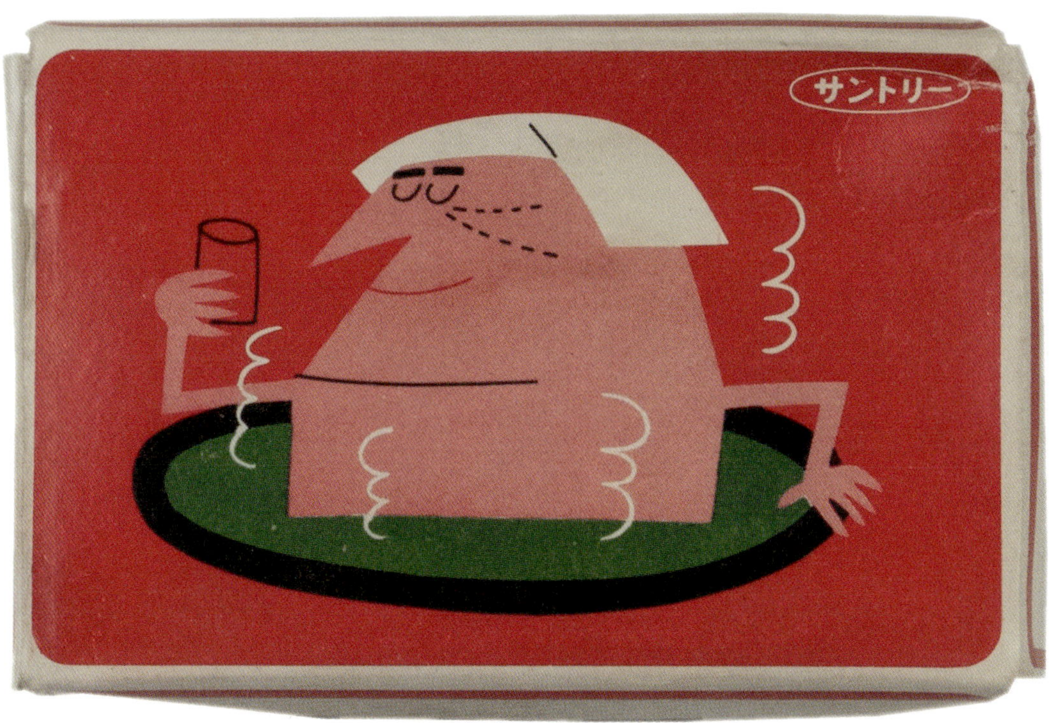

Promotional Uncle Torys soap from the mid-1960s—an early example of cross-branding between Suntory and Mitsuwa Soap ミツワ石鹸.

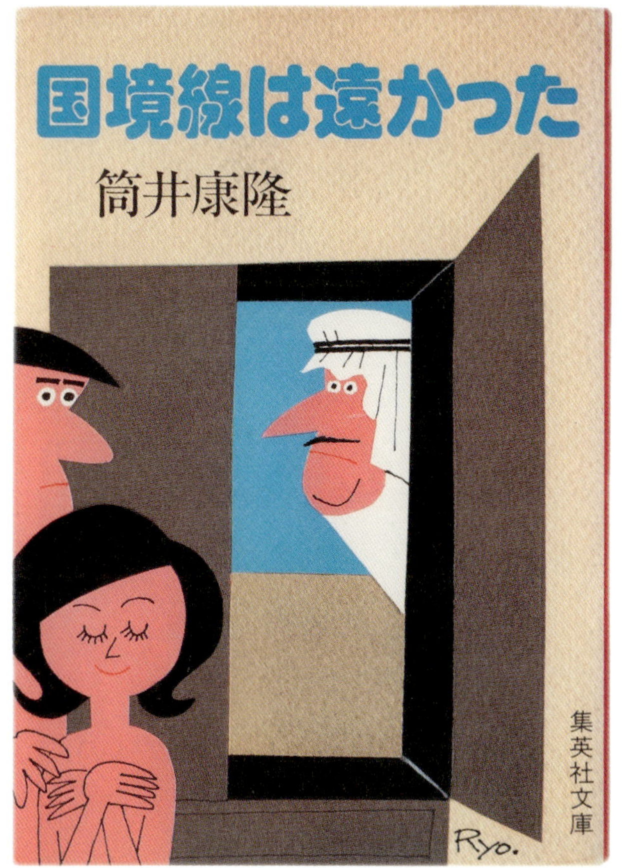

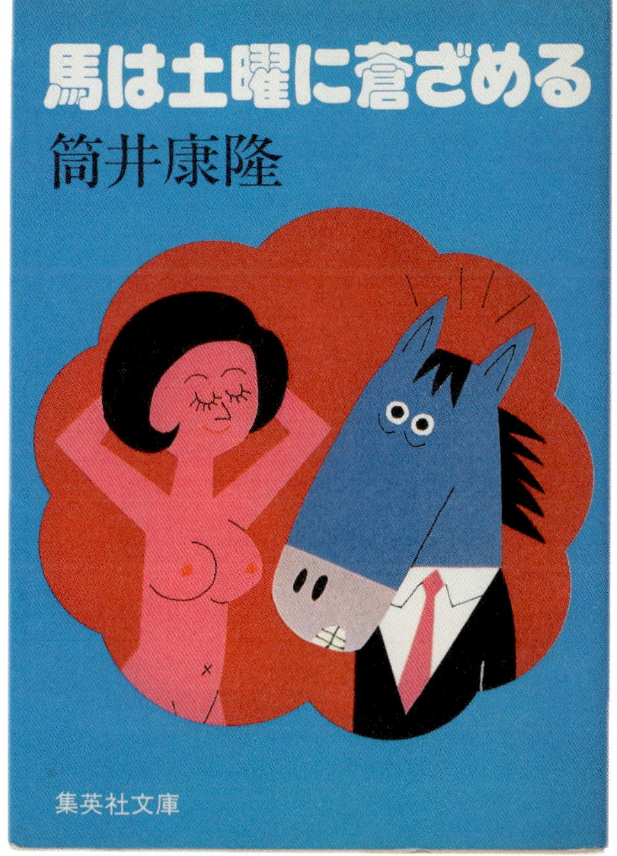

Left: ***The Border Was Quite Far Away*** **国境線は遠かった, Tsutsui Yasutaka 筒井康隆** (Tokyo: Shueisha 集英社, 1981).
Right: ***The Horse Turns Pale on Saturday*** **馬は土曜に蒼ざめる, Tsutsui Yasutaka 筒井康隆** (Tokyo: Shueisha 集英社, 1978).

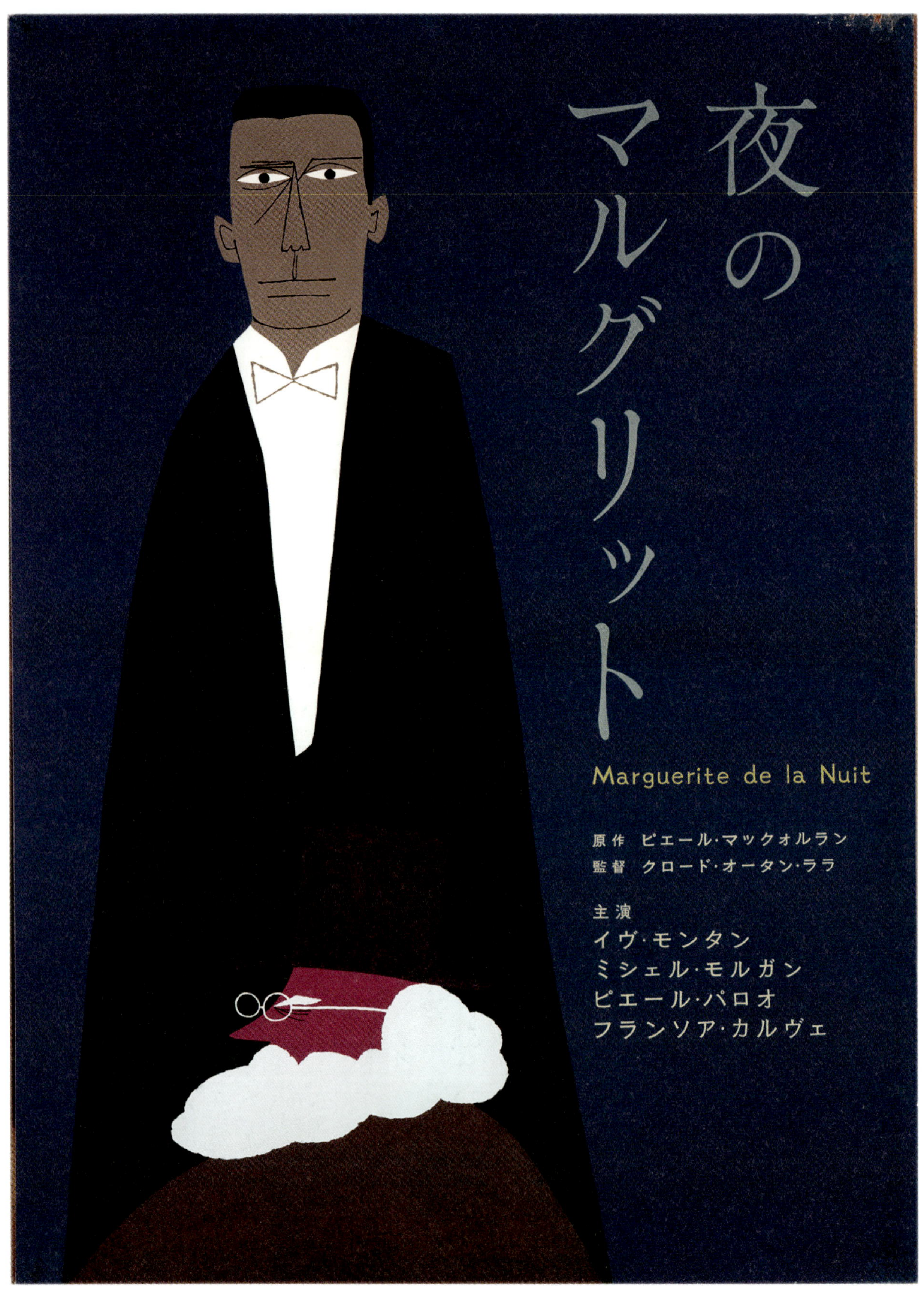

***Marguerite de la Nuit* 夜のマルグリット** poster by Wada Makoto 和田誠, for which he won the 1957 Japan Advertising Artists Club Award.

WADA MAKOTO 和田誠

1936–2019

Wada Makoto was born in Osaka and graduated from Tama Art University, having studied under Sugiura Hisui. In 1957 he received the seventh Japan Advertising Artists Club Prize for his "Night Marguerite" 夜のマルグリット poster design, the first in an incredible string of awards for his work in advertising, illustration, writing, and design. Wada was a prolific designer of book and magazine covers. While still a student, he created a series of speculative illustrated designs for jazz LPs inspired by the work of Blue Note Records' designer Reid Miles, and these were exhibited in the eighth Japan Advertising Artists Club exhibition.

After graduating, he turned down a job offer at the advertising agency Dentsū to join the advertising agency Light Publicity in 1959, having previously produced a film for Toshiba via the company on a freelance basis. The same year, he won a design competition held by the Japan Tobacco and Salt Public Corporation 日本専売公社 for the design of Hi-Lite, a brand of filter cigarettes which became incredibly popular after it debuted publicly in 1960. He designed the logo for the Japan Socialist Party and numerous advertising campaigns for Toray and Canon while at Light Publicity.

Wada was a co-founder of the Tokyo Illustrators' Club in 1964, alongside Yokoo Tadanori, Uno Akira, and others, though the group would disband in 1970. He was one of the participants in the 1965 exhibition *Persona*.

Wada left Light Publicity in 1968 and founded his own studio in Tokyo's Aoyama district. He was selected as a judge for the 1969 Japan Advertising Artists Club awards and exhibition and was present for the student revolt that disrupted the judging sessions and led to the dissolution of the JAAC.

Wada worked across film and publishing and is renowned for his minimal and whimsical style of illustration. He had a prolific career, having designed the covers of the magazines *Weekly Sankei* 週刊サンケイ starting in 1973 and *Weekly Bunshun* 週刊文春 from 1977 until his death, amongst a diverse array of other projects.

Besides designing multiple film posters, he directed a number of full-length feature films, and also worked as a producer and director of anime films, videos, and video games for Nintendo. He authored, illustrated, and designed over 200 books over the course of his lifetime.

References:

Kamekura, Yūsaku, Nagai Kazumasa, Tanaka Ikkō, and Fukuda Shigeo. *4-GD Poster and Mark / Yūsaku Kamekura Kazumasa Tanaka Kazumasa Nagai Shigeo Fukuda*. Tokyo: Yomiuri Shimbun, 1987.

Segi, Shin'ichi, Tanaka Ikkō, and Hiroshi Sano. *Nissenbi no Jidai = The Epoch of the Japan Advertising Artists Club: Nihon No Gurafikku Dezain 1951–70*. Tokyo: Toransuāto, 2000.

Wada, Makoto, and Tanaka Ikkō. *Makoto Wada*. Tokyo: Ginza Graphic Gallery, 1996.

Wada, Makoto. *Sotei Monogatari*. Tokyo: Chūōkoron, 2020.

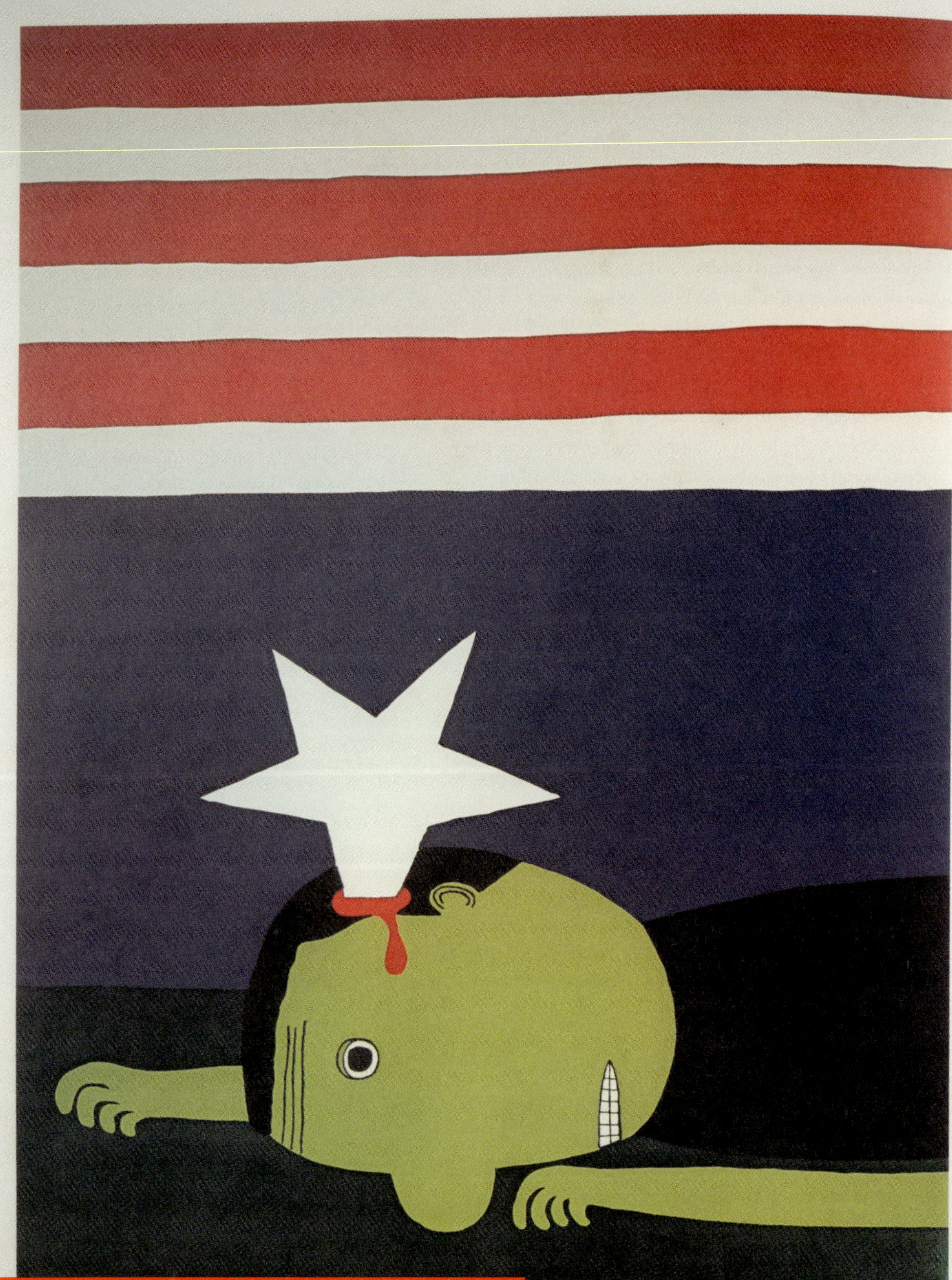

Posterland ポスターランド, Wada Makoto 和田誠 (Tokyo: Kodansha 講談社, 1976).
A large-scale collection of Wada's poster designs throughout the years.

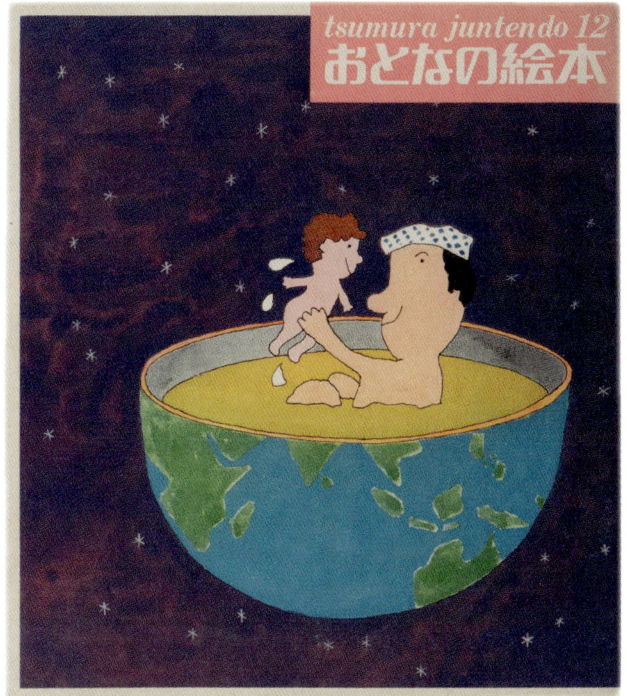

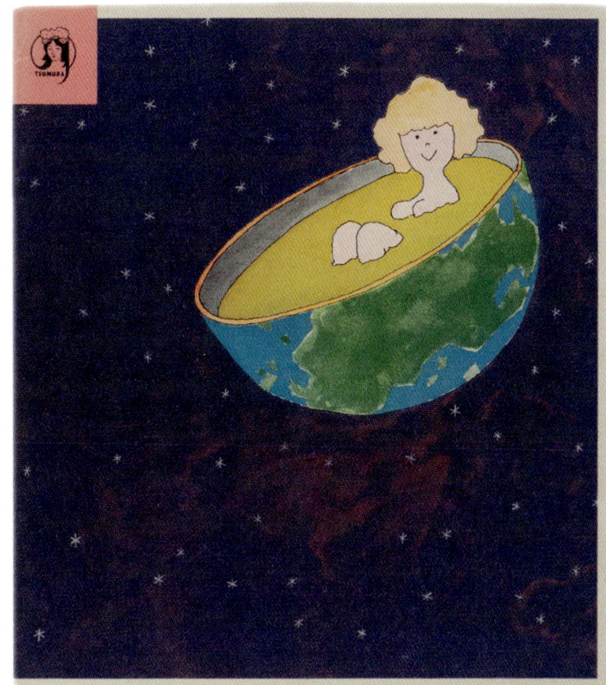

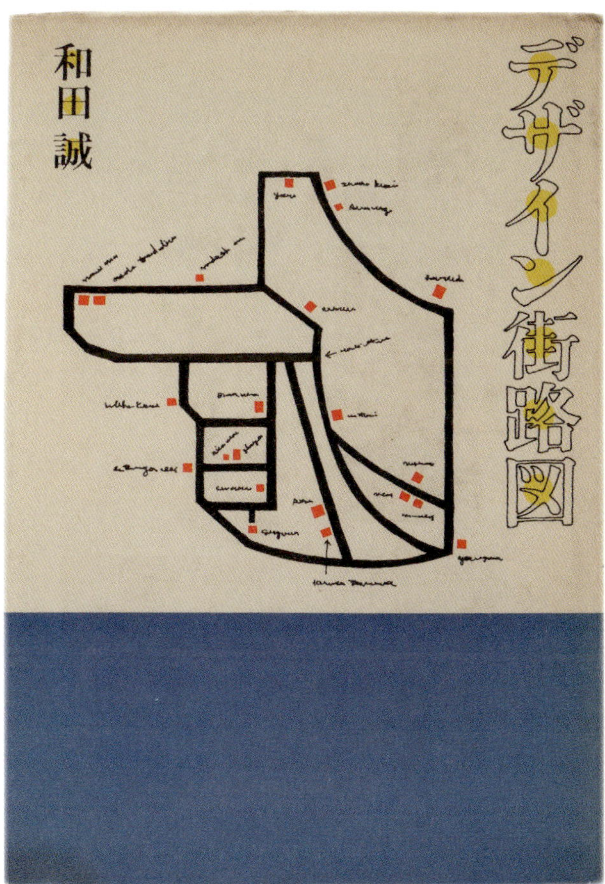

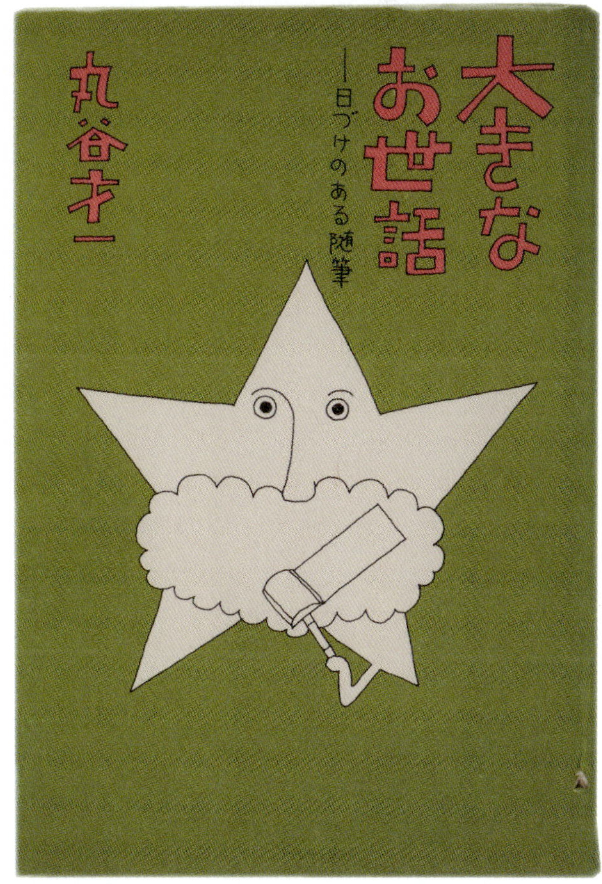

Clockwise from top left: Cover and back cover from ***Tsumura Juntendo* 順天堂 No. 12**, published in 1970, a promotional magazine for the magazine's eponymous college in Tokyo; ***None of Your Business* 大きなお世話, Maruya Saiichi 丸谷才一** (Tokyo: Asahi Shimbun朝日新聞社, 1975); ***Design Street Map* デザイン 街路図, Wada Makoto 和田誠** (Tokyo: Shobunsha 昭文社, 1973), a collection of essays and interviews by Wada Makoto, including interviews of Yokoo Tadanori 横尾忠則, Ishioka Eiko 石岡瑛子, and Yumura Teruhiko 湯村輝彦.

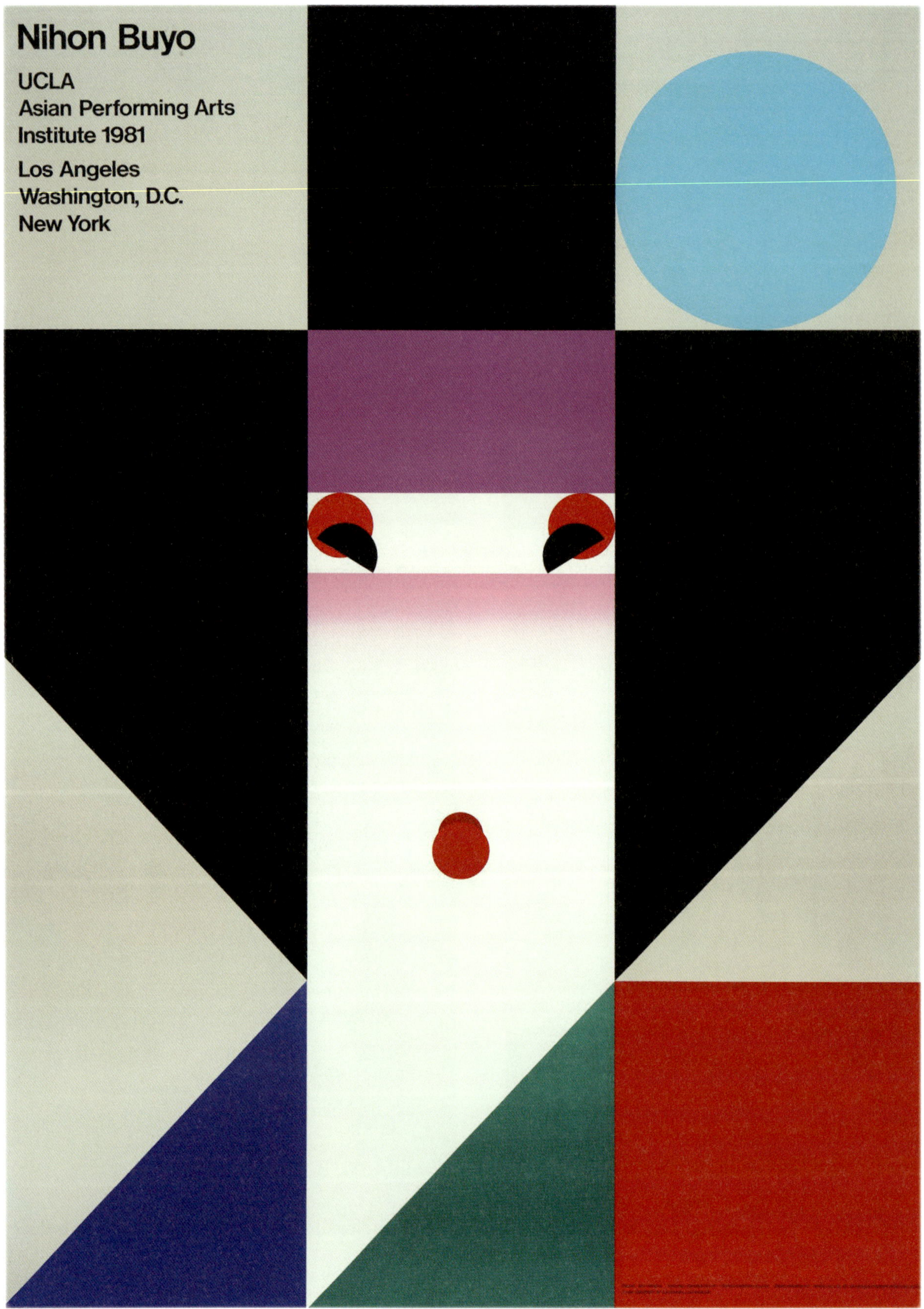

Nihon Buyo poster, Tanaka Ikkō 田中一光, University of California Los Angeles, 1981.

TANAKA IKKŌ 田中一光

1930–2002

"Japanese graphic design has a tendency to deviate from its basic function of transmitting information."[1]
- Tanaka Ikkō

Tanaka Ikkō was born in Nara and graduated from the Kyoto College of Fine Arts. After graduation, he initially worked at the Kanegafuchi textile company for two years, and then he joined the Osaka newspaper *Sankei Shimbun* 産経新聞 in 1952. Five years later, Tanaka moved to Tokyo and joined the advertising agency Light Publicity.

Tanaka was incredibly active in both the Kansai and Kantō regions of Japan, designing posters for the Kanze Noh theater in Osaka and for a number of corporations in Tokyo.

Tanaka participated in the World Design Conference in 1960, designing the WoDeCo event poster. He was one of the co-founders of the Nippon Design Center, a consortium of designers and advertisers working alongside corporations, and he founded his eponymous design studio in 1963. Tanaka also co-curated the 1965 exhibition *Persona*.

Tanaka was one of the six contestants invited to submit work for the 1964 Olympic logo design competition, alongside Inagaki Kōichiro, Kamekura Yūsaku, Kōno Takashi, Nagai Kazumasa, and Sugiura Kōhei. While his logo design was not chosen, Tanaka would go on to be one of the main designers of the 1964 Olympic identity, designing the Olympic medals and the signage for the games. Tanaka won a design competition for the longer variant of Peace cigarettes, allowing him more financial security and the ability to move his design studio into more expansive quarters in the Kita-Aoyama area of Tokyo.

After the dissolution of the Japan Advertising Artists Club in 1970, there was a giant gap in the social culture of graphic design in Tokyo—where once there were regular meetings and events, for two years there was a void. In 1972, Tanaka founded the cultural venue Off Design, partially as a space where designers might meet. He co-founded Tokyo Designer's Space (TDS), a gallery within Off Design where designers could exhibit their work. In 1976, TDS instigated a five-month series of exhibitions called *One Day One Show*, wherein TDS members would show their work for only twenty-four hours in the space. The work shown was constantly in flux, with a new designer featured each day of the five months.

Tanaka was appointed Creative Director of monolithic printing corporation DaiNippon Printing's Ginza Graphic Gallery (GGG), Tokyo's leading graphic design exhibition space, in 1986. Tanaka designed the logo for the GGG and created the template for the gallery's long-running book series.

Tanaka would go on to become Creative Director for the Seibu Saison Group—a holding company that owns a number of department stores and railway lines—and would execute a large number of projects for them across branding, packaging, interior design, and advertising campaigns. He designed the company's logo and Futura-inspired custom typeface in 1982, as well as the identity for Seibu's department store Loft in 1984.

Tanaka designed the identity for fashion designer Mori Hanae, created an expansive body of work for Issey Miyake, and designed the logos for *Expo '85* in Tsukuba and *World City Expo Tokyo '96*.

In 1979, Tanaka was asked by the Seiyu Group, a supermarket chain founded in 1946, to provide the creative direction for a new retail venture that differed from typical consumption patterns in Japanese society at that time.

Japanese customers were used to paying a premium for branded goods, resulting in the formation of a mass-luxury market in which possessing expensive, exclusive goods seemed to be a necessity rather than a desire. Tanaka's vision was to focus on the curation of high-quality merchandise and ensure that nothing sold by this new initiative was over-packaged. His idea was that the products were mostly generic, brand-free, and anonymous—a protest against luxury goods' excessive labeling and expensive price tags. While it was fashionable at the time to buy a brand-name product regardless of its usefulness, Tanaka and his team anticipated that a growing part of the population would choose functionality, affordability, and quality over marketing gimmickry, exorbitant price tags, and status symbols.

Tanaka collaborated with marketing consultant Koike Kazuko 小池一子 to cultivate the market positioning of this new product line through copywriting, and later with interior designer Sugimoto Takashi 杉本貴志 to curate inviting retail spaces.

1 Patricia Jane Graham, *Japanese Design: Art, Aesthetics & Culture* (North Clarendon, VT: Tuttle Publishing, 2014), 224.

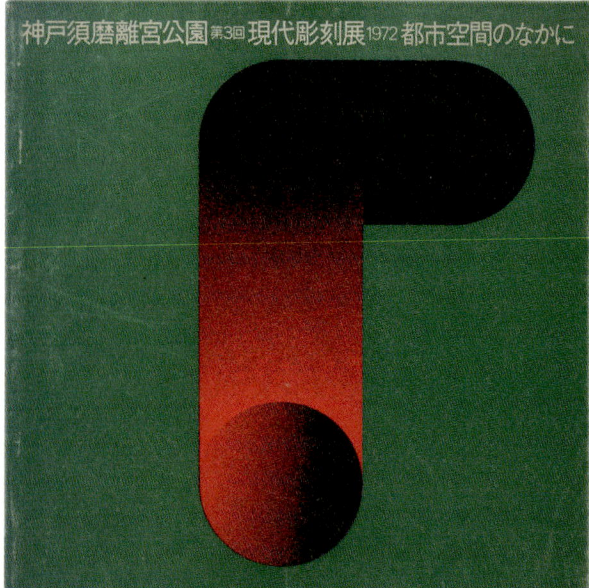

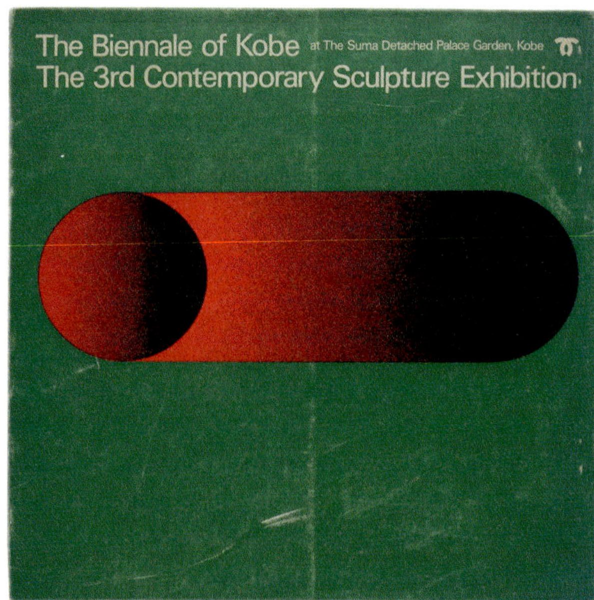

Front and back cover catalog design for ***The Biennale of Kobe: 3rd Contemporary Sculpture Exhibition***, designed by Tanaka Ikko in 1972.

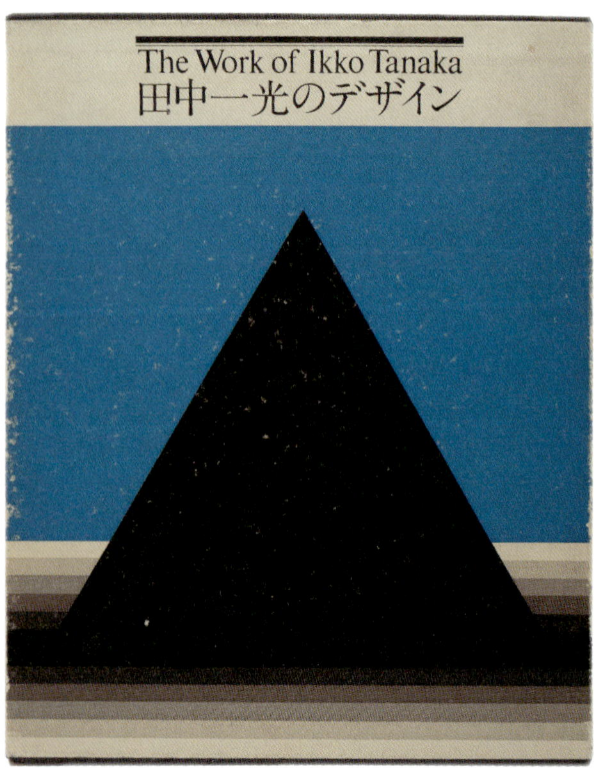

***The Work of Tanaka Ikko* 田中一光のデザイン, Tanaka Ikkō 田中 一光, (Tokyo: Shinshindou 駸々堂, 1975).** A large-scale, 214-page monograph devoted to Tanaka's assorted graphic design projects.

Four kanji came up in their meetings, namely 無印良品 ("Mujirushi Ryōhin" or "no brand good product"), and this became the name of the venture, though it has been referred to as MUJI in the West since 1999.

Tanaka was the first Creative Director of MUJI from 1980 until 2000. Tanaka was involved at every touchpoint of the MUJI project, managing each aspect of the brand including strategy, advertising, packaging, and broadcast direction. He led the brand from humble beginnings as a product line of nine household goods and thirty-one food products sold at Seiyu supermarkets, to a veritable army of standalone retail stores that dot the Japanese landscape selling a vast array of food, clothing, stationery, and household goods. The brand is recognized for being affordable yet offering quality, minimalist-designed goods with a Japanese aesthetic.

Tanaka's most iconic work—the Rinpa 琳派 school of painting-inspired 1981 "Nihon Buyō" poster, was created for a dance event at the University of California Los Angeles at the request of Tanaka's longtime associate, critic and and organizer Katsumi Masaru. Katsumi had given Tanaka his first big professional break in 1958, selecting his work for the cover of the first issue of his new magazine, グラフィックデザイン *Graphic Design*. It was Katsumi again who selected Tanaka as one of the competitors for the 1964 Olympic logo competition and to work on the design for the Olympics, and with whom Tanaka would co-curate *Persona*.

1 Graham, Patricia Jane. *Japanese Design: Art, Aesthetics & Culture*. Tokyo: Tuttle Publishing, 2014.

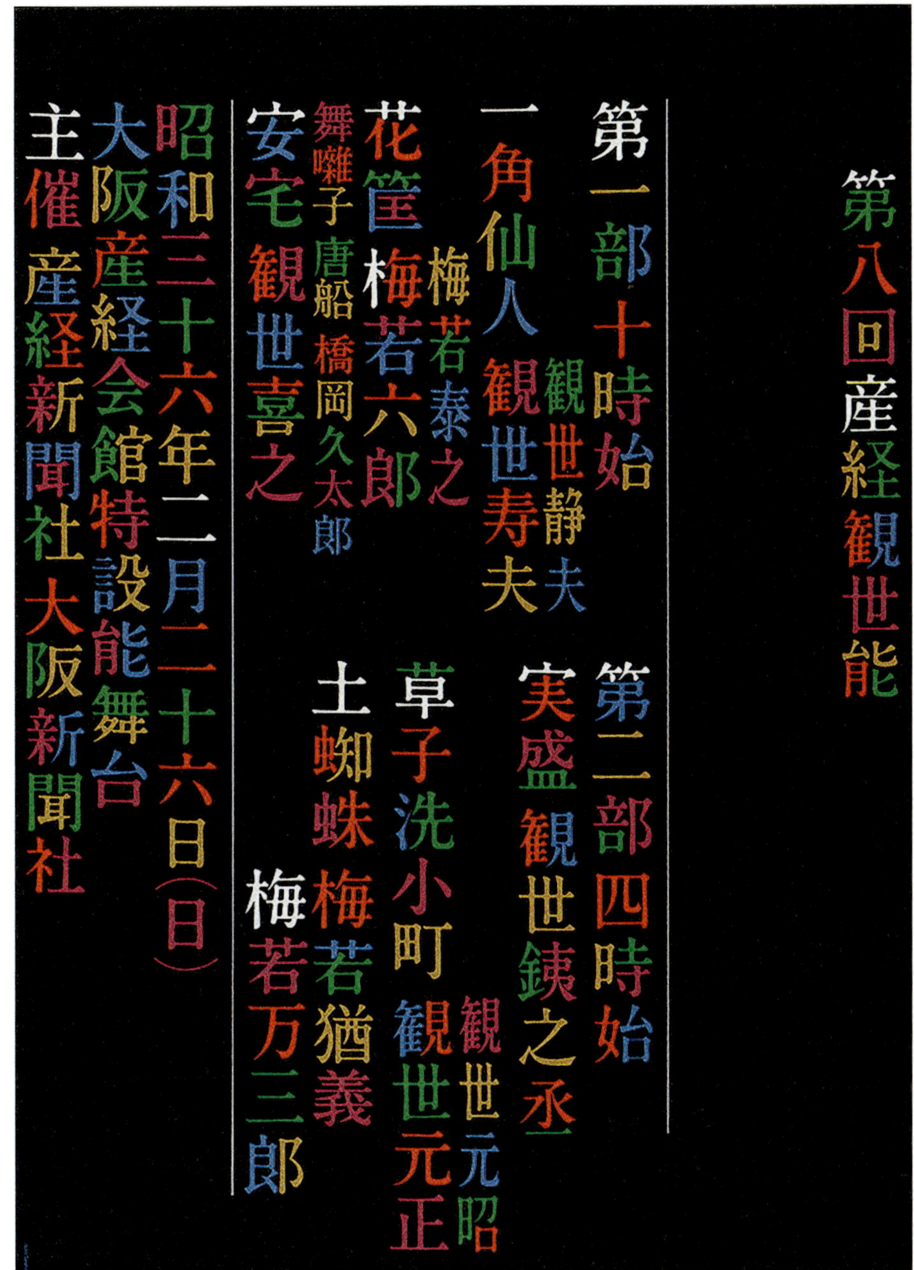

Promotional poster for the ***8th Sankei Kanzei Noh performance*** from 1961.

Tanaka's 1986 logo design for **Ginza Graphic Gallery**, Dai Nippon Printing Co., Ltd's graphic design exhibition space.

Throughout the 1980s and '90s, Tanaka created assorted interpretations of the abstracted geometric profiles of kabuki performers. He was a rigorous typographer and lifelong lover of the typeface Bodoni, for which he designed the complementary mincho typeface Kocho with his longtime client, the type foundry Morisawa, in 1993.

Tanaka's work is best understood through his articulation of a high level of abstraction, structural geometry, playful use of color, and simplified versions of traditional Japanese forms.

References:

Kamekura, Yūsaku, and Ayao Yamana. *Gurafikku Dezain no Seiki: Bunshō to Danwa to Sakuhin De kōsei: Meiji Sedai Yamana Ayao Sugiura Hisui Kara shōwa Sedai Made*. Tokyo: Bijutsu Shuppansha, 2008.

Segi, Shin'ichi, Tanaka Ikkō, and Hiroshi Sano. *Nissenbi no Jidai = The Epoch of the Japan Advertising Artists Club: Nihon No Gurafikku Dezain 1951–70*. Tokyo: Toransuāto, 2000.

Tanaka, Ikkō, Mitsuo Katsui, and Hiroshi Kashiwagi. *Nihon no Bukku Dezain 1946–95 = Book Design in Japan 1946–95*. Tokyo: Ginza Graphic Gallery, 1996.

Tanaka, Ikkō. *Tanaka Ikkō*. Tokyo: Ginza Graphic Gallery, 1993.

Tanaka, Ikkō. *Tanaka Ikkō: dentō to Konnichi No Dezain = Tanaka Ikko: Design of Tradition and Today*. Tokyo: Toransuāto, 1998.

Traganou, Jilly. "Tokyo's 1964 Olympic Design as a 'Realm of [Design] Memory.'" *Sport in Society* 14, no. 4 (2011): 466–81. https://doi.org/10.1080/17430437.2011.565925.

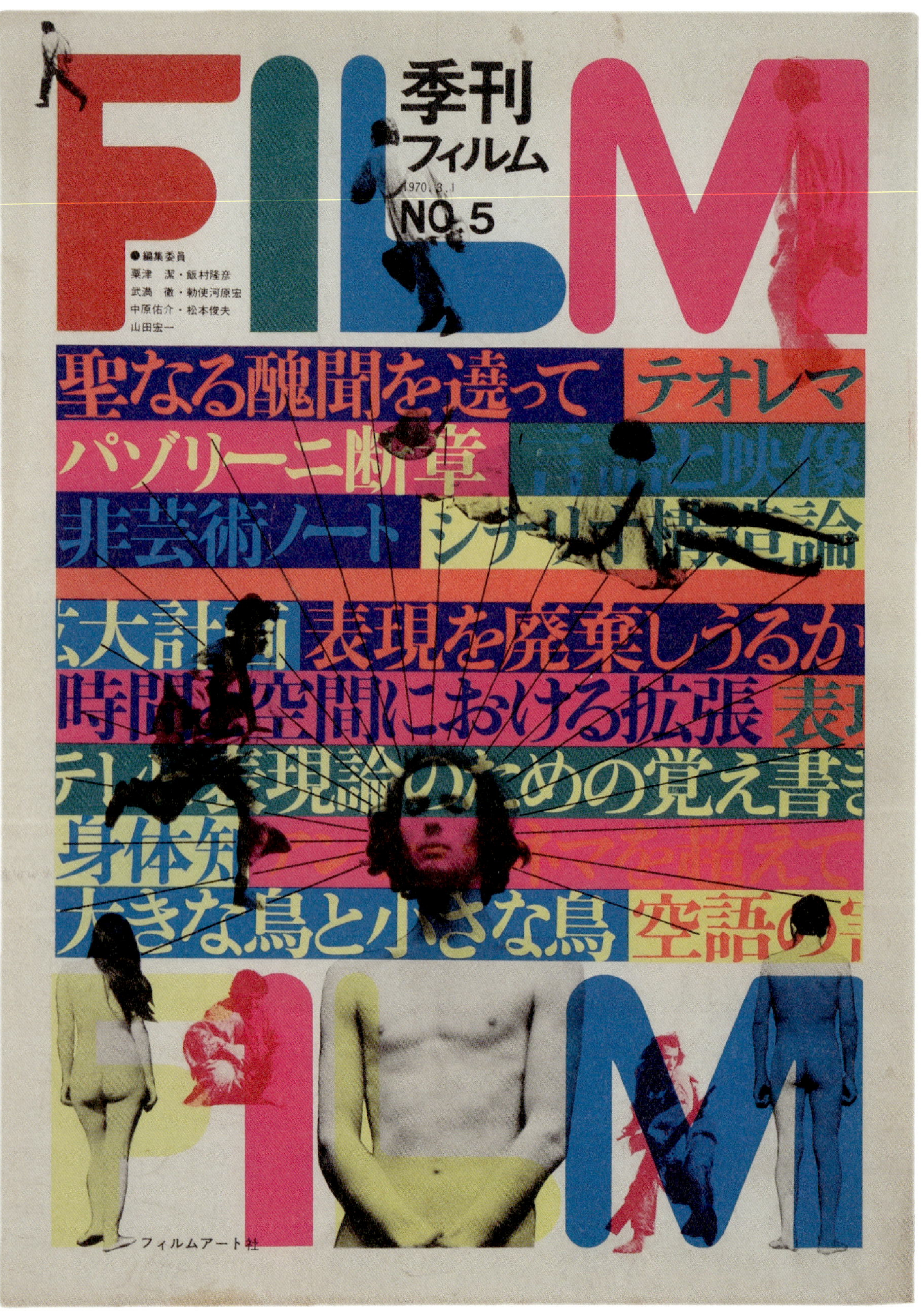

Magazine cover for ***FILM Quarterly*** **季刊 FILM** No. 5 (Tokyo: Film Art-sha フィルムアート社, 1970) created in collaboration between Awazu Kiyoshi 粟津潔 and fellow designer Enomoto Ryoichi 榎本了壱, marrying psychedelic spot colors with photographic collage and illustration.

AWAZU KIYOSHI 粟津潔

1929–2009

Awazu Kiyoshi was largely self taught, and he started working as a graphic designer in 1954, designing sketches for posters and doing paste-up for the Independent Film Advertising Club 独立映画宣伝部 as a part-time employee. His first poster design was for Murayama Tomoyoshi's Shinkyo Gekidan theater troupe, which led to work for other troupes such as Zenshinza and Shinseisazuka. This was followed by a number of years in which he created posters for film studios such as Dokuritsu Eiga and Nikkatsu, quickly gaining notoriety for his deft mixture of illustration, custom lettering, and detailed typography.

Awazu's 1955 Japan Advertising Artists Club award-winning poster *Give Back Our Sea* 海を返せ depicted a fisherman barred from his trade due to the effects of pollution caused by the American military. The poster was a timely and culturally resonant piece of socioeconomic critique which established the concept of designer as advocate of social causes. His posters for the 1957 documentary *The Crying Whales* and the 1957 play *Chuji Kunisawa* further cemented Awazu's position as a young designer to watch.

Awazu spent the rest of the 1950s and the 1960s refining his folk-influenced style, experimenting with color and form, and investigating the possibilities of chance processes, after an encounter with composer John Cage. Awazu consistently declined invitations to join advertising agencies and larger design studios—a bold move at the time. He worked as a lecturer at Kuwasawa Design School from 1961 to 1964, then taught at Musashino Art University as Associate Professor from 1964 through 1970.

He participated in the incredibly popular 1965 exhibition *Persona* at the Matsuya Ginza department store, having been invited by curator and JAAC stalwart Tanaka Ikkō. Awazu exhibited posters and book cover designs that showed his interest in working for cultural institutions and his subjective and intuitive approach to graphic design and illustration.

Awazu frequently collaborated with architects, infusing some of Japan's national monuments with a proto-hippie folk sensibility that eschewed the hard edges of Modernism for an organic massing of lines and naturalistic form. Awazu found a kindred spirit in the ideas and company of architect Kurokawa Kishō 黒川紀章, with whom he would found the hybrid architecture and graphic design movement Metabolism 新陳代謝, whose aims included the exploration of physical, spatial, and graphic megastructures built up through organic biological growth.

The 1960s saw Awazu continuing his work in film, creating fascinating poster designs for the avant-garde film *The Woman in the Dunes* in 1964, and *Kwaidan*, an adaptation of four traditional Japanese ghost stories as popularized by journalist, amateur ethnologist, and writer Patrick Lafcadio Hearn. Freewheeling formal experimentation influenced by Pop Art and '60s counterculture from both abroad and home in Japan also found their way into Awazu's work, observable in his bold color schemes, raw linework, and eclectic typography. Traces of Ben Shahn's illustrative approach and lettering pop up in Awazu's work in the 1960s, as do elements of Push Pin Studios' appropriation of "olde timey" decorative advertising cuts and a compositional approach influenced by Yokoo Tadanori. Awazu was obsessed with concentric linework, and many of his projects rely upon overprinting for dazzling optical effects.

Having been canonized for his early works, Awazu veered into graphic left-field in the late '60s and '70s. His visual experiments in the realms of architecture and theater from this period incorporate the excitement of British paper architects Archigram and Eduardo Paolozzi married with the decorative elements of ukiyo-e expressed through the medium of coarse-grained silkscreen. Traditional motifs are filtered through a contemporary lens that can be disturbing, at times—dismembered heads emitting copious bodily fluids and the omnipresent crows of Tokyo crying tears of shame, interleaved with expressive hand-drawn characters, their strokes swollen and collapsing upon themselves. Some of the most striking compositions include a number of magazine covers that Awazu created in collaboration with fellow designer Enomoto Ryōichi 榎本了壱 (1947–) for *FILM Quarterly* 季刊 or *FILM* magazine, combining psychedelic spot colors with photographic collage and illustration.

Throughout the 1970s and 1980s, Awazu remained devoted to the poster as a form of graphic expression. At the time, public perception and appreciation shifted from "pure" graphic design to multimedia, advertising-based, big-budget initiatives such as those produced by art director Ishioka Eiko for the Parco department store chain, spanning film, print, and broadcast.

1 Kurokawa, Kisho, Kiyoshi Awazu, Kiyonori Kikutake, and Noburo Kawazoe. *Metabolism: the Proposals for a New Urbanism*. Tokyo: Bijutsu Shuppan Sha, 1960.

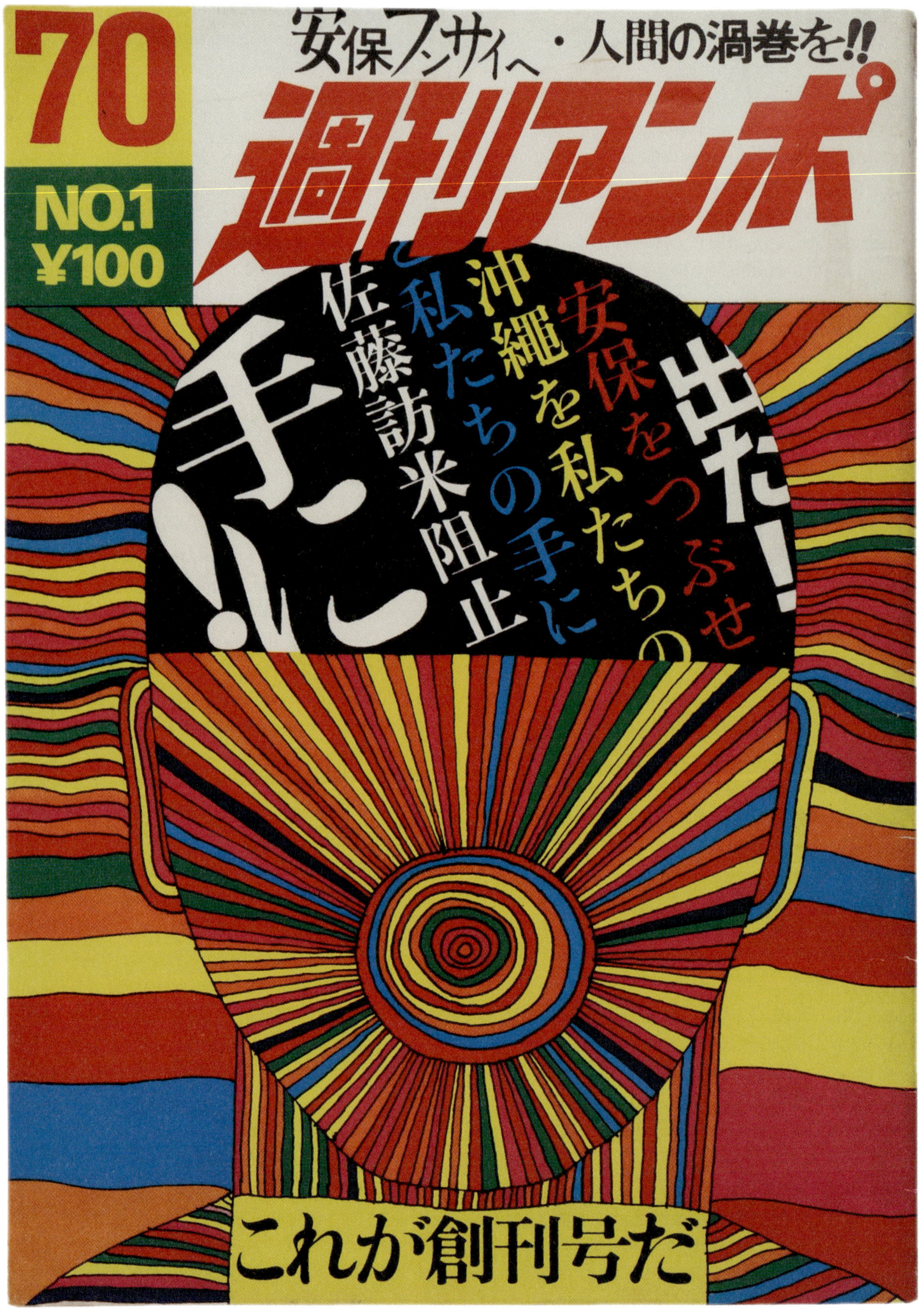

Awazu's cover for the debut issue of the political magazine ***Weekly Anpo*** **週刊アンポ**, published in 1969.

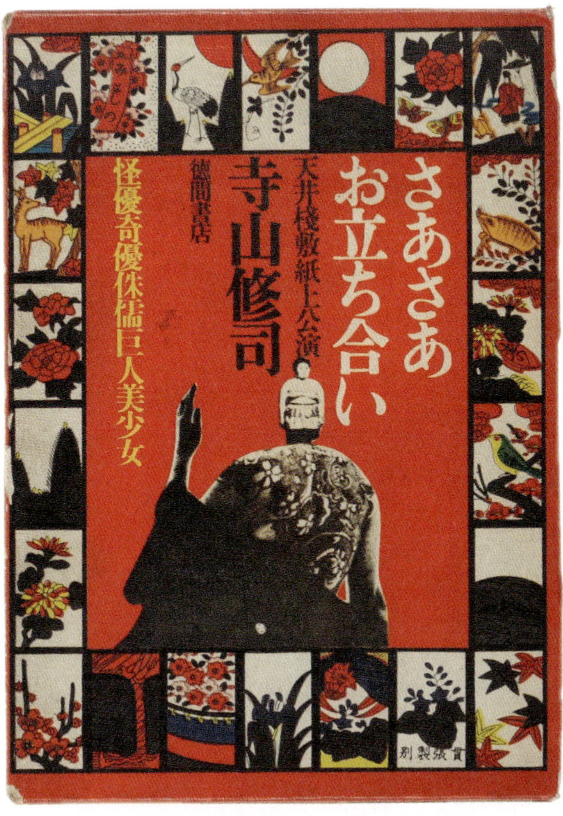

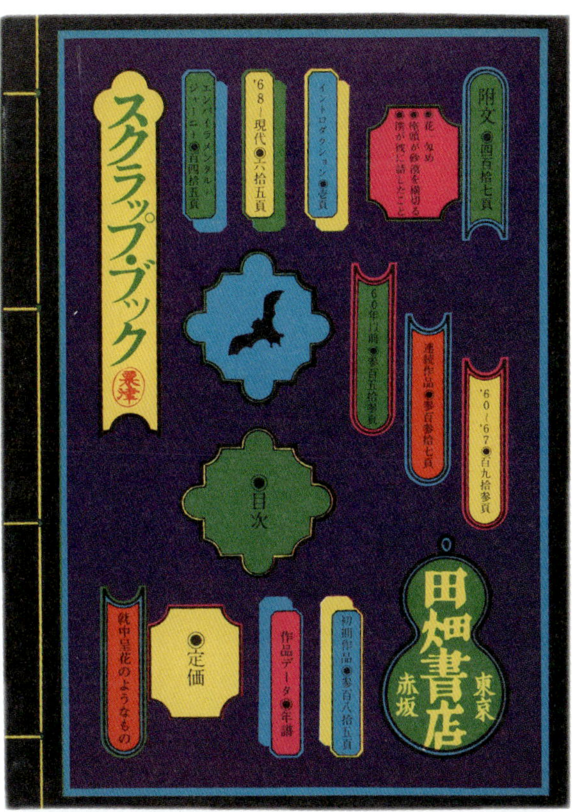

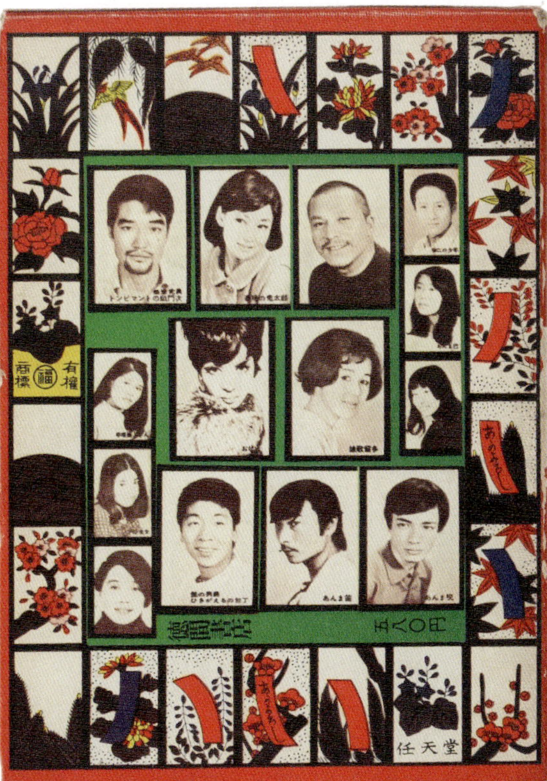

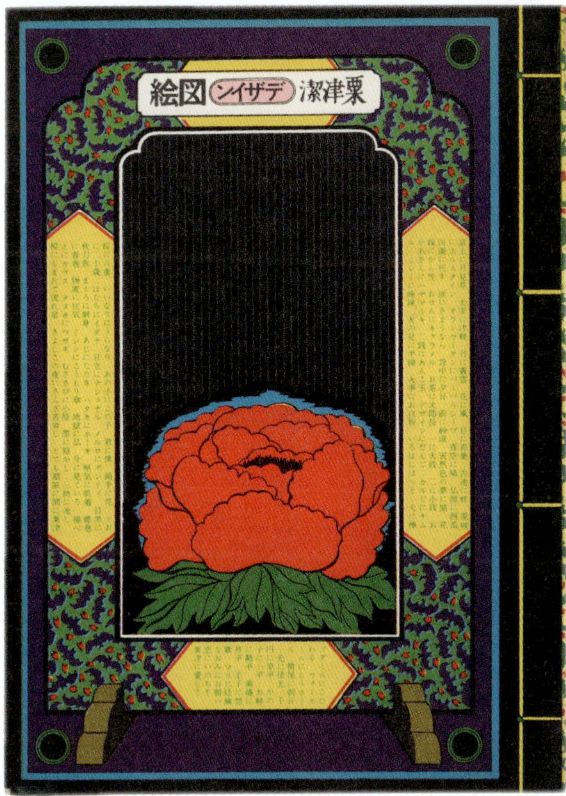

Above: ***Come Witness the Tenjo Sajiki Performance on Paper* さあさあお立ち合い　天井桟敷紙上公演　怪優奇優侏儒巨人美少女, Terayama Shūji 寺山修司 (Tokyo: Tokuma Shoten 徳間書店, 1968).** Design by Awazu Kiyoshi 粟津潔 with photography by Moriyama Daido.

Above and following page: Front cover, back cover and spreads from ***Kiyoshi Awazu Scrapbook* 粟津潔デザイン図絵 (Tokyo: Tabata Shoten 田畑書店, 1971).** A mammoth, 459-page, highly illustrated book that is a visual feast of Awazu's mid-period work, sheathed in a printed wraparound cardboard sleeve.

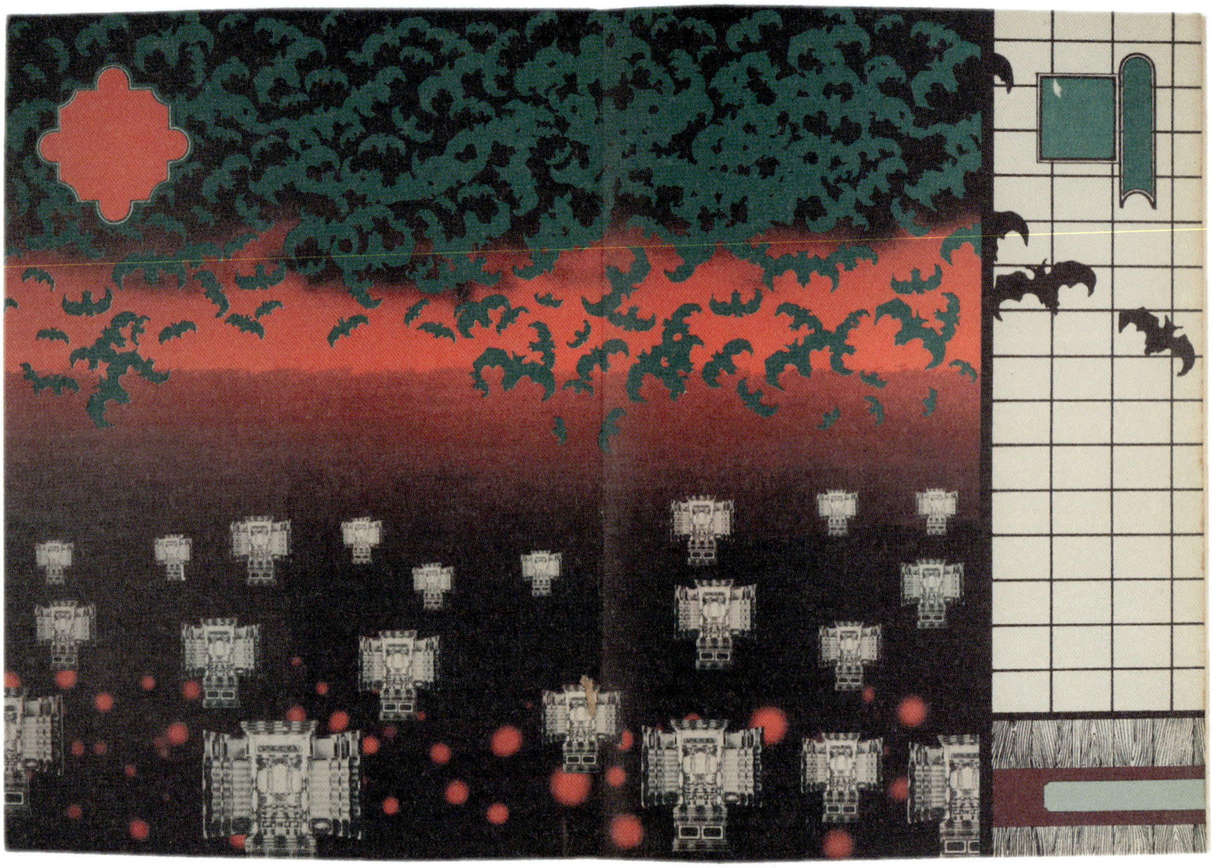

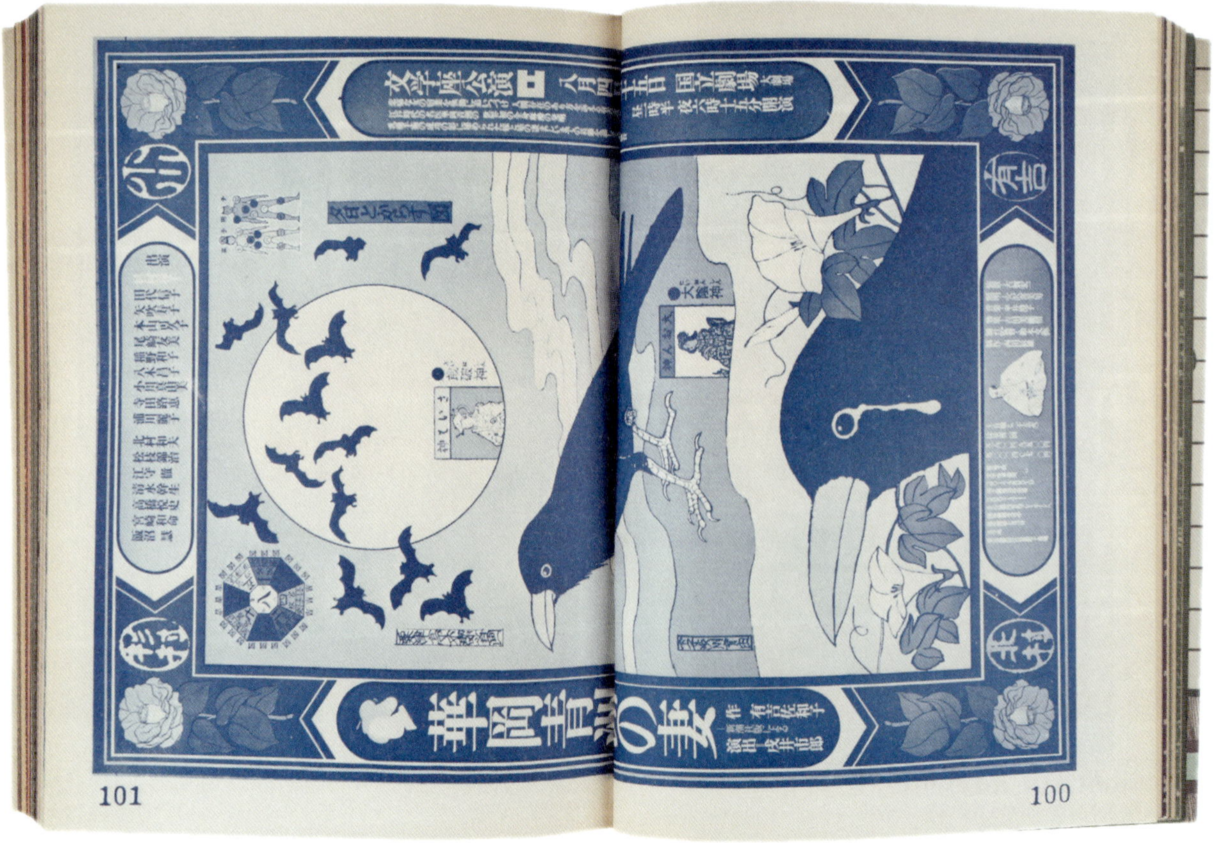

While Japan's design industry moved wholesale to a fascination with the gloss and sheen of the photograph and the airbrush, Awazu battered away via pen, brush, ink, and press type, creating virtual cosmoses of flattened figure/ground relations.

Despite being out of step with visual trends at that time, Awazu had established himself as a force to be reckoned with, and commissions continued with an increased focus on collaborative projects in the field of architecture. The most notable of these projects was Awazu's exterior design scheme for the Nibankan Building in the Kabukicho red-light district of Shinjuku. Reminiscent of proposed early-Modern Japanese kiosk designs, the Nibankan Building's various planes are pasted with bright colors and geometric shapes—like a Pop Art painting fragmented and vomited on a simplified, though not simplistic, multi-planar structure.

Designed by 109 Building architect Takeyama Minoru 竹山実, the Nibankan Building in Shinjuku was featured on the cover of Charles Jencks's breakthrough 1977 book, *The Language of Post-Modern Architecture*. The collaborative, formal approach and holistic graphic treatment were an early precursor to the hyper-decorative tendencies of other Postmodern architects. Included in the architectural plan was a proposal to revisit the graphic treatment at five-year intervals, and to revisit the pop colors and shapes even more regularly. Adventurous and forward-thinking, the re-skinning of the building was meant to mirror the constant change that is innate to the vibrant Kabukicho district.

Nestled in nearby Harajuku since 1964, the Awazu design office chugged away—Awazu and an assistant working through each day's assignments, breaking for extended games of Go amidst the fumes of Cow Glue, Awazu's adhesive of choice. He preferred the clear, very, very permanent sealant for paste-up in lieu of the then-typical rubber cement. In 1988, the studio quietly packed up and relocated to a remote part of Kawasaki, where Awazu had Kyoto Station architect Hara Hiroshi build him a palatial modern home with an in-house studio amongst the rice fields and rolling hills of Kanagawa. From his new home, Awazu continued his assorted activities, exhibiting internationally, taking on design commissions, sculpting, and screenprinting.

In 2000, Awazu became the first Director of the Toppan Printing Corporation's Printing Museum, and the ardent independent contractor and longtime educator finally became a "company man." Awazu steered the museum, situated in the industrial Edogawabashi district, to numerous awards and an enhanced status amongst cultural institutions in Tokyo. Meanwhile, he continued to research and exhibit actively, exploring a long-held interest in the petroglyphs of Native Americans, which culminated in an exhibition on the subject. A number of his works are held in the permanent collection of the 21st Century Museum of Contemporary Art, Kanazawa.

Awazu passed away in 2009 in Kawasaki.

References:

Awazu, Kiyoshi. *Awazu Kiyoshi: kōya no Gurafizumu*. Tokyo: Firumu Ātosha, 2007.

Awazu, Kiyoshi, and Nakahara Yūsuke. *Awazu Kiyoshi sakuhinshū = Kiyoshi Awazu*. Tokyo: Kōdansha, 1978.

Awazu, Kiyoshi. *Insatsu Hakubutsushi*. Tokyo: Toppan insatsu, 2001.

Lynam, Ian. "Glue Vapors & Go: The Life of Awazu Kiyoshi." *Néojaponisme*. Néojaponisme, December 11, 2012. https://neojaponisme.com/2012/12/11/glue-vapors-go-the-life-of-awazu-kiyoshi/.

Kamekura, Yusaku, and Ayao Yamana. *Gurafikku Dezain no Seiki: Bunshō to Danwa to Sakuhin De kōsei: Meiji Sedai Yamana Ayao Sugiura Hisui Kara shōwa Sedai Made*. Tōkyō: Bijutsu Shuppansha, 2008.

Kurokawa, Kisho, Kiyoshi Awazu, Kiyonori Kikutake, and Noburo Kawazoe. *Metabolism: The Proposals for a New Urbanism*. Tokyo: Bijutsu Shuppan Sha, 1960.

Segi, Shin'ichi, Tanaka Ikkō, and Hiroshi Sano. *Nissenbi no Jidai = The Epoch of the Japan Advertising Artists Club: Nihon No Gurafikku Dezain 1951–70*. Tokyo: Toransuāto, 2000.

Shibukawa, Hoyoshi, and Ryoichi Enomoto. "Memory of Kiyoshi Awazu." *Idea* 58, no. 340 (May 2010): 213–20.

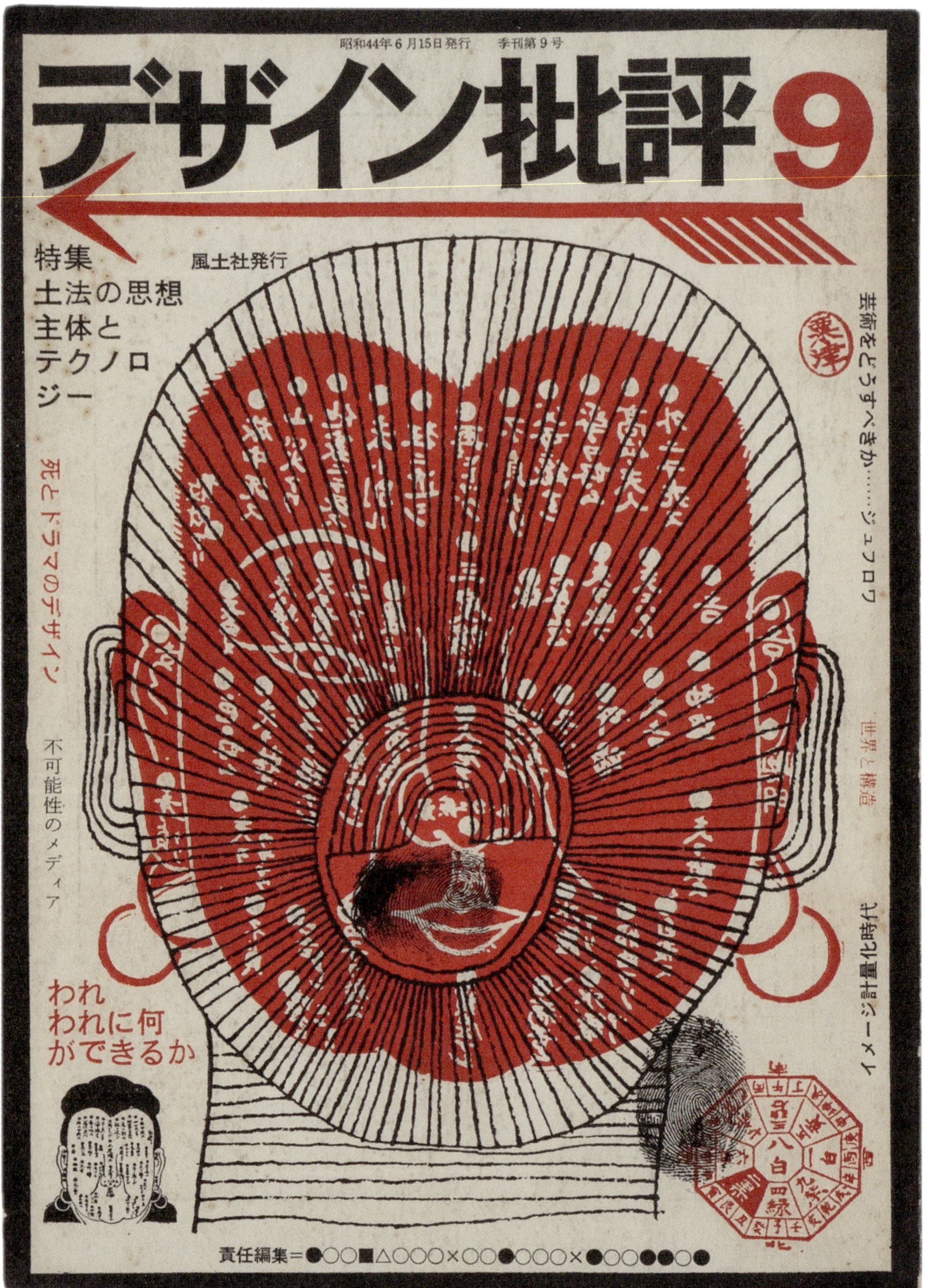

Design Review デザイン講評 No. 9 (Tokyo: Fudosha 風土社, 1969).

The King of Circle かがくのとも, Tanikawa Shuntaro 谷川俊太郎 (Tokyo: Fukuinkan Shoten 福音館書店, 1971). A largely psychedelic picture book for young children encouraging them to embrace science in an array of rounded forms, from records to boulders. Design and illustration by Awazu Kiyoshi 粟津潔.

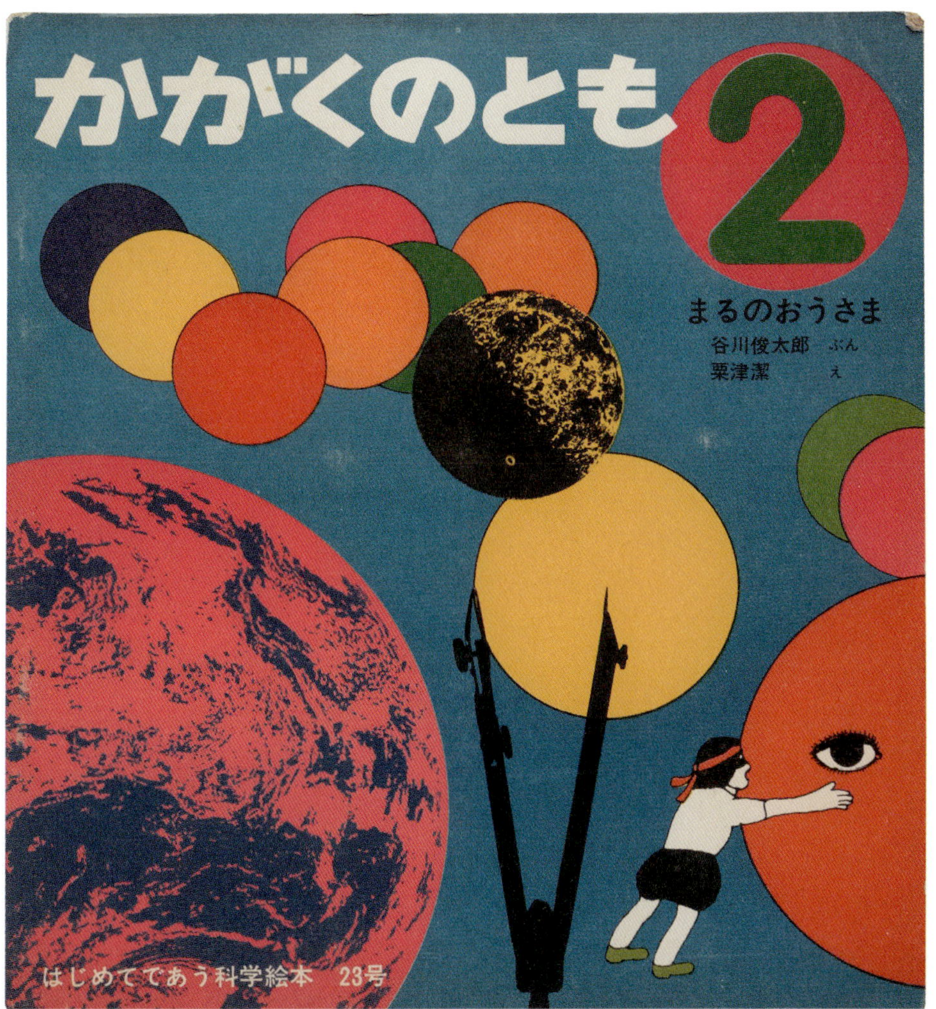

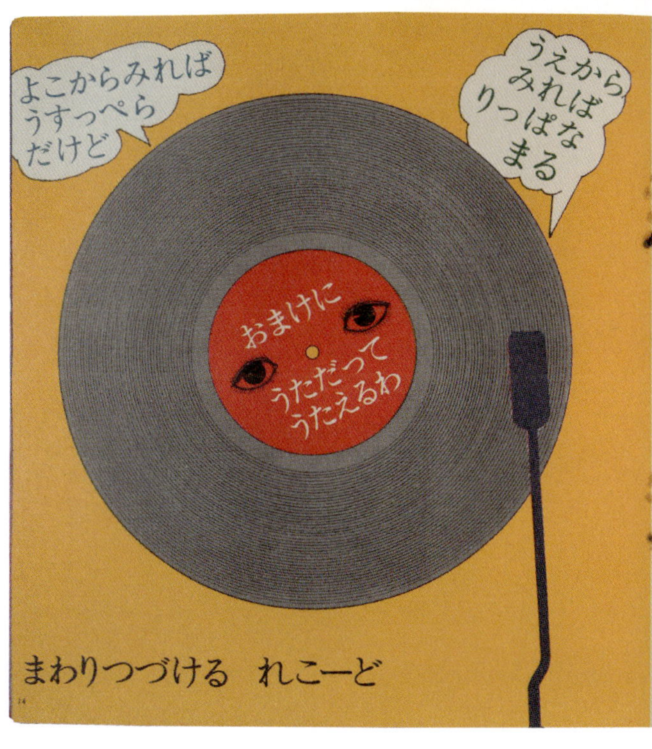

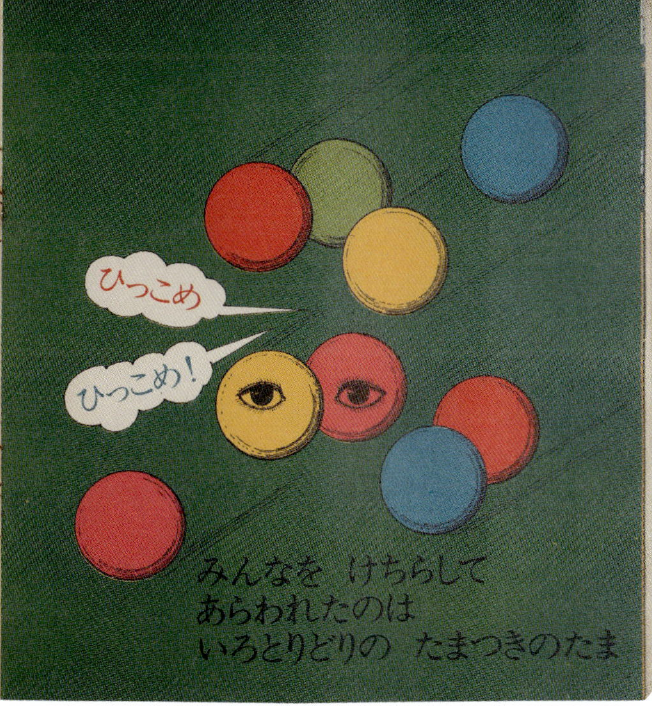

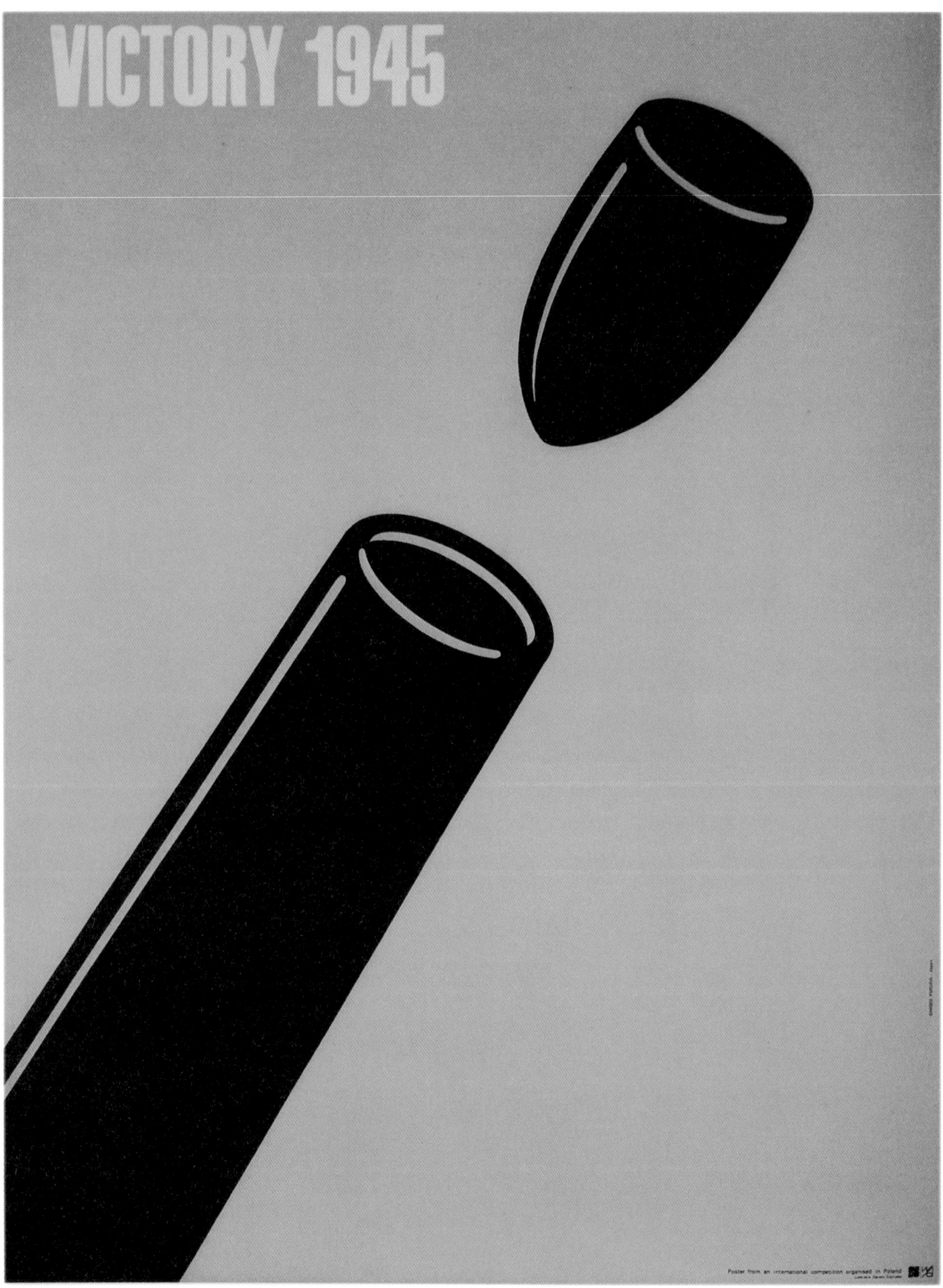

Victory 1945 **poster by Fukuda Shigeo 福田繁雄**, 97.0 x 67.0 cm, winner of the 30th Annual Warsaw International Poster Competition in 1975.

FUKUDA SHIGEO 福田繁雄

1932–2009

"I believe that in design, thirty percent dignity, twenty percent beauty, and fifty percent absurdity are necessary."
- Fukuda Shigeo[1]

Fukuda Shigeo was born in 1932 to a family of toy manufacturers. He studied at the Tokyo National University of Fine Arts and Music, earning a Japan Advertising Artists Club prize in their fifth exhibition in 1955 prior to graduation. He immediately took up employment in the food products company Ajinomoto in 1956 before becoming freelance two years later. Fukuda's career was a lauded one—he would participate in exhibitions all over the globe every year from 1965 on, for nearly the entirety of his career, either as exhibitor or judge.

In the 1960s, Fukuda developed a deep interest in optical illusions, writing for the *Asahi Shimbun* and *Idea* on the topic, and carving out an iconic, high-contrast signature graphic style for which he would become known globally.

American designer Paul Rand helped organize Fukuda's first international solo exhibition in 1967 at the IBM Gallery in New York, which was followed by subsequent solo shows in Japan, Poland, China, and Argentina.

Rand said of Fukuda, "Playfulness, the language of pleasure and understanding, needs no interpreters. Its appeal is to the intellect, to the imagination. This, perhaps more than any other attribute, seems best to describe Shigeo Fukuda."

Fukuda's most well-known poster, 1975's *Victory 1945*, features a cannon with its shell inverted, emphasizing the senselessness of war. This type of illustrative playfulness was manifest in all Fukuda's signature work, from hundreds of iterations on the theme of "shaking hands," to an Earth Day poster from 1982 which featured an ax sprouting a tiny branch from its handle. Fukuda was a master of the "Big Idea" approach to advertising design—visual metaphors doing the heavy lifting. His aesthetic trickery was expressed in his domestic space, as well—Fukuda's house on the outskirts of Tokyo had a false red door that was only one-point-two meters high. The actual door was concealed in the wall of the house and sported a giant sculpture of a fried-egg in the backyard.

Fukuda was as commercially successful as he was prolific. He worked on multiple high-profile projects, including posters for Japanese textile firms in the early 1960s, the identity for the *1970 World Expo* in Osaka, campaigns for National/Panasonic, and a redesign of the Seibu department store identity in Tokyo in 1976. While renowned for his illustration-based poster work, Fukuda was also masterful in the use of photographic collage techniques, evident in his *Expo '70* poster designs.

Between 1982 and 1984, Fukuda was Visiting Professor of Design at Yale University in the US. Fukuda was inducted into the Art Directors Club (ADC) Hall of Fame in New York in 1987, the first Japanese designer to be honored by that institution. There is a permanent installation of Fukuda's works in the Ninohe Civic Center in Iwate Prefecture.

1 Steven Heller, "Shigeo Fukuda, Graphic Designer, Dies at 76," *The New York Times* (January 20, 2009): https://www.nytimes.com/2009/01/20/arts/design/20fukuda.html.

References:

Heller, Steven. "Shigeo Fukuda, Graphic Designer, Dies at 76." *The New York Times*. The New York Times, January 20, 2009. https://www.nytimes.com/2009/01/20/arts/design/20fukuda.html.

Kamekura, Yūsaku, and Ayao Yamana. *Gurafikku Dezain no Seiki: Bunshō to Danwa to Sakuhin De kōsei: Meiji Sedai Yamana Ayao Sugiura Hisui Kara shōwa Sedai Made*. Tokyo: Bijutsu Shuppansha, 2008

Kamekura, Yūsaku, Nagai Kazumasa, Tanaka Ikkō, and Fukuda Shigeo. *4-GD Poster and Mark / Yūsaku Kamekura Kazumasa Tanaka Kazumasa Nagai Shigeo Fukuda*. Tokyo: Yomiuri Shimbun, 1987.

Nagai, Kazumasa, Mitsuo Katsui, and Masayoshi Nakajo. "Obituary: Tsunehisa Kimura, Shigeo Fukuda." Edited by Kiyonori Muroga and Toshiaki Koga. *Idea* 57, no. 335 (July 2009): 177–84.

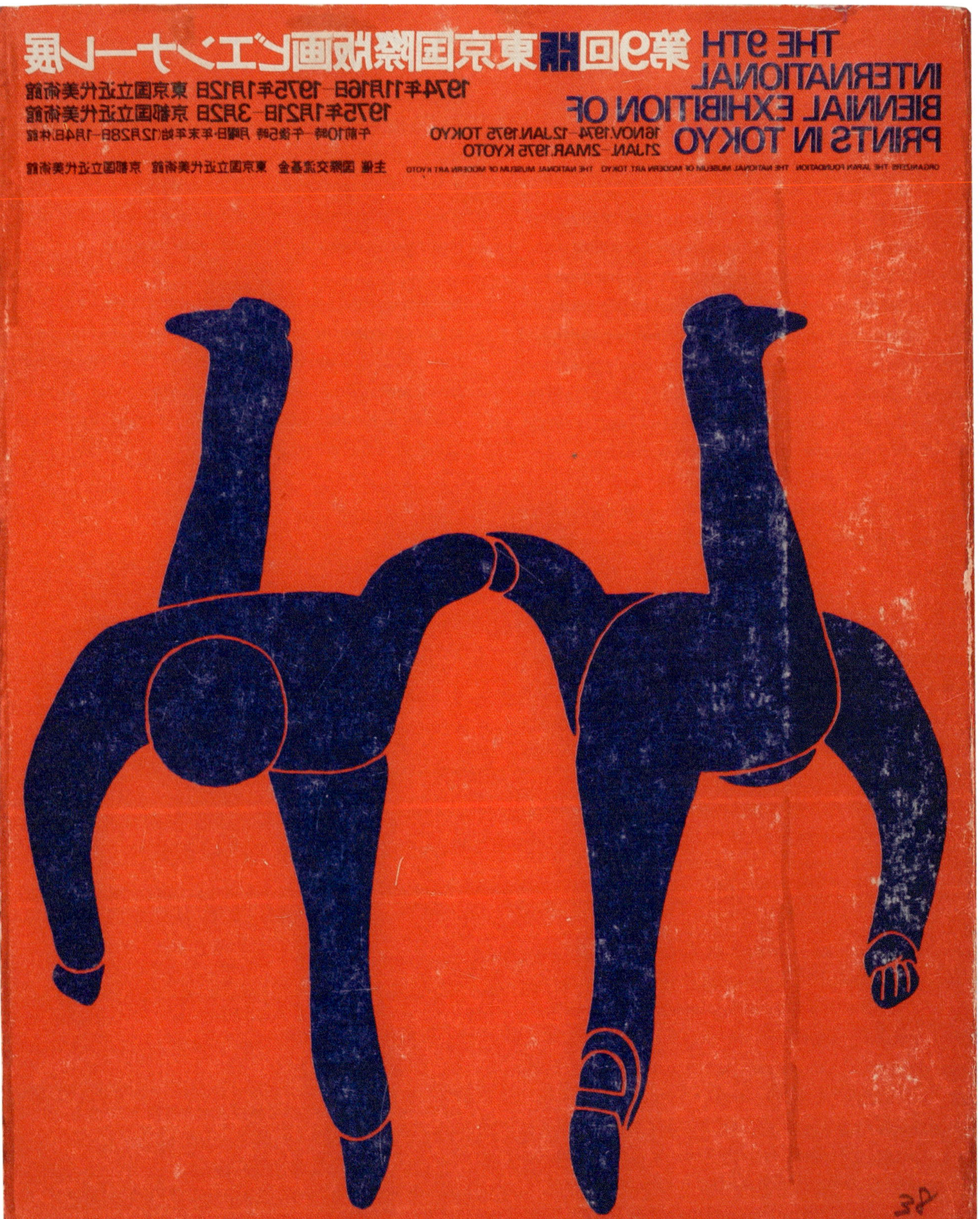
第9回東京国際版画ビエンナーレ展
1974年11月16日–1975年1月12日 東京国立近代美術館
1975年1月21日–3月2日 京都国立近代美術館
主催 国際交流基金 東京国立近代美術館 京都国立近代美術館
THE 9TH INTERNATIONAL BIENNIAL EXHIBITION OF PRINTS IN TOKYO
16 NOV. 1974 – 12 JAN. 1975 TOKYO
21 JAN. – 2 MAR. 1975 KYOTO
ORGANIZERS: THE JAPAN FOUNDATION THE NATIONAL MUSEUM OF MODERN ART TOKYO THE NATIONAL MUSEUM OF MODERN ART KYOTO

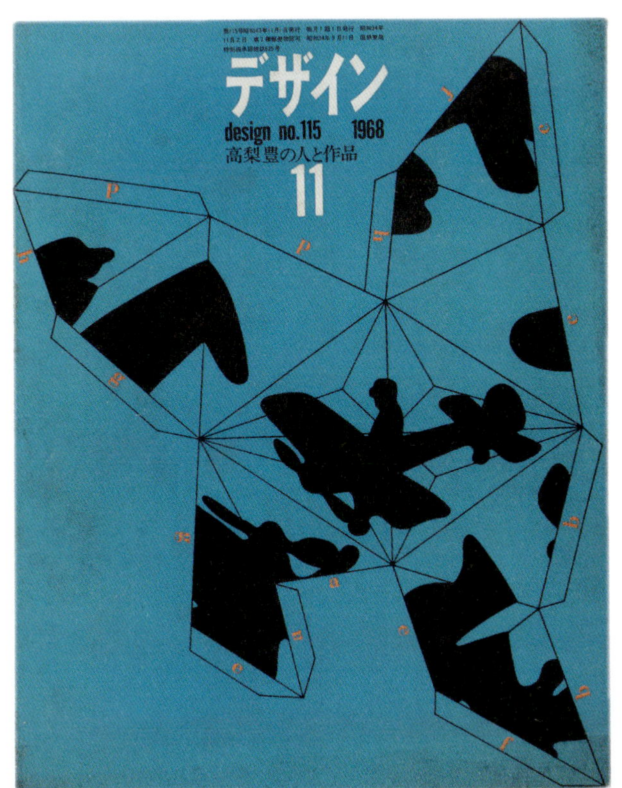

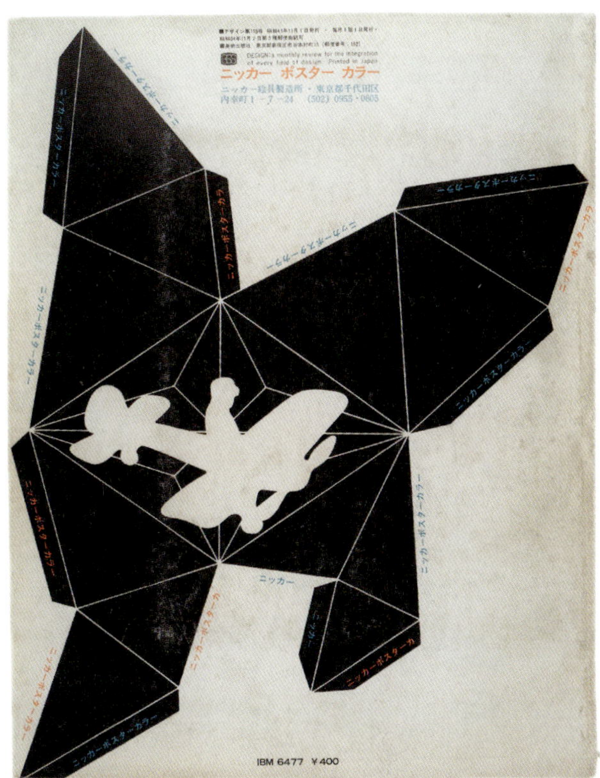

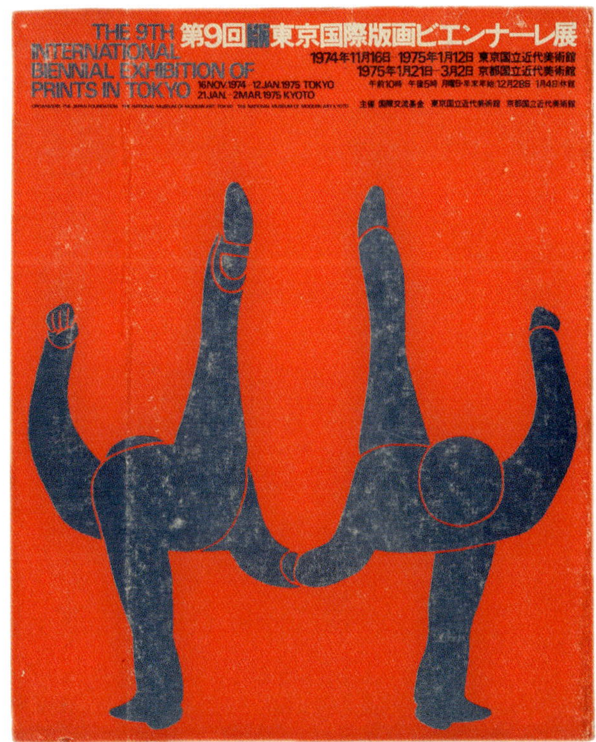

Top: Front and back cover designs for ***Design* デザイン No. 115** (Tokyo: Bijutsu Shuppansha 美術出版社, 1968).
Opposing page and bottom: ***9th International Biennial Exhibition of Prints in Tokyo* catalog** (Tokyo: National Museum of Modern Art / Yomiuri Shimbun 国立近代美術館／読売新聞, 1975).

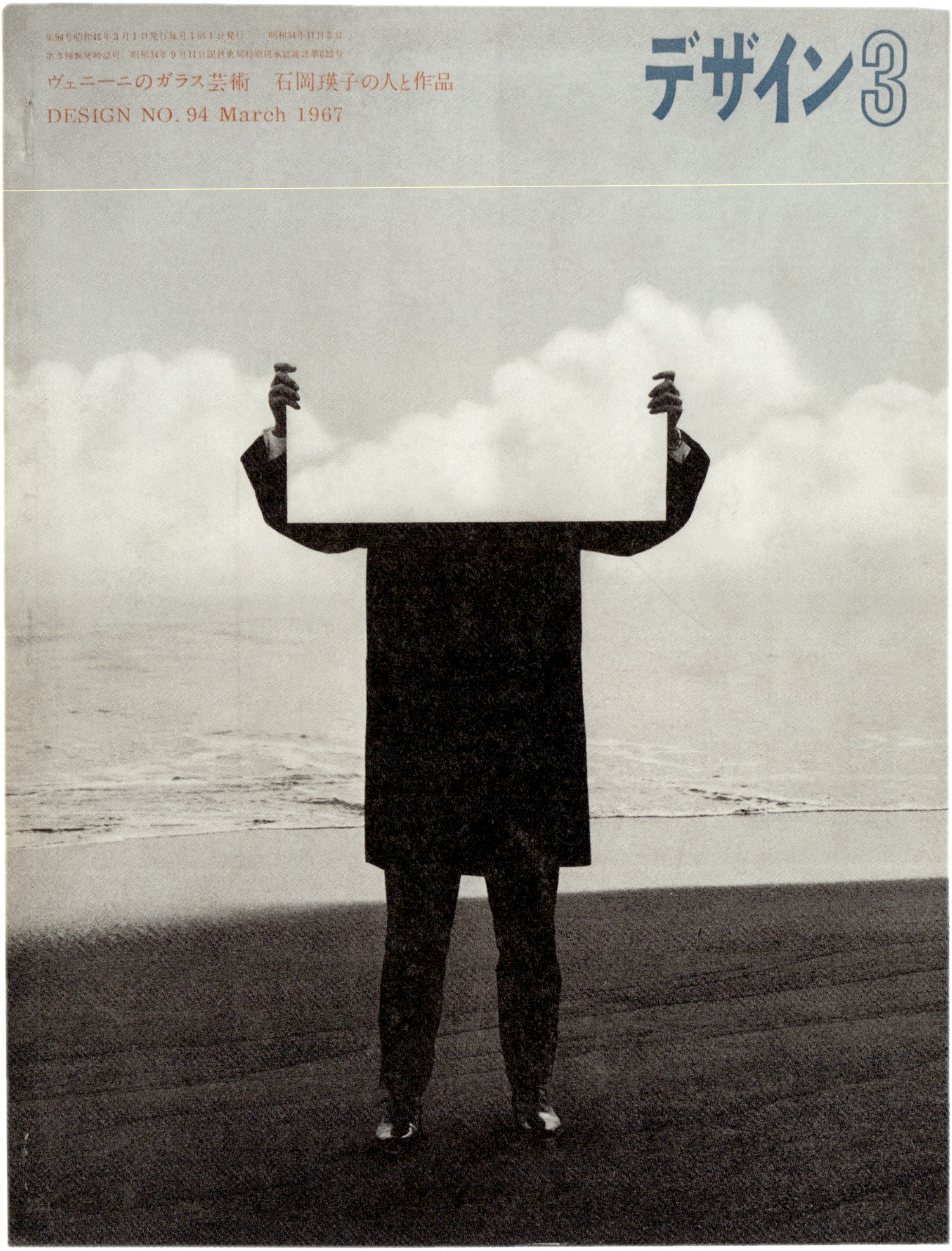

第94号昭和42年3月1日発行毎月1回1日発行　昭和34年11月2日
第3種郵便物認可　昭和34年9月11日国鉄東局特別扱承認雑誌第625号

ヴェニーニのガラス芸術　石岡瑛子の人と作品

DESIGN NO. 94 March 1967

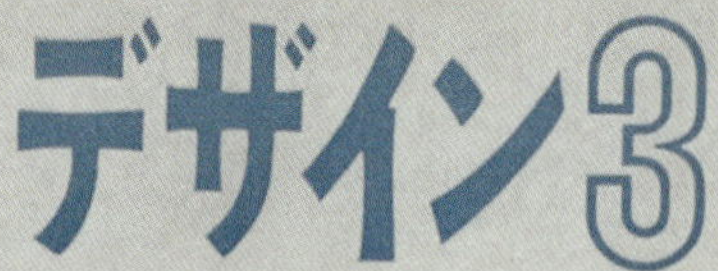

Front cover design for ***Design* デザイン No. 94 (Tokyo: Bijutsu Shuppansha 美術出版社, 1967)** by Hosoya Gan 細谷巖.

HOSOYA GAN 細谷巖

1935–

Hosoya Gan was born in Kanagawa Prefecture. In 1954, he joined advertising agency Light Publicity, where he worked as an Art Director and is currently the Representative Director. Hosoya participated in the groundbreaking 1965 *Persona* exhibition at the Matsuya Ginza department store.

In 1966, Hosoya was one of the competitors in the private competition for the design of the 1972 Sapporo Winter Olympics logo, though his submission would lose out to Nagai Kazumasa. Hosoya designed a kinetic typographic poster for the 1972 Olympics.

Hosoya was the art director for *Global Architecture* magazine throughout the 1970s and 1980s and worked on the advertising for iconic Japanese products from Otsuka Pharmaceutical, including the energy bar Calorie Mate and the sports drink Pocari Sweat.

In 1979, Hosoya designed the logo for the Seibu Lions baseball team based on Tezuka Osamu's character Kimba the White Lion. He was awarded the Medal with Purple Ribbon in 2001.

In 2009, Hosoya held a career retrospective exhibition titled *Last Show* at the Ginza Graphic Gallery in Tokyo. Two books of Hosoya's art direction have been published, alongside a slim book from the GGG series of monographs.

References:

Hosoya, Gan. Hosoya Gan. Tokyo: Ginza Graphic Gallery, 2009.

Hosoya, Gan. *Hosoya Gan No Dezain rōdo 69*. Tokyo: Hakusuisha, 2004.

Kamekura, Yūsaku, and Ayao Yamana. *Gurafikku Dezain no Seiki: Bunshō to Danwa to Sakuhin De kōsei: Meiji Sedai Yamana Ayao Sugiura Hisui Kara shōwa Sedai Made*. Tokyo: Bijutsu Shuppansha, 2008.

Segi, Shin'ichi, Tanaka Ikkō, and Hiroshi Sano. *Nissenbi no Jidai = The Epoch of the Japan Advertising Artists Club: Nihon No Gurafikku Dezain 1951–70*. Tokyo: Toransuāto, 2000.

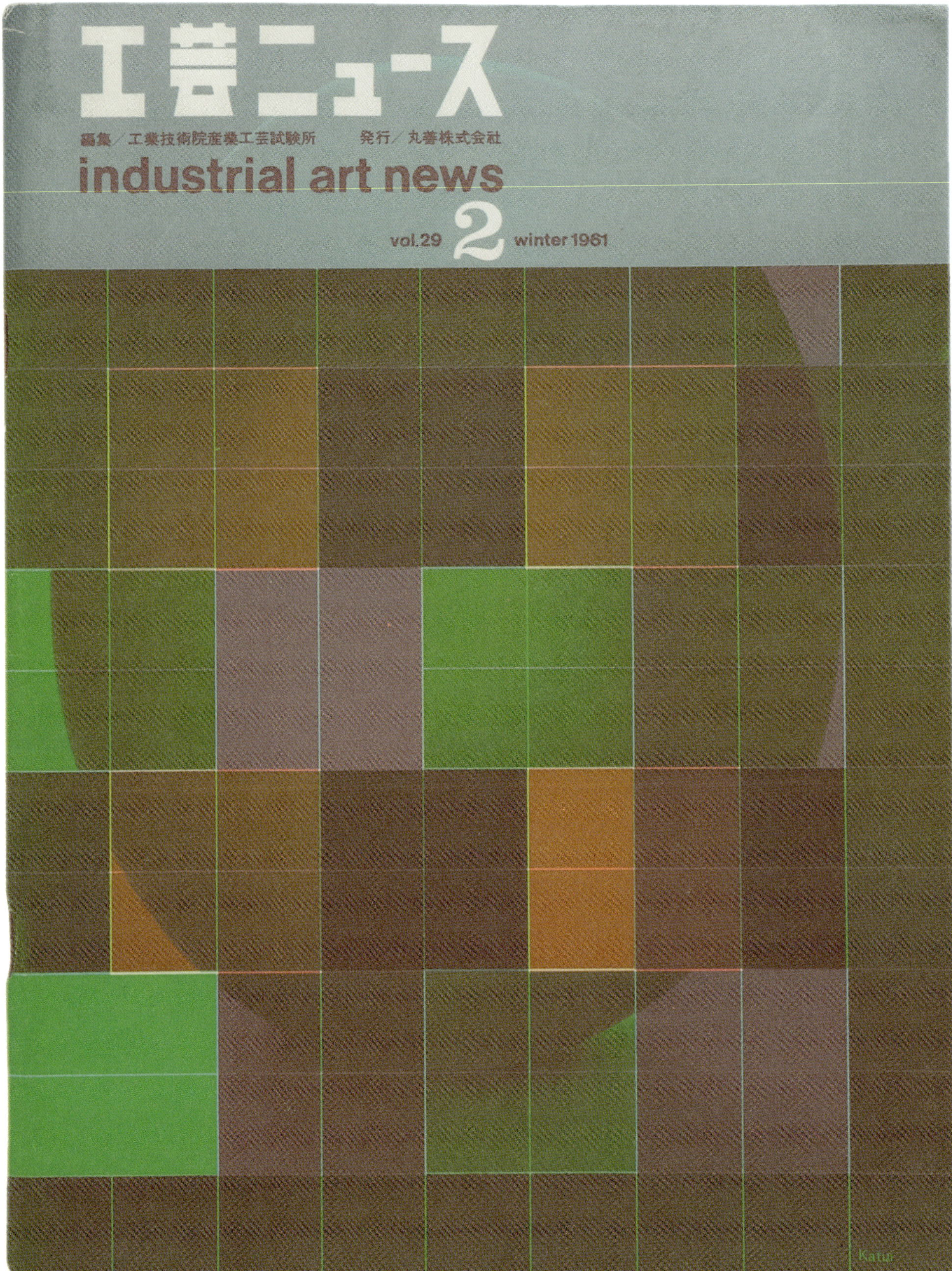

Cover design by Katsui Mitsuo 勝井三雄 for ***Industrial Art News*** **(Kōgei News) 工芸ニュース,**
Vol. 29 No. 2, edited by Industrial Arts Institute (IAI) (Tokyo: Maruzen, 1961).

KATSUI MITSUO 勝井三雄

1931–2019

Katsui Mitsuo was born in Tokyo and attended Tokyo University of Education. In 1956, he joined the food products company Ajinomoto, where he worked for five years before starting his own firm in 1961. Alongside colleague Nagai Kazumasa, Katsui joined the 21 Association in Tokyo in 1959, exploring notions of design and culture.

Katsui became a lecturer at Tokyo University of Education (now the National University of Tsukuba) in 1961, joined the faculty of Tokyo Zokei University in 1966, and in 1987 became faculty at Musashino University.

Katsui was brought on by organizer Katsumi Masaru to work alongside Yamashita Yoshirō on the 1964 Tokyo Olympic logo identity guidelines—the first planned document to unify the aesthetics of the Olympic games in history. The guidelines specified color palettes, typographic palettes, and logo usage for the Tokyo Olympics.

Katsui would go on to participate in the 1965 *Persona* exhibition at the Matsuya Ginza department store in Tokyo and would exhibit in a host of subsequent exhibitions in the late 1960s. Katsui served as art director of the *Japan World Exposition* in Osaka in 1970, the *International Ocean Exposition* in Okinawa in 1975, and the *International Exposition of Science and Technology* in Tsukuba in 1985. He has held numerous exhibitions around the world and in Japan.

In 1984, Katsui was invited to lecture and judge at the Eleventh Brno Design Biennial. Katsui was awarded the Medal with Purple Ribbon in 1996. From 2009 to 2012, he was Chairman of the Japan Graphic Designers Association and has served as its Executive Director since. Katsui served on the selection committee for the 2020 Olympic logo design.

Katsui was an early adopter of digital technology for creating graphic design work, and his use of gradated color fields, fine line work, and ambient abstraction are all signature aspects of his output.

References:

Kamekura, Yūsaku, and Ayao Yamana. *Gurafikku Dezain no Seiki: Bunshō to Danwa to Sakuhin De kōsei: Meiji Sedai Yamana Ayao Sugiura Hisui Kara shōwa Sedai Made*. Tokyo: Bijutsu Shuppansha, 2008.

Katsui, Mitsuo. *Yōhen Tenmoku Aruiwa Kokoro*. Tokyo: Hakusuisha, 2020.

Segi, Shin'ichi, Tanaka Ikkō, and Hiroshi Sano. *Nissenbi no Jidai = The Epoch of the Japan Advertising Artists Club: Nihon No Gurafikku Dezain 1951–70*. Tokyo: Toransuāto, 2000.

Tanaka, Ikkō, Mitsuo Katsui, and Hiroshi Kashiwagi. *Nihon no Bukku Dezain 1946–95 = Book Design in Japan 1946–95*. Tokyo: Ginza Graphic Gallery, 1996.

第71号昭和40年5月1日発行
毎月1回1日発行
昭和34年11月2日第3種郵便物認可
昭和34年9月11日
国鉄東局特別扱承認雑誌第625号

5 DESIGN NO.71 1965 デザイン

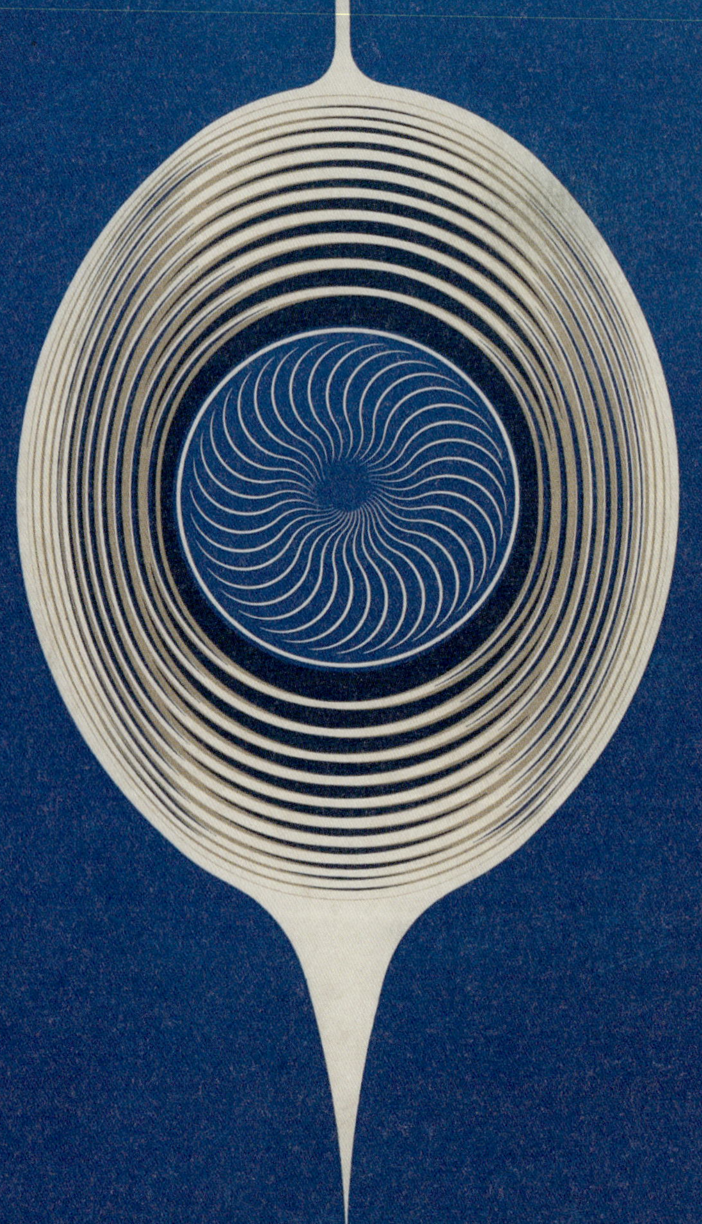

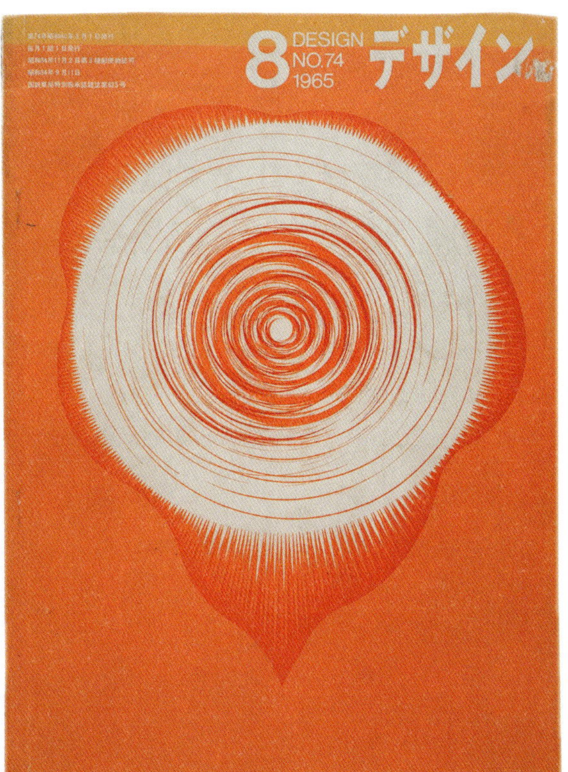

Left: Front cover design for ***Design* デザイン No. 71** (Tokyo: Bijutsu Shuppansha 美術出版社, 1965) Above: Front cover design for ***Design* デザイン No. 74,** (Tokyo: Bijutsu Shuppansha 美術出版社, 1965).
Below: Cover for ***Industrial Art News* (Kogei News) 工芸ニュース, Vol. 31 No. 4, edited by Industrial Arts Institute (IAI), Tokyo** (Tokyo: Maruzen, autumn 1963). All designed by Nagai Kazumasa 永井一正.

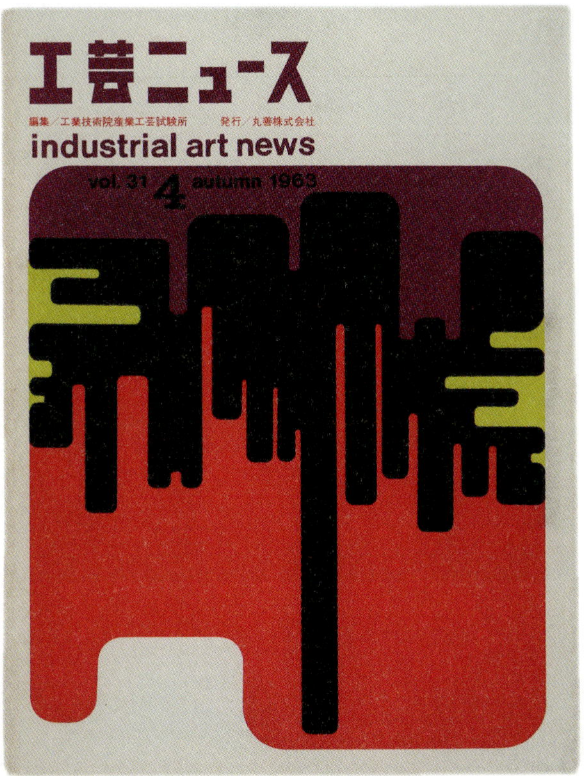

NAGAI KAZUMASA 永井一正

1929–

Nagai Kazumasa was born in Osaka. He briefly attended Tokyo College of Art, studying sculpture, then left due to an eye condition and returned to Osaka to recover. He joined Yamato Textiles in 1951 as an assistant designer, learning the trade on the job. Nagai became enamored with the Kansai journal *Press Art* and developed a friendship with fellow Osakan designer Tanaka Ikkō, with whom he would found the A Club, a study group for designers in Osaka, in 1952.

In 1953, Nagai joined the Japan Advertising Artists Club, and in 1959 he joined the 21 Association in Tokyo. He joined longtime friend Tanaka Ikkō as one of the founding members of the Nippon Design Center in Tokyo in 1960.

Nagai was one of the competitors nominated to submit to the 1964 Tokyo Olympic logo design competition but whose design was not selected. The following year, Nagai would design the logo for Asahi Breweries, then Japan's largest beer producer, and in 1966 he was given another shot at designing an Olympic logo in a private competition for the upcoming 1972 Olympics in Sapporo: Nagai's submission won out over seven others.

In 1973 Nagai designed the logo for the Expo '75 in Okinawa, and in 1975 he became President of the Nippon Design Center. Nagai was awarded the Medal with Purple Ribbon in 1989, and a decade later he received The Order of the Rising Sun, Gold Rays with Rosette. He was inaugurated as Chairman of the Japan Graphic Design Association in 1994 and was on the Tokyo Olympic Design Committee responsible for choosing Sano Kenjirō's 佐野研二郎 ill-fated design for the 2020 Olympics in 2015.

References:

Kamekura, Yūsaku, Nagai Kazumasa, Tanaka Ikkō, and Fukuda Shigeo. *4-GD Poster and Mark | Yūsaku Kamekura Kazumasa Tanaka Kazumasa Nagai Shigeo Fukuda*. Tokyo: Yomiuri Shimbun, 1987.

Kamekura, Yūsaku, and Ayao Yamana. *Gurafikku Dezain no Seiki: Bunshō to Danwa to Sakuhin De kōsei: Meiji Sedai Yamana Ayao Sugiura Hisui Kara shōwa Sedai Made*. Tokyo: Bijutsu Shuppansha, 2008.

Nagai, Kazumasa. *Kazumasa Nagai: Design Life*. Tokyo: Rikuyo-Sha Publishing, 1994.

Nagai, Kazumasa. *Posutā Bijutsukan*. Tokyo: Kabushiki Kaisha Rikuyōsha, 2013.

Segi, Shin'ichi, Tanaka Ikkō, and Hiroshi Sano. *Nissenbi no Jidai = The Epoch of the Japan Advertising Artists Club: Nihon No Gurafikku Dezain 1951–70*. Tokyo: Toransuāto, 2000.

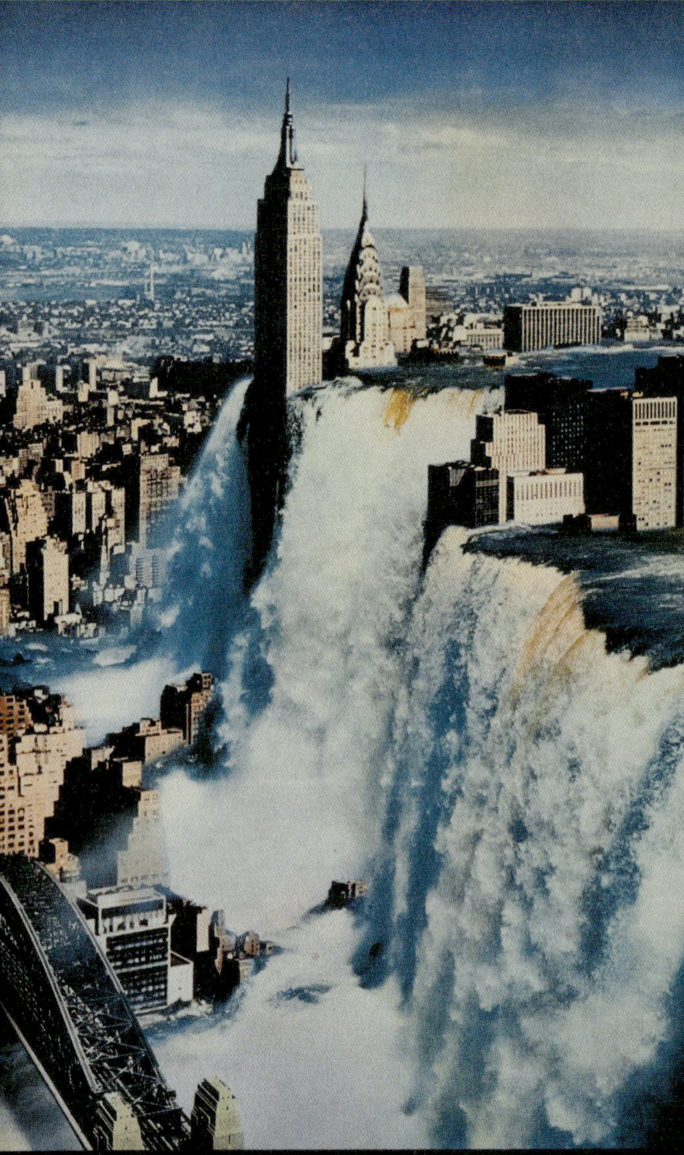

This and opposing page: cover design and images from ***Kimura Camera: Tsunehisa Kimura's Visual Scandal*** **キムラカメラ 木村恒久のヴィジュアル・スキャンダル** (Tokyo: PARCO Publishing PARCO 出版, 1981).

KIMURA TSUNEHISA 木村恒久

1928–2008

Kimura Tsunehisa was born in Osaka and graduated from Osaka City Crafts School's drawing department. Kimura enlisted in the Navy after graduation but was not deployed, as the war ended shortly thereafter. He would win a number of design awards early in his career, and he participated in the design research committee A Club alongside fellow designers Tanaka Ikkō, Katayama Toshihiro, and Nagai Kazumasa.

Kimura worked for the Nippon Design Center from 1960 until becoming a freelancer in 1964. The following year, he participated in the Persona exhibition at the Matsuya Ginza department store.

Kimura became an associate professor at Tokyo Zokei University in 1968; that same year, he became heavily involved in photomontage, work which would largely define the remainder of his career. He published a book and held an exhibition of his photomontage works called *Kimura Camera - Visual Scandal* by Tsunehisa Kimura at Parco View between 1978 and 1980. Kimura would go on to hold a number of other solo exhibitions internationally and domestically.

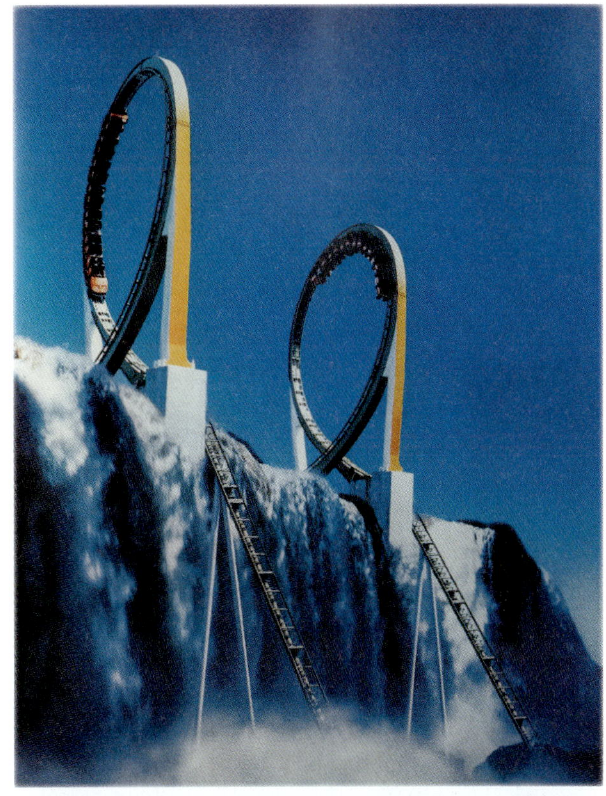

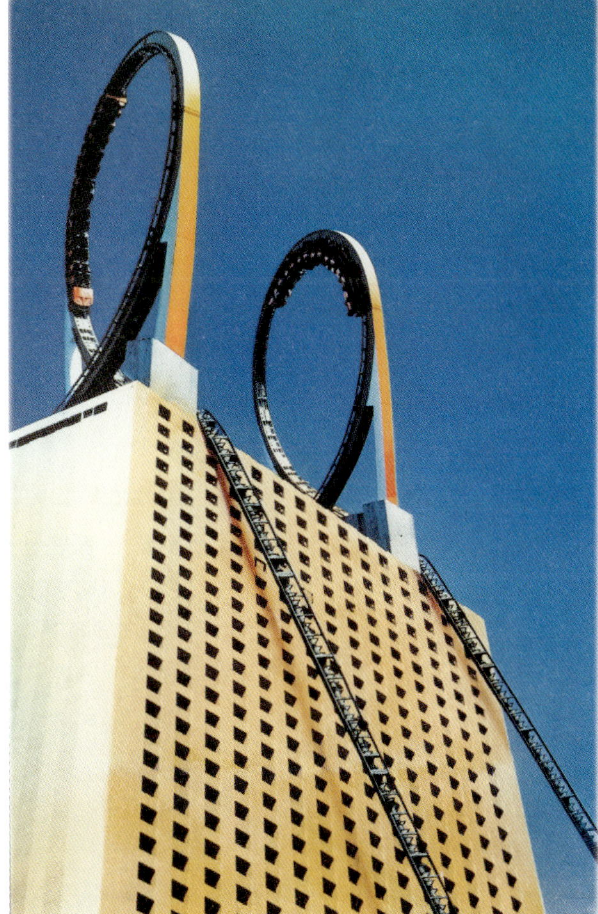

References:

Kamekura, Yūsaku, and Ayao Yamana. *Gurafikku Dezain no Seiki: Bunshō to Danwa to Sakuhin De kōsei: Meiji Sedai Yamana Ayao Sugiura Hisui Kara shōwa Sedai Made*. Tokyo: Bijutsu Shuppansha, 2008.

Kimura, Tsunehisa. *Kimura Camera*. Tokyo: Parco Shuppan, 1980.

Nagai, Kazumasa, Mitsuo Katsui, and Masayoshi Nakajo. "Obituary: Tsunehisa Kimura, Shigeo Fukuda." Edited by Kiyonori Muroga and Toshiaki Koga. *Idea* 57, no. 335 (July 2009): 177–84.

Segi, Shin'ichi, Tanaka Ikkō, and Hiroshi Sano. *Nissenbi no Jidai = The Epoch of the Japan Advertising Artists Club: Nihon No Gurafikku Dezain 1951–70*. Tokyo: Toransuāto, 2000.

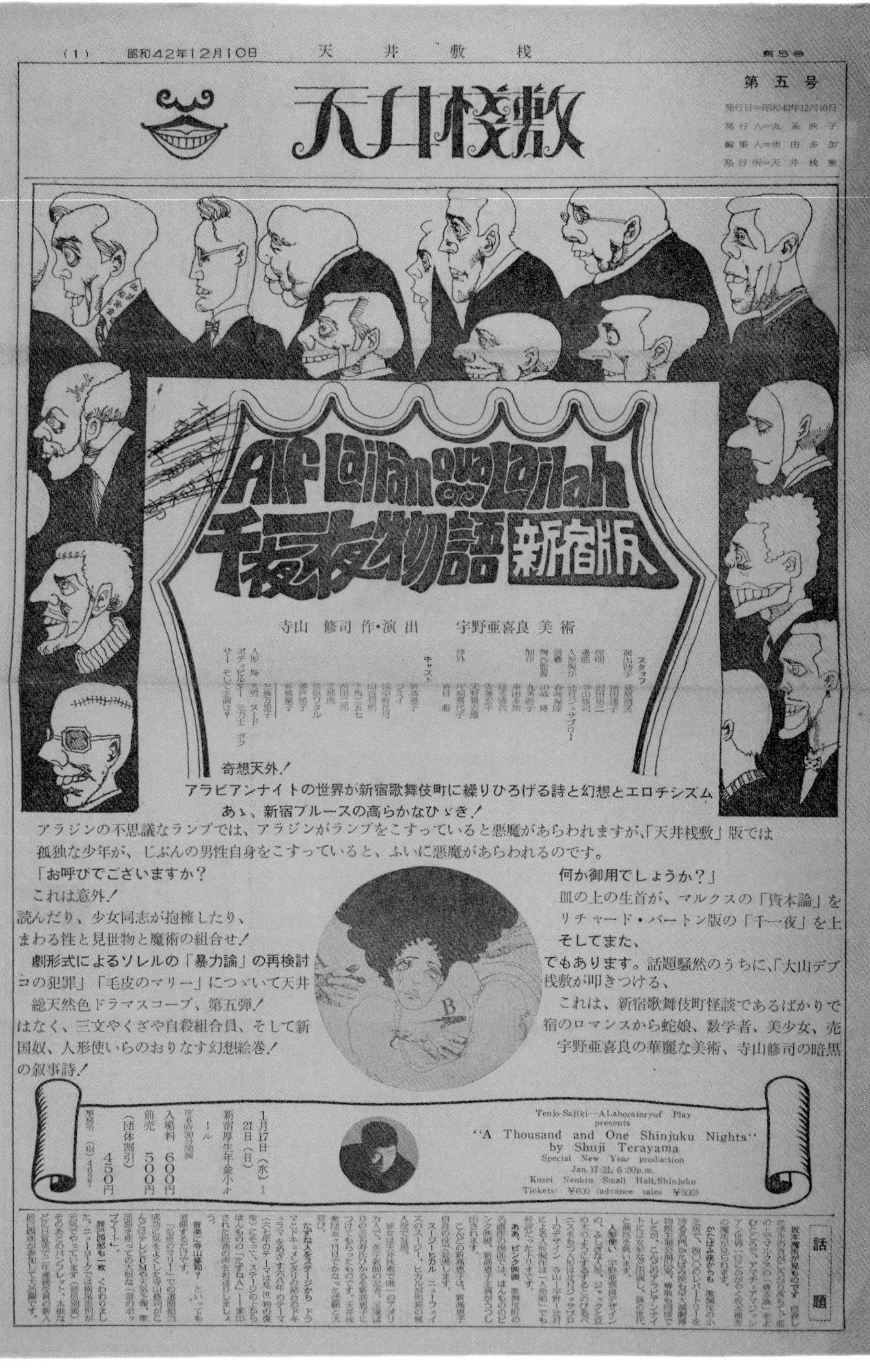

(1)　昭和42年12月10日　天　井　敷　桟　第5号

天井桟敷

第五号

発行日＝昭和42年12月10日
発行人＝九 条 映 子
編集人＝東 由 多 加
発行所＝天 井 桟 敷

Alf Laylah wa Laylah
千夜一夜物語 新宿版

寺山　修司 作・演出　　宇野亜喜良 美術

スタッフ

キャスト

奇想天外！

アラビアンナイトの世界が新宿歌舞伎町に繰りひろげる詩と幻想とエロチシズム

あゝ、新宿ブルースの高らかなひゞき！

アラジンの不思議なランプでは、アラジンがランプをこすっていると悪魔があらわれますが、「天井桟敷」版では孤独な少年が、じぶんの男性自身をこすっていると、ふいに悪魔があらわれるのです。

「お呼びでございますか？　何か御用でしょうか？」

これは意外！

皿の上の生首が、マルクスの「資本論」を読んだり、少女同志が抱擁したり、リチャード・バートン版の「千一夜」を上まわる性と見世物と魔術の組合せ！

そしてまた、劇形式によるソレルの「暴力論」の再検討でもあります。話題騒然のうちに、「大山デブコの犯罪」「毛皮のマリー」につゞいて天井桟敷が叩きつける、総天然色ドラマスコープ、第五弾！

これは、新宿歌舞伎町怪談であるばかりではなく、三文やくざや自殺組合員、そして新宿のロマンスから蛇娘、数学者、美少女、売国奴、人形使いらのおりなす幻想絵巻！

宇野亜喜良の華麗な美術、寺山修司の暗黒の叙事詩！

1月17日（水）～21日（日）
新宿厚生年金小ホール
夜6時30分開演
入場料　600円
前売　500円
（団体割引）　450円
事務所（41）4627

Tenjo-Sajiki—A Laboratory of Play
presents
"A Thousand and One Shinjuku Nights"
by Shuji Terayama
Special New Year production
Jan. 17-21, 6:30p.m.
Kosei Nenkin Small Hall, Shinjuku
Tickets: ¥600 (advance sales ¥500)

話題

Tenjō sajiki **天井桟敷** No. 5 (Tokyo: Tenjō sajiki 天井桟敷, December 10, 1967).
Promotional tabloid newspaper for the Tenjō Sajiki underground theater troupe, designed by Uno Akira 宇野亜喜良.

UNO AKIRA 宇野亜喜良

1934–

Uno Akira was born in Aichi Prefecture and graduated from Nagoya City Crafts High School's Design School. Uno's father operated an interior design company and encouraged his son to paint from an early age. After graduating, Uno's work was exhibited by the Japan Advertising Artists Club in 1953 and awarded in 1956. The same year, Uno went to work for the beverage manufacturer Calpis, later moving to the Nippon Design Center in 1960, where he worked on posters, advertising, and other projects for the chemical company Asahi Kasei.

Ondine, Uno's breakout collaborative book with photographer Hosoe Eikoh 細江英公, was released in an edition of 300 by Tokyo photography publisher Genkosha 玄光社 in 1963. The book is an erotic melange of often overprinted illustration and photographic art directed by designer Miyanaga Iwao 宮永磐夫. *Ondine*'s subject was the actress and sex symbol Enami Kyoko 江波杏子, and the book interleaved Uno's sensual illustrations with Hosoe's high-contrast black-and-white photography.

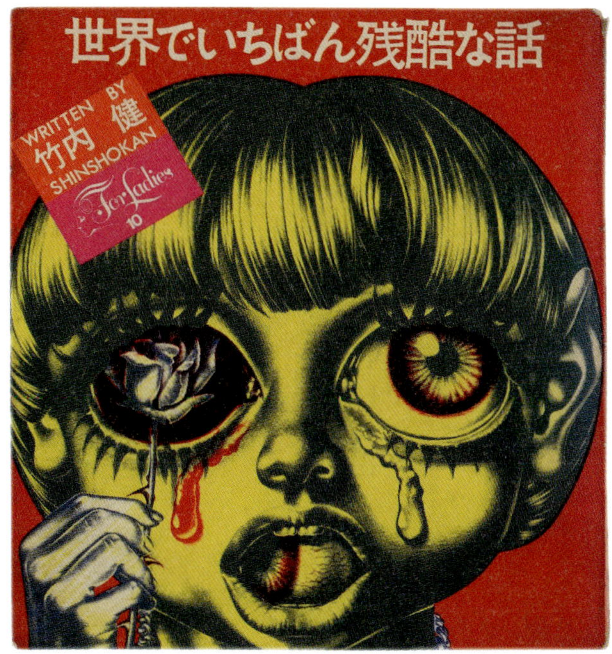

The Most Cruel Story in the World, Angel of the Rose 世界でいちばん残酷な話, Takeuchi Ken 竹内健 (Tokyo: Shinshokan 新書館, 1966).

In 1964, Uno joined Studio Ilfil, a collaborative studio with Yokoo Tadanori and 1964 Olympic pictogram designer Harada Tsunao. In 1965, Uno founded the Tokyo Illustrators' Club (now the Tokyo Illustrators Society) with Yokoo Tadanori, Wada Makoto, and others and went freelance. Uno exhibited in the Persona exhibition in 1965 at Matsuya Ginza.

Uno's poster and program designs for the Tenjō Sajiki 天井桟敷 theater troupe were incredibly significant in the late 1960s and early 1970s, as they mirrored the turbulent youth cultures of that era. His extravagant posters for the dramatic work of playwright and director Terayama Shūji 寺山修司 attracted much attention to the group, winning Uno multiple design awards.

A central figure in the 1960s poster art and illustration scene alongside Yokoo Tadanori, Tanaami Keiichi 田名網敬一, and Awazu Kiyoshi, Uno has been prolifically published in assorted monographs, featuring his sensuous and often grotesque stylized sexual portraiture. Uno's expressive style of dress, carnal artwork, and trademark shaved eyebrows made him into a cultural icon. His lurid pen and pencil depictions of gaunt young women wearing too much eyeliner, fantastical animals that mix multiple species, and ghostly renderings of the macabre, all held together with delicate watercolor washes, stand out from the work of his peers from the 1960s. Still active today, he often signs his work "Aquirax," attempting to impart a French sensibility to his often baroque compositions.

References:

Goodman, David. *Angura: Posters of the Japanese Avant-Garde*. New York, NY: Princeton Architectural Press, 1999.

Kamekura, Yūsaku, and Ayao Yamana. *Gurafikku Dezain no Seiki: Bunshō to Danwa to Sakuhin De kōsei: Meiji Sedai Yamana Ayao Sugiura Hisui Kara shōwa Sedai Made*. Tokyo: Bijutsu Shuppansha, 2008.

Kuwahara, Shigeo, and Hiroyuki Sasame. *Japan Avangyarudo: Angura Engeki Kessaku posutā Hyaku = Japan Avantgarde: 100 Poster Masterpieces from Underground Theatre*. Tokyo: Paruko Entateinmento Jigyōkyoku, 2004

Muroga, Kiyonori, and Toshiaki Koga. "Le Cahier De Coquelicots: The Collected Drawings of Aquirax Uno." *Idea* 54, no. 315 (March 2006): 5–56.

Shuri, Yuki, and Shinju Onuki. *Kakimoji no Dezain*. Tokyo: Graphic-sha, 2017.

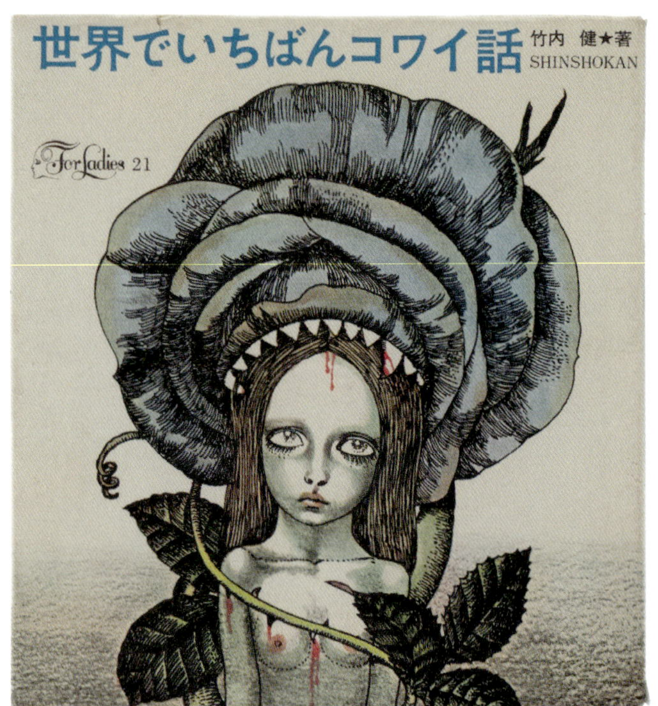

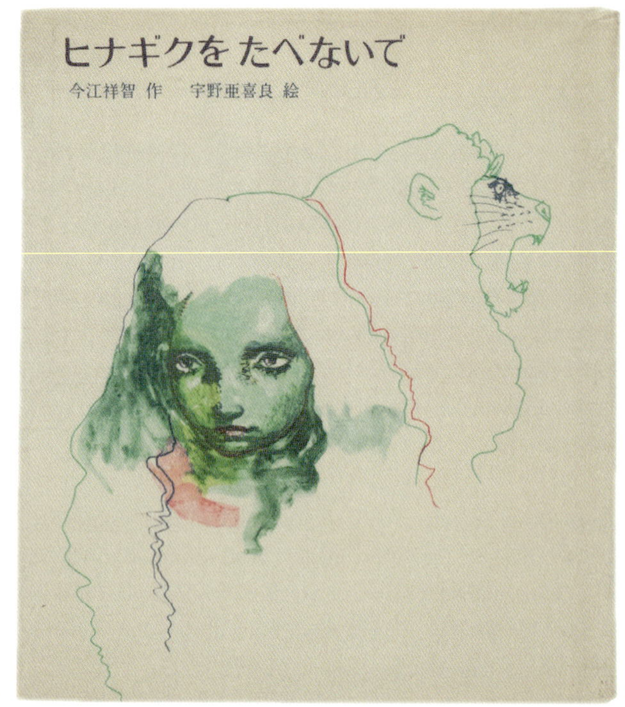

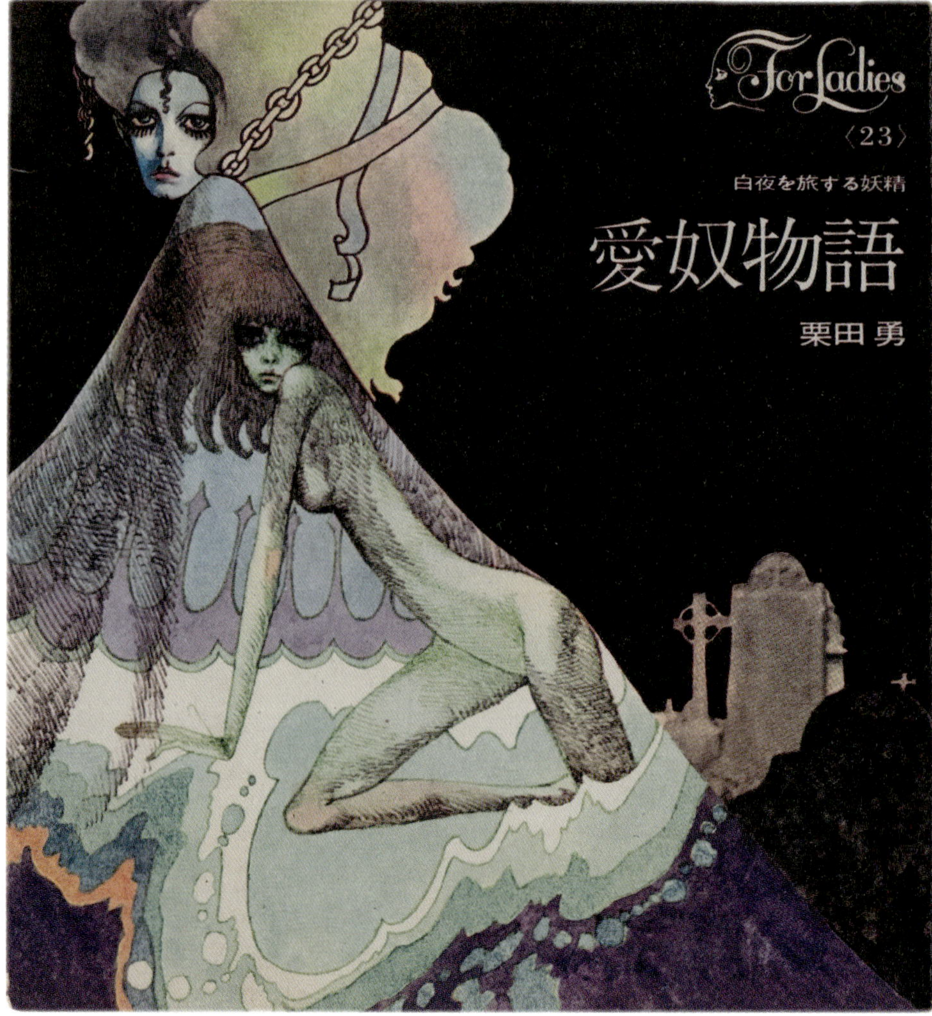

Clockwise from top left: ***The Most Scary Story in the World, Rose Devil*** **世界でいちばんコ ワイ話, Takeuchi Ken 竹内健** (Tokyo: Shinshokan 新書館, 1968); ***Don't Eat Daisies*** **ヒナギク をたべないで, Imae Yoshitomo 今江祥智 文** (Tokyo: Kaiseisha 偕成社, 1974); ***Love Story: Fairy Traveling in the Midnight Sun*** **愛奴物語ー白夜を旅する妖精, Kurita Isamu 栗田勇** (Tokyo: Shinshokan 新書館, 1969). All designed and illustrated by Uno Akira 宇野亜喜良.

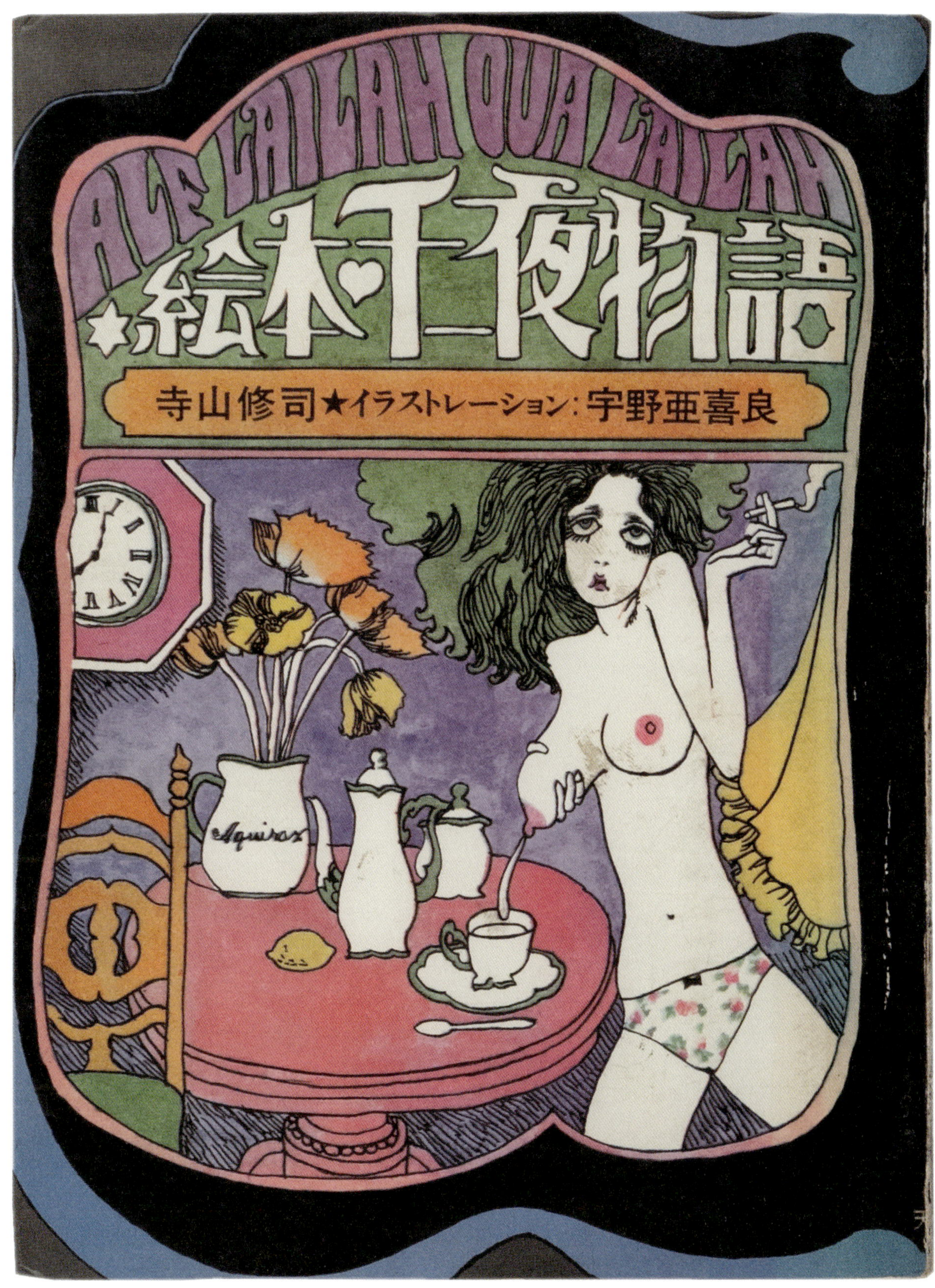

Book cover design by Uno Akira 宇野亜喜良 for ***Senichiya Monogatari*** **絵本·千一夜物語, Terayama Shuji 寺山修司** (Tokyo: Tensei Shuppan 天声出版: 1968).

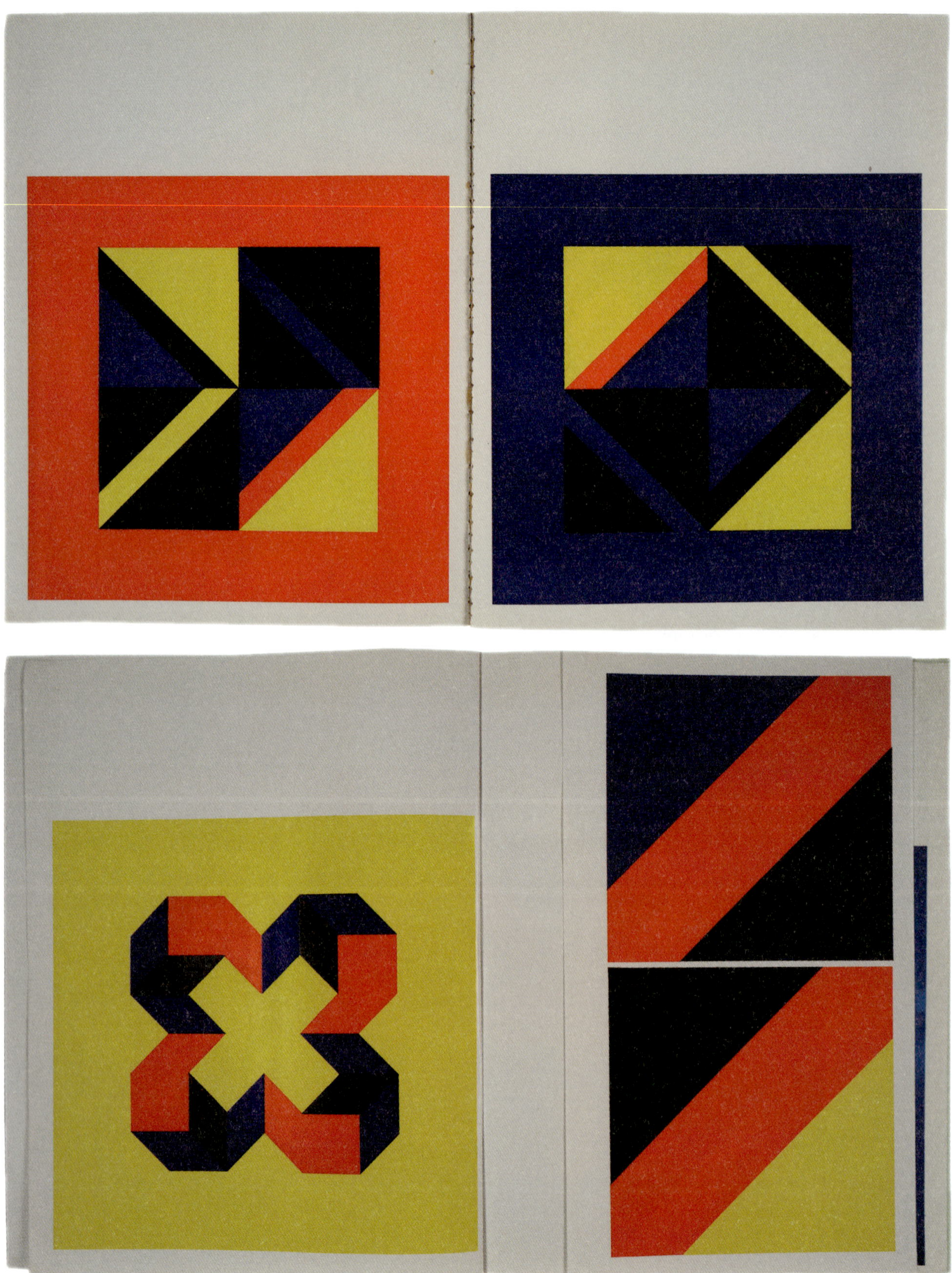

"Square & Movement" より, a twelve-page feature in ***Design* デザイン No. 140** (Tokyo: Bijutsu Shuppansha 美術出版社, 1970) showcasing Katayama's modernist approaches to form-based geometric construction.

KATAYAMA TOSHIHIRO 片山利弘

1928–2013

Katayama Toshihiro was born in Osaka and became a largely self-taught graphic designer, artist, and sculptor. Katayama joined the design-oriented groups A Club and the 21 Society in the early 1950s, researching the relationships between design and modern culture. He joined the Nippon Design Center in 1960, working under the direction of Kamekura Yūsaku on a range of advertising and packaging for Nikon Camera products. While at the Nippon Design Center, the bilingual Katayama came in contact with staff from the Swiss pharmaceutical giant Geigy and was invited to join their company in 1963. Working in Switzerland from 1963 to 1966, Katayama created a variety of promotional design work for Geigy and had his first solo exhibition at the Herman Miller store in Basel. This was followed by a solo exhibition traveling to Zurich, Geneva, Bern, and Winterthur.

In 1965, Katayama participated in the *Persona* exhibition held at the Matsuya Ginza department store, at the request of fellow Osaka native Tanaka Ikkō. The following year, Katayama moved to the United States to design for the Carpenter Center for the Visual Arts at Harvard University. He began teaching a course called Visual Studies there the following year. Katayama later was appointed director of the Carpenter Center for Visual Arts and served in that position from 1990 to 1995.

Katayama was a devout modernist, yet his work was often provocative in its use of geometric form and optical effects: "His aim is to parry and eliminate, always saying with the barest essentials more than would be said with much encumbrance and ornament."[1]

In 1974, Katayama designed the book project *Three Notations/ Rotations*, a boxed set of rotatable graphic/typographic compositions, with Mexican poet Octavio Paz. Katayama held a solo exhibition at the AIGA (American Institute of Graphic Arts) Gallery in New York in 1978.

Throughout the 1980s and 1990s, Katayama would design a wide range of interiors, sculptures, and environmental design schemes for Japanese corporations such as Mitsui Sumitomo, Panasonic, Japan Tobacco, and many others. Working alongside landscape architect Cynthia Smith, Katayama redesigned Porter Square in Cambridge, Massachusetts, making the high-traffic area a safer, more inclusive public space for pedestrians and cyclists.

In 1995, Katayama exhibited his *30 Years Retrospective—Farewell Show* at Harvard University. In 2009, a book of Katayama's Harvard University students' projects was published by Kyoto University of Art and Design.

1 Barth Schwartz, "Form from Process," *The Harvard Crimson* (December 7, 1967): 12.

References:

Kamekura, Yūsaku, and Ayao Yamana. *Gurafikku Dezain no Seiki: Bunshō to Danwa to Sakuhin De kōsei: Meiji Sedai Yamana Ayao Sugiura Hisui Kara shōwa Sedai Made*. Tokyo: Bijutsu Shuppansha, 2008.

Muroga, Kiyonori, and Makie Kubo. "In Memory of Toshihiro Katayama." *Idea* 61, no. 358 (May 2013): 194–97.

Nomiyama, Sakura. "About Toshihiro Katayama." *Idea* 1, no. 380 (January 2018): 112–33.

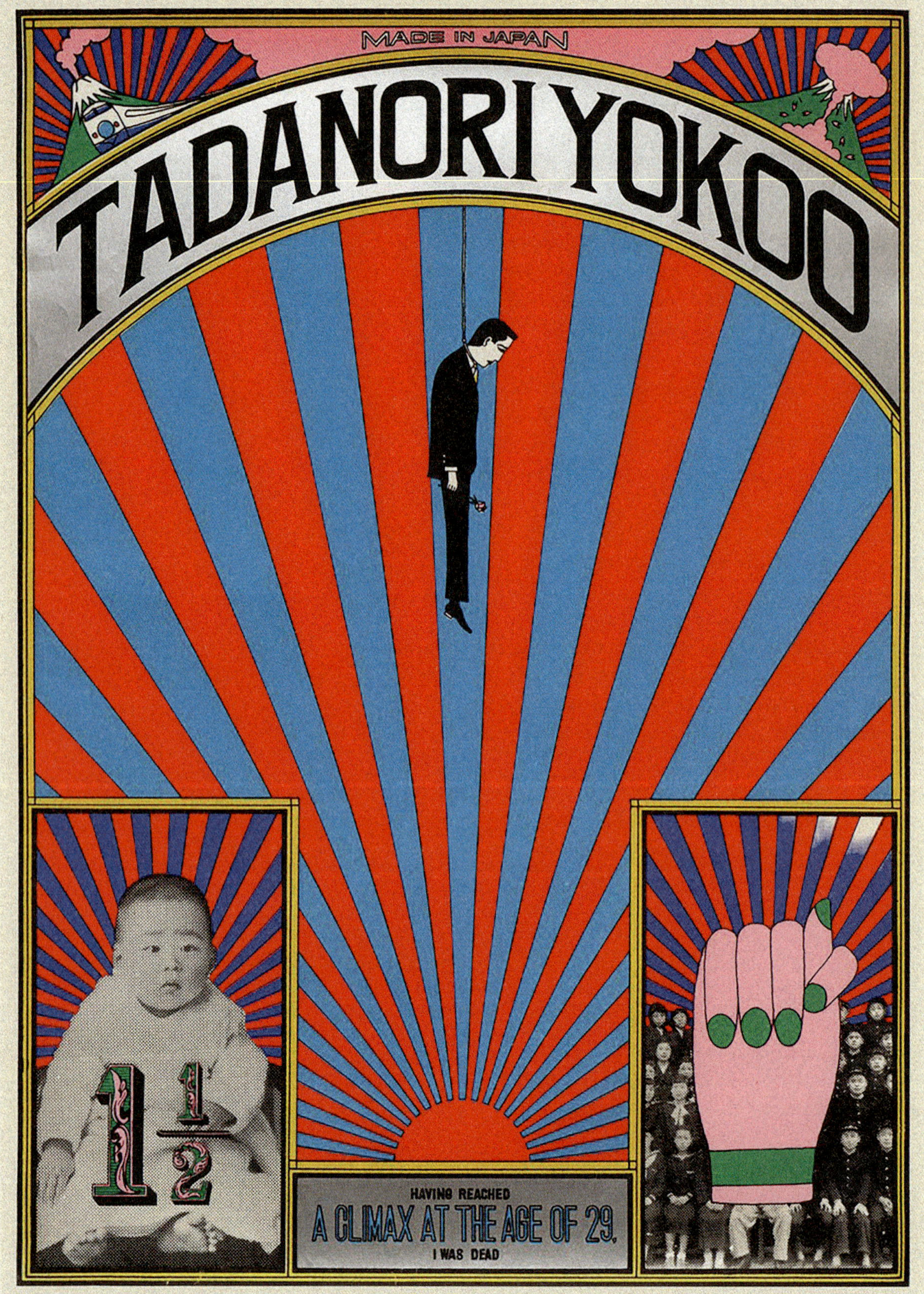

Made in Japan, Tadanori Yokoo, Having Reached a Climax at the Age of 29, I Was Dead, Yokoo Tadanori 横尾忠則, 1965.

YOKOO TADANORI 横尾忠則

1936–

Yokoo Tadanori is the most famous graphic designer that the country of Japan has produced to date. Yokoo is best known for his groundbreaking poster designs of the 1960s, but he also created a giant array of music packaging in the 1970s and 1980s. Yokoo's work blew open the doors to multiple generations of Japanese graphic designers working with a postmodern approach and aesthetic, and carrying on with many of the themes Yokoo established in the 1960s and 1970s. Yokoo's work defines the intersection of art and design, and it continues to inform expressions of creativity in Japan and around the globe today.

Yokoo was born in Nishiwaki, a relatively small city in Hyōgo Prefecture—about a three-and-a-half-hour train ride from Kyoto today. As a teenager, his ambitions were to work at a post office and to paint in his spare time. After a few years designing posters and wrapping paper for the Chamber of Commerce in Nishiwaki while also contributing to the newspaper Kobe Shimbun, Yokoo was offered membership in the Japan Advertising Artists Club in 1956. He moved to Tokyo in 1960, and he joined the Nippon Design Center after being invited by Tanaka Ikkō. Shortly after, he broke his right thumb and was unable to work for the first ten months of what would be a four-year tenure with the organization, leaving Yokoo feeling quite guilty toward Tanaka for the mishap.

In 1964, Yokoo founded Studio Ilfil, a collaborative studio with Uno Akira and Harada Tsunao. He founded the Tokyo Illustrators' Club with Uno Akira, Wada Makoto, and others the following year. This period of collaborative and individual work for Ilfil was an exciting time, as each member began his career as a stage and graphic designer for the theater through the group.

Yokoo worked on the design of the 1964 Olympic icons as a member of one of the design teams led by Yamashita Yoshirō. He was paid in tickets to the Games, a rite of passage for many in the JAAC.

Yokoo found further low-paid yet groundbreaking work for the magazine *Hanashi no Tokushū* 話の特集 (Nipponsha), changing the masthead/logo design with each issue. Meanwhile, Yokoo's poster designs for independent theaters in Tokyo were becoming exceedingly popular, as they diverged from the foreshortened, flattened, abstract graphic style of post-WWII Japanese graphic design. Inspired by early Japanese packaging and its use of motifs from Japanese printmaking, package design, Chinese ornament, and Victoriana, Yokoo's work stood out from that of his peers.

Yokoo's breakout moment was his contribution to the Persona exhibition held in 1965 at the Matsuya department store in Tokyo's upscale Ginza shopping district. The poster, *Made in Japan, Tadanori Yokoo, Having Reached a Climax at the Age of 29, I Was Dead*, was a mix of messages from the youngest participant in the show. The rising sun motif, a symbol of both Japanese imperialism and reference to early Modern packaging, was made wry and ironic. Mount Fuji is pictured with a *shinkansen* 新幹線 bullet train—which had made its debut just a year prior—speeding past while twin Mount Fujis stand adjacent, simultaneously erupting and being bombed. Yokoo's portrait photo at age one-and-a-half is shown, as is a childhood class photo overlaid with an illustration of a hand with its thumb covered by the index finger—the Japanese symbol for lying.

The centerpiece is a cartoon portrait of the designer as an adult, a rose in hand, dangling from a noose. Designers didn't do this kind of stuff in the 1960s: political commentary about imperialism and national development, representations of suicide, much less talking about yourself turning thirty years old. Posters were supposed to be for *clients*. This level of self-expression was unheard of in graphic design at the time, both in Japan and around the world.

Yokoo's posters in *Persona* and afterwards were dynamic, shocking, sensual, and proto-psychedelic, and they offered visual passion that other Japanese graphic design did not at the time, having been stuck in modernist "problem-solving" territory for the previous decade and a half.

That initial poster, along with a number of others that featured copious nudity, political expression, and grotesque violence, propelled Yokoo Tadanori into the pop culture stratosphere in Japan. What Yokoo's work presented was something deep: the deployment of an innate personal skew on graphic design combined with the acumen of an individual who had worked in screen printing prior to professionalizing as a designer. By utilizing visual metaphors, metonymy, allegory, collage, intuition, personal history, and chance processes—and slamming it all together—Yokoo created design that, looking backward, disrupted the continuum of graphic design history as we know it. Contemporary histories of graphic design situate the birth of Postmodernism in the late 1970s in Western Europe and North America, yet Yokoo was creating postmodern work more

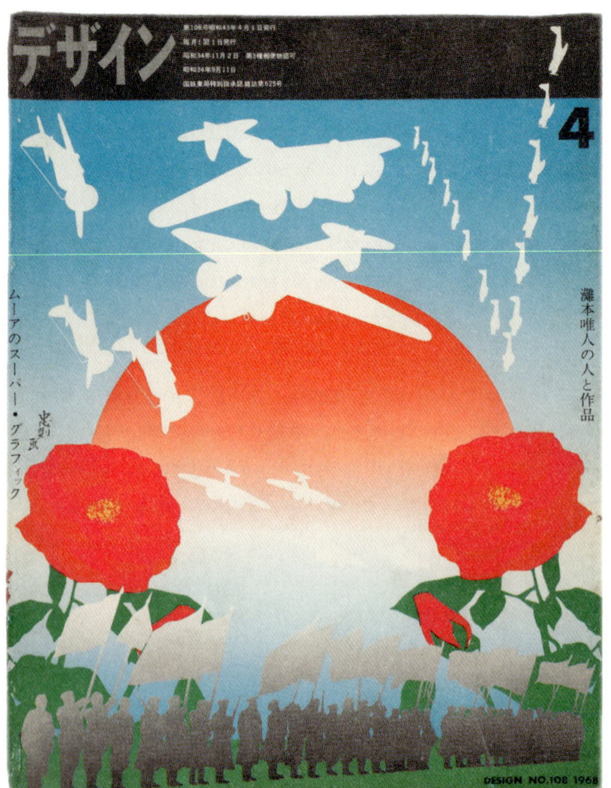

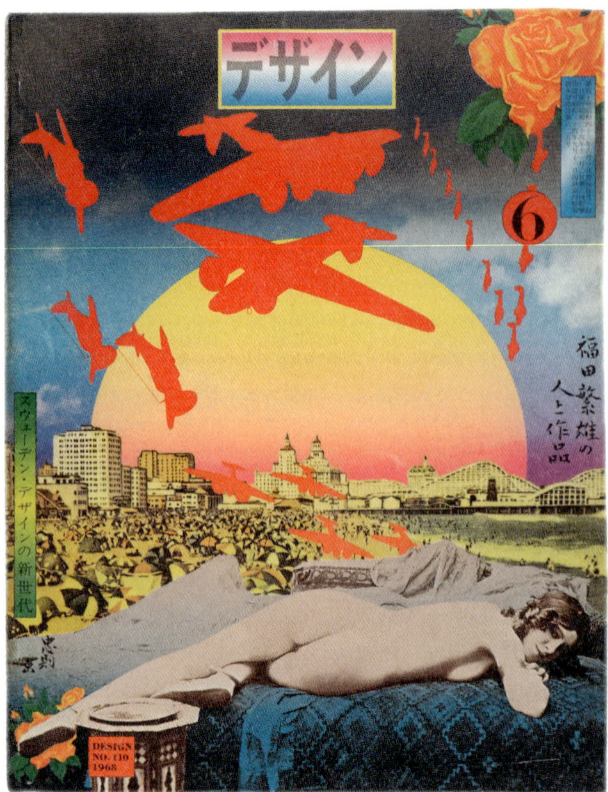

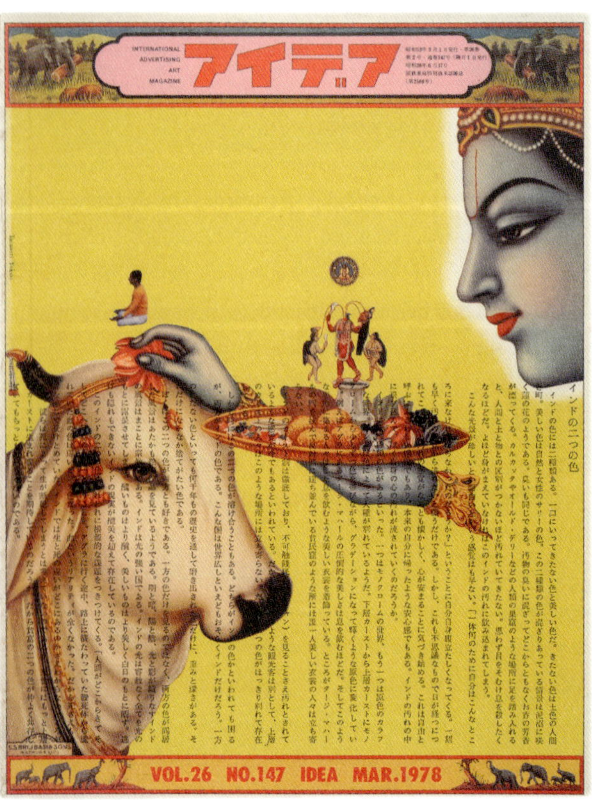

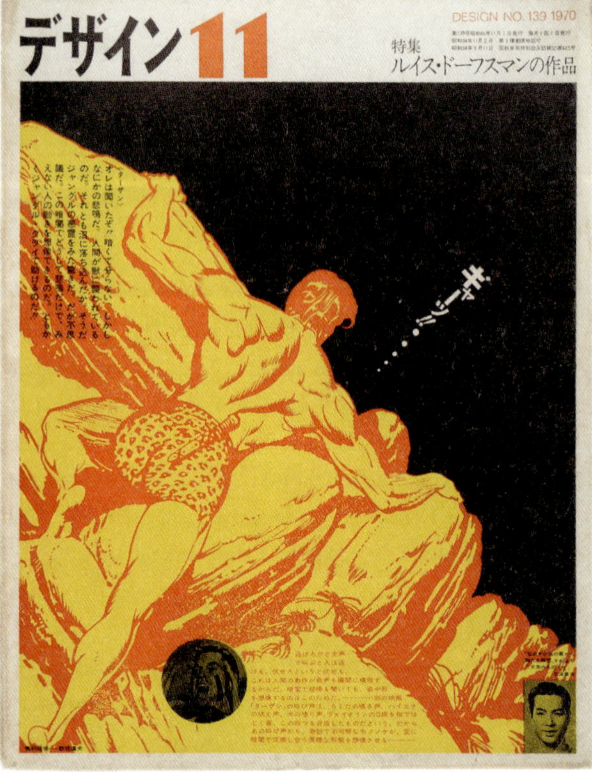

Clockwise from top left: Front cover design for ***Design* デザイン No. 108** (Tokyo: Bijutsu Shuppansha 美術出版社, 1968); front cover design for ***Design* デザイン No. 110** (Tokyo: Bijutsu Shuppansha 美術出版社, 1968); cover design for ***IDEA* アイデア No. 147** (Tokyo: Seibundo Shinkosha 誠文堂新光社, 1978); front cover design for ***Design* デザイン No. 133** (Tokyo: Bijutsu Shuppansha 美術出版社, 1970).

Top: Soundtrack album cover design for the popular TV show ***Mu* ムー** (Tokyo: Polydor, 1977).
Bottom: **Santana *Amigos*** LP cover (Tokyo: Columbia, 1976).

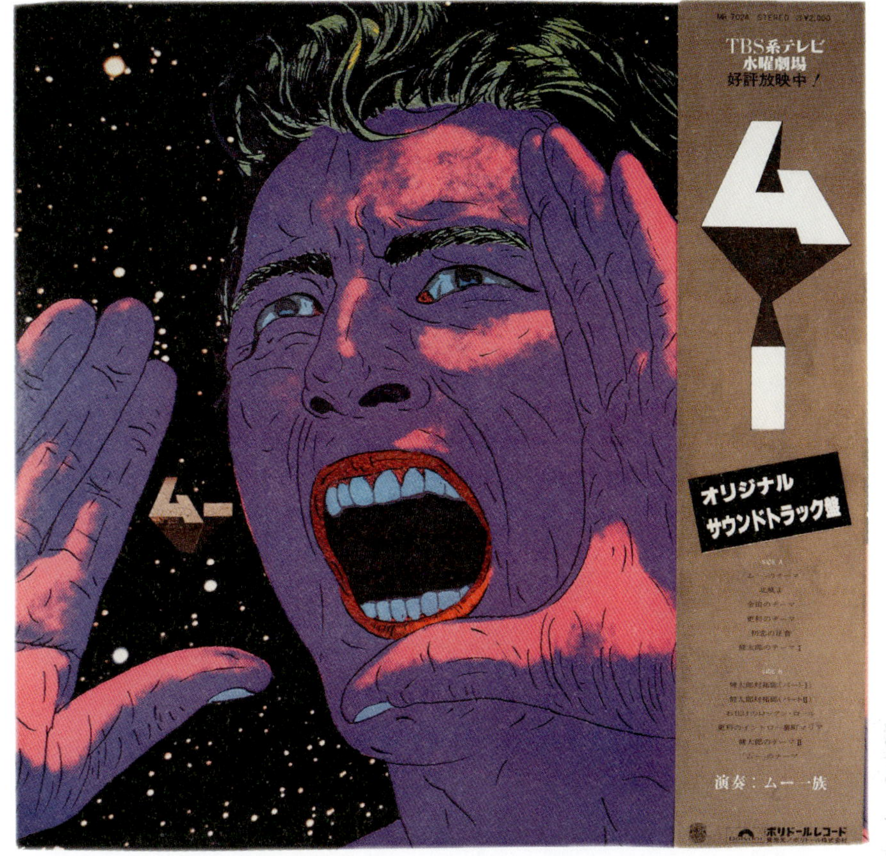

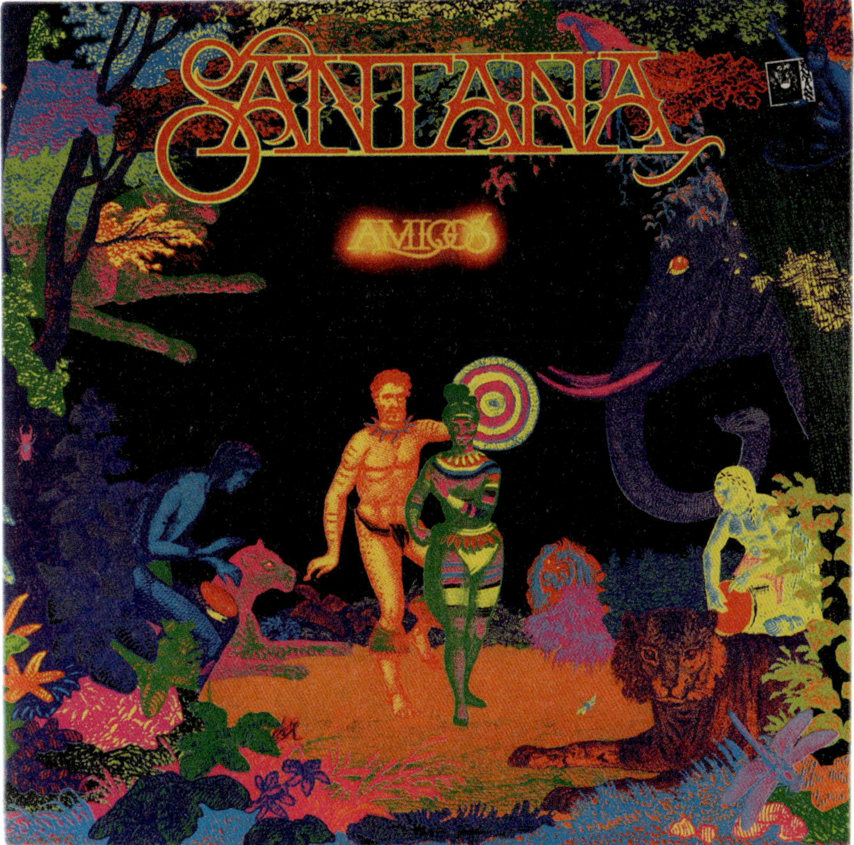

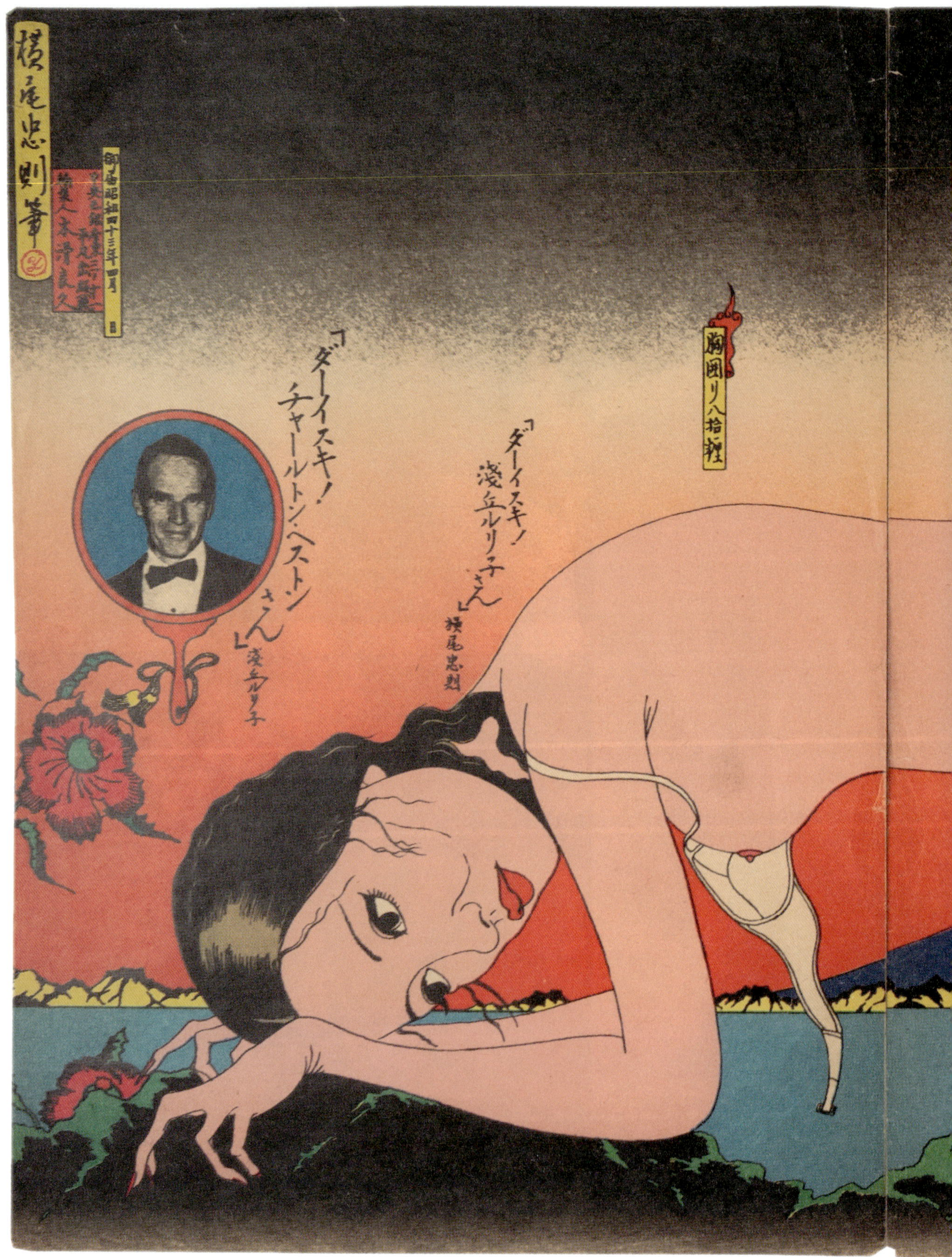

胸囲り八拾糎
「ダーイスキ！浅丘ルリ子さん」横尾忠則
「ダーイスキ！チャールトン・ヘストンさん」浅丘ルリ子
御届昭和四十三年四月　日
横尾忠則筆

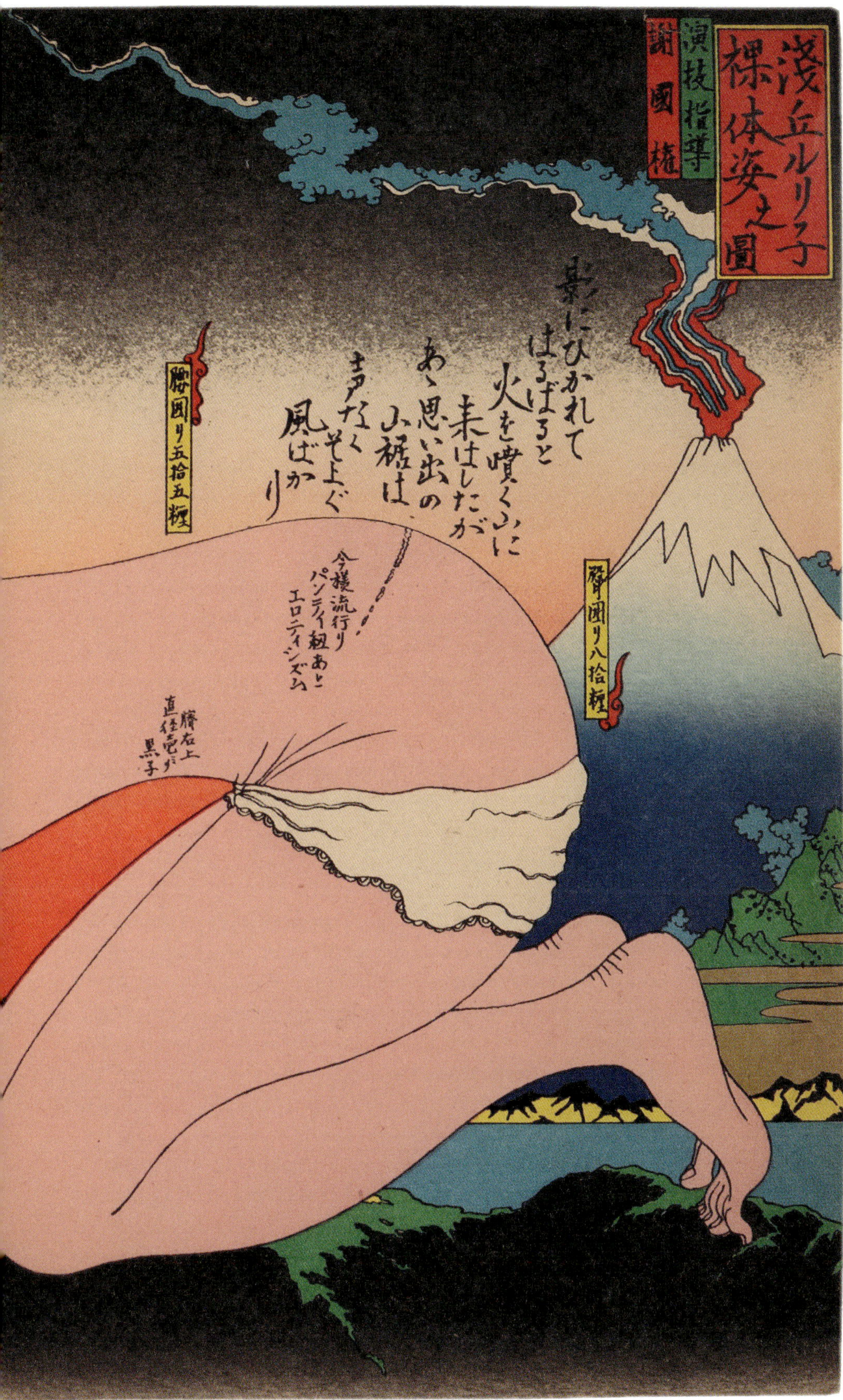

***Landscape with Madonna* 浅丘ルリ子裸体姿之圖**, Yokoo's 1968 homage to his *Diary of A Shinjuku Thief* co-star Asaoka Ruriko 浅丘ルリ子, over which she would threaten to sue him over for portraying her both in the nude and as a trite individual.

Of note is the smiling onlooker wearing a bowtie in the composition—an image of American actor Charlton Heston, who is saying "daisuki." (This expresses that he very much likes what he sees.) The composition was originally printed in the May 6,1968, issue of the magazine ***Heibon Punch* 平凡パンチ**.

than a decade before the term was applied to graphic design. Yokoo's work disrupts common understandings of graphic design history. Japan may have been late to adopt the language of Westernized modern graphic design, but Postmodernism via Yokoo arrived a dozen years earlier than in graphic design in the West.

Additionally, Yokoo's work from the 1960s was laden with *meaning*, while the individuals in the psychedelic movement in San Francisco, with whom he is often lumped in, were profoundly literal in their work.

In 1967, he designed the cover for the seven-inch single for the band The Happenings Four—a lounge-influenced Group Sounds band. The record features hand-colored photos of the band members, along with pseudo-psych lettering and a sprinkling of decorative elements. On a poster for the play *John Silver*, Yokoo printed a carefully lettered, handwritten apology to the director for producing the poster after opening night. Yokoo was cast as "Birdie," a young Japanese book thief, in Nagisa Oshima's 大島渚 divisive 1968 agitprop film *Diary of a Shinjuku Thief* 新宿泥棒日記.

For the design of Mishima Yukio's 三島由紀夫 posthumous 1969 book *Immoral Education Course* 不道徳教育講座, Yokoo painted on the bodies of a pair of naked women and inscribed them with verses. The photographer Hosoe Eikoh shot pictures of the pair, before Yokoo recolored the photograph akin to a blacklight being shone on the female duo, juxtaposing the figures with taught, angular bilingual lettering.

Yokoo designed the jackets for a number of notable records over the next few years, including Takakura Ken's *Deluxe* and Fuji Junko's *Red Peony Gambler*, both soundtracks to popular film stars' records, bringing him even further into the Japanese public eye. His designs evoked the rogue *yakuza* ヤクザ appeal of both records. Each featured illustrations of the film stars in character, mixing pop colors with Yokoo's own deft Japanese calligraphy, and offset with gradated colors inspired by traditional ukiyo-e printmaking.

The year 1969 also saw the release of the *Opera "From the Works of Tadanori Yokoo,"* a hybrid psych/enka/experimental album by Ichiyanagi Toshi 一柳慧, Yoko Ono's first husband and former student of John Cage. This double picture disc is an homage to Yokoo's early graphic works and is a powerhouse of design and indeterminate music.

Yokoo would design an onslaught of book and manga covers, illustrate books and magazines, and stay immensely, immensely busy throughout 1969. He designed the cover for the music LP *Kokoro No Uramado* 心の裏窓 by Asaoka Ruriko 浅丘ルリ子, an immensely popular actress tied to the Nikkatsu film company who acted alongside a bevy of Japan's most talented actors at that time (including Shishido Jo 宍戸錠, perhaps the first actor to have surgically implanted cheeks so that he resembled a squirrel). The album featured a mind-blowing bee's-eye view of Asaoka, one of postwar Japan's greatest sex symbols. It stands as one of Yokoo's greatest graphic works—a singular piece of Brutalist collage. Two years later, Yokoo produced an illustrated poster depicting a prone, naked Asaoka, for which she would threaten to sue.

In the meantime, much bigger things were afoot. The United States and Japan had both signed the Treaty of Mutual Cooperation and Security between the United States and Japan 日本国とアメリカ合衆国との間の相互協力及び安全保障条約, or Anpo 安保 for short. Anpo was later ratified between the US and Japan in Washington in January 1960, allowing for the United States' continued use of Japanese territories for a decade-long period. Yokoo had participated in anti-Anpo demonstrations in 1960 and was a long-time opponent to American occupation. In 1969, Yokoo drew satirical illustrations of Japanese Prime Minister Satō Eisaku 佐藤榮作, which were rejected by *TIME* magazine but were repurposed for the leftist political protest magazine *Weekly Anpo* 週刊アンポ.

Yokoo's politicization emboldened graphic design students to violently protest the 1969 judging session of a Japan Advertising Artists Club meeting and earned Yokoo long-lasting enmity from JAAC elders Kamekura Yūsaku and Tanaka Ikkō, Yokoo's longtime mentor, who later wrote dismissively of Yokoo. Despite this, Yokoo spoke glowingly of his former mentor in *Idea* for Tanaka's obituary in 2002.

Yokoo remained a busy and incredibly sought-after designer through the 1970s. In 1970, he released the book *The Complete Tadanori Yokoo* 横尾忠則全集, a Bible-sized paean to his career to date, filled with sensual and provocative imagery and writings by the young design star. Yokoo designed a teenager's bedroom worth of posters for international rock acts including Earth, Wind & Fire; The Beatles; Emerson, Lake & Palmer; Cat Stevens; and Tangerine Dream. Yokoo became known to the international music industry, including record labels in the US and Europe, through this poster work. In these posters,

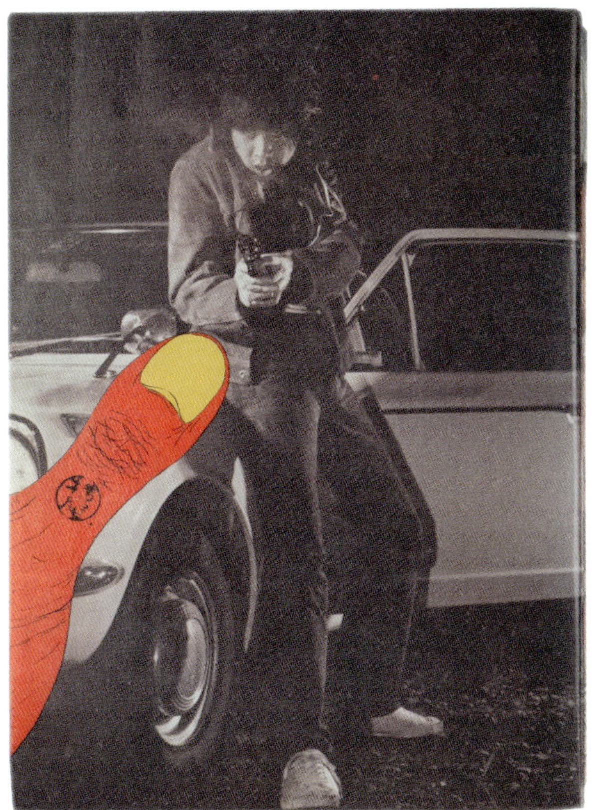

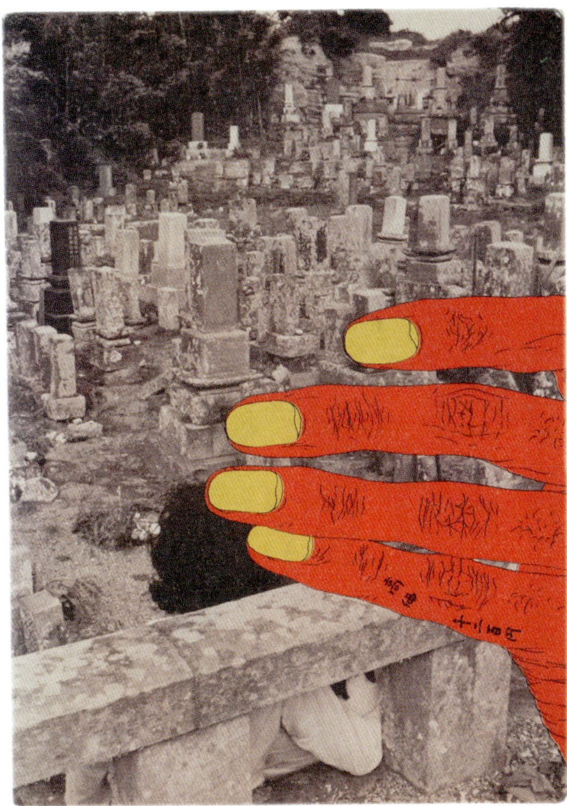

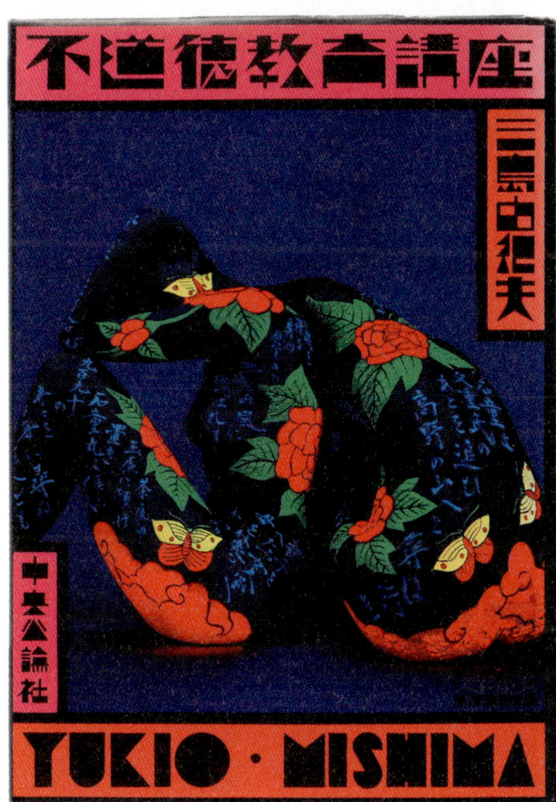

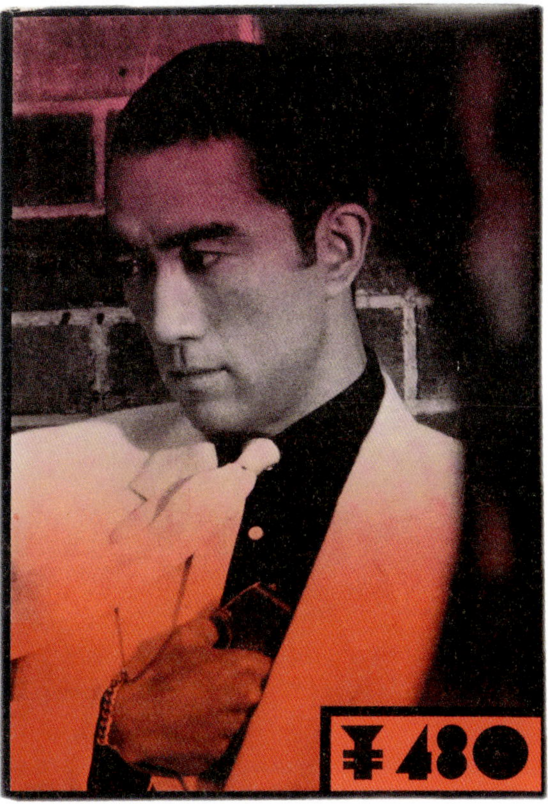

Top: front and back cover of ***Diary of Yokoo Tadanori* 一米七〇糎のブルース 横尾忠則日記, Yokoo Tadanori 横尾忠則** (Tokyo: Shinshokan 新書館, 1969). Bottom: ***Immoral Education Course* 不道徳教育講座, Mishima Yukio 三島由紀夫** (Tokyo: Chuōkōron-sha 中央公論社, 1969).

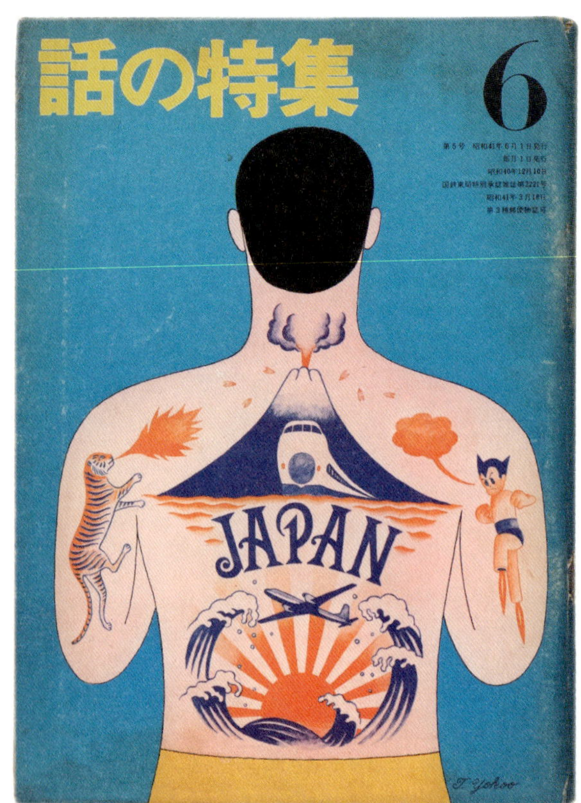

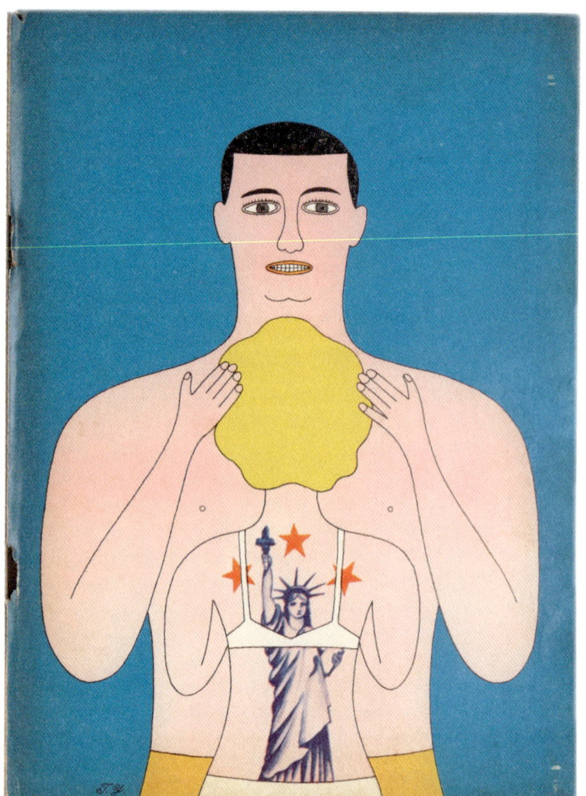

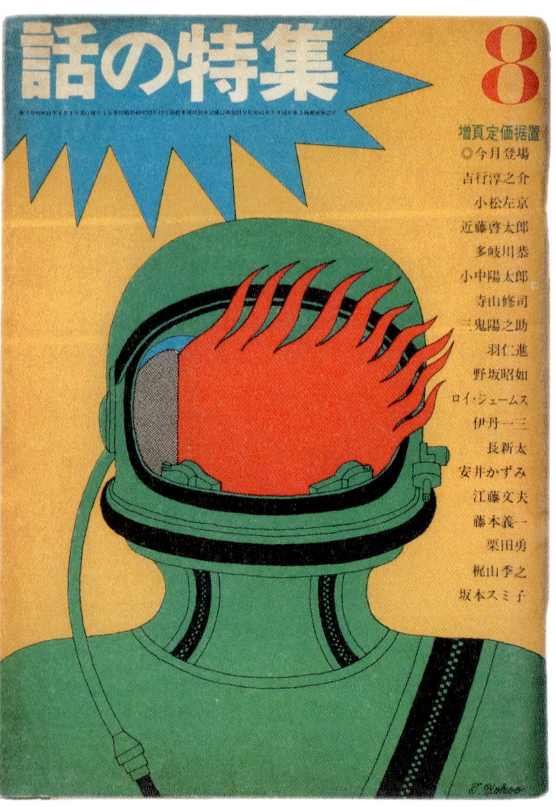

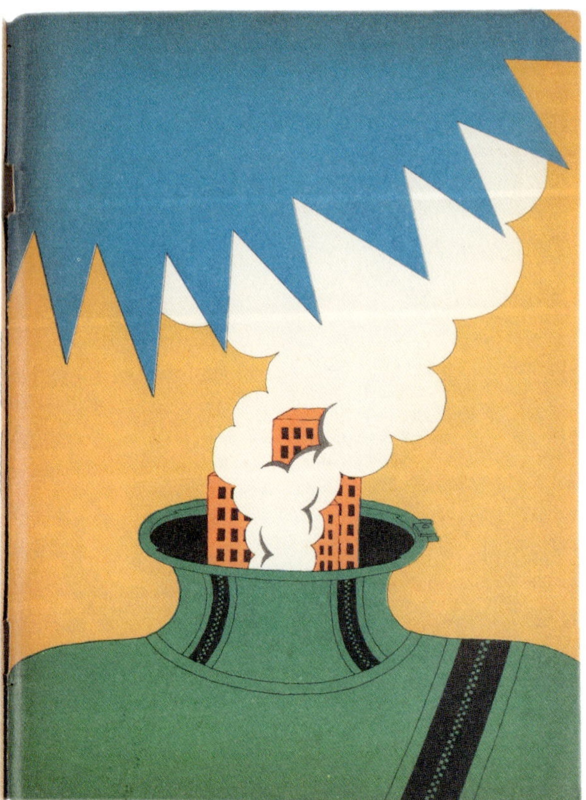

This page and second following: Assorted cover and inside back cover designs from the first edition of the magazine ***Hanashi no Tokushu*** **話の特集** (Tokyo: Nippon-sha, 1966).

Yokoo shifted from hand-wrought illustration to collage. Icons of history and geography are juxtaposed with pop stars of the day—the contextualization of musicians into scenes in Babylon, Egypt, and anonymous wild jungles boosting the pop stars' gravitas.

Yokoo's design for *Lotus*, a 1974 Santana live album recorded in Japan, became highly popular. The record sleeve featured a photograph of a Buddha in repose against an illustration of a red lotus, with circular gradient chakras floating around the composition, nestled within a fisheye-lensphotograph of a rising sun. This was complemented by lettering that riffs on the forms of the Devanagari language. The record reflected Yokoo's fascination with Indian imagery at the time, along with his interest in meditation, the occult, and extraterrestrial life. These themes would loom largely in other projects, particularly his 1974 covers for *Shinjuku Play Map* #5 and #6 and *Idea* #147.

The imagery used on *Lotus* was revisited in Miles Davis's 1975 *Agharta* double LP, a live record put to tape in Japan. Davis asked Yokoo to create album artwork that extended the themes Yokoo established on Santana's *Lotus*. Interestingly, the album design for *Lotus* is actually about the mythical subterranean utopia known as Agharta, while the cover for Davis's album is an oddball mashup of the eponymous hollow world/Middle Earth utopia with allusions to the lost city of Atlantis, UFOs, and Afrofuturism. The cover shows two women perched on the edge of a jungle, with a megalopolis splayed out in the background. The gatefold sleeve within the album explains Yokoo's visuals in detail:

> *"During various periods in history, the supermen of Agharta came to the surface of Earth to teach the human race how to live together in peace and save us from wars, catastrophe, and destruction. The apparent sighting of several flying saucers soon after the bombing of Hiroshima may represent one visitation. The UFO shown here symbolizes a similar connection."*

Yokoo's next big record project was Santana's *Amigos* album, released in 1976. The imagery continues the visual story from *Agharta*, with a psychedelic-looking Mayan man and woman again standing on a jungle cliff—this time surrounded by old advertising imagery of drumming "natives," wild animals, and, looming behind, a black void reminiscent of the Lotus album. On the interior, images of Jesus, Buddha, and Kali are set against spacescapes, full-bleed floods of gold printing, an Archigram-esque diagram of a concert in a pyramid, and live shots from a Santana concert in an arena.

Yokoo's exploration of alternate realities didn't stop there—his next album cover design was for the 1977 soundtrack of the popular TV show *Mu* ムー, later retitled *Mu Tribe* ムー族, by Gō Hiromi 郷ひろみ and Kiki Kirin 樹木希林. Yokoo designed the opening sequence for the television show, one of the rare examples of his work in motion since the 1960s.

Yokoo also designed the 1978 cover of the Hosono Haruomi 細野晴臣 LP *Cochin Moon*, an experimental "electro-exotica" album which was meant to sonically illustrate an unreleased Bollywood film. The album was meant to be a collaboration, and the duo traveled to India for inspiration, but Hosono wound up having to produce the album solo, as Yokoo was the victim of diarrhea during their travels in India and was, for the most part, confined to the hotel from which the album took its title.

The final installment of Yokoo's idealized/alternate futures for record packaging from the 1970s was the design of synthesizer musician Tomita Isao's 冨田勲 seminal 1978 album, *The Bermuda Triangle*. The front cover of the original pressing is bisected diagonally with a looming half-moon/half-geodesic dome, a collaged gold high-heeled foot pressing on the artist's name, and a religious icon overlooking the ruins of a Roman forum. The bottom features collaged Caucasian people holding hands, all looking down on a Superstudio-influenced axonometric grid that is overlaid on a landscape, the bottom cells of which have the words "Pyramid Sounds" lettered within. A Roman column with a Rococo anti-pattern frames the right side, while the left shows another small cropped landscape with a darkened window pasted on it.

Yokoo's body of work showing inner worlds over the first two decades of his career is perhaps his greatest gift to culture. He demonstrated that the real way out is to go in, by designing objects that showed as much of his dreams as they did of himself.

In the 1980s, Yokoo transitioned from graphic design toward painting, producing works such as the *Y-Roads* series: portraits of desolate forked intersections, often mystically illuminated by streetlight, with the occasional stray dog or apparition.

Yokoo has overseen the opening of two museums in his name within his lifetime; The Yokoo Tadanori Museum of Contemporary Art, which opened in 2012, and Teshima Yokoo House in collaboration with architect Yuko Nagayama on Teshima island in the Seto Inland Sea, which opened in 2013.

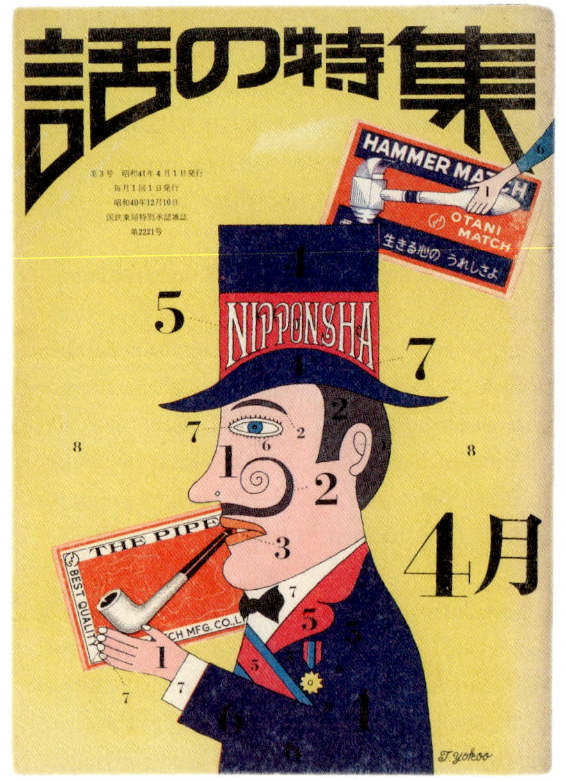
話の特集
第3号 昭和41年4月1日発行
毎月1回1日発行
昭和40年12月10日
国鉄東局特別承認雑誌
第2221号
HAMMER MATCH
OTANI MATCH
生きる心の うれしさよ
NIPPONSHA
THE PIPE
BEST QUALITY
4月
T. Yokoo

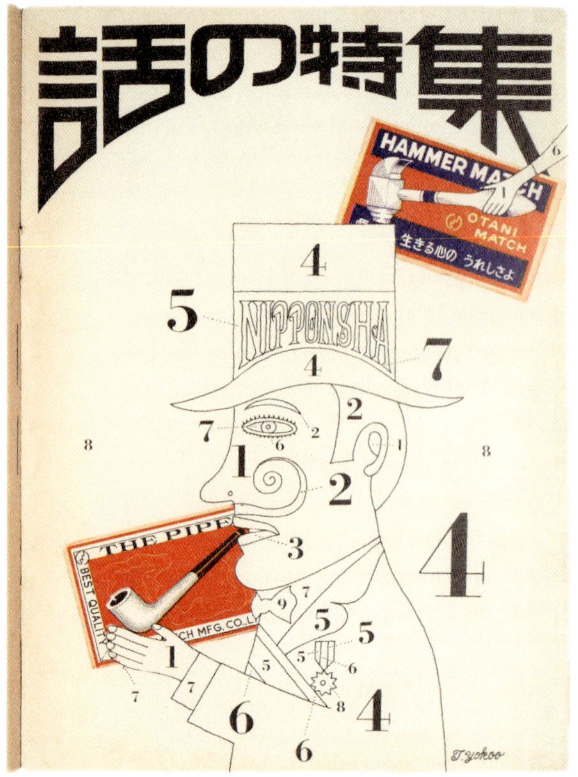
話の特集
HAMMER MATCH
OTANI MATCH
生きる心の うれしさよ
NIPPONSHA
THE PIPE
BEST QUALITY
T. Yokoo

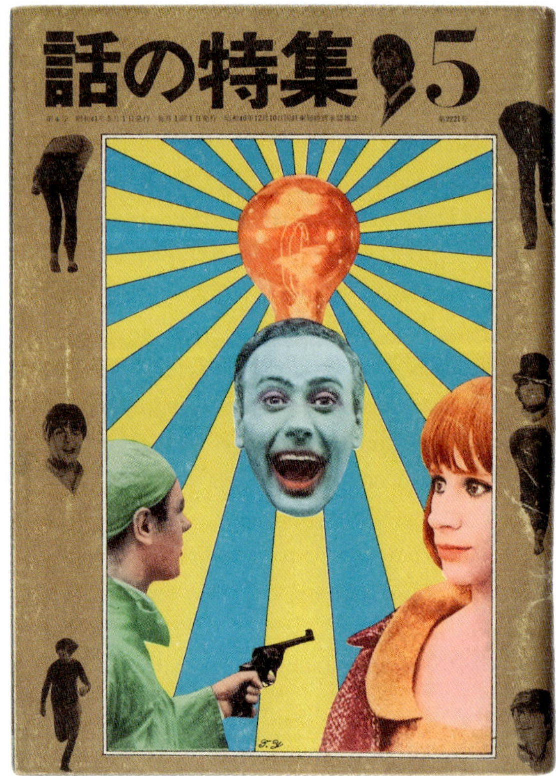
話の特集 5

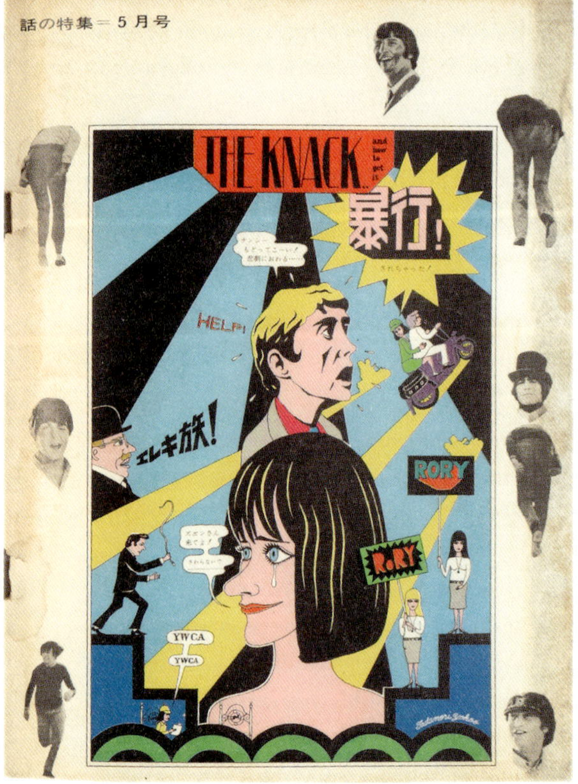
話の特集＝5月号
THE KNACK
暴行!
HELP!
エレキ族!
RORY
YWCA

Cover for ***The Sun*** **(Taiyo) 太陽 No. 114 (Tokyo: Heibonsha 平凡社, December 1972).** This issue features an expansive and explicit collaboration between Yokoo and photographer Shinoyama Kishin 篠山紀信 devoted to the life and times of writer Ōzaki Shirō 尾崎士郎.

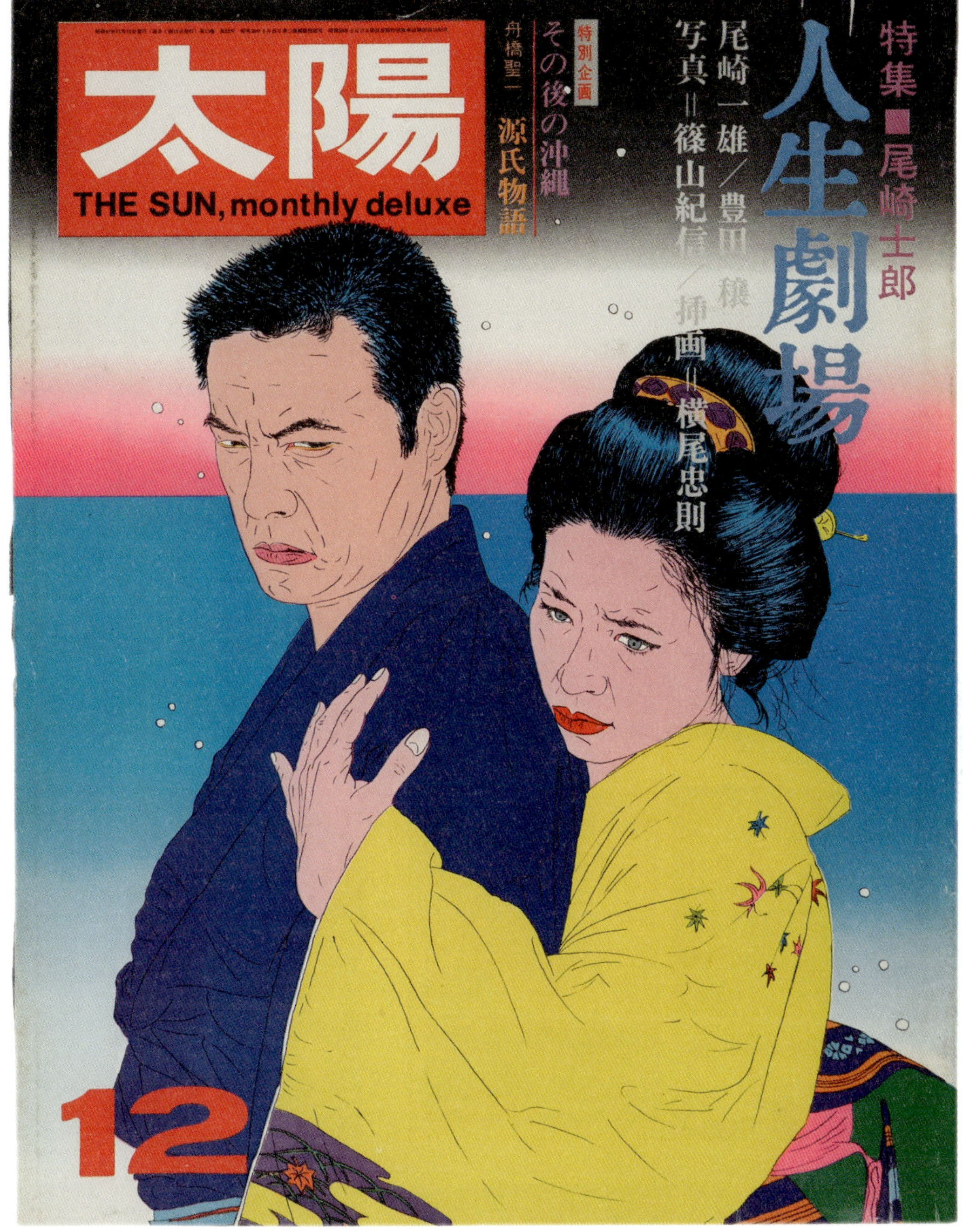

References:

Goodman, David. *Angura: Posters of the Japanese Avant-Garde*. New York, NY: Princeton Architectural Press, 1999.

Kamekura, Yūsaku, and Ayao Yamana. *Gurafikku Dezain no Seiki: Bunshō to Danwa to Sakuhin De kōsei: Meiji Sedai Yamana Ayao Sugiura Hisui Kara shōwa Sedai Made*. Tokyo: Bijutsu Shuppansha, 2008.

Kuwahara, Shigeo, and Hiroyuki Sasame. *Japan Avangyarudo: Angura Engeki Kessaku posutā Hyaku = Japan Avantgarde: 100 Poster Masterpieces from Underground Theatre*. Tokyo: Paruko Entateinmento Jigyōkyoku, 2004.

Lynam, Ian. "The Album Design of Yokoo Tadanori." Red Bull Music Academy Daily, June 8, 2015. https://daily.redbullmusicacademy.com/2015/06/yokoo-tadanori-album-design/.

Muroga, Kiyonori. "Tadanori Yokoo 196X: Selected Works from the 1960s and 1970s." *Idea* 1, no. 342 (September 2010): 5–122. .

Traganou, Jilly. "Tokyo's 1964 Olympic Design as a 'Realm of [Design] Memory.'" *Sport in Society* 14, no. 4 (2011): 466–81. https://doi.org/10.1080/17430437.2011.565925.

Yokoo, Tadanori, and Tōno Yoshiaki. *Yokoo Tadanori = Tadanori Yokoo*. Tokyo: Kabushiki Kaisha Chikuma Shobō, 1971.

Yokoo, Tadanori. *Bōken'ō Yokoo Tadanori = Tadanori Yokoo Be Adventurous!* Tokyo: Kokusho Kankōkai, 2008.

Yokoo, Tadanori. *Tadanori Yokoo: Complete Book Designs*. Tokyo: PIE, 2013.

Yokoo, Tadanori, and Noriyuki Shimizu. *Yokoo Tadanori zenposutā = The Complete Posters of Tadanori Yokoo*. Tokyo: Kokusho Kankōkai, 2010.

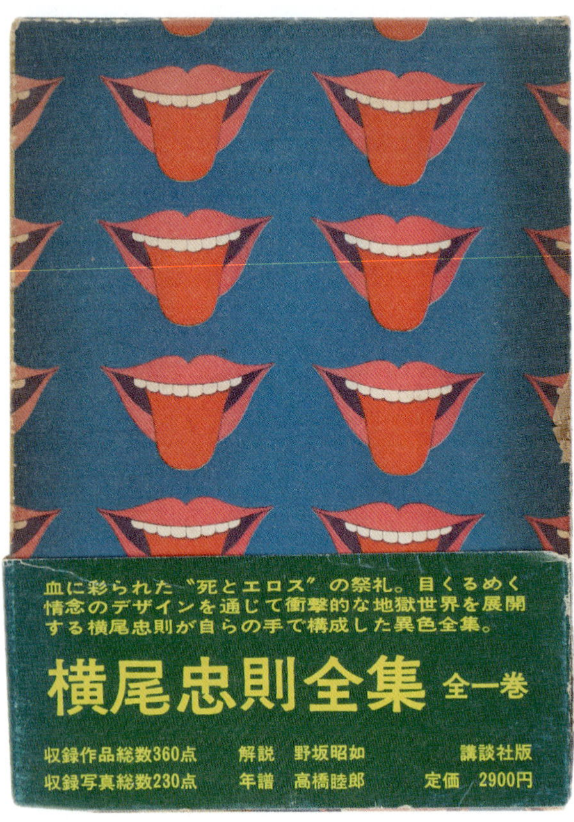

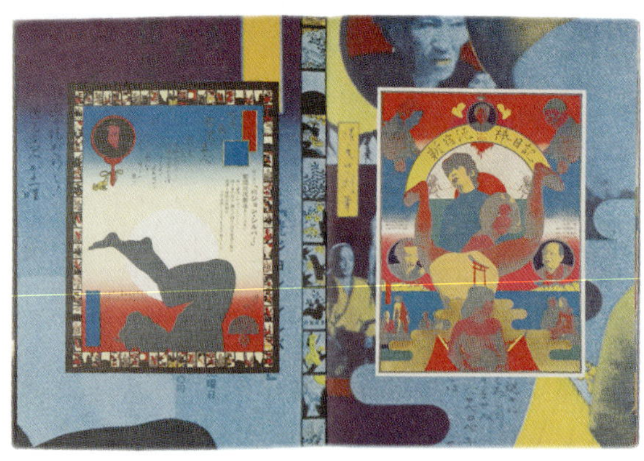

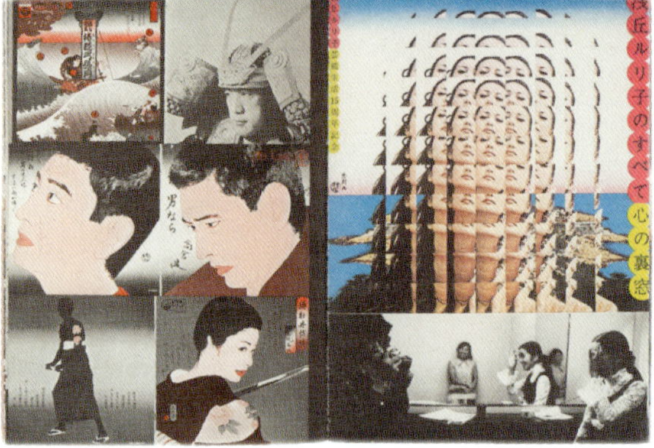

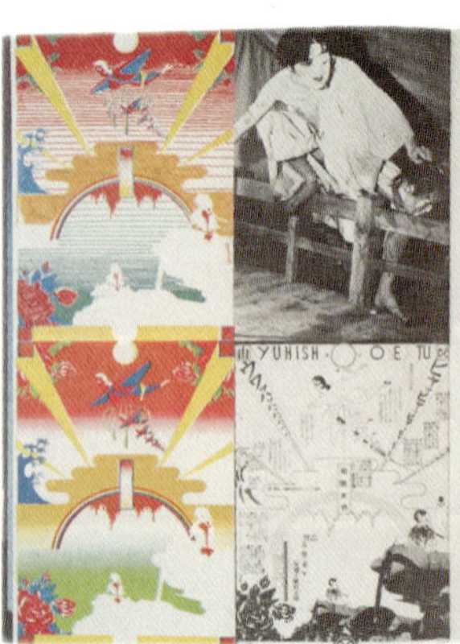

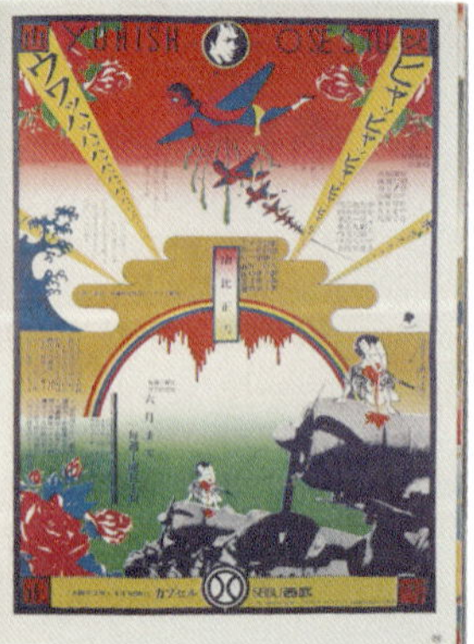

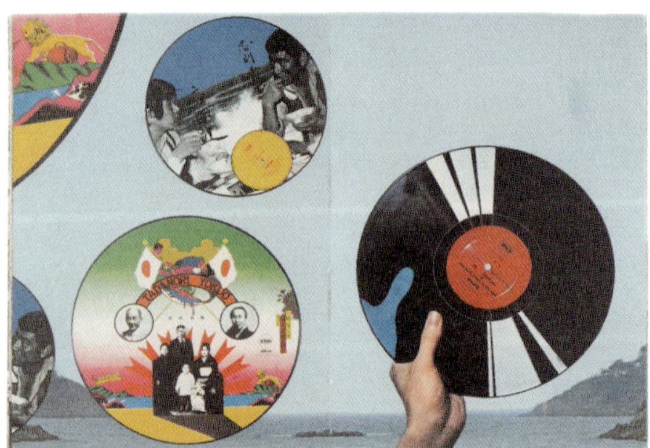

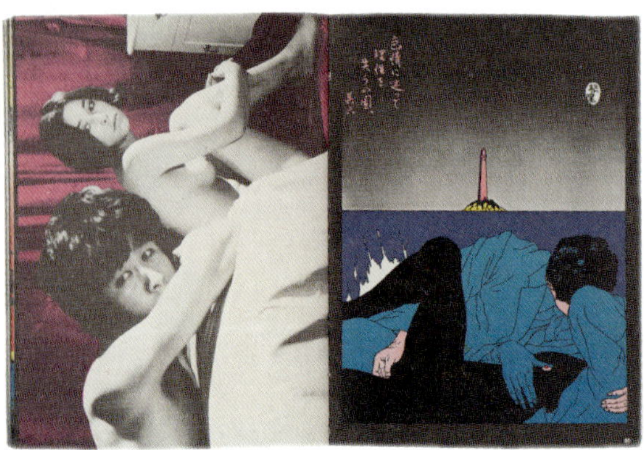

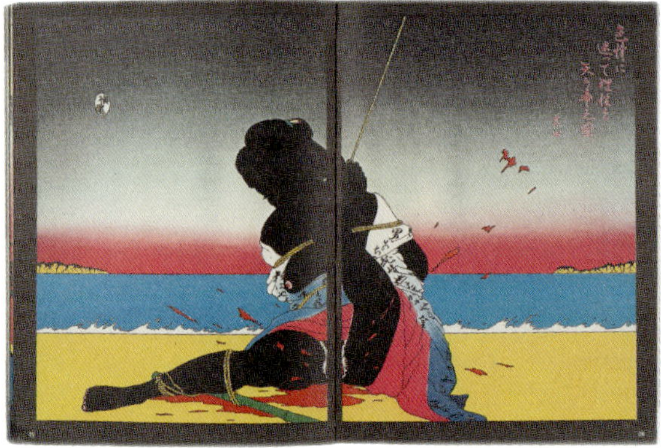

Covers and spreads from ***The Complete Tadanori Yokoo* 横尾忠則全集, Yokoo Tadanori 横尾忠則** (Tokyo: Kodansha 講談社, 1971).

ANGURA アングラ

Yokoo Tadanori, Uno Akira, Hirano Kōga, Kushida Mitsuhiro 串田光弘, and other designers gained notoriety largely because of their affiliation with the avant-garde *Angura* theater movement アングラ演劇, also known as *shōgekijō* 小劇場 or "The Little Theater" movement. (The term "Angura" is a conflation of the words "andaaguraundo engeki アンダーグラウンド演劇" or "underground theater.") Angura materialized in the early 1960s, in a politicized reaction to the structural and ideological limitations of the modern theater movement known as Shingeki 新劇 (literally, "new theater"), which was initially popularized in the 1920s.

In the 1960s, many young Shingeki troupe members tired of being forced to wait years for a starring role or provide any input into productions due to the troupes' hierarchical organizational structures. The tension was exacerbated by younger members' support of student protest groups whose politics differed from those of the organizing body Shingekijin Kaigi 新劇人会議 (Shingeki Workers Association), which officially sided with the Japan Communist Party. Nearly the entire Shingeki community rallied to protest the revision of the Anpo US-Japan Security Treaty, leading to violent street battles with right-wing counter-protest groups in which many Shingeki members were injured. The experience of revolutionary direct action emboldened many Shingeki members to start their own theater movement, giving birth to Angura—a wild and radical form of theater that broke with the conventions of the far-more-restrained Shingeki movement. Angura productions were held in large tents and other unconventional venues, and they utilized direct audience interaction and dramatic, often grotesque, costumes, makeup, and set designs. Productions' storylines featured confounding plots and sequencing, overt sexuality, left-wing politics, and explicit violence.

It was against this backdrop that young graphic designers created some of the most dynamic and shocking visual design, creating posters, leaflets, playbills, and stage sets for legendary directors such as Terayama Shuji 寺山修司, Kara Jūrō 唐十郎, and Suzuki Tadashi 鈴木忠志.

Angura graphic designers were working among a wider, multidisciplinary community and movement, within which aesthetics flowed from medium to medium. Many graphic designers were simultaneously working as stage designers and thus directly influencing how audience participants were visually consuming theater troupes' productions. Designers were in direct collaboration with directors—a far cry from typical client/designer relationships. In many ways, Angura productions were some of the highest points of designer-as-culture-maker in Japan.

Despite the politically leftist origins of Angura, the portrayal of gender in theater productions and their assorted ephemera tended toward hypermasculine depictions of male characters and objectified, hypersexualized representations of women in various states of undress. In a 2006 essay, Australian academic Vera Mackie lamented, "Visual culture associated with the underground theater movement of 1960s Japan consistently displays a fascination with the female body as spectacle,"[1] noting that the assorted Angura groups "seem to have developed without the benefit of the feminist ideas which were developing at the time."[2]

References:

Goodman, David. *Angura: Posters of the Japanese Avant-Garde.* New York, NY: Princeton Architectural Press, 1999.

Kuwahara, Shigeo, and Hiroyuki Sasame. *Japan Avangyarudo: Angura Engeki Kessaku Posutā Hyaku = Japan Avantgarde: 100 Poster Masterpieces from Underground Theatre.* Tokyo: Paruko Entateinmento Jigyōkyoku, 2004.

1 Vera C. Mackie, "The Spectacle of Woman in Japanese Underground Theatre Posters," *Performance Paradigm*, No. 2 (2006): 91–101, https://ro.uow.edu.au/artspapers/1000/.

2 Ibid.

HIRANO KŌGA 平野甲賀

1938–2021

Hirano Kōga (often transliterated as Hirano Kouga) was born in Seoul, Korea, the son of Japanese citizens posted in Japan's then-colony. In 1957, Hirano began his studies in art and design at Musashino Art School, the predecessor to Musashino Art University, where he studied under Hara Hiromu. In 1960, while still a student, Hirano won the Japan Advertising Artists Club Special Prizes for his design work for Oe Kenzaburo's 大江健三郎 book *Leap Before You Look*. Upon graduation, he joined Takashimaya department stores' advertising department, where he worked until 1964.

That year, Hirano began producing posters, flyers, and stage sets for independent theaters in Tokyo, particularly for the June Theater Troupe 六月劇場 which later morphed into the Black Tent Theatre 黒テント劇場 in 1968. The troupe's leftist repertoire included sociopolitical plays that embodied subcultural opposition to war, capitalism, and social conformity. Hirano's posters and programs associated with the Angura theater movement were highly stylized, provocative, and visually seductive.

From 1964 until 1991, Hirano was the lone book cover designer for the counterculture publishing company Shobunsha, for whom he designed over 6,000 book covers in a variety of styles. Hirano also designed the publishing house's rhinoceros logo. Shobunsha has published a wide variety of literature spanning much of postwar contemporary culture, and Hirano's cover designs for Shobunsha incorporate dozens of different stylistic approaches.

In 1973, Hirano worked as the art director of *Wonderland* ワンダーランド, renamed *Treasure Island* 宝島, one of Japanese youth culture's canonical publications exploring rock, jazz, and theater in the early 1970s. Starting in the 1980s, Hirano began using free-form hand lettering of his own design, inspired by early avant-garde lettering models from both Japan and the West.

Through this combination of disparate work, Hirano developed an assortment of stylistic approaches that used illustration, photomontage, and layering of multilingual typography and lettering.

In 1978, Hirano joined the experimental folk band Suigyū Gakudan 水牛楽団 with composer, critic, and pianist Takahashi Yuji 高橋悠治, performing Pan-Asian protest songs in Thai and Japanese. He also worked with Takahashi's monthly journal *Suigyū Tsūshin* 水牛通信 as both a designer and an occasional editor. After touring internationally in Asia, Europe, and Russia, Hirano ended his involvement with the journal and the band in 1987.

Hirano wrote at length about the history of Japanese lettering and design for *Idea* magazine. In 1984, Hirano won the Kōdansha Publishing Culture Awards and Book Design Award. He had career-spanning exhibitions at Musashino University, the Ginza Graphic Gallery in Tokyo, and Kyoto's DDD Gallery. In 2007, he released the digital typeface Koga Grotesque, culled from the "greatest hits" of his hand lettering.

Hirano co-founded first Studio Iwato and subsequently Theatre Iwato, small DIY theaters in the Kagurazaka district of Tokyo, where a range of theatrical productions were staged between 2005 and 2013. The following year, Hirano moved to the island of Shōdoshima in Kagawa Prefecture, where he ran the occasional publishing house Sono Fune Ni Notte その船にのって.

From his time working as one of the most vital and expressive visual mouthpieces of 1960s resistance culture to his death in 2021, Hirano's body of work is widely admired for its depth, complexity, historical reference, and intellectualism.

References:

Goodman, David. *Angura: Posters of the Japanese Avant-Garde*. New York, NY: Princeton Architectural Press, 1999.

Hirano, Kōga. *Hirano Kōga*. Tokyo: DNP Bunka Shinkō Zaidan, 2017.

Hirano, Kōga. *Hirano Kōga Sōtei no Hon*. Tokyo: Riburopōto, 1985.

Hirano, Kōga. *Hirano Kōga To*. Tokyo: Nītopēpā, 2020.

Kuwahara, Shigeo, and Hiroyuki Sasame. *Japan Avangyarudo: Angura Engeki Kessaku Posutā Hyaku = Japan Avantgarde: 100 Poster Masterpieces from Underground Theatre*. Tokyo: Paruko Entateinmento Jigyōkyoku, 2004.

Tsuno, Kaitaro, Yuji Takahashi, and Osamu Torinoumi. "Kouga Hirano: Letters and Movements." *Idea* 59, no. 345 (March 2011): 1–80.

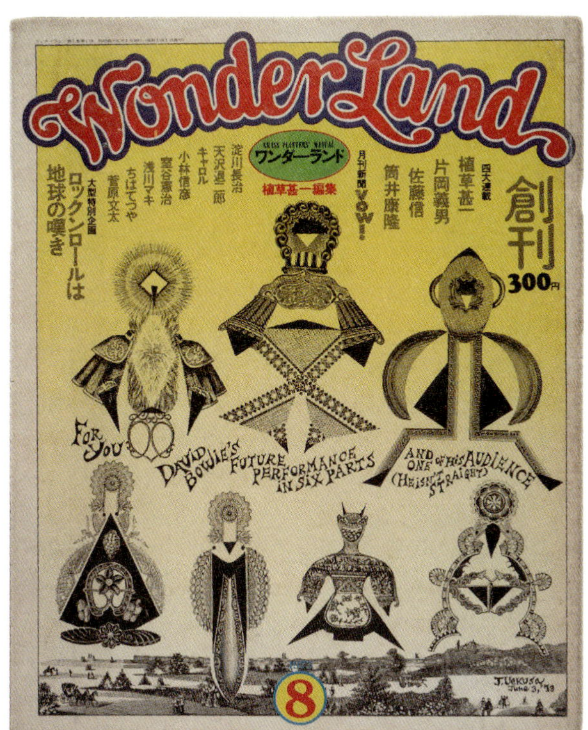

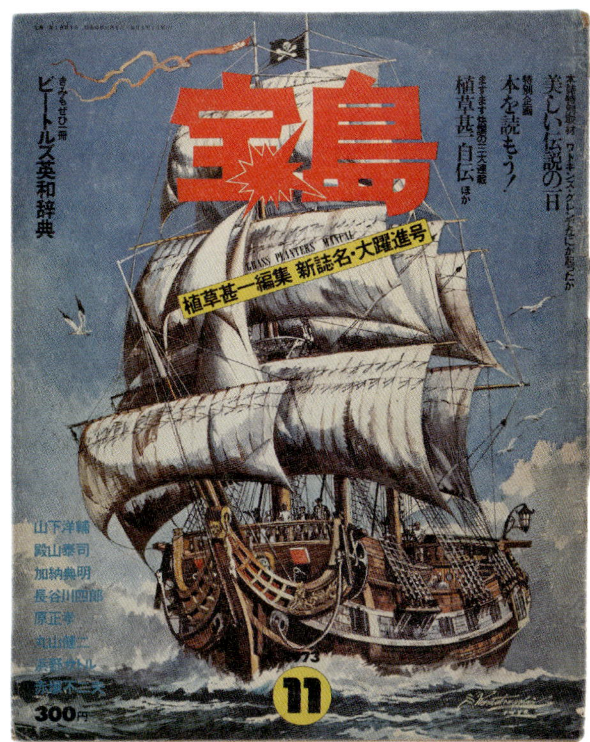

Cover designs for ***Wonderland* ワンダーランド** (renamed ***Treasure Island* 宝島** starting with the third issue), one of Japan's youth culture's canonical publications exploring rock, jazz, and theater in the early 1970s.

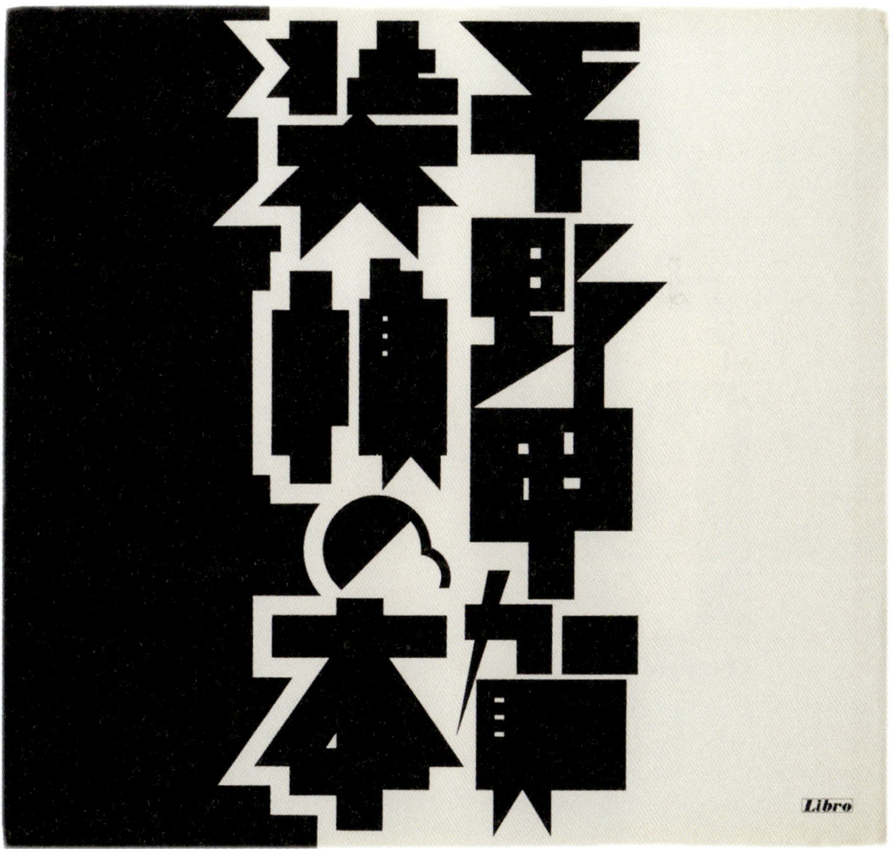

***The Book Design of Kōga Hirano* 平野甲賀 装幀の本** (Tokyo: Libroport, 1985). A then-comprehensive collection of book jacket and poster designs by Hirano, with an extensive interview by fellow designer Sugiura Kōhei at the rear of the book.

KUWAYAMA YASABURO 桑山弥三郎

1937–2017

Kuwayama Yasaburō was born in Niigata Prefecture. He graduated from Musashino Art School. While in school, Kuwayama formed the design team Group Taiposu (Group Typos) with classmates Ito Katsukazu 伊藤勝一, Hayashi Takao 林隆男, and Nagada Katsuya 長田克己.

Kuwayama participated in establishing DOCCO Design Inc., a design studio located in Shibuya, Tokyo, that works across type design, corporate identity, packaging, and brochure design. He taught type design at Asagaya Art Academy from 1969 to 1974 and taught typography at Musashino Art University from 1970 to 1979.

In 1969, he opened the Kuwayama Type Design Office, where he released the modular typeface family Taiposu タイポス, created with Group Taiposu through the type foundry and typesetting technology company Sha-ken for photo-typesetting. The Taiposu system was outlined in Kuwayama's book, *Lettering & Design* レタリングデザイン, published in 1969 by Tokyo publishing company Graphic-sha. The book features a robust historical telling of both Latin and Japanese display typeface design and includes sections on custom lettering and application in print, as environmental signage, and on screen. The book was reprinted a number of times through the 1980s.

Kuwayama went on to design over 100 full typefaces, with an additional 300 typefaces devoted to numerals alone. His typefaces have been used for the logos of major corporations such as Nissan, ANA, Toshiba, Ajinomoto, Mitsui Home, and countless others.

Kuwayama was the author and designer of over sixty books about design, lettering, logos, and marks. His book series *Trademarks & Symbols*, *Trademarks & Symbols of the World Volume 1: The Alphabet in Design*, *Trademarks & Symbols of the World Volume 2: Design Elements*, *Trademarks & Symbols of the World Volume 3: Pictogram & Sign Design*, and *Trademarks & Symbols of the World Volume 4: European Trademarks* are iconic collections of logotypes and trademarks which were published and repackaged by assorted publishers in the United States and Europe.

Above and opposite: ***Lettering & Design* レタリングデザイン** (Tokyo: Graphic-sha グラフィック社, 1969).

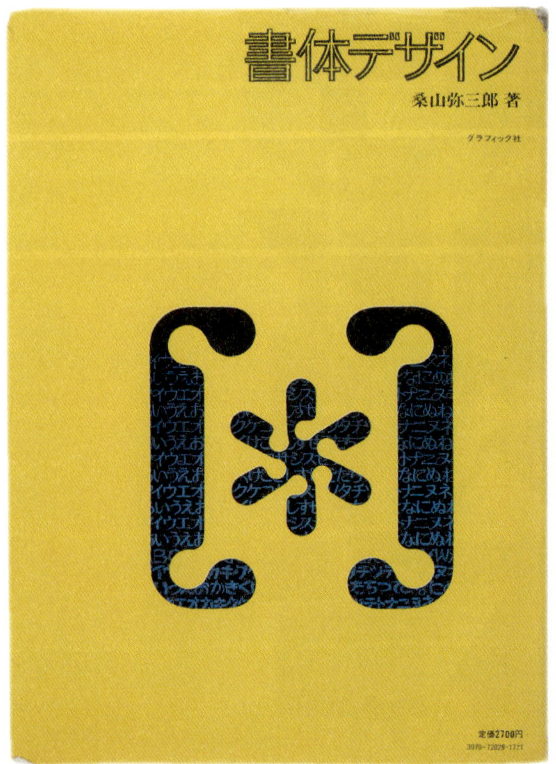

Above and opposite: ***Type Design* 書体デザイン** (Tokyo: Graphic-sha グラフィック社, 1972).

References:

Kamekura, Yūsaku, and Ayao Yamana. *Gurafikku Dezain no Seiki: Bunshō to Danwa to Sakuhin De Kōsei: Meiji Sedai Yamana Ayao Sugiura Hisui Kara shōwa Sedai Made*. Tokyo: Bijutsu Shuppan-sha, 2008.

Kuwayama, Yasaburō. *Retaringu Dezain = Lettering and Design*. Tokyo: Gurafikkusha, 1969.

Kuwayama, Yasaburō. *Shotai Dezain*. Tokyo: Graphic-sha, 2020.

Mukai, Yuichi. "Taiposu." *Idea* 56, no. 329 (July 2008): 151–66.

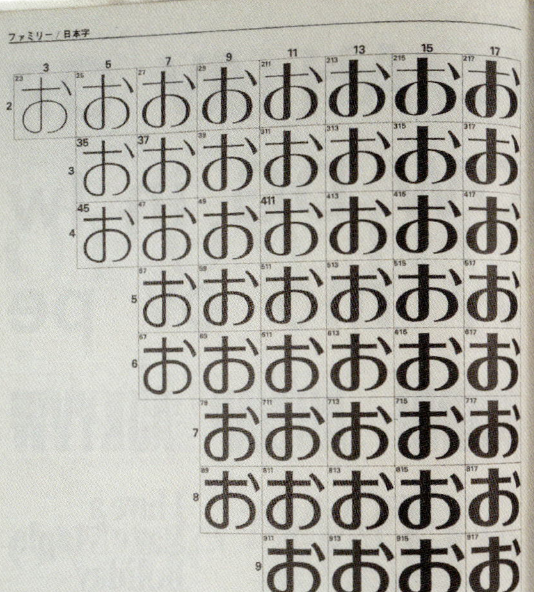

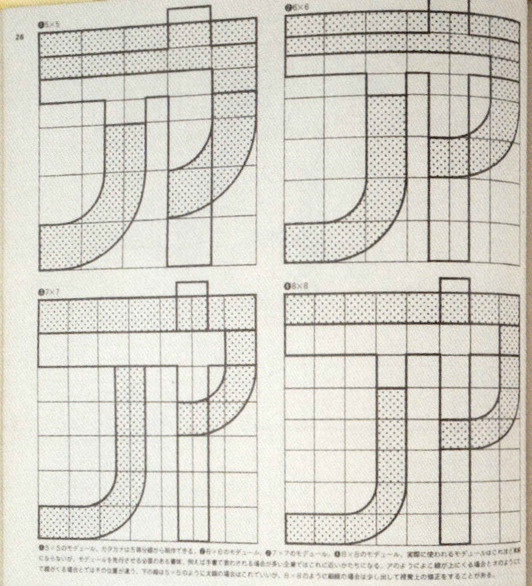

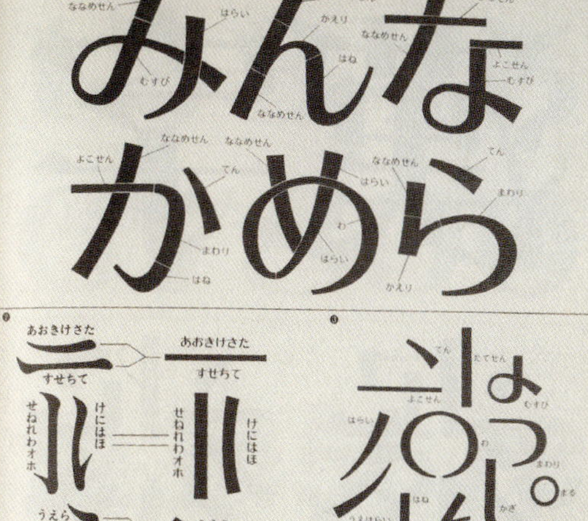

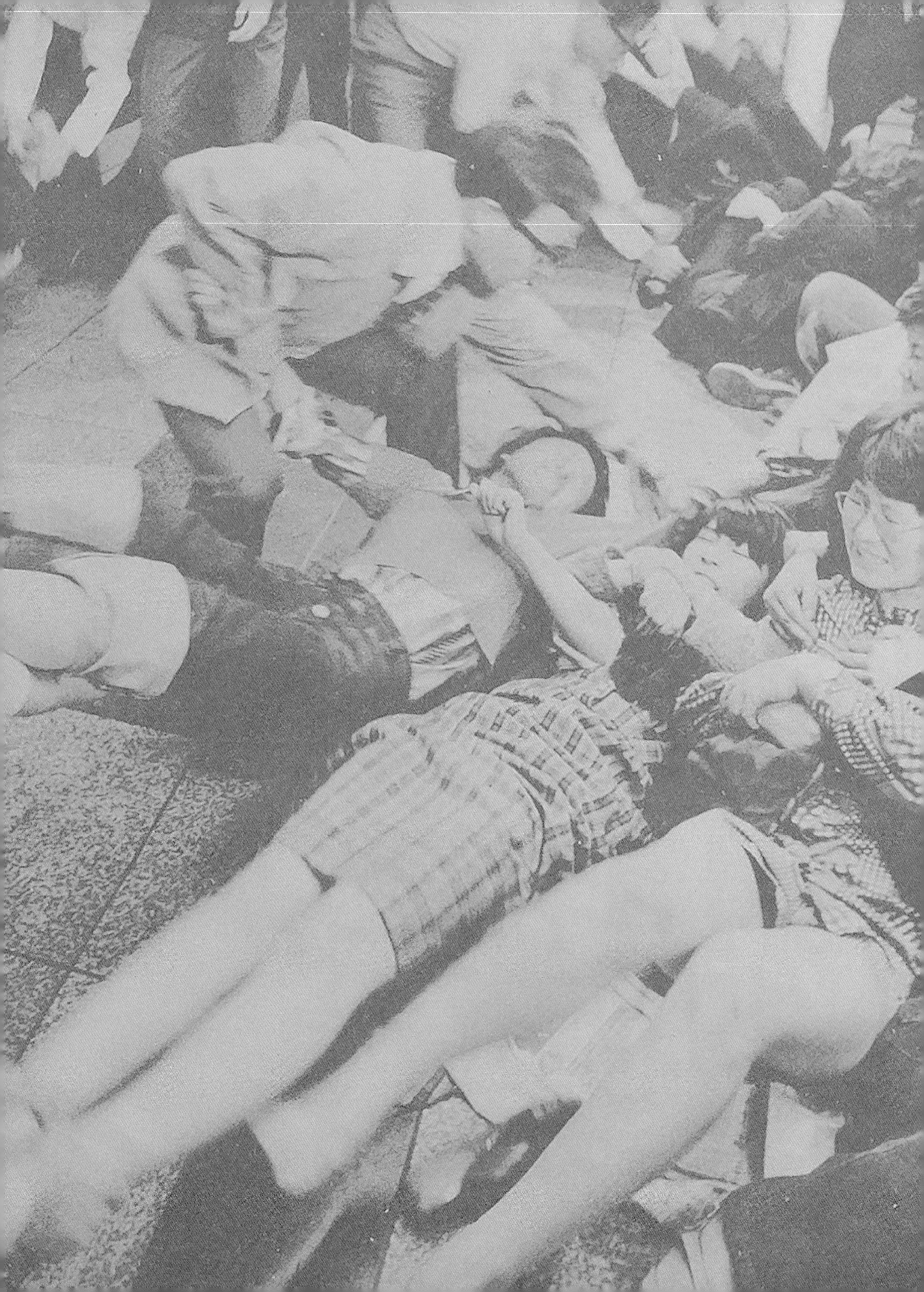

the rise of ribu

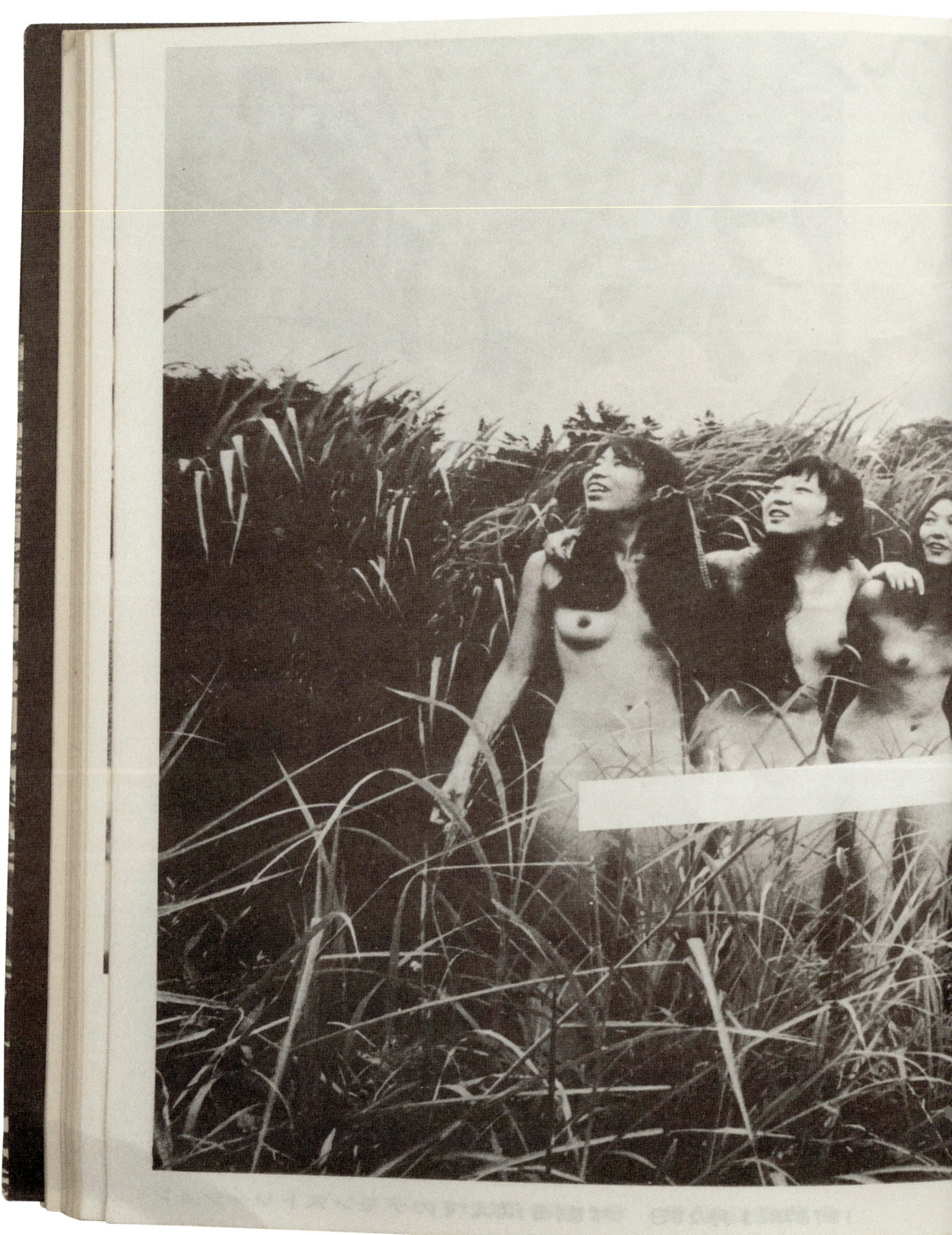

A photographic spread from the 1971 inaugural issue of ***Onna • Eros* 女・エロス** depicting nude Ribu activists in solidarity during the very first Ribu camping convention.

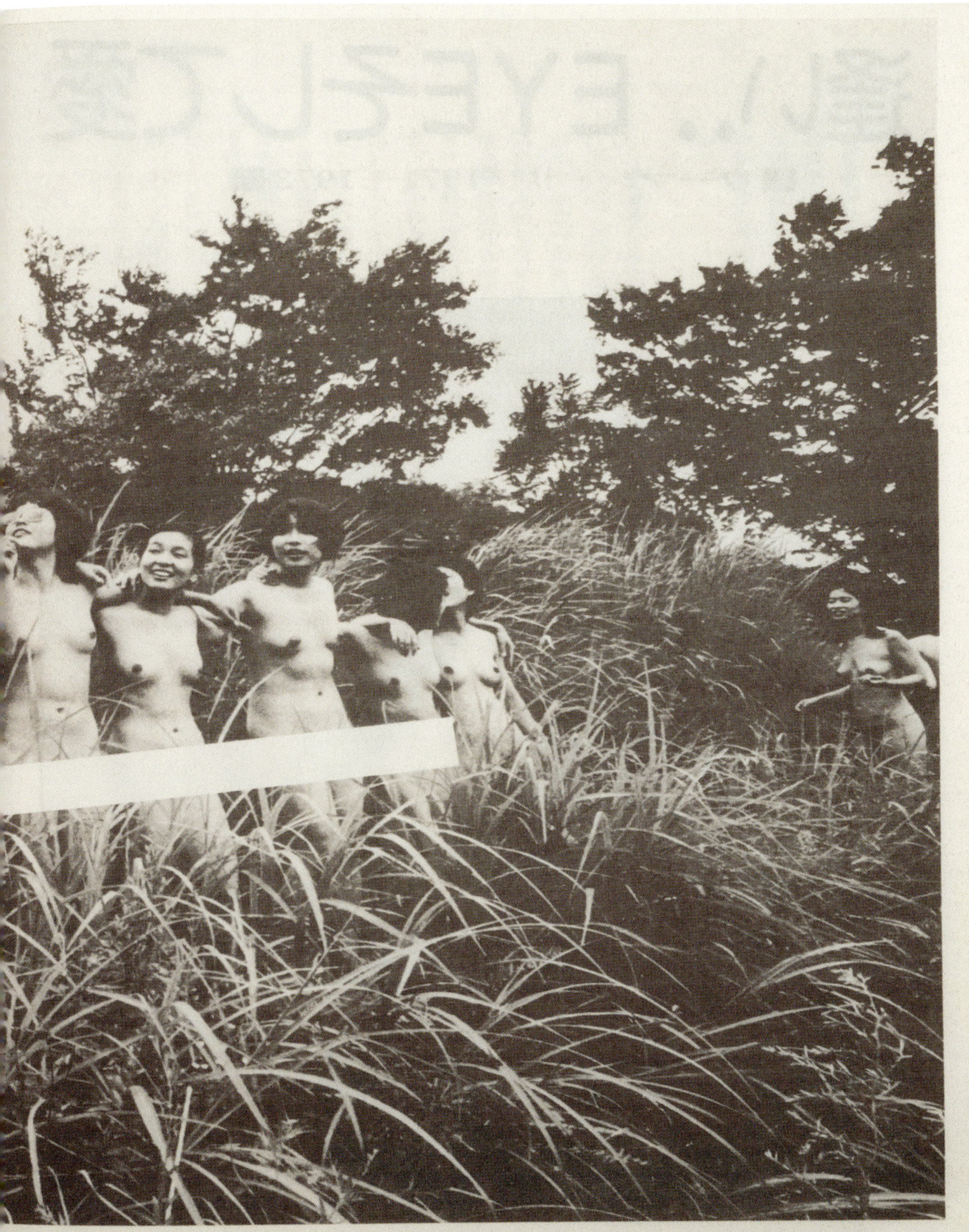

1971年 8月　第一回リブ合宿（長野県）

The Rise of Ribu

The mid-1960s saw Japan engaging on a global scale in its export of industrial and manufactured goods. Japan industrialized later than many Western nations and was therefore able to avoid many of the developmental mishaps that occur during rapid scaling of production. This, combined with consistent wage increases for the Japanese labor force, strategic patent acquisitions, improvement to multiple classes of foreign-origin products, and high levels of both private and public investment and savings paved the way to a vastly enhanced economy in the 1970s and 1980s.

The middle of 1970 saw the emergence of Ūman Ribu ウーマンリブ, representing "Women's Lib(eration)" in katakana. Traditional roles of marriage and family were harshly criticized by Ūman Ribu activists such as Tanaka Mitsu 田中美津 and the Gurūpu Tatakau Onnatachi グループ戦う女達 (Group of Fighting Women), who maintained that the social and cultural structure of Japan oppressed not only women but also men.[1] Various Ūman Ribu-oriented groups issued comprehensive critiques of Japanese society that spanned economics, socioeconomic class structures, and historically based, patriarchal cultural constructs.

In 1972, Ūman Ribu organizers co-founded the Ribu Shinjuku Center リブ新宿センター, a women-run women's shelter and center for feminist activism in Tokyo, where women could receive legal assistance and counseling on reproductive health. In many ways, members of the more than fifty Ribu cells that spread throughout Japan were far more radical than Western feminists, with some holding pro-infanticide positions and espousing extremes of sexual liberation. Yet the movement occasionally tended toward more conservative ideologies: when individuals associated with the Ribu movement translated the American books *Women's Liberation: Blueprint for the Future* (1971) and *Our Bodies, Ourselves* (1974) into Japanese, they intentionally omitted the chapters devoted to lesbian identity. It wasn't until the 1980s that the text on lesbian identity from the 1984 edition of *Our Bodies, Ourselves* was included as a two-page insert in the Japanese publication.[2]

The cover of the first edition of the English-language *Our Bodies, Ourselves* features a photograph of three women of differing generations holding a placard reading "Women Unite," surrounded by awkward hand lettering. The cover of the first Japanese edition is both more abstract and more aesthetically refined: "女", the kanji for *woman*, is the largest character in the title, offset by an orange spot-color illustration of a sun against a striped silver background.

Collectively, the members of the Ribu Shinjuku Center began producing the radical feminist magazine *Onna·Eros* 女・エロス in 1973; it was published by the Tokyo-based left-wing Shakai Hyōronsha 社会評論社 publishing group. In *Onna·Eros*, numerous contributors sought to eliminate the prewar stratification of women by age, class, and occupation and instead align them all under the term *onna* 女 (women). The first issue of the magazine covered wide-ranging topics under the general theme of "Unsettling the Marital System." The issue included historical examinations of global expressions of feminism, a reprint of Hiratsuka Raichō's manifesto from the first issue of the *Seitō* journal in 1911, a feature on progressive feminist groups in the United States, op-ed essays on the preference of many women to remain single and on the liberation of sex, and an essay on lesbian identity.

The cover design for the first issue of *Onna·Eros* was executed by Yamauchi Shizuka 山内静香, who was also responsible for the masthead logo that would be used throughout the entire print run of the magazine. The journal's editorial design was handled by Kyoka Asuka 狂花飛鳥. Professionally typeset, *Onna·Eros* legitimized the Ribu movement in print. The phototype layouts integrated photographs and illustrations from contributors, spot illustrations, and photographic sections depicting members of the movement speaking at Ribu conferences, pursuing direct action through "die-in" public protests, and being physically assaulted by males. Of note is a photograph printed across a double-page spread in the magazine's inaugural issue: it shows ten naked Ribu-associated women, the majority arm in arm, standing in a copse of trees amid tall, wild grasses during the first Ribu camping convention (women only, members of the press included) in 1971—women together, in nature. Accompanying the photograph were illustrations by Usu Nanami 薄奈々美 and inline illustrations by Kusano Mutsuko 草野むつ子 and Kunii Isako 国井功子.

1 Setsu Shigematsu, *Scream from the Shadows: The Women's Liberation Movement in Japan* (Minneapolis: University of Minnesota Press, 2012), 78–79.

2 Boston Women's Health Book Collective and Judy Norsigian, *Our Bodies, Ourselves: A Book by and for Women*, trans. Akiyama Yōko, Kuwahara Kazuyo, and Yamada Mitsuko (Tokyo: Gōdō Shuppan, 1984), 98.

Onna · Eros was only one of scores of Ribu-oriented publications that emerged from all over Japan under the name *onna no mini-comi* 女のミニコミ or "women's mini communication"—"mini communication" being the opposite of "mass communication." These included titles such as the Tokyo letterpress-printed booklet *This Road* この道ひとすじ; the Osaka-based *From Women to Women* 女から女たちへ; translations of essays culled from the first two issues of the periodical *Notes*, edited by the Canadian-American writer Shulamith Firestone; and the Tokyo journal *Neo-Ribu* ネオリブ. The often-gritty analogue aesthetics of handwrought illustration, printmaking, hand lettering, and press type; the small-press approach; and the organic distribution networks of the original onna no mini-comi were—in essence—proto-zines, as much as short books.

The most vocal leader of the Ribu movement, Tanaka Mitsu 田中美津, ceased publishing and participating in public activism in 1975, when she moved to Mexico after visiting a United Nations conference there. She lived there for four years and became a single mother during that time. In her absence, the Ribu Shinjuku Center closed in 1977, though Ribu-oriented publications continued in earnest. *Onna · Eros* ceased publication in 1983, but other publications continued through the early 2010s. Kuno Ayako 久野綾子 (a Ribu member from Nagoya who had been present at the first camping convention) published fifty-nine issues of the A5-sized, seventy-page zine *Woman's Mutiny* おんなの叛逆 between 1971 and 2013. It began with a print run of 2,000 copies, though the last issue saw the number reduced to 500.

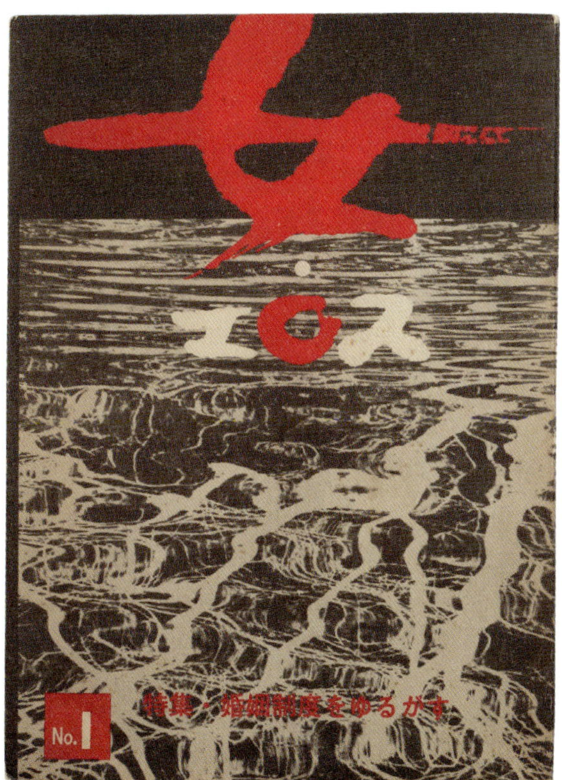

Cover of the first issue of ***Onna • Eros* 女・エロス** designed by Yamauchi Shizuka 山内静香 in 1971.

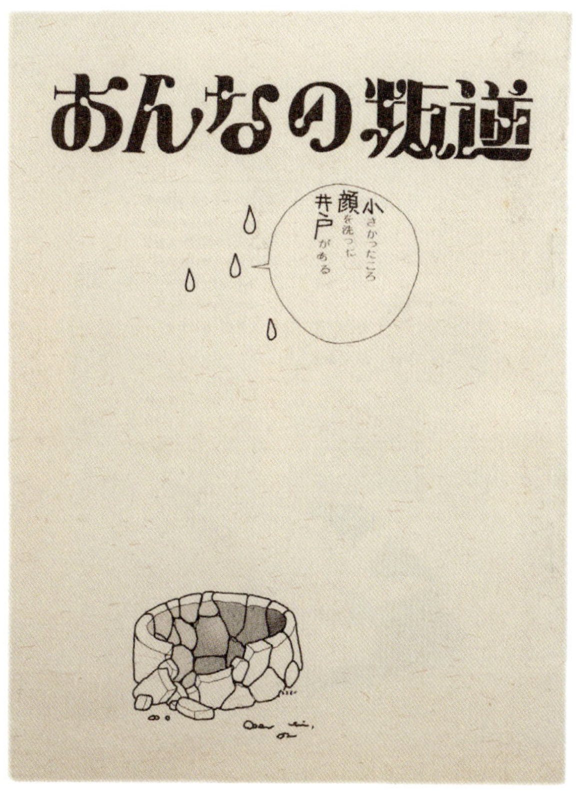

Cover of the fourth issue of the independent journal ***Woman's Mutiny* おんなの叛逆**, published in Nagoya.

References:

Clammer, John, Brian Moeran, and Lisa Skov. "Consuming Bodies: Constructing and Representing the Female Body in Contemporary Japanese Print Media." Essay. In *Women, Media and Consumption in Japan*, 197–219. London: Routledge, 2013.

Tanaka, Keiko. "Japanese Women's Magazines: The Language of Aspiration." Essay. In *The Worlds of Japanese Popular Culture: Gender, Shifting Boundaries and Global Cultures*, edited by D. P. Martinez, 120–22. Cambridge, MA: Cambridge University Press, 1998.

シンポジウム・現代の発見

40年9月13日 10月5日 京都国立国際会館 主催 日本カルチベイションセンター 後援 朝日新聞社

1

意味:このひとつの織物は

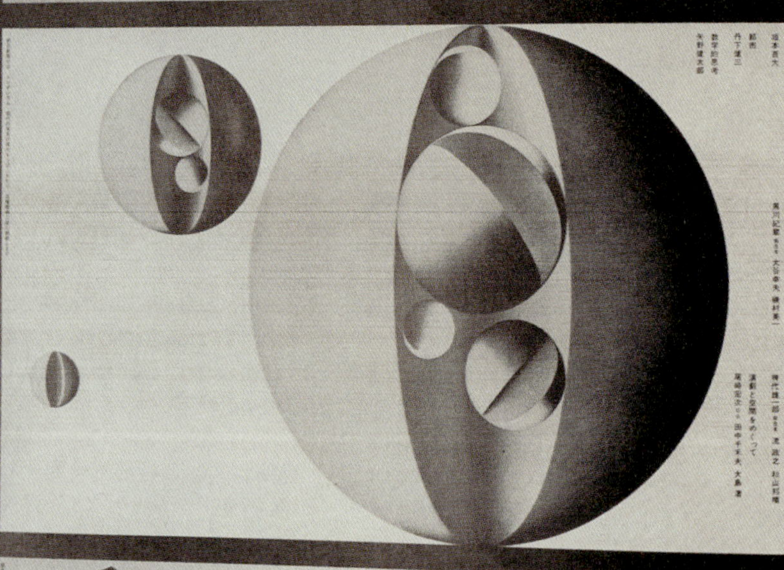

シンポジウム・現代の発見

40年9月13日 10月5日 京都国立国際会館 主催 日本カルチベイションセンター 後援 朝日新聞社

7

陽にかけ昇る技術思想

Japan Advertising Artists Club's 15th JAAC competition-winning series of posters designed by Ishioka Eiko in 1965 for a fictional event series called "Symposium: A Finding of Our Times," published in **"Symposium: A Finding of Our Times,"** published in ***Design* デザイン No. 94** (Tokyo: Bijutsu Shuppansha 美術出版社, 1967).

ISHIOKA EIKO 石岡瑛子

1938–2012

Ishioka Eiko was born in 1938 in Tokyo. Her father was a graphic designer who discouraged her from entering the field, but she went on to study design at Tokyo University of the Arts. After graduating in 1961, she worked as a designer for the cosmetics company Shiseido for five years, having demanded equal pay to her male colleagues. Ishioka won the Japan Advertising Artists Club's fifteenth JAAC competition/exhibition in 1965 for a series of posters for a fictional event series called "Symposium: A Finding of Our Times." This was the first time that a woman was awarded the JAAC Prize—the highest award in Japanese graphic design at that time. Ishioka wrote that the posters were inspired by the site where the symposia might be held (the International Conference Hall in Kyoto) and that the three-dimensional forms displayed in the poster were abstractions of the site that served to highlight the assorted discussions that might be held by a wide range of professionals across the arts and humanities. That same year, Ishioka won an Art Directors Club Bronze prize for her work art-directing Shiseido's Honey Cake magazine advertisements—ads in which the cosmetics company's premium soap was treated like actual cake, with the bars of soap cut with knives and sections carved out with utensils.

Ishioka was appointed art director at CBS Sony Records in 1968, working on numerous record packaging, advertising, and public relations projects, though she maintained a part-time role at Shiseido through the following year. Ishioka established her graphic design and art direction practice, the Eiko Ishioka Design Office, in 1970, rapidly attracting a number of clients. Ishioka designed the initial poster for Expo '70, and her poster *POWER NOW* was exhibited at and remains in the collection of MoMA.

She began working as an art director for the department store chain Parco, envisioning and executing consecutive advertising campaigns as the chain expanded from its flagship location in Ikebukuro to Shibuya and beyond starting in 1973. Her relationship with Parco lasted until 1983, and during her tenure she worked with a diverse array of influential women, mixing races and cultural heritages in her representations of contemporary women.

Parco's business model was divergent from that of earlier department stores, as president Masuda Tsūji 増田通二 set out to cultivate a department store that "curated" the assorted retail shops within Parco in lieu of offering manufactured goods. In this way, Parco's profits were based on retail rental costs instead of the sale of goods. Ishioka selected women from assorted races and cultures to cast her vision of the woman of the future. She was critical of the social and cultural roles of Japanese women in the 1970s and 1980s, believing them to be passive and subservient in thought and action. Ishioka cultivated advertising campaigns populated with women from all over the world that highlighted their strengths and personalities, hoping to inspire women in Japan to have more agency in their lives. Her work for Parco included these images of women in scenes and settings that were rich with connotation and lyrical in their use of color and form. In this way, Ishioka carved new methodologies for creating visual meaning in the Japanese advertising and design landscape, neither working in modernist "problem-solving" modes nor exploring the often self-referential and historical reinterpretation methods used by the popular younger designers of the 1960s. Ishioka created work that was redolent with emotion, as she used the notion of "atmosphere" to conjure imaginative scenes in her advertising and broadcast work.

Ishioka co-directed a 1979 television commercial for Parco filmed by Kurigami Kazumi 操上和美 with a Sakamoto Ryuichi 坂本龍一 soundtrack. In the commercial, she instructed American actress Faye Dunaway to spin and then eat a hard-boiled egg over the course of ninety seconds while wearing a mourning dress. Connotatively, the power of this commercial lies in presenting footage of a famous foreign actress-as-widow locking eyes with the audience and doing whatever she pleased. Dunaway is consuming—and doing so with obvious pleasure—despite the tragedy that might be surrounding her. The death of the symbolic husband means nothing—there is only the woman and the egg: the object of desire.

Ishioka's power as a conceptual creative director came to full form across her broadcast and print campaigns for Parco. Another 1979 Parco advertising campaign starred popular singer Sawada Kenji 沢田研二, adorned only in makeup, lying prone on the water's edge of an ocean beach at night, waves lapping at his naked body as he stared at the camera. One more campaign from 1979 again featured Faye Dunaway, clad in a pleated cloak and ornate pleated headdress, flanked by two half-naked prepubescent girls (incidentally Ishioka's nieces) with the ad slogan "Can West Wear East?" 西洋は東洋を着こなせるか. The gazes of all three female subjects were directed dead-on at the audience.

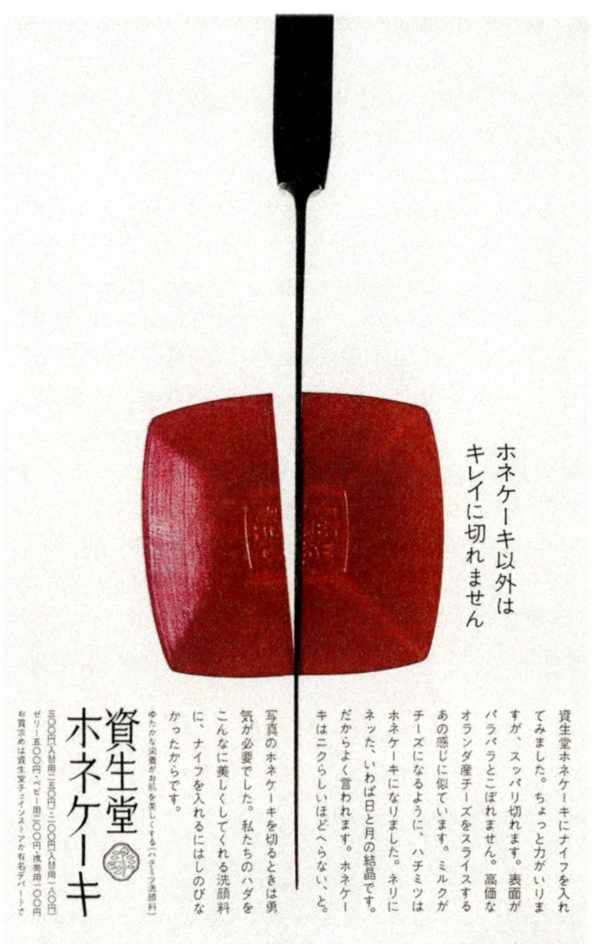

Ishioka's breakout 1964 magazine advertisement for Shiseido's Honeycake ホネケーキ soap.

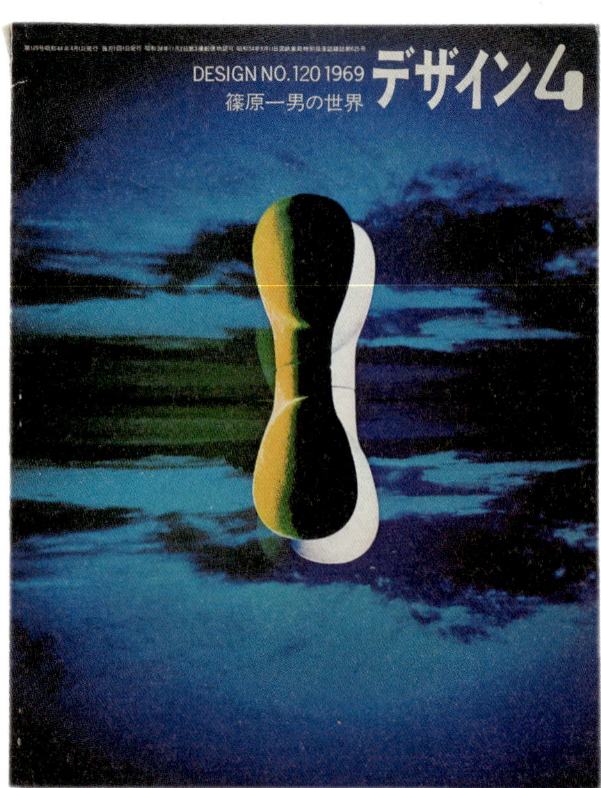

Cover design with photographer Ogawa Takayuki 小川 隆之 for ***Design* デザイン No. 120** (Tokyo: Bijutsu Shuppansha 美術出版社, 1969).

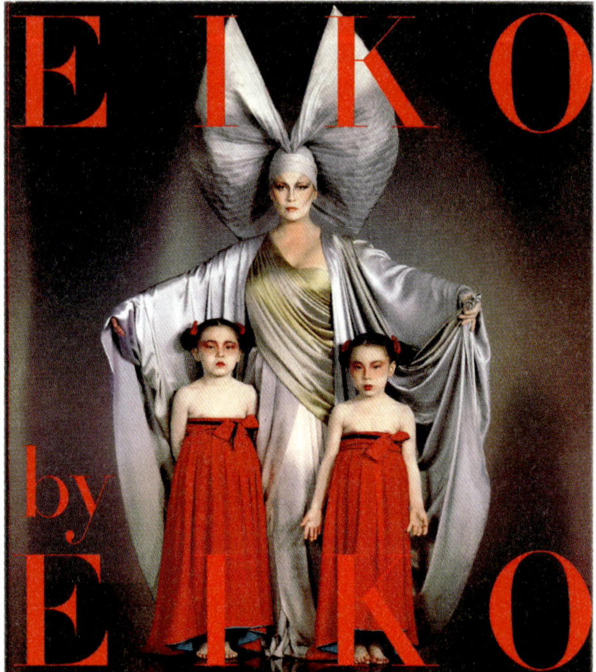

***Eiko by Eiko*, Ishioka Eiko** (New York: Callaway Editions, 1983). Ishioka's monograph.

Ishioka collaborated regularly with Leni Riefenstahl, the controversial creator of wartime Nazi propaganda films, whom Ishioka would use to film and photograph women all over the globe for successive Parco campaigns. Ishioka would go on to design two books of Riefenstahl's photography of the Nuba, various indigenous peoples in Sudan.

Throughout the 1970s, Ishioka worked on a wide variety of freelance projects, including the branding and packaging design for GOM, product designer Kurokawa Masayuki's 黒川雅之 range of rubber and metal ashtrays, lighters, pens, and coasters for NY MoMA, and branding and packaging for the Kissa Sport footwear brand. She was the art director for the fiction anthology magazine *Shosetsu Yasei Jidai* 野性時代, and she created a wide variety of Japanese brands' corporate identities, including the holding company Tokyu, logos for sports teams like the Houston Rockets, and award-winning packaging for musicians like Miles Davis. Her design for Davis's album *Tutu* would garner her a Grammy Award for Best Music Packaging Design.

Ishioka's work exploited the latest technologies, and her facility with analog layout and the airbrush enabled her to create a wide variety of sophisticated visual expressions, many of which celebrated the human figure, in particular the female form.

Following the abrupt shuttering of her design studio and a fifteen-month sabbatical in the United States to replenish her creative energies, Ishioka published her first monograph, *Eiko by Eiko, Eiko Ishioka: Japan's Ultimate Designer*, in 1983 in simultaneous English and Japanese versions. The large-format, full-color book, featuring the photograph of Faye Dunaway and the two girls from her 1979 Parco campaign prominently on the cover, helped introduce Ishioka to countless new clients and audiences globally and expanded her practice.

Ishioka's stunning work on the Japanese posters for the 1979 Francis Ford Coppola film *Apocalypse Now* had caught Coppola's eye and led him to hire Ishioka as a costume and stage designer for his 1992 film *Dracula*. She had previously worked as the designer for the film *Mishima: A Life in Four Chapters* with director Paul Schrader in 1985, for which she received an award at Cannes. Ishioka designed the costumes for a number of later productions for the Dutch Opera, Cirque du Soleil, and others. Ishioka directed the music video "Cocoon" and art directed the LP *Vespertine* for Icelandic singer Bjork in 2002 and worked as a costume designer on four of Indian director Tarsem Singh's films, including *The Cell*. She also designed the costumes for the opening ceremony of the 2008 Beijing Olympic Games.

The first female Japanese graphic designer to be recognized on the global stage, Ishioka passed away in 2012 at age seventy-three.

References:

Ishioka, Eiko. *Eiko by Eiko: Japan's Ultimate Designer*. New York, NY: Callaway, 1983.

Ishioka, Eiko. *Ishioka Eiko*. Tokyo: Ginza Graphic Gallery, 2020.

Ishioka, Eiko, and Francis Ford Coppola. *Eiko: On Stage*. New York, NY: Callaway, 2000.

Kamekura, Yūsaku, and Ayao Yamana. *Gurafikku Dezain no Seiki: Bunshō to Danwa to Sakuhin De Kōsei: Meiji Sedai Yamana Ayao Sugiura Hisui Kara shōwa Sedai Made*. Tokyo: Bijutsu Shuppansha, 2008.

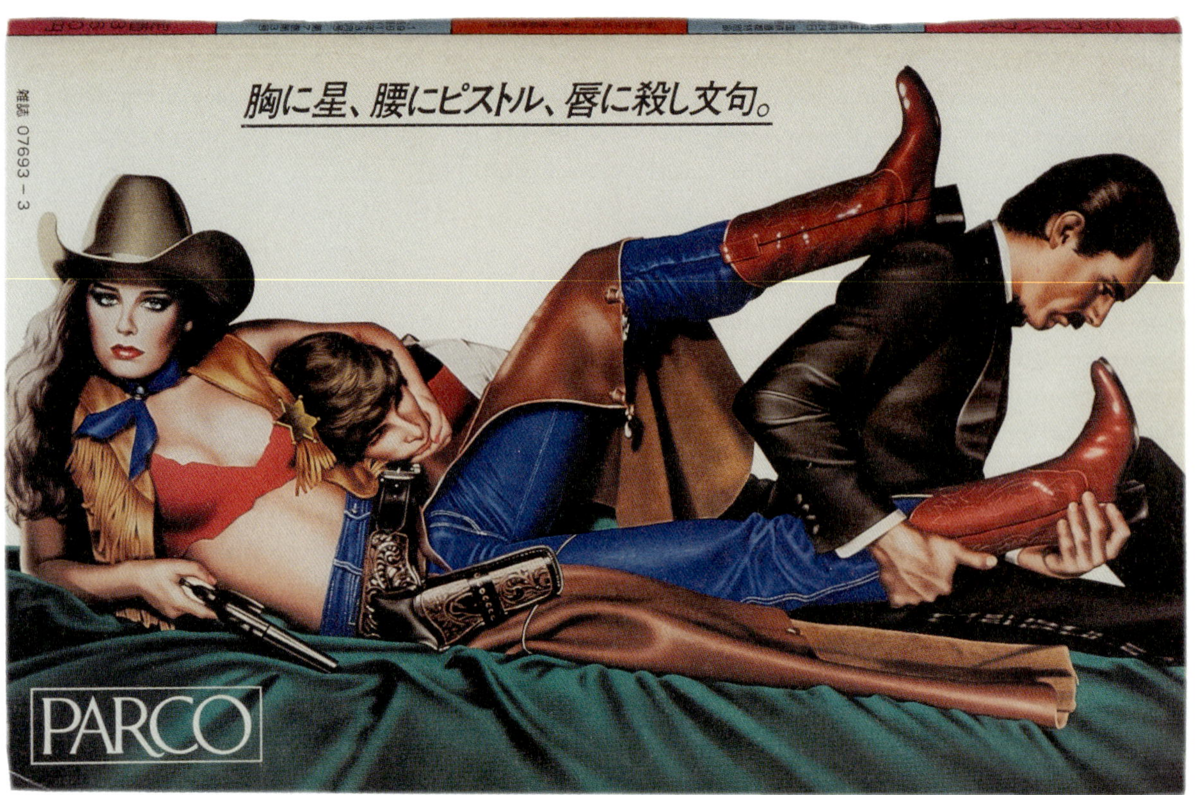

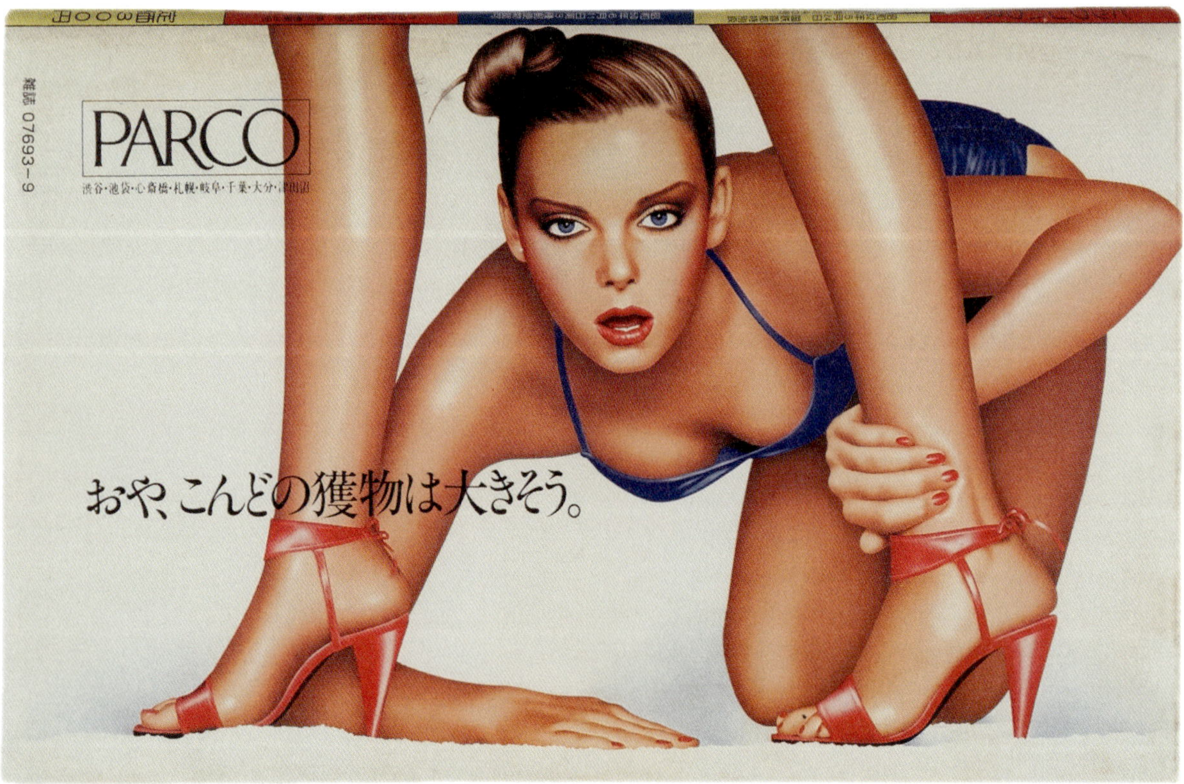

Parco advertisements illustrated by Yamaguchi Harumi 山口はるみ from the back covers of assorted issues of the magazine *Bikkuri House* ビックリハウス (Tokyo: Parco Publishing Parco 出版, 1978–1979).

YAMAGUCHI HARUMI 山口はるみ

1941–

Yamaguchi Harumi was born in Matsue in Shimane Prefecture. She attended Tokyo National University of Fine Arts and Music studying painting. After graduating, Yamaguchi joined the Seibu department stores' promotion department, where she worked as an illustrator in their visual communication center for three years.

Yamaguchi began her career as an independent illustrator participating in the work of the Parco department stores' newly opened advertising and promotions department. Yamaguchi began using the airbrush as her main illustration tool in 1972 and quickly became Japan's preeminent airbrush illustrator throughout the 1970s and 1980s. Her work for Parco was incredibly popular—her illustrations echoed historic interpretations of department stores as centers for culture as much as retailing.

At Parco, Yamaguchi worked alongside two other women—art director Ishioka Eiko and copywriter Koike Kazuko—for three years to create advertising and design. Parco president Masuda Tsūji 増田通二 patronizingly referred to the trio as his "three daughters" who were able to imbue the department store with an aura of ineffable cool. Masuda's 2005 biography, *The Opening Bell Has Rung: Welcome to the Theater Masuda* 『開幕ベルは鳴った—シアター·マスダへようこそ』, contains this anecdote:

The influence of the three daughters, each "possessors of strong individualism and cool decisiveness" were essential to successfully devising the framework for Parco's image strategy. It was an intentional choice to use women to deliver advertising that would be appealing to women.

According to Yamaguchi's representative art gallery in Tokyo, Nanzuka Underground:

Parco had soon focused on "women" as a major driving source behind Japanese society of the 1970s and onward, further succeeding in diverting this power to the business sector. Yamaguchi's female figures are far from notions of eroticism as portrayed allegedly through male eyes in the form of pin-ups. On the contrary, the women themselves appear to joyously celebrate their own sexuality and existence. Furthermore, the images of women partaking in boxing, baseball, and skateboarding which Yamaguchi had illustrated in the 70s, could be interpreted as an ironic gesture towards a male-dominant society at a time prior to the establishment of the Equal Employment Opportunity Act in 1985; an era when women were unable to equally advance into society.[1]

In 2001, Japanese sociologist and feminist Ueno Chizuko commented on Yamaguchi's oeuvre in a monograph dedicated to the illustrator's work, writing that "while appearing to adhere to the scenario of male-tailored eroticism, Yamaguchi deconstructs male desire through her exaggerative depictions. As a consequence, the female body is Idealized to a realm unreachable by male hands."[2]

Yamaguchi's work is worth consideration for having put forth a feminist perspective in advertising prior to the establishment of Japan's Equal Employment Opportunity Act in 1985, and for the brazen approach to public objectification of the female body that she utilizes in her work.

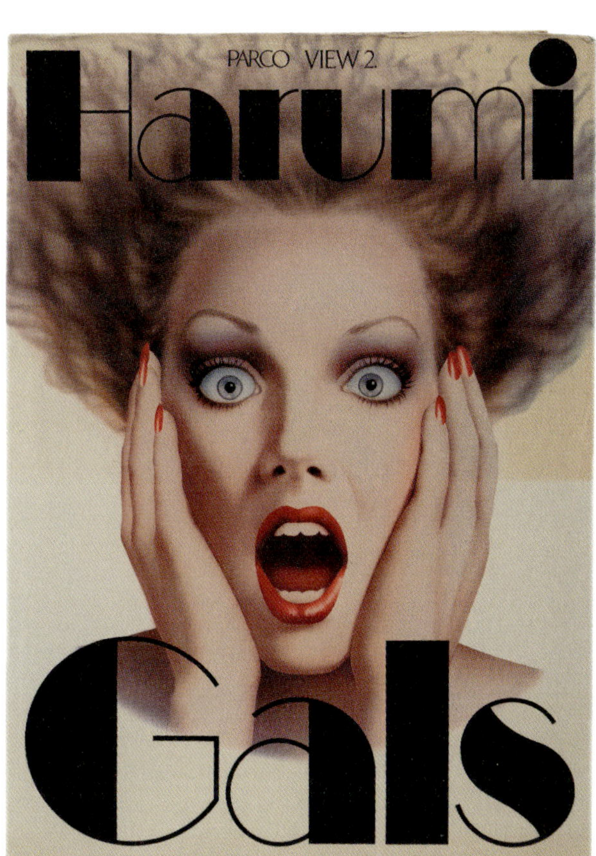

Cover of ***Harumi Gals*** (Tokyo: Parco Publishing Parco 出版, 1978). Designed by Yamaguchi with Yokoo Tadanori.

1 "Harumi Yamaguchi " Harumi Gals," Nanazuka, Nanzuka, February 2015, https://nug.jp/en/exhibitions/2015harumiYamaguchi/press-release.

2 Dal Chodha. "The Japanese Artist Who Remade Girl Power for Modern Women." AnOther. AnOther Magazine, April 19, 2017. https://www.anothermag.com/art-photography/9751/the-japanese-artist-who-remade-girl-power-for-modern-women.

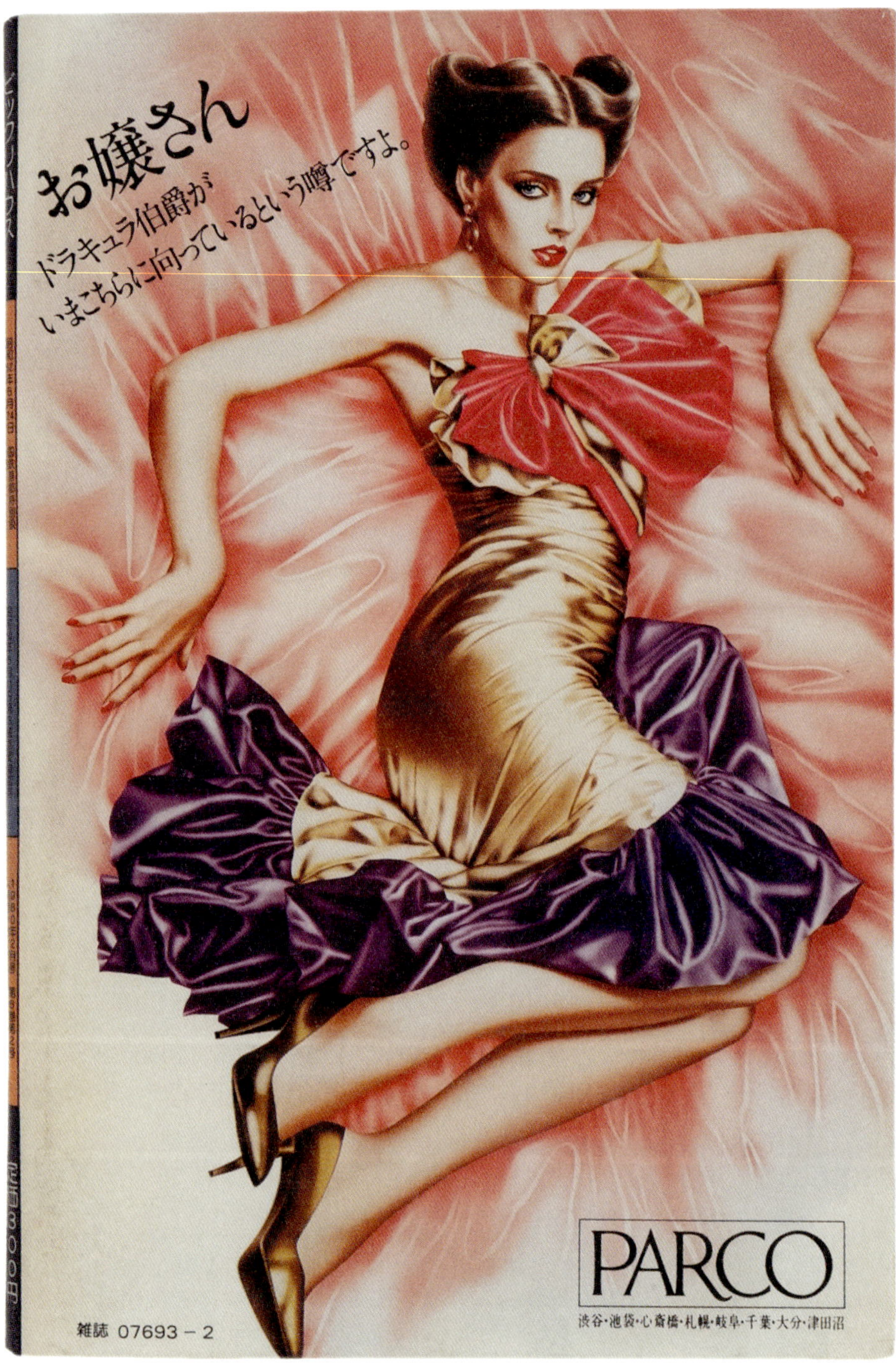

Parco advertisement from the back cover of ***Bikkuri House* ビックリハウス** (Tokyo: Parco Publishing Parco 出版, 1979).

Yamaguchi's monograph *Harumi Gals* was published by Parco in 1978. Yamaguchi is a Tokyo ADC Award winner, was a long-time member of Tokyo Illustrators Society, and has exhibited internationally, and her work is in the collection of MoMA in New York City.

References:
Yamaguchi, Harumi. *Harumi Gals*. Tokyo: Parco Shuppan, 1978.

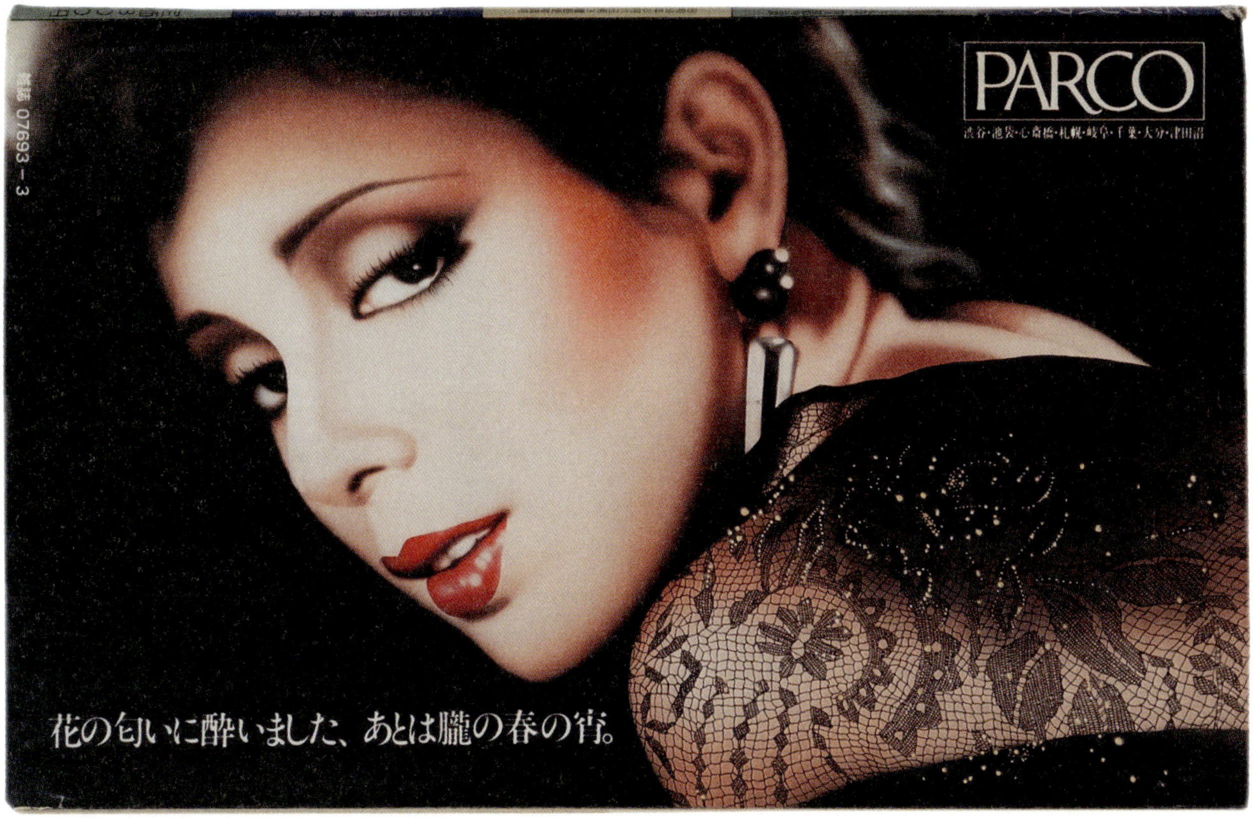

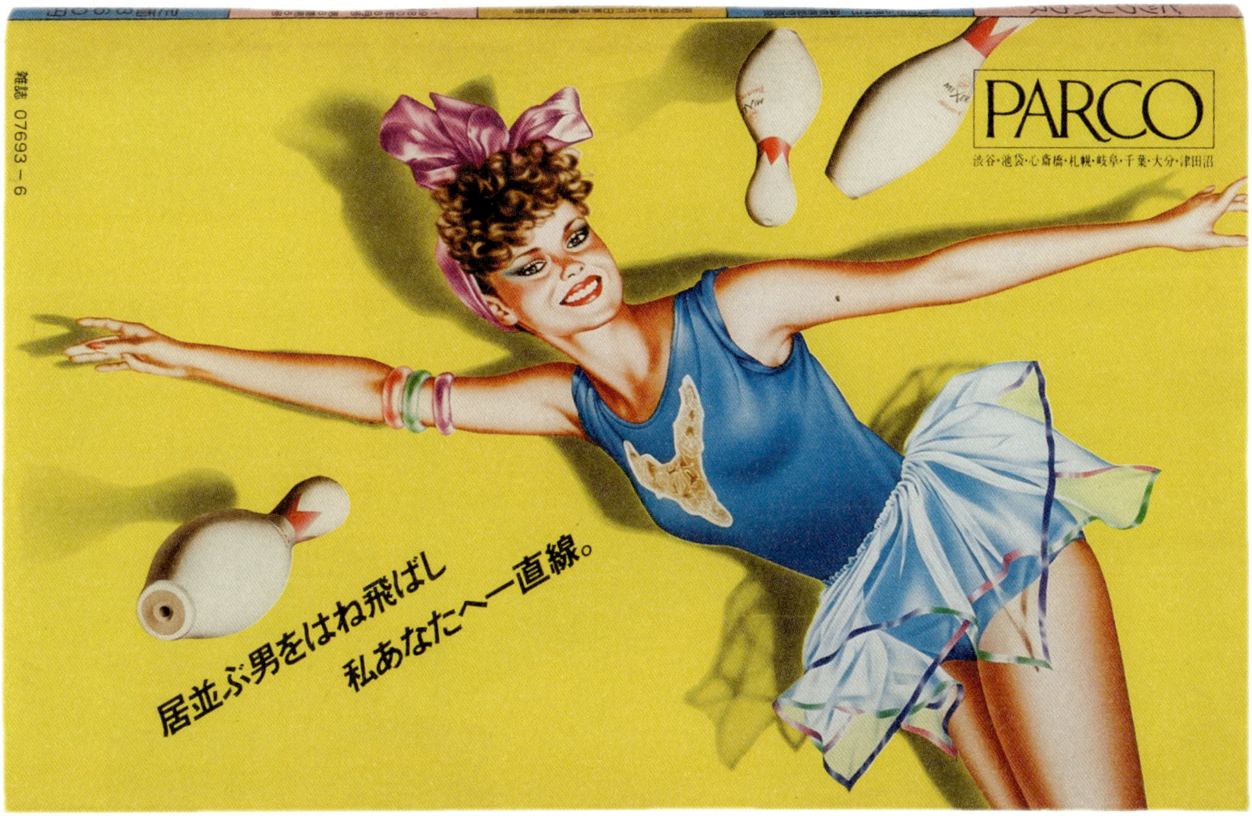

Parco advertisements illustrated by Yamaguchi Harumi 山口はるみ from the back covers of assorted issues of the magazine ***Bikkuri House* ビックリハウス** between 1978 and 1979 published by Parco Publishing Parco 出版 in Tokyo.

MATSUNAGA SHIN 松永真

1940–

Matsunaga Shin was born in Tokyo in 1940 and attended the Design Department of the Tokyo National University of Fine Arts and Music, graduating in 1964. He worked in the cosmetics corporation Shiseido's advertising and design division after graduation, where, alongside Nakamura Makoto and Ishioka Eiko, Matsunaga helped steer the brand's design in a more casual, lifestyle-oriented direction.

Matsunaga left in 1971 to start his own design business. His career has spanned corporate identity, packaging, and poster design. Some of his more notable works include the corporate identity design for the fashion brand Issey Miyake, Blendy instant coffee products, Calbee snacks, the Benesse Group, Bandai toys, Can Chu-Hi malt liquor, and Scottie tissue. Matsunaga has been awarded the Japan Advertising Artists Club Special Prize and the Mainichi Design Award, and he was recognized at the twelfth International Biennale in Warsaw, Poland. He has also won the Japan Ministry of Education's Art Encouragement Prize and the JAAC Prize Yamana Award.

He has held solo exhibitions in Poland, the former Yugoslavia, New York, Puerto Rico, Belgium, and Slovenia. His designs are in the permanent collections of numerous museums around the world, including MoMA in New York.

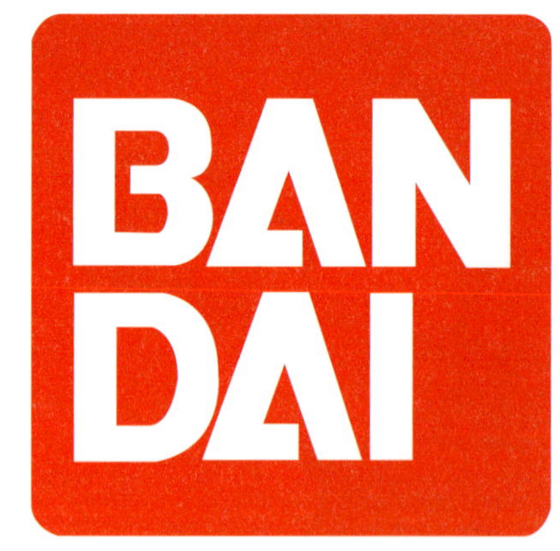

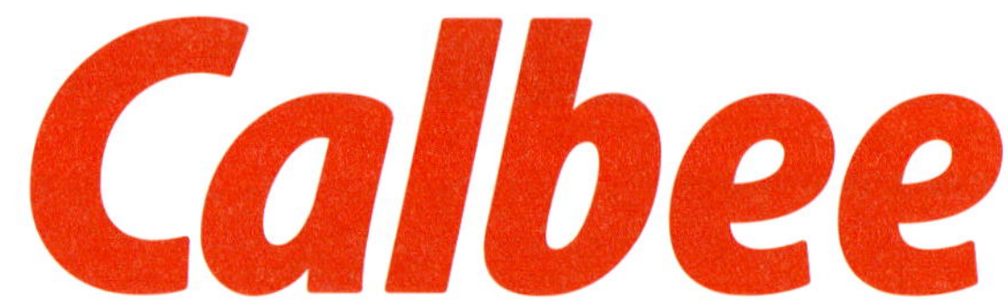

References:

Matsunaga, Shin, and Usuda Shōji. *Matsunaga Shin*. Tokyo: DNP Bunka Shinkō Zaidan, 2013.

Shiseido, *Bi to Chi no Mīmu Shiseidō, Shiseido Meme Katarogu = Shiseido 1872–1998*. Tokyo: Shiseidō, 1998.

Sachi, Kaneda. "The Imaging Strategy of Shiseido in the 1930s: Analyzing Visual Magazines That Represented Corporate Identity." *Design History* 1, no. 14 (2016).

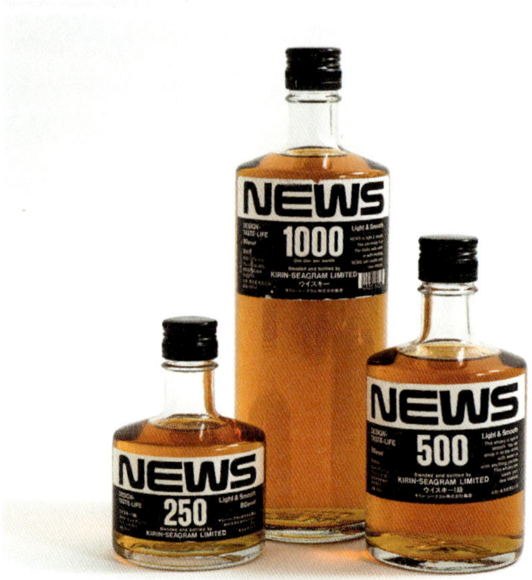

From top: Logos for toy manufacturer **Bandai** and snack food company **Calbee**, and 1985 packaging design for Kirin Seagram's **NEWS** brand whiskey.

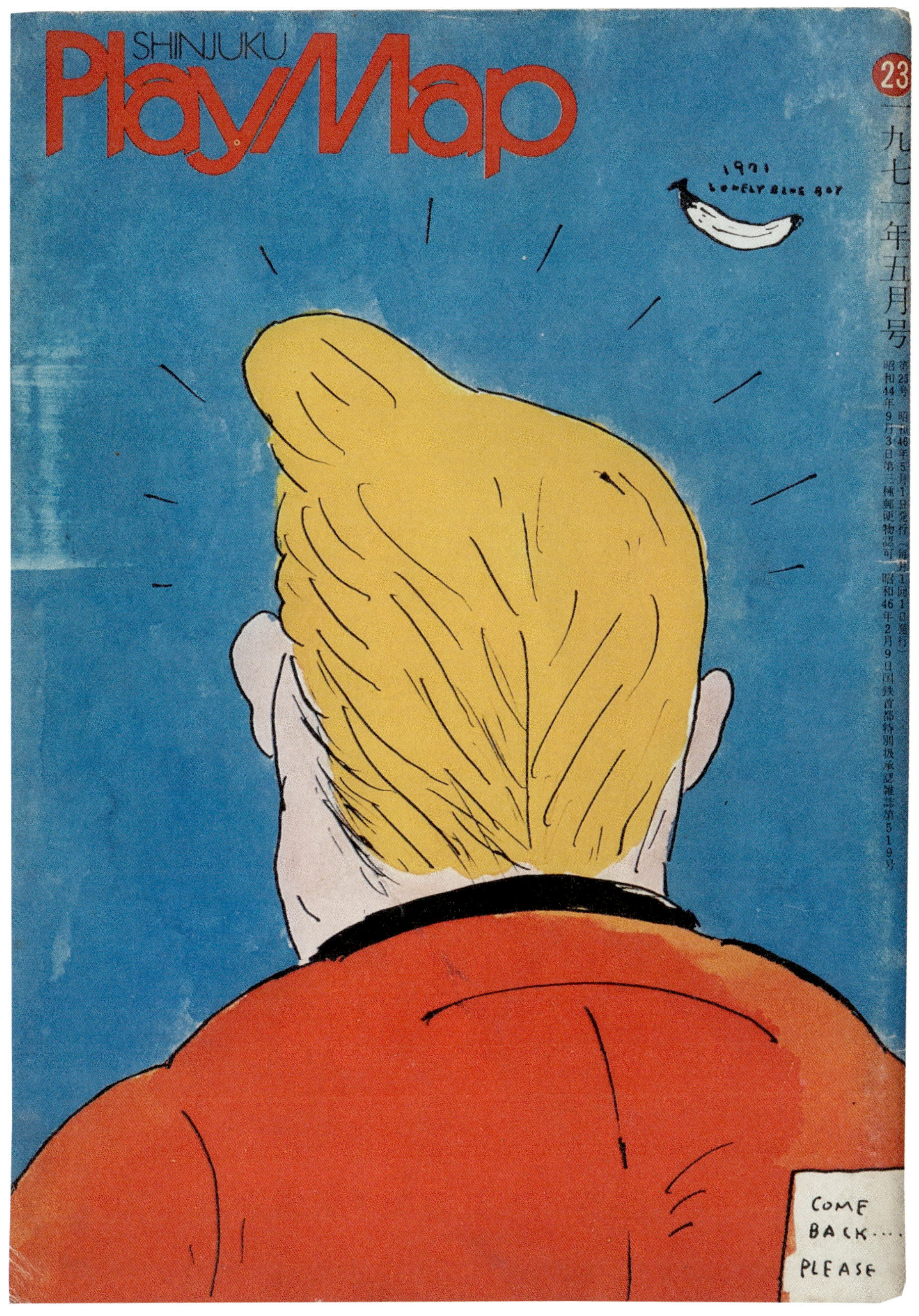

Cover illustration/design and interior illustration for ***Shinjuku Play Map*** 新宿プレイマップ No. 23 (Tokyo: Shinjuku PR Committee 新都心新宿PR委員会, 1971).

Yumura Teruhiko 湯村輝彦 illustrated a story written by his business partner Itoi Shigesato 糸井重里 about a flying penguin hunting for swim trunks, published as a sweet and very silly children's book called ***Sayonara, Penguin* さよならペンギン** (Tokyo: Subaru Shobō すばる書房, 1976). The book became an instant bestseller due to the humorous and melancholy nature of the book.

YUMURA TERUHIKO 湯村輝彦

1942–

Yumura Teruhiko was born in Tokyo to a relatively wealthy family, his father was the manager of the Meijiza 明治座, a theater that specialized in kabuki performances. He studied at Tama Art University under Yamana Ayao and was regarded as a taciturn and volatile student who resented completing design work according to his faculty's guidelines. These offenses delayed his graduation, though the graduation works themselves would be featured in *Idea* that year as an outstanding example of design and illustration work by a recent graduate.

Yumura won a handful of awards in the late 1960s and cycled through a number of design studios, first as an employee and eventually as co-founder. He established his design studio Original Flamingo Studio in 1975 alongside copywriter Itoi Shigesato 糸井重里, fellow hybrid illustrator/designer Nagai Hiroshi 永井博, and others. In 1976, Yumura and Itoi published their first children's book, *Sayonara Penguin* さよならペンギン, about a penguin looking to buy some swimwear. The following year, Yumura and Itoi were invited to contribute to the cult manga compendium *Garo* カロ, and they created a disturbing serialized manga called *Penguin Gohan* ペンギンごはん, again featuring a penguin, though one prone to libidinous violence and antisocial behavior.

Yumura's visual work is representative of *heta-uma* 下手上手 aesthetics—"heta" meaning "of poor skill" or "awkward," whereas "uma" means "good"—the term heta-uma is an abbreviation of the saying "一見ヘタのようだが実はウマい" (ikken heta no yōdaga jitsuwa umai), meaning "Looks bad at first but is actually good". Despite being able to render illustrations elegantly, Yumura chose to create work that appears shaky, inelegant, and on the border of being a rough sketch drawn in everyday indelible marker. His use of garish, clashing colors, shabbily cut screentone, and messy application of color looks like the work of an amateur, but it is wholly intentional. The popularity of Yumura's work helped push heta-uma visuals into popular public consciousness.

Yumura has been heavily involved in advertising art direction, illustration, editorial design, and the design of music packaging. He has published a number of books on topics as wide-ranging as suffering from hemorrhoids and male pattern baldness.

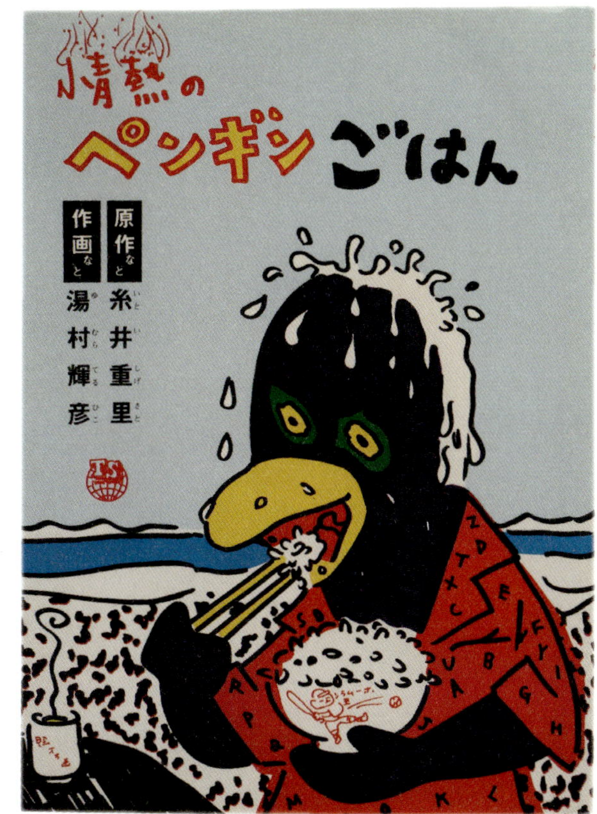

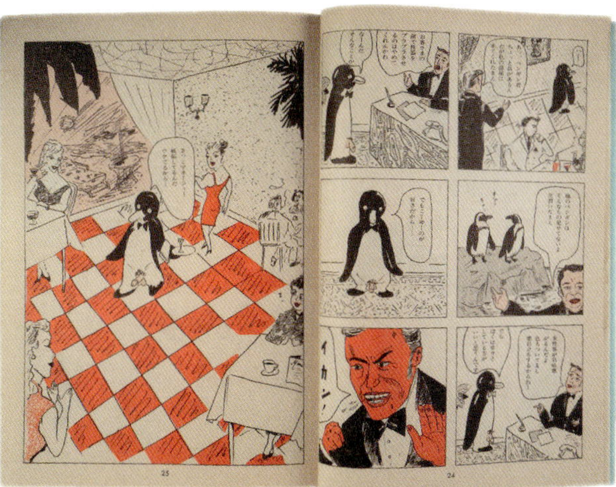

Jōnetsu no pengin gohan (*Passionate Penguin Rice*) 情熱のペンギンごはん, Itoi Shigesato 糸井重里, Yumura Teruhiko 湯村輝彦 (Tokyo: Joho Center Shuppan-kyoku 情報センター出版局, 1980).
Shortly after the publication of *Sayonara, Penguin* さよならペンギン, disillusioned with relative fame and success, the duo began working on the serialized manga *Penguin Gohan* (*Penguin Rice*) ペンギンごはん originally published in 1976 in the alternative manga *Garo*, depicting the life of a misanthropic, ultra-violent, and sexually depraved penguin. The collected Penguin Gohan comics were published in 1980 as *Passionate Penguin Rice*.

References:
Kawamura, Yōsuke, and Teruhiko Yumura. *Kawamura Yōsuke vs. Yumura Teruhiko: Kokkyō o Keshisaru Shisen = Works of Yosuke Kawamura*. Tokyo: Shōgakkan, 1984.

Itoi, Shigesato, and Teruhiko Yumura. *Kanpon Jōnetsu no Pengin Gohan*. Tokyo: Chikuma Shobō, 1993.

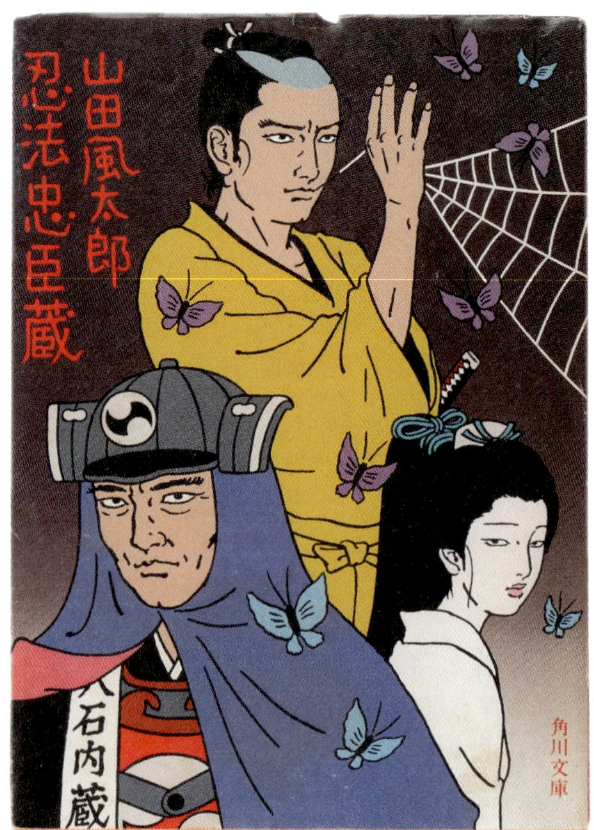

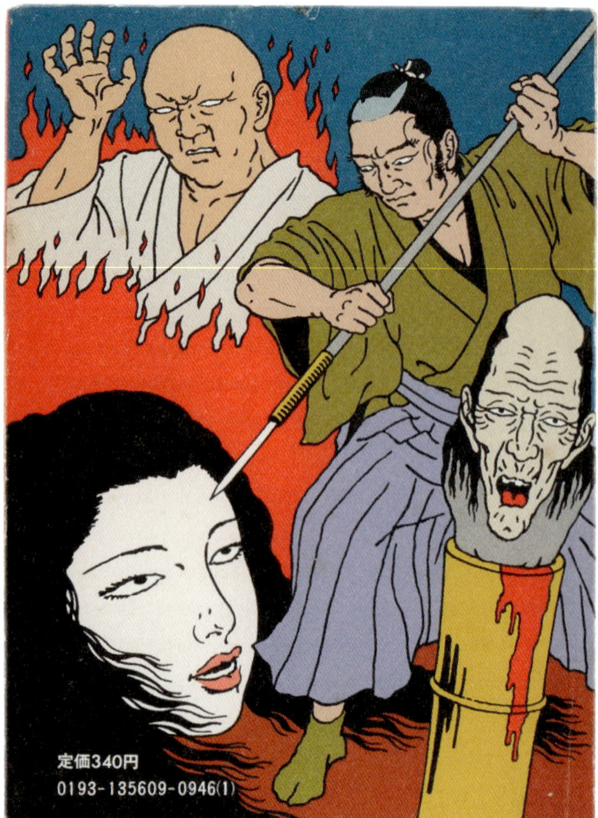

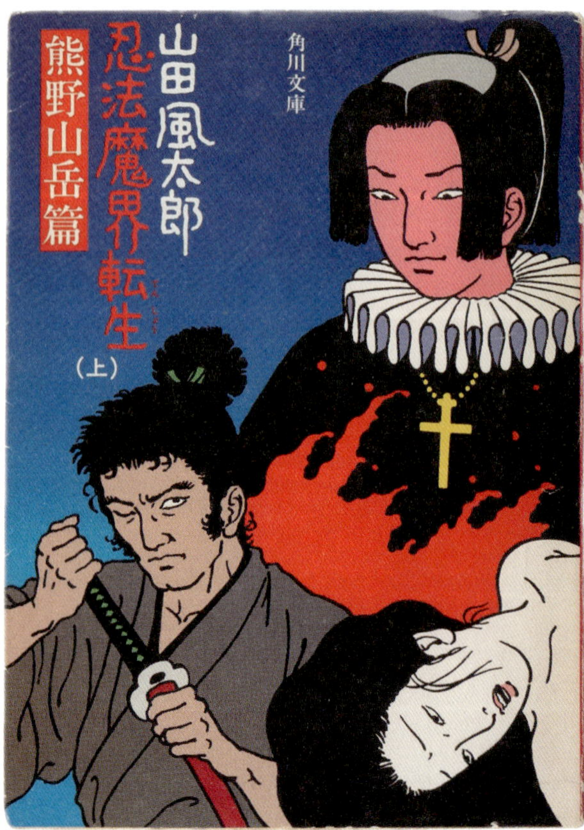

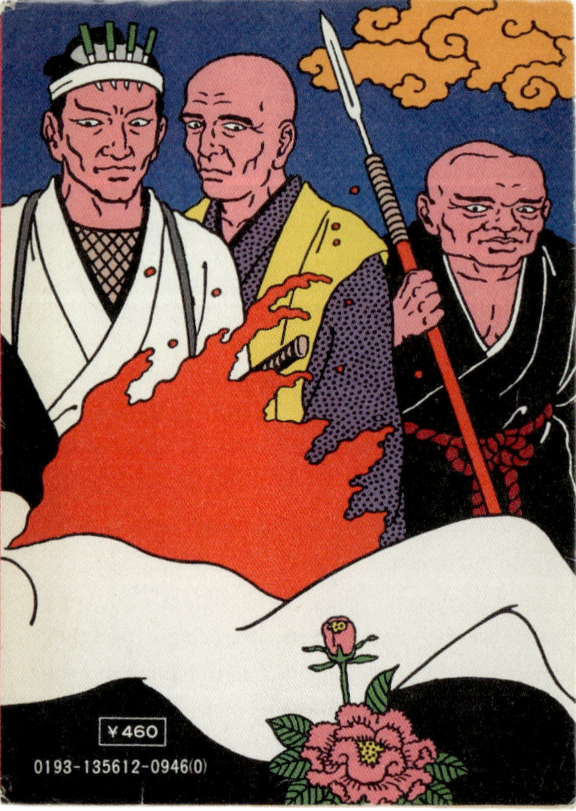

A variety of cover designs for volumes of the ninja-oriented literature of Yamada Fūtaro 山田風太郎 published by Kadokawa Shoten 角川書店 from the mid-1970s through the mid-1980s.

SAEKI TOSHIO 佐伯俊男

1945–2019

Saeki Toshio was born in Miyazaki Prefecture and was raised largely in Osaka. Saeki moved to Tokyo in 1969 and rose to prominence in the 1970s, regularly contributing illustrations to the magazine *Heibon Punch* 平凡パンチ and designing book covers for the publishing company Kōdansha, all sprinkled with his trademark high-contrast, lurid illustration style.

Saeki contributed an erotic illustration that was used on the cover of John Lennon and Yoko Ono's LP *Some Time in New York City* in 1972. Since the 1970s, Saeki regularly published anthologies of his illustration work and exhibited his work globally. His artwork and prints explore a mix of the supernatural, the erotic, and the grotesque, often mercilessly flaunting sexual transgression.

References:

Jansen, Charlotte. "Meet the Master of Japanese Erotica You've Never Heard Of." Artsy. Artsy, April 17, 2017. https://www.artsy.net/article/artsy-editorial-meet-master-japanese-erotica-heard.

Saeki, Toshio, and Noriko Tetsuka. *1970, Toshio Saeki*. Tōkyō: Seirin Kōgeisha, 2006.

Yeung, Kylie. "Obituary: Toshio Saki (1945–2019)." *ArtAsiaPacific*. Art Asia Pacific, January 20, 2020. http://artasiapacific.com/News/ObituaryToshioSaeki19452019.

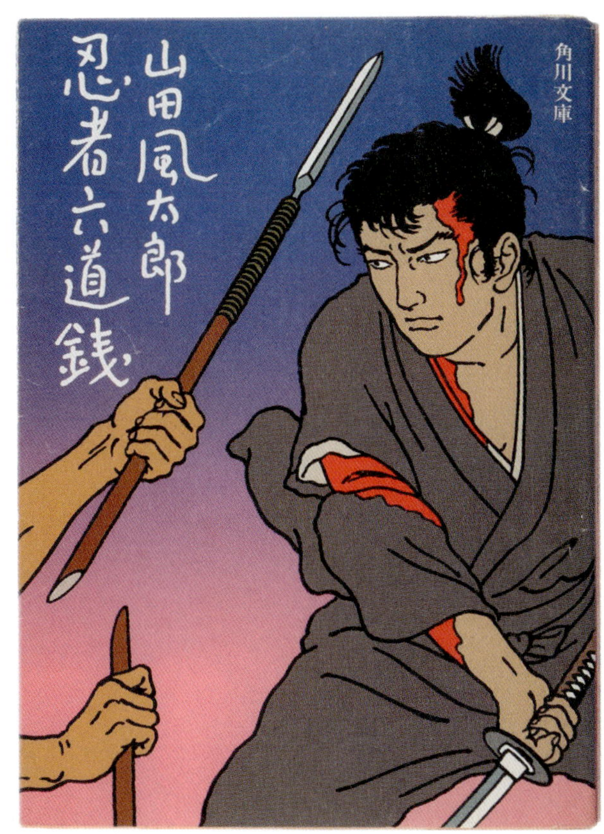

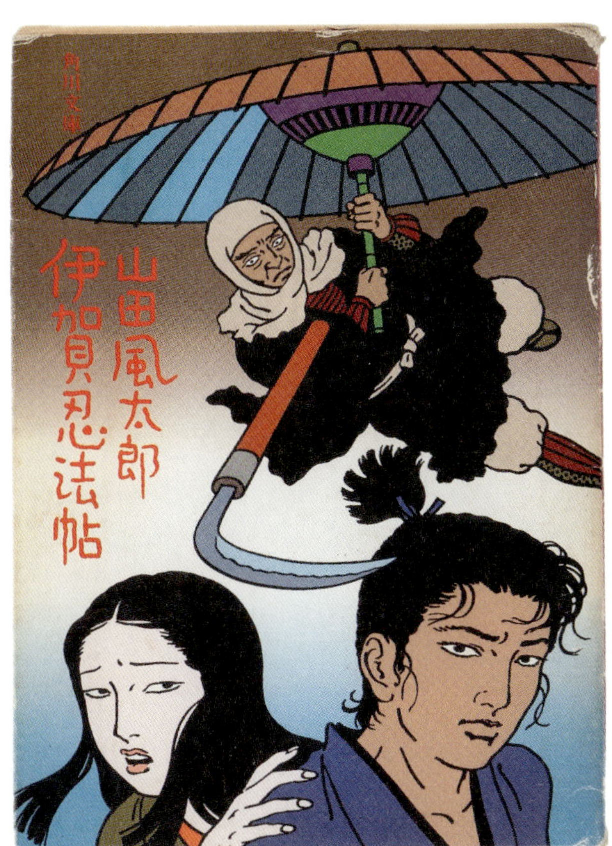

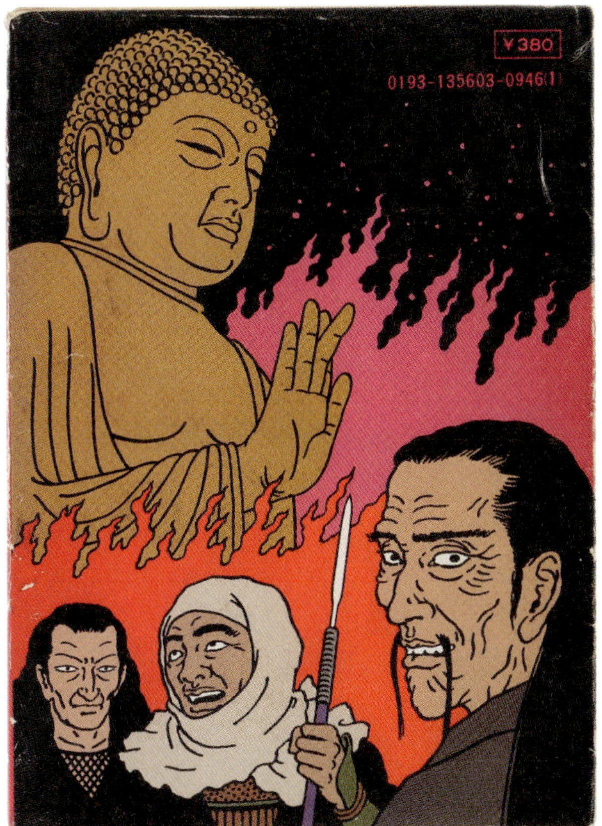

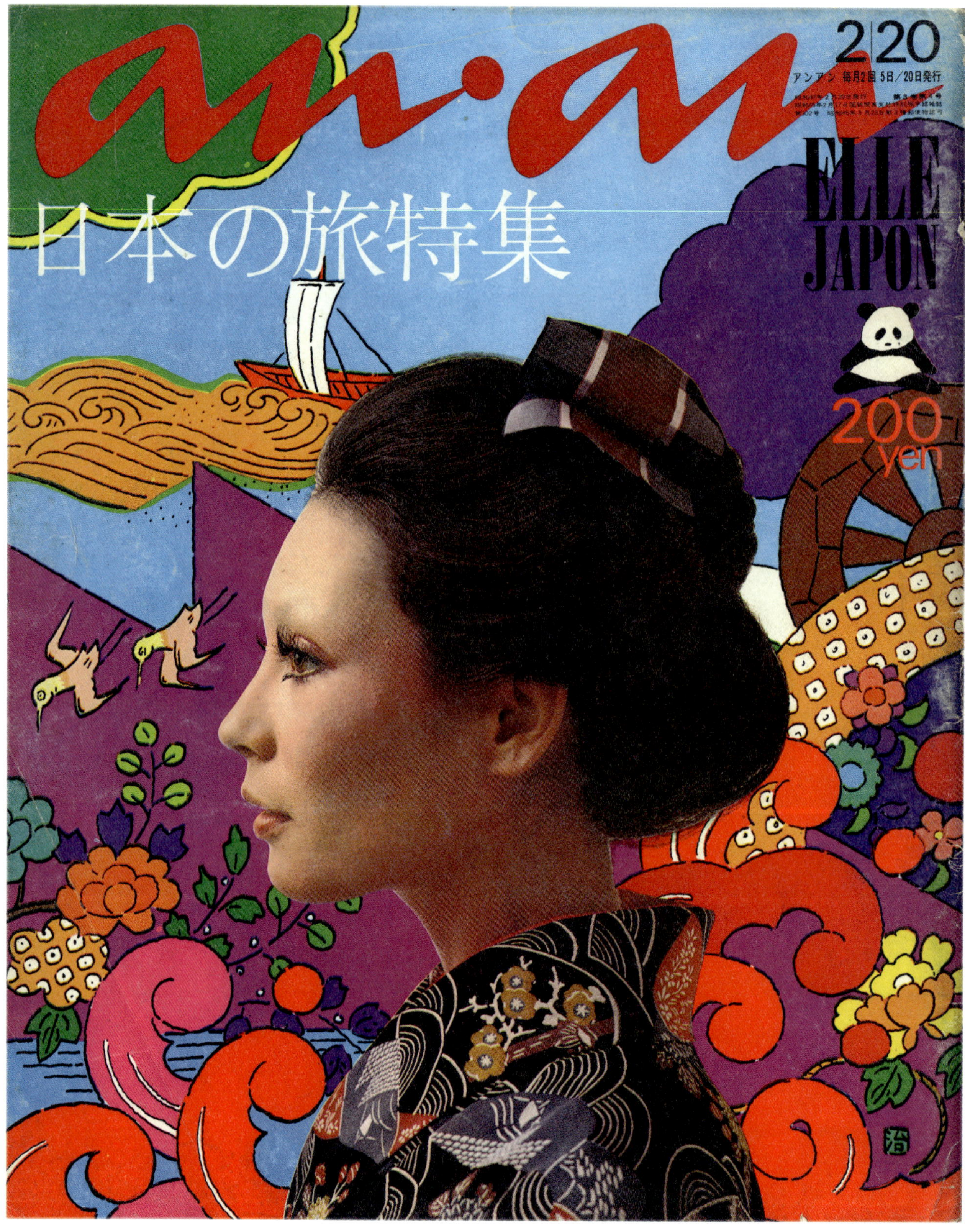

Cover illustration by Harada Osamu 原田治 for ***An•An* No. 47** (Tokyo: **Heibonsha 平凡社, 1972**). Art direction by Horiuchi Seiichi.

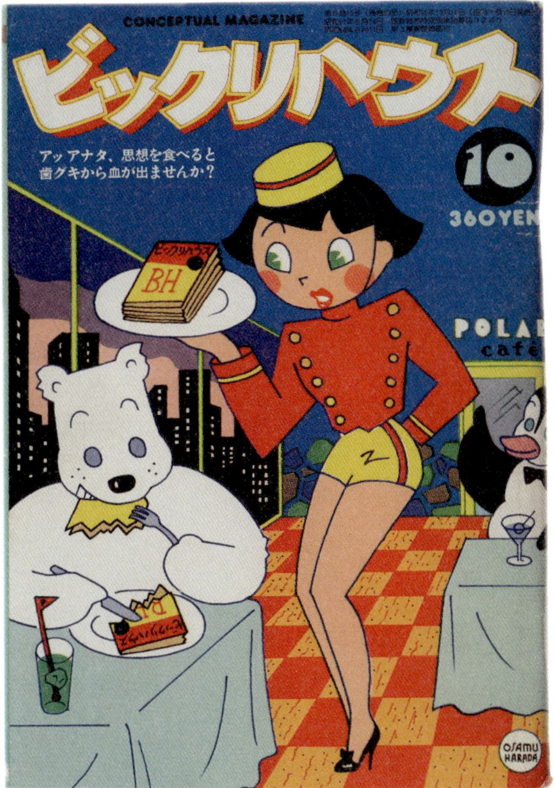

Cover design for subculture magazine ***Bikkuri House* ビックリハウス,**
Vol. 59 (Tokyo: Parco Publishing Parco 出版, 1980).

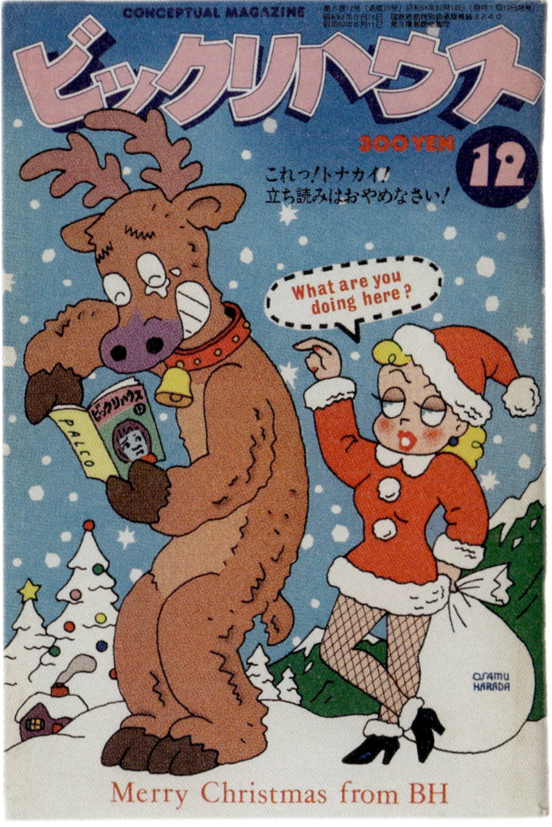

Cover design for subculture magazine ***Bikkuri House* ビックリハウス,**
Vol. 69 (Tokyo: Parco Publishing Parco 出版, 1980).

HARADA OSAMU 原田治

1946–2016

Harada Osamu was born in Tokyo to a family that ran assorted import/export businesses. He studied graphic design at Tama Art University and, after graduation, heavily influenced by the work of Push Pin Studios, he relocated to New York City to soak up the American "vibe" and further develop his portfolio. Harada returned to Japan the following year, finding work as a hybrid freelance illustrator and designer. This began with a series of lettering and illustration treatments in both retro and contemporary styles for the women's fashion and lifestyle magazine *An An*, at the request of art director Horiuchi Seiichi 堀内誠一. Harada would go on to design logos and characters for Calbee brand potato chips, the Japanese subsidiary of Mister Donut, and the English-language cram-school chain ECC.

In 1975, Harada began releasing his own line of assorted products known as Osamu Goods, each emblazoned with his historically influenced illustration and typography. Osamu Goods' towels, tote bags, keychains, and household goods became incredibly popular with teenage women and were hallmarks of design and consumerism in Japanese culture in the 1980s.

References:

Harada, Osamu, Setagaya Bungakukan, and Setagaya Bunka Zaidan. *Osamu's A to Z: Harada Osamu no Shigoto*. Tokyo: Aki Shobo, 2019.

Harada, Osamu. Osamu Goods Story. *Osamu Goods*, January 7, 2020. https://www.osamugoods.com/story/vol032.html.

Itoi, Shigesato. "堀内さん。" ほぼ日刊イトイ新聞. *Hobo Nikkan Itoi Shinbun*, January 4, 2017. https://www.1101.com/horiuchi/.

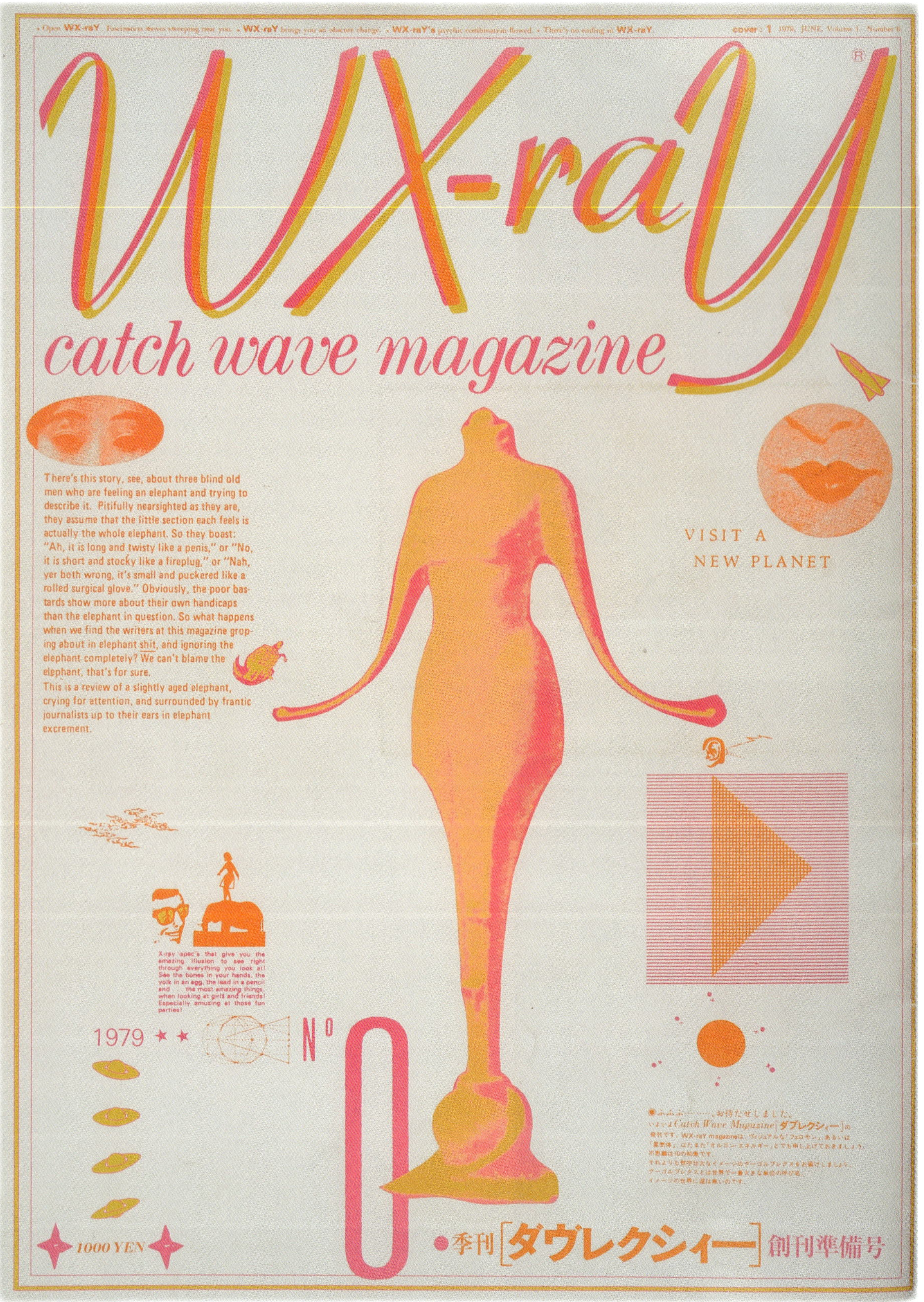

This spread: The lone 1979 issue of the oversize magazine ***WX-raY*** created by the editorial graphic design studio WXY, composed of Harata Heikichi 羽良多平吉, Orui Makoto 大類信, and Nakayama Gin'o 中山銀士.

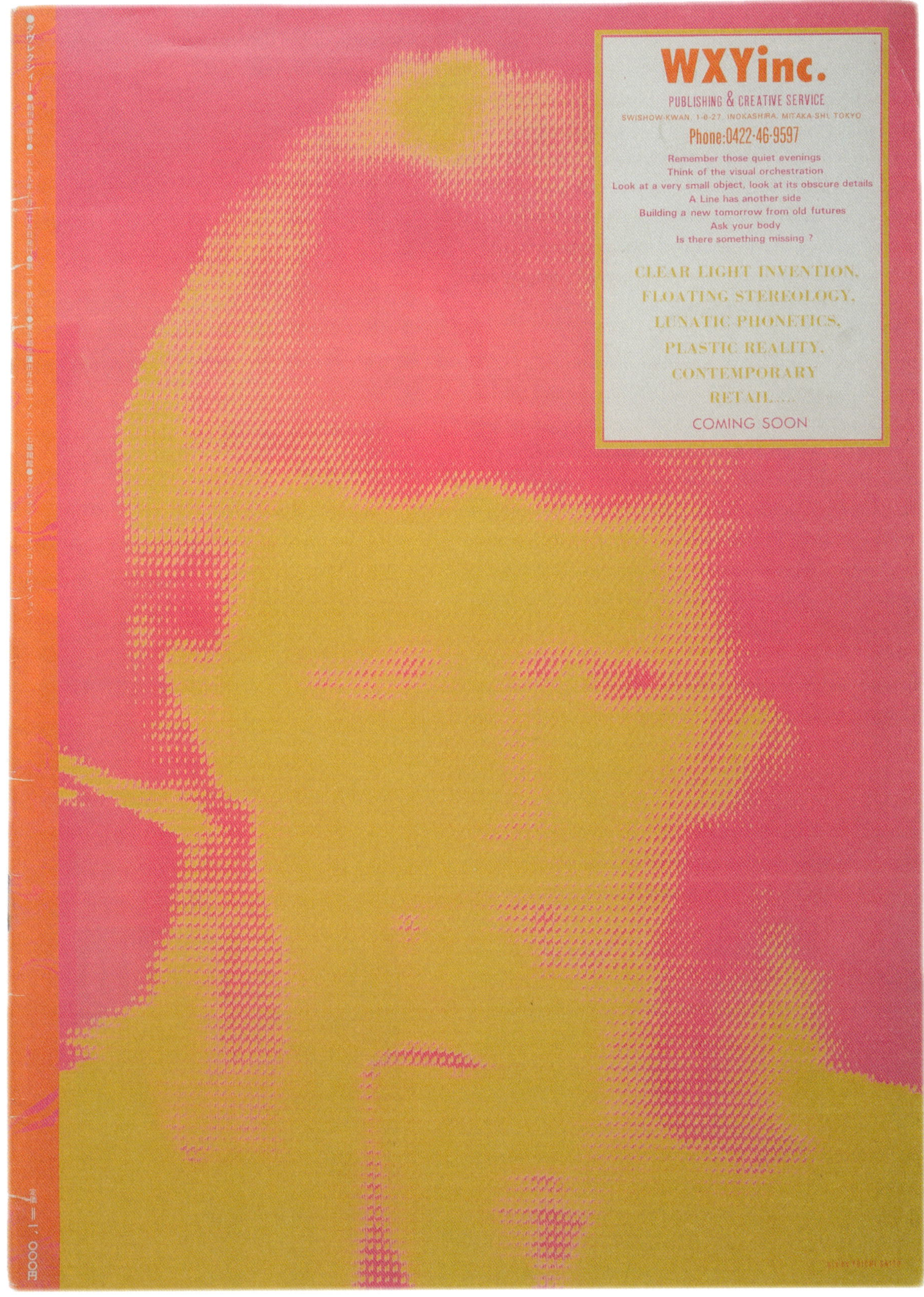
WXYinc.
PUBLISHING & CREATIVE SERVICE
SWISHOW-KWAN, 1-8-27, INOKASHIRA, MITAKA-SHI, TOKYO
Phone:0422-46-9597
Remember those quiet evenings
Think of the visual orchestration
Look at a very small object, look at its obscure details
A Line has another side
Building a new tomorrow from old futures
Ask your body
Is there something missing ?
CLEAR LIGHT INVENTION,
FLOATING STEREOLOGY,
LUNATIC PHONETICS,
PLASTIC REALITY,
CONTEMPORARY
RETAIL....
COMING SOON

HARATA HEIKICHI 羽良多平吉

1947–

Harata Heikichi (often stylized as Harata HeiQuiti and Harata HeiQuicci) was born in Tokyo and graduated from Tokyo National University of Fine Arts and Music with a major in Visual Design. Initially influenced by designers like Sugiura Kohei and Yokoo Tadanori, Harata worked as a freelance graphic designer and quickly developed his signature style of visual parataxis, conscientiously combining disparate imagery and typography in order to create new semantic meaning.

In the early 1970s, Harata worked first on the magazine *ZOO* and then on the magazine *Shinjuku Play Map*, leading to a large body of commissions in editorial design, from which he gained a strong following. His early visual works included editorial design for Japanese underground subculture magazines like *Yū 遊*, *Heaven*, and *Variete*. Harata created the visual design for the albums *Solid State Survivor* and *Public Pressure* by the legendary Japanese music group Yellow Magic Orchestra, a band that embodied the zeitgeist of Japanese New Wave graphic design and visual art in the 1980s.

In 1979 Harata formed the editorial graphic design studio WXY with Ōrui Makoto 大類信 and Nakayama Gin'o 中山銀士, and the trio published the oversize magazine *WX-raY*. While only one issue was published, it sparked a wave of self-initiated and self-published media by graphic designers. *WX-raY*'s use of vibrant color, halftone texture, and atmospheric, expressive typography made Harata a cult star in Japanese graphic culture. Harata's design for *Solid State Survivor*, featuring photography by Sukita Masayoshi 鋤田正義, led to many more commissions, including record covers and tour posters for the hit Japanese pop duo Pink Lady in 1980 and Japanese tour posters for the German electropunk band Deutsch Amerikanische Freundschaft (DAF) in 1982. Harata also worked as art director and editorial designer for the fantasy literature magazine *Somnium* in the early 1980s.

In 1985, Harata became a part-time lecturer in editorial design at Joshibi University of Art & Design 女子美術大学. Harata opened his own design studio, EDiX, in 1989 and began exploring the possibilities of digital graphic design; freed from the constraints of phototypesetting, Harata's compositions became increasingly atmospheric, complex, and lyrical. In the 1990s, Harata designed the monthly avant-garde manga anthology magazine *Garo* ガロ. Harata's covers for the manga explore both graphic and semantic space—when stacked together, each of *Garo*'s monthly issues reveals a panoramic composition by year.

"When the whole of his career is assessed, many regard him as the visual forerunner of contemporary Japanese visual subcultures. Harata developed and practiced his own book design methodology "Shoyō-Sekkei"—literally translated, the aggregate parts are: sho (book) + yō (vessel) + sekkei (architectural plan). No mere conflation, the yo element simultaneously means "outlook"—referring not only to modern Western "form and content" philosophies but a more holistically comprehensive overview of the total architecture of the book-as-object and how readers will interact with a book project as both object and media.

After years of applied research examining the relationship of digital tools, writing, and media, Harata's interests have shifted toward an examination of the ambiguity and concreteness of "shiro," the Japanese word which represents both white and emptiness. At the core of Harata's practice is a desire for a unified methodology of total design that dissuades deconstruction or fragmentation. Heavily reliant upon the compound, juxtapositional nature of the Japanese language, Harata's work is worth prolonged examination."

- Muroga Kiyonori 室賀清徳

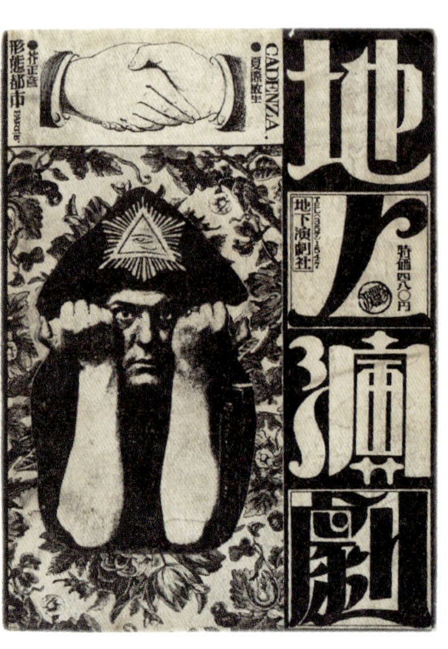

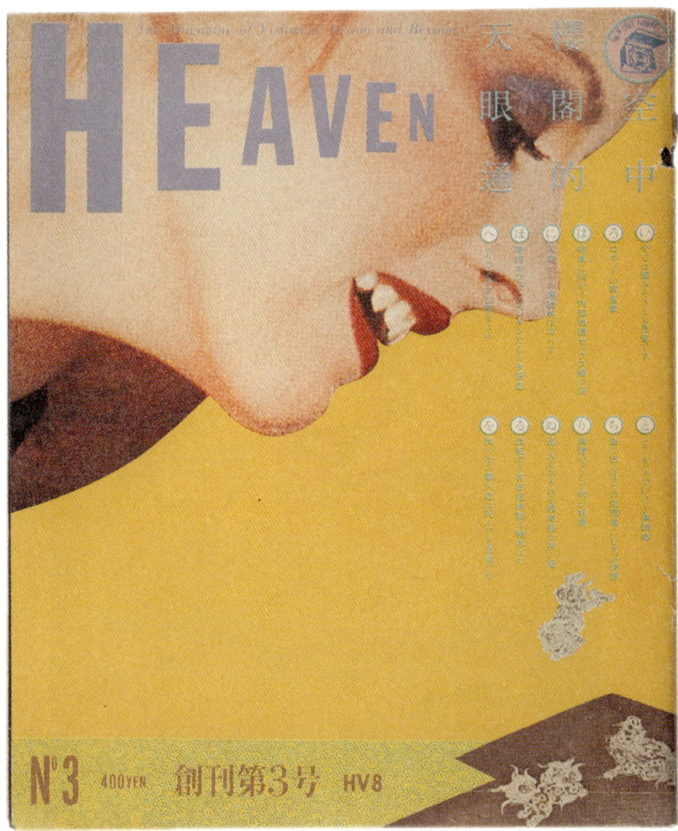

Above and below: Covers of ***HEAVEN***, the self-proclaimed "underground intellectual magazine" published from 1980–1981. *HEAVEN* was initially published in 1979 as *X-Magazine* and was renamed *X-Magazine Jam* the same year. These early issues were strictly sold in vending machines nationally, so that the content might not be censored or restricted according to pornography rules of the day. *X-Magazine* and *X-Magazine Jam* relied on the appearance of softcore pornography of the time, with explicit covers and photographic features, in order to fund the editors' desired subcultural content, notably features on drugs, mysticism, Zen, cult cinema, punk rock, fantasy literature, the occult, parody, and professional wrestling, amongst other topics. Eleven issues of the precursor magazines were published, and the magazine was relaunched as *HEAVEN* in 1980, with Harata jettisoning the overtly sexual graphics for the appearance of a new wave magazine. Nine issues of *HEAVEN* were published prior to the magazine surrendering to editorial infighting and staff turnover. *HEAVEN* and its precursors have been the subject of numerous academic and subcultural publications since the magazine's demise.

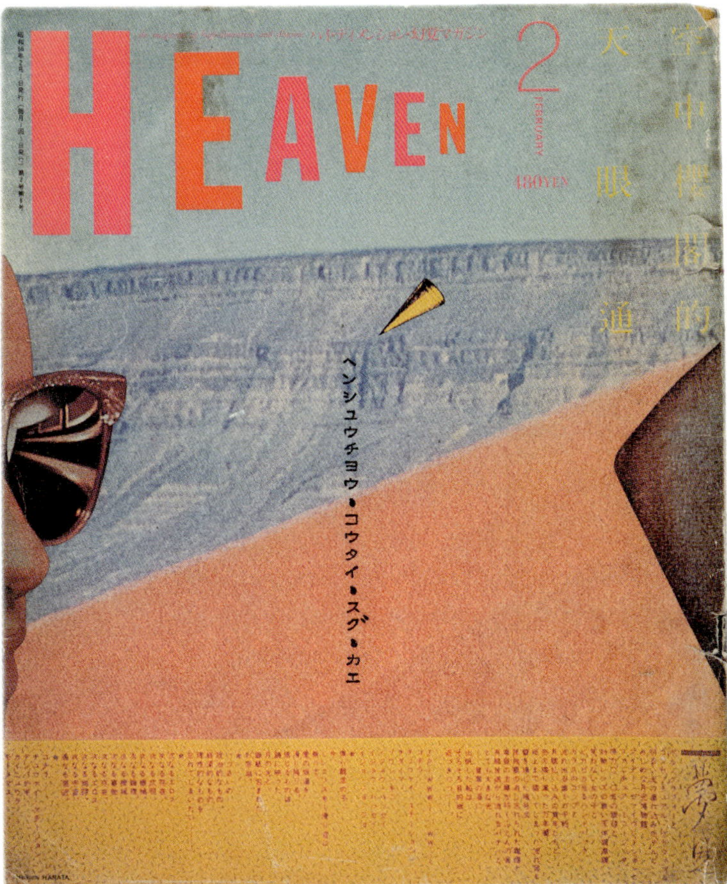

References:

Muroga, Kiyonori. "HeiQuiti Harata: Yes, I See." *Idea* 1, no. 347 (May 2011): 1–251.

Opposite: ***Chika-engeki*** **(Underground Theater) 地下演劇** (Tokyo: Chika-engekisha 地下演劇社, 1970). A subcultural magazine designed and largely edited by Harata the same year he graduated from university and dedicated to the theater movements of that era.

ORUI MAKOTO 大類信

1949–

Ōrui Makoto attended Kuwasawa Design School and worked for assorted design and advertising companies for three years before going freelance. In 1978, Orui began working for the magazine *Yū* 遊 and met fellow designer Harata Heikichi there. The duo began working for *Rockin' On* magazine and used the name WXY inc. for their design endeavors alongside Nakayama Gin'o 中山銀士 and others. They made the self-published magazine *WX-raY* to enhance their portfolio and soon attracted clients such as the bands Sheena and the Rokkets and Pink Lady with their hybrid punk/new wave approach to graphic design and illustration. In 1979, Orui worked simultaneously on the redesign of the magazine *Takarajima* 宝島 and editorial design for the magazine *Pomp* ポンプ and provided illustration work for stories written by Itasaka Gen 板坂元 for the newspaper *Yomiuri Weekly*.

Orui worked on a number of book titles for the rock-and-roll lifestyle publisher Hachiosha 八曜社 throughout the 1980s, while also designing hybrid culture/pornography magazines that were only sold through vending machines. Starting in 1982, Orui began crediting his work to his new solo design studio, Fiction Inc, working for publications such as the culture and literary magazine *SALE2*. He started a retail shop called Bondage: Tokyo Japan from inside of his studio in 1987, selling bondage-related goods, photography books, and Western publications, inspired by a recent trip that he had made to Paris. Orui opened THE deep, a gallery in Nogizaka in Tokyo in 1990, later moving to Shibuya in 1994.

In 2001, Orui became the art director of the French fashion and lifestyle magazine *Purple* for a handful of years, and in 2006 he discontinued his editorial design work for *Rockin' On* (reappearing briefly in 2014 to contribute the design for *Rockin' On*'s Lou Reed memorial issue). Orui moved to Paris, where he pursues the making of ceramics and running his latest venture, Radical Silence Production, publisher of the irregular art journal *THE international* and distributes foreign publications within Japan.

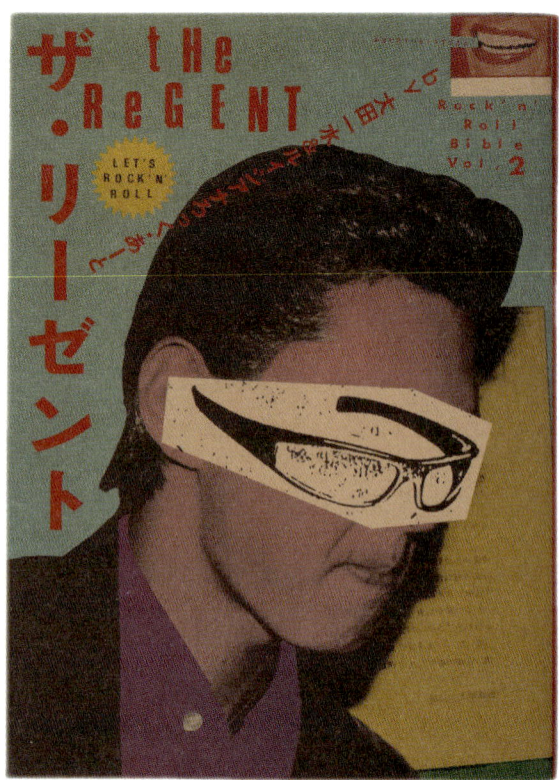

Above and below: ***The Regent* ザ・リーゼント, Ōta Issui 大田一水 (Tokyo: Hachiosha 八曜社, 1982).** "Regent" is the Japanese term for the pompadour hairstyle, one of Japan's grandest signifiers of youth rebellion. This highly illustrated book charts the development of the hairstyle.

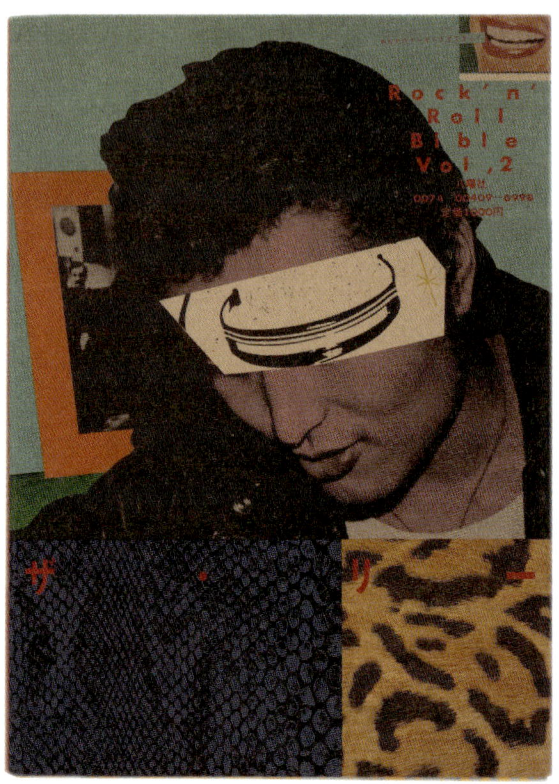

References:

Barbora, and Kiyonori Muroga. "Design of Makoto Orui: Tendencies and Measures." *Idea* 1, no. 363 (March 2014): 106–108.

Barbora, and Kiyonori Muroga. "Memorandum About Makoto Orui." *Idea* 1, no. 363 (March 2014): 107–14.

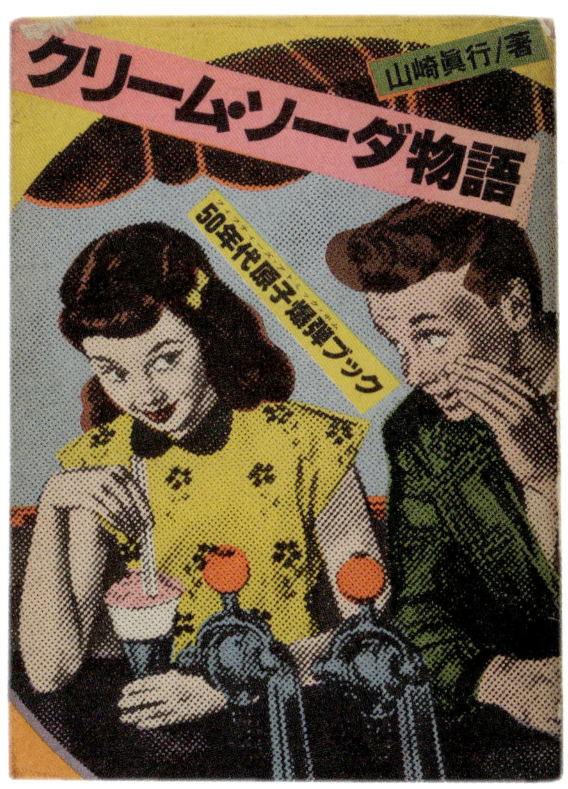

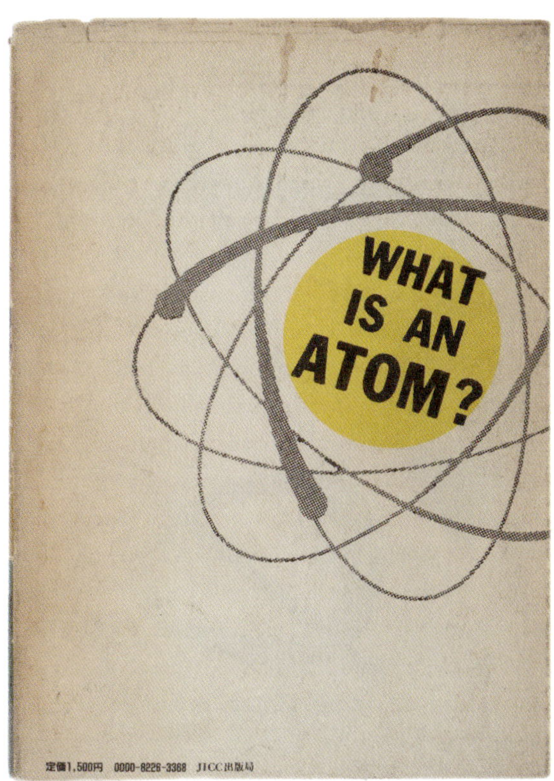

Clockwise from top left: Front and back cover, spreads from ***Cream Soda Monogatari*** **クリームソーダ物語, Yamada Masayuki 山崎 眞行** (Tokyo: JICC Shuppansha JICC出版局, 1982). A highly graphic book exploring the aesthetics of "the atomic age" of the 1950s.

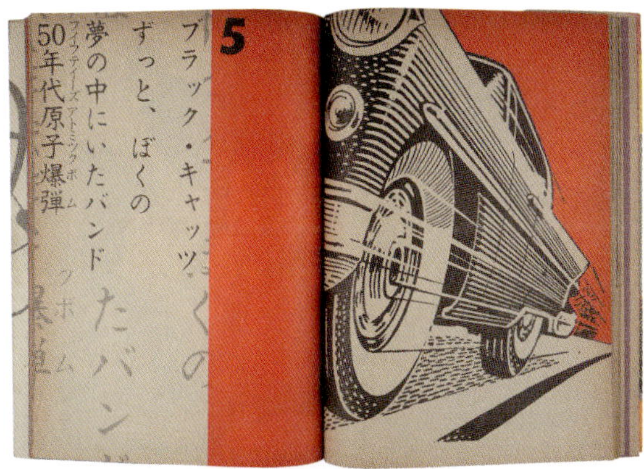

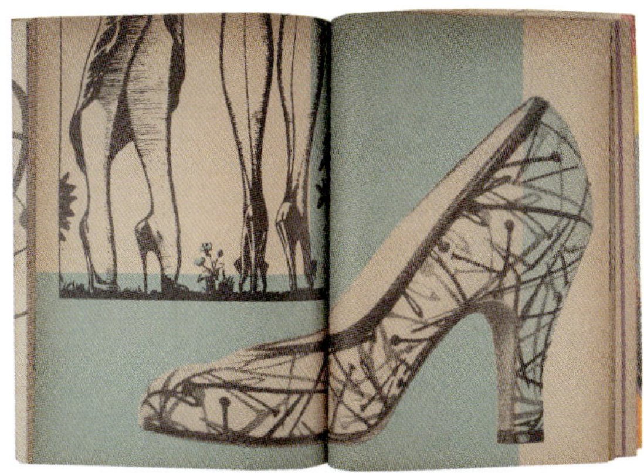

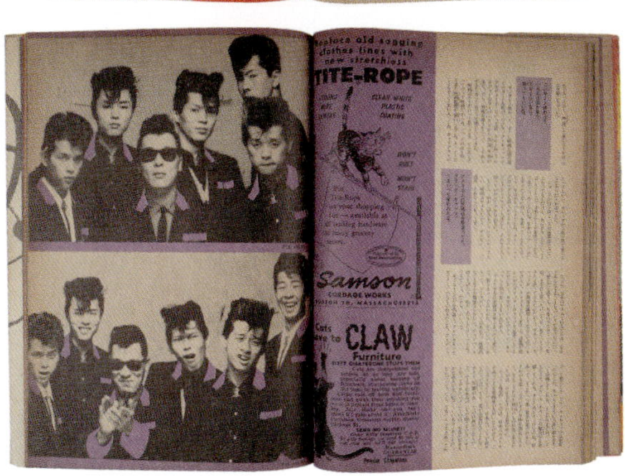

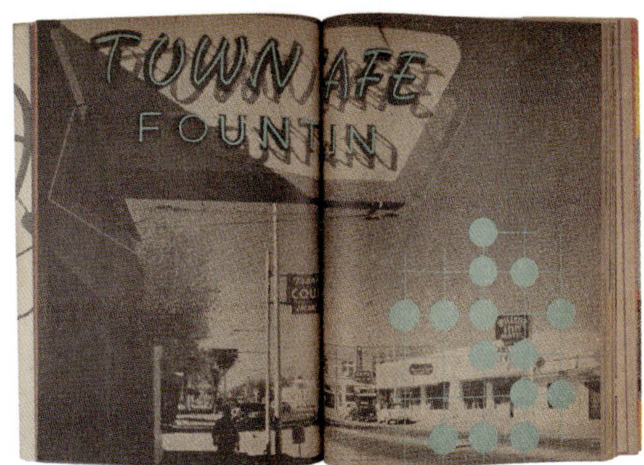

ASABA KATSUMI 浅葉克己

1940–

Asaba Katsumi was born in Kanagawa Prefecture. After studying at Kuwasawa Design School and working for Light Publicity, he founded the Katsumi Asaba Design Studio in 1975.

Asaba is renowned for his highly connotative and playful hand-drawn lettering and identity design. He has designed the logos for innumerable corporations and lettering for a wide array of exhibitions and publications, and he has art directed popular advertising campaigns for Suntory, Seibu Department Stores, and Misawa Homes. Asaba designed the logo of the Democratic Party of Japan and the official poster for the 1998 Olympic Winter Games in Nagano. He has received many awards, including the Japan Academy Prize for Outstanding Achievement in Art Direction, the Yūsaku Kamekura Design Award of the Japan Graphic Designers Association (JAGDA), and the Medal with Purple Ribbon from the Government of Japan.

He is a committee member of the Tokyo Art Directors Club, chairman of the Tokyo Type Directors Club, president of JAGDA, and representative of Japan to the Alliance Graphique Internationale. He is a visiting professor at Tokyo Zokei University and Kyoto Seika University and president of Kuwasawa Design School.

He is a councilor of the Japan Table Tennis Association and is ranked at the sixth level in the sport. In the spring of 2013, he was awarded the Order of the Rising Sun, Gold Rays with Rosette from the Government of Japan for his contributions to culture and the arts.

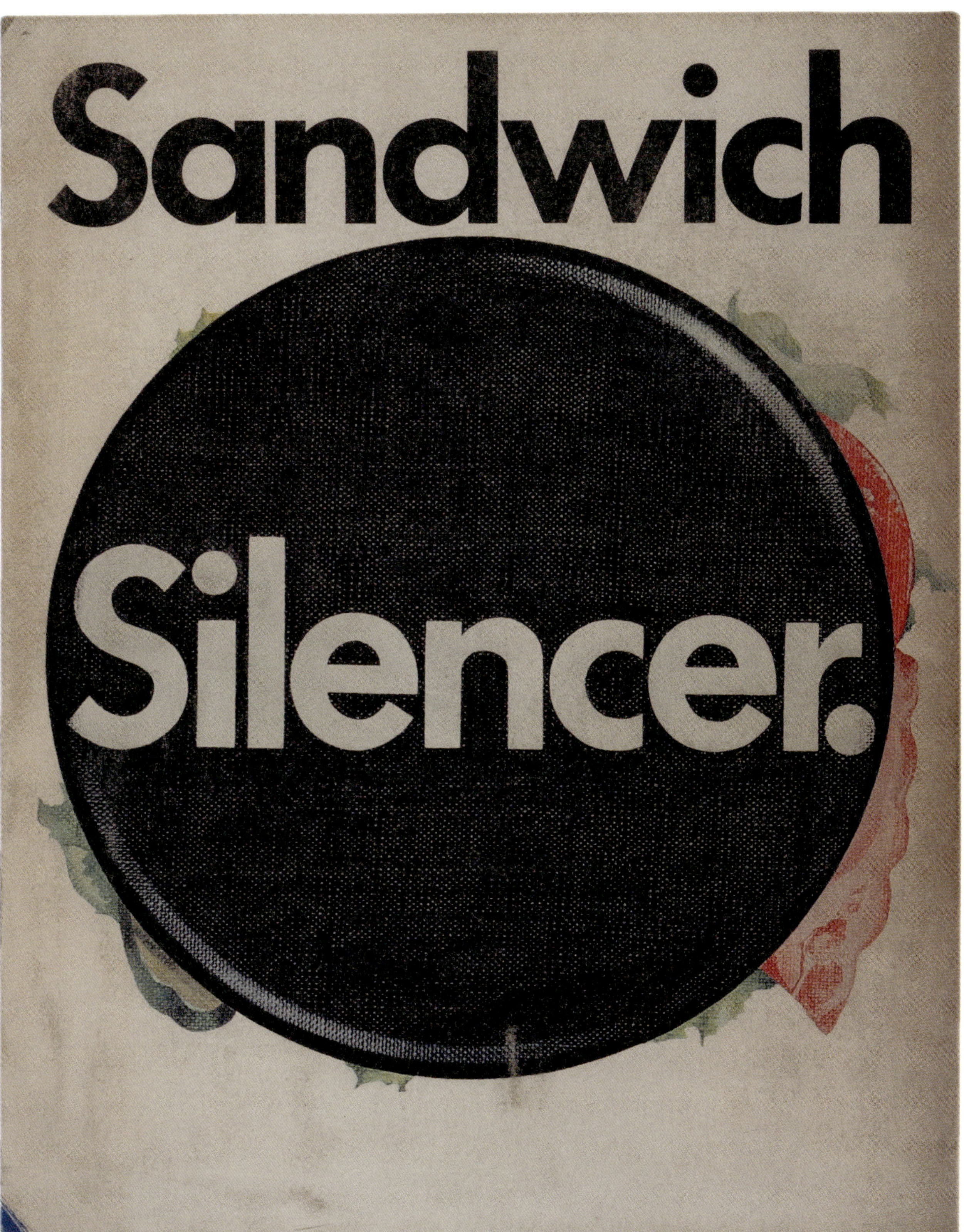

Sandwich Silencer, the lone publication from the lauded design, art, and literature collective Silencer **(Tokyo: Ouritsu-Shuppan 王立出版,1974)**. Silencer was composed of sixteen members: Asaba Katsumi 浅葉克巳, Kanoh Noriaki 加納典明, Konishi Keisuke 小西啓介, Kuramata Shirō 倉俣史朗, Sakurai Ikuo 桜井郁男, Nagatomo Keisuke 長友啓典, Kuroda Seitaro 黒田征太郎, Kamijō Takahisa 上條喬久, Sukita Masayoshi 鋤田正義, Takahashi Minoru 高橋稔, Tomura Hiroshi 戸村浩, Higurashi Shinzō 日暮真三, Aoba Masateru 青葉益輝, Nagahama Osamu 長浜治 , Shiine Yamato 椎根和, and Itō Takamichi 伊藤隆道.

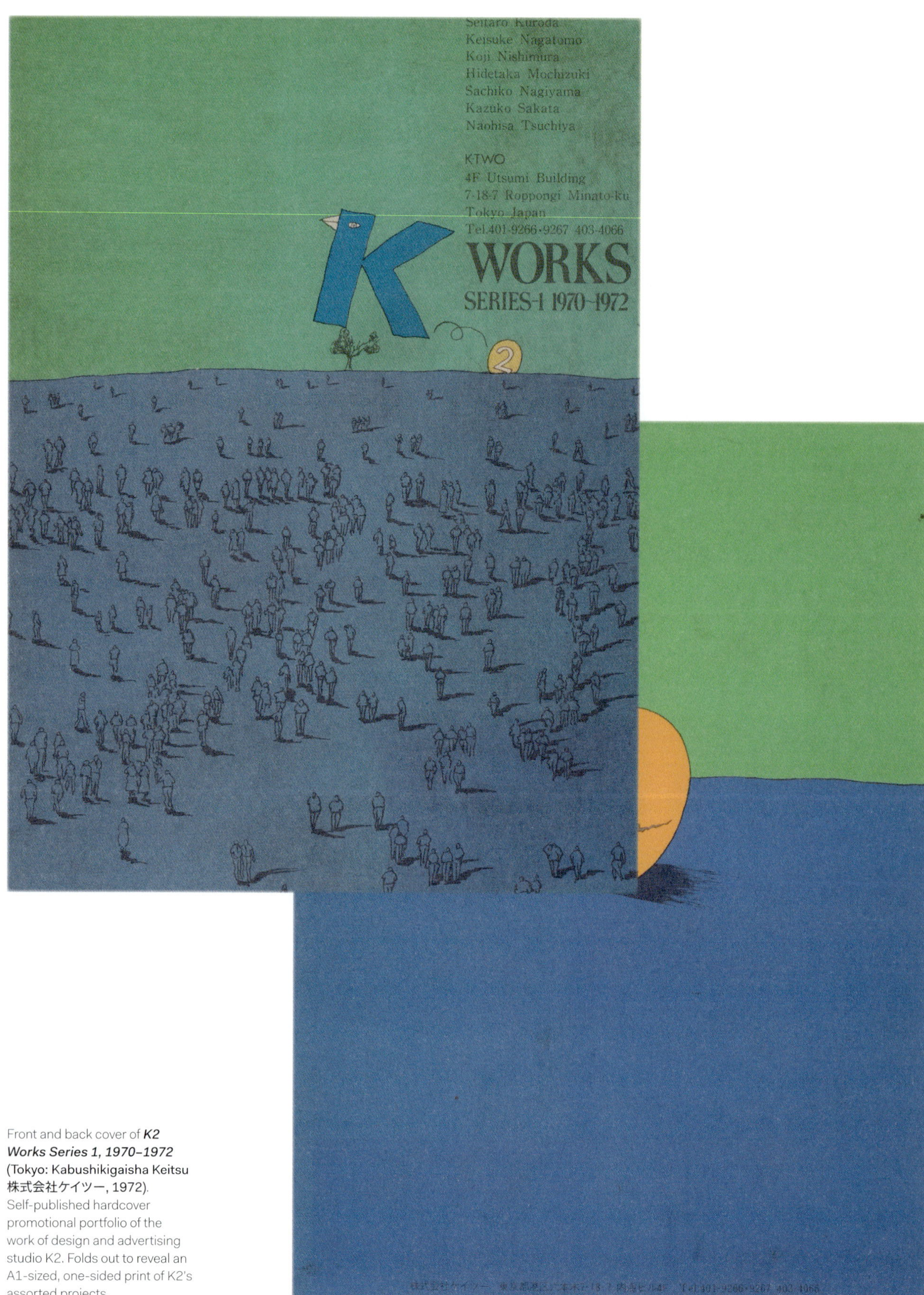

Front and back cover of ***K2 Works Series 1, 1970–1972*** (Tokyo: Kabushikigaisha Keitsu 株式会社ケイツー, 1972). Self-published hardcover promotional portfolio of the work of design and advertising studio K2. Folds out to reveal an A1-sized, one-sided print of K2's assorted projects.

K2:

KURODA SEITARO 黒田征太郎

1939–

NAGATOMO KEISUKE 長友啓典

1939–2017

Kuroda and Nagatomo, both born in Osaka in 1939, established the design and illustration studio K2 in 1969, winning the Warsaw International Poster Biennale the same year. Previously, Nagatomo had graduated from the Kuwasawa Design School in 1961 and then joined the Nippon Design Center, where he worked as a designer under art director Yamashiro Ryūichi. Kuroda, a high school dropout, had worked at Hayakawa Yoshio's design office. The pair were introduced by Hayakawa and Tanaka Ikkō and struck up a fast friendship, leading to the formation of their studio.

K2 employed a number of talented designers, copywriters, and illustrators at their Roppongi office, including Nishimura Kōji 西村浩二 and Tsuchiya Naohisa 土屋直久 in their early years, and they published the bound poster/portfolio *Works Series 1: 1970–1972*. By 1972, their staff briefly expanded to include thirty members, and they opened an office in Osaka for a few years to pursue work associated with the Osaka World Expo.

K2's body of work included editorial design and illustration, promotional design, packaging design, poster design, and corporate identity. Their early projects included explorations of expressive typography and lettering, freewheeling illustration, and a masterful approach to photomontage.

Both Nagatomo and Kuroda were members of the design, art, and literature collective Silencer alongside fellow designer Asaba Katsumi and photographer Sukita Masayoshi 鋤田正義, and they had work published in the group's 1970 compendium, *Sandwich Silencer*. The book was largely bilingual and was printed in full color with sections devoted to each of Silencer's members. Silencer held three exhibitions of experimental work and launched their own bar briefly.

K2 collaborated on a number of pictorial books, and the partners also put out solo publications. Their commercial practice grew to encompass logo and set design for broadcast television, including the *This is Good Morning Asahi* おはよう朝日です television program from 1994 to 2003. They designed the corporate identity design for Kintetsu Railways, the poster design for the Nagano Paralympics, and multiple editorial direction projects. Nagatomo worked as a Visiting Professor at Tokyo Zokei University and advisor to the Graduate School of Design at Nihon Kōgakuin College 日本工学院.

K2 held a retrospective exhibition at Tokyo's Ginza Graphic Gallery in 1996.

Nagatomo passed away in 2017, and Kuroda currently resides in Kitakyushu in the south of Japan after living in the United States for a number of years.

References:

Asaba, Katsumi, Tenmei Kano, Shiro Kuramata, Keisuke Nagatomo, Seitarō Kuroda, Takahisa Kamijou, Masayoshi Sukita, Hiroshi Tomura, Shinzo Higurashi, and Masuteru Aoba. *Sandwich Silencer*. Tokyo: Ouritsu-Shuppan-Sha, 1974.

Kuroda, Seitarō, and Keisuke Nagatomo. *K2: Kuroda Seitarō, Nagatomo Keisuke*. Tokyo: Ginza Graphic Gallery, 1996.

Kuroda, Seitarō, and Keisuke Nagatomo. *Sorosoro Iikana Seitaro Kuroda / Keisuke Nagatomo K2 Cultural Monument Book*. Tokyo: Kōdansha, 1982.

Ishihara, Yoshihisa, Seitarō Kuroda and Keisuke Nagatomo. "Seitarō Kuroda and Keisuke Nagatomo K2." In *1979 Nen Tokyo Dezainazu Supe-su = 1979 Tokyo Designers Space*, 43–45. Tokyo: Seibundo Shinkosha, 1979.

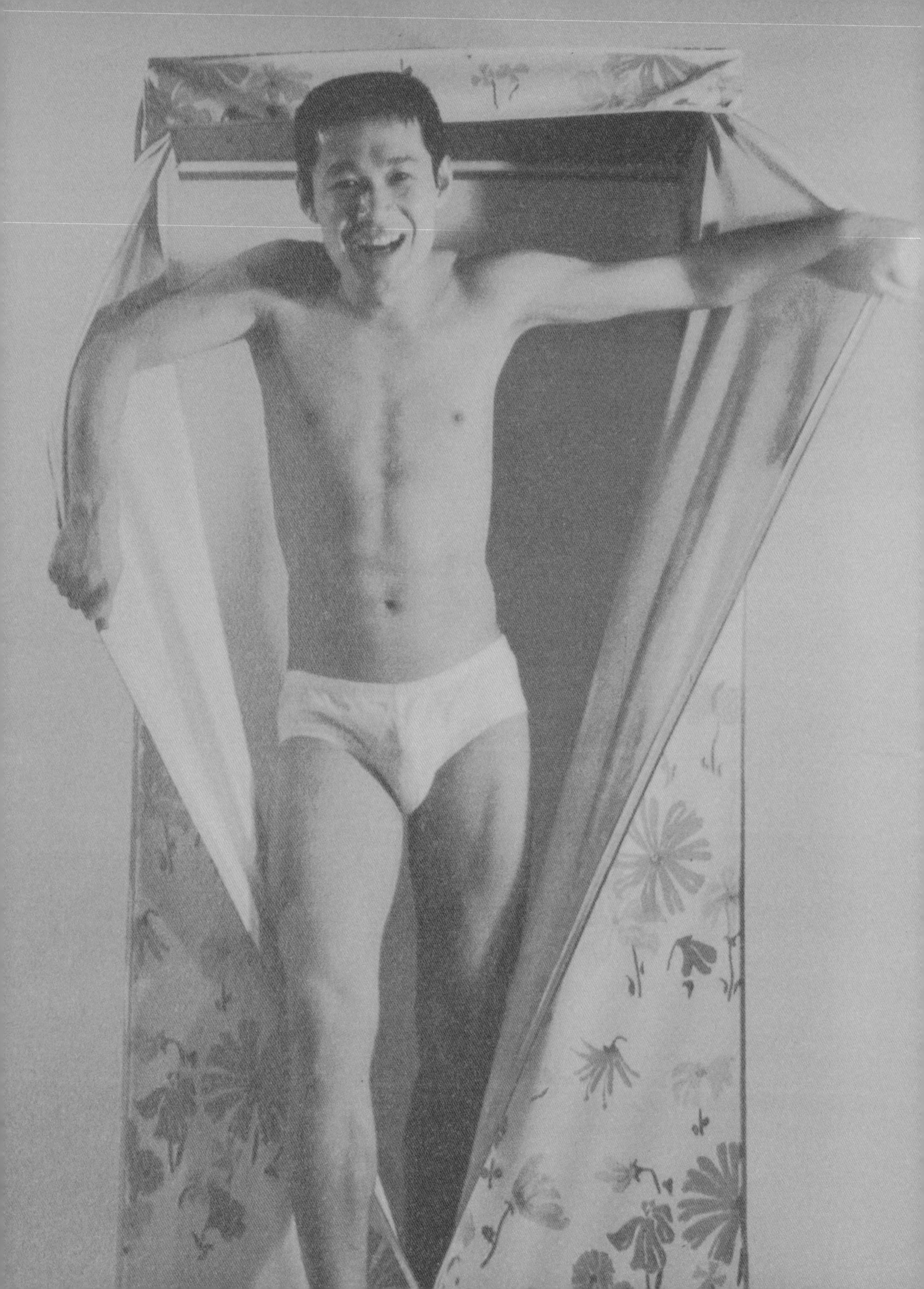

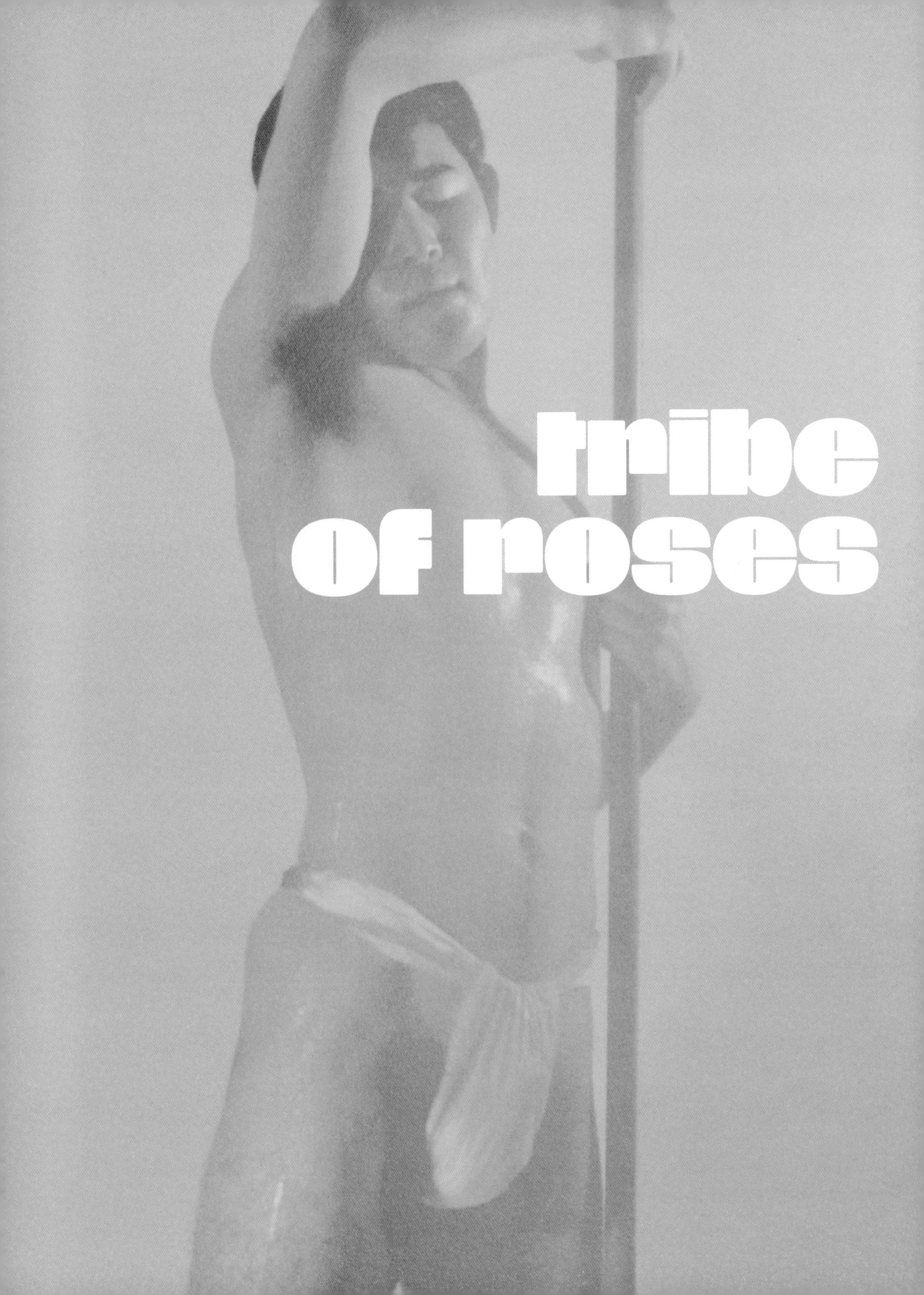

tribe of roses

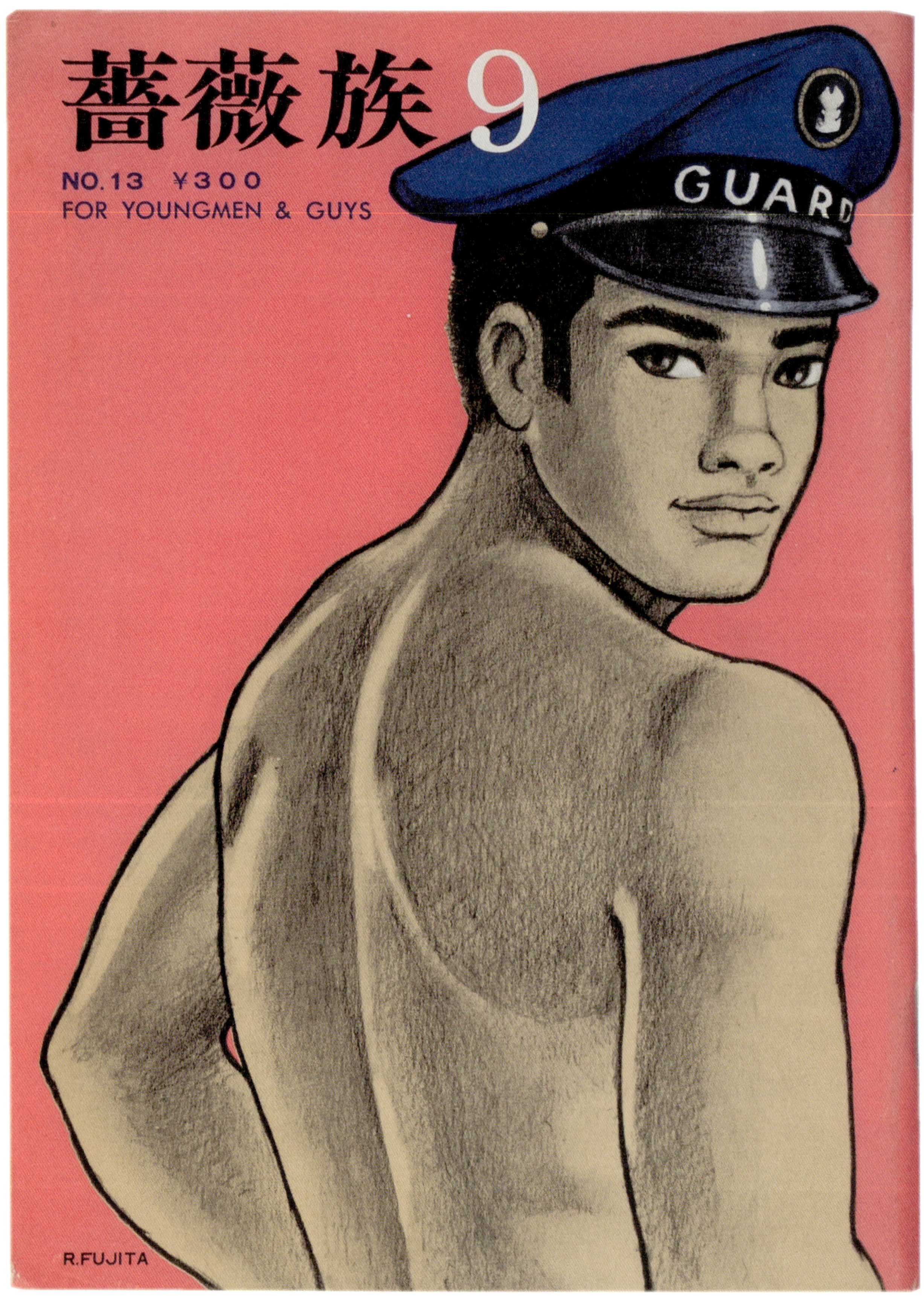

Cover of ***Barazoku* 薔薇族, September issue** (Tokyo: Dainishobō 第二書房, 1973). Cover design by Fujita Ryu 藤田竜.

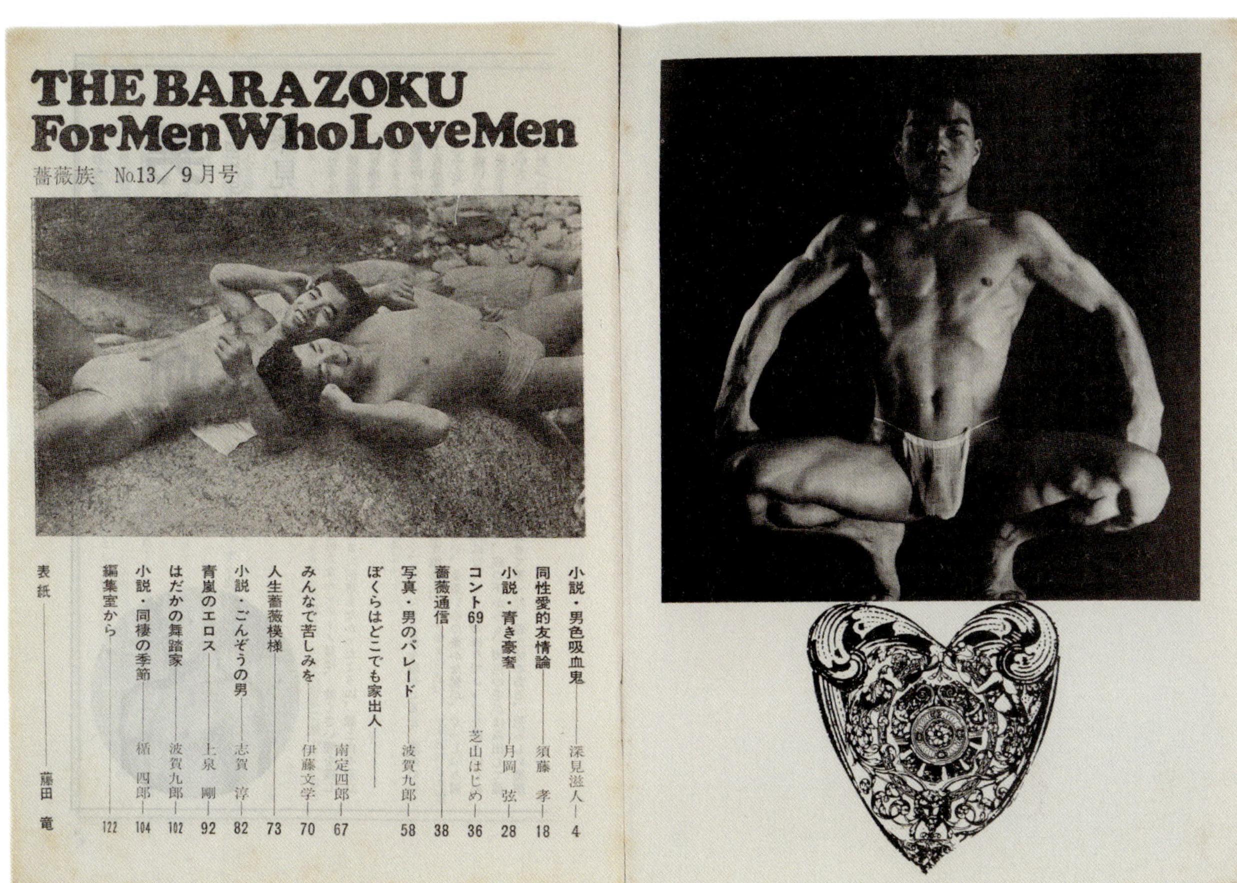

THE BARAZOKU
ForMenWhoLoveMen
薔薇族　No.13／9月号

Spread from ***Barazoku* 薔薇族, September issue**
(Tokyo: Dainishobō 第二書房, 1973).

Tribe of Roses

Barazoku 薔薇族 (Tribe of Roses), Japan's first commercially circulated gay men's magazine, was released in 1971 by the heterosexual publisher Itō Bungaku 伊藤文學 of Dainishobō 第二書房. Earlier publications such as the subscription-only *Adonis* アドニス and *Bara* 薔薇 predated *Barazoku*, however *Barazoku* was the first magazine to be available nationally via mainstream booksellers.

Itō had previously published a number of books for gay audiences in Japan, such as *Homo Techniques: Sex Life between a Man and another Man* ホモテクニックー男と男の性生活 and *Lesbian Techniques: Sex Life between a Woman and another Woman* レスビアンテクニックー女と女の性生活. While the publisher was an ally to the Japanese queer community, *Barazoku*'s editors were gay, specifically Fujita Ryu 藤田竜 and Mamiya Hiroshi 間宮浩. Fujita had worked for Nakahara Jun'ichi's Himawari and was an experienced writer, editor, illustrator, and graphic designer. Fujita designed the very first issue of *Barazoku* and also illustrated the cover. Another frequent contributor was Fujita's longtime partner, Naitō Rune 内藤ルネ. Naitō was also a former employee of Nakahara Jun'ichi and the illustrator of the girl's magazine *Junior Soleil*.

The inclusion of Fujita and Naitō's illustration work would prove to be instrumental to *Barazoku*'s success. Their cheerful yet erotic illustrations of men were highly appealing to the magazine's fan base and were the next step in the evolution of the Japanese *kawaii* かわいい or 可愛い ("cute") aesthetic. (As noted by contemporary graphic designer and writer Masaki Ray 真崎嶺, "The term 'kawaii' is etymologically rooted in ideas of pity—meaning something that is so helpless that it is endearing."[1]) These transformational aesthetics were largely pioneered by Fujita and Naitō's former employer Nakahara, notably his pixie-faced illustrations of children with bright, oversized eyes and slightly enlarged heads. Naitō, often working under the pseudonyms Daisuke and Sahara Sam,

1 Lynam, Ian, and Ray Masaki. Ian Lynam and Ray Masaki in conversation. Personal, May 21, 2022. (Note: The first known instance of this flipped usage was by Kishi Tamaki in 1914.)

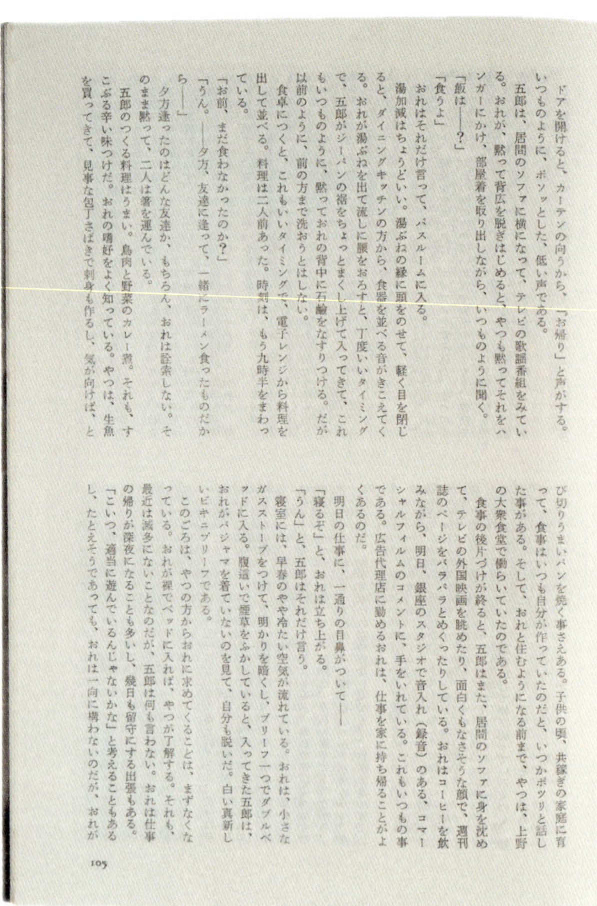

ドアを開けると、カーテンの向うから、「お帰り」と声がする。いつものように、ボソッとした、低い声である。

五郎は、居間のソファに横になって、テレビの歌謡番組をみている。おれが、黙って背広を脱ぎはじめると、やつも黙ってそれをハンガーにかけ、部屋着を取り出しながら、いつものように聞く。

「飯は――？」

「食うよ」

おれはそれだけ言って、バスルームに入る。

湯加減はちょうどいい。湯ぶねの縁に頭をのせて、軽く目を閉じると、ダイニングキッチンの方から、食器を並べる音がきこえてくる。おれが湯ぶねを出て流しに腰をおろすと、丁度いいタイミングで、五郎がジーパンの裾をちょっとまくし上げて入ってきて、これもいつものように、黙っておれの背中に石鹸をなすりつける。だが以前のように、前の方まで洗おうとはしない。

食卓につくと、これもいいタイミングで、電子レンジから料理を出して並べる。料理は二人前あった。時刻は、もう九時半をまわっている。

「お前、まだ食わなかったのか？」

「うん。――夕方、友達に逢って、一緒にラーメン食ったものだから――」

夕方逢ったのはどんな友達か、もちろん、おれは詮索しない。そのまま黙って、二人は箸を運んでいる。

五郎のつくる料理はうまい。鳥肉と野菜のカレー煮。それも、すこぶる辛い味つけだ。おれの嗜好をよく知っている。やつは、生魚を買ってきて、見事な包丁さばきで刺身も作るし、気が向けば、とび切りうまいパンを焼く事さえある。子供の頃、共稼ぎの家庭に育って、食事はいつも自分が作っていたのだと、いつかボツリと話した事がある。そして、おれと住むようになる前まで、やつは、上野の大衆食堂で働らいていたのである。

食事の後片づけが終ると、五郎はまた、居間のソファに身を沈めて、テレビの外国映画を眺めたり、面白くもなさそうな顔で、週刊誌のページをパラパラとめくったりしている。おれはコーヒーを飲みながら、明日、銀座のスタジオで音入れ（録音）のある、コマーシャルフィルムのコメントに、手をいれている。これもいつもの事である。広告代理店に勤めるおれは、仕事を家に持ち帰ることがよくあるのだ。

明日の仕事に、一通りの目鼻がついて――

「寝るぞ」と、おれは立ち上がる。

「うん」と、五郎はそれだけ言う。

寝室には、早春のやや冷たい空気が流れている。おれは、小さなガスストーブをつけて、明かりを暗くし、ブリーフ一つでダブルベッドに入る。腹這いで煙草をふかしていると、入ってきた五郎は、おれがパジャマを着ていないのを見て、自分も脱いだ。白い真新しいビキニブリーフである。

このごろは、やつの方からおれに求めてくることは、まずなくなっている。おれが裸でベッドに入れば、やつが了解する。それも、最近は滅多にないことなのだが、五郎は何も言わない。おれは仕事の帰りが深夜になることも多いし、幾日も留守にする出張もある。「こいつ、適当に遊んでいるんじゃないかな」と考えることもあるし、たとえそうであっても、おれは一向に構わないのだが、おれが

105

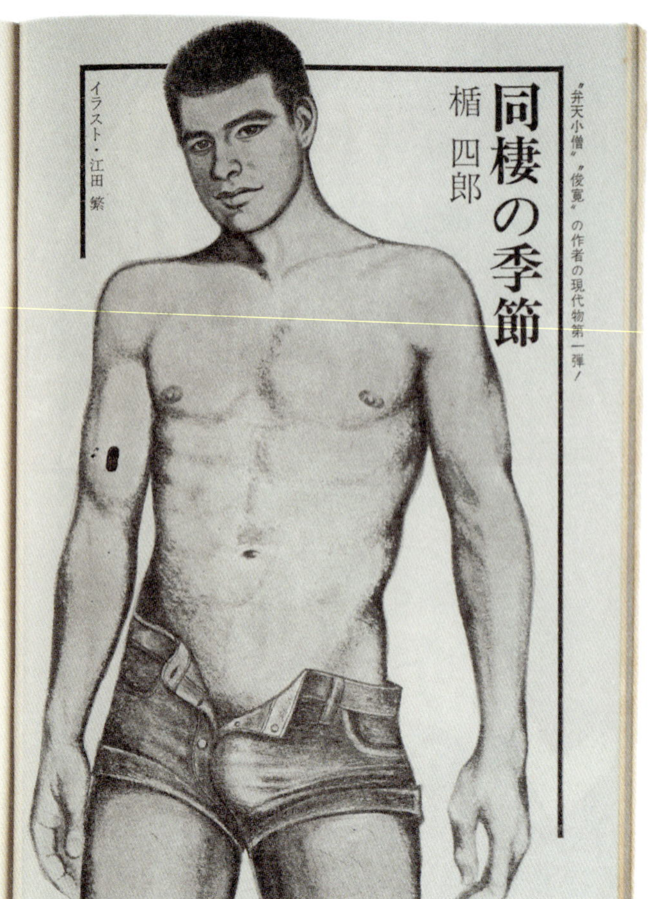

"弁天小僧""俊寛"の作者の現代物第一弾！

同棲の季節

楯 四郎

イラスト・江田 繁

took Nakahara's visual imprint further, emphasizing the distortions of his subjects' physiology and trailblazing the kawaii aesthetic both for *Barazoku* and for other productions. The *Barazoku* illustrators' intentional stylistic enlarging of characters' heads and eyes and diminishing of aspects of the rest of the body emphasized the "cute" aspect of kawaii as it is known globally today.

The first issue of *Barazoku* sold 10,000 copies immediately and showed mainstream booksellers that queer literature could be profitable. A typical issue of the magazine was around 124 pages (though later issues would become inflated to approximately 300 pages in the late 1970s), consisting of literature, interviews, advice columns, demonstrative "how-to" articles, community news, and personal ads—the personal ads being how the magazine made much of its revenue. The ads were placed by readers seeking relationships, romance, meetups, and sex, yet they featured no addresses in print, in order to protect advertisers' safety. The editors of *Barazoku* personally connected each individual who responded to the advertisements, working as an integrated and simultaneous dating service. Each issue of *Barazoku* featured copious photographs of fit and sporty younger men, both nude and clothed, yet it was not considered a pornographic magazine by many, despite the simulations of sex often depicted within.

Barazoku paved the way for competing queer magazines with national distribution that would further connect gay men across Japan, including *Adon* アドン, launched in 1974 by former *Barazoku* writer Minami Sadashirō 南定四郎, and *Sabu* さぶ, founded by editor Sakuragi Tetsurō 櫻木徹郎.

References:

Itō, Bungaku. *Barazoku henshūchō*. Tokyo: Gentōsha, 2006

McLelland, Mark J. "Sons, Brothers, Fathers and Lovers: Amae in Japanese Gay Personal Ads." In *Male Homosexuality in Modern Japan Cultural Myths and Social Realities*, 134–36. Richmond, Virginia: Taylor & Francis, 2005.

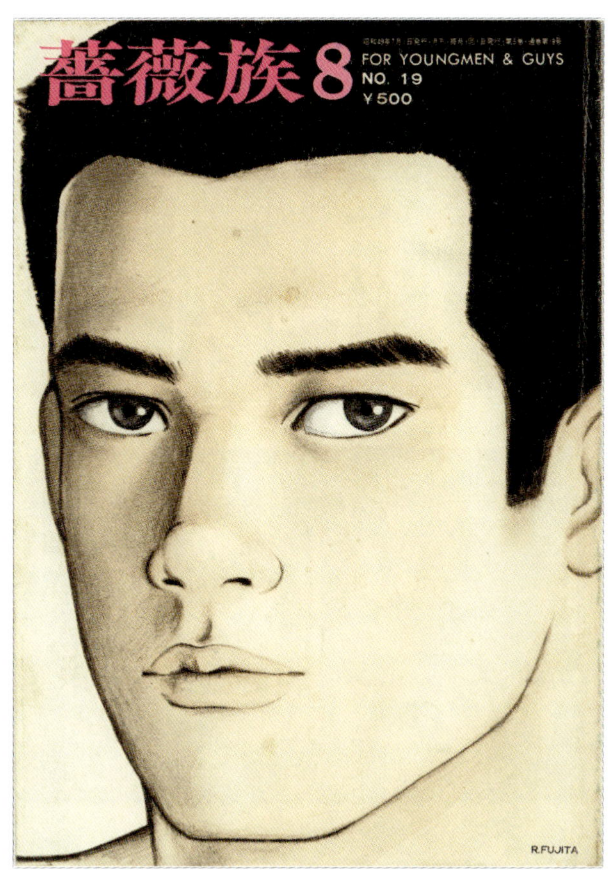

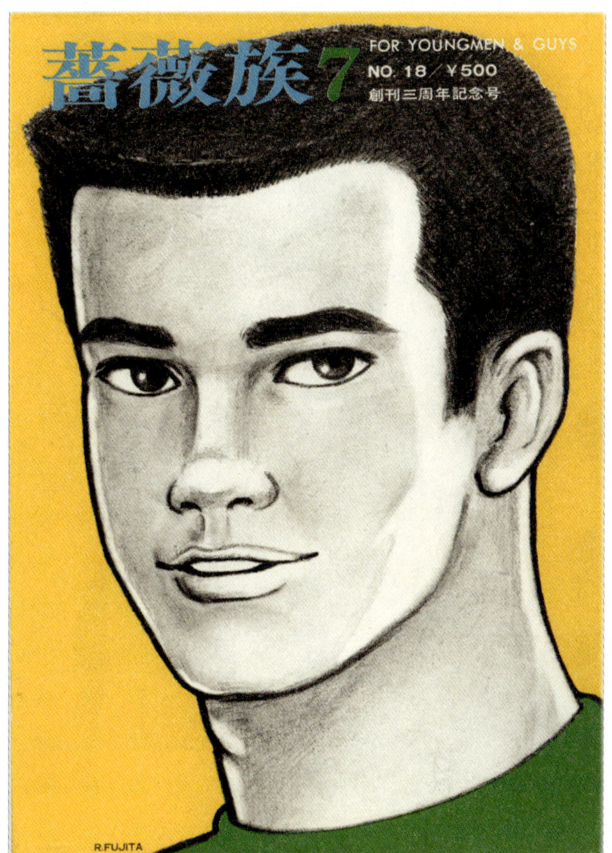

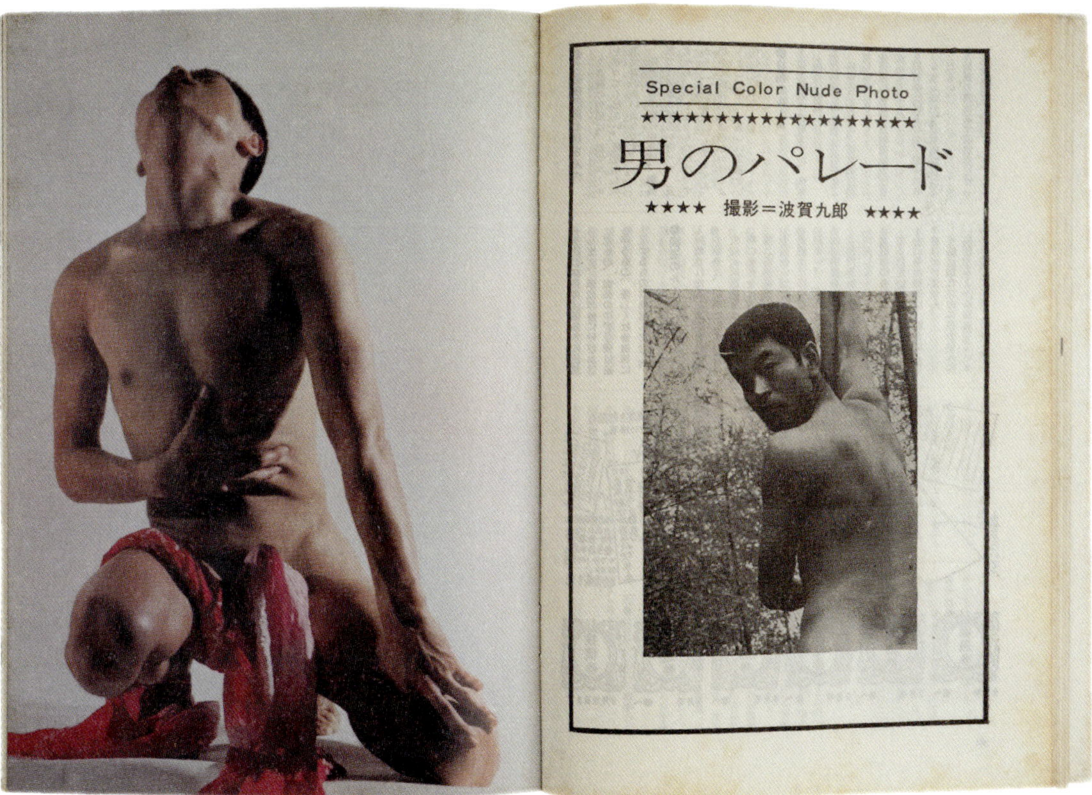

Covers and spreads from various 1970s issues of ***Barazoku* 薔薇族** published by Dainishobō 第二書房. Cover designs by Fujita Ryu 藤田竜.

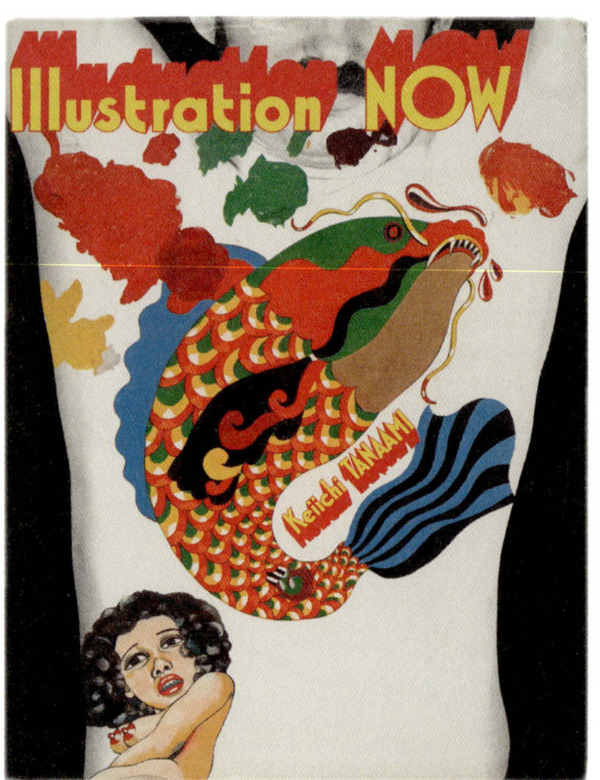

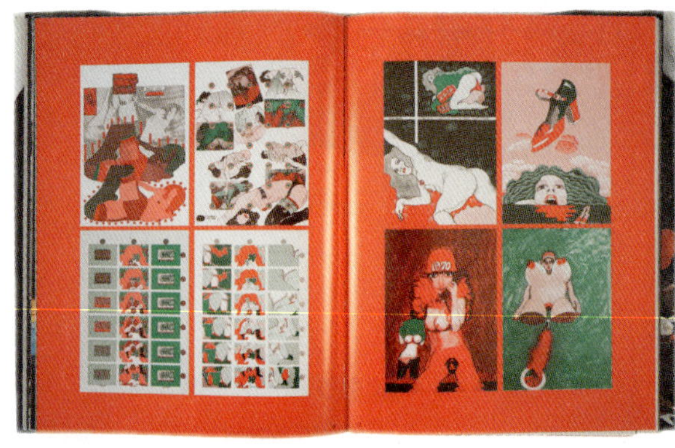

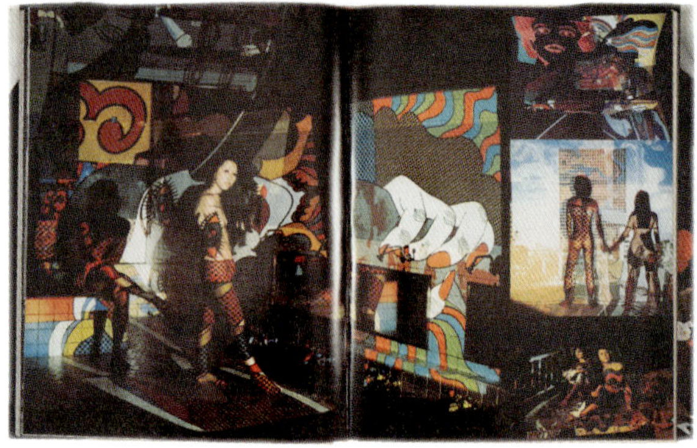

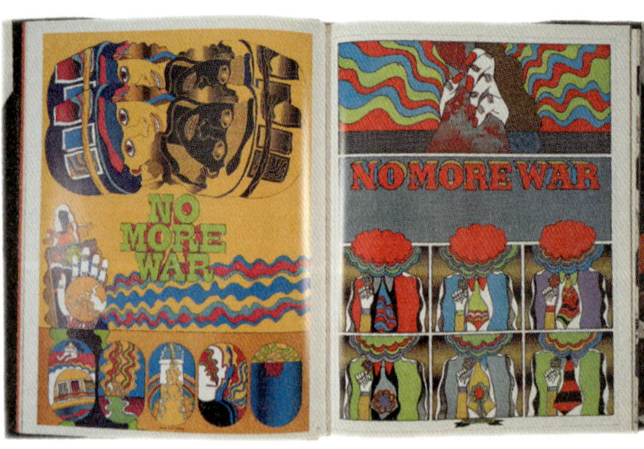

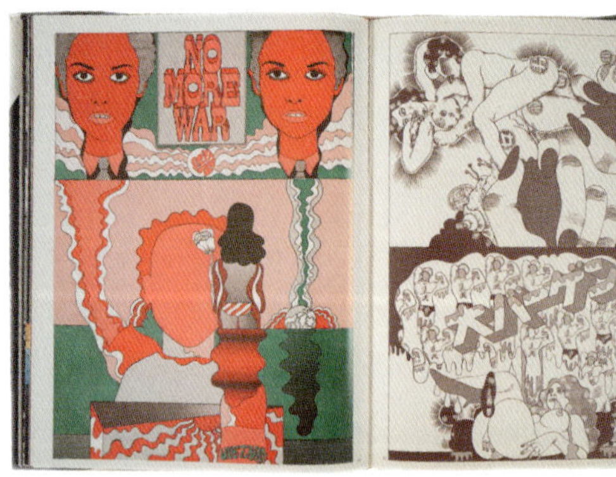

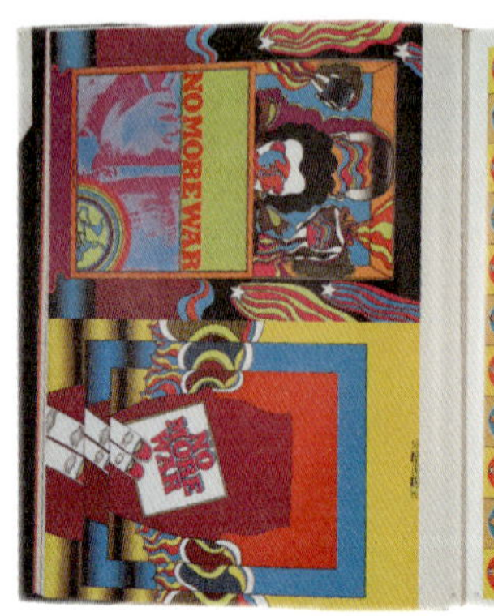

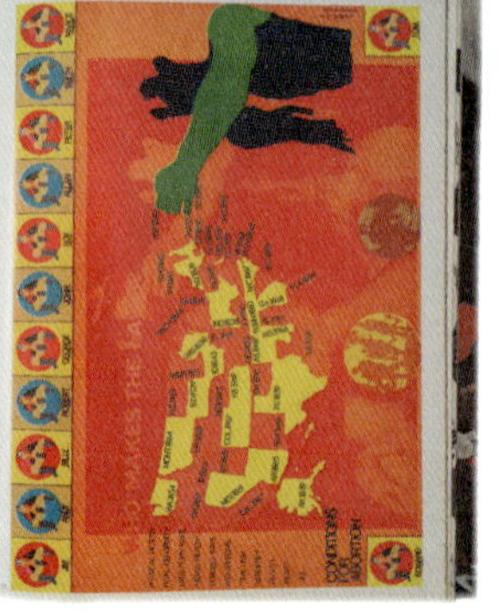

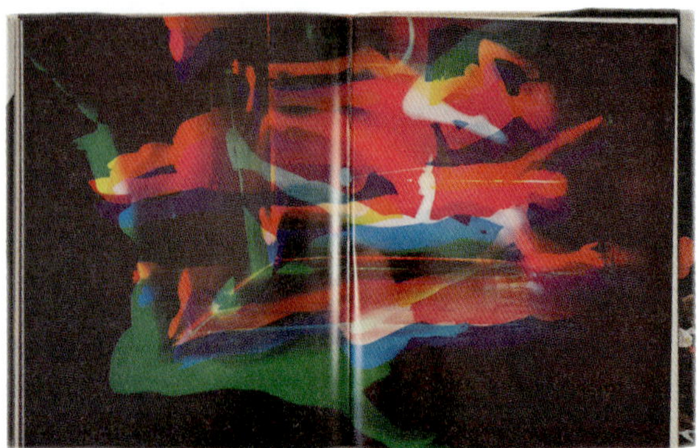

Illustration NOW Tanaami Keiichi Illustration NOW 田名網 敬一 (Tokyo: Rippu Shobou 立風書房, 1975).
Designed by Horiuchi Seiichi, this volume is dedicated to the sensual, psychedelic work of Tanaami.

TANAAMI KEIICHI 田名網敬一

1936–2024

Tanaami Keiichi was born in Tokyo into a family involved in the sale of textiles. Tanaami's family was opposed to his decision to become an artist or designer, as their "only concept of artists at the time was that they were 'dirty, womanizing, drunken derelicts living in poverty.'"[1] He was allowed to attend Musashino Art University on the condition that he study commercial art and design so that a "real job" would await him upon graduation. Exceeding his family's expectations, Tanaami's first large professional project was the art direction for *Mademoiselle* magazine, completed while still enrolled in university. Before graduating in 1958, Tanaami also won an award from the Japan Advertising Artists Club and was invited to become a member by mentor Awazu Kiyoshi.

Upon graduation, Tanaami took a job at the advertising agency Hakuhodo, though he would quit two years later to become freelance. Tanaami developed a style of collaging his own illustration with that of panels and textures from American comics and high-contrast photography, overlaying it all with booming display typography. He visited New York in 1967 and experienced a range of Andy Warhol's works, which inspired him to work across multiple media and to pursue a career as both a designer and an artist.

In the 1960s and 1970s, Tanaami designed the Japanese album covers for LPs by Jefferson Airplane and the Monkees and worked in animation, inspired by the work of illustrator, designer, and animator Yanagihara Ryōhei. He created three dozen animated analog short films during this time, holding screenings in Japan, Canada, Germany, and the US.

He became the first art director for the Japanese magazine *Monthly Playboy* 月刊プレイボーイ in 1975 and his experiences visiting the Playboy Mansion and Warhol's Factory that same year would lead Tanaami to create new bodies of work which explored "antisocial themes, critiques of the system, and the liberation of sexual expression." His 1976 exhibition *Super Orange of Love* was shut down by the police on the opening day due to the pornographic nature of much of the work.

Tanaami developed pulmonary edema in 1981 and was hospitalized for months—he would experience hallucinations during that time due to being heavily medicated, and the experience reinvigorated him: "I found a connection between being conscious of death so close to myself and to being alive, and that became the powerful energy that supported my creativity."

Tanaami exhibited internationally numerous times in the 1980s through the 2010s, his work again receiving critical acclaim. A few dozen monographs of his work have been published internationally, and throughout the 2000s, Tanaami continued to create commercial work, most notably for fashion brands such as Adidas, Mary Quant and Paul Smith.

In 1991, Tanaami became faculty at Kyoto University of Art and Design.

References:

Bold, Audrey. "Interview: Keiichi Tanaami." Gadabout. Gadabout, April 22, 2012. http://gadaboutmag.com/interview-keiichi-tanaami/.

Tanaami, Keiichi. *Tanaami Keiichi*. Tokyo: Ginza Graphic Gallery, 2006.

Tanaami, Keiichi. "Keiichi Tanaami." Nanzuka Underground, 2011. https://keiichitanaami.com/en/bio.html.

Tsuda, Rasa. "Interview with Keiichi Tanaami: Finding Pleasure under Hard Circumstances." Azito Art. Azito Art, April 2, 2015. http://azito-art.com/topics/finding-pleasure-under-hard-circumstances-interview-with-keiichi-tanaami/.

1 Nanzuka Underground. "Biography." Keiichi Tanaami. Nanzuka Underground. https://keiichitanaami.com/en/bio.html.

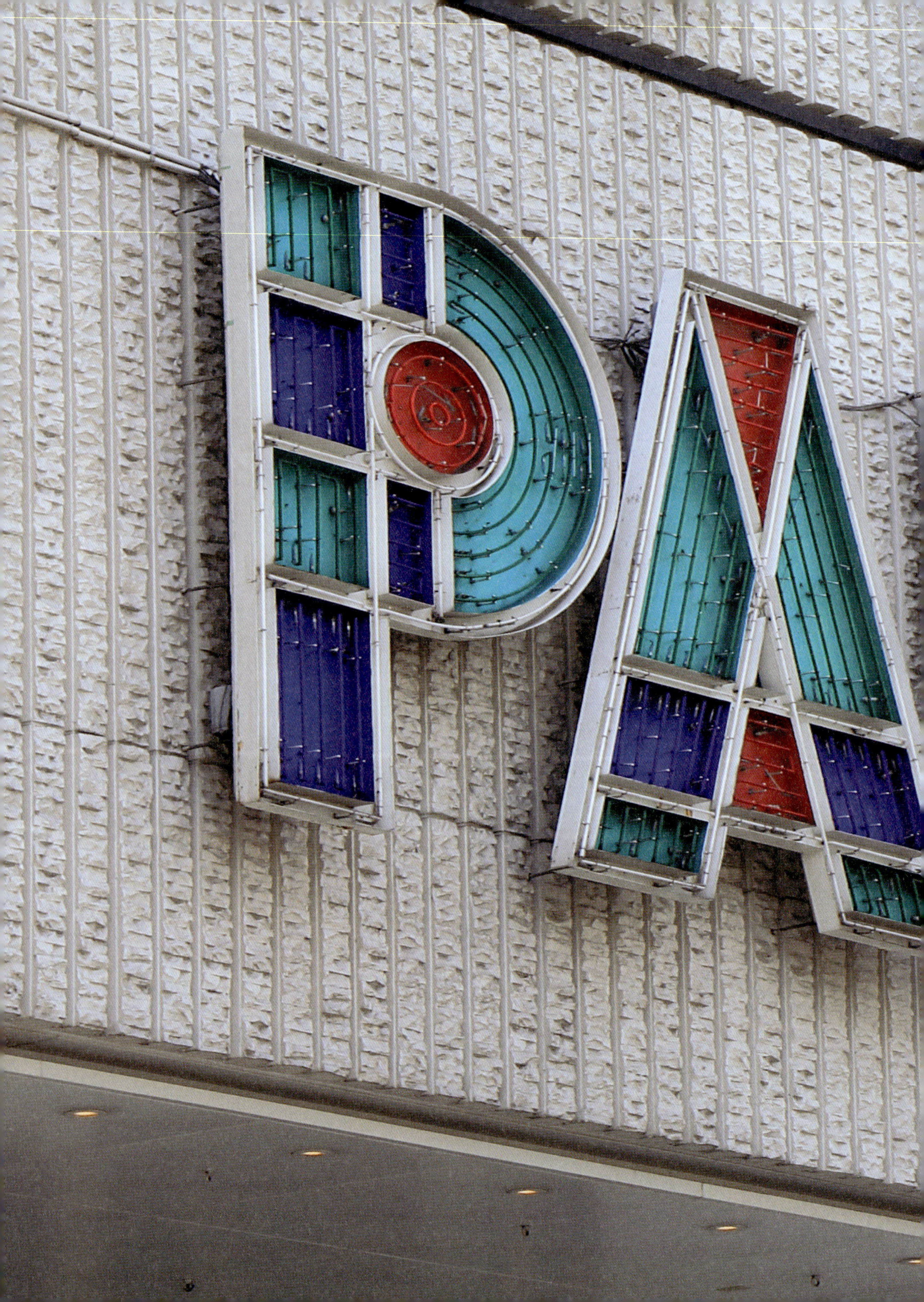
PA

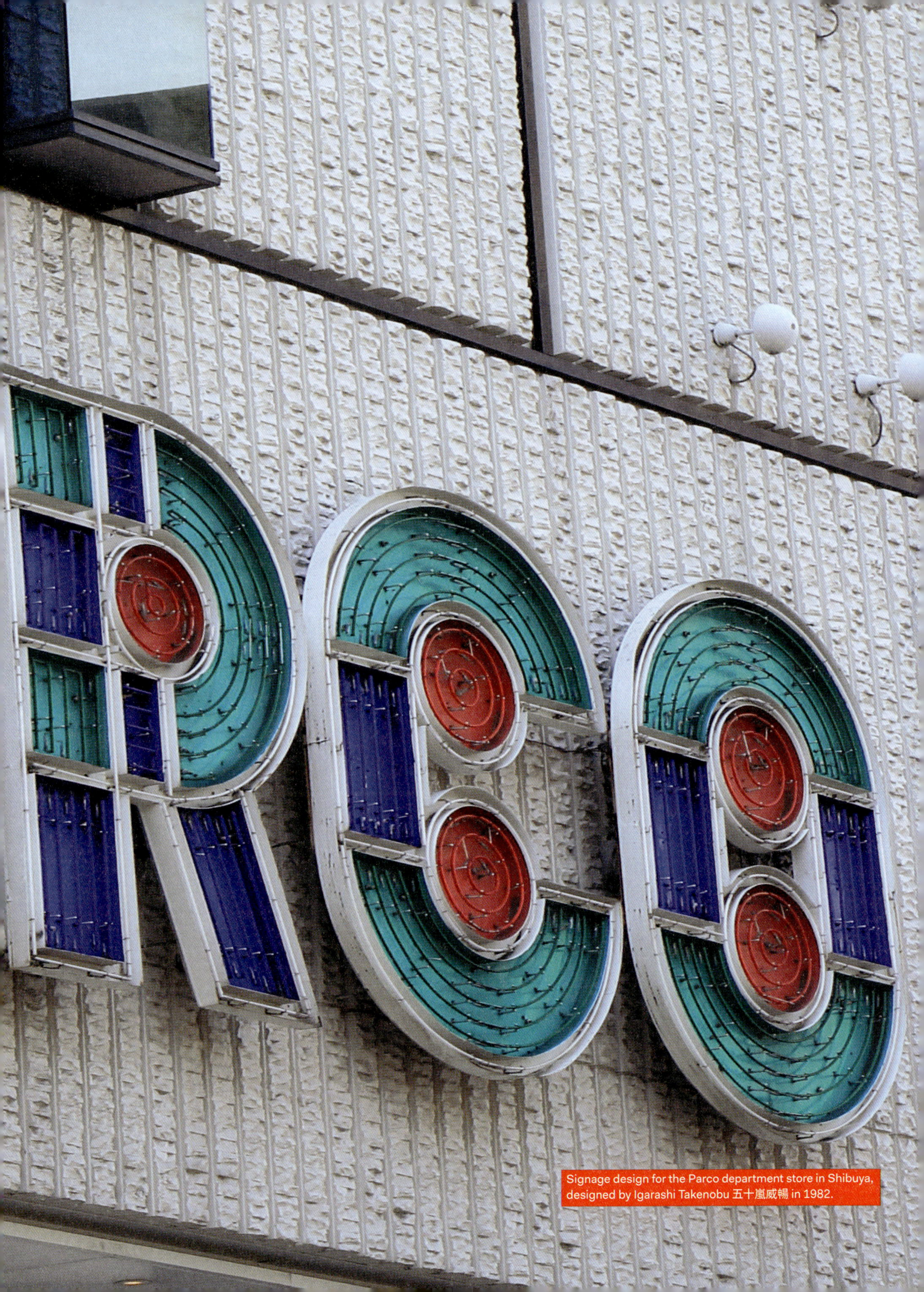

Signage design for the Parco department store in Shibuya, designed by Igarashi Takenobu 五十嵐威暢 in 1982.

IGARASHI TAKENOBU 五十嵐威暢

1944–

Born in Hokkaido in 1944, Igarashi graduated from Tama Art University in 1968 and completed his postgraduate studies at the University of California in 1969. He would go on to teach at UCLA after being the Head of the Design Department at Tama Art University, following in the footsteps of his predecessors Sugiura Hisui and Yamana Ayao.

Igarashi designed visual identity programs for Japanese clients such as Meiji Milk Products Co., Suntory Holdings, Mitsui Bank, and Tama Art University. He also designed numerous projects for international clients like MoMA, for whom he designed eight consecutive calendars featuring his iconic axonometric alphabets.

Regarding his practice, Igarashi writes that his "approach to design and sculpture has always wavered between my wish to do something useful for society, and my desire to create something beautiful with my own hands. In my opinion, there are three essential things in work: passion, challenge, and discovery. Without that, work gets boring; with that, work is enjoyable. Artwork that is enjoyable also results in success."[1]

Igarashi's seminal work for the Parco buildings' signage in Shibuya and Chōfu are masterpieces and icons of Japanese graphic design—two-dimensional layers given three-dimensional form and space. His 1987 book *Igarashi Alphabets: From Graphics to Sculptures* is an eclectic exploration of extrusion-based style that delights to this day.

In 1994, Igarashi ended his twenty-five years of design work and moved to Los Angeles to become a sculptor. He moved to Hokkaido in 2004, where he has been producing various installation-based artworks.

References:

Igarashi, Takenobu, and Sakura Nomiyama. *Takenobu Igarashi A–Z*. London: Thames and Hudson, 2019.

Igarashi, Takenobu. "Profile." Takenobu Igarashi. Takenobu Igarashi, 2015. http://www.takenobuigarashi.jp/profile.

Igarashi Takenobu, *Igarashi Alphabets from Graphics to Sculptures*, Zürich: ABC-Verlag, 1987.

1 Igarashi, Takenobu. "Introduction." Essay. In *Takenobu Igarashi: Design and Fine Art*, 12–13. New York: Graphis, Inc, 2018.

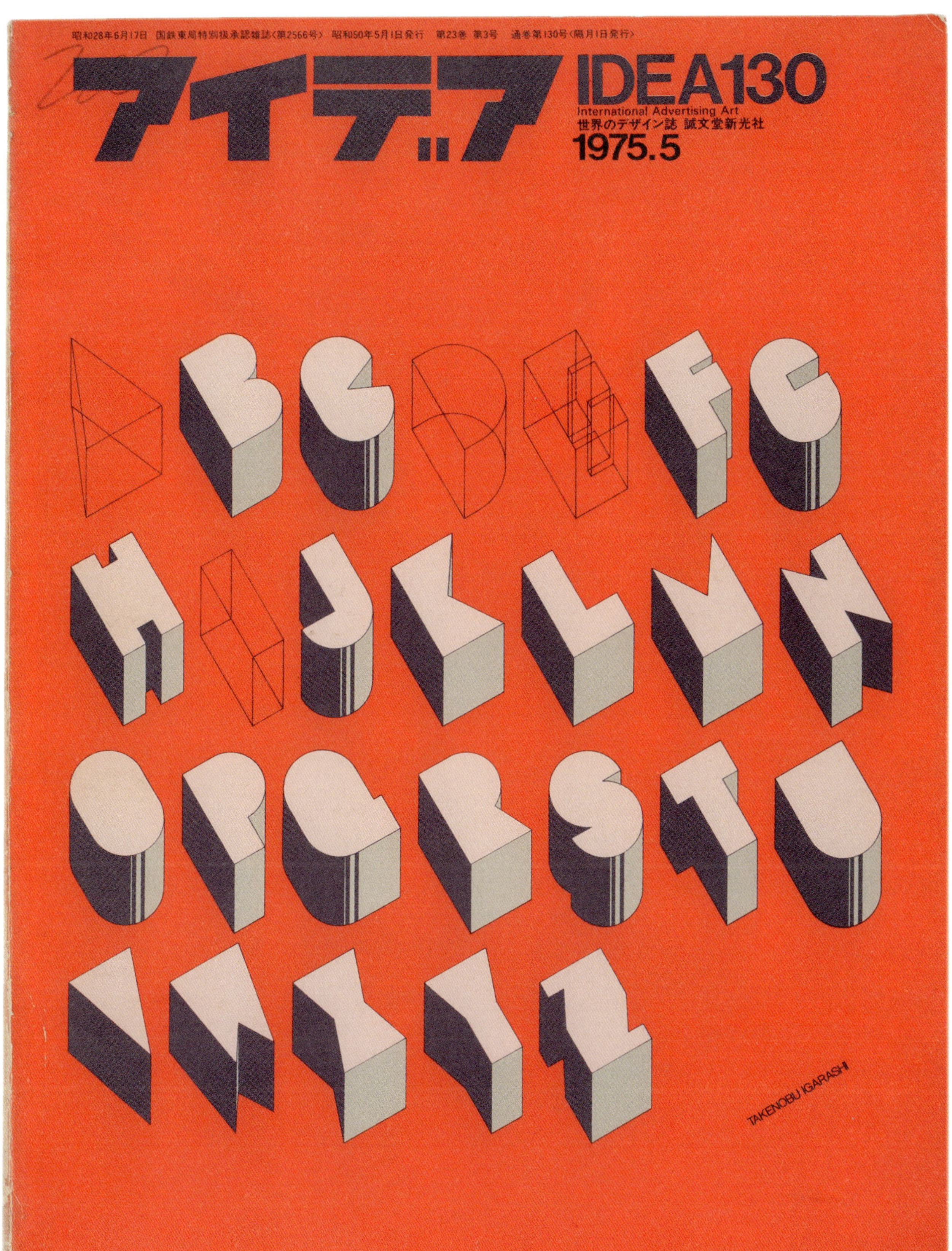

Cover design by Igarashi Takenobu 五十嵐威暢 for ***IDEA* アイデア No. 130** (Tokyo: Seibundo Shinkosha 誠文堂新光社, 1975). This cover design is typical of Igarashi's use of isometric or axonometric lettering.

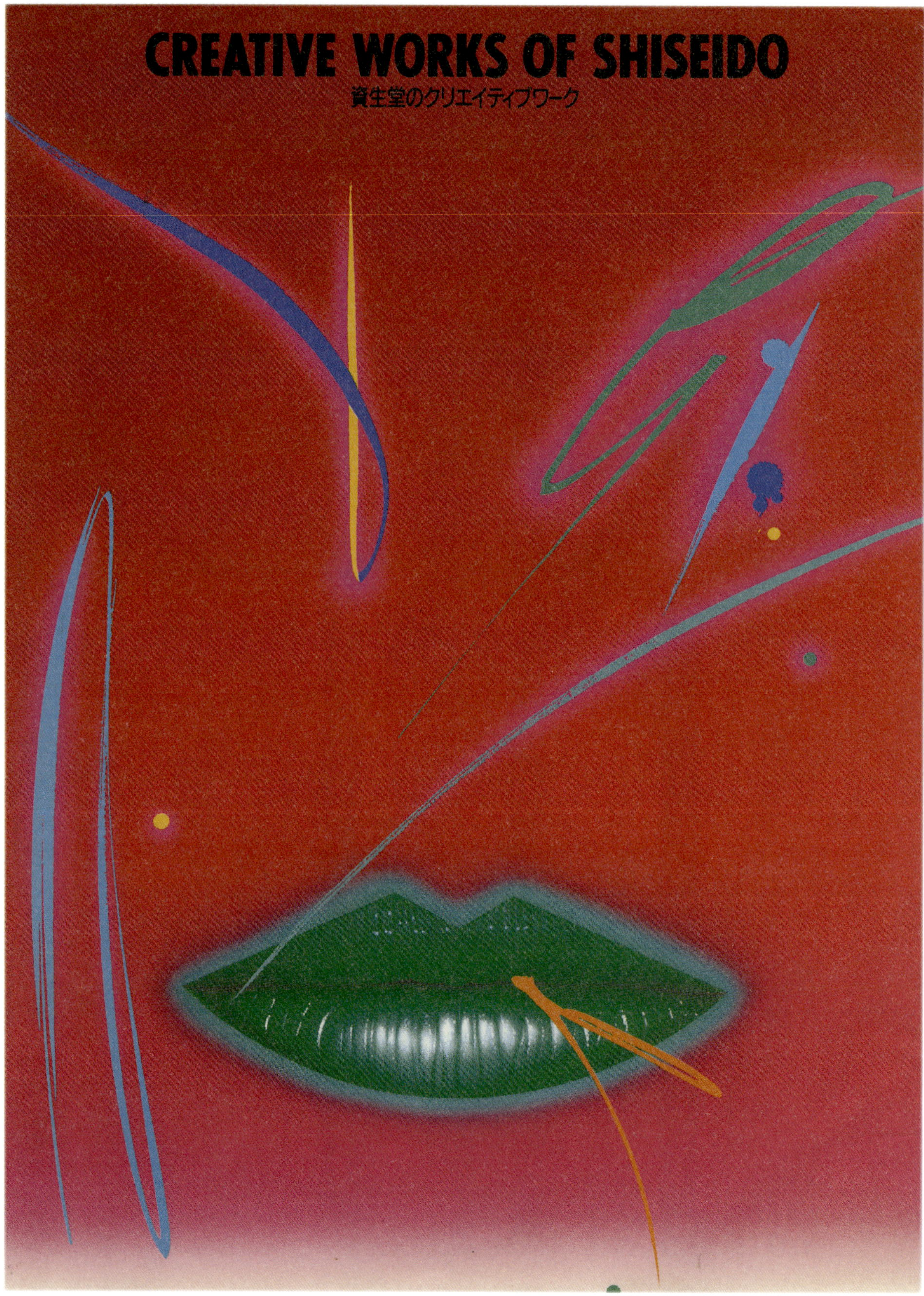

Creative Works of Shiseido with cover illustration by Sato Koichi 佐藤晃一 (Tokyo: Kyuryudo 求龍堂, 1985).

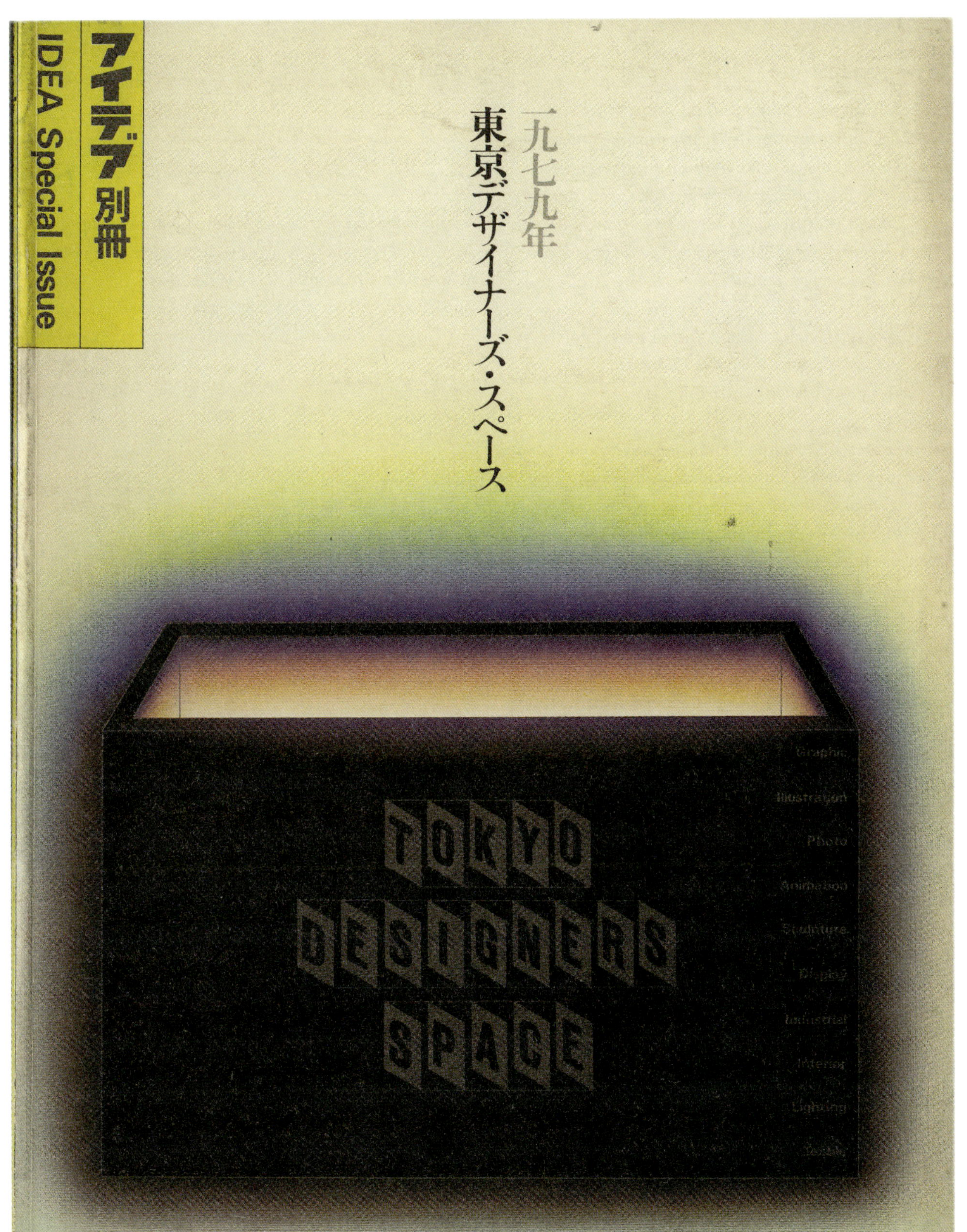

A "Special Issue" of ***Idea* アイデア** with cover illustration by Sato Koichi 佐藤晃一 **(Tokyo: Seibundo Shinkosha 誠文堂新光社, 1979).**

SATŌ KOICHI 佐藤晃一

1944–2016

Satō Koichi was born in Takasaki City in Gunma Prefecture in 1944. He graduated from the Design Department of Tokyo National University of Fine Arts in 1969. After working briefly for Shiseido after graduation, Satō went freelance in 1971, opening his own studio. His clients included theatrical groups, German fashion designer Jurgen Lehl, Mitsukoshi department stores, and Takeo Paper, amongst others.

Satō became a part-time lecturer at Tokyo University of the Arts in 1982 and was appointed to a full professorship at Tama Art University in 1995, where he worked until 2015.

Satō's work is replete with both futuristic imagery and traditional Japanese motifs. His best-known poster designs feature haunting, abstract, luminescent visual forms that are highly connotative—it is as if his compositions are emanating the metaphysical. His poster and book cover designs elude concrete statements, opting instead to *suggest* rather than depict. This poetic approach to expressing the metaphysical, inspired by his interests in haiku, music, and theater and his childhood infatuation with science, exude a visual poetry in step with the Japanese understanding of nonverbal communication. For Satō, even the quietest moment communicated meaning through his work, as did his sometimes delicate and sometimes vibrant use of gradated color.

A haiku practitioner, Satō harnessed the multivarious approach to emotion and scene-setting that is inherent in haiku poetry, wringing out profound emotion in his visual work and bringing the metaphysical to his compositions. His work is bound up in dichotomies, that of yore and that of the present, the natural and the artificial, light and dark, and cold and heat.

Early on in his career, Satō confronted his influences head on, creating a series of posters both in homage and in imitation of his design hero, Yokoo Tadanori. Regarding these early works, Satō wrote:

> *"Generally speaking, this is an age where we are cautioned against being imitative. If we take a close look at Japanese culture and many other cultures as well, we notice that imitation has always been one of the most important factors to make a culture evolve. In my view, it is important to trace the courses our precursors took in order empirically to test our own knowledge. I think so because it is important to accumulate empirical knowledge in evaluating the process of creating designs in our own styles. Only by doing so can we get the feel of the results of our efforts to create designs in our own styles. We will never be able to do so if we are content to steal others' ideas that fit our tastes. We can study really hard only by experiencing by ourselves the whole process of our precursors' creative work."*

Satō won the Mainichi Design Award in 1991, the Japanese Ministry of Education's Art Encouragement Prize in 1998, and a number of international poster competitions in Brno, Lahti, Helsinki, Warsaw, Essen, Moscow, Hong Kong, New York, and Toyoma. His work is included in many major museum collections.

Satō retired from Tama Art University in 2015 and died in 2016 at age seventy-one.

References:

Ishihara, Yoshihisa, and Koichi Sato. "Koichi Sato." In *1979 Nen Tokyo Dezainazu Supasu = 1979 Tokyo Designers Space*, 48–52. Tokyo: Seibundo Shinkosha, 1979.

Sato, Yoshiaki. "Spirit and Nature of Koichi Sato." *Idea* 1, no. 375 (October 2016): 103–4.

Taguchi, Atsuko. "Koichi Sato in Tama Art University." *Idea* 1, no. 375 (October 2016): 105–6.

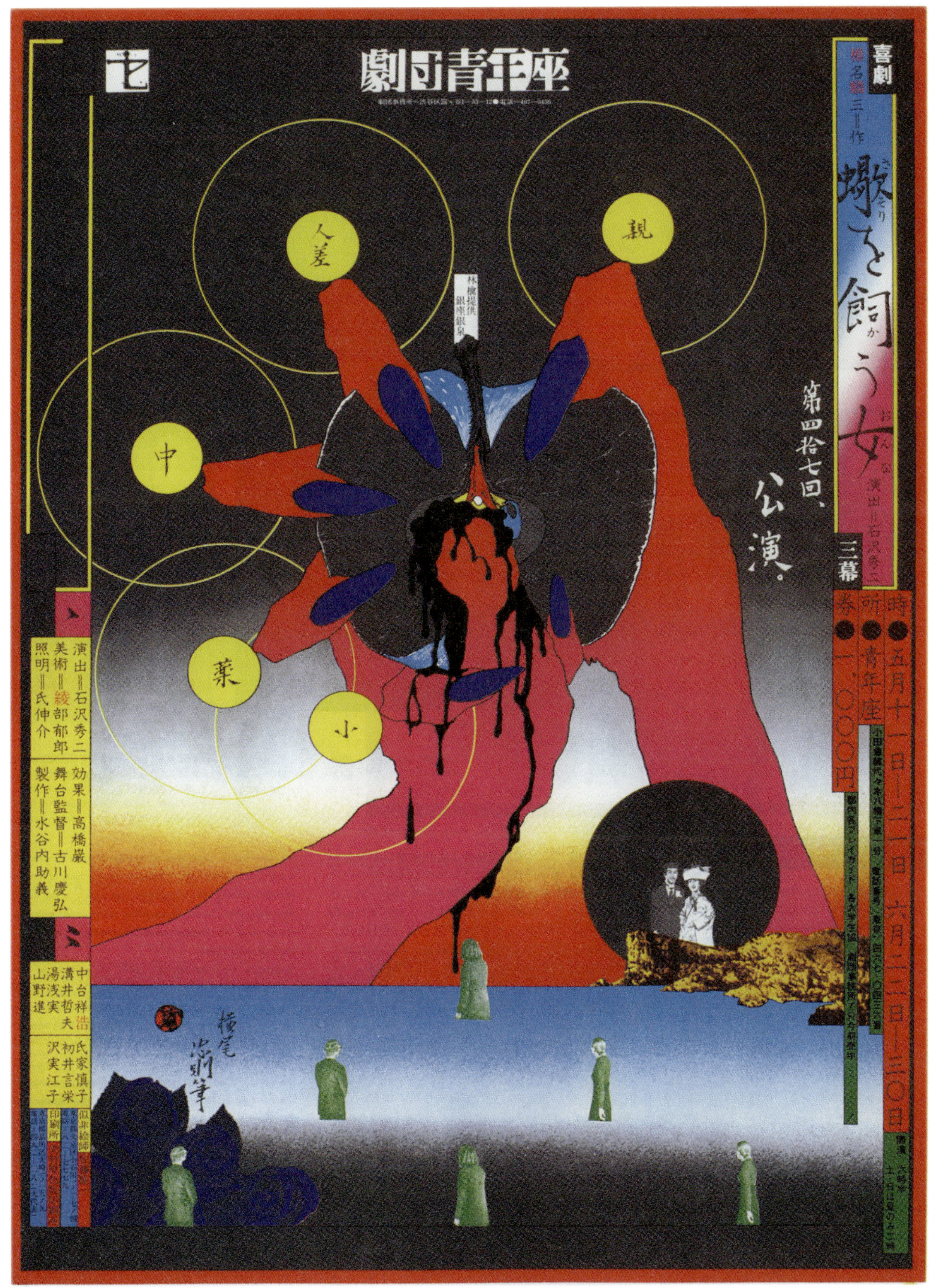

One of Sato Koichi's posters in homage to Yokoo Tadanori.

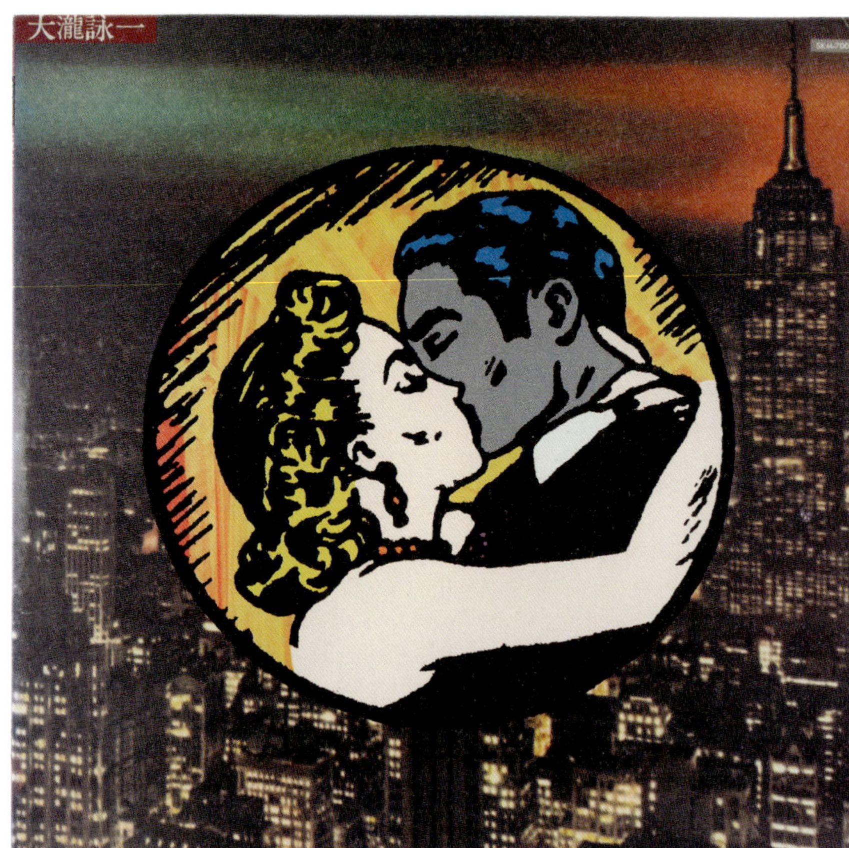

Ohtaki Eiichi, *Eiichi Ohtaki's Go Go Niagara! LP* (Tokyo: Niagara Records, 1976). Designed by WORKSHOP MU!!

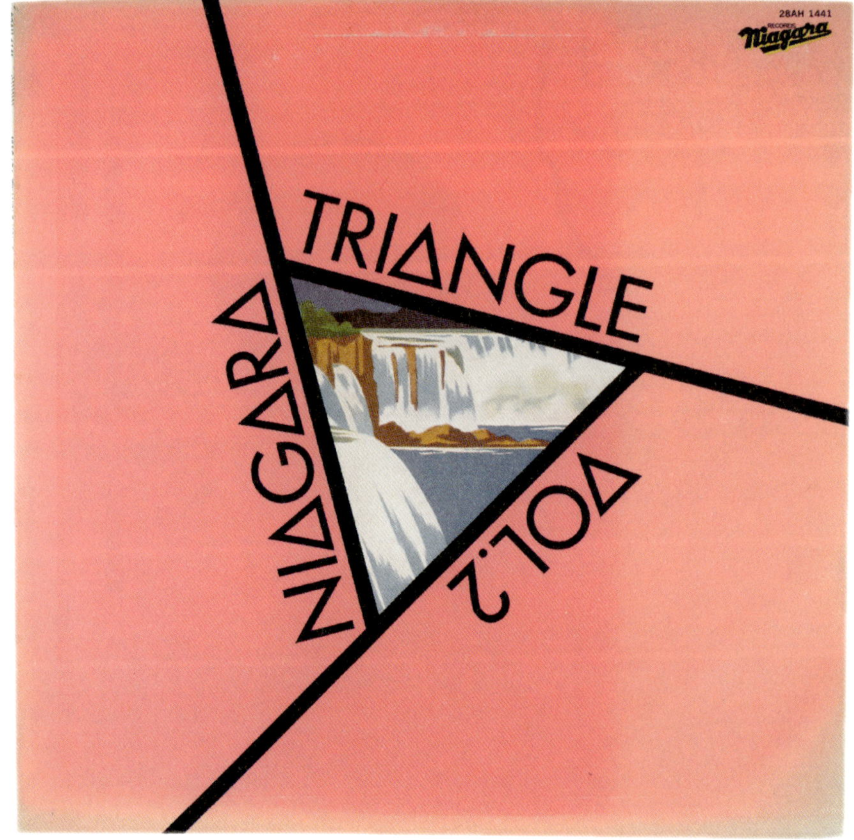

Niagara Triangle, *Volume 2* LP (Tokyo: Niagara Records, 1982). Designed by WORKSHOP MU!!

WORKSHOP MU!!: MANABE TATSUHIKO 眞鍋立彦, NAKAYAMA YASUSHI 中山泰 & OKUMURA YUKIMASA 奥村靫正

The three members of the design studio WORKSHOP MU!!—founder/president Manabe Tatsuhiko, Nakayama Yasushi, and Okumura Yukimasa—were drawn together through their love for antiques and American culture.

Manabe was born in 1946 in Fukuoka but later moved to Tokyo with his family, where they settled in the northwest part of the city, close to the United States Air Force housing area Grant Heights. Manabe would spend his childhood riding his bicycle to Grant Heights and soaking up as much American culture as he could. During his senior year in high school, he met the Hokkaido-born Nakayama while taking art classes at Ochanomizu Art School, and the two would go on to attend Kuwasawa Design School. At Kuwasawa, they met fellow student Okumura, also born in 1947, though he'd grown up in Aichi as the son of a businessman who was passionate about Nihonga painting. The trio's influences were quite wide-ranging, from Raymond Loewy, to underground American cartoonists, to Andy Warhol, to traditional Japanese art and culture. Fanatical music lovers, their range of interests would inspire the future studio to become one of the groundbreaking music packaging design studios in Japan from the 1970s onward.

Manabe, Nakayama, and Okumura specialized in graphic design at Kuwasawa, three students in a ten-person program which was largely taught by working designers. On a school trip to Kyoto, the three students bonded over their love for antiques. Okumura had been working at a family friend's antique shop in the Aoyama district and began curating and selling antiques with Manabe and Nakayama at that time, selling pieces at rock festivals and to interested collectors. Manabe and Nakayama founded WORKSHOP MU!! in 1969, Manabe leaving behind a job as an assistant at Kuwasawa, and Nakayama quitting a job at a Shinjuku design studio. The pair were joined by Okumura the following year, as he had been following his passion as an antique dealer and broker previously. From their first office in Aoyama, they began working in retro-styled pop collage-based compositions with materials from vintage American magazines from the 1930s through the 1950s. Manabe's future wife, Fukushima "Miiko" Masako, a fellow Kuwasawa graduate, was instrumental in the formation and early years of the studio, helping to make ends meet financially by working as a model while the small studio gained momentum.

WORKSHOP MU!!'S first client projects were for a newly founded independent record label called Mushroom. The connections that the studio members made working on Mushroom projects would help guide the rest of their careers, notably through their working relationship with musician and producer Hosono Haruomi, later of the notable bands Happy End はっぴいえんど and Yellow Magic Orchestra. WORKSHOP MU!! moved to a pair of American-style houses in the "American Village" section of Sayama in Saitama in 1971, with one house functioning as the studio and the other as living quarters for the three men and one woman. The rent was cheap and the space was ample—their client and collaborator Hosono moved into their neighborhood, and within a few years nearly the entirety of the "American Village" was occupied by members of WORKSHOP MU!!'s circle of friends. Studio work was executed by a handful of apprentices over the years, including Tachibana Hajime 立花ハジメ, who would go on to have successful dual careers as both a musician and a designer, and the photographer Mike Nogami 野上眞宏, who would move to New York in the late 1970s and pursue photography there.

WORKSHOP MU!!'s early projects were a mix of vernacular graphics and staged photography—their interest in 1950s postwar American visual culture was as much a part of their fashion statements at that time (Hawaiian shirts, saddle shoes, sukajan nylon-and-silk bomber jackets, blue jeans, and greased-up pompadours) as it was the impetus for their design work. Their LP cover and packaging designs for Kosaka Chu, the Sadistic Mika Band, and Asada Hiroshi explored assorted American design tropes, from the employment of Hawaiian shirt patterns to postcard-style illustrated display lettering. The trio used recycled illustrations from the 1950s to great effect for the design of the literary journal Politea and for the debut LP by Ohtaki Eiichi. It was this aesthetic that would help define the visual style surrounding Ohtaki and Hosono's band Happy End, the first rock band in Japan to sing completely in Japanese and whose commercial success paved the way for future Japanese popular music.

One of the most lasting visual contributions that WORKSHOP MU!!! offered was the art direction and design for Ohtaki's record label, Niagara. The label's visual inspiration was from the packaging and advertisements for a brand of laundry starch called Niagara. The design of Ohtaki's solo album *Niagara Moon* is a re-creation of a Niagara starch box, though with modifications of the text on the cover and the addition of a few new visual elements, notably a retro illustration of a couple admiring

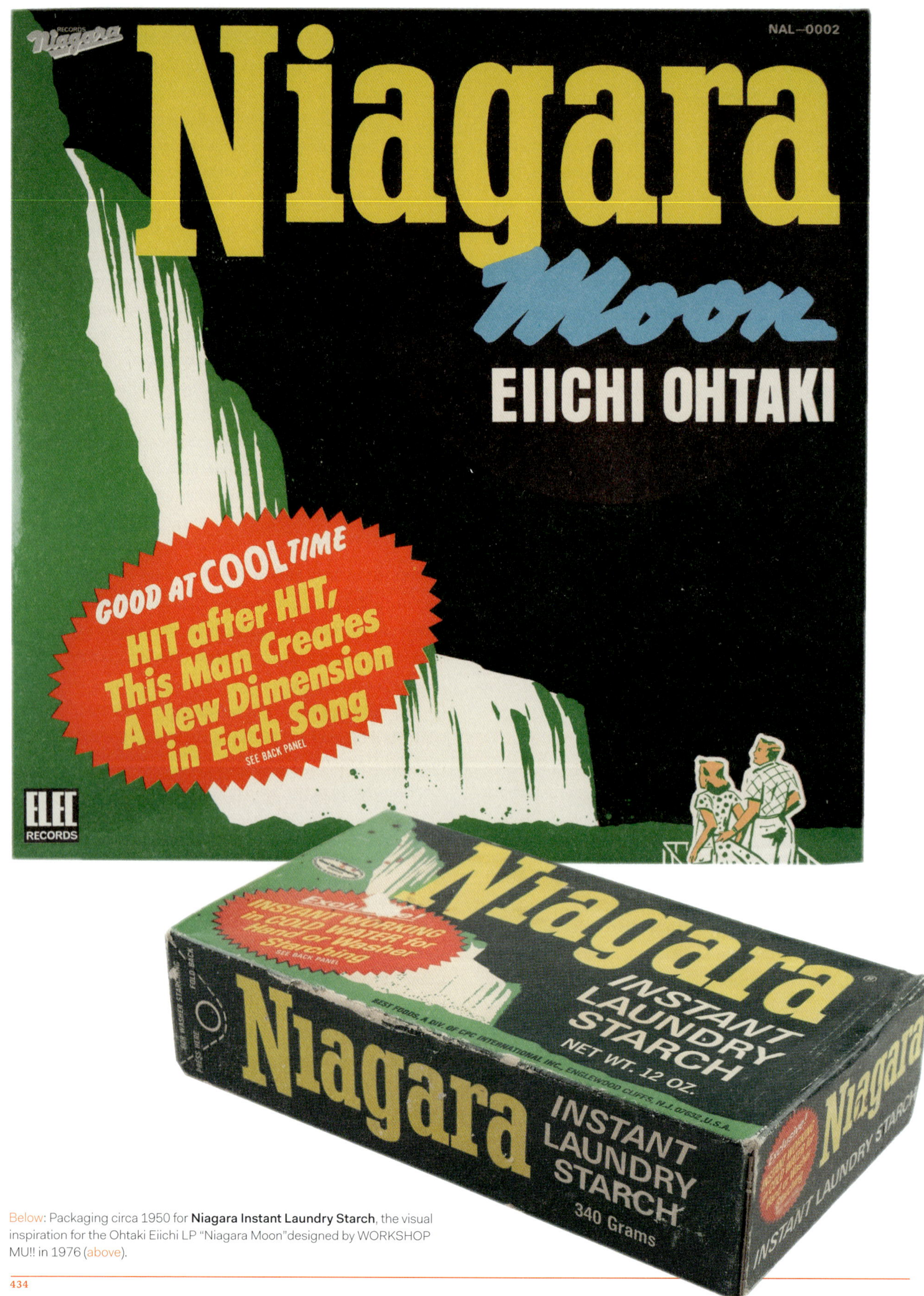

Below: Packaging circa 1950 for **Niagara Instant Laundry Starch**, the visual inspiration for the Ohtaki Eiichi LP "Niagara Moon"designed by WORKSHOP MU!! in 1976 (above).

Niagara Falls in the lower right-hand corner. This act of appropriation foreshadowed similar Postmodern moves in the West by a handful of years.

WORKSHOP MU!! dissolved amicably in 1976, with each of the designers pursuing solo careers. Nakayama continued designing the Niagara Records catalog, creating a visual feast of retro aesthetics. Manabe worked on projects for VAN Jacket, a definitive Tokyo fashion brand, and became the director of DO!FAMILY, a clothing line and associated shop in Harajuku. Okumura designed iconic album covers for bands like Tin Pan Alley and Checkers, though he is best known for his album cover designs for Yellow Magic Orchestra's LPs *BGM* and *Technodelic*, which feature imagery appropriated from a turn-of-the-century Russian journal. Okumura founded his own practice, The Studio Tokyo Japan, Inc., in 1977, teaches at Joshibi University of Art and Design, and was the first known designer to use desktop publishing to produce design work in Japan commercially in 1989.

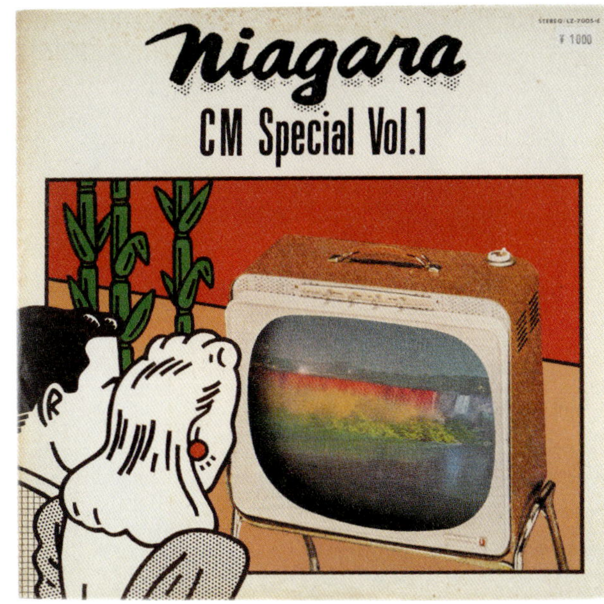

V/A, ***Niagara CM Special Volume 1*** compilation LP (Tokyo: Niagara Records, 1981). Designed by WORKSHOP MU!!

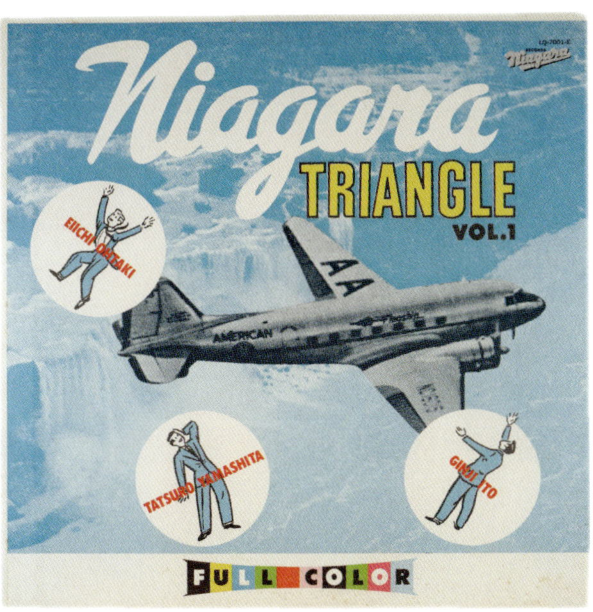

Niagara Triangle, "Volume 1" LP, (Tokyo: Niagara Records, 1976). Designed by WORKSHOP MU!!

References:
Murakami, Ryū. *Post: Poppu aato no Aru Heya*. Tokyo: Kōdansha, 1986.

Nogami, Mike, and Nagisawa Ohkawa. *Workshop Mu: Designing from 1970 and Forever*. Tokyo: Shufu no Tomosha, 2006.

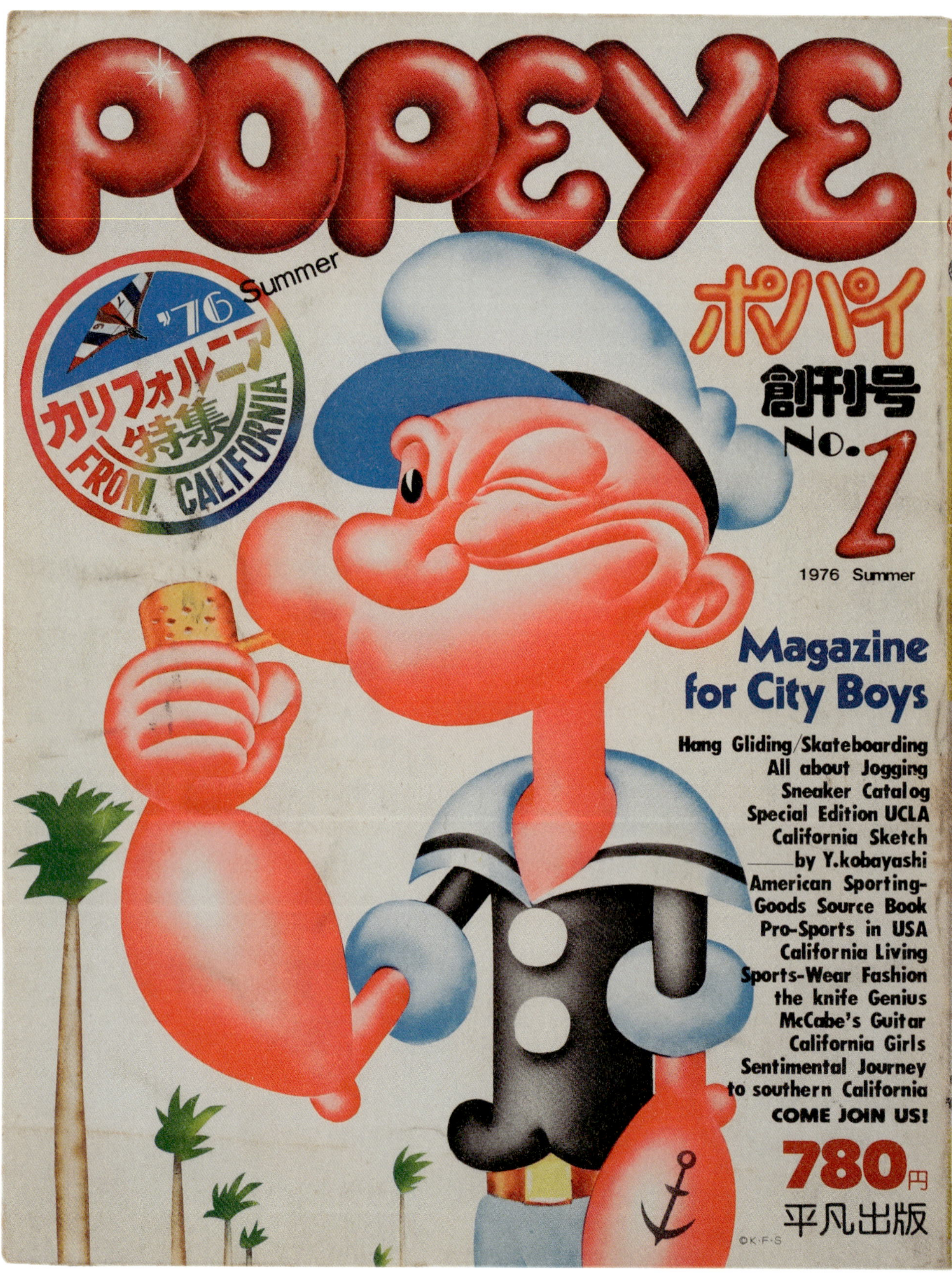

The inaugural issue of ***Popeye* ポパイ** published by Heibonsha 平凡社 in 1976, with the subtitle "Magazine for City Boys" and billed as "Men's An An" on the inside cover. This first issue is a guide to the Southern California lifestyle, introducing sports like skateboarding and hang gliding and showcasing assorted fashion items and brands, and includes geographic guides.

HORIUCHI SEIICHI 堀内誠一

1932–1987

Horiuchi Seiichi was born in Tokyo. He attended Nihon University's Primary School 日本大学第一高等学校 and spent his childhood in Rainbow Studio, the graphic design business run out of tenement houses owned by his father, Horiuchi Haruo 堀内治雄. Rainbow Studio was inspired by and modeled after the elder Horiuchi's time working at Tada Hokuu's Sun Studio, one of Japan's first design studios.

Horiuchi joined the Isetan Department Store's publicity department in Shinjuku, in 1947 at the age of fourteen and worked there for nine years, designing window displays, props, advertisements, and packaging. Horiuchi was heavily involved in the design and production of Isetan's publicity magazine, *Bouquet* ブーケ, starting in 1951, and in 1953 he began designing the entire magazine himself.

He was involved in the design and art direction of a number of other magazines in the mid-1950s, such as *ARS Camera* ARS カメラ, *Camera Club* カメラクラブ, and Minolta's monthly promotional photography magazine, *Rokkor* ロッコール. In these photography-themed publications, any pages not featuring photography tended to use Horiuchi's illustration or abstract geometric compositions.

Horiuchi left Isetan in 1956 and co-founded the company Ad Center in 1957, working across editorial design, packaging design, and illustration. Ad Center was notable in that, beyond design work, the company also specialized in the planning stages of advertising for print, radio, and television. One of Ad Center's main clients was Heibonsha 平凡社, the publisher of the prominent men's lifestyle and fashion magazine *Heibon Punch* 平凡パンチ, which had taken Japan by storm with its appeal to youth and emerging salarymen alike. *Punch*'s editorial focus during the turbulent '60s was on consumption in lieu of politicization, and it operated as a brand and style manual for youth fashions. Horiuchi worked on *Punch*'s fashion pages, art directing, designing, and writing copy since the magazine's auspicious launch in 1964.

Horiuchi art directed the spin-off magazine *Weekly Heibon Punch for Girls* from 1968 to 1970 and the magazine's relaunch as *An An* アンアン in 1970, for which he provided the total art direction and design for what would become an icon in the Japanese publishing scene. *An An* featured fashion photography of both male and female Japanese models shot in exotic locales around the world. Each issue balanced nuanced typography, pop illustration, and vibrantly colored hand lettering. Horiuchi was awarded the Tokyo Art Directors Club Prize for his work for *An An* in 1971, though the magazine was operating financially in the red.

Horiuchi departed Ad Center in 1969 and went freelance, focusing on editorial design work, including the magazine *Chi to Bara* 血と薔薇 (*Blood & Roses*), the "Revue of Eroticism, Homosexuality, Sadism, Masochism, Fetishism, Narcissism, Infantilism, Magic, the Occult, New Humor, Complexes and the Psychic"—this subhead emblazoned in French on the cover of each issue. *Chi to Bara*'s debut featured a highly sexualized photographic feature of writer and novelist Mishima Yukio portraying the Christian martyr Saint Sebastian alongside a text written by Mishima calling for "a moral revolution." The cover of the second issue depicted a nude male's lower torso clad in a chastity belt with one leg in black pantyhose topped with a ribbon of black silk. Only four issues of *Chi to Bara* were published, but each was incredibly shocking, offering "an outlet for readers suffering from complexes and for readers suffering from too few"—a bounty of both eros and cruelty in each issue.

Following his pioneering work for *An An*, Horiuchi created the logo design, art direction, and illustration for the men's fashion magazine *Popeye* in 1976. *Popeye* launched with an issue devoted to Californians' lives and lifestyles, featuring a vibrant fluorescent-pink illustration of the spinach-munching sailor under a three-dimensional pink-bubble-lettered masthead with a row of palm trees in the background. As with many of his projects, Horiuchi included detailed hand-drawn maps of his travels through featured locales. Throughout his tenure as art director and designer of assorted titles published by Heibonsha, locations as wide-ranging as Italy, Mexico, France, and Los Angeles would be dissected under Horiuchi's gaze and dedicated to paper.

In 1980, he undertook the same scope of labor for the first issue of the sibling men's lifestyle magazine *Brutus*, designing the logo, art directing the magazine, and occasionally providing lively illustrations for features within. *Brutus* became the blueprint for urban lifestyle magazines in Japan, with Horiuchi regularly contributing from abroad, as he had relocated full-time to France right before *Brutus*'s launch. An accomplished photographer, Horiuchi would fill in for photographers as needed if none were on location.

Horiuchi also designed the logotype and did some art direction for *Olive*, the "Magazine for City Girls," since its launch in 1982. Originally, *Olive* was published as a special edition of *Popeye* aimed at a younger demographic than *An An*, to ensnare the hearts and wallets of younger female consumers.

Publishing *Brutus* and *Popeye* for men to match different demographics (*Popeye* for younger men and *Brutus* for older men) and *An An* and *Olive* for varied demographics for women was a strategic move on Heibonsha's part, with Horiuchi art directing for the appropriate gender, age, and income category—often through the mail. Horiuchi's approach was largely formulaic, in that each issue consisted of a mix of lifestyle photography, product-catalog documentation of current trends, and documentation of a foreign or domestic locale.

Horiuchi was a prolific writer, illustrator, and designer of picture books for children—his first title, *Blanky the Black Horse* くろうまブランキー, was published in 1958 and was followed by a score of other popular books numbering 110 in total.

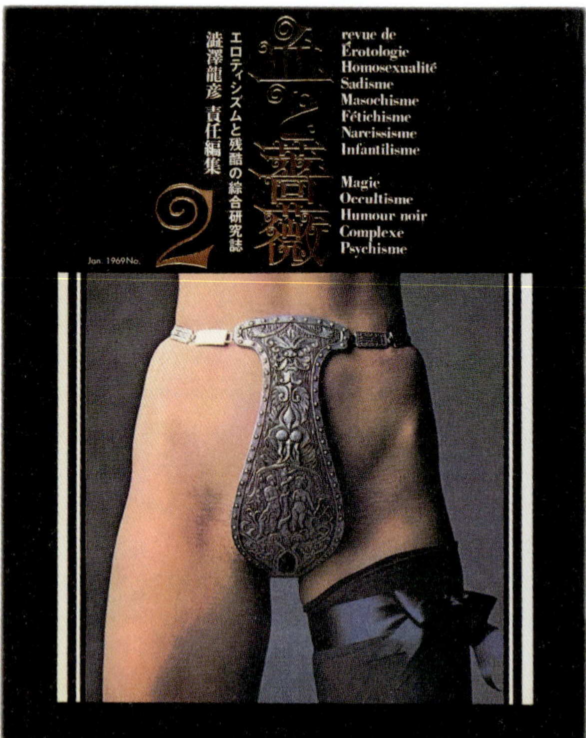

Above: Cover of the second issue of ***Chi to Bara* 血と薔薇**, or ***Blood & Roses***, the "Revue of Eroticism, Homosexuality, Sadism, Masochism, Fetishism, Narcissism, Infantilism, Magic, the Occult, New Humor, Complexes and the Psychic" (Tokyo: Tensei Shuppan 天声出版, 1969). The cover features a male figure's shorn lower torso clad in a chastity belt with a stocking and ribbon adorning one leg.

Below: ***Chi to Bara* 血と薔薇** Issue No. 1 (Tokyo: Tensei Shuppan 天声出版, 1968) opens with an iconic photo shoot of author Mishima Yukio 三島由紀夫 recreating the legend of Saint Sebastian in pin-up form.

References:

Horiuchi, Seiichi. *Horiuchi Seiichi, 1932-1987: Zasshi to Ehon no Sekai*. Hiratsuka-shi: Hiratsuka-shi Bijutsukan, 1999.

Horiuchi, Seiichi. *Chichi no Jidai Watakushi No Jidai: Waga Editoriaru Dezainshi*. Tōkyō: Magajin Hausu, 2007.

Itoi, Shigesato. "Horiuchi-san." ほぼ日刊イトイ新聞. Hobo Nikkan Itoi Shinbun, January 4, 2017. https://www.1101.com/horiuchi/.

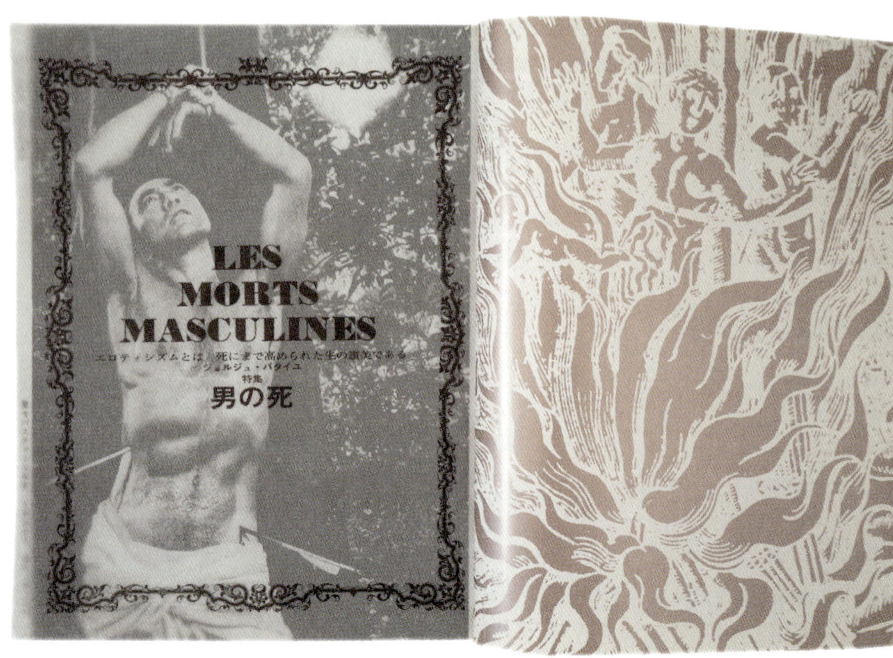

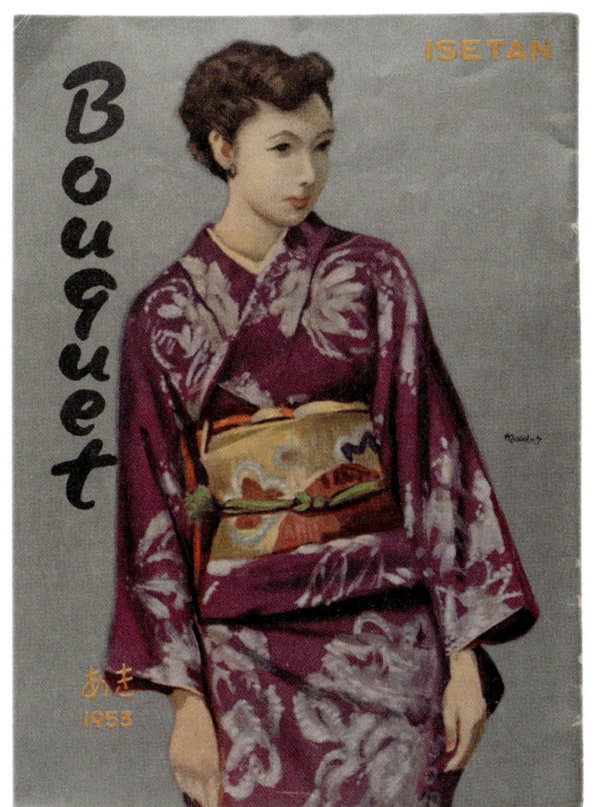

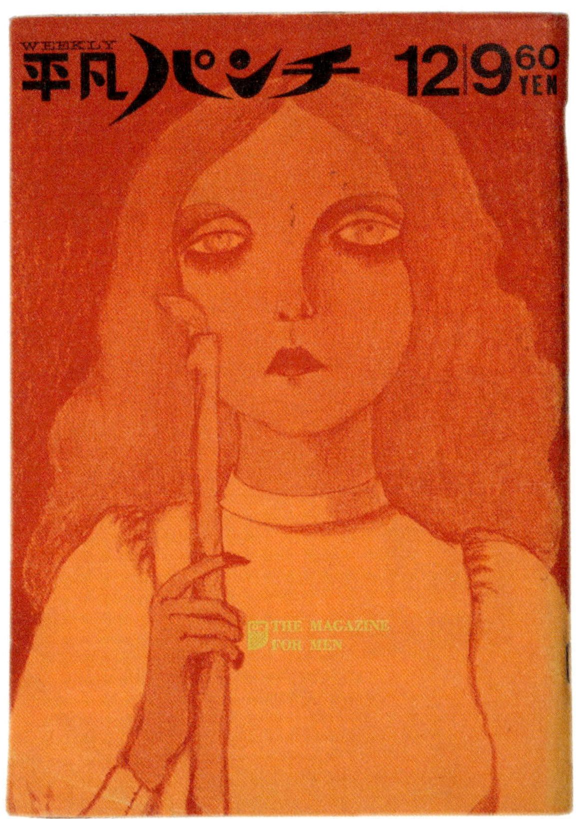

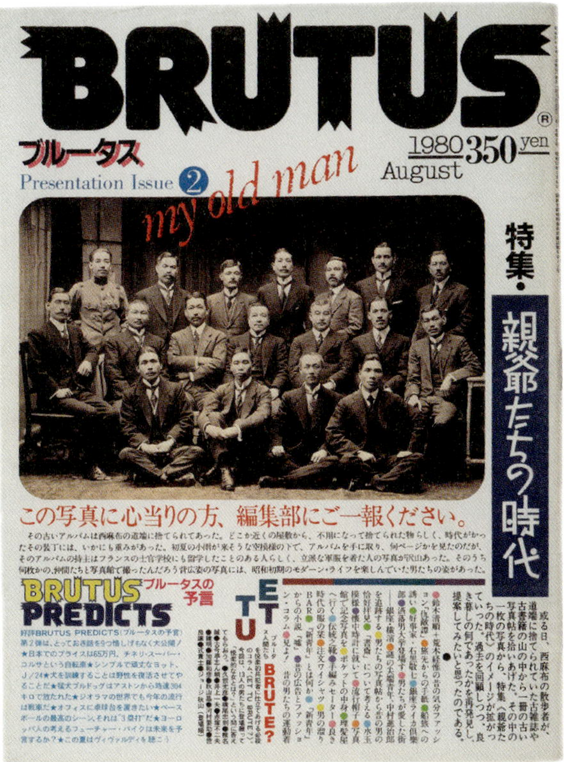

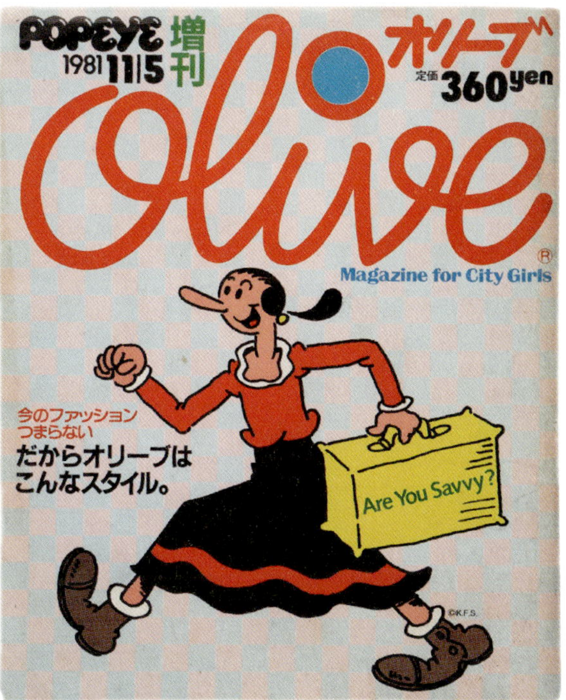

Clockwise from top left: ***Bouquet* ブーケ, Fall issue (Tokyo: Isetan 伊勢丹, 1953)**; ***Weekly Heibon Punch* 刊平凡パンチ Vol. 236, (Tokyo: Heibonsha 平凡社, 1968)**; ***Brutus* ブルータス No. 2 (Tokyo: Heibonsha 平凡社, 1980).**; the inaugural 1981 issue of ***Olive* オリーブ (Tokyo: Heibonsha 平凡社, 1981)**, published with the subtitle "Magazine for City Girls," was released as an "extra issue" of the magazine *Popeye* ポパイ in an attempt to market lifestyle and fashion to an urban and suburban, upper-middle-class, teenage, female target audience.

conclusion

Brace-u

Conclusion

So much has happened in Japanese graphic design since 1975: the rise of video game culture, the advent of emoji, and the explosive proliferation of graphic design due to the desktop-publishing revolution. The past near-fifty years is so rich that it should be cataloged in its own book. Graphic design in Japan continues to thrive today, perhaps in spite of itself. Wages for designers are usually lower than in the United States and Western Europe, yet there is a pride and a sense of history and dignity in the culture of graphic design in Japan that is often elevated above design culture in the West.

Perhaps this is due in large part to documentation—there is value to history in Japan that is both implicit and explicit. The history of architecture in Japan is one of near-constant building and razing in lieu of preservation. The history of Japanese graphic design is perhaps the opposite—Japan is a book culture, one that is obsessed with printed matter, and the culture of Japanese graphic design is preserved in print simultaneously as documentation and as artifact. This has somehow happened despite firebombings, earthquakes, nuclear attacks, tsunami, and countless other disasters.

Saddled with subtropical weather patterns, the Japanese climate is not good for print. Monasteries and libraries prior to the Meiji Restoration took to airing books outside on days with dry weather. Perusing antiquarian books in Tokyo's lively Jimbōchō bookselling district, even the most casual observer will come across volumes riddled with the bored holes of worms and insects that have eaten trails through innumerable pages from history. Yet, somehow, so much survives despite the heat, the humidity, the pests, and the disasters, both natural and unnatural. Jimbōchō itself is a testament to a culture invested in this curious form of history.

The same can be said for publishing in Japan and the myriad books devoted to graphic design. It has been said that there is a book for literally every topic, sub-topic, or micro-topic in Japan, and this obsession with culture has helped keep the history of graphic design alive here. The printing companies that survived the Great Kanto Earthquake of 1923 now dominate Japan's printing industry and far, far beyond. *Idea*, first published in 1953, still counts as one of the top graphic design magazines in the world, devoted to graphic design in all its contemporary and historical forms.

The Japanese design aesthetic continues to evolve and grow, as does an investment in the history of Japanese graphic design culture. It has taken the work of countless individuals to help document graphic design in Japan—from the birth of Japan's first graphic design studio as founded by Tada Hokuu to the groundbreaking editorial design work done by Horiuchi Seiichi, the son of one of Tada's employees.

There is history here, and this is just one variation on it. There are not enough women represented here. There is a lack of representation of queer voices, foreign voices, immigrant voices, and ethnically diverse voices.

In short, there is still work to be done.

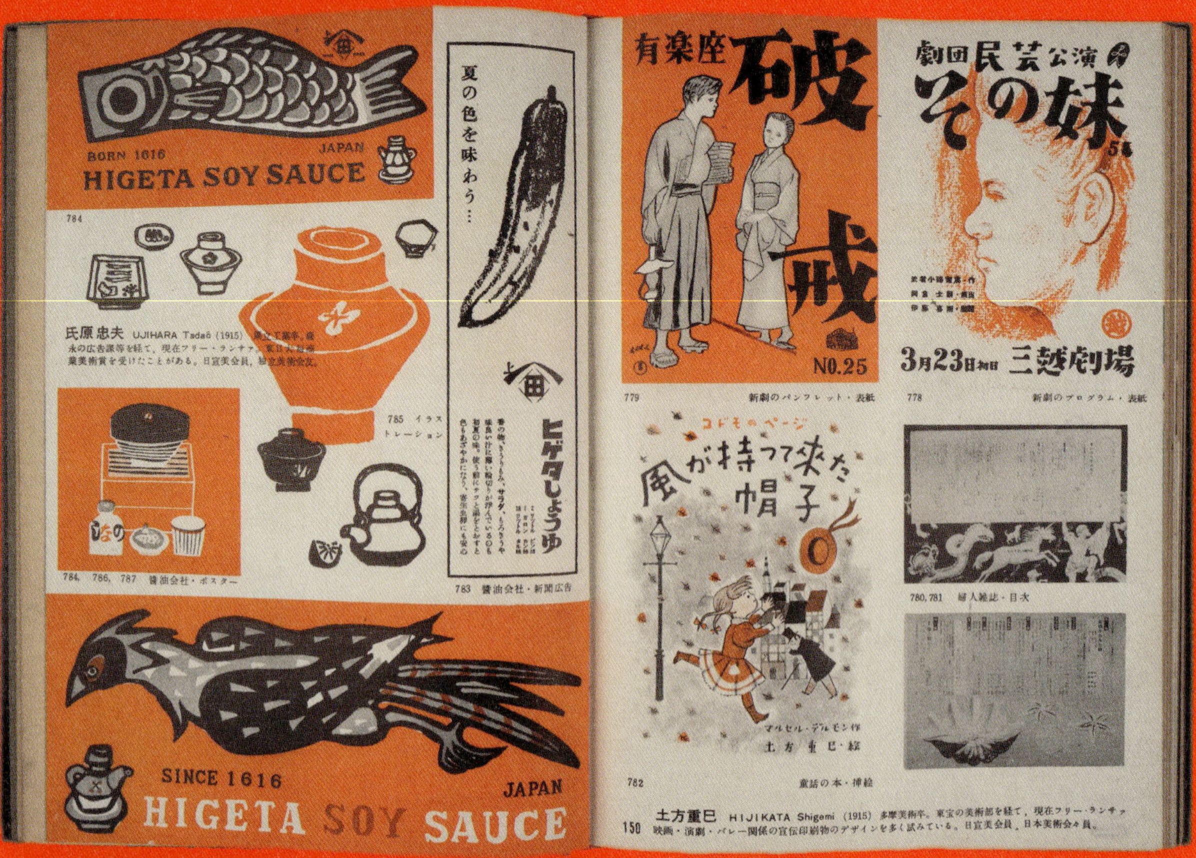

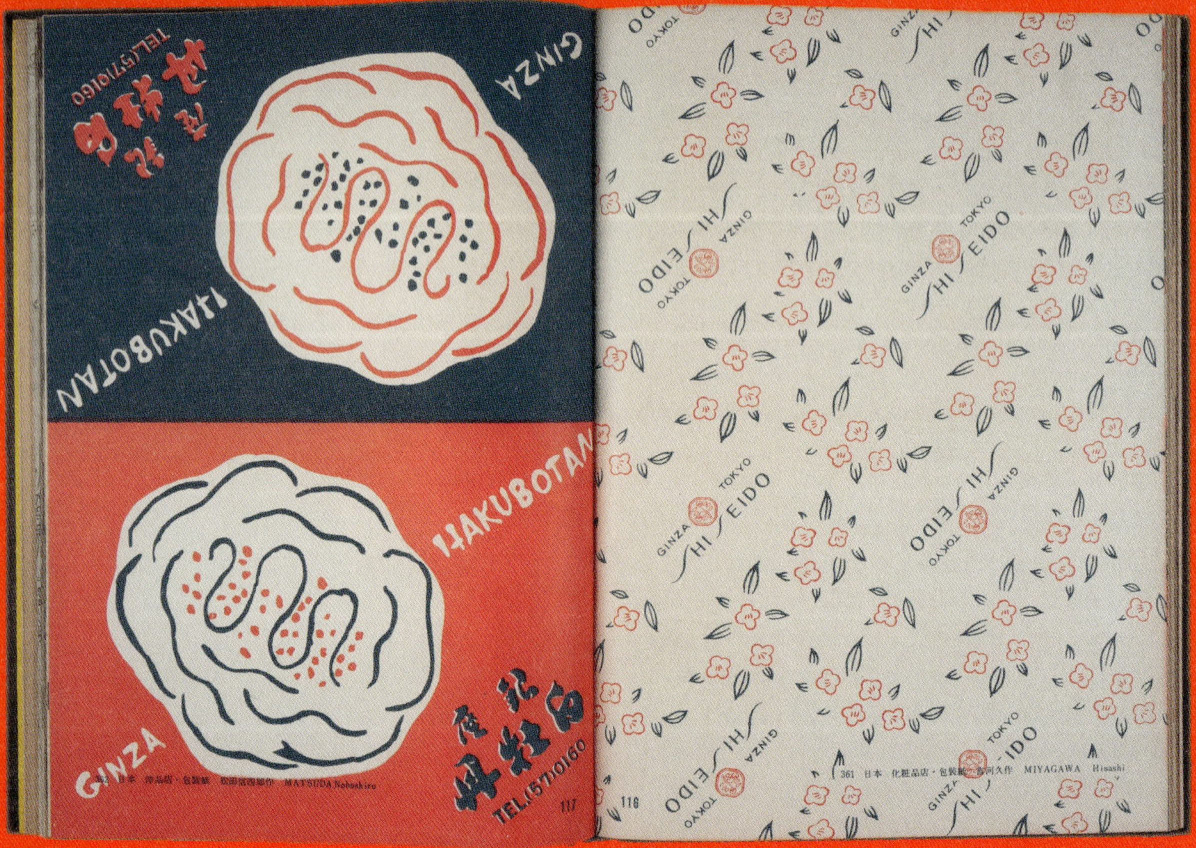

Spreads from *Shōgyō Dezain Zenshū* 商業デザイン全集 No. 5 (The World's Commercial Design) (Tokyo: David-sha ダヴィッド社, 1954).

Glossary

A Club Aクラブ: design study group founded in 1952
Ainu アイヌ: indigenous people of Japan
Alliance Graphique Internationale (AGI): private international design club
Angura アングラ演劇: underground theater movement
anime アニメ: Japanese animation
Art Nouveau: an international style of art, architecture, and applied art influenced by Japanese ukiyo-e printmaking
bijinga 美人画: artwork depicting beautiful women
bokashi ぼかし: gradated printing
chiyogami 千代紙: graphic, repetitive designs applied to paper
Chuo Kōbo 中央工房: wartime propaganda publisher
collotype コロタイプ: photographic printing process
cut カット: spot illustration
dezain デザイン: design
dōga 童画: painting and illustration for children in their formative years, especially fairy tales and children's literature
dōjinshi 同人誌: mini-comics
Edō: the name of Tokyo prior to 1868
***Front*:** wartime propaganda magazine
***Fujin Gahō* 婦人画報:** magazine for women
***Gebrauchsgrafik*:** historic German commercial art and graphic design magazine
Ginza 銀座: upscale area of Tokyo
Ginza Graphic Gallery ギンザ グラフィック ギャラリー: graphic design-oriented exhibition space run by DaiNippon Printing founded in 1986
Greater East Asia Co-Prosperity Sphere 大東亜共栄圏: Japanese interwar empire
gurafikku dezain グラフィックデザイン: graphic design (1950s–present)
Hakubakai 白馬会: artists' society led by arts educator Kuroda Seiki 黒田清輝
***Hanatsubaki* 花椿:** a Shiseido publication
hanga 版画: printmaking
***Heibon Punch* 平凡パンチ:** defunct lifestyle magazine for men
Heibonsha 平凡社: Tokyo-based publishing company
hidari yokogaki 左横書き: left-to-right horizontal orthography
hiragana 平仮名: Japanese syllabary mostly used to indicate prefixes and grammatical word endings, but also used to represent entire words
Hochschule für Gestaltung Ulm (HfG Ulm): German design university which operated from 1953 to 1968
***Idea* アイデア:** contemporary Japanese graphic design magazine founded in 1953
Isetan 伊勢丹: Japanese department store chain
Japan Advertising Artists Club (JAAC) 日本宣伝美術会: postwar graphic design organization
Japan Graphic Designers Association (JAGDA): graphic design organization formed in 1978
kamon 家紋: family crests
kanji 漢字: writing system imported to Japan from China in the fourth century BC
katakana 片仮名: Japanese syllabary used for foreign loanwords, country names, and proper names of foreigners
kimono 着物: Japanese T-shaped, wrapped-front garment with square sleeves and a rectangular body
kinema moji キネマ文字: high contrast display characters for poster and magazine cover work within the theater industry
kōan 考案: the mental and intellectual articulation of a design concept to be executed
***Kogei News* 工芸ニュース:** industrial design magazine
***Kōkokukai* 広告界:** early graphic design magazine, predecessor to Idea
kamishibai 紙芝居: street corner storytelling art form
kanban 看板: commercial sign
kunten 訓点: circular, square, triangular and derivative marks which are used to suggest the pronunciation and meaning of lesser-known characters
kurashi 暮し: everyday life
***Kurashi no techo* 暮しの手帖:** cultural magazines for women
Manchukuo 満州国: occupied Manchuria
manga マンガ: Japanese comic books and graphic novels
Medal with Purple Ribbon 紫綬褒章: Japanese government awards given to individuals who have contributed to academic and artistic developments, improvements and accomplishments
Metabolism 新陳代謝: Japanese architecture and graphic design group
migi yokogaki 右横書き: right-to-left horizontal orthography
Mingei 民芸: folk crafts
Mitsukoshi 三越: a Tokyo kimono retailer turned international department store
Modernologio 考現学: archeology of the present day
moga モガ: 1920s term for "modern girl" signifying a modern woman
moji 文字: characters
mon 紋: official crests
Morisawa 株式会社モリサワ: Osaka-based digital type

foundry and technology company

MUJI 株式会社良品計画: Japanese retail company

nihonga 日本画: Japanese art

***Nippon*:** wartime propaganda magazine

Nippon Design Center 日本デザインセンター: advertising and design company

Nippon Kōbo 日本工房: wartime propaganda publisher

Norakuro のらくろ: propaganda cartoon character

Parco: Japanese department store chain

***Persona* ペルソナ:** graphic design exhibition in 1965

pochibukuro ポチ袋: printed gift-giving money envelopes

***Press Art* プレスアルト:** defunct Kansai-based graphic design journal

omoshirogara 面白柄: novelty patterned fabrics

romaji ローマ字: Latin characters

Seibundo Shinkosha (Seibundo) 誠文堂新光社: Tokyo-based publishing company, publisher of *Kōkokukai* and *Idea*

senden zasshi 宣伝雑誌: propaganda magazines

senjafuda 千社札: honorific seals to be applied to shrines

sensōgara 戦争柄: propaganda patterned fabrics

shin-hanga 新版画: early 20th century printmaking movement which maintained the division of labor of the ukiyo-e system

Shiseido 資生堂: cosmetics corporation

shōgyō bijutsu 商業美術: commercial art (term from 1920s–1930s)

shōgyō dezain 商業デザイン: commercial design (term from 1940s)

shōjo 少女: young women who are older than "girls" yet whose heterosexual virginity is still intact

shufu 主婦: housewife

shunga 春画: erotic ukiyo-e prints

sōsaku hanga 創作版画: early 20th century printmaking movement focused on self-expression

Takashimaya 髙島屋: Japanese department store chain

tategaki 縦書き: right-to-left vertical orthography

Tōhōsha 東方社: wartime propaganda publisher

Tokyo Art Directors Club 東京アートディレクターズクラブ: design organization founded in 1952

typofoto: historic German term for the integration of photography, typography, and illustration

ukiyo-e 浮世絵: genre of Japanese painting and printmaking which flourished from the 17th to 19th centuries

ūman ribu ウーマンリブ: Japanese women's liberation movement

USSR in Construction (SSSR na stroike): Russian propaganda magazine designed by Alexander Rodchenko and Varvara Stepanova

woodblock: carved pieces of wood used for relief printing

yōga 洋画: Western art

World Design Conference (WoDeCo): design conference held in Tokyo in 1960

yukata 浴衣: unlined cotton summer kimono, worn in casual settings

zuan 図案: the physical execution of a design

zuan moji 図案文字: display lettering from the 1920s and 1930s

Periods of applicable Japanese history

Heian 平安時代: 794–1185

Kamakura 鎌倉時代: 1185–1333

Muromachi 室町時代: 1336–1573

Azuchi-Momoyama 安土桃山時代: 1573–1600

Edo 江戸時代 / Tokugawa 徳川時代: 1603–1867

Meiji 明治時代: 1868–1912

Taishō 大正時代: 1912–1926

Shōwa 昭和時代: 1926–1989

Heisei 平成時代: 1989–2019

Reiwa 令和時代: 2019–

Additional references

Bing, Siegfried, and Robert Koch. *Artistic America, Tiffany Glass, and Art Nouveau*. Cambridge, MA: MIT Press, 1970.

Bogdanova-Kummer, Eugenia. *Bokujinkai: Japanese Calligraphy and the Postwar Avant-Garde*. Leiden: Brill, 2020.

Bullock, Julia C., Ayako Kano, and James Welker. *Rethinking Japanese Feminisms*. Honolulu, HI: University of Hawaii Press, 2018.

Bungō No sōtei. Tōkyō: Nihon Hōsō Shuppan Kyōkai, 2008.

Chong, Doryun, Michio Hayashi, and Fumihiko Sumitomo. *From Postwar to Postmodern: Art in Japan, 1945-1989*. New York, NY: Museum of Modern Art, 2012.

Clammer, John, Brian Moeran, and Lisa Skov. "Consuming Bodies: Constructing and Representing the Female Body in Contemporary Japanese Print Media." Essay. In *Women, Media and Consumption in Japan*, 197–219. London: Routledge, 2013.

Culver, Annika A. *Glorify the Empire: Japanese Avant-Garde Propaganda in Manchukuo*. Vancouver, BC: Univ Of Brit Columbia Pr, 2013.

Earhart, David C. *Certain Victory: Images of World War II in the Japanese Media*. London: Routledge, 2015.

Fraser, James Howard, Steven Heller, and Seymour Chwast. *Japanese Modern: Graphic Design between the Wars*. San Francisco: Chronicle Books, 1996.

Germer, Andrea, and Reiko Ogawa. "Japan: Gender Studies in Transnational Perspective." *Geschlecht und Gesellschaft Handbuch Interdisziplinäre Geschlechterforschung*, 2019, 1483–92. https://doi.org/10.1007/978-3-658-12496-0_148.

Herdeg, Walter. "Graphis Annual 138/139." *Visual Art and Design in Japan* 14, no. 138/139 (1968): 20. https://doi.org/10.2307/3186778.

Huffman, Jeff. *Family Crests of Japan*. Berkeley, CA: Stone Bridge Press, 2007.

Ikuta, Makoto. *Nihon no Bijutsu Ehagaki 1900-1935: Meiji Umare No Retoro Modan*. Kyōto-shi: Tankōsha, 2006.

Jackson, Anna. *Kimono: the Art and Evolution of Japanese Fashion: the Khalili Collections*. London: Thames and Hudson, 2020.

Jansen, Marije, Elise Wessels, May Meurs, and Gerard Forde. *Japan: Modern: Japanese Prints from the Elise Wessels Collection*. Amsterdam: Rijksmuseum, 2016.

Katashio, Jiro. "A Record of the Rise of Media." *Vignette: Typography Journal* 00 (December 2001).

Kida, Takuya. *Yōkoso Nihon e: 1920-30-Nendai no tsūrizumu to Dezain = Visit Japan: Tourism Promotion in the 1920s and 1930s*. Tōkyō: Tōkyō Kokuritsu Kindai Bijutsukan, 2016.

Kuwahara, Shigeo, and Hiroyuki Sasame. *Japan Avangyarudo: Angura Engeki Kessaku posuta Hyaku = Japan Avantgarde: 100 Poster Masterpieces from Underground Theatre*. Tōkyō: Paruko Entateinmento Jigyōkyoku, 2004.

Lucken, Michael. *Imitation and Creativity in Japanese Arts: from Kishida Ryūsei to Miyazaki Hayao*. New York, NY: Columbia University Press, 2016.

Mackie, Vera. "Genders, Sexualities and Bodies in Modern Japanese History." *Routledge Handbook of Modern Japanese History*, 2017, 348–60. https://doi.org/10.4324/9781315746678-25.

Mason, Richard Henry Pitt, and John Godwin. Caiger. *A History of Japan*. Boston: Tuttle Publishing, 2004.

Masuda, Kingo. "A Historical Overview of Art Education in Japan." *The Journal of Aesthetic Education* 37, no. 4 (2003): 3–11.

Nishimura Morse, Anne, Kendall H. Brown, and J. Thomas Rimer. *Art of the Japanese Postcard: the Leonard A. Lauder Collection at the MFA, Boston*. Boston, MA: MFA Publications, 2004.

Ohki, Sadako, and Adam Haliburton. *The Private World of Surimono = Surimono No Shiteki Sekai: Japanese Prints from the Virginia Shawan Drosten and Patrick Kenadjian Collection*. New Haven: Yale University Art Gallery, 2020.

Pate, Alan Scott. *Kanban: Traditional Shop Signs of Japan*. San Diego, CA: Princeton University Press, 2017.

Rimer, J. Thomas., and Toshiko M. McCallum. *Since Meiji: Perspectives on the Japanese Visual Arts, 1868-2000*. Honolulu: University of Hawaii Press, 2012.

Suzuki, Michiko. *Becoming Modern Women: Love and Female Identity in Prewar Japanese Literature and Culture*. Stanford, CA: Stanford University Press, 2010.

Tipton, Elise K, and John Clark. *Being Modern in Japan: Culture and Society from the 1910s to the 1930s*. Honolulu, HI: University of Hawaii, 2000.

COLOPHON:

Set Margins' no. 54

Fracture: Japanese Graphic Design 1875–1975

Ian Lynam

ISBN: 978-1-942884-39-2

Edited by Louise Rouse & Chris Palmieri

Copy edited by Angela Paladino

Proofread by Joshua Hansell & Ren Makishima

Design by Ian Lynam | ianlynam.com

Photography by Steve White II, unless otherwise noted

Endpaper images by YueQi Wang from her notes for the final exam in the class Japanese Graphic Design History at TUJ

Image production by Iori Kikuchi & Eglif Pascal Santoso

Image rights acquisitions by Ren Makishima

Type:

Axis / Type Project

Dolly Pro / Underware

Fakt Pro / TypeBy

Onick / Wordshape

Orly Stencil / TypeBy

Ryumin Pro / Morisawa

More: japanesedesignhistory.com

Set Margins' no. 54

setmargins.press

I am indebted to a wide array of generous individuals who helped make this book a reality. Thanks to the Research Department at Temple University Japan Campus—foremost to former Director Professor Mariko Nagai, former staff Anais DiCroce, and Emily Proulx—and the administration of TUJ—notably the late Assistant Dean Jonathan Nelson Wu and former Associate Dean Alistair Howard—for providing research funds that were put into place for field research and student research assistants. A bevy of incredible researchers worked alongside me and helped out in a myriad of ways, including Ren Makishima, Masaki J. Finch, Jarod Hodge, Naoko Kato, Iori Kikuchi, Nicole Ann Kimura, Emiko Nishiwaki, Hikari Otomo, Eglif Pascal Santoso, and Lucas Tokuda. I owe thanks to my colleagues at TUJ, Vermont College of Fine Arts and CalArts past and present—to former VCFA MFA in Graphic Design Program Directors Jennifer Renko and Danielle Dahline, and former Dean Matthew Monk for providing travel and research funding.

Thanks to the score of institutions that have invited me to speak and share this research over the past number of years. Thank you to Yuki Kameguchi, Jeri Blocker, Hannah Smith, Michael Scaringe, Patrick Tsai, Madoka Nishi, Ranko Nagata, Michael Razic, Naomi Razic, Evan Mast, Maggie Barnes, Eric Mast, Taro Nettleton, Renna Okubo, Thien Huynh, Ryan Seuffert, Kirsten Seuffert, Raymundo Reynoso, Christine Villa, Takayuki Kubota, Jimmy Luu, Kaoru Sakurai, Shinya B. Watanabe, Aggie Toppins, Kyle Broyles, Yuki Kurita Broyles, Briar Levit, Chris Ro, Yunim Kim, Jess Mantell, Geoff Kaplan, Jeremy Freeman, Gail Swanlund, Lars Harmsen, Akiko Yamagami, Francisco Laranjo, James Chae, Mark Anderson and Kurumi Kido. I owe a tremendous debt to my parents, Bill Lynam and Maria Lynam, and my beloved nephew, Kyle Evan Lynam Jr. and his family. Thanks to Kenichi Kameguchi and Reiko Kameguchi for putting up with so many moldy boxes in their genkan over the years. Thank you, Chris, Louise, Angela, Yuki, Ren, and Josh for helping make this book what it is.

Yuki, thank you for your constant support—I never could have pursued this book without you. This book is dedicated to *you*.

This book and the research behind it would never have been possible without initial prompting from Kiyonori Muroga. Muroga-san glibly told me over a decade ago that "he knew" I'd write a Japanese graphic design history book one day, and without that challenge, I never would have taken this up.

(Of course, he doesn't remember having said this at all today.)

I am blessed with hundreds of friends all over the globe who contributed to this project, often without knowing it. You are probably one of them—thank you.

The names in this book follow the Japanese order of surname first. Additionally, plural conjugation follows Japanese conjugation. One kimono is "one kimono." Two kimonos are "two kimono."

A sizable part of me feels loath to publish this—the world has become so small and keeps getting smaller. I hope that with this project I might honor the culture that I have lived in for the past two decades and help facilitate wider cultural understanding.

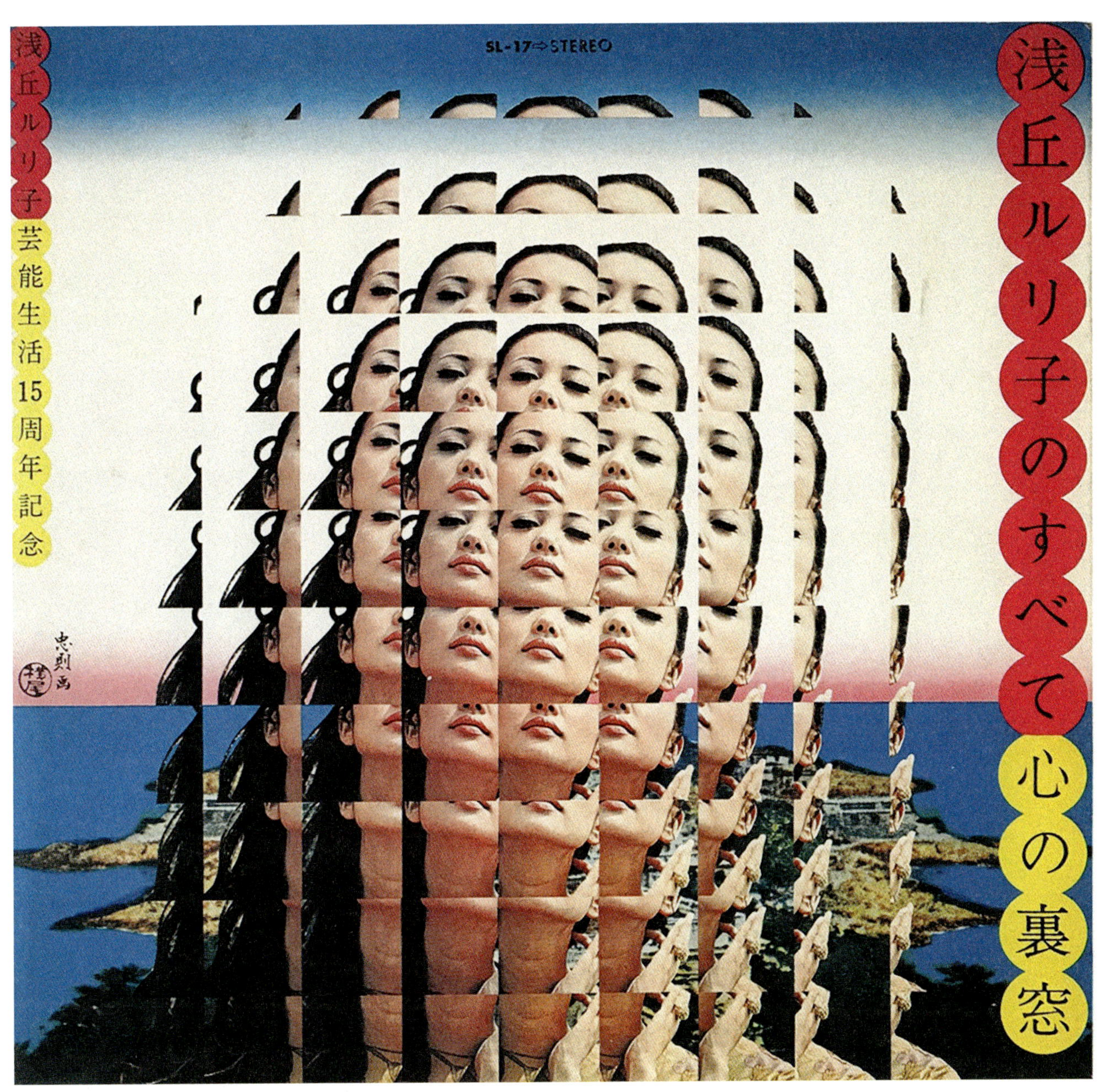

Asaoka Ruriko 浅丘ルリ子 - 心の裏窓 *Kokoro no Uramado* 心の裏窓 LP cover
(Tokyo: Teichiku テイチク, 1969). Designed by Yokoo Tadanori 横尾忠則

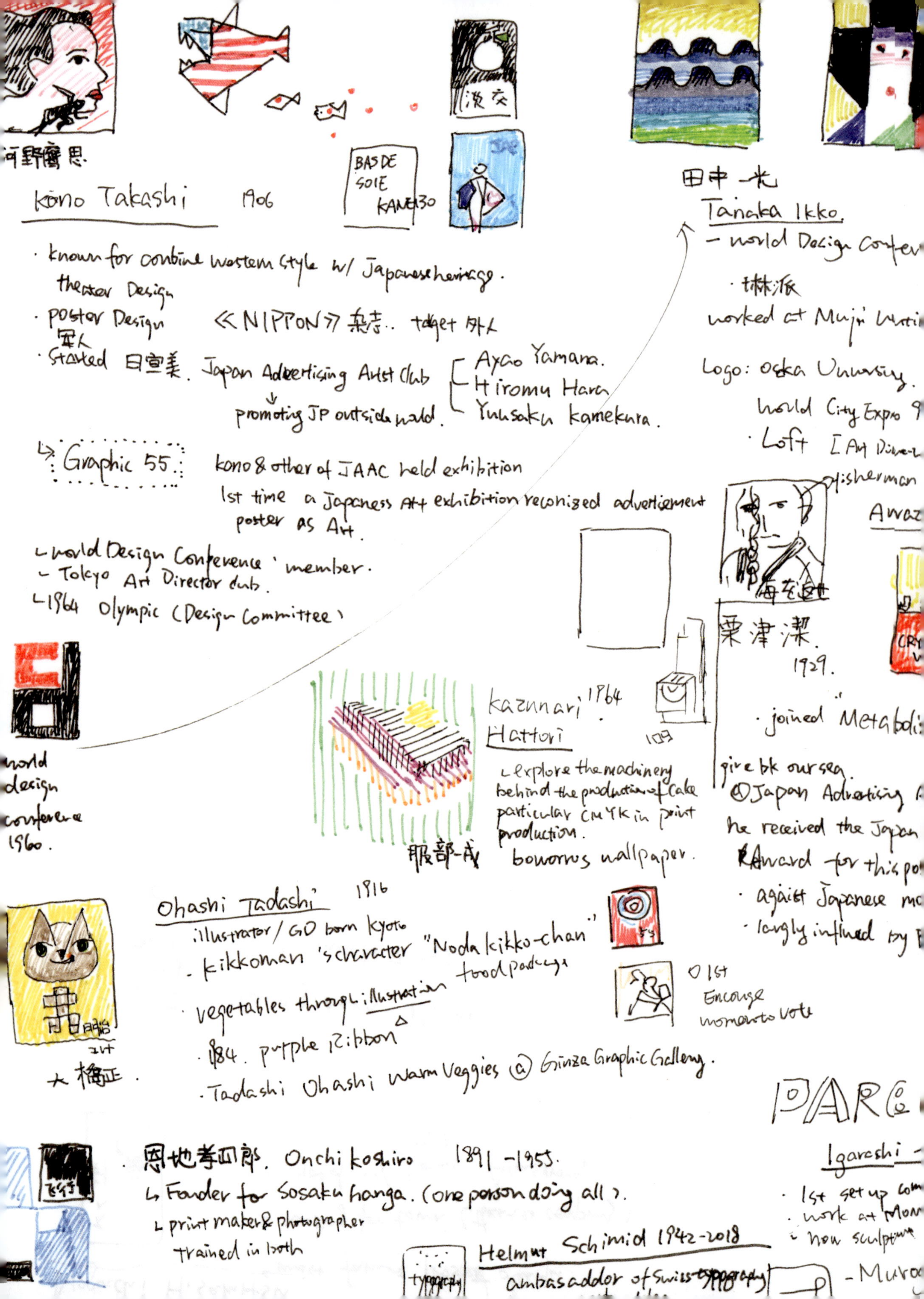
河野鷹思
Kono Takashi 1906
BAS DE SOIE KANEBO
淡交
· known for combine western style w/ Japanese heritage.
theater Design
· poster Design «NIPPON» 杂志.. target 外人
军人
· Started 日宣美. Japan Advertising Artist Club
promoting JP outside world.
Ayao Yamana.
Hiromu Hara
Yuusaku kamekura.
Graphic 55
kono & other of JAAC held exhibition
1st time a Japaness Art exhibition reconized advertisement poster as Art.
world Design Conference member.
Tokyo Art Director club.
1964 Olympic (Design Committee)
world design conference 1960.
田中一光
Tanaka Ikko.
world Design Confer
琳派
worked at Muji
Logo: Osaka University
world City Expo
Loft
fisherman
Awaz
栗津潔.
1929.
· joined "Metaboli
give bk oursea
Japan Advertising
he received the Japan
Award for this po
· against Japanese
· largly inflned by
kazunari Hattori 1964
109
explore the machinery behind the production of cake particular CMYK in print production.
bowerrus wallpaper.
服部一成
Ohashi Tadashi 1916
illustrator / GD born kyoto
· kikkoman 's character "Noda kikko-chan"
food package
vegetables through illustration
184. purple Ribbon
· Tadashi Ohashi warm Veggies @ Ginza Graphic Gallery.
大橋正.
1st
Encourge womens to vote
PARCO
恩地孝四郎. Onchi koshiro 1891 -1955.
Founder for Sosaku hanga. (one person doing all).
print maker & photographer
Trained in both
Helmut Schimid 1942-2018
ambassador of Swiss typography
typography
Igarashi
1st set up
work at MoM
now sculpture
Muro